# Maples of the World

# Maples of the World


D. M. van Gelderen
P. C. de Jong
H. J. Oterdoom

*photographs by J. R. P. van Hoey Smith*

Theodore R. Dudley, Ph.D., Scientific Editor



**TIMBER PRESS**
*Portland, Oregon*

All photos by J. R. P. van Hoey Smith unless otherwise noted.



ISBN 0-88192-000-2

Printed in Hong Kong

TIMBER PRESS, INC.
The Haseltine Building
133 S.W. Second Avenue, Suite 450
Portland, Oregon 97204-3527, U.S.A.

Library of Congress Cataloging-in-Publication Data

Gelderen, D. M. van.
Maples of the world / D. M. van Gelderen, P. C. de Jong, H. J. Oterdoom ; photographs by J. R. P. van Hoey Smith.
p. cm.
Includes bibliographical references (p. ) and index.
ISBN 0-88192-000-2
1. Maple. I. Jong, P. C. de (Piet C.) II. Oterdoom, H. J. (Herman John) III. Title.
QK495.A17G44 1994
583'.28--dc20 92-46361
CIP

# Contents

*Species color plates follow page 112; hybrid and cultivar color plates follow page 272.*

# Foreword

If you have a garden you almost certainly have an *Acer.* That friendly and accommodating plant is represented throughout the temperate zone of the Northern Hemisphere. There are so many maples that they may well occupy more space in dendrological reference books and nursery lists than any other genus excepting *Rhododendron.* There has been very little literature on the Aceraceae, however, though invaluable articles are to be found in Bean, Krüssmann, and Rehder, in addition to the work of J. D. Vertrees.

The present volume, the result of the joint efforts of several of the best specialists over many years, fills an obvious gap and should be of the greatest interest to all lovers of trees.

Roger de Candolle
*Late President of the*
*International Dendrology Society*

# Preface

In 1975, the late J. D. Vertrees visited Europe and met the future authors of this book, three years before Timber Press published his well-known *Japanese Maples.* During his visit Vertrees urged his Dutch maple friends to write a book on the entire genus. After some deliberation, the three of us agreed to accept this challenge.

Information about the genus *Acer* lies scattered in many publications. Bringing order to this diverse body of information, often dealing with only one or two aspects of the genus, proved to be a time-consuming and tedious undertaking. In fact, it has taken us about 16 years to accomplish the task of reclassifying the genus and collating all the information, both published and unpublished.

The difficulties, drawbacks, and disadvantages of a multiauthored book are well known. Differences of style and approach to the subject cannot be avoided. We trust the reader will not be inconvenienced and will find that we have resolved most of these problems.

This book contains something of interest for everyone—whether botanist, nursery professional, gardener, or dendrologist. It is our aim that readers may find answers to complicated taxonomic questions as well as information on trees suitable for their landscapes.

The authors are indebted to Mr. J. D. Vertrees, Dr. T. Delendick, and Dr. T. R. Dudley for their invaluable advice and cooperation, and for reading the manuscript and making many corrections.

Should this book stimulate an interest in this splendid genus, then we will be more than adequately rewarded.

D. M. van Gelderen
Dr. P. C. de Jong
Dr. H. J. Oterdoom

# Acknowledgments

The authors wish to thank the following individuals for their assistance in preparing this manuscript:

Mrs. Inez Langevoort-de Maaré, who prepared the line drawings;
Dr. Thomas Delendick, who guided the preparation of the species chapter and provided other valuable suggestions;
Dr. Theodore R. Dudley, who solved many difficult taxonomic problems in his role as scientific editor and gave this manuscript his peer review;
Dr. Elizabeth C. Dudley, who copyedited the manuscript and made our work much easier;
The late Mr. J. D. Vertrees, who provided valuable suggestions for the cultivar chapter;
Mr. Wang Dajun, former director of the Shanghai Botanic Garden, who provided English translations of Chinese sources, thus making available to us much information on little-known Chinese species;
Professor M. Yokoi of the Faculty of Horticulture, Chiba University, Matsudo, Japan, who gave his generous assistance with Japanese names;
Mrs. A. van Rhijn-van der Veer, who computerized and corrected the bibliography;
Dr. D. O. Wijnands, who solved several taxonomic problems and wrote the appendix on *Acer mono* versus *Kalopanax;*
Mr. Dirk van Gelderen, who compiled the index;
Mrs. P. Sprado, who corrected and translated Japanese names;
Mrs. H. J. J. van Gelderen-Esveld, without whose initial pushing this book would never have been written;
Mr. Richard Abel, who believed in us and generously shared his expertise in publishing throughout the many years this manuscript was in the making.

*Were I to await perfection, my book would never be finished.*

Tai T'ung, 13th-century scholar
THE SIX SCRIPTS: PRINCIPLES OF CHINESE WRITING

*May what is said correctly be free of nasty reprimands, and may the mistakes made by ignorance be corrected by more qualified persons.*

Diodorus Siculus

*[A]ll the Particulars contained in this Book cannot be found in any one Piece known to me, but ly scattered and dispersed . . . and so this may serve to relieve those Fastidious Readers . . . not willing to take the Pains to search them out.*

John Ray
THE WISDOM OF GOD MANIFESTED IN THE WORKS OF CREATION

Chapter 1

# Maples in Nature and in the Garden

DR. H. J. OTERDOOM

For an all too brief period each autumn the woods of North America and the Orient, and many gardens throughout the temperate world, are ablaze with scarlet, gold, and yellow when maples, the most spectacular of all trees, adorn the countryside. Maples delight the eye, provide one of nature's finest sweets, and hold their own as timber with even the mighty oaks. Throughout the ages people have been enchanted with this magnificent and versatile genus of trees known as *Acer.*

## HISTORY OF MAPLE NAMES

The word *acer* derives from the Proto-Indo-European word *ac,* meaning "sharp, to be sharp, to sharpen," and seems to represent the sound of sharpness. *Ac* is found in many Greek and Latin words, including *acropolis, akouo* (to hear, or more literally, to prick up one's ears), *acutus, acacia, aculeata,* and others.

The word's association with the genus *Acer* possibly comes from the pointed leaves associated with maples, a feature that is reflected also in the German synonym *Spitzblatt.* In Russian, maples are called *òstrolistnyj klejën,* meaning "sharp-leaved." Loudon (1838) offers an alternative explanation for how the word *ac* became associated with the genus *Acer*: because the wood of some *Acer* species is extremely hard, it was much sought after for making pikes and lances. Thus the genus was named after the shape of these instruments.

The Dutch common name for the field maple, *Spaanse aak,* is revealing, for in it we not only recognize the root word, but we also find an intimation of the origin of the English word for *oak,* representing an entirely different genus of trees.

*Acer,* interestingly, is used in Latin in the neuter form. This usage contrasts with the general rule in Latin that the names of trees, as well as those of women, islands, countries, and cities, are always feminine. For some reason the neuter form was well established by the time of Christ (see Ovid's *Amores* I, XI, 26, 27, and 28).

Accepted since antiquity, the name *Acer* was officially assigned to the genus by Linnaeus in *Species Plantarum* (1753). Linnaeus chose not to coin a new name for the genus, something he did in many other cases and for which he was reproached by his contemporaries. So firmly was the name *Acer* established in the minds of botanists that Linnaeus found no purpose served by departing from traditional usage.

Prior to assigning the name *Acer* to the genus, Linnaeus had listed four *Acer* species in *Hortus Cliffortianus,* published in 1737:

1. *Acer majus,* a synonym of *A. montanum,* by reference to Dodonaeus's *Stirpium Historiae, Pemptades Sex,* cited as "Dod. pempt." with an incorrect page number. Linnaeus's extremely short method of annotation resulted in the change of the title of Dodonaeus's book in this and all the writings to come. *Acer majus* is a synonym of *A. pseudoplatanus* L.

2. *Acer platanoides,* with *A. montanum* and *A. majus* as synonyms. Linnaeus reports this species as growing in his native Sweden.

3. *Acer campestre,* with the synonyms *A. minus* or *A. vulgare, minore folio.* Linnaeus cites this species as growing in Germany, Holland, England, Gallia, Italia, and Helvetia.

4. *Acer maximum* is a synonym of *Acer negundo.* Linnaeus warns the reader that this species should not be confused with *Vitex negundo!* In *Species Plantarum* Linnaeus applies the name *Acer negundo,* referring to the resemblance of this maple's leaves to those of *Vitex negundo.*

By the time Linnaeus officially assigned the name *Acer* to the genus, he listed nine species of *Acer,* with a considerably modernized binomial nomenclature. This was quite a remarkable change for 16 years. Linnaeus's spelling of *A. pensylvanicum* differs from the spelling of the state of its habitat: according to the rules of nomenclature, an incorrectly spelled name is perpetuated forever. (For another example, compare *Wisteria,* named for U.S. anatomist Caspar Wistar).

Through the ages there has been much confusion about the identity and names of maples. This confusion extends even to different genera, such as *Carpinus,* which is considered a third species of *Acer* by Dodonaeus (1583). The genus *Platanus* was also sometimes confused with *Acer.* Theophrastus (372–c. 287 B.C.), a Greek philosopher and natural scientist, warned of this confusion in his *Enquiry into Plants* and mentioned several other Greek names: *Glinon, Sphendamnos,* and *Zygia.*

The Russian common name for maple is *kljen.* The Polish *klon* and the Lithuanian *klevas* also derive from the Greek *gleinos* or *gleinon,* as do the Medieval Latin *clenus,* the Middle High German *linboum* or *limboum,* and the Lower High German *lehne.* In the German languages this name was transferred to the genus *Tilia.* In Sweden and Norway the indigenous Norway maple is called *Lönn;* in Denmark, *Lon;* and in Gotland, *Lünd.*

John Evelyn wrote about maples in *Sylva* (1664):

> The maple (*Acer*) was of old held in equal estimation with the *Citron;* . . . But there is a larger sort, which we call *Sycamor.* The *Sycamor* is much more in reputation for its shade than it deserves; for the leaves which fall early (like those of the *Ash*) turn to *Mucilage,* and putrify with the first moisture of the season; so as they contaminate and mar our Walks, and therefore (by my consent) to be banished from all curious Gardens and Avenues. There is in Germany a better sort of *Sycamor* than ours, wherewith they make *Saddle-trees,* and divers other things of use; our own is excellent for *Cart* and *Plow-timber,* being light, tough, and not much inferior to *Ash* itself.

It is a pity that the name *sycamore* should have been adopted in England for *Acer pseudoplatanus* L., because it conceals the fact that this tree is a typical member of its genus. When the tree was introduced into Britain from central Europe in or before the 16th century, it was confused with the sycamore of the Bible, which actually is an Eastern fig tree with a somewhat similar leaf, *Ficus sycomorus,* growing in Egypt, Syria, and other nearby countries. Further, the Scots (and the French) confused this great maple with the plane tree and to this day still call both tree and timber *plane.* To complete the confusion, North Americans call their plane tree,

*Platanus occidentalis,* a *sycamore,* while the French apply the name *plane* to the Norway maple. The English botanist John Gerard (1633) objected to the name *sycamore* in his herbal: "This is now commonly (yet not rightly) called the Sycomore tree. And seeing use will have it so, I think it were not unfit to call it the bastard *Sycomore.*"

The meanings of most *Acer* specific names are evident. For example, *rufinerve,* with rust-colored hairs on the veins; *platanoides* and *pseudoplatanus,* with leaves like *Platanus. Cappadocicum* and *tataricum* obviously are names of regions where certain trees were found. *Ginnala* derives from the colloquial name given by people living along the Amur River in northeastern Asia. Several so-called mountain maples exist in the world (i.e., their common name locally is mountain maple). One in central United States is known as *A. spicatum,* but another, the Rocky Mountain maple, is called *A. glabrum.* In Europe the classic mountain maple (German *Bergahorn*) of the Swiss and Austrian Alps is *A. pseudoplatanus.*

## NATIVE HABITAT AND DISTRIBUTION OF MAPLES

Inhabitants of the Northern Hemisphere, maples are at home in the temperate climate of North America and Eurasia but enter the tropics in southeast Asia. In Indonesia they cross the equator on Java and some of the lesser Sunda Islands. They are found in the mountains of the Philippines, Sumatra, Borneo (Kalimantan), Celebes (Sulawesi), and Malaysia. They also occur in the Mediterranean climate of California and the Mediterranean Sea area. From temperate Europe and a small strip in northern Africa, maples spread across the Balkans, Cyprus, Crete, Lebanon, Turkey, Iraq, Iran, Afghanistan, and Pakistan and then along a rather narrow corridor in the Himalayas. They fan out from China to southeast Asia, Japan, Korea, Manchuria, eastern Siberia, Sachalin, and the Kurile Islands. They are found in the southern Asiatic region of the Commonwealth of Independent States (the former Soviet Union) and in regions of China, especially in Sichuan, Yunnan, and Hubei provinces, which possibly is their center of origin.

In North America maples occupy the entire United States save the tip of Florida and southwestern California. They occupy all the temperate regions of Canada and reach the southernmost part of the Alaska panhandle, south of latitude 59°. *Acer glabrum* ssp. *douglasii* extends along streams and in sheltered ravines through the Rocky Mountains into Alberta, to the head of the Lynn Canal, which is the northernmost point of this species's distribution. Local and disjunct populations, considered as relict displacements from the Pleistocene when they were forced to retreat southward before the oncoming ice sheets, are found in Mexico and Guatemala. Other tree species native to the North American continent, such as ponderosa pine (*Pinus ponderosa*), Douglas fir (*Pseudotsuga menziesii*), sweet gum (*Liquidamber styraciflua*), and white pine (*Pinus strobus*), display the same tendency to form population pockets in Mexico and Central America.

"Widely distributed, but nowhere abundant" is true of maples in all parts of their range. They were most abundant in the Miocene from 25 to 5 M.Y.B.P. (Million Years Before Present). As both the wood and the pollen wall of maple are perishable (more so than those of most other trees), it is difficult to assemble data about the distant past of maples through paleobotanical research.

A remarkable characteristic of *Acer* is that various species live together (sympatry) within each other's range without hybridizing. Stebbins (1977) writes that populations of sugar maple (*A. saccharum*) and red maple (*A. rubrum*) live together over considerable areas but remain reproductively distinct. The two species, which apparently are incapable of exchanging genes under natural conditions, enjoy the highest density of all maples in their natural habitat. A comparable pair in Europe is *A. pseudoplatanus* and *A. platanoides.* The absence of hybrids between these two pairs is marked and results from different flowering periods. The same absence of natural hybrids can be seen in Japan in southern Kyushu where occasionally *A.*

*micranthum* and somewhat more often *A. mono* and *A. rufinerve* are found in small groves of *A. sieboldianum.* In central Honshu, Japan, groves of *A. japonicum* and *A. shirasawanum* are interspersed with the ubiquitous *A. mono* and *A. palmatum,* often with *A. argutum* and sometimes with *A. crataegifolium.* In northeast Kyushu on the slopes of Mount Kuju (1764 m/5788 ft), shrubby *A. diabolicum* grows among large specimens of *A. nipponicum* and *A. carpinifolium.*

Quite a different matter is evidenced by the seemingly similar *Acer rubrum* of North America and *A. pycnanthum* of Japan. These species have been separated by thousands of kilometers and the Pacific Ocean for 7 million years. They hardly possess any differences despite the opportunity for distinct evolutionary development. To the best of our knowledge, no experiments in hybridizing these two species have been undertaken.

Sharing this peculiar global distribution is *Acer rufinerve* of Japan, which has a rather similar counterpart in the eastern half of North America, *A. pensylvanicum* (moosewood maple). The most conspicuous difference between these two species is their autumn color: the Japanese maple is red and its North American counterpart is yellow. Both have rust-colored hairs on their veins!

Another pair of rather similar maples is *Acer japonicum* in Japan and *A. circinatum* in the Pacific Northwest of North America. *Acer caudatum* ssp. *ukurunduense* of northern Japan, the Kuriles, and eastern Asia (Manchuria, Sachalin, and the Ussuri region) and *A. spicatum* in North America demonstrate similar affinities, although the leaf underside of the Asian species is much hairier. Both species occur on moist, rocky hillsides in the shade of other trees and are truly arborescent only on the western slopes of the mountains in some parts of their ranges. Another pair is *A. campestre,* the field maple of Europe, the Mediterranean, and southwest Asia, and *A. miyabei* of Hokkaido, Japan's northernmost island.

The genus *Acer* displays a marked tendency to have vicarious species. If populations occupying separate areas are clearly descended from an immediate common ancestor and are sufficiently distinct in external morphology to the extent that systematists can always tell them apart, they may be known as *vicarious* species. This pattern may be seen in the affinities between *A. platanoides* of Europe and Asia Minor and *A. cappadocicum* in eastern Turkey, which is distinguished in China as *A. cappadocicum* ssp. *sinicum.* In northern China *A. longipes* ssp. *amplum* and *A. truncatum* are present, while *A. mono* is very abundant in Japan where it has many subspecies but uncommon in central northern China. Yet another vicarious set of species is the snakebark maple group, with a number of related species in the Himalayas, China, and Japan, and one representative, *A. pensylvanicum,* in eastern North America. *Acer pseudoplatanus* grows in continental Europe and the Balkans, but is related to *A. heldreichii* from the Balkans, and to *A. heldrechii* ssp. *trautvetteri* and *A. velutinum* in Turkey, the Caucasus, and northern Iran.

Vast areas of southern Europe are occupied by *Acer campestre,* and many different local but formalized scientific names have been given by regional botanists. The Mediterranean species *A. monspessulanum* extends well into Asia Minor, the Caucasus, the Near East, and Iran. A subspecies recognized by botanists in the former Soviet Union but considered as synonymous with the species by U.S. botanists is *A. monspessulanum* ssp. *ibericum* in the Caucasus (Georgia). The vicarious species to the east is *A. pentapomicum* of Afghanistan and Kashmir. *Acer negundo* is very widespread in North America, extending from southern Canada into the United States from coast to coast, and south into Mexico and the Guatemalan mountains. It has established itself far beyond its natural range in many parts of Canada and the United States and exhibits its weedy characteristics in some of its far-flung subspecies in Europe and Asia where it was imported and has naturalized. *Acer negundo* is intermediate between the very variable vicarious species and those like *A. rubrum.*

Unlike the red and silver maples, the sugar maple (*Acer saccharum*) has evolved subspecies to fill different niches on the vast North American continent. The recognized subspecies of *A. saccharum* are subspecies *floridanum, grandidentatum, leucoderme, nigrum, ozarkense,* and *skutchii,* although not all taxonomists agree with this classification.

## CHARACTERISTICS OF MAPLES

All *Acer* species are woody plants ranging from small shrubs to trees of the largest dimensions, such as the Oregon maple (*A. macrophyllum*) in North America, *A. pseudoplatanus* in the mountains of central Europe, and *A. velutinum* in the eastern parts of the Caucasus and northwest Iran. The latter species was described in a Vedic passage as the mighty maple, soaring upwards to 37 m (120 ft) or more, and with leaves 30 cm (1 ft) wide. In the Himalayas, *A. oblongum* reaches great dimensions. To North American and European maple lovers it may seem rather odd that even *A. palmatum* in Japan can attain 25 m (82 ft) in height. Most maples are deciduous, only a few are evergreen. Leaf arrangement always is opposite. As Cronquist (1968) remarked, most members of the genus "look so much like maples."

Maples were undoubtedly introduced into cultivation for their many beautiful characteristics: flowers, bark (e.g., *Acer griseum;* the snakebark maple), and spectacular autumn colors. Viewing the autumn colors in northeastern United States and southern Canada is one of the preeminent pilgrimages undertaken annually by North Americans. *Acer saccharum* and *A. rubrum* set fire to the landscape with oranges, reds, and purples, and in western North America, *A. circinatum,* the vine maple, and *A. macrophyllum,* the Oregon maple, hardly do less to glorify the autumnal hills.

In Japan *Acer palmatum* and *A. japonicum* set the hills, parks, and gardens alight with their fiery red leaves. In the Himalayas and central China they also bring some color to the environment. European maples are not as gorgeous in color, though *A. platanoides* and *A. campestre* can have nice yellows and oranges and sometimes purples. In southern Scandinavia and eastern Europe *A. platanoides* colors well. In southeast Europe *A. tataricum* has red samaras early in summer and brick-red leaves in autumn. In the eastern regions of the former Soviet Union, *A. tataricum* ssp. *ginnala* produces the reds of autumn.

Maples are admired in spring for the red young shoots of most trees. The anthers of the male flowers of *Acer diabolicum* are a fine red. The flaking cinnamon-colored bark of *A. griseum* presents a stunning appearance throughout the year, coupled with good red autumn foliage. The three-lobed foliage of *A. cissifolium* from Japan, *A. triflorum* from Korea, and *A. henryi* and *A. sutchuenense* from China can always be counted on for good red color in autumn.

Maples do not suffer from continent-wide blights as do chestnuts and elms nor are they ever eaten bare by caterpillars as are oaks. It may be that maples are relatively free of such diseases and pests because of their scattered distribution pattern.

## TIME OF MAPLE FLOWERING

Generally speaking, maples flower much earlier in their development than do oaks and beeches, but great differences in age of flowering occur between sections within *Acer.* Some maples, such as those in section *Acer* or *A. nipponicum* (section *Parviflora*), do not flower until the trees have reached 20 years of age. Other maples, such as those in section *Macrantha,* may flower when only 5 years old. *Acer sinopurpurascens* (section *Lithocarpa*) flowers when only a few years old and a foot (30 cm) high.

Most maples are intermediate between these extremes, but there are no specific rules for determining the age of flowering. Most species flower in the spring, during April and May. Very early to flower, however, are species such as *Acer tegmentosum* and the North American species *A. rubrum* and *A. saccharinum,* which have ripened seeds by early summer or late spring (May), depending on the locality and climate.

Most maples are insect-pollinated, producing only about 1000 pollen grains per single flower. On the other hand, wind-pollinated birches, oaks, poplars, ashes, and elms produce about 10,000 grains of pollen per flower. The relatively small quantity of pollen produced is one reason why *Acer* pollen is infrequently found as microfossils.

## USEFUL MAPLE PRODUCTS

### Maple Wood

The wood of *Acer* is a typical sapwood type: cream-colored, unimpregnated by tannins. Tannin impregnation not only yields colored heartwood typical of most trees but also makes wood weather resistant. Maple wood decomposes quickly when placed in contact with soil or exposed to weather.

According to Virgil, author of the *Aeneid,* maple planks (*trabibus . . . acernis*) were used in building the Trojan horse and maple wood (*solio . . . acerno*) was used for the floor.

Today *Acer saccharum* is the hardwood widely used and preferred in North America for floors and walls in homes, bowling alleys, gymnasia, and so forth. It is also used as interior beams in building construction, as well as for furniture. The softer wood derived from *A. macrophyllum, A. rubrum,* and *A. saccharinum* is tooled for kitchen utensils and wooden tools.

*Acer pseudoplatanus* (sycamore) provides the most famous and distinguished use of maple wood—the back, sidewalls, and pegs of violins. Only the table (or belly) of this musical instrument is made from pine or spruce (*bois de résonance*).

### Maple Honey

Several species of maple are known for the honey they yield, which is characterized by a pale amber, sometimes greenish color; unremarkable flavor and aroma; and slow, fine granulation. Measured in kilograms per hectare or in pounds per acre, the honey-producing potential of various genera can be grouped into six classes (Crane 1975):

| | | |
|---|---|---|
| Class 1: 0–25 | Class 3: 51–100 | Class 5: 201–500 |
| Class 2: 25–50 | Class 4: 101–200 | Class 6: over 500 |

Among the plants with the highest honey potential are perennial and shrubby species of the Asclepiadaceae, Boraginaceae, Compositae, Dipsacaceae, Hydrophyllaceae, Labiatae, Leguminosae, Onagraceae, Scrophulariaceae, and Verbenaceae (*Vitex negundo* var. *incisa*), and the tree genera *Acer* and *Tilia.* Species from eight other plant families, including the Aceraceae, are in Class 6. *Acer campestre* belongs to Class 6 and *A. platanoides* to Class 4. The honey potential of *A. pseudoplatanus* is given as 4–6 in England and Wales. Nothing is known about other species of *Acer.*

Batra (1985) reports that *Acer rubrum* (red maple) is an important early spring food resource for honeybees and other insects since the flowers develop before the leaves appear and contain abundant pollen grains. Entomophilous characteristics include abundant nectar yield from exposed nectaries on the floral discs and a delicately sweet fragrance.

### Maple Syrup

A much more famous maple product is maple syrup, which European immigrants to North America learned to make from Native Americans. When taken from the tree, maple sap is crystal clear and does not taste sweet; its sugar content usually is only about 1 percent but can reach 3 percent for "very good trees." Not only did the early North American settlers learn how to collect maple sap and produce maple sugar, but more importantly they learned that *Acer saccharum* provided a substitute for very expensive cane sugar. Breaking out of dormancy, this species produces sap between mid-December and bud expansion in the spring. The sap flow is temperature dependent, occurring only following a rise in ambient temperature during the day and a fall in temperature at night. The rate of flow reduces as temperature decreases, but then increases again the next day with temperature increase. Sap is collected through a hollow tap driven into the tree trunk. When boiled down, 8 gallons (30 liters) of sap produce one gallon (4 liters) of syrup.

*Acer saccharum* ssp. *saccharum* is the major taxon of importance in the maple syrup industry, though *A. saccharum* ssp. *nigrum, A. rubrum,* and even *A. saccharinum* have spring sap flows rich in sugars. The latter three species are less frequently tapped because of their lower sugar concentrations. Most maple syrup is now produced in Quebec, Canada, and in a number of U.S. states, including New Hampshire, Vermont, New York, West Virginia, and Ohio. Chinese correspondents report that *Acer* species in China yield a sweet sap also (T. R. Dudley, pers. com.).

Free-standing trees are much more productive than forest trees. While the mechanism of sap rising is poorly understood, it appears that a water pumping mechanism in the roots and xylem, which subsides when the tree comes into leaf, is the driving agent. There is a substantial literature on the growing and tapping of maple trees, and the reduction of the collected sap into sugar, to which the reader can refer for complete details of this process.

### Biochemicals from Maples

Few biochemicals of any significance as compounds either useful or harmful to humans are derived from maples. Indeed, the genus *Acer* has occupied a very modest place through the ages in herbals and chemistry books. The Greek physician Dioscorides does not mention it nor do medicinal plant books from China and Japan (Duke & Ayensu 1985).

Maple syrup urine disease appears in modern medical literature, but the name refers only to the color of urine produced by patients. Maple bark stripper's disease is caused by the fungus *Cryptostroma corticale,* which causes sooty bark disease in maples as well as other plants. In humans the disease is characterized by a hypersensitive reaction to fungal spores, as are related immunological reactions induced by such agents as moldy hay (farmer's lung) and so forth. The condition is completely relieved by eliminating the fungal spores.

Many maples contain saponins in the form of glycosides. These chemical agents possess insect repellent and even insecticidal properties, thus sometimes protecting the wood against termites. *Acer rubrum* leaves are known to have caused the death of cattle and horses in West Virginia, and recently cancer chemotherapeutic drugs were derived from *A. negundo;* the active compound comes from triterpenoid saponins (Lewis & Elvin-Lewis 1977).

## LANDSCAPING WITH MAPLES

The principal use of maples is for landscaping private and public gardens and parks, and for street and roadside plantings. In these settings maples offer much beauty. The selection of fine landscape trees possessing a wide variety of features is unsurpassed in this genus, which offers small trees or large; flowers before the leaves appear; handsome stem designs; beautiful leaf forms and colors; and a spectacular show of color in the autumn. The last characteristic is well-known to many people, but the full landscaping potential of *Acer* is much more extensive than is generally recognized.

As in every human activity, fashion far too often dictates the landscape use of plants. Yet, it is a cause of wonder that the beauty of maples is hardly exploited by gardeners or landscape architects. For example, consider the extensive landscape possibilities in *Acer palmatum* alone. Only a few cultivars are seen with any regularity, while most remain hidden in the gardens and arboreta of connoisseurs. Further, a great number of species, such as *A. distylum* or *A. diabolicum*, are hardly ever seen. The former, with its lindenlike leaves and fine butter-yellow autumn color, and the latter, with its fine red male flowers in spring, are splendid trees. *Acer mono* and *A. cappadocicum* ssp. *lobelii*, with their cover of yellow flowers before the leaves appear, are hardly ever seen outside of specialist collections. The same can be said of *A. opalus.*

Although the most conspicuous and colorful autumn trees of North America—*Acer saccharum* and *A. rubrum*—are not as spectacular and exuberant in Europe, they nevertheless give a fine display in most years, and there are many other maples, especially the eastern Asian maples, that are not as climate-dependent to present a fine autumn show. Given a sunny position, *A. palmatum* 'Osakazuki' always displays fine red color late in October. Other species that deserve greater use include *A. caesium* ssp. *giraldii*, *A. capillipes*, *A. caudatum* ssp. *ukurunduense*, *A. cissifolium*, *A. crataegifolium*, *A. davidii*, *A. griseum*, *A. heldreichii* ssp. *trautvetteri*, *A. maximowiczianum*, *A. micranthum*, *A. rufinerve*, *A. tegmentosum*, and *A. triflorum*, to name but a few. All are available in specialist nurseries, which can propagate a particular species if it is not in stock.

## Maples for Large Gardens

Species most suitable as specimen or accent trees in large gardens (1 ha/2.5 acres or more) include the following species with their subspecies and varieties: *Acer caesium*, *A. cappadocicum*, *A. heldreichii*, *A. hyrcanum*, *A. mono*, *A. monspessulanum*, *A. obtusifolium*, *A. opalus*, *A. platanoides*, *A. pseudoplatanus*, *A. saccharum*, *A. sempervirens*, and *A. velutinum*. With accent on form and color, not on height, *A. japonicum* (especially cultivars 'Aconitifolium' and 'Vitifolium'), *A. pseudosieboldianum*, *A. sieboldianum*, and *A. shirasawanum* are recommended.

*Acer campbellii* and its subspecies *flabellatum* are recommended for warmer regions, and for subtropical areas *A. calcaratum* and *A. elegantulum* are superior. *Acer erianthum* is hardy enough for temperate regions. *Acer fabri* and the larger *A. laevigatum* are also suitable for tropical areas, as is *A. laurinum*. The latter, a giant with a beautiful white coloring on the undersides of the leaves, is even more startling than the silver maple, *A. saccharinum*. *Acer rubescens* is a good accent tree for warm regions, and *A. pentaphyllum*, a rather rare but fine plant, is suitable for warm regions that seldom experience frost.

For lawn accent, all members of section *Macrantha*, the snakebark maples, are suitable: *A. capillipes*, *A. caudatifolium*, *A. crataegifolium*, *A. davidii*, *A. laisuense*, *A. micranthum*, *A. morifolium*, *A. pectinatum*, *A. pensylvanicum*, *A. rubescens*, *A. rufinerve*, *A. sikkimense*, *A. tegmentosum*, and *A. tschonoskii*. *Acer nipponicum* also serves well as a large accent tree.

Moderately growing species include *Acer caudatum* ssp. *ukurunduense* and *A. spicatum*, which are among the hardiest species in the entire genus; *A. distylum*; *A. griseum*; *A. mandshuricum*; *A. maximowiczianum*; *A. sutchuenense*; and *A. triflorum*.

*Acer rubrum*, *A. pycnanthum*, and *A. saccharinum* are large accent and background trees. *Acer sinopurpurascens*, *A. sterculiaceum*, and *A.sterculiaceum* ssp. *franchetii* are outstanding species also.

For a beautiful spring display of male flowers, *Acer diabolicum* is a good choice. *Acer macrophyllum* is a giant maple and the only species in series *Macrophylla* of section *Lithocarpa* with gorgeous orange autumn color and beautiful yellow flowers in the spring.

*Acer paxii*, an evergreen, is very much like *A. buergerianum* but is suitable only for subtropical regions as is the large *A. oblongum*. *Acer carpinifolium* is a fine medium-sized tree that turns yellow in autumn. It tends, however, to become weedy when male and female trees are grown together.

The recommendation of Carpenter et al. (1975) regarding maples is worth repeating: "By planting maples alone it would be possible to represent a large part of the world in a single landscape design." The reader may rest assured that I and my coauthors wholly endorse this view and would only add that such a landscape would make a great garden as well! We must confess, however, such a planting would be too much of a good thing if every landscape was designed following this principle.

## Maples for Small Gardens

Either of two approaches can be pursued when using maples in a small gardens (less than 1 ha/2.5 acres). In the first approach the same trees planted in larger gardens may be planted but in smaller numbers, perhaps only one tree. The maxim "less is more" should be followed in this approach. An attractive example can be found in the gardens of Knighthayes Court in southern England, where a single *Acer pseudoplatanus* 'Brilliantissimum' dominates a small garden area.

A second option is to plant several of the smaller maples that grow no more than about 25 ft (8 m) high. These include all cultivars of *Acer palmatum* and all the snakebark maples, which are hardly ever disappointing.

*Acer glabrum* and the closely related *A. acuminatum, A. argutum, A. barbinerve,* and *A. stachyophyllum* are all lovely small trees.

## Maples for Public Gardens

Maples suitable for public parks and gardens can be selected from among virtually all the species in the genus. Landscape architects should consider planting groups of maples using a variety of species to create differences in form, size, texture, and color. With repetition, balance, and emphasis, many landscape objectives may be served.

Apart from the usual green, maple colors include red or yellow, and some selections and cultivars bear variegated silver-green or golden-green leaves. It is interesting that variegated trees are detested by some, but appreciated by others—another case in which "beauty is in the eye of the beholder."

Several other cultivars of *Acer pseudoplatanus* bear yellow or piebald colors. For instance, *A. pseudoplatanus* 'Leopoldii', with yellow fields and streaks on its leaves, was much in vogue a century ago. Today we see very large trees of this cultivar in the parks and gardens of Europe, especially around old towns where the city walls once stood. A companion cultivar is *A. pseudoplatanus* 'Simon Louis Frères', with pink and yellow patches on the leaves, although today for some reason this cultivar is no longer used.

*Acer platanoides* 'Drummondii', with a great deal of yellow in the leaves, is still widely planted in parks and camping sites. *Acer platanoides* 'Globosum' produces a medium-sized tree with a round, compact top.

Companion trees can be found in section *Palmata* series *Palmata,* and include the following species with their subspecies: *A. ceriferum, A. circinatum, A. duplicatoserratum, A. japonicum, A. palmatum, A. pauciflorum, A, pseudosieboldianum, A. pubipalmatum, A. robustum, A. shirasawanum,* and *A. sieboldianum.* Vertrees (1978b) provides a full account of these species and their cultivars. In summary, it is safe to say that only a very few *Acer* species and cultivars are unsuitable for landscape use.

## Maples as Street Trees

Maples are widely used as street and roadside trees in Europe, North America, China, and Japan. In metropolises like Paris and Berlin, maples were widely used in the 19th century. In 1935 *Acer platanoides* and *A. pseudoplatanus* accounted for 18 percent of the street trees in Berlin and in 1959 still represented 17 percent of the plantings. They were second only to *Tilia* with 41 and 44 percent, respectively.

Generally speaking, maples resist high winds well. *Acer pseudoplatanus* is quite wind resistant and thus much planted along the western coast of England and in northern and western Scotland to protect gardens and houses from Atlantic gales. Sometimes, however, it is detested for its weedy properties. *Acer saccharinum,* unhappily, has brittle branches, which can be a nuisance, although the cultivar 'Pyramidale' seems to be free of this fault.

Maples are widely used in France as roadside trees. In the countryside, *Acer pseudoplatanus* is often planted alternately with medium-sized trees of the purple *Prunus cerasifera* 'Nigra', while the silver-green *Acer negundo* 'Variegatum' is often interspersed with a purple *Prunus* in villages. Red hues derived from *A. platanoides* 'Schwedleri' and 'Reitenbachii' are used to give color to the esplanade in the center of Helsinki, Finland, and *A. pseudoplatanus* 'Atropurpureum', with a purple leaf underside, is a beloved street tree in The Netherlands. *Acer platanoides* is frequently used as a street tree in The Netherlands. Regrettably, this is not an appropriate use of this beautiful tree, which often damages sidewalks and streets with its large superficial roots. Sometimes *A. cappadocicum* is planted for its pure yellow autumn color. The only nuisance it presents is its suckering habit, a characteristic it shares with *A. cissifolium.*

In North America sugar maples (*Acer saccharum*) have been planted as roadside and shade trees in large numbers since colonial times. This species has not proved to be adaptable for suburban and urban plantings as it is intolerant of higher temperatures and soil compaction, two factors that can lead to maple decline.

In China *Acer truncatum* is used as a street tree in the large cities, and in Japan and Korea (as in Pretoria, South Africa) *A. buergerianum* is widely planted along the city streets, seemingly insensitive to pollution. The latter tolerates a great deal of pruning and lopping, yet remains a beautiful tree. Interestingly, it is also used for bonsai, as is *A. palmatum* ssp. *matsumurae.*

## Maples for Warm or Cold Sites

The only truly tropical maple is *Acer laurinum* from Indonesia, Malaysia, and the Philippines. Species that grow in nearly tropical or subtropical localities include *A. buergerianum* ssp. *ningpoense, A. calcaratum, A. campbellii* ssp. *sinense, A. caudatifolium, A. coriaceifolium, A. elegantulum, A. fabri, A. oblongum, A. oliverianum* ssp. *formosanum, A. paxii, A. sikkimense* ssp. *sikkimense,* and *A. tonkinense.* A list of this length will surely surprise those who think that maples are native only to cold- or warm-temperate regions.

Somewhat less tender but not entirely hardy are *Acer campbellii* ssp. *flabellatumcer, A. pentaphyllum,* and *A. rubescens.* Any of these do well in USDA plant hardiness zone VII or above.

In colder sites, *Acer caudatum* ssp. *ukurunduense, A. ginnala, A. negundo,* and *A. spicatum* tolerate the temperatures of zone II; *A. pensylvanicum, A. platanoides, A. rubrum, A. saccharinum,* and *A. saccharum* do well in zone III; and *A. campestre, A. tataricum,* and *A. tegmentosum* can be used in zone IV. *Acer mandshuricum* can also be used in zone IV, but it is a special case. It is very hardy, thriving in Finland, for example, but cannot stand the treacherous spring frosts that occur after leafing out. It seems to think that winter is over after the easing of the extreme cold. It also requires hot summers to ripen off the wood and cannot tolerate long warm autumns that extend into December. It would probably do well in the continental climate of Canada and the United States.

## Maples for Wet or Very Dry Sites

Because maples are very accommodating plants, they cope very well with dryness or wetness throughout a large range.

*Acer rubrum* tolerates wet sites very well, and *A. pycnanthum* in Japan grows in very wet conditions. Many species have riverbanks, valleys, or rich bottomlands as their natural habitats. *Acer saccharum* ssp. *floridanum* grows in wet woods, and *A. rubrum* var. *drummondii* from the southern United States grows in deep swamps.

*Acer circinatum* is occasionally seen in dry sites. The Mediterranean species, such as *A. hyrcanum, A. monspessulanum, A. obtusifolium, A. opalus, A. sempervirens,* and *A. syriacum* (syn. *A. obtusifolium*) survive well in hot and dry summers, although they benefit from mild and wet winters.

## Maples for Special Soils

As a rule, maples are not particular regarding soil properties. For example, *Acer campestre,* often thought of as a calcicole, does equally well in acid soil. *Acer pseudoplatanus* has even been used in the colonization of power station ash heaps in Great Britain. A regular supply of water is their major requirement.

*Acer rubrum* prefers a lower pH, acidic substrate. While it will grow in somewhat alkaline soils, it will not develop the characteristic gorgeous autumn color. *Acer campestre* and *A. monspessulanum,* on the other hand, like limey (alkaline) soils (pH above 7), but they will do as well in slightly acid soils. Because maples are very tolerant trees it is worth trying to grow them in a variety of garden settings.

Chapter 2

# Propagation of Maples

D. M. VAN GELDEREN

Before exploring the propagation of individual *Acer* species, several general principles should be stated to provide perspective. First, all species of *Acer* may be propagated from seed. Unfortunately, however, viable seed is not always available, and as a consequence many species sold in the trade are propagated by vegetative means. Second, all named cultivars must be propagated vegetatively. Third, a group of species or hybrids (a grex) should not be propagated or distributed under a cultivar name (as has been done in the past with *A. davidii* 'George Forrest', *A. davidii* 'Ernest Wilson', and others). Fourth, it is wise to propagate formae vegetatively if the propagules are to be distributed to botanical collections or in commerce, because formae often do not breed true. Fifth, all the known methods of vegetative propagation can be used to propagate maples. Some methods are very useful and satisfying for amateur propagators, while other, more demanding methods are restricted to professional growers as they require special equipment not always readily available to amateurs.

While it is not the purpose of this book to explain the principles of propagating woody plants (it is assumed that the reader understands the basic techniques), some methods are more suited to individual species and clones than are others.

## METHODS OF PROPAGATION

### Seed

Growing maples from seed is generally an easy procedure. Most species produce viable seed, which is usually harvested in September–October, depending upon weather conditions. Seed collected slightly green in early September typically germinates better the following spring (e.g. *Acer campestre*). The collector should be aware, however, that several species produce parthenocarpic fruits. Such species produce what looks like a wonderful crop of fruit but one that is very disappointing when the nutlets are opened. *Acer griseum* is the most infamous species in this regard. Several species are dioecious; that is, solitary trees cannot produce viable seed. Only when several trees of both sexes are growing closely together can one expect a good crop. Well-known examples are *Acer carpinifolium* and *A. diabolicum*. Some species produce seed that germinates readily the following spring, while others require a stratification period of 12–18 months or more.

Seed must be harvested in the early autumn, but not before mid-September. After collection it can be either sown immediately in frames or stored for sowing in the spring. However the seed is stored, it is essential to keep it cool and fresh. It should not be stored in plastic bags for any protracted length of time; paper bags are usually better.

When seed is collected in the autumn, the embryo is not fully developed, so it is necessary to keep the seed moist and damp to permit maturation. Under no circumstances should seed be dried (e.g., laid out in the sun) or the embryo may be damaged. All stored seed requires proper conditions of humidity. The amateur gathering only a small quantity of seed should place it in a polyethylene bag with moist (not wet) peat, tie and label the bag, then store the seed in a refrigerator at about 40°F (5°C). Storing seed in sharp sand immediately after collection is a good and widely used method to improve rate of germination, but collectors should beware that a few seeds usually germinate unexpectedly early. Also, it is important to protect seed stored in sand from mice.

If the seed is sown immediately after harvesting, the soil should be covered with dry, sharp, clean sand to avoid undesired moss growth. Self-picked seed usually germinates freely the following spring, but seed bought from commercial sources often germinates slowly or not at all the following spring because it has been dried too much. Such seed must be stratified a year in moist sand. If dry seed must be sown, it is wise to soak it for a few hours before sowing. Seed with a very hard, woody nutlet, like that of *Acer griseum* and its allies, must always be stratified for at least a year.

Small quantities of seeds or seeds of rare species are preferably sown in trays or boxes. Large quantities of the commoner species may be sown in beds in the nursery. Good garden soil should be used or a medium available in the trade if suitable soil is not available. Beds, trays, and frames must be well-drained as lack of oxygen in the soil considerably stunts seedling development. Soil pH is also important. If sandy, soil should have a pH of about 5.5; if loamy, 6.0; and if peaty, 4.5. If the pH is too low, the rooting system will not develop well, resulting in weak growth. The soil should be reasonably free of weed seeds. Once again, beware of mice; they adore maple seed.

Seeds must not be sown too deeply and never deeper than the diameter of the nutlets. Usually the seeds germinates in April, so the tiny seedlings must be protected against late spring frosts. During the summer the seedbeds and trays must be kept clean with all weeds removed while still small. Seedlings of most species will easily grow 40–60 cm (18–24 in) tall, and some fast-growing species will produce seedlings well over 1 m (39 in) in height in the first year.

Seedlings may be attacked by the *Pythium* fungus, which causes them to wilt. To control this fungus, the seedlings should be sprayed four to six times with a good fungicide. Those seeds sown too deeply are especially prone to attack by *Pythium.*

Seedlings are lifted in November and can be planted in the nursery the following spring. They may also be lifted and potted after they have developed their first true leaves, although subsequent growth is reduced. Usually seedlings of scarce or valuable species are potted in March before they leaf out and treated as container-grown plants. It is preferable to place these liners in a lath-house, providing shade and protection against the hot sun, strong winds, and other unfavorable weather conditions.

Seedlings must be well watered in dry spells, and it is often best to keep them in a cool greenhouse for several weeks or months. They can be brought into a lath-house when their root systems are well developed.

## Layering

Vegetative propagation of maples is carried out in several ways. Probably the simplest and cheapest means is by layering. Practically every maple species may be propagated by layering, making this a very convenient method for amateur gardeners. Nevertheless, the method has some distinct disadvantages: not only is it very time-consuming, but the production of any significant quantity of new plants is not possible unless large numbers of mother-plants (stools) are used.

Only a few maple species and cultivars can be propagated economically by layering—mainly the cultivars of *Acer saccharinum* and *A. cappadocicum.* For this purpose stools are formed, the branches are pinned to the soil, and the young shoots are earthed up. Usually the rooted layers can be removed from the stools a year later. In earlier years, tens of thousands of *Acer palmatum* 'Atropurpureum' were produced by layering, but the technique has been abandoned in most commercial nurseries in favor of more modern methods of propagation.

## Cuttings

A second method of vegetative propagation involves taking softwood cuttings. Many species of maple are easily propagated in this way. If cuttings are taken in June or July, the rooting percentage is usually quite high. Alternatively, stock plants can be brought into growth in the greenhouse in early spring (February–March). Softwood cuttings taken and rooted this early will frequently develop new growth before autumn. However, such cuttings die, not infrequently, during the winter.

Hardwood cuttings are not a reliable method of propagation. Thus cuttings must be taken before hard wood develops. The leaves must be undamaged and free of any fungus or insect eggs. Cuttings from mother plants growing in the open should be made in early summer, while cuttings from forced mother plants can be made earlier in the year.

Cuttings are prepared by leaving two to three pairs of leaves and one pair of buds at the base of each cutting. The cuttings must be superficially wounded by removing a very thin slice of the bark at the base. They should be disinfected with a fungicide and then dipped in rooting hormone (1 percent indolebutyric acid in talcum powder) before being inserted in trays containing a medium of 2:1 peat and sharp sand. The freshly inserted cuttings should be covered with the thinnest available polyethylene sheet. Once the cuttings have rooted, the trays can be moved to another place in the greenhouse for hardening off.

Rooted cuttings must show new growth during the summer before being pricked out. Lacking such new growth, they usually do not survive, and if they do, they grow poorly and later often collapse. The new growth vigorously activates regrowth the next spring, particularly with cultivars of *Acer palmatum.*

A significant disadvantage of propagation by cuttings is that all the roots are clonal. A number of species and cultivars, including *Acer palmatum,* do not form vigorous trees on their own roots. Furthermore, *Verticillium dahliae* (wilt disease) can cause very serious losses in *A. palmatum* cultivars. Some well-known cultivars such as 'Atropurpureum' and 'Bloodgood' are quite susceptible. Clonal plants on clonal roots are far more susceptible those grafted on species rootstock. In this author's opinion, commercial propagation of cultivars of *A. palmatum* by cuttings is to be avoided, although many growers have a different view.

## Grafting

Grafting, a third and very important method of vegetative propagation, is done at different times of the year and with a variety of techniques, depending upon the grower's preference. The usual technique is side grafting on potted rootstocks. Unfortunately, grafting is neither easy nor successful for the typical amateur gardener. It is better left to professional nursery personnel.

Budding to produce vigorous long whips suitable for growing into well-formed trees for both street plantings and gardens is possible on a large scale. Grafting is also a good method for producing shrubs of *Acer negundo* cultivars.

The selection of a suitable rootstock is of critical importance in grafting. Rootstocks must be selected from species in the same section if the graft is to take. All cultivars should preferably be grafted on seedlings of the parent species.

Rootstocks used for summer grafting must be potted early in the spring in clay or rigid plastic pots 7 cm (3 in) in diameter. These rootstocks require much attention as they dry out easily. Before planting them in a good potting medium, the roots must be carefully pruned. Alternatively, transplanted seedlings of first quality with a well-developed root system make excellent rootstocks. One week before grafting starts, potted rootstocks must be lifted and brought to the greenhouse to dry for a week or so to decrease sap flow. All leaves must be removed from the rootstock to force sap to the scion.

The grafting technique used is the same in summer and winter. Rubber ties are better than string. Most growers graft "Dissectum types" on 30- to 35-cm (12- to 14-in) rootstocks. In my opinion, this is not wise; rather, the graft must be placed as low as possible so the graft wound will disappear into the soil. One-year-old grafts of Dissectum types must be staked for the first 2 years to obtain a straight central stem. If very strong, long understocks are disposed, it is possible to graft Dissectum types and other weeping forms on 100- to 120-cm (40- to 47-in) standards, thus producing little trees.

Grafting can also be undertaken in February. If it is done in a greenhouse, the rootstocks need not be potted in advance but may be potted and grafted at the same time. The advantages of winter grafting are that there is no need for scions with undamaged leaves and that the rootstocks can be used immediately after potting. The major disadvantage is that the unified grafts must be kept in the greenhouse until mid-May to avoid late frosts. The greenhouse must be heated, which increases the costs quite considerably.

For winter grafting the scions must be taken in frost-free weather conditions. To avoid problems, it is wise to use every good day in December before Christmas to cut scions that can then be stored in a cold storage chamber at 2°C (36°F), well packed in polyethylene bags, until the rootstocks have broken dormancy and are prepared for grafting. The scions cut must be first choice, young twigs of the current year, with three to four undamaged, well-developed pairs of buds in winter. Beware of insect eggs, which hatch readily in the greenhouse and can destroy young grafts. Two-year-old wood can be taken for dwarf forms or for densely branched cultivars.

Grafted plants must be kept in the greenhouse for 8–10 weeks for winter grafts and 4–6 weeks for summer grafts, depending on weather conditions. The grafts should be covered with the thinnest possible polyethylene sheet to retain moisture, rather than placing them under a mist system, which only encourages *Verticillium.* Typically, about 4 weeks after grafting in July, the scions are unified and can be carefully hardened off. Once hardened off they can be either repotted in larger clay pots and planted outside, or stored in their 7-cm (3-in) pots in a tunnel or a frame for repotting early the following spring. Of course, they also can be potted in rigid containers or planted directly in the field. The latter method has been largely abandoned in recent years due to losses in the field.

Cultivars of *Acer palmatum* may be grafted in either summer or winter. July is a good month to graft because the scions have ripened their first growth but are not yet too woody. It is essential that the scions have undamaged leaves. Usually three to four pairs of leaves are sufficient. This is particularly important in plants whose nodes are long, as a reasonable scion length may have grown no more leaves. Scions of the dwarf forms will usually have more leaf pairs.

Summer grafting of maples other than cultivars of *Acer palmatum* and *A. japonicum* is done the same way, except that the process is initiated 4–6 weeks later, as scions of fast-growing cultivars need more time to ripen. Consequently, grafting is done in September. The same procedure can be repeated in February.

Hardwood grafting is employed for only a few slow-growing cultivars of *Acer pseudo-*

*platanus,* as a rule. The procedure is done in the same way as for *Prunus, Malus,* and other genera, and the results are quite variable. Hardwood scions are suitable for grafting both in the greenhouse and outside. Outside winter grafting, for example, is widely done with *Acer pseudoplatanus* 'Brilliantissimum'.

## PROPAGATION OF INDIVIDUAL SPECIES AND CULTIVARS

***A. acuminatum.*** This species is preferably propagated by seed. As the species is dioecious, it is very important to ascertain that the harvested fruit contains viable seed. Softwood cuttings taken in June usually give good results. Grafting on *A. spicatum* is possible, but the results are usually poor.

***A. argutum.*** This species is preferably propagated by seed, but as it is dioecious, verify that the seed is viable. Cuttings taken in early summer root well, and grafting on *A. spicatum* is easy.

***A. barbinerve.*** See ***A. argutum.***

***A. buergerianum.*** This species is easily propagated by seed, but make sure the seed is viable. Chinese or Japanese seed is usually good, but fruit of garden origin is often parthenocarpic. All cultivars of this species can be grafted on *A. buergerianum* seedlings, preferably in July. Cuttings taken in June–July usually root easily, but overwintering can be difficult. Rooted cuttings should be potted in early spring or later the same summer.

***A. caesium.*** This rare species is usually propagated by seed. Try to obtain seed from its natural habitat; seed merchants in India supply it regularly. Grafting on *A. pseudoplatanus* and *A. caesium* ssp. *giraldii* is possible, but usually leads to poor results.

***A. campbellii*** and its subspecies. Grafting on *A. palmatum* yields good results. Propagation by seed is preferable, but only occasionally possible as true seed is usually not available.

***A. campestre.*** Seed procured from commercial sources usually must be stratified after soaking as it is too dry and too deeply dormant. Freshly collected seed will partially germinate the following spring and the balance the next spring. All cultivars must be grafted on *A. campestre* rootstock, either in summer or winter, in the greenhouse. Some slow-growing forms may be propagated by cuttings. The few tree forms, such as 'Elsrijk', are budded in early summer. The purple-leaved clones like 'Red Shine' and 'Royal Ruby' grow faster when budded than when grafted in the greenhouse, but they do not easily form well-branched shrubs. All the vigorous cultivars can be layered.

***A. capillipes.*** This species is easily grown by seed. Be certain of the provenance of the mother tree as the species hybridizes easily in gardens with related species. Superior forms of *A. capillipes* can be better propagated by cuttings, which root easily, or grafted on any seedling in section *Macrantha.*

***A. cappadocicum*** and its subspecies. The species and its subspecies *lobelii* are usually grown from seed. Budding of the subspecies usually gives bad results. Grafting on *A. platanoides* is rather easy. The cultivars are often propagated by layering as they easily form stools, which produce many layers. *Acer cappadocicum* ssp. *sinicum* is usually grafted in the summer in a greenhouse. Seed of this subspecies is hardly ever available.

***A. carpinifolium.*** This species is always propagated by seed. Attention must be paid to the germination rate of the harvested fruit. When no seed is available, layering is the only suitable method. Grafting is impossible as no compatible understock is known. The species' only cultivar can be grafted on it.

***A. caudatifolium.*** As seed is not available, this species is always and easily grafted on any seedling of section *Macrantha.*

***A. caudatum*** and its subspecies. See ***A. spicatum.*** If no seed is available, grafting on *A. spicatum* seedlings is a good alternative.

***A. circinatum.*** This species is easily grown from seed, but do not let the seed dry out as the germination rate can become very low. Seed of garden origin is of the same quality as collected wild seed. Cultivars of this species must be grafted on *A. palmatum,* which is, strangely enough, a better rootstock than *A. circinatum* itself.

***A. cissifolium.*** This species is usually propagated by layering. Almost all plants in cultivation are female, so viable seed is uncommon. It is preferable to select male and female trees in such cases and to plant a group in an arboretum. Plants grow easily from cuttings.

***A.*** × ***conspicuum.*** This hybrid and its cultivars are easily grafted on any seedling of section *Macrantha.* Cuttings are possible but not easy; because the leaves and internodes of this hybrid are quite large, cuttings wilt easily.

***A. coriaceifolium.*** Propagation by seed is the only method.

***A.*** × ***coriaceum.*** This hybrid can be grafted without difficulty on *A. pseudoplatanus.*

***A. crataegifolium.*** Propagation by seed is preferable, and seed of garden origin can be used as this species does not hybridize freely. Grafting the species and its cultivars on seedlings of section *Macrantha* is reasonably easy.

***A. davidii*** and its subspecies. This variable species is very easily grown from seed, but usually the seedlings are hybrids or so variable that it is not wise to plant them as true *A. davidii* unless carefully checked. These seedlings are, in fact, useful only as rootstocks for all the species and cultivars of section *Macrantha.* Good clones of *A. davidii,* its subspecies *grosseri,* and its cultivars must be vegetatively propagated by means of cuttings or grafting. The best time for grafting is early September when the scions are well ripened. It is important to control the root system of the rootstocks in the pot before grafting as poorly rooted rootstocks die easily the following winter. Cuttings taken in July usually root rather well, but regrowth in spring can be problematic. Only *A. davidii* 'Serpentine' strikes easily from cuttings and regrows well the following spring.

***A. diabolicum.*** This species is very difficult to propagate. Viable seed is almost never available because the species is dioecious, and grafting on related species is impossible because there is no good species in this section that can be used as a rootstock. Only the remotely related *A. pseudoplatanus* and *A. rubrum* can be used, and the results are usually very poor.

***A. distylum.*** This species is easily grown from seed. Seed of garden origin is perfectly satisfactory, but only occasionally available. Cuttings can be used when no seed is available, but regrowth is difficult.

***A. erianthum.*** This species can be grown from seed, which is occasionally available. Grafting on *A. palmatum* is a good substitute.

***A. glabrum*** and its subspecies. This species and its subspecies can be grown from seed, but seed is only rarely available. Seed collected in the wild usually germinates well, but due to the hard coat takes 2 years to do so. Propagation by cuttings is difficult as *A. glabrum* and its allies lose their leaves early in the autumn and undamaged leaves are hard to find in July. The current year's wood ripens very early.

***A. griseum.*** This species produces abundant fruits, but unfortunately most of them are empty as the species has an unusually strong tendency to form parthenocarpic fruit. Fruits must be examined carefully before sowing. It is wise to break open 50 or more to see whether the harvested fruits possess embryos. Stratifying is essential. The stratified seed can be sown in October to avoid damage to germinating seedlings in early spring frosts. Propagation by cuttings is possible but unreliable and economically unacceptable. Layering can be used to produce a few plants for friends.

***A. grosseri.*** See ***A. davidii.***

***A. heldreichii*** and its subspecies. This species and its subspecies are propagated preferably from seed, but unhybridized seed of garden origin is almost never obtainable. Seedlings of putative hybrid origin are now named *A.* × ***pseudo-heldreichii.*** Some seeds do come true and the resulting seedlings can easily be distinguished from hybrids. Grafting on *A. pseudoplatanus* is a good substitute for growing from seed. Clonally propagated trees are worthy of a place in collections.

***A. henryi.*** See ***A. cissifolium.*** This species is propagated by layering, and also from seed. Wild seed is sometimes available from local sources.

***A. hyrcanum.*** This rare tree must always be propagated from seed. Grafting is unsatisfactory as there is no appropriate rootstock. The species is compatible with *A. pseudoplatanus,* but the results from grafting are poor.

***A. japonicum*** and its cultivars. This species and its cultivars are usually grafted on *A. palmatum* in July or February. There are no particular exceptions to this rule. Seed of true *A. japonicum* is almost never available, so grafting is the only method available. Cuttings are very poor so never grown.

***A. laevigatum*** and its allies. When no seed is available, which is usually the case, all species from the series can be grafted on *A. palmatum.* These species are easy to raise from cuttings and the results are good. Overwintering may be difficult, however, as all species of this series are tender.

***A. longipes*** and its subspecies. Here again seed is quite scarce. Grafting on *A. platanoides* is a good possibility if the potted rootstocks have developed a good root system. Cuttings are unsuccessful. Layering might be possible, but is not practiced.

***A. macrophyllum.*** This species is generally grown from seed which is readily available. The few cultivars should preferably be grafted on the species itself rather than on *A. platanoides.*

***A. mandshuricum.*** It is very difficult to obtain viable seed of this rare species. The few seeds available from botanic gardens are usually old and dry. To make propagation by seed still more difficult, most fruits are parthenocarpic. Grafting on *A. griseum* has proved unsuccessful to date. Cuttings are possible.

***A. maximowiczianum.*** See ***A. griseum.***

***A. micranthum.*** This species is propagated preferably by seed, but seed is only occasionally available. Grafting on seedlings of any species of section *Macrantha* is quite easy.

***A. mono*** and its subspecies. Since seed is only rarely available, this species and its allies are usually propagated by grafting on *A. platanoides.* It is wise to graft as low as possible since *A. platanoides* is more vigorous than *A. mono* and suckers appear regularly. These suckers can take over the whole plant until the *A. mono* cultivar is lost. This is especially true with the variegated cultivars. Seeds of *A. mono* ssp. *okamotoanum,* which are rarely available, have an embryo problem, so few germinate. The subspecies may be grafted on *A. platanoides.*

***A. monspessulanum*** and its allies. Seed collected in the wild usually germinates fairly well, while seed of garden origin is often parthenocarpic. Seeds of the subspecies are extremely difficult to obtain, so the only remaining possibilities are growing from cuttings, which is difficult, or grafting on seedlings of *A. monspessulanum,* which are scarce. *Acer pseudoplatanus* can be used as a rootstock but it produces poor plants; suckering and weak grafting wounds are usual. *Acer opalus* might possibly be a good rootstock, but this species is also rare in cultivation and only rarely used as a rootstock.

***A. negundo*** and its allies. The universal rootstock is *A. negundo.* All cultivars and subspecies are grafted or budded on this species. The strong-growing cultivars are usually budded, producing good long whips the following year that are quite suitable for standard trees. Budding should be done very early, preferably in mid-June, so the budded scions develop a small new shoot the same summer; otherwise losses the following winter can be considerable. Slow-growing forms can be grafted in the greenhouse in July or in February. Grafting produces bushy plants for shrubby forms. Cuttings of *A. negundo* and its cultivars root easily, but are not grown on a large scale.

***A. nikoense*** (syn. *A. maximowiczianum*).

***A. nipponicum.*** The only method to propagate this rare species is by seed, but seed is rarely available as there are very few mature trees in cultivation and many fruits are parthenocarpic. Although the fruits are formed in large clusters, only a few are good and they dry out easily and lose their viability quickly.

***A. oblongum.*** This species is propagated by seed or by grafting on *A. buergerianum.*

***A. obtusifolium.*** This species is propagated preferably by seed, which germinates easily, but is rather hard to obtain. Grafting on *A. monspessulanum* is possible, but rather difficult.

***A. oliverianum*** and its allies. The species can be propagated from seed, but usually it and its allies are propagated by grafting onto *A. palmatum.*

***A. opalus*** and its subspecies. If no seed is available, the only means of propagating is by grafting on *A. pseudoplatanus* or *A. monspessulanum,* which is rather difficult. Seed of garden origin is usually not viable. Propagation by cutting is not done as the wood of this species ripens so quickly that softwood cuttings simply are not present.

***A. palmatum*** and its allies. The species itself is grown from seed, but most of the seedlings serve as a rootstock for the cultivars. It is preferable to graft all the cultivars and the results are usually quite good. Grafting can be done twice a year in July and February. It is essential to use scions with undamaged leaves. Only a few strong-growing cultivars are commercially propagated from cuttings. Plants of the dissected and variegated cultivars on their own roots almost always fail to grow into good plants.

***A. pectinatum*** and its subspecies. This species is propagated preferably from seed. Unfortunately almost all the subspecies are rare and good seed is almost never available. Only subspecies *forrestii* is occasionally grown from seed. To remain true, three subspecies—*taronense, maximowiczii,* and *laxiflorum*—must be grafted on any seedling of section *Macrantha.* This grafting is rather easy if good, ripened scions are taken.

***A. pensylvanicum.*** This species is propagated from seed. Although grafting on *A. pseudoplatanus* is sometimes done, it should be avoided. The few cultivars can be grafted on the species itself.

*A. pentaphyllum.* This rare species does not produce viable seed, so it is usually propagated by cuttings, which are successful. Grafting, however, is the better method and has been done on *A. pseudoplatanus, A. rubrum,* and *A. saccharinum* with good results. *Acer buergerianum* might provide a good rootstock, but it has not been tried. Grafts on *A. palmatum* fail.

***A. platanoides*** and its cultivars. The species is very easily grown from seed. All cultivars can be budded onto the species, especially when whips are required. Side-grafting in the greenhouse is also easy when shrubs are needed. It is better to graft in September than in February. In The Netherlands, winter grafting is only done with scions sent from other countries, and not on a commercial scale.

***A. pseudoplatanus.*** See ***A. platanoides*** as the commercial methods of propagation are much the same. Always use *A. pseudoplatanus* for the rootstock, for budding, and for side-grafting. Hardwood grafting is used for the widely grown cultivars 'Brilliantissimum' and 'Prinz Handjery', both on 120- to 180-cm (47- to 71-in) rootstock. The whips need not necessarily be placed outside, as good grafts with hardwood scions can be done in the greenhouse, placing the whips outside in April or May.

***A. pseudosieboldianum.*** The species and its allies can easily be grafted on *A. palmatum.* Growing plants from seed is also possible, but viable and reliable seed is hardly ever available.

***A. pycnanthum.*** This rare tree from Japan may be propagated by seed, which ripens and is harvested very early in the summer, but seed is rarely available, and there are no mature trees in Europe or North America producing viable seed. Cuttings are possible, but this species can easily be grafted onto *A. rubrum* in the greenhouse, or budded.

***A. rubescens.*** When seed is available, it is preferable to propagate this species by seed. Grafting on any hybridized seedling of section *Macrantha* is also possible and quite easy.

***A. rubrum*** and its allies. This species can be grown from seed, which ripens and must be harvested very early in June. Viability decreases very quickly, so the freshly harvested seed must be sown immediately. Seeds germinate quickly and the young seedlings may grow 30 cm (12 in) the first summer. These seedlings may be used as rootstocks for the many cultivars of *A. rubrum,* or grown as whips for future trees.

Cultivars of *A. rubrum* can be propagated by layering or by grafting. Budding is also possible, but must be done rather early as severe winter damage can occur sometimes if the cultivars are budded on true *A. rubrum.* It is very important to mark the true cultivars as there is very little difference between the juvenile leaves of the rootstock and cultivars. The same holds true for grafted plants.

***A. rufinerve.*** This common species is generally propagated by seed, which is quite easily obtained. Cultivars are grafted onto the species or onto any other seedling of section *Macrantha.*

***A. saccharinum.*** See ***A. rubrum.*** Almost all cultivars are propagated by layering, which is quite productive and easy. The layers usually root in one summer, and, even with only a few roots, they transplant successfully.

***A. saccharum*** and its allies. This maple is generally propagated by seed in North America. In Europe, where viable seed is not easily obtained, this species and its allies are sometimes propagated by layering or from seedlings imported from the United States, but because importing maple plants into Great Britain is prohibited, British growers import seed from the United States. Budding is not practiced in Europe. The many subspecies can theoretically be propagated by seed, but this practice is only very occasionally possible. It is much better to avoid doubtful plants and to graft subspecies and cultivars on *A. saccharum.* Results are often rather poor when grafting is done on *A. saccharinum* and usually bad when done on *A. pseudoplatanus.* The latter rootstock should be avoided if possible as its suckers grow more strongly than the scion. Sometimes, however, there is no better alternative. Grafting is preferably done in September.

***A. sempervirens.*** Grafting on *A. monspessulanum* is a good substitute when no seed is available. Although grafting on *A. pseudoplatanus* is also possible, the results are usually poor.

***A. shirasawanum*** and its allies. These species can be grafted on *A. palmatum* as easily as if they were cultivars of *A. palmatum.*

***A. sieboldianum*** and its cultivars. Grafting onto *A. palmatum* rootstock is the easiest and most certain way to propagate this species and its cultivars. Seed is often of doubtful origin and hybridizes freely with related species.

***A. sinopurpurascens.*** See ***A. diabolicum.***

***A. spicatum.*** This species is easily propagated from seed, but, unfortunately, seed is only occasionally available. Propagation by cuttings produces strong plants.

***A. stachyophyllum*** and its subspecies. Most fruits are parthenocarpic and do not contain viable seed. When the seed is good, it germinates easily and the seedlings grow quite vigorously in the first year. If no seed is available, cuttings taken in June–July are usually successful.

***A. sterculiaceum*** and its subspecies. This group causes considerable difficulties. All the subspecies are dioecious, so seed is seldom available unless several trees are growing together, which is almost never the case. Grafting is quite difficult, as there is no suitable rootstock in this section. The only possibility is grafting on *A. pseudoplatanus,* which is more or less successful. Layering is also problematic, as the branches are stiff and brittle. The same is true for cuttings, which are practically impossible to root.

***A. tataricum*** and its subspecies. *Acer tataricum* and subspecies *ginnala* are easily grown from seed. The other subspecies are better grafted on subspecies *ginnala* to keep them true, as seed of garden origin seldom comes true. The few cultivars can easily be rooted from cuttings or grafted on seedlings of subspecies *ginnala.*

***A. tegmentosum.*** This species is propagated by seed, which is occasionally available. Grafting on any seedling of section *Macrantha* is no problem.

***A. triflorum.*** See ***A. griseum.*** Grafting onto *A. rubrum* has succeeded once, though the resulting plant, which flourishes in the Esveld Aceretum, Boskoop, The Netherlands, still throws a few suckers.

***A. truncatum*** and its allies. This species and its allies are propagated preferably by seed. The cotyledons of the species, which are not visible, remain under the soil surface, and the true leaves develop immediately when the seedlings appear above ground. This is the safest way to check if a seedling is truly *A. truncatum.* When no seed is available, grafting on *A. platanoides* is possible, but the results are usually rather poor.

***A. tschonoskii*** and its subspecies. Whenever possible this species and its subspecies are propagated by seed, but grafting on any seedling of section *Macrantha* is a good substitute.

***A. velutinum*** and its allies. These species are propagated preferably by seed. Grafting on *A. pseudoplatanus* can be done, but only a small percent of the grafts take.

***A.* × *zoeschense.*** This hybrid is propagated by grafting on *A. campestre* or by layering. Layers root easily.

Chapter 3

# Maple Diseases and Pests

DR. H. J. OTERDOOM

This chapter provides a general account of the ills to which maples are heir. The discussion is deliberately general for two reasons. First, to deal in detail with all the causes of the ills and misfortunes of maple trees worldwide, this book would assume proportions of a multivolume encyclopedia. So many, and usually local, are the environmental factors, diseases, insects, and so forth that can cause problems, a complete treatment in this book would be quite out of place. Second, the remedies for these ills differ widely, not just from one region of the world to another, but from one nation or state to the next. The reasons for these differences in both diagnosis and treatment range from differing disease and insect populations, through differing environmental conditions and differing traditional practices, to differing governmental regulatory policies. Further, the principles of identification and treatment change with time. Readers faced with a declining or manifestly unhappy tree are strongly encouraged to contact a local horticulturist for assistance.

With this explanation and recommendation to seek local advice for both diagnosis and treatment, let us turn to some general considerations relating to the health and viability of maples.

## ENVIRONMENTAL AGENTS

Maples in temperate climates are seldom impacted negatively by environmental agents. They are not especially vulnerable to high temperatures, frost, drought, gales, pollution, and so forth. Red (*Acer rubrum*) and silver (*A. saccharinum*) maples tolerate excessive water more readily than other species. Sugar maple (*A. saccharum*) is susceptible to so-called maple decline, seen in built-up areas and probably caused by soil compaction, although it is possible that nematodes and the use of salt in winter to clear roads of ice and snow also play a part.

Maples resist wind well. *Acer pseudoplatanus* is used in western and northern Great Britain along the coastal areas and in the offshore islands to bear the brunt of Atlantic gales. The densely ramified, adventitious roots, which often grow rather deep, give these trees a solid foothold.

In alkaline soils, chlorosis sometimes develops as a result of iron deficiency. Norway (*A. platanoides*), red, silver, and sugar maples seem particularly sensitive, but in general maples are not particular as to soil pH.

Squirrels may wound young red and sugar maple trees to drink the sap, but human beings cause the most extensive and continued damage with mowing machines, weedkillers and other chemicals, vandalism, and so forth. Nevertheless, the widespread human abuse of trees and all flora is not confined to maples.

## VIRAL AGENTS

While maple mosaic (maple mottle), peach rosette virus of maple, tobacco ringspot, and other viral diseases have been recorded, virus infections of maple are not common. Trees infected with a virus may be stunted, with dense green foliage, but not all viruslike symptoms are caused by viruses. Some eriphyid mites and aphids cause feeding damage that resembles virus symptoms, as do some nutrient imbalances. A multitude of genetic abnormalities also causes viruslike changes in color, pigment distribution, and growth forms. Finally, deformities produced by hormone weedkillers often resemble viral symptoms.

For ease of identification, the symptoms of most virus diseases can be placed in four categories:

1. Lack of chlorophyll formation in normally green organs
2. Dwarfing or inhibition of growth
3. Distorted growth of all or part of the plant
4. Necrotic areas and lesions

Light green areas on leaves or yellow or white flecks take a variety of forms. If the affected areas are relatively large and appear in a random, patchwork fashion, the symptom is called a *mosaic* or *mottle.* If the affected tissue develops open rings or ellipses, the pattern is called a *ringspot,* or, if the circles or ellipses are closed, it is called a *blotch.* A linear form is known as a *line pattern.*

Virus infections may affect the normal growth habit, resulting in a variety of atypical formations of plant parts. Affected leaves may twist and curl or become blistered or puckered, usually resulting from the normal growth of uninfected cells near those dying. Witches' brooms may be formed, branches may be flattened (fasciation) or limp, rubbery and unable to support themselves.

A tree infected by a virus will often live for many years after becoming infected. The virus may go completely unnoticed by the average homeowner and often by all but the trained plant pathologist.

## BACTERIAL AGENTS

Bacterial leafspot caused by *Pseudomonas acris* is seen in California on the leaves of Oregon maple (*Acer macrophyllum*). Crown gall caused by *Agrobacterium tumefaciens* is unknown in maples, as is fire blight (*Erwinia amylovora*). Clearly, few bacteria harm maples.

## FUNGAL AGENTS

### Sooty Molds

Sooty molds are caused by several species of fungi of various genera but primarily by dark-colored *Actinomyces* of the order Dothideales. These fungi, such as *Capnodia* (*Fumago*) and *Limacinia,* are not parasitic but live on "honeydew," the sugary deposit formed on plant parts from the droppings of insects, particularly aphids and scale. The fungal growth—black, papery layers that can be peeled off the underlying leaf—is so abundant that it gives the leaf the typical black, sooty appearance that also blocks much light from the plant. The presence of this sooty mold fungi is not usually a significant indication of the health of the plant but does indicate the presence of insects and may warn of a severe aphid or scale problem. Sooty molds can be identified easily by the black, sooty mycelial growth that can be completely wiped off a leaf or stem with a moistened cloth, paper, or hand, leaving a clean, healthy-looking plant surface underneath. No control measures are necessary against this fungus.

## Tar Spot

Tar spot caused by the fungus *Rhytisma acerinum* is one of the most striking fungal infections on maple leaves. Red and silver maples are commonly infected in the eastern United States. In Europe *Acer pseudoplatanus* is susceptible and *A. platanoides* is affected only in Finland, where *A. pseudoplatanus* does not occur. As a rule, tar spot is not a serious problem, and maples grown in large cities with some air pollution escape this unsightly infection.

*Rhytisma punctatum* is another leaf spot fungus causing speckled tar spot on leaves. The minute, black spotting occurs on many species along the Pacific Coast in North America, but tar spot caused by *R. acerinum* is rare in that region. Groups of raised spots about the size of a pinhead appear on the upper side of the leaf.

## Cankers

Fungi of the genus *Nectria* may cause cankers. *Nectria cinnabarina* is widespread as a hardwood saprophyte and occasionally becomes parasitic, causing either cankers around wounds and the bases of dead branches or die-back of twigs and branches—especially in the United States but also in Europe. Reddish fungal fruiting bodies develop in large numbers.

Trunk cankers of box elder (*Acer negundo*), Norway maple, red maple, and sugar maple occur in North America from the Great Lakes states to the Northeast and to Quebec, Canada. Often they are caused by the fungus *Futypella parasitica*. Trees in the 2.5–9 cm (1–3 in) diameter class, especially those not growing optimally, are often killed, while those over 12.5 cm (5 in) in diameter are seldom killed. The disease is damaging only to stands containing a high proportion of sugar maple. A dead branch stub is usually present in the center of a canker. Initial infection occurs when a tree is young. Cankers on trunks can rarely be eradicated by surgical methods once they have become extensive, but cankers on branches can be destroyed by removing and discarding the affected branch. Removing dead branches and avoiding unnecessary injury to the tree are probably the best means of preventing canker formation. Beware of the barrier zones made by the tree (see the many Shigo references in the Bibliography for further discussion of this point).

## Verticillium

One of the most widespread diseases of *Acer* is *Verticillium* wilt, which occurs not only in cultivars of *Acer palmatum* but also in native forests across the United States. It has been seen in a hedge row in Japan. It often occurs as a twig die-back but does not kill the tree. The disease is caused by *Verticillium dahliae* and *V. albo-atrum*, which are the same according to North American mycologists but different according to European experts. *Verticillium* propagules can survive in the soil for up to 13 years (Dickinson & Lucas 1977). Several forms of this very important maple parasite have been distinguished (Phillips & Burdekin 1982). The first is a chronic wilt. Progressive wilting of the foliage and crown die-back lead to the death of the crown, usually within a few years but sometimes within the season of infection. The second form is an acute wilt in which all the foliage of the crown suddenly wilts and dies, generally in late summer, and hangs dried and withered on the tree after normal leaf fall. In the third form, described by Strong (1936), trees are apparently healthy at the end of the season, but fail to flush the following spring. All three forms of the disease have been observed in Britain by Piearce (1972).

Apart from remaining viable for many years as a propagule in the soil, this pathogen colonizes roots of many species in which it does not cause disease, behaving as a saprophyte. This ability to colonize appears to be important in maintaining the infection potential of the organism. A significant population increase occurs only after colonization in a susceptible plant. As yet, there is no defense against this fungus. Nursery owners have found that grafted Japanese maples, especially *Acer palmatum,* have a higher resistance to *Verticillium* than those on their own roots. The soil can be disinfected both by chemicals and by heat or steam.

### Other Fungal Agents

*Ganoderma* rot may lead to rapid decline of trees along city streets. In Europe it is very rare, but the fruiting body of this polypore fungus is often used in flower arrangements in Japan. Other polypores may cause heartrot but the trees are not without defenses (Shigo 1983, 1985).

Sapstreak was first found in the United States in 1944 in North Carolina. The fungus *Ceratocystis coerulescens* is the cause of this disease, which kills trees from the top down.

Trunk decay caused by *Valsa leucostomoides* is seen in the New England states in sugar maples.

Sooty bark disease, caused by *Cryptostroma corticale,* is seen as a saprophyte on sugar maple logs in the United States and Canada, causing maple bark stripper's disease, a pulmonary ailment in humans. In Great Britain the disease has been found on *Acer pseudoplatanus* in the London area, where it seems to be encouraged by hot summers.

*Fusarium, Botrytis,* and *Pythia* are serious threats, as they are everywhere in the world in every species of plant. Frost damage or a drought may initiate an attack. Thickly crowded seedlings are especially susceptible (damping off). The best thing growers can do to control these threats is to create the best possible growing environment for their plants. It is also advisable to destroy sick plants.

Maples are occasionally attacked by *Armillaria mellea,* though they are not particularly susceptible to it. This scourge is known as honey or shoestring fungus. There is no consensus about the virulence of this parasite. Usually it only attacks and kills trees weakened by drought or waterlogging, but this is true of most pests and diseases. Currently it is presumed that four or five distinct subspecies of differing virulence exist.

Other maple diseases caused by fungi are *Phomopsis* blight, seen in Norway maples used as street trees in the United States.

Powdery mildews in maples are seldom serious.

## GALLS

Galls result from the pathological development of plant tissue and are induced by the stimulus of a parasitic organism. The stimulus is believed to be a growth-regulating chemical produced by the parasite, as normal cells are again produced if the parasite leaves the host or dies. Each gall-making species causes an excrescence structurally different from all others. Thus a gall-making organism can be identified without actually being seen, by observing the structure of the gall and by noting the species of host plant.

Galls seldom lead to serious problems in maples. About 95 percent of the known galls are caused by nematodes, mites, and insects. The remaining 5 percent are caused by bacteria, fungi, and viruses. Galls may develop on any of the actively growing parts of plants, from root tips to the growing points of the shoots.

Maple spindle gall caused by *Vasates aceris-crumena* occurs most frequently on sugar maple. Maple bladder gall mite, *Vasates quadripes,* is most common on silver and red maple. Both spindle and bladder galls occur on the upper sides of the leaves. Sometimes leaf distortion occurs in heavy infestations. Many eryphyid mite species produce galls on maples in Europe. These are often seen as brick-red, rounded or pointed excrescences about 5 mm (0.2 in) long on the upper leaf surface.

*Acer pseudoplatanus* can harbor root galls.

## INSECTS

Maples are not particularly subject to serious insect infestations. Comprehensive information about insects can be found in Johnson and Lyon (1976, 1988).

The Amur maple, *Acer tataricum* ssp. *A. ginnala,* is among host plants of the fourlined plant bug, *Poecilocapsus lineatus,* which is widely distributed in the northern United States and Canada. Other insects found in North America include the boxelder bug, *Leptocoris trivittatus,* colonizing *A. negundo.* Similar to it is *Leptocoris rubrolineata,* which is found only in the Pacific states. None of these insects have yet appeared in Europe.

### Aphids

The most common plant insect pests are aphids, and maples, too, do not escape their interest. The most serious population build-up of aphids occurs in the spring when the sap flow is strongest and its amino acid content highest. Young trees of many species can be dismally maimed by aphids. Interestingly, maples are host to aphid populations that do not transmit disease and as a consequence have gone unnoticed for ages. This is borne out by the following stories.

The aphid *Periphyllus californiensis* was first identified on *Acer palmatum* at the University of California at Berkeley by a Japanese botanist. Subsequent investigation proved that it is a common inhabitant of *A. palmatum* and its relatives in eastern Asia.

Another aphid, *Drepanosiphum oregonensis,* was discovered for the first time on *Acer macrophyllum* in western North America. It eventually turned out to be native to the eastern Mediterranean region on *A. monspessulanum* and *A. opalus,* though it was unknown until discovered in North America.

Aphid species often are monophagous, living on a particular species of tree. Under some circumstances, however, a specific aphid will reside on related maples, although only temporarily. Thus each maple species has particular aphids living on it. Only one species of the genus *Drepanosiphum* is polyphagous. It feeds on most maple species, as does *Periphyllus testudinacea.*

Most aphid species living on trees move to a secondary host during the summer, but those specific to maples never do. Aphids occurring on milk sap maples (section *Platanoidea*), for example, do not exhibit a summer diapause but simply move to the petioles or even the roots. According to Dr. Hille Ris Lambers (pers. com.), aphids seldom transfer fungi and diseases to maples as their manner of piercing the leaf tissue, without injecting a chemical, precludes this secondary infection.

Maple species are host to aphids belonging to the genera *Drepanaphis* and *Periphyllus,* of which large populations can develop due to the absence of natural control organisms. When maples are heavily infested by aphids, copious amounts of honeydew secreted by the insects collect on leaves and objects beneath them. Leaves covered with honeydew collect dust and dirt, or, when sooty mold develops, the affected leaves may stop functioning and drop prematurely. It is not uncommon for silver and Norway maple to nearly defoliate in the United States.

The woolly alder aphid, *Prociphilus tessalatus,* produces white, waxy filaments prolifically, the distinctive sign of its presence on infested plants. Its biology is of special interest to the naturalist: two hosts are required, alder and silver maple.

## Comstock Mealybug

Another maple enemy is the Comstock mealybug, *Pseudococcus comstockii,* which is believed to have originated in Asia, though it was first reported in the United States in 1918 at two distant points—California and New York. Plant injury is caused by the removal of sap and the formation of knots and adventitious growth.

## Scales

Other insects that feed on maples are the scales, including cottony cushion scale, *Icerya purchasi;* cottony maple scale, *Pulvinaria innumerabilis;* and cottony maple leaf scale, *Pulvinaria acericola.* These insects do not usually occur in the same area. The maple leaf mealy bug or maple phenacoccus, *Phenacoccus acericola,* is found from the northeastern United States west to Minnesota and south to Tennessee. Another species attacking maples is *Pulvinaria floccifera,* which has two common names in North America: cottony camellia scale and cottony taxus scale. The black scale, *Saissetia oleae,* is one of the most common and destructive soft scales in California, Florida, and the Gulf states. It is a common pest of greenhouse-grown plants in many other states. Its host list is extremely long and includes maples.

A new menace to trees in urban areas in the United Kingdom is horse chestnut scale, *Pulvinaria regalis,* which was first recorded in 1964 and has since spread from eastern Britain to towns throughout southern England and the Midlands. The highest level of infestation occurs on trees growing in difficult sites, such as by sidewalks or along tarmac roads. This epidemic confirms that most diseases and pests attack unthrifty trees. We are, perhaps, beginning to see concrete evidence of what arboriculturists have been preaching for years: trees are not likely to thrive when forced to grow too close to new buildings, by sidewalks, or in car parks due to compaction of the root soil, nutrient deficiencies, and drainage problems.

Many other scales attack maples. They are difficult to distinguish so readers should turn to local horticulturists or entomologists for identification and recommended procedures.

## Leafhoppers

Leafhoppers are strange-looking creatures with bizarre forms. Some have been described as resembling miniature dinosaurs. They suck sap with their sharp mouthparts, but injury to plants is caused primarily by the females when they split young bark in preparation for egg laying. Of the confirmed feeding hosts, lime (*Tilia* species), beech (*Fagus* species), hornbeam (*Carpinus* species), oak (*Quercus* species), cherry (*Prunus* species), sumac (*Rhus* species), hickory (*Carya* species), and horse chestnuts (*Aesculus* species) appear to be most common, with limes supporting significantly larger populations than the species which gives the pest its common name, maple leafhopper (*Alebra albostriella*).

Plant injury occurs in three ways: by destruction of the chlorophyll, by removal of plant fluids, and by winter egg deposition. Leafhoppers feed continually on a leaf and, during nymphal development, remove or destroy from one-third to one-half of the chlorophyll. The injured leaves often drop prematurely. Fungal diseases (often stem cankers) enter the wood when the tissues are cut by the leafhopper's egg-laying apparatus. Such diseases kill the already weakened plant.

Most insects feed on the phloem, but leafhoppers and cicadas feed either on the phloem or the xylem. The xylem-feeders have adapted to the dilute quality of xylem sap by evacuating large amounts of water while feeding. It rains, even on a clear day, under infested trees.

## White Fly

In addition to aphids (Aphididae), scales (Coccoideae), and hoppers (Cicadellidae), white flies may be found on maples. *Aleurochiton forbesii* is one of the few species of white fly found in the northern United States. It occurs exclusively on maples and feeds on the undersides of the leaves. It rarely causes measurable damage to its host, and little is known about its biology and behavior.

## Lacebugs

There are at least 27 species of lacebugs in the genus *Corythucha* that feed on deciduous trees and shrubs. Most have very specific host preferences. Maples luckily are only favored by the birch lacebug, *C. pallipes* (syn. *C. betula*, syn. *C. cyrta*). The adults are beautifully sculptured, resembling an intricate, lacy network. They range from 3 to 6 mm (0.1–0.2 in) in size. All lacebugs overwinter as adults in bark crevices, branched crotches, or similarly protected areas of their host, and all generally show the same life cycle. They arouse from hibernation at about the time of leaf development. Eggs are attached to the underside of a leaf with a brown sticky substance. Within a few days the eggs hatch and nymphs begin feeding on the leaf underside. With sucking mouthparts they pierce the epidermis and withdraw fluids and cell contents, causing characteristic chlorotic flecks that are visible on the upper surface of the leaf. The nymphs only remotely resemble the adults. A complete cycle from egg to adult requires about 30 days, so several generations occur each year. In late summer all stages may be found feeding together and their dark, varnishlike excrement may cover most of the undersides of the leaves from which all food-manufacturing tissue has been devoured.

## Thrips

Long a pest of certain greenhouse plants, the greenhouse thrip, *Heliothrips haemorrhoidalis,* also damages woody ornamentals, including maples in southerly latitudes. Unlike most thrips, the greenhouse thrip feeds on leaves rather than on blossoms, buds, or growing shoots. Both immature and adult thrips live in dense colonies and feed by puncturing plant cells with their specialized mouthparts to withdraw cell sap. Their feeding causes a flecking, bleaching, or silvering of the affected leaves. Damaged foliage becomes papery and wilts, then drops prematurely. Fully as important as direct feeding injury by *Heliothrips* is the production of vast quantities of a varnishlike excrement that collect on the foliage and create an unsightly appearance.

## Borers

These insects feed inside roots, trunks, branches, or twigs. Usually the borer is in the larval stage of development, although some beetles also are borers. Eggs are deposited in bark crevices on scar tissue or, in a few cases, below the bark surface, by the adult female during spring, summer or fall, depending on the species. After hatching, the larvae penetrate the bark and the underlying wood. When they reach the wood they cannot be controlled.

As with any disease or pest, unthrifty trees are most readily affected. Treating bark wounds is not considered necessary. Most trees cope with attack by compartmentalizing any tissue damaged by enemies (Shigo 1985). Newly transplanted trees can be protected with burlap wrappings.

## Root Weevils

These insects, of which there are many species, do no particular damage to maples. The adults are beetles, feeding at night on the leaves, doing little damage to the host. On the other hand, the larvae or grubs living in the soil among the roots are highly destructive. Root weevils are not found on maples in Europe.

Damage to plants in overwintering seedling flats prior to transplanting has been reported in the United States (Vertrees 1978). Fall transplantation eliminates this problem. Serious losses occur in grafting pots. Growing the one-year understock in small containers for a second season gives the larvae the opportunity to feed in the pots, thereby causing serious damage to the 2-year understock. Soil drenches or potting-up 2-year-old stock the fall prior to grafting prevents this loss. Young transplanted grafts and seedling selections are also subject to this threat in nursery beds. Mature trees are rarely endangered by root weevils, and, if damage occurs, it is usually limited and easily overcome by the tree.

Container-grown nursery stock and, in some cases, bonsai plants are subject to the threat of root damage. Close inspection to locate this potential problem is advisable. Root inspection in late fall or early winter will reveal the presence of grubs or damaged roots.

To sum up the impact of diseases and pests on maples, prevention is the best means for dealing with damage to plants, be it environmental, viral, bacterial, fungal, or by insects. Improving any favorable element in the tree's situation—proper fertilization, watering during dry spells, periodic spraying for leaf-chewing insects and blighting fungi, and proper pruning of infested or weakened branches—is the best remedy.

Chapter 4

# Structure of Maples

DR. H. J. OTERDOOM and DR. P. C. DE JONG

The principal morphological characteristics of maples are summed up in Table 1, which is elaborated on in this chapter.

## FLOWERS

Flowers of most *Acer* species have five sepals, five petals, eight stamens, and a bicarpellate ovary (Table 1). Four-merous flowers with four stamens are found in a few species. Slight deviations from these typical numbers frequently occur, especially in the number of stamens. Five, ten, or twelve stamens are not uncommon. There is a tendency for the flowers opening last to be 4-merous flowers instead of the usual 5-merous and to have fewer stamens.

In dioecious taxa, female flowers may lack stamens, while male flowers usually have at least a trace of an ovary; however, the male flowers of *Acer negundo* show no trace of an ovary. The flowers of *A. carpinifolium* usually have no visible rudimentary ovaries when in flower, but undifferentiated female primordia can often be seen in the buds.

Tricarpellate ovaries are found infrequently, suggesting that the present bicarpellate anatomy was derived from an earlier 3-carpellate progenitor, as is seen in Hippocastanaceae and Sapindaceae, two related families. Occasionally, an increase in the number of carpels is found; for example, *Acer saccharum*, 4-carpellate fruit; *A. platanoides*, 4- and 5-carpellate fruits; and *A. pseudoplatanus*, 4-, 5-, and 8 carpellate fruits. Pax (1885), Koidzumi (1911), and Hall (1951) suggest that the 5-merous flower originally had 5-carpellate ovaries.

De Jong (1976) found that ovaries consisting of four or more carpels are always fasciated and have two to three connate styles. Fasciated flowers with a still higher number of carpels were observed (*Acer henryi* with 13 carpels and *A. tataricum* ssp. *ginnala* with 17), but these have several free styles. Such polycarpellate flowers are marked by an increase in other floral parts as well. The irregular arrangement and the fasciation of ovaries with four or more carpels probably indicates that a 3-carpellate ovary is primitive, and higher numbers are genetic departures from this structure.

In *Acer diabolicum*, a dioecious species, the male flowers have connate perianths. Several authors have reported flowers of *A. saccharum* in which the corolla is absent. From studies of herbarium specimens it may be concluded that the perianth is usually 5-lobed, but occasionally 6- to 8-lobed. Flowers of *A. saccharinum* usually are considered to be apetalous.

It is possible that a connate perianth resulted from compression of the floral axis. This compression brought the sepals and petals together in one whorl in the same way as the two stamen whorls.

TABLE 1. Variation of selected morphological characters in *Acer*.

| Section | Series | Number of floral parts | | | Position of the disc[1] | Inflorescences | | Nutlet[4] | Parthenocarpic tendency[5] | Folding manner of the cotyledons[6] | Leaf type[7] | Pairs of bud scales |
|---|---|---|---|---|---|---|---|---|---|---|---|---|
| | | Sepals | Petals | Stamens | | Type[2] | Arrangement[3] | | | | | |
| I *Parviflora* | *Parviflora* | 5 | 5 | 8 | I | I | I | C | W | I | 5–6 | 2 |
| | *Caudata* | 5 | 5 | 8 | A–I | I | I | F,V | W | A | 5–6 | 2–3 |
| | *Distyla* | 5 | 5 | 8 | A | I | I | C | M | I | 10 | 2 |
| II *Palmata* | *Palmata* | 5 | 5 | 8 | E | I | I | C | M | I | 6,7 | 4 |
| | *Sinensia* | 5 | 5 | 8 | E | I | I | C | W–M | I | 5,6,7 | 4 |
| | *Penninervia* | 5 | 5 | 8 | E | I | I | C | W–M | I | 10 | 4 |
| III *Wardiana* | | 5 | 5 | 8 | A | I | I | F | M? | ? | 5 | 2 |
| IV *Macrantha* | | 5 | 5 | 8 | I | III | II | F,(C) | M | A | 5,6,9 | 2 |
| V *Glabra* | *Glabra* | 5 | 5 | 8 | A | II–III | II | F,V | S | A | 3–5 | 2–4 |
| | *Arguta* | 4 | 4 | 4–6 | A | III | II,IV | F,V | S | A | 5,9 | 2–3 |
| VI *Negundo* | *Negundo* | 4–5 | — | 4–5 | — | III–V | III | F,V | S | A | 2 | 2–3 |
| | *Cissifolia* | 4 | 4 | 4 | A | III | III | F,V | S | A | 3 | 2 |
| VII *Indivisa* | | 4–5 | 4–5 | 4–6 | A | III | I | F | S | A | 10 | 9–13 |
| VIII *Acer* | *Acer* | 5 | 5 | 8 | E | II | I | C | M | I | 6 | 5–10 |
| | *Monspessulana* | 5 | 5 | 8 | E | II | I | C | S | I | 5,6,(9) | 8–12 |
| | *Saccharodendron* | 5 | 0(–2) | 8 | E | II | II | C | S | I | 5,6 | 6–9 |
| IX *Pentaphylla* | *Pentaphylla* | 5 | 5 | 8 | E | II | I | C | ? | ? | 8 | 4–8 |
| | *Trifida* | 5 | 5 | 8 | E | II | I | C | S | I | 5,9 | 4–8 |
| X *Trifoliata* | *Grisea* | 5–6 | 5–6 | 10–13 | E–A | III | II | C | S | I | 3 | 11–15 |
| | *Mandshurica* | 5 | 5 | 10–12 | A | II–III | II | C | S | I | 3 | 10–12 |
| XI *Lithocarpa* | *Lithocarpa* | 5 | 5 | 8 | A | III | IV | C,V | S | I | 5,6 | 8–12 |
| | *Macrophylla* | 5–6 | 5–6 | 9–12 | A | II | I | C | S | A | 6 | 5–8 |
| XII *Platanoidea* | | 5 | 5 | 8 | A | II | I | F | M | A | 5,6,9 | 5–8 |
| XIII *Pubescentia* | | 5 | 5 | 5 | A | II | II | F | M | A | 5,6 | 6–10 |
| XIV *Ginnala* | | 5 | 5 | 8 | E | II | II | F,V | M | A | 4,5,9 | 5–10 |
| XV *Rubra* | | 5 | 0(–3),5 | 4–6 | —,I | IV | IV | C | W | A | 5–6 | 4–7 |
| XVI *Hyptiocarpa* | | 5 | 5 | 5–12 | A | II–III | IV | C | W | ? | 10 | 7–11 |

[1] E = extrastaminal, A = amphistaminal, I = intrastaminal.
[2] See Figure 4.1
[3] I = terminal, II = terminal + lateral, III = lateral, partly mixed buds, IV = lateral.
[4] C = convex, F = flat, V = veined.
[5] W = weak, M = moderate, S = strong.
[6] I = incumbent, A = accumbent.
[7] See Figure 4.8

## Inflorescences

The genus *Acer* is characterized by five basic types of inflorescence as shown in Figure 4.1. The distribution of these inflorescences is shown in Table 1. The inflorescence part that is most difficult to describe is the ramification of the rachis. The lowermost secondary axes are opposite, in keeping with the opposite leaf position of the vegetative shoot. This passes into scattered branching towards the top of the inflorescence; sometimes there is a transitional zone of one or two whorls with three to eight secondary axes. When the lowermost secondaries are rather long, their tertiary branching may correspond to that of the secondary branching of the rachis. The continued branching of the axis sometimes results in a monochasium consisting of cincinni (from the Latin *cincinnus,* a curl, referring to a tight, unilateral scorpioid cyme) that are generated by branching on the node of the lowermost bracteole ($\alpha$-prophyll) of the secondary, tertiary, and following axes (see type I inflorescence in Figure 4.1). The number of flowers of these cincinni varies from 2 to 14. Depending on the

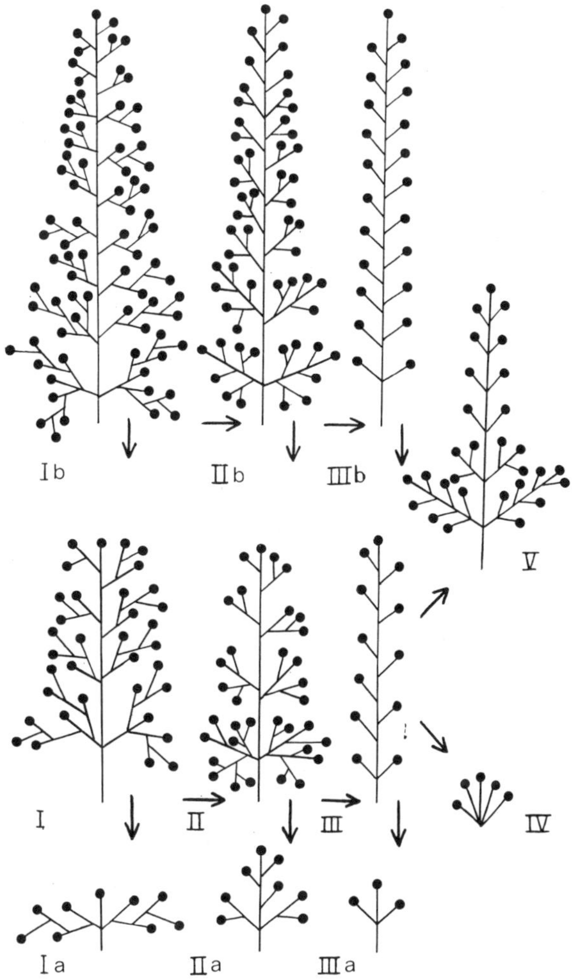


FIGURE 4.1. The five basic types of inflorescence in *Acer:* (I) compound inflorescence with cincinni; (II) compound inflorescence with cincinni reduced; (III) racemes; (IV) umbel; and (V) compound raceme. (Key: *a* = reduced rachis; *b* = elongated rachis; and *c* = reduction of *b* to a raceme from a compound inflorescence.) The arrows indicate possible evolutionary trends.

length of the rachis, two extremes of the type I inflorescence can be distinguished: type Ia with a very short rachis (*Acer circinatum*) and type Ib with a very long rachis (Fig. 4.1).

Type II represents the most common *Acer* inflorescence. Most secondary axes carry two or more tertiary axes (Fig. 4.1). These occasionally develop into small cincinni carrying three to four flowers. As in the type I inflorescence, extremes with a very short or an elongated rachis can be distinguished in type II (Fig. 4.1). *Acer pseudoplatanus* is an example of an elongated type II inflorescence: its inflorescences have tertiary axes that are partly inserted on the rachis by shortening the secondary axes (Fig. 4.2).

The inflorescence of type III is a raceme with terminal flowers (Fig. 4.1). Extremely short and long racemes are classed as types IIIa and IIIb, respectively.

Type IV inflorescence is a sessile umbel (Fig. 4.1). As Table 1 indicates, this inflorescence type is found only in section *Rubra* (Figs. 4.3, 4.4, 4.5).

Type V represents a compound raceme, found in male specimens of *Acer negundo.* The puzzling classification of the inflorescence of this species is closely related to the development of its generative shoot (see below).

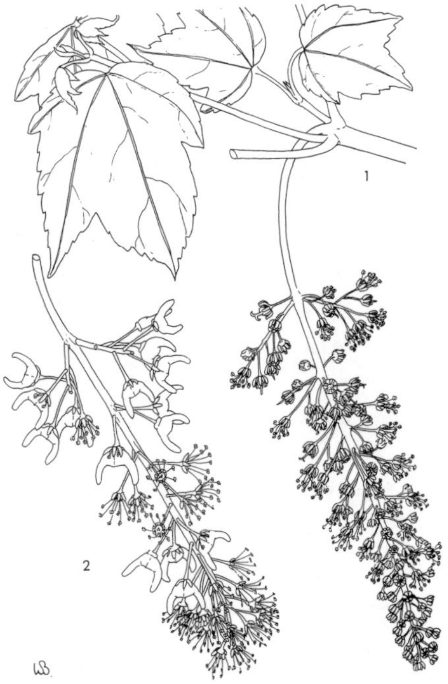


FIGURE 4.2. *Acer pseudoplatanus* L. is an example of duodichogamy (flowering type C): (1) flowering branchlet with inflorescence at the end of the ♂$_{\mathrm{I}}$ phase (22 May 1969); and (2) inflorescence during ♂$_{\mathrm{II}}$ phase (3 June 1969). ×1. [Wag. B. G. no. 11480.]

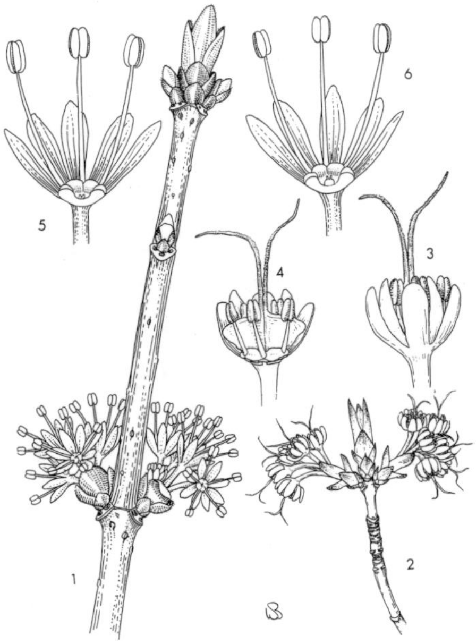


FIGURE 4.3. Dioecious specimens of *Acer rubrum* L.: (1) branchlet, ♂ inflorescence (×3); (2) branchlet, ♀ inflorescence (×2); (3) ♀ flower (×6); (4) ♀ flower with perianth partly removed (×6); and (5, 6) ♂ flower longitudinal section. [1, 5: 'Schlesingeri', Wag. B. G. no. 11472; 2–4: 'Sanguineum', Wag. B. G. no. 7809; 6: Wag. B. G. no. 7811.]

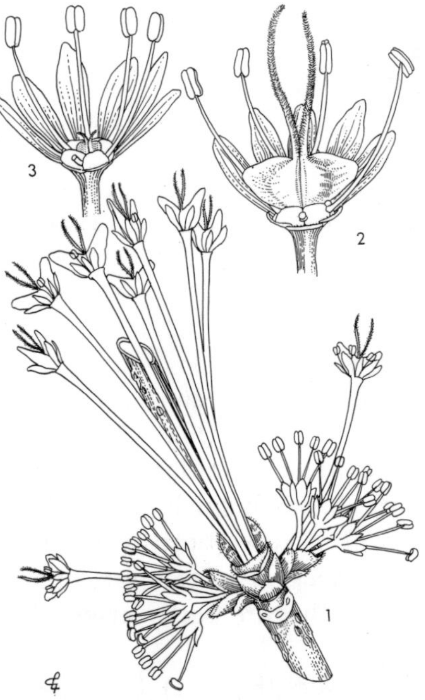


FIGURE 4.4. Polygamous specimen of *Acer rubrum* L.: (1) branchlet, with three inflorescences developed from one axillary bud, showing protogyny forced into flowers indoors (×3); (2) ♀ flower (×9); and (3) ♂$_{\mathrm{II}}$ flower (×9). Wag. B. G. no. 1757.

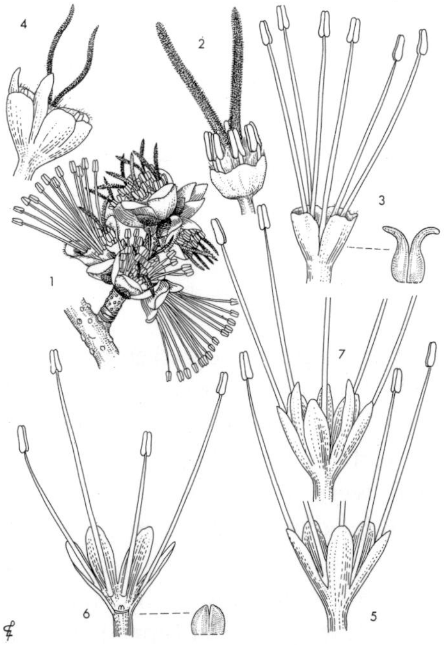


FIGURE 4.5. *Acer saccharinum* L: (1) branchlet with ♂, ♀, and androgynous inflorescences (×2); (2) ♀ flower (×6); (3) ♂ flower (×6) and abortive pistil (×24); (4) ♀ flower with two petals (×6); (5) ♂ flower with sepals nearly free (×6); (6) ♂ flower longitudinal section (×6) and abortive pistil (×24); (7) ♂ flower with three petals. [1–3: 'Eugeia', Wag.; 4: 'Bowlespark', Wag.; 5–7: 'Schwerinii', Wag. B. G. no. 13276.]

For all five inflorescence types, the position or arrangement of the inflorescence at the generative shoots and the companion leaves are distinguishing elements for classification. Four distinct positions from which inflorescences emerge from the shoots can be identified: terminal, terminal and lateral, lateral with partly mixed buds, and lateral (see Table 1).

In most species, inflorescences from mixed flower and shoot buds of the previous year predominate. Depending on the pairs of accompanying leaves, Ogata divided these taxa into four groups: Group I contains inflorescences that emerge almost exclusively from terminal buds on vigorous long shoots of the previous year. Group II inflorescences emerge from lateral buds on long shoots. Section *Trifoliata* could be placed in this group, but the female specimens of section *Glabra* series *Arguta* give rise to much confusion. Their inflorescences develop mainly from terminal buds on short, lateral, two-leaved branches. Ogata (1967) spoke of mixed lateral buds and Murray (1970c) spoke of mixed terminal buds. The present author found inflorescences mainly developed from terminal buds on short shoots, but also from lateral buds on mostly long shoots (group II). Groups III and IV develop inflorescences from lateral buds on short shoots only. The distinction between them lies in the occurrence of more or less mixed buds in group III. These mixed buds have leaflets which usually drop prematurely. In section *Negundo* they occur predominantly on female trees.

## Calyx and Corolla

Within the genus *Acer* the corolla shows distinct variations in shape and color, in addition to reduction and fusion with the calyx. A number of species have flowers with white or whitish petals, contrasting markedly with the green or reddish sepals (e.g., sections *Palmata* and *Parviflora* and series *Cissifolia* of section *Negundo*). The most striking contrasts are seen in species of the southern range of section *Palmata* (e.g., *A. campbellii, A. erianthum, A. laevigatum,* and *A. tonkinense*), whose flowers have recurved red or reddish sepals and 3- to 5-lobed white petals that are rolled inward. The long, smooth petals in section *Parviflora* series *Caudata* and section *Negundo* series *Cissifolia* contrast markedly with the small, inrolled, hairy sepals.

In most of the remaining taxa the petals have the same yellowish, greenish, or occasionally reddish color as the sepals. Usually there are only small variations in size, hairiness, and curvature among them. Male flowers grow larger during anthesis by elongation of the petals.

## Stamens

The rather irregular whorl of eight stamens is thought to have developed from two whorls of five stamens each. As in all flowers, the development of the nectarial disc strongly influences the ultimate arrangement of the stamens. Flowers with ten stamens have five episepalous stamens, each enclosed by a disc lobe at their base. These observations seem to indicate a reduction of episepalous stamens.

## Pollen

*Acer* species do not produce the large quantities of pollen characteristic of *Alnus, Betula, Pinus,* and Quercus species. As maple trees have never grown in extremely dense stands and because their pollen walls (sporopollenin) are more perishable than those of most trees, microfossil pollen studies have not been particularly helpful in paleobotany. Pollen grains of living species have been more commonly studied (e.g., Biesboer 1975).

Maple pollen grains are generally tricolporate, radially symmetrical, isopolar, and prolate to nearly spheroidal. The amb (from the Latin *ambitus,* meaning contour, circumference) of a pollen grain viewed with one of the poles uppermost is rounded and triangular. The apocolpi (area at the pole) is only 2–9 $\mu$m in diameter. Colpi (longitudinal, usually more or less distinctly delimited apertures) extend nearly to the poles, are fairly broad (2–10 $\mu$m) with tapering ends, and have a smooth or slightly granular membrane. Ora are circular when present. The sexine (outer layer) is striate, rugulose, granular, or reticulate, and usually thicker than the nexine (the layer inside or below the sexine). The lirae, rugulae, and muri are generally rounded in outline (ridges); 0.5–1.5 μm wide; elongate or short; straight, curved, or sharply bent; and often branched, interweaving, anastomosing, or oriented in various directions. The grains are tectate (roofed). The baculae (more or less perpendicular or radial rods or rodlike elements supporting the roof) are distinct. The size of pollen grains varies from 22 μm in *Acer micranthum* to 55 μm in *A. macrophyllum.* The tricolporate taxa are *Dipteronia* and sections *Parviflora* and *Palmata,* supporting the view of the original pollen character (i.e., the more primitive form) of *Acer.*

Pollen morphology studies of the Aceraceae have provided little additional evidence for delimiting existing sections except for a few instances. The striate sexine pattern predominates (Fig. 4.6). *Acer carpinifolium,* with atypical leaves resembling those of *Carpinus,* also has a distinctly granular sexine, quite different from the usual pattern in the Aceraceae (Fig. 4.7).

Pollen investigations of two closely related families, the Sapindaceae and Hippocastanaceae, reveal a predominance of striate sculpturing similar to that of maples. The identification of maples and their species by pollen examination does not, in general, seem feasible.

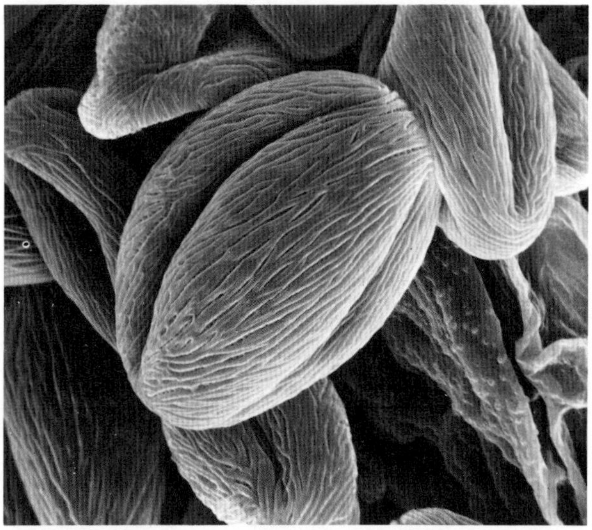

FIGURE 4.6. Pollen of *Acer pectinatum* ssp. *laxiflorum* (Kew) shows the striate sexine pattern typical for the Aceraceae. ×2500

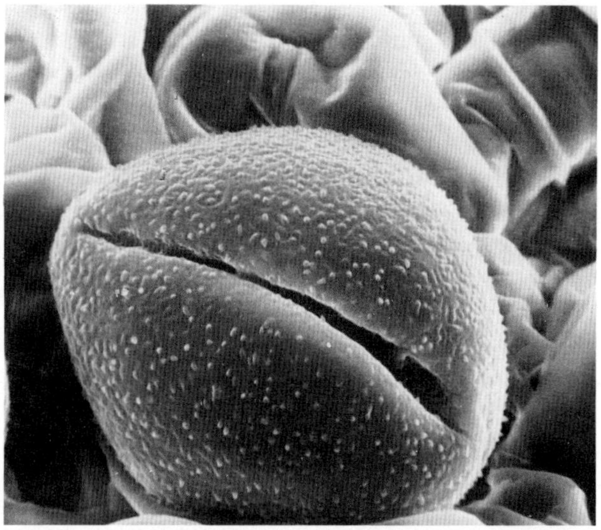

FIGURE 4.7. Pollen of *Acer carpinifolium* (Wageningen) is distinctly granular sexine. ×3700

## Honey Disc

Depending on the insertion of the stamens, the location of the disc may be extrastaminal, intrastaminal, or, sometimes rather indistinctly, amphistaminal (Table 1). Several taxonomists have pointed to this variation as an important characteristic for distinguishing among species. Pax (1885) introduced the terms *extrastaminalia* and *intrastaminalia.* However, he employed them for only half of the genus and did not maintain the usage in his monograph of 1902.

Koidzumi (1911) placed all of Pax's sections in extrastaminalia and intrastaminalia divisions. This general division was also adopted by Rehder (1927) and Momotani (1962b) in their keys. Nakai (1915b) followed Koidzumi, but placed section *Platanoidea* in a separate group, the *Circumstaminalia.* Section *Negundo* series *Negundo* and *Acer saccharinum* of section *Rubra* lack floral discs.

The amphistaminal disc displays wide morphological variation, and the taxa possessing this type of disc are not usually closely related. The disc edge may be entire (the stamens being inserted in the center, as in section *Platanoidea*), or lobed (the stamens in the center of the lobes, as in section *Parviflora* series *Caudata*), or more or less enclosed between the lobes (e.g., section *Parviflora* series *Distyla* and section *Pubescentia*).

The disc is usually glabrous, but in some species it is more or less pubescent: *Acer campbellii, A. erianthum, A. garrettii, A. laevigatum, A. tonkinense,* and *A. tutcheri.* Slightly hairy discs occur in *A. fabri, A. laurinum, A. nipponicum,* and *A. wardii.*

Many authors (e.g., Pax, Koidzumi, Nakai, and Pojárkova) considered the mode of staminal insertion in the disc phylogenetically important. The common type, and the most primitive, in *Acer,* as well as in *Dipteronia, Aesculus,* and nearly all sapindaceous genera is extrastaminal. The shift of stamen insertion to the middle or outer margin of the disc very probably developed in more than one taxon, because the present taxa with amphistaminal or extrastaminal discs are only remotely related.

In some dioecious taxa (e.g., section *Indivisa,* section *Glabra* series *Arguta,* and section *Negundo* series *Cissifolia*) the insertion of the stamens varies between the outer margin and the middle of the disc, probably because some of the stamens are inserted higher due to the absence of the (aborted) pistil. In two wind-pollinated taxa the honey disc is absent.

## Style and Stigma

The size of the stigmas on flowers of some taxa seems to be clearly related to their anemophilous nature (e.g., *Acer negundo, A. rubrum,* and *A. saccharinum*). The stigmas are enlarged by being fully split, doubling the pollen-receptive surface.

The flowers of several other species also have rather short styles and long stigmas. In these taxa, which flower before or during the emergence of the leaves, wind pollination is obviously an asset. Examples include sections *Macrantha, Trifoliata, Lithocarpa,* and *Acer* (*A. monspessulanum, A. opalus,* and *A. saccharum*), all of which flower early.

Wide variations in style and stigma length also occur within species. Flowers of *Acer macrophyllum,* for example, usually have short styles and long stigmas, though flowers with long styles and short stigmas have been found on some herbarium specimens. Similar variations occur in sections *Acer, Ginnala,* and *Platanoidea.*

## Parthenocarpic Tendency

After flowering, male flowers immediately fall off. On the other hand, female flowers show parthenocarpic development of the ovary, at least initially. This is especially evident in the dioecious species.

On the basis of their sexual expression (monoecious or dioecious), the species of *Acer* can be divided into five groups: a stage representing the original mode of sexual expression, three stages of development from primitive parthenocarpy, and a stage in which flowers are completely dioecious. The first group is composed of dichogamous species, which mainly flower in a male-female-male sequence (duodichogamy). The aborted pistils of the male flower, flowering before the female phase, are smaller than those of male flowers after the female phase. This mode of sexual expression is also evident in related primitive taxa, such as *Dipteronia* (Aceraceae), *Aesculus* (Hippocastanaceae), and several sapindaceous genera. It is believed to be the original mode of sexual expression in *Acer.* Representatives of this group are found in section *Parviflora* series *Parviflora,* section *Palmata* series *Sinensia* (partly), and section *Parviflora* series *Caudata.* Other characteristics of these taxa are the large compound inflorescences with cincinni, developing mainly from mixed terminal buds; the small entomophilous flowers with distinct calyces and corollas; flowering one month after bud burst; their parthenocarpic tendency; and the presence of few bud scales.

The second group is composed of dichogamous species in which half of the population flowers protogynously while the remaining individuals produce protandrous, duodichogamous, and/or male inflorescences (heterodichogamy). Cross pollination is favored. This state of affairs is controlled primarily by environmental conditions as annual variations are common. Anthesis (flowering) starts simultaneously with, or shortly after, bud burst. Genetic male flowers, if present, form a low percentage of the population. This mode of sexual expression is the most common in the genus and occurs in sections *Platanoidea, Palmata* (in part), *Ginnala, Pentaphylla* series *Trifida, Acer* series *Acer* and *Saccharodendron,* and *Parviflora* series *Distyla.*

A third group is intermediate between the dichogamous species (group II) and the completely dioecious species (group I). The protogynous individuals are partly replaced by female individuals. The ratios of female to male flowers vary between the species and populations of a species. The evolution to male individuals is complete or nearly so. In the latter case protandry still occurs, but the small inflorescences tend to flower completely male in most years. Protogynous individuals often produce few, if any, female flowers. Although the data are rather incomplete for this group, it is clear that the evolution to male individuals is completed much earlier than the evolution to female individuals. Species of this group are found in sections *Rubra, Hyptiocarpa, Glabra* series *Glabra,* and *Acer* series *Monspessulana.* These taxa tend to develop lateral inflorescences, to often flower before leaf development, and to manifest various stages of development to anemophily (wind pollination).

The fourth group is basically a protandrous flowering group in which the individuals do not produce a second sequence of male flowers and protogyny is never observed. The inflorescences are small racemes that usually produce unisexual flowers. Individual trees in the wild usually flower completely male or female, but cultivated trees observed for more than 10 years produced flowers of both sexes. Androgynous flowers, if present, always flower protandrously. Sexual expression appears to be strongly dependent on environmental and internal factors. The male and female flowers on one tree are often distributed on separate branches, which frequently flower simultaneously and self-pollinate (geitonogamy). Detached branches of some male flowering trees flower completely female if forced into flower one month before anthesis occurs on branches outdoors. This mode of sexual expression is found in section *Macrantha* series *Tegmentosa* and *Acer maximowiczianum* (syn. *A. nikoense*) and probably is an early specialization. It should be noted that in section *Parviflora* series *Parviflora* (group I), the second phase male flowers are rare.

The fifth group is composed of dioecious species located in sections *Indivisa, Lithocarpa, Negundo,* and *Glabra* series *Arguta.* These species represent less than 10 percent of the genus. With the exception of section *Indivisa,* in which female flowers have rudimentary stamens, the female flowers of these other species lack stamens. Male flowers in all sections and series usually have small, abortive pistils. The inflorescences are very small and, with the exception of section *Indivisa* and female species of section *Glabra* series *Arguta,* are exclusively produced from lateral buds with few leaf primordia. Unpollinated female flowers develop parthenocarpically. In addition to the evolution to dioecy, the genus *Acer* tends toward wind pollination. This development seems to have been favored by climatic conditions in certain parts of its habitat and is most pronounced in the early flowering species of eastern North America, where one taxon, series *Negundo,* is definitely wind pollinated.

Most maples flower just as the leaves appear, but flowers of *Acer japonicum, A. monspessulanum, A. opalus, A. platanoides, A. rubrum,* and *A. saccharinum* appear before the leaves. Pax (1885) was of the opinion that this characteristic, which makes a considerable contribution to the beauty of the tree, represents the original nature of maples in the Tertiary period.

## FRUITS AND SEEDS

The distinctive winged fruits, called *samaras,* are as much the hallmark of maples as acorns are of oaks. Maple fruits consists of 2 one-seeded mericarps (samara dicarpellata).

Ogata (1967) considers the shape of the nutlets, as he calls them, a most important means for identification of species, though others (including the present authors) believe that only the most knowledgeable acerologist can derive much help from them. Mai (1984), however, after studying maple fruits, differentiated sections and series on the basis of carpomorphological characteristics.

Maple seeds (nutlets) are round, usually flattened, and with smooth, hairy, or veined surfaces (Table 1). The largest seeds are about 0.5 cm (0.25 in) in diameter. The larger the seed, the larger the wing.

It should be noted that the fruits of some taxa are occasionally parthenocarpic, in which case the seedpod remains empty (Table 1). Parthenocarpy, thought to be an advanced characteristic, is very obvious in dioecious species. Their seedless, empty fruits are practically indistinguishable from seed-bearing fruits. If the wall of the nutlet is heavily lignified (woody), as is often the case with *Acer griseum* and *A. maximowiczianum,* it is difficult to determine which seeds can be successfully sown, so the pods must be cut open in random samples.

In normal development, the embryo fills the cavity of the fully grown fruit and also determines the form of the capsule (i.e., flat or more round).

The form of the wing differs by species, as can the angle at which the two wings are placed relative to each other. Some make an angle of 180° (e.g., *Acer campestre*), while others are parallel (*A. griseum*).

Rehder (1905) classified the way the cotyledons are folded in the seed as either incumbent or accumbent. Incumbent cotyledons are usually found in convex locules, while accumbent cotyledons usually appear in concave or flat locules (Table 1). Some species having accumbent cotyledons and convex locules, such as *A. macrophyllum* and *A. rufinerve,* depart from this correlation, their fruits containing a brown material that partly fills the cavity. The cotyledons are green, except those of species with very thick-walled fruits (e.g., section *Trifoliata*). Incumbent cotyledons are found in *Acer, Integrifolia, Lithocarpa, Palmata,* and *Parviflora,* while accumbent cotyledons are found in sections *Glabra, Indivisa, Macrantha, Negundo, Parviflora* (series *Caudata*), *Rubra,* and *Trifoliata.* The fruits of sections *Hyptiocarpa* and *Pentaphylla* have not been classified.

The seed wall is extratestal (i.e., the protective layer is in the outer epiderm). The mesophyll usually has a layer of small crystal cells, and the pericarp assumes the protective function of the seed coat. There is no arillus.

Two ovules are found in each locule, but only one develops after fertilization. Occasionally mericarps with two seeds have been observed.

Seeds of *Acer rubrum* and *A. saccharinum* germinate immediately at maturity in early summer. Very often they sprout lying on top of the soil. The seeds of most other species, on the other hand, germinate very early the following spring—February or March. Germination may be impeded in seeds enveloped by thick ligneous pericarps and thus require another year. Ingram (1975) reported germination of *A. laxiflorum* (syn. *A. pectinatum* ssp. *laxiflorum*) seeds 10–12 years following the death of the original tree.

In the absence of wind the samara does not get far from the tree. Ridley (1930) found that *Acer niveum* (syn. *A. laurinum*) samaras, which weigh 100 mg (0.154 grain), could float in the air for some days. The trees of this species are large and widely dispersed in the Javanese mountains, where the wind is strong enough to transport their samaras for up to 40 km (25 miles).

Nearly all species demonstrate epigeal germination (i.e., the cotyledons are the first leaves seen above the soil after germination). Exceptions are *Acer saccharinum* and *A. truncatum,* where the cotyledons remain under the surface of the soil, in which case the first leaves seen are the first pair of true leaves, the cotyledons emerging afterwards.

Maple seeds do not remain viable for long since they dry out very readily. Tylkowski (1985), noting this extreme sensitivity to water loss, described a successful method for keeping the germinative capacity for 18 months: store the seeds in tightly sealed containers at −3°C (27°F) with a high initial water content of about 50 percent of the fresh weight of the seeds.

## STEM

All members of the genus *Acer* are woody plants, varying from small shrubs to lofty trees. Most are trees of small to medium height. The well-developed boles of larger trees display different configurations in their bark that are a great help in distinguishing various species: compare the fine ridgy bark of *A. platanoides* with the flaky bark of *A. pseudoplatanus* and the smooth bark of *A. cappadocicum*. Only *A. truncatum* has very rough bark. *Acer griseum* is unique in the genus, with cinnamon- to red-colored bark shed in large, thin flakes, as in birch.

The common name, snakebark maples, derives from the beautiful longitudinal stripes on 2-year-old twigs and older branches. The white stripes are formed by wax produced to protect the tree against loss of moisture. Some of the one-year-old twigs of *Acer giraldii* (*A. caesium* ssp. *giraldii*), *A. rufinerve*, and *A. tegmentosum* have a beautiful, glaucous, waxy bloom.

## BUD SCALES

Although scale leaves and bracts are indistinguishable from leaf primordia, when fully developed they have many fewer parts than the leaves. They are frequently related to leaves by intermediate forms. Indeed, in the spring very small leaves on top of the inner bud scales, more or less in the form of the true leaves, can be seen. Their ontogeny (individual development) is marked by an early promotion of the lower parts of the leaf primordium (anlage) in relation to the upper part, after which all development ceases (Strassburger 1976).

Ogata (1967) considers the number of bud scales an important distinguishing characteristic of *Acer* species. He distinguishes, somewhat arbitrarily, five categories. Some sections have a fixed number of two, three, or five pairs of bud scales, but with increasing numbers the variations become wider and more frequent (Table 1).

The bud scales expand with the leaves in spring, the innermost becoming the largest and sometimes developing leaflets at their top. These bud scales are capable of photosynthesis, but soon fall off the branch or twig (they are caducous). *Dipteronia* (the other genus in Aceraceae) has no bud scales.

## LEAVES

Several maple species derived their names from foliar characteristics: *Acer acuminatum, A. barbatum* (syn. *A. saccharum* ssp. *floridanum*), *A. barbinerve, A. carpinifolium, A. catalpifolium* (syn. *A. longipes* ssp. *catalpifolium*), *A. cissifolium, A. crataegifolium, A. flabellatum* (syn. *A. campbellii* ssp. *flabellatum*), *A. glabrum, A. grandidentatum* (syn. *A. saccharum* ssp. *grandidentatum*), *A. macrophyllum, A. oblongum, A. palmatum, A. pentaphyllum, A. platanoides, A. pseudoplatanus, A. rufinerve, A. truncatum, A. velutinum,* and the now obsolete name *A. villosum* (syn. *A. sterculiaceum*). Pax (1885) made several sectional designations on the basis of leaf form: *Indivisa, Palmata,* and *Trifoliata.*

The typical maple leaf is palmately 5-lobed, about as wide as long or somewhat longer than wide, but the number of lobes varies from no lobes at all, as in *Acer carpinifolium, A. davidii, A. distylum, A. oblongum, A. sikkimense,* and *A. tataricum;* to three lobes, as in *A.*

*monspessulanum* and *A. pentapomicum;* to three lobes with two very tiny lobes at the base of the leaf, as in *A. capillipes, A. pensylvanicum,* and *A. rufinerve;* to 13 lobes, as in *A. japonicum* (Fig. 4.8). A group of east Asian maples and one species in North America have pinnate leaves, with three leaflets most of the time; the North American species *Acer negundo* has five and, in some cases, seven leaflets. Table 1 shows the various leaf types common to *Acer.*

Most maples are deciduous, but a few are evergreen or nearly so—*Acer obtusifolium* and *A. sempervirens.* Most evergreen species are native to Southeast Asia and the Himalayan region: *A. coriaceifolium, A. fabri, A. laevigatum, A. laurinum,* and *A. oblongum.*

*Acer velutinum* and *A. sterculiaceum* have an indumentum on the undersides of the leaves. Most maples have hairs in the axils of the veins, usually most conspicuous near the petioles. In some cases the specific color of the hairs is reflected in the name of the species; for example, *A. rufinerve,* meaning reddish veins, is so named because of the hair color.

Stipules are absent, with one exception—*Acer saccharum* ssp. *nigrum.* The color of the first leaves in spring is often red or red-brown. The red, yellow, or orange leaf colors in the fall, particularly marked in *A. saccharum,* are a hallmark of the genus.

The leaf arrangement of the genus is always opposite, a diagnostic characteristic. If the leaves are alternate, then the plant is not a maple. The twigs and branches repeat the opposite arrangement of the leaves, growing in opposite pairs.

Vegetative buds develop during the summer in the axils of the petioles (leaf stalks). The lower ends of these petioles are often thickened (the pulvinus). In several species the new buds are completely hidden by these pulvini; the buds of section *Macrantha* are stalked.

The buds generally are in opposite pairs (decussate) with one bud at the twig ends, leading to monopodial branching. Some sections, however, also have a pair of buds at the twig ends, as in section *Palmatum,* which departs from the monopodial growth habit.

There is no distinguishable, external difference between flower and vegetative shoot buds; dissection is necessary for comparison.

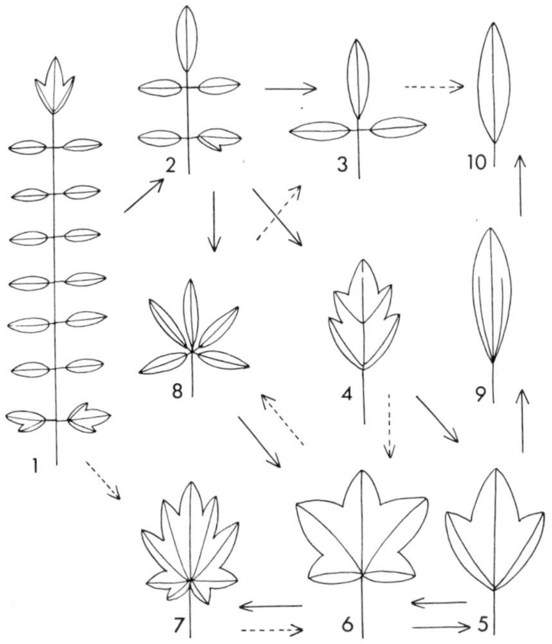


FIGURE 4.8. Basic leaf types in the *Aceraceae:* (1) pinnate (*Dipteronia*); (2) pinnate; (3) trifoliolate; (4) pinnatilobed; (5) trilobed; (6) 5-palmatilobed; (7) 7- to 11-palmatilobed; (8) palmatifoliolate; (9) entire, with strong basal veins; and (10) entire, pinnately veined. The arrows indicate possible evolutionary trends; dotted arrows indicate developments less probable in the case of *Acer.*

## ROOTS

*Acer* roots are much-branched, providing stability for the tree in high winds, and adventitious. No taproot is developed after the seedling stage. Like the roots of many other trees, maple roots have vesicular-arbuscular mycorrhizae (i.e., endomycorrhizae). These fungi are of great benefit to the tree; the relationship is symbiotic. Phosphorus, in particular, is taken up by the fungus; thus, the poorer the soil is in phosphorus, the better the mycorrhizae function in providing this chemical to the tree. The mycorrhizae also assist in the uptake of other minerals such as sulfur and potassium. The trees in turn supply the fungi with sucrose and other carbohydrates that they are unable to synthesize. Fertilizing has a negative effect on the mycorrhizal population.

## WOOD

Maple wood is fine-grained due to the nature of the xylem vessels, which are evenly distributed (diffuse-porous) in the annual ring produced during each spring and summer and which are more nearly uniform in size throughout the growth ring than those in either ring-porous or semi-ring-porous patterns (Figs. 4.9, 4.10). Other trees such as oak, ash, and elm are ring-porous: the portion of the annual ring produced in the early spring has much larger vessels, producing differentiation in the one-year ring (Fig. 4.11). The capacity of the xylem vessels to transport liquids in ring-porous trees can be up to 10 times greater than that of diffuse-porous trees. The xylem vessels of ring-porous trees become useless after 2–3 years; those in diffuse-porous genera remain functional for many more years, thereby making up for their lesser transport capacity.

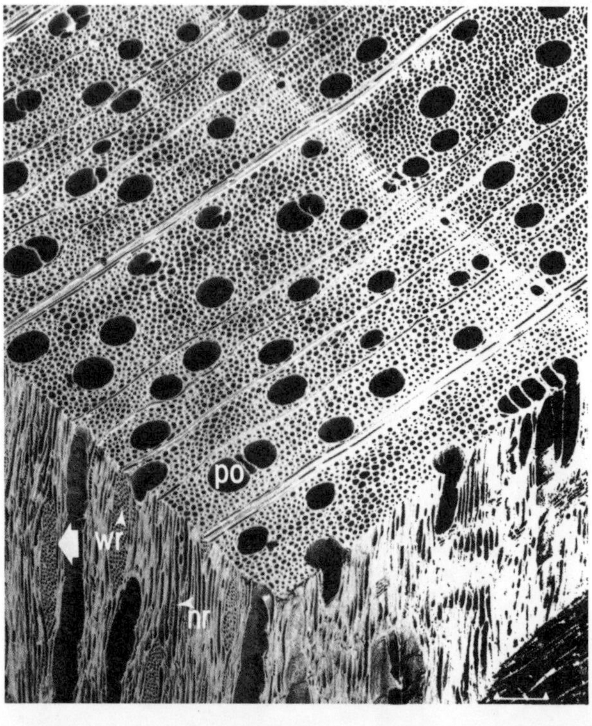


FIGURE 4.9. A scanning electron micrograph of the sugar maple, Acer saccharum, reveals that two sizes of rays are found in this species, the larger rays being as wide or wider than the pores. Key: wr = wide ray; nr = narrow ray. From Core, Cote, and Day (1979), *Wood Structure and Identification* (Syracuse University Press, Syracuse, New York). Used with permission.

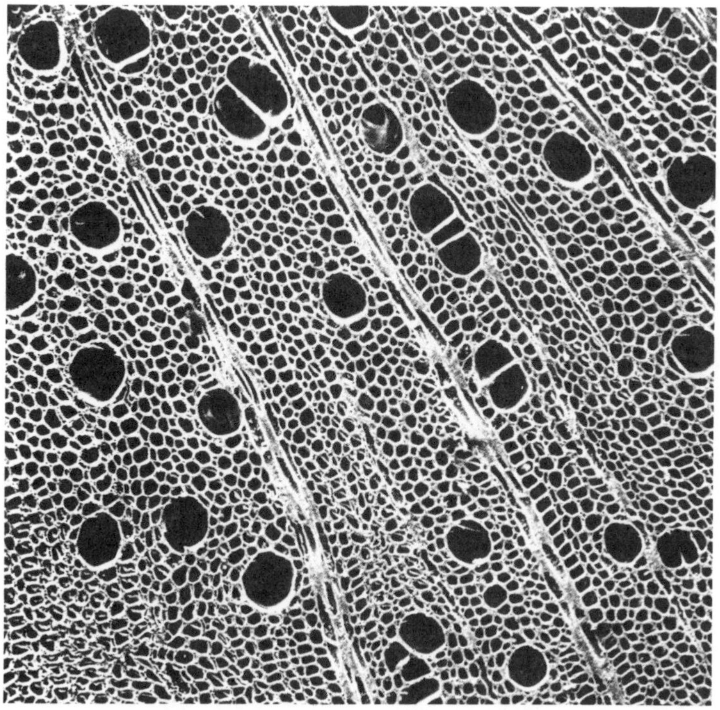

FIGURE 4.10. Tranverse section of the stem of sycamore, *Acer pseudoplatanus,* showing practically the same diffuse porous structure as the sugar maple, *A. saccharum,* in Figure 4.9.

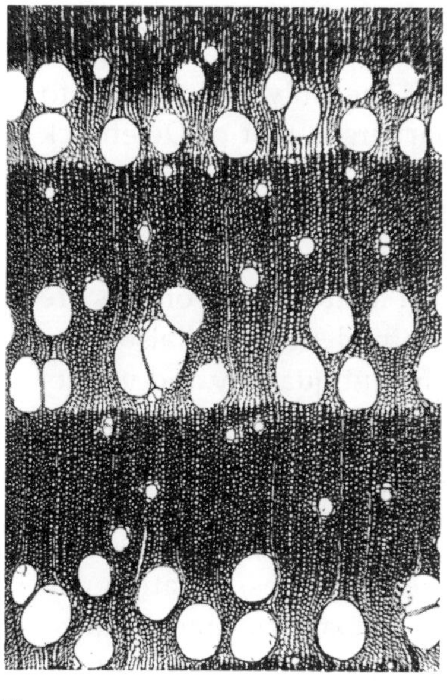

Ring-porous
*Fraxinus nigra,* 14X
Black ash
Other examples:
*Quercus* spp.
*Carya* spp.

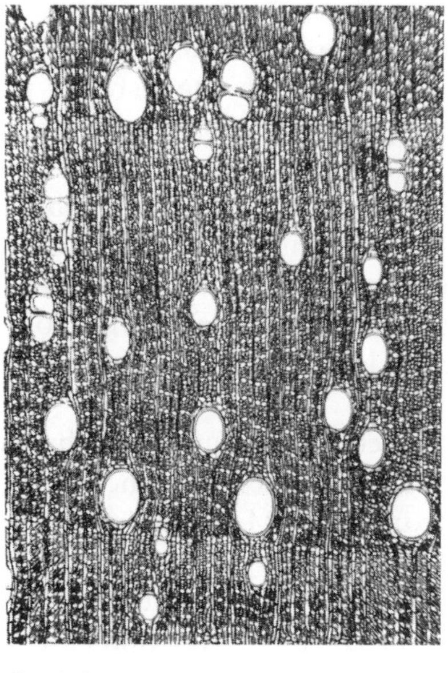

Semi-ring-porous
*Diospyros virginiana,* 14X
Persimmon
Other examples:
*Juglans* spp.
*Salix nigra*

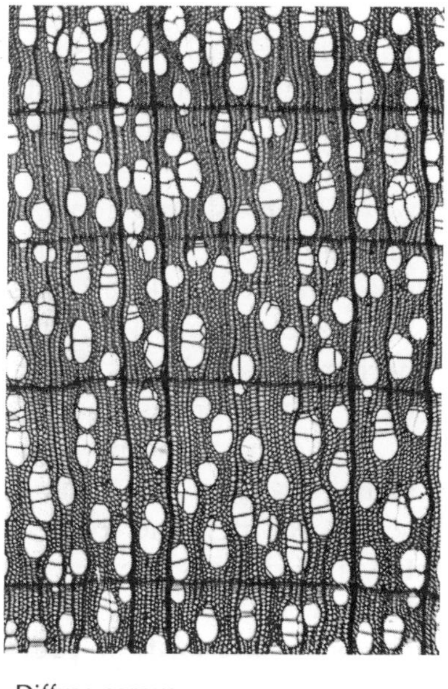

Diffuse-porous
*Betula alleghaniensis,* 14X
Yellow birch
Other examples:
*Tilia americana*
*Acer* spp.

FIGURE 4.11. Examples of hardwood groupings based on pore size change across the growth increment. Maple wood, like that of yellow birch, is fine-grained due to the even distribution of xylem vessels (diffuse-porous), which are smaller than their counterparts in ring-porous wood. From Core, Cote, and Day (1979), *Wood Structure and Identification* (Syracuse University Press, Syracuse, New York). Used with permission.

## CYTOLOGY

The basic chromosome number in the genus *Acer* is 13. This is called the *haploid* number, and is the chromosome count present in the gametes—the pollen and egg cells. When the male and female gametes unite (fertilization) after pollination, the shared chromosome count is called the *diploid* number. The diploid number for most species of *Acer* is $2n = 26$. However, some species are tetraploid; that is, the number of chromosomes is doubled and written as $4n = 52$. Other species are hexaploid, with $6n = 78$.

On the basis of their chromosome number, *Acer* species can be divided into two groups. Group 1 includes seven maples with $2n = 52$, 78, or 104:

| | Polyploid Chromosome Number (2*n*) | | |
|---|---|---|---|
| Species | 52 | 78 | 104 |
| *A. carpinifolium* | • | | |
| *A.* × *freemanii* | | • | |
| *A. pseudoplatanus* | • | | |
| *A. pycnanthum* | | • | |
| *A. rubrum* | | • | • |
| *A. saccharinum* | • | | |
| *A. velutinum* | • | | |

All other members of the genus belong to Group 2: $2n = 26$.

## CHEMISTRY

The use of biochemicals to identify, differentiate, or relate taxa is a relatively new approach in systematic botany. Thus, little is known of the chemistry of maples. The only major work to date studying the taxonomy of the genus *Acer* with biochemical markers is that of Delendick (1981).

The most commonly studied biochemicals are the phenol derivatives called *flavonoids.* The range of discrete chemical structures in flavonoids affords many characteristics useful as independent checks on classification systems based on morphological features. Flavonoids are remarkably stable. They are readily and easily derived from old or young leaves, and also from herbarium specimens. They occur in leaves of all *Acer* species in sufficient quantity and variety to be useful for systematic purposes.

The usual morphological characteristics considered by systematic botanists are apetaly, sympetaly, presence or absence of floral discs, presence of latex, pollen form, aperture, and sculpture, trichome configuration under SEM (Scanning Electron Microscopy), inflorescence types, bud scale number, type of fruit pericarp, cotyledon folding, petiole types, venation pattern, wood anatomy, leaf margins, leaf shapes, and phyllotaxy. Correlations among these characters are far from precise. Likewise, the correlations found by biochemical analyses (e.g., between primitive and derived [advanced] characteristics) are not perfect, though tendencies can be identified.

It is peculiar that a very conspicuous maple characteristic—the frequent red color in both the young shoots and in autumn leaves—has not yet been studied in depth. Everyone agrees that cyanide-3-glucosides (anthocyanins) produce this coloration, although it is lacking in some species. The chemical properties of anthocyanins have been little investigated due to difficulties encountered in their isolation, and their general instability, especially in aqueous solution (Hradzina, in Harborne & Mabry 1982).

The appearance of fall coloration is thought to be caused by high sugar production during the photosynthetic period and by lower metabolic rates and/or reduced transport during cool nights, resulting in a steady increase in the concentration of sugars in the photosynthetic tissues. Deficiency of important minerals such as phosphorus also results in an increase in anthocyanin content in plants. Nitrogen seems to reverse anthocyanin production.

The synthesis of anthocyanins is, as are most processes in plants, light-dependent. Anthocyanins accumulate in the vacuoles of epidermal or subepidermal tissues in plants and are responsible for the pink, red, purple, and blue colors present in flowers, leaves, and fruit. Several factors are involved in this color expression, the most important being the pH of the cell sap in the vacuole, the nature of the aglycone, the extent of glycolation, the concentration of anthocyanins and other flavonoids in the vacuole, and metal-complexing.

Present knowledge of the physiological properties of anthocyanins does not permit firm conclusions concerning their function. In the spring they capture blue light, the richest in energy for building chloroplasts and chlorophyll. It has also been suggested that anthocyanins provide protection against ultraviolet radiation, which is highest in spring, but this does not account for autumnal coloration when ultraviolet light is reduced and energy for metabolism is not needed.

In Delendick's (1981) survey, 130 chemical compounds (flavonoids and some simpler phenolics) were found in the Aceraceae, distributed among 188 species and a number of cultivars. One dramatic result of this comprehensive investigation is the discovery that *Acer japonicum* 'Aureum' is really *A. shirasawanum* 'Aureum'. Once Delendick announced his conclusion, it became clearly evident to others that the morphology of the two plants is identical, but prior to that many acerologists had simply "sailed along" using the incorrect name. This episode proves again that taxonomists should not accept traditional views without first exploring them in depth to fully understand the underlying fundamentals.

Delendick's (1981) study also proved the following:

1. The familial relationship between the Sapindaceae, the Hippocastanaceae, and the Aceraceae. All three are members of the Sapindales and share the ability to synthesize branched-chain $C_6$ and $C_7$ cyclopropane amino acids.
2. That *Acer campbellii* ssp. *campbelli* and ssp. *flabellatum* are similar.
3. That each maple species produces a stable and reproducible flavonoid profile.
4. The existence of a great difference between flavonoid patterns of the cotyledons and those of the true leaves.
5. That ellagic acid is a common compound present in most Aceraceae, but is absent in section *Rubra,* the derived taxa (sections *Indivisa* and *Negundo*), the species *A. campestre,* and the genus *Dipteronia.*
6. That the leaves of practically all *Acer* species produce kaempferol and quercetin.
7. That aceritannin is only found in the leaves of sections *Rubra* and *Ginnala.*
8. That glycoflavones have a very restricted distribution in the Aceraceae; a pair of apigenin-C-glycosides is shared by *Acer carpinifolium* (section *Indivisa*) and *Dipteronia.*
9. That flavonol-*O*-glycosides are absent (regarded as primitive) in two of the three series of section *Parviflora,* series *Parviflora* and *Distyla;* in sections *Ginnala, Trifoliata,* and *Hyptiocarpa;* and in the highly derived sections *Rubra* and *Negundo,* as well as in the genus *Dipteronia.* Flavonol-*O*-glycosides are regularly present in species of every section, but are absent in *Acer henryi* (section *Negundo* series *Cissifolia*) and in several species of section *Palmata.* They occur so infrequently in *A. carpinifolium* and the

species of section *Glabra* series *Arguta* that their absence in these may be considered characteristic.

10. That isorhamnetin compounds are restricted to section *Negundo* and section *Lithocarpa* series *Macrophylla.*
11. That aside from a few species in section *Palmata,* the only species that lack quercetin-3-*O*-rhamnoside are members of sections *Negundo* and *Lithocarpa.*
12. That the chemistry of section *Macrantha* does not reflect the subdivision of this section into three series, as proposed by various authorities (Pojárkova, Ogata, Murray, and Momotani).
13. That within section *Negundo,* series *Cissifolia* differs chemically from series *Negundo.*
14. That some of the most interesting and varied chemistry is found in section *Palmata,* one of the largest sections. At one extreme in some characteristics is *Acer palmatum;* at the other end is *A. japonicum.* Chemical characteristics, however, do not support the division of the section into series.
15. That the profile of the three species in section *Rubra* is indistinguishable from the profile of species in section *Ginnala.*
16. That series *Pentaphylla* of section *Pentaphylla* has a great deal in common with the other series, *Trifida.*
17. That *Acer buergerianum* 'Jako Kaede' is not a maple at all. Its chemical profile is unlike that of any maple examined. Vertrees (1972) had previously found that cuttings of this cultivar rooted readily, a phenomenon not common in maples, and Tanai (1978a, 1978b), looking at leaf venation patterns, determined this cultivar to be *Premna japonica,* a shrubby species of the Verbenaceae and a tropical plant.
18. That series *Saccharodendron* is related to series *Monspessulana* and *Acer.*
19. That section *Lithocarpa* appears to be closely related to section *Trifoliata* and series *Macrophylla* of section *Lithocarpa.*
20. That series *Macrophylla* is related to series *Lithocarpa,* the New World counterpart of this eastern Asian group, and that these species belong in section *Lithocarpa.*
21. That *Dipteronia* shares some flavonoids with *Acer carpinifolium.* The chemistry of *Dipteronia sinensis,* for example, is very much like that of most *Acer* species. In fact, there are several derived *Acer* species whose chemistry is further removed from the typical (i.e., flavonol) *Acer* pattern than is that of *Dipteronia.*

The terms *primitive* and *advanced* (or *derived*) are not absolute, but represent relative character states. They cannot be used in connection with results deriving from the simpler chemical compounds (e.g., phenolics, amino acids, carbohydrates) in precisely the same way in which they are applied to morphological characteristics. Floral parts—free versus connate or adnate; presence of a part versus its reduction or absence; actinomorphy versus zygomorphy—are useful characteristics that are generally recognized as end points of derivational series. They are so consistently correlated with character continuities or discontinuities that are considered primitive or advanced that the particular states themselves have come to be regarded as primitive or advanced, within the context of the evolution of the angiosperms. Morphological characteristics have acquired absolute instead of relative value through common usage.

One can place the flavonoids in a structural or biosynthetic sequence, but such ordering is hardly analogous to a morphological sequence. There is no continuum from one chemical profile to another comparable to that found in morphological features. A 3-hydroxyflavone is not a flavone but a flavonol; a flavonol-7-glycoside represents separate entity-variation on a theme—rather than a gradual development. Moreover, many morphological features (especially those of floral morphology) have a genetically controlled development that is quite complex as compared to the genetic factors governing the presence of various flavonoid classes. Simple mutations may stimulate or negate the synthesis of individual biochemical compounds, but although some biosynthetic steps are apparently under multiallelic control, control of flavonoid synthesis is hardly to be compared to the multigenic control of many morphological characteristics.

Hypotheses formulated to explain the status of flavonoids as phylogenetic markers have relied on correlations with morphological states. For example, Bate-Smith (1962, 1974) hypothesized that the presence of leucoanthocyanins, or, in more recent usage, proanthocyanins, is a primitive feature as these flavonoids are commonly associated with woodiness. Since then Sporne (1969, 1980) has reinforced the notion of the primitive character of proanthocyanins by correlation with a fairly extensive list of other primitive characters, but primitive or advanced characters in plants are hardly ever completely associative. No plant taxon has only primitive or only advanced features. Stipules, for example, are viewed as primitive, yet the presence of stipules has a positive correlation with only 10 of the 24 features listed as primitive.

A further complication arising from using correlations involving flavonoids is that, as compared with morphological features, the distributions of individual flavonoid compounds are still far from well known. Even in those groups where a substantial number of species have been examined, the survey is often biased towards temperate groups.

Delendick (1981) cites Gornall and Bohm, who recognized two chemical trends in the angiosperms: a reduction in structural complexity (following a reverse direction along biosynthetic pathways) and diversification (with the flavonoid nucleus undergoing progressive elaboration). As a result Gornall and Bohm distinguished among flavonoid character states that are primitive, advanced, and highly advanced. This is certainly a more realistic outlook (as it is for morphological characteristics), considering the enormous number of angiosperms and the complexity of evolutionary pathways.

## ALLELOPATHY

Allelopathy describes the harmful effects, direct or indirect, of one plant on another through the production of chemical compounds that are diffused into the environment. Such chemicals are emitted from either above- or underground parts of the plant. Allelopathy must be clearly distinguished from other environmental factors that affect plants sharing the same habitat, such as competition for water, minerals, and light. In allelopathy, chemical compounds directly reduce competition by creating a toxic environment in which other plants cannot thrive.

Probably the best known case of allelopathy is that of the walnut (*Juglans*). The compounds produced and diffused to the environment by this genus are notorious: few plant species can grow and reproduce in the immediate vicinity of trees of this genus, and its potency has been known at least from Roman times.

The genus *Acer* shares with numerous other genera an allelopathic domination, although it is not as virulent as the domination of *Juglans*. For example, *Acer saccharum* trees in North American forests produce substances allelopathic against seedlings of other trees, so that newly germinated seedlings of black spruce, *Picea mariana;* tamarack, *Larix laricina;* jack pine, *Pinus banksiana;* white spruce, *Picea glauca;* northern white cedar, *Thuja occidentalis;* and yellow birch, *Betula alleghaniensis,* are repressed exponentially when grown in *Acer saccharum* root exudate (Barrett 1980). Other inhibitory *Acer* species, from the most to the least active, are *A. campestre, A. platanoides* and ssp. *turkestanicum, A. pseudoplatanus, A. tataricum* and ssp.*ginnala, A. cappadocicum, A. negundo,* and *A. saccharinum.*

Allelopathic compounds also come into play in grafting and budding. Scions and rootstock must be from closely allied species to prevent biochemical rejection. Allelopathic relations should also be considered in selecting mixtures of *Acer* species for ornamental or forest plantings. Allelopathic activity may even, in part, account for the diffuse populations of members of the genus. It may be speculated that, unless winds can carry the samaras well away from the parent plant or others in the vicinity, the seedlings have virtually no opportunity to sprout and mature.

Chapter 5

# Paleobotany and Evolution of Maples

DR. H. J. OTERDOOM

To understand the evolution and history of maples one must begin by locating and interpreting the many fossils within the context of their present distribution throughout the world and their interrelationships in the various modern habitats. The first comprehensive paleobotanic review of the genus *Acer* was undertaken by Pax (1885, 1886). A more recent account, confined to European fossils, was completed by Walther (1972).

The angiosperms, of which *Acer* is one of thousands of genera, originated in the early Cretaceous, about 120 M.Y.B.P. (Million Years Before Present). They had dispersed across the surface of the planet by the end of this period, about 67 M.Y.B.P. This rapid conquest of flowering plants was made possible not only by geological and climatic conditions, but also by their intrinsically superior dispersal capacities and by the evolution of efficient dispersers and pollinators. From the early Cretaceous to the Miocene, eastern Asia and North America were connected by Beringia, a very broad land link between eastern Siberia and Alaska. The earth was much warmer then than at present. The tropics were twice as large, the polar regions were temperate, and no permanent ice sheets existed anywhere. Large inland shallow seas occupied extensive areas on the large continents, and many present-day continental regions were below sea level because the oceans were higher. These conditions persisted well into the Miocene (25–5 M.Y.B.P.).

Fossil maples have been found only in the Northern Hemisphere (a list of fossils is given at the end of this chapter). The first maplelike trees were found in the Upper (i.e., youngest) Cretaceous, about 100 M.Y.B.P., with 73 other genera of angiosperms in Alaska. The first maple fossil discovered in eastern North America was *Acer amboyense,* which Newberry (1896) found in the New Jersey Raritan Formation of the late Cretaceous. These maples did not look much like modern species. The principal fossil remnants discovered were leaves, fruits, wood macrofossils, and pollen microfossils.

About 90 M.Y.B.P. *Acers* species lived in Greenland, Iceland, Spitsbergen, and Alaska. These species are thought to have derived from a center of origin, diversity, and distribution in central and western China—in the modern provinces of Hubei, Sichuan, and Yunnan—although no fossils have been discovered in this region.

In the Pliocene (5–1.7 M.Y.B.P.), when the earth began to cool—heralding the onset of the Quaternary with its ice ages—maples disappeared from the circumpolar areas, retreating to present-day temperate regions. A gap was created in the great arc of deciduous forest around the North Pacific. These forests were replaced by boreal, coniferous forests and even tundra. Tropical species of many genera disappeared from the British Isles as temperatures dropped to values comparable to the present.

With knowledge of the vegetative retreat from the poles one can understand the obvious floristic and paleofloristic affinities of the eastern parts of Asia and North America. A pupil of Linnaeus by the name of Halenius was the first to call attention to this floristic relationship (1750). Ever since, botanists have speculated about the mechanism underlying this phenomenon. Pax called attention to several closely related species of *Acer* paired between eastern Asia and eastern North America. *Acer spicatum* of North America (from Labrador to Saskatchewan, and southward to northern Georgia and Iowa) closely resembles *A. caudatum* ssp. *ukurunduense* of northern Japan, Manchuria, and the southern Kuriles. The latter was at one time treated as a botanical variety or form of the distant North American species. Section *Macrantha* consists of species restricted to eastern Asia and one species, *Acer pensylvanicum,* in eastern North America, which is closely allied to the Japanese *A. capillipes* and *A. rufinerve.* The main difference between *A. rufinerve* and *A. pensylvanicum* is autumn leaf color: the Japanese species is red; the North American species is yellow. Some early authors considered all these species conspecific.

Section *Negundo,* characterized by 3- to 7-foliolate leaves, is comprised of species distributed in eastern Asia and virtually the entire North American continent. The two Asiatic species are *Acer henryi* of central China and *A. cissifolium* of Japan. Their closest relative is the North American species *A. negundo.* Another, still more striking, pair is *A. rubrum* of North America and *A. pycnanthum,* which is confined to a small area on central Honshu, the largest island of Japan. Although separated by several thousand miles and several million years, these two maples can hardly be distinguished as different species.

There is a similar relationship between *Acer circinatum,* distributed from British Columbia to northern California, and *A. japonicum,* of Honshu and Hokkaido islands, Japan. Both are native from the upper parts of the temperate zone to the lower parts of the subalpine zone and both share (1) rich autumn colors and (2) the development of specially adapted fruit and seed dispersal.

It is interesting that these presently disjunct tree species are matched by disjunct populations of phytophagous insects that feed upon them. For example, there is a strong resemblance between the eastern Asian and the eastern North American species of *Cerambycidae* (longhorn beetles), a family of fairly host-specific wood borers.

The oldest known specimens of *Acer* are found in the Upper Cretaceous North American flora of the Amboy clays in southern California. Fossils of maples from the Paleocene and Eocene epochs (65–38 M.Y.B.P.) have not been found in significant numbers. One hundred and thirty-five species of plant fossils, including *Acer,* have been identified in the Middle Eocene Green River flora in southwest Wyoming. These macro- and microfossils accumulated in a vast lake that extended across southwest Wyoming and adjacent parts of Colorado and Utah.

The oldest maple species found in Europe is *Acer haselbachensis* from the Eocene-Oligocene border (about 38 M.Y.B.P.). Fossils of *A. tricuspidatum* Braun (1845), are also found in Europe, most frequently in the Upper Oligocene to Lower Pliocene (40–16 M.Y.B.P.), with the exception of the Middle Miocene, which probably was too warm for this species in section *Rubra.* Microfossils of pollen are reported by Chester et al. (1967) from the former Soviet Union in the Oligocene (e.g., *A. platanoides*). In some deposits from the Upper Oligocene, *A. paleosaccharinum* Stur (1867), related to modern *A. saccharum,* is the dominant maple, but it disappears altogether after the Lower Miocene.

Maples came into their own in the Miocene. The Mascall flora of the Miocene, excavated from sediments in east-central Oregon between Dayville and Mount Vernon, includes 70 species of temperate trees, of which *Acer bolanderi* Lesquereux (1878) is the most abundant maple. Modern species closely related to this ancient species include *A. saccharum* ssp. *grandidentatum* and *A. saccharum* ssp. *leucoderme.* Also found in this fossil flora was *A. negundoides* MacGinitie (1933), related to *A. negundo* and *A. henryi,* the latter native to central China.

Many paleo-species disappeared during and following the Pliocene (5–1.7 M.Y.B.P.) as a result of climatic deterioration. This is especially true in Europe where plants had little opportunity to migrate southward due to the east–west structure of the mountains in central Europe. In contrast, the north–south structure of the North American mountains and vast areas in China, and the wide-open steppes of eastern Asia afforded plants the opportunity to retreat before the advancing ice sheets.

In Europe *Acer integrilobum* Weber (1852), probably related to *A. cappadocicum,* is found in disjunct periods: Lower–Middle Miocene, the Upper Miocene, and again at the Miocene–Pliocene border. *Acer integrilobum* is presumed to be a member of section *Platanoidea.* The related fossil *A. integerrimum* (Vivani) Massalongo (1859), sometimes found in abundance, is the presumed ancestor of *A. cappadocicum.* This fossil maple is found in the middle of the Lower Miocene, but more frequently in the Upper Pliocene. *Acer sancta-crucis* Stur (1867) is occasionally found in strata from the middle European Tertiary, and clearly belongs to section *Palmata. Acer rueminianum,* found in the Lower Miocene of central Europe and in the Upper Oligocene of Switzerland, cannot be related to any modern species. *Acer decipiens* Heer (1859), found in the Lower and Upper Miocene and in the Lower and Upper Pliocene, is a near relative of the present-day *A. monspessulanum.* Fossils of *A. crenatifolium* Ettingshausen (1869), considered the most probable ancestor of *A. hyrcanum,* are present in the Middle and Upper Miocene and in the Lower Pliocene.

Walther (1972) suggests the fossil maple *Acer engelhardtii* is related to the modern species *A. kwangsiense,* which, according to him, is identical to *A. tonkinense.* He also believes the fossil *A. integrilobum* is related to *A. longipes.* Both modern species now grow in the wild only in China and Vietnam.

The modern view of the evolution of the genus *Acer* is presented by Firsov (1982) and summarized here. In light of the modern distribution of the genus *Acer,* we can conclude that the place of origin and distribution must be central, southwest, and western China—the modern provinces of Hubei, Sichuan, and Yunnan. Present populations suggest that the genus radiated in three directions from this center: westward along the Himalayas into Persia, Afghanistan, and Asia Minor, and subsequently to the Balkans and Europe; southward into Indo-China, Malaysia, Indonesia, and the Philippines; and northeast into Manchuria, Korea, Japan, and eastern Siberia, from which it crossed Beringia into North America, western Greenland, Iceland, and Spitsbergen. *Acer* reached the apex of its development in the Miocene. Its trees were most abundant not only in the number of species and individuals, but also in distribution, for they covered the largest land mass ever attained by the genus.

*Acer* was adversely affected by the Pleistocene glaciations, especially in Europe. In North America the genus was pushed southward, giving rise to modern disjunct pockets as far south as Guatemala. After the glacial period broke the continuous areas of the ancient taxa, the final formation and fixation of the numerous geographic taxa occurred. However, most evolution and development had taken place before the catastrophe of the Pleistocene.

One of the most striking events in the history of the genus *Acer* was the tendency to develop flowers of one gender, even though some taxa vary the gender in one inflorescence from male to female or female to male. Only a few species are fully dioecious (e.g., *A. negundo*). This transformation was accomplished by reducing the number of floral parts. However, the reduction in flower parts also led to the loss of the nectarial disc, resulting in inefficient wind pollination rather than pollination by nectar-seeking insects.

It may be assumed that the original maple flower lost two stamens of the epipetalous whorl early on because primitive related taxa (e.g., *Dipteronia*) display the same loss. In some taxa, especially those with a 6-merous perianth, the number of stamens increased to 9–13; in others, especially those with a 4-merous perianth, the epipetalous whorl is often completely eliminated (see Table 1 in Chapter 4).

As mentioned in Chapter 4, Pax (1885), Koidzumi (1911), and Pojárkova (1933) considered the mode of staminal insertion in the disc to be phylogenetically significant. Pojárkova assumed that an amphistaminal disc, as in the Sapindaceae, was the most common type, and she ascribed this form to the Aceraceae. The common type in *Acer,* however, and in *Aesculus, Dipteronia,* and nearly all sapindaceous genera, is extrastaminal and was certainly present in the original maple flowers.

The major trends in the evolution of flowering and sexual expression in *Acer*—from insect-pollinated to wind-pollinated and from monoecy to dioecy—were first described by Pax (1885). All authors refer, in this connection, to *A. negundo,* the single species of the genus in which both developments have been completed.

Other trends in the evolution of the genus are less significant though still meaningful. One example is the form of the leaves. Walther (1972) mentions this change of leaf form in the fossil species *Acer tricuspidatum* from the Late Oligocene to the Early Pliocene. The evolution required all 20 million years of the Miocene (Fig. 5.1). The impression derived from paleobotanic studies is that 3-lobed maples were initially much more abundant than 5-lobed maples. The rather sudden broadening leaf base leads to the view that 5-lobed leaves of maples evolved from the 3-lobed.

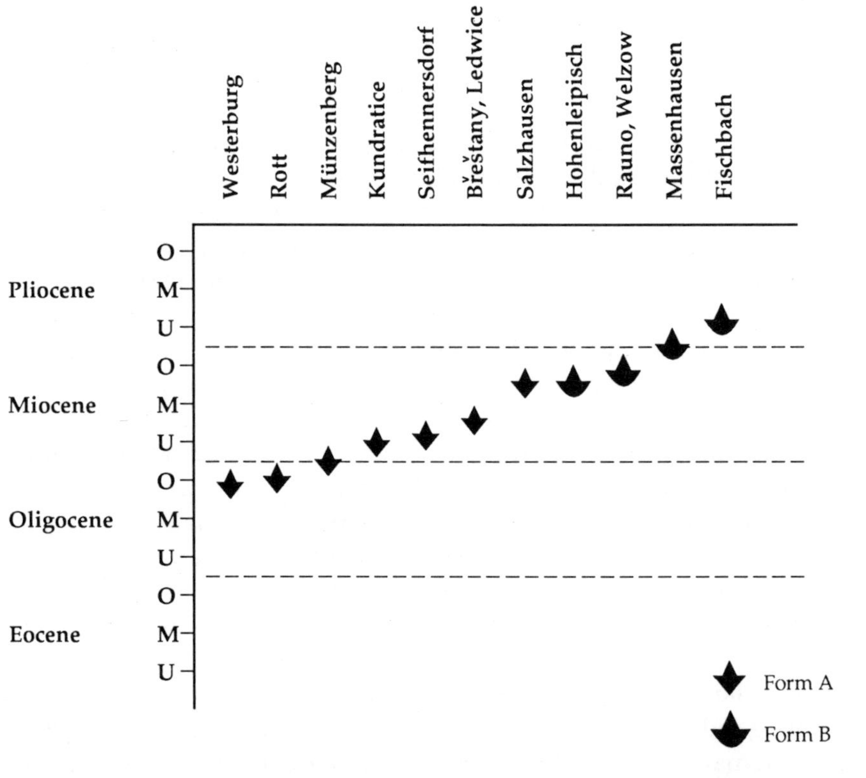


FIGURE 5.1. Changes in the basal parts of the leaf in *Acer tricuspidatum* during the Middle European Tertiary (Walther, 1972). Used with permission.

Since its original description, *Dipteronia* has been classed within the Aceraceae, and there has been continuing discussion about giving it a separate status or even possibly excluding it from this family. *Dipteronia* and *Acer* are believed to have diverged very early. Fossil leaflets and fruits of the former are among the earliest fossils of both Asia and North America, and the genus appears to be closer to the presumed common sapindaceous ancestor than to *Acer,* especially in foliar morphology and pollen type. The recently reported chromosome number for *Dipteronia* ($2n = 20$) is further evidence of a closer relationship with the Sapindaceae than with the Aceraceae. The haploid number ($x = 13$) that characterizes the Aceraceae is very uncommon in the Sapindaceae. Chemically, however, *Dipteronia* possesses a typical advanced *Acer* pattern.

## List of Fossil *Acer*

*Acer acutelobatum* Ludwig (1860)
*Acer alvordense* Axelrod (1944)
*Acer ambiguum* Heer (1878)
*Acer amboyense* Newberry (1896)
*Acer ampelophyllum* Saporta (1862)
*Acer angustifolium* Heer (1883)
*Acer aquidentatum* Lesquereux (1878)
*Acer aquilum* Chaney (1920)
*Acer aquimontanum* Unger (1854)
*Acer arcticum* Heer (1877)
*Acer beckerianum* Goeppert (1852)
*Acer bendirei* Lesquereux (1889)
*Acer bilinicum* Ettingshausen (1869)
*Acer bolanderi* Lesquereux (1878)
*Acer boloense* Massalonga (1851)
*Acer borussicum* Caspary (1887)
*Acer brachyphyllum* Heer (1859)
*Acer bruckmannii* Heer (1859)
*Acer chaneyi* Knowlton (1926)
*Acer coloradense* McGinitie (1953)
*Acer columbianum* Chaney & Axelrod (1959)
*Acer completum* Chaney (1920)
*Acer corneliae* Massalonga ex Saporta (1879)
*Acer crassinervium* Ettingshausen (1869)
*Acer crassipes* Heer (1859)
*Acer crenatifolium* Ettingshausen (1869)
*Acer cytisifolium* Goeppert (1855)
*Acer dasycarpoides* Heer (1859)
*Acer debilum* Huzioka & Suzuki (1954)
*Acer decipiens* Heer (1859)
*Acer decurrens* Lamotte (1952)
*Acer engelhardtii* Walther (1972)
*Acer eupalmatum* Koidzumi ex Endo (1934)
*Acer eupterigium* Unger (1847)
*Acer florigerum* Cockerell (1908)
*Acer florinii* Hu & Chaney (1940)
*Acer florissantii* Kirchner (1898)
*Acer fragile* Knowlton (1917)
*Acer fremontense* Lamotte (1952)
*Acer gargueiri* Saporta (1865)
*Acer gaudinii* Schimper (1874)
*Acer giganteum* Goeppert (1852)
*Acer gigas* Knowlton (1902)
*Acer glabroides* R. Brown (1937)
*Acer glandilosum* Massalongo (1859)
*Acer gracile* Saporta (1867)
*Acer gracilescens* Lesquereux (1883)
*Acer granatense pliocenicum* Saporta (1873)
*Acer grossedentatum* Heer (1859
*Acer haselbachensis* Walther 1972
*Acer heerii* Massalongo (1858)
*Acer heterodentatum* McGinitie (1953)
*Acer hilgendorfii* Nathorst (1883)
*Acer inaequale* Heer (1877)
*Acer inaequaterale* Saporta (1866)
*Acer inaequilobum* Kovats (1856)
*Acer incisum* Heer (1859)
*Acer indivisum* Weber (1852)
*Acer integerrimum* (Vivani) Massalongo (1859)
*Acer integrilobum* Weber (1852)
*Acer integrum* Borissova-Bekrjasheva ex Pojárkova (1949)
*Acer islandicum* Heer (1869)
*Acer isolobum* Massalongo (1859)
*Acer italicum* Massalongo (1859)
*Acer jurenakii* Stur (1867)
*Acer kirchnerianum* Knowlton (1916)
*Acer klipsteinii* Ettingshausen (1868)
*Acer knowltonii* Brown (1940)
*Acer kokangenense* Endo (1950)
*Acer koreanicum* Endo (1950)
*Acer limburgense* Godwin (1956)
*Acer maginii* Rerolle (1885)
*Acer magnum* Velenovsky (1881)
*Acer majus* sensu Caspary (1865), non Gray
*Acer massiliense* Saporta (1865)
*Acer mchenryi* Hu & Chaney (1940)
*Acer medianum* Knowlton (1902)
*Acer megalopteryx* Unger (1847)
*Acer meisenense* Endo (1950)
*Acer merriamii* Knowlton (1902)
*Acer meunzenbergense* Ludwig (1860)
*Acer micranthum* sensu Caspary (1881), non Siebold & Zuccarini

*Acer middlegatei* Axelrod (1956)
*Acer minus* Knowlton (1902)
*Acer minutifolium* Chaney (1920)
*Acer minutum* Hollick (1892)
*Acer miocaudatum* Hu & Chaney (1940)
*Acer miodavidii* Hu & Chaney (1940)
*Acer miofranchetii* Hu & Chaney (1940)
*Acer mysticum* Kirchner (1898)
*Acer narbonense* Saporta (1865)
*Acer negundoides* McGinitie (1933)
*Acer nicolai* Boulay (1890)
*Acer nordenskiolii* Nathorst (1883)
*Acer obligopteryx* Saporta (1889)
*Acer obliquum* Pimenov ex Pojárkova (1949)
*Acer obtusilobum* Unger (1847)
*Acer oeynhausianum* Goeppert (1855)
*Acer oligondontum* Heer (1869)
*Acer opuloides* Heer (1859)
*Acer orbum* Lamotte (1952)
*Acer oregonianum* Knowlton (1902)
*Acer osmontii* Knowlton (1902)
*Acer otopteryx* Goeppert (1852)
*Acer palaeo-campestre* Ettingshausen (1870)
*Acer palaeo-diabolicum* Endo (1950)
*Acer palaeo-miyabei* Maedler (1939)
*Acer palaeo-palmatum* Langeron (1901)
*Acer palaeo-platanoides* Endo (1950)
*Acer palaeo-saccharinum* Stur (1867)
*Acer parschlugianum* Unger (1847)
*Acer patens* Braun ex Unger (1850)
*Acer paucidentatum* Hollick (1897)
*Acer pegasinum* Unger (1847)
*Acer perditum* Cockerell (1908)
*Acer pictoides* Baikov ex Pojárkova (1949)
*Acer platyphyllum* Braun ex Unger (1850)
*Acer pleistocenicum* Penhallow (1890)
*Acer pliocaenicum* Saporta ex Berry (1923)
*Acer pliocenicum* Chaney (1933)
*Acer ponzianum* Gaudin (1858)
*Acer populites* Ettingshausen (1869)
*Acer populifolium* Krasnov (1911)
*Acer primaevum* Saporta (1862)
*Acer pristinum* (Newberry) Pax (1902)
*Acer productum* Braun (1851)
*Acer protensum* Braun (1851)
*Acer proto-distylum* Endo (1950)
*Acer proto-miyabei* Endo (1950)
*Acer proto-trifidum* Tanai (1952)
*Acer pseudocampestre* Unger (1847)
*Acer pseudocarpinifolium* Endo (1950)
*Acer pseudo-chrysophyllum* Lesquereux (1878)
*Acer pseudo-creticum* Ettingshausen (1851)
*Acer pseudo-monspessulanum* Unger (1847)
*Acer quinquelobum* Saporta (1865)
*Acer radiatum* Braun (1845)
*Acer recognitum* Saporta (1867)
*Acer ribifolium* Goeppert (1855)
*Acer rueminianum* Heer (1859)
*Acer sachalinum* Heer (1878)
*Acer sancti-crucis* Stur (1867)
*Acer santagatae* Massalongo (1859)
*Acer saskatchewanense* Dawson (1876)
*Acer saxonicum* Unger ex Pax (1885)
*Acer scharlokii* Caspary (1886)
*Acer schimperi* Heer (1859)
*Acer schmalhausenii* Palibin (1901)
*Acer schumannii* Conwentz (1886)
*Acer sclerophyllum* Heer (1859)
*Acer scottiae* McGinitie (1933)
*Acer secretum* Lesquereux (1872)
*Acer septilobatum* Oliver (1934)
*Acer sepultum* Andrae (1855)
*Acer sibiricum* Herer (1878)
*Acer siifolium* Goeppert (1852)
*Acer sphendaminum* Massalongo (1859)
*Acer sturii* Engelhardt (1881)
*Acer subcampestre* Goeppert (1855)
*Acer subintegrilobum* Ettingshausen (1887)
*Acer subpictum* Saporta (1873)
*Acer subrecognitum* Barolle (1885)
*Acer subtenuilobatum* Langeron (1901)
*Acer succineum* Caspary (1880)
*Acer sugawarai* Endo (1951)
*Acer tenuilobatum* Saporta (1867)
*Acer terra-caeruleae* Caspary (1887)
*Acer torontoniense* Penhallow (1907)
*Acer trachyticum* Kovats (1856)
*Acer triaenum* Massalongo)
*Acer triangulilobum* Goeppert (1855)
*Acer tricuspidatum* Braun (1845)
*Acer trifoliatum* sensu Braun (1845), non Rafinesque
*Acer trilobum* Lamotte, non Moench (1952)
*Acer tyrellii* Smiley (1963)
*Acer visibile* Hollick (1936)
*Acer vitifolium* sensu Unger (1845)
*Acer voltianum* Massalongo (1851)
*Acer vivarium* Knowlton (1899)
*Acer yabei* Endo (1950)

Chapter 6

# Taxonomy and Reproductive Biology of Maples

DR. P. C. DE JONG

Students of the taxonomy of *Acer* include a long and distinguished group of plant scientists. Despite their enormous body of knowledge and data, several taxa are still poorly defined. The affinities of numerous taxa, mainly within the sections, remain unclear. Modern research, especially in biochemistry, has clarified some obscure relationships, but other recent data, in turn, have brought previously accepted views into question. These new taxonomic research methods and data have proved not only the complexity of the genus but also the importance and inadequacies of a purely morphological approach.

Several recently proposed classifications differ substantially from one another and also reveal different species concepts. The classification presented in this volume focuses on species concepts, and, as a result of extensive biological, taxonomic, and nomenclatural research on *Acer,* proposes 14 new combinations: one new varietal combination, 12 new subspecific combinations, and one new sectional combination. These new combinations are indicated by the Latin *comb. nov.* or *comb. & stat. nov.* wherever appropriate, and the basionym is presented in the text of the following taxonomic treatment. The new name combinations in this volume that propose nomenclatural rank and status are as follows:

*A. campbellii* ssp. *sinense* (Pax) de Jong

*A. campbellii* ssp. sinense var. *longilobum* (Fang) de Jong

*A. campbellii* ssp. *wilsonii* (Rehder) de Jong

*A. davidii* ssp. *grosseri* (Pax) de Jong

*A. longipes* ssp. *amplum* (Rehder) de Jong

*A. longipes* ssp. *catalpifolium* (Rehder) de Jong

*A. longipes* ssp. *firmianioides* (Cheng ex Fang) de Jong

*A. mono* ssp. *okamotoanum* (Nakai) de Jong

*A. platanoides* ssp. *turkestanicum* (Pax) de Jong

*A. pseudosieboldianum* ssp. *takesimense* (Nakai) de Jong

*A. sikkimense* ssp. *metcalfii* (Rehder) de Jong

*A. stachyophyllum* ssp. *betulifolium* (Maximowicz) de Jong

*A. tataricum* ssp. *aidzuense* (Franchet) de Jong

Section *Wardiana* (de Jong) de Jong

## HISTORICAL SURVEY OF CLASSIFICATION SYSTEMS

The genus *Acer* was created by Tournefort in 1700. Linnaeus (1737a) accepted *Acer* as a distinct genus in the first edition of his *Genera Plantarum*. Later in *Species Plantarum* (1753) he described nine species, of which *A. pseudoplatanus* is accepted as the type species of the genus.

The first monographs of the genus were written by Lauth (1781), Thunberg (1793), and Spach (1834). However, the most important early monograph was written by Pax, who published two comprehensive papers—the first in 1885 (continued in 1886) and the second in 1902. By the time the latter paper was published, large herbarium collections from eastern Asia had become available and thus Pax distinguished 114 species arranged into 13 sections. He further grouped the sections into four "categories" and produced a phylogenetic scheme.

The delimitation of the genus led to considerable controversy, mainly about the placement of *Acer negundo*. Several authors placed this species in the separate genus *Negundo* (Boehmer 1760, Moench 1794, de Candolle 1824, Endlicher 1836–1840, Bentham & Hooker 1862, Rydberg 1913, Plowman 1915, and Small 1933). Rafinesque (1833) proposed the name *Negundium* for this taxon. Nieuwland (1911, 1914) and Small (1933) placed other *Acer* species in separate genera. None of these views are currently supported.

The name Aceraceae was first used by Lindley (1836) for an order. Because Jussieu (1789), however, proposed the name Acera for the family, he is considered the founder of the family in keeping with article 18 of the International Code of Botanical Nomenclature (ICBN). Most authors have accepted this family name, which includes *Acer* and the small genus *Dipteronia* Oliver that includes only two species, both native to central and southwestern China. For some time *Dobinea* Buchanan-Hamilton was also included in the Aceraceae (Don 1825, Endlicher 1836–1840, Bentham & Hooker 1862), but at present this genus is placed in the Podoaceae, a small family related to the Anacardiaceae (Willis 1980).

The Aceraceae have been considered part of the order Sapindaceae (Reichenbach 1828, 1834, Horaninov 1847, Gray 1858, Braun 1860, Bentham & Hooker 1862, and Drude 1887), or at least as closely allied to that family and to the Hippocastanaceae (Cronquist 1968, Takhtajan 1969). Palynological studies by Muller and Leenhouts (1976) showed strong affinities between these families. These authors found that "macromorphologically there is no clear demarcation between the Sapindaceae on the one hand and the Aceraceae and Hippocastanaceae on the other." Their diagram of phylogenetic relationships shows the Hippocastanaceae as possibly included in the Sapindaceae tribus Harpullieae (subfamily Dodonaeoideae). They considered the Aceraceae as probably near this tribe.

*Dipteronia* appears closer to the presumed sapindaceous ancestor in most characteristics than to *Acer*. According to Arends and Van der Laan (1979), its chromosome count ($n = 10$) is likely more in keeping with *Aesculus* ($n = 20$) of the Hippocastanaceae and with the Sapindaceae ($n = 10$–$14$) than with that of *Acer* ($n = 13$). All modern students of the family and all standard references refer the Aceraceae to the order Sapindales.

Following Pax, several further taxonomic studies on the genus were undertaken. Of special interest are the studies of Pojárkova (1933b), Momotani (1961, 1962b), Ogata (1967), Murray (1970a–i), de Jong (1976), and Delendick (1981). Various regional taxonomic revisions and surveys of the genus have also been published: for China, Fang (1939, 1966, 1979a,

1979b, 1981a, 1981b), and Hu & Cheng (1948); for Russia and the other republics of the former Soviet Union, Pojárkova (1933a, 1933b, 1949); for Europe, Gams (1925) and Walters (1968); for Indochina, Gagnepain (1950); for Iran, Murray (1969b); for Japan, Miquel (1867a), Koidzumi (1911a, 1911b), and Ogata (1965); for Korea, Nakai (1915a, 1915b); for Malaysia, Bloembergen (1948); for Nepal, Banerji and Das (1971); for North America, Sargent (1891a, 1891b) and Brizicky (1963); for Pakistan, Murray (1975a); and for Turkey, Yaltirik (1967a, 1967b, 1971). In addition, the following authors contributed to the taxonomy and classification or published surveys of the genus: Bean (1970), Desmarais (1952), Ellis (1963), Errico (1957), Firsov (1982), Keller (1942), Koch (1869), Krüssmann (1976a, 1984), Lippold (1968), Mai (1983, 1984), Maximowicz (1880), Nicholson (1881), Rehder (1905, 1907, 1927, 1933, 1949), Santamour (1982a), Schneider (1907, 1909), Schwerin (1893, 1903), Warsow (1903), and Wesmael (1890).

Before Pax (1885) divided the genus into "categories" and sections, other authors had already distinguished separate taxa. Rafinesque (1836) distinguished six subgenera based on the species native to North America. Koch (1869) divided the genus into four "groups." Maximowicz (1880) proposed two sections, *Acer* and *Negundo.*

Pax's "categories" and Koch's "groups" have no taxonomic status, and were based on two specific morphological characters of the flowers: the presence of a honey disc, and the insertion of the stamens on it. The sections were based mainly on leaf, inflorescence, and fruit features. Pax arranged the genus as follows:

| Extrastaminalia | Adiscantha | Perigyna |
|---|---|---|
| Section *Rubra* | Section *Negundo* | Section *Glabra* |
| Section *Spicata* | | Section *Campestria* |
| Section *Palmata* | Intrastaminalia | Section *Platanoidea* |
| Section *Trifoliata* | Section *Macrantha* | Section *Saccharina* |
| Section *Integrifolia* | Section *Indivisa* | Section *Lithocarpa* |

Except for section *Negundo* (Boehmer) Maximowicz, the above sections were first described by Pax.

Rehder (1905) accepted Pax's divisions, but added one new section, *Arguta.* In 1949, however, Rehder reduced all sections except section *Negundo* to series rank under section *Acer.* Koidzumi (1911a) simplified Pax's arrangement to the extent of recognizing only two major "divisions" within *Acer,* Intrastaminalia and Extrastaminalia. He erected five new sections for Japanese species, including two monotypic sections—*Carpinifolia* for *Acer carpinifolium* and *Parviflora* for *A. nipponicum.* Nakai (1915b), in turn, formalized Koidzumi's "divisions" by listing them as subgenera and added his own subgenus *Circumstaminalia.* He removed *Acer ginnala* from Pax's very heterogenous section *Spicata* and placed it in a new section, *Ginnala.*

Pojárkova (1933b) was the first to criticize Pax's system by pointing out the heterogeneity of many sections. She proposed a more natural grouping of the genus into 17 sections, 4 of which were new; in each section 1–5 series were distinguished, yielding a total of 32. Pojárkova reclassified the species of Pax's heterogeneous section *Spicata* into three sections. However, she included *Acer campestre* and *A. miyabei* from Pax's section *Campestria* in section *Platanoidea.* She was the first to associate some Old and New World taxa: series *Lithocarpa* (syn. series *Villosa* Pojárkova) with series *Macrophylla;* series *Monspessulana* with series Saccharodendron (syn. series *Saccharum* Pojárkova); and series *Arguta* with series *Glabra.*

Momotani (1962b) later divided the genus into three subgenera: *Acer, Negundo,* and *Carpinifolia.* He arranged 13 sections in subgenus *Acer,* including one new section, *Macrophylla.* He proposed a very natural grouping of the genus, except for the heterogeneous section

*Integrifolia,* which contains species with entire leaves and was further sorted out by Fang (1966) and Ogata (1967).

Fang's studies of Chinese maples spanned half a century (1932, 1939, 1966, 1979, 1981). In his revision published in 1966, he proposed one new section, *Hyptiocarpa,* and accepted Hu and Cheng's (1948) section *Pentaphylla.* His treatment of the genus combines the concepts of Pojárkova and Rehder, but he was unaware of Momotani's publications. In my opinion his division of the genus is rather artificial (i.e., his subgenus *Negundo* includes all maples with compound leaves).

Ogata (1967) made a careful study of wood anatomy and morphology. As a result he eschewed distinctions at the subgeneric level, recognizing 25 sections. He gave much attention to phylogeny, but some interesting taxa from western and southeastern Asia, important for phylogenetic or taxonomic reasons, were not adequately available to him and he was unaware of Fang's 1966 publication.

The main objectives to which Murray (1970a) addressed his study of the genus were (1) to assess previous classifications of the family, (2) to determine the correct status for each name, and (3) to classify each entity in an orderly arrangement. The major portion of Murray's thesis (which is not a valid publication) is a catalogue of about 5000 epithets arranged in alphabetical order. He proposed seven subgenera with four sections and 35 series. The subgenera were based mainly on morphological differences in flowers and inflorescences (especially the arrangements of the latter on the twigs) and the mode of sexual expression (monoecious or dioecious). In distinguishing taxa of lower rank, particularly the series, leaf morphology was used as the principal criterion. The flowers were superficially described as 4- or 5-merous with no further attention to the morphology of sepals and petals, the number of stamens, and the mode of staminal insertion. The inflorescences were roughly described as corymbose, paniculate, or racemose. The disregard of important phylogenetic characteristics of bud scales, flowers, and inflorescences, and the importance given to leaf morphology resulted in a very artificial classification of the genus, and Murray's approach is in marked contrast to that of other students of his generation. In fact, he did not change his classification after the papers of Ogata (1967) and de Jong (1976) were made available to him. These only induced him to propose two more new subgenera and one new section in volume 13 of his privately published periodical *Kalmia* (1983). Murray's catalogue (the thesis) of published *Acer* names is, however, virtually complete to 1970 and has become an important reference tool for later students of the genus.

In 1976 de Jong published a comprehensive study of flowering and sexual expression in the genus. His systematic scheme comprises 14 sections of which 9 are subdivided into two or three series:

Section *Acer*
- Series *Acer*
- Series *Monspessulana* Pojárkova
- Series *Saccharodendron* (Rafinesque) Murray

Section *Platanoidea* Pax
- Series *Platanoidea*
- Series *Pubescentia* Pojárkova

Section *Palmata* Pax
- Series *Palmata*
- Series *Sinensia* Pojárkova
- Series *Penninervia* Metcalf

Section *Macrantha* Pax
- Series *Tegmentosa* Pojárkova

Series *Wardiana* De Jong
Section *Parviflora* Koidzumi
Series *Parviflora*
Series *Distyla* (Ogata) Murray
Series *Ukurunduensia* de Jong
Section *Trifoliata* Pax
Section *Rubra* Pax
Section *Ginnala* Nakai
Section *Lithocarpa* Pax
Series *Lithocarpa*
Series *Macrophylla* Pojárkova
Section *Negundo* (Boehmer) Maximowicz
Series *Negundo*
Series *Cissifolia* (Koidzumi) Momotani
Section *Glabra* Pax
Series *Glabra*
Series *Arguta* (Rehder) Rehder
Section *Integrifolia* Pax
Series *Trifida* Pax
Series *Pentaphylla* (Hu & Cheng) Murray
Section *Indivisa* Pax
Section *Hyptiocarpa* Fang

De Jong also studied the distribution patterns of these sections (Table 2). His study of the sequences of male and female flowers within inflorescences and remarks by the artists who illustrated the flowering branches led to more study of *Acer* flowers and inflorescences and later to further work on the taxonomy and phylogeny of the genus. Although this classification was adopted by Krüssmann (1976a, 1984) and Firsov (1982), a somewhat different sectional analysis is presented by de Jong in the present volume, one which takes into account the biochemical studies of Delendick (1981) and Santamour (1982a) and the carpomorphologic studies of Mai (1983, 1984) (see "Taxonomic Synopsis" later in this chapter).

TABLE 2. Geographic distribution of *Acer* species per section (de Jong, 1976).

| Section | Europe & Western Asia | Central & Eastern Asia | China | Japan | Western North America | Eastern North America | Total area |
|---|---|---|---|---|---|---|---|
| I *Acer* | 8 | 1 | 1 | | | 1(+1) | 10(+1) |
| II *Platanoidea* | 4 | 13(+6) | 9(+5) | 2 | | | 15(+6) |
| III *Palmata* | | 29(+11) | 20(+9) | 5 | 1 | | 30(+11) |
| IV *Macrantha* | | 15(+4) | 7(+2) | 4(+1) | | 1 | 16(+4) |
| V *Parviflora* | | 3 | 1 | 3 | | 1 | 4 |
| VI *Trifoliata* | | 5(+4) | 5(+4) | | | | 5(+4) |
| VII *Rubra* | | 1 | | 1 | | 2 | 3 |
| VIII *Ginnala* | 1 | 2(+2) | 1(+1) | 1(+1) | | | 3(+2) |
| IX *Lithocarpa* | | 4(+6) | 3(+4) | 1 | 1 | | 5(+6) |
| X *Negundo* | | 2 | 1 | 1 | 1 | 1 | 3 |
| XI *Glabra* | | 4(+1) | 1(+1) | 1 | 1 | | 5(+1) |
| XII *Integrifolia* | | 8(+6) | 8(+6) | | | | 8(+6) |
| XIII *Indivisa* | | 1 | | 1 | | | 1 |
| XIV *Hyptiocarpa* | | 3(+4) | 2(+3) | | | | 3(+4) |
| Genus **ACER** | 13 | 90(+44) | 59(+34) | 20(+2) | 4 | 6(+1) | 111(+45) |

( ) insufficiently known taxa: (sub) species or synonyms

Delendick (1981) developed an intensive interest in the taxonomy of the genus while engaged in research on the chemistry of *Acer* flavonoids. His critical review of previous classifications, especially those of Ogata (1967) and de Jong (1976), led him to propose 20 sections arranged in five groups. Some of de Jong's series were given sectional rank following Ogata and Murray (1970a). Delendick's classification is as follows:

Section *Parviflora* Koidzumi
  Series *Parviflora*
  Series *Caudata* Pax
  Series *Distyla* (Ogata) Murray
Section *Macrantha* Pax
Section *Glabra* Pax
Section *Arguta* Rehder
Section *Indivisa* Pax
Section *Negundo* (Boehmer) Maximowicz
Section *Cissifolia* Koidzumi
Section *Palmata* Pax
Section *Ginnala* Nakai
Section *Rubra* Pax
Section *Hyptiocarpa* Fang
Section *Oblonga* (Hu & Cheng) Delendick
Section *Pentaphylla* Hu & Cheng
Section *Platanoidea* Pax
Section *Pubescentia* (Pojárkova) Ogata
Section *Acer*
Section *Goniocarpa* Pojárkova
Section *Saccharina* Pax
Section *Trifoliata* Pax
Section *Lithocarpa* Pax
Section *Macrophylla* Momotani

Delendick's series *Caudata* of section *Parviflora* is synonymous with de Jong's series *Ukurunduensia* (of 1976), a nomenclatural problem discussed later in this chapter under section *Parviflora*.

In a paper dealing with his research on the chemistry of the peroxidase activity of isoenzymes in cambial tissues, Santamour (1982a) tested the classifications of Rehder (1949), Murray (1970a), and de Jong (1976). His work involved the chemistry of about 50 species. While his results certainly are of interest, they are of limited value, particularly above the level of section. Santamour found affinities between series *Acer* and series *Monspessulana* (*A. hyrcanum* and *A. opalus*) of section *Acer; A. campestre* and *A. platanoides* of section *Platanoidea; A. rubrum* and *A. saccharinum* of section *Rubra; A. buergerianum* of series *Trifida* and *A. pentaphyllum* of section and series *Pentaphylla* (as seen by this present volume); and further between the taxa of section *Ginnala* (i.e., the complex species *A. tataricum* as seen by this present volume). Other taxa showed rather different patterns; for example, subspecies *saccharum* and *grandidentatum* of *A. saccharum; A. monspessulanum* and *A. opalus* of series *Monspessulana* (section *Acer*); *A. distylum* and *A. spicatum* of section *Parviflora;* and *A. griseum* and *A. mandshuricum* of section *Trifoliata.*

In 1983 Mai published the results of his study of the endocarps of European and western Asian taxa. Due to the differences in endocarps of *Acer campestre, A. platanoides,* and *A. cappadocicum,* he revived Pojárkova's concept of distinguishing series *Campestria* within section *Platanoidea.* He further retained series *Pubescentia* within section *Platanoidea,* despite observed similarities to species of other sections. Finally, series *Monspessulana* of section *Acer* was given sectional rank as section *Goniocarpa.* Although Mai's study involved only a small part of the genus, his remarks on the development of endocarps during the evolution of the genus are of great importance in understanding the phylogeny of maples.

In 1984 Mai published a further paper on the same subject that covered the whole genus. While acknowledging the necessity of incorporating all morphological characters as well as paleobotanic studies in constructing a natural scheme, he found that differences in carpomorphological characters permitted the determination of sections and series. He further separated the genus into four phylogenetic clusters (*Abstammungsgemeinschaft*) that, in his opinion, could be considered as subgenera. His taxonomic treatment is nomenclaturally incorrect in part and does not take into account Delendick's research and classification scheme. Compared to his 1983 paper, Mai's 1984 classification gives *Pubescentia* sectional rank, discounting affinities with section *Platanoidea,* and treats the series *Arguta, Ukurunduensia, Grisea,* and *Macrophylla* as separate sections. (Further comments on his classification are included in the notes added to the description of the sections proposed in this present volume, as well as in the phylogenetic discussion.) While Mai's arrangement of series is not followed in the present volume, his studies give a better understanding of the phylogeny of the genus and clarify some uncertain affinities. His classification of the genus is as follows:

- Subgenus *Acer (aceroide Abstammungsgemeinschaft)*
  - Section *Acer*
    - Series *Acer*
    - Series *Saccharodendron*
  - Section *Goniocarpa*
    - Series *Monspessulana*
  - Section *Pentaphylla*
    - Series *Pentaphylla*
    - Series *Trifida*
  - Section *Hyptiocarpa*
    - Series *Decandra*
  - Section *Rubra*
    - Series *Eriocarpa*
    - Series *Rubra*
- Subgenus *Carpinifolia (spicatoide Abstammungsgemeinschaft)*
  - Section *Parviflora*
    - Series *Parviflora*
    - Series *Distyla*
  - Section *Arguta*
    - Series *Arguta*
    - Series *Ukurunduensia*
  - Section *Glabra*
    - Series *Glabra*
  - Section *Macrantha*
    - Series *Tegmentosa*
    - Series *Rufinervia*
    - Series *Wardiana*
  - Section *Palmata*
    - Series *Palmata*
    - Series *Sinensia*
    - Series *Penninervia*

Section *Pubescentia*
Series *Pubescentia*
Section *Ginnala*
Series *Tatarica*
Section *Indivisa*
Series *Carpinifolia*
Subgenus *Sterculiacea (campestroide Abstammungsgemeinschaft)*
Section *Platanoidea*
Series *Platanoidea*
Series *Campestria*
Section *Trifoliata*
Series *Grisea*
Series *Macrophylla*
Section *Lithocarpa*
Series *Lithocarpa*
Series *Diabolica*
Subgenus *Negundo (negundoide Abstammungsgemeinschaft)*
Section *Negundo*
Series *Negundo*

## PHYLOGENETIC CONCEPTS

As already described, several authors have not only classified the genus but also constructed phylogenetic schemes. Pax's classification (1885) was based upon a limited number of morphologic characters. Indeed, his four categories were distinguished only on the basis of insertion orientation of the stamens on the honey disc and the absence of the discs. Koidzumi (1911b), in turn, used only a limited number of morphological characteristics. Pojárkova (1933) was the first to produce a phylogenetic scheme, which is still of use (see Fig. 6.1), and the first to associate some New and Old World taxa complexes. She also advanced the view that a laticiferous petiole and an amphistaminal disc were the most primitive characteristics.

Momotani (1961) was the first to give much attention to the number of bud scales as an important morphological feature for classification and phylogeny. His studies of *Acer* chemistry (1962b) led him to conclude that *A. nipponicum* of section *Parviflora* is very close to *A. rufinerve* of section *Macrantha.* For want of affinity to any other taxa he placed *A. carpinifolium* in a separate subgenus.

Ogata (1967) had a great interest in infrageneric relations but noted that the absence of several ancient "forms" that may have linked the present sections made it difficult to unravel the correct interrelations of the sections. He distinguished six groups within the genus that differ markedly from one another phylogenetically:

Group A
Section *Macrantha* (primitive)
Section *Parviflora*
Section *Palmata*
Section *Glabra*
Section *Negundo*
Section *Rubra*
Section *Ginnala*

Group B
- Section *Platanoidea*
- Section *Pubescentia*

Group C
- Section *Acer* (excluding *A. sempervirens*)

Group D
- Section *Oblonga*
- Section *Trifoliata*
- *A. sempervirens* of section *Acer*

Group E
- Section *Lithocarpa*
- Section *Hyptiocarpa*

Group F
- Section *Indivisa*

The use of some of these sections and groups in the present volume is not precisely according to Ogata's concepts as his data for section *Hyptiocarpa* and series *Monspessulana* of section *Acer* were limited and consequently their use in this grouping was highly speculative. Important characteristics employed in Ogata's grouping include the number of bud scales, the shape of the nutlets, features of wood anatomy, the arrangement of inflorescences on the shoots, leaf type, and the staminal insertion in the disc. Ogata considered section *Macrantha* as most primitive and hence closest to the ancestral type, and section *Palmata* as rather remotely related to the remaining sections of Group A.

Rather than propose a phylogenetic scheme, de Jong (1976) published a number of remarks on intersectional affinities. He pictured the original *Acer* as a tree bearing large, compound inflorescences with terminally and laterally arranged cincinni that developed from mixed buds. The entomophilous flowers were 5-merous with eight stamens inserted on the inner side of the disc. Anthesis commenced one month or later after bud expansion. Following anthesis, male flowers first dropped stamens and sepals, followed a short time later by the pedicels. The trees were monoecious and sexual expression mainly protandrous, more exactly duodichogamous (a male-female-male sequence). Further, the buds possessed only a few bud scales and the plants had little tendency to develop parthenocarpic fruits. The leaves are visualized as being pinnately veined. On the basis of this description of the original maple, de Jong considered some taxa of section *Parviflora* as closest to the ancestral type.

Delendick's (1981) scheme was not published as a complete classification; instead he distinguished five groups. He proposed to demonstrate not only the enormous number of characteristics and tendencies that must be considered and understood to construct a complete affinity outline, but also to emphasize the complexity and incompleteness of the data. His chemical investigations confirmed de Jong's concept of the phylogenetic development of morphological characteristics. Delendick's groups have no taxonomic status, though the sections follow his classification of the genus:

Group I
- Section *Parviflora*

Group II
- Section *Palmata*

Group III
- Section *Ginnala*
- Section *Rubra*
- Section *Hyptiocarpa*

Group IV
- Section *Platanoidea*
- Section *Oblonga*
- Section *Pentaphylla*
- Section *Acer*
- Section *Goniocarpa*
- Section *Saccharina*
- Section *Trifoliata*

| | |
|---|---|
| Section *Lithocarpa* | Section *Glabra* |
| Section *Macrophylla* | Section *Arguta* |
| Section *Pubescentia* | Section *Cissifolia* |
| Group V | Section *Negundo* |
| Section *Macrantha* | Group VI |
| Section *Indivisa* | Section *Dipteronia* |

Delendick's focus on the affinities of section *Ginnala* with sections *Rubra* and *Hyptiocarpa* as derived taxa is a new concept. He further considered section *Indivisa* as a distant relative of sections *Arguta* and *Macrantha,* devoting over 20 pages of his thesis to this topic. The significant points of his thesis are as follows:

1. Chemically, *Dipteronia* reflects a typical *Acer* pattern. Although evolutionarily advanced, it is no more so than the species in series *Ukurunduensia* (syn. series *Caudata*) of section *Parviflora* or section *Palmata.*
2. In its foliar morphology and pollen type, *Dipteronia* is closer to the presumed common sapindaceous ancestor than it is to *Acer.* Its colporate pollen, which has been considered a primitive feature, is similar to pollen types in sections *Palmata* and *Parviflora.*
3. The species in section *Palmata* can be divided into two chemical types, a division inconsistent with existing series concepts. Delendick further discovered several species with either an intermediate chemistry or individuals within a species possessing one or the other of two types. In the absence of chemical and palynological data for many Chinese species, including primitive species such as *Acer tonkinense,* this finding may be significant in providing an explanation of these differing chemistries and of relationships between species.
4. Section *Ginnala* has an affinity to sections *Rubra* and *Hyptiocarpa.* Although Ogata (1967) first suggested a relationship between sections *Rubra* and *Ginnala,* a view supported by their chemistry and one in which section *Rubra* is the more advanced of the two, Delendick cautiously associates sections *Hyptiocarpa* and *Rubra.* He advanced this new concept on the basis of the fruit type being common with *Acer saccharinum* and a chemistry on the whole primitive, but with similarities to that of section *Rubra.*
5. The taxa of group IV show affinities in their phytochemistry as well as in morphological characteristics. Section *Trifoliata* has a rather primitive biochemistry and an equal affiliation with sections *Lithocarpa, Acer,* and *Saccharina.* Delenick placed the puzzling section *Pubescentia* near section *Platanoidea* and intermediate between that section and series *Monspessulana* of section *Acer.*
6. The chemistry of the rather heterogenous group V shows that section *Macrantha* is poorly related to the other sections of this group. Chemically this section differs slightly from section *Glabra,* and in several aspects seems to derive from rather independent evolutionary lines. Series *Cissifolia* of section *Negundo* shows strong affinities with section *Glabra,* and especially with its series *Arguta.* Biochemically the series *Cissifolia* and *Negundo* of section *Negundo* specialize along different lines. The arrangement of section *Indivisa* in this group is surprising, as it has long been believed that *A. carpinifolium* had no obvious relatives within the genus. Delendick recognized a relationship with series *Arguta,* although fairly distant.

Tanai (1978a) examined the venation of *Acer,* using the cleared leaf method, to precisely compare with extant fossil species. He produced a "tree" of probable phylogenetic relationships that varies considerably from the trees of Ogata, de Jong, and Delendick. Tanai's work is of interest by virtue of its treatment of the fossil data of the recognized taxa.

Mai's 1983 study of the endocarp and its relation to the history of the genus was based on the view that the swollen convex endocarp is a primitive characteristic. The endocarps of species in section *Oblonga* seemed closer to the original ancestor than to those of series *Monspessulana.* Mai found strong similarities in the endocarps of sections *Ginnala* and *Glabra,* especially series *Arguta.* He further suggested a link of section *Platanoidea* through *A. campestre* to section *Trifoliata* and a possible link of section *Pubescentia* to section *Macrantha.* Mai (1984) concluded that series *Ukurunduensia* (syn. series *Caudata* in the present volume) and *Parviflora* contain those species possessing the most primitive endocarps, a view based in part on the similarities between the endocarps of series *Ukurunduensia* and those of the genus *Dipteronia.* Mai's classification of section *Ginnala* within subgenus *Carpinifolia* gives this group a clear resemblance to Ogata's (1967) group A and also supports Delendick's placement of group *Ginnala-Rubra-Hyptiocarpa* near section *Parviflora* and group *Glabra-Macrantha-Negundo-Indivisa.* Although Mai placed section *Pubescentia* within the subgenus *Carpinifolia* because of its supposed affinities with section *Macrantha,* this placement may support possible affinities with the group *Ginnala-Rubra-Hyptiocarpa.* All these taxa (except section *Ginnala*) show similarities in the tendency toward reduction of floral parts, the insertion of the stamens on the disc, and the arrangements of the inflorescences on the shoots.

The affinities among Mai's subgenera remain rather unclear. The basic position of series *Pentaphylla* within his subgenus *Acer* is notable, as is the placing of series *Monspessulana* near series *Trifida* instead of series *Acer.* Mai did not include *Acer caesium* in his study and it is quite possible that the carpomorphological character of this species might change his view. The placement of sections *Hyptiocarpa* and *Rubra* within the subgenus *Acer* reveals the limits of such single character studies, and the placement of section *Macrantha* within the subgenus *Carpinifolia* is more or less consistent with the schemes of Momotani (1962b) and Ogata (1967). Ogata considered section *Macrantha* as the most primitive group, while Momotani found a close affinity to series *Parviflora* of section *Parviflora* through *A. rufinerve.*

In de Jong's view, section *Palmata* possesses more primitive characteristics than does section *Macrantha,* and Mai's (1984) work lends further support to the affinities of section *Macrantha* to both sections *Palmata* and *Parviflora.* Thus in the present volume section *Wardiana* is placed somewhat intermediate between sections *Palmata* and *Macrantha,* a position that sets section *Macrantha* apart from Delendick's group V. Delendick's classification and phylogeny of the genus are based on a thorough study of former schemes and the significant results of his research on *Acer* biochemistry. As already suggested, these new data clarify some concepts about the genus, but at the same time increase the complexities associated with it. De Jong (1976) proposed his series to demonstrate a common ancestry, but Delendick only retained the series sequence in section *Parviflora.* Delendick's series represent the very primitive taxa and do not lead to an organization of the genus from a common ancestor. Therefore, the present volume distinguishes series, but not to the degree proposed by de Jong in 1976.

## INFRAGENERIC CLASSIFICATION OF *ACER* PROPOSED IN THE PRESENT VOLUME

- Section *Parviflora* Koidzumi
  - Series *Parviflora*
  - Series *Distyla* (Ogata) Murray
  - Series *Caudata* Pax
- Section *Palmata* Pax
  - Series *Palmata*
  - Series *Sinensia* Pojárkova
  - Series *Penninervia* Metcalf
- Section *Wardiana* (de Jong) de Jong, comb. & stat. nov.
- Section *Macrantha* Pax
- Section *Glabra* Pax
  - Series *Glabra*
  - Series *Arguta* (Rehder) Rehder
- Section *Negundo* (Boehmer) Maximowicz
  - Series *Negundo*
  - Series *Cissifolia* (Koidzumi) Momotani
- Section *Indivisa* Pax
- Section *Acer*
  - Series *Acer*
  - Series *Monspessulana* Pojárkova
  - Series *Saccharodendron* (Rafinesque) Murray
- Section *Pentaphylla* Hu & Cheng
  - Series *Trifida* Pax
  - Series *Pentaphylla*
- Section *Trifoliata* Pax
  - Series *Grisea* Pojárkova
  - Series *Mandshurica* Pojárkova
- Section *Lithocarpa* Pax
  - Series *Lithocarpa*
  - Series *Macrophylla* Pojárkova
- Section *Platanoidea* Pax
- Section *Pubescentia* (Pojárkova) Ogata
- Section *Ginnala* Nakai
- Section *Rubra* Pax
- Section *Hyptiocarpa* Fang

This new classification of the genus proposed by de Jong contains some adaptations of his earlier (1976) work and some new concepts from the papers of Delendick (1981), Santamour (1982a), and Mai (1984). The isolated position of *Acer wardii* within the genus is acknowledged by the acceptance of section *Wardiana.* Although *A. wardii* exhibits some resemblance in its morphological characteristics to several species of section *Palmata,* it is quite different from other species in that section. For example, within section *Palmata* the honey discs are always extrastaminal and the bud scales always 4-paired, but *A. wardii* has an amphistaminal disc and two pairs of bud scales. The chemistry of *A. wardii,* however, supports the placement of the new section near section *Palmata.* Although Delendick's research points out the artificiality of the series distinguished in section *Palmata,* they are maintained in the present volume to separate, for the present, an original and a more derived group.

Section *Pubescentia* remains one of the most poorly known taxa of the genus. Its fruits were not available to Delendick, but, as pointed out by Mai (1984), they resemble those found in section *Macrantha,* those of some taxa in the complex species *A. mono* (section *Platanoidea*), and those of *A. rubrum* (section *Rubra*).

Both Delendick (1981) and Santamour (1982a) support the placement of Pojárkova's series *Mandshurica* and *Grisea* in section *Trifoliata.* Consequently, though with some reservations, the present volume includes these series in the same place. It is possible this placement of the section will need to be changed following further studies of the more primitive *Acer sutchuenense* in series *Mandshurica.*

Delendick's phylogenetic concept is of great value for a better understanding of *Acer* and its long history and his division of the genus into five groups is fully accepted in the present volume as the basis for a new phylogenetic scheme shown in Figure 6.1. This figure, which shows the placement of sections and series and their relation to *Acer*'s most primitive ancestor, is not intended to present a definite genealogical tree for the genus, but rather is an effort to

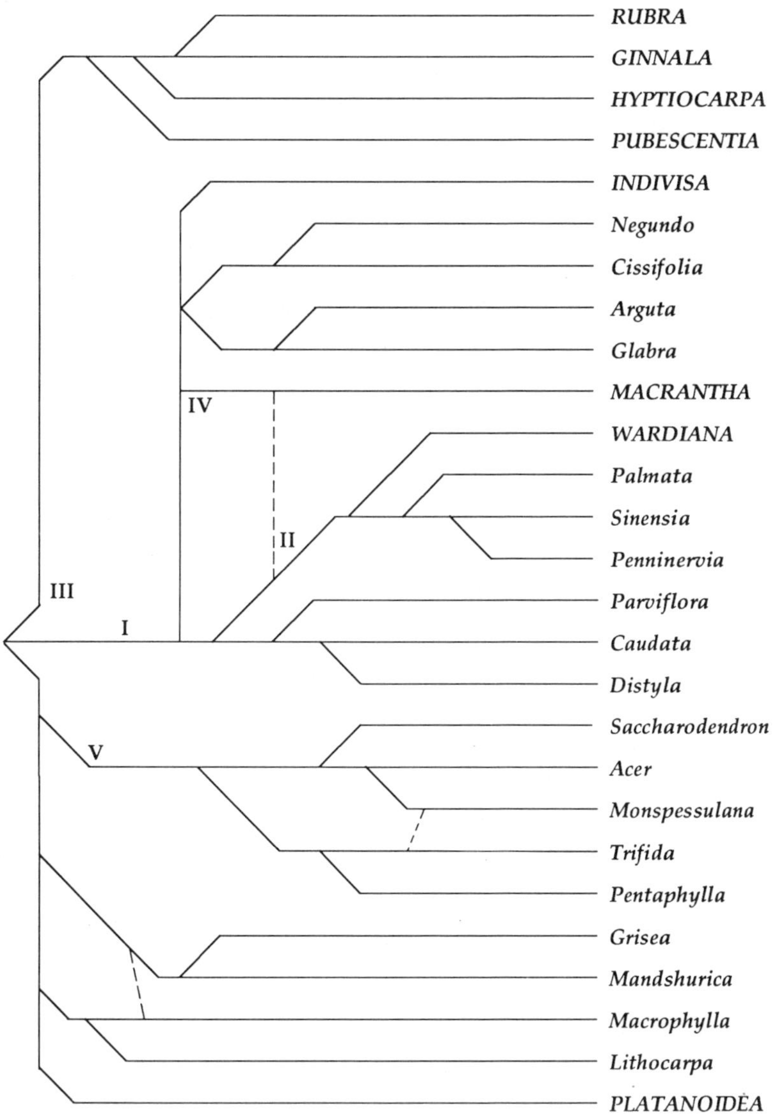


FIGURE 6.1. Phylogenetic scheme for the genus *Acer* based on the work of Pajárkova, but with groups I–V as distinguished by Delendick (except *Pubescentia.* Section names are given in capital letters, series in lowercase; dotted lines indicate other possible affinities.

represent in visual form the concept of the possible evolution of the genus adhered to by the three authors of the present volume. It and the phylogenetic scheme in Figure 6.1 reflect the extraordinary number and complexity of tendencies within and between taxa, many of which appear to have evolved independently into various infrageneric categories. For example, of Delendick's five main groups, some of the taxa retain the primitive extrastaminal honey discs, yet in all groups a shift toward amphistaminal or intrastaminal discs is evident. Further, in at least four groups a clear evolutionary trend from monoecy to dioecy and from terminal to lateral inflorescences can be traced. In addition, the parthenocarpic tendency is restricted to two of the groups.

A swollen endocarp typically indicates a parthenocarpic development, which certainly is a derived characteristic. Hence Mai's theory (1983) of the evolution of the endocarp is considered unlikely. Though data available for *Acer* are extensive, the history of the genus becomes more complex as more data are developed. New methods, including cladistic and numerical taxonomy, may help in developing a decisive picture but more anatomical, phytochemical, and paleobotanical data will be of greatest use.

Here then rests the case for the arrangement of the sections and most of the series in the genus as proposed above. These taxa are presented in this volume as natural groups, and clearly within each taxonomic group the reader will discern the adaptations intrinsic to each section, in part, as co-evolving with others.

## THE CONCEPT OF SPECIES

Various authors dealing with the genus *Acer* have held differing views as to the limitations required to define species. Some recognized several micro-species in such complex species as *A. campestre* (Dendrovski 1973, 1974b), *A. miyabei* and others (Fang 1939, 1966), and *A. pentapomicum* and others (Pojárkova 1933). Others separated complex species using the device of geographic or ecologic subspecies or varieties—*A. saccharum* (Rousseau 1940, Desmarais 1952); *A. glabrum* (Keller 1942); *A. palmatum* (Koidzumi 1911a); *A. caesium, A. cappadocicum, A. opalus, A. pentapomicum, A. truncatum,* and others (Murray 1969a, 1970a); *A. negundo* and others (Wesmael 1890). None of these authors based their species criteria on the morphological features of flowers and inflorescences, mode of sexual expression, or compatibility studies. Instead, leaf characteristics, fruit variability (especially the angle between the wings), geographical distributions, and, occasionally, special habitat preference were the major criteria used. Although leaves are very useful for identification, they often are extremely variable as a result of age, habitat, and vitality, even on the same plant. Much value is often attached to the degree, composition, and placement of indumentum, pubescence, and so forth, but these features may disappear throughout the season and may vary within populations.

The studies of Dansereau and Lafond (1941) and Desmarais (1947, 1952) loom very large in the concept of species used in this book. These authors studied the leaf characters of the sugar maple, *Acer saccharum,* and the related taxa, *A. floridanum, A. grandidentatum, A. leucoderme,* and *A. nigrum* in the field. The occurrence of more than one of these taxa at the same site resulted in the discovery of a great number of individuals showing intermediate and recombining characteristics, previously described under an assortment of species, varieties, and formae names. Consequently, Desmarais (1952) combined all these closely related taxa in one species, *A. saccharum,* with the other taxa as subspecies. He considered *A. saccharophorum* to be the correct species name, but now most people have gone back to *A. saccharum,* with *A. saccharophorum* as a synonym. This does not detract from the point he made about the related taxa being subspecies.

Murray (1969a, 1970a, 1977) also identified several similarly complex species distributed throughout the genus and published them in his own privately published journal, *Kalmia.*

Some of his combinations cannot be accepted today, mainly due to distinct differences in the morphology of the reproductive organs. For example, *Acer cissifolium* differs from *A. henryi* not only by virtue of disjunction in geographic distribution but also in the properties of its petals, such as length, color, and dehiscence time; *A. garrettii* and *A. laurinum* vary in the number of stamens (8–12 versus 4–6); and *A. mono* and *A. truncatum* vary in the manner of seed germination (epigeal versus hypogeal) and texture of mature bark (smooth versus very rough). However, following Murray, several complex species are distinguished in the present volume, all of them involving a number of geographic subspecies.

It has been difficult to define the species delimitation of several taxa, especially some from Asia, for lack of herbarium specimens and cultivated plants. As a consequence, some taxa recognized in this work as species are probably members of complex species or are clustered as subspecies of a complex species, and some of these placements and combinations may in time prove to be untenable. The status of many varieties also remains unclear due to inadequate information about their occurrence in the wild, and a number of them known only in cultivation might better be treated as cultivars.

## KEY TO THE SECTIONS AND SERIES

1. Leaves simple .......... 7
   Leaves compound .......... 2
2. Leaves trifoliolate or pinnate .......... 3
   Leaves palmatifolioate, 5(–7) leaflets ... Section **Pentaphylla** series **Pentaphylla**
3. Bud scales 2- to 4-paired .......... 5
   Bud scales 10- to 15-paired .......... Section **Trifoliata**
4. Leaflets subentire to lobulate, lateral leaflets subsessile, fruits villose .......... Series **Grisea**
   Leaflets serrulate, lateral leaflets stalked, fruits glabrous ... Series **Mandshurica**
5. Inflorescences terminal and axillary: flowers 5-merous, stamens .......... Section **Glabra** series **Glabra**
   Inflorescences axillary; flowers 4-merous, stamens 4–6; dioecious .......... Section **Negundo**
6. Leaves trifoliolate; flowers with petals and honey discs; Asia.. Series **Cissifolia**
   Leaves pinnate, 3–7 leaflets; flowers apetalous, honey disc wanting; North America .......... Series **Negundo**
7. Bud scales 2- to 4-paired .......... 8
   Bud scales 5- or more paired .......... 17
8. Bud scales always 2-paired, valvate .......... 11
   Bud scales 2- to 4-paired .......... 15
   Bud scales always 4-paired, terminal buds usually wanting.... Section **Palmata**
9. Leaves undivided, coriaceous, persistent .......... Series **Penninervia**
   Leaves 3- to 13-lobed .......... 10
10. Leaves 3- to 7-lobed; inflorescences mostly large and erect, pedicles of postanthesis male flowers partly dropped; nutlets mostly without veins, pericarp thin; subtropical areas .......... Series **Sinensia**
    Leaves 5- to 13-lobed, suborbicular; inflorescences rather small, peduncles mostly pendant, pedicels of postanthesis male flowers completely dropped; nutlets mostly veined; temperate areas .......... Series **Palmata**
11. Inflorescences racemes or small corymbs, the latter with opposite secondary axes and large bracts, 10–25 flowers .......... 12
    Inflorescences large corymbs with cincinni, 20–400 flowers...Section **Parviflora**

12. Shoots striped, axillary buds stalked, inflorescences racemose . . . . . . . . . . . . . . . . . . . . . . . . . . . . . . . . . . . . . . . . . . . . . . . . . . . . . . . . . . . . Section **Macrantha**
Shoots with stiff hairs; inflorescences with distinct bracts and opposite secondary axes . . . . . . . . . . . . . . . . . . . . . . . . . . . . . . . . . . . . . . . . Section **Wardiana**
13. Leaves undivided; inflorescences erect; nutlets veined; Japan . . . Series **Distyla**
Leaves 3- to 5- (to 7-) lobed . . . . . . . . . . . . . . . . . . . . . . . . . . . . . . . . . . . . . . . . . . 14
14. Leaves 3-lobed, large; inflorescences large, peduncles drooping; nutlets globose; Japan . . . . . . . . . . . . . . . . . . . . . . . . . . . . . . . . . . . . . . . . . . . . . . . . . Series **Parviflora**
Leaves 3- to 5- (to 7-) lobed; inflorescences erect, pedicels of postanthesis male flowers partly dropped; nutlets small, rather flat . . . . . . . . . . . . . . Series **Caudata**
15. Inflorescences large, erect, with small cincinni; flowers with narrow petals, twice as long as the sepals; nutlets small, not strongly veined; parthenocarpic tendency low to moderate . . . . . . . . . . . . . . . . . . . . . . . . . . . . . . . . . Series **Caudata**
Inflorescences small, racemose or corymbose; petals as long as the sepals; nutlets strongly veined, parthenocarpic tendency strong . . . . . . . Section **Glabra**
16. Inflorescences terminal and axillary from mixed buds; flowers 5-merous, stamens 8; western North America . . . . . . . . . . . . . . . . . . . . . . . . . . . Series **Glabra**
Dioecious; male inflorescences axillary from leafless buds, female inflorescences terminal and axillary from mixed buds; flowers 4-merous, stamens 4–6; East Asia . . . . . . . . . . . . . . . . . . . . . . . . . . . . . . . . . . . . . . . . . . . . . . . . . . . Series **Arguta**
17. Inflorescences terminal and axillary from mixed buds . . . . . . . . . . . . . . . . . . . 20
Inflorescences axillary from leafless buds. . . . . . . . . . . . . . . . . . . . . . . . . . . . . . . 18
18. Leaves undivided, coriaceous . . . . . . . . . . . . . . . . . . . . . . . . . Section **Hyptiocarpa**
Leaves lobed, chartaceous . . . . . . . . . . . . . . . . . . . . . . . . . . . . . . . . . . . . . . . . . . . . . 19
19. Bud scales 4- to 7-paired; inflorescences in clusters, fasciculate-umbellate; perianth red or green-red, stamens 5. . . . . . . . . . . . . . . . . . . . . . . . Section **Rubra**
Bud scales 8- to 12-paired; inflorescences racemose; perianth yellow-green, stamens 8–12 . . . . . . . . . . . . . . . . . . . . . . . . . . . . . . . . . . . . . . . . . . Series **Lithocarpa**
20. Leaf petioles laticiferous; honey discs amphistaminal, stamens 8–12. . . . . . . . 21
Leaf petioles not laticiferous; honey discs extrastaminal, stamens 8, or amphistaminal, stamens 5 . . . . . . . . . . . . . . . . . . . . . . . . . . . . . . . . . . . . . . . . . . . . . . . . . 22
21. Inflorescences with pendant peduncles, rachises long; stamens 8–12; nutlets keeled, convex; western North America . . . . . . . . . . . . . . . . Series **Macrophylla**
Inflorescences erect; stamens 8; nutlets flat; Europe, Asia . . . . . . . . . . . . . . . . . . . . . . . . . . . . . . . . . . . . . . . . . . . . . . . . . . . . . . . . . . . . . . . . . . . . . . . . . . . Section **Platanoidea**
22. Leaves undivided, biserrate, chartaceous; inflorescences racemose; dioecious; nutlets flat. . . . . . . . . . . . . . . . . . . . . . . . . . . . . . . . . . . . . . . . . . . . . Section **Indivisa**
Inflorescences corymbose; monoecious (sometimes male specimens) . . . . . . 23
23. Leaf margins entire to coarsely serrate; nutlets spherically convex and often keeled, or flat . . . . . . . . . . . . . . . . . . . . . . . . . . . . . . . . . . . . . . . . . . . . . . . . . . . . . 24
Leaf margins biserrate; nutlets elliptically convex, veined . . . . . Section **Ginnala**
24. Stamens 8, discs extrastaminal; nutlets convex, often keeled. . . . . . . . . . . . . . . 25
Stamens 5, discs amphistaminal; nutlets flat . . . . . . . . . . . . . Section **Pubescentia**
25. Leaves undivided to 3-lobed, usually coriaceous, persistent; flowers whitish yellow, petals narrow,longer than sepals, stamens not well-exserted; parthenocarpic tendency, strong. . . . . . . . . . . . . . . . . . . . . . . . . . . . . . . . . . . . . . Series **Trifida**
Leaves 3- to 7-lobed, rarely unlobed, chartaceous, sometimes coriaceous and persistent; flowers green-yellow, petals rather broad, as long as sepals, stamens well-exserted; parthenocarpic tendency strong to moderate . . . . . . Section **Acer**

26. Flowers apetalous, calyces connate, long, pendant pedicels; eastern North America........................................ Series **Saccharodendron**
Flowers with non-connate corolla and calyces ......................... 27
27. Leaves large, 5- to 7-lobed, chartaceous, inflorescences large; flowers on rather short pedicels; parthenocarpic tendency moderate .............. Series **Acer**
Leaves variable, 3- to 5-lobed, chartaceous, sometimes coriaceous and persistent; inflorescences moderate to small; flowers on long pendant pedicels, somewhat shorter on evergreen taxa; parthenocarpic tendency strong............
......................................... Series **Monspessulana**

## I. Section *Parviflora* Koidzumi (1911a)

This section includes three distantly related series that represent primitive, relict taxa of *Acer*. In its present delimination the section was first recognized by Momotani (1962b). The rejection of *A. spicatum* as the type species of section and series *Spicata* leaves section *Parviflora* as the oldest name. The chemotaxonomic studies of Delendick (1981) affirmed the primitive status of the taxa. Santamour's (1982a) studies revealed rather different isoenzyme profiles for *A. distylum* and *A. spicatum*, so he distinguished them as distinct sections. Mai (1984) placed series *Ukurunduensia* (*Spicata* sensu Mai) in a separate section together with series *Arguta*. He further concluded from his carpomorphological studies that, within the genus, series *Ukurunduensia* (syn. series *Caudata*) exhibited the most affinities with the genus *Dipteronia*, a relationship supported by Delendick.

All taxa in this section bear colporate pollen, the original type in *Acer* and the type also found in section *Palmata* to which section *Parviflora* is remotely related. Series *Parviflora* of section *Parviflora* possesses affinities with section *Macrantha* that Momotani (1962a) and Mai (1984) recognized through *A. rufinerve*.

Series *Ukurunduensia* (syn. series *Caudata*) possesses the most primitive features and shares some morphological characteristics with sections *Palmata* and *Wardiana*. De Jong (1976) proposed series *Ukurunduensia* as a new name, rejecting *Caudata*, which, according to Bean (1970), was based on *A. caudatum* sensu Pax, a synonym of *A. acuminatum*. Delendick (1981) presented arguments for accepting series *Caudata* based on the lectotype of *A. caudatum* Wallich; however, this was without comment on the notes in Bean (1970), which were based on specimens in the Wallich herbarium. The present volume recognizes series *Caudata* Pax, placing series *Ukurunduensia* in synonymy.

## II. Section *Palmata* Pax (1885)

This section in its present alignment was recognized by Ogata (1967). Although the taxa in it form a natural group, this section is somewhat heterogeneous as a result of various specializations. It is characterized by four pairs of bud scales and frequently aborted terminal buds. Together with section *Parviflora* this section represents the most primitive maples. Both sections produce colporate pollen and have a primitive chemistry.

Series *Sinensia*, containing the more primitive taxa, remains somewhat artificial by virtue of intermediate taxa. The phytochemical data of Delendick (1981) revealed two main types: the "japonicum" and the "palmatum." Accordingly, Delendick rejected any series. His research, however, involved only a few of the species in the section and also mentioned intermediate characteristics. As Delenick noted, this section needs further study to unravel its complex phylogeny. The taxa in the primitive series *Sinensia* are not well studied. For example, *A. tonkinense* may well be considered as very primitive: it has large trilobate leaves; very large inflorescences with many-flowered cincinni; small flowers each with a reflexed, red calyx;

lobed, white petals; and hairy honey discs. Similar to some other species in this series, postanthesis male flowers fall with a part of the pedicels.

It is possible that series *Palmata* presently contains several lines that are not closely related. Some species in it are characterized by a marked increase in the number of leaf lobes.

Series *Penninervia* differs principally from series *Sinensia* in the persistent, unlobed leaves. As far as is known, the seedlings exclusively develop unlobed leaves. Mai (1984) maintained series *Penninervia,* but he found that its endocarps were very similar to those of series *Sinensia.*

De Jong believes that section *Wardiana* is a rather closely related, but quite distinct, taxon. Through section *Wardiana,* section *Palmata* has affinities with section *Macrantha.*

## III. Section *Wardiana* (de Jong) de Jong, comb. & stat. nov.

Basionym: section *Macrantha* series *Wardiana* de Jong, *Flowering and Sex Expression in* Acer. *A Biosystematic Study,* Mededel. Landbouw. Wageningen *76–2*:144. 1976.

De Jong (1976) originally proposed this section as a monotypic series within section *Macrantha.* W. W. Smith (1917), who described the single species, *Acer wardii,* noted its distinctive characteristics—the long bracts and the amphistaminal discs—and suggested some affinity to *A. sinense* (section *Palmata* series *Sinensia*). Most authors have included this species in section *Macrantha* (series *Macrantha*), except Rehder (1927), who placed it in section *Palmata.* Rehder's concept was adopted by Delendick (1981), who found some similarities in the chemistry, but depended especially upon specific morphological characters. Mai (1984) maintained *Wardiana* as a series within *Macrantha* despite the endocarp similarities between section *Wardiana* and series *Sinensia* of section *Palmata.*

*Acer wardii* apparently is not in cultivation, and only herbarium material was available for study. Its pollen, seedlings, and chromosome number are unknown. On the basis of Delendick's chemical data and the plant's morphology, this taxon is given new sectional rank. The species is characterized by long inflorescence bracts, amphistaminal floral discs, and two pairs of bud scales. These features distinguish it from section *Palmata,* although it shares some characters with sections *Palmata* and *Parviflora* (e.g., the abscission of stamens, and inflorescences with small cincinni). No data at present indicate a close affinity to either sections *Parviflora* or *Macrantha.* In the phylogenetic scheme presented in this volume, section *Wardiana* is placed in the group containing section *Palmata,* but at the end of section *Palmata* and before section *Macrantha.*

## IV. Section *Macrantha* Pax (1885)

This section contains only closely related taxa. The further divisions proposed by Pojárkova (1933b) and accepted by many authors, including Momotani (1962b), Fang (1966), Ogata (1967), and Murray (1970c), are unnecessary; these distinctions are based primarily on leaf morphology.

While *Acer micranthum* and *A. tschonoskii* differ slightly from the other taxa in the section, the differences are inconsequential; however, *A. tschonoskii* seems to hold a key position within the section. A flowering tree was observed in 1985 on which male flowers were produced after the females flowered. This phenomenon had never before been recorded for taxa in this section. On the basis of carpomorphological characteristics, Mai (1984) distinguished a series *Rufinervia,* following Momotani's proposal based on biochemical characteristics. Both Mai and Momotani considered this section as close to series *Parviflora* by virtue of a link through these proposed series.

In the present volume the number of species in this section is radically reduced from previous works. Most of the species were proposed by Murray (1970d, 1977, 1979); two proposed combinations are added, however, and Murray's complex and expanded species, *A. tegmentosum,* is not accepted. Delendick's phytochemical study confirmed the close affinities of the taxa within section *Macrantha* and the need for further revisional work. Within no other section of the genus do the species so easily hybridize in collections, and there is some evidence that introgressive hybridization may also occur in the wild. Delendick placed section *Macrantha* in the group containing sections *Glabra, Negundo,* and *Indivisa.* De Jong agrees that section *Macrantha* has some affinities, though rather distant, to section *Glabra,* but notes that the two sections diverge somewhat and that section *Macrantha* has clear affinities with Delendick's groups I and II. *Acer rufinerve* is the only species outside of Delendick's groups I and II with colporate pollen.

### V. Section *Glabra* Pax (1885); amend. Momotani (1962b)

Pojárkova (1933b) first recognized the affinities of both series in this section, as the taxa bear strong resemblances in most morphological characteristics, but she gave each series sectional rank. Momotani (1962b), however, proposed this section as it is employed in the present volume.

While phytochemical data largely support these affinities, some taxa diverge, thus posing further questions. Series *Arguta* is the more advanced in its dioecy and reduction of floral parts, but phytochemically seems to be more primitive, displaying similarities with series *Cissifolia* of section *Negundo* (Delendick 1981). Mai (1984) also viewed series *Arguta* as less advanced, and arranged it, together with series *Ukurunduensia* (syn. series *Caudata*) of section *Parviflora,* in a separate section.

Section *Glabra* appears to have affinities to section *Macrantha,* but both sections represent independent, parallel evolutionary lines. Section *Glabra* also resembles section *Lithocarpa* in specialization and geographical distribution: both have a rather primitive, monoecious series in western North America and a more specialized, dioecious series in eastern Asia.

### VI. Section *Negundo* (Boehmer) Maximowicz (1880)

This section includes two highly specialized series, both dioecious. Their close affinities were first recognized by Momotani (1962b) and Murray (1970b), who included them as separate sections in the subgenus *Negundo.* Most authors have given these taxa sectional rank, but recently Mai (1984), on the basis of carpomorphological characteristics, found no reason to do so. Consequently, he only distinguished series *Negundo.* He further considered that section *Negundo* is remotely related to series *Ukurunduensia* (syn. series *Caudata*). Delendick (1981) and Santamour (1982a) confirmed the affinities between the series of section *Negundo.*

Delendick (1981) also found affinities between series *Cissifolia* of section *Negundo* and series *Arguta* of section *Glabra.* He further reported rather different phytochemical profiles for *A. henryi* and *A. cissifolium,* which Murray (1966) had combined. Both species share most morphological characters, but differ in their corollas. *Acer cissifolium* has long, narrow, yellow petals, while *A. henryi* has rather small, whitish petals, most of which fall off before or during anthesis. In the present volume these taxa are accepted as distinct species, a view supported by Mai (1984).

### VII. Section *Indivisa* Pax (1885)

This monotypic section is generally considered to be derived and without any clear affinities. Momotani (1962b) distinguished it as the subgenus *Carpinifolia,* which was accepted by Murray (1970a). Mai (1984) and Ogata (1967) recognize section *Ginnala* as the nearest ally. Delendick (1981) found that the chemical profile of *A. carpinifolium* is not derived to the same extent as its floral and foliar morphology. Phytochemically, section *Indivisa* is somewhat more advanced than either section *Macrantha* or series *Arguta* of section *Glabra.* The pollen morphology of *A. carpinifolia* also differs from that of all other species.

## VIII. Section *Acer*

In accordance with the ICBN, this section, containing the type species of the genus, *Acer pseudoplatanus,* must be named section *Acer.* In de Jong's view it consists of three series, the affinities of which were first recognized by Pojárkova (1933b). The resemblances among the series include morphology of reproductive organs, leaves, bud scales, and seedlings, as well as phytochemistry.

Series *Acer* is closely related to series *Monspessulana,* as was confirmed by Delendick (1981) and Santamour (1982a). Mai (1984), however, does not agree with this view and stated that the only affinity of series *Monspessulana* was with series *Trifida* of section *Pentaphylla.* He placed series *Monspessulana* in a separate section (*Goniocarpa*), at the same time retaining the third series, *Saccharodendron* in section *Acer.* Series *Saccharodendron* is slightly more advanced in its phytochemistry, but otherwise parallels the other two series of section *Acer.* Despite these clear and close affinities, in the case of series *Acer* and *Monspessulana,* Delendick preferred giving them sectional rank.

Series *Acer* is synonymous with Pojárkova's section *Gemmata.* Despite the strong affinities of the five species of this series, Pojárkova proposed three series that were adopted by Murray (1970c). Most authors consider *Acer pseudoplatanus* to be the most primitive species of the series. Delendick (1981) stated in this connection:

> Morphologically one can state a reduction series (inflorescence, lamina lobing) from *A. pseudoplatanus* through *A. heldreichii/A. trautvetteri* to *A. velutinum/A. caesium/A. giraldii.* This morphological series is reflected only slightly in the chemistry. The flavonoid profiles of *A. pseudoplatanus* and *A. heldreichii/A. trautvetteri* are virtually identical, while *A. velutinum* is chemically intermediate between the latter pair and *A. caesium/A. giraldii.* It may be possible to regard this sequence (*pseudoplatanus/heldreichii/velutinum, et al.*) as an evolutionary one.

The inflorescences of *A. pseudoplatanus* are derived, in de Jong's opinion, from the typical corymb as found in section *Acer* and related sections. Within series *Acer, A. caesium* differs with its keeled nutlets and small seeds that bear a strong resemblance to those of series *Monspessulana* and section *Pentaphylla.* On the basis of morphological characteristics, de Jong concludes that Delendick's proposed sequence does not represent a reduction series and that the true sequence is very likely the reverse of that proposed by Delendick (1981).

Series *Monspessulana* contains the taxa of Pojárkova's section *Goniocarpa.* Murray (1970a, 1979) arranged these taxa in four heterogeneous species, which are accepted by Firsov (1982) and by de Jong in the present volume. The deciduous taxa show some development toward anemophily; anthesis occurs before leaf development, and they bear pendant flowers with long, thin pedicels, exserted stamens, and large stigmas. The semi-evergreen taxa have small inflorescences that resemble those of series *Acer.* Murray (1983a), following Ogata (1967), proposed a separate section, *Orientalia,* for these semi-evergreens.

Series *Saccharodendron* is synonymous with Pax's (1885) section *Saccharina,* which was accepted by most authors. This taxon is characterized by its apetalous flowers. In other morphological characters the series strongly resembles series *Monspessulana.* Murray (1970b) adopted Rafinesque's (1836) subgenus *Saccharodendron* for this taxon. Santamour (1982a) criticized the assignment of this taxon as a series within section *Acer.* His phytochemical research failed to reveal any affinities between series *Saccharodendron* and the other two series in this section. However, de Jong believes his results for the subspecies of *A. saccharum* are confusing. For example, *A. saccharum* ssp. *grandidentatum* differed from the other subspecies, but also had similarities with *A. opalus* of series *Monspessulana.* Mai (1984) found close affinities between series *Saccharodendron* and *Acer* in the morphology of the endocarps.

The present volume follows Desmarais (1952), Murray (1970a, 1980a), and Mai (1984) in accepting one complex species, *Acer saccharum,* in series *Saccharodendron.* However, Murray (1981) reverts back to accepting the subgenus *Saccharodendron* Rafinesque (1836) and reaccepts section *Saccharina* Pax (1885).

## IX. Section *Pentaphylla* Hu & Cheng (1948)

This section contains two rather closely related series, *Pentaphylla* and *Trifida.* De Jong (1976) included series *Pentaphylla* in section *Integrifolia,* based on the strong resemblance of branches, bud scales, inflorescences, honey discs, and fruits with their counterparts in series *Trifida.* Delendick (1982) found that the name *Integrifolia* for this section had been invalidated by Fang (1966), who selected *A. laevigatum* as the lectotype. This species is now assigned to series *Penninervia* of section *Palmata.* Delendick correctly proposed the name *Oblonga,* but his section *Oblonga* only contained the taxa of series *Trifida.* In the delimitation of the section proposed in the present volume, Hu and Cheng's (1948) *Pentaphylla* must be given priority over Delendick's series *Oblonga.*

The chemical data of Delendick (1981) and Santamour (1982a), and Mai's (1984) study of the endocarps, provide further support for the clear affinities between these series of section *Pentaphylla*. The taxa of series *Trifida* appear to form a natural group of closely related species, but few of them have been thoroughly studied. Section *Pentaphylla* appears to be rather primitive and has affinities with section *Acer.*

## X. Section Trifoliata Pax (1885)

Species in this section are easily recognized by their trifoliate leaves, large numbers of bud scales, and 3-flowered inflorescences. *Acer sutchuenense* has a many-flowered, corymbose inflorescence; it represents the most primitive member of this section and is set apart in series *Mandschurica* by its amphistaminal floral discs. However, *A. sutchuenense* has very rarely been brought into cultivation and has not been well studied. It is commonly seen as related to *A. mandshuricum,* but de Jong believes their relationship is fairly distant. In addition to the distinct morphology of *A. sutchuenense,* this species lacks the cavity at the junction of the nutlets that characterizes the fruits of *A. mandshuricum.*

Pojárkova (1933b) proposed the two series *Grisea* and *Mandshurica,* which were not generally accepted, certainly not by de Jong (1976). However, the phytochemical data of Delendick (1981) and Santamour (1982a) provide additional reasons for accepting Pojárkova's arrangement. Mai (1984) did not concur in the need for these series, but his carpomorphological studies led him to transfer series *Macrophylla* of section *Lithocarpa* to section *Trifoliata.* Delendick (1981) considers section *Trifoliata* to be somewhat intermediate between sections *Acer* and *Lithocarpa.* Mai (1984) discovered affinities between section *Trifoliata* and his series *Campestria* of section *Platanoidea.*

The trifoliate leaves of the section were interpreted by de Jong (1976) as rather primitive, but Delendick (1981) believes they are a derived characteristic from trilobate leaves.

## XI. Section *Lithocarpa* Pax (1885)

The two somewhat remotely related series of this section, series *Lithocarpa* and *Macrophylla,* were proposed by Pojárkova (1933b). They occupy distinct geographic areas but bear similar reproductive organs.

Series *Lithocarpa* includes the most specialized taxa of the section: they are dioecious and develop their inflorescences from leafless lateral buds. Delendick (1981) found the series morphologically and chemically advanced and closely related to series *Macrophylla.* However, he assigned sectional rank to both taxa.

Several authors noted the heterogeneity of series *Lithocarpa.* Some of its taxa, such as *Acer sinopurpurascens* (de Jong 1976), have laticiferous petioles. The male flowers of *A. diabolicum* have connate perianths, so Momotani (1962b) placed the species in a separate series called *Diabolica,* a placement supported by Fang (1966) and Mai (1984). Ogata (1967) considered *A. thomsonii* (syn. *A. sterculiaceum* ssp. *thomsonii*) as somewhat apart phylogenetically from *A. diabolicum.* However, Murray (1970a) distinguished *A. thomsonii* as a subspecies of his large complex species *A. sterculiaceum.* He also (1969) proposed a separate subgenus *Sterculiacea* and a series *Sterculiacea* for the taxa of series *Lithocarpa.*

Series *Macrophylla* is morphologically less advanced than series *Lithocarpa.* Delendick (1981), however, found that the former has chemically much in common with section *Negundo,* making series *Macrophylla,* from the chemical point of view, one of the most advanced taxa in *Acer.* Mai (1984) transferred series *Macrophylla* to section *Trifoliata,* rather remotely allied to his section *Lithocarpa.* According to Delendick (1981) the affiliation of section *Trifoliata* is about equally between section *Lithocarpa* and section *Acer.* Mai (1984) found that section *Lithocarpa* has close affinities to section *Platanoidea.*

## XII. Section *Platanoidea* Pax (1885)

The species in this rather primitive section are closely related and can be considered a natural group, without any series. The phytochemistry and the fruits of *Acer campestre* and *A. miyabei* are somewhat different, but not sufficiently so to require a separate series *Campestria* as proposed by Pojárkova (1933b) and supported by others, including Murray (1970a) and Mai (1984), who identified a series *Campestria* as a basic element within his "campestroid phylogenetic cluster" and with affinities to section *Trifoliata.*

Murray (1970a) greatly reduced the number of species in this section, an approach concurred with in the present volume although not all of his proposed combinations are accepted.

De Jong (1976) included a series *Pubescentia* in section *Platanoidea,* as originally proposed by Pojárkova (1933b). Delendick's (1981) phytochemical data do not support a clear affinity with this section, so the present volume follows Delendick and accepts section *Pubescentia.* Section *Platanoidea* shares a characteristic phytochemical compound (an aceritannin analogue, Delendick's compound 100) with series *Lithocarpa* of section *Lithocarpa.* These two sections are also unusual in their laticiferous petioles and amphistaminal discs.

## XIII. Section *Pubescentia* (Pojárkova) Ogata (1967)

The taxa in this section are rather advanced within the genus. They bear flowers with five stamens and amphistaminal discs, which are somewhat lobed. The inflorescences, for the most part, are corymbose and develop from mixed terminal buds. Small racemes develop from leafless lateral buds. The fruits show some similarities with those in sections *Macrantha* and *Platanoidea,* particularly some infraspecific taxa of *A. mono,* and with *A. rubrum* of section *Rubra.*

Section *Pubescentia* includes a complex species, *Acer pentapomicum,* as distinguished by

Murray (1970a, 1975) from central Asia, and *A. pilosum* from northeastern China. Pojárkova (1949) first understood the affinities between these two species, but *A. pilosum* is not well studied and is no longer in cultivation. In his original description of *A. pilosum,* Maximowicz (1880) included a drawing of a branchlet with racemose inflorescences developed from leafless lateral buds. By virtue of this picture, Rehder (1927) included this species in section *Lithocarpa* (series *Lithocarpa*), a placement adopted by Momotani (1962b) and Murray (1970a). The inflorescences are mainly corymbose, but small, racemose inflorescences may develop from lateral buds.

Ogata (1967) gave Pojárkova's series *Pubescentia* sectional rank, a placement accepted by Delendick (1981) and Mai (1984). Murray (1970c) first placed series *Pubescentia* in section *Goniocarpa;* later (1983a) he distinguished a subgenus for this taxon. Pojárkova (1933b) and de Jong (1976) distinguished a series *Pubescentia* within section *Platanoidea.*

Delendick (1981) placed section *Pubescentia* in his group IV near section *Platanoidea,* further suggesting an intermediate position between section *Platanoidea* and series *Monspessulana* of section *Acer.* Mai's (1984) carpomorphological studies did not reveal affinities of section *Pubescentia* to section *Platanoidea,* thus he placed the former near section *Macrantha.* In the present volume, section *Pubescentia* is placed in Delendick's group III, suggesting affinities with the group *Ginnala-Rubra-Hyptiocarpa* by virtue of similar tendencies (e.g., reduction of stamens, amphistaminal discs, and lateral inflorescences).

### XIV. Section *Ginnala* Nakai (1915)

In de Jong's view this section is monotypic, containing one large, complex species, *Acer tataricum,* which in turn consists of a number of closely related intraspecific taxa with the widest geographical distribution of any species of the genus. Momotani (1962a) and Delendick (1981) found slight differences in the chemistry of the interspecific taxa, but morphologically, and especially in their reproductive organs, there are no clear specific distinctions. Mai (1984) observed a slight variation of endocarps, which in his opinion justified specific rank for some taxa, such as *A. aidzuense* (Franchet) Nakai. Ogata (1967) was the first to describe affinities of this rather primitive section with section *Rubra,* an observation supported by Delendick's research on the flavonoids.

In the present volume, sections *Rubra* and *Hyptiocarpa,* and perhaps *Pubescentia,* are seen as more advanced taxa originating from a common ancestor near section *Ginnala.* Mai (1984) does not recognize such affinities. His studies resulted in placing section *Ginnala* near series *Ukurunduensia* (syn. series *Caudata*) of section *Parviflora* and series *Arguta* of section *Glabra,* with the further supposition of remote affinities to section *Indivisa.*

### XV. Section *Rubra* Pax (1885)

This section is highly specialized and consists of hexaploid and octoploid taxa. De Jong does not believe this homogeneous section should be divided into two series, *Eriocarpa* and *Rubra,* as originally proposed by Pojárkova (1933b) and supported by Murray (1970a) and Mai (1984). The taxa included share a high degree of resemblance in morphological characters and mode of reproduction. Evolution toward anemophily is most advanced in *Acer saccharinum,* with apetalous flowers lacking honey discs. Delendick (1981) and Santamour (1982a) discovered strong affinities in the phytochemistry of *A. rubrum* and *A. saccharinum,* two North American species that occasionally hybridize in the wild and in cultivation. These hybrids were only recognized recently. Murray (1969) named the hybrid *A.* × *freemanii* after its discoverer O. M. Freeman (1941). When de Jong published his studies in 1976 he did not recognize this hybrid. The flowers captioned *A. saccharinum* (Wageningen B. G. no. 13276) and depicted in figure 27 of his paper were collected from a clone, long in cultivation in The

Netherlands. Now known as *A.* × *freemanii* 'Elegant', this clone has free sepals and 0–3 free petals.

Ogata (1967) first described some affinity between sections *Rubra* and *Ginnala,* a relationship supported by Delendick's (1981) chemical research. Mai's (1984) work does not support Ogata's affinities, and accordingly he placed sections *Ginnala* and *Rubra* in different clusters. His endocarp studies, however, did indicate that section *Rubra* has some affinities with section *Hyptiocarpa,* thus supporting the findings of de Jong (1976) and Delendick (1981).

### XVI. Section *Hyptiocarpa* Fang (1966)

The species of this section and their affinities are not well understood. There is a large variation among the species in both the number of stamens and the insertion of the honey discs. The taxon with a southern distribution has five (or four to eight) stamens and glabrous discs. The taxon with a northern distribution has eight (or up to twelve) stamens and hairy discs. The fruits in this section are rather similar to those of *A. saccharinum* of section *Rubra* with often only one carpel developing. The rudiments of the other carpel are easily overlooked. This offers further proof of the complete absence of any parthenocarpic tendency.

Due to the similarities in morphology, moderately supported by phytochemistry, Delendick (1981) placed this section in a group with sections *Ginnala* and *Rubra.* Mai's (1984) investigations also support an affinity to section *Rubra* and further to series *Acer* of section *Acer.* The paucity of data about the two taxa in this section is illustrated by Fang's (1966) proposal to place two series in this section, while placing part of the taxa in his series *Trifida* of section *Pentaphylla* (i.e., *A. garrettii* and *A. laurinum*). Ogata (1967) proposed two sections for the taxa contained in the section. Murray (1969a) first distinguished only a single complex species in section *Hyptiocarpa.* Later, however, he (1983) adopted Ogata's proposals by placing this section in a separate subgenus. The inflorescences of section *Hyptiocarpa* show the same evolutionary tendencies as observed in section *Pubescentia:* large inflorescences are corymbose, while small ones are racemose.

## REPRODUCTION

### Seed Dormancy

While delayed seed germination is characteristic of the genus, it is a derived state. The best-known species departing from this norm—by germinating immediately after ripening—are *Acer rubrum* and *A. saccharinum* of section *Rubra* from northeastern North America. These species flower very early in spring and have ripe fruits before the end of May. The unlignified pericarp of *A. saccharinum* fruit lacks any mechanism to delay germination until the following year. In this respect, the seed of *A. rubrum* is better protected and can be stored to the next season, although it typically germinates the same summer in the wild.

Our knowledge of the germination behavior of other species possessing a thin, unlignified pericarp is rather meager. According to Mrs. Satrapadja of the Botanic Gardens, Bogor, Indonesia (personal communication), it is very likely that the seed of *Acer laurinum* (section *Hyptiocarpa*) from Southeast Asia will germinate immediately. Experience has shown that the seeds of the related *A. distylum* and *A. nipponicum* of section *Parviflora* dry out very quickly and must be sown immediately upon ripening or stored in sand after harvesting until the next spring. Interestingly, none of the species mentioned above develop parthenocarpic fruits. In the case of *A. laurinum* and *A. saccharinum* the seedless mericarps of fully grown fruit are hardly visible and are sometimes shed earlier (Fig. 6.2). In contrast, the seedless fruits of species with a strong parthenocarpic tendency are practically indistinguishable from seed-bearing fruits.

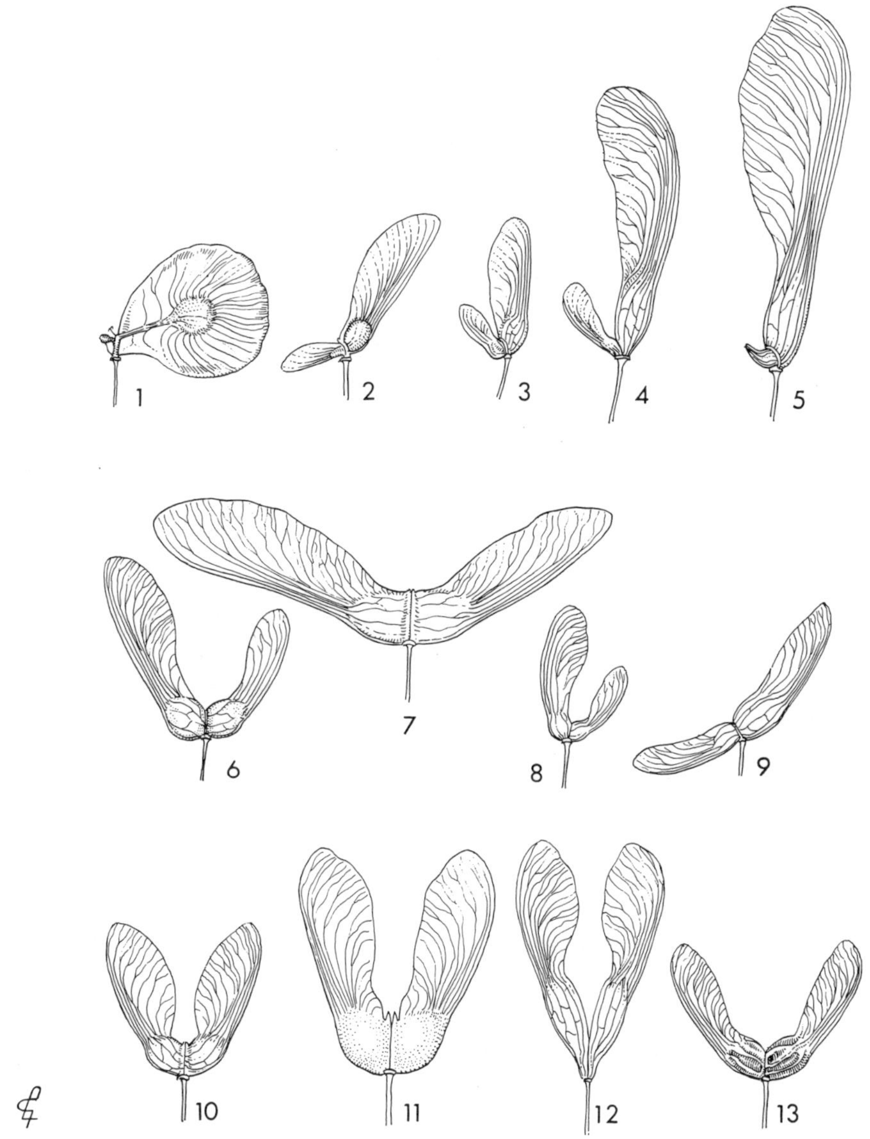


FIGURE 6.2. One-seeded samaras with various degrees of parthenocarpic development of the seedless mericarp (×5/6); parthenocarpic tendency is weak in 1–5, moderate in 6—9, and strong in 10—13: (1) *Dipteronia sinensis* Oliv. (De Jong 266); (2) *Acer tonkinense* Lecomte (Stewart & Cheo 613); (3) *A. rubrum* L. (De Jong 405); (4) *A. saccharinum* L. (Mazzeo 995); (5) *A. laurinum* Haskarl (Chun & Tso 43433); (6) *A. pseudoplatanus* L. (De Jong 330); (7) *A. platanoides* L. (De Jong 634); (8) *A. rufinerve* S. & Z. (De Jong 503); (9) *A. circinatum* Pursh. (De Jong 211); (10) *A. opalus* Mill. (De Jong 83); (11) *A. griseum* (Fr.) Pax (De Jong 260); (12) *A. negundo* L. (Vrugtman 1067); (13) *A. stachyophyllum* Hiern. (De Jong 350).

The fruits of such seeds (e.g., *A. griseum*) develop an especially thick, woody pericarp and demonstrate extended seed dormancy. Sometimes it is possible to distinguish seed-bearing fruits from seedless ones by their relatively late ripening. Nonetheless, before harvesting it is advisable to dissect some fruits to establish the presence of viable embryos.

The longest dormancy develops in sections *Glabra* and *Trifoliata,* in section *Lithocarpa* series *Lithocarpa,* and in some species of section *Palmata.* Germination usually only takes place in the second or third spring following sowing. The seeds of almost all other species germinate the spring after autumn or early spring sowing. In dry, cold storage germination can be delayed for at least another year.

## Juvenile Stage

The seedlings of nearly all *Acer* species first develop a pair of unlobed leaves following the cotyledons. The only exceptions are the many-lobed species in section *Palmata,* which develop lobulate leaves as the first true leaves. By the end of the first season, and surely by the second year, the seedlings of most species have leaves resembling, in most aspects, those of adult specimens. The principal difference is in the degree of indumentum. The leaves of young plants of some species may completely lack hairs.

The young plants of a few species bear leaves different from those of adults for several years. This characteristic is particularly noticeable in series *Trifida* of section *Pentaphylla* (*Acer buergerianum* and *A. oblongum*). *Acer oblongum* has entire adult leaves, but trilobulate juvenile ones. Some leaves of a specimen of *A. oblongum* planted in the Royal Botanic Gardens at Kew, Great Britain, at the beginning of this century are still trilobulate. However, this undoubtedly atypical tree has not yet flowered, probably due to the cool climate. Some species in section *Macrantha* that normally bear unlobed leaves produce trilobulate leaves as young plants and frequently on vigorous shoots of mature plants as well. Trilobulate leaves have never been observed on seedlings of species in section *Indivisa* and series *Penninervia* of section *Palmata.*

De Jong observes that first flowering varies from 3–20 years within the genus. Very early flowering is a characteristic of *Acer rubrum* (section *Rubra*) and *A. spicatum* (section *Parviflora*), several species in section *Macrantha,* most species of section *Glabra,* and some species in Sections *Palmata* and *Platanoidea.* On the other hand, some species of section *Acer,* section *Pentaphylla, A. macrophyllum* (section *Macraphylla*), *A. nipponicum, A. pycnanthum,* and *A. saccharinum* (all in section *Rubra*) are relatively late to flower.

## Flowering and Sexual Expression

One of the attractive features of many maple species is their flowering. This is especially true for those species that flower before the leaves: *A. rubrum* (section *Rubra*), *A. monspessulanum* (section *Acer*), *A. diabolicum* (male plants only, section *Lithocarpa*), *A. platanoides* (section *Platanoidea*), and *A. opalus* (section *Acer*). As the flowers themselves are small and rather inconspicuous, the very interesting rhythmic course of flowering, with phases of male and female flowers, has remained rather obscure and unnoticed.

The flowering patterns are remarkable, particularly in light of the variability within the genus, and give evidence of the genus's evolution from monoecious to dioecious taxa. Within *Acer* no less than five evolutionary stages of flowering can be distinguished, and each stage has living representatives. The flower buds of the purely monoecious species develop normally until a specific time before anthesis that is unique to each species. From that time all trees, part of a population, or sometimes just branches of individual trees, pass through a critical period, starting from the oldest flower buds, in which pistil abortion leads to functional male flowers. This critical period may be from 5 months to only a few days before the opening of the flower buds and results in a phase of male flowers. When pistil development remains undisturbed, ripening of the stamens does not occur. The filaments do not elongate and the anthers remain closed, which results in functionally female flowers.

The remarkably detailed account found in Linnaeus's *Genera Plantarum* (1742) of the development of these two types of morphologically bisexual flowers within the same inflorescence is still useful:

> Flores, in eadum umbella Hermaphroditi, saepe duplicis generis: inferiores Hermaphroditi feminei, quorum antherae non dehiscunt, sed pistillum mox in fructum excrescit; superiores Hermaphroditi masculi, quorum antherae pollen pluunt, pistilla vero non accrescunt, sod decidunt.

Linnaeus obviously observed that despite the presence of both sexual organs only one or the other ever functioned. He clearly labeled the flowers as either male or female. He also recognized the differing positions of the male and female flowers within the inflorescence (respectively "inferiores" and "superiores"). Why Linnaeus's detailed description of the flowers remained unnoticed by most botanists, and particularly by students of the genus *Acer* such as Pax (1902), Schneider (1909), Koidzumi (1911), and Ogata (1967), remains unclear.

De Jussieu (1789) commented first about the rhythmic flowering of male and female flowers in stages ("flexes" or waves). The first detailed description of these stages was that of Wahlenberg (1820). He observed that the inflorescences on some trees of *Acer platanoides* bore only male flowers while others bore only female flowers at the beginning of anthesis, and in the course of flowering some flowers of the other sex were produced. Wittrock (1886) undertook the first extensive study of the flowering of *Acer* and recorded observations during different years in a large number of *A. platanoides,* street trees in Stockholm, Sweden. He noticed that about half the trees started with a male phase that was generally followed by a female phase. This female phase, in a few cases, was in turn followed by a male phase. Conversely, the other half of the trees produced a female phase first that was always followed by a male phase. Wittrock called the various combinations *Infloreszenztypen.*

Macleod (1894) was the first to discover that the ovaries in male flowers, produced before a female phase, were more radically reduced than those produced in male flowers following the female phase. De Jong (1976) called these two types male I and male II, respectively. He studied the development of these flowers before anthesis and found that pistil abortion in the two types is caused by different factors. In the case of protandry (male flowers first), a primitive characteristic of *Acer* and related taxa, the explanation is rather difficult and will be discussed later, but the case of male flowers following the female phase (male II flowers) is rather easily explained. Pistil abortion is caused by strong competition for nutrients by female flowers (buds) and fruits. This was proven by removing female flower buds from *A. pseudoplatanus* (section and series *Acer*) some days before anthesis, which led to a new generation of female flowers. This phenomenon also may be observed in several other genera, such as *Cleome* and *Musa.*

The rhythmic course of flowering of maples usually involves the whole tree as was first pointed out by Vogler (1906), who along with Haas (1933) determined that nearly all the trees of *A. platanoides* studied repeated the same sequence of male and female phases year after year. In later years several authors published similar observations, in some cases using other species (e.g., Gabriel, 1968, for *A. saccharum;* and Scholz, 1960, for *A. pseudoplatanus*). De Jong (1976) studied most of the genus, using living plants of about 30 species that were observed for 3–5 years and herbarium specimens for the remaining species. Figure 6.3 shows all the reported flowering types, although types G–L were only occasionally found and mainly involved species bearing large inflorescences, notably *A. pseudoplatanus.* It is clear that rhythmic flowering within a population of the same species with protandrous and protogynous (female flowers first) individuals favors cross-fertilization. Isolated monoecious flowering trees produce viable seeds. Self-sterility, occasionally mentioned in the literature, has never been observed by the present author.

## Evolution of Flowering and Sexual Expression

The major trends in the evolution of flowering (inflorescence types) and sexual expression in *Acer,* from entomophily to anemophily and from monoecy to dioecy, are very obvious and have been described by various authors, beginning with Pax in 1885. All authors, in commenting on this evolutionary sequence have focused on *A. negundo* (section *Negundo* series *Negundo*), the single species of the genus where anemophily and dioecy are fully realized.

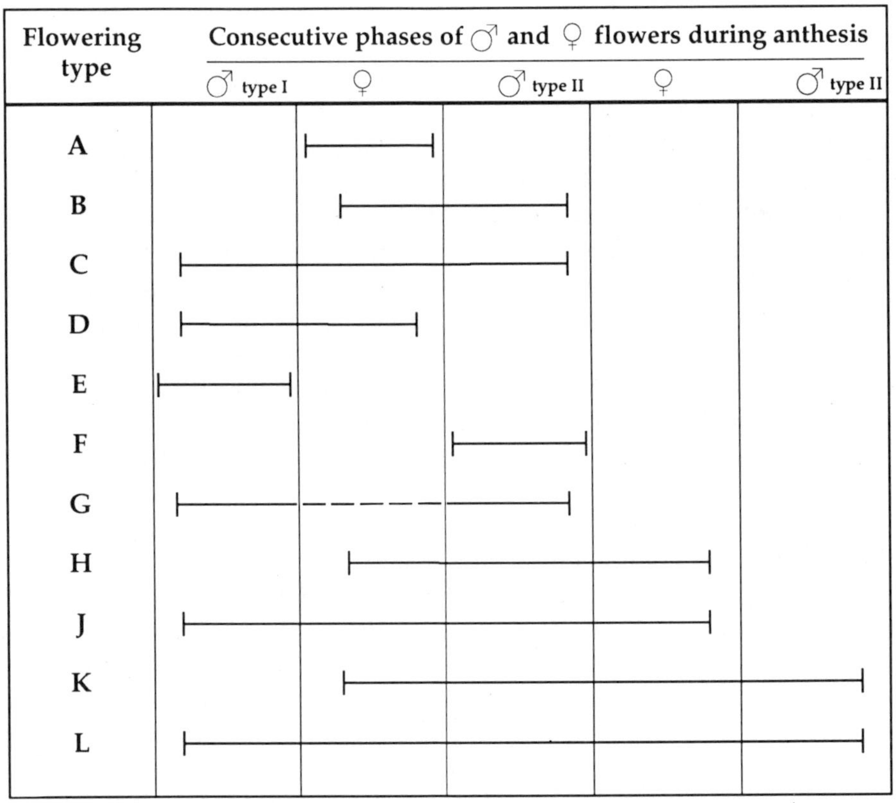


FIGURE 6.3. Flowering types of *Acer* inflorescences: A = inflorescence consists of female flowers; B = inflorescence produces female flowers first followed by phase of male flowers; C = inflorescence produces flowers in three sonsecutive phases—male–female–male; D = inflorescence produces male flowers first followed by phase of female flowers; E = inflorescence consists of male flowers; F = inflorescence consists of type II male flowers, mostly found together with flowering type B. Line length, representing a single inflorescence, gives no correlation with the real size of number of flowers. Sources: A, C, E (p.p.) after Wittrock (1886); B, D after Wittrock (1886), modified by Correns (1928).

De Jong (1976) noticed some species within sections *Palmata* and *Parviflora,* which still flower in the manner of the presumed "original" maple (i.e., duodichogamously—male-female-male—flowering type C). Most species studied were found to fall between the primitive mode and completely dioecy. De Jong distinguished five evolving stages, one of which departs slightly from the main trend and will be discussed more extensively (see "An Apparently Dioecious System" below).

**The Primitive Mode of Flowering (Duodichogamy).** The most primitive mode of sexual expression in *Acer* is the male-female-male sequence, corresponding to flowering type C, and known as duodichogamy. The same sequence also occurs in related primitive taxa of the Hippocastanaceae (*Aesculus parviflora*), Sapindaceae (*Allophyllus* and others) and *Dipteronia* of the Aceraceae. *Acer nipponicum* and possibly *A. tonkinense* (section *Palmata,* series *Sinensia*) retain this mode to the present. However, in the former species the second phase, the wave of male II flowers, is mostly lacking as, often, are the female flowers, but all individuals start anthesis with male (I) flowers. *Acer spicatum* and *A. caudatum* ssp. *ukurunduense* (section *Parviflora*) are predominantly duodichogamous, with a small part of the population protogynous. The first phase of male flowers (male I flowers) probably results from intensive competition for nutrients and hormones between flower buds of the developing inflorescences. This leads to pistil abortion in the majority of the flower buds, starting with the oldest. The timing of the appearance of the female phase during anthesis is strongly governed by environmental conditions. For example, low temperatures appear to favor development of female (and bisexual) flowers.

This primitive mode of flowering is rare within the genus. It is confined to portions of sections *Palmata* and *Parviflora* and involves taxa that flower late in the season and have multiflorous inflorescences with cincinni. These taxa display many other primitive characteristics in their morphology, palynology, and chemistry as well.

**Protogynous Flowering (Dichogamy).** Dichogamy is directly derived from duodichogamy and is found in a number of species in which part of the population is protogynous. The female sexual expression of individuals in these species is less dependent on environmental conditions than in duodichogamy. In the case of *A. pseudoplatanus* (many plants were studied over many years), it was found that about 10 percent of the protogynous plants produced in one or more years a small number of protandrous inflorescences (flowering type C). We might guess that the benefits of the occurrence of protogynous flowering individuals is about 50 percent at present. The percentage increase may have developed with the evolution of decreasing sizes of inflorescences, which led to the reduction of the male II phase, and even of the female phase on the protandrous flowering individuals (flowering types D and E, respectively). Today, the majority of *Acer* species are in this stage of flowering evolution.

A number of species possessing primitive characteristics (e.g., large inflorescences and a relatively late flowering time) have a rather low proportion of protogynous individuals. For example, in *Acer spicatum* about 14 percent (10 out of 82 herbarium specimens collected in the wild) and in *A. caudatum* ssp. *A. ukurunduense* about 10 percent (3 out of 30) of the populations flower protogynously. Other species displaying low percentages of protogyny were found in series *Penninervia* and *Sinensia* of section *Palmata.*

The extensive data collected by a large number of students over a wide range of species have revealed that while the proportion of protogynous flowering individuals varies widely, the total never exceeds 50 percent. Sections *Palmata, Ginnala, Pentaphylla, Pubescentia, Trifoliata* in part and section *Acer* series *Acer,* section *Pentaphylla* series *Distyla,* section *Lithocarpa* series *Macrophylla,* section *Acer* series *Saccharodendron* and section *Parviflora* series *Caudata* are presently in this stage of evolution.

**Genetically Male Individuals.** A further step towards dioecy was first shown by protandrous flowering trees. At some period in evolution they failed to produce female flowers, and became genetically male. Such trees sometimes occur in dichogamous populations but in very low percentages. The opportunity to increase the number of male individuals developed from conditions in which protandrous individuals were no longer able to produce a male II stage, and seldom produced female flowers. This evolutionary tendency was favored by further reductions in the size of the inflorescences.

At present there are taxa which have nearly completed the evolution to male trees. Within these taxa there are a few female individuals, but the largest portion of the population remains protogynous. In this stage of evolution environmental conditions often determine the ratios of flower types within any given population in any given year. Examples of these taxa are sections *Hyptiocarpa* and *Rubra,* series *Glabra* of section *Glabra* and series *Monspessulana* of section *Acer.*

**Complete Dioecy.** From the stage marked by male and protogynous trees some taxa finally evolved into complete dioecy. This stage is best exemplified by *A. negundo.* The androecium of the female flowers in this stage is completely absent (e.g., in section *Negundo,* series *Arguta* of section *Glabra* and series *Lithocarpa* of section *Lithocarpa*). In section *Indivisa* the female flowers still possess rudimentary stamens.

From observations of *Acer sterculiaceum* and *A. diabolicum* (both in section *Lithocarpa,* series *Lithocarpa*) and with information from R. A. Banks, Hergest Croft, Herefordshire, England, I and my coauthors have determined that male plants on rare occasions produce a few fruits and female plants infrequently produce viable seeds without cross-pollination. Botanists generally view dioecy as an advanced evolutionary stage and monoecy as more primitive. *Acer negundo* is evidently a most successful species as it has established itself in many parts of the world after introduction. No other dioecious species of *Acer* seems to have profited by being sexually more advanced, nor have they proved to be more competitive than monoecious taxa in natural populations.

**An Apparently Dioecious System.** The sexual expression of a small part of the genus does not appear initially to have any obvious relation to any one of the stages discussed above. Such species are found in section *Macrantha,* and *Acer maximowiczianum* of section *Trifoliata.* The trees bear small racemes with either male of female flowers, but in some years some of the branches produce flowers of the opposite sex. This phenomenon could be easily overlooked, and the often observed irregular fruiting has not been associated with this variability in the floral sexual expression.

Observations made over an extended number of years have confirmed that all individuals of the taxa named above are basically protandrous and, with one exception (*A. tschonoskii*), are unable to produce male flowers after a female phase (male II flowers). De Jong (1976) found that sex determination had not occurred by one month before flowering. When he forced detached branches into flower at least one month before normal flowering, he obtained only female flowers. The direct cause of pistil abortion remains unclear, but it always manifested itself first in the oldest buds of inflorescences in the most advanced state of development. It was clear that a relatively late floral initiation and any retardation in development favored escape from abortion. Retardation might result from competition of developing fruits and from weakening of the trees by injury.

Hibbs (1978) conducted further field observations of this phenomenon in *A. pensylvanicum.* He found that young trees growing in open sites produced predominantly male flowers. Older individuals, particularly those in crowded or otherwise deleterious circumstances, were marked by sex-shifts to the female condition. Many old trees, when they fruited heavily were not able to survive crowded, stressed conditions. These observations throw light on the natural functioning of sexual expression in this species. Its unusual mode derives directly from the original duodichogamous condition mediated by a substantial reduction in the size of the inflorescences.

There are other direct links between section *Macrantha* and the primitive sections *Palmata* and *Parviflora* which lend further support to the view that this mode of sexual expression relates directly to the original duodichogamous flowering.

Such an explanation does not account for the case of *A. maximowiczianum.* Direct links with duodichogamous taxa are rather unlikely. Observations showed that young individuals were male or female, but not predominantly male. The frequency of monoecious plants was rather low. Some older trees continued to produce exclusively male flowers in most years, which is exceptional within section *Macrantha.* The loss of the ability to produce male flowers after the female phase (male II flowers) probably reduced the contribution of protogynous individuals in reproduction, leading to an elimination of this type and prevention of the rise of genetically female individuals.

In other taxa of the genus the ability to produce male II flowers also has disappeared but in a later stage of evolution and after the rise of genetically male individuals. This development has resulted in complete dioecy.

## TAXONOMIC SYNOPSIS

compiled by D. M. van Gelderen

Division: Embryophyta/Siphonogama
Subdivision: Angiospermae
Class: Dicotyledonae
Order: Sapindales
Family: Aceraceae Jussieu (1789, as *Acera*)
Genus: *Acer* L. (1753).

*Acer* is classified into 16 sections, 8 of which are further subdivided into 19 series. These sections and series accommodate 230 taxa: 124 species, 95 subspecies (including the typical subspecies), 8 varieties, and one forma.

I. Section *Parviflora* Koidzumi (1911)
1. Series Parviflora
*A. nipponicum* Hara (1938)
2. Series *Distyla* (Ogata) Murray (1983)
*A. distylum* Siebold & Zuccarini (1845)
3. Series *Caudata* Pax (1886)
*A. caudatum* Wallich (1830) ssp. *caudatum*
*A. caudatum* ssp. *multiserratum* (Maximowicz) Murray (1982)
*A. caudatum* ssp. *ukurunduense* (Trautvetter & Meyer) Murray (1966)
*A. spicatum* Lamarck (1786)
II. Section *Palmata* Pax (1885)
4. Series *Palmata*
*A. ceriferum* Rehder (1911)
*A. circinatum* Pursh (1814)
*A. duplicatoserratum* Hayata (1911)
*A. japonicum* Thunberg ex Murray (1784)
*A. palmatum* ssp. *amoenum* (Carrière) Hara (1954)
*A. palmatum* ssp. *matsumurae* Koidzumi (1911)
*A. palmatum* Thunberg ex Murray (1784) ssp. *palmatum*
*A. pauciflorum* Fang (1932)
*A. pseudosieboldianum* (Pax) Komarov ssp. *pseudosieboldianum*
*A. pseudosieboldianum* ssp. *takesimense* (Nakai) de Jong comb. & stat. nov.
*A. pubipalmatum* Fang (1932)
*A. robustum* Pax (1902)
*A. shirasawanum* Koidzumi (1911) var. *shirasawanum*
*A. shirasawanum* var. *tenuifolium* Koidzumi (1911)
*A. sieboldianum* Miquel (1865)
5. Series *Sinensia* Pojárkova (1933)
*A. calcaratum* Gagnepain (1948)
*A. campbellii* Hooker & Thomson ex Hiern in Hooker f. (1875) ssp. *campbellii*
*A. campbellii* ssp. *chekiangense* (Fang) Murray (1977)
*A. campbellii* ssp. *flabellatum* (Rehder) Murray (1977)
*A. campbellii* ssp. *sinense* (Pax) de Jong, comb. & stat. nov.
*A. campbellii* ssp. *sinense* var. *longilobum* (Fang) de Jong, comb. & stat. nov.
*A. campbellii* ssp. *wilsonii* (Rehder) de Jong, comb. & stat. nov.
*A. chapaense* Gagnepain (1948)

*A. confertifolium* Merrill & Metcalf (1937)
*A. elegantulum* Fang & Chiu (1979)
*A. erianthum* Schwerin (1901)
*A. fenzelianum* Handel-Mezzetti (1933)
*A. kuomeii* Fang & Fang f. (1966)
*A. kweilinense* Fang & Fang f. (1966)
*A. lanpingense* Fang & Fang f. (1966)
*A. linganense* Fang & Chiu (1979)
*A. mapienense* Fang (1979)
*A. miaoshanicum* Fang (1966)
*A. olivaceum* Fang & Chiu (1979)
*A. oliverianum* ssp. *formosanum* (Koidzumi) Murray (1969)
*A. oliverianum* Pax (1889) ssp. *oliverianum*
*A. schneiderianum* Pax & Hoffman (1922)
*A. shangszeense* Fang & Soong (1966)
*A. sichourense* (Fang & Fang f.) Fang (1979)
*A. sunyiense* Fang (1966)
*A. taipuense* Fang (1966)
*A. tonkinense* ssp. *kwangsiense* (Fang & Fang f.) Fang (1979)
*A. tonkinense* ssp. *liquidambarifolium* (Hu & Cheng) Fang (1979)
*A. tonkinense* Lecompte (1912) ssp. *tonkinense.*
*A. tutcheri* Duthie (1908)
*A. wuyuanense* Fang & Wu (1979)
*A. yaoshanicum* Fang (1979)

6. Series *Penninervia* Metcalf (1932)

*A. cordatum* Pax (1889)
*A. crassum* Hu & Cheng (1948)
*A. erythranthum* Gagnepain (1948)
*A. eucalyptoides* Fang & Wu (1979)
*A. fabri* Hance (1884)
*A. hainanense* Chun & Fang (1966)
*A. kiukiangense* Hu & Cheng (1948)
*A. laevigatum* Wallich (1830)
*A. lucidum* Metcalf (1932)
*A. oligocarpum* Fang & Hu (1979)
*A. sino-oblongum* Metcalf (1932)
*A. yinkunii* Fang (1966)

III. Section *Wardiana* (de Jong) de Jong, comb. & stat. nov.

*A. wardii* W. W. Smith (1917)

IV. Section *Macrantha* Pax (1885)

*A. capillipes* Maximowicz (1867)
*A. caudatifolium* Hayata (1911)
*A. crataegifolium* Siebold & Zuccarini (1845)
*A. davidii* Franchet (1885) ssp. *davidii.*
*A. davidii* ssp. *grosseri* (Pax) de Jong, comb. & stat. nov.
*A. laisuense* Fang & Hu (1966)
*A. micranthum* Siebold & Zuccarini (1845)
*A. morifolium* Koidzumi (1914)
*A. pectinatum* ssp. *forrestii* (Diels) Murray (1977)
*A. pectinatum* ssp. *laxiflorum* (Pax) Murray (1977)

*A. pectinatum* ssp. *maximowiczii* (Pax) Murray (1977)
*A. pectinatum* Wallich ex Nicholson (1881) ssp. *pectinatum*
*A. pectinatum* ssp. *taronense* (Handel-Mazzeti) Murray (1977)
*A. pensylvanicum* L. (1753)
*A. rubescens* Hayata (1911)
*A. rufinerve* Siebold & Zuccarini (1845)
*A. sikkimense* ssp. *metcalfii* (Rehder) de Jong, comb. & stat. nov.
*A. sikkimense* Miquel (1867) ssp. *sikkimense*
*A. tegmentosum* Maximowicz (1857)
*A. tschonoskii* ssp. *koreanum* Murray (1977)
*A. tschonoskii* Maximowicz (1886) ssp. *tschonoskii*

V. Section *Glabra* Pax (1885); amend. Momotani (1962)

7. Series *Glabra*

*A. glabrum* ssp. *diffusum* (Greene) Murray (1971)
*A. glabrum* ssp. *douglasii* (Hooker) Wesmael (1890)
*A. glabrum* Torrey (1828) ssp. *glabrum.*
*A. glabrum* ssp. *neomexicanum* (Greene) Murray (1970)
*A. glabrum* ssp. *siskiyouense* Murray (1983)

8. Series *Arguta* (Rehder) Rehder (1949)

*A. acuminatum* Wallich ex D. Don (1825)
*A. argutum* Maximowicz (1867)
*A. barbinerve* Maximowicz (1867)
*A. stachyophyllum* ssp. *betulifolium* (Maximowicz) de Jong, comb. & stat. nov.
*A. stachyophyllum* Hiern in J. Hooker (1875) ssp. *stachyophyllum*

VI. Section *Negundo* (Boemer) Maximowicz (1880)

9. Series *Negundo*

*A. negundo* ssp. *californicum* (Torrey & Gray) Wesmael (1890)
*A. negundo* ssp. *interius* (Britton) A. & D. Loeve (1954)
*A. negundo* ssp. *mexicanum* (DC.) Wesmael (1890)
*A. negundo* L. (1753) ssp. *negundo.*

10. Series *Cissifolia* (Koidzumi) Momotani (1962)

*A. cissifolium* (Siebold & Zuccarini) K. Koch (1864)
*A. henryi* Pax (1889)

VII. Section *Indivisa* Pax (1885)

*A. carpinifolium* Siebold & Zuccarini (1845)

VIII. Section *Acer*

11. Series *Acer*

*A. caesium* Wallich ex Brandis (1874) ssp. *caesium*
*A. caesium* ssp. *giraldii* (Pax) Murray (1969)
*A. heldreichii* Orphanides ex Boissier (1856) ssp. *heldreichii*
*A. heldreichii* ssp. *trautvetteri* (Medvedev) Murray (1982)
*A. pseudoplatanus* L. (1753)
*A. velutinum* Boissier (1846)

12. Series *Monspessulana* Pojárkova (1933)

*A. hyrcanum* Fischer & Meyer (1837) ssp. *hyrcanum*
*A. hyrcanum* ssp. *intermedium* (Pančić) Bornmüller (1894)
*A. hyrcanum* ssp. *keckianum* (Pax) Yaltirik (1967)
*A. hyrcanum* ssp. *reginae-amaliae* (Orphanides ex Boissier) Murray (1970)
*A. hyrcanum* ssp. *sphaerocarpum* Yaltirik (1967)
*A. hyrcanum* ssp. *stevenii* (Pojárkova) Murray (1969)

*A. hyrcanum* ssp. *tauricolum* (Boissier & Balansa) Yaltirik (1967)
*A. monspessulanum* ssp. *assyriacum* (Pojárkova) Rechinger f. (1969)
*A. monspessulanum* ssp. *cinerascens* (Boissier) Yaltirik (1967)
*A. monspessulanum* ssp. *ibericum* Yaltirik (1967)
*A. monspessulanum* ssp. *microphyllum* (Boissier) Bornmüller (1914)
*A. monspessulanum* L. (1753) ssp. *monspessulanum*
*A. monspessulanum* ssp. *oksalianum* Yaltirik (1967)
*A. monspessulanum* ssp. *persicum* (Pojárkova) Rechinger f. (1969)
*A. monspessulanum* ssp. *turcomanicum* (Pojárkova) Murray (1969)
*A. obtusifolium* Sibthorp & Smith (1809)
*A. opalus* ssp. *hispanicum* (Pourret) Murray (1969)
*A. opalus* ssp. *obtusatum* (Willdenow) Gams (1925)
*A. opalus* P. Miller (1768) ssp. *opalus*
*A. sempervirens* L. (1767)

13. Series *Saccharodendron* (Rafinesque) Murray (1970)
*A. saccharum* Marshall (1785) ssp. *saccharum*
*A. saccharum* ssp. *floridanum* (Chapman) Desmarais (1952)
*A. saccharum* ssp. *grandidentatum* (Torrey & Gray) Desmarais (1952)
*A. saccharum* ssp. *leucoderme* (Small) Desmarais (1952)
*A. saccharum* ssp. *nigrum* (Michaux f.) Desmarais (1952)
*A. saccharum* ssp. *ozarkense* Murray (1978)
*A. saccharum* ssp. *skutchii* (Rehder) Murray (1975)
*A. saccharum* var. *rugelii* (Pax) Rehder (1900)
*A. saccharum* var. *schneckii* Rehder (1913)
*A. saccharum* var. *sinuosum* (Rehder) Sargent (1919)

IX. Section *Pentaphylla* Hu & Cheng (1948)

14. Series *Pentaphylla*
*A. pentaphyllum* Diels (1931)

15. Series *Trifida* Pax (1886)
*A. buergerianum* Miquel (1865) ssp. *buergerianum*
*A. buergerianum* ssp. *formosanum* (Hayata) Murray & Lauener (1967)
*A. buergerianum* ssp. *ningpoense* (Hance) Murray (1982)
*A. coriaceifolium* Léveillé (1912)
*A. discolor* Maximowicz (1880)
*A. fengii* Murray (1977)
*A. oblongum* Wallich ex DC. (1824)
*A. paxii* Franchet (1886)
*A. shihweii* Chun & Fang (1966)
*A. sycopseoides* Chun (1932)
*A. wangchii* ssp. *tsinyunense* Fang (1979)
*A. wangchii* Fang (1966) ssp. *wangchii*
*A. yuii* Fang (1934)

X. Section Trifoliata Pax (1885)

16. Series *Grisea* Pojárkova (1933)
*A. griseum* (Franchet) Pax (1933)
*A. maximowiczianum* Miquel (1867)
*A. triflorum* Komarov (1901)

17. Series *Mandshurica* Pojárkova (1933)
*A. mandshuricum* Maximowicz (1867)
*A. sutchuenense* Franchet (1894)

XI. Section *Lithocarpa* Pax (1885)
18. Series *Lithocarpa*
*A. diabolicum* Blume ex Koch (1864)
*A. leipoense* Fang & Soong (1966)
*A. sinopurpurascens* Cheng (1931)
*A. sterculiaceum* ssp. *franchetii* (Pax) Murray (1969)
*A. sterculiaceum* Wallich (1830) ssp. *sterculiaceum*
*A. sterculiaceaum* ssp. *thomsonii* (Miquel) Murray (1969)
19. Series *Macrophylla* Pojárkova ex Momotani (1962)
*A. macrophyllum* Pursh (1814)
XII. Section *Platanoidea* Pax (1885)
*A. campestre* L. (1753)
*A. cappadocicum* Gleditsch (1785) ssp. *cappadocicum*
*A. cappadocicum* ssp. *divergens* (Pax) Murray (1978)
*A. cappadocicum* ssp. *lobelii* (Tenore) Murray (1982)
*A. cappadocicum* ssp. *sinicum* (Rehder) Handel-Mazzetti (1933)
*A. cappadocicum* ssp. *sinicum* var. *tricaudatum* (Veitch ex Rehder) Rehder (1914)
*A. longipes* ssp. *amplum* (Rehder) de Jong, comb. nov.
*A. longipes* ssp. *catalpifolium* (Rehder) de Jong, comb. nov.
*A. longipes* ssp. *firmianioides* (Cheng ex Fang) de Jong, comb. & stat. nov.
*A. longipes* Franchet ex Rehder (1905) ssp. *longipes*
*A. miyabei* ssp. *miaotaiense* (Tsoong) Murray (1969)
*A. miyabei* Maximowicz (1888) ssp. *miyabei*
*A. mono* Maximowicz (1857) ssp. *mono*
*A. mono* ssp. *mono* f. *ambiguum* (Dippel) Rehder (1939)
*A. mono* ssp. *okamotoanum* (Nakai) de Jong, comb. & stat. nov.
*A. mono* var. *mayrii* (Schwerin) Nakai (1930)
*A. nayongense* Fang (1979)
*A. platanoides* L. (1753) ssp. *platanoides*
*A. platanoides* ssp. *turkestanicum* (Pax) de Jong, comb. nov.
*A. tenellum* Pax (1889)
*A. tibetense* Fang (1939)
*A. truncatum* Bunge (1833)
XIII. Section *Pubescentia* (Pojárkova) Ogata (1967)
*A. pentapomicum* Stewart ex Brandis (1874)
*A. pilosum* Maximowicz (1880)
XIV. Section *Ginnala* Nakai (1915)
*A. tataricum* ssp. *aidzuense* (Franchet) de Jong, comb. & stat. nov.
*A. tataricum* ssp. *ginnala* (Maximowicz) Wesmael (1890)
*A. tataricum* ssp. *semenovii* (Regel & Herder) Murray (1982)
*A. tataricum* L. (1753) ssp. *tataricum*
XV. Section *Rubra* Pax (1885)
*A. pycnanthum* Koch (1864)
*A. rubrum* L. (1753)
*A. saccharinum* L. (1753)
XVI. Section *Hyptiocarpa* Fang (1966)
*A. garrettii* Craib (1920)
*A. laurinum* Hasskarl (1843)

Chapter 7

# Maple Species and Infraspecific Taxa

D. M. VAN GELDEREN

In the following systematic treatment of the species, subspecies, and varieties of *Acer*, the descriptions have been grouped into 16 sections, which are further broken down into series, if any (see "Taxonomic Synopsis" in Chapter 6). A brief description of the section and/or series precedes the descriptions of the species and infraspecific taxa, which have been arranged alphabetically by series and which include the following information:

1. The valid botanical name, authority, and date of publication, followed by the basionym, if applicable, and any invalid synonyms.
2. Location of the type specimen. Herbarium abbreviations are given in Appendix 5.
3. Common name(s) in English, followed by other languages.
4. Latin basis for epithet and its meaning.
5. Publications in which an illustration of the taxon is found, preceded by plate number(s), if any, corresponding to color photographs of the taxon in the present volume. Parenthetical numbers at the end of each plate caption refer to the location of the photograph as listed in Appendix 7. Full citations to sources are given in the Bibliography.
6. Morphological characteristics of the species, including habit, leaves, inflorescences, flowers, fruits, and bark and buds.
7. Hardiness rating, based on the U.S. Department of Agriculture Plant Hardiness Zone Map (see Appendix 6).
8. Autumn color.
9. Natural distribution of the species.
10. Chromosome number (if known).
11. Short descriptions of subspecies, varieties, forma, and cultivars, when (1) differing in minor characteristics, (2) not in cultivation, or (3) not described more fully in a separate entry. In most cases, fuller descriptions of the cultivars are given in Chapter 9.
12. Source(s) of information about the species.
13. Paragraph summary of highlights of the species.

## SECTION PARVIFLORA Koidzumi (1911)

TYPE SPECIES: ***Acer nipponicum*** Hara (1938).
HABIT: Deciduous trees and shrubs.
LEAVES: 3-, sometimes 5- to 7-lobed or undivided, chartaceous, margins serrate.
BUD SCALES: 2-, sometimes 3-paired.
INFLORESCENCES: Large corymbose, elongated rachises with cincinni, terminal and axillary, 35–400 flowers.
FLOWERS: 5-merous; perianths green-white; stamens mostly 8; discs amphi- or intrastaminal, slightly ferrugineous, pubescent.
FRUITS: Parthenocarpic tendency low.
SERIES: *Parviflora, Distyla, Caudata.*
REFERENCE: De Jong 1976.

Section *Parviflora* has relationships to sections *Glabra* and *Macrantha.* All series in section *Parviflora,* and especially series *Caudata,* display the characteristics of the primitive maple except for the leaves.

SERIES PARVIFLORA (Koidzumi) Pojárkova (1933)
TYPE SPECIES: ***Acer nipponicum*** Hara (1938).
HABIT: Trees, with rather thick branches.
LEAVES: Large, 3- to 5-lobed, margins doubly serrate.
BUD SCALES: Always 2-paired, more or less valvate, green-red.
INFLORESCENCES: Very large, paniculate-corymbose, 150–400 or more flowers.
FLOWERS: Perianths small, glabrous; discs intrastaminal, slightly ferruginous, pubescent.
FRUITS: Nutlets large, globose, densely ferruginous, pubescent when young, many underdeveloped nutlets on each truss.
SEEDLINGS: Cotyledons large, narrowly oblong, apices truncate.
SPECIES: *Acer nipponicum* Hara (1938).
REFERENCE: De Jong 1976.

This monotypic series consists of *Acer nipponicum,* which is endemic to Japan and rare in cultivation. The species forms a medium-sized tree with large deciduous leaves.

SECTION: *Parviflora* SERIES: *Parviflora*
ACER NIPPONICUM Hara (1938)
SYNONYMS
- *A. parviflorum* Franchet & Savatier (1878), non Ehrhart.
- *A. pensylvanicum* ssp. *parviflorum* (Franchet & Savatier) Wesmael (1890).
- *A. crassipes* sensu Pax (1902), non Heer.
- *A. spicatum* var. *ukurunduense* sensu Léveillé (1906), non Maximowicz.
- *A. pictum* var. *parviflorum* Schneider (1922).
- *A. brevilobum* Hesse ex Rehder (1938).

TYPE: AAH, as *A. crassipes.*
COMMON NAMES: Nippon maple, Tetsu kaede, Tetsu noki.
EPITHET: *Nipponicus,* from Nippon (Japan).
ILLUSTRATIONS: Plate 1; de Jong (1976), Koidzumi (1911b), Krüssmann (1965a), Kurata 1964–1976, Satake et al. (1989), Vertrees (1987).
HABIT: A small- or medium-sized tree in its native habitat, often up to 20 m tall but only 10–12 m in cultivation, openly branched; young shoots greenish and stout, with juvenile brownish hairs, later becoming glabrous; bark smooth, greenish brown.
LEAVES: Shallowly 5-lobed and deeply cordate, 12–25 cm across, lobes broadly ovate, shortly acuminate, middle lobe large, outer lobes much smaller, rusty pubescent beneath, becoming more glabrous in the summer; margins serrate; petioles 8–15 cm long.
INFLORESCENCES: Very long, paniculate-corymbose, terminal, trusses up to 30–40 cm long.
FLOWERS: 5-merous, yellow-green, appearing with the leaves, rather late in the season—the end of June—making this the last *Acer* to flower. Large inflorescences first produce only male flowers, and in some years female flowers are completely absent; when female flowers are produced, they appear mainly in the inflorescences of a few branches.
FRUITS: Samaras obtuse, 3–5 cm long, ferruginous and pubescent; wing margins wavy, not flat; fruits borne on long-stalked trusses about 20–30 cm, often sterile with only weak, flat nutlets; viable seeds are found as firm, large, round nutlets, about 1 cm in diameter. Variability of flowering results in very irregular fruiting.
HARDINESS: Zone V.
AUTUMN COLOR: Golden yellow to brown-yellow, soon curling.
DISTRIBUTION: Endemic to Japan, in mountain

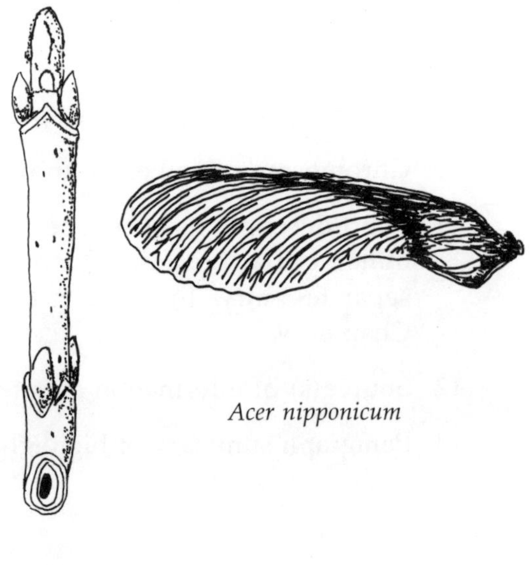

*Acer nipponicum*

forests on Honshu and Shikoku, also on Kyushu Island, at 900–1800 m.
REFERENCES: Bean (1970), de Jong (1976), Koidzumi (1911), Krüssmann (1976a), Kurata (1964–1976), Murray (1970c), Ogata (1965a), Rehder (1986 facs.), Vertrees (1987).

One of the rarer hardy maples in cultivation. A very few mature trees occur in collections. Probably the best specimen is growing in the Zuiderpark, The Hague, The Netherlands. This tree was purchased just before World War II from the nursery of H. A. Hesse, Weener, Germany, under the synonym *Acer brevilobum*, by the late famous dendrologist S. G. A. Doorenbos, director of the Municipal Parks and Gardens of The Hague. It is now about 13 m tall, with a large crown, and has become a very handsome tree, with huge leaves that are somewhat rusty on the undersides. The tree develops huge panicles of fruits. In some years a fair crop can be harvested. The seeds lose their viability quickly, so fresh seed must be sown as soon as possible.

At first glance, *Acer pensylvanicum* seems to be allied but is not. *Acer nipponicum* is an isolated species in the genus, and cannot be confused with any other maple on close inspection. The panicles are particularly distinctive, up to 40 cm long. Ogata (1967) reports seeing inflorescences of 400–600 flowers.

Propagation by seed is the only means currently available. Cuttings have never struck and grafting on several other species as understock has not been successful.

*Acer nipponicum* certainly deserves to be planted much more widely. In the coming years young trees will become available in the trade, propagated from the Zuiderpark tree. Quite a few young trees grow in several collectors' gardens in Great Britain and other European countries; all of these are seedlings of the Zuiderpark specimen. Other trees are being grown successfully in the United States from seedlings grown and distributed by Brian Mulligan of the University of Washington arboretum in Seattle. Some seedlings are growing in the Royal Botanic Garden in Edinburgh, derived from an adult tree in Dawyck Garden, Scotland. There is also a young tree in the Botanic Garden in Copenhagen, Denmark, which is not derived from the Dutch tree.

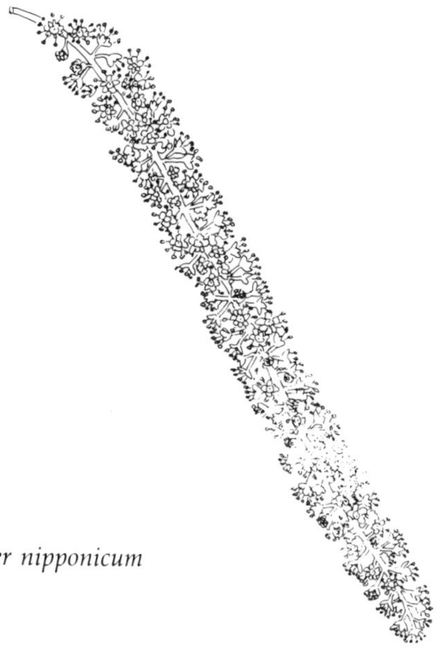

*Acer nipponicum*

Seedlings from the Zuiderpark specimen have already borne viable seeds, so this species will be far more popular and available in the near future. There appears to be very little variability in the seedlings; at present no aberrant seedlings have been observed, and the species remains without cultivars.

SERIES DISTYLA Murray (1970)
TYPE SPECIES: ***Acer distylum*** Siebold & Zuccarini (1845).
HABIT: Deciduous trees or large shrubs, small to medium height.
LEAVES: Undivided, deeply cordate; margins crenate.
BUD SCALES: Always 2-paired, valvate, brownish pubescent.
INFLORESCENCES: Upright, ferruginous pubescent, 35–70 flowered.
FLOWERS: Sepals hairy; discs lobed; stamens inserted between the lobes.
FRUITS: Nutlets on erect racemes, elliptic-convex, strongly ferruginous pubescent when young.
SEEDLINGS: Cotyledons narrowly elliptic.
SPECIES: *Acer distylum* Siebold & Zuccarini (1845).
REFERENCE: De Jong 1976.

This is a monotypic series, including only *Acer distylum* from Japan, a very distinctive species that grows as a small tree or large shrub, with entire, unlobed, deciduous leaves. It has some value as a garden plant, but is rare in cultivation.

SECTION: *Parviflora* SERIES: *Distyla*
ACER DISTYLUM Siebold & Zuccarini (1845)
TYPE: NBV, collected by Keiske in Japan; lectotype per Miquel (1865).
COMMON NAMES: Lindenblättriger Ahorn, Hitotsuba kaede, Maruba kaede.
EPITHET: *Distylus*, with 2 styles.
ILLUSTRATIONS: Plate 2; Koidzumi (1911), Krüssmann (1976a), Kurata (1964–1976), Ogata (1965a), Satake et al. (1989), Vertrees (1987).
HABIT: A treelike shrub to 10 m tall under favorable conditions, otherwise a much smaller shrub,

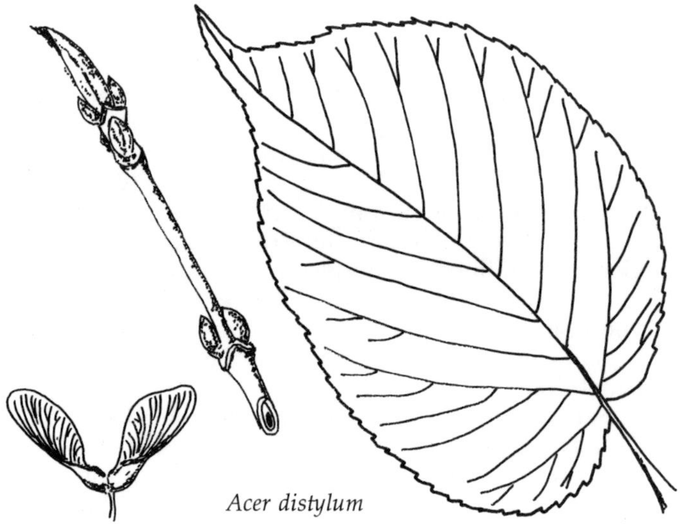

*Acer distylum*

rather densely branched; branches yellowish gray, somewhat corky.
LEAVES: Not unlike the leaves of *Tilia* or linden; ovate, not lobed, 10–15 cm long and 5–8 cm wide, gray-green, deeply cordate; apices acuminate, finely serrated, asymmetrical; undersides pale green, shining and glabrous, pinkish gray when young.
FLOWERS: Yellow on very erect spikes, small, nodding from the erect pedicels.
FRUITS: Borne on conspicuous erect racemes; nutlets with rounded wings about 3 cm long.
BARK AND BUDS: Bark gray-yellow, somewhat forked; buds stalked (valvate).
HARDINESS: Zone VI.
AUTUMN COLOR: Golden yellow or gold-brown.
DISTRIBUTION: Endemic to Japan, northern half of Honshu.
SUBSPECIES: None.
CULTIVAR: 'Fuiri kouri kaede', a variegated clone, not known in Europe or North America, but reported to be in cultivation in Japan.
REFERENCES: Bean (1970), Krüssmann (1976a), Kurata (1964–1965), Murray (1970c), Ogata (1965), Pax (1902), Rehder (1986 facs.), Veitch (1904), Vertrees (1987).

This species is endemic to Japan, growing on fertile soils in the northern part of Honshu, but even there it is rather rare. Charles Maries introduced it in 1879 to Great Britain for Veitch Nursery, although Siebold and Zuccarini made the description in 1865. This distinct and easily recognized species cannot be confused with any other maple.

It is a very interesting small tree, quite unlike any other maple with its silvery green, entire leaves that look like those of a peculiar linden. It is a treelike shrub under favorable conditions, with yellow-gray branches. The leaves are ovate and unlobed and somewhat "dusty" when young. The new growth has an attractive pinkish color. It flowers relatively late, as do the other species of this section, at the beginning of June. The erect inflorescences and the flowers resemble those of *Acer spicatum* and *A. caudatum* ssp. *ukurunduense*, but are somewhat smaller. The flowers are greenish white and resemble those of section *Macrantha*, especially *A. tschonoskii*.

*Acer distylum* is rather rare in Great Britain, but good specimens can be found in several gardens and collections. Outside Great Britain it is very rarely cultivated. It is usually propagated by seed, which is not easy to obtain. It can be propagated by cuttings, but the rooted cuttings are fragile and hard to transplant. Therefore, it is rare in the trade and only available from a few specialized nurseries.

SERIES CAUDATA Pax 1886
TYPE SPECIES: ***Acer caudatum*** Wallich (1830).
HABIT: Small trees or shrubs.
LEAVES: 3- to 5-, sometimes to 7-lobed, pubescent beneath or glabrous; margins serrate.
BUD SCALES: 2-, sometimes 3-paired.
INFLORESCENCES: Upright, 50–200 flowers; pedicels of postanthesis male flowers partly caducous.
FLOWERS: Petals narrow, white, twice as long as the hairy, greenish sepals; discs lobed, partly amphistaminal, partly intrastaminal; postanthesis male flowers drop petals and stamens first.
FRUITS: Nutlets small, veined, with one side convex and the other concave.
SEEDLINGS: Cotyledons small, narrowly elliptic.
SPECIES AND INFRASPECIFIC TAXA
*Acer caudatum* Wallich (1830) ssp. *caudatum*.
*Acer caudatum* ssp. *multiserratum* (Maximowicz) Murray (1970).
*Acer caudatum* ssp. *ukurunduense* (Trautvetter & Meyer) Murray (1966).
*Acer spicatum* Lamarck (1786).
REFERENCE: De Jong (1976).

This series includes only two species, one of them quite complex. The North American *Acer spicatum* is remarkably uniform, but its Asian counterpart, *A. caudatum*, now includes *A. ukurunduense* Trautvetter & Meyer. As these taxa are very rare in cultivation, more research is needed to determine their status. All are small trees or large shrubs, with deciduous 3- to 5- or 7-lobed leaves. They are valuable garden plants.

SECTION: *Parviflora* SERIES: *Caudata*
ACER CAUDATUM Wallich (1830) ssp. CAUDATUM
SYNONYMS
*Acer acuminatum* sensu Dippel (1892).
*A. papilio* King (1896).
TYPE: BM; lectotype chosen by Dr. H. Hara;

formerly *Wallich, 1225,* K, now rejected.
COMMON NAMES: Aoba.
EPITHET: *Caudatus,* like a tail.
ILLUSTRATIONS: Plate 3; Fang (1981a), Krüssmann (1976a).
HABIT: A medium-sized tree to 7–10 m tall, with ash-gray (never red), smooth stems; bark rougher than in subspecies *ukurunduense,* in some cases even slightly fissured or peeling in small flakes.
LEAVES: 5-lobed, 7–12 cm across, lobes triangular, coarsely and acutely saw-toothed, with finely serrate teeth; undersides with a more or less persistent covering of yellowish hairs; petioles about 7–10 cm long.
FLOWERS: On erect spikelike panicles of staminate flowers; the main axes of the inflorescences, peduncles, and pedicels all hairy.
FRUITS: Fruiting racemes about 12 cm long; fruits 3–4 cm long including the nutlet; wings ascending; pedicels 3–7 mm long.
BARK AND BUDS: Bark ash-gray (never red as in subspecies *ukurunduense*), smooth; buds pubescent.
HARDINESS: Zone IV.
AUTUMN COLOR: Yellow.
DISTRIBUTION: Eastern Himalayas and Upper Burma; also found in Manchuria, Korea and northern Japan.
CHROMOSOME NUMBER: $2n = 26$, as *A. caudatum* (Krikieb 1957, Wright 1957, Mehra et al. 1972).
SUBSPECIES
- ssp. *caudatum,* the typical subspecies.
- ssp. *multiserratum* (Maximowicz) Murray (1970).
- ssp. *ukurunduense* (Trautvetter & Meyer) Murray (1966).

REFERENCES: Banerji & Das (1971), Bean (1970, 1988), Dippel (1892), Fang (1981a), Krüssmann (1976a), Murray (1970c), Pax (1902), Rehder (1905, 1986 facs.), Schneider (1912).

A very rare and handsome tree with a very confusing nomenclature. Its nearest relatives are *Acer spicatum* and *A. caudatum* ssp. *ukurunduense.* Both these taxa differ from *A. caudatum* ssp. *caudatum* by their red branches and stems, which later turn to a mixture of gray and red. The leaves of *A. caudatum* differ from both these taxa, being almost orbicular, with 5–7 lobes, while the leaves of both *A. spicatum* and *A. caudatum* ssp. *ukurunduense* are longer than wide.

The inflorescences, flowers, and fruits of subspecies *ukurunduense* and typical *Acer caudatum* are very similar. This strong resemblance and the morphological characteristics make for a great deal of confusion in this complex species.

True *Acer caudatum* is very rare in cultivation, with only a few gardens reporting having it in their collections. Practically none of them could be satisfactorily confirmed. A few years ago wild-collected seed arrived in Holland; the young plants looked very promising and true to type, but died.

*Acer caudatum* ssp. *ukurunduense*

In *Acers in Nepal* Banerji and Das (1971) note:

> *A. papilio* is distributed in Eastern Himalaya at 3,300 to 4,000 m and it extends to East Nepal. There are no collections that we have come across from West Nepal. Neither is there any record of the species further west. According to King (loc. cit.) [1896], "this species has been confused with *A. pectinatum* Wall. and *A. caudatum* Wall.; it is at once distinguished from both by its paniculate inflorescence, that of *A. caudatum* being fasciculate, while that of *A. pectinatum* is a few-flowered simple raceme ..." We are in full agreement with King, as these differences are clear and prominent; thus, we are surprised to find that Pax treated this species as a synonym of *A. caudatum.* Cowan & Cowan (loc. cit.) [1929] have recognised the species as distinct from others. We also have noted the difference in the shape of the petals.

Despite Desmond Clarke's argument in Bean (1970) that the name *Acer caudatum* should be rejected in favor of *A. papilio* King, there is no good reason to accept the name *A. papilio* as the valid name for the entire complex. The objective of the authors of this work is to accept complex taxa as species. Hence, *A. caudatum* is better brought together with *A. caudatum* ssp. *ukurunduense* as a species and *A. papilio* as a synonym. The argument in Bean is cited in full (with slight editing) by way of reference:

> *A. caudatum* is ambiguous: The name *A. caudatum* starts from Wallich. He included under it two sets of herbarium material which he had previously regarded as representing two distinct species. These he had catalogued in the East India Company's Herbarium as *A.*

*caudatum* (no. 1225) and *A. pectinatum* (no. 1226). In his account of *A. caudatum* Wallich made clear that he had come to regard this material as representing a single variable species—*A. caudatum*—and cited *A. pectinatum* as a synonym. In fact, his earlier judgement was the correct one. No. 1226 is a distinct species, *A. pectinatum.* No. 1225 is, with one exception mentioned below, *A. acuminatum,* a species validly described by David Don some years earlier. Wallich's description of *Acer caudatum* is clearly compounded of these two species. As for the specimen figured under t.132, there is nothing to match it in the Kew Herbarium, but it is nearest to a specimen of *A. pectinatum* in Hooker's herbarium and is not *A. caudatum* as understood by Rehder (i.e., *A. papilio*). This confusion would have been resolved if Wallich had designated a type for *A. caudatum,* but he did not do so, and there is no way of deducing one from his account. Rehder (1905) applied the name *A. caudatum* Wall. to *A. papilio,* but excluded Wallich's description of the staminate flowers (which refers to *A. acuminatum*) and the synonym *A. pectinatum.* But what is left of Wallich's *A. caudatum* is impossible to identify. Nor did Rehder deal with the material upon Wallich based his account; he makes no mention of the nos. 1225 and 1226, and the only specimen he cited for *A. caudatum* is one collected by J. D. Hooker in Sikkim, and the only specimen of this group in Hooker's herbarium is *A. pectinatum.*

It should be added that one of the collections in the Wallich herbarium under no. 1225 seems to be *A. papilio.* It is sterile and mounted with a flowering specimen which is clearly *A. acuminatum.* Even if the sterile piece is really *A. papilio,* there is no reason to take it as the holotype of *A. caudatum,* unless it be that it is the one specimen that might answer to Wallich's descriptions of the leaves; in fact it does not agree well with his description. It will be therefore evident that the name *A. caudatum* Wall. has been so confused that it is best abandoned. The valid name for *A. caudatum* sensu Rehder is *A. papilio* King (*Journal As. Soc. Bengal* [1896] 65:115).

In 1988 Desmond Clarke's opinion changed, and in Bean (1988, vol. 5) he points out that *Acer caudatum* has to be preserved as the valid name of this species and that *A. papilio* should be sunk in synonymy. Hara (1975) chose a lectotype of this species, which is in the British Museum. No true *A. caudatum* is present in *Wallich 1225* (Kew Herbarium).

SECTION: *Parviflora* SERIES: *Caudata*

ACER CAUDATUM ssp. MULTISERRATUM (Maximowicz) Murray (1970)

BASIONYM: *A. multiserratum* Maximowicz (1889).

SYNONYMS

*A. erosum* Pax (1889).

*A. caudatum* var. *prattii* Rehder (1905).

TYPE: Syntypes LE; G. N. Potanin, Gansu Province, China; Mor-ping—Wuping; flur. Lumbu; Idshu-shan.

EPITHET: *Multiserratus,* with many incisions—referring to the leaves.

HABIT: A tree, usually many-stemmed, to 10 m tall, very much like *A. caudatum* ssp. *ukurunduense,* with a gray stem.

LEAVES: 5-lobed, 8–12 cm across, lobes triangular, the central lobe longer, undersides glabrous not pubescent; margins serrate.

FLOWERS: On erect spikes.

FRUITS: Fruiting racemes about 10 cm long; wings ascendent, 3–4 cm long.

BARK AND BUDS: Very similar to *A. caudatum* ssp. *ukurunduense.*

HARDINESS: Zone V.

DISTRIBUTION: Gansu to Yunnan provinces, China, where it is a common tree.

REFERENCES: Bean (1970), Fang (1981a), Murray (1970c), Rehder (1986 facs.).

This subspecies, for which no records of trees in cultivation can be found, is intermediate between subspecies *caudatum* and *ukurunduense.* It is quite possible that when it is introduced and better known, it may be reclassified as a synonym of subspecies *ukurunduense.* A tree under this name in the Botanic Garden of Copenhagen, Denmark, has not been verified and might well be *Acer caudatum* ssp. *ukurunduense.*

*Acer caudatum* var. *prattii* is rejected as a variety and is considered to be synonymous with subspecies *multiserratum.* Its distribution in Sichuan Province, China, lies within the range of subspecies *multiserratum* in Gansu to Yunnan provinces, China. The vegetative and floral characteristics of variety *prattii* are identical with those of subspecies *multiserratum.*

SECTION: *Parviflora* SERIES: *Caudata*

ACER CAUDATUM ssp. UKURUNDUENSE (Trautvetter & Meyer) Murray (1966)

BASIONYM: *A. ukurunduense* Trautvetter & Meyer (1856).

SYNONYMS

*A. ukurunduense* var. *pilosum* Nakai (1856).

*A. dedyle* Maximowicz (1857).

*A. spicatum* var. *ukurunduense* (Trautvetter & Meyer) Maximowicz (1859).

*A. spicatum* var. *ussuriense* Budischev (1867).

*A. spicatum* ssp. *ukurunduense* (Trautvetter & Meyer) Pax (1889).

*A. lasiocarpum* Léveillé & Vaniot (1906).
*A. ukurunduense* var. *sachalinense* Nakai (1915).
TYPE: LECB; F. Schmidt, Sachalin.
COMMON NAMES: Arahaga, Arahana, Hozaki kaede, Ogara bana.
EPITHET: *Ukurunduensis,* from Ukurundu (Manchuria), China, one of the regions in which the tree grows.
ILLUSTRATIONS: Plate 4; Fang (1981a), Krüssmann (1976a), Kurata (1964–1976), Satake et al. (1989).
HABIT: A small tree or treelike shrub to 7–8 m tall; like *A. spicatum* in shape; young branches orange-gray to red, later gray-yellow, slightly pilose; sparsely branched.
LEAVES: 5- to 7-lobed, 5–8 cm across, intensely hairy beneath, lobes deep; margins coarsely lobulate, tapering to long mucros at apices.
INFLORESCENCES: Corymbose, upright, many-flowered.
FLOWERS: Pale yellow to white, closely resembling those of *A. spicatum.*
FRUITS: Samaras 2.5–4 cm long in corymbs, few on individual trusses since many flowers do not set any seeds.
BARK: Rough, somewhat fissured when mature, sometimes peeling.
HARDINESS: Zone IV.
AUTUMN COLOR: Yellow.
DISTRIBUTION: Manchuria to Hubei Province, China, to 600 m. Also in Japan on Honshu and Hondo islands, in thickets on sunny slopes and along streams. A dwarfish expression grows in Sachalin. Introduced about 1900.
CHROMOSOME NUMBER: $2n = 26$ (Krikieb 1957, Wright 1957).
REFERENCES: Bean (1970), Fang (1981a), Koch (1869), Krüssmann (1976a), Kurata (1964–1976), Murray (1970c), Ogata (1965), Pax (1902), Pojárkova (1933b), Schneider (1892).

This is a rare plant and not always correctly labeled in cultivation. It is a treelike shrub, up to 10 m tall, that is very much like *Acer spicatum,* its close ally, in its habit and leaf shape. The leaves of *A. caudatum* ssp. *ukurunduense* are intensely tomentose, while those of *A. spicatum* are fully glabrous (an important characteristic in the field). The leaves of subspecies *caudatum* are almost orbicular and not as hairy; nor are the branches as reddish, while the bark is more fissured.

*Acer caudatum* ssp. *ukurunduense* will grow under any soil or moisture conditions, from very wet to rather dry. In stony situations along river-banks it grows as a shrub, and in Sachalin and on the Kurile Islands it grows as an almost prostrate shrub.

This maple is seldom found in collections. It is not often offered in the trade, and when it is, is often not the true subspecies. It can be propagated by seed. Grafting is possible on *Acer spicatum* seedlings as understock. Softwood cuttings also strike successfully.

SECTION: *Parviflora* SERIES: *Caudata*

ACER SPICATUM Lamarck (1786)

SYNONYMS
*A. parviflorum* Ehrhart (1789).
*A. montanum* Aiton (1789).
*A. pumilum* Bartram (1792).
*A. rugosum* de Vos (1887).
TYPE: P.
COMMON NAMES: Mountain maple.
EPITHET: *Spicatus,* bearing a spike—referring to the large spikelike inflorescences.
ILLUSTRATIONS: Koidzumi (1911), Krüssmann (1976a).
HABIT: A large shrub or, rarely, a small tree, sparsely branched; branches reddish to gray; bud scales few, reddish; young, vigorously growing branches and shoots red.
LEAVES: 3- to 5-lobed, 6–12 cm long and wide; bases cordate, rugose-puberulous above; undersides fully glabrous; margins coarsely doubly-serrate; petioles 4–6 cm long.
INFLORESCENCES: Paniculate-racemose, terminal, suberect.
FLOWERS: Yellow-green, small, trusses 8–15 cm long, appearing in May–June; petals long, narrow and white; male flowers shed petals and stamens before the flowers drop.
FRUITS: Samaras about 2.5 cm long, wings divergent, turning red in autumn.
BARK AND BUDS: Young shoots red, 2-year-old wood red spotted with gray, older wood fully gray.
HARDINESS: Zone III.
AUTUMN COLOR: Clear yellow to orange and sometimes red.
DISTRIBUTION: In the United States and Canada, from Newfoundland to Saskatchewan, Iowa, Michigan, and Pennsylvania to northern Georgia in the Appalachians. Almost always shrubby in forest borders in rocky and moist situations.
CHROMOSOME NUMBER: $2n = 26$ (Krikieb 1957, Wright 1957).
SUBSPECIES: None.

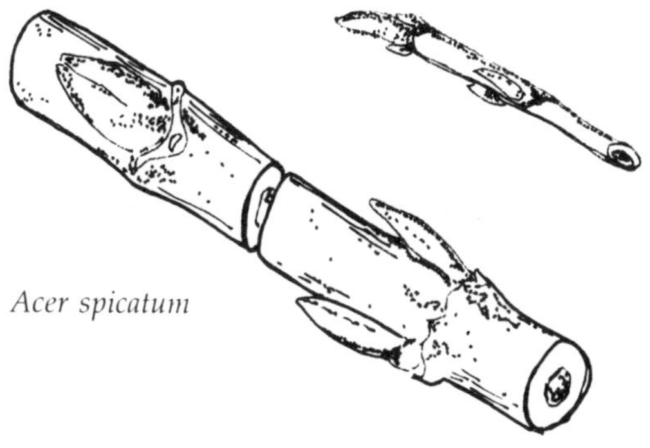

*Acer spicatum*

CULTIVARS: None; this is a remarkably uniform species.
REFERENCES: Bean (1970), Dippel (1892), Elwes & Henry (1908), Koch (1869), Koidzumi (1911), Krüssmann (1976a), Murray (1970c), Pax (1902), Rehder (1986 facs.).

This species was extremely rare in European cultivation at the beginning of this century, but was reintroduced about 1905 by Elwes from seed collected near Ottawa, Canada. Its first introduction had been by Archibald, Duke of Argyll, about 1775. Lamarck described it in 1786.

A well-known synonym, *Acer montanum* (sensu Aiton, non Garsault), dates from 1789. This name is also incorrectly applied to *A. pseudoplatanus. Acer spicatum* is easily confused with *A. caudatum* ssp. *ukurunduense,* its closest relative. The most important differences between these two species are the fully glabrous leaves of *A. spicatum* and the distinctive hairiness of *A. caudatum* ssp. *ukurunduense.* The latter is also similar, but its leaves are much more orbicular. There is a resemblance to *A. argutum,* but *A. spicatum* twigs are less red, with more deeply impressed venation.

*Acer spicatum* is a multistemmed or shrubby tree with elegant, 3- to 5-lobed leaves and deep impressed veins. The young shoots are often a beautiful red, later turning to gray with red flecks, with the branches becoming gray-brown and somewhat fissured. It is easily propagated from seed and is available from time to time in the nursery trade. Seedlings of *A. spicatum* can be used as an understock for grafting closely related species. It also strikes from cuttings taken early in the summer.

## SECTION PALMATA Pax (1885)

TYPE SPECIES: ***Acer palmatum*** Thunberg ex Murray (1784).
HABIT: Deciduous or partly evergreen trees and shrubs.
LEAVES: 3- to 13-lobed or unlobed, chartaceous or coriaceous; margins serrate, sometimes entire; apices obtuse.
BUD SCALES: Always 4-paired.
INFLORESCENCES: Corymbose with cincinni terminal and, less frequently, axillary; pedicels of postanthesis male flowers often partly dropped.
FLOWERS: 5-merous; sepals red or green-red; petals mostly white and rolled inward; stamens 8; discs extrastaminal.
FRUITS: Nutlets elliptical-globose, never empty, parthenocarpic tendency low to moderate.
SEEDLINGS: Cotyledons usually narrowly oblong.
SERIES: *Palmata, Sinensia, Penninervia.*
REFERENCE: De Jong (1976).

Section *Palmata*—especially series *Sinensia,* which deviates from the original maple described above only in its aborted terminal buds, the lobed leaves, and the four pairs of bud scales—is primitive. On the basis of morphological characteristics, the section is very close to section *Parviflora,* but this was not established by the experiments of Momotani (1962a, 1962b, 1962c) who only studied some species of the more specialized series *Palmata.* Probably the section has been somewhat distinct from the remaining taxa since the phylogenetic beginning of the genus.

### SERIES PALMATA Pax

TYPE SPECIES: ***Acer palmatum*** Thunberg ex Murray.
HABIT: Deciduous trees and shrubs; terminal buds usually abortive.
LEAVES: 5- to 9-lobed, or up to 13-lobed, suborbicular, chartaceous; margins serrate.
INFLORESCENCES: With 5–25 flowers; pedicels of postanthesis male flowers completely dropped.
FLOWERS: Petals mostly white, sometimes reddish; stamens of postanthesis male flowers drop first.
FRUITS: Nutlets mostly veined, parthenocarpic tendency moderate.
SPECIES AND INFRASPECIFIC TAXA
- *A. ceriferum* Rehder.
- *A. circinatum* Pursh.
- *A. duplicatoserratum* Hayata.
- *A. japonicum* Thunberg ex Murray.
- *A. palmatum* ssp. *amoenum* (Carrière) Hara.
- *A. palmatum* ssp. *matsumurae* Koidzumi.
- *A. palmatum* Thunberg ex Murray ssp. *palmatum.*
- *A. pauciflorum* Fang.
- *A. pseudosieboldianum* (Pax) Komarov ssp. *pseudosieboldianum.*
- *A. pseudosieboldianum* ssp. *takesimense* (Nakai) de Jong, comb. & stat. nov.
- *A. pubipalmatum* Fang.
- *A. robustum* Pax.
- *A. shirasawanum* Koidzumi var. *shirasawanum.*
- *A. shirasawanum* var. *tenuifolium* Koidzumi.
- *A. sieboldianum* Miquel.

REFERENCE: De Jong (1976).

This series includes 11 species, some with several subspecies, varieties, or forms. They are all medium-sized trees or large shrubs, with deciduous, palmately lobed leaves. Most are of outstanding beauty (Plate 5). With the exception of one species from North America, all are endemic to eastern Asia. A few species are not in cultivation and are not well-known.

PLATE 1. *Acer nipponicum.* Fruiting branch. (15)

PLATE 2. *Acer distylum.* Flowering branch. (15)

PLATE 3. *Acer caudatum* ssp. *caudatum.* Fruiting branch. (15)

PLATE 4. *Acer caudatum* ssp. *ukurunduense.* Fruiting branch. (15)

PLATE 5. *Acer palmatum* and *Cercidiphyllum japonicum.* Old specimen trees. (12)

PLATE 6. *Acer circinatum.* (17)

PLATE 7. *Acer japonicum.* Typical leaves. (15)

PLATE 8. *Acer palmatum* ssp. *amoenum.* Leaves. (15)

PLATE 9. *Acer palmatum* ssp. *matsumurae.* Leaves. (15)

PLATE 10. *Acer palmatum* ssp. *palmatum.* Leaves. (15)

PLATE 11. *Acer pseudosieboldianum* ssp. *pseudosieboldianum.* Well-developed leaves. (8)

PLATE 12. *Acer pseudosieboldianum* ssp. *takesimense.* Typical leaves, with silky hairs when young. (15)

PLATE 13. *Acer shirasawanum* var. *shirasawanum.* Leaves with erect fruits. (15)

PLATE 14. *Acer sieboldianum.* Autumn colors. (45)

PLATE 15. *Acer calcaratum.* Mature leaves. (15)

PLATE 16. *Acer campbellii* ssp. *flabellatum.* Young leaves. (14)

PLATE 17. *Acer campbellii* ssp. *sinense*. Young shrub in the greenhouse. (15)

PLATE 18. *Acer campbellii* ssp. *wilsonii*. Typical 3-lobed leaves. (13)

PLATE 19. *Acer elegantulum*. Young plant cultivated from wild-collected seed (courtesy of Wang Dajun). (15)

PLATE 20. *Acer erianthum*. Leaves and flowers. (8)

PLATE 21. *Acer oliverianum* ssp. *formosanum*. Young leaves. (15)

PLATE 22. *Acer oliverianum* ssp. *oliverianum*. Leaves of a young tree. (15)

PLATE 23. *Acer tonkinense* ssp. *kwangsiense*. Mature leaves. Grown from wild-collected seed (courtesy of Wang Dajun). (15)

PLATE 24. *Acer laevigatum*. Unlobed, slightly wavy leaf margins. (15)

PLATE 25. *Acer lucidum.* Leathery, unlobed leaves. (15)

PLATE 26. *Acer capillipes.* Fruiting branch. (10)

PLATE 27. *Acer capillipes.* Snakebark, a typical trunk of this species. (33)

PLATE 28. *Acer caudatifolium.* Young leaves. (15)

PLATE 29. *Acer crataegifolium.* Fruiting specimen. (20)

PLATE 30. *Acer davidii* ssp. *davidii.* Typical unlobed leaves and fruits. (15)

PLATE 31. *Acer davidii* ssp. *grosseri.* Branch with mature leaves. (15)

PLATE 32. *Acer davidii* ssp. *grosseri.* Typical snakebark trunk. (4)

PLATE 33. *Acer pectinatum* ssp. *forrestii.* Fruiting branch. (15)

PLATE 34. *Acer pectinatum* ssp. *maximowiczii.* Flowering branch. (20)

PLATE 35. *Acer pectinatum* ssp. *taronense.* Mature leaves. (15)

PLATE 36. *Acer pensylvanicum.* Trunk and leaves in the fall. (29)

PLATE 37. *Acer rubescens.* Young leaves on a small plant. (15)

PLATE 39. *Acer rufinerve.* Autumn colors. (19)

PLATE 40. *Acer sikkimense* ssp. *sikkimense.* Leathery unlobed leaves. (15)

PLATE 38. *Acer rubescens.* A heavy trunk of this rare species. (5)

PLATE 41. *Acer tegmentosum.* Fruiting branch. 43)

PLATE 42. *Acer glabrum* ssp. *douglasii.* Fruiting branch. (15)

PLATE 43. *Acer glabrum* ssp. *glabrum.* Typical mature leaves. (15)

PLATE 44. *Acer acuminatum.* Natural habitat in Milke Danda Range in eastern Nepal.

PLATE 45. *Acer argutum.* Detail of shrub, reticulate leaves. (15)

PLATE 46. *Acer barbinerve.* Male and female plant together. (15)

PLATE 47. *Acer stachyophyllum* ssp. *betulifolium.* Suckers. (15)

PLATE 48. *Acer stachyophyllum* ssp. *stachyophyllum*. Mature leaves. (7)

PLATE 49. *Acer negundo* ssp. *californicum*. Typical hairy leaves. (15)

PLATE 50. *Acer negundo* ssp. *interius*. Photo by Peter Del Tredici. (6)

PLATE 51. *Acer negundo* ssp. *negundo*. Fruiting branches. (7)

PLATE 52. *Acer henryi.* Fruiting branch. (43)

PLATE 53. *Acer caesium* ssp. *giraldii.* Mature leaves. (15)

PLATE 54. *Acer heldreichii* ssp. *trautvetteri.* Trees along a road in Turkey.

PLATE 55. *Acer heldreichii* ssp. *trautvetteri.* Fruiting branch with conspicuous red samaras. (37)

PLATE 56. *Acer pseudoplatanus.* Old tree growing in the wild near Klosters, Switzerland.

PLATE 57. *Acer velutinum.* Flowering branch. (34)

PLATE 58. *Acer hyrcanum* ssp. *hyrcanum.* Mature tree growing in the wild in eastern Turkey.

PLATE 59. *Acer hyrcanum* ssp. *hyrcanum.* Fruiting branch in natural habitat in Kasnak, Turkey.

PLATE 60. *Acer hyrcanum* ssp. *intermedium.* Detail of leaves. (15)

PLATE 61. *Acer hyrcanum* ssp. *keckianum.* Leaf detail from a tree in natural habitat in Kasnak, Turkey.

PLATE 62. *Acer hyrcanum* ssp. *sphaerocarpum.* Fruiting branch in natural habitat in Kasnak, Turkey.

PLATE 63. *Acer hyrcanum* ssp. *tauricolum.* Fruiting branch in natural habitat in Kasnak, Turkey.

PLATE 64. *Acer monspessulanum* ssp. *microphyllum.* Leaf detail. (15)

PLATE 65. *Acer monspessulanum* ssp. *monspessulanum.* Mature tree in its natural habitat in Turkey.

PLATE 66. *Acer monspessulanum* ssp. *monspessulanum.* Flowering branch. (38)

PLATE 67. *Acer monspessulanum* ssp. *monspessulanum.* Fruiting branch. (38)

PLATE 68. *Acer monspessulanum* ssp. *turcomanicum.* Mature leaves. (41)

PLATE 69. *Acer obtusifolium.* Leaf detail. (25)

PLATE 70. *Acer opalus* ssp. *obtusatum.* Mature leaves. (15)

PLATE 71. *Acer opalus* ssp. *opalus.* With a rough, fissured bark. (46)

PLATE 72. *Acer opalus* ssp. *opalus.* Leaf detail. (4)

PLATE 73. *Acer sempervirens.* Grafted young plant, collected in the wild on Crete. (15)

PLATE 74. *Acer sempervirens.* Grafted plant, from the tree in the Jardin des Plantes in Paris. (15)

PLATE 75. *Acer saccharum* ssp. *saccharum.* Tree in its autumn color growing wild in the United States.

PLATE 76. *Acer saccharum* ssp. *saccharum.* Flowering branches. (36)

PLATE 77. *Acer saccharum* ssp. *leucoderme.* Branch in autumn color. (42)

PLATE 78. *Acer saccharum* var. *schneckii.* Leaf detail and trunk.

PLATE 79. *Acer pentaphyllum.* Flowering branch. (24)

PLATE 80. *Acer buergerianum* ssp. *buergerianum.* Adult, mature leaves. (27)

PLATE 81. *Acer buergerianum* var. *ningpoense.* Fruiting branch. (26)

PLATE 82. *Acer coriaceifolium.* Young plant, grown from wild-collected seed. (15)

PLATE 83. *Acer oblongum.* Fully unlobed, leathery leaves. (15)

PLATE 84. *Acer griseum.* Splendid trunk of the Paperbark maple. (46)

PLATE 85. *Acer griseum.* Autumn color. (4)

PLATE 86. *Acer maximowiczianum.* Tree. (43)

PLATE 87. *Acer maximowiczianum.* Autumn color. (15)

PLATE 88. *Acer triflorum.* Mature leaves and fruits. (15)

PLATE 89. *Acer triflorum.* Typical trunk, differing from *A. griseum.* (4)

PLATE 90. *Acer mandshuricum.* Mature leaves. (30)

PLATE 91. *Acer diabolicum.* Mature leaves. (15)

PLATE 92. *Acer sinopurpurascens.* Young leaves. (4)

PLATE 93. *Acer sinopurpurascens.* Flowering branch, male. (4)

PLATE 94. *Acer sterculiaceum* ssp. *franchetii.* Mature leaves. (8)

PLATE 95. *Acer sterculiaceum* ssp. *sterculiaceum.* Fruiting branch. (15)

PLATE 96. *Acer sterculiaceum* ssp. *thomsonii.* Huge young leaves. (15)

PLATE 97. *Acer campestre.* Young tree with corky bark. (46)

PLATE 98. *Acer campestre.* Three-lobed leaves. (34)

PLATE 99. *Acer cappadocicum* ssp. *divergens.* Small-leaved tree. (39)

PLATE 100. *Acer cappadocicum* ssp. *lobelii.* Columnar tree. (25)

PLATE 101. *Acer cappadocicum* ssp. *sinicum* var. *tricaudatum*. Young leaves. (15)

PLATE 102. *Acer miyabei* ssp. *miyabei*. Mature leaves. (15)

PLATE 103. *Acer mono* ssp. *mono*. Fruiting branch. (7)

PLATE 104. *Acer mono* ssp. *okamotoanum*. Fruiting branch.

PLATE 105. *Acer platanoides* ssp. *platanoides.* Mature tree growing in the wild at Zirl, Switzerland.

PLATE 106. *Acer platanoides* ssp. *turkestanicum.* Mature leaves. (15)

PLATE 107. *Acer tenellum.* Mature, 3-lobed leaves. (15)

PLATE 108. *Acer truncatum.* Heavily fissured trunk. (16)

PLATE 109. *Acer truncatum.* Fruiting branch. (25)

PLATE 110. *Acer pentapomicum.* Young specimen. (15)

PLATE 111. *Acer pentapomicum.* Mature leaves. (15)

PLATE 112. *Acer tataricum* ssp. *aidzuense.* Fruiting branch. (15)

PLATE 113. *Acer tataricum* ssp. *ginnala.* Huge specimen tree. (20)

PLATE 114. *Acer tataricum* ssp. *ginnala.* Flowering branch. (20)

PLATE 115. *Acer tataricum* ssp. *tataricum.* Fruiting branch with red samaras. (43)

PLATE 116. *Acer tataricum* ssp. *tataricum.* Adult tree. (31)

PLATE 117. *Acer pycnanthum.* Leaves. (15)

PLATE 118. *Acer rubrum.* Tree in autumn color. 48)

PLATE 119. *Acer rubrum.* Autumn colors. (43)

PLATE 120. *Acer saccharinum.* (4)

PLATE 121. *Acer laurinum.* Tropical species. (15)

SECTION: *Palmata* SERIES: *Palmata*

## ACER CERIFERUM Rehder (1911)

TYPE: A, collected in 1907 by *E. H. Wilson, 1934,* Fang Hsien, Hubei Province, China; isotypes FI, W.

EPITHET: *Ceriferus,* covered with. wax.

HABIT: A tree to 12 m tall; branches waxy gray.

LEAVES: 5- to 7-lobed, 6–9 cm across, suborbicular, lobes ovate-acuminate, sharply serrate, pubescent along the veins beneath; petioles pubescent, about 3 cm long.

INFLORESCENCES: Corymbose, terminal.

FLOWERS: Not seen.

FRUITS: Samaras 2.5 cm long, horizontal; nutlets villose.

BARK AND BUDS: Bark smooth, not fissured; bud scales few, 6 or more.

HARDINESS: Zone VII (?).

DISTRIBUTION: Western Hubei, China; only one specimen seen, at 1500 m.

REFERENCES: Fang (1981a), Murray (1970c), Sargent (1913).

Rehder described this species in 1911 from a collection made by E. H. Wilson in western Hubei Province, China. It is extremely rare and only reported to have been at the U.S. National Arboretum. According to Chinese sources, this species may be conspecific with *Acer robustum,* also very rare. It is also related to *A. sieboldianum,* with which it shares the pubescence of the leaves but is easily distinguished by 7–11 lobed leaves.

SECTION: *Palmata* SERIES: *Palmata*

## ACER CIRCINATUM Pursh (1814)

SYNONYMS

*A. virgatum* Rafinesque (1836).
*A. macounii* Greene (1902).
*A. modocense* Greene (1902).

TYPE: PH, collected by Meriwether Lewis & William Clark.

COMMON NAME: Vine maple.

EPITHET: *Circinatus,* coiled inward from the tip.

ILLUSTRATIONS: Plate 6; de Jong (1976), Krüssmann (1976a), Vertrees (1987).

HABIT: Commonly a densely branched shrub or small tree, sometimes more than 10 m tall; branches glabrous, brown to pale green, often speckled with white; young shoots somewhat "sticky."

LEAVES: 7- to 9-lobed with regular lobes, almost circular in general outline, heart-shaped at the base, doubly serrated, pale green; juvenile leaves somewhat hairy, puberulous beneath, becoming glabrous.

FLOWERS: About 1 cm across, borne on small corymbose clusters, with purple-red sepals and white petals.

FRUITS: Samaras horizontal, 3–5 cm long, red when young, very conspicuous; nutlet flat and wrinkled, germinating easily.

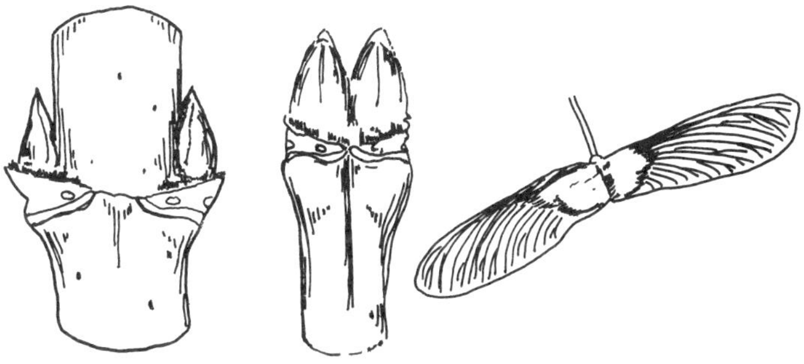

*Acer circinatum*

BARK AND BUDS: Young branches and stems often fresh green with white spots, sticky, later gray to fawn, or reddish on the sunlit side.

HARDINESS: Zone V.

AUTUMN COLOR: Very brilliant red-orange, depending on the locality of the tree. The thickets in Washington and Oregon, USA, are a sea of color in October.

DISTRIBUTION: British Columbia, Canada, through Washington and Oregon, penetrating to northern California, USA; on riverbanks in the Cascade Range, Oregon, to 2000 m, often forming impenetrable thickets.

CHROMOSOME NUMBER: $2n = 26$.

VARIETY: var. *fulvum* J. Henry (1915), flowers yellow; reduced to a forma by Murray (1981), f. *fulvum* (Henry) Murray.

CULTIVARS: Several (see Chapter 9).

REFERENCES: Bean (1970), Dippel (1892), van Gelderen (1969), de Jong (1976), Krüssmann (1976a), Murray (1970c, 1981a), Rehder (1986 facs.), Vertrees (1987).

Pursh described the vine maple in 1814, and it was introduced to Europe in 1826. Several names have been given to this species, but they are now placed in synonymy.

The brilliant autumn colors of this gorgeous inhabitant of the West Coast of North America splash the forest with flames of red, orange, and yellow. It is sometimes a small tree, but more commonly a shrub of irregular habit with many twisted branches. It forms dense thickets and layers freely. The leaves are suborbicular, 7- to 9-lobed, and light green. Their shape is the model for the distinctive rank of majors and lieutenant-colonels in the U.S. Army.

In cultivation this species can be confused with two Japanese species, *Acer japonicum* and *A. pseudosieboldianum.* Both Japanese species have leaves similar to *A. circinatum;* the latter, however, is always somewhat sticky and has a stiffer habit.

*Acer circinatum* is easily propagated from seed, and the seedlings are very uniform. If no seed is available, grafting on *A. palmatum* is a good alternative method of propagation. The few cultivars of *A. circinatum* can also be grafted on *A. palmatum* understock which, curiously enough, is a better understock than *A. circinatum* itself.

A natural variety with yellow flowers, variety *fulvum,* was found by J. Henry in 1915, but seems to have since disappeared. An expression with dissected leaves was found in the wild by Mr. Monroe about 1960. It is treated as a cultivar and propagated by grafting.

As it is common in the Pacific Northwest, this species is often offered in the trade there. It is less readily available in Europe and eastern North America, but it can be found in specialized nurseries. It and its cultivars are highly recommended as valuable garden plants that deserve to be planted more widely.

SECTION: *Palmata* SERIES: *Palmata*

## ACER DUPLICATOSERRATUM Hayata (1911)

SYNONYMS

*A. palmatum* subvar. *formosanum* Koidzumi (1911).

*A. palmatum* ssp. *pubescens* (Li) Murray (1978).

TYPE: Taiwan, Taitung Hsien, Mataranchi (N. Konishi) 1902; A, PE.

EPITHET: *Duplicatoserratus,* doubly serrate.

ILLUSTRATION: Liu (1962).

HABIT: A small tree, with branches and shoots pubescent.

LEAVES: 5- to 7-lobed, pubescent beneath.

FLOWERS: Not seen.

FRUITS: Not seen.

HARDINESS: Zone VI (?).

AUTUMN COLOR: Not seen.

DISTRIBUTION: Endemic to northern and central Taiwan, locally in deciduous forests at 1200–2000 m.

VARIETY: var. *chinense* C. S. Chang (1990), leaves as in the species, fully glabrous; Anhui Province, China.

REFERENCES: Chang (1990), Fang (1981a), Li (1963a), Liu (1962), Murray (1970a, 1977).

This Taiwanese member of the *Acer palmatum* complex was named *A. duplicatoserratum* by Hayata in 1911 and was thought to be endemic to Taiwan. Koidzumi regarded it as a variety of *A. palmatum,* and Li named it *A. palmatum* var. *pubescens* in 1952. Murray changed its status to a subspecies in 1978, but Fang (1981a) agreed with Hayata and treated this taxon as a distinct species. Chang (1990) investigated the Taiwanese and Chinese complex of *A. palmatum* thoroughly and concluded that this taxon was a distinct species.

After having studied Chang's publication, the authors of the present volume agree with this opinion. When we previously considered this taxon to be a subspecies of *Acer palmatum,* we thought it strange that no trace of pubescence could be seen in any of the very numerous cultivars of *A. palmatum,* except on freshly developed or juvenile leaves. Indeed, it is the pubescence that distinguishes *A. duplicatoserratum* from its allies in the *A. palmatum* complex. At one time we believed that pubescence was an aberrant characteristic and that it might be possible to include this species in *Acer sieboldianum.* However, the leaves with 7–9 lobes serve to separate the taxon from its former status as a subspecies of *A. palmatum,* and the flavonoid complement of *A. duplicatoserratum* is distinct in comparison to Japanese and Korean *A. palmatum* subspecies, due to the absence of flavones and glycoflavones. Since this taxon is distinct morphologically, chemically, and geographically, it is treated in this volume as a distinct species, in accordance with the opinions of Fang and Chang (see Chang 1990, 555).

*Acer duplicatoserratum*

SECTION: *Palmata* SERIES: *Palmata*

ACER JAPONICUM Thunberg ex Murray (1784)

SYNONYMS

*A. circumlobatum* Maximowicz (1867).
*A. japonicum* var. *macrophyllum* hort. ex Nicholson (1881).
*A. palmatum* var. *macrophyllum* hort. ex Nicholson (1881).
*A. circumlobatum* var. *insulare* Pax (1886).
*A. insulare* Pax (1892), non Makino.
*A. kobakoense* Nakai (1931).
*A. japonicum* var. *kobakoense* (Nakai) Hara (1936).
*A. japonicum* var. *insulare* (Pax) Ohwi (1953).

TYPE: UPS, collected by *C. P. Thunberg.*

COMMON NAMES: Ha uchiwa kaede, Hobako ha uchiwa, Meigetsu kaede, Shinano uchiwa.

EPITHET: *Japonicus,* from Japan.

ILLUSTRATIONS: Plate 7; Fang (1981a), Koidzumi (1911), Krüssmann (1976a), Kurata (1964–1976), Satake et al. (1989), Vertrees (1987).

HABIT: A tree in its native habitat, and a large treelike shrub in cultivation, up to 8–10 m tall; branches reddish to gray; shoots glabrous and not sticky.

LEAVES: Suborbicular, 8–15 cm across, 7-, 9-, or even 11-lobed; sinuses often shallow; basal lobes connivent; margins serrate; lobes incised to less than half the diameter of the leaf; petioles 3–5 cm long, often slightly pubescent.

FLOWERS: Purplish red in rather long drooping corymbs, very conspicuous, appearing before the leaves in April.

FRUITS: Samaras erect to divergent, often pubescent, 3 cm long, always hanging under the leaves.

BARK AND BUDS: Bark gray and smooth, not fissured; bud scales few.

HARDINESS: Zone V.

AUTUMN COLOR: Orange-scarlet, speckled with yellow, often very conspicuous.

DISTRIBUTION: Mountain forests in northern Japan—Hokkaido and almost the entire island of Honshu—at 900–1800 m.

CHROMOSOME NUMBER: $2n = 26$.

VARIETIES

var. *insulare* (Pax) Ohwi (1953), samara wings spreading horizontally, but otherwise similar to the typical variety; growing on Honshu; Japanese names are "Shinano ha uchiwa" or "O meigetsu;" Ohwi reported this natural variety which is no longer considered distinct, but is treated as a synonym of the species; not in cultivation; plants labeled "Meigetsu" or "Itaya" in some nurseries are indistinguishable from the species, but may be the same as this variety.

var. *kobakoense* (Nakai) Hara (1936), leaves with simple lobes and more closely together than the typical variety, otherwise very similar; growing on Hokkaido; Japanese name is "Kobako ha uchiwa"; Ohwi reported this natural variety which is no longer considered distinct, but is treated as a synonym of the species; not in cultivation.

var. *stenolobum* Hara (1936), samaras densely hairy.

var. *villosum* Koidzumi (1911), leaves villous, tomentose beneath.

CULTIVARS: Many (see Chapter 9).

REFERENCES: Bean (1970), Dippel (1892), Fang (1981a), van Gelderen (1969), Krüssmann (1976a), Kurata (1964–1976)7, Murray (1970c), Ogata (1965), Pax (1902), Rehder (1986 facs.), Veitch (1904), Vertrees (1987).

Murray described this species in 1784, based on Thunberg's work, then unpublished. Since then, many synonyms have appeared in the literature. A common one is *Acer circumlobatum,* which equates to *A. japonicum* as figured by Koidzumi (1911).

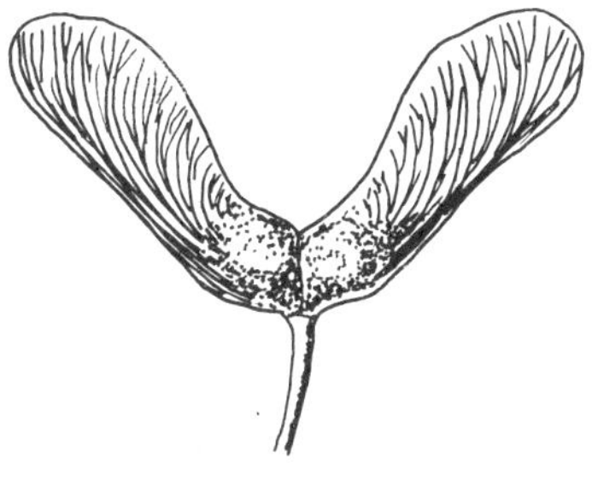

*Acer japonicum*

This species is not easily confused with other maples, save possibly for *Acer pseudosieboldianum*; however, *A. japonicum* grows quite unlike that species, much looser and very open. When *A. japonicum* is in flower, it is quite distinctive, having bright red flower trusses.

*Acer japonicum* is found extensively in cultivation, although, strangely, the true species is not readily available. It has many cultivars in cultivation, although not nearly as many as *A. palmatum*. Some authors recognize two to three natural varieties, but these apparently are not in cultivation. Some varieties may be considered synonyms of the species, or perhaps formae (i.e., f. *villosum* [Koidzumi] Hara [1954]).

Many plants labeled 'Vitifolium' in Europe are actually the species itself. The cultivars are valuable garden plants, and their autumn color can be very brilliant, depending on the origin of the specimen.

Propagation by seed is rather easy, although occasionally the seeds do not germinate freely. Grafting on *Acer palmatum* is a possible alternative.

SECTION: *Palmata* SERIES: *Palmata*

ACER PALMATUM ssp. AMOENUM (Carrière) Hara (1954)

BASIONYM: *A. amoenum* Carrière (1867).

SYNONYMS

- *A. palmatum* var. *coreanum* Nakai (1914).
- *A. palmatum* var. *heptalobum* Rehder (1938).
- *A. palmatum* var. *amoenum* (Carrière) Ohwi (1953).

EPITHET: *Amoenus,* lovely.

ILLUSTRATIONS: Plate 8; Kurata (1964–1976), Lee (1979), Satake et al. (1989).

HABIT: A tree, occasionally a treelike shrub, to 10 m tall or more, usually taller than wide but not always; branches glabrous, reddish green when young, gray when mature, with white dots or lenticels, not always present.

LEAVES: Usually 7-lobed, the basal lobes sometimes very small, 6–15 cm across, lobes about half the diameter of the leaf blades; margins serrate; petioles 3–5 cm long.

INFLORESCENCES: Corymbose, terminal.

FLOWERS: Small, blooming in May; sepals red; petals cream.

FRUITS: Samaras 3–5 cm long, wings often distinctively colored, nutlets rounded.

BARK AND BUDS: Bark smooth, only very occasionally fissured, as in 'Arakawa' or 'Nishiki gawa'; shoot buds paired.

HARDINESS: Zone V.

AUTUMN COLOR: Yellow to orange, often very brilliant.

DISTRIBUTION: Mountainous regions of Japan, Korea, and China, in the same regions as subspecies *palmatum*.

CHROMOSOME NUMBER: $2n = 26$.

CULTIVARS: Many (see Chapter 9).

REFERENCES: Koidzumi (1911), Krüssmann (1976a), Murray (1970c), Ogata (1965), Vertrees (1987).

This subspecies is rarely found in cultivation under its own name, and if found, is of clonal origin. The numerous cultivars are much better known.

SECTION: *Palmata* SERIES: *Palmata*

ACER PALMATUM ssp. MATSUMURAE Koidzumi (1911)

SYNONYMS

- *A. palmatum* subvar. *intermedium* Schwerin (1893).
- *A. palmatum* var. *palmatilobum* Koidzumi (1911).
- *A. palmatum* var. *palmatipartitum* Koidzumi (1911).
- *A. palmatum* var. *spontaneum* Koidzumi (1911).
- *A. matsumurae* (Koidzumi) Koidzumi (1925).

EPITHET: *Matsumurae,* after Jinzo Matsumura, a Japanese professor of botany, 1856–1928.

ILLUSTRATIONS: Plate 9; Kurata (1964–1976), Satake et al. (1989), Vertrees (1987).

HABIT: A large shrubby tree to 10 m tall and often as wide or even wider; branches gray-brown, smooth; young shoots often red to reddish green.

LEAVES: 7- to 9-lobed, very deeply incised almost to the base, 5–10 cm across, distinctively colored; margins doubly serrate; lobes often have long acuminate apices.

INFLORESCENCES: Corymbose, terminal.

FLOWERS: Small, blooming in May; sepals reddish; petals cream.

FRUITS: Samaras 3–5 cm long, divergent; nutlets rounded.

BARK AND BUDS: Bark smooth; buds at twig ends always in pairs.

HARDINESS: Zone V.

AUTUMN COLOR: Red, orange to yellow, very brilliant.

DISTRIBUTION: Mountainous regions of Japan, together with subspecies *palmatum*.

CHROMOSOME NUMBER: $2n = 26$.

CULTIVARS: Many (see Chapter 9).

REFERENCES: Van Gelderen (1983), Koidzumi (1911), Kurata (1964–1976), Murray (1970c), Vertrees (1987).

This subspecies is rare in cultivation and mostly of clonal origin in collections.

SECTION: *Palmata* SERIES: *Palmata*

ACER PALMATUM Thunberg ex Murray (1784) ssp. PALMATUM

SYNONYMS

*A. polymorphum* var. *palmatum* (Thunberg) Koch (1853).
*A. formosum* Carrière (1867).
*A. jucundum* Carrière (1867).
*A. japonicum* var. *polymorphum* (Siebold & Zuccarini) Veitch (1867).
*A. palmatum* var. *thunbergii* Pax (1886).
*A. polymorphum* var. *thunbergii* (Pax) Dieck (1886).
*A. palmatum* var. *spectabile* Koidzumi (1911).
*A. palmatum* var. *amabile* Koidzumi (1911).
*A. polymorphum* sensu Siebold & Zuccarini (1845), non Spach (1934).

TYPE: Syntype UPS, collected by *C. P. Thunberg*, Japanese garden origin.

COMMON NAMES: Japanese maple, Érable du Japon, Fächerahorn, Iroha momiji, Iwato beni, Kaede noki, Momiji, Tako kaede.

EPITHET: *Palmatus*, in the form of a hand.

ILLUSTRATIONS: Plate 10; Fang (1981a), Koidzumi (1911), Krüssmann (1976a), Kurata (1964–1976), Satake et al. (1989), Vertrees (1987).

HABIT: A tree or treelike shrub to 10 m tall and occasionally twice as wide; branches glabrous, reddish when young, gray-brown after some years, occasionally with irregular stripes; extremely variable.

LEAVES: 5- to 7-lobed (the typical expression is always 5-lobed), palmate, apices tapered, 5–10 cm long and wide; lobes lanceolate, doubly serrate; upper surfaces fresh green, lower surfaces paler, often slightly pubescent when young; petioles green, 2–5 cm long. Extremely variable; many cultivars have different colors and variegations.

INFLORESCENCES: Small, corymbose, terminal.

FLOWERS: Small, appearing in May/June; sepals red-purple; petals creamy white.

FRUITS: Samaras 1 cm long, often underdeveloped, divergent, ripening in September; fruits among the smallest in the genus. Cultivars often bear larger seeds with deeply colored samaras.

BARK AND BUDS: Usually green to gray-brown, though many cultivars have different colored bark; buds always in pairs.

HARDINESS: Zone V.

AUTUMN COLOR: Yellow-orange, often very brilliant.

DISTRIBUTION: Widespread in Japan, Korea, Taiwan, eastern China. In Japan in the mountains of Azuma Fukushima, also on Shikoku and Kiyushu to the south; on Honshu Island at 100–1100 m.

CHROMOSOME NUMBER: $2n = 26$.

SUBSPECIES

ssp. *amoenum* (Carrière) Hara (1954), leaves 5- to 7-lobed, fruits large.
ssp. *matsumurae* Koidzumi (1911), leaves deeply divided almost to the base, margins serrate.
ssp. *palmatum*, the typical subspecies.

CULTIVARS: Over 250 named cultivars (see Chapter 9).

REFERENCES: Bean (1976), Bijhouwer (1926), Dippel (1892), Fang (1981a), van Gelderen (1969, 1979, 1983), Koch (1869), Koidzumi (1911), Krüssmann (1976a), Kurata (1964–1976), Murray (1970c), Ogata (1965), Pax (1885, 1902), Rehder (1986 facs.), Thunberg (1784), Vertrees (1987).

*Acer palmatum* is certainly the most important ornamental maple in cultivation. It and its numerous cultivars can be admired in almost every garden and park. Enormous trees can be found in Japan as well as in several European and North American gardens. This species has been in cultivation for centuries in Japan, China, and Korea. The Japanese gardeners selected a large number of different expressions (mostly now called cultivars), some of great beauty and very different from the wild species.

Murray published three "species" of this taxon, based on Thunberg's work, then unpublished: *Acer palmatum*, *A. septemlobum*, and *A. dissectum*. The green-leaved types were introduced to Great Britain about 1830. Several years later, Philip von Siebold, a military physician in the service of the government of The Netherlands–Indies, visited Japan and sent many cultivars back to his nursery in Leiden, The Netherlands. Many descriptions were provided by Professor Zuccarini of Munich, Germany, and in 1845 Siebold and Zuccarini published their results. Zuccarini recognized six "varieties" within his *A. polymorphum*—*A. decompositum*, *A. dissectum*, *A. linearilobum*, *A. palmatum*, *A. septemlobum*, and *A. sessilifolium*—confused by the many differences among the leaves of *A. polymorphum*, which sometimes occurred on the same or very similar plants. After the affinities of these different plants became known, Thunberg's earlier (1783) name of *A. palmatum* was recognized as valid.

Of the Japanese introductions in Siebold's nursery, Witte (1860), curator of the Botanic Garden of Leiden, The Netherlands, wrote: "We admired the very many different species or varieties at Mr. von Siebold's nursery. It is not yet known whether they are hardy. All of them are very beautiful." Siebold (1864) offered them for sale in the journal *Flore des Serres* described by Van Houtte (1857, 1861, 1865) under such forms as 'Atropurpureum', 'Palmatifidum', 'Roseo-marginatum' and 'Versicolor'. All these original selections are still in cultivation, which proves the good taste of buyers like van Houtte and Verschaffelt in Ghent, Belgium, as well as King Wilhelm of Württemberg (now part of Germany).

The confusion of the species names was considerable. Famous dendrologists and taxonomists, such as Koch and Regel, maintained *Acer polymorphum* as a valid species name and included *A. sessilifolium* Siebold & Zuccarini (1845), and often several forms of *A. japonicum,* under *A. polymorphum.* André (1870a) used the name *A. palmatum* for the whole group for the first time in 1870.

Siebold's first maples came to England about 1881, while other maples came directly from Japan to England. Nicholson described 13 distinct cultivated varieties or cultivars in 1881 in *Gardener's Chronicle.* Pax (1885) finally brought order out of chaos by recognizing the name *Acer palmatum* Thunberg ex Murray as the correct one based on priority and nomenclatural typification, thus bringing the double use of *A. polymorphum* and *A. palmatum* to an end. Pax's names were used in the second edition of *Die natürlichen Pflanzenfamilien III* (Engler and Prantl 1907) and became the basis for the present usage of the name *A. palmatum.*

About 1900, Japanese botanists began using their Japanese cultivar names in place of Latinized names. This caused a great deal of confusion in the Western world, as many of these cultivars were thought to be quite new when in fact they were already in cultivation under other names. Today the use of the Japanese cultivar names (not common names) is an accepted procedure, and they are usually more precise and provide better "separations" than the Latin names. It will always be difficult, however, for Western writers to avoid misspelling these Japanese names. For example, Oh isami, O-isami, and Oosami refer to the same cultivar, and Deshiojo, Deshojo, and Desojo are three spellings for the same cultivar. Westerners also confound the chaos by using transliterated Japanese common or colloquial names as cultivar names. A Japanese common name is different from a Japanese cultivar name.

Listed below are the former botanical names of *Acer palmatum* taxa and their currently correct names:

var. *amabile* Koidzumi (1911) = included in ssp. *palmatum*
var. *amoenum* (Carrière) Ohwi = ssp. *amoenum* (Carrière) Hara (1954)
var. *dissectum* (Thunberg) Miquel = 'Dissectum'
f. *eudissectum* Schwerin (1896) = 'Dissectum'
subvar. *eupalmatum* Schwerin (1893) = ssp. *palmatum*
subvar. *formosanum* Koidzumi (1911) = *A. duplicatoserratum*
*A. formosum* Carrière (1867) = ssp. *palmatum*
f. *formosum* (Carrière) Koch (1867) = ssp. *palmatum*
ssp. *genuinum* Koidzumi (1911) = ssp. *palmatum*
f. *genuinum* Miquel (1870) = ssp. *palmatum*
var. *heptalobum* Rehder (1938) = included in ssp. *amoenum*
subvar. *heterolobum* Koidzumi (1911) = ssp. *matsumurae*
var. *hortense* Koidzumi (1911) = ssp. *matsumurae*
f. *illustre* Koch (1867) = included in ssp. *amoenum*
subvar. *intermedium* Schwerin (1893) = included in ssp. *matsumurae*
f. *latialatum* (Nakai) Hara (1954) = included in ssp. *palmatum*
var. *linearilobum* Miquel (1867) = 'Linearilobum'
var. *matsumurae* Koidzumi (1911) = ssp. *matsumurae*
var. *multifidum* Koch (1864) = Dissectum group
f. *normale* Schwerin (1893) = ssp. *palmatum*
*A. ornatum* = 'Ornatum'
subvar. *palmatilobum* Koidzumi (1911) = included in ssp. *matsumurae*
var. *palmatipartitum* Koidzumi (1911) = ssp. *matsumurae*
var. *palmatisectum* Koidzumi (1911) = 'Ornatum'
var. *palmatum* = ssp. *palmatum*
var. *pubescens* Li (1953) = *A. duplicatoserratum*
var. *quinquelobum* Koch (1864) = ssp. *palmatum*
ssp. *septemlobum* sensu Koidzumi (1911) = ssp. *amoenum*
var. *septemlobum* sensu Koch (1864) = included in *Kalopanax*
var. *spectabile* Koidzumi (1911) = ssp. *palmatum*
var. *spontaneum* Koidzumi (1911) = ssp. *matsumurae*
var. *thunbergii* Pax = ssp. *palmatum*

*Acer palmatum* is easily recognized, although it is often confused with *A. japonicum* in the trade. Few other species have similar correlated characteristics, and the few species that could be confused are much rarer (e.g., *A. oliverianum* and *A. shirasawanum*). Some authors, such as Ogata, split the species into three to four separate species, but the authors of the present volume maintain *A. palmatum* as one species with the following recognized subspecies: *amoenum, matsumurae,* and *palmatum.*

Nakai ex Hyams (1967) considered the Korean plants as a variety of the species, but today *Acer palmatum* is considered indigenous to Korea, China, and Japan, and Korean and Japanese plants are indistinguishable. An expression available in the trade is called 'Koreanum', but it is uncertain whether this treelike bush with large, 7-lobed leaves and good autumn color is a true Korean plant. In this volume it is treated as a cultivar.

*Acer palmatum* is easily grown from seed, which breeds true when harvested from typical and isolated trees. The many cultivars must be propagated by grafting on seedling understock, which may be done both summer and winter under good greenhouse conditions. Several cultivars can be propagated by cuttings, although regrowth in the following spring can be very difficult. It is also possible to sow seeds of cultivars; they do not breed true, but they germinate freely and can produce very interesting forms for selection purposes. Inconspicuous seedlings can be used as understock. Seed harvested from Dissectum cultivars may produce seedlings with finely dissected leaves.

SECTION: *Palmata* SERIES: *Palmata*

## ACER PAUCIFLORUM Fang (1932)

TYPE: *R. C. Ching 1790,* Chen-chion, Zhejiang Province, China; K.

EPITHET: *Pauciflorus,* few-flowered.

ILLUSTRATION: Fang (1981a, as *A. changhwaense*).

HABIT: A shrub not exceeding 3–4 m tall; branches often glaucous.

LEAVES: Orbicular, 5-lobed, up to 6 cm across, lobes oblong, doubly serrate; petioles short, 1 cm long, pilose, purplish.

INFLORESCENCES: Corymbose, villose, few-flowered.

FRUITS: Samaras 2 cm long, erect.

HARDINESS: Zones VI–VII.

DISTRIBUTION: Zhejiang Province, China, at 200–300 m.

VARIETY: var. *changhwaense* Fang & Fang f. (1966), leaves yellow, pubescent; type PE.

REFERENCES: Fang (1981a), Murray (1970c).

Little is known about this species, which was described by Fang in 1932. Apparently, it is not in cultivation in the Western world. It is mentioned in a few dendrological works, but further information is not available.

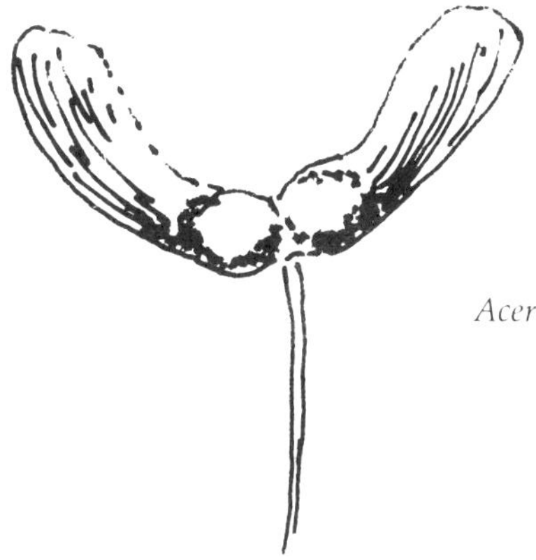

*Acer pauciflorum*

SECTION: *Palmata* SERIES: *Palmata*

## ACER PSEUDOSIEBOLDIANUM (Pax) Komarov (1904) ssp. PSEUDOSIEBOLDIANUM

BASIONYM: *A. circumlobatum* var. *pseudosieboldianum* Pax (1886).

SYNONYMS

*A. parvifolium* Buditschev (1864).
*A. sieboldianum* var. *mandshuricum* Maximowicz (1886).
*A. japonicum* var. *nudicarpum* Nakai (1909).
*A. ishidoyanum* Nakai (1915).
*A. palmatum* var. *pilosum* Nakai (1919).
*A. microsieboldianum* Nakai (1931).

TYPE: Syntypes *C. J. Maximowicz,* Port Bruce (Vladivostok), Russia; LE, W.

COMMON NAMES: Keijo hautiwa, Kuwagata hautiwa.

EPITHET: *Pseudosieboldianum,* combination of *pseudo,* meaning "false," and *sieboldianum,* thus implying a plant very similar in appearance to *A. sieboldianum.*

ILLUSTRATIONS: Plate 11; Fang (1981a), Krüssmann (1976a), Vertrees (1987).

HABIT: A small tree or shrub to 8 m tall and even wider; openly branched; branches gray, striped blackish, not unlike those of *A. japonicum;* young shoots slightly sticky, long, slender, with a whitish bloom.

LEAVES: 9- to 11-lobed, 10–14 cm across; bases cordate, lobes lanceolate-palmate, doubly serrate, undersides covered with silky white hairs when young, dark green above, shed very late in autumn and often staying on the tree during mild winters; petioles 3–5 cm long.

INFLORESCENCES: Corymbose, terminal.

FLOWERS: Appearing before the leaves; sepals reddish purple; petals cream.

FRUITS: Samaras about 3 cm long, divergent, brown to purplish. Some specimens vary in the shape of the samaras and the shape of the leaf bases, giving rise to varietal names such as variety *ambiguum* Nakai, and variety *macrocarpum* Nakai.

HARDINESS: Zone IV.

AUTUMN COLOR: Yellow, orange, or red and in combinations, often brilliant.

DISTRIBUTION: Manchuria, Ussuri River, China; Korea, in mixed forests on well-drained and stony soil.

CHROMOSOME NUMBER: $2n = 26$.

SUBSPECIES

ssp. *pseudosieboldianum,* the typical subspecies.
ssp. *takesimense* (Nakai) de Jong, comb. & stat. nov.

VARIETIES

var. *ambiguum* Nakai (1915), leaves truncate to cordate.
var. *koreanum* Nakai (1909), samara wings parallel.

*Acer pseudosieboldianum*
ssp. *pseudosieboldianum*

var. *lanuginosum* Nakai (1931), leaves and samaras woolly.
var. *macrocarpum* Nakai (1915), samaras horizontal.

REFERENCES: Bean (1970), Fang (1981a), van Gelderen (1969), Krüssmann (1976a), Murray (1970c), Pojárkova (1933), Rehder (1986 facs.), Vertrees (1987).

*Acer pseudosieboldianum* is a rather rare maple. Its orbicular leaves are similar to those of *A. japonicum* and *A. sieboldianum,* the only two species with which *A. pseudosieboldianum* may be confused. However, the habit of *A. japonicum* is much stiffer and sturdier and its shoots are much shorter. *Acer sieboldianum* bears smaller leaves, 7- to 9-lobed and softly pubescent, especially when young, and its habit of is also more upright and firm.

*Acer pseudosieboldianum* has not been clearly defined. Several of its synonyms attest to variation, such as *A. circumlobatum* var. *pseudosieboldianum, A. circumlobatum* var. *mandshuricum* and others. Several varieties have been described by Nakai. Pax reduced *A. pseudosieboldianum* to a variety of *A. circumlobatum,* a name now sunk in synonymy. Komarov gave *A. pseudosieboldianum* specific rank in 1904. Nakai (1918) also described *A. takesimense* and stated that it is close to *A. pseudosieboldianum.* Material under the name *A. takesimense* looks rather different from *A. pseudosieboldianum* and appears closer to *A. palmatum.* There is not sufficient authentic material to clarify this matter definitively, but in the present volume *A. takesimense* is tentatively placed here as a subspecies.

*Acer pseudosieboldianum* can be propagated by seed, but it is only occasionally available. Grafting on potted understock of *A. palmatum* is a good means of propagating typical plants.

The garden merit of this species must not be overestimated as it often has a floppy and loose habit. Its leaves turn brown weeks before they are shed in very late in autumn, making the tree unattractive. Many varieties and cultivars of *Acer japonicum* and *A.palmatum* make much better garden plants.

SECTION: *Palmata* SERIES: *Palmata*
ACER PSEUDOSIEBOLDIANUM ssp. TAKESIMENSE (Nakai) de Jong, comb. & stat. nov.
BASIONYM: *A. takesimense* Nakai (1918), *Notulae ad Plantas Japonicae et Koreae XVII, Bot. Mag. Tokyo* 32: 107. 1918.
TYPE: *T. Nakai 4418,* in rupibus Dodong, Ullung-do, South Korea; TI.
COMMON NAMES: Seom Tanpung Namu (meaning "Island-growing maple tree").
EPITHET: *Takesimensis,* from Takeshima (Ullung-do), South Korea.
ILLUSTRATIONS: Plate 12; Lee (1979).
HABIT: A shrubby tree; heavily branched, more so than typical *A. pseudosieboldianum;* young branches and twigs green with reddish tips.
LEAVES: Smaller than those of the species and rather similar to those of *A. palmatum,* 11-lobed, 8–12 cm across, slightly pubescent when young; margins serrate, not hairy; petioles about 6 cm long, narrowing into the leaf bases, hairy when young, glabrous when mature.
FRUITS: Small, samaras parallel, not hairy.
HARDINESS: Zones V–VI (?).
AUTUMN COLOR: Yellow.
DISTRIBUTION: Ullung-do, a small Korean island in the East China Sea.
REFERENCES: Lee (1979), Murray (1970c), Nakai (1918).

This very rare subspecies was recently introduced to a few nurseries in Europe, so there is very little evidence yet as to how it behaves in cultivation. The general appearance is like a smaller version of *Acer pseudosieboldianum* ssp. *pseudosieboldianum.*

*Acer pseudosieboldianum* ssp. *takesimense*

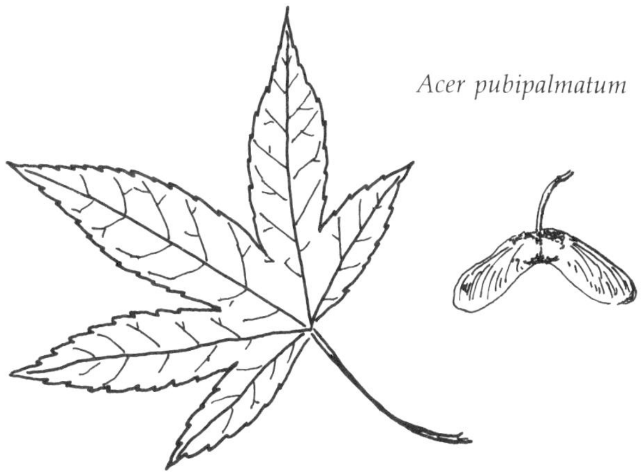

*Acer pubipalmatum*

SECTION: *Palmata* SERIES: *Palmata*
ACER PUBIPALMATUM Fang (1932)
TYPES: Syntypes *S. Chen 493, K. R. Tsoong 392,* eastern Zhejiang Province, China; PE; HHBG.
EPITHET: *Pubipalmatus,* like a hairy hand.
ILLUSTRATION: Fang (1981a).
HABIT: A tree 10–12 m tall; branches tomentose to glabrescent.
LEAVES: Deeply 5- to 7-lobed, 6–9 cm across; margins doubly serrate, truncate to subcordate; veins canescent beneath; petioles 2.5–5 cm long.
INFLORESCENCES: Corymbose, villose.
FLOWERS: Sepals purple; petals cream.
FRUITS: Samaras pubescent, divergent, about 2.5 cm long.
DISTRIBUTION: Zhejiang Province, China, at 700–1000 m.
VARIETY: var. *pulcherrimum* Fang & Chiu (1979), not in cultivation in Europe or North America.
REFERENCES: Chang (1990), Fang (1981a), Krüssmann (1976a), Murray (1970c).

This species is not known to be cultivated in the West, and is subsequently poorly known. It is cultivated in the Hangzhou Botanic Garden in Hangzhou, China. Wild-collected seeds received in 1982 did not germinate.

According to Chang (1990), this species is closely related to *Acer duplicatoserratum* var. *chinense,* with similar flavonoids and morphology. *Acer pubipalmatum* has smaller fruits, very deeply lobed leaves, and densely pubescent ovaries.

SECTION: *Palmata* SERIES: *Palmata*
ACER ROBUSTUM Pax (1902)
SYNONYMS
*A. anhweiense* Fang & Fang f. (1966).
*A. campbellii* ssp. *robustum* (Pax) Murray (1977).
TYPE: *Giraldi 2116,* Shaanxi Province, China; FI; isotypes BM, A.

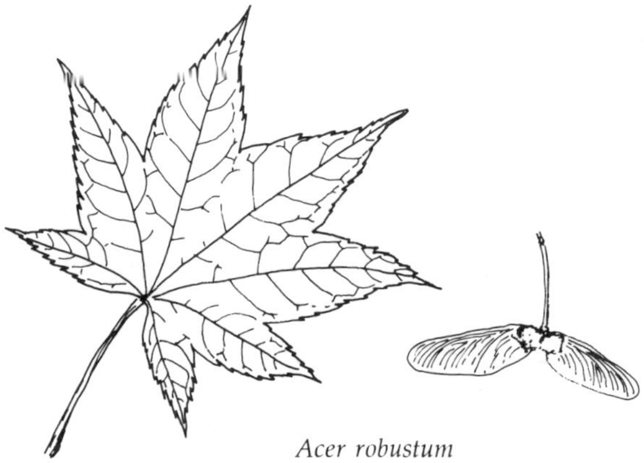

*Acer robustum*

EPITHET: *Robustus,* robust.
ILLUSTRATION: Fang (1981a).
HABIT: A tree or treelike shrub to 10 m tall; branches brown to purplish.
LEAVES: 7- to 9-lobed, 7–10 cm across, lobes ovate and acuminate, finely serrate, outer lobes small, shining green on both sides with silky hairs on the undersides; bases cordate.
INFLORESCENCES: Corymbose, terminal.
FLOWERS: Dark red.
FRUITS: Samaras up to 6 cm long, much larger than those of *A. palmatum.*
HARDINESS: Zone V.
AUTUMN COLOR: Red.
DISTRIBUTION: Hubei, Anhui, and Yunnan provinces, China, at 1000–2000 m.
VARIETIES
var. *honanense* Fang (1979).
var. *minus* Fang (1979).
REFERENCES: Fang (1981a), Krüssmann (1976a), Murray (1970c, 1977), Rehder (1986 facs.), Sargent (1913), Schneider (1912).

This is an extremely rare plant, and there are only a few reports of it in cultivation. An old plant in Tharandt, Germany, has been reported under this name, but it is uncertain whether it is the true species.

The almost-round leaves of this species are similar to those of *Acer campbellii,* and while the two species are related, it is difficult to determine how this species differs from its relatives since living material is not available. Plants grown from seed turned out to be some form of *A. japonicum.*

According to Murray this species is also related to *Acer pubipalmatum,* a species not in cultivation, but differs from it by both its larger leaves and seeds. *Acer robustum* differs from *A. palmatum* in its larger fruits and larger sepals and tepals. Young fruits are reported to be purple.

Fang (1981a) mentions variety *honanense* and variety *minus,* although it is difficult to determine whether these are merely minor variants unworthy of taxonomic recognition.

SECTION: *Palmata* SERIES: *Palmata*

## ACER SHIRASAWANUM Koidzumi (1911) var. SHIRASAWANUM

SYNONYM: *A. japonicum* f. *microphyllum* Siesmayer (1889).
TYPE: Syntypes *G. Koidzumi,* Nikko Hakone-yama, Honshu, Japan; KYO, L, TI.
COMMON NAMES: O itaya meigetsu, Oo-hauchiwa kaede.
EPITHET: *Shirasawanus,* after Japanese botanist Homi Shirasawa (1868–1947).
ILLUSTRATIONS: Plate 13; Koidzumi (1911), Krüssmann (1976a), Kurata (1964–1976), Ogata (1965), Satake et al. (1989), Vertrees (1987).
HABIT: A small tree to 15 m tall in its native habitat and half that in cultivation, often wider than high; branches glabrous, often tipped with small whitish dots; bud scales few; trunk gray to grayish brown.
LEAVES: 9- to 11-lobed, 9–12 cm across, orbicular, canescent to glabrous, lobes acuminate and sharply toothed or doubly so, bases cordate, with tufts of hair in the axils; margins often tinted reddish; petioles about 5 cm long.
INFLORESCENCES: Corymbose, upright, terminal.
FLOWERS: Upright, appearing with the leaves in May; sepals purple, petals whitish.
FRUITS: Samaras about 2–3 cm long, in small clusters; nutlets round, in erect, small trusses standing above the leaves, 6–10 fruits per truss.
HARDINESS: Zone V.
AUTUMN COLOR: Clear yellow.
DISTRIBUTION: Japan, southern Honshu, Shikoku Kantoo district, at 1200–1800 m.
VARIETIES
var. *shirasawanum,* the typical variety.
var. *tenuifolium* Koidzumi (1911), leaves pubescent and somewhat more deeply incised than those of the species.
CULTIVARS: Several (see Chapter 9).
REFERENCES: Delendick (1983), Koidzumi (1911), Krüssmann (1976a), Kurata (1964–1976), Murray (1970c), Ogata (1965), Rehder (1986 facs.), Vertrees (1987).

*Acer shirasawanum* var. *shirasawanum*

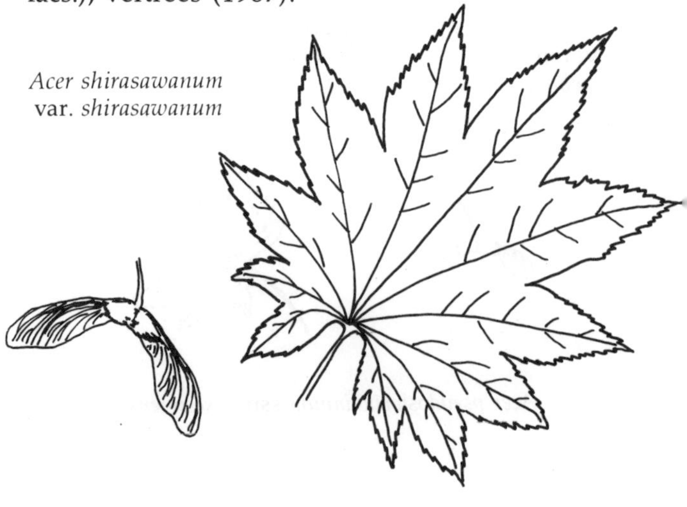

This very handsome species was described by Koidzumi in 1911 and is not as rare in cultivation as once believed. There are several old specimens in European gardens which previously were misidentified. *Acer shirasawanum* grows into a large shrubby, well-branched tree with very attractive leaves whose golden autumn color is quite charming. Flowers and fruit stand upright, a very conspicuous feature of this species.

*Acer shirasawanum* can be confused with *A. sieboldianum* and also with cultivars of *A. japonicum* or *A. palmatum.* It does not have the pubescent leaves of *A. sieboldianum,* which in turn lacks the reddish tinged leaf margins of *A. shirasawanum.* Both *A. japonicum* and *A. pseudosieboldianum* are much more open trees, with stouter branches. A typical feature of *A. shirasawanum* is the presence of tiny white dots (punctae) on branches and leaves, especially in early summer.

Investigation by Delendick (1983) clearly indicates that some well-known cultivars of *Acer japonicum* belong to *A. shirasawanum.* Cultivars 'Aureum' and 'Microphyllum' have the same erect flowers and fruits and also the same leaf shape, making them quite different from true *A. japonicum. A. shirasawanum* 'Palmatifolium' has long been in cultivation, and its name cannot be traced. Old trees of this selection are in Kalmthout, Belgium, and in Hergest Croft, Kington, Great Britain, where they exhibit the same autumn colors as the species.

*Acer shirasawanum* can be propagated by seed, but garden seed is often hybridized and should be avoided. Seedlings of 'Microphyllum' breed true, even if harvested from a garden. Grafting on *A. palmatum* is easy and a preferred method of propagation.

SECTION: *Palmata* SERIES: *Palmata*

## ACER SHIRASAWANUM var. TENUIFOLIUM Koidzumi (1911)

SYNONYM: *A. tenuifolium* (Koidzumi) Koidzumi (1916).

TYPES: Syntypes *G. Koidzumi,* Nikko, Fuji, Kiso-Ontakesan, Japan; KYO, TI.

COMMON NAME: Hino uchiwa kaede.

EPITHET: *Tenuifolius,* with narrow, fine leaves.

ILLUSTRATIONS: Kurata (1964–1976), Ogata (1965), Satake et al. (1989), Vertrees (1987).

HABIT: A small tree or shrub to 8–10 m tall; branches reddish to gray.

LEAVES: 7- to 9-lobed, 5–8 cm across, lobes rhombic-lanceolate and rather deeply cleft to the middle of the blades; margins doubly serrate, pubescent beneath, with silky hairs; bases cordate; petioles 3–5 cm long.

INFLORESCENCES: Corymbose, terminal.

FLOWERS: Pale yellow with purplish sepals, appearing in May.

*Acer shirasawanum* var. *tenuifolium*

FRUITS: Samaras 2.5 cm long, wings ascending; nutlets rounded.

BARK AND BUDS: Buds always in pairs at shoot ends; bud scales few.

HARDINESS: Zone V.

AUTUMN COLOR: Golden yellow.

DISTRIBUTION: Mountains of central and southern Japan, the southern part of Fukushima throughout Honshu and Shikoku.

REFERENCES: Koidzumi (1911), Kurata (1964–1976), Murray (1970c), Ogata (1965), Vertrees (1987).

It is questionable whether this taxon deserves varietal rank or species recognition. Koidzumi placed it as a variety under *Acer shirasawanum* in 1911, but raised it to specific rank in 1916.

A very rare plant, it is only known to the authors of the present volume from North American material supplied by J. D. Vertrees. The Botanic Garden of Rogow, Poland, was growing seedlings in 1986, and the Milde Arboretum in Bergen, Norway, has a plant likely to have been derived from the same source. In Trebah, a garden in Cornwall, UK, is a large tree.

This variety is a small, somewhat openly branched tree whose leaf margins are provided with distinctive silky hairs. It differs from *Acer shirasawanum* in the presence of these silky hairs. It is easily grafted on *A. palmatum* understock. Seed is rarely available and then only from garden origin. This beautiful garden plant, with its golden yellow autumn color, should be more readily available.

SECTION: *Palmata* SERIES: *Palmata*

ACER SIEBOLDIANUM Miquel (1865)

SYNONYMS

*A. japonicum* var. *sieboldianum* (Miquel) Franchet & Savatier (1878).

*A. polymorphum* var. *kaempferi* Späth (1879).

*A. palmatum* var. *kaempferi* Späth ex Schwerin (1893).

TYPE: *Ito Keiske*, Figo, Japan; L.

COMMON NAMES: Aiai gasa, Itaya meigetsu, Kibana uchiwa kaede, Ko hau uchiwa kaede (meaning "small-leaved form").

EPITHET: *Sieboldianus*, after German botanist and physician P. F. von Siebold (1796–1866).

ILLUSTRATIONS: Plate 14; Koidzumi (1911), Krüssmann (1976a), Kurata (1964–1976), Ogata (1965), Vertrees (1987).

HABIT: An erect-growing small tree to 10 m tall, not unlike some specimens of *A. japonicum;* branches and branchlets canescent or even tomentose, thinner and more closely set than in *A. japonicum;* young wood somewhat sticky.

LEAVES: 7- to 11-lobed, 6–9 cm across, orbicular, hairy at the axils, dark green, often with darker lobes, lobes doubly serrate, bases cordate to truncate; petioles 2.5–4 cm long, canescent.

INFLORESCENCES: Densely corymbose, terminal, slightly hairy.

FLOWERS: Pale yellow, rather small.

FRUITS: Small, samaras 1.5–2 cm long, ascending and glabrescent.

BARK AND BUDS: Bark gray and smooth.

HARDINESS: Zones III–IV.

AUTUMN COLOR: Coppery red to dark glistening red.

DISTRIBUTION: Japan, in mountain forests on Shikoku, Kiyushu, and Honshu. Also in the northern parts of Japan from sea level to 900 m, on moist and open sites. Very abundant in the southern part of Kiyushu.

CHROMOSOME NUMBER: $2n = 26$.

VARIETIES

var. *microphyllum* Maximowicz (1886), leaves 3–4 cm across; also regarded as a form, f. *microphyllum* (Maximowicz) Hara (1954).

var. *tsushimense* Koidzumi (1911), leaves 7-lobed, sinuses deep.

var. *yezoense* Miyabe & Tatewaki (1938), leaves 10–14 cm across.

CULTIVARS: Several (see Chapter 9).

REFERENCES: Bean (1970), Dippel (1892), van Gelderen (1969), Koidzumi (1911), Krüssmann (1976a), Kurata (1964–1976), Murray (1970c), Ogata (1965), Pax (1902), Rehder (1986 facs.), Veitch (1904), Vertrees (1987).

*Acer sieboldianum* was described by Miquel in 1865. Found in many North American and European gardens, this species can also be grown in Sweden and Norway, where cultivars of *A. palmatum* fail. It is very hardy and can be grown in all kinds of climates. It forms forests in its Japanese habitat and prefers moist and open situations.

A very handsome garden plant, it is relatively common. Its chief features are the attractive erect habit and its beautiful dark green leaves which have darker, sometimes reddish borders. Juvenile leaves have tufts of hairs in the axils. These 7- to 11-lobed leaves are conspicuously doubly serrate and their autumn color is dark to glistening red or even gold-copper.

*Acer sieboldianum* can be confused with some of its relatives, such as small-leaved forms of *A. japonicum* and some cultivars of *A. palmatum,* but its erect habit and pubescent leaf undersurfaces and petioles distinguish it from *A. palmatum.* The pubescence often disappears during the summer, but the doubly serrate leaf margins also distinguish *A. sieboldianum* from *A. palmatum* ssp. *palmatum.*

This plant can be propagated from seed, but garden seed is not always true. It is better to purchase grafted specimens derived from a genuine plant whose understock is *A. palmatum.* Grafting is easily done in February or July in a well-equipped greenhouse.

Some varieties have been recognized by Japanese botanists, although they are not in cultivation. However, there are several garden forms with Japanese names. The very small-leaved 'Sode no uchi' is almost a natural bonsai, and 'Kinugasa yama' is a splendid plant by virtue of its pubescent leaves. Possibly the variety (or forma) *microphyllum* is identical with 'Sode no uchi', but as no living material of variety *microphyllum* is known to exist, the issue remains unresolved.

SERIES SINENSIA Pojárkova (1933)

TYPE SPECIES: ***Acer campbellii*** ssp. ***sinense*** (Pax) de Jong, comb. & stat. nov. (syn. *A. sinense* Pax)

HABIT: Deciduous trees; terminal buds often abortive.

LEAVES: 3- to 7-lobed, chartaceous but sometimes coriaceous; margins usually serrate but sometimes entire.

INFLORESCENCES: Large, usually elongated rachises, 20–250 flowers; pedicels of postanthesis male flowers partly dropped.

FLOWERS: Sepals often somewhat recurved; petals often lobed; discs sometimes pubescent.

FRUITS: Parthenocarpic tendency low.

SPECIES AND INFRASPECIFIC TAXA

*A. calcaratum* Gagnepain.

*A. campbellii* Hook. f. & Thomson ex Hiern in Hooker f. ssp. *campbellii.*

*A. campbellii* ssp. *chekiangense* (Fang) Murray.

*A. campbellii* ssp. *flabellatum* (Rehder) Murray.

*A. campbellii* ssp. *sinense* (Pax) de Jong, comb. & stat. nov.
*A. campbellii* ssp. *sinense* var. *longilobum* (Fang) de Jong, comb. & stat. nov.
*A. campbellii* ssp. *wilsonii* (Rehder) de Jong, comb. & stat. nov.
*A. chapaense* Gagnepain.
*A. confertifolium* Merrill & Metcalf.
*A. elegantulum* Fang & Chiu.
*A. erianthum* Schwerin.
*A. fenzelianum* Handel-Mazzetti.
*A. kuomeii* Fang & Fang f.
*A. kweilinense* Fang & Fang f.
*A. lanpingense* Fang & Fang f.
*A. linganense* Fang & Chiu.
*A. mapienense* Fang.
*A. miaoshanicum* Fang.
*A. olivaceum* Fang & Chiu.
*A. oliverianum* ssp. *formosanum* (Koidzumi) Murray.
*A. oliverianum* Pax ssp. *oliverianum.*
*A. schneiderianum* Pax & Hoffman.
*A. shangszeense* Fang & Soong.
*A. sichourense* (Fang & Fang f.) Fang.
*A. sunyiense* Fang.
*A. taipuense* Fang.
*A. tonkinense* ssp. *kwangsiense* (Fang & Fang) Fang.
*A. tonkinense* ssp. *liquidambarifolium* (Hu & Cheng) Fang.
*A. tonkinense* Lecompte ssp. *tonkinense.*
*A. tutcheri* Duthie.
*A. wuyuanense* Fang & Wu.
*A. yaoshanicum* Fang.

REFERENCE: De Jong (1976).

This series includes mainly deciduous trees from subtropical regions, primarily China and surrounding countries. The leaves are 3- to 5-lobed, rather large, and deciduous.

In the present volume some well-known species have been reduced to subspecific rank due to their close affinities, and several newly described Chinese species have been tentatively accepted, although it is not yet possible to examine them as living plants. Type specimens, of course, are available for examination in Chinese herbaria. Both P. C. de Jong and D. M. van Gelderen point out that maintaining the many taxa described as species is in conflict with their aim of composing large and variable taxa as one species.

However, as it may seem physically impossible to visit and check these taxa in Chinese herbaria, these imperfectly known species should be maintained as valid species until further information and specimens for study become available. Probably many will be sunk into synonymy when living material is introduced into Western horticulture and the type specimens are evaluated.

SECTION: *Palmata* SERIES: *Sinensia*

## ACER CALCARATUM Gagnepain (1948)

SYNONYMS

*A. isolobum* Kurz (1872), non Massalongo (1859).
*A. osmastonii* Gamble (1908).
*A. craibianum* Delendick (1978).
*A. wilsonii* ssp. *burmense* Murray (1978).

TYPE: Burma, *A. Kurz 1365;* K (as *A. isolobum*).
EPITHET: *Calcaratus,* spurred.
ILLUSTRATIONS: Plate 15; Delendick (1978, as *A. craibianum*), Valder (1975, as *A. tonkinense*).
HABIT: A tree of medium height, with glabrous branches, fresh green; young shoots very vigorous, up to 100 cm long.
LEAVES: 3-lobed, 20–25 cm long and 7.5–11 cm wide, lobes acuminate, lateral lobes 6–14 cm long, glabrous, dark olive green above and paler green beneath, bases rounded to subcordate; margins entire or slightly serrate; petioles 2–4 cm long.
INFLORESCENCES: Corymbose, terminal.
FLOWERS: 5-merous, cream to yellow.
FRUITS: Not known.
HARDINESS: Zones VIII–X.
AUTUMN COLOR: Yellow-orange.
DISTRIBUTION: Burma, in the hills between Mong Kai and Mong Wa; Thailand, including regions such as Phu Miang and Doi Khun Pong; and Sikkim, India.
CULTIVARS: None.
REFERENCES: Delendick (1979, 1980), Murray (1978b), Shimizu et al. (1981).

The story of this rare species is very complex. Gagnepain described it in 1948 and separated it from *Acer isolobum,* which had been described by Kurz in 1872 and later became a homonym of *A. isolobum* Massalongo. Kurz based his description on sterile material collected in Pegu, Burma. Gamble named the taxon *A. osmastonii* in 1908, but the taxon remained poorly known, as no flowers or fruits were collected and, while the herbarium material at Kew is plentiful, it cannot solve this problem.

In 1978 Delendick substituted the name *Acer craibianum* for *A. isolobum* Kurz, and Murray included *A. wilsonii* (listed in the present volume as *A. campbellii* ssp. *wilsonii*). Murray cited *A. isolobum* Kurz as having strong affinities with *A. osmastonii,* but requiring a new name if considered a valid species; it is the basis of his combination *A. wilsonii* ssp. *burmense.* Murray presents no reasons or data to support this treatment, but presumably the leaf outline, common to these taxa, was critical. While there certainly are affinities between *A. craibianum* and *A. campbellii* ssp. *wilsonii,* the affinities between *A. craibianum, A. calcaratum, A. osmastonii,* and other species of this section are equally strong. In fact, close affinity between *A. osmastonii* and *A.*

*calcaratum* is so clear, the former is currently regarded as a possible hybrid. Shimizu et al. (1981) put the taxa *A. calcaratum*, *A. craibianum* and *A. osmastonii* together as one species with *A. calcaratum* as the valid name. Delendick now agrees with this treatment, and his *A. craibianum* is a synonym of *A. calcaratum.* Meanwhile, *A. osmastonii* is considered a synonym of *A. calcaratum* in the present volume.

The distributions of *Acer campbellii* ssp. *wilsonii* and *A. calcaratum* do not overlap, the former being widespread in China and the latter being found only in Thailand and adjacent Burma. The two taxa are very effectively separated by the towering mountain ranges of western Yunnan Province. Since they are readily distinguishable on the basis of their foliar morphology, it is preferable to maintain them as distinct.

*Acer calcaratum* may be distinguished from *A. campbellii* ssp. *wilsonii* by its leaf shape and size. Leaves of the former are basally 3-lobed, the lobes spreading at 60–90°, while those of the latter are 3-lobed above the middle, with the veins diverging at less than 45°, and occasionally with two additional basal lobules. In addition, the leaves of *A. campbellii* ssp. *wilsonii* are much smaller than those of *A. calcaratum.*

Several years ago J. D. Vertrees of Roseburg, Oregon, USA, sent a plant of *Acer calcaratum,* bearing the epithet *A. craibianum,* to Boskoop, The Netherlands. It was successfully grafted on *A. palmatum,* but is no longer in cultivation in The Netherlands, although one or two specimens may survive in Great Britain. The species is too tender for the climate of western Europe, except perhaps in some very sheltered gardens in Cornwall or Ireland. It might also do well in moist southern parts of the United States. It is hoped that the few cultivated specimens will produce flowers and fruits. Further details about the introduction of this species can be found under *A. tonkinense,* the incorrect name under which *A. calcaratum* started its journey to Western gardens.

SECTION: *Palmata* SERIES: *Sinensia*

ACER CAMPBELLII Hook. f. & Thomson ex Hiern (1875) ssp. CAMPBELLII

TYPE: *W. Griffith,* Sikkim; K.

EPITHET: *Campbellii,* after Dr. D. H. Campbell, a botanist, explorer, and colleague of Dr. J. D. Hooker.

ILLUSTRATIONS: Fang (1981a), Krüssmann (1976a).

HABIT: A tree to 30 m tall in native habitat but much smaller in cultivation; young shoots reddish brown and glabrous; branches gray-brown.

LEAVES: Young leaves bronze-red soon turning to olive-green, 5- to 7-lobed, palmate, 12–20 cm across, lobes equally ovate-caudate, serrulate, tending to terminate in a slender acuminate point, bases truncate or cordate, nearly completely glabrescent, vein axils tufted with whitish hairs beneath; petioles reddish, 4–8 cm long.

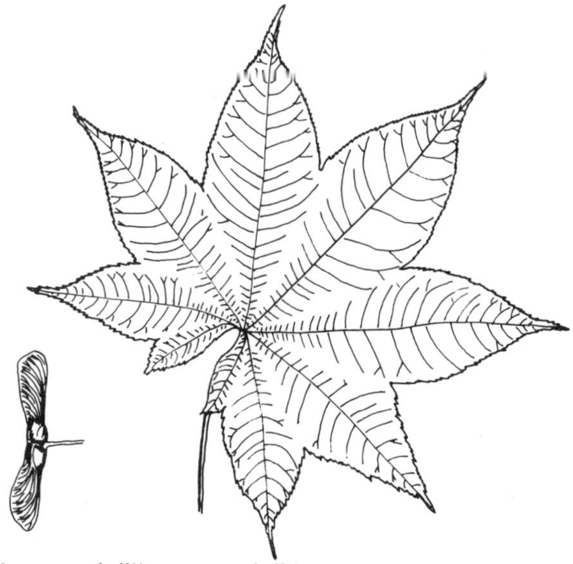

*Acer campbellii* ssp. *campbellii*

FLOWERS: Terminal on slender panicles up to 15 cm; sepals yellowish; petals white, small; floral discs and ovaries hairy.

FRUITS: Glabrous, 4–6 cm across; samara wings spreading to an angle of about 150°.

BARK AND BUDS: Mature stems and trunks gray-green, smooth, not rough, often like *A. palmatum* and its allies; young wood covered with a white bloom.

HARDINESS: Zones VII–VIII.

AUTUMN COLOR: Golden yellow or sometimes fiery red.

DISTRIBUTION: Darjeeling, Sikkim, the Himalayas, and western China, to 3000 m, on the banks of streams and often on rough places. Frequently found in Nepal together with *A. pectinatum, Magnolia campbellii, Populus glauca,* and *Taxus wallichiana.* Large trees grow in the valleys of Barum Khola and Kasua Khola. Also occasionally found in Upper Burma and North Vietnam in the valley of Chapa.

CHROMOSOME NUMBER: $2n = 26$.

SUBSPECIES

- ssp. *campbellii,* the typical subspecies.
- ssp. *chekiangense* (Fang) Murray (1977); basionym is *A. wilsonii* var. *chekiangense* Fang (1932); leaves chartaceous, 5-lobed, remotely serrate, petioles densely yellow pubescent; synonym is *A. sinense* ssp. *chekiangense* (Fang) Murray (1969).
- ssp. *flabellatum* (Rehder) Murray (1977).
- ssp. *sinense* (Pax) de Jong, comb. & stat. nov.
- ssp. *wilsonii* (Rehder) de Jong, comb. & stat. nov.

VARIETY: var. *serratifolium* Banerji (1961), leaf veins pubescent beneath.
CULTIVARS: None.
REFERENCES: Bean (1970), Fang (1981a), Gagnepain 1950, Hillier (1973), Krüssmann (1976a), Lancaster (1976), Murray (1970c, 1977), Pax (1902), Rehder (1986 facs.), Schneider (1912).

Unfortunately, this very beautiful and interesting species is too tender for most regions of Europe and North America. It can be planted in the milder regions of Great Britain, in sheltered gardens in The Netherlands and Belgium, and in the Pacific Northwest, California, and Florida in the United States. Hardier specimens seem to exist, but there are no recognized clonal names. Several young plants cultivated from Nepalese seed grew well in Boskoop, The Netherlands, but their hardiness was no better than usual. Another good specimen grows in the Westonbirt Arboretum in Gloucestershire, Great Britain. It survived the hard winter of 1984–1985 and even produced viable seed in the autumn of 1985.

*Acer campbellii* forms a small tree and in less favorable conditions grows into a sizable shrub. In its native habitat it reaches a height of about 30 m; this size has not yet been attained in cultivation. Its large, glossy, olive-green leaves are palmately lobed, each lobe ending in a slender point.

Subspecies *campbellii* is easily confused with subspecies *flabellatum,* its closest ally. The latter seems to be a smaller, hardier tree with slightly smaller leaves than those of *Acer campbellii.* Some other plants formerly treated as species, such as *A. sinense* and *A. wilsonii,* are included here as subspecies under *A. campbellii.* The variability within and between these taxa is tremendous, yet they all seem to "merge" into one another.

*Acer campbellii* can be propagated by seed or grafted on seedlings of *A. palmatum.* Grafting produces superior specimens.

*Acer campbellii* ssp. *campbellii* var. *serratifolium*

SECTION: *Palmata* SERIES: *Sinensia*

## ACER CAMPBELLII ssp. FLABELLATUM (Rehder) Murray (1977)

BASIONYM: *A. flabellatum* Rehder (1905).
SYNONYMS
*A. campbelli* ssp. *heptaphlebium* (Gagnepain) Murray (1977).
*A. heptalobum* Diels (1931).
TYPE: Lectotype *A. Henry 6900;* syntypes *E. H. Wilson 708, 1232,* Hubei Province, China; K; P; W.
EPITHET: *Flabellatus,* fan-shaped.
ILLUSTRATIONS: Plate 16; Fang (1981a), Gagnepain (1950).
HABIT: A small tree, often only a large shrub, 6–9 m tall; stout, sturdy branches; young stems gray-green.
LEAVES: 7-lobed, the outer lobes small, very regular, serrate, distinctly acuminate, upper sides dark and shining green, with a paler green below; young leaves often with a reddish hue, disappearing when mature; petioles 4–5 cm long.
FLOWERS: On slender panicles; floral discs and ovaries glabrous (hairy in *A. campbellii* ssp. *campbellii*).
FRUITS: Samaras about 3 cm long, brownish, spreading almost horizontally; nutlets firm and round.
BARK AND BUDS: Distinctly gray-green, older stems olive, with some traces of stripes.
HARDINESS: Zone VII.
AUTUMN COLOR: Yellow.
DISTRIBUTION: Hubei and Sichuan provinces, China, in acid soils at 1800–2600 m. Also occurring in Yunnan Province, northern Laos, and Vietnam.
CHROMOSOME NUMBER: $2n = 26$.
VARIETY: var. *yunnanense* (Rehder) Fang (1939), leaves sharply serrulate; the Yunnan and Upper Burma variety of *A. campbellii* ssp. *flabellatum;* synonym is *A. campbellii* var. *yunnanense* Rehder (1905), more tender than subspecies *flabellatum,* rare in cultivation, and differing in its bristle-tipped teeth on sharply serrate leaf margins.
REFERENCES: Bean (1970), Fang (1981a), Gagnepain (1950), Krüssmann (1976a), Murray (1970c, 1977), Rehder (1986 facs.).

This remarkably beautiful subspecies of *Acer campbellii* has distinctive, shining, large palmate leaves. The tree's somewhat exotic appearance distinguishes it from other allied maples. It is a tree or large shrub with gray-green branches that are twigged like many shrubs of *A. palmatum,* to which this species is closely related.

Rehder described *Acer campbellii* ssp. *flabellatum* (as *A. flabellatum*) in 1905, and Wilson introduced it in 1907. Its closest ally is *A. campbellii* ssp. *campbellii,* which is more tender and much rarer. Recent new introductions of *A. campbellii* ssp. *flabellatum* from Nepal seem to be slightly hardier than earlier introductions. Subspecies *flabellatum* is easily confused with subspecies *campbellii*, but the former's leaf margins are more serrate, and its ovaries are hairy instead of glabrous. Also very closely related and possibly synonymous in the opinions of van Gelderen, de Jong, and Oterdoom, is *A. heptalobum* Diels (1931), which is not to be confused with *A. palmatum* 'Heptalobum', a very different plant altogether. *Acer heptalobum* is native on Mount Chicha in Yunnan Province, China, and in Annam, Laos, and Tonkin.

*Acer heptaphlebium* Gagnepain (1948), which is not in cultivation, is treated as a synonym. Its leaves are pubescent in vein axils when young, and its ovaries are pubescent, like those of subspecies *campbellii*. Both taxa could be merged with *A. campbellii* ssp. *flabellatum*. Murray combined *A. heptaphlebium* as a subspecies under *A. campbellii* in 1977. One geographical variety has been described as variety *yunnanense*, a more southerly and more tender type with about the same leaves. Recent biochemical research has shown that *A. campbellii* and its subspecies are possibly the same. They differ only morphologically and perhaps should be merged into one grex species.

SECTION: *Palmata* SERIES: *Sinensia*

ACER CAMPBELLII ssp. SINENSE (Pax) de Jong, comb. & stat. nov.

BASIONYM: *A. sinense* Pax in Hooker's *Icones Plantarum* 19: tab. 1897, note 1. 1889.

SYNONYMS

- *Liquidambar rosthornii* Diels (1900).
- *A. chingii* Hu (1930).
- *A. sinense* var. *iatrophifolium* Diels (1931).
- *A. bicolor* Chun (1948).
- *A. sinense* ssp. *chingii* (Hu) Murray (1977).

TYPE: *A. Henry 5831*, Hubei Province, China (original destroyed in Berlin during World War II); BM; E; P; W.

EPITHET: *Sinensis*, Chinese.

ILLUSTRATIONS: Plate 17; Fang (1981a), Krüssmann (1976a).

HABIT: A small tree to 10 m tall; bark rough, gray; branches thin and green, glabrous; young growth reddish.

LEAVES: 5-lobed, thick and coriaceous, 9–12 cm across, bases slightly cordate, lobes triangular-ovate, margins remotely serrate, glabrous above, hair tufts in vein axils beneath; petioles 3–5 cm long, red.

INFLORESCENCES: Terminal, paniculate, about 15 cm long.

FLOWERS: Yellow-green, appearing with the leaves.

FRUITS: Samaras 2 cm long, connivent, subhorizontal to acute.

HARDINESS: Zone VIII.

AUTUMN COLOR: Yellow.

DISTRIBUTION: Hubei and Sichuan provinces, China, at 1500–2000 m. Very widespread, forming thickets.

CHROMOSOME NUMBER: $2n = 26$.

VARIETIES

- *A. campbellii* ssp. *sinense* var. *longilobum* (Fang) de Jong, comb. & stat. nov.; basionym is *A. sinense* var. *longilobum* Fang (1939), leaves narrowly elongated.
- *A. sinense* var. *brevilobum* Fang (1939), lobes short; synonym is *A. prolificum* Fang).
- *A. sinense* var. *concolor* Pax, leaves larger, underside green.
- *A. sinense* var. *microcarpum* Metcalf (1942), samaras 1 cm.
- *A. sinense* var. *pubinerve* (Rehder) Fang (1932), veins pubescent, 3-lobed.
- *A. sinense* var. *undulatum* Fang & Wu (1979).

CULTIVARS: None.

REFERENCES: Bean (1970), Fang (1981a), Krüssmann (1976a), Murray (1970c, 1977, 1981b), Pax (1902), Rehder (1986 facs.), Sargent (1913), Schneider (1912).

*Acer campbellii* ssp. *sinense*, which is very rare in cultivation, is closely allied to subspecies *campbellii* and subspecies *flabellatum*. The tree is very tender and, unlike its relatives, can be planted only in very sheltered gardens. In the present volume it is treated as a subspecies under *A. campbellii*, while Chinese specialists maintain it as a species.

*Acer campbellii* ssp. *sinense* can grow into a small tree, but remains a shrub in cooler climates. Its leaves are thick and coriaceous, and stiffer than those of subspecies *campbellii* and *flabellatum*. They also have a whitish bloom on the undersides. As so little material is available, it is hard to specify the practical field characteristics separating it from its allies.

*Acer campbellii* ssp. *sinense*

Propagation by seed is limited by seed availability for this rare subspecies. Grafting on *Acer palmatum* is a realistic possibility. Attempts have been made to obtain fresh seed from China, where it grows in Sichuan and Hubei provinces as a small tree. Fang recognized several varieties, none of which are in cultivation. It is uncertain whether the varieties listed above should be maintained, but there is insufficient material available in Western horticulture and herbaria to make this decision.

Several seedlings of this subspecies were brought to Europe from China, but only one of them survived the cold winter of 1984–1985. This plant, growing in Vasterival Gardens (owned by Princess Sturdza), near Dieppe, France, died back to ground level, but young shoots appeared in June 1985 were grafted on *Acer palmatum* rootstock. The resulting plants are now about 2 m tall and grow vigorously.

This subspecies has also been grown from seeds originating in Beijing Botanic Garden. The seedlings match the French plant quite closely, but the distinguishing characteristics are still in a juvenile state. The author saw this subspecies often in W. Sichuan; it resembles *A. oliverianum*.

*Acer bicolor* Chun (1948) is considered a synonym of *A. campbellii* ssp. *sinense*, and is a synonym of *A. sinense* var. *iatrophifolium* Diels (1933). It is not known in Western horticulture.

*Acer chingii* Hu (1930) was reduced to a subspecies of *A. sinense* by Murray in 1977. The drawings available led the authors to place it as a synonym of *A. campbellii* ssp. *sinense*.

SECTION: *Palmata* SERIES: *Sinensia*

## ACER CAMPBELLII ssp. WILSONII (Rehder) de Jong, comb. & stat. nov.

BASIONYM: *A. wilsonii* Rehder, in C. S. Sargent, *Trees & Shrubs*:105, t. 79. 1905.

SYNONYM: *A. angustilobum* H. Hu (1931).

TYPE: *E. H. Wilson 303*, Hubei Province, China; holotype A; K; W.

EPITHET: *Wilsonii*, after botanist E. H. Wilson (1876–1930).

ILLUSTRATIONS: Plate 18; Fang (1981a), Krüssmann (1976a).

HABIT: A shrub or small tree; branches green or purplish to brown; young shoots thin.

LEAVES: Distinctly 3-lobed, 8–10 cm across, basal lobes when present much smaller than the central one; margins entire or remotely serrate; bases rounded to subcordate; petioles 3–4 cm long.

INFLORESCENCES: Paniculate, terminal.

FLOWERS: Yellowish green.

FRUITS: Samaras 2.5 cm long, wings horizontal; nutlets ovoid.

HARDINESS: Zone VI.

DISTRIBUTION: Hubei, Yunnan, Zhejiang, Guangdong, and probably other provinces, China, at 1200–1800 m.

CHROMOSOME NUMBER: $2n = 26$.

VARIETIES

- var. *kwangtungense* (Chun) Fang (1939), young leaves, branches, and samaras yellowish pilose; from Guangdong Province, China.
- var. *longicaudatum* (Fang) Fang (1979).
- var. *obtusum* Fang & Wu (1979).

CULTIVARS: None.

REFERENCES: Bean (1970), Fang (1981a), Krüssmann (1976a), Murray (1970c), Rehder (1986 facs.), Sargent (1913), Schneider (1912).

This subspecies was discovered by A. Henry in Yunnan and by E. H. Wilson in Hubei in 1900. In 1907 it was introduced to the Arnold Arboretum, where Alfred Rehder described it in honor of the famous horticulturist Ernest H. Wilson.

This beautiful but little-known maple is well worth a place in a maple collection. Although a small or large tree in the wild, in cultivation it is only a shrub. It has distinctly 3-lobed leaves with small basal lobes and round bases.

*Acer campbellii* ssp. *wilsonii* is easily distinguished from its allies, subspecies *campbellii* and *flabellatum*, by its distinctive round bases and small basal lobes. The leaves of its allies, in contrast, are orbicular and have differently shaped lobes.

It is very difficult to obtain this subspecies in the trade—seed is almost never available and grafting on *Acer palmatum* is difficult. Summer grafts are not often successful because the scions must have undamaged leaves. Winter grafting is also difficult due to the thin young wood, which ripens quite late and is susceptible to the fire fungus *Nectria cinnabarina*.

*Acer wilsonii* is now tentatively placed as a subspecies under *A. campbellii*, but it might not be as closely allied to subspecies *campbellii* as it is to the other subspecies *flabellatum* and *sinense*.

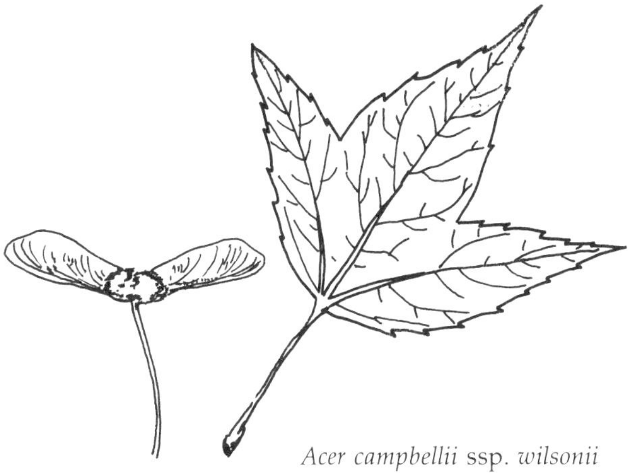

*Acer campbellii* ssp. *wilsonii*

SECTION: *Palmata* SERIES: *Sinensia*

## ACER CHAPAENSE Gagnepain (1948)

TYPE: *Pételot 5824;* Chapa, Tonkin, North Vietnam; P.
EPITHET: *Chapaensis,* after Chapa, a Vietnamese region or valley.
ILLUSTRATION: Gagnepain (1950).
HABIT: A tree of medium size with brownish branches, glabrous.
LEAVES: 3- to 5-lobed, 5–15 cm across, almost orbicular, glabrous, with five main veins and short lateral veins, bases truncate; margins subentire to sinuate; petioles slender, 1–4 cm long.
FLOWERS: Not seen.
FRUITS: Samaras diverge at 45°, 4 cm long; nutlets striped or veined, 5 mm across, flat as in section *Platanoidea.*
HARDINESS: Zones VIII–IX.
DISTRIBUTION: Chapa, North Vietnam.
CHROMOSOME NUMBER: $2n = 26$.
CULTIVARS: None.
REFERENCES: Gagnepain (1950), Murray (1970c).

This species apparently is not cultivated in the West. Murray placed it in section *Palmata* series *Sinensia,* and other botanists place it in section *Platanoidea.* It seems to be very close to *Acer campbellii* ssp. *flabellatum,* but as there is no material available to determine relationships, it is treated in this volume as a separate species. It must be pointed out, however, that it is a very doubtful taxon.

It is probably a tree with irregular leaves whose petioles are irregular in length.

*Acer chapaense*

SECTION: *Palmata* SERIES: *Sinensia*

## ACER CONFERTIFOLIUM Merrill & Metcalf (1937)

SYNONYMS
*A. wilsonii* var. *serrulatum* Dunn (1908).
*A. oliveranum* var. *serrulatum* (Dunn) Rehder (1911).
*A. johnedwardianum* Metcalf (1942).
*A. tutcheri* ssp. *confertifolium* (Merrill & Metcalf) Murray (1977).
*A. confertifolium* var. *serrulatum* (Dunn) Fang (1979).

TYPE: *W. T. Tsang 21407;* Yam-na-shan, Guangdong Province, China. BM; K; P; original holotype A.
EPITHET: *Confertifolius,* with leaves set closely together.
HABIT: A shrub about 1 m tall, low and dense, with numerous branches and few bud scales; twigs slender, glabrous; young growth green.
LEAVES: 3-lobed, 2.5–5 cm across; margins crenate; petioles 2.5 cm long; leaf blades coriaceous, many clustered at the top of the twigs; bases cordate, usually divided nearly obtusely to half the length of the leaf blade; main veins prominent below.
INFLORESCENCES: Terminal.
FLOWERS: Few; other characteristics unknown.
FRUITS: Samaras few, obtuse, 2 cm long, reddish purple, diverging at an obtuse angle.
BARK AND BUDS: Bark scabrous, dark gray.
HARDINESS: ?
DISTRIBUTION: Fujian and Guangdong provinces, China, at low altitudes.
CULTIVARS: None.
REFERENCES: Fang (1981a), Murray (1970c, 1977).

*Acer confertifolium* is probably not in cultivation, certainly not in the Western world. It was described by Metcalf in 1937 and known earlier under other names, including *A. wilsonii* var. *serrulatum* and *A. oliverianum* var. *serrulatum.*

It is very probably close to *Acer oliverianum* and is described as a densely branched low shrub with 3-lobed leaves. It is not closely related to *A. serrulatum* Hayata from Taiwan, which has 5-lobed leaves, grows rather quickly into a treelike shrub, and is a synonym of *A. oliverianum* ssp. *formosanum* (Koidzumi) Murray.

SECTION: *Palmata* SERIES: *Sinensia*

## ACER ELEGANTULUM Fang & Chiu (1979)

TYPE: Syntypes *Y. Y. Ho 23101, 23021, 23024,* Changhua, Zhejiang Province, China; IBSC.
EPITHET: *Elegantulus,* of elegant habit.
ILLUSTRATIONS: Plate 19; Fang (1981a).
HABIT: A tree to 15 m tall but often not taller than 9 m.
LEAVES: Thin, papery, 5-lobed, somewhat broader than long, 7–10 cm across, basal lobes much smaller than ovate or triangular-ovate central and side lobes; small mucro at apices.

Acer elegantulum

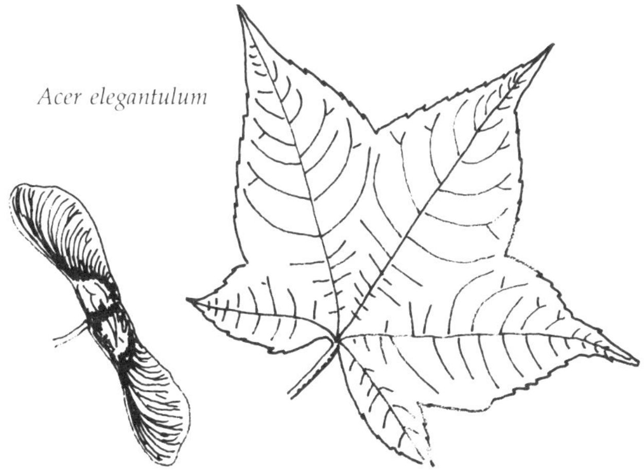

INFLORESCENCES: Paniculate.
FLOWERS: Andromonoecious, sepals 5, green, oblong-ovate, dark green, twice as long as the petals; stamens 5.
FRUITS: Samaras pale yellow, about 4 cm long, almost horizontal; nutlets swollen, 6 mm thick.
BARK AND BUDS: Bark scabrous, dark brown.
HARDINESS: Zones VII or VIII.
DISTRIBUTION: Zhejiang and Jiangxi provinces, China, at 700–1000 m.
VARIETIES
var. *elegantulum*, the typical variety.
var. *macrurum* Fang & Chiu (1979), samaras smaller, only 1–1.5 cm long.
CULTIVARS: None.
REFERENCE: Fang (1981a).

Seeds of this species were distributed to several European nurseries and gardens by the Shanghai Botanic Garden in about 1985 and five years later some plants were available for morphological study. The seedlings grew and developed quickly to compact shrubs, about 2 m tall in 1990. The description of the species matches these plants, with the exception that the central lobe of the leaf is clearly longer than the outer lobes. The plants have not yet flowered. They may not be hardy, except in favorable climatic conditions.

SECTION: *Palmata* SERIES: *Sinensia*
ACER ERIANTHUM Schwerin (1901)
SYNONYMS
*A. oxyodon* Franchet ex Fang (1939), pro syn.
*A. stachyanthum* Franchet ex Fang (1939), pro syn.
TYPE: *A. Henry 8989*, Sichuan Province, China; P.
EPITHET: *Erianthus*, with wool-covered flowers.
ILLUSTRATIONS: Plate 20; Fang (1981a), Krüssmann (1976a).
HABIT: A shrub or sometimes a small tree to 6–8 m tall; young stems green to olive-green, older wood gray, almost glabrous, with small whitish dots.
LEAVES: 5- to 7-lobed, of thin texture, 6–12 cm across, lobes prominently triangular, argutely toothed, dark green above, undersides with conspicuous white tufts of silky hairs, bases slightly cordate, veins somewhat grooved.
INFLORESCENCES: Slender panicles, 5–10 cm long.
FLOWERS: Yellowish, after the development of the leaves, stamens long, ovaries felted with silky hairs.
FRUITS: Samaras horizontal, up to 3 cm long; nutlets downy when young, glabrous when mature.
BARK AND BUDS: Bark gray and smooth, not splitting.
HARDINESS: Zone V.
AUTUMN COLOR: Yellow, but often browning and curling early in the autumn.
DISTRIBUTION: Sichuan, Guangxi, and Hubei provinces, China, in mountainous regions at 2000–3000 m.
CULTIVARS: None.
REFERENCES: Bean (1970), Fang (1981a), Krüssmann (1976a), Murray (1970c), Pax (1902), Rehder (1986 facs.), Sargent (1913), Schneider (1912), Schwerin (1901).

Graf von Schwerin described *Acer erianthum* in 1901. Wilson brought it to Europe in 1901 among his collections for Veitch Nursery. Augustine Henry discovered it earlier as his herbarium specimen *Acer 8989*.

A rare maple from China, this species is a member of section *Palmata* but at first glance appears rather different. It is found in cultivation only occasionally. It is a small tree or shrub with 5- to 7-lobed leaves of a thin, almost papery texture, with grooved veins. Its leaves are easily sunburned (in its native habitat it grows in partial shade), so for good results it needs a well protected place in the garden.

It is readily propagated from seed, but seed is only rarely available. Grafting on *Acer palmatum* is also possible, but less desirable as it does not strike very well. It has no cultivars or subspecies.

SECTION: *Palmata* SERIES: *Sinensia*
ACER FENZELIANUM Handel-Mazzetti (1933)
SYNONYM: *A. tonkinense* ssp. *fenzelianum* (Handel-Mazzetti) Murray (1969).
TYPE: *Fenzl 44*, Chapa, Tonkin, North Vietnam; W.
EPITHET: *Fenzelianus*, after Austrian botanist E. Fenzl (1808–1879).
ILLUSTRATIONS: Fang (1981a), Gagnepain (1950).
HABIT: A tree to 15 m tall; branches smooth, olive to gray, with large brown lenticels.
LEAVES: 3-lobed or tridentate, subcoriaceous, 7.5–15 cm long and as wide, bases rounded to subcordate; petioles 3–5 cm long, densely tomentose, gray to yellow-brown.
INFLORESCENCES: Few-flowered, short corymbs.

Acer fenzelianum

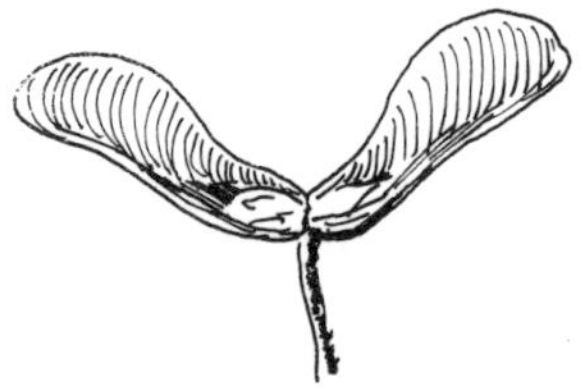

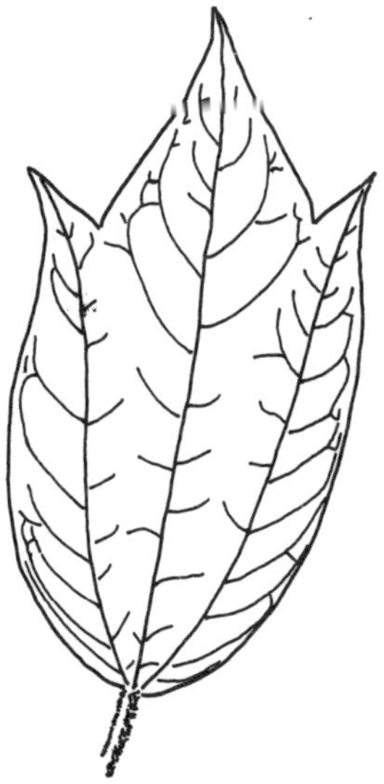

(Its relative, *A. tonkinense,* has very long corymbs, with many flowers.)
FLOWERS: 5-merous.
FRUITS: Samaras medium-sized; nutlets woody, in very small trusses, unlike *A. tonkinense,* which has soft nutlets on long racemes.
BARK AND BUDS: Bark gray, smooth.
HARDINESS: Zone VIII.
DISTRIBUTION: North Vietnam at 1100–1500 m, and southern Yunnan Province, China, at 1000–1500 m.
CULTIVARS: None.
REFERENCES: Fang (1981a), Gagnepain (1950), de Jong (1976), Murray (1970c).

Hardly any further information is available on this species. Its relationship to *Acer calcaratum* and *A. tonkinense* is obvious. It is not in cultivation.

SECTION: *Palmata* SERIES: *Sinensia*

ACER KUOMEII Fang & Fang f. (1966)

TYPE: *K. M. Fang 11818,* Sichou Hsien, Fadou, Yunnan Province, China; PE.
EPITHET: *Kuomeii,* from Kuo Mei, the given name of the original collector of the species.
ILLUSTRATION: Fang (1981a).
HABIT: A small tree to 8 m tall.
LEAVES: 5- to 7-lobed, 11–13 cm across, basal lobes much smaller; margins moderately toothed; apices acuminate.
INFLORESCENCES: Paniculate.
FRUITS: Samaras small, spreading at a 120° angle.
HARDINESS: Zones VII–VIII.
DISTRIBUTION: Yunnan Province, China, at 1200–2000 m.
CULTIVARS: None.
REFERENCE: Fang (1981a).

This is possibly a synonym of *Acer campbellii* ssp. *sinense* (Pax) de Jong. It is not in cultivation.

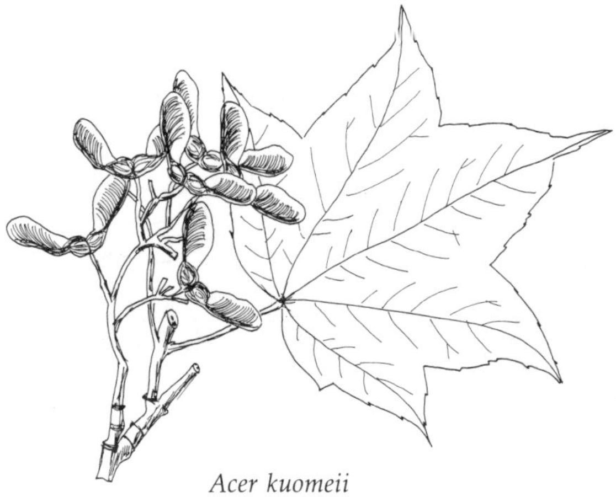

Acer kuomeii

SECTION: *Palmata* SERIES: *Sinensia*

ACER KWEILINENSE Fang & Fang f. (1966)

TYPE: *Kwangfu Exp. No. 429,* Lung-sheng Haien, Guangxi Province, China; IBSC; isotypes IBK, PE, SZ.
EPITHET: *Kweilinensis,* after Guilin (formerly Kweilin), a district of Guangxi Province, China.
ILLUSTRATION: Fang (1981a).
HABIT: A shrub or small tree to 6–7 m tall.
LEAVES: 5-lobed, lobes up to half the leaf blade, 5–8 cm long and 7–10 cm wide, pubescent in the underside of vein axils.
INFLORESCENCES: Erect panicles.
FLOWERS: Andromonoecious; sepals green-purplish; petals pale green; stamens 8, glabrous; ovaries densely yellowish villose.
FRUITS: Samaras 4–5 cm, almost horizontal; wings falcate.
HARDINESS: Unknown.
DISTRIBUTION: Guangxi Province, China, on hills, at 1000–1500 m.
CULTIVARS: None.
REFERENCES: Fang (1966, 1981a), Murray (1970c).

According to Murray, *Acer kweilinense* is very closely related to *A. erianthum.* As no living Western material is available for comparison and we have no access to the Chinese herbaria at this writing, we tentatively retain *A. kweilinense* as a species. It is not known in Western horticulture.

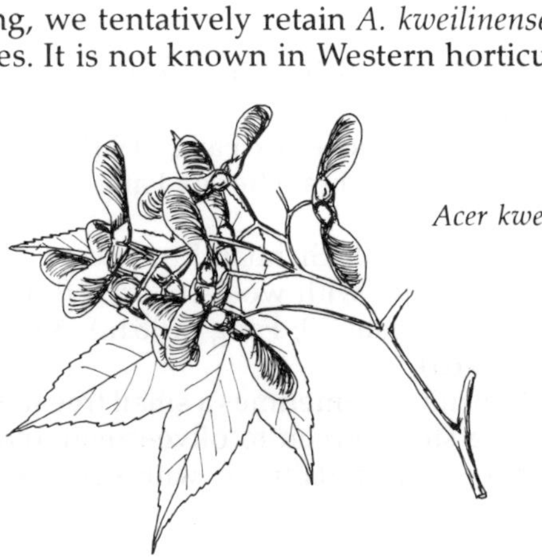

Acer kweilinense

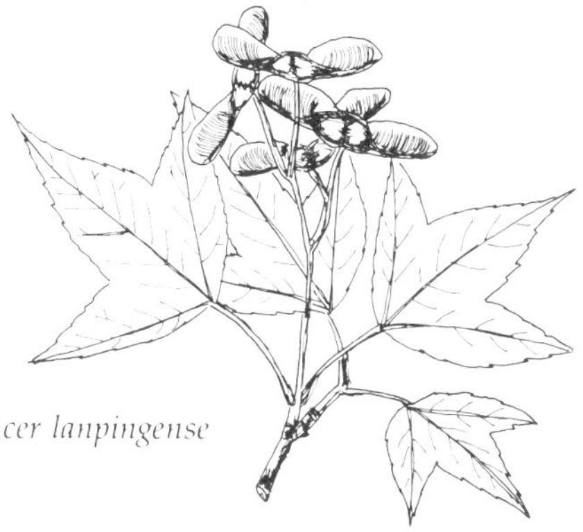

*Acer lanpingense*

SECTION: *Palmata* SERIES: *Sinensia*

ACER LANPINGENSE Fang & Fang f. (1966)

TYPE: *P. J. Mao 272,* Lan Ping Hsien, northwest Yunnan Province, China; PE.

EPITHET: *Lanpingensis,* after Lan Ping, a district in Yunnan Province, China.

ILLUSTRATION: Fang (1981a).

HABIT: A tree to 10–15 m tall.

LEAVES: 3-lobed, 4–6 cm long and 5–7 cm wide, lobes coarsely serrate; petioles 3–5 cm long.

INFLORESCENCES: Corymbose.

FLOWERS: In small corymbs, otherwise unknown.

FRUITS: Samaras 2–3 cm long, almost horizontal.

HARDINESS: Unknown.

DISTRIBUTION: Lan Ping District, Yunnan Province, China, in mountainous regions up to 2600 m.

CULTIVARS: None.

REFERENCES: Fang (1966, 1981a), Murray (1970c).

According to Murray and the original description by Fang & Fang f., this species is closely related to *Acer tutcheri.* It is not known in Western horticulture, and the lack of living specimens or herbarium material makes confirmation difficult, as *A. tutcheri* also is not in cultivation. *Acer lanpingense* is here maintained as a species until more information becomes available.

SECTION: *Palmata* SERIES: *Sinensia*

ACER LINGANENSE Fang & Chiu (1979)

TYPES: Syntypes *Y. Y. Ho 21134, 21178, 21261, 21337, 22011, 22123, 30948, 20991,* Lingan Hsien, Zhejiang Province, China; HHBG.

EPITHET: *Linganensis,* after Lingan, a district in Zhejiang Province, China.

ILLUSTRATION: Fang (1981a).

HABIT: A large shrub to 5–7 m tall; branches waxy, greenish blue.

LEAVES: 5- to 7-lobed (sometimes up to 9-lobed), lobes serrate, 5–8 cm across, glabrous on both sides except for tufts at vein axils below.

FLOWERS: Petals larger than the sepals; ovaries densely tomentose.

FRUITS: Wings almost horizontal.

DISTRIBUTION: China, at 600–1300 m.

CULTIVARS: None.

REFERENCES: Fang (1979a, 1981a).

This species seems to be close to *Acer pseudosieboldianum.* It is not in cultivation.

SECTION: *Palmata* SERIES: *Sinensia*

ACER MAPIENENSE Fang (1979)

SYNONYM: *A. gracile* sensu Fang & Fang f. (1966), non Saporta (1867).

TYPE: *W. P. Fang 1607,* Mapien Hsien, Sichuan Province, China; PE.

EPITHET: *Mapienensis,* after Mapien, a district in Sichuan Province, China.

ILLUSTRATION: Fang (1981a).

HABIT: A deciduous tree to 10 m tall; twigs slender, glabrous; young growth green to purplish.

LEAVES: 5-lobed or remotely 7-lobed, 8–10 cm across, margins finely serrate, veins rather prominent, bases truncate or rarely cordate; lobes oblong or oblong-ovate, acute at apices, slightly curved; undersides pale green and comose on vein axils, main veins 5, conspicuous above, slightly elevated beneath; petioles about 2 cm, slender.

*Acer linganense*

*Acer mapienense*

FLOWERS: About 15–20 flowers on racemes 14–17 cm long and usually drooping.
FRUITS: Samaras spreading at an angle of 150°, wings rather large, about 2–3 cm, in racemes 10–15 cm long.
BARK AND BUDS: Bark smooth, purplish brown.
HARDINESS: Probably zones VI–VII.
DISTRIBUTION: Sichuan Province, China, in mountainous regions at 2000–2500 m.
CULTIVARS: None.
REFERENCES: Fang (1981a), Murray (1970c).

This species is closely allied to *Acer campbellii* ssp. *flabellatum* and might be included in it when adequate material is available.

SECTION: *Palmata* SERIES: *Sinensia*

ACER MIAOSHANICUM Fang (1966)

TYPE: *C. S. Chun 16275,* Ta Miao Shan Hsien, North Guangxi Province, China; IBSC.
EPITHET: *Miaoshanicus,* after Miao Shan, a district in northern Guangxi Province, China.
ILLUSTRATION: Fang (1981a).
HABIT: A shrub 3–5 m tall.
LEAVES: 5- to 7-lobed, 7–10 cm long and 7–12 cm wide; lobes short, broad; margins finely serrate; outer lobes underdeveloped.
INFLORESCENCES: Paniculate, intensely purple, glabrous, up to 10 cm long.
FLOWERS: Unknown.
FRUITS: Samaras 3–5 cm long, spreading out at an angle of about 90°.
HARDINESS: Probably zones VI–VII.
DISTRIBUTION: Hills in Guangxi Province, China, up to 900 m.
CULTIVARS: None.
REFERENCES: Fang (1966, 1981a), Murray (1970c).

According to Murray, *Acer miaoshanicum* is very closely related to *A. erianthum,* and Fang (1966) places it close to *A. kweilinense,* which is very closely related to *A. erianthum* as well.

The species is not in cultivation in the West, but the author has seen it in Sichuan. It clearly differs from *A. erianthum* by its purplish leaves. *Acer miaoshanicum* must be retained as a valid species until more information becomes available.

*Acer miaoshanicum*

SECTION: *Palmata* SERIES: *Sinensia*

ACER OLIVACEUM Fang & Chiu (1979)

TYPE: Syntypes *Y. Y. Ho 21114, 21116,* Tien mu Shan, Lingan Hsien, Zhejiang Province, China; HHBG.
EPITHET: *Olivaceus,* olive green.
HABIT: A tree to 10 m tall or taller; twigs nearly terete, purple or purplish green.
LEAVES: 5-lobed, 7–8 cm across, papery, nearly cordate or truncate at bases, with acuminate apices; lobes regularly cleft, 3.5 cm long, pale olive green, comose at the veins on the undersides.
INFLORESCENCES: Short-paniculate.
FLOWERS: Andromonoecious; sepals 5, ovate, purplish green, 3 mm long, pilose inside; petals 5, pale white.
FRUITS: Samaras 3 cm long, spreading to an angle of about 120°, wings incurved, long-elliptic; nutlets globular, 5 mm long, veins obvious.
BARK AND BUDS: Bark scabrous, purplish green or pale brown.
HARDINESS: Unknown.
DISTRIBUTION: Zhejiang, southern Anhui, and eastern Jiangxi provinces, China, at 200–1000 m.
CULTIVARS: None.
REFERENCE: Fang (1981a).

This species seems to be rather closely allied to *Acer oliverianum.* There is no material available in Europe for comparison, so it is maintained as a species until further investigation is possible.

SECTION: *Palmata* SERIES: *Sinensia*

ACER OLIVERIANUM ssp. FORMOSANUM (Koidzumi) Murray (1969)

BASIONYM: *A. oliverianum* subvar. *formosanum* Koidzumi (1911).
SYNONYMS
*A. oliverianum* var. *nakaharae* Hayata (1911).
*A. oliverianum* f. *longistaminum* Hayata (1911).
*A. oliverianum* f. *microcarpum* Hayata (1911).
*A. serrulatum* Hayata (1911).
TYPE: *Nakahara 161,* Chosokei, Cheelung, Taiwan; TI; syntypes *Hayata 3136,* Taiwan.
COMMON NAME: Itomaki shima momiji.
EPITHET: *Formosanus,* from Formosa (now Taiwan).
ILLUSTRATIONS: Plate 21; Koidzumi (1911), Liu (1962).
HABIT: A tree up to 20 m tall, much larger than its Chinese counterpart subspecies *oliverianum;* branches reddish and glabrous.
LEAVES: 5-lobed, palmate, 7 cm long and 9–10 cm wide, almost circular, glabrous on both sides, larger and stouter than those of the species, bases cordate; lobes of the same regular shape, 5–7 cm long; petioles glabrous, 1.5–3 cm long; vigorous young plants often have much larger purple leaves, with lobes up to 10 cm long and coarsely toothed margins.
INFLORESCENCES: In terminal, corymbose umbels.

*Acer oliverianum* ssp. *formosanum*

FLOWERS: Yellow, appearing with the leaves; petals 5, rounded.
FRUITS: Samaras almost horizontal, obovate, 2.5 cm long including nutlets, diverging at an angle of 90–120°.
HARDINESS: Zones VII–VIII.
AUTUMN COLOR: Yellow.
DISTRIBUTION: Very widespread on Taiwan, and the largest species of *Acer* on the island; common in forests at 1000–2000 m.
CULTIVARS: None.
REFERENCES: Bean (1970), Fang (1981a), Koidzumi (1911), Krüssmann (1976a), Liu (1962), Murray (1970c).

This is a vigorously growing tree on Taiwan. It is reported as not very hardy, though its hardiness has not been tested, as there are very few adult plants in collections. Unfortunately, this subspecies is too tender for planting in exposed gardens. It can be used in temperate regions of Great Britain and North America.

There are plants in cultivation under the name *Acer serrulatum* Hayata, a synonym of this subspecies. There has been some confusion with *A. serrulatum*, as *A. wilsonii* var. *serrulatum* (Dunn) Rehder is a synonym of *A. confertifolium*, which, however, may not be in cultivation.

SECTION: *Palmata* SERIES: *Sinensia*

ACER OLIVERIANUM Pax (1889) ssp. OLIVERIANUM

SYNONYM: *A. campbellii* ssp. *oliverianum* (Pax) Murray (1977).
TYPE: *A. Henry 6512* (original destroyed in Berlin in World War II); K; G; BM.
EPITHET: *Oliverianus*, after English botanist Daniel Oliver (1830–1916).
ILLUSTRATIONS: Plate 22; Fang (1981a), Koidzumi (1911), Krüssmann (1976a).
HABIT: A small tree or well-branched shrub to 8–10 m tall; young branches glabrous; young shoots green to purplish.
LEAVES: 5-lobed, palmate, 5–12 cm across, almost cordate at bases, lobes ovate, fresh green on both sides, very finely serrate, totally glabrous except for down along vein axils when young.
INFLORESCENCES: Terminal, corymbose, 4–10 cm long.
FLOWERS: Small, whitish, appearing with the leaves; sepals purplish green; petals white.
FRUITS: Samaras subhorizontal, wings 2.5 cm long and 1 cm wide; fruits glabrous.
BARK AND BUDS: Bark dark gray with some brown, smooth.
HARDINESS: Zones VI–VII.
AUTUMN COLOR: Yellow to brownish.
DISTRIBUTION: Hubei and Yunnan provinces, China, in mountainous regions at 1500–2000 m.
SUBSPECIES
- ssp. *oliverianum*, the typical subspecies.
- ssp. *formosanum* (Koidzumi) Murray (1969), leaves larger than those of the typical subspecies.

CULTIVARS: None.
REFERENCES: Bean (1970), Elwes & Henry (1908), Fang (1981a), Koidzumi (1911), Krüssmann (1976a), Murray (1970c, 1977), Pax (1902), Rehder (1986 facs.).

A small tree, *Acer oliverianum* is occasionally found in gardens. It was discovered by Augustine Henry and described by Pax in 1889. Wilson introduced it for Veitch Nursery in 1901.

It has rather large, palmately lobed leaves and is easily mistaken for a robust, green-leaved *Acer palmatum*. Normally the bark of *A. oliverianum* is greener than that of *A. palmatum*. The leaves of *A. oliverianum* are entirely glabrous. In fact, it is intermediate between *A. palmatum* and *A campbellii*, among others. Vigorously growing young plants are prone to a dieback of their long shoots in severe winters.

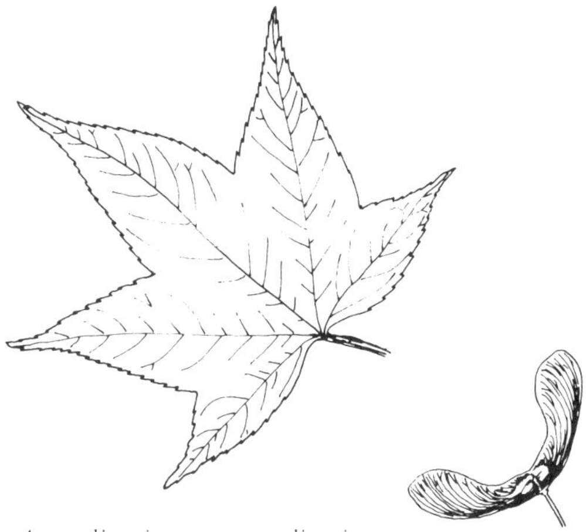

*Acer oliverianum* ssp. *oliverianum*

This subspecies is difficult to propagate from seed. Most failures are due seed that is too dry and too old. If seed is freshly collected and sown immediately, some success may be expected. The subspecies is also easy to graft on *A. palmatum,* so it can be made available.

A magnificent tree of this subspecies, about 60 years old and 12 m tall, is growing in the Zuiderpark in The Hague, The Netherlands. Another specimen is present in Westonbirt Arboretum, Great Britain.

SECTION: *Palmata* SERIES: *Sinensia*

## ACER SCHNEIDERIANUM Pax & Hoffmann (1922)

SYNONYM: *A. campbellii* ssp. *schneiderianum* (Pax & Hoffmann) Murray (1977).

TYPE: *C. K. Schneider 1281,* Kalapa to Liuhen, Sichuan Province, China; E; K; W.

EPITHET: *Schneiderianus,* after German botanist Camillo K. Schneider (1876–1951).

HABIT: A small tree to 6 m tall; young branches dark gray, current year's growth green or purple; twigs slender, glabrous.

LEAVES: 5-lobed, remotely serrate, chartaceous, somewhat glabrescent beneath, lobes obovate and shortly acuminate, 7–8 cm across, bases nearly cordate or truncate; petioles up to 5 cm long, red and flattish, glabrous or pilose.

INFLORESCENCES: In many-flowered, terminal corymbs.

FLOWERS: Andromonoecious, small, greenish yellow.

FRUITS: Samaras purplish red when young, pale yellow when mature; wings oblong or oblong-ovate, 6–7 mm wide, horizontally spreading; nutlets nearly globular, nerves prominent.

BARK AND BUDS: Smooth, gray or purplish.

HARDINESS: Zone VI (?).

DISTRIBUTION: Sichuan and Yunnan provinces, China, in mountains to 2800 m.

VARIETIES

var. *pubescens* Fang & Wu (1979), leaves pubescent.

var. *schneiderianum,* the typical variety.

CULTIVARS: None.

REFERENCES: Fang (1981a), Krüssmann (1976a), Murray (1970c, 1977).

*Acer schneiderianum* is yet another species not in cultivation in Western horticulture. It was described in 1922 by Pax and Hoffmann, and reported by Fang (1981a), the Chinese *Acer* specialist.

It is said to be a small tree and much like *Acer campbellii.* Until additional material becomes available, *A. schneiderianum* will be kept apart from the former species, even though it eventually might be synonymous.

SECTION: *Palmata* SERIES: *Sinensia*

## ACER SHANGSZEENSE Fang & Soong (1966)

TYPE: *S. C. Chun 5088,* Guangxi Province, China; IBSC.

EPITHET: *Shangszeensis,* after Shangsze, a district in Guangxi Province, China.

ILLUSTRATION: Fang (1981a).

HABIT: A small tree to 10 m tall; branches green to purplish black; twigs strong and glabrous; young growth green to purplish.

LEAVES: 7-lobed, coriaceous, glabrous, 9–12 cm across, bases cordate, lustrous green above, undersides pale green; lobes oblong-ovate or triangular-ovate; apices acuminate; margins crenulate; petioles up to 6 cm long, purplish and robust.

INFLORESCENCES: Corymbose, terminal.

FLOWERS: Sepals purplish; petals pale yellow; ovaries pilose.

FRUITS: Samaras about 3 cm long, falcate and purplish, diverging obtusely; nutlets nearly ovate, 8–10 mm thick.

BARK AND BUDS: Bark pale black.

HARDINESS: Zone VII.

DISTRIBUTION: Southwestern Guangxi Province, China, at 800–1000 m, on Mount Shiwandashan.

VARIETIES

var. *anfuense* Fang & Soong (1979), larger leaves and samaras.

var. *shangszeense,* the typical variety.

CULTIVARS: None.

REFERENCES: Fang (1981a), Murray (1970c).

At present, there is no living material of this species growing in the Western world. The species seems to be close to *Acer campbellii* and *A. campbellii* ssp. *flabellatum. Acer shangszeense* var. *shangszeense* is also related to the rather well-known *A. erianthum.* It is evaluated as a separate species until living material becomes available and comparative herbarium material has been located.

*Acer shangszeense*

*Acer sichourense*

SECTION: *Palmata* SERIES: *Sinensia*
ACER SICHOURENSE (Fang & Fang f.) Fang (1979)
BASIONYM: *A. angustilobum* var. *sichourense* Fang & Fang f. (1966).
TYPE: *K. M. Feng 11514*, Hsiangping shan, Sichour Hsien, Yunnan Province, China; PE, KUN.
EPITHET: *Sichourensis*, after Sichour, a district in Yunnan Province, China.
ILLUSTRATION: Fang (1981a).
HABIT: A tree to 10–15 m tall.
LEAVES: 5-lobed, palmate, the two basal lobes strongly underdeveloped, other lobe apices acuminate, 6–8 cm long and almost as wide, bases rounded or slightly subcordate.
FLOWERS: Not seen.
FRUITS: Samaras about 4 cm long, rather narrow, diverging at an angle of 90°, in short racemes.
HARDINESS: Zones VII–VIII.
DISTRIBUTION: Yunnan Province, China, in mountainous regions at 1200–1800 m.
CULTIVARS: None.
REFERENCE: Fang (1981a).

This species seems allied to *Acer campbellii* ssp. *wilsonii* and ssp. *sinense*. No living material is available. Eventually it might be included in *A. campbellii* ssp. *wilsonii*.

SECTION: *Palmata* SERIES: *Sinensia*
ACER SUNYIENSE Fang (1966)
TYPE: *C. S. Li 90716*, Sun-yi Hsien, Guangdong Province, China; IBSC.
EPITHET: *Sunyiensis*, after Sun-yi, a district in Guangdong Province, China.
HABIT: A small tree, sometimes large shrub, to 3 m tall.
LEAVES: 3- (to 5-) lobed, almost orbicular, 10–12 cm across.
FLOWERS: Unknown.
FRUITS: Samaras 3.5 cm long; wings acutely divergent, falcate, 1.2 cm wide.
HARDINESS: Unknown.
DISTRIBUTION: Guangdong Province, China.
CULTIVARS: None.
REFERENCES: Fang (1966, 1981a), Murray (1970c).

Fang considers this species very close to *Acer sinense* (*A. campbellii* ssp. *sinense*), and Murray agrees. There is no living material available in Western horticulture. When more knowledge and collections of this species become available it will most probably become a synonym of *A. campbellii* ssp. *sinense*.

SECTION: *Palmata* SERIES: *Sinensia*
ACER TAIPUENSE Fang (1966)
TYPE: *L. K. Li 202503;* Taipu Hsien, Guangdong Province, China; IBSC.
EPITHET: *Taipuensis*, after Taipu, a district in Guangdong Province, China.
HABIT: An evergreen tree about 5–10 m tall; branches purplish to dark green.
LEAVES: 3-lobed, coriaceous, 10–14 cm across, lobes caudate-lobulate; margins undulate; petioles up to 6 cm long, purple.
INFLORESCENCES: Paniculate, 15 cm long, glabrous.
FLOWERS: Not seen.
FRUITS: Samaras 3–5 cm long, horizontal.
HARDINESS: Unknown.
DISTRIBUTION: Eastern part of Guangdong Province in southeastern China.
CULTIVARS: None.
REFERENCES: Fang (1981a), Murray (1970c).

This is another taxon not yet in cultivation in the West. Its botanical status cannot be confirmed until additional herbarium and living materials become available. Possibly it is close to *Acer campbellii* ssp. *wilsonii*. Fang (1966) placed this taxon in his section *Oblonga*, subsection *Trifida* (formerly subsection *Buergeriana*), but in 1981 he allied it to *A. wilsonii*. Evergreen species are uncommon in series *Sinensia*, hence the uncertain position for this species in the classification proposed in the present volume.

SECTION: *Palmata* SERIES: *Sinensia*
ACER TONKINENSE Lecompte (1912) ssp. TONKINENSE
TYPE: *Bon*, Ninh-Binh, North Vietnam; P.
EPITHET: *Tonkinensis*, after Tonkin, North Vietnam.
ILLUSTRATION: Fang (1981a), de Jong (1976).
HABIT: A small tree or large shrub to 8–10 m tall; branches olive to green or purplish; twigs terete, waxy-pruinose, glabrous.
LEAVES: Shallowly 3-lobed or tridentate, leathery, 10–15 cm long and 7–11 cm wide; lobes more or less elliptic; apices acute; margins entire; bases round to subcordate; nerve axils tufted beneath; petioles 3 cm long; juvenile leaves coarsely serrate.
INFLORESCENCES: Paniculate, terminal, multiflowered.
FLOWERS: Sepals and anthers red; petals lobed, white; discs hairy.
FRUITS: Samaras 3 cm long, wings subhorizontal,

*Acer tonkinense* ssp. *tonkinense*

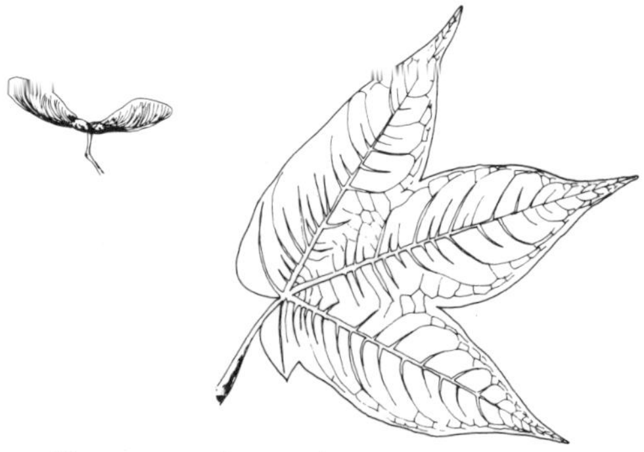

*Acer tonkinense* ssp. *kwangsiense*

falciform; nutlets almost ovate, 8 mm long and 6 mm wide.
BARK AND BUDS: Bark dark brown, smooth.
HARDINESS: Zone VIII–IX.
AUTUMN COLOR: Orange-yellow to red.
DISTRIBUTION: Guangxi and Yunnan provinces, China, at low altitudes; Tonkin, North Vietnam.
SUBSPECIES
- ssp. *kwangsiense* (Fang & Fang f.) Fang (1979); basionym is *A. kwangsiense* Fang & Fang f. (1966); leaves larger, 12–17 cm across, margins remotely serrate; see Plate 23.
- ssp. *liquidambarifolium* (Hu & Cheng) Fang (1979); basionym is *A. liquidambarifolium* Hu & Cheng (1948); leaves evenly lobed, 8–14 cm across.
- ssp. *tonkinense,* the typical subspecies.

CULTIVARS: None.
REFERENCES: Delendick (1979), Fang (1981a), de Jong (1976), Krüssmann (1976a), Murray (1970c), Valder (1975).

This very rare species was introduced into cultivation in 1985. Ten years prior to its introduction, Valder (1975) of Sydney University, Australia, wrote about a plant called *Acer tonkinense* that turned out to be *A. calcaratum* (which see).

In 1985 seed of *Acer tonkinense* ssp. *kwangsiense* was received and distributed in North American and Europe through the courtesy of Wang Dajun, emeritus curator of the Shanghai Botanic Garden, China. About 25 plants are now growing in The Netherlands, and several have been distributed to collections all over the world.

*Acer tonkinense* has the longest inflorescences of any species in series *Sinensia,* with many flowers on each terminal panicle. It is a tree with leathery, subcoriaceous, shallowly 3-lobed leaves, whose margins are entire. The cotyledons are large (1–2 cm across) and round rather than thin and lance-shaped, as is usual in species of this section. This feature suggests affinity to section *Macrantha.*

*Acer tonkinense* ssp. *liquidambarifolium*

SECTION: *Palmata* SERIES: *Sinensia*

## ACER TUTCHERI Duthie (1908)

SYNONYM: *A. oliverianum* var. *tutcheri* (Duthie) Metcalf ex Lee (1935).
TYPE: *W. J. Tutcher,* Lantao Island, Hong Kong; K.
EPITHET: *Tutcheri,* after Dr. Tutcher, a botanist and curator of the Hong Kong Botanic Garden.
HABIT: A small tree to 10 m tall; branches glabrous, purplish brown; twigs terete, pale green or purplish green.
LEAVES: 3-lobed, 5–10 cm across, subcoriaceous; lobes triangular-ovate, serrulate; bases round to subtruncate; vein axils tufted with hairs beneath; petioles about 3 cm long.
INFLORESCENCES: Terminal, short-corymbose or paniculate, 2–3 cm long.
FLOWERS: Andromonoecious, yellowish, appearing after leaves have developed; discs slightly villose; ovaries densely white pilose; petals obovate; sepals yellowish green, ovate-oblong, obtuse.
FRUITS: Samaras 2.5–3 cm long, diverging obtusely, spreading nearly horizontally, purplish; nutlets swollen, nearly ovate, 5 mm thick.
BARK AND BUDS: Bark purplish brown.
HARDINESS: Zones VII–VIII.
DISTRIBUTION: Hong Kong; Guangdong, Guangxi, and Yunnan provinces, China; with Chinese and Taiwanese variations, at 2500 m.

*Acer tutcheri*

VARIETIES: None in cultivation, although three have been described.
- var. *formosanum* Murray (1977), Taiwan.
- var. *serratifolium* Fang (1966), leaves 3- to 55-lobed, margins serrate; from Guangdong Province, China.
- var. *shimadai* Hayata (1911), samaras small; from Taiwan.

CULTIVARS: None.
REFERENCES: Fang (1981a), Koidzumi (1911), Li (1977), Murray (1970c, 1971).

This species is not in cultivation in western Europe or North America. It is reported to be a small tree, rather closely related to *Acer oliverianum*, with glabrous branches and 3-lobed leaves that are 5–10 cm across. It may be quite close to plants labeled *A. serrulatum*, a synonym of *A. oliverianum* ssp. *formosanum*. Living and herbarium materials are necessary to decide whether this is true or not.

SECTION: *Palmata* SERIES: *Sinensia*

## ACER WUYUANENSE Fang & Wu (1979)

TYPE: *C. H. Li & C. Chen 2204163*, Wuyuan Hsien, Jiangxi Province, China; LBG.
EPITHET: *Wuyuanensis*, after Wuyuan Hsien, Jiangxi Province, China.
ILLUSTRATION: Fang (1981a).
HABIT: A tree 5–7 m tall; twigs slender, glabrous, pale green or pale purplish green.
LEAVES: 5-lobed, 7–9 cm across, the basal lobes usually much smaller, other lobes parted obtusely to slightly below the middle of blades; apices acuminate; bases subcordate; blades dark green and glabrous above, pale purplish green when dried.
FLOWERS: Andromonoecious, in few-flowered racemes; sepals 5, pale purplish green, 2 mm long; petals 5, white.
FRUITS: Samaras horizontal; nutlets flattened, 3 cm long.
BARK AND BUDS: Bark dark gray, dark brown or purplish; winter buds very small.
HARDINESS: Zone VI (?).
DISTRIBUTION: Jiangxi Province, China, at 500–1200 m.

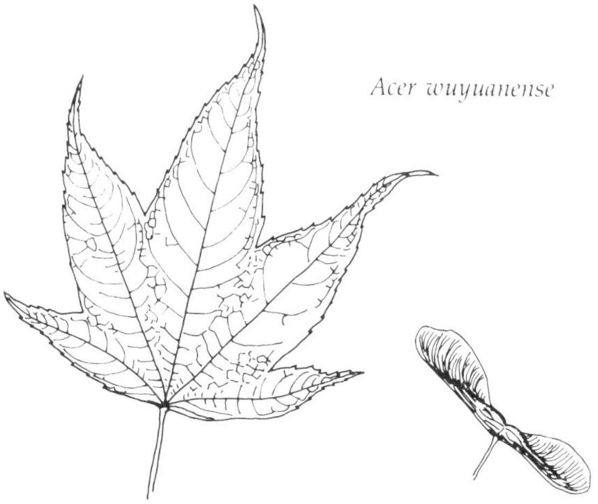

*Acer wuyuanense*

VARIETIES
- var. *trichopodum* Fang & Wu (1979), with smaller leaves and samaras; undersides of leaves and petals yellowish pilose.
- var. *wuyuanense*, the typical variety.

CULTIVARS: None.
REFERENCE: Fang (1981a).

This species is very closely allied to species such as *Acer oliverianum* and *A. elegantulum*, and to a lesser degree to *A. campbellii*. Seeds were received at Castle Howard, York, Great Britain, and some germinated in the spring of 1989. It is not yet possible to determine whether the status of this species is correct.

SECTION: *Palmata* SERIES: *Sinensia*

## ACER YAOSHANICUM Fang (1979)

TYPE: *S. S. Sin 21179*, Hsiangchow Hsien, Yaoshan region, Province, China; IBSC.
EPITHET: *Yaoshanicus*, after Yaoshan, a mountainous region in Guangxi Province, China.
ILLUSTRATION: Fang (1981a).
HABIT: A deciduous tree, slender, glabrous; twigs thin; older wood about 2 mm thick.
LEAVES: 3- to 5-lobed, apices acuminate, thin,

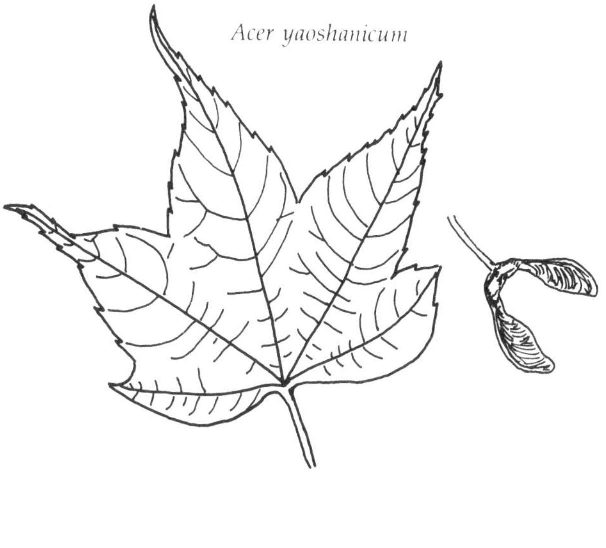

*Acer yaoshanicum*

papery, outline rotund, 4–4.5 cm long and 5–6 cm wide, bases cordate, green above, olive beneath.
FLOWERS: In few-flowered inflorescences.
FRUITS: Samaras small, only 1.5 cm long, in small trusses about 5 cm long; wings about 5 mm long, diverging at an acute angle. purplish nutlets 2 mm in diameter.
BARK AND BUDS: Bark dark gray or pale black.
DISTRIBUTION: Eastern part of Guangxi Province, China, at 1600–2000 m.
CULTIVARS: None.
REFERENCE: Fang (1981a).

No further information is available on this new species, which might be allied to *Acer campbelli* ssp. *sinense.* Fang (1979) reports it as being allied to *A. sinense* Pax and *A. chingii* Hu.

SERIES PENNINERVIA Metcalf
TYPE SPECIES: ***Acer laevigatum*** Wallich.
HABIT: Trees partly evergreen; terminal buds usually abortive.
LEAVES: Unlobed, coriaceous; margins entire to serrate.
INFLORESCENCES: Large, usually elongated rachises, 20–250 flowers; pedicels of postanthesis male flowers partly dropped.
FLOWERS: Sepals often somewhat recurved; petals often lobed; disc sometimes pubescent.
FRUITS: Parthenocarpic tendency low.
SPECIES
*A. cordatum* Pax.
*A. crassum* Hu & Cheng.
*A. erythranthum* Gagnepain.
*A. eucalyptoides* Fang & Wu.
*A. fabri* Hance.
*A. hainanense* Chun & Fang.
*A. kiukiangense* Hu & Cheng.
*A. laevigatum* Wallich.
*A. lucidum* Metcalf.
*A. oligocarpum* Fang & Hu.
*A. sino-oblongum* Metcalf.
*A. yinkunii* Fang.
REFERENCE: De Jong (1976).

This series includes mainly subtropical or tropical trees, with evergreen, rarely deciduous, unlobed leaves. It shares some morphological characteristics with series *Sinensia* (namely, inflorescences, flowers, and fruit). Many of the 12 species in this series are not in cultivation so little is known about them. Some of them may be sunk in synonymy or reduced in rank under other species or infraspecific taxa when more herbarium and living materials become available.

All the species of this series are endemic to China and are only suitable as garden plants if planted in very sheltered locations in warm temperate or subtropical areas.

SECTION: *Palmata* SERIES: *Penninervia*
ACER CORDATUM Pax (1889)
SYNONYM: *A. laevigatum* ssp. *cordatum* (Pax) Murray (1978).
TYPE: *A. Henry 7721,* Hubei Province, China (original destroyed in Berlin in World War II); lectotype K; isotypes A, K, G.
EPITHET: *Cordatus,* heart-shaped.
ILLUSTRATIONS: Engler & Prantl (1907), Krüssmann (1976a), Pax (1902).
HABIT: A tree or large shrub 3–10 m tall, up to 13 m tall in native habitat; young stems gray and glabrous.
LEAVES: Persistent, ovate, unlobed, 6 cm long and 3.5 cm wide, 3-veined, upper surfaces brilliant green, undersides bluish green; margins remotely serrate; bases cordate; apices acuminate; petioles 1–1.5 cm.
FLOWERS: Very small, in glabrous, reddish corymbs.
FRUITS: Samaras 2.5 cm long, wings spreading at a wide angle.
BARK AND BUDS: Bark gray and smooth.
HARDINESS: Zones VII–VIII.
DISTRIBUTION: Hubei, Zhejiang, and Fujian provinces, China, in mountainous areas at 500–1200 m.
VARIETIES
var. *cordatum,* the typical variety.
var. *microcordatum* Metcalf (1932), with smaller leaves.
var. *subtrinervium* (Metcalf) Fang; basionym is *A. subtrinervium* Metcalf; leaves 3-nerved.
REFERENCES: Fang (1981a), Krüssmann (1976a), Murray (1970c, 1977), Pax (1902).

Pax described this species, which is very rare in cultivation. A specimen at Bodnant Gardens, Wales, died in the winter of 1981–1982.

It is difficult to determine whether varieties *microcordatum* and *subtrinervium* deserve varietal rank, as adequate material is unavailable, and comparative studies still need to be done.

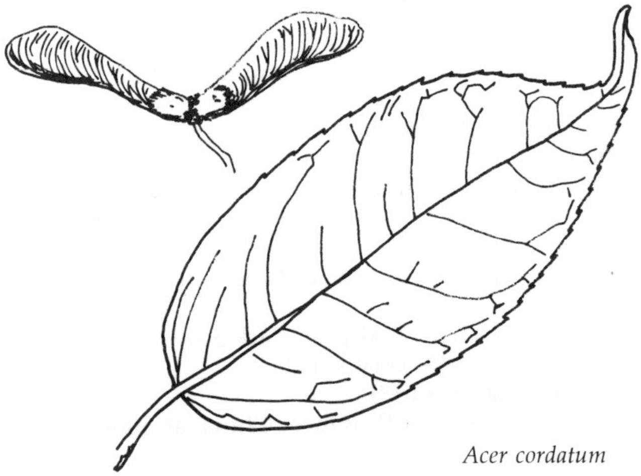

*Acer cordatum*

SECTION: *Palmata* SERIES: *Penninervia*

ACER CRASSUM Hu & Cheng (1948)

TYPES: PE; K; syntypes *Wang 87087, 88839,* Fooning, Yunnan Province, China.

EPITHET: *Crassus,* thick, fat.

ILLUSTRATION: Fang (1981a).

HABIT: A small tree 10–12 m tall; branches brown to gray, bud scales many.

LEAVES: Coriaceous, elliptic-oblong, 9–15 cm long and 2.5–4 cm wide, penniveined, lustrous green above, glaucous beneath; margins entire; petioles thick, 1 cm long.

INFLORESCENCES: Paniculate, terminal, villous.

FLOWERS: 5-merous.

FRUITS: Samaras 2.5–5 cm long, reddish, somewhat villous.

HARDINESS: Zones VII–VIII.

DISTRIBUTION: District of Foo-ning, Yunnan Province, China, at about 1000 m.

REFERENCES: Fang (1981a), de Jong (1976), Murray (1970c).

This species is not in cultivation in the West, but T. R. Dudley reports that it was in cultivation in China at the Hangzhou Botanic Gardens. It is a small tree with coriaceous, oblong leaves not unlike those of *Acer laevigatum.*

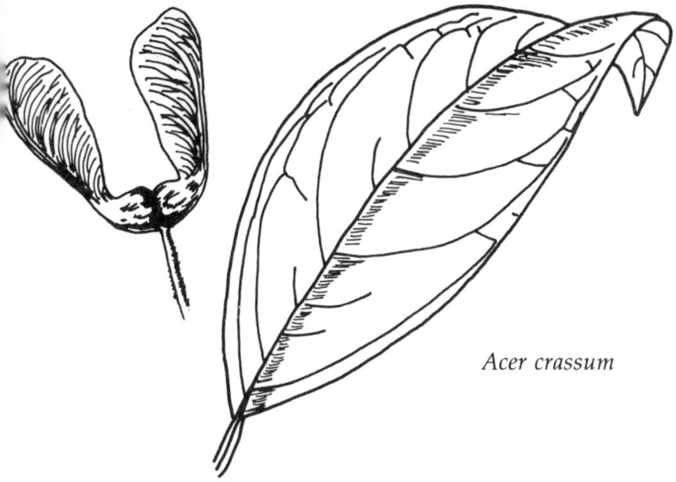

*Acer crassum*

SECTION: *Palmata* SERIES: *Penninervia*

ACER ERYTHRANTHUM Gagnepain (1948)

TYPE: Syntypes *Poilane 239833, 30049,* Quang-tri Province, Annam, Vietnam; P.

EPITHET: *Erythranthus,* red flowering.

ILLUSTRATION: Gagnepain (1950).

HABIT: A tree to 12 m tall; main stems 35 cm in diameter; branches and stems greenish brown.

LEAVES: Unlobed, entire, broadly lanceolate, 6–12 cm long and 2–3 cm wide; apices acuminate; margins entire.

FLOWERS: 5-merous, reddish, in short corymbs.

FRUITS: Samaras 4–5 cm long, spreading at an angle of about 135°; nutlets thick, 5–8 mm in diameter.

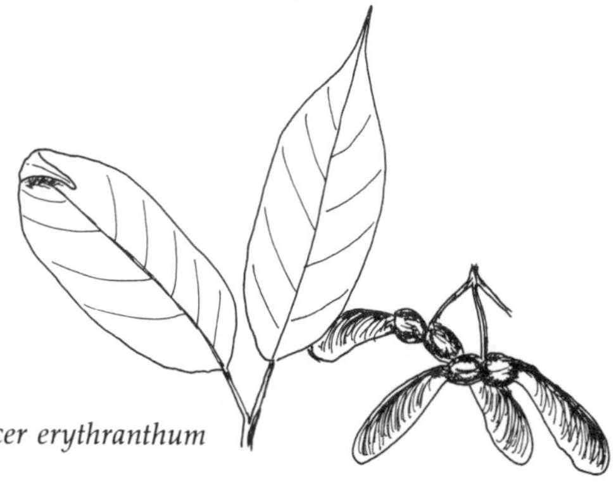

*Acer erythranthum*

DISTRIBUTION: Mountains of Braian, Dong-temple, province of Quang-tri in Annam, Vietnam.

REFERENCES: Gagnepain (1950), Murray (1970c).

This species from Vietnam is not in cultivation in the West. According to Murray it is very close to *Acer laevigatum,* a view supported by others. It must be recognized as a species until further living or herbarium material becomes available.

SECTION: *Palmata* SERIES: *Penninervia*

ACER EUCALYPTOIDES Fang & Wu (1979)

TYPE: *Exp. Pl. Tshing-heu & Tibet 5977,* Xizang Province, Ne-ma-mu Hsien; HNWP; PE.

EPITHET: *Eucalyptoides,* like *Eucalyptus.*

ILLUSTRATION: Fang (1981a).

HABIT: A tree to 15–20 m tall.

LEAVES: Unlobed, oblong-elliptic, 8–15 cm long, 4–6 cm wide, lower surfaces glaucous; petioles purple, up to 5 cm long.

INFLORESCENCES: Corymbose, up to 7 cm long.

FRUITS: Samaras yellow-green, 2–3 cm long, distinctly spreading at an angle of 150°; wings falcate, very narrow, 5–8 mm wide; nutlets 3 mm in diameter.

HARDINESS: Zones VI–VII.

DISTRIBUTION: Xizang Province (formerly Tibet), China, in mountainous areas to 2200 m.

REFERENCE: Fang (1981a).

Possibly this species should be transferred to section *Pentaphylla* as it seems related to *Acer wangchii.*

*Acer eucalyptoides*

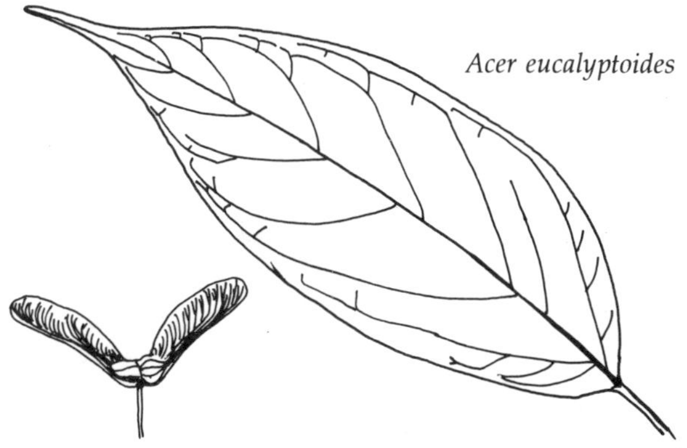

SECTION: *Palmata* SERIES: *Penninervia*

## ACER FABRI Hance (1884)

SYNONYMS

*A. reticulatum* Champion (1851), pro parte.
*A. laevigatum* var. *fargesii* Veitch (1904).
*A. fargesii* (Veitch) Rehder (1905).
*A. laevigatum* var. *reticulatum* (Champion) Rehder (1905).
*A. prainii* Léveillé (1912).
*A. fabri* var. *rubrocarpum* Metcalf (1932).
*A. laevigatum* ssp. *reticulatum* (Champion) Murray (1977), pro parte.

TYPE: *E. Faber 22220,* Lo-fau-shan, Guangdong Province, China; K; HK.

EPITHET: *Fabri,* after Rev. Ernst Faber, who collected the plant in China 1887–1891.

ILLUSTRATIONS: Fang (1981a), Krüssmann (1976a).

HABIT: A tree in native habitat to 20 m tall, never more than 8–10 m tall in favorable conditions in cultivation, mostly evergreen, sometimes deciduous; young stems thin, red at first, gray-green when ripening, glabrous.

LEAVES: Fully unlobed, oblong, 5–15 cm long and 3–4 cm wide, shining dark green on both sides, leathery; apices acuminate; margins entire or very finely serrated, never toothed; bases cuneate (differing in this characteristic from *A. cordatum,* which has cordate leaf bases); petioles 2–3 cm long.

INFLORESCENCES: Paniculate, erect, terminal, 4–6 cm long.

FLOWERS: 5-merous, red, on short lateral branches, with purple sepals and white petals.

FRUITS: Samaras about 1–3 cm long, reddish-purplish, obtuse; wings with a wide angle; nutlets rounded, beautifully red in an upright position.

BARK AND BUDS: Bark smooth and gray.

HARDINESS: Zones VII–VIII.

DISTRIBUTION: Hong Kong, eastern Himalaya, and China in Fujian, Hubei, Sichuan, Hainan, Guangdong, Guangxi, and Zhejiang provinces.

*Acer fabri*

VARIETIES

var. *fabri,* the typical variety.
var. *gracillimum* Fang (1979), leaves 4–4.5 cm long and 2–2.5 cm wide; petals 1 cm long; fruits 3 cm long; samaras 1.8–2 cm long and borne only 2–3 per inflorescence.
var. *megalocarpum* Hu & Cheng (1948), samaras 6 cm long.
var. *virescens* Fang (1932), leaves villose; samaras large.

REFERENCES: Bean (1970), Elwes & Henry (1908), Fang (1981a), Krüssmann (1976a), Murray (1970c, 1977), Oterdoom (1982), Rehder (1986 facs.).

This tender species from southern China is suitable only for the very mildest regions of Great Britain, Ireland, and North America. It was described by Hance in 1884, and introduced to Great Britain in 1901 by E. H. Wilson.

*Acer fabri* grows into a tree 8–10 m high in cultivation and reaches twice that height in its native habitat. Its leaves are fully unlobed and oblong, not unlike those of *A. laevigatum,* with which *A. fabri* can be confused. However, the leaves of the former are more undulate and their margins are not so entire as in true *A. fabri,* which is also more evergreen and, unfortunately, more tender than *A. laevigatum.* Fine specimens are found in Guangdong Botanical Garden.

*Acer fabri* is also allied to *A. cordatum,* from which it differs in its cuneate leaf bases, and local populations in Hong Kong have been called *A. reticulatum.* Some varieties have been recognized by Chinese botanists that differ mainly in the size of the samaras.

This species can be propagated from seed and grafted on *Acer palmatum.* Grafting on its nearest ally, *A. laevigatum,* has been done successfully several times.

SECTION: *Palmata* SERIES: *Penninervia*

## ACER HAINANENSE Chun & Fang (1966)

TYPE: *C. S. Liu 25444,* Hainan Province, China; PE.

EPITHET: *Hainanensis,* after Hainan, a province (and an island) of China north of the South China Sea.

ILLUSTRATION: Fang (1981a).

HABIT: An evergreen tree to 10 m tall.

LEAVES: Unlobed, 5–7 cm long and 2.5–4 cm wide; apices acute, coriaceous, slightly acuminate.

INFLORESCENCES: 5–6 cm long, paniculate.

FLOWERS: Light yellow, andromonoecious, sparsely pilose; pedicels very slender.

FRUITS: In short clusters; samaras spreading to an angle of 135°; nutlets 5 mm thick.

BARK AND BUDS: Bark dark brown or gray, young growth purplish green.

HARDINESS: Zone VIII, or even more tender.

DISTRIBUTION: Hainan and Guangdong provinces, China, at 500–1400 m.

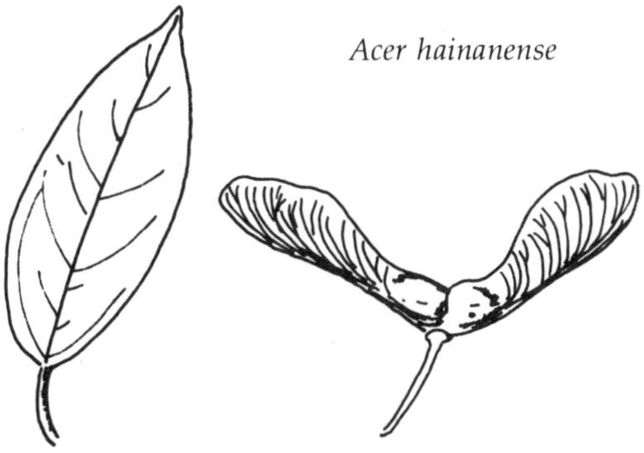
*Acer hainanense*

REFERENCE: Fang (1981a).

This species is not known in cultivation in the West, although it is present in Guangzhou and Hangzhou botanic gardens. It is probably closely allied to *Acer cordatum* and *A. laevigatum*.

SECTION: *Palmata* SERIES: *Penninervia*

ACER KIUKIANGENSE Hu & Cheng (1948)

TYPE: *T. T. Yu 19444,* Kiukiang Valley, Guangdong Province, China; PE.
EPITHET: *Kiukiangensis,* after Kiukiang, a valley in Guangdong Province, China.
ILLUSTRATION: Fang (1981a).
HABIT: A tree or large shrub to 12 m tall.
LEAVES: Persistent, ovate and unlobed, 7–9 cm long and 2.5–4 cm wide; petioles short.
FLOWERS: Not seen.
FRUITS: Not seen.
HARDINESS: Unknown.
REFERENCES: Fang (1981a), Murray (1970c).

Murray considers this species a synonym of *Acer cordatum,* without giving reasons. As no living or herbarium material is available, it is treated as a species in the present volume.

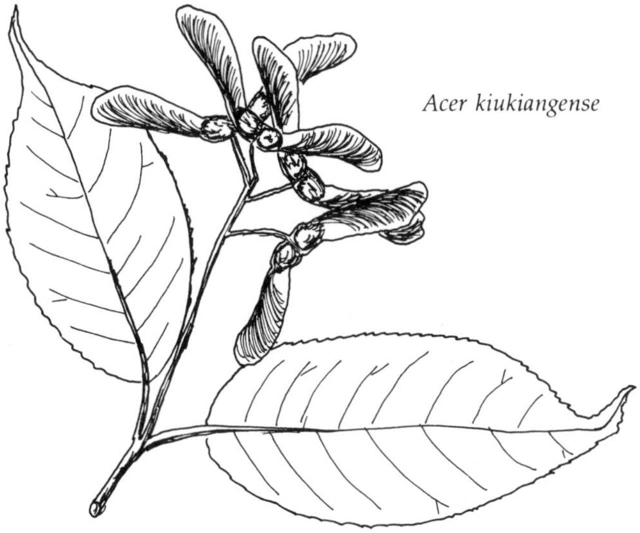
*Acer kiukiangense*

SECTION: *Palmata* SERIES: *Penninervia*

ACER LAEVIGATUM Wallich (1830)

SYNONYMS
- *A. laevigatum* ssp. *reticulatum* (Champion) Murray, pro parte.
- *A. reticulatum* Champion (1851), pro parte.
- *A. laevigatum* var. *angustum* Pax (1886).
- *A. oblongum* var. *angustum* (Pax) Wesmael (1890).

TYPE: *N. Wallich 1223,* Nepal; K; PH.
EPITHET: *Laevigatus,* smooth.
ILLUSTRATIONS: Plate 24; Fang (1981a), Gagnepain (1950), Krüssmann (1976a).
HABIT: A tree 10–15 m tall, with a rounded crown; branches and stems olive green or sometimes purplish, smooth.
LEAVES: Persistent, lanceolate-oblong, 3-veined at the bases, 8–15 cm long and 3.5 cm wide, unlobed, olive green, reticulate, glabrous above, some tufts of hairs in the vein axils beneath; margins entire or serrate when young; petioles about 1 cm long.
INFLORESCENCES: Corymbose-paniculate, terminal.
FLOWERS: Yellow.
FRUITS: Samaras purplish, upright, 4–7 cm long.
BARK AND BUDS: Young shoots rather like those of *A. palmatum.*
HARDINESS: Zones VII–VIII.
AUTUMN COLOR: Yellow, but very often coloring only when the tree is placed in an unfavorable site, after which the leaves may drop.
DISTRIBUTION: Southeast Asia, Sichuan Province, Nepal; also throughout central and southeastern China to Hong Kong. In mountain forests at 1600–2000 m, but not forming thickets by itself.
CHROMOSOME NUMBER: $2n = 26$.

VARIETIES
- var. *dimorphifolium* (Metcalf) Fang & Hu (1966), close to *A. fabri,* with rougher leaves, margins entire, unlobed, base oval; from Fujian Province, China.

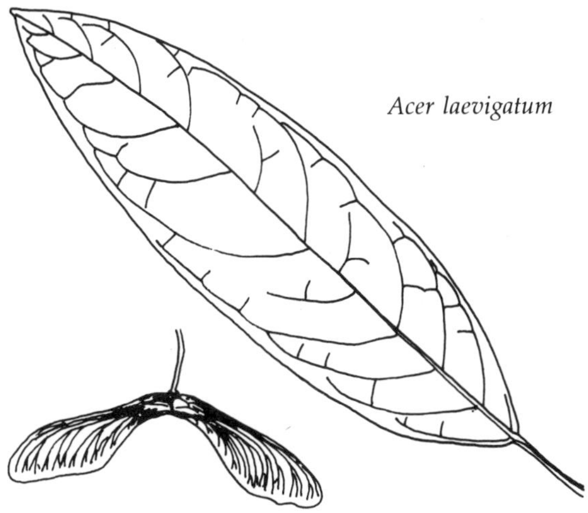
*Acer laevigatum*

var. *laevigatum*, typical variety.
var. *salweenense* (W. W. Smith) Cowan ex Fang (1939), leaves pubescent; Xizang and Yunnan provinces, China, and North Burma.

REFERENCES: Bean (1970), Fang (1981a), Gagnepain (1950), Krüssmann (1976a), Murray (1970c), Oterdoom (1982), Pax (1902), Rehder (1986 facs.).

A tender species from southeastern Asia, *Acer laevigatum* was described by Wallich in 1830 and is only rarely found in gardens in very mild regions in southern England, Ireland, and North America.

It grows into a tree that has long lanceolate leaves with remotely toothed leaf margins. Juvenile leaves have markedly serrate margins.

This species can only be confused with *Acer fabri*, its closest relative, which is also very rare. *Acer erythranthum*, with less entire margins, can hardly be distinguished from either *A. fabri* or *A. laevigatum*, but is maintained here as a species, as any living material is not available for close examination. Thus, while *A. fabri*, *A. erythrantheum*, and *A. laevigatum* are treated separately in the present volume, they might one day be merged into one species (i.e., *A. laevigatum*).

Propagation by seed is possible, but grafting on *Acer palmatum* produces stronger plants.

SECTION: *Palmata* SERIES: *Penninervia*

## ACER LUCIDUM Metcalf (1932)

TYPE: *K. P. To & E. H. Groff 104*, Guangdong Province, China; PE No. 2864; A.
EPITHET: *Lucidus*, shining.
ILLUSTRATION: Plate 25.
HABIT: A tree to 5–6 m tall; branches red-brown to gray; bud scales few.
LEAVES: Persistent, somewhat leathery, 7–10 cm long and 2.5 cm wide, lanceolate, lustrous green above, glaucous beneath; margins entire; petioles short, 1–2 cm long.
INFLORESCENCES: Corymbose.
FLOWERS: Yellow.
FRUITS: Samaras erect, 2.5 cm long.
HARDINESS: Zone VIII.
DISTRIBUTION: Guangdong Province, China, at 800–1200 m.
REFERENCES: Fang (1981a), Murray (1970c).

At one time this Chinese species was introduced into cultivation at Boskoop, The Netherlands, but the two plants died suddenly, so the species was lost to cultivation. *Acer lucidum* is reported to be a tree, with a rust brown bark and persistent leaves, much longer than wide, of the same shape as those of *A. fabri*.

SECTION: *Palmata* SERIES: *Penninervia*

## ACER OLIGOCARPUM Fang & Hu (1979)

TYPE: *Exp. Pl. Tsingh & Tibet 3063*, Xizang, Tesing Bridge, Mei-to Hsien, China; PE.
EPITHET: *Oligocarpus*, with few fruits.
HABIT: A deciduous tree to 10–12 m tall; twigs terete; young growth pale green.
LEAVES: Entire, unlobed, 8–10 cm long and 4 cm wide, with shortly acuminate mucros, few-veined.
INFLORESCENCES: Corymbose, slender.
FLOWERS: Not seen.
FRUITS: Samaras glabrous, small, diverging at an angle of about 90°; few fruits to a cluster, frequently only 2–4; nutlets swollen, 8 mm in diameter.
BARK AND BUDS: Bark gray.
HARDINESS: Zones VII–VIII.
DISTRIBUTION: Southern Xizang Province, China.
REFERENCE: Fang (1981a).

This species is closely related to *Acer cordatum* and might be included in the latter taxon when living material becomes available for comparison. Fang & Hu (1979) state that their *A. oligocarpum* is allied strongly to *A. kiukiangense*, but is noticeably different from it by having leaves with fewer veins, corymbose and slender infructescences with only 2–4 fruits, and glabrous samaras diverging at an acute angle.

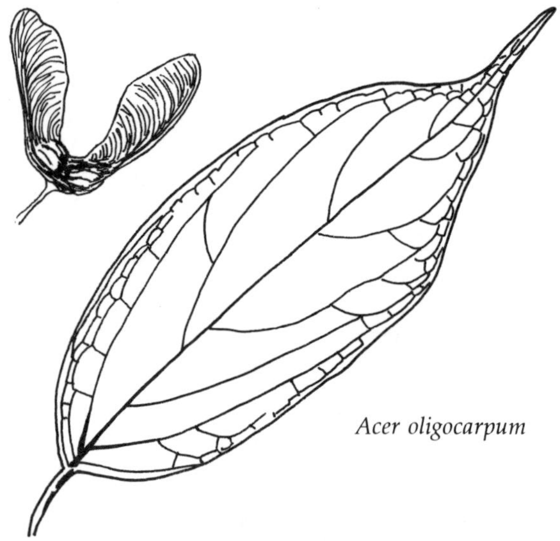

*Acer oligocarpum*

SECTION: *Palmata* SERIES: *Penninervia*

## ACER SINO-OBLONGUM Metcalf (1932)

SYNONYM: *A. oblongum* sensu Bentham (1861) non Wallich ex DC.
TYPE: Syntypes *Wright 72*, Hong Kong at A; *Ford*, Hong Kong at K.
EPITHET: *Sino-oblongus*, combination of *Sino*, meaning "Chinese" and *oblongum*, implying a Chinese *A. oblongum*.

ILLUSTRATION: Fang (1981a).
HABIT: A small tree 5–7 m tall; branches purplish brown, bud scales few; twigs slender, glabrous; young growth thin, purplish; old branches with ovate lenticels.
LEAVES: Elliptic, coriaceous, persistent, 6–8 cm long and 2 cm wide, glaucous beneath; apices acuminate; bases rounded; margins entire; petioles 2.5 cm long.
INFLORESCENCES: Corymbose, terminal.
FLOWERS: Yellow-green, andromonoecious; sepals 5, ovate-oblong; petals 5, oblanceolate.
FRUITS: Samaras 2 cm long, convex; wings acute; nutlets swollen, 8 mm thick.
HARDINESS: Zones VII–VIII.
DISTRIBUTION: Guangdong Province and southern China in coastal areas, and Hong Kong.
REFERENCES: Fang (1981a), Krüssmann (1976a), Murray (1970c), Oterdoom (1982).

*Acer sino-oblongum* is not closely related to *A. oblongum,* as the latter species is placed in section *Pentaphylla,* not in section *Palmata*. The species is believed not to be in cultivation in Europe or North America, but it was seen in the Botanic Garden of Guangzhou by members of the International Dendrology Society during their 1981 tour of China. It is a small tree with persistent, coriaceous, elliptical leaves.

The similarity of the names *Acer oblongum* and *A. sino-oblongum* may be confusing. However, once a name has been validly published, a plant must be called by its scientific name, not by any implied meaning or common name.

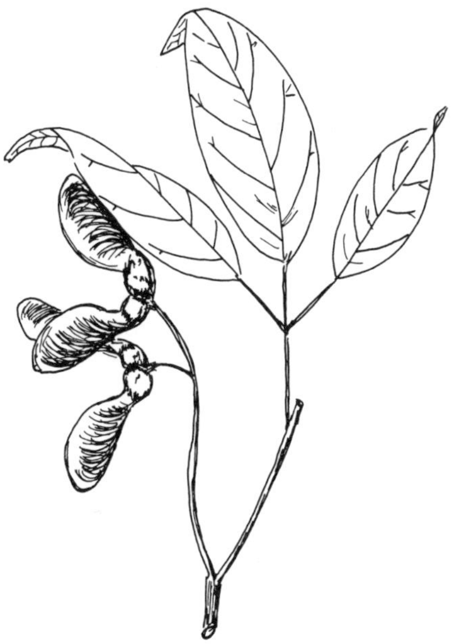

*Acer sino-oblongum*

SECTION: *Palmata* SERIES: *Penninervia*

ACER YINKUNII Fang (1966)

TYPE: *Yin Kun Lee, Po 1546,* Tu-an Hsien, western Guangxi Province, China; IBSC.
EPITHET: *Yinkunii,* after Yin Kun Lee Po, who first collected this species.
ILLUSTRATION: Fang (1981a).
HABIT: A small tree 3–5 m tall; branches purplish gray to brown; bud scales imbricate; young growth purplish.
LEAVES: Oblong-ovate, 3–6 cm long and 1.5–2 cm wide, glaucuous beneath; nerves inconspicuous; apices caudate-attenuate, 2 cm long; margins entire and undulate; bases rounded to broadly cuneate; petioles 2.5 cm long, purplish.
INFLORESCENCES: Corymbose, 2–2.5 cm long.
FLOWERS: Purplish, sparsely pilose. Other flower characteristics not known.
FRUITS: Samaras purplish, suberect, 2.5 cm long; nutlets ovoid and 7 mm thick.
BARK AND BUDS: Old bark has elliptic lenticels.
HARDINESS: Zones VII–VIII.
DISTRIBUTION: Western Guangxi Province, China, at 1000–2000 m.
REFERENCES: Fang (1981a), Murray (1970c).

*Acer yinkunii* is close to *A. cordatum,* maybe even synonymous, but no living material is available for comparison, and it is not possible at this time to investigate the pertinent herbarium specimens.

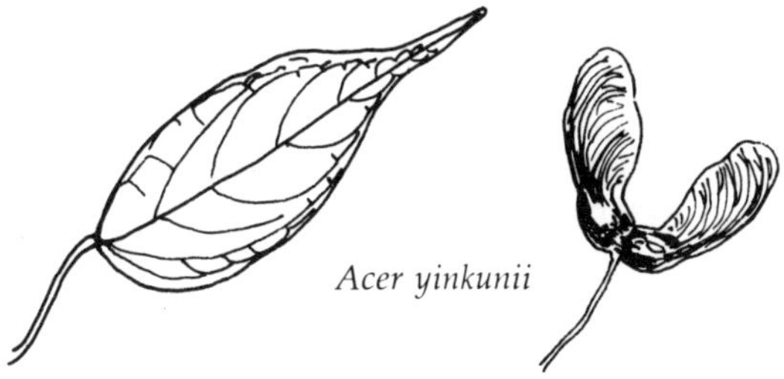

*Acer yinkunii*

## SECTION WARDIANA (de Jong) de Jong, comb. &. stat. nov.

BASIONYM: *Acer,* section *Macrantha* series *Wardiana* de Jong, Meded. Landb. Wageningen 76(2):147. 1976.
TYPE SPECIES: ***Acer wardii*** W. W. Smith (1917).
HABIT: Small trees or shrubs; young shoots with stiff hairs.
LEAVES: 3-lobed; margins serrulate.
INFLORESCENCES: Upright corymbose, with small cincinni; secondary axes opposite; bracts very distinct.
FLOWERS: Perianths red, reflexed at close of anthesis; discs amphistaminal; postanthesis male flowers shed stamens first.
FRUITS: Nutlets rather flat.

SPECIES: *A. wardii* W. W. Smith.
REFERENCE: De Jong (1976).

This newly established section includes only one aberrant species that has some characteristics of the sections *Palmata* and *Macrantha. Acer wardii* is a small tree from Upper Burma (now Myanmar) and Yunnan Province, China, and is not in cultivation in the West.

SECTION: *Wardiana*
ACER WARDII W. W. Smith (1917)
SYNONYM: *A. mirabile* Handel-Mazzetti (1924).
TYPE: *F. Kingdon Ward 1614,* Upper Burma; E.
EPITHET: *Wardii,* after English plant hunter Frank Kingdon Ward (1885–1958).
ILLUSTRATION: Fang (1981a).
HABIT: A small tree to 10 m tall, purplish branches.
LEAVES: 3-lobed, 6–9 cm across; lobes ovate-triangular, opules attenuate-caudate to 3 cm long; margins serrulate; bases subcordate; vein axils rufous-pilose beneath; petioles purplish, 3–5 cm long.
INFLORESCENCES: Paniculate-racemose, terminal and lateral, with large bracts, similar to inflorescences in section *Palmata* but differing by having amphistaminal discs and two pairs of bud scales.
FLOWERS: Purplish, with a reflexed perianth; male flowers drop the stamens first.
FRUITS: Samaras purplish, 2–3 cm long, wings obtuse; nutlets flat.
BARK AND BUDS: Bark inconspicuously striped; buds valvate.
HARDINESS: Zone VII or VIII.
AUTUMN COLOR: Not seen.
DISTRIBUTION: Upper Burma; Yunnan Province and eastern Xizang, China; and Assam, to 3000 m.
REFERENCES: Bean (1970), Fang (1981a), de Jong (1976, 1977), Krüssmann (1976a), Murray (1970c).

*Acer wardii* grows in the mountainous regions of the Chinese-Burmese border. Frank Kingdon Ward discovered it in 1914, and George Forrest, a Scottish plant explorer, introduced it to Great Britain, where it proved to be tender.

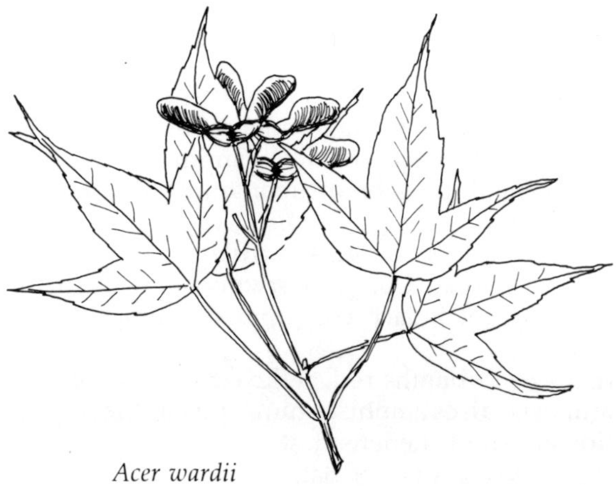
*Acer wardii*

Today it is a very rare species—only a few arboreta have ever listed it in their collections. A tree at Trewithen Gardens, Cornwall, Great Britain, died in the winter of 1962–1963, and now this species is probably no longer in cultivation in the West. It is not available in the trade.

The species was described by Professor W. W. Smith, who considered it near to *Acer campbellii* ssp. *sinense.* However, it differs in some morphological characteristics from the latter and the other species of section *Palmata.* De Jong places it here in a new section, *Wardiana,* separated from section *Macrantha.* Delendick included it in section *Palmata,* a view unacceptable to the present author. The species of section *Palmata* all have some morphological characteristics in common, which is not the case in *A. wardii. Acer wardii* differs by having two pairs of bud scales and extrastaminal discs, and does not have the terminal buds typical of section *Palmata.*

*Acer wardii* is an aberrant relative of the snakebark maples, although it differs from them (de Jong 1976). It grows into a small tree bearing 3-lobed leaves and purplish flowers in terminal trusses.

## SECTION MACRANTHA Pax

**TYPE SPECIES: *Acer pensylvanicum*** L.
HABIT: Deciduous trees, more often shrubs; branches often with white stripes; axillary buds stalked.
LEAVES: Undivided or 3- to 5-, sometimes 7-lobed, often caudate-acuminate; margins serrate.
BUD SCALES: Always 2-paired, valvate, red or green-red.
INFLORESCENCES: Racemose, rarely corymbose, terminal and axillary, 10–25 flowered.
FLOWERS: 5-merous; perianth green-yellow or reddish; discs intrastaminal; stamens 8.
FRUITS: Nutlets convex, more often rather flat, one side convex, the other side convex with a hole in the center or concave, parthenocarpic tendency variable—weak to modest.
SEEDLINGS: Cotyledons small, elliptic.
SPECIES AND INFRASPECIFIC TAXA

- *A. capillipes* Maximowicz
- *A. caudatifolium* Hayata
- *A. crataegifolium* Siebold & Zuccarini
- *A. davidii* Franchet ssp. *davidii.*
- *A. davidii* ssp. *grosseri* (Pax) de Jong, comb. & stat. nov.
- *A. laisuense* Fang & Hu.

*A. micranthum* Siebold & Zuccarini.
*A. morifolium* Koidzumi (1914).
*A. pectinatum* ssp. *forrestii* (Diels) Murray.
*A. pectinatum* ssp. *laxiflorum* (Pax) Murray.
*A. pectinatum* ssp. *maximowiczii* (Pax) Murray.
*A. pectinatum* Wallich ex Nicholson ssp. *pectinatum.*
*A. pectinatum* ssp. *taronense* (Handel-Mazzetti) Murray.
*A. pensylvanicum* L.
*A. rubescens* Hayata.
*A. rufinerve* Siebold & Zuccarini.
*A. sikkimense* ssp. *metcalfii* (Rehder) de Jong, comb. & stat. nov.
*A. sikkimense* Miquel ssp. *sikkimense.*
*A. tegmentosum* Maximowicz.
*A. tschonoskii* ssp. *koreanum.*
*A. tschonoskii* Maximowicz ssp. *tschonoskii.*

REFERENCE: De Jong (1976).

Commonly known as the snakebark maples, these important trees in horticulture form a fairly homogeneous group. All are small trees or large shrubs, with deciduous leaves and conspicuously white-striped bark.

Section *Macrantha* includes 14 species, with several subspecies. The Japanese species and the one North American species are easily distinguishable, but the Chinese species, which are situated in the Himalayas, are still in a state of evolution and diversification. Several taxa formerly regarded as species have been reduced to subspecific rank.

SECTION: *Macrantha*

ACER CAPILLIPES Maximowicz (1867)

SYNONYM: *A. pensylvanicum* ssp. *capillipes* (Maximowicz) Wesmael (1890).

TYPE: *Tschonoski,* Senano, Honshu, Japan; isotypes BM; E; G.

COMMON NAMES: Ashibosa urinoki, Hosoe kaede, Roter Schlangenhaut-Ahorn, Urika nishiki.

EPITHET: *Capillipes,* hair foot, referring to the stalks of the samaras, which are as thin as hair.

ILLUSTRATIONS: Plates 26, 27; Bean (1970), Hunt (1978a), de Jong (1977), Koidzumi (1911), Krüssmann (1976a), Kurata (1964–1976), Satake et al. (1989).

HABIT: A tree or sometimes a large shrub with several stems, to 12 m tall in native habitat, not as tall in cultivation; densely branched; slender long shoots on strongly growing specimens.

LEAVES: 3- to 5-lobed, although sometimes the leaves seem to be unlobed, dark green, red when unfolding, 6–12 cm long and almost as wide, bases subcordate, lobes conspicuously triangular with slender apices, side lobes much shorter, doubly serrate and glabrous; veins and petioles usually red.

FLOWERS: Greenish white in pendant, slender racemes, 6–12 cm long; male and female flowers usually appear on different branches; some branches bear many fruits, while others bear none.

*Acer capillipes*

FRUITS: Numerous, small, short-winged, glabrous, 1.5–2.5 cm long; wings somewhat rounded at tips, underdeveloped, spreading almost horizontally.

BARK AND BUDS: Bark very distinctive, with white stripes on a reddish green surface, fading to faintly white stripes on a green background in older trees; leaf buds often on short stalks; young shoots purplish red, not waxy, glabrous.

HARDINESS: Zone V.

AUTUMN COLOR: Crimson to dark red, occasionally orange.

DISTRIBUTION: Japan, mountain forests Chichibu Range, Honshu, and Shikoku islands.

CHROMOSOME NUMBER: $2n = 26$ (Santamour 1971).

VARIETY: var. *fujisanense* Koidzumi (1911), leaves 5-lobed; lobes smaller than in the species.

REFERENCES: Bean (1970), Hillier (1973), Hunt (1978a), de Jong (1977), Koidzumi (1911), Krüssmann (1976a), Kurata (1964–1976), Murray (1970c), Ogata (1965), Rehder (1986 facs.), Veitch (1904), Vertrees (1978, 1987).

One of the best of its section, *Acer capillipes,* described by Maximowicz in 1867, is quite common. It can be found in many collections, but not always under its proper name. One of the best specimens grows in the Winkworth Arboretum, Godalming, Great Britain.

Professor C. S. Sargent introduced this species about 1892 to the Arnold Arboretum, Jamaica Plain, Massachusetts, USA, and sent young plants to the Royal Botanic Gardens, Kew, Great Britain.

Young plants, especially, have a remarkable

"red" appearance. This species usually grows as a many-stemmed, treelike shrub. The bark has the typical white stripes on a green-red background. The petioles are red, as are the veins of the leaves. The leaves are dark green and usually reddish when unfolding, 3- to 5-lobed with the triangular lobes having slender apices.

The species is easily propagated by seed, which must be harvested from isolated trees, as they can hybridize readily with related species such as *Acer davidii* and *A. davidii* ssp. *grosseri*. Propagation by cuttings made in July is also easy.

This species can be confused with several related species, especially *Acer davidii* ssp. *davidii* or ssp. *grosseri*. These taxa have different, glabrous leaves with differing lobes, or no lobes at all. Another related species, *A. morifolium*, endemic to Yakushima, Japan, has mostly unlobed leaves. *Acer rubescens* also has similar leaves, but sheds them much later in the season.

*Acer capillipes* is a valuable garden plant and can by planted almost everywhere. It is one of the best, hardiest, and most undemanding species of *Acer*. In 1969 it received the Award of Garden Merit from the Royal Horticultural Society, Wisley.

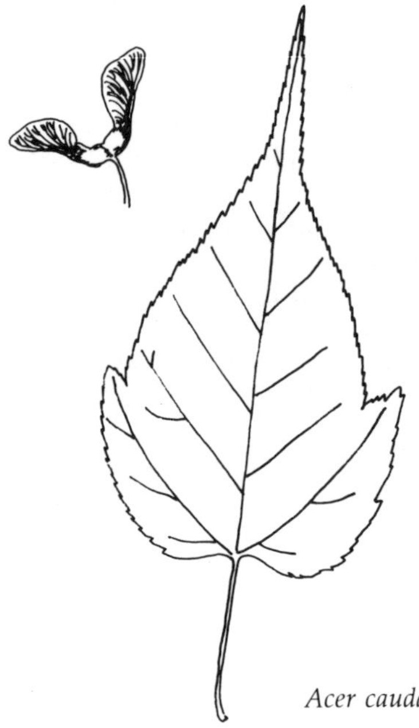

*Acer caudatifolium*

SECTION: *Macrantha*

ACER CAUDATIFOLIUM Hayata (1911)

SYNONYMS

*A. insulare* Makino (1910).
*A. kawakamii* Koidzumi (1911).
*A. morrisonense* Hayata (1911).
*A. ovatifolium* Koidzumi (1911).
*A. kawakamii* var. *taiton-montanum* (Hayata) Li (1952).
*A. capillipes* var. *insulare* (Makino) Murray (1977).
*A. pectinatum* ssp. *formosanum* Murray (1977).

TYPES: Hondo, Guikosan, Taiwan; isotypes G; NY.
COMMON NAME: Kawakami-maple.
EPITHET: *Caudatifolius*, with long tapering leaf tops.
ILLUSTRATIONS: Plate 28; Koidzumi (1911, as *A. ovatifolium*), Krüssmann (1976a), Li (1963a), Liu (1962).
HABIT: A small slender tree to 10–12 m tall, much shorter in cultivation, sometimes open or densely branched with glabrous, thin-textured stems.
LEAVES: Ovate, 8–12–15 cm long, acuminate, sharply double-toothed, pubescent when young, lobed on young shoots, almost unlobed on mature shoots; petioles red or green.
FLOWERS: In racemose umbels, somewhat purplish.
FRUITS: Samaras 2.5–3 cm long, wings obtuse, nutlets small (0.5–0.8 cm long) and flat.
BARK AND BUDS: Bark on mature shoots striped with white lines on a reddish green stem; buds valvate.
HARDINESS: Zone VII.
AUTUMN COLOR: Yellow.
DISTRIBUTION: Taiwan, in mountain forests at 2500–3000 m, but also found at lower elevations.
REFERENCES: Bean (1970, as *A. rubescens*), de Jong (1977), Krüssmann (1976a), Liu (1962), Murray (1970c, 1977).

This very rare species in cultivation is markedly different from its relatives and is often grown under an incorrect name. Sometimes it may be found labeled as *Acer kawakamii*, a synonym.

*Acer caudatifolium* has rather small, narrow, dull green papery leaves, with long apices. The leaves unfold very early in the spring, and greenish yellow flowers also appear very early, in March. The tree, which is densely branched with green twigs and branches that do not show many stripes on their bark, requires shelter and can be grown in gardens where protected sites are available. It is easily propagated by grafting on any seedling of section *Macrantha*.

*Acer caudatifolium* is not easily confused with other related species due to the long, tapered, caudate apices of its leaves. It is comparable only to *A. pectinatum* ssp. *forrestii* in some expressions, but this taxon is very different in many other characters. Murray's view that this species is better placed under *A. pectinatum* as subspecies *formosanum* is not accepted in the present volume. The living material presently in Europe, introduced by J. G. S. Harris in 1971, shows few affinities with *A. pectinatum*.

SECTION: *Macrantha*
ACER CRATAEGIFOLIUM Siebold & Zuccarini (1845)

SYNONYM: *A. crataegifolium* f. *typicum* Schwerin (1893).
TYPES: Syntypes *von Siebold, Maximowicz, Tschonoski;* Nagasaki, Senano, Japan; L.
COMMON NAMES: Hawthorn maple, Ao uri, Hana kaede, Hon uri, Shira hashi noki, Shira kaede, Me urinoke, Yama kaede.
EPITHET: *Crataegifolius,* with leaves like those of the genus *Crataegus.*
ILLUSTRATIONS: Plate 29; Koidzumi (1911), Krüssmann (1976a), Kurata (1964–1987), Satake et al. (1989), Vertrees (1987).
HABIT: A small tree or many-branched shrub, erect-growing, sometimes to 8 m tall; branchlets purplish green with inconspicuous white stripes, glabrous.
LEAVES: Ovate, bases truncate or cordate bases, 5–7 cm long, dark bluish green, irregularly serrate, often 3-lobed, sometimes 5-lobed, glabrous except when quite young, markedly larger on vegetative shoots than on fertile branches; margins quite notched when young.
FLOWERS: Almost white, in small, somewhat erect racemes, 3–4 cm long, produced with the first spring leaves.
FRUITS: Small and glabrous, 1.5–2 mm long, often sterile due to poor pollination; samaras purplish red, wings only 1 cm long or less, spreading almost horizontally.
BARK AND BUDS: Striped with green or whitish green on a purple bark; buds valvate.
HARDINESS: Zone VI.
AUTUMN COLOR: Dark red, not very attractive.
DISTRIBUTION: Central and southern Japan, in moist mountainous regions.
CHROMOSOME NUMBER: $2n = 26$ (Darlington & Wylie 1955).
VARIETIES
var. *crataegifolium,* the typical variety.
var. *macrophyllum* Hara (1934), with larger leaves to 15 cm long.
CULTIVARS: A few (see Chapter 9).
REFERENCES: Bean (1970), Dippel (1892), de Jong (1977), Koidzumi (1911), Krüssmann (1976a), Kurata (1964–1976), Murray (1970c), Pax (1902), Rehder (1986 facs.), Veitch (1904), Vertrees (1978, 1987).

The name of this species suggests affinity with the leaves of the hawthorn, although in reality this is only remotely the case. The species was described by Siebold and Zuccarini in 1845. Maries introduced it in 1879, together with other Japanese species, for Veitch Nursery, Exeter, Great Britain. It has no synonyms; nevertheless, it is occasionally misnamed with other "valid" epithets.

*Acer crataegifolium* occasionally grows into a small tree, but usually is a rather dense shrub with dark purplish red branches that have the stripes typical of species in section *Macrantha.* The rather small, dark bluish green leaves have irregular lobes; mature leaves are often unlobed. The margins are purplish. The autumn color is usually an unattractive blackish red, sometimes a good orange.

Because of poor seed germination, this species is available only occasionally in the trade. Propagation by cuttings is possible; grafting on understock of any species in the section is, of course, no problem.

A very charming, variegated cultivar, 'Veitchii', can be successfully grafted on understock of any species in the section. *Acer crataegifolium* var. *macrophyllum* grows faster than the species, becoming a large bushy shrub up to 5–6 m tall. The leaves are at least twice as large as the typical variety, but have the same bluish green color.

SECTION: *Macrantha*
ACER DAVIDII Franchet (1885) ssp. DAVIDII

SYNONYMS
*A. cavaleriei* Léveillé (1912).
*A. laxiflorum* var. *ningpoense* Pax (1902).
*A. sikkimense* var. *davidii* (Franchet) Wesmael (1890), pro parte (vide Murray 1977).
*A. sikkimense* var. *serrulatum* Pax (1886) (see Murray 1977).
TYPE: *Fr. David 1869,* Moupine, Sichuan Province, China; P.
COMMON NAMES: Father David's maple, Davids-Ahorn (in German).
EPITHET: *Davidii,* after Father Armand David, French missionary and botanist (1826–1900).
ILLUSTRATIONS: Plate 30; Harris (1983), de Jong (1977), Krüssmann (1976a), Mitchell (1972).
HABIT: A tree, sometimes with several trunks, to 15 m tall, usually somewhat higher than wide; young stems often reddish with white stripes; branches and stems striped green and white when mature.
LEAVES: Ovate-oblong, 7–15 cm long and 3—6 cm wide, dark green with reddish, glabrous, crenate margins; bases slightly cordate; veins parallel and prominent; mature leaves on short lateral branches, always unlobed; young leaves on long shoots (vigorously growing) usually slightly or fully lobed; almost all leaves on young plants (2- to 4-years-old) are lobed.
FLOWERS: 5-merous, light yellow, glabrous, on pendulous racemose corymbs; female corymbs longer than males. An entire branch will be either male or female, and these same branches may have flowers of the opposite sex in alternating or random successive years.

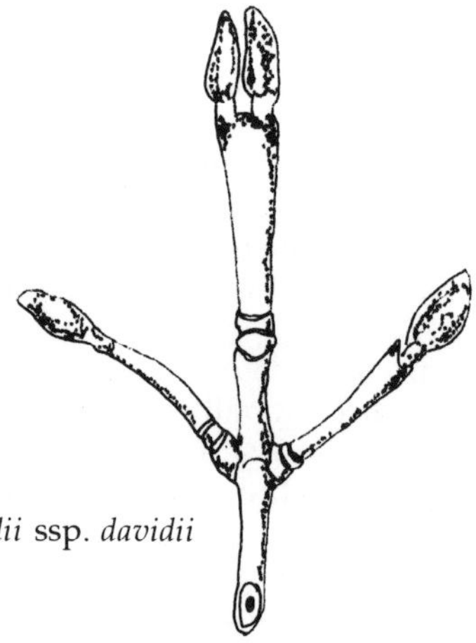

*Acer davidii* ssp. *davidii*

FRUITS: About 3 cm long, sometimes shorter; samaras almost horizontal; nutlets small and flattened.
BARK AND BUDS: Green or reddish green striped with white; buds valvate.
HARDINESS: Zones V–VII.
AUTUMN COLOR: Yellow and red, somewhat irregular.
DISTRIBUTION: Widely distributed in central and western China—Yunnan, Hubei, Sichuan, Henan, and many other provinces—at 1200–3000 m, on acid, generally moist soils. Scattered with other trees and woody plants.
CHROMOSOME NUMBER: $2n = 26$ (Santamour 1971).
SUBSPECIES
ssp. *davidii,* the typical subspecies.
ssp. *grosseri* (Pax) de Jong, comb. & stat. nov., leaves clearly lobed.
VARIETY: var. *horizontale* Pax (1902), with horizontal samaras; Shaanxi, China.
CULTIVARS: 'George Forrest', 'Ernest Wilson', and several others (see Chapter 9).
REFERENCES: Bean (1970), de Jong (1977), Krüssmann (1976a), Murray (1970c), Pax (1902), Rehder (1986 facs.), Sargent (1913), Veitch (1904).

*Acer davidii,* described by Franchet in 1885, is one of the best known members of section *Macrantha* and grows in many collections and gardens, although not always under its proper name: sometimes as *A. grosseri* and even as *A. capillipes.*

Father David, a French missionary to whom we owe many Chinese plant introductions, discovered this species, and E. H. Wilson rediscovered it in the Kyu Hills at 1500–2000 m altitude. Maries introduced it from Chang, Hubei Province, China, to Great Britain for Veitch Nursery in 1879.

*Acer davidii* usually becomes a moderately large tree or treelike shrub. Trees with 3–5 trunks are quite common. The habit is more or less open and vase-shaped. A beautiful specimen with good fastigiate habit grows in the Cantonspark in Baarn, The Netherlands; it is labeled *A. grosseri* (is *A. davidii* ssp. *grosseri*) but does not match that taxon.

This species seems to be good for street planting. It likes acid soils, but grows in other soil types as well. It has the reputation for bearing fully unlobed leaves, but this is not always true, and there are many exceptions. Young healthy plants, growing vigorously, usually have more or less heavily lobed leaves. In fact, unlobed leaves can only be found on mature trees on short branches—almost never on long new shoots. Neither seedlings nor plants grafted from a specimen growing at Kew display unlobed leaves when young. The stems of this species are beautifully striped, white on a greenish red bark.

*Acer davidii* is easily propagated from seed harvested from isolated, well-identified trees. Grafting clones of this species is easily done on any seedling or hybridized seedling of section *Macrantha.*

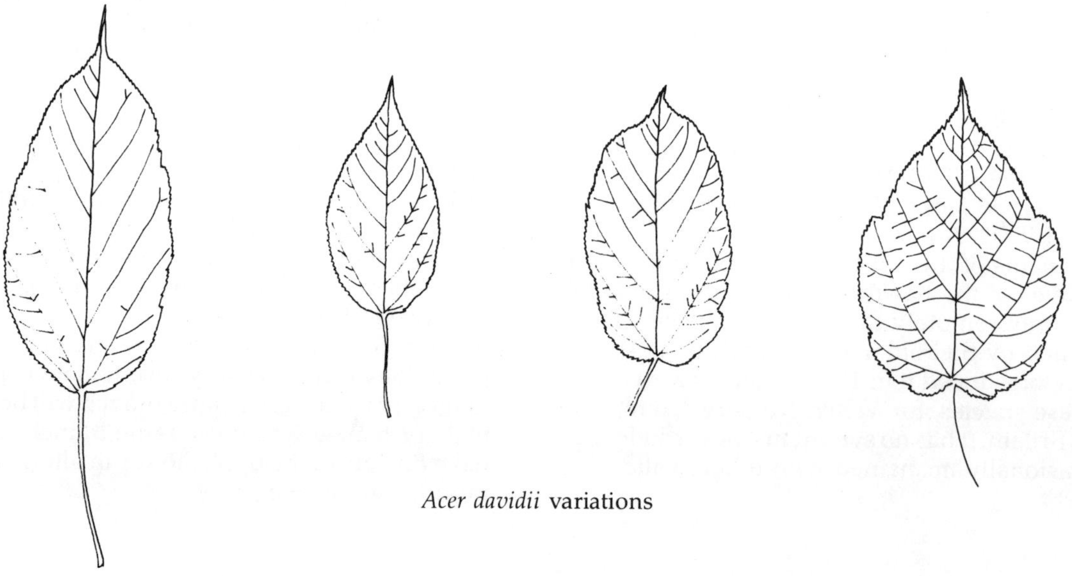

*Acer davidii* variations

Two "grexes" of *Acer davidii*, 'Ernest Wilson' and 'George Forrest', were not original clones, as a few English nurseries sold their own selected seedlings from among these "grexes." Neither named cultivar has unlobed leaves when young. The plants sold under 'Ernest Wilson' normally present a greener appearance than those sold under 'George Forrest', which have redder stems.

A plant of *Acer davidii* 'George Forrest' in Westonbirt Arboretum is, or was, incorrectly labeled as *A. forrestii* under F. 22239. The arboretum also has a plant of *A. davidii* 'Ernest Wilson', at the junction of Mitchell and Morlay drives, which is a Maries or perhaps a Wilson introduction. Another beautiful tree grows in the Gardens of Villa Taranto, Pallanza, Italy, bearing the probably incorrect name *A. davidii* var. *horizontale*. It is a very wide growing plant, with shiny, unlobed young leaves.

Messrs. W. J. Hooftman of Boskoop, The Netherlands, found a chance seedling of *Acer davidii* with smaller olive-green leaves and a very distinctive dark red bark with white stripes. This new selection is called 'Serpentine'. Its inflorescences suggest the influence of *A. crataegifolium*, as do the leaves. One wonders, however, how such a hybrid can originate when so few plants of *A. crataegifolium* are in cultivation. It might possibly be an unhybridized variant of *A. davidii* from a very northerly province.

The maples in section *Macrantha* originating from the western part of China include *Acer davidii* ssp. *davidii*, *A. davidii* ssp. *grosseri*, and *A. sikkimense* ssp. *metcalfii*. The affinities between these taxa are very close, and it is often very difficult to properly separate living material. The wealth of herbarium material does not support several different, localized, geographical species. *Acer davidii* is the oldest and best-known name for this taxon, but in this volume Murray's view of uniting *A. sikkimense* and *A. davidii* into one species is rejected.

SECTION: *Macrantha*

ACER DAVIDII ssp. GROSSERI (Pax) de Jong, comb. & stat. nov.

BASIONYM: *A. grosseri* Pax (1902).

SYNONYMS

*A. pavolinii* Pampanini (1910).
*A. hersii* Rehder (1922).
*A. grosseri* var. *hersii* (Rehder) Rehder (1933).
*A. tegmentosum* ssp. *grosseri* (Pax) Murray (1966).
*A. tegmentosum* var. *hersii* (Rehder) Murray (1980).

TYPE: *Giraldi 2121*, Shaanxi Province, China; FI.
EPITHET: *Grosseri*, after German botanist W. C. H. Grosser (1869–1942).
ILLUSTRATIONS: Plates 31, 32; de Jong (1976), Krüssman (1976a), Rehder (1933).
HABIT: A small tree, or more frequently a large shrub, to 10 m tall and often as wide; young stems green striped with white; mature branches less conspicuously striped.
LEAVES: Almost triangular-ovate, bases cordate, about 7 cm long and wide, quite often 3-lobed or almost unlobed, green, very variable; lobes small, short-acuminate, doubly serrate; undersides of juvenile leaves sometimes with brown hairs.
FLOWERS: Yellow, borne on pendulous racemes about 5–8 cm long. On most trees one branch bears only male flowers and another branch bears only females. However, these branches may change the sex of their flowers from one year to the next.
FRUITS: Samaras about 1–2 cm long; nutlets small, rounded, almost horizontal.
BARK AND BUDS: Conspicuously striped, gray-green, never reddish.
HARDINESS: Zone V.
AUTUMN COLOR: Yellow.
DISTRIBUTION: Northern and central China, in the provinces of Hunan and Shaanxi.
CHROMOSOME NUMBER: $2n = 26$ (Santamour 1971).
CULTIVARS: None selected to date.
REFERENCES: Bean (1970), de Jong (1976, 1977), Krüssmann (1976a), Murray (1970c, 1976a), Rehder (1986 facs.).

*Acer davidii* ssp. *grosseri*, discovered by Giraldi in Shaanxi Province, China, was described by Pax in 1902 and introduced to Europe about 1927 through the Arnold Arboretum.

Murray (1969) placed it as a subspecies of *Acer tegmentosum* in 1969, but this is incorrect. *Acer grosseri* does not deserve specific rank and must be placed under *A. davidii*, to which it is most closely related morphologically, as subspecies *grosseri*.

This tree, which is rather widely planted in collections but usually labeled incorrectly as *Acer hersii* or *A. grosseri hersii*, produces a very "green" impression. It is a small, many-branched tree or frequently a large shrub, 7–10 m high, with beautifully white-striped bark. Its leaves are almost triangular, 7–9 cm across, and 3-lobed or only sparingly lobed. This subspecies is easily confused with less typical expressions of *A. davidii*, or with related species such as *A. pectinatum* ssp. *laxiflorum*. It varies considerably, since it hybridizes rather freely with related taxa. Solitary stock plants often produce fairly uniform offspring, but seedlings produced by trees labeled *Acer hersii* are usually very variable.

It is recommended that this subspecies be propagated vegetatively by grafting on any seedling of section *Macrantha*.

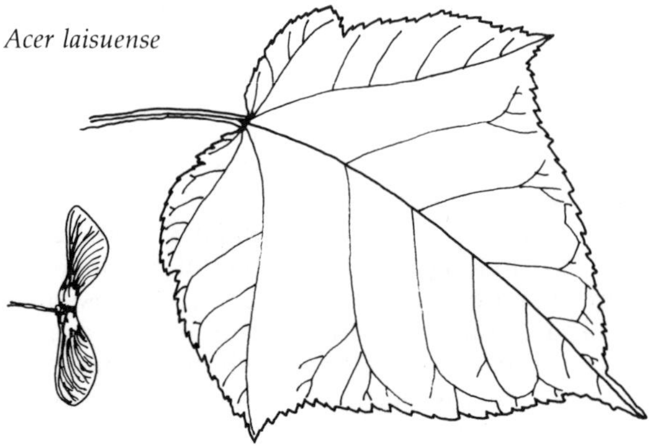

*Acer laisuense*

*Acer micranthum*

SECTION: *Macrantha*
ACER LAISUENSE Fang & Hu (1966)
TYPES: *D. P. Ho 45918,* Lai-su-ku, Sichuan Province, China; PE; isotype SZ.
EPITHET: *Laisuensis,* after Laisun, a district in Sichuan Province, China.
ILLUSTRATION: Fang (1981a).
HABIT: A tree 6–12 m tall.
LEAVES: 3- to 5-lobed, rounded, 10–12 cm long and wide; margins crenulated.
FLOWERS: In long racemes, similar to those of *A. tegmentosum.*
FRUITS: Samaras firm, with rounded nutlets, in trusses about 10 cm long.
HARDINESS: Unknown.
DISTRIBUTION: Northwestern Sichuan Province, China.
REFERENCES: Fang (1981a), Murray (1970c).

This species is not in cultivation in the West. It is said to be close to both *Acer tegmentosum* and *A. pectinatum.* When living material and herbarium specimens become available, this species might become a synonym of another Asiatic species, such as *A. tegmentosum.* It is originally described (Fang, 1966) as differing from that species by having dentate leaves, smaller fruits that are 20–22 mm long, and longer pedicels that are 10–12 cm long.

SECTION: *Macrantha*
ACER MICRANTHUM Siebold & Zuccarini (1845)
TYPE: *Siebold,* Japan; L.
COMMON NAME: Ko mine kaede.
EPITHET: *Micranthus,* with small flowers.
ILLUSTRATIONS: De Jong (1976), Koidzumi (1911), Krüssmann (1976a), Kurata (1964–1976), Satake et al. (1989), Vertrees (1978, 1987).
HABIT: A small tree or large shrub to 8 m tall, heavily branched; bark glabrous; young stems thin.
LEAVES: 5-lobed, sometimes even 7-lobed, deeply lobed, 5–7 cm long and wide, glabrous on both surfaces, or occasionally with minor hair tufts in the vein axils; lobes acuminate, connivent, nearly enclosing the sinuses; margins serrate; petioles 2–4 cm long.
FLOWERS: Yellowish green, very small, in terminal racemes 3–5 cm long; appearing in May.
FRUITS: Samaras almost horizontal or spreading in a wide angle, 1–2 cm long; nutlets glabrous.
BARK AND BUDS: Purplish to green with inconspicuous white stripes; buds valvate.
HARDINESS: Zone VI.
AUTUMN COLOR: Red to orange-yellow, occasionally golden yellow.
CHROMOSOME NUMBER: $2n = 26$ (Bolkhovskikh 1969).
DISTRIBUTION: Mountainous forests on Honshu, Shikoku and Kyushu islands, Japan, at 700–1800 m.
REFERENCES: Bean (1970), de Jong (1976, 1977), Koidzumi (1911), Krüssmann (1976a), Kurata (1964–1976), Murray (1970c), Rehder (1986 facs.), Vertrees (1978, 1987).

*Acer micranthum,* described by Siebold and Zuccarini in 1845, was introduced to Europe about 1879. It is one of the most beautiful maples for small gardens (although actually quite rare), growing into a moderate-sized shrub and only occasionally into a small tree. It is easily confused with related species such as *Acer tschonoskii,* but the latter has a more open habit. Usually *A. micranthum* is heavily branched, the twigs mostly red or sometimes yellow-red. The leaves are set densely together and are quite variable, especially on young plants. Juvenile leaves on vigorous shoots have often the same shape as leaves of *A. tschonoskii,* but the leaves of mature trees are much more deeply incised. The dense branching is only found in *A. micranthum* and, to a lesser degree, in *A. pectinatum* ssp. *maximowiczii,* but in the latter the leaves are larger and not so deeply divided. The flowers and fruits of *A.*

*micranthum* are much smaller than those of all its relatives, and when in flower it is easy to distinguish.

This species is easily propagated by cuttings or by grafting on any seedling of section *Macrantha.* Propagation by seed is also possible, but the germination percentage is invariably quite low.

In the Hillier Arboretum there is a plant called *Acer micranthum* f. *candelabrum,* which is of larger habit and has larger leaves than the species; its origin is unknown and the name is not published. Most probably it is a seedling. It is published in the present volume with an English description. Clearly it is not a forma but rather a cultivar, 'Candelabrum'.

SECTION: *Macrantha*
## ACER MORIFOLIUM Koidzumi (1914)

SYNONYMS
- *A. insulare* auct. non Makino (1910).
- *A. caudatum* sensu Ito & Matsumura (1920), non Wallich.
- *A. capillipes* var. *morifolium* (Koidzumi) Hatusima (1954).
- *A. capillipes* ssp. *insulare* (Makino) Murray (1977).

TYPE: Makino, Kyushu, Kagoshima, Yakushima; MAK.
COMMON NAMES: Shima uri kaede, Yakushima ogarabana, Yakushima onaga kaede.
EPITHET: *Morifolius,* with leaves resembling those of the genus *Morus.*
ILLUSTRATIONS: Kurata (1964–1976), Liu (1962).
HABIT: A treelike shrub to 10–12 m tall; trunks green with white stripes; shoots slender, long-growing, reddish.
LEAVES: Mostly unlobed, or only remotely lobed, ovate-cordate, veined beneath, of the same texture as *A. capillipes.*
FLOWERS: Yellowish white in short racemes, similar to *A. capillipes.*
FRUITS: Numerous, small and short-winged, 1.5–2 cm long; samaras immature on material seen.
BARK AND BUDS: Bark green with white stripes, rather conspicuous.
HARDINESS: Zones VI–VII.
AUTUMN COLOR: Yellow.
DISTRIBUTION: Yakushima, Tanegashima and Ryukyu islands, Japan.
REFERENCES: Kurata (1964–1976), Liu (1962), Murray (1970c, 1977).

*Acer morifolium* is not in cultivation in Europe or North America. Plants under this name or one of its synonyms are so far invariably incorrectly labeled and difficult to identify. Sometimes they are hybrids of *A. capillipes,* with (almost) unlobed leaves.

In September 1990 two small, grafted plants came into The Netherlands, having been purchased at a Japanese nursery. It is presently impossible to identify them definitively.

*Acer morifolium*
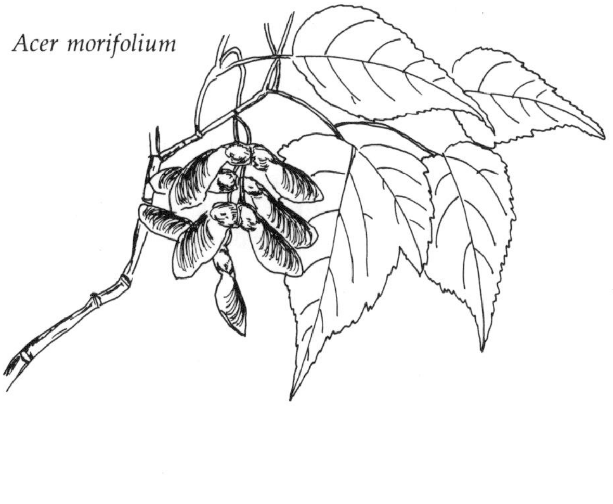

SECTION: *Macrantha*
## ACER PECTINATUM ssp. FORRESTII (Diels) Murray (1977)

BASIONYM: *A. forrestii* Diels (1912).
SYNONYMS
- *A. laxiflorum* sensu Rehder (1911), non Pax.
- *A. forrestii* f. *caudatilobum* Rehder (1933).
- *A. forrestii* var. *minor* W. W. Smith in Fang (1933), pro syn.
- *A. grosseri* var. *forrestii* (Diels) Handel-Mazzetti (1933).

TYPES: *Forrest 2106,* Yunnan Province, China; holotype E; isotypes A, K.
EPITHET: *Forrestii,* after Scottish plant hunter George Forrest (1873–1932).
ILLUSTRATIONS: Plate 33; de Jong (1976), Mitchell (1972).
HABIT: A slender tree or treelike shrub 7–12 m tall, quite often as wide; young stems purplish or red, sometimes green, glabrous, often beautifully striped with white; sparsely branched with graceful, spreading branches.
LEAVES: Mostly 3- to 5-lobed, more or less heart-shaped, slender pointed, bases finely serrate, 6–14 cm long and 2.5–4 cm wide, glaucescent beneath; side lobes triangular, sometimes almost unlobed on flowering shoots; petioles red, occasionally with hair tufts at the axils when young.
FLOWERS: Brownish green or purplish red, produced with the young leaves; on few-flowered racemes.
FRUITS: Samaras 1.5 cm wide, spreading horizontally; nutlets flattish; fruits glabrous, many parthenocarpic.
BARK AND BUDS: Variable bark, often beautifully striped, purplish to green, occasionally bright red.
HARDINESS: Zones V–VI.
AUTUMN COLOR: Variable, sometimes orange, often yellow-brown and not very attractive.
DISTRIBUTION: Lichiang Range in northern Yunnan

Province, China, growing in open situations in mixed forest.

CULTIVARS: 'Alice' and two others (see Chapter 9).

REFERENCES: Bean (1970), Fang (1981a), de Jong (1976, 1977), Krüssmann (1976a), Murray (1970c, 1977), Sargent (1913).

George Forrest introduced this subspecies in 1906, having discovered it in the mountains of the Lichiang Range, northern Yunnan Province, China.

One of the more difficult taxa to identify correctly, it is rather rare and is often mislabeled or misnamed. It is easily confused with several variants of *Acer davidii* ssp. *grosseri, A. capillipes,* and *A. pectinatum* ssp. *pectinatum.* Rehder and Wilson (in Sargent 1913) considered it synonymous with *A. laxiflorum,* but this is not the case, and Handel-Mazzetti placed it as a variety under *A. grosseri* in 1933. As this taxon has many affinities to *A. pectinatum,* it is treated here as a subspecies under *A. pectinatum,* the placement originally proposed by Murray (1977).

*Acer pectinatum* ssp. *forrestii* forms a slender and open tree or treelike shrub, often beautifully striped with white. Its leaves are usually 5-lobed with slender lobe points. Unlike those of *A. davidii* ssp. *grosseri* and not more than 4–5 cm wide, they are also dissimilar from those of *A. capillipes,* which are much wider. The petioles are red, as in *A. capillipes.* On good specimens of subspecies *forrestii* the petals are purplish red. On the other hand, there are brownish green-looking expressions.

Propagation by cuttings is recommended to maintain the integrity of the subspecies. Grafting on any species from section *Macrantha* is also possible. Nevertheless, the subspecies is only occasionally available in the trade. Unfortunately, plants from *Acer davidii* 'George Forrest' are sometimes supplied in the trade in place of subspecies *forrestii.* This poor nursery practice causes unnecessary confusion as the two plants are quite different.

Only one forma, *caudatilobum,* had been recognized, and it is now reduced to synonymy.

SECTION: *Macrantha*

ACER PECTINATUM ssp. LAXIFLORUM (Pax) Murray (1977)

BASIONYM: *A. laxiflorum* Pax (1902).

TYPES: Lectotype *Pratt 838,* Sichuan Province, China; K; BM, G, MOAR, NY; syntypes *Faber,* Mount Omei, Sichuan Province, China; A, NY, W.

EPITHET: *Laxiflorus,* with loose flowers.

ILLUSTRATIONS: Krüssmann (1976a), Nakai (1914).

HABIT: An upright-growing tree of moderate size, 6–12 m tall; young stems glabrous, reddish green or green with rather inconspicuous white stripes.

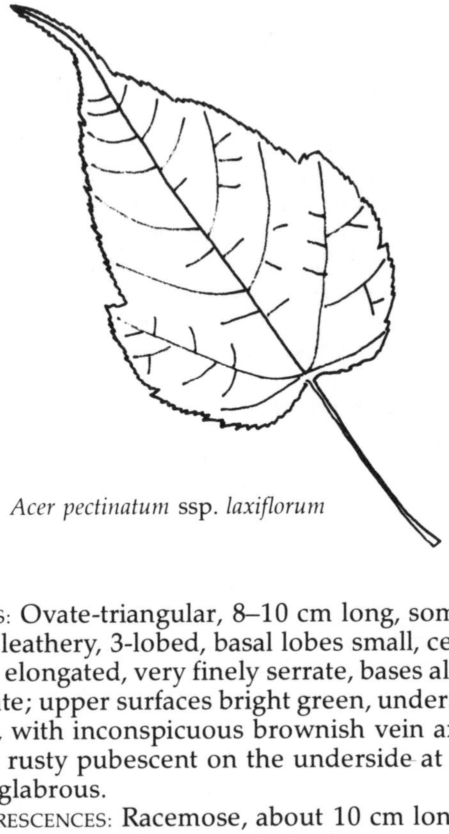

*Acer pectinatum* ssp. *laxiflorum*

LEAVES: Ovate-triangular, 8–10 cm long, somewhat leathery, 3-lobed, basal lobes small, central lobes elongated, very finely serrate, bases almost cordate; upper surfaces bright green, undersides paler, with inconspicuous brownish vein axils; veins rusty pubescent on the underside at first, later glabrous.

INFLORESCENCES: Racemose, about 10 cm long, pendulous, developing with the leaves.

FLOWERS: Large, dark reddish to brown-yellow. Flowers on one branch are all of one sex, as is often seen in this section.

FRUITS: Samaras nearly horizontal, 3 cm long, often spreading at a right angle.

BARK AND BUDS: Faintly striped bark, stems usually green; buds valvate.

HARDINESS: Zone VI.

AUTUMN COLOR: Yellow.

DISTRIBUTION: China, mountains in Sichuan and Yunnan (?) provinces. Also on Emei shan (Mt. Emei) and near Kangding (Tatsien lu).

CHROMOSOME NUMBER: $2n = 26$ (Mehra 1972).

VARIETIES

- *A. laxiflorum* var. *dolichophyllum* Fang (1982 & 1981), refers to variety *longiphyllum* in an attempt to make the whole name Greek and etymologically pure.
- *A. laxiflorum* var. *integrifolium* Fang (1932), leaves subentire.
- *A. laxiflorum* var. *longilobum* Rehder (1911), leaves 5- lobed; central lobe somewhat longer than the outer lobes. A plant is present in Dawyck Gardens, Scotland; whether it can be maintained as a variety can only be determined by more study of the very scarce material.
- *A. laxiflorum* var. *longiphyllum* Fang (1932), leaves 20 cm long; veins pilose.

REFERENCES: Bean (1970), Fang (1981a), de Jong (1977), Krüssmann (1976a), Murray (1970c, 1977), Pax (1902), Rehder (1986 facs.), Sargent (1913).

*Acer laxiflorum* is best placed as a subspecies under *A. pectinatum*, a placement proposed by Murray (1977), together with the related taxa *A. forrestii*, *A. maximowiczii* and *A. taronense*.

*Acer pectinatum* ssp. *laxiflorum* is an upright-growing tree of moderate size, which may also grow as a multistemmed shrub. It bears basally lobulate or even almost unlobed leaves, similar to those of *A. davidii* ssp. *davidii* or subspecies *grosseri*, although the central lobe of *A. pectinatum* ssp. *laxiflorum* is much longer. The leaves are fresh green with few traces of red in the petioles.

Grafting is relatively easy on any species of section *Macrantha*. However, care should be taken to propagate the true *Acer pectinatum* ssp. *laxiflorum*. Quite a number of plants under the name of *A. laxiflorum* actually represent *A. capillipes* and, having been distributed by a German nursery, are established in numerous European gardens. These misidentified plants obviously are not true to name, and care must be taken not to propagate them as *A. pectinatum* subsp. *laxiflorum*. One of the few true-to-name specimens in Europe is found at Trewithen, Cornwall, Great Britain. There is also a good specimen in the Dawyck Gardens, Scotland.

Fang recognized two natural varieties, not known in the West, both listed under *Acer laxiflorum*. The four varieties listed above may all someday be sunk into synonymy.

SECTION: *Macrantha*

ACER PECTINATUM ssp. MAXIMOWICZII (Pax) Murray (1977)

BASIONYM: *A. maximowiczii* Pax (1889).
SYNONYM: *A. urophyllum* Maximowicz (1889).
TYPES: Lectotype *Henry 6857*, Hubei Province, China (original destroyed in Berlin [B)] during in World War II); K; isotypes BM, E, P, NY.
EPITHET: *Maximowiczii*, after Russian botanist and plant hunter K. J. Maximowicz (1827–1891).
ILLUSTRATIONS: Plate 34; Fang (1981a).
HABIT: A small tree or large shrub; bark gray or greenish with inconspicuous white stripes, glabrous.
LEAVES: Quite variable on the same tree; 3- to 5-lobed, 5–8 cm long, middle lobes acuminate, others acute, margins serrate, bases subcordate, vein axils tufted rusty beneath and often glaucous; petioles 5–6 cm long, reddish.
INFLORESCENCES: Racemose, terminal.
FLOWERS: Yellow-green.
FRUITS: Samaras small, obtuse, on short stalks, horizontal, about 3 cm long.

*Acer pectinatum* ssp. *maximowiczii*

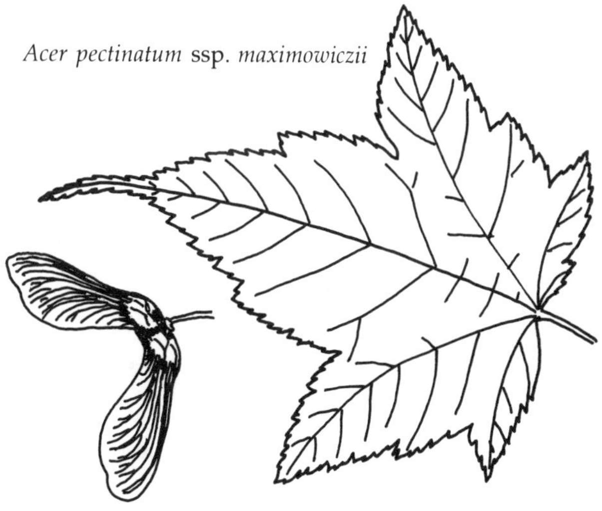

BARK AND BUDS: Bark inconspicuously white-striped; branches of young trees are red to purple, especially in winter.
HARDINESS: Zone V.
AUTUMN COLOR: Yellow.
DISTRIBUTION: Hubei, Gansu, and Sichuan provinces, China.
REFERENCES: Bean (1970), Fang (1981a), de Jong (1977), Krüssmann (1976a), Murray (1970c), Rehder (1986 facs.).

Pax described the basionym of this subspecies from Chinese specimens collected by A. Henry and the Russian botanist and explorer Potanin, but Wilson introduced the subspecies to Great Britain as *Acer laxiflorum*, now a subspecies of *A. pectinatum*.

*Acer pectinatum* ssp. *maximowiczii* is usually a small tree, but can also grow as a rather large shrub with several stems with striped bark. Young twigs are usually purplish red. Its leaves are rather variable, even on the same plant, a feature it shares its close relatives, the other subspecies of *A. pectinatum*. Many authors considered this subspecies as related to *A. micranthum* and *A. tschonoskii*, placing all three in the former series *Micrantha* within section *Macrantha*. In fact, it is difficult to separate this subspecies from its allies, as there is so little living and herbarium material with which to compare it. *Acer tschonoskii* has a more open habit and larger, more wavy leaves, while the leaves of *A. micranthum* are more deeply cut than those of *A pectinatum* ssp. *maximowiczii*.

Propagation is not at all difficult. Cuttings taken in July root readily. Propagation by seed is also possible, but true seed is almost never available. Grafting on seedlings of any species of section *Macrantha* is also easy.

An entirely different maple, *Acer maximowiczianum* (formerly *A. nikoense*), might cause confusion due to its specific epithet.

SECTION: *Macrantha*
ACER PECTINATUM Wallich ex Nicholson (1881) ssp. PECTINATUM

TYPES: *Wallich 1226,* from eastern Himalayas; K; isotypes BM, G.
EPITHET: *Pectinatus,* like a comb.
ILLUSTRATION: Pax (1902).
HABIT: A tree in its native habitat, only a large shrub in cultivation; young branches glabrous, reddish or brownish; mature branches have inconspicuous white-gray stripes.
LEAVES: 5-lobed (or 3- to 5-lobed), with only small basal lobes, 7.5–14 cm long and 5–8 cm wide, central lobe very long relative to other lobes; lobes triangular, acuminate, regularly and doubly serrate; vein axils tufted beneath; petioles red, 7–8 mm long.
FLOWERS: Whitish yellow, on racemes.
FRUITS: Samaras 2–2.5 cm long, almost horizontal, on racemes 7–10 cm long.
BARK AND BUDS: Bark inconspicuously striped.
HARDINESS: Zones VI–VII.
AUTUMN COLOR: Yellow.
DISTRIBUTION: Himalayas, Bhutan, Nepal, upper Burma, and possibly Yunnan and Sichuan provinces, China.
SUBSPECIES
ssp. *forrestii* (Diels) Murray.
ssp. *laxiflorum* (Pax) Murray.
ssp. *maximowiczii* (Pax) Murray.
ssp. *pectinatum,* the typical subspecies.
ssp. *taronense* (Handel-Mazzetti) Murray.
CULTIVARS: A few (see Chapter 9).
REFERENCES: Bean (1970), Fang (1981a), de Jong (1977), Krüssmann (1976a), Murray (1970c).

Various former species such as *Acer forrestii, A. laxiflorum, A. maximowiczii,* and *A. taronense* were grouped by Murray in 1977 as subspecies under *A. pectinatum,* which is the oldest valid name in this group. These infraspecific assignments are accepted in the present volume.

*Acer pectinatum* ssp. *pectinatum*

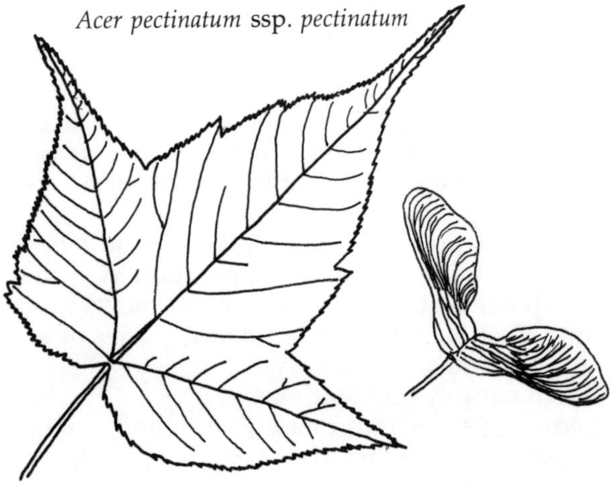

This very beautiful but somewhat tender small tree is found in a few collections. It has a slender habit and does not often show much of its snakebark character. The leaves often have distinctive fiery red petioles, not unlike those of *Acer tschonoskii* or *A. pectinatum* ssp. *forrestii.* The leaves of *A. pectinatum* differ from those of subspecies *forrestii* by having broader lobes with sharp apices.

*Acer pectinatum* is only occasionally available in the trade. It can be propagated by seed, which is almost never available. Grafting on any species from section *Macrantha* is a good substitute and also a good means by which to propagate the hardier variants and maintain the purity of the species. Most of the young plants now growing in various collections are grafted specimens. Sometimes plants labeled *A. pectinatum* are in fact slightly aberrant forms of *A. pectinatum* ssp. *forrestii.*

This handsome maple deserves more extensive use as it is beautiful in somewhat sheltered gardens.

SECTION: *Macrantha*
ACER PECTINATUM ssp. TARONENSE (Handel-Mazzetti) Murray (1977)

BASIONYM: *A. taronense* Handel-Mazzettii (1924).
SYNONYMS
*A. chienii* Hu & Cheng (1948).
*A. chloranthum* Merrill (1941).
TYPE: *Handel-Mazzetti 9385,* Taron River (Upper Irrawaddy), Yunnan Province, China; WU; isotype A.
EPITHET: *Taronensis,* from the Taron River, Yunnan Province, China.
ILLUSTRATIONS: Plate 35; Fang (1981a).
HABIT: A medium, erect-growing tree to 15 m tall; branches thin, purplish brown to reddish with faint stripes; bud scales ciliate.
LEAVES: 5-lobed, ovate, 4–10 cm long and 3–8 cm wide, lobes triangular ovate, with tapered apices, basal lobes much shorter, dark green above, brown tufts at the axils beneath as in *A. rufinerve;* margins doubly serrate; leafing out early in the season; juvenile, vigorously growing leaves not pubescent.
INFLORESCENCES: Racemose, terminal.
FLOWERS: Yellow-green.
FRUITS: Samaras purplish, 3 cm long; wings obtuse, glabrous, spreading at a right angle or wider.
HARDINESS: Zone VI.
AUTUMN COLOR: Yellow.
DISTRIBUTION: Northeast Burma; Sichuan, Yunnan, and eastern Xizang provinces, China; in mountainous regions.
REFERENCES: Bean (1970), Fang (1981a), de Jong

(1977), Krüssmann (1976a), Murray (1970c, 1977).

This subspecies is very rare in cultivation. It was discovered by Austrian botanist Friedrich Handel-Mazzetti, in the valley of the Taron River, a tributary of the Irrawaddy in northern Burma. Forrest introduced the species in 1924 from seed collected along the Chinese-Burmese border.

There is, unfortunately, considerable confusion within and between herbaria specimens. One of the very few trees in cultivation is found at Caerhays Castle, Cornwall, Great Britain, where it was incorrectly identified as *Acer rufinerve* (George Forrest #24264). The few plants growing in other gardens as *A. pectinatum* ssp. *taronense* were probably propagated from the Caerhays specimen, including all plants distributed by Dutch nurseries.

*Acer pectinatum* ssp. *taronense* is closely allied to *A. pectinatum* ssp. *forrestii,* but differs by having shorter leaf blades with shorter apices, and small tufts of hairs on the vein axils, not unlike *A. rufinerve.* In other respects it is quite different from *A. rufinerve,* not only in leaf shape, but also in leaf color: subspecies *taronense* has reddish leaves while *A. rufinerve* has bluish leaves. There is also a considerable difference in the seed: *A. rufinerve* has round bullet-shaped nutlets with small wings, while *A. pectinatum* ssp. *taronense* has ovate nutlets tapering into the wings.

*Acer pectinatum* ssp. *taronense* is easily propagated by grafting on any species of section *Macrantha.* Propagation by softwood cuttings has also proven successful. Vegetatively propagated plants are surprisingly hardy in the European coastal countries; seedlings from other sources may prove to be less hardy.

*Acer pectinatum* ssp. *taronense*

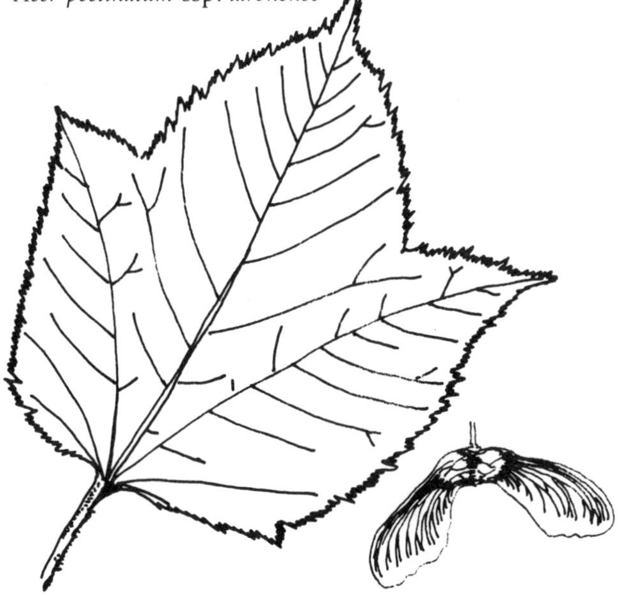

SECTION: *Macrantha*

ACER PENSYLVANICUM L. (1753)

SYNONYMS

*A. striatum* Duroi (1771).
*A. canadense* Marshall (1785).
*A. tricuspifolium* Stokes (1812).
*A. pensylvanicum* var. *integrifolium* G. Don ex Koch (1853).

TYPE: *P. Kalm,* "Habitat in Pennsylvania," LINN sp. *#1225.13;* LINN.

COMMON NAMES: Moosewood, Striped maple, Pennsylvanischer Ahorn, Streifen-Ahorn

EPITHET: *Pensylvanicus,* from Pennsylvania; the epithet is correctly written with one *n* as Linnaeus made the original error which, according to the ICBN, must be maintained.

ILLUSTRATIONS: Plate 36; de Jong (1976, 1977), Krüssmann (1976a).

HABIT: A small tree or treelike shrub to 10–12 m tall and often as wide (in rough conditions as scrub), generally slender trunked, rather open in cultivation (often more erect in the wild), only sparsely branched; branches conspicuously striped with rather wide white stripes; young shoots salmon-pink, also striped with white.

LEAVES: 3-lobed, obovate, 12–20 cm long and wide, lobes short and shallowly crenate, undersides somewhat rusty when young; margins doubly serrulate; bases cordate; petioles 3.5 cm long, with brownish hairs when young.

INFLORESCENCES: Racemose, terminal, pendulous.

FLOWERS: 5-merous, yellow-green, appearing after the leaves.

FRUITS: Samaras short, 1 cm long, obtuse, flat, in short umbels.

BARK AND BUDS: Strikingly striped bark; buds valvate.

HARDINESS: Zones IV–V (–VII).

AUTUMN COLOR: Golden yellow.

DISTRIBUTION: Eastern North America: cool north-facing slopes of the Appalachians, Upper Great Lakes to Nova Scotia, eastern Canada, west to Minnesota and south to Georgia.

CHROMOSOME NUMBER: $2n = 26$ (Santamour 1971).

CULTIVARS: A few (see Chapter 9).

REFERENCES: Bean (1970), Dippel (1892), Elwes & Henry (1908), de Jong (1976, 1977), Koch (1869), Krüssmann (1976a), Linnaeus (1753), Murray (1970c), Pax (1902), Pojárkova (1933), Rehder (1986 facs.), Schneider (1912), Veitch (1904).

One of the most striking of all maples, this species is becoming more popular in horticulture. It is the only species of snakebark maple native to North America; all other species are Asiatic. Fossils of maple trees from several different taxonomic sections have been discovered, mainly in Europe and Asia, but none of section *Macrantha.*

In its native habitat it is usually a small tree or

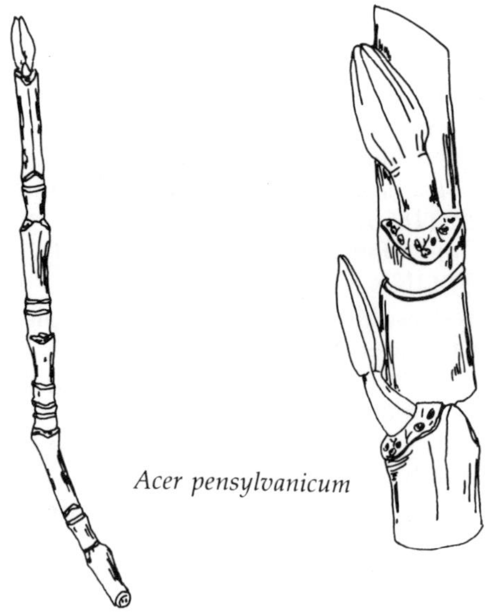

Acer pensylvanicum

shrub growing with *Betula alleghaniensis, Tsuga canadensis, Fagus grandifolia, Carya,* and *Picea.* It is also found with *Acer sacchanum* and *A. rubrum* as an undergrowth. It was introduced to Europe in 1755 and is one of the few species of *Acer* described by Linnaeus (1753).

*Acer pensylvanicum* deserves a place in many gardens if only for having the most striking bark of all species of section *Macrantha,* especially in winter when the bark becomes reddish with wide, white distinctive stripes. It has a handsome shape, which integrates well into landscapes, and a brilliant golden yellow autumn color. It has the largest leaves of all the species in section *Macrantha* and is usually, but not always, openly branched. Thus it is not easily confused with other maples, even its relatives such as *A. capillipes* or *A. davidii* ssp. *grosseri.* It is common in *Acer* collections and is frequently found in gardens and parks, often as a treelike, many-stemmed tall shrub.

*Acer pensylvanicum* is easily propagated by seed. If the seed is not hybridized, it comes true to the species. Some commercial nurseries bud this species on *A. pseudoplatanus,* but this produces weak plants with the understock suckering heavily. Grafting on any species of section *Macrantha* is a much better method of propagation if seed is not available.

One very beautiful cultivar, 'Erythrocladum', has conspicuous salmon-red twigs in winter. Unfortunately, this fine plant is very hard to propagate, and thus is almost never available. There is a huge tree of this cultivar in Knighthayes Court Gardens, Tiverton, Great Britain.

SECTION: *Macrantha*

## ACER RUBESCENS Hayata (1911)

SYNONYM: *A. morrisonense* sensu Li (1963), non Hayata.

TYPE: *Konishi #A.*[11] at 2500 m, Batai-ankei, Taiwan; TNS.

EPITHET: *Rubescens,* reddish.

ILLUSTRATIONS: Plates 37, 38; Liu (1962).

HABIT: A tree to 20 m tall; branches and bark distinctively white-striped, glabrous.

LEAVES: 3- to 5-lobed or remotely unlobed, 6–15 cm long and 5–7 cm wide, very variable in shape, with tapering apices, almost evergreen, not dropping before December; more lobed and always glabrous on vigorously growing shoots, but smaller, less lobed, and slightly pubescent in spring on short older side shoots.

FLOWERS: Yellow-green, on short racemes.

FRUITS: On short racemes, samaras 2–3 cm long almost diverging horizontally; nutlets flattened.

BARK AND BUDS: Distinctively striped bark; buds valvate.

HARDINESS: Zone VII (VIII).

AUTUMN COLOR: Yellow.

DISTRIBUTION: Taiwan, in mountain forests up to 2000–2500 m.

CULTIVAR: One (see Chapter 9).

REFERENCES: Bean (1970), de Jong (1977), Liu (1963), Murray (1970c).

This beautiful maple is very rare. A mature tree grows in Trewithen Gardens, Cornwall, Great Britain, labeled incorrectly as *Acer morrisonense;* it originated from seed collected by *Yashiroda, no. 109* in Taiwan.

Li (1963) placed *Acer morrisonense* in synonymy under *A. rubescens,* but Murray does not agree, saying that it is distinct from *A. rubescens* per its holotype (Hara 1970). He places it in synonymy under *A. caudatifolium.*

Acer rubescens

This tree has a beautifully striped trunk. Young leaves on vigorously growing branches have large lobes. The shape of juvenile leaves is comparable to that of *A. capillipes* leaves. Slender ovate leaves have few lobes on mature branches. Offspring of the Trewithen are nearly evergreen: the leaves never drop before December, and the plants leaf out very early in the season. The petioles are beautifully red.

Unfortunately, this species is not sufficiently hardy for garden use in cold temperate zones, and must be given a well-sheltered place in the garden, except in the mildest regions of the Great Britain, New Zealand, Australia, and North America. It is easily propagated by grafting on species of section *Macrantha.*

SECTION: *Macrantha*
ACER RUFINERVE Siebold & Zuccarini (1845)
SYNONYMS
*A. pensylvanicum* ssp. *rufinerve* (Siebold & Zuccarini) Wesmael (1890).
*A. cucullobracteatum* Léveillé & Vaniot (1906).
TYPE: Syntypes Siebold, Keiske, Japan; L.
COMMON NAMES: Ao kaede, Ao momiji, Izuka, Komori kaede, Konji noki, Rostnerviger Ahorn, Uri noki, Urihada kaede
EPITHET: *Rufinervis,* with rusty colored veins.
ILLUSTRATIONS: Plate 39; Koidzumi (1911), Krüssmann (1976a), Kurata (1964–1976), Mitchell (1972), Satake et al. (1989), Vertrees (1987).
HABIT: A tree or treelike shrub to 15 m tall, not broader than 5–7 m; branches green to silvery green, with distinctive white stripes, no trace of red.
LEAVES: 3- to 5-lobed, 6–15 cm across, dark green, undersides pale green with tufts of rusty hairs (that disappear in summer) in vein axils; tufts not present on vigorously growing shoots; margins doubly serrate; bases cordate; veins impressed on the upper surfaces; petioles 3–6 cm long.
INFLORESCENCES: Racemose, terminal.
FLOWERS: Pale green, appearing after the leaves.
FRUITS: Samaras small, about 2 cm long; nutlets rounded and thick.
BARK AND BUDS: Bark distinctively white-striped on green, not reddish, trunk; buds valvate.
HARDINESS: Zone V.
AUTUMN COLOR: Reddish to orange-yellow.
DISTRIBUTION: Honshu, Shikoku, Kiyushu and Yakushima islands, Japan, in mountain forests up to 2500 m.
CHROMOSOME NUMBER: $2n = 26$ (Darlington 1955).
CULTIVARS: A few (see Chapter 9).
REFERENCES: Bean (1970), Dippel (1892), Elwes & Henry (1908), de Jong (1977), Koidzumi (1911), Krüssmann (1976a), Kurata (1964–1976), Murray (1970c), Ogata (1965), Rehder (1986 facs.), Veitch (1904), Vertrees (1978, 1987).

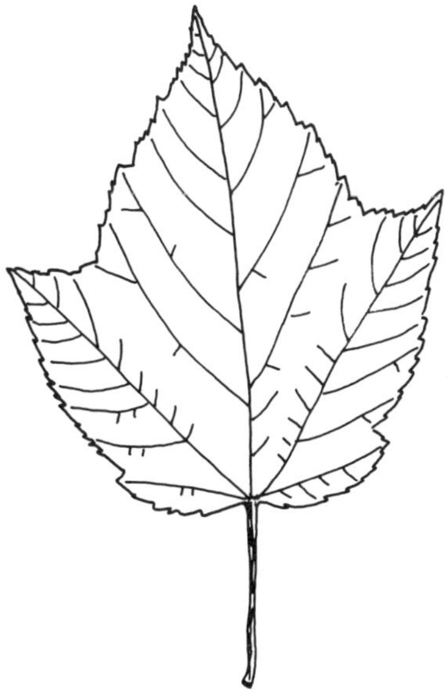

*Acer rufinerve* (from a vegetative shoot)

*Acer rufinerve* is probably the most common snakebark maple in cultivation. It was introduced from Japan by Charles Maries for Veitch Nursery in 1881.

Momotani states (in Ogata, 1965, 1967) that *Acer rufinerve* is more closely related to *A. nipponicum* than any other species of section *Macrantha. Acer nipponicum* does indeed show certain similarities to *A. rufinerve,* though the inflorescences and flowers are totally different from those of *A. rufinerve.* Attempts were made to graft *A. nipponicum* on *A. rufinerve,* but the results were quite unsatisfactory.

*Acer rufinerve* has a very "green" appearance, and indeed only a few snakebark maples are so green. It is easily distinguished from its nearest relatives, such as *A. tegmentosum,* a very sparsely branched tree, which has a much "bluer" bloom (glaucous) on its branches. Another very green ally is *A. davidii* ssp. *grosseri,* which lacks the bluish bloom on the wood but whose leaves are unlike those of *A. rufinerve.* The leaves of *A. rufinerve* are distinctively 3- to 5-lobed with doubly serrate margins. The branches of young trees are glabrous and covered with a bluish bloom with no trace of red. The wood on mature trees develops white stripes without any trace of red.

This plant is usually propagated by seed, and since it does not hybridize easily, garden seed can be used. The seed should be stored in sand and sown early in the following spring, to avoid dormancy, as with *Acer campestre.*

There are several cultivars, one of which is 'Albo-limbatum', with silver- or white-edged margins; it is quite common, but not very striking (see Chapter 9).

SECTION: *Macrantha*
ACER SIKKIMENSE ssp. METCALFII (Rehder) de Jong, comb. & stat. nov.
BASIONYM: *A. metcalfii* Rehder, *Journal Arnold Arboretum* 14:222.1933.
SYNONYMS
*A. davidii* var. *trilobatum* (Diels) Lee (1935).
*A. kiangsiense* Fang & Fang f. (1966).
TYPES: Lectotype *Lingnan University (Canton Christian College) 12135,* F. Metcalf, Guangdong, Tring-tan Mountain near Iu, China; A; isotypes BM, A; syntype *S. S. Sin 298,* southern Hunan, A.
EPITHET: *Metcalfii,* after U.S. botanist and explorer F. P. Metcalf (1892–1955).
ILLUSTRATION: Rehder (1933).
HABIT: A tree to 10 m tall; bark smooth; branches glabrous and indistinctly striped.
LEAVES: 3-lobed, 8–15 cm across, caudate-acuminate, leathery and reticulate on both sides; margins coarsely serrate; petioles 3 cm long.
INFLORESCENCES: Racemose, terminal.
FLOWERS: Not seen.
FRUITS: Samaras obtuse, 3 cm long; nutlets 6 mm wide, on 4–6 fruited racemes, 5–6 cm long.
BARK AND BUDS: Bark indistinctly striped; bud scales smooth.
HARDINESS: Zones VII–VIII.
DISTRIBUTION: Guangdong, Hunan, and Jiangxi provinces, China.
REFERENCES: Fang (1981a), de Jong (1977), Murray (1970c), Rehder (1933).

Very little is known about this taxon; apparently it is not in cultivation and no living material has been seen. Rehder states that it is closely related to *Acer davidii* ssp. *grosseri,* but here it is considered to be closer to *A. sikkimense* (formerly *A. hookeri*).

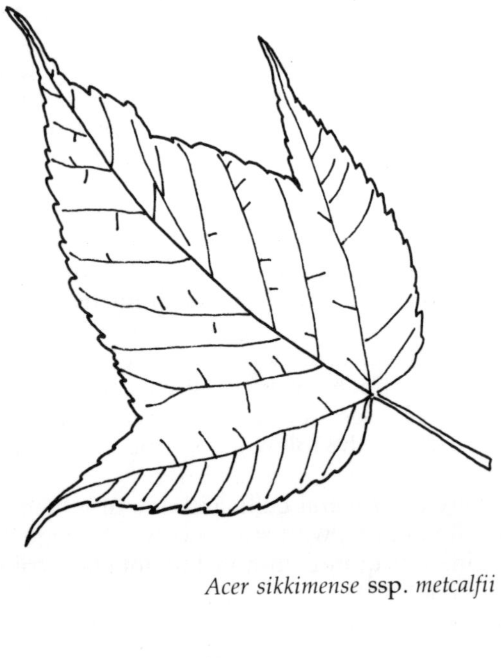

*Acer sikkimense* ssp. *metcalfii*

SECTION: *Macrantha*
ACER SIKKIMENSE Miquel (1867) ssp. SIKKIMENSE
SYNONYMS
*A. hookeri* Miquel (1867).
*A. sikkimense* ssp. *davidii* (Franchet) Wesmael (1890), pro parte excl. *A. hookeri* (vide Murray 1977).
*A. sikkimense* ssp. *hookeri* (Miquel) Wesmael (1890).
*A. cordifolium* hort. Kew (1894), non Moench.
*A. griffithii* hort. Kew (1894).
TYPES: *Hooker & Thomson f. #3,* Sikkim; holotype BM; isotypes G, W, FI.
EPITHET: *Sikkimensis,* from Sikkim (Kingdom) Province, India, in the Himalayas.
ILLUSTRATIONS: Plate 40; Fang (1981a), Krüssmann (1976a), Lancaster (1976).
HABIT: A tree in native habitat to 12 m tall; young stems and shoots red, slightly striped with white, glabrous. Reported as sometimes growing epiphytically in native habitat in the Himalayas.
LEAVES: Ovate, 8–15 cm long and 5–10 cm wide, unlobed or occasionally 3-lobed, very shiny green, almost leathery, not thin (Krüssmann 1976a). apices acuminate, bases cordate margins crenate, subentire or finely serrulate; petioles slender, 3–5 cm long.
INFLORESCENCES: Small, terminal racemes.
FLOWERS: Small, greenish, appearing with the leaves.
FRUITS: Samaras about 2 cm, at a right angle, on racemes 12–15 cm long; nutlets firm and round.
BARK AND BUDS: Bark slightly white-striped; buds valvate.
HARDINESS: Zone VIII.
AUTUMN COLOR: Unknown.
DISTRIBUTION: Eastern Himalayas, Sikkim, Bhutan, Assam, North Burma, in mountain forests at 2500–3000 m. Also in Yunnan Province, China.
CHROMOSOME NUMBER: $2n = 26$ (Mehra 1972).
SUBSPECIES
ssp. *metcalfii* (Rehder) de Jong, comb. & stat. nov.
ssp. *sikkimense,* the typical subspecies.
VARIETIES
var. *serrulatum* Pax (1886), margins serrulate; not in cultivation; probably should be merged with the species, which is very variable.
*A. hookeri* var. *majus* Pax, with leathery leaves.
*A. hookeri* var. *orbiculare* Fang & Wu (1979), with almost-round leaves.
REFERENCES: Bean (1970), Dippel (1892), Fang (1981a), de Jong (1977), Krüssmann (1976a), Murray (1970c), Pax (1902), Rehder (1986 facs.), Schneider (1912).

*Acer sikkimense* was described by Miquel in 1867. Wesmael (1890) later placed *A. hookeri* as a

*Acer sikkimense* ssp. *sikkimense*

subspecies under it. Research by de Jong in the herbaria of Kew and the British Museum led him to conclude that *A. sikkimense* must be merged with *A. hookeri.* Many herbaria sheets of both *A. hookeri* and *A. sikkimense* are available; they demonstrate that the differences between these species are so unimportant and inconsistent that there is not sufficient reason to separate them. A close relative, the former *A. metcalfii,* has now been placed as a subspecies under *A. sikkimense,* as it demonstrates adequate correlated differential characteristics distinct from subspecies *sikkimense.*

*Acer sikkimense* is a very beautiful species of snakebark maple, but unfortunately it is also very tender. It has unlobed, shining green leaves that are almost evergreen and do not drop until it becomes very cold. In mild winters or in greenhouses they do not drop until the new leaves develop. In its native habitat this is a small-or medium-sized tree with a faintly striped trunk, like some other members of section *Macrantha.* Stems and branches of young trees are quite glabrous and only indistinctly striped.

This species can be propagated by seed. Propagation by cuttings has not been tried, but should be possible. It is worth noting that grafting on seedlings of several species of section *Macrantha* has failed so far, possibly due to the low quality of the scions.

This species can only be planted in the mildest parts of Great Britain, North America, New Zealand, and Australia, and then only in very sheltered gardens. Young plants are extremely tender and must be kept frost-free through the winter.

Two varieties—var. *majus* and var. *orbiculare* of *Acer hookeri*—are mentioned with this subspecies because *A. hookeri* is no longer recognized as a species. New combinations seem superfluous because these two taxa, not in cultivation, may be reduced to synonymy, when living material becomes available and when comparative studies are done with herbaria specimens.

SECTION: *Macrantha*

ACER TEGMENTOSUM Maximowicz (1857)

SYNONYM: *A. pensylvanicum* ssp. *tegmentosum* (Maximowicz) Wesmael (1890).

TYPE: *Maximowicz,* Moktschala, Amur, eastern Siberia, Russia; LE.

COMMON NAME: Amur'scher Ahorn.

EPITHET: *Tegmentosus,* meaning "covered, hidden."

ILLUSTRATIONS: Plate 41; Fang (1981a), Krüssmann (1976a), Nakai (1909).

HABIT: A small tree or large shrub to 10 m tall, sparsely branched; branches purple to gray-green, with whitish stripes on the glabrous bark; young shoots glabrous, intensely bluish (glaucous), later slightly striped with white.

LEAVES: 3- to 5-lobed, 10–18 cm across, hexagonal, margins doubly serrate, fresh green; lobes acuminate, glabrescent; petioles 3–8 cm long; young leaves appear very early in spring.

INFLORESCENCES: Pendulous-racemose, terminal, 7–10 cm long.

FLOWERS: Yellow-green, appearing as early as April, together with the leaves or slightly earlier; often unisexual.

FRUITS: Samaras about 3 cm long; wings subhorizontal.

BARK AND BUDS: Bark faintly striped white, but less conspicuous than those on *A. rufinerve* or *A. pensylvanicum;* buds valvate.

HARDINESS: Zones IV–V.

AUTUMN COLOR: Yellow.

DISTRIBUTION: In moist locations and along the banks of the Amur and Ussuri rivers in Russia, and in mountainous regions of North Korea and Manchuria.

REFERENCES: Fang (1981a), de Jong (1977), Krüssmann (1976a), Koch (1869), Murray (1970c), Nakai (1909), Pojárkova (1933), Rehder (1986 facs.).

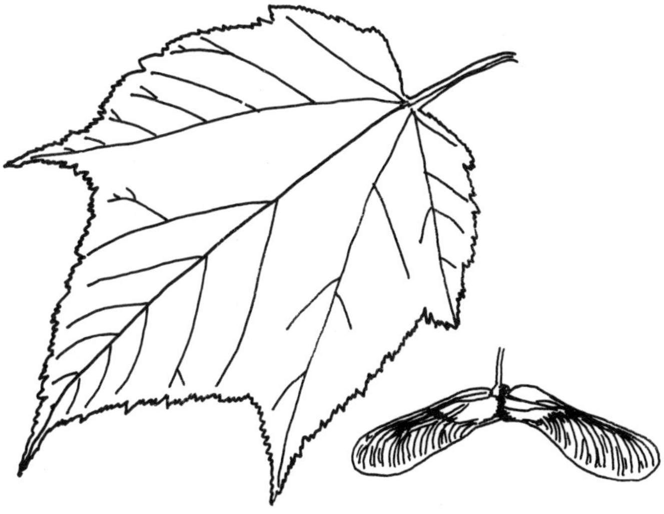

*Acer tegmentosum*

Maximowicz described this species in 1857, but Wesmael (1890) placed it as a subspecies under *Acer pensylvanicum,* to which it is rather closely (e.g., the inflorescences, flowers and fruits are similar), but *A. tegmentosum* is definitely a distinct species. The two are geographically widely separated, and the blue bloom is absent in *A. pensylvanicum* but always prominently present in *A. tegmentosum.* Very good specimens, both male and female, grow in Seattle at the University of Washington Arboretum.

A small tree with purplish to gray-green stems, *Acer tegmentosum* is sparsely branched and striped with white. The leaves are 10–18 cm across, hexagonal and 3- to 5-lobed. The name *tegmentosum* signifies that the inflorescences grow from the "hook" of the bud scales or that the bud scales, leaves, and branches are covered with a bloomy wax (glaucous).

*Acer tegmentosum* can be mistaken for *A. rufinerve,* as it has the same bluish wax on its branches, but it is waxier than *A. rufinerve.* The leaves are similar, differing mainly in size: those of *A. tegmentosum* are larger than those of *A. rufinerve.* A very important difference is that *A. tegmentosum,* a far more open and leggy shrub, leafs out very early in the spring and flowers at least 4–5 weeks earlier than *A. rufinerve.* The seeds are round, like those of *A. rufinerve,* but softer and smaller. This maple does not form forests but grows in mixed vegetation.

As it does not often set viable seed, this species is hard to find in the nursery trade. Grafting on *Acer rufinerve* works well and is occasionally done by specialists. It should be noted that this species may suffer from late spring frosts.

SECTION: *Macrantha*

ACER TSCHONOSKII ssp. KOREANUM Murray (1977)

SYNONYMS

*A. tschonoskii* var. *rubripes* Komarov (1904).
*A. komarovii* Pojárkova (1949).

TYPES: *E. H. Wilson 10700,* North Korea, Hamgyong-Pukto, Chongjin, Kyongsong; holotype A; isotype BM.

EPITHET: *Koreanus,* from Korea.

HABIT: A small tree or treelike shrub; branches dark green to gray, striped with white; bark of young shoots often coral red turning greenish yellow in summer.

LEAVES: 5-lobed, 5–18 cm long, 4–6 cm wide, lobes acute, less caudate than in subspecies *tschonoskii;* petioles red.

INFLORESCENCES: Racemose, terminal.

FLOWERS: Yellowish.

FRUITS: Samaras 3 cm long, in racemes with usually only a few fruits per infructescence; wings obtuse.

*Acer tschonoskii* ssp. *koreanum*

BARK AND BUDS: Conspicuously red young shoots and twigs, especially in winter, older branches green to gray with stripes; buds valvate.

HARDINESS: Zones IV–V.

AUTUMN COLOR: Yellow to orange.

DISTRIBUTION: Mountains of North and South Korea, also in northern China (Manchuria). The former variety *rubripes* was the sole representative in the Sorak Mountains of northeastern South Korea.

REFERENCES: Fang (1981a, as *A. komarovii*), Murray (1977), Pojárkova (1933b).

Pojárkova (1949) named this plant *Acer komarovii.* It has thinner and more incised leaves than those of the species. Komarov (1904) described variety *rubripes,* with brilliant red twigs and even more acuminate apices, from Manchuria and North Korea. Seedlings of *A. tschonoskii* also display this characteristic from time to time, so this variety might only be a geographical variant. Murray (1971) considered *A. komarovii* and *A. tschonoskii* var. *rubripes* to be synonymous, and described subspecies *koreanum* with less caudate lobes, growing only in Korea and China (Manchuria), and not in Japan.

SECTION: *Macrantha*

ACER TSCHONOSKII Maximowicz (1886) ssp. TSCHONOSKII

SYNONYMS

*A. pellucidobracteatum* Léveillé & Vaniot (1906).
*A. tschonoskii* f. *macrophyllum* (Nakai) Sugimoto (1961).

TYPES: Syntypes *Tschonoski,* Nikko, Province Nambu, Japan; LE; isotype P; Tanaka, Japan; TNS.

COMMON NAMES: Hakusan momiji, Mine kaede.

EPITHET: *Tschonoskii,* after Japanese botanist

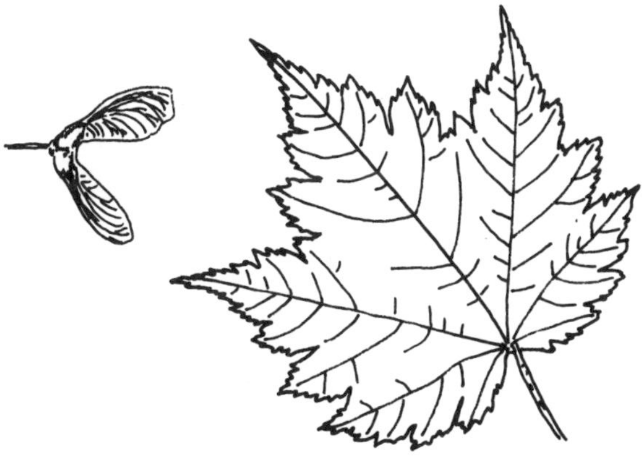

*Acer tschonoskii* ssp. *tschonoskii*

Tschonoski (1841–1925), who was a collector for Maximowicz.
ILLUSTRATIONS: Fang (1981a), Koidzumi (1911), Krüssmann (1976a), Ogata (1965), Nakai (1909), Satake et al. (1989).
HABIT: A shrub or small tree in native habitat to 10 m tall, with glabrous branches.
LEAVES: 5-lobed or rarely 7-lobed, 5–10 cm long and 4–6 cm wide, lobes rhombic, apices attenuate, margins incised, bases cordate; vein axils tufted with red-brown hairs when young; petioles red, 3–5 cm long.
INFLORESCENCES: Racemose, terminal, to 10 cm long, with only a few fruits.
FLOWERS: Yellowish, 6–10 per inflorescence, occurring late (at the end of May), but earlier than for *A. micranthum.*
FRUITS: Samaras 3 cm long, wings obtuse.
BARK AND BUDS: Bark purple or reddish, with inconspicuous white stripes; buds valvate.
HARDINESS: Zones IV–V.
AUTUMN COLOR: Yellow to deep red.
DISTRIBUTION: Northern Japan—on Honshu and Hokkaido islands—in mountain forests, widespread from 1400 m to the timberline (2500 m).
CHROMOSOME NUMBER: $2n = 26$ (Darlington 1955).
SUBSPECIES
  ssp. *koreanum* Murray (1977), endemic to Manchuria and Korea.
  ssp. *tschonoskii,* the typical subspecies.
VARIETY: var. *australe* Momotami (1962); apparently not in cultivation.
REFERENCES: Bean (1970), de Jong (1977), Koidzumi (1911), Krüssmann (1976a), Murray (1970c), Ogata (1965), Pojárkova (1933b), Rehder (1986 facs.), Vertrees (1978, 1987).

This species grows randomly and as isolated plants. It is a small tree or a slender shrub, to 10 m tall. Its distinct leaves have long tapered apices and beautiful red petioles. The leaf margins are coarsely incised. The leaves are the same shape as those of *A. pectinatum,* but the lobes are quite different. Most of the snakebark maples do not have these long, tapered central lobes, so there is little danger of confusion with other species.

*Acer tschonoskii* is a very beautiful and desirable plant, worthy of a place in more gardens. It should be made more readily available in the trade.

## SECTION GLABRA Pax amend. Momotani

TYPE SPECIES: ***Acer glabrum*** Torrey (1828).
HABIT: Deciduous trees and shrubs.
LEAVES: Chartaceous, undivided, 3- to 5-lobed, sometimes partially trifoliolate; margins serrate.
BUD SCALES: 2- to 4-paired.
INFLORESCENCES: Small, racemose or corymbose, terminal and sometimes exclusively axillary, 10–25 flowers.
FLOWERS: 4- or 5-merous, yellowish; discs amphi- to extrastaminal.
FRUITS: Nutlets flat, glabrous, strongly veined, parthenocarpic tendency strong.
SEEDLINGS: Cotyledons small, obovate.
SERIES: *Glabra, Arguta.*
REFERENCE: De Jong (1976).

Section *Glabra* resembles section *Lithocarpa* in specialization and geographic distribution. Both have a rather primitive monotypic series in western North America and a more specialized dioecious series in eastern Asia. Section *Glabra* is related to section *Parviflora* and perhaps to *Macrantha.*

### SERIES GLABRA

TYPE SPECIES: ***Acer glabrum*** Torrey.
HABIT: Shrubs or small trees.
LEAVES: 3- to 5-lobed or partly trifoliolate.
BUD SCALES: 2- to 4-paired.
INFLORESCENCES: Corymbose or racemose, terminal and axillary.
FLOWERS: 5-merous; stamens 8.
SPECIES AND INFRASPECIFIC TAXA
  *A. glabrum* ssp. *diffusum* (Greene) Murray.
  *A. glabrum* ssp. *douglasii* (Hooker) Wesmael.
  *A. glabrum* Torrey ssp. *glabrum.*
  *A. glabrum* ssp. *neomexicanum* (Greene) Murray.
  *A. glabrum* ssp. *siskiyouense* Murray.
REFERENCE: De Jong (1976).

Series *Glabra* is monotypic, containing only *Acer glabrum* and its subspecies. They are mainly shrubs with 3- to 5-lobed leaves, indigenous to the western part of North America. *Acer glabrum* is in cultivation, although uncommon.

SECTION: *Glabra* SERIES: *Glabra*

ACER GLABRUM ssp. DOUGLASII (Hooker) Wesmael (1890)

BASIONYM: *A. douglasii* Hooker (1847).

SYNONYMS

*A. barbatum* sensu D. Douglas ex Hooker (1831), non Michaux.

*A. subserratum* Greene (1902).

TYPE: Syntypes *D. Douglas,* Rocky Mountains, USA; *D. Douglas,* Blue Mountains, USA; K.

EPITHET: *Douglasii,* after Scottish plant hunter David Douglas (1799–1834).

ILLUSTRATIONS: Plate 42; Krüssmann (1976a).

HABIT: A shrub or treelike shrub to 6 m tall; young shoots erect, attractively scarlet red; mature branches gray, rather densely branched.

LEAVES: Mostly 3-lobed, somewhat shallowly lobed, 5–10 cm wide or, rarely, smaller; lobes shortly acuminate, central lobes broadly ovate.

FLOWERS: Yellow-green, often dioecious, in terminal, short corymbs.

FRUITS: Samaras broader than those of subspecies *glabrum.*

BARK AND BUDS: Young shoots distinctly dark red; buds small.

HARDINESS: Zone V.

AUTUMN COLOR: Clear yellow.

DISTRIBUTION: North America, Alaska to Oregon, along riverbanks in the mountainous regions. Abundant in the southern part of the Cascade Range and in the province of Alberta, Canada.

REFERENCES: Bean (1970), Dippel (1892), Krüssmann (1976a), Murray (1970), Pax (1902), Rehder (1986 facs.).

*Acer glabrum* ssp. *douglasii* inhabits northern California from the Cascade Range to the Siskiyou Mountains, and extends also into Alaska. While it can be confused with *A. glabrum* ssp. *glabrum,* its leaves are almost always 3-lobed and more serrate than those of the species. This interesting maple deserves wider use. It was named to honor the famous plant hunter David Douglas.

SECTION: *Glabra* SERIES: *Glabra*

ACER GLABRUM Torrey (1828) ssp. GLABRUM

SYNONYMS

*A. glabrum* var. *tripartitum* (Torrey & Gray) Pax (1886).

*A. tripartitum* Nuttall ex Torrey & Gray (1838).

*A. glabrum* var. *monophyllum* (Schwerin) Pax (1902).

*A. glabrum* f. *trisectum* Sargent (1921).

TYPE: *Dr. James,* Rocky Mountains, about latitude 40°, USA; NY.

COMMON NAMES: Rock maple, Rocky Mountain maple.

EPITHET: *Glabrus/glaber,* glabrous.

*Acer glabrum* ssp. *glabrum*

ILLUSTRATIONS: Plate 43; Harris (1983), Krüssmann (1976a).

HABIT: A large shrub or sometimes a small tree with purplish red young stems; bud scales few; branchlets glabrous, often fastigiate.

LEAVES: 3- to 5-lobed to subtrifoliate, 6–15 cm across, glabrous, lobes acuminate and doubly toothed, shiny green above, light green or bluish on the undersides, without down; margins serrate; petioles red, 3–5 cm long.

FLOWERS: Yellow-green, on terminal, few-flowered corymbs, appearing in April.

FRUITS: Samaras erect and acute-angled, 3 cm long.

BARK AND BUDS: Young stems conspicuously purplish, older bark gray and sometimes slightly fissured; buds very small.

HARDINESS: Zone IV.

AUTUMN COLOR: Clear yellow to orange-yellow.

DISTRIBUTION: Rocky Mountains of North America on riverbanks and also as undergrowth in forests. Also occurring in the Black Hills of South Dakota. Subspecies *douglasii* occurs in the Cascade Range of Oregon, and subspecies *siskiyouense* in the Siskiyou Mountains of southern Oregon and northern California.

SUBSPECIES

ssp. *diffusum* (Greene) Murray (1971), with smaller leaves.

ssp. *douglasii* (Hooker) Wesmael (1890), a Western form and the most important subspecies.

ssp. *neomexicanum* (Greene) Murray (1970), leaves trifoliate.

ssp. *siskiyouense* Murray (1983), with rhombic leaves.

VARIETIES

var. *greenei* Keller (1942), with very small leaves.

var. *torreyi* (Greene) Smiley (1921), leaves 5-lobed.

FORM

f. *bicolor* Pax (1886), a name used by Pax for both white and yellow variegated clones but one that is illegitimate under the present code.

CULTIVAR: One (see Chapter 9).

REFERENCES: Bean (1970), Dippel (1892), Krüssmann (1970a), Murray (1970c, 19811, 1983a), Pax (1902), Rehder (1986 facs.).

This species inhabits the western part of the United States from the coast of Oregon and Washington to the Rocky Mountains. It is not very abundant in its habitat and is relatively rare in cultivation. It was described by Torrey in 1828.

*Acer glabrum* forms a treelike shrub with reddish gray branchlets; young shoots are purplish. The leaves are small, 3- to 5-lobed, and shining green with reddish petioles. The tree is recognizable by its thin and variable leaves. While *A. glabrum* could be mistaken for *A. tataricum,* the latter species does not have purplish stems.

The species is propagated by seed, which germinates freely, or by softwood cuttings.

SERIES ARGUTA (Rehder) Rehder

TYPE SPECIES: ***Acer argutum*** Maximowicz (1867).

HABIT: Deciduous trees and shrubs.

LEAVES: Undivided or 3- to 5-lobed.

INFLORESCENCES: On males, axillary from leafless buds; on females, terminal and axillary from mixed buds.

FLOWERS: 4-merous, dioecious, stamens 4–6, few female flowers.

SPECIES AND INFRASPECIFIC TAXA

- *A. acuminatum* Wallich ex D. Don.
- *A. argutum* Maximowicz.
- *A. barbinerve* Maximowicz.
- *A. stachyophyllum* ssp. *betulifolium* (Maximowicz) de Jong, comb. & stat. nov.
- *A. stachyophyllum* Hiern ssp. *stachyophyllum.*

REFERENCE: De Jong (1976).

This series includes four species, one of which is Japanese (*Acer argutum*). The other species occur in the Himalayas, West Pakistan, Korea, and China. They are large shrubs with 3- to 5-lobed or almost unlobed leaves. Most of these species are in cultivation.

SECTION: *Glabra* SERIES: *Arguta*

ACER ACUMINATUM Wallich ex D. Don (1825)

SYNONYMS

- *A. caudatum* Nicholson (1881), non Wallich (1830).
- *A. sterculiaceum* Koch 1869), non Wallich (1830).

TYPE: Syntype *Wallich 1225,* pro parte, Srinagar, India; K; PH.

EPITHET: *Acuminatus,* tapering gradually or abruptly from inwardly curved sides to a long, slender point.

ILLUSTRATIONS: Plate 44; Murray (1975a).

HABIT: A small tree to 6–7 m tall or a large, erect shrub about 4–6 m tall; young stems smooth, purplish.

LEAVES: 3- to 5-lobed, the basal lobes insignificant, leaf blades 6–12 cm long and about as wide; lobes triangular; apices acuminate, with long and slender tails (acumens), sharply toothed, often double-toothed; undersides with whitish hairs initially, later glabrous.

FLOWERS: 4-merous; male flowers in corymbs, female flowers in short umbels.

FRUITS: Samaras 3–4 cm long, wings spreading at a right angle, on simple and lax racemes 12–20 cm long.

BARK AND BUDS: Young shoots purplish red, somewhat downy; bud scales in pairs.

HARDINESS: Zones V–VI.

AUTUMN COLOR: Yellow-orange, not very distinctive.

DISTRIBUTION: Western part of the Himalayas in Nepal. Also in West Pakistan, Kashmir near Srinagar, and Kamroop.

REFERENCES: Bean (1970), Dippel (1892), Hillier (1965), Krüssmann (1976a), Murray (1970c), Pax (1902), Rehder (1986 facs.).

The name *Acer acuminatum,* given by Danish botanist Nathaniel Wallich, was first published by Don in 1825. The species was introduced into cultivation in 1845. Bean (1970) states:

> *Acer acuminatum* was described by David Don from a specimen collected at Srinagar by a native collector, employed by N. Wallich, who was the Superintendent of the Botanic Garden at Calcutta. Don took the name from one of Wallich's letters. The name does not occur in Wallich's lists, but material under the name *A. caudatum* agrees with *A. acuminatum.* All the material under nr. 1225 (*A. caudatum*) is *A. acuminatum.* When Wallich described his *A. caudatum,* he cited also nr. 1225, therefore *A. caudatum* Wall. consist in part of *A. acuminatum.*

Further details are given in the present volume in the description for *A. caudatum* Wallich (1831).

*Acer acuminatum* grows into a small, slender tree with smooth purplish stems, and can also be a wide shrub not much higher than 4–6 m tall. It is hardy in moderate climates. It can be confused with several species of section *Macrantha,* such as *A. pectinatum* or *A. tschonoskii,* but it lacks the distinctively striped bark and valvate buds typical of section *Macrantha.* Its leaf lobes are triangular, prolonged at the apices, forming long and slender points (hence the name *acuminate*). This long apex is also found on leaves *A. pectinatum* and subspecies *forrestii.*

As *Acer acuminatum* is a dioecious species, ripe and viable seed is difficult to obtain. If any fruits are borne, they are almost always empty. It is possible to propagate the species from softwood cuttings; however, these do not root easily. Grafting is difficult, as no appropriate root stock is available.

Schwerin wrote in one of his valuable contributions on *Acer* that at the end of the 19th century plants of *Acer acuminatum* (or plants bearing this name) were grafted on *A. negundo,* sold as small standard trees, and incorrectly identified as *A. laevigatum.* This seems rather fantastic and, in fact, cannot be true as grafting *A. acuminatum* on *A. negundo* does not seem possible. Schwerin also wrote that he grafted *A. acuminatum* onto *A. pseudoplatanus,* which seems more likely, as *A. pseudoplatanus* accepts many kinds of maples.

*Acer argutum*

SECTION: *Glabra* SERIES: *Arguta*

ACER ARGUTUM Maximowicz (1867)

SYNONYMS

*A. diabolicum* ssp. *argutum* (Maximowicz) Wesmael (1890).

*A. palmatum* var. *plicatum* Léveillé (1906).

TYPE: *Tschonoski,* Senano, Nambu, Japan; holotype LE; isotype BM; F.

COMMON NAMES: Asanoha kaede, Miyama momiji.

EPITHET: *Argutus,* sharply pointed.

ILLUSTRATIONS: Plate 45; Koidzumi (1911), Krüssmann (1976a), Kurata (1964–1976), Satake et al. (1989).

HABIT: A small, deciduous tree up to 6 m tall, often only a large shrub, with erect branches; young shoots scarlet, often with reddish hairs or downy; mature branches speckled red and gray, later completely gray.

LEAVES: 6–12 cm long and as wide or sometimes narrower, 5-lobed, noted for reticulate veins; lobes ovate with double-toothed margins; undersides downy, especially on the whitish veins; leaf blades may shrivel in hot sun.

FLOWERS: Greenish yellow, dioecious; male flowers borne on racemes before the leaves unfold, female flowers on solitary racemes in the leaf axils.

FRUITS: Samaras small, spreading horizontally, borne on slender stalks, few to a corymb; seeds about 2 cm long; nutlets flat and veined.

BARK AND BUDS: Bark red on young trees, gray on mature trees, young shoots as red as the twigs of *Cornus alba,* most branches with insignificant whitish stripes, color darkens in winter.

HARDINESS: Zones IV–V.

AUTUMN COLOR: Golden yellow.

DISTRIBUTION: Mountain forests in Japan, especially on Honshu (in the southern two-thirds) and Shikoku islands, at 600–1000 m, growing along small rivers and streams.

CULTIVARS: None.

REFERENCES: Bean (1970), Dippel (1892), Elwes & Henry (1908), Koidzumi (1911), Krüssmann (1976a), Kurata (1964–1976), Murray (1970c), Rehder (1986 facs.), Veitch (1904).

*Acer argutum* was described by the famous Russian botanist Maximowicz in 1867, and was introduced by Maries for Veitch Nursery in 1881. Nine years later Wesmael put this species as a subspecies under *Acer diabolicum,* but there is no affinity between these taxa. Seedlings named as *A. diabolicum,* another Japanese species, were received in The Netherlands in 1978, and proved to be *A. argutum.* It is remarkable how misidentifications have such long lives.

This is certainly one of the more graceful shrubs of this section. It forms a rather tight and upright shrub, or even a small tree. The young shoots and branchlets are often brilliantly scarlet, especially on young plants. The leaves have distinctive reticulate veins that cover the leaf blades, similar to the leaves of *Acer spicatum* and *A. caudatum* ssp. *ukurunduense.* The species, however, is not easily confused with other species. Only *A. spicatum* bears some resemblance, but its wood is not nearly so red and its older wood is always gray.

*Acer argutum* prefers a moist, cool location and is perfectly hardy. Unfortunately, it is only occasionally available in the trade. It can be propagated by seed, but since it is dioecious, viable seed can only be harvested from a group of several plants, which is almost never possible. Propagation by cuttings is a good substitute. Cuttings must be taken in July and can be rooted with the aid of hormones, although this can be a difficult procedure. Grafting on *A. pseudoplatanus* has been done, but the take rate is low and there are many suckers from the understock.

SECTION: *Glabra* SERIES: *Arguta*

ACER BARBINERVE Maximowicz (1867)

SYNONYMS

*A. diabolicum* ssp. *barbinerve* (Maximowicz) Wesmael (1890).

*A. megalodum* Fang & Su (1979).

TYPE: K. J. *Maximowicz,* Ussuri, China (Manchuria); LE.

EPITHET: *Barbinervis,* with bearded veins.

ILLUSTRATIONS: Plate 46; Fang (1981a, as *A. megalodum*), Krüssmann (1976a), Pojárkova (1933b).

HABIT: A small deciduous, androdioecious tree or large shrub to 10 m tall, with several stems; bark smooth and gray; young shoots green or very rarely reddish.

LEAVES: Thin, 5-lobed, roundish or ovate with long and slender apices, sharply and coarsely toothed, 5–12 cm long and almost as wide, occasionally larger on long shoots, dark green and somewhat downy when young, undersides softly hairy with some tufts of hairs in vein axils (hence its name: "bearded veins"); bases heart-shaped; petioles long, up to 6 cm.

FLOWERS: Yellowish; on male trees, in clusters of 4–6; in female trees, in racemes about 5–6 cm long at the end of two-leafed branchlets.

FRUITS: Samaras spreading at an angle of about 120°; fruits 4–6 cm long, usually not viable if from solitary trees.

BARK AND BUDS: Stems greenish; young shoots downy, not unlike its relative, *A. argutum;* buds valvate.

HARDINESS: Zone IV.

AUTUMN COLOR: Yellow.

DISTRIBUTION: Southeastern Manchuria, valleys of the Upper Ussuri; and Shaanxi Province, China. Also Korea.

*Acer barbinerve*

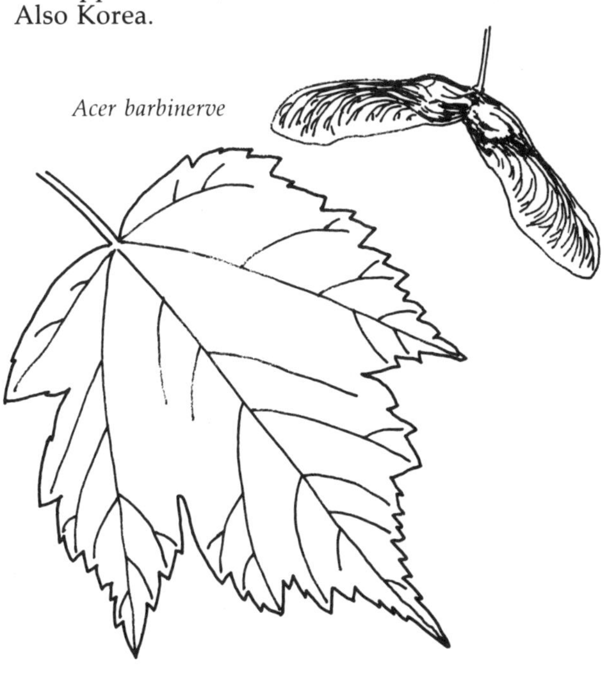

VARIETY: var. *glabrescens* Nakai (1914), with glabrous leaves; growing in Korea, but not in cultivation in the West.

REFERENCES: Bean (1970), Fang (1981a), Krüssmann (1976a), Murray (1970c), Pojárkova (1933b), Rehder (1986 facs.).

*Acer barbinerve* was discovered in 1867 and introduced to Great Britain about 1890. Maximowicz made the diagnosis, but Wesmael brought the species under *A. diabolicum* in 1890.

*Acer barbinerve* is closely related to *A. argutum,* though much rarer. It differs from this ally in leaf shape, having slender apices, and in never displaying the scarlet twigs. The sharp- and coarsely toothed leaves are thin. *Acer barbinerve* forms a small tree or merely a large shrub of the same habit and appearance as *A. argutum,* or *A. stachyophyllum.* The branchlets and stems are gray or greenish.

Propagation is best accomplished by seed, but as this species is androdioecious, viable seed is hard to obtain. The propagation methods suitable for *Acer argutum* are recommended for this species. As this maple is extremely rare in collections, there is little possibility of purchasing it in the trade.

In 1979 Fang & Su described *Acer megalodum.* From analysis and drawings (Fang 1981a) of this species, it will probably turn out to be synonymous with *A. barbinerve. Acer megalodum* is not in cultivation nor are herbarium specimens available. However, the available description matches that of *A. barbinerve.* Only the drawings of *A. megalodum* are different in some respects, especially the leaf serration. The fruits of *A. megalodum* appear to be spreading at a 45° angle, while those of *A. barbinerve* are almost horizontal. This, however, is not a consequential difference. Fang clearly states that *A. megalodum* and *A. barbinerve* are closely related. For these reasons *A. megalodum* is not considered a true species in the present volume, but rather is regarded as a synonym of *A. barbinerve.*

SECTION: *Glabra* SERIES: *Arguta*

ACER STACHYOPHYLLUM Hiern (1875)

SYNONYM: *A. tetramerum* Pax (1889).

TYPE: Syntypes *Griffith,* Bhutan, *Hooker f.* Sikkim, Lachoon Valley.

EPITHET: *Stachyophyllus,* from *stachys,* meaning ear of grain, spike. Spike-leaved.

ILLUSTRATIONS: Fang (1981a), Krüssmann (1976a), Pax (1902, as *A. tetramerum*).

HABIT: A small, erect-growing tree, with several stems growing closely together; branches brownish yellow to orange-brown; usually suckers, which is very unusual for maples.

LEAVES: Ovate, unlobed to 3-lobed, 5–8 cm long, margins incised to lobulate, glaucous beneath,

pubescent in the petiole axils; petioles 2 cm long.
INFLORESCENCES: Racemose, terminal.
FLOWERS: Yellowish, dioecious, stamens 4.
FRUITS: Samaras 2–5 cm long, wings acute, borne on short racemes, often parthenocarpic.
BARK AND BUDS: Bark indistinctly striped; bud scales valvate.
HARDINESS: Zone V.
AUTUMN COLOR: Yellow.
DISTRIBUTION: Himalayas, from Sikkim to Hubei Province, central China, in mountain forests to 3000 m.
CHROMOSOME NUMBER: $2n = 26$ (Mehra 1972).
SUBSPECIES

- ssp. *betulifolium* (Maximowicz) de Jong, comb. & stat. nov.; basionym is *A. betulifolium* Maximowicz, *Plantae Chinenses Potaninae, Acta Horti Petropoli* 11:108. 1889; with much smaller leaves; originally described from Gansu Province, China; very rare; suckers freely once established. Several former varieties of *A. tetramerum,* such as variety *haopingense* and variety *dolichurum* Fang & Wu, could possibly be included in this new subspecies, which is somewhat variable; Plate 47.
- ssp. *stachyophyllum,* the typical subspecies; Plate 48.

VARIETY: var. *pentaneurum* (Fang & Hu) Fang (1979), a Chinese taxon unknown in cultivation; Fang (1979) considers *A. muliense* Fang & Hu (1966) a synonym of this variety.
REFERENCES: Bean (1970), Fang (1981a), Krüssmann (1976a), Murray (1970c), Pax (1902), Rehder (1986 facs.), Schneider (1912), Veitch (1904).

*Acer stachyophyllum* ssp. *stachyophyllum*

This species is much better known by as *Acer tetramerum,* the name given it by Pax (1889) and the name under which Wilson introduced the species in 1901. Hiern's (in Hooker 1875) type material of *A. stachyophyllum* proved to be identical with *A. tetramerum.* Thus the name *A. stachyophyllum* must be adopted as it has priority.

This small, erect-growing, multistemmed or even fastigiate tree has a somewhat untidy habit. The leaves are small, 5–7 cm long, 3- to 5-lobed with incised lobes, deep green and somewhat glaucous beneath, with a yellow autumn color. The tree usually sets many sterile fruits, but from time to time enough male flowers are produced for a good crop of viable seed. These are borne in rather long, drooping trusses.

*Acer stachyophyllum* is distinguished from *A. argutum* and *A. barbinerve,* its close relatives, by the fastigiate growth. The leaves of *A. argutum* also differ in their reticulate veins and *A. barbinerve* has much more coarsely serrate leaf margins.

Both the species and its subspecies are easily propagated from softwood cuttings. Often viable seed is not available, and there is no fitting understock for grafting. From time to time the species is available in the trade, but some feel it has little ornamental value, so it may always be a rather rare tree.

## SECTION NEGUNDO (Boehmer) Maxim.

TYPE SPECIES: ***Acer negundo*** L. (1753).
HABIT: Deciduous trees or shrubs.
LEAVES: Chartaceous, compound, trifoliolate or pinnate, 5–7 foliolate; margins entire or remotely dentate.
BUD SCALES: 2- to 3-paired.
INFLORESCENCES: Racemose or compound racemose, axillary from leafless buds or accompanied by 1–2 pairs of small leaves, which drop precociously, with 15–50 flowers.
FLOWERS: 4-merous, dioecious; stamens 4–6, absent in female flowers.
FRUITS: Nutlets small, elliptic-spherical to rather flat, veined, parthenocarpic tendency strong.
SEEDLINGS: Cotyledons narrowly oblong.
SERIES: *Negundo, Cissifolia.*
REFERENCE: De Jong (1976).

Section *Negundo* has two highly specialized, closely related series, which still have the original pinnate leaves and a low number of bud scales. Affinities to other sections are not very clear. The section probably represents a very early taxon.

SERIES NEGUNDO
TYPE SPECIES: ***Acer negundo*** L.
LEAVES: Pinnate, sometimes to 9-foliolate.
BUD SCALES: 2-, more often 3-paired.
INFLORESCENCES: Racemose or compound racemose on long drooping peduncles.
FLOWERS: Apetalous, greenish, discs absent, anemophilous, anthesis before leaf development.
SPECIES AND INFRASPECIFIC TAXA
*A. negundo* ssp. *californicum* (Torrey & Gray) Wesmael.
*A. negundo* ssp. *interius* (Britton) A. & D. Loeve.
*A. negundo* ssp. *mexicanum* (DC.) Wesmael.
*A. negundo* L. ssp. *negundo.*
REFERENCE: De Jong (1976).

Series *Negundo* has only one species with four subspecies. The species has a vast range throughout North America and is also naturalized in large areas of China. It is very common in cultivation. The dioecious trees bear large compound leaves.

SECTION: *Negundo* SERIES: *Negundo*
ACER NEGUNDO ssp. CALIFORNICUM (Torrey & Gray) Wesmael (1890)
BASIONYM: *Negundo californicum* Torrey & Gray (1838).
SYNONYMS
*A. californicum* (Torrey & Gray) D. Dietrich (1849).
*A. negundo* var. *parishianum* Kuntze (1891).
*Negundo aceroides* var. *californicum* (Torrey & Gray) Sargent (1889).
*Rulac californicum* (Torrey & Gray) Nieuwland (1911).
*A. negundo* var. *arizonicum* Sargent (1919).
TYPE: *David Douglas,* California, USA; K.
EPITHET: *Californicus,* from California.
ILLUSTRATION: Plate 49.
HABIT: A tree to 25 m tall, with strongly pubescent branches.
LEAVES: Trifoliolate, often up to seven leaflets, each leaflet 4–8 cm long, ovate, more serrate and lobed than the typical subspecies; juvenile leaves covered with a thick, pubescent tomentum; adult leaves covered with whitish hairs.
FLOWERS: Very much like those of *A. negundo* ssp. *negundo.*
FRUITS: Samaras yellowish, slightly pubescent, produced in abundance on long, drooping racemes.
BARK AND BUDS: Bark darker colored than in the typical subspecies; buds covered with a dense tomentum.
HARDINESS: Zones V–VI.
AUTUMN COLOR: Yellow.
DISTRIBUTION: In valleys and riverbanks in middle and southern California, together with *Alnus, Salix* and *Platanus* species. Also growing in Arizona in moist situations.
VARIETY: var. *texanum* Pax (1886), young shoots slightly tomentose, leaves trifoliolate, broadly elliptic, juvenile leaves irregularly serrate, puberulent beneath; occurs in Arizona, Texas, and Missouri, but apparently is not in cultivation; intermediate between subspecies *negundo* and *californicum.*
CULTIVARS: Several (see Chapter 9).
REFERENCES: Bean (1970), Elwes & Henry (1908), Koch (1869), Krüssmann (1976a), Murray (1970c).

In several botanic gardens plants are mistakenly labeled as this subspecies and are instead representatives of subspecies *negundo.* The very conspicuous hairiness distinguishes subspecies *californicum* at a glance from its allies. It is widespread in California, where it occurs in thickets and windbreaks, along riverbanks, and even in densely populated areas.

SECTION: *Negundo* SERIES: *Negundo*
ACER NEGUNDO ssp. INTERIUS (Britton) A. & D. Loeve (1954)
BASIONYM: *A. interior* Britton (1908).
SYNONYMS
*A. kingii* Britton (1908).
*Rulac interius* (Britton) Nieuwland (1911).
*R. kingii* (Britton) Nieuwland (1911).
*Negundo interius* (Britton) Rydberg (1913).
*N. kingii* (Britton) Rydberg (1913).
TYPE: *Underwood & Selby 11,* Ouray near Durango, Colorado, USA; holotype NY.
EPITHET: *Interius,* in the inner part, referring to the natural distribution range of the species.
ILLUSTRATION: Plate 50.
HABIT: A tree, with puberulent branches, rarely glabrous.
LEAVES: Trifoliolate, thin, glabrous beneath or slightly hairy at midribs, coarsely lobulate; leaflets long, petiolulate.
FLOWERS: Not seen, but most probably like subspecies *negundo.*
HARDINESS: Zone V.
FRUITS: Not seen, but probably like subspecies *negundo.*
DISTRIBUTION: Rocky Mountains and the Plains, from Saskatchewan, Canada, south to New Mexico, USA.
REFERENCES: Krüssmann (1976a), Murray (1970c).

This poorly described and unknown subspecies is rarely found in cultivation. Its status as a subspecies is maintained for the same reasons already discussed for several Chinese species in section *Palmata,* series *Sinensia.* A huge tree is growing in the Arnold Arboretum, USA, and younger plants are in the Botanic Garden of Hamburg, Germany.

Some taxa, such as *Acer negundo* ssp. *interius*

and many Chinese species, cannot be studied more intensively, as they are often provided with only poor descriptions and limited, inadequate drawings. Furthermore, herbarium specimens are rarely available. Often it is prudent, after examining the descriptions and illustrations available, to sink these taxa into synonymy, until better materials become available that clearly demonstrate a higher status or rank. (Some might argue, however, that it is more prudent, after examining the descriptions and illustrations available, to treat these taxa as species or as sundry infraspecific ranks until better materials become available that might clearly demonstrate that treating them as synonyms is more appropriate.)

SECTION: *Negundo* SERIES: *Negundo*

ACER NEGUNDO ssp. MEXICANUM (DC.) Wesmael (1890)

BASIONYM: *Negundo mexicanum* DC. (1824).

SYNONYMS

*A. ternatum* DC. (1824).
*A. mexicanum* (DC.) Pax (1886).
*Rulac mexicanum* (DC.) Nieuwland (1911).
*A. serratum* Pax ex Standley (1923).

TYPE: Syntypes *Uhde 1140; Hegewich; Schiede 1829,* Mexico; B (destroyed); G.

EPITHET: *Mexicanus,* from Mexico.

HABIT: A tree; young shoots almost glabrous.

LEAVES: Trifoliolate, leaflets the same size, elliptical, 6–8 cm long and 2.5–3 cm wide, dark green, much paler beneath, densely tomentose beneath; margins serrate.

FLOWERS: Female flowers on long panicles, male flowers on long pedicellate, short racemes.

HARDINESS: Zones VI–VII.

FRUITS: Borne on long panicles, glabrous.

DISTRIBUTION: Mountains of central Mexico and Guatemala.

REFERENCES: Krüssmann (1976a), Murray (1970c).

*Acer negundo* ssp. *mexicanum* apparently is not in cultivation. It has long been known in the literature and is one of the very few maples first described by Augustin Pyramus de Candolle (1778–1841), the great ancestor of the famous family of botanists from Geneva, Switzerland.

SECTION: *Negundo* SERIES: *Negundo*

ACER NEGUNDO L. (1753) ssp. NEGUNDO

SYNONYMS

*Negundo aceroides* Moench (1794).
*Negundium fraxinifolium* Rafinesque (1808) nomen nudum.
*Negundo fraxinifolium* (Stokes) DC. (1824).
*Acer trifoliatum* Rafinesque (1836).
*A. lobatum* Rafinesque (1836).
*A. negundo* ssp. *typicum* Wesmael (1890).

*Acer negundo* ssp. *negundo*

*A. negundo* ssp. *vulgare* (Pax) Schwerin (1893).
*Rulac negundo* (L.) Hitchcock (1894).
*Acer fauriei* Léveillé (1906).
*Rulac nuttallii* Nieuwland (1911).
*Acer orizabense* (Rydberg) Standley (1923).

TYPE: *LINN 1225.7;* LINN, "Habitat in Virginia."

COMMON NAMES: Ash-leaved maple, Box elder, Eschenahorn.

EPITHET: *Negundo,* an old generic name for *Acer,* used by J. Ray in 1698 and derived from the similarity to *Vitex negundo.*

ILLUSTRATIONS: Plate 51; de Jong (1976), Krüssmann (1976a).

HABIT: A tree of rapid growth, often with more than one trunk, 12–20 m tall, occasionally even taller; branches brittle, fully glabrous, covered with a glaucous bloom when young.

LEAVES: 3–7 foliolate, sometimes to 9-foliolate, leaflets ovate, 5–10 cm long and 3–5 cm wide, olive-green to fresh green; margins remotely dentate to subentire; outer leaflet often 3-lobed; petioles 6–10 cm long.

INFLORESCENCES: Lateral.

FLOWERS: Pale green, dioecious; male flowers usually in clusters of four, stamens often purplish; female flowers consisting of two whitish stigmas on long pendulous racemes.

FRUITS: Samaras erect to acute, yellowish, in long drooping racemes, very often sterile, produced abundantly.

BARK AND BUDS: Greenish olive to bluish when young.

HARDINESS: Zones III–V (–VIII, for very southerly expressions).

AUTUMN COLOR: Yellow.

DISTRIBUTION: Indigenous to Canada, often forming immense impenetrable thickets; also along edges of roadsides. Found also in mixed forests in the eastern and middle regions of the United States, on riverbanks, westward to the Rocky Mountains, south to Guatemala. Naturalized in eastern China.

CHROMOSOME NUMBER: $2n = 26$ (Darlington 1955, Santamour 1965).

SUBSPECIES

ssp. *californicum* (Torrey & Gray) Wesmael (1890).
ssp. *interius* (Britton) A. & D. Loeve (1954).
ssp. *mexicanum* (DC.) Wesmael (1890).

ssp. *negundo*, the typical subspecies.
CULTIVARS: Many (see Chapter 9).
REFERENCES: Bean (2970), Dippel (1892), Elwes & Henry (1908), de Jong (1976), Koch (1869), Krüssmann (1976a), Linnaeus (1753), Murray (1970c), Pax (1902), Pojárkova (1933b), Rehder (1986 facs.).

Box elder is a very common maple in North America. It is widely planted in Europe and North America, and is also very commonly naturalized throughout the United States and in large areas of China, and Central and South America. Linnaeus used the species name *negundo* after J. Ray, who proposed it as a generic name for *Acer* in 1698. There are many synonyms due to the extreme variability of the leaves and the very wide natural distribution.

The box elder may form large trees marked by rapid growth with long, 3–7 (–9) foliolate leaves, not unlike *Fraxinus excelsior.* The species is dioecious; if planted alone, female trees normally produce enormous quantities of parthenocarpic fruits. The branches are brittle, and the quality of the timber is rather poor.

*Acer negundo* is not easily confused with other species, except perhaps *A. cissifolium* from Japan or its ally *A. henryi* from China, both belonging to the same section as *A. negundo,* but a different series. These two Asiatic taxa of series *Cissifolia* have different leaf shapes, while *A. negundo* has smaller leaflets. The branches are green in *A. negundo,* except in subspecies with glaucous twigs, and not reddish gray as in *A. cissifolium. Acer negundo* also forms a larger tree than its relatives.

*Acer negundo* has been in cultivation since the time North American plants were being introduced to Europe. It has many cultivars. Due to its vast natural distribution range there are several named botanical variations, the most important is *A. negundo* ssp. *californicum,* which has heavily pubescent leaves and is native to western California. The pubescence is persistent during the summer.

This maple, so easily propagated from seed, is the understock for its many cultivars. Propagation is by budding in early summer or by grafting on potted understocks in July, or in February in a heated greenhouse.

SERIES CISSIFOLIA (Koidzumi) Momotani
TYPE SPECIES: ***Acer cissifolium*** (Siebold & Zuccarini) Koch (1864).
LEAVES: Trifoliolate.
BUD SCALES: 2-paired.
INFLORESCENCES: Racemose; rachises long; 15–30 flowers.
FLOWERS: 4-merous, sepals and tepals distinct, greenish white or yellow, 4–6 stamens, disc amphistaminal.
SPECIES
*A. cissifolium* (Siebold & Zuccarini) K. Koch.
*A. henryi* Pax.
REFERENCE: De Jong (1976).

This small series includes two species. The Chinese *Acer henryi* was reduced to subspecific rank under *A. cissifolium* by Murray (1966) as these taxa appear to be closely related, but the present authors disagree. Both species are small, dioecious trees with deciduous, compound leaves. Both are known in horticulture, and *A. cissifolium* is an especially valuable garden plant.

SECTION: *Negundo* SERIES: *Cissifolia*
ACER CISSIFOLIUM (Siebold & Zuccarini) Koch (1864)
BASIONYM: *Negundo cissifolium* Siebold & Zuccarini (1845).
SYNONYMS
*A. fraxinifolium* var. *cissifolium* Veitch (1876).
*A. negundo* var. *cissifolium* (Siebold & Zuccarini) Mouillefert (1895).
*Crula cissifolia* (Siebold & Zuccarini) Nieuwland (1911).
TYPE: *P. F. von Siebold,* Hakone, Japan; L.
COMMON NAMES: Amahogi, Amakuki, Amako kaede, Cissus-blättriger Ahorn, Mitsude kaede.
EPITHET: *Cissifolius,* with *Cissus*-like leaves.
ILLUSTRATIONS: Koidzumi (1911), Krüssmann (1976a), Kurata (1964–1976), Satake et al. (1989).
HABIT: A rather small tree, occasionally a large shrub, to 12 m tall; branches mostly gray, sometimes green; young stems speckled with red; juvenile shoots hairy, later glabrous.
LEAVES: Compound trifoliolate with three leaflets borne on slender petiolules, leaflets 6–9 cm long, obovate or oval, apices acute, coarsely and irregularly toothed, glabrous, except for some tufts at the vein axils on undersides.
INFLORESCENCES: Densely racemose, pendulous, glabrous.
FLOWERS: Yellow-green, 4-merous, dioecious, pedicillate, very small, on pedicels 3–5 mm long, produced in May.
FRUITS: Samaras about 3 cm long, obliquely ovate, 1 cm wide, forming an angle of about 60°; fruits produced very profusely in long slender corymbs, almost always parthenocarpic since male and female trees are seldom planted together.
BARK AND BUDS: Bud scales few.
HARDINESS: Zone V.
AUTUMN COLOR: Yellow to orange-yellow.
DISTRIBUTION: Japan, in mountain forests, from southern Hokkaido to central Kyushu.
CHROMOSOME NUMBER: $2n = 26$ (Mehra 1972).
CULTIVARS: Very few (see Chapter 9).

REFERENCES: Bean (1970), Dippel (1892), Koidzumi (1911), Krüssmann (1976a), Kurata (1964–1976), Murray (1970c), Pax (1902), Rehder (1986 facs.), Schwerin (1901), Veitch (1904), Vertrees (1978, 1987).

This maple with *Cissus*-like leaves belongs to the trifoliated group of section *Negundo* and not to section *Trifoliata,* as mentioned in some dendrological books. Siebold and Zuccarini published the description in 1845 as *Negundo cissifolium.* Koch transferred it to the genus *Acer* in 1864.

Native to Japan where it forms small forests on Hokkaido Island, this species was introduced to Europe before 1870. It forms a small tree or occasionally a large shrub. The leaves are trifoliated (i.e., consisting of 3-petiolulate leaflets borne on petioles) and olive-green, often tinged with yellow-orange when young. The autumn color is often very good, yellow to orange-yellow. The species does not like dry sites and should be given good shelter in cold and windy situations.

This maple is dioecious; viable seed is almost never obtainable due to solitary planting. Most plants in cultivation are female and were propagated by layering. The majority of nurseries offering this species possess only female stock plants. Schwerin reported in 1901 that his plants always flowered male, just the opposite of the plants presently in cultivation.

Now generally available in the trade, this maple plays a modest role in landscaping in Europe. It can easily be confused with *Acer henryi,* which is much greener, has more coarsely toothed leaflets, and is glabrous.

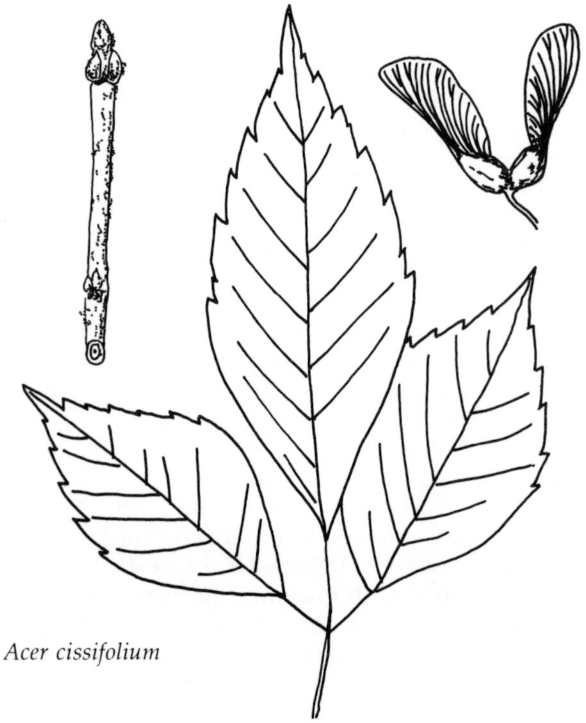

*Acer cissifolium*

SECTION: *Negundo* SERIES: *Cissifolia*

## ACER HENRYI Pax (1889)

SYNONYMS

*A. henryi* var. *serratum* Pampanini (1910).
*Crula henryi* (Pax) Nieuwland (1911).
*Acer henryi* f. *intermedium* Fang (1932).
*A. stenobotrys* Franchet ex Fang (1939).
*A. cissifolium* ssp. *henryi* (Pax) Murray (1966).

TYPE: Lectotype *A. Henry 5644-B,* Hubei Province, China: K.

EPITHET: *Henryi,* after Irish plant hunter Augustine Henry (1857–1930).

ILLUSTRATIONS: Plate 52; Fang (1981a), Krüssmann (1976a).

HABIT: A small tree or frequently a large shrub to 10 m tall and as wide; young shoots hairy and green, becoming smooth and olive-green when mature.

LEAVES: Trifoliolate, 5–10 cm long, variably entire or remotely serrate toward apices, green on both sides with fairly long acuminate apices; leaflets elliptical, often basally oblique; laterals often nearly sessile to subsessile; petioles to 10 cm or longer.

FLOWERS: Sessile on slender, hairy spikes, produced before the leaves, dioecious; petals almost white and shed very early during anthesis.

FRUITS: Samaras about 2 cm, almost horizontal, almost sessile; fruits in drooping racemes about 10–15 cm long, abundant on the tree; most seeds not viable since male trees are usually not in the same garden as females.

BARK AND BUDS: Green to olive-green.

HARDINESS: Zone V.

AUTUMN COLOR: Beautifully yellow with red.

DISTRIBUTION: Central China, Hubei and Sichuan provinces.

REFERENCES: Bean (1970), Fang (1981a), Krüssmann (1976a), Murray (1970c), Pax (1902), Rehder (1986 facs.).

*Acer henryi* was discovered by A. Henry, described by Pax in 1889, and introduced in 1903 by E. H. Wilson for Veitch Nursery in Great Britain. Murray placed it as a subspecies under *A. cissifolium* in 1966, a classification not accepted in the present volume. The two taxa are closely allied, however, and can be confused.

Rather rare in cultivation, *Acer henryi* grows in several collections. Some trees were labeled *A. sutchuenense* instead of *A henryi* due to an introduction confusion created by E. H. Wilson. There are several fine fruiting specimens in the U.S. National Arboretum, Washington, DC, which were originally collected as seed in the Shennongjia forest District of Hubei Province, China, by the 1980 Sino-American Botanical Expedition to western Hubei.

The leaves of *Acer henryi* usually consist of 3 leaflets and are only faintly toothed. *Acer*

*Acer henryi*

*cissifolium* usually has 5 leaflets and is more clearly dentate. *Acer henryi* also lacks the conspicuous yellowish orange color in the young growth, which is so attractive in *A. cissifolium.* Seedlings of both species are very similar in the serration of the leaflets. With age, *A. henryi* demonstrates a reduction of serrations resulting in faintly serrate or entire leaflets. On adult trees of *A. henryi,* only vigorous shoots are clearly serrate. Furthermore, leaflets of *A. henryi* are darker green, becoming purplish in the summer.

The species is dioecious, but as it is often planted alone, viable seed is rarely available, due to its parthenocarpic and sterile fruits. Propagation is possible by layering or by viable seed, if available. The species is not often available in the nursery trade. Major points of merit are its beautiful autumn color and the interesting long, pendulous racemes of the usually sterile fruits.

Murray's (1966) combination of *Acer cissifolium* ssp. *henryi* was premature and without benefit of detailed analyses of the inflorescences and floral structures of both taxa. There is no doubt that these taxa are closely allied, although geographically isolated, and that in all probability they had a common ancestor. Many features that differentiate *A. henryi* from *A. cissifolium* are, in fact, presented in the foregoing accounts of these taxa. The view of these taxa as separate and distinct species is further reinforced by careful study and comparison of living plants in their native habitats and in cultivation, as well as by evaluating many herbarium collections. Of particular significance are the facts that the taxa have different types of inflorescences and different floral morphologies. In addition, the flowers of *A. cissifolium* are strongly pedicellate, while those of *A. henryi* are sessile. The leaflets of *A. cissifolium* are, for the most part, always strongly serrate-dentate, while those of *A. henryi* are entire or only randomly and irregularly serrate toward the apices.

It is not surprising that the late Professor Fang Wen-pei (1981a) recognized *Acer henryi* in his final account of the Aceraceae and treated *A. cissifolium* ssp. *henryi* (Pax) Murray as a synonym. The present author concurs fully with de Jong's (1976) statement:

> Murray (1966) combined *A. cissifolium* from Japan and *A. henryi* from C. China. Both species agree in most morphological characters but vary in the corolla of the flowers. *A. cissifolium* has long, narrow, yellow petals, while *A. henryi* has whitish petals, which mostly drop before or during anthesis. Although both species were successfully crossed, spontaneous hybridization in collections may rarely occur. The present author does not accept them as conspecific.

The lectotype, *Acer henryi, 5644-B,* from Hubei Province, China, was selected by Fang during a research trip to the Royal Botanic Gardens, Kew, who later (1939) published this conclusion.

## SECTION INDIVISA Pax

TYPE SPECIES: ***Acer carpinifolium*** Siebold & Zuccarini.

HABIT: Small deciduous trees or shrubs.
LEAVES: Undivided; veins unicostate; lateral veins parallel as in *Carpinus;* margins doubly serrate.
BUD SCALES: 9- to 13-paired, brown.
INFLORESCENCES: Racemose, terminal and axillary from mixed buds, 10–20 flowered.
FLOWERS: 4-merous, dioecious; perianths greenish yellow; stamens usually 6; discs amphistaminal-intrastaminal.
FRUITS: Nutlets narrowly elliptic-spherical to rather flat, glabrous, parthenocarpic tendency strong; cotyledons narrowly oblong, acuminate.
SPECIES: *A. carpinifolium* Siebold & Zuccarini.
REFERENCE: De Jong (1976).

Section *Indivisa* is the most specialized section of the genus (dioecious, unlobed leaves, simple racemes, many bud scales, tetraploid) and without any clear affinities to any other section. The fruits resemble those of section *Negundo,* but parthenocarpic fruits are flat.

*Acer carpinifolium* is an isolated species, placed in a separate monotypic section. There are no close relatives. It is usually a small tree or large shrub, with deciduous, undivided leaves. It is well-known in cultivation and used as a garden plant.

SECTION: *Indivisa*

ACER CARPINIFOLIUM Siebold & Zuccarini (1845)

SYNONYMS

*A. binatum* Siebold ex Koch (1864).

*A. japonicum* var. *carpinifolium* Siesmayer (1888).

TYPE: *P. F. von Siebold,* Japan; L.

COMMON NAMES: Hornbeam maple, Arahago, Chidorinoki, Hainbuchen-Ahorn, Shira-side, Tsuba-noki, Yamashiba-kaede.

EPITHET: *Carpinifolius,* leaves like those of *Carpinus* (hornbeam).

ILLUSTRATIONS: Koidzumi (1911), Kurata (1964–1976), Krüssmann (1976a), Vertrees (1987).

HABIT: A small tree or large shrub to 10 m tall, densely branched, upright growing but not fastigiate; branchlets thin, glabrous.

LEAVES: Oblong, unlobed, occasionally 8–12 cm long and 4–6 cm wide, doubly serrate and densely covered with silky hairs when young, especially on the veins, very similar to leaves of *Carpinus japonica.*

FLOWERS: Greenish, androdioecious, stamens 5–6, flowering in May; borne in racemes, on long, slender pedicels.

FRUITS: Wings about 2 cm long, curved like a bow; nutlets flat and rather small, about 1 cm long.

BARK AND BUDS: Dark gray-brown and not fissured.

HARDINESS: Zone III.

AUTUMN COLOR: Very often a good golden yellow or rich brown.

DISTRIBUTION: Japan, in mountain forests up to subalpine heights, growing together with *Fraxinus spaethiana* and *Pterocarya rhoifolia.*

CHROMOSOME NUMBER: $2n = 52$ (Darlington 1955).

CULTIVAR: One (see Chapter 9).

REFERENCES: Bean (1970), Koidzumi (1911), Krüssmann (1976a), Kurata (1964–1976), Murray (1970c), Pax (1902), Rehder (1986 facs.), Veitch (1904), Vertrees (1978, 1987).

Maries introduced this species for Veitch Nursery in 1879, but it was described by Siebold and Zuccarini in 1845.

This peculiar maple resembles a hornbeam more than a maple. It leaves are remarkably similar to those of *Carpinus betulus* and *C. japonica,* not only in texture but also in size; however, the leaves of *Acer carpinifolium* are always opposite, whereas those of *Carpinus* are alternate. *Acer carpinifolium* forms a small tree or large shrub, often to 7–8 m tall, sometimes of tight habit and at other times of slender and open habit. As they are dioecious, male and female plants must be planted closely together to obtain viable seed.

*Acer carpinifolium* cannot be confused with any other maple, being the only member of section *Indivisa.* The autumn color is often brilliantly yellow. It is not readily available in the trade, one reason being that viable seed is difficult to obtain. Seed invariably germinates very early in the season, often as early as February, especially when sown in a cool greenhouse. The species can be propagated by layering and by cuttings, although the regrowth of rooted cuttings is difficult.

This species is an interesting plant for every maple lover due to its unusual appearance. A valuable characteristic is its extreme hardiness. It grows on all types of soil, but tends to grow leggy and slender in woodland conditions.

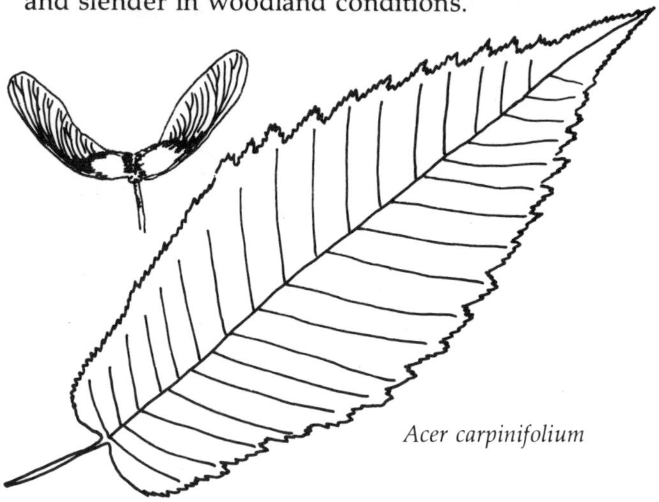

*Acer carpinifolium*

## SECTION ACER

**TYPE SPECIES:** ***Acer pseudoplatanus*** L. (1753).

HABIT: Deciduous trees or shrubs, occasionally almost evergreen (*A. sempervirens*).

LEAVES: 3- to 5-lobed; margins coarsely crenate to dentate, sometimes entire.

BUD SCALES: 5- to 13-paired, imbricate, gray-brown.

INFLORESCENCES: Corymbose, terminal and axillary.

FLOWERS: 5-merous; perianths yellowish green, often somewhat closed during anthesis; stamens usually 8; filaments long, exserted in male flowers; discs extra-staminal.

FRUITS: Nutlets ovoid, often keeled, parthenocarpic tendency strong, sometimes moderate.

SEEDLINGS: Cotyledons narrowly oblong, apices obtuse or truncate.

SERIES: *Acer, Monspessulana, Saccharodendron.*

REFERENCE: De Jong (1976).

Section *Acer* appears related to section *Pentaphylla,* series *Trifida,* and section *Trifoliata,* and rather remotely related to sections *Ginnala, Lithocarpa,* and *Platanoidea.* Relationships to all taxa with five and more bud scales may exist, except with section *Indivisa.*

Of the three series in section *Acer,* series *Monspessulana* and *Saccharodendron* are more specialized than series *Acer* (e.g., reduction of the corolla, sex expression, anemophily, parthenocarpy).

SERIES ACER

TYPE SPECIES: ***Acer pseudoplatanus*** L.

HABIT: Deciduous trees; young branches and buds rather thick.

LEAVES: Mostly 5-lobed, chartaceous; margins coarsely serrate.

BUD SCALES: 5- to 10-paired.

INFLORESCENCES: Rather large, 25–150 flowered.

FRUITS: Nutlets ovoid, globose, occasionally somewhat keeled, parthenocarpic tendency moderate.

SPECIES AND INFRASPECIFIC TAXA

*A. caesium* Wallich ex Brandis ssp. *caesium.*
*A. caesium* ssp. *giraldii* (Pax) Murray.
*A. heldreichii* Orphanides ex Boissier ssp. *heldreichii.*
*A. heldreichii* ssp. *trautvetteri* (Medvedev) Murray.
*A. pseudoplatanus* L.
*A. velutinum* Boissier.

REFERENCE: De Jong (1976).

Four species with their subspecies are placed in series *Acer,* including the type species, *A. pseudoplatanus.* They are all large trees, with 3- to 5-lobed, deciduous leaves. Most are from western Asia and Europe, all are well known in cultivation, and some are important in horticulture.

SECTION: *Acer* SERIES: *Acer*

ACER CAESIUM Wallich ex Brandis (1874) ssp. CAESIUM

SYNONYMS

*A. molle* sensu Pax (1890).
*A. luteolum* Borbas (1891).

TYPE: *N. Wallich,* "Northwest Himalayas, from the Indies to Nepal, at 2000–3000 m, scattered in mixed forests, mostly in shady valleys"; K.

EPITHET: *Caesius,* bluish.

ILLUSTRATIONS: Krüssmann (1976), Murray (1975a).

HABIT: A tree to 25 m tall in native habitat, rarely more than 15 m tall in cultivation, shaped not unlike *A. pseudoplatanus;* young shoots, often short and stout, with a bluish bloom, turning brown at maturity; trunk slightly fissured, golden brown.

LEAVES: 5-lobed, rather thin, 18–25 cm wide and 15–18 cm long, bases cordate, apices somewhat tapered, typically crowded at the end of the shoot (especially on young plants still forming vigorous shoots); margins finely toothed; undersides somewhat glaucous, not prominently veined; occasionally 3-lobed or with remote outer lobes.

FLOWERS: Monoecious, sepals and tepals greenish white; borne in upright corymbs.

FRUITS: Samaras 4–5 cm long, wings rectangular; nutlets dark red-brown, hard, thick.

BARK AND BUDS: Bark smooth, but peeling on old trees (as with *A. pseudoplatanus*); buds dark brown, somewhat crowded at the end of vigorous shoots.

HARDINESS: Zone V.

AUTUMN COLOR: Yellow.

DISTRIBUTION: Mountain forests in Sichuan and Yunnan provinces, China, at 2000–3000 m. Also in Kashmir and Nepal (only reported in the western part). This species has a disjunct distribution and does not occur in Sikkim or Bhutan.

CHROMOSOME NUMBER: $2n = 26$ (Santamour 1988); $2n = 52$ (tetraploid, reported by Mehra 1969).

SUBSPECIES

ssp. *caesium,* the typical subspecies.
ssp. *giraldii* (Pax) Murray (1969).

REFERENCES: Bean (1970), Krüssmann (1976a), Murray (1970c), Pax (1902), Stainton (1972).

*Acer caesium* was described by Brandis in 1874. This typical subspecies from the Himalayas and western China grows into a stately tree in both its native habitat and in cultivation. In fact, it is the Himalayan counterpart of its ally *A. caesium* ssp. *giraldii* from Shaanxi and Yunnan provinces, China. The latter has a very conspicuous bloom on its shoots, but the leaves are not crowded at the shoot ends. Murray (1969) included *A. giraldii* as a subspecies under *A. caesium,* which is accepted here.

*Acer caesium* ssp. *caesium* is relatively poorly known and deserves much wider use. The tree has more or less the same form as *A. pseudoplatanus,* but does not reach the same size in cultivation. The young shoots show a hint of bluish bloom. The leaves are somewhat crowded at the ends of vigorous young shoots. Mature shoots are golden brown. The beauty of this tree makes it worthy of a place in parks or large gardens. It is hardy in most regions, but only a few nurseries are offering it in the trade.

Propagation can be done by seed, as seed is occasionally available in the trade. If no seed is available, it is also possible to graft superior types or expressions on potted understock of *A. pseudoplatanus.* Budding in summer is also possible.

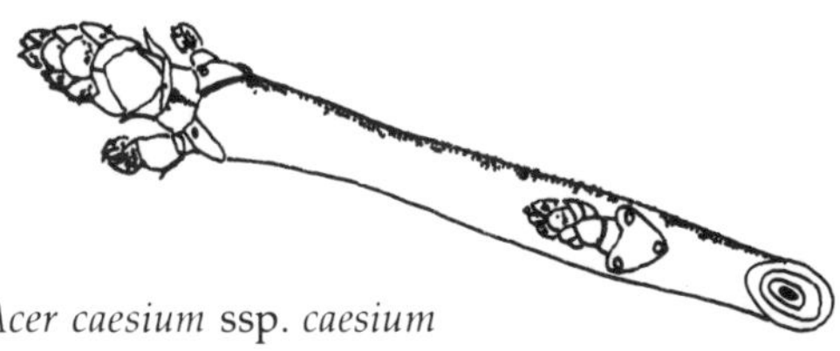

*Acer caesium* ssp. *caesium*

*Acer caesum* ssp. *giraldii*

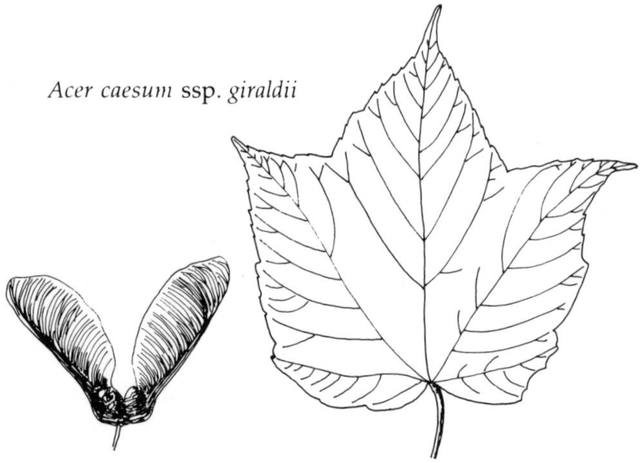

SECTION: *Acer* SERIES: *Acer*

ACER CAESIUM ssp. GIRALDII (Pax) Murray (1969)

BASIONYM: *A. giraldii* Pax (1902).

TYPES: Syntypes *Giraldi 2115, 2136,* Shaanxi Province, China; FI.

EPITHET: *Giraldii,* after Giraldi, an Italian missionary and botanist who worked in Shaanxi Province, China, from 1890–1895.

ILLUSTRATIONS: Plate 53; Fang (1981a), Harris (1983).

HABIT: A tree to 10–12 m tall, shaped similar to subspecies *caesium,* with stout branches, rather openly branched; young shoots conspicuously covered with a bluish white bloom, disappearing in the 2nd-3rd year, bark turning dark brown and somewhat peeling.

LEAVES: 3- to 5-lobed, 15–22 cm across, bases subcordate, lobes with rounded apices, shining green, blue-green beneath, not crowded at the top of the shoot as on subspecies *caesium,* rarely appearing before mid-May; margins remotely toothed.

FLOWERS: Greenish white, monoecious; on upright racemes.

FRUITS: Samaras to 6 cm long, wings parallel; nutlets thick and rounded.

BARK AND BUDS: Bark dark brown, but young shoots distinctively bluish white.

HARDINESS: Zone V.

AUTUMN COLOR: Rich yellow.

DISTRIBUTION: Northern and western China; Shaanxi Province; also in Yunnan Province as solitary trees.

REFERENCES: Bean (1970), Fang (1981a), Murray (1970c).

*Acer giraldii* was described by Pax in 1902, and Murray placed it as a subspecies under *A. caesium* in 1969.

The most interesting feature of this rare maple is the bluish white bloom covering the new growth. It is a few-branched, open tree, with more or less the same habit as its relative, *A. caesium* ssp. *caesium.* Subspecies *giraldii* cannot be confused with subspecies *caesium,* as the latter does not show the bluish white bloom, and the leaves of subspecies *giraldii* are not crowded together as with subspecies *caesium.* The leaves of subspecies *giraldii* are large, and 3- to 5-lobed with long petioles.

This subspecies is very rare in the trade, since trees in cultivation rarely produce viable seed. This subspecies is widely cultivated in cities and villages of Shaanxi Province, and can be observed in its natural habitat in the Qinling Mountains. Grafting is possible on *A. pseudoplatanus,* but is difficult. Growth is weak, especially during the first 2–3 years after grafting. The understock suckers rather heavily, and frequently the young grafts die back.

This is truly an attractive tree and valuable for both horticulturists and botanists. There are no cultivars.

SECTION: *Acer* SERIES: *Acer*

ACER HELDREICHII Orphanides ex Boissier (1856) ssp. HELDREICHII

TYPES: Syntypes *T. H. H. Heldreich, T. G. Orphanides,* Mount Parnassus, Kyllene, Greece; E; W.

COMMON NAMES: Balkan maple, Greek maple, Griechischer Ahorn.

EPITHET: *Heldreichii:* after T. H. H. von Heldreich (1822–1902), director of the Botanic Gardens of Athens, Greece.

ILLUSTRATION: Krüssmann (1976a).

HABIT: A rather large tree to 15 m or more; trunk smooth, with few fissures; stems and shoots gray-brown, glabrous; lenticels oblong.

LEAVES: 3- to 5-lobed, 8–15 cm long and wide, deeply divided almost to the bases, thin textured, uppersides shining dark green, undersides paler; margins coarsely toothed; petioles reddish, 4–6 cm long, glabrous. Leaves on trees growing in the Greek mountains are often smaller than those in more northerly habitats such as Yugoslavia, Bulgaria, and Albania.

FLOWERS: Yellow, on large, erect, terminal corymbs; monoecious, appearing at the end of May.

FRUITS: Samaras 3–5 cm, obtuse-angled.

BARK AND BUDS: Bark like that of remaining smooth longer than any other species of this series; buds darker than those of *A. pseudoplatanus.*

HARDINESS: Zone V.

AUTUMN COLOR: Golden yellow.

DISTRIBUTION: Northern Greece, as well as in the mountains of Albania, Yugoslavia (Serbia, Hercegovina, Montenegro), and Bulgaria.

CHROMOSOME NUMBER: $2n = 26$ (Santamour 1988)

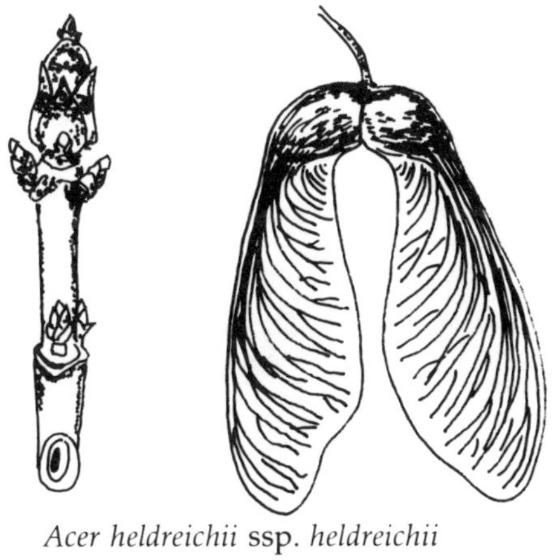

*Acer heldreichii* ssp. *heldreichii*

SUBSPECIES
ssp. *heldreichii,* the typical subspecies.
ssp. *trautvetteri* (Medvedev) Murray (1982).
VARIETY: var. *macropterum* (Visiani) Pax (1886), like the typical subspecies, but with larger samaras; chromosome number is $2n = 26$ (Santamour 1980); present in Botanic Garden, Zagreb, Croatia.
REFERENCES: Dippel (1892), Elwes & Henry (1908), Krüssmann (1976a), Murray (1976c), Pax (1902), Rehder (1986 facs.), Schneider (1912).

*Acer heldreichii* was described by Boissier in 1856. This species has a remarkable absence of synonyms.

It inhabits southeastern Europe, with trees growing in the Greek mountains often having smaller leaves than those growing in Serbia, Montenegro, or Hercegovina of Yugoslavia. This species also grows in the Albanian mountains and in Bulgaria.

It is a moderate-sized tree closely related to *Acer pseudoplatanus,* with the same habit but different leaves. The leaves are 3- to 5-lobed, deeply divided, and of a rather thin texture. The petioles are usually reddish or even red. The leaf shape is not unlike that of subspecies *trautvetteri* or even *A. pseudoplatanus* 'Palmatifidum'. Subspecies *heldreichii* can be easily mistaken for its close ally, subspecies *trautvetteri.* In fact, it is often difficult to determine what taxon it is in the field. The top leaflet is almost free from the two side leaflets, which are somewhat less deeply divided. As a general rule, subspecies *trautvetteri* has black buds which can only be seen clearly in the autumn or winter. The lobes are also not so deeply divided as in true subspecies *heldreichii.* The two subspecies meet and overlap in Turkey.

Propagation is easy from seed harvested from solitary specimens. Hybrids occur readily with related taxa such as subspecies *trautvetteri* or *A. pseudoplatanus.* In fact, quite a few trees labeled *A. heldreichii* are hybrids of uncertain origin and are sometimes labeled *A.* × *pseudo-heldreichii,* a validly described, naturally occurring hybrid (Fukarek & Celjo 1959). Grafting on *A. pseudoplatanus* is also easy and is useful in maintaining particular "true" trees.

SECTION: *Acer* SERIES: *Acer*

## ACER HELDREICHII ssp. TRAUTVETTERI (Medvedev) Murray (1982)

BASIONYM: *A. trautvetteri* Medvedev (1880).
SYNONYMS
*A. insigne* sensu Nicholson, non Boissier & Buhse (1881).
*A. insigne* var. *trautvetteri* (Medvedev) Pax (1886).
TYPE: *E. R. von Trautvetter,* Caucasus, Tblisi, Georgia.
COMMON NAMES: Redbud maple, Kaukasus-Ahorn.
EPITHET: *Trautvetteri:* after E. R. von Trautvetter (1809–1889), director of the Botanic Garden in St. Petersburg, Russia.
ILLUSTRATIONS: Plates 54, 55; Krüssmann (1976a).
HABIT: A large tree with a rounded crown, to 15–17 m tall; branches red-brown to gray; bud scales imbricate; young branchlets green, turning red in autumn; leaf buds blackish.
LEAVES: Deeply 5-lobed, cordate, 10–15 cm across, lobes ovate, dark green above, glaucous beneath; margins coarsely dentate to lobulate; petioles 6–15 cm long, red or reddish; young leaves (often with intact bud scales) conspicuously red.
INFLORESCENCES: Paniculate, terminal, appearing after the leaves, to 15 cm long.
FLOWERS: Yellow.
FRUITS: Samaras red, large, to 7 cm long, wings parallel; ripe nutlets brown.
BARK AND BUDS: Bark of main stems smoothly gray; inner bud scales often bright red.
HARDINESS: Zone V.
AUTUMN COLOR: Yellow to brown.
DISTRIBUTION: Northeastern Turkey and the Caucasus. Mixed with *Abies* and *Sorbus* spp. on the edges of alpine meadows; does not form its own forests.
CHROMOSOME NUMBER: $2n = 26$ (Santamour 1988).
REFERENCES: Bean (1970), Elwes & Henry (1908), Krüssmann (1976a), Murray (1970c, 1982b), Pojárkova (1933b), Rehder (1986 facs.), Schneider (1912), Schwerin (1900).

This subspecies of *Acer heldreichii* is a large tree native to eastern Turkey and the Caucasus. It replaces *A. pseudoplatanus* in those areas.

The taxon was discovered in the Caucasus by Radde in 1864, identified with *Acer platanoides* by Trautvetter, and introduced for Van Volxem's Nurseries in 1866. It was described for the first time in *Botanical Magazine,* 1866, as *A. insigne* Boissier & Buhse. Later the Radde herbarium material proved to be a mixture with *A. velutinum,* and Medvedev renamed the part that was not *A.*

*velutinum* as *A. trautvetteri,* based on an 1880 a Trautvetter collection. Pax attached this name again to the now synonymous name *A. insigne* as a variety in 1886. *Acer insigne* Boissier & Buhse (1860) is now treated as a synonym of *A. velutinum* (1846).

The current treatment of this taxon was inevitable, due to its mixed geographical distribution and the difficulty in distinguishing subspecies *trautvetteri* properly from subspecies *heldreichii.* Further investigation indicates that the feature of dark buds is not universally consistent. This fact provides additional reason to include the former *A. trautvetteri* as a subspecies of *A. heldreichii.*

This subspecies is the characteristic tree of the Colchic Region in the Caucasus, where it grows at altitudes up to 2500 m. It is often mixed with *Abies nordmanniana* and *Sorbus* species at the edges of alpine meadows.

The tree reaches 20–25 m in height and has a large crown. The leaves are deeply 5-lobed, 12–15 cm across or sometimes larger on vigorous young trees. The winter buds are dark, almost black. The petioles are often conspicuously red. The tree leafs out relatively late, later than its relatives, usually not before mid-May.

It is difficult to separate this subspecies from its closest relative, *Acer heldreichii* ssp. *heldreichii.* The distinguishing features of the latter are the less darkly colored winter buds, and the lighter green, differently shaped, and softer textured leaves. Subspecies *trautvetteri* is also rather difficult to distinguish from *A. pseudoplatanus,* from which it differs mainly in its dark buds and its far more deeply divided leaves. Hybrid trees with intermediate characteristics are frequently planted in gardens, and labeled *A. heldreichii* ssp. *trautvetteri.* These hybrids are usually among subspecies *heldreichii,* subspecies *trautvetteri,* and/or *A.* × *pseudoplatanus.* It was not unusual in the past to harvest hybrid seed from trees in botanic gardens or parks, as the parental species were often planted closely together. Such progeny are often labeled as *A. pseudo-heldreichii.* Unlike its relatives, subspecies *trautvetteri* is very showy when the buds expand, due to the red inner bud scales. Another relative is *A. velutinum,* but this species is easily distinguished from subspecies *trautvetteri* by its huge leaves with rounded lobes.

*Acer heldreichii* ssp. *trautvetteri* is easily propagated by seed, but attention should be paid to the origin of the seed, because of the hybridity potentials. If necessary, grafting on *A. pseudoplatanus* is easy to do, and the resulting tree grows quickly.

This subspecies is available in the trade from time to time. The red petioles are attractive, as are the unfolding new leaves and the glistening red samaras appearing in early winter.

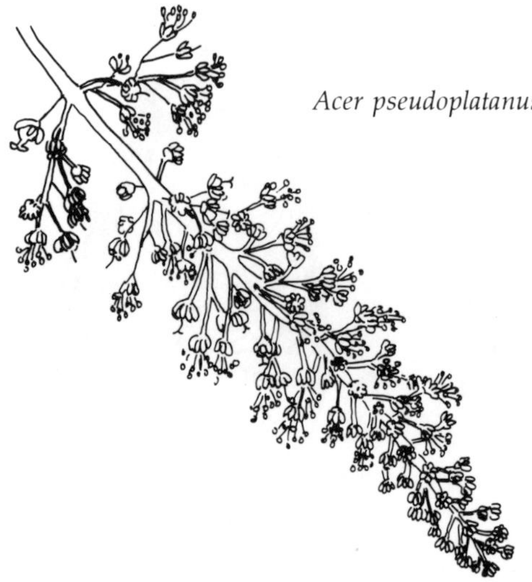

*Acer pseudoplatanus*

SECTION: *Acer* SERIES: *Acer*

## ACER PSEUDOPLATANUS L. (1753)

SYNONYMS

*A. montanum* Garsault (1764).
*A. opulifolium* Thuillier (1799), non Villars (1786).
*A. procerum* Salisbury (1796).
*A. ramosum* Schwerin (1895).
*A. sericeum* Schwerin (1895).
*A. platanophyllum* St. Lager ex Keegan (1909).

TYPE: *LINN 1225.5;* LINN. "Habitat in Helvetiae, Austriae montanis."

COMMON NAMES: Sycamore maple, sycamore, Acero, Aer, Aschér (Rhaetoro-manic), Bergahorn, Erable sycomore, Gewone Esdoorn, Valbirk.

EPITHET: *Pseudoplatanus:* a false plane (*Platanus*) tree.

ILLUSTRATIONS: Plate 56; Krüssmann (1976a), de Jong (1976).

HABIT: A large tree with a wide, often somewhat irregular crown, to 25 m tall and almost as wide; young branches green to gray-brown, with green buds.

LEAVES: Variable in size and color, 3- to 5-lobed, rounded, 8–15 cm across, ovate, acute to obtuse, olive-green above, glaucous to reddish beneath, nerves often pubescent, bases cordate; margins denticulate; petioles 6–15 cm long, often reddish; first pair of leaves ovate, unlobed, and cordate at the bases. Leaves may be larger or pale green to dark shining green; sometimes they are disfigured by the fungus *Rhytisma acerinum,* which does not appear to weaken the tree.

INFLORESCENCES: Racemose-paniculate, pendulous, terminal, 10–15 cm long trusses, appearing after the leaves.

FLOWERS: 5-merous, yellow-green, monoecious.

FRUITS: Samaras 5 cm long, well developed, erect; nutlets ovoid, convex. Cotyledons 3–4 cm,

sessile, oblong, entire.
BARK AND BUDS: Bark peeling in small scales, fissuring in large strips; bud scales few, green with a dark margin.
HARDINESS: Zone IV.
AUTUMN COLOR: Yellow to brown.
DISTRIBUTION: Europe, especially in mountainous regions: Germany (Harz), Russia (Crimea, Caucasus), Spain (Pyrenees), France (Cantabrian Mountains), Swiss Alps, Bosnia, northern Greece, and the Carpathian mountains in Poland, Slovakia,and Romania. The extreme easterly limit is around the Caspian Sea. It is not native to the British Isles, Belgium, The Netherlands, northwest France, northern Germany, or Scandinavia. It is, however, flourishing in these countries and naturalizes abundantly.
CHROMOSOME NUMBER: $2n = 52$ (polyploid) (Darlington 1955).
VARIETIES: In earlier years many so-called natural varieties and formae were recognized, though none are accepted in this volume. In the last 30 years of the 19th century particularly, several botanists gave such status to the many slight differences of growth habit, but most of these names have been sunk in synonymy since the natural differences are insufficiently constant to maintain the plants as natural formae, varieties, or subspecies. Furthermore, many forms were named solely on the basis of cultivated or nursery-origin plants—these automatically are to be treated as cultivars (see Chapter 9). A few of these former varieties, now included in the species, are nevertheless obviously different enough to mention separately, though they usually are not clonal:

var. *macrocarpum* Spach (1834), samaras 5–6 cm long, subhorizontal.

var. *microcarpum* Spach (1834), samaras small, 2–4 cm long, apices convergent; synonym is f. *distans* Rikli (1903).

var. *tomentosum* Tausch (1829), leaves pubescent beneath; occurs rather frequently in southern Italy and Dalmatia.

FORMS

f. *erythrocarpum* (Carrière) Pax (1864), fruits red; occurs in the wild in central Europe; name founded on a tree in cultivation in a French nursery (*Revue Horticole* 1864, 171), thus is treated as a cultivar (see Chapter 9).

f. *purpureum* (Loudon) Rehder (1949), leaf undersides more or less purple; frequently observed in the wild; see Bean 1970 for further details.

f. *variegatum* (Weston) Rehder (1949), a name generally applicable to a group of variegated trees of the species that frequently occur in the wild and also in seedbeds in cultivation (from wild-collected seed); wild seedlings with variegated leaves were often sold under this name a century ago, so most of the older clones, now properly named, derive from these origins; large trees still growing in England at Petersham Lodge in Richmond and at Guisborough Park in Yorkshire, but the tallest specimen is at Linton Park, Kent, Great Britain.

CULTIVARS: Many (see Chapter 9).
REFERENCES: Bean (1970), Dippel (1892), Elwes & Henry (1908), de Jong (1976), Krüssmann (1976a), Linnaeus (1753), Murray (1970c), Pax (1902), Pojárkova (1933b), Rehder (1986 facs.), Yaltirik (1967a).

The sycamore maple is the most common of all *Acer* species in Europe. It is the type species for *Acer* published by Linnaeus (1753). As with *A. platanoides,* many geographical forms and varieties have been reduced into direct synonymy of the species. All specimens of *A. pseudoplatanus* recorded from eastern Anatolia, Turkey, have proved to be *A. heldreichii* ssp. *trautvetteri.*

In its wild state this species does not form forests, but occurs as more or less isolated groups of trees, only forming a uniform forest in Thüringen, Germany. The tree usually forms a part of *Betula* and *Abies* forests. It grows up to altitudes of about 2000 m and forms shrubs up to the timberline.

Its closest relatives are *Acer heldreichii* ssp. *heldreichii* and ssp. *trautvetteri,* but these have different leaves, with much more deeply cleft lobes. The buds of both subspecies are blackish rather than green. *Acer pseudoplatanus* has pendulous paniculate inflorescences.

In cultivation, hybrids between *Acer heldreichii* ssp. *trautvetteri* and *A. pseudoplatanus* frequently occur. A number of hybrid trees can be found in various arboreta, sometimes labeled correctly as *A.* × *pseudo-heldreichii* Fukarek & Celjo (1959).

No subspecies or varieties of *Acer pseudoplatanus* are accepted in the present volume, although many varieties are described in the literature. These taxa might be treated as formae, but many of them may also deserved only cultivar status. Article 28 of the ICBN states that plants brought from the wild into cultivation retain the names that are applied to the same taxa growing in nature. Seedlings grown in gardens, and thus not found in the wild, get cultivar names.

*Acer pseudoplatanus* is easily propagated by seed and often becomes a weed in gardens and parks. It is not affected by spring frosts and likes a good soil, even calcareous soils, but does not grow well in extremely wet conditions. Most of the cultivars have to be grafted on seedlings or budded in summer.

It is likely that the oldest cultivated tree is at

Kippenross near Dublane, Scotland. The records of this estate indicate that this tree must now be well over 500 years old, but it is not certain whether this tree is still alive (records from Henry & Elwes, 1906). There is also a tree behind the Burnam Hotel at Dunkeld, Scotland, which is reported to be over 1000 years old, but this report is unconfirmed.

The timber of the sycamore maple is white, close-grained, and moderately hard. It is used for many purposes, including small furniture, toys, tools, and brushes. Special trunks are used for musical instruments, especially violins Veneer from this species is widely used in the furniture industry.

SECTION: *Acer* SERIES: *Acer*

ACER VELUTINUM Boissier (1846)

SYNONYMS

*A. insigne* Boissier & Buhse (1860), non Nicholson.

*A. pulchrum* hort. ex Nicholson (1881).

*A. insigne* var. *obtusilobum* Freyn & Sintenis (1902).

TYPES: Holotype *Aucher-Eloy 4293-A,* Gilan, Iran; G; isotypes W, G.

COMMON NAMES: Velvet maple, Samt-Ahorn.

EPITHET: *Velutinus,* velvetlike.

ILLUSTRATIONS: Plate 57; Krüssmann (1976a), Schwerin (1894).

HABIT: A large tree to 25 m tall or taller; branches glabrous, brown to gray, rather stout; buds imbricate, lateral buds distinctly stalked; young branchlets green, becoming reddish, also glabrous.

LEAVES: 5-lobed, 15–25 cm across, glaucous beneath or with a yellow-brown tomentum along the nerves, bases almost cordate, lobes ovate; margins coarsely serrate to lobulate; petioles 10–25 cm long.

INFLORESCENCES: 8–12 cm long, corymbose-paniculate, terminal, erect.

FLOWERS: Yellowish green, appearing after the leaves.

FRUITS: Samaras 3–6 cm long, stout, erect to obtuse, in short umbels; nutlets tomentose and globose, smaller than those of the other species of this series.

HARDINESS: Zone V.

AUTUMN COLOR: Yellow.

DISTRIBUTION: Caucasus, on mountains of Talysch (Gilan), common in forests from sea level to 600 m. Also growing wild in the northern provinces of Glulan and Astrabad, Iran.

CHROMOSOME NUMBER: $2n = 26$ (Santamour 1988); other references record $2n = 52$ (polyploid).

VARIETIES

var. *glabrescens* (Boissier & Buhse) Murray (1969), with glabrous leaves.

var. *vanvolxemii* (Masters) Rehder (1938), with leaves glaucous beneath, larger than those of variety *glabrescens,* nerves pubescent; an eastern variant from Kakhetie, Georgia, Eastern Caucasus, where it grows in mountain forests at low elevations in river valleys; originally collected by G. van Volxem from near Lagodechi, central Caucasus, and brought to Kew Gardens.

CULTIVAR: One (see Chapter 9).

REFERENCES: Bean (1970), Dippel (1892), Elwes & Henry (1908), Krüssmann (1976a), Murray (1970c), Pax (1902), Rehder (1986 facs.), Schneider (1912).

*Acer velutinum,* the velvet maple, is one of the largest maples; very few species grow faster or taller. It is used as a street tree in Russia and Belarus, not only as the species, but also in the glabrous form, formerly known as *A. insigne,* but now correctly identified as *A. velutinum* var. *glabrescens* (Boiss. & Buhse) Murray.

It grows to a huge tree of 25 m tall with large leaves, surpassed in size only by *Acer macrophyllum.* It has been known for many years, but is surprisingly rare in horticulture. It can hardly be confused with any other maple, due to its huge leaves with rounded lobes.

*Acer velutinum* can be propagated readily from seed, but when no seed is available, budding on *A. pseudoplatanus* is an acceptable method. Extremely large-leaved garden specimens could be propagated vegetatively and treated as cultivars, if necessary.

It seems wisest to treat the varieties *glabrescens* and *vanvolxemii* as varieties when they are propagated from original seed. Good clones must be propagated vegetatively and separately named.

As previously mentioned with *Acer pseudoplatanus,* one cannot give original wild-collected variants the same name if treated as cultivars. When similar variations are of garden origin, or when a solitary aberrant plant is found in the wild, a cultivar name may be given. Many so-called forms (*formae*) named in the early years of this century were not forms at all, but only incidentally aberrant specimens discovered in cultivation. Large numbers of such taxa are now treated as cultivars, retaining the original name, capitalized.

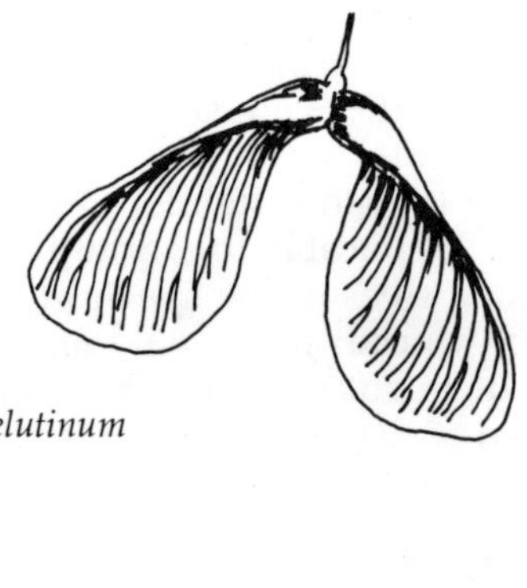

*Acer velutinum*

SERIES MONSPESSULANA Pojárkova (1933)
TYPE SPECIES: ***Acer monspessulanum*** L. (1753).
HABIT: Trees or shrubs, deciduous or partly evergreen.
LEAVES: Usually 3-, sometimes 5-lobed or unlobed, often coriaceous; margins entire to coarsely serrate.
BUD SCALES: 8- to 12-paired.
INFLORESCENCES: With 10–50 flowers, usually on long pendulous pedicels.
FRUITS: Nutlets keeled-convex, parthenocarpic tendency strong.
SPECIES AND INFRASPECIFIC TAXA
- *A. hyrcanum* Fisch. & Meyer ssp. *hyrcanum.*
- *A. hyrcanum* ssp. *intermedium* (Pančić) Bornmüller.
- *A. hyrcanum* ssp. *keckianum* (Pax) Yaltirik.
- *A. hyrcanum* ssp. *reginae-amaliae* (Orphanides ex Boissier) Murray.
- *A. hyrcanum* ssp. *sphaerocarpum* Yaltirik.
- *A. hyrcanum* ssp. *stevenii* (Pojárkova) Murray.
- *A. hyrcanum* ssp. *tauricolum* (Boissier & Balansa) Yaltirik.
- *A. monspessulanum* ssp. *assyriacum* (Pojárkova) Rechinger.
- *A. monspessulanum* ssp. *cinerascens* (Boissier) Yaltirik.
- *A. monspessulanum* ssp. *ibericum* Yaltirik.
- *A. monspessulanum* ssp. *microphyllum* (Boissier) Bornmüller.
- *A. monspessulanum* L. ssp. *monspessulanum.*
- *A. monspessulanum* ssp. *oksalianum* Yaltirik.
- *A. monspessulanum* ssp. *persicum* (Pojárkova) Rechinger.
- *A. monspessulanum* ssp. *turcomanicum* (Pojárkova) Murray.
- *A. obtusifolium* Sibthorp & Smith.
- *A. opalus* ssp. *hispanicum* (Pourret) Murray.
- *A. opalus* ssp. *obtusatum* (Willdenow) Gams.
- *A. opalus* Miller ssp. *opalus.*
- *A. sempervirens* L.

REFERENCE: De Jong (1976).

Five species with their subspecies belong to series *Monspessulana.* They are small trees or large shrubs, with deciduous or evergreen leaves. Several subspecies are not known in cultivation, and others are quite rare.

SECTION: *Acer* SERIES: *Monspessulana*
## ACER HYRCANUM Fischer & Meyer (1837) ssp. HYRCANUM

SYNONYMS
- *A. campestre* var. *hyrcanum* (Fischer & Meyer) Loudon (1842).
- *A. opulifolium* Ledebour (1842), non Villars.
- *A. tauricum* hort. ex Kirchner (1864).
- *A. barbatum* sensu Gordon (1873), non Michaux.
- *A. caucasicum* hort. ex Nicholson (1881).
- *A. ibericum* hort. ex Nicholson (1881), non Willdenow.
- *A. italum* ssp. *hyrcanum* (Fischer & Meyer) Pax (1886).
- *A. opalus* var. *hyrcanum* (Fischer & Meyer) Rehder (1914).
- *A. opalus* ssp. *hyrcanum* (Fischer & Meyer) Murray (1977).

TYPE: *C. A. von Meyer;* LE.
COMMON NAME: Balkan-Ahorn.
EPITHET: *Hyrcanus,* after Hyrcania, a Persian province.
ILLUSTRATIONS: Plates 58, 59; Krüssmann (1970c), Murray in Rechinger (1969), Pojárkova (1933b).
HABIT: A medium-sized tree or multistemmed shrub to 10–12 m tall.
LEAVES: Very variable, 5-lobed, often lobulate, 3–10 cm across, coarsely toothed, green above, glaucous beneath, upper lobes rectangular; basal leaves small and ovate; petioles to 10 cm long, reddish.
FLOWERS: Yellow-green, in glabrous, short corymbs, appearing with the leaves.
FRUITS: Glabrous, samaras erect to connivent, 3 cm long.
BARK AND BUDS: Bark dark gray-brown, hairy when young, soon glabrous; buds imbricate.
HARDINESS: Zones IV–V.
AUTUMN COLOR: Yellow.
DISTRIBUTION: Balkan mountain forests in Croatia, Serbia, Bosnia, and Montenegro of Yugoslavia; also in western Asia (i.e., Turkey, western Iran, Lebanon); mixed with *Juniperus excelsa, Quercus sessiliflora,* and *Q. ehrenbergii.*
CHROMOSOME NUMBER: $2n = 26$ (Santamour 1988).
SUBSPECIES
- ssp. *hyrcanum,* the typical subspecies.
- ssp. *intermedium* (Pančić) Bornmüller (1925), leaves with bluish undersides; extremely rare in collections and only occasionally available in the trade; includes f. *cordisectum.*
- ssp. *keckianum* (Pax) Yaltirik, with almost sessile leaves; found in Turkey and Lebanon, growing with the famous cedars of Lebanon.
- ssp. *reginae-amaliae* (Orphanides ex Boissier) Murray.
- ssp. *sphaerocarpum* Yaltirik.
- ssp. *stevenii* (Pojárkova) Murray, a rather well-known subspecies from the Crimea; treated in Russian publications as a separate species.
- ssp. *tauricolum* (Boissier & Balansa) Yaltirik, found in Turkey and Lebanon.

REFERENCES: Bean (1970), Dippel (1892), Koch (1869), Krüssmann (1976a), Murray (1970c, 1978b), Pax (1902), Pojárkova (1933b), Rehder (1986 facs.), Schneider (1912), Schwerin (1900), Yaltirik (1969).

*Acer hyrcanum* has been known for many years. It was described by Fischer & Meyer in 1837 and is named after the Persian province of Hyrcania. Its classification is complicated by its many synonyms, which have arisen from the variability of the typical subspecies and the other subspecies. Many specific names have been given to taxa which are now recognized as subspecies or varieties.

It usually grows into a large shrub and occasionally into a tree. The leaves are somewhat similar to those of *Acer campestre,* but they do not have milky sap. There is a certain similarity with *A. monspessulanum,* but the leaves of that species are far more leathery, and their leaf lobes are always rounded or even almost absent. The leaves of *A. hyrcanum* are definitely 5-lobed, usually about 5–7 cm across, but occasionally larger. Its petioles are also much longer than those of *A. monspessulanum.*

*Acer hyrcanum* can be propagated by seed, but it is almost never available. It is a rare maple and missing in most collections. Its tendency to set parthenocarpic fruits is also strong. Grafting is possible on *A. pseudoplatanus* and *A. monspessulanum,* but the understock suckers freely and grows too strongly for the scion.

*Acer reginae-amaliae* is here treated as a separate subspecies. Its leaves are similar to those of *A. hyrcanum* ssp. *hyrcanum,* but a great deal smaller; in fact, few maples have smaller leaves. Murray (1977) recombined *A. hyrcanum* and all of its *subspecies, formae,* and *varietates* under *A. opalus* Miller, a view which is not accepted here.

SECTION: *Acer* SERIES: *Monspessulana*

### ACER HYRCANUM ssp. INTERMEDIUM (Pančić) Bornmüller (1925)

SYNONYMS

- *A. hyrcanum* var. *cordisectum* (Borbas) Bornmüller (1894)
- *A. intermedium* Pančić (1871).
- *A. italum* var. *serbicum* (Pax) Pax 1886.
- *A. intermedium* var. *cordisectum* Borbas (1891).
- *A. italum* f. *cordisectum* (Borbas) Pax (1893).

TYPE: *J. Pančić* Serbia (Botanical Institute of the University of Belgrad, Serbia—without acronym).

EPITHET: *Intermedium,* intermediate.

ILLUSTRATION: Plate 60.

HABIT: A large, rather densely branched shrub with dark gray-brown branches.

LEAVES: 5-lobed, often lobulate, 3–8 cm wide, coarsely toothed, undersides markedly bluish.

FLOWERS: Similar to the flowers of the species.

FRUITS: Glabrous, samaras more or less erect, virtually identical to the species.

HARDINESS: Zones IV–V.

AUTUMN COLOR: Yellow.

DISTRIBUTION: Central Balkan Plateau.

REFERENCE: Murray (1970c).

This subspecies differs from subspecies *hyrcanum* by the bluish color of the undersides of the leaves. The forma *cordisectum* is included in this taxon.

Pax (1902) regarded this taxon as only a minor variant of his *Acer italum* ssp. *hyrcanum,* fully stated as *A. italum* ssp. *hyrcanum* var. *hyrcanum* f. *intermedium* (Pančić) Pax (1886). It is in cultivation in The Netherlands.

SECTION: *Acer* SERIES: *Monspessulana*

### ACER HYRCANUM ssp. KECKIANUM (Pax) Yaltirik (1967)

BASIONYM: *A. italum* var. *keckianum* Pax (1893).

SYNONYM: *A. hyrcanum* f. *tomentellum* (Pax) Simonkai (1908).

TYPE: *Aescherson & Sintenis 583,* Mount Ida near Edremit, western Turkey; E; K; G.

EPITHET: *Keckianum,* after Austrian botanist Karl Keck (1825–1894).

ILLUSTRATION: Plate 61.

HABIT: A small shrubby tree or shrub to 4–5 m tall and about as wide.

LEAVES: 5-lobed, lobulate, 3–6 cm wide, coarsely toothed, sometimes sessile, undersides markedly tomentose; petioles much shorter than counterparts in the typical subspecies.

FLOWERS: As in the typical subspecies.

FRUITS: Same size and shape as in subspecies *hyrcanum.*

HARDINESS: Zones IV–V.

AUTUMN COLOR: Yellow.

DISTRIBUTION: Mountainous regions in Lebanon and western Turkey, to 2000 m, mostly as scrub.

REFERENCES: Krüssmann (1976a), Murray (1970c), Schwerin (1900).

This subspecies differs from subspecies *hyrcanum* by having smaller leaves with hairy undersides, and very short petioles. It grows in Lebanon and western Turkey together with *Cedrus libani, Quercus libanii, Ostrya carpinifolia,* and *Juniperus drupacea.* It is in cultivation in The Netherlands, but still scarce and too young for a final determination.

Schwerin observed several trees and shrubby trees in a few villages in Lebanon (Baruk and Massar El Fachar), where cattle were not allowed in the mountains. Elsewhere, however, the plants were eaten and deformed by sheep and goats, along with other flora.

SECTION: *Acer* SERIES: *Monspessulana*

### ACER HYRCANUM ssp. REGINAE-AMALIAE (Orphanides ex Boissier) Murray (1970)

BASIONYM: *A. reginae-amaliae* Orphanides ex Boissier (1853).

*Acer hyrcanum* ssp. *reginae-amaliae*

SYNONYMS
*A. monspessulanum* var. *reginae-amaliae* (Boissier) Wesmael (1890).
*A. orientale* f. *quinquenerve* Vierhapper (1919).
TYPES: *T. Orphanides 408,* Styx, Mount Chelmos, Greece; holotype G; isotypes P, BM, E, FI.
EPITHET: *Reginae-Amaliae, Königin Amalia:* after Queen Amalia of Greece (1812–1875), wife of King Otto.
HABIT: A shrub to 2–3 m tall, rather twiggy, of the same form as subspecies *hyrcanum* but with much thinner shoots.
LEAVES: Very small, 5-lobed with undulate margins, 5–15 mm across, of a firm texture; margins slightly serrate; basal lobes often underdeveloped, especially on the smallest leaves.
FLOWERS: Not seen.
FRUITS: Not seen.
HARDINESS: Zone V.
AUTUMN COLOR: None.
DISTRIBUTION: Greece and Western Turkey in dry and stony places.
REFERENCES: Bean (1970), Murray (1970c).

Despite its very small leaves, the smallest in the genus, this xeromorphic shrub is not sufficiently different from *Acer hyrcanum* to give it specific rank. It is a subspecies of *A. hyrcanum,* and not related to *A. monspessulanum.*

There is a puzzling collection from Turkey (circa 1970, through Vertrees) producing plants with 5-lobed, very small leaves with undulate, slightly serrate margins. Fast-growing shoots produce leaves that are slightly larger, but never exceeding 1.5–2 cm. Plants from these Turkish seeds (P. H. Davis, 13685) growing in the Esveld Aceretum, Boskoop, The Netherlands, and labeled *A. monspessulanum* "from Turkey," match the above description. The seed probably originated from the Royal Botanic Garden, Edinburgh, Scotland. Yaltirik (1967) comments about this *Davis 13685* collection as a note following *A. sempervirens:*

> In its distinctive wood anatomy and elongate nutlets, this gathering resembles *A. sempervirens* not *A. hyrcanum* .... It approaches the Greek *A. reginae-amaliae* Orph. ex Boiss.... More material is needed of this interesting plant, which in many ways is morphologically intermediate between *A. sempervirens* and *A. hyrcanum* subsp. *tauricolum.*

No garden claims to have mature plants of subspecies *reginae-amaliae.* Additional materials are needed for further study of these related taxa.

SECTION: *Acer* SERIES: *Monspessulana*
ACER HYRCANUM ssp. SPHAEROCARPUM Yaltirik (1967)
TYPE: Holotype *P. Davis 15715,* Antalya, southern Turkey; E.
EPITHET: *Sphaerocarpus,* with globose fruit.
ILLUSTRATION: Plate 62.
HABIT: A densely branched shrub.
LEAVES: 5-lobed, 3–5 cm across; no further description available.
FLOWERS: Not seen.
FRUITS: Samaras very small, not exceeding 1 cm in length.
HARDINESS: Zone V.
DISTRIBUTION: Southern Turkey.
REFERENCES: Murray (1970c), Yaltirik (1967b).

This recently described subspecies differs from subspecies *hyrcanum* by its very small, 1-cm long samaras. It is now in cultivation.

SECTION: *Acer* SERIES: *Monspessulana*
ACER HYRCANUM ssp. STEVENII (Pojárkova) Murray (1969)
BASIONYM: *A. stevenii* Pojárkova (1933).
TYPE: *Stankov, 1917,* Crimea, Ukraine; LE.
EPITHET: *Stevenii,* after German botanist Christian von Steven (1781–1867).
HABIT: A small, shrubby tree to 4 m tall.
LEAVES: 5-lobed, dark bluish green above and paler beneath, with pilose veins; lobes shallowly caudate acuminate.
FLOWERS: Same form and shape as subspecies *hyrcanum.*
FRUITS: About 3–4 cm long, samaras connivent; nutlets flat.
HARDINESS: Zone V.
DISTRIBUTION: Crimea-Ukraine, in a small wooded area in the Utchan Gorge of the Ai Petri Mountains.
REFERENCES: Krüssmann (1976a), Murray (1970c).

This rare, small tree differs from subspecies *hyrcanum* mainly by its bluish green leaves, which are tomentose beneath and have abruptly acuminate lobes. It is very rare in cultivation; from time to time seed is offered by botanic gardens in Russia and Ukraine. Unfortunately, this seed does not germinate due to its dryness; quite often it is too old or stored too long.

SECTION: *Acer* SERIES: *Monspessulana*
ACER HYRCANUM ssp. TAURICOLUM (Boissier & Blanche) Yaltirik (1967)
BASIONYM: *A. tauricolus* Boissier & Blanche (1856).
TYPES: Syntypes Turkey, *T. Kotschy 342;* Castelli Gulek Taure Alicici, 1843; *Balansa 982,* Bostante Tchai et Kamechli Tchai, 1856; K, E, BM, G, W.
SYNONYMS
*A. reygassei* Boissier & Blanche (1856).

*A. hyrcanum* var. *reygassei* (Boissier & Blanche) Boissier (1867).
*A. italum* var. *tauricolum* (Boissier & Blanche) Pax (1886).
*A. italum* var. *acutilobum* Schwerin (1893).

EPITHET: *Tauricolum,* inhabitant of the Taurus Mountains, Anatolia. Boissier's intended meaning of the Taurus Mountains (on the north coast of Anatolia, along the Black Sea) is a misnomer since the distribution of this taxon is in the Anti-Taurus Mountains of southern Anatolia, Lebanon, and western Syria.
ILLUSTRATION: Plate 63.
HABIT: A small tree or shrub to 5–6 m tall.
LEAVES: 5-lobed, dark green above, slightly tomentose beneath, later glabrous, 5–10 cm across, more deeply incised than those of subspecies *hyrcanum* or subspecies *keckianum;* lobes acuminate to rounded, coarsely toothed; petioles long, reddish.
FLOWERS: As in subspecies *hyrcanum.*
FRUITS: As in subspecies *hyrcanum.*
BARK AND BUDS: Bark brown.
HARDINESS: Zone V.
DISTRIBUTION: Anti-Taurus Mountains in southern Turkey (Anatolia), western Syria, and Lebanon.
REFERENCES: Krüssmann (1976a), Murray (1970c, 1974b), Schneider (1912), Schwerin (1900).

This is a very rare, small tree, differing from its relatives by its larger leaves, long petioles, and acuminate leaf lobes. It is very rare in cultivation, not reported in any garden in Europe or North America.

A seedling plant in the Esveld Aceretum, Boskoop, The Netherlands, labeled *Acer hyrcanum* f. *tomentellum,* is definitely not that forma (i.e., ssp. *keckianum*), but is very close to the description of *A. hyrcanum* ssp. *tauricolum.* The plant is still too young to determine whether it is identical with this subspecies.

SECTION: *Acer* SERIES: *Monspessulana*
### ACER MONSPESSULANUM ssp. ASSYRIACUM (Pojárkova) Rechinger f. (1969)

BASIONYM: *A. assyriacum* Pojárkova (1933).
TYPE: *J. F. N. Bornmüller 1006,* Kuh-Sefin, near Erbil, Iraq; LE; W.
EPITHET: *Assyriacus,* from the ancient empire of Assyria, on the plains of the Tigris (including Mesopotamia), now in Iraq and eastern Turkey.
HABIT: A shrub or dense shrublike tree.
LEAVES: 3-lobed, occasionally 5-lobed, dentate on sterile shoots.
FLOWERS: Not seen.
FRUITS: Not seen.
HARDINESS: Zones V–VI.
DISTRIBUTION: Western Iran and northern Iraq.
REFERENCES: Murray (1970c), Rechinger (1969).

This subspecies is not in cultivation in Europe or America and is known only in the literature and herbaria.

SECTION: *Acer* SERIES: *Monspessulana*
### ACER MONSPESSULANUM ssp. CINERASCENS (Boissier) Yaltirik (1967)

BASIONYM: *A. cinerascens* Boissier (1846).
SYNONYM: *A. canescens* Bornmüller ex Stapf (1894).
TYPE: *T. Kotschy 37,* Shiraz, Iran; BM; M; W.
EPITHET: *Cinerascens,* grayish.
ILLUSTRATION: Krüssmann (1970c).
HABIT: Usually a shrub, rather densely branched, not unlike *A. sempervirens;* young shoots tomentose, later glabrous.
LEAVES: Variable in size and shape, 3-lobed, 2–6 cm long, grayish green, blunt, pilose beneath; basal lobes often strongly reduced; margins entire or coarsely toothed.
FLOWERS: Appearing with the leaves in April–May, similar to the typical subspecies.
FRUITS: Samaras almost parallel; nutlets small and hard.
BARK AND BUDS: Bark olive-green with blackish spotting.
HARDINESS: Zones V–VI.
DISTRIBUTION: Southeastern Turkey, Iraq, Lebanon, and western Iran in dry and stony places, scattered as scrub.
VARIETIES: It is not the intent of the present volume to place the following three varieties as comb. nov. under *A. monspessulanum* ssp. *cinerascens.*

*A. cinerascens* var. *boissieri* Schwerin (1898), leaves small, tomentose on both sides.
*A. cinerascens* var. *bornmuelleri* Schwerin (1898), much like subspecies *monspessulanum;* totally glabrous, except young, unfolding leaves tomentose.
*A. cinerascens* var. *paxii* Schwerin (1898), leaves very small, glabrous on both sides; growing in high mountains up to 2700 m.

REFERENCES: Krüssmann (1976a), Murray (1970c), Schwerin (1898).

This subspecies has been known for a long time in the literature and in herbaria. Nevertheless, it could not be found in any living collection in Europe or North America. Efforts should be made to introduce it and its relatives into cultivation. It likes a sunny and dry place. In its native habitat it grows in rocky situations in a warm and dry climate.

SECTION: *Acer* SERIES: *Monspessulana*
### ACER MONSPESSULANUM ssp. IBERICUM (Bieberstein) Yaltirik (1967)

BASIONYM: *A. ibericum* Bieberstein ex Willdenow (1806).
TYPE: Iberia (Georgia).
EPITHET: *Ibericus,* from Iberia, an ancient province of the Roman Empire in the Caucasus in Georgia.

HABIT: Small tree up to 8 m high. Trunk with gray bark. Young shoots glabrous, light brown, the older grayish brown.
LEAVES: 3-lobed, coriaceous, glaucous-green, shiny and glabrous above, paler beneath, densely cobwebby-hairy at first, later sparsely hairy at surface and along the nerves, usually broadening up to 7 cm long and 9 cm wide, rounded or cordate at the base; lobes ovate or triangular, obtuse or acute, usually entire but sometimes strongly dentate at the margin; petioles glabrous, usually longer than the blades.
FLOWERS: Sessile corymbs, pendulous, simply or rarely compound, with glabrous long pedicels; developing simultaneously with the leaves or slightly before them; calyx and corolla yellow, 4-merous, calyx broadly ovate 4–4.5 mm long; petals oblong-ovate, slightly longer than sepals; stamens two times longer than corolla; ovary densely hairy.
FRUITS: Samaras 2.5–3.5 cm long, wings vertical, rarely diverging at an acute angle, dilated above, nuts woody, glabrous outside, hairy inside.
BARK AND BUDS: Buds small, dark, and pointed.
HARDINESS: Zones V–VII, depending on provenance, mountains or lower regions.
DISTRIBUTION: Caucasia, northeastern Turkey, northern and northwestern Iran.
REFERENCES: Pojárkova (1949), Yaltirik (1967), Rechinger (1969), Murray (1970c).

SECTION: *Acer* SERIES: *Monspessulana*

## ACER MONSPESSULANUM ssp. MICROPHYLLUM (Boissier) Bornmüller (1914)

SYNONYMS

*A. microphyllum* Boissier (1846).
*A. syriacum* var. *hermoneum* Bornmüller (1898).
*A. monspessulanum* f. *divergens* Bornmüller (1914).
*A. monspessulanum* f. *micropterum* Bornmüller (1914).
*A. microphyllum* (Boissier) Dinsmore (1931), non Opiz.

TYPE: Lectotype, selected here, *T. Kotschy 240,* Mount Hermon, Lebanon; G, K, BM.
EPITHET: *Microphyllus,* small-leaved.
ILLUSTRATION: Plate 64.
HABIT: A densely branched shrub.
LEAVES: Very small, no other description available.
FLOWERS: Not seen.
FRUITS: Not seen.
HARDINESS: Zone VI.
DISTRIBUTION: Mountains of Lebanon, Palestine, Syria, and southern Turkey.
REFERENCE: Murray (1970c).

This poorly described subspecies is not known in cultivation, and it is uncertain whether it deserves subspecific recognition. As it is indigenous to Turkey, it might be identical or closely related to the puzzling maple already described as *Acer hyrcanum* ssp. *reginae-amaliae.* So little material is available that it is impossible to make any conclusions at this time. Nevertheless, it is very questionable whether the subspecies of *A. monspessulanum* endemic in Lebanon are still present. The collections were made almost 100 years ago and during the last 25 years especially most of Lebanon and adjacent countries have been destroyed or brought in agricultural cultivation.

SECTION: *Acer* SERIES: *Monspessulana*

## ACER MONSPESSULANUM L. (1753) ssp. MONSPESSULANUM

SYNONYMS

*A. trifolium* Duhamel (1755).
*A. trilobatum* Lamarck (1786).
*A. trilobum* Moench (1794).
*A. ibericum* Bieberstein ex Willdenow (1806).
*A. illyricum* (hort. ex Tausch) Reichenbach (1829).
*A. monspessulanum* var. *ibericum* (Willdenow) Tausch (1829).
*A. obtusatum* var. *ibericum* (Willdenow) Loudon (1842).
*A. creticum* Miller, non L.
*A. liburnicum* hort. ex Kirchner (1864).
*A. littorale* hort. ex Nicholson (1881).
*A. talyschense* Radde-Fomin (1931).

TYPE: *LINN #1225.15* "Habitat Monspelii," southern France.
COMMON NAMES: Montpellier maple, Burgenahorn, Dreilappiger Ahorn, Erable de Montpellier, Sestilo.
EPITHET: *Monspessulanus,* from Montpellier, an ancient city in southern France, where the species is abundant.
ILLUSTRATIONS: Plates 65, 66, 67.
HABIT: Variable, small and densely branched tree or large, dense shrub (wild plants in northern sites always as scrub), semi-evergreen or deciduous, 6–12 m tall, occasionally taller, with a rounded crown; branches glabrous, reddish brown to gray.
LEAVES: Extremely variable, coriaceous, 3-lobed, obtuse, 3–5 cm across, dark green, shining, glaucous beneath; margins entire or sometimes serrate; petioles long, 3–5 cm.
INFLORESCENCES: Pendulous, corymbose.
FLOWERS: Yellow-green, flowering in April or May.
FRUITS: Samaras subconnivent, wings reddish, 2–2.5 cm long, carpels glabrous; nutlets small, hard; often parthenocarpic, especially on cultivated specimens.
BARK AND BUDS: Bark sometimes corky; buds small and pointed.
HARDINESS: Zones V–VI.
AUTUMN COLOR: Yellow.

DISTRIBUTION: Mediterranean area: Spain, Portugal, Greece, Italy, Turkey, southern parts of Ukraine and Georgia, southern France, occasionally in Germany in sunny and dry valleys of the rivers Mosel, Rhine, and Nahe; also in the Swiss and French Jura, western Asia, Iran, Morocco and Algeria. Grown in the milder parts of North America. Only the typical subspecies, subspecies *monspessulanum,* is found in Europe.
CHROMOSOME NUMBER: $2n = 26$.
SUBSPECIES
- ssp. *assyriacum* (Pojárkova) Rechinger.
- ssp. *cinerascens* (Boissier) Yaltirik.
- ssp. *microphyllum* (Boissier) Bornmüller.
- ssp. *monspessulanum,* the typical subspecies
- ssp. *oksalianum* Yaltirik.
- ssp. *persicum* (Pojárkova) Rechinger.
- ssp. *turcomanicum* (Pojárkova) Murray.

VARIETIES
- var. *athoum* Bornmüller & Sintenis in Bornmüller (1894), samara wings divergent.
- var. *cassinense* Terracciano ex Bolle (1895), samaras red.
- var. *commutatum* (J. & K. Presl) Steudel (1840), samaras incurved.
- var. *divergens* Coutinho (1895), samara wings divergent.
- var. *villosum* Willkomm & Lange (1880), leaves villose.

FORM: f. *maroccanum* Schwerin (1893), leaf lobes narrowly triangular.
CULTIVARS: Three (see Chapter 9).
REFERENCES: Bean (1970), Dippel (1892), Elwes & Henry (1908), Firsov (1982), Koch (1869), Krüssmann (1976a), Linnaeus (1753), Murray (1970c, 1974b), Pax (1902), Pojárkova (1933b), Rehder (1976 facs.), Schneider (1912), Schwerin (1894, 1898, 1900).

Linnaeus proposed this species in 1753 together with a few other very well-known species such as *Acer campestre, A. negundo, A. pensylvanicum, A. platanoides, A. pseudoplatanus,* and *A. rubrum.* It has been known since the early days of botany and is widespread throughout the entire Mediterranean area. It grows in Ukraine along the Black Sea; occasionally in Germany on sunny and dry sites in the valleys of the rivers Mosel, Rhine, and Nahe; in the French and Swiss Jura; in North Africa (i.e., Morocco and Algeria); and as far east as Iran. It is found in Lebanon, especially the small-leaved variations. In the northerly latitudes of Europe it can only grow as scrub, but is successful in Great Britain, in the Benelux countries, and in the milder parts of Germany, Denmark, southern Sweden, and North America.

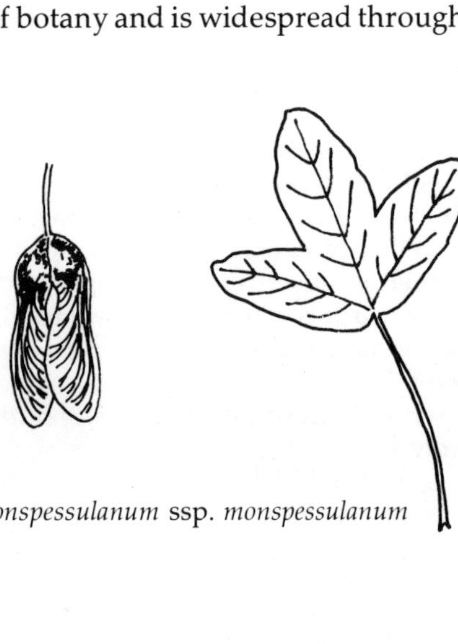

*Acer monspessulanum* ssp. *monspessulanum*

Due to the extensive natural range of this species there are many geographical variants. Modern taxonomy has reduced some of these named forms (*forma*) to cultivar status or to synonymy of the species. There are many synonyms to be found in the literature. Some subspecies, such as subspecies *cinerascens,* with gray-green leaves, have been assigned to *A. orientale multi-auctore* (now *A. sempervirens* or *A. obtusifolium*). Subspecies *turcomanicum,* which has leaves that are rusty-pilose on the undersides, has been recognized by Pojárkova (1949) as a separate species, *A. turcomanicum.*

The names *Acer alpinum* and *A. helveticum* are sometimes encountered. Both, published only once in *A Dutch Handbook for Lovers of Strange and Unusual Plants* (1795) and then without any description, are probably synonyms of *A. monspessulanum.* Reymers found these taxa of *Acer* at lower elevations of the western Alps, and they have been recorded in the handbook of the Société des Sciences Physiques de Lausanne (Switzerland). It is worth noting that there are no subspecies described in the European area, but quite a few in Levant. It is a matter of taxonomic and phytogeographic judgment whether these subspecies, particularly the Turkish ones, are to be maintained.

The species forms a small and densely branched tree; in unfavorable locations it is a shrub with coriaceous, almost leathery leaves, which sometimes are semi-evergreen or entirely deciduous. It can be mistaken for *Acer campestre* or its cultivars, but *A. monspessulanum* does not have the milky sap that is so prevalent in *A. campestre* and its allies. It is also possible to confuse it with *A. sempervirens,* but the latter is usually almost evergreen and has much smaller and often unlobed leaves. It is not widely planted, although it is relatively easy to obtain in the trade. It can be a very useful and pleasant plant in the garden. Trees growing in less than favorable situations tend to set parthenocarpic fruits. One must check for this tendency when harvesting fruits for propagation.

The evergreen cultivar 'Sempervirens' is identical with *Acer sempervirens* L. Subspecies *microphyllum* Boissier (1867), from Lebanon, has tiny leaves and might be related to, or synonymous with, variants belonging to *A. hyrcanum* ssp. *reginae-amaliae.* However, it is treated in this volume as *A. monspessulanum* ssp. *microphyllum* (Boissier) Bornmüller (1914), since little or no comparison materials are available.

During the *Acer* symposium held in 1988 in The Netherlands (organized by the International Dendrological Society), Faik Yaltirik confirmed the difficulties in obtaining the many subspecies of both *A. hyrcanum* and *A. monspessulanum* and in bringing them into cultivation. Hardly any seed can be found, and young seedlings are also scarce in their native habitat where goats and sheep eat them along with the other vegetation. The plants that are left rarely flower due to the hard "pruning" they receive from these animals. The only way to obtain many of these subspecies is to select fine specimens in the summer, then return in winter to cut scions for grafting.

SECTION: *Acer* SERIES: *Monspessulana*

## ACER MONSPESSULANUM ssp. OKSALIANUM Yaltirik (1967)

TYPE: Holotype *H. Kayaçik,* Sarimsak, Andirin, Maras, southeastern Turkey; ISTO (#388).
EPITHET: *Oksalianus,* after E. Muhlis Oksal, a professor and director of the Forest Botany Institute, Istanbul, Turkey.
HABIT: A shrub of moderate size.
LEAVES: 5-lobed, markedly tomentose beneath.
FLOWERS: Not seen.
FRUITS: Not seen.
HARDINESS: Zones V–VI.
DISTRIBUTION: Southeastern Turkey.
REFERENCES: Murray (1970c), Yaltirik (1967b).

This is another subspecies not known in cultivation. The description is very short. Without living material and more herbarium specimens it is not possible to determine whether subspecies *oksalianum* should be maintained at any rank.

SECTION: *Acer* SERIES: *Monspessulana*

## ACER MONSPESSULANUM ssp. PERSICUM (Pojárkova) Rechinger f. (1969)

SYNONYM: *A. persicum* Pojárkova (1933).
TYPE: *J. Bornmüller 3375,* Sha-Kuh Kerman, central Iran; BM; W.
EPITHET: *Persicus,* from Persia (Iran).
HABIT: A shrub.
LEAVES: 3-lobed, up to 3 cm wide.
FLOWERS: Not seen.
FRUITS: Not seen.
HARDINESS: Zones V–VI.
DISTRIBUTION: Central Iran.
REFERENCE: Murray (1970c).

Another subspecies of *Acer monspessulanum,* not known in cultivation. Efforts should be made to introduce all these species and subspecies to Europe or North America. Botanists and horticulturists should become better acquainted with this very confusing group of maples.

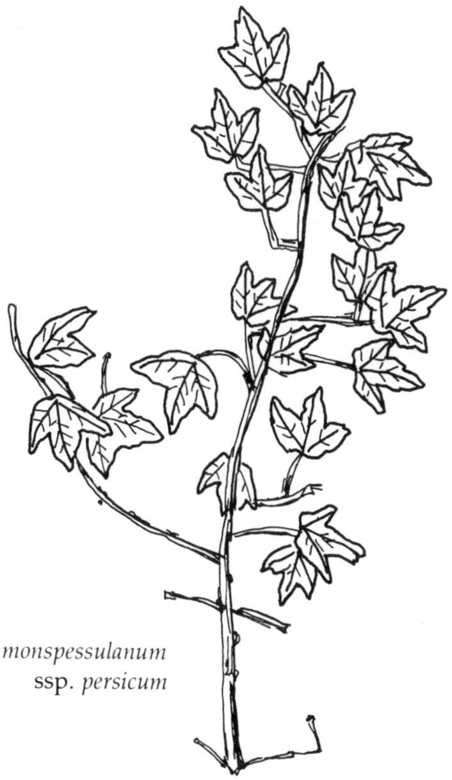

*Acer monspessulanum* ssp. *persicum*

SECTION: *Acer* SERIES: *Monspessulana*

## ACER MONSPESSULANUM ssp. TURCOMANICUM (Pojárkova) Murray (1969)

BASIONYM: *A. turcomanicum* Pojárkova (1932).
SYNONYMS
*A. monspessulanum* var. *divergens* Radde-Fomin (1932), non Coutinho (1895).
*A. latealatum* Radde-Fomin (1932).
*A. luteolatum* Radde-Fomin ex Parsa (1951).
TYPE: *A. Michelson 81,* Kopet-Dag, Turkmeniya; LE.
EPITHET: *Turcomanicum,* from Turkmeniya.
ILLUSTRATION: Plate 68.
HABIT: A rather large, densely branched shrub to 2–3 m tall.
LEAVES: 3-lobed, 3–4 cm long and 3–5 cm wide, leathery, almost evergreen in mild winters, rusty and pilose below; lobes diverging almost horizontally; veins prominent.
FLOWERS: Not seen.
FRUITS: Samaras connivent; nutlets small, hard, often parthenocarpic in unfavorable conditions.
HARDINESS: Zones V–VIII.
AUTUMN COLOR: Not obvious, or slightly yellowish.
DISTRIBUTION: Near the Caucasus Mountains, in Turkmeniya.
REFERENCES: Krüssmann (1976a), Murray (1970c).

This rare plant is not identical with the ambiguous name *Acer monspessulanum* 'Sempervirens', which is the same as *A. sempervirens.* The leaves of subspecies *turcomanicum* are much larger and markedly 3-lobed, in comparison with *A. sempervirens.* Usually its leaves are larger than in the typical subspecies. It is a fully hardy plant, interesting for its shiny leaves; in mild winters it is almost evergreen. It is now in cultivation in The Netherlands, propagated by vegetative means.

SECTION: *Acer* SERIES: *Monspessulana*

## ACER OBTUSIFOLIUM Sibthorp & Smith (1809)

SYNONYMS

*A. orientale* L. (1767).
*A. sempervirens* var. *obtusifolium* (Sibthorp & Smith) Tausch (1829).
*A. syriacum* Boissier & Gaillardot (1856).
*A. syriacum* var. *cyprium* Boissier (1867).

TYPE: *Smith,* Mount Sphaciotica, Crete, Greece; BM; K; G.
EPITHET: *Obtusifolius,* with obtuse leaves.
ILLUSTRATION: Plate 69.
HABIT: A small evergreen tree or rounded shrub to 5–6 m tall in native habitat, usually much shorter in cultivation; twigs and branches glabrous.
LEAVES: Leathery, coriaceous, varying in shape, ovate to 3-lobed and obovate, mostly entire, especially on mature plants, 4–10 cm long and 3–6 cm wide, 3-veined, distinctly bright gray-green.
INFLORESCENCES: Small corymbs on short side shoots.
FLOWERS: Greenish yellow.
FRUITS: Samaras 2 cm long, diverging at an angle of about 60°.
BARK AND BUDS: Bark yellowish olive, smooth.
HARDINESS: Zone VII.
AUTUMN COLOR: Absent.
DISTRIBUTION: Eastern Turkey, Syria, Lebanon, Palestine, and Cyprus, along coastal mountain regions. No longer present on Crete.
CHROMOSOME NUMBER: $2n = 26$ (as *A. syriacum,* Santamour 1988).
REFERENCES: Bean (1970), Krüssmann (1976a), Murray (1970c), Rehder (1986 facs.).

*Acer obtusifolium* is usually described as a variety or synonym of *A. sempervirens,* although there are several reasons not to do so (see under *A. sempervirens*). This taxon is rather well-known under the name *A. syriacum,* a synonym. Plants grown from seed labeled *A. sempervirens* var. *obtusifolium* are identical to the former *A. syriacum.* As there are no discernable differences between plants from Crete—*A. obtusifolium* (now extinct on Crete)—and those from Syria—*A. syriacum*—these two taxa are united in the present volume under *A. obtusifolium,* which is the oldest name. This name is well known and documented and will eliminate the constant confusion with *A. sempervirens* L. (1767) and *A. orientale* L. (1767).

The name *Acer orientale* L. (1767) must be rejected as a later homonym of *A. orientale* L. (1759). More than one species now recognized as being different were included in the 1767 application of *A. orientale.* Moreover, the 1767 description does not fit with living or herbarium materials. The name *A. creticum* L. is also very ambiguous. It has been attached to several taxa, as pointed out by Schneider (1912).

In its native habitat *Acer obtusifolium* grows as scrub and forms huge shrubs or eventually small trees. The leaves are leathery and coriaceous and much larger than those of *A. sempervirens.* The species is reliably evergreen in mild regions, but in cold winters the leaves shrivel and drop off. Usually the plants recover well. It is the hardiest evergreen maple and seldom suffers winter damage in the British Isles. It is rare in gardens and only occasionally available in the trade. When no seed is available it is possible to graft this species on potted understock of *Acer pseudoplatanus* or *A. monspessulanum.*

SECTION: *Acer* SERIES: *Monspessulana*

## ACER OPALUS ssp. HISPANICUM (Pourret) Murray (1969)

BASIONYM: *A. hispanicum* Pourret (1788).

SYNONYMS

*A. granatense* Boissier (1838).
*A. nevadense* Boissier ex Pax (1886).
*A. cadevallii* Marcet (1909).
*A. opalus* var. *africanum* (Pax) Murray (1969).
*A. opalus* f. *microphyllum* Koch.

TYPE: Montserrat.
EPITHET: *Hispanicus,* from Spain.
HABIT: A small tree or treelike shrub, rather densely branched.
LEAVES: Small, 5-lobed, 2.5–6 cm across; lobes blunt; veins pilose beneath.
INFLORESCENCES: Terminal, short umbels with many yellow flowers.
FRUITS: Samaras small, wings divergent; nutlets thick.
BARK AND BUDS: Bark gray-brown; buds dark and small.
HARDINESS: Zone VI.
DISTRIBUTION: Mountains of Spain, primarily the Pyrenees; also in southwestern France.
REFERENCES: Murray (1970c), Walters (1968).

This shrubby tree is, as far as is known, not in cultivation. It is quite doubtful whether variety *africanum* and the so-called species *A. granatense* (cf. Walters 1968) deserve any botanical status other than as synonyms of subspecies *hispanicum.* As there is no living material under these names in cultivation, it is impossible to compare them with living specimens of the other subspecies.

SECTION: *Acer* SERIES: *Monspessulana*

ACER OPALUS ssp. OBTUSATUM (Willdenow) Gams (1925)

BASIONYM: *A. obtusatum* Willdenow (1806).

SYNONYMS

*A. opulifolium* var. *tomentosum* Tausch (1829).
*A. opulifolium* var. *velutinum* Boissier (1867), non *A. velutinum* Boissier (1846).
*A. italum* var. *neapolitanum* (Tenore) Dieck (1885).
*A. italicum* var. *aetnense* Tineo ex Strobl (1885).
*A. opalus* var. *bosniacum* Maly (1906), in syn.

TYPE: "In siccis montosis Hungariae et Croatiae" (de Candolle, *Prodromus* Vol. 1, p. 594, 1824.). De Candolle makes reference to L. Trattinick, *Archiv der Gewächskunde,* Vol. 1 "n. 14 ic." "Type" collections will probably be found in W and G.

COMMON NAME: Bosnian maple.

EPITHET: *Obtusatus,* with short and obtuse lobes.

ILLUSTRATION: Plate 70.

HABIT: A small tree or large, multistemmed shrub to 8 m tall.

LEAVES: Smaller than those of subspecies *opalus,* with shorter, obtuse lobes, undersides tomentose when young; margins slightly toothed; bases more or less cordate.

INFLORESCENCES: Short umbels, very floriferous, appearing before the leaves.

FLOWERS: Yellow.

FRUITS: Samaras 2.5 cm long; fruits in clusters on short, small trusses, glabrous, green, often parthenocarpic on cultivated trees.

BARK AND BUDS: Bark like that of subspecies *opalus.*

HARDINESS: Zone V.

AUTUMN COLOR: Inconspicuous, sometimes yellow-bronze.

DISTRIBUTION: Hungary, Croatia, Serbia, Slovenia, and southern Italy (i.e., Sicily and Calabria); occasionally in North Africa. Very disjunct distribution.

CHROMOSOME NUMBER: $2n = 26$ (Santamour 1988).

REFERENCES: Bean (1970), Dippel (1892), Elwes & Henry (1908), Koch (1869), Krüssmann (1976a), Murray (1970c, 1977), Pax (1902), Rehder (1986 facs.), Schneider (1912).

SECTION: *Acer* SERIES: *Monspessulana*

ACER OPALUS Miller (1768) ssp. OPALUS

SYNONYMS

*A. italum* Lauth (1781).
*A. montanum* Dalechamps ex Lamarck (1786).
*A. opulifolium* Villars (1786).
*A. vernum* Carrière ex Lamarck (1786).
*A. rotundifolium* Lamarck (1786).
*A. apolifolium* Persoon (1805).
*A. opulifolium* var. *opalus* (Miller) Koch (1853).
*A. italicum* Lauche (1880).
*A. rupicolum* Chabert (1910).

TYPE: Acer #8, *P. Miller;* BM.

COMMON NAMES: Italian maple, Erable printanier, Frühlings-Ahorn, loppo.

EPITHET: *Opalus,* misspelling of *Opulus,* an old generic name of *Acer; Viburnum opulus* (Guelder rose) looks like a maple.

ILLUSTRATIONS: Plates 71, 72; Bean (1970), Krüssmann (1976a), Schwerin (1894).

HABIT: A tree to 10–13 m tall, often a shrub in native habitat; young branches glabrous; extremely variable.

LEAVES: Very variable, 3- to 5-lobed, obtuse, 6–15 cm across, undersides glaucous, hairy when young, pubescent on the veins, somewhat "crinkled" when mature, never flat; lobes short and obtusely toothed.

INFLORESCENCES: Terminal, corymbose in short umbels, very floriferous, appearing before or with the leaves; pedicels 3 cm long.

FLOWERS: Yellow.

FRUITS: Samaras erect, 3–5 cm long; wings dark brown, divergent, only slightly narrowed at the base; nutlets thick, often parthenocarpic, especially on cultivated plants.

BARK AND BUDS: Bark smooth and gray, fissured and dark on older trees; bud scales imbricate.

HARDINESS: Zone IV.

AUTUMN COLOR: Not distinctive in cultivation, but sometimes yellow or bronze; in its native habitat, often beautifully reddish to golden brown.

DISTRIBUTION: Jura Mountains in Switzerland and France, on hillsides up to about 1000 m altitude. Also in Burgundy in France, the Pyrenees in Spain, Corsica, the Apennines in Italy, eastward to the Caucasus, Morocco, and Algeria. Associated plants in the Jura are *Buxus sempervirens, Ilex aquifolium, Prunus mahaleb, Quercus pubescens, Sorbus aria,* and *S. torminalis;* more southerly, *Acer monspessulanum* and *Laburnum anagyroides.*

CHROMOSOME NUMBER: $2n = 26$.

SUBSPECIES

ssp. *hispanicum* (Pourret) Murray (1969), a small-leaved specimen found in Spain and the Pyrenees.
ssp. *obtusatum* (Willdenow) Gams, found in mountains of Bosnia and Hercegovina; leaf lobes shorter than lobes of ssp. opalus and leaf texture sturdier, otherwise not very different.
ssp. *opalus,* the typical subspecies.

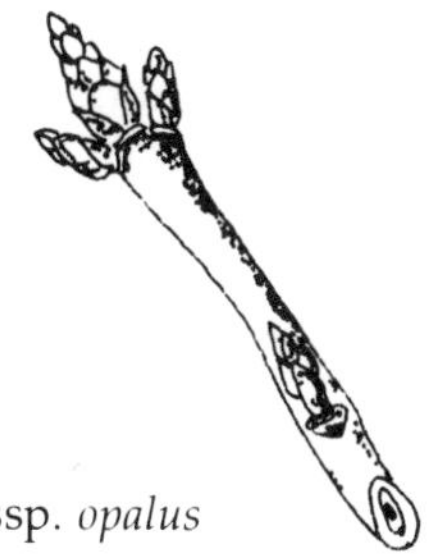

*Acer opalus* ssp. *opalus*

VARIETY: var. *corallinum* Beauverd (1930), samaras coral-red.
REFERENCES: Bean (1970), Dippel (1892), Elwes & Henry (1908), Hegi (1925), Koch (1869), Krüssmann (1976a), Murray (1970c), Pax (1902), Rehder (1986 facs.), Schneider (1912), Schwerin (1894), Walters (1968).

There is much confusion regarding the nomenclature of this species and, consequently, many synonyms. The valid name *opalus*, given by Miller in 1768, was originally used erroneously by Ray in 1688, rather than the correct *opulus. Opalus* actually refers to *Acer italum*, the southern counterpart of *A. campestre* (*Opalus italum*).

One of the few native European species of the genus *Acer, A. opalus* is nevertheless rare in cultivation and even rarer in the trade. It is rather closely allied to *A. monspessulanum*, but is readily distinguished by its much larger leaves and growth habit. At first glance, it is not unlike a small *A. pseudoplatanus*, but closer examination reveals many differences, especially in its inflorescences and seed, denser branching structure, and the absence of any red color in the petioles. An outstanding feature is its striking, very profuse floral display, appearing before the leaves.

Subspecies *opalus* can be propagated by wild-collected seed. Cultivated trees often bear parthenocarpic seed, so seed is hard to get in the trade.

Murray (1977) recombined *Acer hyrcanum* and all its infraspecific taxa to *A. opalus* (i.e., *A. opalus* ssp. *hyrcanum*, ssp. *intermedium*, ssp. *stevenii*, ssp. *tauricolum*, ssp. *tauricolum* f. *keckianum*, ssp. *tauricolum* var. *sphaerocarpum*, ssp. *reygassei*. He also added new *formae:* ssp. *obtusatum* f. *glabrescens*, ssp. *opalus* f. *glaucum*, and ssp. *opalus* f. *pubescens*).

SECTION: *Acer* SERIES: *Monspessulana*

## ACER SEMPERVIRENS L. (1767)

SYNONYMS

*A. orientale* auct. non L.
*A. creticum* auct. non L., non Miller.
*A. heterophyllum* Willdenow (1796).
*A. humile* Salisbury (1796).
*A. willkommii* Wettstein (1889).
*A. monspessulanum* ssp. *orientale* (L.) Wesmael.

TYPE: Yaltirik (1967a) "Described from cultivated material said to have originated in the Levant." If extant, a specimen may be in LINN or S or SBT.
EPITHET: *Sempervirens*, evergreen.
ILLUSTRATIONS: Plates 73, 74; Pax (1902).
HABIT: A small tree or shrub to 6–7 m tall, but very often much shorter, deciduous or partly evergreen; branches usually glabrous. According to Bean (1970), some wild plants on Crete have young twigs covered with a short down; the coauthors of the present volume, however, have never seen this downy pubescence on the leaves and twigs of adult plants.
LEAVES: Variably shaped, often unlobed or indistinctly 3-lobed, very often persistent on dwarf plants, 1–4 cm long and 1–2 cm wide, bright green, quite glabrous on both surfaces; margins entire or shallowly undulated, sometimes with a few small teeth.
FLOWERS: Greenish yellow, on few-flowered corymbs about 1.5 cm long.
FRUITS: Samaras glabrous, 1.5 cm long, sometimes longer, parallel or at an angle of 60°.
HARDINESS: Zones VI–VII.
AUTUMN COLOR: Not present or only a hint of color on old leaves after abscission.
DISTRIBUTION: Eastern part of the Mediterranean area (i.e., Lebanon, western Turkey, Greek archipelago).
FORMS: A number of formae were described in earlier years, but because many different leaf shapes and sizes may be found on the same plant, they cannot be sustained.
REFERENCES: Bean (1970), Krüssmann (1976a), Murray (1970c), Rehder (1986 facs.), Yaltirik (1967b).

Murray's (1970c, 145) description is not accepted in the present volume: "(Type: Tournefort Herb. at P) . . . excluding mention of lvs. being 'subvillous' ('pubescent' in Linne') in error!" Dippel (1892), however, described *Acer sempervirens* as growing on the mountains of the Greek Archipelago and Syria: "It is a densely branched shrub or small tree, with gray or brown bark, growing large. Leaves leathery, 1–4 cm, rounded-ovate, very short petioles, base somewhat cordate." This perfectly describes *A. sempervirens* as we know it today and agree with Schneider (1909, 1912), who wrote:

> It has been impossible for me to clarify the distinctions between *Acer orientale* L. and *Acer creticum* L. . . . *Acer foliis trilobis integerrimus pubescentibus* does not agree with *Acer creticum* or *Acer orientale* sens. Auct. but far more with certain forms of *Acer monspessulanum*. The oldest sure name may be *Acer sempervirens* L.

The close relative of *Acer sempervirens* is *A. obtusifolium* (the former *A. syriacum*, also evergreen, is a synonym), but the leaves of *A. obtusifolium* are larger, 6–10 cm long. The name *A. sempervirens* var. *obtusifolium* is now, obviously, a synonym of *A. obtusifolium*.

There is also a variety *nanum* Tausch (1829), with leaf margins usually entire. Sometimes uncertain names of formae are reduced to cultivar rank, as is frequently done with species such as *A. platanoides, Acer pseudoplatanus*, and others. Following this practice, the typical dwarf expression, vegetatively propagated, could be named *A. sempervirens* 'Nanum'. This is, however, not a practice to encourage; in fact, it is taxonomically inaccurate and encourages coining of Latin cultivar names by nursery professionals, which, if coined since 1 January 1959, are illegitimate.

The nomenclature of this species was pointed out by Yaltirik (1967):

> The nomenclature of this variable species deserves a note. *A. orientale* L. was undoubtedly based on a hairy-leaved plant, well known to Miller. No authentic specimen can be traced and there is no justification for applying the name to a species which always has glabrous leaf blades. The name *A. creticum* merely replaces *A. orientale* and is therefore illegitimate.
>
> The first valid name for our species is *Acer sempervirens* L, based on a dwarf form with entire ovate leaves. Among the wild specimens seen, only Bozakman's gathering has leaves of this type. All the other species have 3-lobed leaves, as in Greece and Crete.

Linnaeus's (1759, 1310) original description of *Acer orientale* reads "*A. fol. trilobis integerrimus pubescentibus.* Mill. dict." The species, however, is hairless, so Linnaeus must have been describing another taxon. Describing *A. sempervirens,* Linnaeus (1767, 128) referred again to Miller: "Acer foliis ovatis integerrimus sempervirentibus. Mill. dictat. Habitat in Oriente." Miller (1759), however, originally described two maples and neither of his descriptions illustrates Linnaeus' binomial nomenclature:

> 10. Acer foliis trilobis integerrimus subvillosis. The eastern Maple with Ivy leaves. This is the Acer orientalis hederae foliis Tournef. Cor. 43.
>
> 11. Acer foliis ovatis integerrimus sempervirentibus Eastern Maple with oval entire leaves, which are evergreen.

Other authors of dendrological works have also struggled to correctly identify this species. Pax, for example, differentiates about six formae based only on herbarium specimens, but since leaves of several shapes are to be found on the same tree, taxonomic recognition of foliar variations is certainly superfluous.

During several visits to Crete the author of this chapter compared and studied hundreds of plants in the wild. He found many more shrubby plants than trees. One explanation is that through hundreds of years of grazing, sheep and goats have destroyed all young seedlings. It was remarkable that at 1500 m and higher, trees to 10 m tall were found, especially on the flanks of Mount Ida in central Crete. Some consistent difference between leaves of shrubs and trees was observed: unlobed leaves were rare on trees. In fact, larger trees usually had 3-lobed leaves, which were more leathery and more persistent than the unlobed leaves of more shrubby plants.

## SERIES SACCHARODENDRON

TYPE SPECIES: ***Acer saccharum*** Marshall (1785).

HABIT: Deciduous trees.

LEAVES: 3- to 5-lobed, sometimes up to 7-lobed, chartaceous; margins entire to coarsely dentate.

BUD SCALES: 6- to 9-paired.

INFLORESCENCES: With 10–60 flowers, on pendulous pedicels, terminal or frequently axillary (and then from leafless buds).

FLOWERS: Apetalous; calyces connate.

FRUITS: Nutlets spherical, parthenocarpic tendency strong.

SPECIES: *A. saccharum.*

REFERENCE: De Jong (1976).

One variable, extremely polymorphic species is placed in this monotypic series, which includes seven subspecies and three varieties, all proposed by Desmarais, Rehder, or Murray. This complex species is native primarily in North America, and extends from subtropical areas in Central America as far south as Guatemala and Mexico to vast areas in the northern United States and in Canada. The leaves are almost always 5-lobed and deciduous.

SECTION: *Acer* SERIES: *Saccharodendron*

## ACER SACCHARUM Marshall (1785) ssp. SACCHARUM

SYNONYMS

- *A. palmifolium* Borkhausen (1800).
- *A. saccharophorum* Koch (1853).
- *A. palmifolium* var. *barbatum* (Michaux) Schwerin (1893).
- *Saccharodendron barbatum* (Michaux) Nieuwland (1914).
- *Acer treleaseanum* Bush (1931).
- *Saccharodendron saccharum* (Marshall) Moldenke (1937).

TYPE: *H. Marshall,* near his home (specimen apparently lost or? at DWC); topotypes *E. Murray;* Marshallton, Pennsylvania, USA, 30 miles west of Philadelphia; A (fide Murray).

COMMON NAMES: Sugar maple, Suikeresdoorn, Sukkerloenn, Zucker-Ahorn.

EPITHET: *Saccharum,* with sugar.

ILLUSTRATIONS: Plates 75, 76; Krüssmann (1976a).

HABIT: A tree to 40 m tall, upright growing; branches gray-brown.

LEAVES: 3- to 5-lobed, usually 5, 8–15 cm across, regularly shaped, apices sharply acute, each lobe with many small and 2–3 larger teeth, upper sides dark green, paler beneath, glabrous; petioles 6–8 cm long.

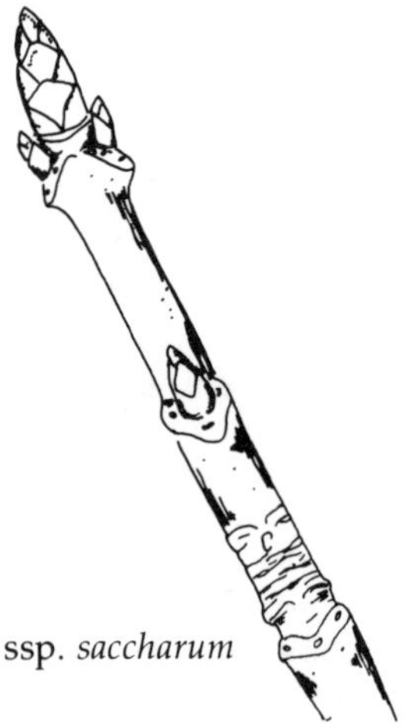

*Acer saccharum* ssp. *saccharum*

INFLORESCENCES: Corymbose, pedicels pendant, pubescent.
FLOWERS: 5-merous, pale yellow, apetalous, appearing before the leaves, unisexual or bisexual.
FRUITS: Samaras U-shaped, often irregular. Trees in cultivation in Europe often bear no fruits at all, or if seeds are present they are not viable.
BARK AND BUDS: Bark rough, but regularly fissured. Bud scales many, imbricate.
HARDINESS: Zone III.
AUTUMN COLOR: Yellow to orange or scarlet, and often all these colors mixed; a most brilliant performance in the fall.
DISTRIBUTION: Eastern North America to Mexico and Guatemala, together with *Tsuga, Betula,* and *Prunus,* forming forests.
CHROMOSOME NUMBER: $2n = 26$ (Darlington et al. 1955); tetraploid, $2n = 52$ (Darlington and others); hexaploid, $2n = 78$, (Santamour 1971); an anomalous $2n = 53$ (Dent 1962, 1963).
CULTIVARS: Many (see Chapter 9).
SUBSPECIES
- ssp. *floridanum* (Chapman) Desmarais.
- ssp. *grandidentatum* (Torrey & Gray) Desmarais.
- ssp. *leucoderme* (Small) Desmarais.
- ssp. *nigrum* (Michaux f.) Desmarais.
- ssp. *ozarkense* Murray.
- ssp. *saccharum,* the typical subspecies.
- ssp. *skutchii* (Rehder) Murray.

VARIETIES
- var. *rugelii* (Pax) Rehder.
- var. *schneckii* Rehder.
- var. *sinuosum* (Rehder) Sargent.

FORMS
- f. *conicum* Fernald (1934), densely conical tree.
- f. *glaucum* (Schmidt) Pax (1902), leaves glaucous beneath.

REFERENCES: Bean (1970), Dippel (1892), Elwes & Henry (1908), de Jong (1976), Koch (1869), Krüssmann (1976a), Murray (1970c, 1975b), Pojárkova (1933b), Rehder (1986 facs.), Trelease (1894).

*Acer saccharum* is the true sugar maple, very widely distributed in North America, where it is famous for producing sap from which maple syrup is made and for its spectacular autumn foliage colors. It was introduced in 1735 to Europe, according to Loudon.

In North America this tree is unsurpassed for its brilliancy and color in the autumn. It is a very variable and complex species. Several former species have now been reduced to subspecific rank under *Acer saccharum.* It grows to a tree of 40 m tall, with a rather upright habit. The leaves are (3- to) 5-lobed and regularly shaped. The lobes are almost divergent. The petioles are long, 6–8 cm, not unlike those of *A. platanoides.*

The sugar maple is easily propagated from North American seed. Trees in Europe seldom flower and almost never produce viable seed. Consequently, European nurseries occasionally propagate good forms by layering.

SECTION: *Acer* SERIES: *Saccharodendron*

## ACER SACCHARUM ssp. FLORIDANUM (Chapman) Desmarais (1952)

BASIONYM: *A. saccharinum* var. *floridanum* Chapman (1860).
SYNONYMS
- *A. floridanum* (Chapman) Pax (1886).
- *A. barbatum* auct. non Michaux, pro parte.
- *A. barbatum* var. *floridanum* (Chapman) Fosberg (1954).
- *A. nigrum* var. *floridanum* (Chapman) Fosberg (1954).

TYPE: *A. W. Chapman,* upland woods, Florida, USA; NY.
EPITHET: *Floridanus,* from Florida.
HABIT: A small tree to 8–12 m tall, occasionally more when growing in favorable conditions.
LEAVES: 5-lobed, 9–15 cm across, lobes obtuse, bases subcordate to truncate, glaucous beneath.
FLOWERS: Yellowish, same shape and size as subspecies *saccharum.*
FRUITS: Samaras U-shaped and tending to be irregular; often only one wing is formed. Seeds often not viable due to parthenocarpy.
BARK AND BUDS: Bark chalky gray and smooth, not fissured.
HARDINESS: Zone V.
AUTUMN COLOR: Yellow.
CHROMOSOME NUMBER: $2n = 26$.
DISTRIBUTION: Southeastern United States in the coastal plains of Florida, Texas, and Mexico.
REFERENCES: Bean (1970, as *A. barbatum*), Murray (1970c), Rehder (1986 facs.).

*Acer saccharum* ssp. *floridanum* (*A. barbatum,* pro parte) is a small tree with obtuse leaf lobes, growing in the coastal plains of southeastern

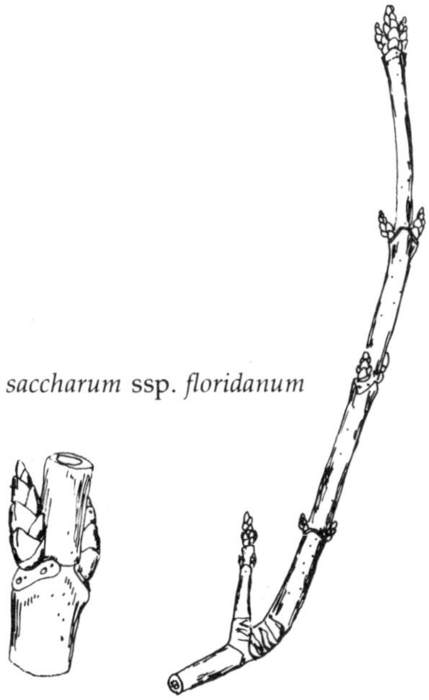

*Acer saccharum* ssp. *floridanum*

North America, and extending to Mexico. It is a rare plant in cultivation. There is much confusion about its name; the synonymous name, *A. barbatum,* includes two mixed taxa. Only the flowers of the original description of *A. barbatum* are correctly placed as subspecies *floridanum,* while the remaining characteristics pertain to *A. rubrum.*

SECTION: *Acer* SERIES: *Saccharodendron*

ACER SACCHARUM ssp. GRANDIDENTATUM (Torrey & Gray) Desmarais (1952)

BASIONYM: *A. grandidentatum* Torrey & Gray (1838).

SYNONYMS

*A. mexicanum* A. Gray (1861).

*A. brachypterum* Wooton & Standley (1913).

*A. nigrum* var. *grandidentatum* (Torrey & Gray) Fosberg (1954).

TYPE: *T. Nuttall,* on Bear River, Utah, in the Rocky Mountains, USA; PH.

COMMON NAMES: Canyon maple, big tooth or hard maple.

EPITHET: *Grandidentatus,* with large teeth on the leaves.

ILLUSTRATION: Barker (1977).

HABIT: A small tree or shrubby tree to 12 m tall, often much shorter, sometimes only a shrub in western Europe; densely branched; branches glabrous, reddish brown.

LEAVES: Distinctly 5-lobed, 5–8 cm across, lobulate, margins entire or with three small basal lobes, shining green above, glaucous beneath, often softly pubescent, often somewhat leathery.

INFLORESCENCES: Corymbose, pendulous, with short pedicels.

FLOWERS: Yellow.

FRUITS: Samaras U-shaped, like those of subspecies *saccharum* but slightly smaller; nutlets rounded, on corymbose umbels.

BARK AND BUDS: Bark gray-brown.

HARDINESS: Zone IV.

AUTUMN COLOR: Splendidly red, scarlet, yellow, and orange.

DISTRIBUTION: In the Rocky Mountains and Utah in the United States, on a north-south axis, at 1500–2500 m. It also grows in Texas and Oklahoma, west to Arizona, and north into Montana; extending south into northern Mexico. Found by Thomas Nuttall along the Columbia and Bear rivers, Utah. Grows on sunny, dry slopes.

CHROMOSOME NUMBER: $2n = 26$.

REFERENCES: Barker (1977), Bean (1970), Dippel (1892), Krüssmann (1976a), Murray (1970c), Rehder (1986 facs.).

This subspecies is confined to the western part of North America and is considered by several botanists to be a species on its own. In this volume, however, the view of Desmarais is accepted, and it is treated as a subspecies of *Acer saccharum.*

In summer it is not conspicuous, but in the autumn it shows splendid colors for several weeks. The mountains in Utah are magnificently colored and offer a sensational view. It is uncommon in European gardens. It is easily propagated by wild seed, or vegetatively by grafting on seedlings of *Acer saccharum.*

Murray (1980, 2) recognized a new taxon, *Acer saccharum* var. *trilobum,* with 3-lobed leaves. Not in cultivation, this variety belongs to subspecies *grandidentatum.*

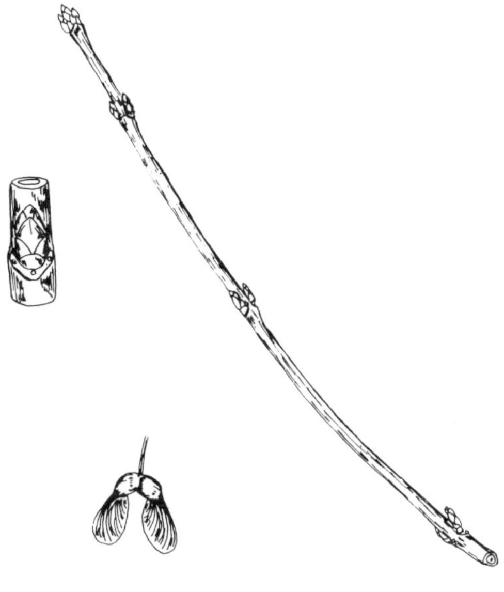

*Acer saccharum* ssp. *grandidentatum*

SECTION: *Acer* SERIES: *Saccharodendron*
ACER SACCHARUM ssp. LEUCODERME (Small) Desmarais (1952)

BASIONYM: *A. leucoderme* Small (1895).
SYNONYMS
*A. floridanum* var. *acuminatum* Trelease (1894).
*A. nigrum* var. *leucoderme* (Small) Fosberg (1954).
TYPE: Lectotype *Small & Heller,* Yadkon Road, Stanley Co., North Carolina, USA; NY.
COMMON NAMES: Chalk maple, Kalkahorn.
EPITHET: *Leucodermis,* with white skin.
ILLUSTRATION: Plate 77.
HABIT: A small tree or occasionally a shrub, to 6–8 m tall, sometimes more, rather densely branched, with a round-topped crown; young shoots thin and glabrous.
LEAVES: 3- to 5-lobed, lobes almost triangular, acute; 5–8 cm across on very vigorous shoots, occasionally larger, usually with 2 large teeth, margins wavy, bases almost cordate, fresh green above, yellow-gray beneath, not glaucous but covered with a prominent, velvety down; petioles glabrous, 4–5 cm long.
FLOWERS: Yellow, appearing in April, on small, few-flowered umbels.
FRUITS: Samaras almost horizontal; nutlets hairy when young, later glabrous, 2 cm long, often parthenocarpic.
BARK AND BUDS: Bark chalky gray.
HARDINESS: Zone V.
AUTUMN COLOR: Yellow, not very conspicuous.
DISTRIBUTION: Southern United States including North Carolina to Florida, Georgia, Alabama, Louisiana, and Arkansas.
REFERENCES: Bean (1970), Krüssmann (1976a), Murray (1970c), Rehder (1986 facs.).

This small tree occasionally is a shrub in cultivation. It differs from its allies mainly by the peculiar velvety down on the undersides of the leaf. Often the leaves are markedly wavy, which is almost never the case in subspecies *saccharum.* The leaves are, in fact, somewhat like those of subspecies *grandidentatum,* but the latter are more leathery and lack the velvety down.

Subspecies *leucoderme* is quite rare in cultivation, and only rarely available in the trade. If no seed is available, grafting is possible on seedlings of any sugar maple.

SECTION: *Acer* SERIES: *Saccharodendron*
ACER SACCHARUM ssp. NIGRUM (Michaux f.) Desmarais (1952)

BASIONYM: *A. nigrum* Michaux (1812).
SYNONYMS
*A. saccharum* var. *pseudoplatanoides* Pax (1902), pro parte.
*A. nigrum* var. *palmeri* Sargent (1921).
TYPE: Michaux Herbarium, P.

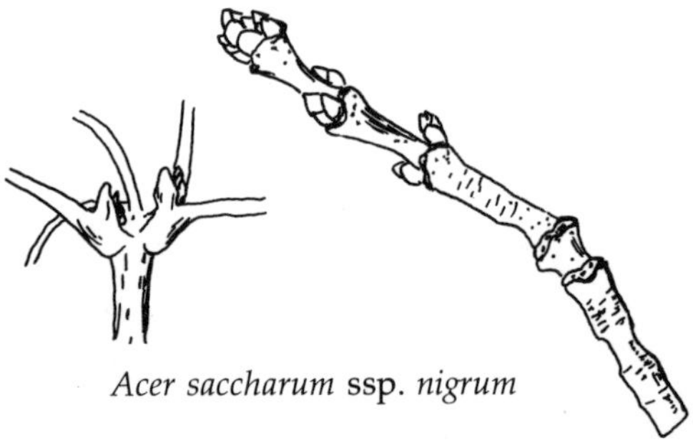
*Acer saccharum* ssp. *nigrum*

COMMON NAMES: Black sugar maple, Schwarz-Ahorn
EPITHET: *Niger,* black.
HABIT: A large tree to 40 m tall in native habitat and usually much smaller in cultivation, with rounded crown; branches pubescent at first; branchlets orange-yellow.
LEAVES: Mostly 3-lobed, occasionally 5-lobed with basal lobes less pronounced, 10–15 cm across on long vigorous shoots but sometimes larger, lobes slightly acuminate, margins undulate, dark green above, yellow-green beneath, partly pubescent on the undersides; petioles bear leaflike stipules that are sometimes quite small or, rarely, absent.
INFLORESCENCES: Corymbose.
FLOWERS: Yellow-green.
FRUITS: Samaras subhorizontal, 3–4 cm long; nutlets rounded.
BARK AND BUDS: Bark very dark, gray-black, furrowed.
HARDINESS: Zone III.
AUTUMN COLOR: Golden yellow.
DISTRIBUTION: Eastern and central North America, together with several *Acer* species, *Carya,* and *Quercus alba;* distributed from Ontario and southern Quebec southward to Kentucky, westward through Michigan to Kansas and Iowa. Grows on calcareous substrates.
CULTIVARS: Very few (see Chapter 9).
REFERENCES: Bean (1970), Dippel (1892), Elwes & Henry (1908), Koch (1869), Krüssmann (1976a), Murray (1970c), Pax (1902), Rehder (1986 facs.).

The black sugar maple is a stately tree growing in eastern and central North America, together with *Acer rubrum, A. saccharinum,* and *A. negundo.* It differs from its allies by its larger leaves, which are similar to those of *A. pseudoplatanus.* Pax noticed this feature when he incorrectly named this tree *A. saccharum* var. *pseudoplatanoides.* The leaves are leathery and have stipules at the petioles, a noteworthy feature since stipules are absent in all other subspecies of *A. saccharum* and in all Aceraceae.

This subspecies is rather rare in cultivation, and few good trees are reported in arboreta. The subspecies is also used to produce maple syrup. The cultivar 'Temple's Upright' ('Monumentale') clearly belongs to this subspecies.

SECTION: *Acer* SERIES: *Saccharodendron*
ACER SACCHARUM ssp. OZARKENSE Murray (1978)

TYPE: *E. J. Palmer 22, 278,* Mcnab, Hempstead County, Arkansas, USA; A; MO; US.
EPITHET: *Ozarkensis,* from the Ozark Mountains in Missouri.
HABIT: A dense tree of the same habit as *A. saccharum* ssp. *grandidentatum.*
LEAVES: 5-lobed, furnished with a horned set of lobules, glaucous beneath.
DISTRIBUTION: Arkansas and Missouri in the United States.
REFERENCE: Murray (1978).

This subspecies is not known in cultivation. A new variety described but not in cultivation is *Acer saccharum* var. *quinquelobulatum* Murray (1982, 17), with 5-lobed leaves, nearly lobulate, lobules round if present. Distributed in Arkansas, Missouri, and Oklahoma, USA, it is related to subspecies *ozarkense.*

SECTION: *Acer* SERIES: *Saccharodendron*
ACER SACCHARUM ssp. SKUTCHII (Rehder) Murray (1975)

BASIONYM: *A. skutchii* Rehder (1936).
TYPE: *A. Skutch 1667,* Nebaj, Quiche, Guatemala; A.
EPITHET: *Skutchii,* after A. F. Skutch, U.S. biologist in Guatemala.
HABIT: A tree to 20 m tall; branchlets glabrous.
LEAVES: 5-lobed, 12–16 cm long and 14–20 cm wide, usually glaucous beneath, bases cordate, veins densely villose-tomentose below.
INFLORESCENCES: Corymbose, strongly branched, glabrous.
FRUITS: Samaras 2.5–4.5 cm long.
DISTRIBUTION: Cloud forests in Guatemala, growing on limestone.
REFERENCE: Murray (1980b).

SECTION: *Acer* SERIES: *Saccharodendron*
ACER SACCHARUM var. RUGELII (Pax) Rehder (1900)

BASIONYM: *A. rugelii* Pax (1886).
SYNONYMS
*A. barbatum* Michaux (1810), pro parte.
*A. subglaucum* var. *rugelii* (Pax) Bush (1931).
TYPES: Syntypes *F. Rugel,* Dendridge & Knoxville, Tennessee, USA; BM; NA; *C. A. Geyer 747,* Missouri, USA; K.
EPITHET: *Rugelii,* after F. Rugel (1806–1878), a German apothecary who became a collector/botanist in the United States.
HABIT: A tree of moderate size.
LEAVES: More papery than those of subspecies *saccharum,* wider than long, 3- to 5-lobed, slightly cordate, undersides glaucous and pubescent; margins entire; bases almost horizontal.
FLOWERS: Yellowish, on small umbels.
FRUITS: Not seen.
DISTRIBUTION: West of the Alleghenies in the United States.
REFERENCES: Bean (1970), Elwes & Henry (1908), Krüssmann (1976a), Murray (1970c), Rehder (1986 facs.).

It is interesting that this variety is hardly found in living collections and nurseries, as it replaces the typical sugar maple in the midwestern United States. It is notable for its more papery leaves, wider than long.

SECTION: *Acer* SERIES: *Saccharodendron*
ACER SACCHARUM var. SCHNECKII Rehder (1913)

SYNONYMS
*A. barbatum* var. *schneckii* (Rehder) Bush (1928).
*A. subglaucum* var. *schneckii* (Rehder) Bush (1931).
TYPE: *C. S. Sargent & Schneck,* Mount Carmel, Wabash Co., Illinois, USA; A.
EPITHET: *Schneckii,* after U.S. botanist J. Schneck (1843–1906).
ILLUSTRATION: Plate 78.
HABIT: A tree to 20 m tall.
LEAVES: 5-lobed; veins on the underside softly pubescent; petioles villose.
FRUITS: Not different from those of subspecies *saccharum.*
DISTRIBUTION: Indiana, Illinois, and Missouri in the United States.
REFERENCES: Krüssmann (1976a), Murray (1970c), Rehder (1986 facs.).

Another variety with a large distribution, *Acer saccharum* var. *schneckii* is rarely found in cultivation. It might be worthwhile to introduce it to the nursery trade. A huge tree with this name in the old arboretum of the Agricultural University in Wageningen, The Netherlands, may not be variety *schneckii.*

SECTION: *Acer* SERIES: *Saccharodendron*
ACER SACCHARUM var. SINUOSUM (Rehder) Sargent (1919)

BASIONYM: *A. sinuosum* Rehder (1913).
SYNONYMS
*A. barbatum* var. *sinuosum* (Rehder) Ashe (1922).
*A. grandidentatum* var. *sinuosum* (Rehder) Little (1944).
*A. nigrum* var. *sinuosum* (Sargent) Fosberg (1954).
TYPE: *S. H. Hastings,* along the Cibolo River, near Boerne, Texas, USA; A.
EPITHET: *Sinuosus,* undulated, with many waves—referring to the leaf margins.
HABIT: A tree of moderate size, much smaller than

subspecies *saccharum.*
LEAVES: 5-lobed, obtuse with subcordate base, 3–5 veins, basal veins to within 1 cm of margins; veins of 5-veined leaves merge into upper lateral veins.
FLOWERS: Not seen.
FRUITS: Not seen.
DISTRIBUTION: Edwards Plateau and western and central Texas in the United States.
REFERENCE: Murray (1970c).

---

## SECTION PENTAPHYLLA Hu & Cheng

TYPE SPECIES: ***Acer pentaphyllum*** Diels (1931).
HABIT: Mostly evergreen trees.
LEAVES: Undivided or 3-lobed, sometimes compound, 5–7 palmatifoliate leaflets, usually glaucous beneath; margins entire to lobulate-serrate.
BUD SCALES: 4- to 8-paired, gray-brown.
INFLORESCENCES: Corymbose, terminal and axillary, 25–75 flowers; bracts distinct.
FLOWERS: 5-merous, perianths yellow-white, petals longer than sepals, usually 8 stamens, discs extrastaminal.
FRUITS: Nutlets keeled convex, parthenocarpic tendency strong.
SEEDLINGS: Cotyledons small, narrowly oblong, acuminate.
SERIES: *Pentaphylla, Trifida.*
REFERENCE: De Jong (1976).

This section displays affinities to sections *Acer, Ginnala, Trifoliata,* and *Lithocarpa* (see also section *Acer*). It has two series, which vary mainly in their leaves, but the monotypic series *Pentaphylla* is not well known.

### SERIES PENTAPHYLLA

TYPE SPECIES: ***Acer pentaphyllum.***
LEAVES: Compound, 5–7 palmatifoliolate; margins serrate to entire.
SPECIES: *A. pentaphyllum* Diels (1931).
REFERENCE: De Jong (1976).

This series is monotypic; its one species has no close relatives and is very distinct. It is in cultivation, but is nevertheless quite rare.

SECTION: *Pentaphylla* SERIES: *Pentaphylla*

### ACER PENTAPHYLLUM Diels (1931)

TYPE: *Jos. Rock 17819,* Muli, Yalung River, Sichuan Province, China; BM; A; W.
EPITHET: *Pentaphyllus,* with five leaves (or, in this case, leaflets).
ILLUSTRATIONS: Plate 79; Fang (1981a), Harris (1983), Krüssmann (1970c), Vertrees (1978).
HABIT: A small tree to 10 m tall, in colder regions a rather small shrub; branches horizontal or almost so; young shoots thin, brownish.
LEAVES: Usually divided into five leaflets, sometimes seven, palmately arranged, united at the petioles, to 8 cm long and about 1 cm wide, oblong-lanceolate, shining green above, glaucous beneath; margins subentire to slightly serrate, often revolute; petioles red, 4–7 cm long.
INFLORESCENCES: Terminal, corymbose, rarely seen.
FLOWERS: Yellow, monoecious.
FRUITS: Samaras about 2 cm long, erect; nutlets convex, light green, almost always parthenocarpic.
BARK AND BUDS: Bark ash-gray, not fissured; buds sharply pointed and blackish.
HARDINESS: Zones VII–VIII.
AUTUMN COLOR: Yellow.
DISTRIBUTION: Yalung Valley, Sichuan Province, western China.
REFERENCES: Bean (1970), Fang (1981a), Krüssmann (1976a), Murray (1970c), Vertrees (1978, 1987).

This is one of the rarest of all cultivated maples. It has no apparent close relatives and is impossible to mistake for any other species. It was discovered by Joseph Rock in 1929, but introduced many years later. A brilliant specimen can be admired in the Strybing Arboretum in Golden Gate Park, San Francisco, California. All plants in cultivation have been derived from this tree and another now vanished.

Its very handsome leaves are divided into five palmately arranged "leaflets" with red petioles. The tree bears fruits abundantly, but they are parthenocarpic and the seeds do not germinate. The only way to propagate the species is by grafting on *A. pseudoplatanus* or *A. saccharinum.* This is difficult, and the results are often very poor. In the near future attempts will be made to propagate it from cuttings.

Unfortunately, *Acer pentaphyllum* is not very hardy and can only be planted outside in sheltered gardens in southwest England, Scotland, and Ireland, southern and far western North America, and regions with comparable climates.

A long-time nurseryman and excellent Japanese horticulturist, Toichi Demoto of Hayward, California, USA, has successfully raised some seedlings of this species. Many years ago, Demoto grafted *A. pentaphyllum* from the trees at Strybing Arboretum, San Francisco. Several have matured sufficiently to flower in his nursery. Some years ago he picked a limited amount of viable seed. Vertrees received three seedlings that are now about 2 m tall. Technically, this achievement provides a different germ plasm highly suitable for hybridizing back to the parent at Strybing.

SERIES TRIFIDA Pax
TYPE SPECIES: ***Acer buergerianum*** Miquel (1865).
LEAVES: Usually persistent, undivided or 3-lobate; margins entire to lobulate-serrate.
SPECIES AND INFRASPECIFIC TAXA
*A. buergerianum* Miquel (1865) ssp. *buergerianum.*
*A. buergerianum* ssp. *formosanum* (Hayata) Murray & Lauener (1967).
*A. buergerianum* ssp. *ningpoense* (Hance) Murray (1982).
*A. coriaceifolium* Léveillé (1912).
*A. discolor* Maximowicz (1880).
*A. fengii* Murray (1977).
*A. oblongum* Wallich ex DC. (1824).
*A. paxii* Franchet (1886).
*A. shihweii* Chun & Fang (1966).
*A. sycopseoides* Chun (1932).
*A. wangchii* Fang (1966) ssp. *tsinyunense* Fang (1966).
*A. wangchii* Fang (1966) ssp. *wangchii.*
*A. yuii* Fang (1934).
REFERENCE: De Jong (1976).

Series *Trifida* is a large series including about 10 species, all of which are Chinese and inhabit warm-temperate and subtropical areas. Many of them are not well known, and a few have not yet been introduced into cultivation. With few exceptions they are large trees that usually bear unlobed, partly persistent leaves. When more living and herbarium materials become available, several species may well be reduced to a lower rank as infraspecific taxa, or sunk into synonymy.

SECTION: *Pentaphylla* SERIES: *Trifida*
ACER BUERGERIANUM Miquel (1865) ssp. BUERGERIANUM
SYNONYMS
*A. trifidum* sensu Hooker & Arnott (1833), non Thunberg.
*A. palmatum* var. *subtrilobum* Koch (1864).
*A. trinerve* Siesmayer (1888).
*A. buergerianum* var. *trinerve* (Siesmayer) Rehder (1922).
*A. subtrilobum* (Koch) Koidzumi (1930).
*A. lingii* Fang (1966).
TYPE: Cultivated in Owari, Japan (Miquel 1867, 469).
COMMON NAMES: Trident maple, Dreizahn Ahorn, Drietand-esdoorn, Hana zakura, Kakunimo, Sankaku kaede, To kaede, Toyama kaede
EPITHET: *Buergerianum,* after J. Buerger (1804–1858), a plant hunter in Japan for the Dutch government.
ILLUSTRATIONS: Plate 80; Fang (1981a), Koidzumi (1911), Krüssmann (1970c), Liu (1962), Vertrees (1978, 1987).
HABIT: A tree to 25 m tall in native habitat but often smaller in cultivation, or a large shrub with a loose and open habit, depending on climate, soil, and exposure of site; stems several; branches glabrous.
LEAVES: 3-lobed, 2.5–6 cm across, undersides glaucous, bases cuneate to rounded, lobes pointing forward, triangular, pendulous (especially in vigorously growing plants); petioles 2.5–6 cm long.
FLOWERS: Whitish, numerous, small, appearing in May, on downy, umbellike corymbs.
FRUITS: Wings small, parallel or convergent; fruits about 2.5 cm long.
BARK AND BUDS: Bark gray-brown, not furcate; few bud scales.
HARDINESS: Zone VI.
AUTUMN COLOR: Olive-green often mixed with scarlet. Later all leaves turn an exquisite orange-yellow. In Korea, the colors of this are as dramatic as those of *A. saccharum* in Canada and the United States.
DISTRIBUTION: Very common in eastern China.
CHROMOSOME NUMBER: $2n = 26$.
SUBSPECIES
ssp. *buergerianum,* the typical subspecies.
ssp. *formosanum* (Hayata) Murray & Lauener (1967).
ssp. *ningpoense* (Hance) Murray (1982).
VARIETIES: None of the following varieties is in cultivation in Europe or the United States.
var. *horizontale* Metcalf (1942), low growing.
var. *kaiscianense* (Pampanini) Fang (1939), leaves deeply 3-lobed.
var. *yentangense* Fang & Fang f. (1966), leaves only 2.5 cm wide.
CULTIVARS: Many (see Chapter 9).
REFERENCES: Bean (1970), Dippel (1892), Fang (1981a), Krüssmann (1976a), Liu (1962), Murray

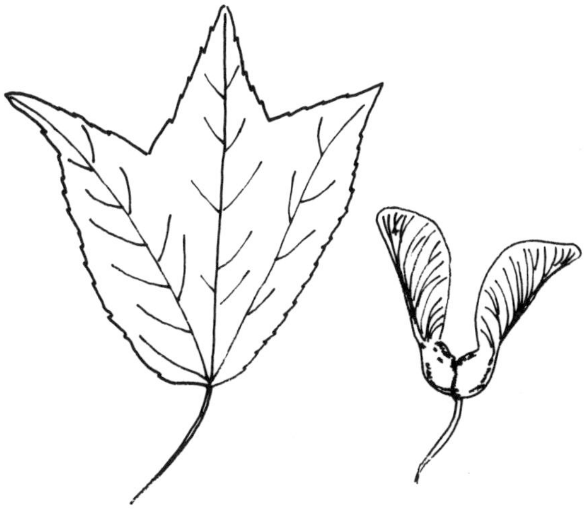

*Acer buergerianum* ssp. *buergerianum*

(1970c, 1981b), Pax (1902), Rehder (1986 facs.), Vertrees (1978, 1987).

*Acer buergerianum,* together with *A. palmatum,* is an important species of *Acer* in China, Taiwan, Korea, and Japan, where it is widely used as a garden and landscaping tree, and as a Penjing/bonsai subject. It is native to eastern China.

The French botanist Miquel described it in 1865. Many variations were assigned names by numerous botanists in the following years, including *Acer trifidum, A. trinerve,* and *A. ningpoense.* Most of these former species have been reduced to subspecific rank, and some are now considered to be synonymous with the species.

De Jong considers *Acer lingii* Fang to be very closely related to, if not identical with, *A. buergerianum.* This conclusion stems from analysis of the descriptions and drawings of both taxa. (Type *A. lingii, P. J. Tsoong 687,* Chow, Fujian Province, China; PE.) Murray also considers *A. lingii* as most probably synonymous with *A. buergerianum.* Unfortunately, there are no herbarium or living materials of *A. lingii* available for study in Europe. Generally, Fang maintains taxa at species rank, whereas the present volume treats many species as large variable taxa (e.g., *A. tataricum, A. pectinatum,* and *A. saccharum*).

*Acer buergerianum* forms small trees or large shrubs in Europe and North America. In Japan and Korea, however, it is used as a street tree on a massive scale. The leaves are shiny, bright green, mostly 3-lobed, and often pendulous on vigorously growing specimens. Its autumn colors can be very good, depending on the locality. The bark is olive-yellow to gray-brown. Fruit is borne in large quantities.

This species is rather difficult to get in the trade and deserves a better treatment, particularly by nursery professionals and by landscapers. It is easily propagated by seed, which must be harvested early in the season and sown immediately. Some trees are self-sterile. Propagation by cuttings from half-ripened wood is possible, but not very easy. It is an important species in horticulture and is suitable for less favorable climates.

Over the centuries, Japanese, Chinese, and Korean horticulturists have developed many cultivars, some of which have been introduced into Europe. Among the most interesting and desirable cultivars are 'Naruto' and 'Tancho'.

The plants growing in Taiwan are assigned a separate name: *Acer buergerianum* ssp. *formosanum.* This taxon is less hardy and cannot be planted in the temperate regions of Europe. It will succeed in the mildest parts of Great Britain and comparable regions.

SECTION: *Pentaphylla* SERIES: *Trifida*

ACER BUERGERIANUM ssp. FORMOSANUM (Hayata) Murray & Lauener (1967)

BASIONYM: *A. trifidum* var. *formosanum* Hayata (1911).

TYPE: *Père L. F. Faurie 65,* Kelung, Taiwan.

COMMON NAME: Taiwan trident maple.

EPITHET: *Formosanus,* from Formosa, now Taiwan.

ILLUSTRATION: Liu (1962).

HABIT: A tree of moderate size, rather heavily branched.

LEAVES: Faintly 3-lobed or fully unlobed, rather variable in shape, somewhat leathery; margins entire.

FLOWERS: Same as those of subspecies *buergerianum.*

FRUITS: Samaras divergent, not connivent as in subspecies *buergerianum.*

BARK AND BUDS: Bark smooth; buds very small, blackish.

HARDINESS: Zone VII.

DISTRIBUTION: Taiwan.

REFERENCES: Liu (1962), Murray (1970c).

This subspecies is distinguished by its leathery leaves. It is not in cultivation in Europe or North America, but is an important tree in Taiwan.

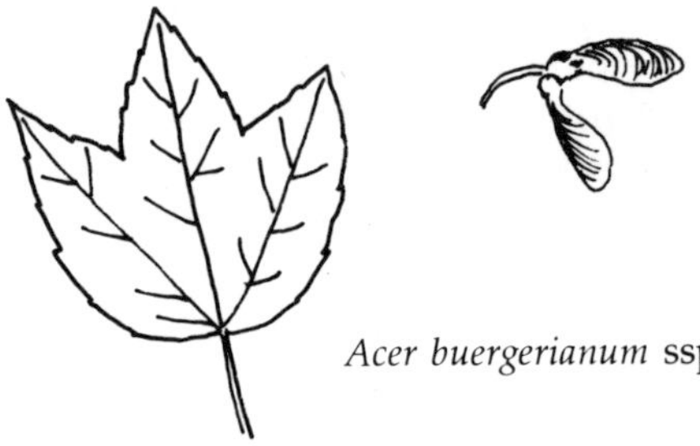

*Acer buergerianum* ssp. *formosanum*

SECTION: *Pentaphylla* SERIES: *Trifida*

ACER BUERGERIANUM ssp. NINGPOENSE (Hance) Murray (1982)

BASIONYM: *A. trifidum* var. *ningpoense* Hance (1873).

SYNONYMS

*A. buergerianum* var. *ningpoense* (Hance) Rehder (1905).

*A. ningpoense* (Hance) Fang (1966).

TYPE: Holotype *R. Swinhoe (Hance Herbarium #17963),* Ningpo, Zhejiang Province, China; BM.

EPITHET: *Ningpoensis,* from Ningpo, a district in Zhejiang Province, China.

ILLUSTRATION: Plate 81.

HABIT: A tree of moderate size, to 15 m tall in favorable situations.

LEAVES: Unlobed or with minor lobes, tri-nerved, leathery, 4–6 cm long and 4–5 cm wide, sometimes evergreen in warm, moist climates, bases

rounded; petioles 2–4 cm long, rather thin.
FLOWERS: Same as those of subspecies *buergerianum,* but with longer stamens.
FRUITS: Samaras divergent; nutlets hard and rounded.
BARK AND BUDS: Bark smooth, gray.
HARDINESS: Zones VI–VIII.
DISTRIBUTION: District of Ningpo in Zhejiang, and adjacent provinces, China.
CULTIVARS: 'Koshi miyasama' and 'Subintegrum'—both currently exist and match the description of the subspecies. Moreover, H. J. Oterdoom saw the subspecies in Guangzhou, China, and confirmed the affinity of both cultivars to it. Found in several botanic gardens in China, 'Subintegrum' also is used in quantity as a street tree in southeastern China (see Chapter 9 for further information).
REFERENCE: Murray (1981b).

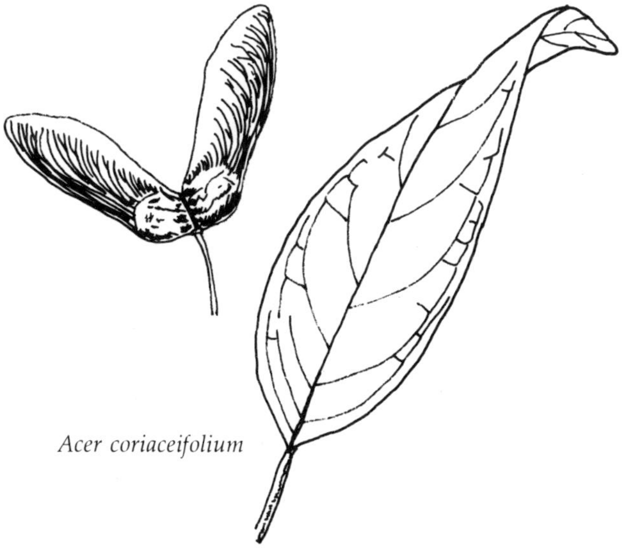
*Acer coriaceifolium*

SECTION: *Pentaphylla* SERIES: *Trifida*

## ACER CORIACEIFOLIUM Léveillé (1912)

SYNONYMS
*A. cinnamomifolium* Hayata (1913).
*A. oblongum* var. *macrocarpum* Hu (1931).
*A. pubipetiolatum* Hu & Cheng (1948), non Fang.
TYPE: *P. J. Cavalerie 3100,* Pin Fa, Yunnan Province, China; E.
EPITHET: *Coriaceifolius,* with leathery leaves.
ILLUSTRATIONS: Plate 82; Fang (1981a), Krüssmann (1970c).
HABIT: An evergreen tree about 10 m tall; stems downy and hairy.
LEAVES: Oblong, 7–12 cm long and 2.5–4 cm wide, gray or yellowish tomentum on the undersides, 3-veined; margins entire; petioles reddish.
INFLORESCENCES: Terminal, corymbose, tomentose.
FLOWERS: 5-merous.
FRUITS: 2.5–5 cm long, obtuse to erect, tomentose.
HARDINESS: Zones VI–VIII.
AUTUMN COLOR: Unknown.
DISTRIBUTION: Yunnan and Guangxi provinces, China, and Taiwan; in tropical regions.
VARIETY: var. *microcarpum* Fang & Chang (1979), with very small fruits.
REFERENCES: Fang (1981a), Krüssmann (1976a), Murray (1970c, 1977).

Léveillé described *Acer coriaceifolium* in 1912 from its habitat in the southern parts of Yunnan Province, China. This tender species is now in cultivation but can be grown only in very mild situations. Mature trees are not yet present. An evergreen tree with oblong and unlobed leaves and a rather slender apex, it is related to *A. oblongum.*

The Botanic Garden of Shanghai sent seeds to several botanic gardens in Europe in 1983 under the name *Acer cinnamomifolium,* which is recognized by Chinese specialists as a separate and distinct species. Young trees are now growing in some collections, but it is too early to say how they will fare.

Fang (1981a) cites *Acer pubipetiolatum* as close to *A. coriaceifolium.* He (Fang, 1966) also recognizes a variety of *A. pubipetiolatum,* var. *pingpienense* Fang & Hu.

SECTION: *Pentaphylla* SERIES: *Trifida*

## ACER DISCOLOR Maximowicz (1880)

TYPE: *Piasezki 1875,* Han River, Gansu Province, China; LE.
EPITHET: *Discolor,* differently colored—referring to the different colors of upper and lower leaf surfaces.
ILLUSTRATION: Maximowicz (1880).
HABIT: A tree with glabrous branches.
LEAVES: Persistent, oblong-ovate, 9–20 cm long and 6–12 cm wide, usually 3-lobed, rarely undivided, shining green above, glaucous beneath; margins remotely dentate; petioles about 3 cm long.
INFLORESCENCES: Corymbose, terminal.
FRUITS: Samaras obtuse.

*Acer discolor*
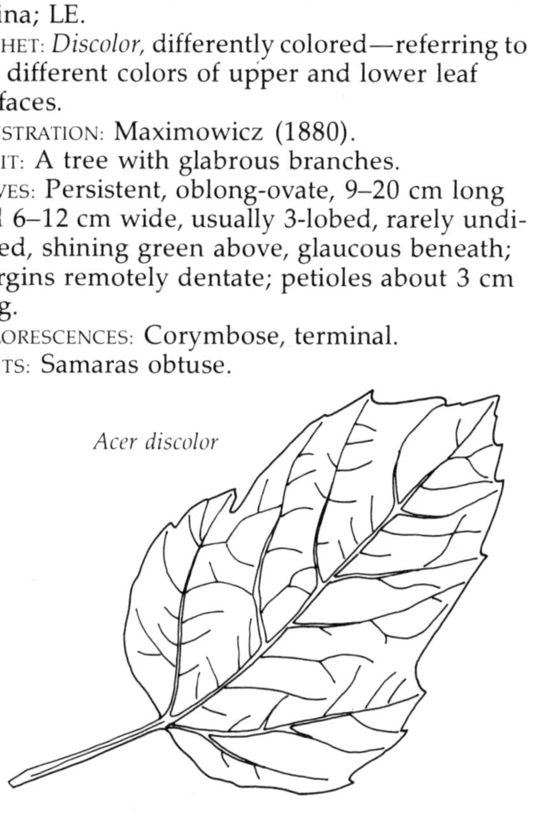

BARK AND BUDS: Bud scales few.
HARDINESS: Zones VII–VIII.
AUTUMN COLOR: Unknown.
DISTRIBUTION: Shaanxi Province, on the river Han, and the northern plains of Gansu and Sichuan provinces, China.
REFERENCES: Fang (1981a), Murray (1970c), Pax (1902), Schneider (1912).

No living material of this species is available. Probably it is very closely allied to *Acer oblongum.* According to Pax (1893), it is close to *A.* × *schwerinii,* but the latter taxon is a hybrid of cultivated origin.

SECTION: *Pentaphylla* SERIES: *Trifida*

ACER FENGII Murray (1977)

TYPES: *K. M. Feng 11383,* Wen-shan Hsien, Dou-i-shuh, Yunnan Province, China; holotype A; isotype PE.
COMMON NAME: Feng's maple.
EPITHET: *Fengii,* after the late Feng Kuo-Mei, a Chinese botanist and discoverer of this species.
HABIT: A tree to 10 m tall; branches sparsely covered with lenticels, dark brown.
LEAVES: Coriaceous, persistent, oblong-ovate, 12–14 cm long and 5–7 cm wide, distinctly reticulate-glabrous above and below, penniveined, reticulations as prominent as in *A. paxii,* gray-green above and brown with tan veins below (Murray); petioles 2.3 cm long.
INFLORESCENCES: Terminal, corymbose and pubescent; peduncles about 6 cm long.
FRUITS: Samaras large, 6 cm long; nutlets about 1 cm, thick, dark brown.
AUTUMN COLOR: Unknown.
DISTRIBUTION: Southwestern China.
REFERENCES: Fang (1981a), Murray (1977, 1982a).

This species is not in cultivation, and there is confusion about it in the literature. Murray (1977) describes it briefly as a tree about 10 m tall, with persistent leaves. It grows in southwestern China and therefore must be rather tender. Murray did not indicate its place within the infrageneric classification nor did he indicate any allied species, but in 1982 he placed it in series *Trinervia* Metcalf. In the present volume it is included in series *Trifida.*

Fang (1981a) lists *Acer fengii* as a synonym of *A. kwangnanense* Hu & Cheng (1948), unfortunately without a drawing, and reported it to be a tree of 15 m tall, with leaves 8–14 cm long and 3–5 cm wide. Murray (1970) writes that *A. kwangnanense* may be a synonym of *A. paxii,* so it is quite possible that *A. fengii* will be included in *A. paxii* once living material becomes available, and herbarium specimens, especially the types, are analyzed.

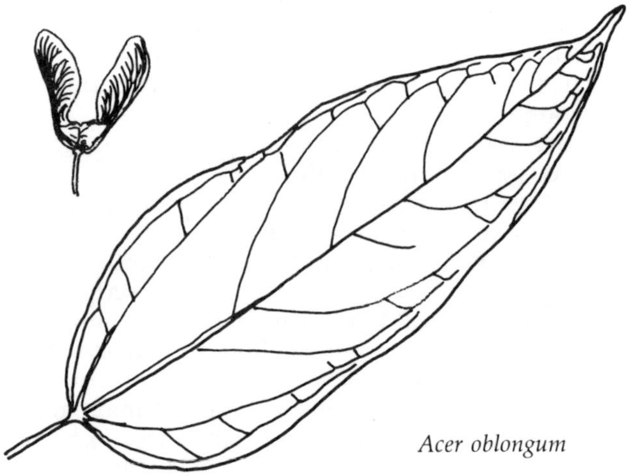

*Acer oblongum*

SECTION: *Pentaphylla* SERIES: *Trifida*

ACER OBLONGUM Wallich ex DC. (1824)

SYNONYMS
- *A. laurifolium* D. Don (1825).
- *A. nepalense* hort. ex Pax (1886).
- *A. nepalense* var. *oblongifolium* hort. ex Wesmael (1890).
- *A. lanceolatum* Molliard (1903).
- *A. albopurpurascens* Hayata (1911).
- *A. hypoleucum* Hayata (1913).
- *A. litseifolium* Hayata (1913).
- *A. discolor* Rehder (1914), non Maximowicz.
- *A. paxii* var. *integrifolium* Léveillé (1915) nomen nudum.
- *A. laikuanii* Ling (1951).

TYPE: *N. Wallich 1222,* Nepal; K; PH.
COMMON NAMES: Flying moth tree, Kusu noha kaede.
EPITHET: *Oblongus,* oblong (i.e., long); greatest width in the middle.
ILLUSTRATIONS: Plate 83; Fang (1981a), Harris (1983), Koidzumi (1911), Liu (1962), Murray (1975a).
HABIT: A tree to 15 m tall in native habitat but much smaller in cultivation; branches glabrous; often evergreen.
LEAVES: Leathery, hard, ovate-lanceolate, without lobes though young plants occasionally bear 3-lobed leaves, apices acuminate, 5–12 cm long and 4–6 cm wide, dark, glossy green above, glaucous beneath, tri-veined; margins almost entire or irregularly crenate. Occasionally some remotely lobed leaves can be observed, notably on the old tree in the Royal Botanic Gardens, Kew, Great Britain.
INFLORESCENCES: Terminal, corymbose, pubescent.
FLOWERS: 5-merous, yellow-green, appearing with the new leaves.
FRUITS: Samaras erect, 2.5 cm long; nutlets angular.
BARK AND BUDS: Bark red-brown to gray, peeling off

in irregular plates.
HARDINESS: Zones VI–VII.
AUTUMN COLOR: Unknown or absent.
DISTRIBUTION: Himalayas, Nepal, Kashmir, western China, on acid soils in mountainous regions, at 600–2000 m, in a diversity of climates.
CHROMOSOME NUMBER: $2n = 26$ (Mehra 1969).
VARIETIES
- var. *concolor* Pax (1889), leaves glaucous on both sides.
- var. *itoanum* (Hayata) Li (1952), with smaller leaves, margins slightly more wavy; growing only on the island of Okinawa.
- var. *laosianum* Lecompte (1912), samara wings concave on inner surfaces; type: Harmand, Bassin d'Attopeu, Laos; P.
- var. *latialatum* Pax (1902), samaras 3 cm long, falcate; described from a tree once growing in Firenze, Italy, reported from the wild; type: *A. Henry 6398,* Hubei Province, China; BM; see Bean (1970, 215).
- var. *membranaceum* Banerji (1963), leaves membranaceous; type: Calcutta Herbarium 331441, Mussoorie, India; CAL.
- var. *microcarpum* Hiern (1875) samaras small; type: *Griffith 935,* Mishmi Hills, E. Bengal, India; BM, G, W.

REFERENCES: Bean (1970), Fang (1981a), Koidzumi (1911), Krüssmann (1976a), Liu (1962), Murray (1970c), Pax (1902), Rehder (1986 facs.), Veitch (1904), Walker (1976).

This species has been known for a long time. The first description dates back to 1824, the same year the species was introduced to Great Britain from the Himalayas. Henry brought Chinese material home in 1900. Due to its vast range and morphological variability, there are many synonyms. One, *A. albopurpurascens,* is sometimes treated as a separate species, as are several others.

This tender species grows as a large tree in its native habitat, but in cultivation grows much smaller. In most northerly gardens it must be treated as a greenhouse plant. It has hard and leathery evergreen leaves, oblong and without lobes. Young vigorous plants occasionally bear 3-lobed leaves, and it is possible to find 3-lobed leaves on mature plants. This characteristic is an indication of the natural genetic variability of the species.

It is used as a street tree in many villages and cities in southeastern China, Hong Kong, and San Diego, California. A specimen of *Acer oblongum,* about 4–5 m tall, can be seen at Kew, where it has survived for many years in spite of its tenderness.

*Acer oblongum* is usually propagated by seed, although propagation by cuttings is possible and may be important for propagation of hardier specimens.

SECTION: *Pentaphylla* SERIES: *Trifida*

## ACER PAXII Franchet (1886)

SYNONYMS
- *A. oblongum* var. *biauritum* W. W. Smith (1915).
- *A. amoenum* Hu & Cheng (1948), non Carrière.
- *A. hilaense* Hu & Cheng (1948).
- *A. kwangnanense* Hu & Cheng (1948).
- *A. paihengii* Fang (1966).

TYPES: Syntypes *Delavay 1, 290, 894,* Yunnan Province, China; P.
EPITHET: *Paxii,* after *Acer* taxonomist F. Pax (1858–1942).
ILLUSTRATIONS: Fang (1981a), Krüssmann (1976a), Pax (1902).
HABIT: A small tree to 10 m tall in native habitat, not unlike *A. buergerianum* but with evergreen leaves; trunk gray and smooth.
LEAVES: Persistent, coriaceous, 3-lobed towards the apices though unlobed leaves also appear on the same tree, 5–7 cm long and 3–5 cm wide, lobes subobtuse to acute, shining dark green above, undersides glaucous; margins entire and wavy; petioles 2–4 cm long, thin.
INFLORESCENCES: Corymbose, terminal.
FLOWERS: Small, white, appearing with the new leaves.
FRUITS: Samaras 2 cm; nutlets globose.
HARDINESS: Zones VII–VIII.
AUTUMN COLOR: Little or absent.
DISTRIBUTION: Southwestern China, in mountain forests of Yunnan Province.
REFERENCES: Bean (1970), Fang (1981a), Krüssmann (1976a), Murray (1970c), Pax (1902).

*Acer paxii* is native to mountainous forests in Yunnan Province, China, where it was discovered by Father Delavay. A rare plant, it is closely related to *A. buergerianum.* It is somewhat tender, especially when young. It grows into a small tree with persistent leathery leaves, 3-lobed towards the apices. Entire leaves appear as well, even on the same shoot. Rehder considers this

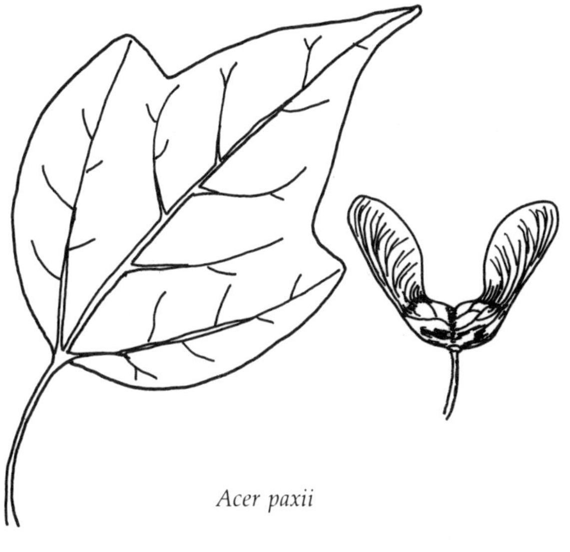

*Acer paxii*

species identical to *A. oblongum* var. *biauritum,* but Fang states that it is a distinct species. The rare *A. fengii* might be conspecific.

*Acer paxii* can only be confused with *A. buergerianum,* but is easily distinguished by its leathery evergreen leaves. It can be propagated by grafting on understock of *A. buergerianum,* if seed is not available.

A large specimen of *Acer paxii* grows in a greenhouse at Blagdon Hall (owned by Viscount Ridley, chairman of the International Dendrology Society) in Northumberland, Great Britain.

SECTION: *Pentaphylla* SERIES: *Trifida*

ACER SHIHWEII Chun & Fang (1966)

TYPE: *Teng, Shi Wei 901,* Ping-Ba Hsien, Kao Fung shan, Guizhou Province, China; IBSC.
EPITHET: *Shihweii,* after Chinese botanist Teng Shi Wei.
HABIT: A large tree to 30 m tall; branches purplish to gray-brown.
LEAVES: Unlobed to slightly lobed, 3-nerved at the base, olive-green above, glaucous beneath, oblong-elliptic, 15–20 cm long and 5–10 cm wide, apices caudate-acuminate; petioles 3–7 cm long.
INFLORESCENCES: Corymbose, terminal.
FRUITS: Samaras 3 cm long, wings diverging obtusely; nutlets purplish brown.
BARK AND BUDS: Buds imbricate.
HARDINESS: Zones VII–VIII.
DISTRIBUTION: Kao-Fung Shan, Guizhou Province, southern China.
REFERENCES: Fang (1981a), Murray (1970c).

This species is not known to be in cultivation in Europe or North America. It grows as a very large tree, unrivalled by any other species of this series. It is probably closely allied to *Acer oblongum.*

SECTION: *Pentaphylla* SERIES: *Trifida*

ACER SYCOPSEOIDES Chun (1932)

SYNONYM: *A. coriaceifolium* ssp. *obscurilobum* Murray (1977).
TYPES: Holotype *R. C. Ching 5336,* N. Luchan Hsien, Tia Lian Shan, Guangxi Province, China; A; isotypes K, LU, US.
EPITHET: *Sycopseoides,* like *Sycopsis,* a genus of the Hamamelidaceae.
HABIT: A small tree; branches yellow-brown, pilose.
LEAVES: Persistent, coriaceous, ovate, 5–8 cm long and 3–5 cm wide, 3-veined, yellow-green above, glaucous and pubescent beneath; margins revolute and briefly 1–2 lobulate; petioles 2.5 cm long; slightly lobed leaves can occur.
INFLORESCENCES: Corymbose, pubescent.
FLOWERS: Yellow.
FRUITS: Samaras and nutlets purple, 3 cm long, wings divergent.
HARDINESS: Zones IX–X (probably).

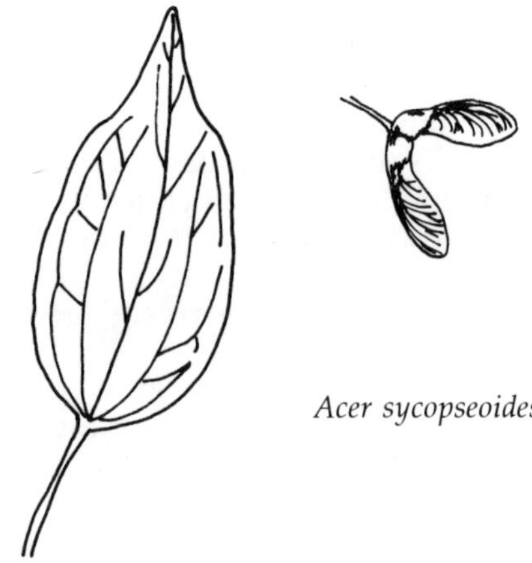

*Acer sycopseoides*

AUTUMN COLOR: Unknown.
DISTRIBUTION: Guangxi Province, southern China.
REFERENCES: Fang (1981a), Murray (1970c, 1977).

This Chinese species, related to *Acer buergerianum* and its allies, has coriaceous, persistent leaves and is reported to have purple fruits and nutlets. Apparently it is not cultivated in Europe or North America.

SECTION: *Pentaphylla* SERIES: *Trifida*

ACER WANGCHII Fang (1966)

TYPE: *C. Wang 43358,* Tien-o Hsien, Guangxi Province, China; IBSC.
EPITHET: *Wangchii,* after Chinese botanist C. Wang.
ILLUSTRATION: Fang (1981a).
HABIT: An evergreen tree to 15 m tall; branches purplish to black-brown.
LEAVES: Lanceolate, coriaceous, about 12 cm long and 3 cm wide, glaucous beneath, with 13–15 conspicuous veins, apices caudate, bases broadly cuneate; margins entire to undulate; petioles purplish, 3 cm long.
INFLORESCENCES: Corymbose, terminal, pedicels densely tomentose.
FLOWERS: Yellow.
FRUITS: Samaras erect, falcate; seeds purplish.
BARK AND BUDS: Bud scales imbricate.
HARDINESS: Probably tender.

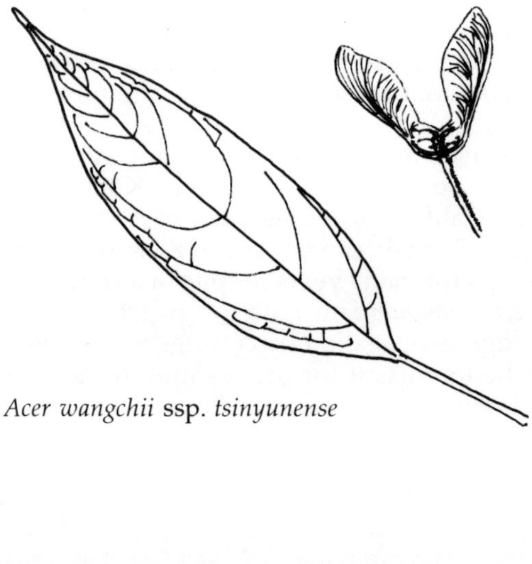

*Acer wangchii* ssp. *tsinyunense*

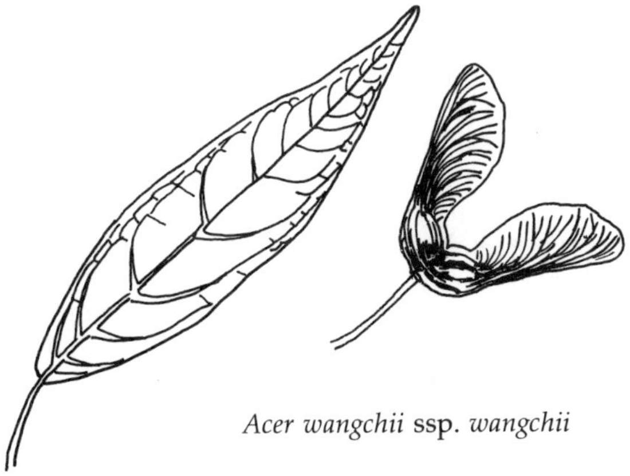

*Acer wangchii* ssp. *wangchii*

DISTRIBUTION: Guangxi Province, China.
SUBSPECIES
- ssp. *tsinyunense* Fang (1979), with narrower leaves.
- ssp. *wangchii,* the typical species.

REFERENCES: Fang (1981a), Murray (1970c).

*Acer wangchii,* a species not known to be in cultivation, is said to be an evergreen tree with lanceolate, coriaceous leaves. It belongs to the many species described by Fang and for which no living material is available, except perhaps in native habitats and the Botanical Institute of Chengdu, Sichuan, China. These species are probably closely allied to *A. oblongum.* Another close relative is *A. yuii.*

SECTION: *Pentaphylla* SERIES: *Trifida*

ACER YUII Fang (1934)

SYNONYM: *A. buergerianum* ssp. *yuii* (Fang) Murray (1982), *Kalmia* 12:17.
TYPE: Holotype *T. T. Yü* 2672, Nan-ping Hsien, Sichuan Province, China; PE.
EPITHET: *Yuii,* after Chinese botanist T. T. Yü.
ILLUSTRATION: Fang (1981a).
HABIT: A small tree to 7 m tall; branches reddish to gray-brown.
LEAVES: 3-lobed, 5–7 cm across, lobes ovate-triangular, acute, margins entire to sinuate, bases rounded, dark green above, yellow-green beneath; nerve axils yellow-pubescent; petioles purplish, 3–5 cm long.
INFLORESCENCES: Corymbose.
FRUITS: Samaras 2.5 cm long, obtuse.
BARK AND BUDS: Bud scales imbricate.
DISTRIBUTION: Sichuan Province, China, at 1800–2000 m.
VARIETY: var. *leptocarpum* Fang & Wu (1979), leaves smaller and thinner, 3.5 cm long and 2.3 cm wide; petioles shorter, only 1–1.5 cm long; fruiting corymbs larger, diverging obtusely or horizontally.
REFERENCES: Fang (1981a), Krüssmann (1976a), Murray (1970c, 1982b).

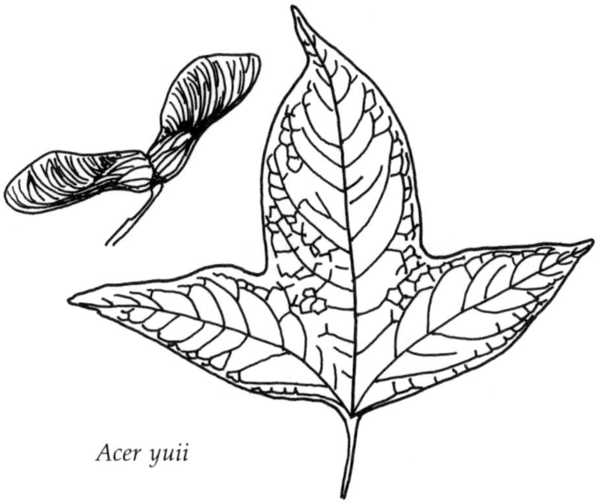

*Acer yuii*

*Acer yuii* var. *leptocarpum*

## SECTION TRIFOLIATA

TYPE SPECIES: ***Acer maximowiczianum*** Miquel (1867).
HABIT: Trees or shrubs, bark sometimes exfoliating.
LEAVES: Trifoliolate, chartaceous; margins subentire to coarsely serrate.
BUD SCALES: 11- to 15-paired, dark gray-brown.
INFLORESCENCES: Mostly 3-flowered, sometimes with up to 25 flowers, racemose or sometimes corymbose, terminal and axillary.
FLOWERS: 5- or 6-merous; perianths yellow-green; stamens 10–13; discs extrastaminal, sometimes amphistaminal.
FRUITS: Nutlets large, spherically convex; pericarps thick, lignified; parthenocarpic tendency strong to very strong.
SEEDLINGS: Cotyledons narrowly ovate.
SERIES: *Grisea, Mandshurica.*
REFERENCE: De Jong (1976).

Section *Trifoliata* is a rather specialized taxon with primitive trifoliolate leaves. The 6-merous perianth possibly indicates a close relationship with section *Lithocarpa.* The section has further affinities to section *Acer* and series *Penninervia* of section *Palmata.*

There is a problem with the type species of section *Trifoliata,* which has a great influence on the correct name for series *Mandschurica.* Fang (1966, 185) deliberately designated *Acer mandshuricum* Maximowicz as the lectotype species of section *Trifoliata,* but Murray (1970) designated *A. maximowiczianum* as the lectotype species. Fang's 1966 designation has priority. If this is adhered to, then series *Mandshurica* becomes series *Trifoliata.* However, Fang (1981) later designated *A. nikoense* (syn. *A. maximowiczianum*) as the lectotype species. This nomenclatural anomaly means there is not a typical series (*Trifoliata*), which is very confusing. This brings the present author back to Murray's (1970) designation (1970), and serves to point out that taxonomists are not always consistent.

SERIES GRISEA Pojárkova
TYPE SPECIES: ***Acer griseum*** (Franchet) Pax (1902).
SPECIES
*A. griseum* (Franchet) Pax (1902).
*A. maximowiczianum* Miquel (1867).
*A. triflorum* Komarov (1901).
REFERENCE: De Jong (1976).

Series *Grisea* includes three species from Japan and China. All are trees or large shrubs with trifoliolate, deciduous leaves. They usually bear heavy crops of woody fruits, and some species have peeling bark. The species are easily distinguishable from one another and are of considerable value for horticulture.

SECTION: *Trifoliata* SERIES: *Grisea*
ACER GRISEUM (Franchet) Pax (1902)
SYNONYMS
*A. nikoense* var. *griseum* Franchet (1894).
*Crula grisea* (Franchet) Nieuwland (1911).
*A. pedunculatum* Hao (1934).
TYPE: Holotype *Père Paul Farges 955,* Sichuan Province, China; P.
COMMON NAMES: Chinese paperbark maple, Papieresdoorn, Zimtahorn.
EPITHET: *Griseus,* gray.
ILLUSTRATIONS: Plates 84, 85; Bean (1970), Fang (1981a),de Jong (1976), Krüssmann (1976a), Pax (1902), Vertrees (1978, 1987).
HABIT: A tree to 15 m tall, of slender habit; young shoots downy and hairy, becoming glabrous when mature.
LEAVES: Trifoliolate; leaflets ovate, 3–8 cm long, incised-lobulate, lateral leaflets oblique, glaucous beneath, olive-green on the upper surfaces; young leaves on strong-growing shoots show pink variegation; petioles hairy.
INFLORESCENCES: Sparsely flowered, pendulous, short fasciculate.
FLOWERS: 5-merous, yellow, often monoecious.
FRUITS: Samaras up to 5 cm long, of very hard texture; nutlets rounded and hairy; seeds mostly parthenocarpic.
BARK AND BUDS: Bark orange-brown to rust-brown, very attractive exfoliation; buds small and dark.
HARDINESS: Zone V.
AUTUMN COLOR: Yellow to orange with scattered scarlet leaves. *Acer griseum* prefers a somewhat shady position; otherwise, the leaves develop black margins during summer and do not show the rich autumn color.
DISTRIBUTION: Widespread in China in the provinces of Shaanxi, Sichuan, Hubei, Henan, Guizhou, Jiangxi, Anhui, and Hunan, now endangered.
CHROMOSOME NUMBER: $2n = 26$ (Darlington 1955).
REFERENCES: Bean (1970), Fang (1981a), de Jong (1978), Krüssmann (1976a), Murray (1970c), Pax (1902), Rehder (1986 facs.), Veitch (1904), Vertrees (1978, 1987).

Franchet described this species in 1894 as a variety of *Acer nikoense* (syn. *A. maximowiczianum*), but Pax gave it specific rank in 1902. Wilson introduced it in 1901 for Veitch Nursery.

The paperbark maple is well known and may be the most splendid of all maples; it certainly is one of the five most outstanding *Acer* species. It forms a small- or medium-sized tree with a brilliant peeling bark, orange-brown in color with beautiful trifoliolate leaves, turning orange-yellow in autumn. It cannot be mistaken for any other maple; its allies lack the peeling bark.

*Acer griseum* must be propagated from seed. Unfortunately, it produces great quantities of parthenocarpic seed; often only one percent of the seed germinates. The fruits are extremely hard and difficult to open and must be stratified in sharp sand for at least a year. It is also possible to sow the seed in boxes. If the seed does not germinate after two seasons, dispose of it. Occasionally a good crop of viable seed occurs. Bulk's nursery in Boskoop, The Netherlands, once had about 50 percent germination, which happens once in a lifetime. Seed viability strongly depends upon the presence and percentage of male flowers during anthesis. Before picking the fruits, note the occurrence of single fruits showing scars of dropped male flowers; this indicates the presence of viable fruit.

This species also can be propagated from softwood cuttings; however, this method requires a great deal of skill. Due to the difficulties with propagation, this spectacular maple is not as readily available as it should be. According to T. R. Dudley, this species is also rather widely planted in China in Beijing, Chengdu, and other major cities, but not as common as *A. buergerianum.*

*Acer griseum* is remarkably uniform in its progeny—no botanical varieties or cultivars have developed.

SECTION: *Trifoliata* SERIES: *Grisea*

ACER MAXIMOWICZIANUM Miquel (1867)

SYNONYMS

*A. nikoense* Maximowicz (1867).
*Negundo nikoense* sensu Nicholson (1881).
*Crula nikoensis* sensu Nieuwland (1911).
*A. shensiense* Fang & Hu (1966).
*A. maximowiczianum* ssp. *megalocarpum* (Rehder) Murray (1969).

TYPE: Syntypes *K. J. Maximowicz,* Naga Gama, Higo and Senano provinces, Japan; L.

COMMON NAMES: Nikko maple, Kocho noki, Meguro, Megusyumi-kaede, Nikko Ahorn.

EPITHET: *Maximowiczianus,* after K. J. Maximowicz (1827–1891), a Russian botanist and plant hunter.

ILLUSTRATIONS: Plates 86, 87; Fang (1981a), Koidzumi (1911), Krüssmann (1976a), Kurata (1964–1976), Satake et al. (1989).

HABIT: A tree to 15 m tall but usually smaller; branches gray; young shoots somewhat purplish and villous; crown flat-topped.

LEAVES: Trifoliolate, leaflets oblong, 5–20 cm long and 2–5 cm wide, oblique, dark green above, glaucous beneath, heavily villous, later becoming more glabrous; margins subentire, ciliate; veins pilose; petioles 4–6 cm long.

INFLORESCENCES: Fasciculate, usually 3-flowered.

FLOWERS: Yellow-green, appearing before the leaves, dioecious, occasionally polygamodioecious.

FRUITS: Samaras 4–5 cm long, erect; nutlets pilose, very woody.

BARK AND BUDS: Bark smooth and gray, not peeling like its close relative *A. griseum;* buds accumulated at shoot apex.

HARDINESS: Zone IV.

AUTUMN COLOR: Reddish orange.

DISTRIBUTION: Japan, in mountain forests on Honshu (southern two-thirds) Kyushu, and Shikoku islands, at 500–1500 m; widely distributed in China in western Hubei and Anhui provinces (Rehder 1913).

CHROMOSOME NUMBER: $2n = 26$ (Darlington 1955).

REFERENCES: Elwes & Henry (1908), Fang (1981a), Koidzumi (1911), Krüssmann (1976a), Kurata (1964–1976), Murray (1969, 1970c), Pax (1902), Rehder (1986 facs,), Sargent (1913), Turrill (1962), Veitch (1904).

This commonly grown tree is usually labeled *Acer nikoense,* and is in fact much better known under that name. Miquel named it *A. maximowiczianum* in 1867, but Maximowicz described an *A. nikoense* a month earlier. In spite of the fact that *A. nikoense* is the older name it must be rejected in favor of *A. maximowiczianum,* as Miquel actually described a species of *Parthenocissus* which he incorrectly diagnosed and named *Negundo nikoense.* A question mark in his original description indicated that he was uncertain if the placement in *Negundo* was correct. On the other hand, Maximowicz described a maple but identified it incorrectly as being identical to Miquel's *Negundo,* which he renamed *A. nikoense.* Miquel realized that Maximowicz's material was not identical with his *Negundo,* correctly considered *A. nikoense* (as a synonym of his *Negundo nikoense*) and attached the name *A. maximowiczianum* to the material that had been incorrectly identified by Maximowicz. Maximowicz's effort to separate *A. nikoense* from the basionym and his neglect of Miquel's reassigned name *A. maximowiczianum* were incorrect. Delendick (1980), while earlier arguing for conserving *A. nikoense* as a valid species name, now agrees that the correct name for this species is indeed *A. maximowiczianum.* Acerologists at last fully concur on this confusing and exasperating matter.

In the practical eye of nursery professionals and gardeners it is a pity that the well-known name *Acer nikoense* must be rejected, as there is also an *A. maximowiczii* Pax (1884), now reduced to subspecific rank as *A. pectinatum* ssp. *maximowiczii.* This taxon, entirely different from *A. maximowiczianum,* is almost always incorrectly described in the literature and on garden labels as *A. maximowiczii.*

Regarding subspecies *megalocarpum* (Rehder) Murray (1969), Rehder (1911) described these plants as variety *megalocarpum,* while Murray considered this geographical expression from China as a subspecies; however, comparison with the Japanese plants does not support this. It is therefore listed in the synonymy.

*Acer maximowiczianum* differs from its close relatives *A. griseum* and *A. triflorum* in its distinct bark and larger leaves. Usually *A. maximowiczianum* grows much taller than either of the others.

This species can be propagated from seed, although the seed often has a poor germination rate. Often the seed is parthenocarpic, as in *Acer griseum.* Most trees produce only all male or all female flowers; when both sexes do occur on the same tree, they usually appear on different branches.

*Acer maximowiczianum* grows in many collections, but is not always easily found in the trade, evidenced by its being listed by only a few nurseries in Europe and North America.

SECTION: *Trifoliata* SERIES: *Grisea*

ACER TRIFLORUM Komarov (1901)

SYNONYMS

*A. triflorum* f. *subcoriaceum* Komarov (1904).
*Crula triflora* (Komarov) Nieuwland (1911).
*A. triflorum* var. *leiopodum* Handel-Mazzetti (1934).
*A. leiopodum* (Handel-Mazzetti) Fang & Chow (1966).
*A. triflorum* ssp. *leiopodum* (Handel-Mazzetti) Murray (1977).

TYPE: Syntype *V. L. Komarov 1051,* North Korea; BM; W; FI.

COMMON NAME: Dreiblütiger Ahorn.

EPITHET: *Triflorus,* having three flowers.

ILLUSTRATIONS: Plates 88, 89; Fang (1981a), Krüssmann (1976a).

HABIT: A tree to 10 m tall in native habitat but often much smaller in cultivation; branches yellow-brown to orange-yellow, not peeling or only slightly so.

LEAVES: Trifoliolate, 3–7 cm long, somewhat pubescent above and glaucous beneath; leaflets obovate-lanceolate; margins entire to coarsely dentate; veins pilose; petioles 3–5 cm long, somewhat pilose.

INFLORESCENCES: Fasciculate, 3-flowered, appearing on short branchlets.

FLOWERS: 5-merous, yellow.

FRUITS: Samaras 3–5 cm long, wings diverging at obtuse angles; nutlets hairy, quite often parthenocarpic.

BARK AND BUDS: Mature bark ash brown, vertically fissured, peeling in small floccose scales, never papery as on *A. griseum;* buds imbricate, sharply pointed.

HARDINESS: Zone V.

AUTUMN COLOR: Very striking golden yellow and orange.

DISTRIBUTION: Shaanxi Province, northern China; Manchuria; and Korea. Grows abundantly in the hills, but does not form forests.

REFERENCES: Bean (1970), Fang (1981a), Krüssmann (1976a), Murray (1970c, 1977), Rehder (1986 facs.).

*Acer triflorum* was introduced to Europe in 1923. It is native to northern China and North Korea, where it is found on a fairly large scale in local nurseries.

This species grows into a relatively small tree of about 10 m in height, rather densely branched, not unlike *Acer griseum,* but lacking the beautiful exfoliating bark of that species. Its trifoliate leaves are very attractive and turn a brilliant golden yellow with orange-red speckles in autumn. Its autumn color is the most beautiful of all trifoliate maples.

It is easily distinguished from its nearest allies, *Acer griseum* and *A. maximowiczianum,* by its ver-

*Acer triflorum*

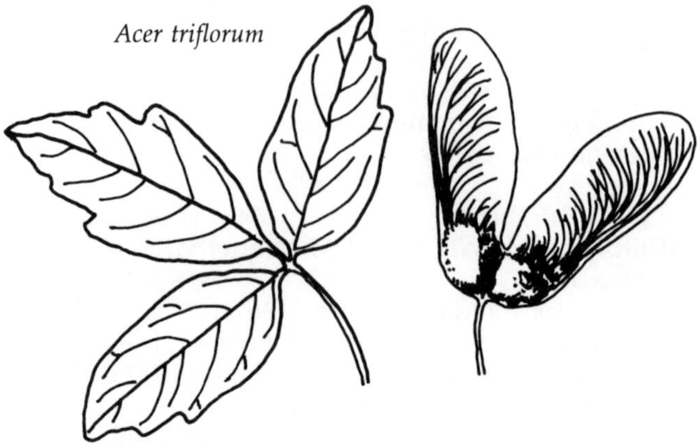

tically fissured and floccose bark. *Acer griseum* has the unique peeling bark, while *A. maximowiczianum* has dark, smooth bark and stiffer, less lobulate leaves.

The fruits of *Acer triflorum* are similar to those of *A. griseum* and *A. maximowiczianum.* Trees have only recently been studied during the flowering period, so the distribution of male and female flowers is uncertain.

As with so many of the species in series *Grisea,* most of its seeds are empty, due to the lack of male flowers. When no viable seed is available, it is possible to graft it on *Acer rubrum,* but the take percentage is low. Of course, grafting on one of its relatives is a better procedure, but none of the trifoliate maples are so proliferate that good understock is available. One known specimen, grafted on *A. rubrum,* is now about 25 years old. Growing in the Esveld Aceretum in Boskoop, The Netherlands, this shrub is about 4 m wide and about 2 m high. From time to time some understock suckers appear. Softwood cuttings also yield poor results.

Murray distinguishes *Acer triflorum* var. *leiopodum* Handel-Mazzetti as *A. triflorum* ssp. *leiopodum* (Handel-Mazzetti) Murray. The differences from *A. triflorum* are so insignificant that de Jong does not accept this but places it into synonymy. Possibly, when herbarium specimens and living material become available, this opinion may be changed, but this seems quite unlikely (see Fang 1966, 264–265); type: Fenzl, Tsingling, southern Shaanxi Province, China; W. The only minor difference that *A. leiopodum* demonstrates from *A. triflorum* is softer pubescent foliage; not a very constant character.

SERIES MANDSHURICA Pojárkova

TYPE SPECIES: ***Acer mandshuricum*** Maximowicz (1867).

SPECIES

*A. mandshuricum* Maximowicz (1867).
*A. sutchuenense* Franchet (1894).

REFERENCE: De Jong (1976).

This series includes two species from China:

one from the north and one from central and west (Sichuan and Hubei). Both are small trees or large shrubs with trifoliolate leaves, the central leaflet being much longer than any in series *Grisea.* Both species lack peeling bark, and their leaves and fruits are not hairy.

SECTION: *Trifoliata* SERIES: *Mandshurica*

ACER MANDSHURICUM Maximowicz (1867)

SYNONYMS

*Negundo mandshurica* (Maximowicz) Budischev (1867).

*Crula mandshurica* (Maximowicz) Nieuwland (1911).

*A. kansuense* Fang & Chang (1966).

*A. mandshuricum* ssp. *kansuense* (Fang & Chang) Fang (1979).

TYPE: *K. J. Maximowicz,* northeast Manchuria (China); LE.

EPITHET: *Mandshuricus,* from Manchuria.

ILLUSTRATIONS: Plate 90; Fang (1981a), Harris (1983), Krüssmann (1970c).

HABIT: A small tree or shrub to 5–6 m tall, sometimes considerably taller; branches glabrous.

LEAVES: Trifoliolate, leaflets oblong-lanceolate, 5–10 cm long and 2.5–3 cm wide, acuminate; central leaflets have the smallest petiolules in the section, obtuse-serrate, dark green above, bluish green beneath, glabrous except on the central veins, which are often pubescent; petioles 4–5 cm long.

INFLORESCENCES: 3-flowered.

FLOWERS: Greenish yellow, 5-merous, strictly male or female, appearing in May.

FRUITS: Samaras about 3 cm long, horizontally spreading, erect; nutlets ovoid.

BARK AND BUDS: Bark smooth, not peeling; buds small and dark.

HARDINESS: Zone IV.

AUTUMN COLOR: Red, often appearing early in autumn.

DISTRIBUTION: Southeastern Manchuria and Gansu Province, China, in mountain forests along the Upper Ussuri River; also in North and South Korea. Very abundant in the region of Vladivostok in eastern Siberia (Russia).

CHROMOSOME NUMBER: $2n = 26$ (Darlington 1955).

REFERENCES: Bean (1970), Fang (1981a), Krüssmann (1976a), Murray (1970c), Pax (1902), Pojárkova (1933b), Rehder (1986 facs.).

Maximowicz described this rare species in 1867. It bears some resemblance to *Acer griseum,* but careful study of its morphological characteristics reveals that it is only remotely related to that species or to the other species of section *Trifoliata.* It was placed in series *Mandschurica* by Pojárkova, together with *A. sutchuenense.* Future studies will shed more light on the characteristics of this heterogenous section.

*Acer mandshuricum* lacks the peeling bark of *A. griseum* and *A. triflorum* and has virtually glabrous leaves and fruits. Its central leaflet is much longer petiolulate than those of other species in this section.

It is very difficult to propagate, viable seed being scarce. Propagation by cuttings is possible, but good stock plants are rare. Grafting on *Acer griseum* is possible, but this method is too expensive for general cultivation; accordingly, it is almost never available in the trade.

SECTION: *Trifoliata* SERIES: *Mandshurica*

ACER SUTCHUENENSE Franchet (1894)

SYNONYMS

*Crula sutchuenensis* (Franchet) Nieuwland (1911).

*A. tienchuanense* Fang & Soong (1966).

*A. sutchuenense* ssp. *tienchuanense* (Fang & Soong) Fang (1979).

TYPE: *Père Paul Farges 955,* Tchen-keou-tin, Sichuan Province, China; P.

EPITHET: *Sutchuenensis,* from Sichuan Province, China.

ILLUSTRATION: Fang (1981a).

HABIT: A shrub or small tree 5–8 m tall; branches purplish to brown; young shoots glabrous.

LEAVES: Trifoliolate, 6–8 cm long, glaucous beneath; leaflets oblong-lanceolate, lateral leaflets oblique; margins remotely serrate; veins sparsely pilose, axils tufted beneath; petioles 6–10 cm long.

INFLORESCENCES: Corymbose, in globular heads.

FLOWERS: Yellowish flowers, monoecious; stamens exserted; occasionally male and female flowers appear on the same tree.

FRUITS: Samaras 3 cm long; nutlets ovoid, very similar to those of *A. mandshuricum;* seed often parthenocarpic.

BARK AND BUDS: Buds imbricate, ciliate.

HARDINESS: Zone V (?).

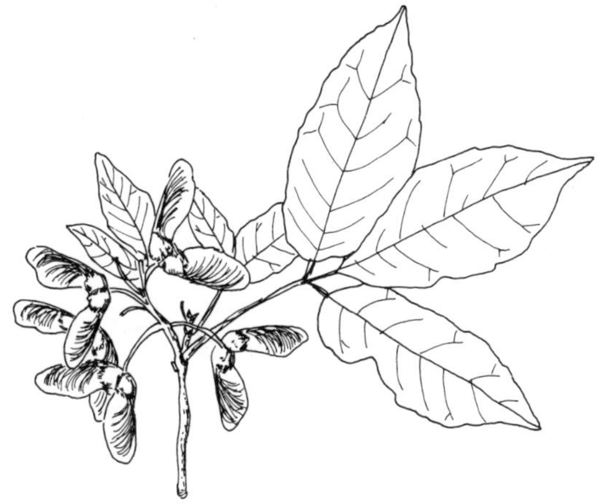

*Acer sutchuenense*

DISTRIBUTION: Hubei and Sichuan provinces, China.
REFERENCES: Bean (1970), Elwes & Henry (1908), Fang (1981a), Krüssmann (1976a), Murray (1970c), Pax (1902), Veitch (1904).

*Acer sutchuenense* is mentioned in many current books on dendrology, although apparently it may no longer be in cultivation. However, it was rediscovered in the wild in Hubei Province, China, in 1980 and introduced into cultivation to the U.S. National Arboretum, having been collected by the Sino-American Botanical Expedition of 1980 in the Shennongjia Forest District (T. R. Dudley, pers. com.).

It was first discovered by Farges at the end of the last century and described by Franchet in 1894. Veitch (1882) states that it was found by Dr. A. Henry. Rehder states that Wilson introduced material under this name, but the specimen proved to be *A. henryi.* A tree "discovered" by J. G. S. Harris at the Tashkent Botanic Garden, in Uzbekistan, is actually *A. henryi.* This might be one reason for its absence in our gardens.

It is a shrub or small tree with glabrous shoots and branches. According to the description, the leaves must be like those of *Acer triflorum,* and its general appearance like *A. henryi.* Its leaves are actually larger and thicker than those of *A. henryi.*

It differs from all other species of this section in having large, many-flowered, corymbose inflorescences. From the study of the few herbarium specimens available (*Farges 995bis, Wilson 639* and *1931*), the species was labeled dioecious, but one sheet of *Wilson 639* in the Kew Herbarium shows inflorescences with male flowers and some inflorescences, developed from leafless axillary buds, with female flowers in bud.

*Acer sutchuenense*

---

## SECTION LITHOCARPA Pax

TYPE SPECIES: ***Acer sterculiaceum*** Wallich (1864) (syn. *A. villosum* Wallich).
HABIT: Large deciduous trees with thick branches.
LEAVES: Large, 3- to 5-lobed, subentire, chartaceous; margins lobulate or entire, sometimes serrate.
BUD SCALES: 5- to 8- to 12-paired.
INFLORESCENCES: Racemose or corymbose, rachises elongated.
FLOWERS: Large, 5-merous; perianth green-yellow; stamens 8–12; discs amphistaminal.
FRUITS: Nutlets keeled convex, usually covered with stiff hairs; parthenocarpic tendency strong.
SEEDLINGS: Cotyledons narrowly oblong, obtuse.
SERIES: *Lithocarpa, Macrophylla.*
REFERENCE: De Jong (1976).

Section *Lithocarpa* contains the rather primitive series *Macrophylla* and the specialized series *Lithocarpa.* Both are related to sections *Acer* and *Trifoliata,* section *Pentaphylla* series *Trifida,* and possibly sections *Hyptiocarpa* and *Platanoidea.* Most species in this section are in cultivation, but few grow in gardens.

### SERIES LITHOCARPA

TYPE SPECIES: ***Acer sterculiaceum*** Wallich.
HABIT: Deciduous trees.
LEAVES: 3- to 5-lobed, subentire; margins remotely dentate to serrulate, sometimes entire; petioles sometimes lactiferous.
BUD SCALES: 8- to 12-paired, gray-brown.
INFLORESCENCES: Racemose, partly corymbose, axillary from leafless buds, 10–20 flowers.
FLOWERS: 5-merous, dioecious; perianth connate (primarily on male specimens of *A. diabolicum* and *A. sinopurpurascens*); stamens 8.
SPECIES
- *A. diabolicum* Blume ex Koch (1864).
- *A. leipoense* Fang & Soong (1966).
- *A. sinopurpurascens* Cheng (1931).
- *A. sterculiaceum* ssp. *franchetii* (Pax) Murray (1969).
- *A. sterculiaceum* Wallich (1830) ssp. *sterculiaceum.*
- *A. sterculiaceum* ssp. *thomsonii* (Miquel) Murray (1969).

REFERENCE: De Jong (1976).

Series *Lithocarpa* is a small and little-known group, including only four species, one with three subspecies. As in section *Macrantha,* the Japanese species is taxonomically well established; the Chinese taxa, however, are complex, with several subspecies, and the characteristics used to distinguish them are rather vague.

SECTION: *Lithocarpa* SERIES: *Lithocarpa*

ACER DIABOLICUM Blume ex Koch (1864)

SYNONYMS

*A. pulchrum* van Houtte (1867).

*A. diabolicum* f. *purpurascens* (Franchet & Savatier) Rehder (1914).

TYPE: *P. F. von Siebold,* Japan; L.

COMMON NAMES: Devil's maple, Hornfrucht-Ahorn, Kaji-kaede, Kiriha-kaede, Oni-momiji.

EPITHET: *Diabolicus,* diabolic—referring to the fruit configuration (i.e., two hornlike, persistent styles are attached to the inner sides of the nutlets between the wings, reminiscent of the horns of a devil) and the stinging hairs, equally on the samaras and nutlets.

ILLUSTRATIONS: Plate 91; Koidzumi (1911), Krüssmann (1976a), Kurata (1964, 1976).

HABIT: A large tree with gray-brown branches to 15 m high, often wider than high; trunk smooth; crown rather heavily branched, stiff.

LEAVES: 10–20 cm across, 5-lobed, cordate or almost truncate at the bases, rough textured, undersides lighter green, prone to break when bent sharply; lobes broadly ovate and rather stiff when mature, with a few large teeth; young leaves sometimes purple-red; young leaves and petioles covered with white silky hairs that usually disappear, remaining only on the petioles and scattered over the leaves.

INFLORESCENCES: Unisexual racemes occur in joints of the previous year's growth.

FLOWERS: Yellow, on short pendulous racemes, strictly unisexual; male flowers with connate perianths, a rare phenomenon in this genus; stamens conspicuously red.

FRUITS: Samaras almost parallel, about 4 cm long; nutlets round, thick, with many whitish bristles; two hornlike, persistent styles attached to the nutlets between the wings.

*Acer diabolicum*

BARK AND BUDS: Bark gray-brown, not fissured; buds dark and stiff.

HARDINESS: Zone IV.

AUTUMN COLOR: Yellow-brown, not conspicuous.

DISTRIBUTION: Mountain forests of Japan, in open, sunny situations. Not in Hokkaido and northern quarter of Honshu.

CHROMOSOME NUMBER: $2n = 26$ (Darlington 1955).

REFERENCES: Bean (1970), Dippel (1892), Elwes & Henry (1908), Koidzumi (1911), Kurata (1964–1976), Murray (1970c), Rehder (1986 facs.), Schneider (1912), Veitch (1904), Vertrees (1978, 1987).

This Japanese species was described as *Acer diabolicum* by Koch in 1864, and was also named *A. pulchrum* by van Houtte in 1867. Maries introduced it to Great Britain in 1881, but the number of trees in cultivation did not increase due to the difficulties of propagation.

The species is easily confused with such closely related species as *Acer sterculiaceum* ssp. *franchetii* or *A. sinopurpurascens.* The former does not have "horns," and the latter is a much smaller tree than *A. diabolicum.*

The tree grows slowly in cultivation, which makes it suitable for smaller gardens. Because of propagation difficulties, however, it will remain only a collector's item. As this species is dioecious, viable seed is rare. A group of about 15 trees is growing in the University of Washington Arboretum in Seattle, Washington. Grafting has been unsuccessful, as there is no suitable understock. The results on *A. pseudoplatanus* are very poor.

The forma *A. diabolicum* f. *purpurascens* (Franchet & Savatier) Rehder (1914) has the same habit of the species, but its young leaves and shoots are purplish red. Späth obtained this forma from Nakai about 1900; however, it is in fact indistinguishable from the species, being merely a male plant and deserving of no formal botanical rank. It is, therefore, sunk as a synonym of the species.

SECTION: *Lithocarpa* SERIES: *Lithocarpa*

ACER LEIPOENSE Fang & Soong (1966)

TYPE: *C. T. Kuan 8460,* Leipo Hsien, southwest Sichuan Province, China; PE.

EPITHET: *Leipoensis,* from Leipo, a district in Sichuan Province, China.

ILLUSTRATION: Fang (1981a).

HABIT: A medium-sized deciduous tree to 10–12 m tall, with sturdy, stout branches; stems glabrous.

LEAVES: 3- to 5-lobed, 15–20 cm across, bases subcordate, apices rounded, upper surfaces dark

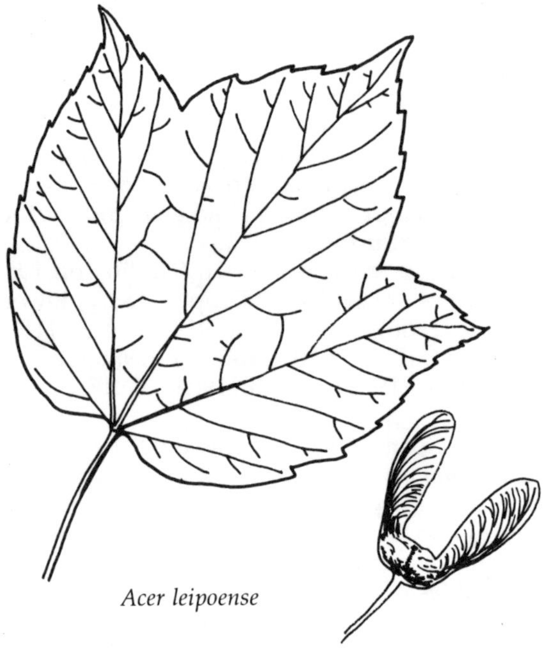

*Acer leipoense*

green, undersides almost white; margins slightly toothed.
FLOWERS: Greenish, in short, dioecious racemes.
FRUITS: Samaras up to 5 cm long; nutlets hairy or only slightly so.
HARDINESS: Zones V–VII.
DISTRIBUTION: Sichuan Province, central China, in mountainous regions, at 1800–2000 m.
SUBSPECIES
- ssp. *leipoense,* the typical subspecies with whitish hairs on leaf undersides; not in cultivation.
- ssp. *leucotrichum* (Fang 1979), with prominent white pubescence on undersides of leaves and on juvenile fruits.

REFERENCE: Fang (1981a).
This species is not in cultivation.

SECTION: *Lithocarpa* SERIES: *Lithocarpa*
## ACER SINOPURPURASCENS Cheng (1931)
SYNONYM: *A. diabolicum* ssp. *sinopurpurascens* (Cheng) Murray (1977).
TYPES: Lectotype *S. Chien 845,* western Tien-Mu Shan, Zhejiang Province, China; A; isotype K; syntypes *W. C. Chang 2424,* Zhejiang Province, China; A, K.
EPITHET: *Sinopurpurascens,* Chinese purplish.
ILLUSTRATIONS: Plates 92, 93.
HABIT: A small tree 6–9 m tall; branches gray to yellowish, green when young.
LEAVES: Deeply 5-lobed, sometimes 3-lobed, remotely dentate to subentire, basal lobes very small, other lobes obovate, wavy, dark green above, glaucous beneath, sparsely pilose; petioles 5–8 cm long, often pubescent, exuding latex when broken.
INFLORESCENCES: Corymbose-racemose; pedicels long.
FLOWERS: Dioecious; lateral sepals purplish red.
FRUITS: Samaras large, 3–6 cm long; nutlets pilose, reddish, usually parthenocarpic.
BARK AND BUDS: Bark gray-brown, smooth; bud scales many, ciliate.
HARDINESS: Zone V.
AUTUMN COLOR: Yellow.
DISTRIBUTION: District of Tien-mu shan, Zhejiang Province, China.
REFERENCES: Fang (1981a), Krüssmann (1976a), Murray (1970, 1977).

Cheng described this species in 1931; Murray placed it as a subspecies under *A. diabolicum* in 1977, a designation not accepted in the present volume.

This slow-growing tree is very rare; the only Dutch specimen is growing in the Trompenburg Arboretum, Rotterdam. Several young trees growing in Europe were grafted from the Trompenburg tree.

The closest relative is *Acer diabolicum,* with which *A. sinopurpurascens* might be confused, although the former is a much larger tree, has the "horn" on each nutlet, and also has smaller leaves. In addition, the flowers of *A. sinopurpurascens* are purplish red, while the female flowers of *A. diabolicum* are yellow, and the male flowers are red.

As it is virtually impossible to get viable seed of *Acer sinopurpurascens,* it should be grafted on *A. sterculiaceum.* This is the best rootstock, but seedlings of this species are rare, too, as are all the species of section *Lithocarpa.* Grafting *A. sinopurpurascens* to *A. pseudoplatanus* is another solution, but usually yields poor results—the plants tend to be weak, and strong growth does not occur until the scion has produced its own roots.

SECTION: *Lithocarpa* SERIES: *Lithocarpa*
## ACER STERCULIACEUM ssp. FRANCHETII (Pax) Murray (1969)
BASIONYM: *A. franchetii* Pax (1889).
SYNONYMS
- *A. schoenermarkiae* Pax (1902).
- *A. franchetii* var. *acuminatilobum* Fang & Chow (1966).
- *A. franchetii* f. *megalocarpum* Fang & Hu (1966).
- *A. franchetii* var. *schoenermarkiae* (Pax) Fang & Chow (1966).
- *A. huianum* Fang & Hsien (1966).
- *A. kungshanense* Fang & Chang (1966).
- *A. lungshengense* Fang & Hu (1966).
- *A. tsinglingense* Fang & Hsien (1966).

TYPE: *A. Henry 6416,* Hubei Province, China; BM; G, K; P; W; A.

EPITHET: *Franchetii,* after French botanist A. R. Franchet (1834–1900).
ILLUSTRATIONS: Plate 94; Fang (1981a), Krüssmann (1976a).
HABIT: A deciduous tree to 15 m high, with sturdy, stout branches; stems glabrous.
LEAVES: 5-lobed, sometimes remotely 3-lobed, 9–15 cm long and as wide, bases slightly cordate, lobes pointing forward, triangular, roughly toothed; petioles long, up to 15 cm; tufts of downy hairs in the leaf axils disappear when mature.
FLOWERS: Yellow-green, dioecious, on racemes borne in joints of the previous season's wood.
FRUITS: Samaras up to 6 cm long, wings spreading at a right angle; nutlets hairy, or only slightly so; seed viable only occasionally.
BARK AND BUDS: Bark gray-brown, smooth.
HARDINESS: Zone V.
AUTUMN COLOR: Yellow.
DISTRIBUTION: Hubei, Yunnan, Guangxi, and Guizhou provinces in China, and Xizang Province in Tibet, in mountainous regions at 1600–3000 m; also grows on Emei shan (Mt. Emei) in Sichuan Province, China.
REFERENCES: Bean (1970), Fang (1981a), Krüssmann (1976a), Murray (1970c), Rehder (1986 facs.), Schneider (1912).

*Acer sterculiaceum* ssp. *franchetii* grows in western, central, and southern China and was introduced by E. H. Wilson for Veitch Nursery in 1901. Pax described this taxon as a species in 1889, but Murray reduced it to a subspecies of *A. sterculiaceum.*

Subspecies *franchetii* can be mistaken for subspecies *sterculiaceum* and *Acer diabolicum,* its nearest allies, or *A. sinopurpurascens. Acer diabolicum,* however, has different seeds and a bluish or purplish hue to its young leaves. *Acer sterculiaceum* ssp. *franchetii* is allied to subspecies *sterculiaceum,* but subspecies *franchetii* has 5-lobed leaves that are more tomentose than the 3-lobed leaves of subspecies *sterculiaceum.* Furthermore, *A. sinopurpurascens* never has 3-lobed leaves. The differences are minor and can be difficult to recognize.

*Acer sterculiaceum* ssp. *franchetii* prefers acid soil and grows slowly. A huge specimen is growing in Westonbirt Arboretum, Great Britain.

All species of section *Lithocarpa* are difficult to propagate as they are almost always dioecious, and rarely is more than one tree planted. Male and female flowers are developed on the same tree only in the most favorable conditions. Grafting on *Acer pseudoplatanus* is difficult, and the resulting growth is usually very poor. Grafting on *A. sterculiaceum* is more successful, but seedlings of the species are only very rarely available.

Chinese botanists recognize several varieties and forms, but the present volume includes these taxa in subspecies *franchetii.* Several newly described taxa, such as *A. tsinglingense* Fang (1966), *A. lungshengense* Fang & Hu (1966), *A. kungshanense* Fang & Chang (1966), and *A. huianum* Fang & Hsien (1960), all indigenous to China, are now merged with *A. sterculiaceum* ssp. *franchetii.* Possibly these are closer to subspecies *sterculiaceum* than to subspecies *franchetii.* Living material and herbarium sheets are completely unavailable in the West, so further study is needed for definitive conclusions.

SECTION: *Lithocarpa* SERIES: *Lithocarpa*
ACER STERCULIACEUM Wallich (1830) ssp. STERCULIACEUM

SYNONYM: *A. villosum* Wallich (1830) non J. & K. Presl.
TYPE: *N. Wallich 1224,* Nepal (1821); BM; K.
EPITHET: *Sterculiaceus,* with leaves like *Sterculia,* a genus of tropical trees and shrubs; also Sterculius, the Roman god of manuring.
ILLUSTRATIONS: Plate 95; Fang (1981a), Krüssmann (1976a).
HABIT: A deciduous tree to 20 m tall, with a large crown; branches thick, stout, dark brown, villous when young.
LEAVES: 3- to 5-lobed, 14–20 cm across, thin textured, subcoriaceous, dull green above, pale green beneath; margins serrate, glabrous; bases cordate; juvenile leaves tomentose on both sides; petioles 5–15 cm long, green.
INFLORESCENCES: Lateral, pendulous, appearing with the leaves in April.
FLOWERS: Dioecious; male flowers in short racemes of about 5–8 flowers, female flowers in pendulous corymbs 10–15 cm long.
FRUITS: On long, pendulous racemes; samaras 3–6 cm long, wings almost horizontal or diverging at an angle of about 45°, depending on the particular tree; nutlets rounded, often parthenocarpic, very villous, staying green much longer than the wings, which turn brown in September.
BARK AND BUDS: Gray-black bark on mature trees slightly fissured; buds imbricate.

*Acer sterculiaceum* ssp. *sterculiaceum*

HARDINESS: Zone V.
AUTUMN COLOR: Yellow-brown.
DISTRIBUTION: Western Himalayas, in mountain forests in Sikkim, Kashmir, and Nepal, at 2300–3000 m.
CHROMOSOME NUMBER: $2n = 26$ (Mehra 1972).
SUBSPECIES
- ssp. *franchetii* (Pax) Murray (1969), leaves mostly 5-lobed.
- ssp. *sterculiaceum,* the typical subspecies.
- ssp. *thomsonii* (Miquel) Murray (1969), leaves remotely serrate, lobes very short.

REFERENCES: Bean (1970), Dippel (1892), Elwes & Henry (1908), Fang (1981a), Koch (1869), Krüssmann (1976a), Murray (1970c), Rehder (1986 facs.), Schneider (1912).

Sir Joseph Hooker introduced this very rare species from Sikkim, and it has been in cultivation since 1835 in Great Britain. Van Volxem introduced it to Germany as early as 1850; however, there are no records of mature trees in that country. Lancaster observed this species in Nepal in 1971, where it grew together with *Magnolia campbellii, Acer campbellii,* and *Sorbus hedlundii.*

*Acer sterculiaceum* ssp. *sterculiaceum* is, unfortunately, better known by its synonym, *A. villosum.* It is hard to distinguish from its nearest allies, the subspecies *franchetii* and *thomsonii.* The leaves of subspecies *franchetii* are 5-lobed, smaller and less villous when young, while the leaves of subspecies *thomsonii* are considerably larger than those of subspecies *sterculiaceum,* which are large, 14–20 cm across, 3- to 5-lobed, and of a rather thin, papery texture. Young leaves are densely tomentose on both sides.

The fruits of *Acer sterculiaceum* ssp. *sterculiaceum* are borne in long pendulous racemes, and they are very often not viable, due to unisexual flowering, unless a male tree is in the direct neighborhood as is the case at the Esveld Aceretum, Boskoop, The Netherlands.

It is possible to graft *Acer sterculiaceum* ssp. *sterculiaceum* on seedlings of *A. pseudoplatanus* but, as with *A. sinopurpurascens,* the results are poor, and such grafts start good growth only when they can form their own roots.

SECTION: *Lithocarpa* SERIES: *Lithocarpa*

## ACER STERCULIACEUM ssp. THOMSONII (Miquel) Murray (1969)

BASIONYM: *A. thomsonii* Miquel (1867).
SYNONYMS
- *A. platanifolium* Griffith (1848), non Stokes.
- *A. villosum* var. *thomsonii* (Miquel) Hiern (1875).

TYPE: *Th. Thomson,* Sikkim; K.
EPITHET: *Thomsonii,* after botanist Thomas Thomson (1817–1878), curator of the Botanic Garden of Calcutta, India, and companion and co-collector with Hooker f. in the Himalayas.
ILLUSTRATION: Plate 96.
HABIT: A large tree to about 15 m high, crown wider than high; branches stout, short, thick.
LEAVES: Very large, 15–30 cm across, 3- to 5-lobed, lobes short; margins remotely serrate.
INFLORESCENCES: Lateral, pendulous, appearing with the leaves.
FRUITS: Samaras 3–5 cm long, wings diverging acutely.
HARDINESS: Zone V.
DISTRIBUTION: Himalayas, Sikkim, Assam, Bhutan.
REFERENCES: Fang (1981a), Krüssmann (1976a), Murray (1970c).

*Acer sterculiaceum* ssp. *thomsonii* is one of the rarest maples in cultivation. It is distinguished from its allies by its very large leaves: the leaves of subspecies *sterculiaceum* are of the same shape but never reach the size of those of subspecies *thomsonii.* A small tree is growing in the Royal Botanic Gardens, Kew, Great Britain.

## SERIES MACROPHYLLA Pojárkova ex Momotani (1962)

TYPE SPECIES: ***Acer macrophyllum*** Pursh (1814).
HABIT: Trees.
LEAVES: Deeply 5-lobed; margins lobulate to entire; petioles lactiferous.
BUD SCALES: 5- to 8-paired, green-red.
INFLORESCENCES: Large, corymbose-paniculate, 30–80 flowered, terminal and axillary.
FLOWERS: 5- to 6-merous, monoecious.
SPECIES: *A. macrophyllum* Pursh.
REFERENCE: De Jong (1976).

The only member of the monotypic series *Macrophylla, Acer macrophyllum* grows in western North America. It is well-known in cultivation and has the largest leaves of all maples.

SECTION: *Lithocarpa* SERIES: *Macrophylla*

## ACER MACROPHYLLUM Pursh (1814)

SYNONYMS
- *A. murrayanum* hort. (1873).
- *A. speciosum* hort. Kew (1894).
- *A. auritum* Greene (1912).
- *A. coptophyllum* Greene (1912).
- *A. dartyophyllum* Greene (1912).
- *A. flabellatum* sensu Greene (1912), non Rehder.
- *A. hemionites* Greene (1912).
- *A. leptodactylum* Greene (1912).
- *A. platypterum* Greene (1912).
- *A. politum* Greene (1912).
- *A. stellatum* Greene (1912).

TYPE: *Lewis and Clark Expedition;* PH.
COMMON NAMES: Bigleaf maple, Oregon maple.
EPITHET: *Macrophyllus,* with big leaves.
ILLUSTRATIONS: De Jong (1976), Krüssmann (1976a).

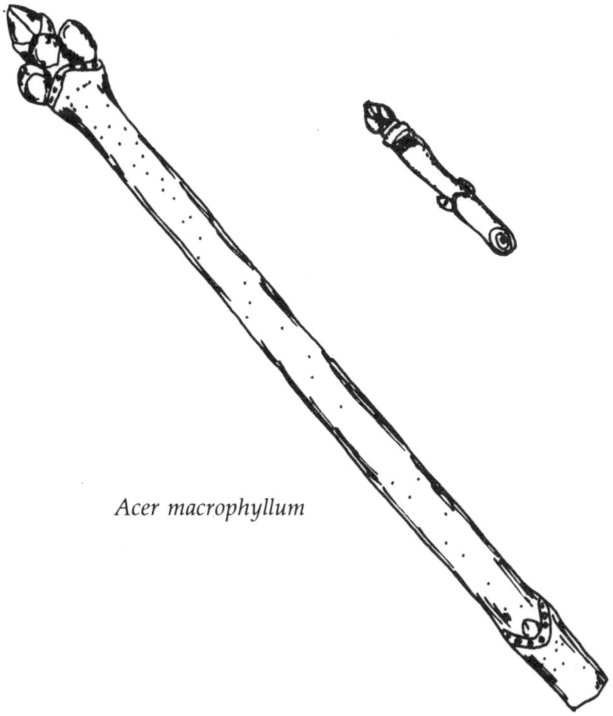

*Acer macrophyllum*

HABIT: A tree to 25 m tall or more, seldom more than 10–12 m tall in Europe; sometimes a treelike, many-stemmed shrub; young branches green and glabrous; older trees form wide, compact, rounded crowns.
LEAVES: Very large, 5-lobed, 20–35 cm wide, lobes obtuse with some large obtuse teeth, bases cordate, shining green above, pale green beneath, often hairy when young; petioles 10–20 cm long, reddish, with milky sap.
FLOWERS: Yellow, on long pendulous racemes or panicles, developing with the young leaves when fully grown, fragrant, appearing in May.
FRUITS: On rather long, pendulous panicles or racemes; samaras horizontal, up to 7 cm long; nutlets have prickly stinging hairs, often in whorls of three (tricarpellate).
BARK AND BUDS: Bark of old trees thick, rough, deeply fissured.
HARDINESS: Zones V–VII.
AUTUMN COLOR: Yellow to orange.
DISTRIBUTION: Alaska to southern California in the United States, as large trees mixed in the conifer forests of the Pacific coast.
CHROMOSOME NUMBER: $2n = 26$.
FORM: f. *rubrifolium* Murray (1981), leaves red when young.
CULTIVARS: Only three (see Chapter 9).
REFERENCES: Bean (1970), Dippel (1892), de Jong (1976), Koch (1869), Krüssmann (1976a), Murray (1970c), Pax (1902), Rehder (1986 facs.), Schneider (1912).

This species, which bears the largest leaves of the entire genus, can grow into a stately tree and is hardly confused with any other maple. It is one of the largest trees growing in the late J. D. Vertrees's Maplewood Nursery, Roseburg, Oregon.

*Acer macrophyllum* has been known for almost 200 years. Pursh described it in 1814, and subsequently several synonyms were published, due to the enormous morphological variation throughout its range—stretching from southern Alaska to southern California. David Douglas introduced it in 1826 to Great Britain, and quite a few beautiful specimens can be found in European gardens, though they never surpass the native trees in size.

The species usually grows as individual understory trees in conifer forests, only occasionally forming forests on its own. Only *Populus trichocarpa* forms larger trees in these regions. Young trees do not always ripen their wood early enough in the season, and dieback of long fleshy shoots occurs occasionally. The tree is otherwise perfectly hardy.

The tree usually bears a heavy crop of seed with stinging hairs that are unpleasant to the touch. It differs in this respect from its allies in this series. This species has a lactiferous sap, but nevertheless does not belong to section *Platanoides.* Its timber is useful for furniture and building purposes.

Propagation is easy from seed. The seed germinates freely, and a one-year-old seedling may grow 1 m high or more.

## SECTION PLATANOIDEA Pax (1885)

TYPE SPECIES: ***Acer platanoides*** L. (1753).
HABIT: Deciduous trees or shrubs.
LEAVES: 3- to 5- to 7-lobed, rarely undivided, chartaceous or somewhat coriaceous; margins entire or remotely dentate to serrate; petioles laticiferous.
BUD SCALES: 5- to 8- or 6- to 10-paired.
INFLORESCENCES: Corymbose, terminal and axillary, mostly from mixed buds.
FLOWERS: 5-merous; stamens 5–8; discs amphistaminal.
FRUITS: Nutlets flat; parthenocarpic tendency moderate.
SEEDLINGS: Cotyledons large, narrowly oblong.
SPECIES AND INFRASPECIFIC TAXA
*A. campestre* L. (1753).
*A. cappadocicum* Gleditsch (1785) ssp. *cappadocicum.*
*A. cappadocicum* ssp. *divergens* (Pax) Murray (1978).

*A. cappadocicum* ssp. *lobelii* (Tenore) Murray (1982).
*A. cappadocicum* ssp. *sinicum* (Rehder) Handel-Mazzetti (1933).
*A. cappadocicum* ssp. *sinicum* var. *tricaudatum* (Veitch ex Rehder) Rehder (1914).
*A. longipes* ssp. *amplum* (Rehder) de Jong, comb. & stat. nov.
*A. longipes* ssp. *catalpifolium* (Rehder) de Jong, comb. & stat. nov.
*A. longipes* ssp. *firmanioides* (Cheng ex Fang) de Jong, comb. & stat nov.
*A. longipes* Franchet ex Rehder (1905) ssp. *longipes.*
*A. miyabei* ssp. *mioataiense* (Tsoong) Murray (1969).
*A. miyabei* Maximowicz (1888) ssp. *miyabei.*
*A. mono* Maximowicz (1875) ssp. *mono.*
*A. mono* ssp. *okamotoanum* (Nakai) de Jong, comb. & stat. nov.
*A. mono* var. *mayrii* (Schwerin) Nakai (1932).
*A. mono* ssp. *mono* f. *ambiguum* (Dippel) Rehder (1939).
*A. nayongense* Fang (1979).
*A. platanoides* L. (1753) ssp. *platanoides.*
*A. platanoides* ssp. *turkestanicum* (Pax) de Jong, comb. & stat. nov.
*A. tenellum* Pax (1889).
*A. tibetense* Fang (1939).
*A. truncatum* Bunge (1833).

REFERENCE: De Jong (1976).

The affinities of section *Platanoidea* and series *Macrophylla* of section *Lithocarpa* are based only on morphological similarities, and need further study. The laticiferous petioles and the amphistaminal discs of section *Platanoidea* and series *Macrophylla* of section *Lithocarpa* probably only indicate a remote relationship. This rather primitive section, *Platanoidea,* does not show close affinities to any other sections.

This section includes large to medium-sized trees with deciduous 3- to 5- to 7-lobed leaves, all having a milky sap in their petioles. This latter characteristic distinguishes section *Platanoidea* from almost all other maples. There are 10 species placed in this section, with almost all their subspecies in cultivation. Some subspecies, varieties, and forms, however, are very rare or not yet in cultivation.

Most species are Chinese, with some representatives in Europe, western Asia, and Japan. There are no North American species.

SECTION: *Platanoidea*

ACER CAMPESTRE L. (1753)

SYNONYMS

*A. vulgare* Borkhausen (1793).
*A. campestre* var. *hebecarpum* DC. (1824)
*A. heterolobum* Opiz (1825).
*A. tomentosum* var. *serotinum* Kitaibel (1864).
*A. campestre* ssp. *leiocarpon* (Wallroth) Pax (1890).
*A. campestre* ssp. *marsicum* (Gussone) Hayek (1921).

TYPE: *LINN no. 1225.14;* LINN.

COMMON NAMES: Common maple, Field maple, Hedge maple, Erable champètre, Feldahorn, Massholder, Spaanse aak, Veldesdoorn.

EPITHET: *Campestris,* from the fields.

ILLUSTRATIONS: Plates 97, 98; de Jong (1976), Krüssmann (1976a).

HABIT: A deciduous tree with a round crown, or a very large shrub with several stems, usually 7–10 (–12) m tall but sometimes to 20 m tall; trees have been found that are 20 m wide and only 5–7 m tall.

LEAVES: 3- to 5-lobed, palmate, up to 12 cm across but usually smaller, wider than long, downy on lower surfaces and somewhat glaucous; margins not toothed, more or less wavy; petioles the same length as blades, exuding a milky sap when broken.

FLOWERS: Yellow-green, on few-flowered, terminal corymbs.

FRUITS: Samaras nearly horizontal, 2.5–5 cm long, wings pubescent; nutlets pilose, very flat.

BARK AND BUDS: Bark brown-gray, corky, becoming scaly and fissured, almost never pubescent.

HARDINESS: Zone IV.

AUTUMN COLOR: Golden yellow or bronze-yellow, rarely brown.

DISTRIBUTION: Widespread in Europe and western Asia; also grows in limited areas of North Africa. Very commonly growing as a shrub, thriving in thickets, sometimes as a tree in the hills or plains, often as undergrowth in forests.

CHROMOSOME NUMBER: $2n = 26$ (Darlington 1955).

SUBSPECIES: Due to the very extensive natural distribution and the enormous variability of this species, it is extremely difficult to establish distinct subspecies. The present volume does not recognize subspecies, although the following have been described in the literature:

ssp. *leiocarpon* (Wallroth) Pax (1890), leaves larger than those of the species, slightly pubescent, margins entire; young branches not corky or only slightly so; occurs in Austria as a tree, but in more northerly locations (i.e., eastern Germany) as a shrub; synonym is var. *austriacum* DC. (1824); a middle-European taxon formerly divided into several varieties and formae (Koch 1869, 534), including subvariety *molle* (Opiz) Koch, a plant with very pubescent leaves and subvariety *sylvestre* (Wenderoth) Koch, with more leathery leaves.

ssp. *marsicum* (Gussone) Hayek (1921), leaves 3- to 5-lobed, lobes subentire, not lobulate;

fruits tomentose to fully glabrous, variable in size, sometimes red; epithet comes from the Marsi, a people residing in the Latium region of middle Italy between the rivers Tiber and Arno; the red-fruited form was formerly called variety *eriocarpum.*

VARIETY: *acuminatilobum* Papp (1954) is, according to Murray, a *nomen in exsiccato* at specific rank and synonymous with *Acer campestre* or possibly belonging to subspecies *leiocarpon.* A publication by Dr. Györffii of Budapest gives further details (Papp 1954). Leaves of this variety were found as fossils in the Matra Mountains of Hungary in the 1940s. Josef Papp, a Hungarian botanist, found a living specimen about 15 m tall. Its leaves seem to be a little more leathery than those of the species. Scions were taken and grafted onto *A. campestre* in the Botanic Garden of Vacratot, Hungary; some still survive. Györffii sent some scions to The Netherlands, but they arrived in poor condition. Nonetheless, they were grafted in March 1985, and the resulting plants do not differ from the species.

CULTIVARS: Many (see Chapter 9).

REFERENCES: Bean (1970), Dippel (1892), Elwes & Henry (1908), Hillier (1965), de Jong (1976), Koch (1869), Krüssmann (1976a), Linnaeus (1753), Murray (1970c), Pax (1902), Rehder (1986 facs.).

*Acer campestre* is one of the few European species, widespread and indigenous to almost all European countries, except Scandinavia and Finland. It is rare in the southern parts of Spain and Portugal, but occurs in North Africa and western Asia.

It grows infrequently in mountainous areas, being usually found on plains, lower hills, steppes, and along riverbanks. Very often it occurs as undergrowth in broadleaved forests.

Linnaeus described *Acer campestre* in 1753. Because this species has a very large distribution, there are numerous geographical forms once recognized as separate species, subspecies, varieties, or forms. Many of these expressions have been reduced to synonymy or are now recognized as cultivars. Quite a few aberrant forms grow in the Balkan countries, but are not endemic to specific areas. In northern Europe, the species is much more uniform.

*Acer campestre* normally grows into large shrubs or flat-topped trees up to 10–12 m tall. The bark is often corky and fissured. The leaves are 3- to 5-lobed and shining green, of various shapes and more or less palmately lobed.

It can hardly be mistaken for any other species except possibly the Japanese *Acer miyabei,* which has larger but similar leaves. *Acer hyrcanum* also has a more or less similar leaf shape, but lacks the milky sap.

A shrubby *Acer campestre* with somewhat hairy leaves is sometimes recognized as subspecies *leiocarpon* (var. *austriacum* [Trautvetter] DC.). Murray accepts this taxon as a subspecies, but it seems better to include it as a synonym of the species. Corky plants have been called *Acer suberosum* or *A. campestre* f. *suberosum,* but these names and subdivisions have been sunk in synonym. As this group is rather variable, only a few members can be regarded as cultivars and propagated vegetatively. The most important of these is 'Austriacum", a tree with softly pubescent leaves (see Chapter 9 for further details).

It is remarkable that this species has little popularity on the Pacific coast of the United States as a hedging plant. Vertrees, the well-known *Acer* grower, grew a perfect hedge at his home in Roseburg, Oregon. The Castle of Schönbrunn in Vienna is also famous for its impressive hedgerows of *A. campestre,* up to 10 m tall. In southern England many hedges are made of this maple interspersed with other plants, including hornbeam and hawthorn. It is also possible to prune this species as topiary, as was done with yew and boxwood during the Baroque period.

The wood is one of the best of its class, of close texture and fine grain. It is, however, seldom used for timber, but rather is occasionally used for small furniture and tools. Several European nurseries and research stations have selected or developed useful cultivars for street trees and reforestation of national forests (see Chapter 9).

*Acer campestre* is readily propagated by seed which, harvested at the end of September, must be planted immediately. Germination normally occurs the following spring. Commercial seed, being much drier, is usually stratified for a year in sharp sand and then sown the following spring.

SECTION: *Platanoidea*

ACER CAPPADOCICUM Gleditsch (1785) ssp. CAPPADOCICUM

SYNONYMS

*A. pictum* auct. non Thunberg (1784).
*A. laetum* C. A. Meyer (1831).
*A. colchicum* Booth ex Gordon (1840).
*A. pictum* f. *caucasicum* Koch (1864).
*A. hederifolium* Ruprecht (1870).
*A. cappadocicum* var. *indicum* (Pax) Rehder (1911).
*A. pictum* var. *colchicum* (Gordon) A. Henry 1908.

TYPES: Tournefort Herbarium at P; lectotype—Murray (1977) chose the foliage illustration in Gleditsch's 1785 work; the typifying copy is at LE.

COMMON NAME: Kolchischer Ahorn.

EPITHET: *Cappadocicus,* after Cappadocia, a Roman province in Anatolia (now Turkey).

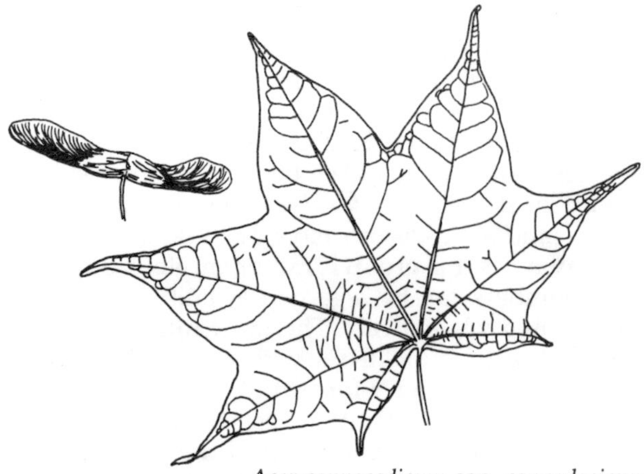

*Acer cappacodicum* ssp. *cappadocicum*

ILLUSTRATIONS: Fang (1981a), Krüssmann (1976a), Murray (1975a).
HABIT: A deciduous tree to 25–30 m tall; young shoots and branches green throughout the second year; vigorous young growth shows a glaucous bloom, later disappearing.
LEAVES: Green when unfolding, sometimes reddish; 5- to 7-lobed, bases cordate, 9–15 cm across, glabrous except for hair tufts in the axils of the veins on the lower surfaces; lobes broadly triangular, extending into caudate points, entire at the margins, sometimes undulate; petioles milky when broken, 5–10 cm long.
FLOWERS: Yellow, in corymbs, about 6–7 cm long.
FRUITS: Wings 3–5 cm long, 2–4 times longer than the nutlets, sometimes underdeveloped, spreading at a wide angle.
BARK AND BUDS: Bark green through 2nd or 3rd year, smooth and gray thereafter.
HARDINESS: Zone V.
AUTUMN COLOR: Brilliant golden yellow.
DISTRIBUTION: Northern Turkey, Caucasia, and Iran. Subspecies *sinicum* is represented in the Himalayas and in China. Found at sea level to 2000 m, usually as isolated trees.
CHROMOSOME NUMBER: $2n = 26$.
SUBSPECIES
ssp. *cappadocicum*, the typical subspecies.
ssp. *divergens* (Pax) Murray (1978).
ssp. *lobelii* (Tenore) Murray (1982).
ssp. *sinicum* (Rehder) Handel-Mazzetti (1933).
CULTIVARS: Three (see Chapter 9).
REFERENCES: Bean (1970), Elwes & Henry (1908), Hillier (1965), Koch (1869), Krüssmann (1976a), Murray (1970c, 1977), Pax (1902), Pojárkova (1933b), Rehder (1986 facs.), Yaltirik, (1967a).

*Acer cappadocicum* was introduced in Europe in 1838. Like all species of section *Platanoidea*, it has a milky sap in the leaves and petioles. It is closely allied to *A. platanoides* and *A. mono*. Its twigs and shoots remain a green color for the first two or three years, which distinguishes it from *A. mono*, whose gray-brown bark is wrinkled or fissured but never green. *Acer platanoides* has a different leaf shape, with more pointed leaves, and differently formed fruits.

There are a large number of synonyms for *Acer cappadocicum*, due to early confusion in its taxonomy. Even today it can be found listed as *A. colchicum* or as *A. laetum*. The name *A. pictum* has also sometimes been misapplied to this species. In fact, *A. pictum* is an invalid name for *A. mono*.

A few former varieties and species are now recognized as subspecies, such as *Acer cappadocicum* ssp. *sinicum* from China, which differs from subspecies *cappadocicum* in having more sharply lobed leaves. A beautiful tree, it is still rare in cultivation.

The very handsome *Acer cappadocicum* ssp. *cappadocicum* is widely used in many gardens and parks. It is a stately tree of 25–30 m tall at maturity, so usually becomes too large for gardens. It adapts to any well-drained soil.

Mature trees produce large amounts of seed. Nevertheless, few nurseries propagate this species from seed. Well-known cultivars, especially 'Rubrum', replace the species. Most of the few cultivars in cultivation are readily available in the trade.

SECTION: *Platanoidea*
ACER CAPPADOCICUM ssp. DIVERGENS (Pax) Murray (1978)
BASIONYM: *A. divergens* Koch ex Pax (1886).
SYNONYMS
*A. quinquelobum* sensu Koch (1869), non Saporta (1865).
*A. lasicum* Schwerin (1898).
TYPES: *K. Koch*, northeast Turkey ("In valle Tschorukthal"), Çoruk Valley in Vil. Artvin: G; topotypes A, G, LE.
EPITHET: *Divergens*, differing in certain characteristics—referring, in this case, to the widely divergent samaras.
ILLUSTRATIONS: Plate 99; Krüssmann (1976a).
HABIT: A treelike shrub or small tree to 10 m tall, usually wider than high and often with more than one trunk; stems yellow-brown.
LEAVES: Mostly 5-lobed but often 3-lobed, 2–5 (to 6–8) cm wide, deeply lobed; lobes ovate; margins entire, obtuse or acuminate; bases somewhat cordate, glabrous, dark green above, paler beneath; veins sharply elevated on upper surfaces.
FLOWERS: Yellow, on very short, few-flowered corymbs.
FRUITS: Samaras horizontal, bent upright, wings diverging at a very obtuse angle; nutlets flattened on both sides.
BARK AND BUDS: Buds small, with apices up to 4 mm, lateral buds up to 3 mm, usually with six red-brown outer scales.

HARDINESS: Zone V.
AUTUMN COLOR: Clear yellow or golden yellow.
DISTRIBUTION: Asiatic part of Turkey (Anatolia), Transcaucasia, on dry and sunny slopes along riverbanks and streams, with shrubby vegetation.
REFERENCES: Bean (1970), Krüssmann (1976a), Murray (1970c, 1977), Pojárkova (1933b), Rehder (1986 facs.).

Pax described this rarely seen Turkish-Caucasian tree as a species; in the present volume it is given subspecific rank under *Acer cappadocicum* as proposed by Murray (1978). Extreme forms merge with subspecies *cappadocicum,* and their distributions and habitats overlap.

Its small *cappacodicum*-like leaves are rather variable in both size and shape. The stems are yellow-brown and not as smooth and gray as in *Acer mono* or subspecies *cappadocicum.* This is a difficult taxon to identify in the field.

*Acer cappadocicum* ssp. *divergens* is rare in cultivation and almost never found in the trade; a very few specialized nurseries supply it. It can be grafted on *A. platanoides* when seed is unavailable.

SECTION: *Platanoidea*
ACER CAPPADOCICUM ssp. LOBELII (Tenore) Murray (1982)
BASIONYM: *A. lobelii* Tenore (1819).
SYNONYMS
*A. platanoides* var. *integrilobum* Tausch (1829).
*A. platanoides* var. *lobelii* (Tenore) Loudon (1838).
*A. lobelii* ssp. *tenorei* Pax (1886).
*A. lobelii* f. *normale* Schwerin (1893).
TYPE: *Michele Tenore,* mountainous woods around Gulf of Naples, Italy; holotype NAP; isotype W.
COMMON NAMES: Italian maple, Lobel maple, Lobel-Ahorn.
EPITHET: *Lobelii,* after French botanist Matthias de L'Obel (1538–1616).
ILLUSTRATIONS: Plate 100; Grootendorst (1969), Krüssmann (1976a).
HABIT: A tree to 20 m tall, with a rather columnar-fastigiate habit; branches glaucous-green, sometimes also purplish brown.
LEAVES: 5-lobed, 12–15 cm wide and as long, dark green, slightly waved; margins entire to undulate; vein axils often tufted with hairs on lower surfaces; lobes subacuminate; bases cordate; petioles 6–10 cm long.
INFLORESCENCES: Corymbose, terminal, and rather short.
FLOWERS: 5-merous, yellow-green, appearing with the leaves.
FRUITS: Samaras often incomplete, wings almost horizontal, glabrous; nutlets rather flat.
BARK AND BUDS: Bark striped longitudinally and very lightly fissured; young shoot have a blue-green bloom; older stems are slightly striped.
HARDINESS: Zone VI.
AUTUMN COLOR: Golden yellow.
DISTRIBUTION: Southern Italy, mountain forests around the Gulf of Naples, and also in the mountains of Calabria.
VARIETY: var. *dissectum* Wesmael, with incised leaves; synonym is *A. cappadocicum* var. *dissectum* (Wesmael) Murray (1977); probably best treated as a cultivar 'Dissectum'; not in cultivation.
REFERENCES: Bean (1970), Dippel (1892), Elwes & Henry (1908), Grootendorst (1969), Koch (1869), Krüssmann (1976a), Murray (1970c, 1977), Rehder (1986 facs.).

This beautiful tree was introduced in European horticulture about 1865. Tenore described it in 1819, but several other authors, including Loudon and Pax, changed its rank. It sometimes has been regarded as a variety of the well-known *Acer platanoides* and even considered a hybrid. In this volume it is considered to be a subspecies of *A. cappadocicum,* having the most westerly distribution of the whole complex.

*Acer cappadocicum* ssp. *lobelii* is a remarkable tree and can be readily recognized by its columnar habit and by the bluish bloom on young shoots. Neither *A. cappadocicum* nor *A. platanoides* grow so pyramidally as a seedling, and both lack the blue bloom. The leaves of subspecies *lobelii* have more undulating margins than those of *A. platanoides* or *A. cappadocicum.*

This subspecies is occasionally available in the trade. The tree is susceptible to mildew, especially in wet summers; although this does not damage the tree, it makes for an untidy appearance.

The cities of Basel, Switzerland, and 's Hertogenbosch, The Netherlands, are currently conducting evaluation trials with this subspecies.

SECTION: *Platanoidea*
ACER CAPPADOCICUM ssp. SINICUM (Rehder) Handel-Mazzetti (1933)
SYNONYMS
*A. cultratum* Wallich (1830).
*A. cappadocicum* var. *sinicum* Rehder (1911).
*A. cappadocicum* var. *cultratum* (Wallich) Fang (1939).
TYPE: Syntypes *A. Henry 10877, E. H. Wilson 1009, 1884, 1925,* Hubei, Sichuan, and Yunnan provinces, China; A; NY; K.
EPITHET: *Sinicus,* Chinese.
HABIT: A large tree, more densely branched than subspecies *cappadocicum,* otherwise of the same general habit and size.
LEAVES: Smaller than those of subspecies

*cappadocicum,* with narrower and longer lobes; 6–10 cm long, mostly 5-lobed, olive-green when young, later sometimes coppery red; lobes tend to be caudate.
FLOWERS: Yellow, on short racemes.
FRUITS: Samaras about twice as long as the nutlets; fruits bright red at maturity, turning to brown, same shape as nutlets of subspecies *cappadocicum.*
BARK AND BUDS: Bark reddish brown, more fissured than that of subspecies *cappadocicum,* often quite like that of *A. mono;* 2nd-year wood remains green.
HARDINESS: Zone V.
AUTUMN COLOR: Golden yellow.
DISTRIBUTION: Himalayas, Hubei, Sichuan, and Yunnan provinces of the China, in mountain forests at 2000–3000 m.
VARIETY: var. *tricaudatum* (see below).
REFERENCES: Bean (1970), Hillier (1965), Krüssmann (1976a), Murray (1970c, 1977), Rehder (1986 facs.).

Ernest H. Wilson introduced *Acer cappadocicum* ssp. *sinicum* from China about 1911, and some years later it was brought to England again from China by the famous Scottish plant hunter George Forrest.

Variety *tricaudatum,* sometimes encountered, belongs to this subspecies. Plants in cultivation as variety *cultratum* are usually Chinese forms and synonymous with *A. cappadocicum* or *A. cappadocicum* ssp. *sinicum.* Their proper place is uncertain at present.

Subspecies *sinicum* forms a tree of moderate size, with a crown often as large as wide. The leaves are of the same shape and size as those of subspecies *cappadocicum,* but the lobes are more pointed, the petioles somewhat longer, and the bark of the tree not as smooth.

This subspecies is rarely seen in gardens and parks and only occasionally in the trade. When no seed is available, it can be grafted on potted understock of *Acer platanoides.*

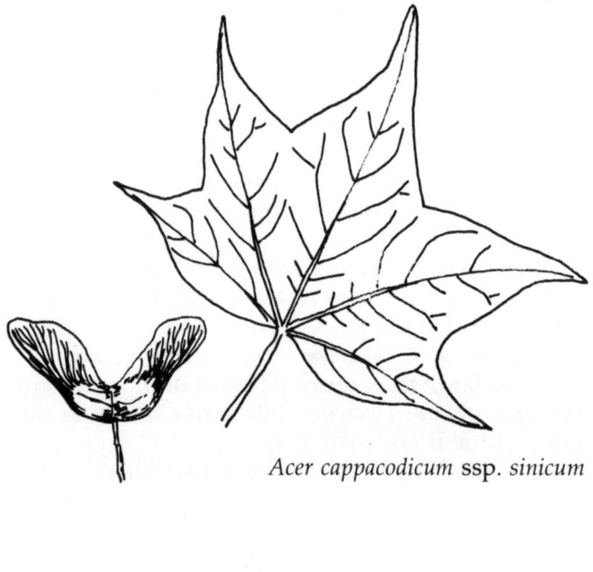
*Acer cappacodicum* ssp. *sinicum*

SECTION: *Platanoidea*
ACER CAPPADOCICUM ssp. SINICUM var. TRICAUDATUM (Veitch ex Rehder) Rehder (1914)
SYNONYMS
*A. laetum* var. *tricaudatum* Veitch (1904).
*A. bodinieri* Léveillé (1912).
*A. pictum* f. *tricuspis* Rehder (1913).
*A. mono* var. *tricuspis* (Rehder) Rehder (1938).
*A. pictum* f. *tricuspis* (Rehder) Fang (1939).
*A. cappadocicum* ssp. *trilobum* Murray (1977).
TYPE: Lectotype *Wilson 234-A (Rehder)*, Hubei Province, China; A; NY; K.
EPITHET: *Tricaudatus,* having three lobes, each long-caudate.
ILLUSTRATION: Plate 101.
HABIT: A tree about 15 m tall and as wide; young shoots purplish, turning to brown-green when mature.
LEAVES: 3- to 5-lobed, the basal lobes often absent or remotely so, 10–15 cm long and 7–10 cm wide, shining green, undersides fresh green; margins entire, slightly undulate; young leaves unfold purple turning green later, rarely 3-lobed.
FLOWERS: As in subspecies *cappadocicum.*
FRUITS: Reddish when immature, of the same shape as those of subspecies *cappadocicum.*
BARK AND BUDS: Bark gray-brown, not fissured, very much like that of subspecies *sinicum.*
HARDINESS: Zone V.
AUTUMN COLOR: Yellow.
DISTRIBUTION: Hubei Province, China.
REFERENCES: Krüssmann (1976a), Murray (1970c).

This variety is still quite rare in cultivation. It differs from subspecies *sinicum* var. *sinicum* by the differently shaped leaves with much smaller basal lobes. Pax treated this variety and several other Chinese forms as *Acer cappadocicum* var. *cultratum,* now included in the synonymy of *A. cappadocicum* ssp. *cappadocicum.*

SECTION: *Platanoidea*
ACER LONGIPES ssp. AMPLUM (Rehder) de Jong, comb. nov.
BASIONYM: *A. amplum* Rehder in Sargent *Plantae Wilsonianae 1:* 86.1911.
SYNONYMS
*A. longipes* var. *tientaiense* Schneider (1907).
*A. amplum* var. *tientaiense* (Schneider) Rehder (1911).
*A. acutum* Fang (1932).
*A. tientaiense* (Schneider) Pojárkova (1933).
*A. cappadocicum* ssp. *amplum* (Rehder) Murray (1977).
TYPES: Lectotype *E. H. Wilson 1906,* Hubei Province, China; A; isotypes B; M; FI; K; W.
EPITHET: *Amplus,* abundant.
ILLUSTRATION: Fang (1981a, as *A. acutum*).
HABIT: A small tree, related to and similar in shape

*Acer longipes* ssp. *amplum*

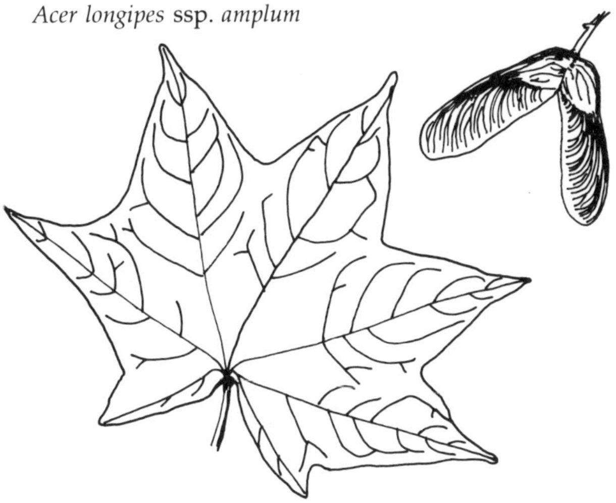

to *A. mono* and *A. cappadocicum,* though always much smaller than *A. cappadocicum;* often wider than high, up to 8 m tall in cultivation and to 20 m tall in native habitat; leaf buds green.
LEAVES: Rather large, glossy green, mostly 5-lobed, somewhat leathery, 8–10–(15) cm long and about as wide; margins entire; middle lobe much larger than the others, often wavy; petioles thin and slender, 5–15 cm long.
FLOWERS: On loose corymbs, 10–20 cm long, with few, yellowish white flowers.
FRUITS: On loose corymbs, with only a few fruits per infructescence; samaras usually underdeveloped, wings spread at a wide angle; seeds flat, like most species of this section.
BARK AND BUDS: Adult trunks dark gray, not unlike *A. platanoides,* with a few glands; young shoots and branches mostly olive-yellow or olive-brown, but sometimes green with whitish spots; all shoots turn the same color when mature.
HARDINESS: Zone V.
AUTUMN COLOR: Dull yellow.
DISTRIBUTION: Western Sichuan and Hubei provinces, China; also in Guangxi Province at 700–2000 m, and in Tien tai Shan, Zhejiang Province at 1000 m.
CHROMOSOME NUMBER: $2n = 26$ (Darlington 1955).
CULTIVAR: One (see Chapter 9).
REFERENCES: Bean (1970), Krüssmann (1976a), Murray (1970c, 1977), Rehder (1986 facs.), Sargent (1913).

*Acer longipes* ssp. *amplum* is a flat-topped tree, to 8 m tall, that is closely related to *A. mono* and *A. platanoides,* with which it can be confused. It differs from the latter by its much smaller habit and smaller leaves, and from the former by its much smoother bark. It forms a dense, shrubby tree to 4–5 m tall. The leaves are dark green, somewhat leathery and rather large. The basal lobes are often insignificant.

Wilson discovered this subspecies in western Sichuan Province, China, in 1901, and Forrest found it in Yunnan and Guangxi provinces. Rehder described it as a species in 1911; Murray included it as a subspecies in *A. cappadocicum* in 1977. It is better included in *A. longipes* as it has almost the same natural distribution and similar leaves. *Acer longipes* is closer to *A. platanoides* than to *A. cappadocicum. Acer amplum* var. *catalpifolium* is now considered to be a distinct subspecies under *A. longipes,* and *A. amplum* var. *tientaiense* is also now included as a synonym of subspecies *amplum.*

It is rather easily propagated by seed, which germinates well. Grafting of superior, selected forms can be done on both *Acer cappadocicum* and *A. platanoides.* It grows in almost every soil, except very chalky. It is only rarely available in the trade.

SECTION: *Platanoidea*
ACER LONGIPES ssp. CATALPIFOLIUM (Rehder) de Jong, comb. nov.
BASIONYM: *A. catalpifolium* Rehder (1911).
SYNONYMS
*A. chunii* Fang (1937).
*A. cappadocicum* ssp. *catalpifolium* (Rehder) Murray (1977).
TYPES: Lectotype *E. H. Wilson 1359,* western Sichuan Province, China; A; isotypes BM; FI; K; NY; W; syntypes *Veitch 3350, Wilson 4082,* western Sichuan Province; K; FI.
EPITHET: *Catalpifolius,* with leaves like *Catalpa.*
ILLUSTRATIONS: Fang (1981a, as *A. chunii*), Krüssmann (1976a).
HABIT: A tree to 30 m tall; young shoots dotted with small lenticels.
LEAVES: Broadly ovate, acuminate, 3-lobed or almost unlobed, 8–25 cm long and 5–15 cm wide, undersides hairy or downy; margins entire.
FLOWERS: 5-merous, yellow-green, on corymbs.
FRUITS: Obtuse, rather large, 5 cm long, wings spreading at a wide angle.
BARK AND BUDS: Bark smooth and gray or even reddish brown.
HARDINESS: Zones VII–X.
DISTRIBUTION: Sichuan and Guangdong provinces, China, at 500–1000 m in low mountainous regions.
REFERENCES: Bean (1970), Krüssmann (1976a), Murray (1970c, 1977), Rehder (1986 facs.), Sargent (1913).

Rehder described this taxon as a species in 1911, and Murray reduced it to subspecific rank in 1977 as *Acer cappadocicum* ssp. *catalpifolium.* It is a rare tree, only recently brought into Great Britain, and not currently otherwise in cultivation in Western gardens. Oterdoom saw trees of this subspecies in the wild in May 1981 on Emeishan (Mt. Emei), Sichuan Province, China, but was not able to bring seed home.

The literature describes it as a fairly large tree, to 20 m tall, with the same general habit as that of *Acer cappadocicum* or *A. mono.* The leaves are very large, mostly 3-lobed or unlobed.

As mature plants are not present in the West, it is impossible to obtain this subspecies in the trade. It promises to be an interesting tree.

SECTION: *Platanoidea*
ACER LONGIPES ssp. FIRMIANIOIDES (Cheng ex Fang) de Jong, comb. & stat. nov.

BASIONYMS
*A. firmianioides* Cheng, Sci. Technol. China 2:35–36.1949, nomen nudum.
*A. firmianioides* Cheng ex Fang, *Acta Phytotax. Sinica 17:* 69. 1979.

TYPE: *W. C. Cheng & C. T. Hwa 740,* Shishuanbana, Lichuan Xian, Hubei Province, China; PE.
EPITHET: *Firmianioides,* with leaves like *Firmiana.*
ILLUSTRATION: Fang (1981a).
HABIT: A tree to 20 m tall.
LEAVES: 3-lobed, 20 cm long and up to 28 cm wide, with entire lobes, larger than leaves of subspecies *amplum.*
FRUITS: Samaras 4.5–5 cm long; fruits large, about 10 cm long including horizontally spreading wings.
HARDINESS: Zones VII–X.
DISTRIBUTION: Native to central China, Shishuanbana, Lichuan Xian, Hubei Province, China, at 1350 m.
REFERENCES: Fang (1981a), Murray (1970c).

Cheng (1949) writes,

This new species differs from its allies in the larger (20 cm long, 28 cm broad) 3-lobed leaves with entire lobes and in the larger (10 cm across) samaras with horizontally spreading wings. A remarkable, distinct species having leaves reminiscent of those of some species of *Firmiana.*

This taxon is now tentatively placed under *Acer longipes,* but might well be sunk in synonymy with *A. longipes* ssp. *catalpifolium,* as living material becomes available and herbarium specimens are studied and compared.

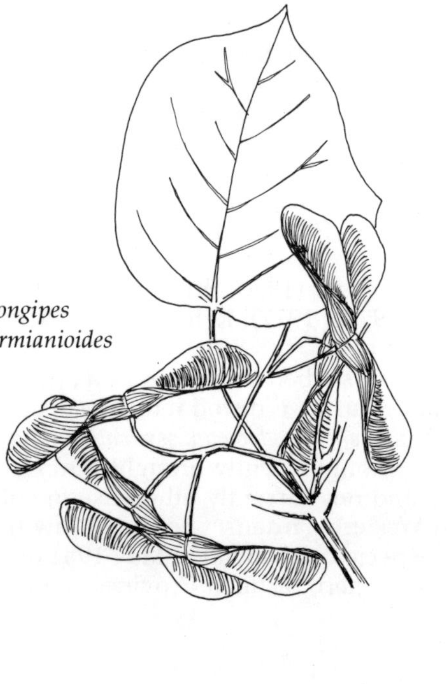

*Acer longipes* ssp. *firmianioides*

SECTION: *Platanoidea*
ACER LONGIPES Franchet ex Rehder (1905) ssp. LONGIPES

SYNONYMS
*A. fulvescens* Rehder (1911).
*A. pashanicum* Fang & Soong (1966).
*A. acutum* Fang var. *tientungense* Fang (1966).
*A. longipes* Franchet ex Rehder var. *nanchuanense* Fang (1979).
*A. longipes* var. *chengbuense* Fang (1979).
*A. longipes* var. *pubigerum* (Fang) Fang (1979).
*A. longipes* var. *weixiense* Fang (1979).
*A. fulvescens* Rehder ssp. *danbaense* Fang (1979).
*A. fulvescens* ssp. *fupingense* (Fang & Hu) Fang & Hu (1979).
*A. fulvescens* ssp. *pentalobum* (Fang & Soong) Fang & Soong (1979).
*A. fulvescens* ssp. *fucescens* Fang (1979).
*A. acutum* var. *quinquefidum* Fang & Chiu (1979).

TYPE: Syntypes *Père Paul Farges,* Sichuan Province, China; K; *E. H. Wilson 327,* Patung, Hubei Province, China; K; E.
EPITHET: *Longipes,* having an elongated point.
ILLUSTRATIONS: Fang (1981a), Harris (1983).
HABIT: A tree to 18 m tall with an umbrellalike habit; branchlets dark brown and smooth when young, silvery and rougher when more mature; crown olive-brown in winter.
LEAVES: Almost invariably 3-lobed, 8–15 cm across, clad with a yellowish down, darker when mature; wild trees sometimes bear leaves without lobes.
FLOWERS: Yellowish, on long racemes.
FRUITS: Samaras incomplete; nutlets flat.
BARK AND BUDS: Olive-brown when young, rather conspicuous.
HARDINESS: Zone V.
AUTUMN COLOR: Clear yellow.
DISTRIBUTION: Western Sichuan Province, China.

SUBSPECIES
ssp. *amplum* (Rehder) de Jong, comb. nov.
ssp. *catalpifolium* (Rehder) de Jong, comb. nov.
ssp. *firmianioides* (Cheng ex Fang) de Jong, comb. & stat. nov.
ssp. *longipes,* the typical subspecies.

VARIETIES: The many varieties and subspecies described by Fang (1966, 1979, 1981a) are cited

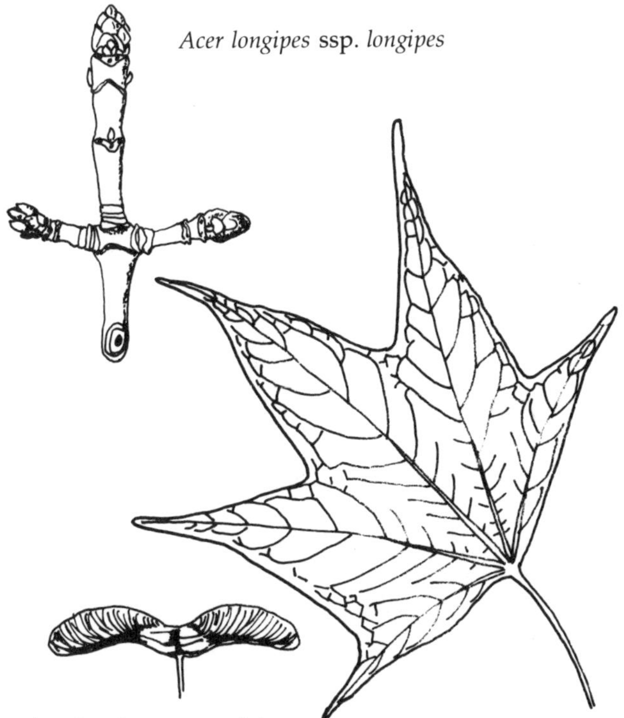

*Acer longipes* ssp. *longipes*

*Acer longipes* var. *weixiense*

as synonyms and are not included here as there is no living material nor any conveniently available herbarium specimens in the West. Some of these taxa will probably be sunk into synonymy.
REFERENCES: Bean (1970), Fang (1981a), Murray (1970c), Rehder (1986 facs.), Schneider (1912).

*Acer longipes* ssp. *longipes* is a very rare cultivated tree, present in only a few collections. Chinese botanists are familiar with *A. longipes,* as it is a very common tree in Sichuan Province. Several new taxa described by Fang, Soong, Cheng, and others from 1932–1981 belong to this group. As no living Chinese material or herbarium specimens are available in Europe or North America, it is very difficult to determine their botanical rank or synonymy. Following the rules of nomenclature, however, *Acer longipes* has priority in this complex.

*Acer amplum* is a subspecies in this complex. It has the same distribution as *A. longipes,* but can rather easily be separated from it by its much smaller habit and differently shaped leaves.

Subspecies *catalpifolium* is quite unknown, and subspecies *firmianioides* is possibly identical with it. Again, as no living or herbarium material of the latter is available in the West, it is almost impossible to form a conclusion.

The drawings in Fang (1981a) show the various leaf shapes of the many species, subspecies, and varieties recognized by the Chinese botanists. It is important to document the names of the various Chinese taxa included in the present volume in *A. longipes,* identifying them as synonyms. It must be remembered that in earlier years many infraspecific taxa of well-known species were described, and a considerable number have been sunk into synonymy.

*Acer longipes* ssp. *longipes* grows to a 18 m tall tree with an umbrella-shaped habit. Its 3-lobed leaves are clad with a yellowish green down, which gives a peculiar olive-green appearance to the leaves. It is closer to *A. platanoides* than to *A. cappadocicum* in respect to bark and flowers. It is fully hardy in England and comparable countries.

Propagation by seed is possible. A tree (labeled *Acer fulvescens*) at Borde Hill Gardens, Great Britain, seems to be the only tree producing viable seed. This seed produces good typical plants which can be propagated by grafting on *A. platanoides.* A specimen in the Esveld Aceretum, Boskoop, The Netherlands, derives from this tree and matches the description fully. It is now 20 years old and 6 m tall, and has not yet flowered.

SECTION: *Platanoidea*
ACER MIYABEI ssp. MIAOTAIENSE (Tsoong) Murray (1969)
BASIONYM: *A. miaotaiense* Tsoong (1955).
SYNONYM: *A. yangjuechii* Fang & Chiu (1979).
TYPE: *T. N. Liou, 11997,* Miaotaitze, Shaanxi Province, China; PE.
EPITHET: *Miaotaiensis,* from Miaotaitze, a county in Shaanxi Province, China.
ILLUSTRATION: Fang (1981a, as *A. yangjuechii*).
HABIT: A small tree.
LEAVES: 3-lobed or remotely 5-lobed, 4–6 cm long and 3–5 cm wide; margins lobulate.
FLOWERS: Yellow-green, on small trusses.
FRUITS: Wings horizontal.
HARDINESS: Zone V (?).
DISTRIBUTION: Shaanxi (subspecies *miaotaiense*) and Zhejiang (*A. yangjuechii*) provinces, China.
REFERENCES: Fang (1981a), Murray (1970c).

This subspecies, first described as a species in 1955, is not in cultivation in the West. It is accepted as a valid subspecies in this volume. When further information and adequate living, herbarium, and type materials become available, it may become synonymous with some other taxon. Its relation to the Japanese *Acer miyabei* ssp. *miyabei* is unclear.

*Acer yangjuechii* Fang & Chiu (1979) is included here as a synonym of *A. miyabei* ssp. *miaotaiense,* although the former occurs in Zhejiang Province in southeastern China, and the latter occurs in northern China in Shaanxi Province. The coauthors of the present volume have compared drawings of these two taxa (cf. Fang, 1981, Plate 16) and concluded that they are

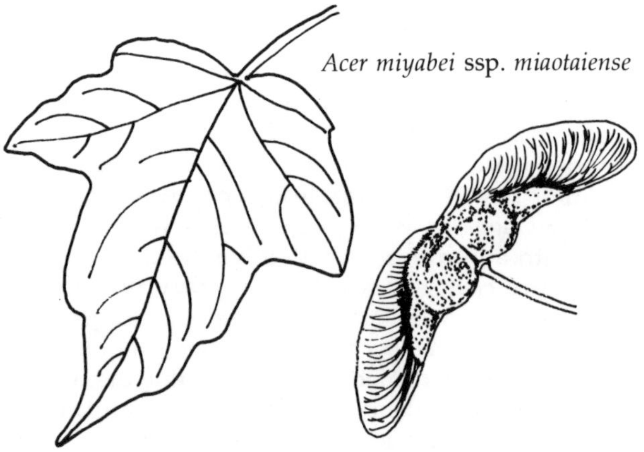

*Acer miyabei* ssp. *miaotaiense*

synonymous, until further information helps to clarify this matter. Of course, study of living materials and taxonomic investigations of the original type collections of these two taxa would be very revealing. After examining living specimens in Zhejiang Province, T. R. Dudley suggests that *A. yangjuechii* be maintained as a separate species or as another subspecies of *A. miyabei.* In 1988 Wang described a glabrous form of subspecies *miaotaiense* as variety *glabrum.*

SECTION: *Platanoidea*

ACER MIYABEI Maximowicz (1888) ssp. MIYABEI

SYNONYMS

*A. hayatae* Léveillé & Vaniot (1906).

*A. shibatai* Nakai (1937).

*A. miyabei* var. *shibatai* (Nakai) Hara (1951).

TYPE: *K. Miyabe,* Niikappu, Province Hidaka, Hokkaido, Japan; TI.

COMMON NAMES: Kuroba itaya, Kurobi-haya, Shibata kaede.

EPITHET: *Miyabei,* after K. Miyabe (1860–1951), Japanese botanist and professor at the University of Sapporo.

ILLUSTRATIONS: Plate 102; Fang (1981a), Koidzumi (1911), Krüssmann (1976a), Kurata (1964–1976), Satake et al. (1989).

HABIT: A tree to 25 m tall, flat-topped; branches gray and pubescent.

LEAVES: 5-lobed or lobulate, 10–15 cm wide, not unlike those of *A. campestre* but larger, olive-green, slightly pilose on both sides, pale green on the undersides, deeply divided on young trees but more truncate at bases on older trees; lobes rather sharply acuminate and somewhat wavy; petioles pubescent.

INFLORESCENCES: Corymbose, terminal, 10–12 cm long, sometimes as short corymbs from leafless axillary buds.

FLOWERS: Yellow-green.

FRUITS: Samaras horizontal, softly pubescent, 2–3 cm long.

BARK AND BUDS: Bark corky.

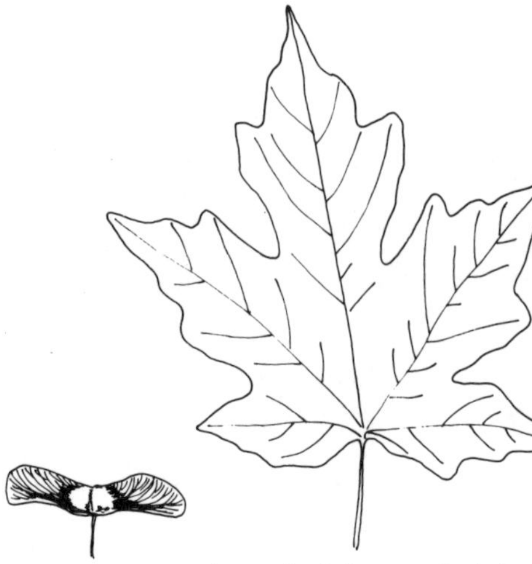

*Acer miyabei* ssp. *miyabei*

HARDINESS: Zone V.

AUTUMN COLOR: Yellow.

DISTRIBUTION: Northern Japan, on riverbanks together with *A. mono.* On Hokkaido in the districts of Ishikari and Hadaki.

SUBSPECIES

ssp. *miaotaiense* (Tsoong) Murray (1969).

ssp. *miyabei,* the typical subspecies.

REFERENCES: Bean (1970), Koidzumi (1911), Krüssmann (1976a), Kurata (1964–1976), Murray (1969, 1970c), Ogata (1965), Rehder (1986 facs.), Veitch (1904), Vertrees (1978, 1987).

Maximowicz published a description of this species in 1888 based on a report from Miyabe, who discovered it. Sargent rediscovered the species in 1892 at Iwanigawa, Hokkaido. A large portion of the ripe seed that he collected was sent to Great Britain in 1895 by the Arnold Arboretum.

Murray recognizes a subspecies *miaotaiense,* not in cultivation, endemic to Shaanxi Province of China. Fang and Chiu described a new species in 1979, *Acer yangjuechii* from Zhejiang Province, which may be synonymous with *A. miyabei* ssp. *miaotaiense.*

The closest relative to *Acer miyabei* ssp. *miyabei* is the European *A. campestre,* but *A. miyabei* is rather easily distinguished by the larger leaves, which are slightly hairy. Both species have corky bark. Some forms of *A. campestre* look very much like *A. miyabei.* Closer examination and reevaluation of type specimens is necessary in these cases.

*Acer miyabei* ssp. *miyabei* perhaps could be used as a small street tree in the same way as *A. campestre. Acer miyabei* is rarely seen in European and North American gardens, and Ogata (1965) reports that it is also rare in Japanese gardens.

This Oriental species and its subspecies are rare in the trade, because they are hard to propagate. Seed is only occasionally available and germinates slowly. Cuttings strike very poorly, so the only vegetative means of propagation is layering or grafting on *Acer campestre.* Grafting is not very successful as 2-year-old plants tend to break away from their understock rather easily.

*Acer miyabei* ssp. *miyabei* was one of the parents of the interspecific garden hybrid *A.* × *hillieri.* The other parent was *A. cappadocicum* 'Aureum'.

SECTION: *Platanoidea*

ACER MONO Maximowicz (1857) ssp. MONO

SYNONYMS

- *A. laetum* var. *parviflorum* Regel (1857).
- *A. pictum* var. *mono* (Maximowicz) Franchet (1884).
- *A. lobelii* var. *mono* (Maximowicz) Wesmael (1890).
- *A. mono* var. *horizontale* Nakai (1912).
- *A. mono* var. *savatieri* (Pax) Nakai (1930).
- ***A. mono* f. *septemlobum* Fang & Soong; see *A. tenellum* var. *septemlobum.***
- *A. mono* var. *tashiroi* Hisauchi (1934).
- *A. mono* var. *trunculatum* Nakai (1953).
- *A. mono* ssp. *savatieri* (Pax) Kitamura (1964).
- *A. truncatum* Bunge ssp. *mono* (Maximowicz) Murray (1969).
- *A. pictum* sensu auct. non Thunberg.

TYPES: *M. Maximowicz,* Pach Tigrsch, Amur, southeastern Siberia, Russia; holotype LE; isotypes MO.

EPITHET: *Mono,* from a Japanese name.

COMMON NAMES: Painted maple, Ao kaede, Itagi kaede, Itaya, Itaya kaede, Shiraki kaede, Tokiwa kaede, Tsuta momiji, Wu Chio Feng, Yorokko kaede.

ILLUSTRATIONS: Plate 103; Krüssmann (1976a), Vertrees (1978, 1987). UPS.

HABIT: A tree to 15 m tall, with glabrous branches, yellow-gray in the 2nd year; crown broadly pyramidal.

LEAVES: 5- to 7-lobed, almost cordate and not unlike those of *A. cappadocicum* and *A. truncatum,* 8–15 cm wide, green on both sides; margins entire; lobes triangular and regularly acuminate; petioles long.

FLOWERS: Yellow, on corymbs 4–6 cm long, appearing with or before the leaves; trees tend to produce all male or all female flowers.

FRUITS: Samaras imperfectly formed, obtuse, wings diverging at a right angle; nutlets flat, the same size as samaras.

HARDINESS: Zone V.

BARK AND BUDS: Bark smooth or unfissured, yellow-gray; buds dark red in winter.

AUTUMN COLOR: Yellow.

DISTRIBUTION: China, Manchuria, Mongolia, southeastern Siberia, Korea, and Sakhalin; also common in Japan on Hokkaido, Honshu, Shikoku, and Kyushu islands.

CHROMOSOME NUMBER: $2n = 26$ (Darlington 1955).

SUBSPECIES

- ssp. *mono,* the typical subspecies.
- ssp. *okamotoanum* (Nakai) de Jong, comb. & stat. nov.

VARIETIES

- var. *mayrii* (Schwerin) Nakai (1930).
- var. *mono,* the typical variety.
- var. *taishakuense* Ogata (1964), leaves pilose.

FORMS

- **f. *ambiguum* (Dippel) Rehder (1939).**
- **var. *marmoratum* f. *dissectum,* probably *A. truncatum* 'Akikaze'.**
- **f. *septemlobum* Fang & Soong (1966), see *A. tenellum* var. *septemlobum.***

CULTIVARS: Several (see Chapter 9).

REFERENCES: Bean (1970), Dippel (1892), Elwes & Henry (1908), Fang (1981a), Kitamura (1972), Koch (1869), Koidzumi (1911), Krüssmann (1976a), Murray (1970c), Ogata (1965), Rehder (1986 facs.), Veitch (1904), Vertrees (1978, 1987).

Maximowicz described *Acer mono* in 1857, Maries introduced it for the first time in 1881, and Wilson brought subspecies *mono* in 1901 from China to the Veitch Nursery in Great Britain. The species was in cultivation in Russia before this introduction to Europe. Murray treats this species as a subspecies of *A. truncatum,* a classification not accepted in the present volume.

*Acer mono* ssp. *mono*

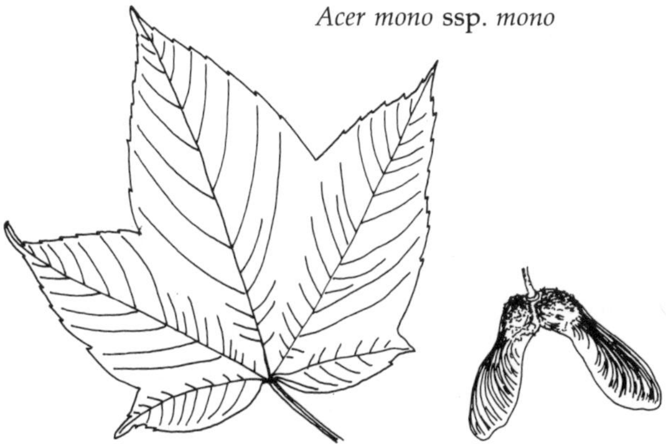

*Acer mono* var. *savatieri*

*Acer mono* has always been a difficult taxon, hence the extensive number of synonyms. Pojárkova, the Russian *Acer* specialist, attempted to split the species in two, calling one-half *A. pictum,* an invalid name of Thunberg—whose species epithet is now attached to *Kalopanax*—and the other half *A. mono.* It is very doubtful whether these are different taxa; however, Pojárkova was very firm in her opinion. Her *A. mono* is described from material collected along the Amur River in Mongolia; her *A. pictum* comes from Japanese material. The type of her *A. pictum,* which is *Kalopanax,* is in the herbarium of the University of Uppsala, Sweden, and the type of her *A. mono* is in the St. Petersburg Herbarium.

*Acer mono* in the sense of Maximowicz is native to northeastern Asia (i.e., China, Manchuria, Korea, and Sakhalin). It is also rather common in Japan, where it grows on Hokkaido, Honshu, Shikoku, and Kyushu islands.

*Acer mono* usually grows into a handsome tree of moderate size. It has a conspicuous, unfissured, smooth bark of a regular yellow-gray color. This bark is one of the best characteristics of this species. The leaves are not unlike those of *A. cappadocicum,* but the lobes are shorter and broader. In fact, the leaves are very variable, and it is impossible to identify a tree only from a couple of leaves. The wings of its fruits are usually underdeveloped. *Acer mono* is easily confused with its nearest relative, *A. cappadocicum,* and sometimes even with *A. platanoides.* The latter has sharply pointed lateral lobules on the lobes, which are absent in *A. mono.* Furthermore, the samaras of *A. platanoides* are usually larger.

This species is readily propagated from seed. European seed can be rather poor, but Chinese seed germinates if still fresh. Seed from botanical gardens is often the result of hybridization. Grafting on *Acer platanoides* is a good means for maintaining "true" types and for propagating cultivars.

*Acer mono* is found regularly in collections, but it is not always properly labeled since it is not always easily recognized. Some variants, like forma *ambiguum,* have a rough bark, and leaves, densely pubescent beneath, with large central lobes and entire margins.

Subspecies *mayrii* is a very rare maple with almost rounded leaves of a thin texture and entirely glabrous. It grows only in Japan and is restricted to regions with a heavy snowfall.

*Acer mono* var. *savatieri* is so similar to subspecies *mono* that it must be synonymous.

Kitamura and Murata (1972) published three new names: (1) *A. mono* var. *marmoratum* (Nicholson) Kitamura, considered in the present volume to be merely a cultivar of *A. truncatum* (see *A. truncatum* 'Akikaze' in Chapter 9); (2) *A. mono* ssp. *taishakuense* (Ogata) Kitamura, a taxon treated later by Ogata (1965a) as a variety, differing mainly in its leaves, which are pilose on the lower surfaces; and (3) *A. mono* ssp. *glaucum* (Koidzumi) Kitamura, treated as a form by Koidzumi (1911) and Murray (1970c) and not distinct enough for subspecific or varietal rank in the present volume.

Dr. D. O. Wijnands, director of the Botanical Gardens of the Agricultural University, Wageningen, The Netherlands, has researched the intriguing, if not mystifying, series of events, publications, misinterpretations, and misidentifications surrounding the usage of the names *Acer mono, A. pictum, Kalopanax pictus,* and *K. septemlobus.* His definitive analysis and resolution of the taxonomic and nomenclatural problems between *A. mono* and *Kalopanax septemlobus* is given in Appendix 4.

SECTION: *Platanoidea*

ACER MONO ssp. OKAMOTOANUM (Nakai) de Jong, comb. & stat. nov.

BASIONYM: *A. okamotoanum* Nakai, in Bot. Mag. Tokyo 31:28.1917.

SYNONYM: *A. okamotoi* Nakai (1915), pro parte excl. partim *A. pseudosieboldiano.*

TYPES: *T. Nakai,* Ullung-do, South Korea; holotype TNS; isotype K.

EPITHET: *Okamotoanus,* derived from the old name for the South Korean island now known as Ullung-do.

ILLUSTRATION: Plate 104.

HABIT: A tree to 10–12 m tall, with a flat-topped crown.

LEAVES: 5- to 7-lobed, 12–15 cm across, broadly ovate, dull green above and light green beneath, reticulate; bases cordate; lobes short, abruptly acuminate; margins entire or nearly so.

FLOWERS: Not seen.

FRUITS: Wings usually connivent, rarely spreading at a right angle, 3.5–4.5 cm long; nutlets flat.

BARK AND BUDS: Bark grayish brown, trunk smooth; buds small, dark brown, enclosed by petiole bases.

HARDINESS: Zones VI–VII.

DISTRIBUTION: Ullung-do, a South Korean island in the Japanese sea. Very rare in nature; some 15 trees were growing on a slope at the northern side of the island.

REFERENCES: Lee (1979), Murray (1970c).

This maple was described in 1917 by Nakai and introduced to Great Britain in 1982 by J. G. S. Harris.

It is endemic to Ullung-do, an island on the upper eastern side of South Korea. Wilson visited the island with Nakai in 1917, but does not appear to have collected seed. The first seeds

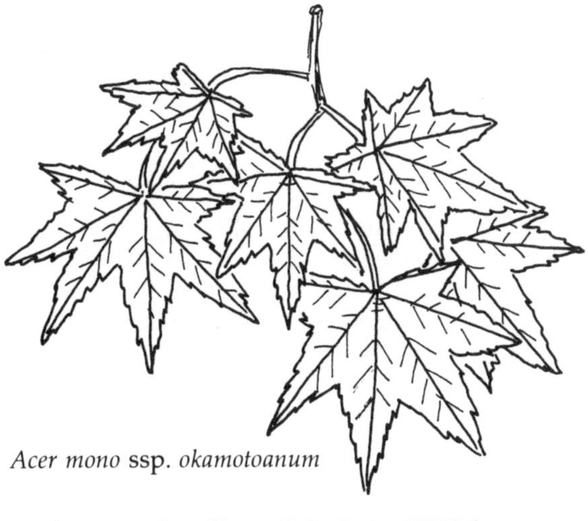

*Acer mono* ssp. *okamotoanum*

were imported to Great Britain in 1980, but none germinated. Scions received in Great Britain from South Korea were grafted on *Acer platanoides*, but failed. Three scions grafted to *A. palmatum* took for a short period, but only one has survived and apparently has its own roots. Harris collected substantial quantities of seed on Ullung-do, but only two plants have survived. Seeds sown at the Royal Botanic Gardens, Kew, Great Britain, from the same collection all failed. This maple appears to have a long "after ripening" period, in contrast to 95 percent (or more) of the other *Acer* species. This characteristic presents difficulties in germination, although there may be many seedlings around the mother trees in the wild. The tree has not been seen in flower.

There is some confusion in the herbarium material of *Acer mono* ssp. *okamotoanum*, which seems to be mixed up with *A. pseudosieboldianum*, a significantly different species. Murray (1970) suggests a strong affinity to *A. truncatum*, which is understandable since he does not recognize *A. mono* as a species but places it as a subspecies of *A. truncatum*.

It is possible to graft this subspecies on seedlings of *Acer mono* or *A. platanoides*. The time of grafting (September) is important as subspecies *okamotoanum* and several other species and cultivars having milky sap earlier in the growing season are difficult to bud when the wood is not ripe.

In 1915 Nakai described a species called *Acer okamotoi* from Ullung-do. The material on which he based this species was mixed with *A. pseudosieboldianum*, which also occurs on Ullung-do. In 1917 Nakai recognized this 1915 error and provided a new name, *A. okamotoanum*, for the part that was not *A. pseudosieboldianum*. However, the synonymy must be completed by adding *Acer okainotoi* Nakai (1915), pro parte, excl. partim *A. pseudosieboldiano*.

SECTION: *Platanoidea*

## ACER MONO var. MAYRII (Schwerin) Nakai (1930)

BASIONYM: *A. mayrii* Schwerin (1901).

SYNONYMS

*A. pictum* var. *mayrii* (Schwerin) Koidzumi (1911).
*A. mono* var. *eupictum* (Pax) Takizawa (1952).
*A. mono* var. *glabrum* (Léveillé & Vaniot) Hara (1954).
*A. truncatum* ssp. *mayrii* (Schwerin) Murray (1969).
*A. cappadocicum* var. *mayrii* (Schwerin) Murray (1977).

TYPES: *H. Mayr, July 1886*, Hokkaido, Japan; isotype A.

COMMON NAMES: Aka itaya, Futa goyama, Sugi moto.

EPITHET: *Mayrii*, after H. Mayr (1865–1911), professor of forestry at the University of Munich, Germany.

ILLUSTRATIONS: Kurata (1964–1976), Satake et al. (1989).

HABIT: A tree or large shrub to 10 m tall, occasionally to 25 m tall in native habitat; branches glabrous to glaucous, later gray to reddish brown.

LEAVES: Mostly 5-lobed, usually without lobules, almost round, thin textured, broadly ovate, green on both sides, entirely glabrous; margins entire; petioles long and glabrous.

FLOWERS: Andromonoecious, greenish white, on corymbs 4–6 cm long, appearing in April–May.

FRUITS: Samaras erect to connivent, 1 cm long, wings small; nutlets flattened.

HARDINESS: Zone V.

AUTUMN COLOR: Yellow.

CHROMOSOME NUMBER: $2n = 26$ (Darlington 1955).

DISTRIBUTION: Northern Japan and Sachalin. Discovered by H. Mayr in 1886 on Hokkaido, restricted to mountainous regions with heavy snowfall.

REFERENCES: Bean (1970), Elwes & Henry (1908), Koidzumi (1911), Krüssmann (1976a), Kurata (1964–1976), Murray (1970c, 1977), Nakai (1932), Rehder (1986 facs.), Schwerin (1901).

*Acer mono* var. *mayrii*

*Acer mono* f. *ambiguum*

SECTION: *Platanoidea*

ACER MONO f. AMBIGUUM (Dippel) Rehder (1939)

BASIONYM: *A. ambiguum* Dippel (1892).

SYNONYMS

*A. pictum* var. *ambiguum* (Dippel) Pax (1893).

*A. dippelii* Schwerin (1893).

TYPE: Apparently there are no extant original specimens. The whereabouts of Dippel's herbarium and type specimens, if they existed at all, are totally unknown.

COMMON NAME: Oni itaya.

EPITHET: *Ambiguus,* doubtful.

ILLUSTRATIONS: Krüssmann (1970c), Kurata (1964–1976).

HABIT: A tree or shrub to 20 m tall with glabrous branches.

LEAVES: 5-lobed, 9–14 cm wide, undersides glaucous; shortly pubescent central lobes much larger than lateral lobes; margins entire.

FLOWERS: Greenish yellow, on short corymbs appearing with the leaves.

FRUITS: Samaras underdeveloped, yellow-brown when mature, nearly erect to ascending; nutlets flat.

BARK AND BUDS: Bark rough, unlike that of *A. mono* ssp. *mono.*

HARDINESS: Zone V.

AUTUMN COLOR: Yellow.

DISTRIBUTION: Japan, widely distributed from Hokkaido through Honshu and Shikoku, forming forests along mountain streams together with *Pterocarya rhoifolia, Aesculus turbinata,* and *Fraxinus* species.

REFERENCES: Dippel (1892), Krüssmann (1976a), Kurata (1964–1976), Murray (1970c), Ogata 1965), Rehder (1986 facs.).

One of the original introductions of the forma bearing this name into the United States is at the Brooklyn Botanic Garden in New York. It has a smooth gray bark. It is possible that this tree is not the true species, does not represent forma *ambiguum,* and has been incorrectly identified for years.

*Acer mono* f. *ambiguum* is widespread and very closely related to subspecies *mono.* It mainly differs in the texture of the bark: subspecies *mono* has smooth bark while forma *ambiguum* has rough bark.

Pax (1901) makes the following observation under *Acer ambiguum* Dippel: "Angeblich aus Ostasien [Japan] stammend, von englischen Baumschulen verbreitet und bisher noch seltene Form; vielleicht nur Kulturform und nicht eigene Art?" This observation provides some evidence that perhaps forma *ambiguum* might well be treated as a cultivar, and trees in the wild are *A. mono* ssp. *mono.*

SECTION: *Platanoidea*

ACER NAYONGENSE Fang (1979)

TYPES: *Pichi Exp., #580,* Naying Hsien, Chuzen Chu, Guizhou Province, China; holotype PE; isotype SH.

ILLUSTRATION: Fang (1981a).

HABIT: A tree to 15 m tall, similar to *A. longipes* ssp. *amplum.*

LEAVES: Inner leaves clearly 3-lobed, 8–12 cm long and 9–11 cm wide; outer leaves often unlobed, densely yellow pilose along veins, softly pubescent beneath.

FRUITS: Samaras 4.5–5 cm long, ovoid to oblong-lanceolate, wings spreading at an obtuse angle; nutlets 1–1.2 cm.

VARIETY: var. *hunanense* (Fang & W. K. Hu) Fang & W. K. Hu (1979), may be synonymous with *A. longipes.*

REFERENCES: Fang (1979a, 1981a).

Possibly this species may be put into the synonymy of *Acer longipes.* As no living or herbarium material is conveniently available, a decision cannot be made at this time.

*Acer nayongense*

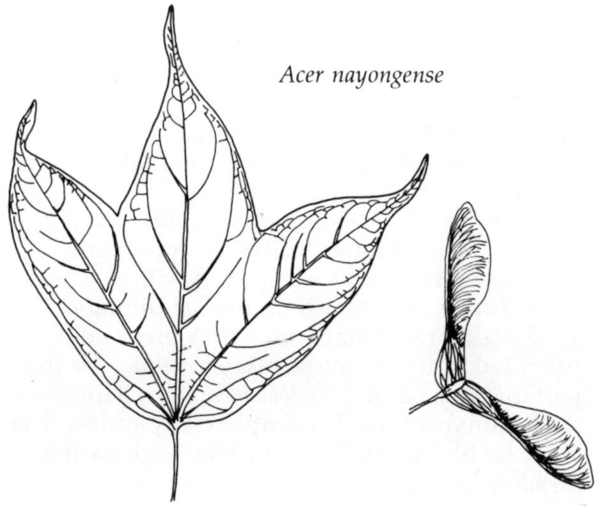

SECTION: *Platanoidea*
ACER PLATANOIDES L. (1753) ssp. PLATANOIDES
SYNONYMS
*A. platanifolium* Stokes (1812).
*A. lactescens* Steudel (1821).
*A. rotundum* Dulac (1867).
*A. laetum* var. *cordifolium* Kanitz (1880).
*A. dasyphyllum* Nicholson (1881).
*A. dobrudschae* Pax (1886).
*A. fallax* Pax (1886).
COMMON NAMES: Norway maple, Erable plane, lonn, lönn, Noorse esdoorn, Platanloenn, Spitzahorn.
TYPE: LINN #1225.11, "Habitat in Europa boreali."
EPITHET: *Platanoides,* like a *Platanus* (called plane tree or sycamore in different areas).
ILLUSTRATIONS: Plate 105; de Jong (1976), Krüssmann (1976a), Ottolander et al. (1879).
HABIT: A tree to 30 m tall and almost as wide, with a round crown; branches glabrous, green to brown, extremely variable.
LEAVES: 5-lobed, 10–25 cm across, upper sides shining green, undersides somewhat glistening, highly variable; lobes caudate, incised dentate and remotely serrate; vein axils hairy; bases hastate or subtruncate; petioles green, 6–20 cm long.
INFLORESCENCES: Corymbose, terminal, many-flowered.
FLOWERS: Yellow-cream, more or less erect, very spectacular; appearing in April before the leaves; cultivars with red leaves often bear reddish flowers.
FRUITS: Samaras 4–7 cm long, well developed; nutlets flat, triangular.
BARK AND BUDS: Bark black-brown, not very fissured, not peeling; bud scales few.
HARDINESS: Zones III–IV.
AUTUMN COLOR: Golden yellow to orange-red.
DISTRIBUTION: Across northern Europe: in Sweden and Norway as far as Tromsö (where tree's habit is shrubby); in Finland up to 62° latitude, in Belarus, Russia, and the Baltic States as far north as Lake Ladoga and as far south as the Crimea and Caucasus but not crossing the Urals; also occurring in the central European countries, but not found in the United Kingdom nor in the coastal countries of the continent, although widely cultivated there and in North America.
CHROMOSOME NUMBER: $2n = 26$ (Santamour 1965); $2n = 26$ and $2n = 39$ (Darlington 1955).
SUBSPECIES
ssp. *platanoides,* the typical subspecies.
ssp. *turkestanicum* (Pax) de Jong, comb. & stat. nov.
CULTIVARS: Many (see Chapter 9).
REFERENCES: Bean (1970), Dippel (1892), Elwes & Henry (1908), de Jong (1976), Koch (1869), Krüssmann (1976a), Linnaeus (19753), Murray (1970c), Ottolander et al. (1979), Pax (1902), Pojárkova (1933b), Rehder (1986 facs.).

*Acer platanoides* is one of the few European species in this section. It is widely known and has been in cultivation for centuries. Linnaeus described it in *Species Plantarum* (1753).

There are two subspecies, but in earlier days a number of geographical and morphological variants were described by various authors. All these names have been reduced to synonymy.

It cannot readily be confused with any other maples. Its closest relatives are *Acer cappadocicum* and *A. mono,* neither of which have lobulate lobes as in *A. platanoides.* The milky sap distinguishes *A. platanoides* from all other maples, except for relatives in section *Platanoides* and series *Macrophylla* of section *Lithocarpa.*

*Acer platanoides* ssp. *turkestanicum* from Turkestan and Afghanistan is somewhat similar but diagnostically different from its closest relative, subspecies *platanoides,* and very rare. The two subspecies occur together in the Crimea and the Caucasus.

*Acer platanoides* grows to a mighty tree with very handsome 5-lobed leaves with remotely but sharply pointed lobes. It can be found in practically every town and village in Europe planted as street or shade trees. It is readily propagated from seed and is the best understock for all its cultivars and some species of the same section.

Numerous selections with green, purple, or brown leaves have been developed for ornamental purposes, particularly in North America (see Chapter 9).

SECTION: *Platanoidea*
ACER PLATANOIDES ssp. TURKESTANICUM (Pax) de Jong, comb. nov. & stat. nov.
BASIONYM: *A. turkestanicum* Pax, in Engler, Das Pflanzenreich *8:*49.1902.
SYNONYMS
*A. lobelii* Bunge (1847), non Tenore.
*A. laetum* var. *regelii* Pax (1902).
*A. lipskyi* Rehder ex Lipsky (1911).
*A. pseudo-laetum* Radde-Fomin (1932).
*A. cappadocicum* ssp. *turkestanicum* (Pax) Murray (1977).
TYPES: *Regel 1884,* mountain woods near Mumynawad, Turkestan, holotype LE; isotypes A; BM.
EPITHET: *Turkestanicus,* from Turkestan.
ILLUSTRATION: Plate 106.
HABIT: A tree similar to subspecies *platanoides* but smaller, to 15 m tall; branches fulvous, glabrous, with reddish brown branchlets, covered with very fine glands when young.
LEAVES: 5- to 7-lobed, occasionally 3-lobed, 10–25

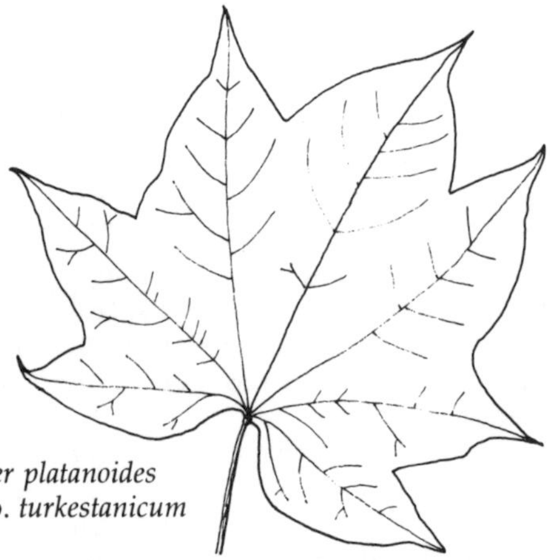

Acer platanoides ssp. turkestanicum

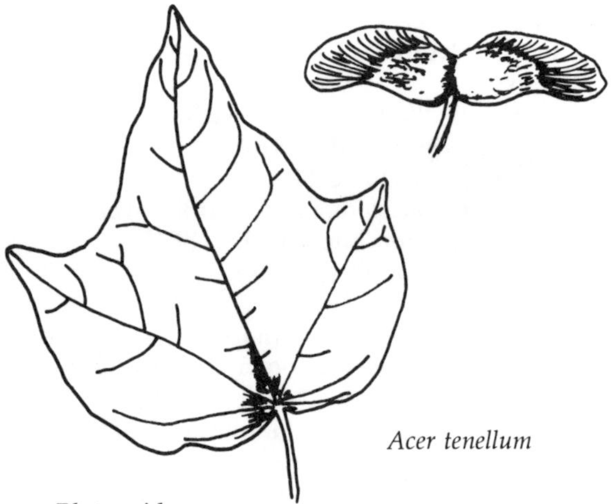

Acer tenellum

cm across; lobes acuminate, triangular; margins entire; bases cordate; blades thick textured, borne on short spurs; vein axils tufted beneath; petioles 5–12 cm long.

INFLORESCENCES: Corymbose, terminal, erect.

FLOWERS: Yellow-green, 10–15 mm across, with purple discs.

FRUITS: Samaras 2.5–5 cm long, broadly falcate or nearly at a right angle, on short corymbs; nutlets flat.

BARK AND BUDS: Bark gray.

HARDINESS: Zone V.

DISTRIBUTION: Northeast Afghanistan and Turkestan, in mountain forests, especially on the plateaus of Tien-shan and Pamu-Alai.

REFERENCES: Krüssmann (1976a), Murray (1970c, 1977), Pojárkova (1933b), Pax (1902).

This is a rather large tree, very similar to subspecies *platanoides;* it bears 5- to 7-lobed leaves, of the same shape but of a thicker texture. From time to time 3-lobed leaves are found on short branches.

This taxon is placed as a subspecies under *Acer platanoides* for the first time, and it may even be synonymous with *A. platanoides,* though this conclusion is not yet supported by sufficient material or conclusive comparisons. It is based on a study of the herbarium material, additional to the type, in K and P. These studies should be continued. Several taxonomists have already reduced *A. platanoides* ssp. *turkestanicum* to varietal rank under *A. cappadocicum* and *A. cappadocicum* ssp. *lobelii.* It is, in fact, much closer to *A. platanoides.*

*Acer platanoides* ssp. *turkestanicum* is quite rare in cultivation, and little living or herbarium material is available. Propagation by seed is possible; otherwise, summer grafting of budding is a good means. Seedling material has been distributed by the Botanic Gardens of the University of Utrecht, The Netherlands, and a few clones have been selected. No cultivar names have been given.

SECTION: *Platanoidea*

## ACER TENELLUM Pax (1889)

SYNONYM: *A. cappadocicum* var. *rotundilobum* Murray (1977), pro parte.

TYPE: Isotypes *A. Henry #5612,* Sichuan Province, China; BM; K; P.

EPITHET: *Tenellus,* delicate, fine in texture.

ILLUSTRATIONS: Plate 107; Fang (1981a), Pax (1902).

HABIT: A small tree or large shrub to 8 m tall; much branched; branches yellowish gray and rather thin.

LEAVES: 5–10 cm across, 3-lobed, side lobes short or even absent on small leaves, shining green on the upper sides, thin, papery; bases cordate; petioles long. The leaves frequently "tremble" in a breeze like those of *Populus tremula* and *P. tremuloides.*

FRUITS: Samaras small; nutlets flat.

BARK AND BUDS: Bark much like that of *A. mono.*

HARDINESS: Zones VI–VIII.

AUTUMN COLOR: Yellow.

DISTRIBUTION: Central China, Yunnan, Sichuan, and Jiangxi provinces, China.

VARIETY: var. *septemlobum* (Fang & Soong) Fang & Soong (1979), with 7-lobed leaves; from Sichuan Province, China; synonym is *A. mono* f. *septemlobum* Fang & Soong (1966). According to Fang (1981a, p. 93), Murray suggested that this variety might belong to *A. cappadocicum* ssp. *sinicum.*

REFERENCES: Bean (1970), Fang (1981a), Krüssmann (1976a), Murray (1970c, 1978a), Pax (1902), Rehder (1968 facs.), Schneider (1912).

This very rare maple was discovered by A. Henry in 1885, described by Pax in 1889 from Sichuan Province, China, and introduced by Wilson in 1901. It can be found in a few gardens in both Great Britain and North America. A good specimen can be found at Borde Hill Gardens in Great Britain incorrectly identified as *Acer mono* var. *tricuspis* (a synonym for *A. cappadocicum* ssp. *sinicum* var. *tricaudatum*).

*Acer tenellum* var. *septemlobum*

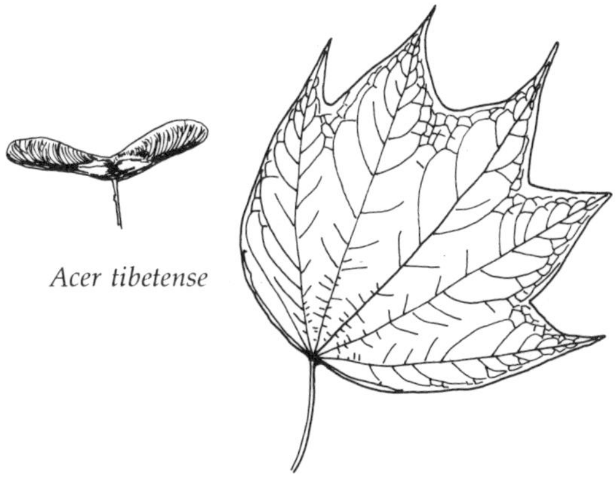

*Acer tibetense*

*Acer tenellum* has small leaves—usually 3-lobed, sometimes 5-lobed or remotely so—and is closely allied to *A. mono,* differing mainly in the size of its leaves. The flowers, having hairy petals, are not like those of *Acer mono.*

As this species is very unusual, it is only occasionally available in the trade. Seed is rarely available, so cuttings are grafted on seedlings of *A. cappadocicum, A. mono,* or *A. platanoides.*

Some authors consider *Acer tenellum* a synonym of *A. cappadocicum* ssp. *sinicum* var. *tricaudatum* (Veitch ex Rehder) Rehder (1914). However, specimens of that variety in cultivation differ greatly from *A. tenellum* as grown in Glasnevin Botanic Garden, Ireland, and elsewhere.

SECTION: *Platanoidea*
ACER TIBETENSE Fang (1939)

TYPES: *F. Kingdon-Ward 10368,* Tibet; holotype BM; isotypes E; MOAR; K.
EPITHET: *Tibetensis,* from Tibet.
ILLUSTRATION: Fang (1979a, 1981a).
HABIT: A tree with purplish to gray branches.
LEAVES: 5-lobed, 5–12 cm across, lobes ovate, caudate-acuminate, basal lobes tend to curve towards the central lobes, dark green above, yellow-gray beneath; margins entire; bases rounded; apices tomentose; petioles 5–8 cm long.
INFLORESCENCES: Corymbose, terminal.
FLOWERS: Green to yellow.
FRUITS: Samaras 2–5 cm long, wings subhorizontal.
BARK AND BUDS: Bud scales few.
HARDINESS: Zone V (?).
DISTRIBUTION: Southeastern Xizang Province, China (formerly called Tibet).
REFERENCES: Fang (1979a, 1981a), Krüssmann (1976a), Murray (1970c).

*Acer tibetense* is a tree with 5-lobed leaves that are 5–12 cm across. There are no records of living specimens in Western arboreta. A native of southeastern Tibet, this species is found in the Rangto Valley and Zayul. This taxon may at a later date become a synonym of *A. longipes.*

SECTION: *Platanoidea*
ACER TRUNCATUM Bunge (1833)

SYNONYMS
*A. pictum* sensu auct. non Thunberg.
*A. laetum* var. *truncatum* (Bunge) Regel (1857).
*A. truncatum* 'Pictum' Siebold (1864).
*A. lobelii* var. *truncatum* (Bunge) Wesmael (1890).
*A. platanoides* var. *truncatum* (Bunge) Gams (1925).
*A. lobulatum* Nakai (1942).

TYPES: *Bunge,* northern China; isotype K; holotype LE.
EPITHET: *Truncatus,* truncate—referring to the shape of the leaf base.
COMMON NAMES: Purpleblow maple, Akajika itaya, Mansen itaya, Shantung maple.
ILLUSTRATIONS: Plates 108, 109; Fang (1981a), Krüssmann (1976a).
HABIT: A small tree to 8–10 m tall, often with twisted branches densely packed together; branches green to purplish or yellow-gray, glabrous, long, slender.
LEAVES: 5- to 7-lobed, somewhat wavy, 6–10 cm across, young leaves often with purplish overtone but later turning olive-green with some purple at the margins; lobes ovate to triangular; apices acuminate; margins almost entire to lobulate; bases cordate or truncate; vein axils tufted beneath; petioles 5–8 cm long.
INFLORESCENCES: Corymbose, terminal.
FLOWERS: Yellow-green, appearing after the leaves in May.
FRUITS: Samaras 3–4 cm long, obtuse, rarely connivent.
BARK AND BUDS: Bark very rough and fissured, more so than on any other maple.
HARDINESS: Zone V.
AUTUMN COLOR: Yellow.
DISTRIBUTION: Northern China as a forest tree; also Amur, Sakhalin, Japan, Korea, Manchuria.
CHROMOSOME NUMBER: $2n = 26$ (Santamour 1971).
VARIETY: var. *paxii* (Schwerin) Murray (1969), leaves pubescent beneath.
CULTIVARS: A few (see Chapter 9).

REFERENCES: Bean (1970), Dippel (1892), Elwes & Henry (1908), Fang (1981a), Krüssmann (1976a), Murray (1970c, 1977), Rehder (1986 facs.), Vertrees (1978, 1987).

*Acer truncatum* is rather abundant in northern China, but rare in Western gardens. Bretschneider introduced it from China to the Royal Botanic Gardens, Kew, Great Britain, in 1881, long after the description by Bunge was made in 1833.

As this species is somewhat difficult to place taxonomically, there are several synonyms and numerous different combinations of names. It has been placed under several species by various authors, but it should be maintained as a distinct species.

Murray considers *Acer truncatum* as the central species of its group, with *A. mono* placed as a subspecies. This classification is not accepted in the present volume. Young seedlings from Chinese seed are much like *A. mono,* but develop differently with age. The trunk of *A. truncatum* is very markedly fissured; this is never the case with *A. mono.*

*Acer truncatum* tends to grow as a shrub in western European climatic conditions. The branches are densely crowded, and young shoots may grow very vigorously. The leaves are of the same shape as those of *A. mono* or *A. cappadocicum,* to which the species is closely related. The leaves of *A. mono* are generally larger and have more truncate bases, while those of *A. cappadocicum* have longer, more acuminate lobes. One of the specific features of *A. truncatum* is that it develops cotyledons under the soil surface, something no other related *Acer* species does. The first things to be seen are the true leaves.

*Acer truncatum* can be grafted on *A. platanoides* if no seed is available.

One of the main avenues in Beijing, China, is planted with splendid trees of this species, which are also found throughout some cities in Shandong and Shaanxi provinces.

## SECTION PUBESCENTIA (Pojárkova) Ogata

TYPE SPECIES: ***Acer pentapomicum*** Stewart ex Brandis (1874).

LEAVES: 3-lobed, somewhat coriaceous, glaucous beneath; margins coarsely serrate; petioles not lactiferous.

BUD SCALES: 6- to 10-paired.

INFLORESCENCES: Terminal or axillary, then partly arising from leafless buds.

FLOWERS: Petals somewhat involuted; stamens mostly 5.

SPECIES

*A. pentapomicum* Stewart ex Brandis (1874).

*A. pilosum* Maximowicz (1880).

REFERENCE: De Jong (1976).

To date only two species are placed in this section, and it is possible they may be merged when more material becomes available and type specimens are studied. Both species lack milky sap in the petioles. They are distributed throughout western Asia and China, but are very rare in cultivation and are poorly known.

SECTION: *Pubescentia*

### ACER PENTAPOMICUM Stewart ex Brandis (1874)

SYNONYMS

*A. pubescens* Franchet (1833).

*A. monspessulanum* var. *turkestanicum* Franchet (1883).

*A. monspessulanum* ssp. *pubescens* (Franchet) Wesmael (1890).

*A. monspessulanum* var. *crenatum* Regel ex Komarov (1896).

*A. regelii* Pax (1902).

*A. fedtschenkoanum* Khrishtofovich (1914).

TYPE: Syntypes *J. L. Stewart 541,* Huzara; *J. L. Stewart 648,* Jhelum Valley, West Pakistan; K.

EPITHET: *Pentapomicus,* original author's misspelling for *pentapotamicus,* meaning Five Rivers.

ILLUSTRATIONS: Plates 110, 111; Murray (1975a), Pax (1902).

HABIT: A shrub or rarely a small tree; branches brown to gray, juvenile branches glabrous, often looking like small, gnarled, shrubby trees.

LEAVES: 3-lobed, thick, very variable, 3–10 cm long and even wider but mostly much smaller, gray-green; margins coarsely serrate; bases subcordate; lobes about half the length of blades; petioles 3–7 cm long.

INFLORESCENCES: Corymbose, terminal; lateral inflorescences occur on leafless, abbreviated shoots.

FLOWERS: 5-merous, yellowish.

FRUITS: Samaras 2.5 cm long, erect; nutlets convex, quite often parthenocarpic.

BARK AND BUDS: Bud scales few.

HARDINESS: Zones V–VI.

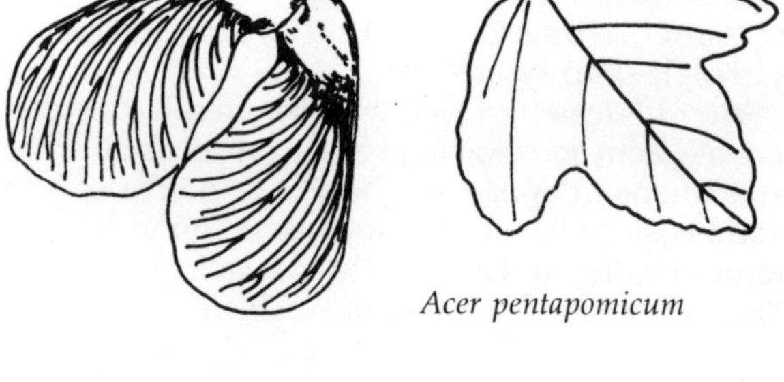

*Acer pentapomicum*

AUTUMN COLOR: Yellow to golden brown.
DISTRIBUTION: Northwest Himalayas, Kashmir, Afghanistan, Turkestan, West Pakistan in dry situations on lower mountains in river basins, growing together with *Juniperus* spp.
CHROMOSOME NUMBER: $2n = 26$ (Santamour 1988)
REFERENCES: Bean (1970), Krüssmann (1976a), Murray (1970c, 1977), Pax (1902), Pojárkova (1933b), Schneider (1912).

*Acer pentapomicum* is a very rare maple, almost never seen in collections in the Western world. It is rather variable, so several names of geographic species are now considered synonymous (*A. pubescens* Franchet, *A. regelii* Pax, *A. fedschenkoanum* Khrishtofovich ).

In Bean (1970) the species name is misspelled as *Acer pentapotamicum.* Desmond Clarke, who was responsible for the nomenclature of *Acer* in that work, indicated that he changed the name to *pentapotamicum* on the "supposition" that the specific epithet indicated its occurrence in the "Five Rivers" area. Brandis (1874) nowhere indicates the derivation of the epithet (which he uses five times in the original publication, as well as later in his book on Indian trees). There is no basis in the ICBN for making such a change. Clarke's conclusion is nice, neat, and almost persuasive, but it is pure speculation with no foundation in fact.

As *Acer pentapomicum* is so rare in collections, it is subsequently rare in the trade. Occasionally seed can be obtained from the wild, but germination has always been very poor. There is a correctly named specimen in the Esveld Aceretum, Boskoop, The Netherlands.

SECTION: *Pubescentia*
ACER PILOSUM Maximowicz (1880)
TYPES: *Piasezki 1876, Ningxia Huizu,* Gansu. In Maximowicz 1880. Province, China; holotype LE; isotypes A, K, MO.
EPITHET: *Pilosus,* with soft hairs.
ILLUSTRATION: Maximowicz (1880).
HABIT: A small tree 6–9 m tall, with thin, reddish or brown-gray branches.
LEAVES: 3-lobed, 4–10 cm wide, subcordate at the bases; lobes oblong-lanceolate, 2.5 cm wide; margins remotely denticulate; middle lobes much longer than laterals, and almost parallel, leathery, dark green above and glaucous beneath; veins pilose beneath; petioles 3–6 cm long, red and pubescent.
INFLORESCENCES: Corymbose, lateral, few-flowered.
FLOWERS: Yellow-green, small.
FRUITS: Samaras small, about 1 cm long, wings ascendant; nutlets pilose and impressed at one side.
HARDINESS: Zone V.

*Acer pilosum*

DISTRIBUTION: Jiangxi, Shaanxi, and Gansu provinces, China.
VARIETIES
- var. *megalophyllum* Fang & Wu (1979), all plant parts larger.
- var. *pilosum,* the typical variety.
- var. *stenolobum* (Rehder) Fang (1966), leaf lobes very short, 0.5 cm wide; basionym is *A. stenolobum* Rehder (1922).

REFERENCES: Fang (1981a), de Jong (1976), Maximowicz (1880), Murray (1970c), Ogata (1967), Pax (1902), Rehder (1986 facs.).

*Acer pilosum* was discovered by Piasezki in 1876 and introduced to the Arnold Arboretum in 1911. There are only two known living specimens in North American arboreta: one at the Arnold Arboretum, the other at the University of Washington Arboretum in Seattle. The latter is labeled *A. regelii* (syn. *A. pentapomicum*), but differs from that species by having less leathery leaves.

## SECTION GINNALA Nakai

TYPE SPECIES: ***Acer ginnala*** Maxim. (1857) (syn. *A. tataricum* ssp. *ginnala* [Maximowicz] Wesmael [1890]).
HABIT: Deciduous shrubs or small trees.
LEAVES: Undivided or 3-lobed, chartaceous; margins serrate.
BUD SCALES: 5- to 10-paired, gray-brown.
INFLORESCENCES: Corymbose, terminal and axillary; bracts distinct.
FLOWERS: 5-merous; perianths greenish white, somewhat involute during anthesis, which occurs after leaves unfold; stamens 8; discs extrastaminal.
FRUITS: Nutlets rather flat, elliptic, strongly veined.
SEEDLINGS: Cotyledons small, elliptic.
SPECIES AND INFRASPECIFIC TAXA
- *A. tataricum* ssp. *aidzuense* (Franchet) de Jong, comb. & stat. nov.
- *A. tataricum* ssp. *ginnala* (Maximowicz) Wesmael (1890).

*A. tataricum* ssp. *semenovii* (Regel & Herder) Murray (1982).
*A. tataricum* L. ssp. *tataricum.*

REFERENCE: De Jong (1976).

This is a rather primitive section without clear relationships. Somewhat related are section *Acer* and series *Trifida* of section *Pentaphyllum.*

Section *Ginnala* is monotypic and includes only one species with four subspecies. All are large Asiatic or European shrubs; occasionally they are trees. The leaves are deciduous, sometimes unlobed. These taxa are too closely related to maintain their specific rank. They are all in cultivation and are useful garden plants.

SECTION: *Ginnala*

ACER TATARICUM ssp. AIDZUENSE (Franchet) de Jong, comb. & stat. nov.

BASIONYM: *A. tataricum* var. *aidzuense* Franchet, Bull. Soc. Bot. France 26:84.1879.

SYNONYMS

*A. ginnala* var. *aidzuense* (Franchet) Pax (1886).
*A. ginnala* var. *yezoense* Koidzumi (1911).
*A. subintegrum* Pojárkova (1933).
*A. aidzuense* (Franchet) Nakai (1935).

TYPE: *Faurie,* Aidzu, Honshu, Japan; P.

COMMON NAME: Karakogi kaede.

EPITHET: *Aidzuensis,* from Aidzue prefecture, Honshu, Japan.

ILLUSTRATION: Plate 112.

HABIT: A large treelike shrub to 10 m tall and as wide, with dense branching; young branches light brown to reddish.

LEAVES: Remotely 3-lobed or almost unlobed, pubescent beneath, fresh green, thin textured, 4–7 cm long and 3–5 cm wide, with no trace of variegation; petioles 2–3 cm long, green.

INFLORESCENCES: Rather short, corymbose.

FLOWERS: Whitish.

FRUITS: Samaras 2–3 cm long, turning brown late, wings parallel; nutlets crinkled.

BARK AND BUDS: Older bark slightly rough.

HARDINESS: Zone IV.

AUTUMN COLOR: Yellow to crimson dotted with yellow.

DISTRIBUTION: Japan, Hokkaido through Honshu and Shikoku, to Kyushu; but not extending to the Kuriles or Sachalin.

REFERENCES: Krüssmann (1976a), Murray (1970c), Ogata (1965, 1967).

*Acer tataricum* ssp. *aidzuense* was described by Franchet in 1879 as a variety of *A. tataricum.* In 1886 Pax placed it under *A. ginnala,* again as a variety. Pojárkova redescribed it, based on a different type, as *A. subintegrum* in 1933. Nakai gave it full specific rank, as *A. aidzuense,* in 1935.

It is closely related to *Acer tataricum* ssp. *tataricum* and subspecies *ginnala,* as evidenced by the nomenclatural confusion. It is intermediate in its morphological characteristics; the leaves are almost unlobed, and the apices not as acuminate as is generally true in subspecies *ginnala.*

The fruits are green with reddish samaras, not browning as early as those of subspecies *tataricum.* Seedlings are remarkably uniform when grown from seed harvested from an isolated specimen.

This subspecies is quite rare in cultivation; a large plant growing in the Zuiderpark, The Hague, The Netherlands, was recently removed by unskilled personnel.

Vegetative propagation is easily accomplished by grafting on *Acer tataricum* ssp. *ginnala* as understock.

SECTION: *Ginnala*

ACER TATARICUM ssp. GINNALA (Maximowicz) Wesmael (1890)

BASIONYM: *A. ginnala* Maximowicz (1857).

SYNONYMS

*A. acinatum* Siebert & Voss (1894).
*A. theiferum* Fang (1966).
*A. ginnala* ssp. *theiferum* (Fang) Fang (1979).

TYPE: *K. J. Maximowicz,* Amur region of Manchuria, China; LE.

COMMON NAMES: Amur maple, Amur-Ahorn, Karakogi kaede.

EPITHET: *Ginnala,* local Amur name for this maple.

ILLUSTRATIONS: Plates 113, 114; Fang (1981a), de Jong (1976), Koidzumi (1911), Krüssmann (1976a), Kurata (1964–1976).

HABIT: A large shrub, occasionally a small tree or a two- to three-stemmed tree to 8–10 m tall; stems rather thin, glabrous, gray to green.

LEAVES: 3-lobed, 4–8 cm long and 3–6 cm wide, dark to dull green, sometimes mottled with white or pink; some unlobed leaves always present; central lobes always the longest; margins revolute crenulate underneath, glabrous, light green; petioles 2.5–5 cm long.

FLOWERS: 5-merous, creamy, in corymbs.

FRUITS: Samaras parallel, 2.5 cm long, connivent; wings often red.

BARK AND BUDS: Bark olive-gray; buds small, inconspicuous.

HARDINESS: Zone IV.

AUTUMN COLOR: Scarlet, dropping soon after coloring.

DISTRIBUTION: Northeastern and northern China, Manchuria, and North Korea; Japan on the islands of Honshu, Shikoku, and Kyushu.

CHROMOSOME NUMBER: $2n = 26$ (Darlington 1955).

CULTIVARS: Several (see Chapter 9).

REFERENCES: Bean (1970), Dippel (1892), Fang (1981a, as ssp. *theiferum*), de Jong (1976), Koch (1869), Koidzumi (1911), Krüssmann (1976a), Murray (1970c), Ogata (1965), Pax (1902), Rehder (1986 facs.), Veitch (1904).

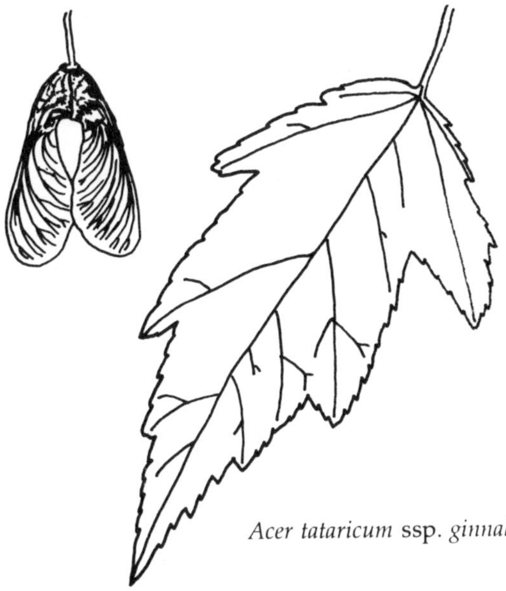

*Acer tataricum* ssp. *ginnala*

*Acer tataricum* ssp. *ginnala* was described (as *A. ginnala*) and introduced by Maximowicz in 1857 to St. Petersburg, Russia. "Ginnala" is the common name for this maple in Manchuria and northern China, hence it should be spelled "ginnala" and not "ginnale" as it sometimes appears.

It usually grows into a large shrub, to 8–10 m tall, but can also form an irregular tree. The leaves are 3-lobed, with some being unlobed, and there are almost always some white and pinkish variegated leaves. The autumn color can be very brilliant, depending upon the selection. The leaves drop soon after coloring. This subspecies can be confused only with subspecies *tataricum*, its nearest relative, which bears unlobed or remotely lobed leaves and never has the peculiar variegation. It is now a very common plant in parks and gardens and widely available in nurseries.

Fang recognizes a variety *theiferum* with unlobed leaves, which has been recently introduced to Europe. Still young, these vigorously growing plants tend to form 3-lobed leaves, so no conclusion can yet be reached as to whether adult trees will also bear unlobed leaves. The present volume does not recognize this variety and considers it to be synonymous with *A. tataricum* spp. *ginnala*.

A few cultivars, most with speckled and variegated leaves, are known but are not readily available. Some new cultivars have been selected for their brilliant autumn colors, such as 'Flame', 'Fire', and the dwarf shrub 'Durand Dwarf'. All these cultivars can easily be propagated by grafting on *ginnala* seedlings or by cuttings in summer.

SECTION: *Ginnala*
ACER TATARICUM ssp. SEMENOVII (Regel & Herder) Murray (1982)

BASIONYM: *A. semenovii* Regel & Herder (1866).

SYNONYMS

*A. ginnala* ssp. *semenovii* (Regel & Herder) Pax (1886).

*A. pusillum* Schwerin (1894).

TYPE: *N. Z. Semenov*, Almaty, Alatau, Uzbekistan; LE.

EPITHET: *Semenovii*, after Russian botanist N. Z. Semenova (1806–1860).

HABIT: A densely branched shrub to 4 m tall, closely related to *A. tataricum* ssp. *ginnala* but smaller; branches and twigs gray-brown.

LEAVES: 3- to 5-lobed, small, 2–3 cm long and 1–2 cm wide, shining green above, glaucous beneath, with no trace of variegation; margins serrate to lobulate; basal lobes large; bases subcordate; petioles 2–3 cm long.

INFLORESCENCES: Corymbose, terminal.

FLOWERS: Pale green.

FRUITS: Samaras connivent-acute, 2.5 cm long.

BARK AND BUDS: Buds small and sharply pointed.

HARDINESS: Zone IV.

AUTUMN COLOR: Yellow.

DISTRIBUTION: North Afghanistan, Bokhara, Uzbekistan; Turkestan, Tien-shan, in mountain forests in the Alatan and Ili areas of Kazachstan in dry, sunny situations, forming shrubby thickets.

REFERENCES: Bean (1970), Dippel (1892), Fang (1981a), Krüssmann (1976a), Murray (1970c, 1982b), Pojárkova (1933b), Rehder (1986 facs.), Schneider (1912), Schwerin (1894).

*Acer tataricum* ssp. *semenovii* is a close relative of both subspecies *tataricum* and subspecies *ginnala*. It was described by the German botanists Regel and Herder in 1866. Both Pax (1886) and Zabel

*Acer tataricum* ssp. *semenovii*

(1878) reduced this species under *A. ginnala* and *A. tataricum* respectively. It is, however, quite distinct and easily separated from both relatives in all morphological characteristics, as well as having much smaller leaves with no traces of variegation such as demonstrated by *A. tataricum* ssp. *ginnala.*

In this volume this plant is regarded as a subspecies of *Acer tataricum. Acer pusillum* Schwerin was thought to be a hybrid between *A. ginnala* and *A. monspessulanum;* it has now been brought under the synonymy of subspecies *semenovii.*

Subspecies *semenovii* grows as a very densely branched shrub. Its leaves are 2–3 cm long and 1–2 cm wide, sometimes slightly leathery. It is found primarily in arboreta; only a few nurseries carry it, as a collector's item.

SECTION: *Ginnala*

ACER TATARICUM L. (1753) ssp. TATARICUM

SYNONYMS

*A. tartaricum* Moench (1785).
*A. cordifolium* Moench (1794).
*A. tartarinum* Poiret (1823).

TYPE: LINN 1225.2, "Habitat in Tataria" Ukraine, Tatarstan.

COMMON NAMES: Tatarian maple, Tatarischer Ahorn.

EPITHET: *Tataricus,* from Tartaria (Tatary), an area in Linnaeus's time that included central Asia and European Russia east of the Don River.

ILLUSTRATIONS: Plates 115, 116; Krüssmann (1976a).

HABIT: A shrub or small tree, with crowded branches, reddish brown to gray-brown.

LEAVES: Unlobed to remotely lobulate but juvenile leaves may have three lobes, 5–10 cm long and almost as wide, broadly ovate; margins doubly serrate; bases subcordate; veins pubescent to nearly glabrescent; petioles 2–5 cm long.

INFLORESCENCES: Paniculate, terminal, erect, appearing with the leaves in May.

FLOWERS: Pale green to white.

FRUITS: Samaras 2 cm long; nutlets rounded and somewhat wrinkled; fruits borne in irregular panicles have red wings during July–August that turn brown as early as September.

BARK AND BUDS: Bark somewhat fissured; buds small and inconspicuous; bud scales few.

HARDINESS: Zone III.

AUTUMN COLOR: Red to brown-red (often absent, as leaves shrivel early in the fall).

DISTRIBUTION: Austria, Hungary, Serbia, Romania, the Caucasus, Ukraine, and Turkey, in sunny, dry situations as forest undergrowth and only occasionally as a solitary tree.

CHROMOSOME NUMBER: $2n = 26$ (Santamour 1971).

SUBSPECIES

ssp. *aidzuense* (Franchet) de Jong, comb. & stat. nov.
ssp. *ginnala* (Maximowicz) Wesmael (1890).
ssp. *semenovii* (Regel & Herder) Murray (1982).
ssp. *tataricum,* the typical subspecies.

VARIETIES

var. *slendzinskii* Raciborski (1888), fruits glabrescent, leaves unlobed.
var. *torminaloides* Pax (1886), leaves 3-lobed; from Russian and Turkish Armenia.

CULTIVARS: Several (see Chapter 9).

REFERENCES: Bean (1970), Elwes & Henry (1908), Koch (1869), Krüssmann (1970a), Linnaeus (1753), Murray (1970c), Pax (1902), Pojárkova (1933b), Schwerin (1900).

*Acer tataricum* is a well-known maple and one of the nine species Linnaeus (1753) described. It is a shrub or small, irregular tree with a densely branched crown and unlobed leaves, 5–10 cm long and almost as wide. Young, vigorous shoots often produce 3-lobed leaves.

This species can only be confused with Amur maple, *Acer tataricum* ssp. *ginnala,* which always has 3-lobed leaves with rather long, acuminate apices and quite often some variegation. These characteristics never occur in *A. tataricum* ssp. *tataricum.*

Currently *Acer tataricum* is considered a complex species, including all the species formerly distinguished in section *Ginnala,* each bearing a close resemblance in the reproductive organs. The vegetative organs, especially the leaves, are very variable. Trees within the natural distribution of subspecies *tataricum* can exhibit lobation of the leaves, while in central China, within the natural environment of subspecies *ginnala,* an unlobed taxon—formerly called *A. theiferum,* is now included as a synonym of subspecies *ginnala.*

Several botanists of the last century (e.g., Pax, Wesmael, Franchet) recognized the similarities within and among the components of this group. However, other botanists (e.g., Nakai, Rehder) treated these taxa at specific rank for many years.

Subspecies *tataricum* grows abundantly in Eastern Europe, from the Steiermark region of Austria through Hungary, Serbia and Romania to the Caucasus and Turkey, and also on Mount Elbrus in the Caucasus, the highest peak in Europe. The tree prefers sunny, dry situations in forest undergrowth, although from time to time it occurs as individuals. Schwerin (1900) reports that *Acer tataricum* is widespread from Odessa to the Crimea and that it has been planted on a large scale as a windbreak in the flat landscape, to provide protection against snowstorms and to retard the drifting of snow on roads and railways.

The species can readily be recognized by the

large clusters of seed, already brown in early September. If sown in October, seed germinates easily the following spring and consequently this plant is readily available in the nursery trade.

## SECTION RUBRA Pax

TYPE SPECIES: ***Acer rubrum*** L. (1753).

HABIT: Deciduous trees, with axillary buds accumulated on fertile shoots.
LEAVES: 3- to 5-lobed, glaucous beneath; margins serrate.
BUD SCALES: 4- to 7-paired, red.
INFLORESCENCES: Fasciculate-umbellate, mostly 5-flowered, axillary from leafless buds.
FLOWERS: 5-merous; perianths red, sometimes green-red; petals and discs sometimes wanting; sepals connate; stamens mostly 5; discs intrastaminal; anthesis before leaf development.
FRUITS: Nutlets small, somewhat convex or large and ovoid, ripening during early summer; parthenocarpic tendency low; seeds germinate immediately.
SEEDLINGS: Cotyledons thick, fleshy, and obovate, or thin and narrowly obovate.
SPECIES
*A. pycnanthum* K. Koch (1864).
*A. rubrum* L. (1753).
*A. saccharinum* L. (1753).
REFERENCE: De Jong (1976).

This is a highly specialized section with unclear relationships. Morphologically it has some similarities with sections *Glabra, Pubescentia,* and even *Hyptiocarpa* (lateral inflorescences, reduction of stamens, discs, seedlings—*Pubescentia*—and fruit—*Hyptiocarpa*).

Section *Rubra* includes three species, all large trees. Two species are endemic to North America, and one is from Japan. They bear 3- to 5-lobed leaves and flower very early. The fruits ripen in May. The North American species are valuable and well-known trees in horticulture; the Japanese species is rare in cultivation.

SECTION: *Rubra*

### ACER PYCNANTHUM K. Koch (1864)

SYNONYMS
*A. rubrum* Koidzumi (1911), non L.
*A. rubrum* var. *pycnanthum* (K. Koch) Makino (1912).
TYPES: *Ito Keisuke,* Japan; isotype L.
COMMON NAMES: Hana kaede, Hana no ki.
EPITHET: *Pycnanthus,* with densely clustered flowers.
ILLUSTRATIONS: Plate 117; Krüssmann (1976a), Kurata (1964–1976), Satake et al. (1989).
HABIT: A tree, much like *A. rubrum,* but usually smaller; branches reddish brown to gray-brown.
LEAVES: Shallowly 3-lobed, suborbicular to ovate, 3–8 cm across, glabrous, shining green above, glaucous beneath; bases subcordate; margins remotely serrate; petioles 3–5 cm long, often reddish.
INFLORESCENCES: Fasciculate, appearing before the leaves, more terminal than those of *A. rubrum,* although lateral inflorescences occur frequently.
FLOWERS: Red.
FRUITS: Samaras erect, 3 cm long, ripening very early in June or July.
BARK AND BUDS: Terminal buds larger than those of *A. rubrum.*
HARDINESS: Zone V.
AUTUMN COLOR: Yellow to red.
DISTRIBUTION: Mountains of Japan on Honshu, in wet places at 400–500 m. Restricted to, and rare in, small areas in Gifu and Nagano prefectures.
CHROMOSOME NUMBER: $2n = 78$, polyploid/hexaploid (Santamour 1965, 1975).
CULTIVARS: Two (see Chapter 9).
REFERENCES: Bean (1970), Krüssmann (1976a), Kurata (1964–1976), Murray (1970c), Ogata (1965, 1967), Rehder (1986 facs.), Vertrees (1978, 1987).

*Acer pycnanthum* is the Japanese counterpart of North American *A. rubrum.* These species can be difficult to separate, especially when the origin of the plants is unknown. They have the same general habit of growing into large trees, although *A. pycnanthum* is somewhat smaller. The leaves of *A. pycnanthum* are also somewhat smaller, more shallowly lobed and suborbicular.

The sites of these species are many thousands of kilometers apart, and it is remarkable that they show so much similarity in their reproductive organs. The flowers of both species are red, appearing just before the leaves and making a striking display. The fruit of both species is produced at the same time very early in the year. The seeds ripen in June/July and lose their viability rather quickly. *Acer pycnanthum* differs from *A. rubrum* in the number of chromosomes—$2n = 74$ for *A. pycnanthum* and $2n = 78$ (hexaploid) or 108 (octaploid), rarely 91 (heptaploid), for *A. rubrum.*

*Acer pycnanthum* grows on Honshu in Japan in wet places at low elevations, and is restricted to a small area in Gifu and Nagano prefectures, where it is rare. Ogata (1965) mentions that a few large specimens have been designated as "natural monuments" by the Japanese government.

*Acer pycnanthum* is largely of interest to the collector, as *A. rubrum* makes a better tree and often has superior autumn colors.

The fruits ripen very early, and must be harvested immediately and sown at once. As there are very few fruiting trees, it seems best to propagate vegetatively from well-documented and correctly identified trees. Grafting on *Acer rubrum* is possible and is practiced by a few specialized nurseries, making the species available from time to time. Most plants in cultivation are grown from an introduction made by J. G. S. Harris in 1971.

SECTION: *Rubra*

ACER RUBRUM L. (1753)

SYNONYMS

*A. carolinianum* Walter (1788).
*A. barbatum* Michaux (1803), pro parte.
*A. sanguineum* Spach (1834).
*Saccharodendron barbatum* (Michaux) Nieuwland (1914), pro parte.
*Rufacer rubrum* (L.) Small (1933).

TYPE: LINN 1225.7, collected by Peter Kalm, habitat in Virginia and Pennsylvania, USA.

COMMON NAMES: Red maple, Megasuri noki, Rode esdoorn, Rot-Ahorn.

ILLUSTRATIONS: Plates 118, 119; de Jong (1976), Krüssmann (1976a).

EPITHET: *Ruber,* red.

HABIT: A large tree with an open crown, to 40 m tall in native habitat, usually not over 20 m tall in cultivation outside of North America; branches brownish red to gray; first-year shoots brown-red.

LEAVES: 3- to 5-lobed, 6–10 cm long, often longer than wide, dark green above, silvery gray underneath, scarlet to orange in autumn; lobes triangular to ovate; margins crenate-serrate.

INFLORESCENCES: Fasciculate, lateral, appearing abundantly before the leaves, very striking.

FLOWERS: Red, monoecious or rarely dioecious.

FRUITS: Samaras erect to connivent, about 2.5 cm long, red when young, ripening in May–June, germinating immediately after falling.

BARK AND BUDS: Trunk rather smooth, not deeply fissured except on very old trees.

AUTUMN COLOR: Brilliant scarlet to orange.

DISTRIBUTION: Eastern United States as far north and west as central Canada and the Dakotas, south to Florida, Texas, and New Mexico; grows on acid soil in moist situations.

CHROMOSOME NUMBER: $2n = 78$; rarely 91 or 108 (hexaploid, septuploid, or octoploid) (Santamour 1965); $F_1$ infraspecific hybrids: $2n =$ 78–91, 98, 104; *A. rubrum* × *saccharinum* (syn. *A.* × *freemanii*) $2n = 78$ (hexaploid).

VARIETIES

var. *drummondii* (Nuttall) Sargent (1884), leaves coriaceous, white beneath, flowers larger than the species; rarely in cultivation, but grows naturally in Arkansas, Texas, Louisiana, and the lower Mississippi Valley to southwestern Indiana and northern Missouri; chromosome number: $2n = 56$ (Santamour).

var. *pallidiflorum* Koch ex Pax (1886), flowers yellowish green; not in cultivation.

var. *tomentosum* Tausch (1829), leaves subtomentose, with exceptionally good colors in autumn; rare in cultivation; (syn. *A. fulgens* hort.).

var. *trilobum* Torrey & A. Gray ex Koch (1853), leaves 3-lobed; native in southeastern United States to Florida; rare; synonym is *A. rubrum* var. *tridens* A. Wood; chromosome number is $2n = 78$ (Ellis 1963).

CULTIVARS: Many (see Chapter 9).

REFERENCES: Bean (1970), Dippel (1892), Elwes & Henry (1908), Grootendorst (1969), de Jong (1976), Koch (1869), Koidzumi (1911), Krüssmann (1976a), Linnaeus (1753), Murray (1970c), Pax (1902), Pojárkova (1933b), Rehder (1986 facs.), Schwerin (1894).

*Acer rubrum* is one of the most common trees in eastern North America and was introduced to Europe in 1656 by Tradescant (Elwes & Henry 1908, 673). It is one of the nine species described by Linnaeus (1753). Its natural distribution includes the whole eastern part of North America, west to Winnipeg in Canada, and the Dakotas and the Great Plains in the United States. It grows together with *Alnus, Carpinus, Larix,* and *Thuja* species, forming thickets and woods.

A glorious tree in North America, where it is called the red maple due to its brilliant autumn colors, it grows to 40 m tall and usually broader when grown under optimum conditions. In European gardens it does not reach these immense sizes, but easily becomes 20 m tall and sometimes as wide. It prefers acid soil. The leaves are 3- to 5-lobed, longer than wide, with undersides conspicuously silvery green, but not as glaucous-silvery as those of *A. saccharinum.*

In cultivation *Acer rubrum* could be confused with its Japanese counterpart, *A. pycnanthum,* since these species are similar and allied. *Acer pycnanthum* is much rarer in gardens, so there is little risk of confusion, particularly with the immense geographic isolation of the natural distributions. Generally speaking, the leaves of *A. pycnanthum* are more shallowly lobed than those of *A. rubrum,* and the latter grows into a much larger tree. It is also possible to confuse *A. rubrum* with *A. saccharinum,* another close relative. *Acer saccharinum* has considerably different leaves that are always more deeply incised and toothed. Its flowers are not red, but greenish.

The red flowers of *Acer rubrum,* occurring freely on naked branches, create an impressive sight. The seed ripens very early in the season and drops in May and June. Sometimes it germinates freely under the tree, and seedlings can be harvested in autumn. The trees are usually unisexual; consequently, for a good crop of seed several trees are needed to insure a male for pollination and seed set.

The autumn color varies from golden yellow to brilliant scarlet, depending on the locality and soil conditions. Trees growing on moist, peaty soils, particularly in southern climates, do not produce as much color since the chlorophyll breakdown begins too late in the season to produce vivid color before leaf fall.

The propagation of selected clones must be done by budding or grafting on seedlings of *Acer rubrum*. If no such seedlings are available, *A. saccharinum* is also suitable as an understock, but this suckers more than *A. rubrum*.

As this tree is so common in North America, the nursery industry and research institutes have done considerable research in selecting exceptionally good forms for landscaping. Among the best are 'October Glory' and 'Red Sunset', both good in European conditions. Because *Acer rubrum* has a very wide natural distribution, a number of botanical/geographic varieties have been described in the past, but the species is rather uniform so only four varieties are considered distinct today. All other names are sunk in synonymy. There is a group of hybrids between *A. rubrum* and *A. saccharinum* called *A.* × *freemanii* Murray (1969). The Dutch cultivar originally described as *A. saccharinum* 'Elegant' is one of these hybrids.

SECTION: *Rubra*

## ACER SACCHARINUM L. (1753)

SYNONYMS

- *A. sylvestre* Young (1783).
- *A. glaucum* Marshall (1785).
- *A. floridanum* hort. ex Lézermes (1788).
- *A. rubrum* var. *pallidum* Aiton (1789).
- *A. dasycarpum* Ehrhart (1789).
- *A. eriocarpum* Michaux (1803).
- *A. tomentosum* Steudel (1821).
- *A. coccineum* Loudon (1842).
- *A. floridum* Loudon (1842).
- *A. macrocarpum* Loudon (1842).
- *A. album* Nicholson (1881).
- *A. palmatum* Nicholson (1881), non Thunberg.
- *A. douglasii* Dieck (1885).
- *A. lutescens* Pax (1886).
- *A. macrophyllum* Pax (1886).
- *A. spicatum* Pax (1886), non Lamarck.
- *Saccharosphendamnus saccharina* (L.) Nieuwland (1914).
- *Argentacer saccharinum* (L.) Small (1933).

TYPE: LINN 1225.10, collected by Peter Kalm, "Habitat in Pensylvania."

COMMON NAMES: Silver maple, Wager's maple, Silberahorn, Zilveresdoorn.

ILLUSTRATIONS: Plate 120; de Jong (1976), Krüssmann (1976a).

EPITHET: *Saccharinus*, with sugar.

HABIT: A tree to 20 m tall in cultivation, to 40 m tall in native habitat, with pendulous branches, often taller than wide; crowns with an open, spreading habit.

LEAVES: Deeply 5-lobed or even divided to the bases, 8–15 cm across, dark green above and glaucous beneath; lobes lobulate with acuminate apices, doubly serrate; central lobes 3-lobulate; petioles 4–6 cm long, thin.

INFLORESCENCES: Corymbose, umbellate, lateral, evident in early spring before the leaves appear.

FLOWERS: Greenish to rose-colored, without petals, most monoecious.

FRUITS: Samaras subhorizontal, 3–5 cm long, ripening early in the summer and germinating immediately after dropping in May–June.

BARK AND BUDS: Bark smooth, orange-brown to gray, with glaucous bloom when young; wood brittle.

HARDINESS: Zone IV.

AUTUMN COLOR: Yellow.

DISTRIBUTION: Eastern North America from Quebec to Florida, west to Minnesota, Kansas, Oklahoma—together with species of *Alnus, Betula, Salix,* and other *Acer* species, including *A. rubrum* and *A. saccharum* ssp. *nigrum*. Never forms forests.

CHROMOSOME NUMBER: $2n = 52$, tetraploid; $F_1$ progeny of *A. saccharinum* × *A. rubrum* (syn. *A.* × *freemanii* Murray) has $2n = 71, 72$ (Santamour 1965).

CULTIVARS: Many (see Chapter 9).

REFERENCES: Bean (1970), Dippel (1892), Elwes & Henry (1908), de Jong (1976), Koch (1869), Krüssmann (1976a), Linnaeus (1753), Murray (1970c), Pax (1902), Rehder (1986 facs.).

The silver maple was introduced to Europe in 1725 by Sir Charles Wager and has become one of the most graceful trees now in cultivation in Europe. It grows to be a stately tree, to 25 m tall in cultivation, often much taller in its native habitat. It is one of nine species described by Linnaeus (1753). A synonym still in use in Europe is *Acer dasycarpum*.

The crowns are built up with graceful, slender, and pendulous branches. The leaves are deeply divided and 5-lobed, rather large, and glaucous beneath. The tree flowers early in the season before the leaves appear, and the seed ripens in May. After dropping, it germinates quickly and abundantly. *Acer saccharinum* frequently forms parthenocarpic seed, especially on solitary trees.

This species can be confused with its nearest relative, *Acer rubrum*, which has red flowers instead of greenish yellow and leaves that are not anywhere near as deeply divided. *Acer rubrum* has denser crowns; the crowns of *A. saccharinum* often are open and lax, and because of brittle wood break up frequently in stormy weather. *Acer saccharinum* is sometimes confused with *A. saccharum* only because of the similarity of their names. Although the name *saccharinum* means "with sugar," this species is not a sugar maple (like *A. saccharum*) and does not yield a sweet sap from which to make syrup or sugar.

This species should not be used as a street tree due to the brittleness of its wood, which does not resist strong wind. In North America, *Acer saccharinum* does not make a good street tree or home garden tree because its root systems rapidly clog storm drains, sewers, sewer lines, and the like. In the United States it is a highly undesirable and noxious tree. Some cultivars, however, produce good street trees. The Dutch clone 'Elegant' is such a cultivar; it belongs to *A.* × *freemanii,* a hybrid group between *A. saccharinum* and *A. rubrum.* Trees of this species are quite often seen in many gardens and parks, but now cultivars are planted more often. The species is readily available in the trade.

## SECTION HYPTIOCARPA Fang (1966)

TYPE SPECIES: ***Acer garrettii*** **Craib** (1920).

HABIT: Evergreen trees, sometimes deciduous.

LEAVES: Undivided, coriaceous, glaucous beneath; margins entire.

BUD SCALES: 7- to 11-paired.

INFLORESCENCES: Corymbose or racemose, axillary from leafless buds.

FLOWERS: 5-merous; perianth yellowish; stamens 4–6 or 8–12.

FRUITS: Nutlets large, ovoid; parthenocarpic tendency very weak.

SPECIES

*A. garrettii* Craib (1920).

*A. laurinum* Hasskarl (1843).

*Hyptiocarpa* is a highly specialized section. Its affinities are indistinct—possibly with sections *Lithocarpa* and *Trifoliata.* This is a small section that includes only two species—one in cultivation and one imperfectly known. When more living and herbarium material becomes available, the two may be merged into one species, *Acer laurinum.*

SECTION: *Hyptiocarpa*

ACER GARRETTII Craib (1920)

SYNONYMS

*A. longicarpum* Hu & Cheng (1948).

*A. machilifolium* Hu & Cheng (1948).

TYPE: *A. G. Garrett 77,* Payap, Thailand; K.

EPITHET: *Garrettii,* after A. G. Garrett (1870–1948), a mycologist in Salt Lake City, Utah.

ILLUSTRATIONS: Fang (1981a), Gagnepain (1950), Krüssmann (1976a).

HABIT: A small tree with reddish or bluish shoots and evergreen leaves.

LEAVES: Persistent, oblong-elliptic, 7–15 cm long and 3–7 cm wide, with bluish undersides, fully unlobed; margins entire; petioles 3–5 cm long.

INFLORESCENCES: Lateral.

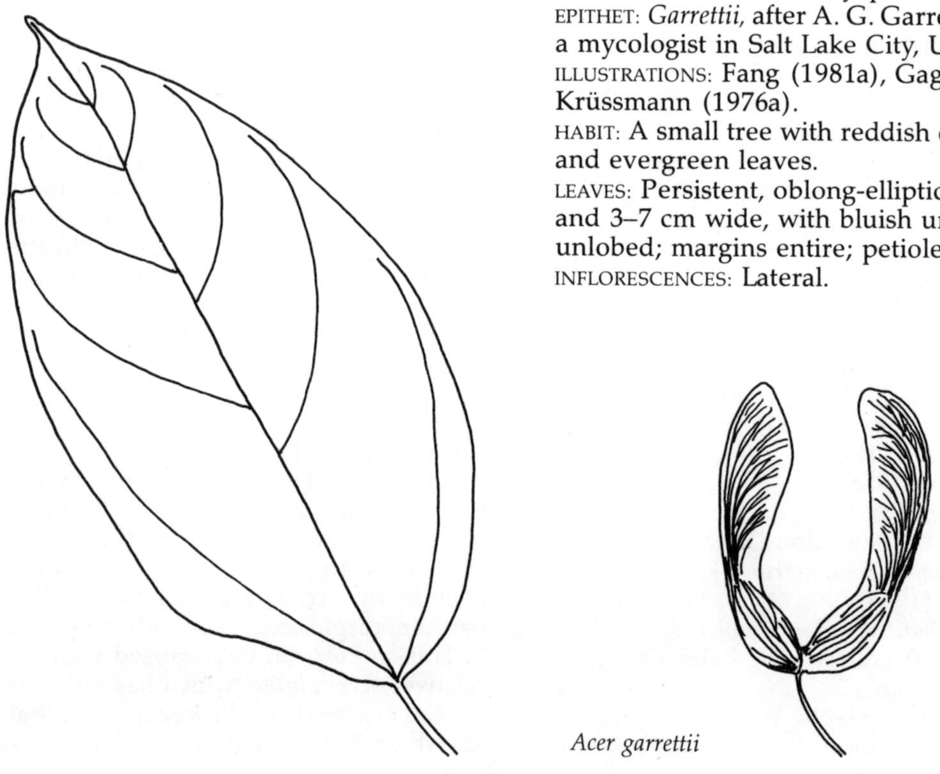

*Acer garrettii*

FLOWERS: 1 cm across, dioecious; stamens 10–12.
FRUITS: Samaras erect, uneven in size, reddish.
HARDINESS: Zones VIII–IX.
DISTRIBUTION: Guangdong and Hainan provinces, China; Thailand; North Annam and Tonkin, Vietnam.
REFERENCES: Fang (1981c), Gagnepain (1950), Krüssmann (1976a), Murray (1969, 1970c).

*Acer garrettii* was described by W. G. Craib in 1920. This tropical species is not known to be in cultivation in Europe or North America, but is present in Guangzhou Botanical Garden, China. It is not suitable for cultivation in cooler latitudes.

It is a small, dioecious tree with reddish branches and persistent oblong-elliptic leaves, not unlike those of *Acer oblongum.*

Some authors include this species in *Acer laurinum,* which is widespread in southeastern Asia. In this volume, the range of *A. garrettii* is confined to the continent of eastern Asia. *Acer laurinum* also inhabits several archipelagoes of southeastern Asia.

SECTION: *Hyptiocarpa*

ACER LAURINUM Hasskarl (1843)

SYNONYMS
- *A. javanicum* sensu Junghuhn (1842).
- *A. niveum* Blume (1845).
- *A. cassiaefolium* Blume (1847).
- *A. philippinum* Merrill (1906).
- *A. curranii* Merrill (1909).
- *A. decandrum* Merrill (1932).
- *A. chionophyllum* Merrill (1941).
- *A. pinnatinervium* Merrill (1941).
- *A. laurinum* ssp. *decandrum* (Merrill) Murray (1977).

TYPE: *Junghuhn,* Java; L.
COMMON NAMES: Walik elar, Wuru dapung, Wuru putih.
EPITHET: *Laurinus,* with evergreen leaves.
ILLUSTRATIONS: Plate 121; Bloembergen (1948).
HABIT: A mighty evergreen tree 25–30 m tall; branches glaucous to purplish.
LEAVES: Persistent, oblong-elliptic, 9–15 cm long and 3–8 cm wide, glaucous beneath, shining green above; margins entire or only very remotely serrate; petioles 3–6 cm long, often grooved.
INFLORESCENCES: Lateral, corymbose, on 2-year-old branchlets.
FLOWERS: Yellowish, dioecious, flowering in spring when most leaves have shed; stamens 10–12.
FRUITS: Samaras erect, 3–7 cm long, unequal, often purplish, acute to obtuse angled.
HARDINESS: Zones VIII–IX.
DISTRIBUTION: Upper Burma and Hainan Province, China; southeast Asia; Malaysia, Indonesia on the islands of Java and Sumatra, Philippines, small Sunda islands to Flores. Grows in mountain forests at 1000–2000 m.
CHROMOSOME NUMBER: $2n = 26$ (Mehra 1972).
REFERENCES: Bloembergen (1948, as *A. niveum*), Murray (1969, 1970c, 1977), Pax (1902).

*Acer laurinum* was named by Hasskarl in 1843. It clearly has a wide natural distribution, considering the great number of synonyms. It grows in primary, rarely secondary or devastated forests, often common but scattered. Trees are easily located by the fallen leaves, which are glaucous.

This tropical species forms mighty trees with evergreen leaves in many parts of southeastern Asia, especially the archipelagoes of the Philipines, Indonesia, and Malaysia. It is now in cultivation in The Netherlands in the Botanical Garden of the University of Groningen (introduced by M. Essers), but nothing is known about its propagation. The tree died shortly after it was transplanted, though seed likely would have germinated if it had been available.

It is remarkable that so little is known about *Acer garrettii* and *A. laurinum,* two tropical species. The former may be considered conspecific with the latter when more comparative material becomes available.

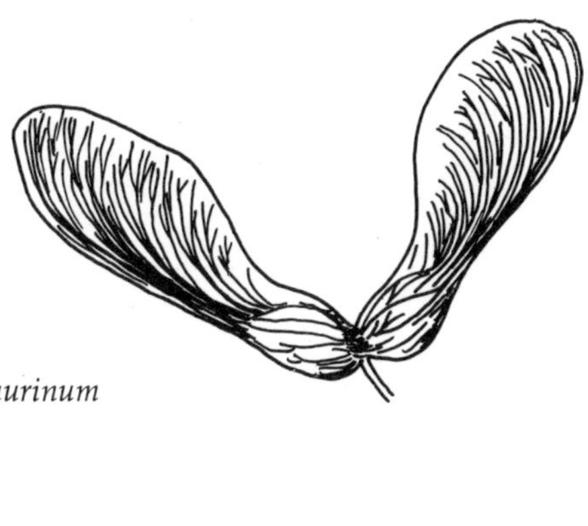

*Acer laurinum*

Chapter 8

# Maple Hybrids[1]

D. M. VAN GELDEREN

The literature records a number of maple hybrids, most from southeastern Europe. The parentage of these hybrids is not always known with certainty, and in several cases the various accounts disagree. It seems unlikely, however, that *Acer* species hybridize freely across sections, especially when one species has laticiferous petioles and the other does not. Closely related species such as *A. opalus* and *A. monspessulanum* tend to hybridize more readily in their natural or cultivated habitats than with less closely related species.

Maple hybrids occur naturally in the wild or they originate in the garden. The latter are relatively new or only recently described. The older hybrids, all described in the 19th century, are *Acer* × *bornmuelleri, A.* × *boscii, A.* × *coriaceum, A.* × *durettii, A.* × *hybridum, A.* × *martinii, A.* × *ramosum, A.* × *rotundilobum, A.* × *dieckii,* and *A.* × *zoeschense.* These form two groups: those with laticiferous petioles, and those without. For example, *A.* × *zoeschense,* a hybrid between *A. campestre* and *A. cappadocicum* ssp. *lobelii,* has laticiferous petioles. Hybrids without milky sap generally have one parent in common—*A. monspessulanum.* The other parent species are *A. pseudoplatanus, A. opalus,* and *A. tataricum.*

*Acer* × *bornmuelleri* does not have any trace of milky sap. Accordingly, the parent cited by Borbas (*A. campestre*) is probably a wrong identification. The general character of *A.* × *bornmuelleri* also shows more influence of *A. opalus* than of *A. campestre.* The female parent is *A. monspessulanum.*

*Acer* × *boscii* has been given several different parentages: *A. monspessulanum* × *A. tataricum* is far more probable than *A. pensylvanicum* × *A. tataricum,* or *A. campestre* × *A. tataricum,* both also given as possibilities.

The parentage of *Acer* × *coriaceum* is given as *A. monspessulanum* × *A. pseudoplatanus.* However, it is clearly a hybrid of *A. monspessulanum* and *A. opalus.* Its buds, leaves, and fruits are all much closer to those of *A. monspessulanum* and *A. opalus* than to those of *A. pseudoplatanus.* Pax assigned the same parents to *A.* × *durettii,* and the strong influence of *A. opalus* is clearly visible.

*Acer* × *dieckii* probably is not a hybrid at all but rather a misidentified and peculiar form of *A. platanoides* (syn. 'Dieckii').

*Acer* × *hybridum* is a very complex taxon with parentages given as *A. opalus* × *A. pseudoplatanus* or *A. opalus* × *A. monspessulanum.* This taxon is comparable with *A.* × *dieckii* and is most

[1]The author wishes to thank Dr. D. O. Wijnands, Agricultural University, Wageningen, The Netherlands, for his assistance and advice in preparing this chapter.

probably nothing but a peculiar form of *A. pseudoplatanus.* There are several different forms.

*Acer* × *martinii* has the same parents as *A.* × *coriaceum* and can be considered synonymous; the same is true for *A.* × *rotundilobum.* One of the parents of the latter hybrid is a subspecies of *A. opalus* ssp. *obtusatum,* but this does not make a difference to its correct nomenclatural position.

*Acer* × *ramosum* is also of doubtful parentage. Schwerin cited it as *A. campestre* × *A. pseudoplatanus,* but that would have meant that a species with laticiferous petioles hybridized with one without laticiferous petioles. It is impossible to check this hybrid for the presence of milky sap as it is unavailable and probably lost to cultivation.

*Acer* × *schwerinii* is another puzzling hybrid that cannot be checked with living material because it is probably lost to cultivation.

The newly described garden hybrids such as *Acer* × *freemanii, A.* × *hillieri, A.* × *pseudo heldreichii,* and *A.* × *conspicuum* do not present such difficulties: their parentages are well known and correct.

At the North Carolina State University, USA, J. C. Raulston has obtained a new group of hybrids by crossing *Acer truncatum* × *A. platanoides.* These hybrids develop to well-formed upright trees with very good fall colors. The influence of *A. platanoides* seems to dominate, and so far no infraspecific name has been published. One cultivar, named 'Keithsform' and traded under the name 'Norwegian Sunset', has excellent fall colors ranging from yellow to red. It has a very good branching structure and may become valuable for street plantings. It attains a height of about 12–15 m and has an oval crown. The dark green leaves are similar to those of *A. truncatum,* but in all other respects this cultivar resembles its other parent. A second cultivar, named 'Warrenred' and traded under the name 'Pacific Sunset', is a smaller tree up to 10 m tall and of finer structure than 'Keithsform'. It has outstanding glossy summer foliage that turns red in fall.

Three doubtful taxa are mentioned here but not described:

1. *Acer* × *guyotii* Beauverd (1920). Parentage: *A. campestre* × *A. opalus.* Syntype: Martigny & Balme, Switzerland. Without description.

2. *Acer* × *langii* Simonkai (1908). Parentage: *A. monspessulanum* × *A. tataricum.* Leaves 6–9 cm wide, obovate, 3-lobed, margins denticulate, subcordate, petioles 3–5 cm long, inflorescences corymbose, samaras erect, 2.5 cm. If the parents of *A.* × *langii* are indeed *A. monspessulanum* × *A. tataricum,* then this hybrid would become a synonym of *A.* × *boscii* Spach.

3. *Acer* × *sabaudum* Chabert (1910). Parentage: *A. opalus* × *A. platanoides.* Syntypes: Gave, Savoy, Longhi, Le Môle, eastern France. Without description. According to Murray, synonymous with *A. opalus.*

Fifteen named interspecific hybrids are discussed in this chapter:

*A. × bornmuelleri* Borbas (1891); probably a synonym of *A. × coriaceum*

*A. × boscii* Spach (1834)

*A. × conspicuum* van Gelderen & Oterdoom (1993)

*A. × coriaceum* Bosc ex Tausch (1829)

*A. × dieckii* (Pax) Pax (1893); probably a synonym of *A. platanoides*

*A. × durettii* Pax (1893); probably a synonym of *A. × coriaceum*

*A. × freemanii* Murray (1969)

*A. × hillieri* Lancaster (1979)

*A. × hybridum* Bosc (1821); probably a synonym of *A. pseudoplatanus*

*A. × martinii* Jordan (1852); probably a synonym of *A. × coriaceum*

*A. × pseudo-heldreichii* Fukarek & Celjo (1959)

*A. × ramosum* Schwerin (1894)

*A. × rotundilobum* Schwerin (1894); probably a synonym of *A. × coriaceum*

*A. × schwerinii* Pax (1893)

*A. × zoeschense* Pax (1886)

ACER × BORNMUELLERI Borbas (1891)

ORIGIN: Naturally occurring.

PARENTAGE: *A. monspessulanum × A. campestre.*

SYNONYMS

*A. × hungaricum* Borbas (1891).

*A. campestre* f. *brachypterum* Borbas ex Schwerin (1893).

TYPE: *J. F. N. Bornmueller,* mountains of Hercegovina, Yugoslavia; BRNU.

EPITHET: *Bornmuelleri,* after J. F. N. Bornmüller (1862–1948), a prolific German botanist and director of the Haussknecht Herbarium, Weimar, for whom the genus *Bornmuelleria* was named.

ILLUSTRATION: Plate 122.

HABIT: A small tree or large shrub with many whorled stems, to 6 m tall.

LEAVES: Mostly 3-lobed, sometimes 5-lobed, wider than long, 2.5–5 cm long and up to 8 cm wide, sparsely pilose to glabrous, very thin textured, somewhat glossy; bases cordate.

FLOWERS: Inflorescences terminal, corymbose, lax.

FRUITS: Samaras spreading horizontally as in *A. campestre;* nutlets 2.5 cm long.

BARK AND BUDS: Shoots fully glabrous, gray-brown; twigs and branches without cork.

HARDINESS: Zone V.

DISTRIBUTION: Mountains of Bosnia-Hercegovina; in northern Greece and over the Balkans; mixed among forests of both parents.

REFERENCES: Krüssmann (1976a), Murray (1970c), Pax (1902), Rehder (1986 facs.), Schneider (1912).

This hybrid is still known in cultivation, being present in the Hillier's Arboretum, Romsey, Great Britain, but is propagated only occasionally. It is rather irregular and small, not unlike *Acer monspessulanum.* Its leaves are also mostly 3-lobed, but the central lobes are much longer than those of *A. monspessulanum.* The leaves are somewhat leathery, similar to *A. × coriaceum.* It seems unlikely, therefore, that the given parentage is correct. The petioles lack any trace of milky sap and suggest relationship more to *A. opalus* than to *A. campestre.*

*Acer opalus* ssp. *obtusatum* is abundant in Hercegovina and sympatric with *A. monspessulanum.* Dr. Zelimir Borzan of the Forestry Faculty of the University of Zagreb says that *A. campestre* is also common in Hercegovina and overlaps in distribution with *A. monspessulanum.* It is quite difficult to decide whether *A. campestre* was involved in this hybrid or not. The morphological characters show no influence of *A. campestre.* If it were true that the parentage of *A. × bornmuellerii* was actually *A. monspessulanum × A. opalus,* then *A. × bornmuelleri* would become a synonym of *A. × coriaceum,* a hybrid of the same parentage but described earlier. The tree in the Hillier Arboretum, which is inferior to *A. × coriaceum* as it is known in horticulture, could be labeled *A. × coriaceum* 'Bornmueller'. Further investigation into the native habitat of this hybrid is necessary to clarify these matters.

ACER × BOSCII Spach (1834)

ORIGIN: Garden.

PARENTAGE: *A. monspessulanum* × *A. tataricum,* or *A. pensylvanicum* × *A. tataricum;* possibly *A. tataricum* × *A. campestre.*

SYNONYMS

*A. lobatum* Bosc ex Spach (1834).

*A. barbatum* sensu Loudon (1838), non Michaux.

TYPE: Unknown at present.

EPITHET: *Boscii,* after French botanist Louis A. G. Bosc (1759–1828).

HABIT: A shrub of medium size or sometimes a small tree, similar to *A. tataricum.*

LEAVES: Broadly obovate, somewhat 3-lobed at the apices, rarely unlobed, 5–7.5 cm long and 2.5–8 (–10) cm wide, very thin textured, pilose to glabrous; bases somewhat cordate; margins coarsely serrate or even double-toothed; petioles thin, about 4 cm long, yellow to red.

INFLORESCENCES: Racemes erect, 4–5 cm long, with only a few flowers.

FLOWERS: Yellowish.

FRUITS: Samaras glabrous, almost parallel, nearly 2.5 cm long.

BARK AND BUDS: Shoots reddish green, downy at first, later glabrous; branchlets dark brown.

HARDINESS: Zone V.

REFERENCES: Dippel (1892), Krüssmann (1976a), Murray (1970c), Pax (1902), Rehder (1986 facs.), Schwerin (1900).

Pax notes in 1902, "This is a cultivated form, almost extinct in the nurseries, it is certainly a hybrid, probably *A. tataricum* × *A. pensylvanicum,* and possibly *A. monspessulanum* × *A. tataricum*" (translated). Koch (1867) noted that he never saw a living plant, as did Graf von Schwerin in 1900, despite substantial efforts to locate one.

It is almost impossible to determine what this hybrid might be. I have never found a trace of this plant. It seems strange that Pax suggests it is a hybrid between a North American and a European species. Especially strange is the fact that in all the descriptions found, the samaras are said to be almost parallel, a conspicuous feature of *Acer monspessulanum.* The uncertainty is compounded by a note that most of the leaves are 3-lobed. Dippel (1892) wrote:

> This plant occurred about 1840 in several gardens in Germany in the region of Mannheim, Darmstadt and Aschaffenburg, but it died out and is now no longer present. One may hope that it will occur again sooner or later. It is supposed to be a dense shrubby tree, not unlike the habit of *A. tataricum* (translated).

Dippel reports it to be a hybrid of *A. tataricum* and *A. campestre.* Rehder (1940) describes the hybrid *A.* × *pusillum* Schwerin (1894) with the parents *A. monspessulanum* and *A. tataricum.* He also states that *A. monspessulanum* × *A. tataricum* is probably a synonym of *A.* × *boscii* K. Koch, and that *A. tataricum* × *A. pensylvanicum* is probably a synonym of *A.* × *boscii* Spach. In 1949 he questionably regards *A.* × *boscii* sensu K. Koch (1860), "pro syn. dub.," non *A.* × *boscii* Spach (1834), as a synonym of *A.* × *pusillum* Schwerin (1894). This confusion cannot be solved in the absence of any living material and type herbarium specimens.

ACER × CONSPICUUM van Gelderen & Oterdoom, hybrida nova

ORIGIN: Garden.

PARENTAGE: *A. davidii* Franchet × *A. pensylvanicum* L.

DESCRIPTION: Hybrida hortensis nova e *Acer davidii* Franch. et *Acer pensylvanico* L. Frutex procerus vel arbor ad 10 m alta. Ramuli laevis glabri. Gemmae hiemales valvatae. Folium petiolatum estipulatum. Lamina 3–5 lobata, apice breviter acuminata, margine serrata, 5–20 cm longa, 5–15 cm lata, laevis glabra vel infra pilis stellatis sparsis tecta. Venae primariae utrinque latere 6–10, supra impressae et subter prominentes pinnatim nervatae. Petiolus 2–10 cm longus, plerumque rubicundus. Inflorescentia terminalia racemosa multiflora, subglabra vel minute pubescentia, 4–15 cm longa. Calyx minutus. Corolla orbiculata 3–5 mm diametro. Fructus glabrus alis late divergentibus.

TYPES: *D. M. van Gelderen,* 1975, Hillier Arboretum, Winchester, Great Britain, and Esveld Aceretum, Boskoop, The Netherlands; holotype WBS.

EPITHET: *Conspicuus,* conspicuous.

HABIT: A slender tree or sparsely branched shrub, up to 10 m tall, occasionally more.

LEAVES: 3- to 5-lobed, basal lobes underdeveloped, apices acuminate, margins serrate, 5–20 cm long 5–15 cm wide, glabrous or sparsely hairy on lower surfaces, pubescence usually disappearing when leaves mature; lateral veins 6–10, slightly impressed; petioles usually reddish, 2–10 cm long, depending on the cultivar.

INFLORESCENCES: In terminal, pendulous, many-flowered racemes, 4–15 cm long, glabrous or slightly pubescent.

FLOWERS: With minute calyxes and orbicular corollas 3–5 mm wide.

FRUITS: Samaras usually short, much like those of *A. davidii;* nutlets flattish, in pendulous racemes.

BARK AND BUDS: Conspicuous white stripes on blue-green or reddish bark; buds valvate.

HARDINESS: Zone V.

AUTUMN COLOR: Golden yellow, sometimes orange-yellow.

CULTIVARS: Four (see Chapter 9).

REFERENCES: Catalogue Firma C. Esveld (1987); correspondence with J. Bond, Regius Keeper of the Royal Windsor Great Park; Hillier & Sons catalogues (1983).

ACER × CORIACEUM Bosc ex Tausch (1829)
ORIGIN: Naturally occurring.
PARENTAGE: *A. monspessulanum* × *A. opalus* ssp. *obtusatum*.
SYNONYMS
*A. creticum* sensu F. Schmidt (1792), non L.
*A. parvifolium* Tausch (1829).
*A. polymorphum* Spach (1834), non Siebold & Zuccarini.
*A.* × *martinii* Jordan (1852).
*A.* × *durettii* Willkomm (1879), nomen nudum.
*A. dealbatum* Dieck (1887).
*A. monspessulanum* var. *quinquelobum* Willkomm & Lange (1893).
*A. trilobatum* hort. ex Kew (1894).
*A. barbatum* Booth ex Schwerin (1894), non Michaux.
*A. monspessulanum* f. *martinii* (Jordan) Rouy & Foucauld (1897).
*A. peronai* Schwerin (1901).
*A. paui* Marcet (1906).
*A. perrierei* Chabert (1909).
*A. guinieri* Chabert (1910).
*A. hyrcanum* sensu Fauret & Maire ex Quezel & Santa (1969), non Fischer & Meyer.
TYPE: Not known.
EPITHET: *Coriaceus*, leathery.
ILLUSTRATION: Plate 123.
HABIT: A small, deciduous tree with a mushroom-shaped habit, to 8–10 m high, with many stiff, stout branches; branchlets glabrous, sometimes slightly sticky.
LEAVES: 3-lobed, sometimes indistinctly 5-lobed, 5–10 cm wide, lustrous, shiny green, coriacous; lobes obtuse and rounded, bases cordate, side lobes occasionally crenate; leafing out very late in the season.
INFLORESCENCES: Corymbose, terminal.
FLOWERS: 5-merous, yellow-green.
FRUITS: Glabrous; samaras 2.5 cm long, wings 1 cm long, diverging at about 60°.
BARK AND BUDS: Bark gray and smooth, like that of *A. opalus;* buds blackish and small, several set together.
HARDINESS: Zone V.
AUTUMN COLOR: Not conspicuous.
DISTRIBUTION: Originally found in southern Europe, especially Croatia and Bosnia-Hercegovina.
REFERENCES: Bean (1970), Dippel (1892), Koch (1869), Krüssmann (1976a), Murray (1970c), Pax (1902), Rehder (1986 facs.), Schneider (1912).

This very valuable small tree of hybrid origin originated on Dalmatian Coast, Croatia, and is poorly known in horticulture to both amateurs and professionals. It is said to be a natural hybrid of *Acer monspessulanum* and *A. opalus*, not of *A. pseudoplatanus* and *A. monspessulanum* as recorded in the original literature. It exhibits very clearly the characteristics of both *A. monspessulanum* and *A. opalus*, but shows no influence of *A. pseudoplatanus*. The bark and buds clearly show the influence of *A. opalus*, and they share almost the same habit.

*Acer × coriaceum* starts into new growth very late in the season, escaping damaging late spring frosts. It can hardly be confused with other maples; only large-leaved forms of *A. obtusifolium* are somewhat similar. The leaves of *A. monspessulanum* are much smaller, while the leaves of *A. opalus* are never so shiny and clearly lobed. This tree should be planted more frequently by landscapers as it is quite suitable for small gardens.

Tausch (1829) provides a description of the synonym *Acer parvifolium*. There are numerous other synonyms, one of the most confusing being *A. creticum* sensu Schmidt (1792), non L.

This hybrid cannot, of course, be propagated from seed, but must be grafted on potted rootstock of *Acer monspessulanum*. Grafted in the greenhouse in early August, potted rootstock takes in 5–6 weeks. The young grafts must be stored in a frame or tunnel, and can be planted out the following spring.

ACER × DIECKII (Pax) Pax (1893)
ORIGIN: Garden.
PARENTAGE: Most probably simply a form of *A. platanoides*.
BASIONYM: *A. lobelii* var. *dieckii* Pax (1886).
SYNONYMS
*A. platanoides* var. *integrilobum* Zabel (1878).
*A. dieckii* f. *integrilobum* (Zabel) Schwerin (1893).
TYPE: Unknown.
EPITHET: *Dieckii*, after G. Dieck (1847–1925), director of Zoeschen Nursery, Berlin, Germany.
ILLUSTRATION: Krüssmann (1976a).
HABIT: A rather large tree to 20–25 m high.
LEAVES: 3- to 4-lobed, or less often 5- to 7-lobed, lobes entire, broadly triangular, usually without lobules, sinuses shallow, broadly rounded, 10–15 cm across, sometimes to 25 cm wide, upper surfaces shiny green, undersides paler, with scattered tufts of brown hairs in the axils, margins entire, bases hastate to truncate.
FLOWERS: Yellow, in rather small corymbs, very much like those of *A. platanoides*.
FRUITS: Glabrous; samaras 5–7.5 cm long, horizontally spreading, wings often underdeveloped.
BARK AND BUDS: Bark gray-brown, not fissured.
HARDINESS: Zone V.
AUTUMN COLOR: Clear yellow.
DISTRIBUTION: Found originally in the Zoeschen Nurseries near Berlin, Germany, as a supposed hybrid between *A. cappadocicum* ssp. *lobelii* and *A. platanoides*.
REFERENCES: Bean (1970), Krüssmann (1976a),

Murray (1970c), Pax (1902), Rehder (1986 facs.), Schneider (1912).

Pax originally described this plant in 1886 as a variety of *Acer lobelii* (*A. cappadocicum* ssp. *lobelii*), but later changed it to the rank of hybrid. He thought it to be a natural hybrid between *A. cappadocicum* ssp. *lobelii* and *A. platanoides*.

*Acer* × *dieckii* is very much like *A. platanoides* in habit and is not erect like *A. cappadocicum* ssp. *lobelii*. The leaves, however, have shorter lobes or are often only 3-lobed. The tree is easily confused with atypical specimens of *A. platanoides* or large-growing forms of *A. cappadocicum* ssp. *lobelii*. Only a few seedlings show the typical (described) leaves of *A.* × *dieckii*; most bear leaves like those of *A. platanoides*. Kew Gardens introduced this plant from the Zoeschen Nurseries, Germany, in 1887.

Probably this tree is not a hybrid at all but only an odd-leaved *Acer platanoides* named 'Dieckii'. It can readily be propagated by grafting or budding on *A. platanoides*.

ACER × DURETTII Pax (1893)

ORIGIN: Garden.

PARENTAGE: *A. monspessulanum* × *A. opalus*, or *A. monspessulanum* × *A. pseudoplatanus*, or *A. pseudoplatanus* × *A. opalus* ssp. *obtusatum* Pax.

SYNONYMS

*A.* × *durettii* Willkomm ex Pax (1893), nomen nudum.

TYPE: Pax does not indicate type.

EPITHET: *Durettii*, after French botanist L. Durett.

ILLUSTRATION: Plate 124.

HABIT: A fairly large tree to 12 m tall; young branches and stems glabrous.

LEAVES: 3- to 5-lobed, coriaceous, often with a couple of lobes at the bases, lobes large and triangular, 5–12 cm wide and 6–9 cm long, glabrous, hairy at the veins, irregularly crenate-serrate, bases cordate; petioles reddish, 2.5–5 cm long.

FLOWERS: Greenish yellow, in pubescent, stalked racemes, 5–8 cm long.

FRUITS: Not seen.

AUTUMN COLOR: Not seen.

CULTIVARS: Two, both probably lost (see Chapter 9).

REFERENCES: Krüssmann (1976a), Murray (1970c), Pax (1902), Rehder (1986 facs.), Schneider (1912), Schwerin (1900).

This hybrid is a reverse cross using the same parents as those of *Acer* × *coriaceum*. Pax thought it a hybrid between *A. opalus* and *A. pseudoplatanus*. It has been misidentified with a number of incorrect names, such as *A.* × *boscii*, *A.* × *hybridum*, and *A.* × *barbatum* Booth ex Schwerin, non Michaux. However, based on received material, we have good reason to consider that *A. monspessulanum* and *A. opalus* are the putative parents.

The coriaceous leaves of this hybrid are thin, like those of *Acer* × *coriaceum*, and small, like those of *A. opalus*. Schwerin reported two cultivars with variegated leaves, both of which have probably been lost to cultivation.

There is a fairly good specimen in the Arboretum Les Barres in Nogent-sur-Vernisson, France. A young tree, grafted from this specimen, grows in the Esveld Aceretum, Boskoop, The Netherlands. If this hybrid ever had to be sunk in synonymy, the cultivar name could be *A.* × *coriaceum* 'Durettii'.

ACER × FREEMANII Murray (1969)

ORIGIN: Garden and naturally occurring.

PARENTAGE: *A. rubrum* × *A. saccharinum*.

TYPE: *E. Murray 344*; garden origin, from clonotype 404–40 at the Arnold Arboretum, Jamaica Plain, Massachusetts, sent by the U.S. National Arboretum in 1944; holotype NA; isotype A.

EPITHET: *Freemanii*, after Oliver M. Freeman (b. 1891), plant breeder at the U.S. National Arboretum.

HABIT: A tree intermediate between both parents, may grow to 20–25 m high, branchlets upright, forming an oval to rounded crown.

LEAVES: Smaller than those of *A. saccharinum* and not as deeply lobed; rather deeply dissected, more than those of *A. rubrum*; sinuses rounded to acute.

FRUITS: Often sterile, due to chromosomal aberrations; samaras 3–6 cm long, not red, striated as in *A. saccharinum*.

BARK AND BUDS: Bark silvery gray, branches gray-brown.

HARDINESS: Zones IV–V.

AUTUMN COLOR: Red and yellow on the same leaves.

DISTRIBUTION: First hybridized in 1933 at the U.S. National Arboretum by O. M. Freeman; dense populations of naturally occurring *A.* × *freemanii* found in Hancock County, northern Maine, by T. R. Dudley.

CULTIVARS: Several (see Chapter 9).

REFERENCES: Grootendorst (1969), Murray (1969, 1981).

*Acer* × *freemanii* was hybridized by Oliver Freeman but later found wild in many areas of the United States where the two parent species are present. It is intermediate between its parents, though it is a better tree than the average *A. saccharinum* seedling and is used as a street tree. Its leaves, though smaller than those of *A. saccharinum* and more deeply dissected, have the same general shape.

Recent studies seem to show that a particular clone of *Acer saccharinum*, called 'Elegant', also belongs to this grex. This clone is correctly called

*A.* × *freemanii* 'Elegant'. However, many plants of 'Elegant' have been sold simply as *A. saccharinum* without a cultivar name.

The clone has been in cultivation in North America and Europe for many years. It has always been propagated vegetatively by layering.

ACER × HILLIERI Lancaster (1979)
ORIGIN: Garden.
PARENTAGE: *A. miyabei* × *A. cappadocicum* 'Aureum'.
TYPE: Hillier's Arboretum, Great Britain.
EPITHET: *Hillieri,* after English nurseryman Sir Harold Hillier (1906–1984).
ILLUSTRATIONS: Lancaster (1979a, 1979b).
HABIT: A small tree, to 8–10 m tall.
LEAVES: 5- to 7-lobed, 10–20 cm across, deeply cordate, lobes ovate, sharply contracting to acuminate tips, three main lobes shouldered with one pair of prominent teeth, glabrous above and beneath except for lines of white hairs along midribs, green and glossy above, paler beneath; petioles slightly pubescent, rather long and slender.
INFLORESCENCES: Corymbs glabrous with scattered pubescence.
FRUITS: Nutlets pubescent and dull; samaras spreading at a wide angle.
BARK AND BUDS: Branches chestnut to reddish brown, turning to grayish brown when mature; buds rounded, bud scales red and shortly ciliate.
HARDINESS: Zone V.
AUTUMN COLOR: Yellow to golden brown.
CULTIVARS: Two—one with green leaves, the other with yellow (see Chapter 9).
REFERENCES: Lancaster (1979a, 1979b).

*Acer* × *hillieri* is a new hybrid from a cross between *A. miyabei* and *A. cappadocicum* 'Aureum' that provided numerous seedlings. The grex was developed at Hillier & Sons, Ampfield, Great Britain. In the early 1930s H. G. Hillier received seed, said to be *A. miyabei,* from Kew Gardens. The resulting trees proved to be hybrids and Roy Lancaster, then curator of the nursery, concluded that the parents were *A. miyabei* and *A. cappadocicum* 'Aureum'. As this plant had not yet been described, Lancaster (1979) published the story and the Latin description. He was convinced of the parentage when he found a second tree of this cross at Hergest Croft that was strikingly similar in form and shape to Hillier's tree, and both parents were found nearby.

The original Hillier plant now bears the cultivar name 'West Hill', while another seedling with leaves shaded yellow in summer is called 'Summergold'. Neither is readily available in the trade, but it is hoped that they will become more popular, as they can be used where *Acer cappadocicum* or its allies grow too large.

The Hergest Croft tree, 'Summergold', was originally planted under the name *Acer miyabei,* but differs considerably in both habit and leaves from this species.

ACER × HYBRIDUM Bosc (1821)
ORIGIN: Garden.
PARENTAGE: *A. opalus* × *A. pseudoplatanus,* or *A. opalus* × *A. monspessulanum;* possibly nothing but an odd expression of *A. pseudoplatanus.*
TYPE: "La pépinière du Roule," Cels-Noisette, France.
EPITHET: *Hybridus,* of hybrid origin.
HABIT: A tree to 15 m tall with a dense, rounded crown; young shoots glabrous, covered with dark brown lenticels.
LEAVES: 3-lobed, bases cordate, 4–9 cm long and wide, unevenly toothed, dark green above and gray-green below.
INFLORESCENCES: Pendulous racemes, 10–15 cm long.
FLOWERS: Yellowish, appearing with the leaves.
FRUITS: Samaras connivent or parallel, 2–3 cm long.
HARDINESS: Zone V.
AUTUMN COLOR: Yellow.
REFERENCES: Bean (1970), Dippel (1892), Grootendorst (1969), Koch (1869), Krüssmann (1976a), Murray (1970c), Pax (1902), Rehder (1986 facs.), Schneider (1912).

There is much confusion about this maple. It is, in fact, very rare, and only a few specimens have been reported, none with a clear description. The leaves are intermediate in form between those of *Acer opalus* and *A. pseudoplatanus* but smaller in size, about 8–10 cm across. So far this plant fits the description made by Spach (1834) with the supposed parents *A. opalus* and *A. pseudoplatanus;* as a mature tree it is closer to *A. opalus* than to the other parent. Koch (1869) stated that he "owns a plant, described by Spach, different from Bosc's plant." He supposed

> that it may be *A. pseudoplatanus* × *A. opalus.* This is a small tree up to 7 m, leaves slightly cordate, 9–12 cm wide, 3-lobed. Flowering raceme about 4 cm long, and fruits always parthenocarpic. Maybe it is even a hybrid with *A. spicatum* (sic). The whole is close to *A. opalus* (translated).

Bosc reports another tree, with smaller leaves, supposed to be a hybrid of *Acer opalus* × *A. monspessulanum.* Its leaves were reported as about 4–10 cm across, but the description is incredibly inadequate and therefore the name becomes a nomen subnudum or a nomen dubium.

Pax wrote (1901), "This is a hybrid, probably no longer present. The name *A.* × *hybridum* is found in many nurseries. It is certainly a hybrid between *A. pseudoplatanus* and *A. opalus,* and the cross *A. pseudoplatanus* × *A. pensylvanicum* seems to be irrational" (translated). For further details, see *A.* × *boscii.*

Two other plants, also called *Acer hybridum,* were grown near Paris at Cels-Noisette, France, by Pépinière du Roule. These trees have apparently disappeared. In England there was an *A. hybridum* in Liverpool (about 1808), and yet another *A. hybridum* Whitney Brames & Milne (1817), both nomina nuda.

Dippel (1892) noted, "This hybrid is mentioned in nursery catalogues regularly and also plants under this name are present in Darmstadt and Mannheim. But they never seem to be genuine, even its parents are not exactly known" (translated). All these confusing premises lead to the likely possibility that *Acer* × *hybridum* might not be infraspecific hybrid at all, but only a peculiar expression or cultivar ('Hybridum') of *A. pseudoplatanus.*

ACER × MARTINII Jordan (1852)

ORIGIN: Naturally occurring.

PARENTAGE: *A. monspessulanum* × *A. opalus.*

SYNONYMS

- *A. monspessulanum* var. *quinquelobum* Willkomm & Lange (1893).
- *A. monspessulanum* f. *martinii* (Jordan) Rouy & Foucauld (1897).
- *A. peronai* Schwerin (1901).
- *A. paui* Marcet (1906).
- *A. perrierei* Chabert (1909).
- *A. guinieri* Chabert (1910).
- *A. hyrcanum* sensu Faurel & Maire ex Quezel & Santa (1963), non Fischer & Meyer.

TYPE: *C. Martin;* LY.

EPITHET: *Martinii,* after Claude Martin (1731–1800), a French missionary to India.

HABIT: A small tree; branches red-brown to gray.

LEAVES: 3- to 5-lobed, 3–9 cm across, margins crenate-serrate, petioles 3–5 cm long, uppersides glabrous, dark green, pubescent when developing; leaves different from those of *A. opalus* in having slender tips on the lobes.

INFLORESCENCES: Corymbs about 5 cm long.

FLOWERS: Appearing with the leaves.

FRUITS: Samaras subhorizontal, light brown.

HARDINESS: Zone V.

DISTRIBUTION: Indigenous to Europe, northern Spain, southern France, the Apennines of Italy, and Yugoslavia—where the two putative parents overlap in distribution.

REFERENCES: Elwes & Henry (1908), Murray (1970c), Rehder (1986 facs.), Schwerin (1901).

Although this hybrid is now considered to be a synonym of *Acer* × *coriaceum,* it is discussed here because of its historical interest. It has the same parentage as *A.* × *coriaceum* and has to be sunk in synonymy, according to the rules of botanical nomenclature.

The original plant could not be traced anywhere in cultivation. Comparison of living materials of *Acer* × *coriaceum, A.* × *bornmuelleri,* and *A.* × *duretti* was not possible.

ACER × PSEUDO-HELDREICHII Fukarek & Celjo (1959)

ORIGIN: Naturally occurring.

PARENTAGE: *A. pseudoplatanus* × *A. heldreichii.*

TYPE: Not known at this time.

EPITHET: *Pseudo-heldreichii,* a false *A. heldreichii.*

HABIT: A large tree with the same habit as the parents.

LEAVES: 5-lobed, 10–15 cm across, slightly wider than long, rather deeply divided—to half the blade length; upper surfaces dark green, with deeper green veins, undersides glaucous or light green.

FLOWERS: Not seen.

FRUITS: On long, pendulous racemes; samaras well-developed, 3–5 cm long.

BARK AND BUDS: Hardly different from either parent; buds not black like those of *A. heldreichii.*

HARDINESS: Zone V.

AUTUMN COLOR: Yellow.

DISTRIBUTION: Populations and individuals occasionally occur in the wild, in those areas where the putative parent species meet, such as in northern Yugoslavia; quite common in horticulture—more common than true *A. heldreichii.* Most seed of *A. heldreichii* is harvested from trees of garden origin, and both parents hybridize freely.

REFERENCES: Fukareck & Celjo (1959), Murray (1970c).

A large specimen of this hybrid grows in the Belmonte Arboretum, Wageningen, The Netherlands.

ACER × RAMOSUM Schwerin (1894)

ORIGIN: Garden.

PARENTAGE: *A. campestre* × *A. pseudoplatanus;* parentage uncertain.

TYPE: Not known.

EPITHET: *Ramosus,* densely branched.

ILLUSTRATIONS: Krüssmann (1976a), Schwerin (1894).

HABIT: A small, upright tree, densely branched; branches dark brown.

LEAVES: 3- to 5-lobed, rounded, 5–9 cm wide, lobes doubly serrate, bases rounded, cordate to subcordate, dark green above, much paler beneath, glabrous, with rusty hairs at the angles of the veins; petioles 7–8 cm long.

INFLORESCENCES: Racemose; corymbs about 8 cm long.

FLOWERS: Yellow-green, like *A. pseudoplatanus;*

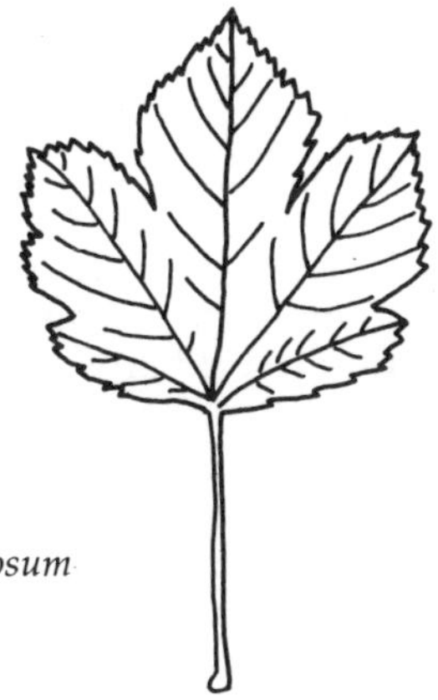
Acer × ramosum

Acer × rotundilobum

stamens thickly covered with whitish hairs.
FRUITS: Samaras subhorizontal, up to 6 cm long.
DISTRIBUTION: Not known in the wild.
HARDINESS: Zone V.
AUTUMN COLOR: Not seen.
REFERENCES: Krüssmann (1976a), Murray (1970c), Pax (1902), Rehder (1986 facs.), Schwerin (1894).

Schwerin (1894) described this hybrid as arising from a cross between *Acer campestre* × *A. pseudoplatanus,* but Pax considered this to be unlikely, as do the coauthors of the present volume. Hybrids between species with laticiferous petioles and those without are most unlikely.

Schwerin found this hybrid in a large quantity of *Acer pseudoplatanus* seedlings in a nursery in Halstenbek, Holstein, Germany. He did not cite a type or publish a Latin description, but he did indicate "spec. novum."

ACER × ROTUNDILOBUM Schwerin (1894)

ORIGIN: Garden.
PARENTAGE: *A. monspessulanum* × *A. opalus* ssp. *obtusatum.*
SYNONYM: *A. barbatum* Booth ex Schwerin (1894), non Michaux.
TYPE: Arboretum Muskau, Germany.
EPITHET: *Rotundilobus,* with rounded lobes.
ILLUSTRATIONS: Plates 125, 126; Krüssmann (1976a).
HABIT: A shrub or small tree; branches reddish with gray lenticels, pubescent when young; new growth red.
LEAVES: 3-lobed, rounded, 5–7 cm across; much thinner in texture, not as hardy, and much more glabrous than those of *A. opalus;* margins somewhat undulate; petioles 4–5 cm long.
FLOWERS: Not seen.
HARDINESS: Zone V.
AUTUMN COLOR: Not seen.
FRUITS: Not seen.
REFERENCES: Bean (1970), Elwes & Henry (1908), Krüssmann (1976a), Murray (1970c), Pax (1902), Rehder (1986 facs.), Schneider (1912).

Named by Schwerin in 1894, the type for this hybrid maple was, or perhaps is still, in the old arboretum of Muskau, Germany, which was founded by Prince Frederik of The Netherlands in the early 1800s. Petzold, a head gardener at the time, coauthored a book on the arboretum (Petzold & Kirchner 1864) but did not cite *Acer × rotundilobum.*

An old tree is growing in Les Barres, France, from which scions were taken to re-introduce this hybrid into the trade. Unfortunately, this effort failed.

ACER × SCHWERINII Pax (1893)

ORIGIN: Garden.
PARENTAGE: *A. crataegifolium* × *A. rufinerve*(?).
SYNONYMS
*A. glaucum* Pax (1893).
*A. veitchii* Schwerin (1894).
TYPE: K, as *A. glaucum;* originally cultivated at the Royal Botanical Gardens, Kew, Great Britain.
EPITHET: *Schwerinii,* after the German dendrologist Graf von Schwerin (1856–1934).
ILLUSTRATIONS: Krüssmann (1976a), Schwerin (1894).
HABIT: A shrub or small tree.
LEAVES: Unlobed to remotely lobed, broadly oblanceolate, 10–15 cm long, bases subcordate, green beneath with hairs when juvenile; petioles 3–5 cm long; sinuses, if present, shallow and acute.
INFLORESCENCES: Corymbose, about 4 cm long.
FLOWERS: Yellowish, appearing with the leaves.
FRUITS: Schwerin's plant flowered regularly, but did not produce viable seed.
BARK AND BUDS: Bark green with clear, white stripes; very much like *A. pensylvanicum.*
HARDINESS: Unknown.
AUTUMN COLOR: Not seen.
REFERENCES: Krüssmann (1976a), Murray (1970c), Pax (1902), Rehder (1986 facs.), Schneider (1912), Schwerin (1900).

*Acer × schwerinii* is said to be a hardy shrub

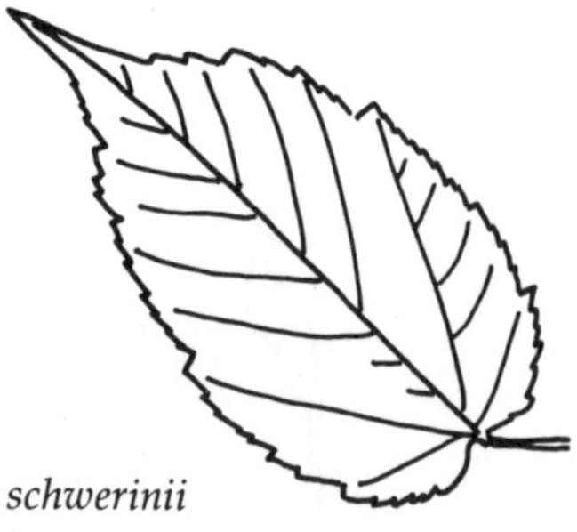

*Acer × schwerinii*

with unlobed or only slightly lobed leaves, very much like *A. pensylvanicum.* Veitch nursery supplied this plant to Schwerin as "Acer sp. from North China." Schwerin called it *A. veitchii,* but suggested that it might be a hybrid between *A. crataegifolium* and *A. rufinerve.* This suggestion is most unlikely, as both *A. crataegifolium* and *A. rufinerve* are Japanese species. *Acer pensylvanicum* is a North American species and cannot be involved, and Pax (1893) one year earlier described this same hybrid as *A. schwerinii.* Fang (1981a) does not mention it as a Chinese taxon.

This hybrid, which is sometimes confused with *Acer campestre* 'Schwerinii', an entirely different plant with purplish red leaves, should be brought back into cultivation and certainly deserves more research. The authors were not able to trace this hybrid.

ACER × ZOESCHENSE Pax (1886)

ORIGIN: Garden.

PARENTAGE: *A. campestre* × *A. cappadocicum* ssp. *lobelii.*

SYNONYMS

*A. campestre* var. *aetnense* hort. ex Koch (1853)
*A. atheniense* hort. ex Nicholson (1881).
*A. neglectum* Lange (1882), non Walpers.
*A. neglectum* var. *zoeschense* (Pax) Schwerin (1894).
*A. aetnense* hort. ex Pax (1902).

TYPE: *Dieck.* In Uechtritz Herbarium, cultivated in a Copenhagen garden.

COMMON NAME: Zoeschener Ahorn.

EPITHET: *Zoeschensis,* after Zoeschen, an old German nursery situated in a village of that name. The nursery was owned by Graf von Schwerin, and the garden's director and head gardener was G. Dieck.

ILLUSTRATION: Plate 127.

HABIT: A medium-sized tree to 15 m tall, often wider than tall, densely branched; branches slightly corky, yellow-brown, minutely pubescent. In other hybrid grexes the branchlets are chestnut brown, turning grayish brown.

LEAVES: 5- to 7-lobed, 10–20 cm across, deeply cordate, lobes acuminate, ovate, sharply contracting to acuminate tips, 3 main lobes shouldered with one pair of prominent teeth, margins entire, glabrous above and beneath except for lines of white hairs along the midribs, lustrous green above, paler beneath; petioles slightly pubescent, 6 cm long, slender.

INFLORESCENCES: Corymbose, terminal, and erect.

FLOWERS: 5-merous, yellow-green, appearing after the leaves.

FRUITS: Samaras pubescent, 3–5 cm long, subhorizontal.

BARK AND BUDS: Bark much less corky than that of *A. campestre.*

HARDINESS: Zone V.

AUTUMN COLOR: Yellow to golden brown.

DISTRIBUTION: A garden hybrid originating in Copenhagen, Denmark.

CULTIVARS: Several (see Chapter 9).

REFERENCES: Bean (1970), Dippel (1892), Krüssmann (1976a), Murray (1970c), Pax (1902), Rehder (1986 facs.).

Originating in Copenhagen, Denmark, about 1880, this hybrid looks more like *Acer campestre* than the other parent: its attractive dark green leaves have a purple hue. The tree is rather easily distinguished from *A. campestre* by its larger leaves, sparser hairs, and the absence of cork on the bark. It is available in the trade and is suitable for smaller parks and especially for narrow streets. It is easily propagated by layering. Grafting and budding on *A. campestre* or *A. platanoides* are also possible. Of its several named cultivars, 'Annae' is by far the best known; it hardly differs from *A. × zoeschense* save that the young leaves are more purple-red when opening.

Chapter 9

# Maple Cultivars

D. M. VAN GELDEREN

Many of the cultivars described in this chapter are old "formae" of wild or cultivated origin described years ago by a number of authors. With the introduction of the *International Code of Nomenclature for Cultivated Plants* in 1953, and the introduction of the coined word "cultivar" for "cultivated variety," the status of most of the names of cultivated origin have been changed to cultivar rank.

A valid cultivar name bears the name of the genus and species in italics and the cultivar name immediately following that combination, in roman type and set off with single quotation marks. It is incorrect to use more Latin names than those validly given to the taxon to which a particular cultivar belongs. For example: *Acer palmatum* 'Osakazuki' and *A. palmatum* ssp. *amoenum* 'Osakazuki' are both correct, as is *A. palmatum* 'Dissectum'. But *A. palmatum dissectum* 'Sekimori' is incorrect because *dissectum* is not a valid name for a subspecies. Professor Masato Yokoi of Chiba University was kind enough to assist the author in determining the best romanized spellings for the names of Japanese cultivars.

"Common" names, so-called, are, regrettably, frequently used in commercial catalogs and advertisements, but certainly have no place in any publication purporting to deal with horticultural or botanical matters in an accurate way.

New introductions should be registered with the International Registrar for unassigned woody genera, Dr. Donald Huttleston, 409 Greenwood Road, Kennett Square, Pennsylvania 19348, USA.

For each cultivar discussed, the name of the introducer is given, as well as the year of introduction and the place of origin, insofar as they are known. References, page numbers, and illustrations are primarily for *Japanese Maples* by J. D. Vertrees: JDV I refers to the first edition, published in 1978; JDV II refers to the second, published in 1987.

The following species, subspecies, and hybrids, listed in alphabetical order, have one or more cultivars:

*Acer buergerianum*
*A. campestre*
*A. cappadocicum*
*A. carpinifolium*
*A. circinatum*
*A. × conspicuum*
*A. crataegifolium*
*A. davidii*
*A. × durettii*
*A. × freemanii*
*A. glabrum*
*A. × hillieri*
*A. japonicum*
*A. longipes* ssp. *amplum*
*A. macrophyllum*
*A. mono*
*A. monspessulanum*
*A. negundo*
*A. palmatum*
*A. pectinatum* ssp. *forrestii*
*A. pectinatum* ssp. *pectinatum*
*A. pensylvanicum*
*A. platanoides*
*A. pseudoplatanus*
*A. pycnanthum*
*A. rubescens*
*A. rubrum*
*A. rufinerve*
*A. saccharinum*
*A. saccharum*
*A. shirasawanum*
*A. sieboldianum*
*A. tataricum* ssp. *ginnala*
*A. tataricum* ssp. *tataricum*
*A. truncatum*
*A. velutinum*
*A. × zoeschense*

## ACER BUERGERIANUM

This is a relatively rare maple in North America and Europe, though widely cultivated in China and Japan, and its cultivars are even rarer. The Japanese name for this species is Tokaede. There are a number of interesting cultivars available that deserve to be better known. The introducers of most cultivars of *Acer buergerianum* are unknown. Most of the cultivars are difficult to propagate, and few are really hardy in northern regions. They usually prefer a rather dry climate in which they tolerate colder temperatures.

**'Akebono'**, see **'Goshiki kaede'**

**'Akebono nishiki'**, see **'Goshiki kaede'**

**'Eastwood Cloud'.** Ron Gordon (1949). JDV II, 150. Shrub, slower growing than the species. The young leaves are almost white, turning through pink and creamy to a pale green. Introduced by P. Cave, New Zealand. A fragile cultivar with interesting foliage and with somewhat stronger growth than 'Wako nishiki'. Zone VII.

**'Elobatum'.** Schwerin (1893). Germany. With unlobed leaves. Not in cultivation (as *A. trifidum* 'Elobatum').

**'Fushima kaede'**, see **'Miyasama'**

**'Goshiki kaede'.** JDV I, 143; JDV II, 150, photo. A dwarfish shrub, not exceeding 1.5–2 m in height. The leaves are much smaller than those of the species, and the central lobes much shorter. They are irregularly variegated; some are entirely green, others are whitish or pink, while others are variegated white or pink. Some whitish leaves turn cream or even yellow when maturing. 'Goshiki' means "five-colored," which is quite appropriate. This delicate and fragile cultivar is difficult both to grow and propagate. It is not hardy. Only occasionally available in the trade. Zones VIII–IX.

**'Integrilobum'**, see **'Subintegrum'** (The name 'Integrilobum' is sometimes used but was never published and is illegitimate.)

**'Iwao kaede'.** JDV I, 144; JDV II, 151. A dense shrub with larger leaves than the species, 6–8 cm long and 7–9 cm wide. They appear very broad as the triangular, blunt-tipped lobes extend acutely at right angles. The young leaves are dark green to bright red, depending on the amount of shade. Mature leaves are dark shiny green and leathery. Sometimes called "rock maple." Very rarely available in the trade. Zones VII–VIII.

**'Jako kaede'.** JDV II, 151. Synonym of *Premna japonica*. Not a maple.

**'Johro kuakame'.** Unregistered Japanese cultivar, imported to The Netherlands in 1991 from Japan. No further description available.

**'Kifu nishiki'.** Yokoi (1989). Japan. A small shrub, densely branched, to 90 cm. Its small leaves are white or cream variegated on the lower half of the leaf blades. Probably tender. Imported to The Netherlands courtesy of M. Yokoi, Chiba University, Japan. There is no entry of this name in previous literature.

**'Koshi miyasama'.** Shibamichi Honten Co. (1975). Japan. A rather strong-growing, shrubby tree, imported to The Netherlands in 1979 from Japan. It grows to about 5–6 m tall and is rather densely branched. The leaves are somewhat leathery, 4–5 cm long and about as wide. Leaves on vigorous long shoots are usually larger. The leaf bases are rounded, the lobes short and blunt. The name has only been found in a Japanese trade-list; it is close to 'Miyasama kaede'. It is now sometimes available in the trade in Europe. Zones VI–VII.

**'Kyuden'.** JDV I, 144; JDV II, 151, photo. A dwarf with very thin twigs, internodes closely set together. The leaves are small, 3 cm long, 2–3 cm wide; leaf bases are cordate, and the leaf shape is ovate to triangular. The side lobes are occasionally absent. Leaves are dark shiny green, leathery, and glaucous beneath. 'Kyuden' means "palace." Difficult to propagate and very rare. Available in the trade in Japan, and sometimes in Europe. Zones VI–VII.

**'Maruba tokaede'.** JDV I, 143; JDV II, 151, photo. Medium-sized tree to 6–7 m tall, rather densely branched. The leaves are leathery in texture and shiny green. They have short, blunt lobes or are almost unlobed. Leaf bases are slightly cordate, main veins prominent, and petioles sturdy, 2–3 cm long. It has very good autumn colors, mainly red to orange and belongs to subspecies *formosanum*. Not available in Europe.

**'Mino yatsubusa'.** JDV I, 144; JDV II, 154, photo. A dwarfish shrub, rather densely branched. The leaves are peculiar, 3-lobed with long and narrow central lobes (Plate 128). The two basal lobes are short and spread at right angles. The long, tapering points of the central lobes are very conspicuous. The blades measure 7–8 cm long and are shiny green; the autumn color can be very good. It is a rare plant, difficult to propagate, and only rarely available in the trade. According to Vertrees, it has also been placed under *A. palmatum*. It is possible, always with difficulty, to graft it on both *A. palmatum* and *A. buergerianum*. Now best considered a cultivar of *A. buergerianum*. Zone VII.

**'Mitsuba kaede'.** JDV I, 145; JDV II, 152. A densely branched shrubby tree, with closely spaced internodes. Leaves of a thin texture, bright green, and about 5–7 cm long and as wide. They are distinctively 3-lobed and T-shaped. The central lobes are twice as long as the basal ones. Autumn color is inconspicuous. The bark is fissured and corky with age. It is hardy and occasionally available in the trade. Zone VI.

**'Mitsuba kaede nishikisiyou'.** This cultivar is indistinguishable from 'Mitsuba kaede' and as the plant has not been described nor the name published, it must be included in that cultivar. It was imported from Japan in 1975.

**'Miyadono'**, see **'Kyuden'**

**'Miyasama'.** JDV I, 143; JDV II, 150. A shrubby plant of moderate size, probably not exceeding 4–5 m. The leaves are dark green, leathery, and glaucous beneath. In very mild winters, they are almost evergreen. Leaf bases are rounded, the lobes short and blunt, from time to time even absent, the leaf thus forming an ovate shape. Autumn color is yellow to orange. 'Miyasama' belongs to subspecies *formosanum,* indigenous to Taiwan, and was formerly called 'Fushimi kaede'. It is widely used for bonsai in Japan. These plants are usually grown from seed and do not deserve this cultivar name.

**'Miyasama kaede'**, see **'Miyasama'**

**'Miyasama kaede yatsubusa'**, see **'Miyasama yatsubusa'**

**'Miyasama yatsubusa'.** JDV I, 145; JDV II, 152, photo. This cultivar is almost identical with 'Miyasama' except for size. It is short and stubby and grows only a few centimeters per year. It is very densely branched with densely packed leaves. Quite rare and only rarely available in the trade. Zones VI–VII.

**'Musk-scented'**, a synonym of *Premna japonica*

**'Naruto'.** JDV I, 146; JDV II, 153, photo. A medium-sized, sturdy shrub, to 3–4 m tall; a twiggy plant with very interesting leaves forming a sharp-pointed T. The central lobes are long-triangular, and the basal lobes spread at right angles. The margins are strongly involute, making the lobes appear much narrower than they really are. The leaf color is a bluish green with glaucous undersides, turning a good yellow in autumn. It can easily be propagated by grafting on seedlings of *A. buergerianum.* Available in the trade. Zone VII.

**'Naruto kaede'**, see **'Naruto'**

**'Nusatoriyama'.** JDV I, 146; JDV II, 153, photo. A special, neat plant, not exceeding 1 m in height. It is very delicate and fragile, difficult to grow. The leaves are almost white in spring and turn to a delicate pink and cream. They are 3–4 cm long and 3-lobed. Because the leaves contain practically no chlorophyll, the plant must be planted in full shade, as its leaves scorch quickly in sunlight. It is difficult to maintain and quite scarce. An interesting plant for the gardener but rarely available, this cultivar is comparable to *A. mono* 'Usugumo' but is by no means identical. A 7- to 9-lobed but otherwise similar plant was called *A. palmatum* 'Nusatoriyama' by Hinkul (1956) and may belong here. Zone VIII.

**'Subintegrum'.** A shrubby tree with leathery leaves, only remotely or slightly 3-lobed. The leaves drop late in the season and are shiny green, glaucous beneath, 5–7 cm long and almost as wide. It is close to 'Koshi miyasama', but not identical, most probably belonging to subspecies *ningpoense.* It is a popular tree in southern China. According to H. J. Oterdoom, who has seen many specimens in China, they differ markedly from typical *A. buergerianum.* 'Subintegrum' is reasonably hardy in the coastal countries of Europe. This is an argument against *A. buergerianum* ssp. *ningpoense* parentage as that tree is supposedly warm-temperate or subtropical. Herbarium specimens look identical. The name 'Subintegrum' is mentioned in Murray's monograph only as, "Type: *Oldham 180,* Nagasaki, Japan; leaves subentire. Basionym: *A. trifidum* f. *subintegrum* Miquel 1867." It is a puzzling plant. Available in the trade. Zones VI–VII.

**'Tancho'.** JDV I, 146; JDV II, 153. Young plants cannot be distinguished from 'Naruto', but mature plants are smaller than that cultivar. It is useful for small gardens. Rarely available in the trade. Zone VII.

**'Tancho kaede'**, see **'Tancho'**

**'Wako nishiki'.** JDV I, 147; JDV II, 154, photo. A dwarf cultivar with tiny, variegated leaves 2 cm long and 1 cm wide. Leaves on young shoots are usually larger. New foliage may be totally white or light green. Like 'Nusatoriyama' it is very difficult to propagate and requires much care and attention. Available in Japan, and now imported to The Netherlands.

## ACER CAMPESTRE

Due to its immense range of distribution, this species shows much variability. All its many cultivars are zone V.

**'Albo-maculatum'.** Schwerin (1901). Germany.

Leaves dotted white. Fruits glabrous. Probably no longer in cultivation.

**'Albo-punctum'.** De Kort (1906). Belgium. Leaves dotted white. Probably no longer in cultivation. Very close to 'Pulverulentum', if not identical.

**'Albo-variegatum'.** Hayne (1822). Great Britain. Leaves variegated white, with large blotches. Fruits pubescent. Probably no longer in cultivation.

**'Angustilobum'.** Schwerin (1901). Germany. Leaf lobes narrower than the species. Probably no longer in cultivation.

**'Argenteo-marginatum'.** Willkomm (1879). Germany. Leaves with white-variegated margins. Very close to 'Albo-variegatum' if not the same. Probably no longer in cultivation.

**'Argenteo-variegatum'.** L. Van Houtte (1885). Gent, Belgium. Leaves variegated white. Very probably identical with 'Argenteo-marginatum' or at least very close. Probably no longer in cultivation.

**'Austriacum'.** De Candolle (1824). Switzerland. Well-branched small tree, to 10 m tall, branches slightly or not at all corky. Leaves rather large, larger than the species, softly pubescent, light green, brilliantly golden yellow in autumn. Leaf margins entire. See also *A. campestre* ssp. *leiocarpon.*

**'Carnival'.** Van Nijnatten (1989). Zundert, The Netherlands. Medium-sized shrub to 3 m tall, rather densely branched; leaves 5-lobed, variegated white and cream. A spontaneous seedling in a large seedbed, this cultivar is similar but not identical to 'Albo-variegatum'. 'Carnival' won an Award of Merit from the Royal Boskoop Horticultural Society in 1989.

**'Compactum', see 'Nanum'**

**'Compactum Nanum', see 'Nanum'**

**'Dusty'.** Kelsey & Dayton (1942). USA. See **'Pulverulentum'.**

**'Eastleigh Weeping'.** Hillier & Sons (1980). Ampfield, Great Britain. A tree of pendulous habit, raised in the Eastleigh Nursery of Hillier & Sons. Leaves like the species; hardly differing from 'Green Weeping', another chance seedling.

**'Elsrijk'.** Broerse (1953). Amstelveen, The Netherlands. Dutch selection from the municipal nurseries of Amstelveen and introduced by C. P. Broerse, the director. This cultivar was selected from a group of 12-year-old trees. 'Elsrijk' is a tree to 12 m tall with an ovoid to conical crown, very densely branched. Leaves small, 4–6 cm across, and dark green. Excellent for narrow streets.

**'Fastigiatum'.** Springer (1930). Wageningen, The Netherlands. Erect tree with a narrow conical crown. Branches very corky. Leaves 5-lobed, tomentose beneath, not differing in shape from the species. Found wild at Neckargemünd in southern Germany. May no longer be in cultivation.

**'Globosum'.** Loudon (1839). Great Britain. See **'Nanum'.**

**'Green Weeping'.** Van Nijnatten (1981). Zundert, The Netherlands. A tree with pendulous branches, found as a chance seedling in beds of *A. campestre;* seedlings raised for forestry purposes in Zundert. Leaves like those of the species, and branches slightly corky. A useful small tree for smaller gardens and cemeteries.

**'Laetum'.** Schwerin (1896). Germany. Tree with upright growth, young branches smooth, new shoots never with reddish tips. Leaves light green. Probably no longer in cultivation.

**'Louisa Red Shine'.** Van den Oever (1989). Haaren, The Netherlands. See 'Red Shine'.

**'Macrophyllum'.** Loddiges (1836). Differing from the species in its larger leaves, 10–15 cm across. Probably no longer in cultivation.

**'Maculatum'.** Groinland (1862). Great Britain. Leaves mottled with white. Probably very close to 'Pulverulentum'. Probably no longer in cultivation.

**'Microphyllum'.** (Opiz) Koch (1853). Germany. Open shrub to 3 m high and wide with very small leaves about 1–2 cm across. Rarely available.

**'Nanum'.** Loudon (1839). Great Britain. Plate 129. Densely branched shrub, to 2–2.5 m high and 2.5–3 m wide (Plate 131). Leaves smaller than the species, 3- to 5-lobed, olive green with reddish margins when young. Flowers very poorly and produces very few seeds. Stronger growing shoots may suddenly appear and must be removed. The young branches are rather brittle. Nice shrub for small gardens, balconies, and big tubs; also suitable for bonsai culture. Can be grafted on *A. campestre* or propagated by softwood cuttings. Propagation by seed sometimes produces dwarf plants. Bean called it 'Globosum', and it is described in *Gartenflora* 42 (1893) under this name, but Loudon described it much earlier, in 1839. De Vos, a famous Dutch nurseryman, received it about 1895 and introduced it only to The Netherlands, and not generally, as stated in Boom's *Nederlandse Dendrologie.* A very large specimen is growing in the Schlosspark at Konopiste, south of Prague, Czech Republic. Another mighty plant grows in the De Dreyen Arboretum of the Agricultural University in Wageningen, The Netherlands.

**'Pendulum'.** Schwerin (1893). Germany. Small tree with pendulous branches. Very rare selection. Probably no longer in cultivation. See **'Eastleigh Weeping'** and **'Green Weeping'.**

**'Postel'.** Kelsey & Dayton (1942). See **'Postelense'.**

**'Postelense'.** Lauche (1896). Germany. Shrub to 3 m tall, with spreading branches. Young leaves golden yellow, greenish yellow when mature (Plate 130). Buds and petioles reddish, fruits glabrous. Tends to burn in full sun. Nice, small tree when grafted on standard. Discovered by von Salisch in Postel, near Militsch in Silesia (Poland), and introduced by R. Lauche. A young and well-placed shrub of this pretty plant, just after leafing out, looks like a flowering *Forsythia.*

**'Pulverulentum'.** Booth ex Kirchner (1859). Germany. Small tree, to 4 m tall, with a large crown, wider than high. Leaves heavily speckled with white, like the species in shape (Plate 131). Half of the blades of some leaves may be green. Long green shoots develop frequently and must be removed regularly. Its origin is unknown, but it was distributed from the old Muskau Arboretum in eastern Germany. It is a nice, small tree, and a good specimen grows in the Belmonte Arboretum, Wageningen, The Netherlands.

**'Punctatissimum'.** Mulligan (1958). Illinois, USA. This plant is growing in the Morton Arboretum, Lisle, Illinois, USA. It is questionable whether it is really different from 'Pulverulentum'. This cultivar and its relatives are not 100 percent stable and seem to be different, but often are not.

**'Punctatum'.** Veitch (1867). Great Britain. See **'Pulverulentum'.**

**'Puncticulatum'.** Schwerin (1893). Germany. Leaves powdered white. Close to 'Pulverulentum'. No longer in cultivation.

**'Queen Elizabeth'.** Studebaker and Lake County Nursery (before 1985). Ohio, USA. Fast growing and developing to a small tree. The slightly pubescent leaves are larger than those of the species, with rounded lobes. Suitable as a small tree in narrow streets or for a high, wind-breaking fence. Very suitable as a street tree by its rather fastigiate habit. Introduced to Europe by A. van Nijnatten, Zundert, The Netherlands. US Plant Patent 4392.

**'Red Shine'.** Van den Oever (1980). Haaren, The Netherlands. Vigorously growing shrubby tree to 4 m tall, rather densely branched. The bark is more corky than its close relative 'Schwerinii'. The leaves are dark purple in the spring, turning a dull, dark greenish red in summer, later becoming dark green. It is showier, more vigorous, and less prone to mildew than the old 'Schwerinii'. It is now readily available in the trade.

**'Royal Ruby'.** Van Nijnatten (1980). Zundert, The Netherlands. Vigorously growing shrubby tree to 5 m tall, rather densely branched. Leaves are purple in the spring, turning to dark green in late summer. Not so showy as 'Red Shine' but grows faster and is suitable for hedges to 4 m tall. A long row of this cultivar, enclosing a garden, is attractive. Free of mildew.

**'Schwerinii'.** Hesse ex Purpus (1897). Germany. Small tree with a narrow crown to 6 m tall. Said to grow vigorously, but this certainly is not always so. Young leaves purple to dark purple, becoming greener in summer. Prone to mildew. Introduced by H. A. Hesse Nurseries in Weener, Germany.

**'Tauricum'.** Loudon (1842). Great Britain. Shrubby plant, usually growing wider than high, to 3–4 m. Leaves 3- to 5-lobed, 5–7 cm across, with acuminate lobes. Zone VII.

**'Tomentosum'.** Willkomm (1879). Germany. Leaves tomentose. Probably no longer in cultivation.

**'William Caldwell'.** Leaman (1980). Great Britain. Small, upright, treelike shrub of dense habit. The leaves are similar to the species in size and shape and color very well in the autumn. Named after William Caldwell of Messrs. Caldwell & Sons Nurseries in Knutsford, Great Britain. Said to be hard to propagate. Not yet available in the trade.

**'Zorgvlied'.** Broerse (1953). Amstelveen, The Netherlands. A Dutch selection from the same group as 'Elsrijk'. It is much the same in appearance but grows into a smaller tree to 10 m tall, with slightly smaller leaves. Seems to be less desirable than 'Elsrijk'.

## ACER CAPPADOCICUM

Of the three known cultivars of this species, only two are in general cultivation.

**'Aureum'.** (Hesse) Rehder (1914). Germany. A moderate tree of the same habit as the species itself, but smaller. The leaves are of the same shape as the species but differ in color. Young leaves are yellow, heavily overlaid with purple that later turns to yellow, becoming light green in late summer (Plate 132). Autumn color is brown-beige. Hesse Nurseries in Weener, Germany, introduced this cultivar as *A. laetum* f. *aureum.* Rehder transferred it to *A. cappadocicum.* Two other synonyms include *A. truncatum* 'Aureum' and *A. truncatum* 'Luteo-variegatum.' Seedlings of *A. cappadocicum* often produce plants with similar leaves. A very beautiful, large specimen is in J. Wieting's nursery in Westerstede, Germany. Zone V.

**'Rubrum'.** Booth Nurseries (1842). Germany. Large tree of the same shape and habit as the species. The young leaves are purple with green undertones, later turning green. Autumn color yellow. A well-known cultivar, suitable as a street tree. Zone V.

**'Tricolor'.** Gouchault (1886). France. Small tree, leaves variegated rose and white on green. Probably no longer in cultivation.

## ACER CARPINIFOLIUM

The hornbeam maple is remarkably constant in its character and not a single cultivar has heretofore been listed. In 1973 one very aberrant plant from a batch of seedlings was selected and has been named.

**'Esveld Select'.** Esveld (1978). Boskoop, The Netherlands. Dwarf, very shrubby, attained a height of 1 m in 10–12 years and 2 m after 20 years. Leaves smaller than those of the species, 4–6 cm long and 2–3 wide, margins strongly serrulate (Plate 133). The plant has a fastigiate habit. Autumn color golden yellow. Rather difficult to propagate; even grafting on seedlings of *A. carpinifolium* is not always successful. Very interesting plant with moderate ornamental value. Zone V.

## ACER CIRCINATUM

The vine maple, very widespread in western North America, is markedly uniform in character. Only in the last few years some cultivars have been selected. They must all be propagated by grafting on seedlings of *Acer palmatum*. All cultivars are zone V.

**'Elegant'.** Mulligan (1958). Washington, USA. A shrub to 6 m, rather openly branched. Leaves of the same size, shape, and autumn colors as the species, but the margins are more incised. This plant was introduced by the Dominion Arboretum, Ottawa, Canada, and published by Mulligan. It is rarely available in the trade but deserves more attention. There is another cultivar called 'Elegant'; see *A.* × *freemanii* in Chapter 8.

**'Glen Del'.** Loucks (1984). Eugene, Oregon, USA. JDV II, 150. A shrub with a narrow, upright habit, not multiple-stemmed as is typical for *A. circinatum*. It grows slowly. The leaves are 5-lobed, divided completely to the center of the leaf, the central lobes much longer than the others. Petioles are red. It was discovered at Del Lane's County Nursery in 1976, first propagated in 1978, and registered and introduced in 1984. Rarely available in the trade.

**'Little Gem'.** Alleyne Cook (1970). Canada. JDV I, 148; JDV II, 155, photo. Derived from a witches' broom. Plant hardly exceeds 1 m in height, very densely branched. Leaves closely set together, 3–5 cm across, of the same shape as the species but much smaller. A very beautiful dwarf shrub, slightly susceptible to sudden twig die-back. Suitable for the rock garden. Only rarely available. Young plants may grow quite fast, to 50 cm a year, but this growth spurt seems to be quite short-lived. Sometimes plants die suddenly without clear reasons.

**'Monroe'.** Mulligan (1974). Washington, USA. JDV I, 149; JDV II, 156, photo. A dense shrub, to 3–4 m, with stiff branches, growing higher than wide but not narrowly. The leaves are deeply incised, 5- to 7-lobed, not unlike the dissected forms of *A. japonicum* or *A. palmatum*, 6–10 cm across, dull green turning to yellow (Plate 134). The cultivar was discovered by W. Monroe of Portland, Oregon, USA, along the Mackenzie River. He layered a branch on the spot and moved the resulting plant to his home in 1965. J. D. Vertrees obtained a second layered plant in 1970 and started propagation by grafting on *A. palmatum*, which is easy. This cultivar is now available in the trade. Unfortunately, it is susceptible to mildew, especially in wet summers.

## ACER × CONSPICUUM

A few cultivars can be grouped under this interspecific hybrid. All are upright yet shrubby trees with beautiful striped bark.

**'Elephant's Ear'.** Bulk (1990). Boskoop, The Netherlands. Large shrub with stout branches, to 8 m high. The color of the bark is purple, striped with white. Leaves very big, especially on young vigorous shoots, 15–30 cm long and 10–20 cm wide, dark green, almost unlobed or shallowly lobed, margins roughly dentate. This cultivar was found in a large batch of seedlings, grown from open-pollinated seed harvested from *A. davidii*, with both *A. pensylvanicum* and *A.* × *conspicuum* 'Silver Vein' nearby in the Esveld Aceretum. Now rarely available. Zone VI.

**'Phoenix'.** Esveld (1986). Boskoop, The Netherlands. Shrub to 4 m; stems are fiery red in winter, striped with white. This very conspicuous feature disappears in summer and the color turns to creamy salmon, as in *A. pensylvanicum* 'Erythrocladum' and *A. palmatum* 'Sangokaku'. The leaves are of the same shape and size as the better-known *A.* × *conspicuum* 'Silver Vein'. It is a chance seedling of 'Silver Vein' that appeared in a seedbed about 1982. Unfortunately, 'Phoenix' is hard to propagate and is prone to sudden die-back. Zone VI.

**'Silver Cardinal'.** Crown Estate Commissioners (1985). Windsor, Great Britain. Huge shrub with snakebark stems and branches, which are red in the juvenile state but green when mature. Leaves variegated when young, with pink and cream, dark green when mature, 5–10 cm long, 3–7 cm wide, broad to narrowly triangular, and with acuminate apices. Margins are irregularly dentate and sometimes with lateral lobes toward the bases. Petioles red. Shown at the Royal Horticultural Society show in London in 1985, it won an Award of Merit. It was a chance seedling of *A. pensylvanicum,* the other parent being unknown, though it could have been *A. davidii* or *A. rubescens.* Unfortunately, it is not yet available in the trade. Zones VI–VII.

**'Silver Vein'.** Hillier & Sons (1975). Ampfield, Great Britain. Medium-sized, slender tree or multistemmed shrub to 10 m tall. Trunks and branches very heavily striped with white on a blue-green bark (Plate 135). Leaves large, 12–20 cm long, 10–15 cm wide, 3-lobed, outer lobes underdeveloped, glabrous, undersides light green (Plate 136). Petioles red, 4–10 cm long. Inflorescences terminal and racemose, up to 15 cm long. This hybrid was found in Hilliers' nurseries about 1960 and named about 1975. It was supposed to be a hybrid between *A. pensylvanicum* and *A. pectinatum* ssp. *laxiflorum;* in fact, it is a seedling from the cross between *A. davidii* 'George Forrest' and *A. pensylvanicum* 'Erythrocladum'. It is a very valuable plant, worthy of a place in a garden. It has the most conspicuous bark of all snakebark maples. Now widely available in the trade. Zones V–VI.

## ACER CRATAEGIFOLIUM

This rather rare species has only a few cultivars, possibly only one.

**'Albo-variegatum'.** Pax (1886). Germany. See **'Veitchii'.**

**'Fueri kouri kaede'**, see **'Veitchii'**

**'Hillieri'.** This name has been seen in some nursery price lists. Most probably it is identical to 'Veitchii'.

**'Meuri kaede no fuiri'.** Ishii Yuga. JDV II, 157, photo. A variegated clone of *A. crataegifolium,* differing from 'Veitchii' by its larger leaves, which are darker green and much less variegated. The white blotches turn to pink in the fall. The variegation is very unstable and often entirely lacking. Zone VI.

**'Meuri ko fuba'**, see **'Meuri kaede no fuiri'**

**'Variegatum'.** Pax (1886). Germany. See **'Veitchii'.**

**'Veitchii'.** Nicholson (1881). Great Britain. Small shrub, to 2–2.5 m high, rather densely branched. Its leaves are smaller than the species, and are pink and white variegated (Plate 137). It is a rare plant and only occasionally seen. As it is rather difficult to propagate it is not generally available in the trade. Zone VI.

## ACER DAVIDII

The variability of this species has led to the selection of several clones that are now in cultivation and propagated vegetatively. Most of them have not yet been described as they are of recent introduction. All are Zones V–VI.

**'Cantonspark'.** De Jong (1980). Doorn, The Netherlands. A Dutch selection, discovered in the Cantonspark of Baarn as a tree labeled *A. grosseri* (a synonym of *A. davidii* ssp. *grosseri*). This cultivar is more suitably placed under subspecies *davidii.* The tree has a rather narrow, fastigiate habit, to 12–15 m high. The trunk is striped with white, as is typical of the species. The leaves are unlobed with some slightly lobed leaves on young shoots, both typical of the species. It is a good tree for narrower streets or smaller gardens and is to be introduced into the trade.

**'Ernest Wilson'.** Keenan (1957). Great Britain. The name was given in 1957; however, the tree has been growing at the Royal Botanic Garden, Edinburgh, since 1907. Tree of moderate size, slightly smaller than the species, to 10–12 m tall with a rounded, rather compact crown, bark beautifully striped with white. Leaves unlobed or slightly lobed, especially on vigorous shoots on young plants. They are of the same shape and size as the species. It fruits abundantly when mature. The tree makes a "green" impression due to the greenish bark and the dark green leaves. Several trees have been sold and named 'Ernest Wilson' although grown from seed. This practice must be avoided as true cultivars can easily be grafted or grown from cuttings. Grafted plants are available in the trade all derived from a specimen in the Esveld Aceretum. Good trees can be seen at Westonbirt Arboretum, Tetbury, Great Britain, and the Royal Botanic Garden, Edinburgh.

**'George Forrest'.** Keenan (1957). Great Britain. Tree of moderate size, with an open and pendulous habit, less high, to 8–10 m, than wide, bark purplish green, striped with white. Leaves larger than 'Ernest Wilson', to 20 cm long, not lobed or slightly lobed on vigorous shoots (Plate 138). This tree makes a "red" impression due to the purplish bark and the crimson-red petioles. This tree has also been sold as seedlings, a practice to be avoided, as the seedlings are not 'George Forrest' (see 'Ernest Wilson'). 'George Forrest' has been confused in the trade with the former *A. forrestii* (syn. *A. pectinatum* ssp. *forrestii*). A good tree grows in the Westonbirt Arboretum, Tetbury, Great Britain; another, in the Royal Botanic Garden, Edinburgh, was planted in 1921. Grafted plants are available in the trade from the Westonbirt tree.

**'Hagelunie'.** Esveld (1992). Boskoop, The Netherlands. A large shrub, up to 10 m tall, with a purplish bark, striped with white. Leaves as in the species, unlobed, young leaves on long vigorous shoots, 3-lobed. Its main feature is the conspicuous bark, especially in winter. Named after the Hagelunie, an insurance company for horticultural enterprise, especially for damages caused by hail, at its hundredth anniversary. This plant has been used as a gift for important customers and suppliers. Only available through the Hagelunie.

**'Horizontale'.** Villa Taranto (before 1959). Intra, Pallanza, Italy. This particular plant, in the gardens of the Villa Taranto, is of a very wide, spreading habit, 4–6 m high but at least 8–10 m wide. Young plants are far more erect, but they soon develop this habit. Young leaves are lobed and are glistening maroon-purple, later changing to dark green. This clone is not identical to or synonymous with *A. davidii* var. *horizontale* Pax (1902), which was so named because of its horizontal samara wings. The name 'Horizontale' was attached to the Villa Taranto plant because of its horizontal habit. It is a remarkable clone and worthy of a place in large gardens. Must be propagated vegetatively. The best means is grafting on any seedling of section *Macrantha.*

**'Karmen'.** Esveld (1985). Boskoop, The Netherlands. A chance seedling that forms a usually multistemmed, small tree to 10 m tall. It bears unlobed leaves, to 15 cm long and only 4–5 cm wide, with long, somewhat acuminate apices. Young leaves may be slightly lobed on vigorous shoots. The leaves are a good brown-maroon when young, becoming dark green when mature. Discovered by P. C. de Jong about 1975 and propagated and introduced by Firma C. Esveld in 1985; named after Karmen Rosalie van Gelderen, granddaughter of this author.

**'Madeleine Spitta'.** Wilfred Fox (1950). Godalming, Great Britain. A fastigiate tree to 12 m tall. This cultivar was raised at the Winkworth Arboretum, Godalming. The name has not been published heretofore and is given to honor the late Madeleine Spitta, involved in the planning of the Winkworth Arboretum. The name has been registered at the Royal Botanic Gardens, Kew, in the inventory of the gardens belonging to the National Trust. It seems that several fastigiate seedlings received this cultivar name. It is rarely available in the trade. The tree found in the Cantonspark in Baarn, The Netherlands, might fit well in this group. This cultivar is in cultivation.

**'Rosalie'.** Esveld (1985). Boskoop, The Netherlands. Nameless but present in the Royal Botanic Gardens, Kew, it has been propagated vegetatively by means of grafting and can be purchased in the trade. The original tree is about 15 m high and is umbrella-shaped. Named after Karmen Rosalie van Gelderen, granddaughter of this author. This tree has a very remarkable blue-purple, striped bark in winter, turning to greenish purple in summer. The leaves are smaller than those of 'Karmen' (Plate 139).

**'Serpentine'.** Hooftman (1976). Boskoop, The Netherlands. Medium-sized shrub, rather erect-growing. Bark purplish red, heavily striped with white. Leaves dark green, almost unlobed, rather small, to 10 cm long and 3–5 cm wide, somewhat brittle and curving (Plate 140). Discovered as a chance seedling in the nursery of W. J. Hooftman, Boskoop, in the early 1970s. It won a Silver Medal at a Flora Nova Show in Boskoop in 1976, where it was shown for the first time. More recent investigation and comparison of flowers, leaves, and fruits indicate a strong resemblance to *A. crataegifolium.* The strong stripes, on the other hand, indicate *A. davidii* influence. The leaves are intermediate between the two. So the plant might be a chance seedling of open-pollinated seed. This theory is weakened by the fact that apparently no plant of *A. crataegifolium* was in the neighborhood. At present a firm conclusion cannot be offered. Theoretically, the plant might be a seedling from plants grown from seed collected in the northernmost part of its habitat in China. A good plant, suitable for small gardens. Available in the trade.

## ACER × DURETTII

Two cultivars from this interspecific hybrid have been recorded. Neither is still in cultivation.

**'Aureo-marginatum'.** Schwerin (1893). Germany. Leaves margined with yellow.

**'Aureo-marmoratum'.** Schwerin (1893). Germany. Leaves flecked and dotted yellow.

## ACER × FREEMANII

All cultivars are zone V.

**'Autumn Blaze'.** Jeffers (1980). Ohio, USA. The original tree is believed to be from Ohio. It is an upright, narrow form, rather fast-growing. Leaves 5-lobed, closely resembling those of *A. saccharinum* and orange in the autumn. In cultivation in both the United States and Europe.

**'Autumn Fantasy'.** Wandell (before 1986). Illinois, USA. The original tree, from central Illinois, was selected by Wandell. It is an upright tree with an oval crown and brilliant autumn colors. The leaves resemble those of *A. saccharinum* more than those of *A. rubrum,* the other hybrid parent.

**'Celebration'.** Lake County Nursery (about 1980). Ohio, USA. An upright tree with columnar branching; up to 15 m in height but rarely wider than 6 m. Leaves resembling those of *A. saccharinum* in shape; leathery and firm in texture. A useful street tree, introduced into Europe by T. van den Oever, Haaren, The Netherlands.

**'Celzam',** see **'Celebration'** (The name 'Celzam' is the valid cultivar name; 'Celebration' is the trademarked name under which it is sold by license-holders.)

**'Elegant'.** Grootendorst (1969). Boskoop, The Netherlands. This cultivar has an interesting story. Originally it was considered an unnamed clone of *A. saccharinum,* propagated by layering and usually sold as that species. Grootendorst subsequently decided it was not identical with the species but of hybrid origin. The crown of 'Elegant' is more compact than that of *A. saccharinum,* and the leaves are slightly more incised; branches ascending; leaves rather small, lobed one-half or more. It is generally available in The Netherlands, but seldom under its correct name. The original plant of this hybrid was at the former nursery De Bie van Aalst, Zundert, The Netherlands. There is another cultivar called 'Elegant' (see *A. circinatum*).

**'Marmo'.** Morton Arboretum (1920). Lisle, Illinois, USA. The original tree is at the Morton Arboretum, but its exact history is not known. It is believed to come from a nursery in Wisconsin. It has an upright, narrow habit and has reached about 25 m in height. The leaves, resembling those of *A. saccharinum* more than *A. rubrum,* are orange to yellow in the autumn.

## ACER GLABRUM

Only one cultivar is recorded, but it is probably no longer in cultivation.

**'Rhodocarpum'.** Schwerin (1910). Germany. Habit like the species. Leaves green, of the usual size and shape. Samaras bright red.

## ACER × HILLIERI

This recently described hybrid currently has two cultivars.

**'Summergold'.** Banks (1979). Great Britain. A moderately sized tree; leaves 5-lobed, yellow, the basal lobes somewhat underdeveloped. It has bright golden leaves in summer and clearly is a cultivar of this hybrid, as pointed out by Lancaster (1979a). Raised by Mr. Banks of Hergest Croft Gardens in Kington, Great Britain, it is now rarely available in the trade. Zone V.

**'West Hill'.** Hillier & Sons (1970). Ampfield, Great Britain. To 10 m in height, leaves dull green, with a very pleasant autumn color. Found in 1930 in a batch of seedlings labeled *A. miyabei.* It was recognized as a hybrid, but the female parent was not known. Roy Lancaster was convinced that it was *A. cappadocicum,* especially when he saw very similar trees in Hergest Croft Gardens, Kington. A large *A. cappadocicum* 'Aureum' grows there very near *A. miyabei.* Very rarely available in the trade. Zone V.

## ACER JAPONICUM

This Japanese maple has a number of cultivars, some of them with fernlike leaves and some with very large leaves. All are zones V–VI. Investigations indicate that several well-known cultivars, including 'Aureum' and 'Microphyllum', need to be transferred to *Acer shirasawanum,* another Japanese species, and they are discussed in the treatment of the cultivars of that species.

**'Aconitifolium'.** Meehan (1888). Great Britain. JDV I, 135; JDV II, 143, photo.
Synonyms
'Fernleaf'. Kelsey & Dayton (1942). Massachusetts, USA.
'Filicifolium'. Yokohama Nurseries (1896). Japan.
'Hau hiwa'. Yokohama Nurseries (1896). Japan.
'Heyhachii'. Matsumara ex Makino (1904). Japan.
'Laciniatum'. Veitch (1904). Great Britain.
'Mai kujaku'. (Name means "dancing peacock.")
'Palmatifidum'. Verschaffelt (1876). Belgium.
'Parsonsii'. Veitch ex Schwerin (1893).
'Veitchii'. Vrugtman (1968). (The name is older.)

Large, shrubby tree, to 15 m tall or occasionally more, often as wide as tall. Bark smooth and gray-brown. Leaves deeply cut, almost to the base in 7- to 11-palmatifid leaflike lobes, margins serrulate, to 15–20 cm across. Petioles green, 5–7 cm long. Autumn color striking scarlet, with gold and orange or even purple-red. One of the most outstanding cultivars for larger gardens. There are few Japanese maples surpassing it in autumnal brilliance. It flowers freely with rather conspicuous red flowers, just before the new leaves appear. Well known in horticulture, excellent specimens of this cultivar can be found in many gardens. It is propagated by grafting on *A. palmatum* and is readily available in the trade. There is some controversy about the nomenclature. Plants of 'Aconitifolium' in the sense meant here are still often labeled as 'Filicifolium'. Zone V.

**'Aconitifolium USA'**, see **'Attaryi'**

**'Angustilobum'.** Koidzumi (1911). Japan. Leaf lobes narrow, apices acuminate. Apparently not in cultivation.

**'Argenteum'.** Lawson (1874). Great Britain. See *A. rufinerve* 'Albo-limbatum'.

**'Ascendens'.** Koidzumi (1911). Japan. Samara wings ascendent. Apparently not in cultivation.

**'Atropurpureum'.** Von Siebold (1856). Germany. A cultivar of *A. palmatum.*

**'Attaryi'.** Vertrees. Roseburg, Oregon, USA. Large, upright shrub or occasionally a small tree to 12 m tall. Bark smooth and gray. Leaves very large, 15–25 cm across, very deeply cleft, to one-half or two-thirds of the blades, 7- to 9-lobed, margins coarsely serrate (Plate 141). Autumn color scarlet or orange-yellow. Petioles green, 5–10 cm long. Flowers red, in nodding clusters. There is some confusion about the nomenclature of this striking cultivar. J. D. Vertrees sent scions from his tree to The Netherlands. The resulting plants were strikingly different from those plants widely known there as 'Aconitifolium', so this clone was given the provisional name 'Aconitifolium USA'. As it is a very attractive plant, it was sold and supplied under this name. Some years later, however, scions were received from elsewhere under the name *A. sieboldianum* 'Attaryi', a then unknown name. It soon became clear that this cultivar did not belong to *A. sieboldianum;* it was identical to 'Aconitifolium USA'. Consequently, the name 'Attaryi' has been transferred to *A. japonicum.* Zone V.

**'Aureum'**, see ***A. shirasawanum* 'Aureum'.**

**'Bigmoon'.** Kelsey & Dayton (1942). USA. See **'Macrophyllum'.** A highly doubtful name.

**'Crassifolium'.** Koidzumi (1911). Japan. Leaves very thick. Probably not in cultivation.

**'Dissectum'.** Bot. Garden Kolding, Denmark. Large shrub, much like 'Green Cascade', but less finely dissected leaves. The name is certainly illegitimate and cannot be traced.

**'Ezono o momiji'**, see under ***A. shirasawarum***

**'Fairy Light'.** Teese (1979). Australia. JDV II, 144. This cultivar is much like 'Green Cascade' but with more dissected leaves. Of slow and irregular growth; the colors are comparable to similar cultivars. Mr. Teese used pollen of a dissected *A. palmatum* in his cross with *A. japonicum* 'Aconitifolium', but no influence of *A. palmatum* is to be seen. Only very rarely in the trade. Zone V.

**'Fernleaf'.** Kelsey & Dayton (1942). USA. See **'Aconitifolium'.**

**'Filicifolium'.** Yokohama Nurseries (1898). Japan. See **'Aconitifolium'.**

**'Filiforme'.** Iseli Nursery (1990). Boring, Oregon, USA. A small, treelike shrub, similar to 'Aconitifolium' but with smaller, fewer-lobed leaves. Autumn color scarlet. This cultivar is mentioned only in the 1990 catalog of the Iseli Nursery, where it is spelled "Filiformis." Both of these Latin cultivar names are illegitimate as they were published after 1 January 1959. Zone V.

**'Flagelliforme Aureum'.** Van Houtte (1885). Belgium. See ***A. shirasawanum* 'Aureum'.**

**'Goldenmoon'.** Kelsey & Dayton (1942). USA. See ***A. shirasawanum* 'Aureum'.**

**'Green Cascade'.** Wright (circa 1955). Canby, Oregon, USA. JDV I, 138; JDV II, 145, photo. Cascading shrub of the well-known "mushroom" habit, like many Dissectum group cultivars of *A.*

*palmatum*. The central shoot requires staking when young to obtain weeping plants. The leaves are very similar to those of 'Aconitifolium' though somewhat smaller. The autumn colors are scarlet, yellow, and orange and are very attractive. This cultivar, developed by Art Wright, is becoming increasingly popular and is available both in the United States and in Europe. Zone V.

**'Ha uchiwa kaede'**, probably a synonym of *A. japonicum*.

**'Hau hiwa'**, see **'Aconitifolium'**

**'Heyhachii'**, see **'Aconitifolium'**

**'Itaya'**. Kingsville Nursery (1942). Maryland, USA. JDV I, 138; JDV II, 145. A large-leaved clone of *A. japonicum*, very close to the species if not identical. Comparable to such cultivars as 'Takinogawa' or 'Vitifolium'. It is a sturdy treelike shrub, usually multistemmed. According to the late J. D. Vertrees, the name 'Itaya' is confusing. This name is also applied as a cultivar name in other species—*A. sieboldianum*, *A. mono*, and *A. truncatum*. The name can also be found in connection with *A. shirasawanum* and *A. mono* ssp. *mayrii*. The old Japanese literature does not clarify this matter. Plants under the name *A. japonicum* 'Itaya' are available in Europe but are identical with those called 'Meigetsu'. According to M. Yokoi, only 'Meigetsu' is legitimate; he considers 'Itaya' and 'Itaya meigetsu' as synonyms, only meaning *A. japonicum* or *A. shirasawanum*. Zone V.

**'Jucundum'**. Hereman (1868). Without description; not in cultivation.

**'Junihitoe'**, see under ***A. shirasawanum***

**'Kaempferi'**. Van Houtte (1885) Belgium.

**'Kakure gasa'**, see ***A. shirasawanum* 'Aureum'**

**'Kasado'**. Koidzumi (1911). Japan. Leaves 13-lobed. Apparently not in cultivation.

**'Kinkakure'**, see ***A. shirasawanum* 'Aureum'**

**'Kinugasayama'**. This cultivar is sometimes placed under *A. japonicum*, but its affinities are much closer to *A. sieboldianum*; with pubescent leaves of similar shape to that species.

**'Kokonoe'**. Koidzumi (1911). Japan. Leaves 13-lobed, orbicular, light yellow-green. Apparently not in cultivation.

**'Kujaku nishiki'**. JDV I, 139; JDV II, 146. The leaves are of the same shape as those of 'Aconitifolium', with white variegation occupying a good part of the dissected lobes. Tender and very difficult to propagate. Not known in Europe. Zone V.

**'Laciniatum'**. Veitch (1904). Great Britain. See **'Aconitifolium'**.

**'Littleleaf'**. Kelsey & Dayton (1942). USA. See ***A. shirasawanum* 'Microphyllum'**.

**'Macranthum'**. Lawson (1874). Great Britain. Leaves 9-lobed. Probably identical with the species. Apparently not in cultivation.

**'Macrocarpum'**. Van Houtte (1893). Belgium. Samaras large. Apparently no longer in cultivation.

**'Macrophyllum'**. Van Houtte ex Schwerin (1893). Germany. Leaves "large." No description. Probably not in cultivation.

**'Macrophyllum Aureum'**. Nicholson (1881). Great Britain. See ***A. shirasawanum* 'Aureum'**.

**'Magnificum'**. Wada (1938). Japan. Possibly idential to 'Macrophyllum'.

**'Mai kujaku'**. JDV I. See **'Aconitifolium'**.

**'Matsuyoi'**. Koidzumi (1911). Japan. See ***A. palmatum* 'Matsuyoi'**.

**'Meckelii'**. Siebold (1864). Germany.

**'Meigetsu'**, see ***A. japonicum***

**'Meigetsu Kaede'**, see ***A. japonicum***

**'Microphyllum'**, see ***A. shirasawanum* 'Microphyllum'**

**'Ogon itaya'**, see ***A. shirasawanum* 'Aureum'**

**'Ogureyama'**, see ***A. shirasawanum* 'Ogureyama'**

**'O isami'**. Koidzumi (1911). Japan. (Alternate spellings: 'Oh isami', 'Oo isami'.) JDV I, 140; JDV II, 147. A treelike shrub, very valuable and one of the most attractive cultivars of this species. It grows to 10 m high and almost as wide. The bark is gray-brown and smooth. Leaves are large, orbicular, and 9- to 13-lobed, rather deeply incised to about half the length of the blade. The tapering ends of the lobes are notched. Leaves easily measure 15–25 cm across. The new growth is olive-yellow to pink, quickly turning dark green. Autumn colors are spectacular—scarlet, gold, yellow, and orange with green. This spectacular cultivar is available in the trade. Zone V.

**'O taki'**. JDV I, 140; JDV II, 147, photo. Medium-sized, sturdy treelike shrub, 4–5 m high and 2–3 m wide. Short shoots bear firm, circular, 9- to 11-lobed, rich dark green leaves. The lobes are divided to the middle of the blades and lie closely together. Autumn colors are very good—rich crimson through orange to yellow. This is a rare tree and only occasionally available. Zone V.

**'Palmatifidum'.** Verschaffelt (1876). Belgium. See **'Aconitifolium'.**

**'Parsonii'.** Veitch (1904). Great Britain. See **'Aconitifolium'.**

**'Platanifolium'.** Van Houtte (1885). Belgium. No description.

**'Princeps'.** Verschaffelt (1864). Belgium. No description.

**'Purpureum'** (As used in the Dutch nursery trade, identical to *A. palmatum* 'Rubrum'.)

**'Rubrum'**, see ***A. palmatum* 'Rubrum'** (USA)

**'Sanguineum'.** Verschaffelt (1864). Belgium. See under ***A. palmatum.***

**'Sayo shigure'**, see under ***A. shirasawanum***

**'Scolopendrifolium'.** Parsons (1887). Great Britain. See ***A. palmatum* 'Linearilobum'.**

**'Taiyu'**, see **'O isami'**

**'Takinogawa'** (Probably *A. japonicum.*) JDV I, 141; JDV II, 148. This name is usually applied to an *A. palmatum* cultivar. There is much confusion about the name, as several different cultivars are labeled 'Takinogawa'. The clone described here was obtained from Maplewood Nursery many years ago and is cultivated in Boskoop, The Netherlands. It has very good autumn colors—gold, yellow, crimson (Plate 142). It is very close to, if not identical with, the species and does not, in fact, deserve clonal or cultivar rank but has been sold under this name in quantity! Zone V.

**'Tenuilobum'.** Koidzumi (1911). Japan. Lobes briefly acuminate. Apparently not in cultivation.

**'Veitchii'.** Vrugtman (1962). Canada. See **'Aconitifolium'.**

**'Viride'.** Verschaffelt (1876). Belgium. Leaves vivid green, no further description. Probably not in cultivation.

**'Vitifolium'.** N. E. Brown (1876). Great Britain. JDV I, 141; JDV II, 148. Treelike shrub, to 15 m high and almost as wide. Bark gray-brown and smooth. The leaves are the same size and shape as those of the species but are somewhat more deeply incised, to half the blade. The autumn colors are brilliant scarlet, orange, crimson, and yellow. This clone is close to the species, and quite often plants labeled 'Vitifolium' clearly represent the species. Magnificent specimens can be seen in the Westonbirt Arboretum, Tetbury, Great Britain. Zone V.

**'Yellow Moon'.** Pennsylvania, USA. See ***A. shirasawanum* 'Aureum'.**

**'Yezo meigetsu kaede'**, see ***A. shirasawanum* 'Microphyllum'**

## ACER LONGIPES ssp. AMPLUM

No cultivars have previously been recorded for this subspecies. About 1980, seeds were harvested in the Zuiderpark, The Hague, The Netherlands, from a tree planted in 1935 called *Acer amplum* var. *tientaiense.* As this variety has been sunk in synonymy, and *A. amplum* reduced to subspecific rank, any new cultivars raised from that seed must be placed under *A. longipes* ssp. *amplum.*

**'Gold Coin'.** Esveld (1985). Boskoop, The Netherlands. A multistemmed, shrubby tree, rather openly branched. A 15-year-old plant is about 2 m high and wide. The bark is gray and smooth, and the leaves are of the same shape and size as those of the species, mostly 5-lobed, the basal lobes often insignificant, 8–12 cm across, petioles thin and slender. Unfolding leaves are purplish, quickly turning to a golden yellow. The color holds very well in summer and hardly scorches in direct sunlight. Autumn color is yellow to whitish. Unfortunately, it is difficult to propagate. This cultivar will be introduced. Zone VI.

## ACER MACROPHYLLUM

The Oregon maple, so prevalent in western North America, has remarkably few cultivars. The three cultivars thus far described are rare in cultivation and only occasionally available in the trade. All are hardy in zone VI.

**'Kimballiae'.** Harrar (1940). Washington, USA. The 8- to 10-cm long leaves of this rare tree are dissected into 3–5 leaflets, 15–20 cm across. It grows slowly and is often only a shrub. The samaras are often tricarpellate. This cultivar was discovered by Snohomish Nursery Co., Washington, USA, and named for Mrs. Frank Kimball.

**'Rubrum'.** Murray (1969). USA. The leaves of this cultivar are reddish bronze when young. It was, or is, in cultivation in the Blake Gardens, University of California, Berkeley. This cultivar name in Latin form is illegitimate since it was published after 1 January 1959.

**'Seattle Sentinel'.** Mulligan (1954). Washington, USA. An erect tree, the same size as the species and with similar leaves. It is not known whether it is still cultivated. No further description is available.

**'Tricolor'.** Schwerin (1893). Germany. An old cultivar, with leaves green to reddish, flecked with white, thus forming a tricolored effect. Similar seedlings are often found in seed batches. These colored forms usually are not stable and lose their color when mature. No longer in cultivation.

## ACER MONO

Only a few cultivars are assigned to this species, and further, there is some confusion as to whether all cultivars placed under *Acer mono* really derive from it. The small-leaved cultivars are more properly placed under *A. truncatum.* Several natural formae are described under the species.

**'Akikaji nishiki'.** Kingsville Nursery. Maryland, USA. List 19. Reported to have dissected leaves. It is more likely that this is a synonym for *A. truncatum* 'Akikaze nishiki'. Zone VI.

**'Akikaze'**, see under ***A. truncatum***

**'Aureum'**, see ***A. cappadocicum* 'Aureum'**

**'Dissectum'.** (before 1899). Yokohama Nurseries Japan. A shrubby tree, to 4 m tall. Leaves green, 7-lobed the lobes slightly dissected. Probably no longer in cultivation. Plants under this name do not have dissected leaf lobes and are apparently false.

**'Futagoyama'.** Koidzumi (1911). Japan. Leaves 5-lobed, small, the lobes irregularly formed, constricted at bases. Probably not in cultivation.

**'Hoshiyadori'.** Kingsville Nursery (1968). Maryland, USA. JDV I, 153; JDV II, 160, photo. A remarkable cultivar with rather large leaves, 5-lobed, sometimes 7-lobed; the central lobe and the two side lobes almost triangular, not unlike typical leaves of *A. mono.* The basal lobes are much smaller or absent. The leaves are irregularly speckled and dotted white and cream. It grows into a small tree or large shrub about 6–7 m high. Unfortunately, it reverts easily and often has long, green shoots that must always be removed. It is somewhat prone to sunburn. It is available in the trade and widely cultivated in Japan. Zone V.

**'Hoshizukiyo'.** JDV I, 153; JDV II, 160. This cultivar, which has rather large leaves, is almost indistinguishable from 'Hoshiyadori'. The leaves are speckled with white and cream and are slightly more intense in color. Not available in the trade.

**'Marmoratum'.** Nicholson (1881). Great Britain. A treelike shrub to 8 m tall. Leaves slightly dotted with white but not nearly so heavily as 'Hoshiyadori' and reverting very easily to totally green (Plate 143). Very rarely available in the trade and not as worthwhile as 'Hoshiyadori'. Zone V.

**'Nikkoense'.** Honda (1932). Japan. A cultivar said to have laciniate lobes and pubescent veins on the leaf undersides. Found in the wild. Not available in the trade.

**'Shufu nishiki'**, see ***A. truncatum* 'Akikaze nishiki'**

**'Tokiwa nishiki'.** JDV I, 154; JDV II, 161. This cultivar is a large shrub to 6–7 m tall and has the typical *A. mono* leaves, 5- to 7-lobed, the central lobes almost triangular. The variegations are quite heavy but not speckled as in 'Hoshiyadori'. Occasionally half the blade is cream or white (Plate 143). This plant is frequently used for landscaping in Japan. It is available in Europe. Zone VI.

**'Tricolor'.** Krüssmann (1959). Germany. See ***A. truncatum* 'Akikaze nishiki'.**

**'Usugumo'.** JDV I, 154; JDV II, 161, photo. According to Vertrees this is a most unusual plant, with batwing-like leaves, 7- to 9-lobed, the triangular and sharply pointed lobes resulting in a large leaf surface. The leaves are 8–11 cm across and thickly speckled with white dots (Plate 144). A narrow strip of white runs along either side of the veins. It is a slow-growing shrub to about 2 m tall at most. It is very rarely available in Europe. Quite a different plant is available with the same name. It bears small pink leaves and grows extremely slowly. Very difficult to propagate and to grow, it is comparable to *A. buergerianum* 'Nusatoriyama', but is by no means identical. Zone VI.

**'Usugumori'**, see **'Usugumo'**

**'Variegatum'.** Nicholson (1881). Great Britain. Leaves green, variegated white and cream. This is probably synonymous with *A. truncatum* 'Akikaze nishiki'.

## ACER MONSPESSULANUM

Only three cultivars have been described, all in the last century, and apparently are no longer in cultivation.

**'Biedermannii'.** Schwerin (1899). Germany. Leaves mottled yellow.

**'Sempervirens'.** Miller ex Lauche (1880). Germany. Leaves ovate, subentire, 2.5–3 cm. May be *A. sempervirens.*

**'Variegatum'.** Groinland (1862). Germany. Leaves variegated, no further description.

## ACER NEGUNDO

Due to the extensive geographic range of this species, three subspecies have been recognized and described. There are a number of cultivars, only a small number of which are now in cultivation. Many have been lost or forgotten.

In 1965 Privalov (Russia) published a list of radiation mutants of *A. negundo* and provided scientific names for all. Since the publication of the *International Code of Nomenclature for Cultivated Plants* in 1959, the use of Latin cultivar names is no longer acceptable. Previous names do, however, figure in some reference works so we note them here though we are uncertain if any are in cultivation:

'Alternophyllotaxe Spirale'
'Appressifolium'
'Bipinnatifolium'
'Brunneo-marginatum'
'Convolutifolium'
'Integrifolium'
'Mixtum Phyllotaxe'
'Obtusifolium'
'Parvifolium'
'Propendifolium'
'Roseo-marginatum'
'Rhytidophyllum'
'Scaphophyllum'
'Strictifolium'
'Verticillate-phyllotaxe'

All cultivars of *Acer negundo* are hardy in zone V. For practical purposes the cultivars are divided into groups:

Group 1a: Young shoots glabrous with bluish down, leaves green

'Albidum'
'Angustifolium'
'Baron'
'Boreale'
'Crispum'
'Discolor'
'Falcatum'
'Giganteum'
'Glaucum'
'Laciniatum'
'Lutescens'
'Nanum'
'Petiolatum'
'Pruinosum'
'Pseudo-californicum
'Pseudocrispum'
'Quinatum'
'Robustum'
'Rozineckianum'
'Rubescens'
'Rubifolium'
'Sensation'
'Subintegrilobum'
'Versicolor'
'Violaceum'

Group 1b: As in Group 1a, but with variegated leaves

'Aureo-limbatum'
'Aureo-maculatum'
'Aureo-marginatum'
'Aureo-variegatum'
'Chrysophyllum'
'Crispum Variegatum' (?)
'Cristatum'
'Elegans'
'Flamingo'
'Guichardii'
'Guttatum'
'Insigne'
'Luteopictum'
'Schwerinii'

Group 2: Young shoots glabrous and not downy

'Auratum'
'Kelly's Gold'
'Nudum'
'Odessanum'
'Serotinum'
'Variegatum'

Group 3: Young shoots tomentose

'Pubescens'

**'Albidum'.** Schwerin (1893). Germany. Vigorous clone; young leaves and branches dull white. Probably no longer in cultivation. (Group 1a)

**'Albo-variegatum'.** Van Houtte (1885). Belgium. See **'Variegatum'.**

**'Angustifolium'.** Schwerin (1893). Germany. Small tree, to 6 m tall, leaflets very different in shape, often quite narrow, always in fives, apices of the central leaflets acuminate. Young shoots downy. Introduced by Dieck, named by Schwerin, now very rare and no longer available in the trade. (Group 1a)

**'Angustissimum'.** Pax (1886). Germany. This is possibly 'Angustifolium'. It is apparently not in cultivation.

**'Argenteo-cinctum'.** Schwerin (1893). Germany. See **'Variegatum'.**

**'Argenteo-limbatum'.** Schwerin (1893). Germany. See **'Variegatum'.**

**'Argenteo-notatum'.** Schwerin (1893). Germany. See **'Variegatum'.**

**'Argenteo-variegatum'.** Schwerin (1893). Germany. See **'Variegatum'.**

**'Argenteo-variegatum Robustum'.** Schwerin (1893). Germany. See **'Variegatum'.**

**'Auratum'.** Späth (1891). Berlin, Germany. Small tree or large shrub, to 6 m tall, branches and shoots glabrous and not downy. Leaves shaped as the species, golden yellow in full sun, paler in the shade, and becoming slightly greener in the later months of the summer and early autumn. For many years this cultivar was thought to be the same as 'Odessanum'. Krüssmann pointed out that this is not the case. True 'Odessanum' has tomentose young shoots and golden yellow leaves. All the plants seen by the authors have glabrous shoots and must be correctly called 'Auratum'. (Group 2)

**'Aureo-limbatum'.** Schwerin (1893). Germany. Most likely this cultivar is identical to the well-known 'Aureo-marginatum'. It has been known under this name since 1893, probably used by Dieck. It is no longer in cultivation. 'Auratum' is a golden yellow-leaved sport of 'Aureo-limbatum'. (Group 1b)

**'Aureo-maculatum'.** Schwerin (1893). Germany. This is also a very old cultivar and very closely related to 'Aureo-marginatum'. As these variegated forms are slightly variable, it is not possible to distinguish them with certainty. It is best to keep these clones under the name 'Aureo-marginatum' or 'Aureo-variegatum'. (Group 1b)

**'Aureo-marginatum'.** Dieck (1885). Germany. A very well-known cultivar. It is often a strong, small tree 8–10 m tall, but frequently is a large shrub. The leaves are of the same shape and size as the species, margined with creamy yellow. Occasionally, yellow leaves are present. An excellent female cultivar, generally available in the trade. Also known as 'Aureo-variegatum', which is a slightly different cultivar and less desirable than 'Aureo-marginatum'. (Group 1b)

**'Aureo-notatum'.** Schwerin (1893). Germany. See **'Aureo-marginatum'** or **'Aureo-variegatum'**

**'Aureo-variegatum'.** Wesmael (1869). Belgium. Introduced by the famous Späth Nurseries, Berlin, Germany, about 1887. A tree 10–12 m tall, its leaves are yellow spotted and partly yellow-margined. Apt to revert to the species. So-called poor forms of 'Aureo-marginatum' may well be identical with 'Aureo-variegatum'. (Group 1b)

**'Aureo-vittatum'.** Schwerin (1894). Germany. See **'Aureo-variegatum'.**

**'Aureum'.** Harrison (1960). USA? An illegitimate name for 'Auratum'.

**'Aureum Odessanum'.** Rothe (1896). Germany. See **'Odessanum'.**

**'Baron'.** McBeath (1982). Canada. A vigorous tree of regular habit, to 20 m tall, sterile and extremely hardy. The leaves are of the typical size and shape. Selected at the Morden Research Station in Canada, from plants growing near Saskatoon, Saskatchewan, it is a good street tree in northerly locations. It can easily be budded on seedling understock. Not yet available in Europe. (Group 1a)

**'Boreale'.** Schroeder (1896). Germany. Reported to be a very winter-hardy form from Moscow. Probably not in cultivation. (Group 1a)

**'Californicum Aureum'.** Levavasseur (1898). France. See **'Odessanum'.**

**'Chrysophyllum'.** Schwerin (1893). Germany. A very vigorous tree of the same shape and size as the species. Leaves 14–16 cm long, with 5 leaflets, ovate-elliptic. The leaflets are 3-lobed or almost trifoliate, and golden yellow-variegated. It is a male, while 'Aureo-marginatum' is a female. It is very rare both in the trade and in collections. (Group 1b)

**'Crispifolium'.** Sudworth (1897). Great Britain. See **'Crispum'.**

**'Crispum'.** Loddiges (1826). Great Britain. Small tree with downy young shoots. Leaves irregularly formed, very pale green, with wavy margins. Probably no longer in cultivation. (Group 1a)

**'Crispum Variegatum'.** Krüssmann (1959). Germany. Krüssmann mentioned this clone as having the same leaves as cultivars with cream margins. He claimed it is common in Dutch parks. We have never seen this cultivar in any garden in The Netherlands and so cannot understand this reference. It is possible that he meant 'Elegans'. As far as is known 'Crispum Variegatum' is not in cultivation, not available in the trade, and was not published before Krüssmann used the name in 1959; accordingly the name is illegitimate. (Group 1b)

**'Cristatum'.** Schwerin (1901). Germany. Reported to have leaves dotted yellow. Apparently no longer in cultivation. (Group 1b)

**'Curly Leaf'.** Kelsey & Dayton (1942) USA. See **'Crispum'.**

**'Densiflorum'.** Schwerin (1896). Germany. Inflorescences said to be very compact. Probably not in cultivation.

**'Dentatum'.** Schwerin (1901). Germany. Leaflet margins dentate. No further description. Probably not in cultivation.

**'Discolor'.** Schwerin (1893). Germany. Reported to be fast-growing. Young shoots whitish. Leaves large, muddy yellow when young, soon becoming green. A female clone not available in the trade. (Group 1a)

**'Dr. Charles Wager'.** Wiegers (1809). Germany. Without description; probably not in cultivation.

**'Elegans'.** Schwerin (1901). Germany. A slow-growing small tree, to 7–8 m tall with a rather dense crown. Leaves smaller than the species, the leaflets somewhat convex, with broad, cream-yellow margins. A very elegant and attractive plant for smaller gardens, occasionally available in the trade. This is a female selection, propagated before 1901 in French nurseries, but not named until 1901 by Schwerin. See also 'Crispum variegatum'. (Group 1b)

**'Elegantissimum'**, see **'Aureo-marginatum'** and **'Variegatum'**

**'Falcatum'.** Schwerin (1896). Germany. Reported to bear incurved, falcate samaras. Apparently not in cultivation. (Group 1a)

**'Flamingo'.** Bastiaanse (1976) (in Van de Laar, 1977, 13–14:74). Oudenbosch, The Netherlands. Small tree or large shrub of about 5–6 m with a rather erect branching habit. Leaves slightly smaller than the species, with 5–7 leaflets, green with clear white to pink margins. Young leaves suffused rather heavily with pink (Plate 145). Young shoots with a bluish down, glabrous. This is a very attractive plant, markedly different from 'Variegatum' due to its pink color, that received an Award of Merit in 1977 in Boskoop, The Netherlands. (Group 1b)

**'Giganteum'.** Schwerin (1893). Germany. A tree with the same shape and habit as the species. Leaves very large, up to 40 cm long, with 7–9 leaflets. (Group 1a)

**'Glaucum'.** Schwerin (1894). Germany. Large tree, young shoots slightly hairy, quickly becoming glabrous; leaves large, dark green. A male selection from 'Violaceum'. No longer available in the trade. (Group 1a)

**'Globosum'.** Wesmael (1890). Belgium. See **'Nanum'.**

**'Goldedge'.** Kelsey & Dayton (1942) USA. See **'Aureo-marginatum'.**

**'Goldspot'.** Kelsey & Dayton (1942) USA. See **'Aureo-variegatum'.**

**'Guichardii'.** Guichard (1889). France. Leaves variegated yellow. Apparently no longer in cultivation. (Group 1b)

**'Guttatum'.** Schwerin (1893). Germany. Small tree, sometimes a shrub. Shoots green and downy. Leaves with 5–7 elongated leaflets, with a green-yellow blotch in the center of each leaflet. Apt to revert to green. No longer available in the trade. (Group 1b)

**'Heterophyllum'.** Späth ex Otto (1883). Germany. See **'Laciniatum'.**

**'Insigne'.** Schwerin (1893). Germany. Small tree, young shoots lack bloom, fully glabrous. Leaves green, centers of leaflets yellowish green. Reverts easily to green. This clone is a sport of 'Aureo-limbatum' and has disappeared from nurseries. (Group 1b)

**'Kelly's Gold'.** Duncan & Davies catalog (1989). New Zealand. Small, deciduous tree, to 5 m tall, with soft golden yellow foliage like 'Auratum'. The color lightens in the autumn. Not yet seen by the authors. (Group 2)

**'Koehneanum'.** Schwerin (1896). Germany. Samara wings overlapping. Probably no longer in cultivation.

**'Laciniatum'.** Kuntze (1867). Germany. Small tree, leaves up to 10 cm, irregularly formed, laciniated to a greater or lesser degree, margins entire and central leaflets not acuminate. Also known as 'Heterophyllum'. No longer available in the trade and extremely rare in collections. (Group 1a)

**'Lombarts'.** Vrugtman (1970). Canada. See **'Variegatum'.**

**'Luteopictum'.** Schwerin (1893). Germany. Rather small tree, to 10 m tall, with brownish purple young shoots, becoming darker in the autumn. Leaves as in the species, but the leaflets have a yellow-green central blotch. There is a strong tendency to produce entirely green leaves. It is an old clone. Only occasionally available in the trade. (Group 1b)

**'Lutescens'.** Schwerin (1893). Germany. A small tree or large shrub, to 10 m, young shoots green, darker at the tips. Leaves consisting of 5 leaflets, ovate, almost as long as wide, light green, turning yellow in summer. Very rare in the trade. 'Auratum' is a better garden plant and has taken its place. (Group 1a)

**'Nanum'.** Willkomm (1879). Germany. Dwarf, a rather small shrub of poor vigor. The leaves are smaller than the species, somewhat convex and irregular, with entire or somewhat coarsely toothed margins. Probably no longer in cultivation. (Group 1a)

**'Nanum Latifolium'**, see **'Nanum'**

**'New California'.** Kelsey & Dayton (1942). USA. See **'Pseudo-californicum'.** (Group 1a)

**'Nudum'.** Schwerin (1893). Germany. The branches of this cultivar are glabrous and olive-green. Probably no longer in cultivation. (Group 2)

**'Odessanum'.** H. Rothe (1890). Odessa, Ukraine. A rather vigorous tree of moderate size, about 8–10 m tall. The young shoots are densely downy. The leaves are of the same shape and size as those of the species, and a nice golden yellow in the full sun; in shade they are lighter green. This attractive cultivar was introduced by H. Rothe and is often confused with 'Auratum', which is far more frequently cultivated. 'Odessanum' seems to have a better habit and might be more desirable. It is not known whether true 'Odessanum' is available but it seems worthwhile to trace it. (Group 2)

**'Parallelum'.** Schwerin (1896). Germany. A weak tree, with samara wings parallel rather than horizontal. Not in cultivation.

**'Pendulum'.** Schwerin (1896). Germany. A tree with pendulous branches. No further description. Probably not in cultivation.

**'Petiolatum'.** Schwerin (1896). Germany. A female clone, of shrubby habit, the green shoots with a white bloom. The leaves are of the same shape as the species, rather large and on very long petioles, to 6–8 cm. The entire leaf may reach 40 cm. No longer available. (Group 1a)

**'Pruinosum'.** Schwerin (1893). Germany. Branches pruinose. No longer in cultivation. (Group 1a)

**'Pseudo-californicum'.** Schwerin (1893). Germany. This group includes all forms with green shoots (never purplish or gray). (Group 1a)

**'Pseudocrispum'.** Schwerin (1893). Germany. A male clone with brown-green young shoots, producing a purple down in autumn. The first leaves are of normal size; later, the basal leaflets become crisped. Very rare in cultivation. (Group 1a)

**'Pubescens'.** Schwerin (1893). Germany. This so-called cultivar is probably nothing but a selection of subspecies *californicum.* Not worthy of any separate rank. (Group 3)

**'Quinatum'.** Schwerin (1893). Germany. Leaves 5-foliolate instead of 7-foliolate. Probably no longer in cultivation. (Group 1a)

**'Rectangulatum'.** Schwerin (1896). Germany. Samaras right-angled. Apparently no longer in cultivation.

**'Robustum'.** Schwerin (1893). Germany. The branches are brown-purple in the autumn. Lost from cultivation. (Group 1a)

**'Rozineckianum'.** Schwerin (1901). Germany. A tree of moderate size with green shoots, densely downy with a white bloom. The almost round leaflets are on short petioles. This tree originated in Czechoslovakia and may still be growing there. It is not available in the trade. (Group 1a)

**'Rubescens'.** Schwerin (1893). Germany. A tree of about the same size as the species. The young shoots are brownish green, later purple. Young leaves reddish, especially the upper pairs of leaflets. Not available in the trade. (Group 1a)

**'Rubifolium'.** Pax ex Schwerin (1893). Germany. Leaves large. Lost from cultivation. (Group 1a)

**'Schwerinii'.** Hybler (1905). Germany. A small tree, with leaves variegated white and rose. This cultivar may be lost from cultivation; it is no longer available in the trade. The more recent 'Flamingo' has the same characteristics. (Group 1b)

**'Sensation'.** J. Frank Schmidt & Son (1980). Oregon, USA. This new cultivar forms a well-branched tree up to 10 m tall. It is regularly built up and of slower growth than the average box elder seedling. The medium green leaves turn brilliant red in the fall. The tree is very hardy and also suitable for street planting. (Group 1a)

**'Serotinum'.** Schwerin (1894). Germany. The branches are pruinose and pubescent. Apparently no longer in cultivation. (Group 2)

**'Silverleaf'.** Kelsey & Dayton (1942). USA. See **'Variegatum'.**

**'Subintegrilobum'.** Schwerin (1901). Germany. Tree; leaflets with entire margins, pale green. Apparently no longer in cultivation. (Group 1a)

**'Variegatum'.** Wiegers (1809). Germany. A small tree to 10 m tall with green shoots, not downy or only slightly so on long, vigorous shoots when young. The leaves are of about the same size as those of the species, broad, creamy white, with broadly serrate margins (Plate 146). Young leaves pinkish, occasionally with entirely white leaflets. It fruits abundantly, but seeds are always sterile, sometimes also variegated white. It appeared as a sport in a nursery in Toulouse, France. The plant grown as 'Elegantissimum' seems to be slightly more variegated. As there is very little material for comparison, the question of whether 'Elegantissimum' is distinct from 'Variegatum' cannot be answered. 'Variegatum' is widely grown and generally available. The tree tends to form branches bearing entirely green leaves. Such branches must be removed as soon as they develop. (Group 2)

**'Versicolor'.** Dieck (1885). Germany. Tree to 12–15 m tall, the young green shoots with a white bloom. The leaves are large, dark green, with light green margins later becoming yellowish. Only leaves grown in the shade remain variegated. It is a male clone, quite rare, and seldom available in the trade. (Group 1a)

**'Violaceum'.** Miller (1826). Great Britain. Tree to 15–20 m tall with branches glaucous to violet. Jäger considered this to be a natural variety as such specimens are common in the Midwest of North America. A vigorously growing tree, young shoots blackish purple with a blue bloom. Leaflets 3–11, commonly 5–7, with soft, silky hairs underneath. (Group 1a)

**'Viridi-marginatum'.** Wesmael (1890). Belgium. See **'Versicolor'.**

**'Yellowleaf'.** Kelsey & Dayton (1942). USA. See **'Auratum'.**

## ACER PALMATUM

Without the invaluable help of the two editions of *Japanese Maples* by J. D. Vertrees, it would have been virtually impossible to compile this list of valid *Acer palmatum* cultivars and invalid or illegitimate cultivar names. Vertrees very accurately described a large number of Japanese cultivars. His nomenclature is followed here, with some exceptions, especially in those names written in Latin form. His Japanese cultivar names are generally followed. As it is superfluous to repeat the up-to-date information contained in Vertrees's editions, the reader is urged to consult them for full descriptions of the cultivars.

Transliterating Japanese names to languages using the Roman alphabet depends greatly on the translator and the language being used. In this work, the English form of transliteration has generally been followed. In earlier years, Pax, van Houtte, Schwerin, and Nicholson rebaptized many of the first introductions with Latin names. Koidzumi and Hayata used both Japanese and Latin names. Indeed, Koidzumi even latinized Japanese words. Under the current system of nomenclature for *A. palmatum*, the Japanese cultivar names are preferable and now widely used. Some may find these names complicated, but such names are quite commonly used in genera such as *Camellia*, *Pinus*, *Paeonia*, and *Prunus* and should create no particular problem for the maple enthusiast.

Lastly, obvious misspellings are not separately listed but are cited, when appropriate, under the correct name.

To comply with the rules of the *International Code of Nomenclature for Cultivated Plants* (1980) and to avoid repetition, the cultivars with valid names are divided into the following seven groups. Most of the groups can be further subdivided on the basis of leaf color. This system of groups has been used in part to cope with the enormous number of names within the species, many of uncertain status. Outstanding cultivars in each group are marked with an asterisk.

### GROUP 1: PALMATUM

Upright shrubs or small trees, with 5- or occasionally 7-lobed leaves, in which case the basal lobes are much smaller. The general leaf shape is like that of subspecies *palmatum*. Fruits of medium to small size.

Group 1a: With green leaves or green with reddish margins

'Acutum'
'Akebono'
'Amagi shigure'
'Ao kanzashi'
*'Aoyagi'
'Arakawa'
*'Aureum'
'Beni kawa'
'Beni yatsubusa'
'Bonnie Bergman'
'Chishio'
'Eddisbury'
'Ibo nishiki'
Issai nishiki
'Jiro shidare'
*'Katsura'
'Kiyohime'
'Kogane nishiki'
*'Koreanum'
'Latilobatum'
'Maiko'
'Maimori'
'Mama'
'Matsuyoi'
'Monzukushi'
'Nishiki gawa'
'Nishiki momiji'
'Nishiki sho'
'Ogi nagashi'
'Orange Dream'
*'Sangokaku'
'Saoshika'
'Saotome'
'Shigarami'
'Tennyo no hoshi'
'Tobiosho'
'Tsuchigumo'
'Ueno homare'
'Ueno yama'
'Volubile'

Group 1b: With purple-red leaves or purple fading to dark green

- 'Aratama'
- *'Atropurpureum'
- 'Atropurpureum Superbum'
- 'Atropurpureum Variegatum'
- 'Beni maiko'
- 'Beni tsukasa'
- *'Chishio Improved'
- 'Crimson Prince'
- 'Deshojo'
- 'Fireglow'
- 'Flushing'
- 'Hyugayama'
- 'Nigrum'
- *'Nuresagi'
- 'Oregon Sunset'
- 'Otome zakura'
- 'Purpureum'
- 'Seigai'
- 'Shaina'
- 'Shin deshojo'

Group 1c: With variegated leaves—pink, cream, or white markings

- 'Andreanum'
- 'Asahi zuru'
- 'Aureo-variegatum'
- 'Beni shichi henge'
- *'Butterfly'
- 'Hanazono nishiki'
- 'Higasayama'
- 'Kagero'
- 'Kagiri nishiki'
- 'Karaori nishiki'
- 'Karasugawa'
- 'Kasen nishiki'
- 'Kingsville Variegated'
- 'Komon nishiki'
- 'Koshibori nishiki'
- 'Marakumo'
- 'Matsugae'
- 'Naruo nishiki'
- 'Nishiki gasane'
- 'Okukuji nishiki'
- *'Oridono nishiki'
- 'Peaches and Cream'
- 'Pulverulentum'
- 'Ryumon nishiki'
- 'Sagara nishiki'
- 'Scottum Roseum'
- 'Seicha nishiki'
- 'Shojo no mai'
- 'Takao'
- 'Tamaori nishiki'
- 'Tricolor'
- 'Tsumabeni'
- *'Tsumagaki'
- *'Ukigumo'
- 'Waka momiji'

GROUP 2: AMOENUM

Upright-growing shrubs or small trees with 7- or occasionally 9-lobed leaves, divided to half the leaf blade or slightly more. The general leaf shape is much like that of subspecies *amoenum*. Fruits of medium size or larger, often in clusters, and red or reddish in color.

Group 2a: With green leaves or green with purple margins

- 'Autumn Glory'
- *'Elegans'
- 'Harusame'
- 'Heptalobum'
- 'Herbstfeuer'
- 'Hogyoku'
- 'Ichigyo ji'
- 'Killarney'
- 'Kinshi'
- 'Kogane sakae'
- 'Lutescens'
- 'Omato'
- *'Osakazuki'
- *'Samidare'
- 'Satzuki beni'
- 'Tana'
- 'Tatsuta'
- *'Utsusemi'

Group 2b: With purple-red leaves or purple fading to dark green

- 'Ariake nomura'
- 'Atropurpureum Novum'
- *'Bloodgood'
- 'Boskoop Glory'
- 'Chikuma no'
- 'Heptalobum Rubrum'
- 'Hessei'
- 'Kingsville Red'
- 'Lozita'
- 'Masumurasaki'
- *'Moonfire'
- 'Muragumo'
- 'Nomura'
- 'O kagami'
- 'Oshio beni'
- 'Rubrum'
- 'Shichi henge'
- 'Shikageori nishiki'
- *'Shojo'
- 'Shojo nomura'
- 'Taimin'
- 'The Bishop'
- 'Tsukubane'
- 'Tsukushigata'
- 'Umegae'
- 'Whitney Red'
- *'Yezo nishiki'

Group 2c: With variegated leaves—pink, white, or cream markings

- 'Hamaotome'
- *'Masukagami'
- 'Wakehurst Pink'
- 'Yubae'

GROUP 3: MATSUMURAE

Large shrubs, only occasionally trees, generally as wide as or wider than high. Leaves 7- or occasionally 9-lobed, deeply divided almost to the base. Leaf margins serrate or incised. General leaf shape like that of *A. palmatum* ssp. *matsumurae.*

Group 3a: With green leaves

- 'Akitsushima'
- 'Green Trompenburg'
- *'Kihachijo'
- 'Kurabeyama'
- 'Mirte'
- 'Mure hibari'
- 'Murogawa'
- *'Nicholsonii'
- *'Omurayama'
- 'Rufescens'
- 'Sazanami'
- 'Seme no hane'
- 'Shiranami'
- 'Tsuri nishiki'
- 'Wou nishiki'

Group 3b: With purple leaves or purple fading to dark green

- 'Akegarasu'
- 'Azuma murasaki'
- *'Beni kagami'
- *'Burgundy Lace'
- 'Chitoseyama'
- 'Iijima sunago'
- *'Inazuma'
- 'Kasagiyama'
- 'Kinran'
- 'Komurasaki'
- 'Ogon sarasa'
- 'Oshu beni'
- 'Oshu shidare'
- *'Sherwood Flame'
- 'Shigure bato'
- 'Shigurezome'
- 'Shinonome'
- 'Sumi nagashi'
- *'Trompenburg'
- *'Yasemin'
- 'Yugure'

Group 3c: With leaves of other colors

- 'Beni shigitatsu sawa'
- 'Matsukaze'
- 'Ogi nagashi'
- 'Shigitatsu sawa'
- 'Taimin nishiki'
- 'Tama nishiki'
- 'Yubae'

GROUP 4: DISSECTUM

Generally mushroom-shaped shrubs or gnarled trees (with some exceptions such as 'Seiryu'), to 4 m high, often wider than high. Leaves 7-lobed, deeply divided to the base. Each lobe doubly incised or serrate, which gives the "lacy" or fern-like appearance typical of this group; containing all the Dissectum group. Botanically this group belongs to subspecies *matsumurae,* but it is different enough from group 3 cultivars to maintain as a separate group.

Group 4a: With green leaves

- 'Ao shidare'
- *'Dissectum'
- *'Dissectum Flavescens'
- 'Dissectum Palmatifidum'
- 'Dissectum Paucum'
- 'Dissectum Unicolor'
- 'Ellen'
- *'Filigree'
- 'Germaine's Gyration'
- 'Kiri nishiki'
- 'Orangeola'
- 'Sekimori'
- 'Suisei'
- 'Sunset'
- 'Uchiwa nagashi'
- 'Waterfall'

Group 4b: With purple or brown leaves, sometimes fading to green

- 'Baldsmith'
- 'Barrie Bergman'
- 'Beni fushigi'
- 'Beni shidare'
- 'Brocade'
- *'Crimson Queen'
- 'Dissectum Nigrum'
- 'Dissectum Rhodophyllum'
- 'Dissectum Rubrifolium'
- 'Dissectum Rubrum'
- 'Dissectum Superbum'
- *'Garnet'
- 'Hatsushigure'
- 'Inaba shidare'
- 'Mioun'
- 'Octopus'
- *'Ornatum'
- 'Pendulum Julian'
- 'Red Dragon'
- 'Red Filigree Lace'
- 'Shojo shidare'
- 'Stella Rossa'
- *'Tamukeyama'
- 'Watnong'

Group 4c: With variegated leaves

'Ariadne'
'Beni shidare Tricolor'
'Dissectum Roseo-marginatum'
*'Dissectum Variegatum'
*'Goshiki shidare'
'Ruth Murray'
'Toyama nishiki'

## GROUP 5: LINEARILOBUM

Upright shrubs, slow-growing to 4 m tall, but often much smaller. Leaves 7-lobed, the lobes narrowed to the main vein or almost so, deeply divided to the base. This group is without botanical status, as this form of *A. palmatum* does not occur in the wild. It belongs to subspecies *palmatum*, but is sufficiently different from group 1 to be maintained as a separate group.

Group 5a: With green leaves

'Angustilobum'
'Ao shime no uchi shidare'
'Chirimen nishiki'
'Karukaya'
'Koto no ito'
*'Linearilobum'
'Miyagino'
'Rhodoneurum'
'Shinobuga oka'
'Takinogawa'
*'Villa Taranto'

Group 5b: With purple or brown leaves

'Aka shime no uchi'
'Atrolineare'
'Beni otake'
'Beni ubi gohon'
'Enkan'
'Keiser'
*'Red Pygmy'
'Willow Leaf'

## GROUP 6: DWARF, BONSAI, AND PENJING

This group contains all the dwarf cultivars suitable for bonsai/penjing culture, or for tubs and pots. Normally none exceed 1 m in height, but there are exceptions. Some cultivars grow very densely but are not true dwarfs. Generally they are very slow growing shrubs with small leaves of various shapes.

'Akita yatsubusa'
'Aoba jo'
'Beni hime'
*'Beni komachi'
'Chishio'
'Coonara Pygmy'
*'Corallinum'
'Coral Pink'
'Crippsii'
'Dwarf Shishi'
'Garyu'
'Goshiki kotohime'
'Hanami nishiki'
'Hoshi kuzu'
'Hupp's Dwarf'
'Iso chidori'
*'Kamagata'
'Kashima'
'Kotohime'
'Kotoito komachi'
*'Kurui jishi'
'Little Princess'
*'Mikawa yatsubusa'
*'Mizu kuguri'
'Murasaki hime'
'Murasaki kiyohime'
'O jishi'
'Okushimo'
'Otohime'
'Pixie'
'Ryuzu'
'Seigen'
'Sekka yatsubusa'
'Sharp's Pygmy'
'Shishigashira'
'Tamahime'
'Tsukumo'
'Wilson's Pink Dwarf'
'Yuri hime'

## GROUP 7

Cultivars fitting within none of the above groups.

'Hagaromo'
'Hazeroino'
'Koshimino'
'Momenshide'
'Nana segawa'
*'Seiryu'
'Wabito'

In the following alphabetical listing of *Acer palmatum* cultivars and synonyms, each legitimate cultivar is provided with the name of the introducer and the year of introduction, if known. No attribution has been given for invalid or illegitimate cultivar names, unless the name is still commonly used. (Many of these can be found in Murray's 1970 dissertation, *Monograph of the Aceraceae.*) Almost all the cultivars are hardy in zone V; only those more tender are assigned a hardiness zone number.

**'Acutum'.** Koidzumi (1911). Japan. Samara wings acutely angled, otherwise like the species. Probably no longer in cultivation. (Group 1a)

**'Adlerschwanz'.** Schwerin (1893). Germany. See **'Dissectum Rubrifolium'.**

**'Akai washino o'.** Krüssmann (1959). Germany. See **'Ornatum'.**

**'Akaji'**, see ***A. truncatum* 'Akaji'**

**'Akaji nishiki'**, see ***A. truncatum* 'Akaji nishiki'**

**'Akane'.** Kobayashi. Japan. No description. Imported in 1991 from Japan to The Netherlands.

**'Aka no shichigosan'**, see **'Shime no uchi'**

**'Akashigata'**, see **'Dissectum Rubrifolium'**

**'Aka shigitatsu sawa'**, see **'Beni shigitatsu sawa'**

**'Aka shime no uchi'.** Chikinsho (1710). Japan. JDV I, 92; JDV II, 98, photo. This beautiful cultivar is rather dwarfed and falls in between 'Atrolineare' and 'Red Pygmy'. It grows into a rather small, treelike shrub to 3 m tall, somewhat twiggy and upright. The leaves are purple-red, later turning to a reddish brown-bronze. They are of the typical shape of the Linearilobum group, with narrowly linear lobes, cleft to the bases. It is only occasionally seen in horticulture; most of the plants actually are 'Atrolineare' (Group 5b). That different, much greener cultivar is in cultivation in Europe and is very similar to 'Linearilobum'. It is hard to determine what this is, possibly 'Aome no udu'. (Group 5b)

**'Aka washino o'**, see **'Ornatum'** and **'Dissectum Rubrifolium'**

**'Akebono'.** Dickson (1887). Great Britain. JDV II, 149. Probably nothing but the species, with paler green leaves. Apparently no longer in cultivation. There is also a cultivar of *A. buergerianum* bearing this name, which means "day dawn." (Group 1a)

**'Akegarasu'.** Koidzumi (1911). Japan. JDV I, 46; JDV II, 52. Large upright shrub, to 5 m or more. Leaves rather large and deeply divided, rich purple-red in spring, later more bronze-red. Petioles rather long, dark red. This is a good cultivar in the large group of so-called 'Atropurpureums' and was first mentioned in *Kaede Binran* (*Japanese Maple List*) of 1882. The name means "the crows at dawn." It is sometimes available in the trade. (Group 3b)

**'Akita yatsubusa'.** Greer Gardens (1989). Eugene, Oregon, USA. Small shrub with dark green leaves, having slightly curved edges. It forms a dense, tight shrub, suitable for small gardens and bonsai. Available in the United States. Zone VI. (Group 6)

**'Akitsushima'.** Koidzumi (1911). Japan. Leaf lobes 7–9, incised. Very probably nothing more than subspecies *matsumurae*. No longer in cultivation. (Group 3a)

**'Akitsuta'.** Koidzumi (1911). Japan. Leaf lobes narrow at the bases. Probably not in cultivation.

**'Albo-marginatum'.** Nicholson (1881). Great Britain. See **'Matsugae'.**

**'Albo-variegatum'.** Pax (1886). Germany. See **'Versicolor'.**

**'Amagi shigure'.** JDV II, 53. Low-growing shrub, densely branched. Leaves small, orbicular, green with orange-yellow tones in the fall. (Group 1a)

**'Amatum'.** Wesmael (1890). Belgium. See **'Ornatum'.**

**'Ampelopsifolium'.** Schwerin (1893). Germany. See **'Tsuri nishiki'.**

**'Andreanum'.** Siebert & Voss (1894). Germany. Said to have pink leaves with green veins. Apparently not in cultivation. (Group 1c)

**'Angustilobum'.** Koidzumi (1911). Japan. Another superfluous name for a clone in the Linearilobum group. It is not possible to determine whether this plant differs from 'Shime no uchi' and its close allies. Probably not in cultivation. (Group 5a)

**'Aoba'.** Schwerin (1893). Germany. See **'Caudatum'.**

**'Aoba fue'.** Schwerin (1893). Germany. See **'Volubile'.**

**'Aoba jo'.** JDV II, 100. Good dwarf shrub with largish leaves. Leaf lobes acuminate, blades dark green, turning to yellow. Suitable for bonsai, occasionally available in the trade. (Group 6)

**'Aoba no fue'.** Yokohama Nurseries (1898). Japan. Leaves 7-lobed, with serrulate margins. Not in cultivation under this name and most likely synonymous with 'Volubile'.

**'Aoba shidare'**, see **'Ao shidare'**

**'Ao hichi gosan'**, see **'Shinobuga oka'**

**'Ao kanzashi'.** Japan. Recently introduced, this green-leaved, sturdy shrub is said to grow to a modest size. Leaves small, slightly incurved or convex, 5-lobed. (Group 1a)

**'Aokii'.** Späth (1892). Germany. See **'Versicolor'.**

PLATE 122. *Acer* × *bornmuelleri.* Mature leaves. (28)

PLATE 123. *Acer* × *coriaceum.* Mature leaves. (15)

PLATE 124. *Acer* × *durettii.* Three-lobed leaves. (15)

PLATE 125. *Acer* × *rotundilobum.* Old tree. (11)

PLATE 126. *Acer* × *rotundilobum*. Mature leaves. (18)

PLATE 127. *Acer* × *zoeschense*. Mature leaves. (15)

PLATE 128. *Acer buergerianum* 'Mino yatsubusa'. Unusually shaped leaves, dwarfish growth. (23)

PLATE 129. *Acer campestre* 'Nanum'. Dwarf form of the common Field maple. (22)

PLATE 130. *Acer campestre* 'Postelense'. Yellow-leaved form of the Field maple. (15)

PLATE 131. *Acer campestre* 'Pulverulentum'. White-powdered leaves. (15)

PLATE 132. *Acer cappadocicum* 'Aureum'. Golden-yellow leaves in the spring. (15)

PLATE 133. *Acer carpinifolium* 'Esveld Select'. The only cultivar of this species. (15)

PLATE 134. *Acer circinatum* 'Monroe'. Leaves deeply dissected. (15)

PLATE 135. *Acer* × *conspicuum* 'Silver Vein'. Conspicuously striped trunk. (15)

PLATE 136. *Acer* × *conspicuum* 'Silver Vein'. Mature leaves. (15)

PLATE 137. *Acer crataegifolium* 'Veitchii'. Leaves variegated with pink. (15)

PLATE 138. *Acer davidii* 'George Forrest'. Selection of the species. (18)

PLATE 139. *Acer davidii* 'Rosalie'. Leaves unlobed. (15)

PLATE 140. *Acer davidii* 'Serpentine'. Small-leaved form, densely branched. (15)

PLATE 141. *Acer japonicum* 'Attaryi'. Very large shrub or tree with dissected leaves. (15)

PLATE 142. *Acer japonicum* 'Takinogawa'. Good autumn color on leaves of this large, treelike shrub, which hardly differs from the species. (15)

PLATE 143. *Acer mono* 'Tokiwa nishiki'. Dwarf shrub with variegated leaves. (15)

PLATE 144. *Acer mono* 'Usugumo'. Compact-growing shrublet with marmorated leaves. (15)

PLATE 145. *Acer negundo* 'Flamingo'. Pink-variegated young leaves. (15)

PLATE 146. *Acer negundo* 'Variegatum'. White-variegated leaves and sterile fruits. (4)

PLATE 147. *Acer palmatum* 'Asahi zuru'. (15)

PLATE 148. *Acer palmatum* 'Atrolineare'. (21)

PLATE 149. *Acer palmatum* 'Atropurpureum'. (30)

PLATE 150. *Acer palmatum* 'Azuma murasaki'. (25)

PLATE 151. *Acer palmatum* 'Beni shichi henge'. (15)

PLATE 152. *Acer palmatum* 'Beni shigitatsu sawa'. (15)

PLATE 153. *Acer palmatum* 'Butterfly'. (15)

PLATE 154. *Acer palmatum* 'Corallinum'. (4)

PLATE 155. *Acer palmatum* 'Dissectum'. (50)

PLATE 156. *Acer palmatum* 'Dissectum Flavescens' (right) and 'Dissectum' (left), with 'Ornatum' (center). Mature trees. (15)

PLATE 157. *Acer palmatum* 'Filigree'. (15)

PLATE 158. *Acer palmatum* 'Goshiki kotohime'. (15)

PLATE 159. *Acer palmatum* 'Goshiki shidare'. (15)

PLATE 160. *Acer palmatum* 'Hagaromo'. (9)

PLATE 161. *Acer palmatum* 'Heptalobum Rubrum'. In autumn color. (3)

PLATE 162. *Acer palmatum* 'Higasayama'. (15)

PLATE 163. *Acer palmatum* 'Kamagata'. (15)

PLATE 164. *Acer palmatum* 'Karasugawa'. (15)

PLATE 165. *Acer palmatum* 'Kurui jishi'. (35)

PLATE 166. *Acer palmatum* 'Masukagami'. (15)

PLATE 167. *Acer palmatum* 'Matsukaze'. (15)

PLATE 168. *Acer palmatum* 'Mikawa yatsubusa'. (15)

PLATE 169. *Acer palmatum* 'Nicholsonii'. (15)

PLATE 170. *Acer palmatum* 'Nigrum'. (15)

PLATE 171. *Acer palmatum* 'Nishiki gasane'. (15)

PLATE 172. *Acer palmatum* 'Okushimo'. (25)

PLATE 173. *Acer palmatum* 'Oridono nishiki'. (15)

PLATE 174. *Acer palmatum* 'Ornatum'. (44)

PLATE 175. *Acer palmatum* 'Red Filigree Lace'. (15)

PLATE 176. *Acer palmatum* 'Sangokaku'. (40)

PLATE 177. *Acer palmatum* 'Seiryu'. (32)

PLATE 178. *Acer palmatum* 'Shigitatsu sawa'. (21)

PLATE 179. *Acer palmatum* 'Trompenburg'. (4)

PLATE 180. *Acer palmatum* 'Ukigumo'. (15)

PLATE 181. *Acer palmatum* 'Villa Taranto'. (21)

PLATE 182. *Acer palmatum* 'Yasemin'. (15)

PLATE 183. *Acer pectinatum* 'Alice'. Pink variegations appearing during summer. (15)

PLATE 184. *Acer pectinatum* 'Sparkling'. Erect-growing shrub, leaves with red petioles. (15)

PLATE 185. *Acer platanoides* 'Crimson King'. Leaves and fruits. (15)

PLATE 186. *Acer platanoides* 'Drummondii'. White-variegated leaves. (7)

PLATE 187. *Acer platanoides* 'Pyramidale Nanum'. Slow-growing columnar tree. (2)

PLATE 188. *Acer platanoides* 'Walderseei'. Leaves powdered white. (28)

PLATE 189. *Acer pseudoplatanus* 'Atropurpureum'. Purple-red underside of leaves. (4)

PLATE 190. *Acer pseudoplatanus* 'Brilliantissimum'. Young, salmon-pink leaves. (4)

PLATE 191. *Acer pseudoplatanus* 'Erythrocarpum'. Red samaras. (7)

PLATE 192. *Acer pseudoplatanus* 'Nizetii'. Leaves heavily speckled with white. (27)

PLATE 193. *Acer pseudoplatanus* 'Worley'. Yellow leaves in summer. (39)

PLATE 195. *Acer rufinerve* 'Albo-limbatum'. Variegated leaves. (46)

PLATE 194. *Acer rubrum* 'Scanlon'. Columnar tree. (21)

PLATE 196. *Acer saccharum* 'Brocade'. Deeply dissected leaves. (15)

PLATE 197. *Acer saccharum* 'Newton Sentry'. Very narrowly growing tree. (50)

PLATE 198. *Acer saccharum* 'Sweet Shadow Cut-Leaf'. With dissected leaves. (47)

PLATE 199. *Acer saccharum* 'Temple's Upright'. Columnar tree. (21)

PLATE 200. *Acer shirasawanum* 'Aureum'. Very old specimen (center of photo). (15)

PLATE 201. *Acer shirasawanum* 'Aureum'. Branching at the foot of a very old specimen. (15)

PLATE 202. *Acer shirasawanum* 'Microphyllum'. Fruiting branches. (15)

PLATE 203. *Acer truncatum* 'Akikaze nishiki'. Variegated foliage. (15)

PLATE 204. *Acer palmatum*. Autumn colors. (49)

PLATE 205. *Acer palmatum* cultivars. Autumn colors. (49)

PLATE 206. *Acer palmatum.* Golden leaves lit by the sun. (49)

PLATE 207. Westonbirt Arboretum's famous Maple Glade. (46)

**'Ao no shichigosan'**, see **'Shinobuga oka'**

**'Ao shichi gosan'**, see **'Ao shime no uchi'**

**'Ao shidare'.** Koidzumi (1911). Japan. JDV I, 63; JDV II, 69. A spreading shrub, about 2 m wide, with cascading branches. The leaves are of the normal Dissectum group shape, but somewhat less incised. It is darker green than the usual cultivars in this group, as can easily be seen when grouped with several others. 'Sekimori' and 'Kiri nishiki' are very close. Very rare in the trade. Zone VI. (Group 4a)

**'Ao shime no uchi'.** Yokohama Nurseries (1896). Japan. See **'Shinobuga oka'.**

**'Ao shime no uchi shidare'.** JDV I, 89; JDV II, 95. This cultivar is quite similar to 'Shino buga oka' but is more pendulous in habit and does not exceed 2 m in height. The branches spread more than is usual in this group; most grow more upright. Leaves deep green and narrowly lobed, almost like grass. The leaves turn yellow to golden in the autumn. Rare in cultivation and in the trade. (Group 5a)

**'Aoyagi'.** *Japanese Maple List* (1882). JDV I, 47; JDV II, 53, photo. A very pleasing upright shrub to 8 m or sometimes more, with a fresh-green bark; very attractive in winter, especially when combined with 'Sangokaku', its counterpart with brilliant red twigs. The leaves are small and pale green, and the shrub is rather densely branched. It is identical to 'Ukon'. The autumn color is a very attractive yellow. The name means "green willow," and the shrub is popular in cultivation and available in the trade. Zone VI. (Group 1a)

**'Arakawa'.** Kobayashi. (1970). Japan. JDV I, 127; JDV II, 135, photo. This is a vigorous, shrubby tree to 6 m or more. Usually the Japanese maples are planted for their attractive foliage, but this cultivar is used for its unusually rough, quite corky bark. This bark develops on 5- to 6-year-old plants, becoming more prominent with age. The leaves are normally shaped, and color is an attractive yellow in the autumn. In JDV II this cultivar still bears the name *A. palmatum* "rough bark maple." This is inconsistent with the rules of nomenclature, and as the name 'Arakawa' is in synonymy, and not elsewhere used, we accept 'Arakawa' as the only valid cultivar epithet. Rare in cultivation and only occasionally available in the trade. Zone VI. (Group 1a)

**'Aratama'.** Vertrees. Roseburg, Oregon, USA. JDV I, 76; JDV II, 100. A bud sport of 'Komurasaki' with fine, brick-red leaves, rather large with stout lobes, separated to the center of the leaf. The color is deeper in the center of the leaf; the margins are sharply toothed. A very rare cultivar with very short growth nodes and quite twiggy and sturdy. Makes a good dwarf shrub and one of the few dwarfs with red foliage. Twelve-year-old plants are less than 1 m high. This cultivar was incorrectly described in JDV I. Zone VI. (Group 1b)

**'Argenteo-maculatum'.** Siebold (1864). Germany. See **'Versicolor'.**

**'Argenteo-marginatum'.** Koch (1869). Germany. See **'Matsugae'.**

**'Argenteo-variegatum'.** Kingsville Nursery. USA. See **'Versicolor'.**

**'Argenteum'.** Weber. Germany. See **'Versicolor'.**

**'Ariadne'.** Esveld (1991). Boskoop, The Netherlands. A chance seedling, discovered in a large batch of open-pollinated seedlings. It forms a shrub, probably 2 m tall and at least as wide. The deeply cleft leaves are less "lacy" than other cultivars of this group and are heavily variegated pink and white, and green and purple. Their autumn colors are brilliant. Named after Vezna Ariadne van Gelderen, granddaughter of this author, this cultivar is to be introduced into the trade in 1993–94. Zone VI. (Group 4c)

**'Ariake nomura'.** JDV I, 47; JDV II, 53. An upright, red-leaved seedling from 'Nomura', a well-known clone with brown-red leaves, from which it is hard to distinguish. 'Ariake nomura' is slightly more brown-red in spring and brighter crimson in the autumn. Rare in cultivation. Zone VI. (Group 2b)

**'Asahi beni zuru'**, see **'Asahi zuru'**

**'Asahi juru'** (incorrectly pronounced), see **'Asahi zuru'**

**'Asahi kaede'**, see *A. mono* **'Dissectum'** (*Japanese Maple List,* 1882)

**'Asahi nomura'**, see **'Asahi zuru'**

**'Asahi zuru'.** Wada (1938). Japan. JDV I, 104; JDV II, 112, photo. This is a vigorous, upright shrub, to 6–7 m high. The leaves are quite like the species but with pink and white variegations scattered over the plant (Plate 147). Vigorous young plants often have no variegation, but older plants, when planted in a poor situation, become very attractive. As there are several cultivars with this configuration, it is better to plant this cultivar only in those cases where a strong plant is needed. The more fragile 'Orido no nishiki' is, for example, much finer and of the same type. 'Asahi zuru' is found in several collections under the name 'Versicolor'. The name means "maple of the morning sun." Available in the trade. Zone VI. (Group 1c)

**'Asaji'.** Koidzumi (1911). Japan. Said to be 7-lobed

and with pilose veins. Apparently not in cultivation. Possibly 'Asahi zuru'.

**'Asanoha'.** Koidzumi (1911). Japan. With 9-lobed leaves having serrate margins, probably a cultivar of subspecies *matsumurae*. Apparently not in cultivation.

**'Asashi yama'.** Dickson (1887). Great Britain. Leaves with bronze-purple margins. Unknown in cultivation.

**'Atrodissectum'**, see **'Nicholsonii'**

**'Atrolineare'.** Schwerin (1893). Germany. JDV I, 89; JDV II, 95, photo. Upright, rather compact shrub, to 4 m or more, and somewhat densely branched. The leaves have lobes that are very narrow, though leaves with wider lobes may be found occasionally, and their color is dark purple, turning a bronze-green in summer (Plate 148). The autumn color is attractively yellow. Strong shoots on young plants may sometimes produce leaves with wider lobes. It is the tallest of its group, but there are several semidwarf forms as well. The nomenclature is very confused. Some names much in use are 'Linearilobum Purpureum', 'Scolopendrifolium', and 'Scolopendrifolium Purpureum'. It is quite common in cultivation. Zones V–VI. (Group 5b)

**'Atropurpureum'.** C. Wattez Nursery (before 1910). Woudenberg, The Netherlands. JDV I, 48; JDV II, 54, photo. This very common maple, widely known and appreciated in horticulture, is cultivated in quantity and is the most important of all Japanese maples. The name is a difficult matter. Nursery professionals the world over use this cultivar name for different clones and even for seedling plants. Most of the plants sold under this name were derived from an excellent clone, grown in The Netherlands, of unknown origin. It is not even certain whether this clone is an original Japanese plant. Thousands of seedlings have been sold as 'Atropurpureum', both in North America and Europe, but this does not change the fact that these populations cannot be sold under any cultivar name. They might better be named forma *atropurpureum*, to distinguish them from the true, vegetatively propagated clonal plants. An article by van Gelderen (1969) points out that this particular clone might be identical with 'Oshio beni', which is not so. This 'Atropurpureum' originated most probably in the nursery of Constant Wattez in Woudenberg, The Netherlands, where it has been propagated by layering for many years. It is not possible, for practical reasons, to produce a new name. Hundreds of thousands of plants have been sold and planted as 'Atropurpureum', and the confusion would be immense. The 'Atropurpureum' contemplated in this description is a well-branched shrub, to 8–10 m tall (Plate 149). The leaves are mainly 5-lobed, but 7-lobed leaves occur frequently. They are rich purple in spring, becoming even darker in early summer and turning to a glistening and brilliant scarlet-red in the autumn. Several other cultivars under the name of 'Atropurpureum' have now been identified under their true Japanese name and are treated alphabetically in this listing. Generally planted and readily available in the trade. (Group 1b)

**'Atropurpureum Laciniatum'**, see **'Laciniatum Purpureum'**

**'Atropurpureum Novum'.** Koster & Sons (1914). The Netherlands. JDV I, 54; JDV II, 60, photo. Robust shrub to 7 m tall with huge leaves, to 10 cm across, mostly 5-lobed with 2 small basal lobes. The color changes rather quickly to a "dirty" brown-green in summer. The autumn color can be attractive, but not always. In the United States this cultivar is used for quick growth. In Europe it is of little importance and becoming rare. Rarely available in the trade. (Group 2b)

**'Atropurpureum Superbum'.** JDV I, 47; JDV II, 53. A good, upright shrub, to 5–6 m. Its leaves are darker than those of 'Atropurpureum' but otherwise of the same shape and size. It is likely that the newer 'Bloodgood' and 'Atropurpureum Superbum' can easily be confused in the spring. The summer color of 'Bloodgood', however, is darker, and it is also less densely branched. This cultivar was imported from Japan into The Netherlands under this name, probably sprouted out of the fantasy of the exporter or importer. The name has not been traced before 1970, the year of introduction in Boskoop, and thus may be an illegitimate cultivar name. As it is of recent introduction it is not often seen but will be available in the trade. Zone VI. (Group 1b)

**'Atropurpureum Variegatum'.** Yokohama Nurseries (1898). Japan. JDV I, 118; JDV II, 126. A rare maple of the same shape and habit as the common 'Atropurpureum' but with crimson variegations. It is of little importance. (Group 1b)

**'Aureo-maculatum'.** Dickson (1887). USA. See **'Aureo-variegatum'.**

**'Aureo-variegatum'.** Van Houtte (1885). Belgium. JDV I, 105; JDV II, 113. Smaller than the species, this cultivar forms a treelike shrub to 8–10 m, with light green leaves bearing little variegation. In the autumn the variegation seems to become somewhat stronger. It is a rather disappointing plant with insufficient variegation. (Group 1c)

**'Aureum'.** Nicholson (1881). Great Britain. JDV I, 48; JDV II, 54, photo. A rather fast-growing, upright shrub, to 8 m. Its small leaves are of the same shape as the species, but they are attractively yellow with a tiny touch of scarlet at the margins. The new growth formed in summer is more yellow and the plants turn a really brilliant, golden yellow in September–October. There is a slight tendency to form dead young wood, as the young shoots are thin and do not always harden off sufficiently in the autumn. Some pruning of the plant is therefore necessary. Rare in horticulture but it can be purchased from time to time. Zone VI. (Group 1a)

**'Aureum Variegatum'.** Hillier & Sons (1928). Great Britain. See **'Aureo-variegatum'.**

**'Autumn Glory'.** De Belder (1954). Belgium. JDV I, 48; JDV II, 54. R. de Belder, owner of the Kalmthout Arboretum, Belgium, introduced some seedlings with very brilliant autumn colors. These plants have proved to be very inconsistent in their coloring on various soils. Vegetatively produced plants show little or no color. They are treelike and have 5- to 7-lobed leaves, incised about half of the leaf blade as in subspecies *amoenum.* (Group 2a)

**'Azuma murasaki'.** *Japanese Maple List* (1882); JDV I, 76; JDV II, 82, photo. Large shrub, of the same height and width, rather densely branched, attaining about 5 m. Leaves dark purple in spring, becoming greenish purple in summer and scarlet in the autumn (Plate 150). The undersides are always dark green. The new leaves have a fine pubescence, which gives them a "silvery" quality. Leaves deeply divided, the lobes incised. It is an attractive plant and deserves wider planting. Grows in some collections, sometimes available in the trade. Zone VI. (Group 3b)

**'Baldsmith'.** Buchholz Nursery (1990). Gaston, Oregon, USA. This cultivar in the Dissectum group has the usual dissected leaves. The color is unusual for this group, being orange-red, turning to yellow in autumn. Available in the United States. Zone VI. (Group 4b)

**'Barrie Bergman'.** Bergman (1969). Pennsylvania, USA. Belongs to the Dissectum group; leaves rust-red on green. Cultivar never registered. Probably no longer in cultivation. (Group 4b)

**'Benakaide'.** Dickson (1887). USA. Leaves purple, turning to green. Apparently no longer in cultivation. Possibly a misspelling of 'Beni kaede'.

**'Beni fushigi'.** Greer Gardens (1988). Eugene, Oregon, USA. Large shrub, broader than high. Leaves dark red and strongly dissected. Available in the trade in North America and introduced to Europe. (Group 4b)

**'Beni hime'.** JDV II, 100. This is one of the smallest dwarfs with reddish foliage. Leaves are of the palmatum type. It is a very attractive, somewhat delicate plant. Rather difficult to propagate, hence only very rarely available. (Group 6)

**'Beni kaede'.** As pointed out at 'Benakaide' this is a "mystery" plant; the naming of Dickson is doubtless erroneous, but a proper description of 'Beni kaede' ("Red maple") cannot be supplied.

**'Beni kagami'.** Angyo Maple Nursery (1930). Japan. JDV I, 76; JDV II, 82, photo. Quite vigorous when young, later slower growing; large shrub, to 8 m, with pendulous branches cascading to the ground. The long, slender shoots give this cultivar an irregular shape when young. The leaves are deeply divided, and the lobes are incised, purple-red when young, turning brown-red in summer. Good autumn color of a fresh crimson. Reported to be a seedling from 'Nomura'. The name means "red mirror." This is a good plant for larger gardens as it needs space. Rare in gardens, but becoming more popular with increased availability. (Group 3b)

**'Beni kawa'.** Greer Gardens (1987). Eugene, Oregon, USA. Large, upright-growing shrub or small tree. Its bark is coral-red in winter, like 'Sangokaku', and reported to be even redder than that cultivar. Leaves are rather small, fresh green with a golden yellow autumn color. Still rare in the trade. Zone VI. (Group 1a)

**'Beni komachi'.** Vertrees (1975). Roseburg, Oregon, USA. JDV I, 94; JDV II, 109, photo. Very nice dwarf maple of about 2 m with leaves of a most unusual brilliant red when unfolding. The leaves are deeply divided, nearly to the petiole, and the lobes are widely and openly spreading, the basal lobes extending backward. The color changes to a bluish green in summer, but the scarlet tones appear again in the autumn. The name means "the beautiful, red-haired little girl." It is a good cultivar for creating bonsai. This cultivar won a Silver Medal at a Royal Boskoop Horticultural Society Show in 1978. Its green counterpart is 'Kamagata'. It is still very rare in gardens in Europe but will be a collector's gem in the future as it hopefully will be available on a broader scale. It is difficult to propagate, as the young wood is very thin. Zone VI. (Group 6)

**'Beni maiko'.** JDV I, 94; JDV II, 109, photo. The name means "red, a dancing girl." A medium-sized shrub up to 2 m or slightly more, very thin-wooded. In poor conditions it grows very slowly. The small leaves are dark scarlet-pink when unfolding, a most attractive color; the lobes are somewhat wrinkled. During summer the color changes to a bluish green, not unattractive, and the tips of the shoots are brownish red. There are a number of cultivars with this type of leaf, including 'Deshiojo', 'Shindeshiojo' or 'Chishio Improved', and 'Otome zakure'. All are attractive, but 'Beni maiko' surely is one of the best. 'Corallinum' belongs also to this type but grows slower. In cold winters, some long, not fully ripened shoots may die back. Found only occasionally in gardens and rarely available in the trade. Zone VI. (Group 1b)

**'Beni no tsukasa'**, see **'Beni tsukasa'**

**'Beni otake'.** Wood (1980). USA. The outstanding feature of this cultivar is its bamboolike appearance; it has very long, narrow, 5- to 7-lobed leaves that are a deep purple-red. It is an attractive, upright plant suitable for landscaping. Introduced by TC Plant, Inc., Hillsboro, Oregon, USA. Not available in Europe. Zone VI. (Group 5b)

**'Beni seigen'.** Yokohama Nurseries (1896). Japan. See **'Corallinum'.**

**'Beni shichi henge'.** Angyo Maple Nursery (1967). Japan. JDV I, 105; JDV II, 113, photo. A rather slow-growing shrub of about the same height and width, about 2–3 m. Openly branched, young shoots brown, thin, and fragile. The leaves are very attractive, green with silver margins, speckled with brown-red, sometimes covering half the blade or an entire lobe (Plate 151). The name means "red and changeful." This cultivar is difficult to propagate and so is not readily available in the trade. Zone VI. (Group 1c)

**'Beni shidare'.** Yokohama Nurseries (1896). Japan. JDV I, 64; JDV II, 70. One of the many closely allied cultivars of the red Dissectum group. This particular cultivar is said to be identical with 'Dissectum Atropurpureum'—a name, however, that covers a wide range of red-leaved Dissectum cultivars, all with good to splendid autumn color. The maple sold under the name 'Dissectum Atropurpureum' usually is 'Ornatum'. It is our opinion that nursery professionals must avoid 'Dissectum Atropurpureum' as a cultivar name. This is entirely possible, as all the cultivars in trade have clear-cut names. The only exception might be 'Ornatum', as this name has long been in use in the whole of Europe, save Great Britain, and in the United States (see Bean, *Trees and Shrubs Hardy in the British Isles*). 'Beni shidare' is very close to 'Ornatum', but it has somewhat more pendulous branches so has a more cascading appearance. The leaves are identical. The name means "red and pendulous." (Group 4b)

**'Beni shidare Tricolor'.** Angyo Maple Nursery (1967). Japan. JDV I, 64; JDV II, 70, photo. This name is illegitimate under the *ICNCP* rules, which forbid mixing languages. This cultivar differs from the preceding in its variegated leaves and tendency to grow less vigorously, to about 1.5 m wide. The base color is more greenish red than in 'Beni shidare', and the finely dissected lobes are variegated with white, cream, or pink. It is slow-growing and rather fragile, and requires extra attention and care. Vertrees calls this cultivar 'Beni shidare Variegated' (see also 'Toyama nishiki'). Zones VI–VII. (Group 4c)

**'Beni shidare Variegated'.** An illegitimate cultivar name. See **'Beni shidare Tricolor'.**

**'Beni shigitatsu sawa'.** JDV I, 103/104; JDV II, 111–112, photo (as 'Aka shigitatsu sawa'). Shrub to 4 m tall, about as high as wide. Leaves tricolored, whitish green and pink, especially attractive in early autumn, deeply divided, mostly 7-lobed (Plate 152). Of modest growth and well worth a place in the garden. It is very close to 'Shigitatsu sawa' or 'Reticulatum', but much redder. Sometimes available in the trade. Zone VI. (Group 3c)

**'Beni tsukasa'.** JDV I, 106; JDV II, 114, photo. Very attractive shrub of medium height, about 5–6 m. Young growth is dark pinkish red, later turning to a peach- or yellow-red. In late summer the color darkens but some variegation remains visible. The leaves are smaller than those of the species, but of the same shape. The wood is thin and fragile. A fine plant for a small garden. Zone VI. (Group 1b/c)

**'Beni ubi gohon'.** Buchholz Nursery (1990). Gaston, Oregon, USA. Dwarfish shrub, upright growing. The long, narrowly lobed leaves are bright purple-red. Available in the USA. Zone VI. (Group 5b)

**'Beni yatsubusa'.** JDV II, 101. Rather strongly and densely growing, this so-called dwarf is not really a dwarf. The name means "red and dwarfish." Leaves are small, 5-lobed, fresh green, larger on vigorous shoots. Fall colors usually red or crimson. (See also description and discussion under 'Chishio'.) (Group 1a)

**'Bicolor'.** Siebold (1864). Germany. Leaves dark red, variegated with pink. Probably no longer in cultivation.

**'Bishop'**, see **'The Bishop'**

**'Bloodgood'.** Bloodgood Nurseries. Long Island, New York, USA. JDV I, 49; JDV II, 55, photo. 'Bloodgood' has become very popular; it bears the darkest leaves of all the cultivars. The leaves are usually 5-lobed with 2 tiny basal lobes. The color remains the same during the entire year, and there is no special autumn color. Save in very dry climates, the leaves do not turn greenish purple in summer, as do others. The fruits are also attractive, with red wings, and hang in clusters for an extended time. The shrub grows upright, to 6–7 m, and is rather narrow. Young plants do not branch well, so heavy pruning is necessary to form attractive plants. F. Vrugtman of Hamilton, Canada, suggests that this is a very old Dutch cultivar, sold to the Bloodgood Nursery by the long-closed firm of Messrs. Ebbinge & van Groos of Boskoop, The Netherlands. This is a well-known and useful cultivar and is quite common in the trade. (Group 2b)

**'Bloodleaf'.** Kelsey & Dayton (1942). USA. See **'Atropurpureum'.**

**'Bloodvein'.** Kelsey & Dayton (1942). USA. See **'Atrolineare'.**

**'Bonfire'**, see **'Seigai'** and *A. truncatum* **'Akaji nishiki'**

**'Bonnie Bergman'.** Bergman (1969). Pennsylvania, USA. Leaves 5- to 7-lobed, scarlet in autumn. Apparently not available in the trade. (Group 1a)

**'Boskoop Glory'.** Greer Gardens (1985). Eugene, Oregon, USA. Strong, large shrub to 8 m. Leaves dark wine-red, lobes cleft to half the blade. It keeps its color very well but does not show much autumn color. It was introduced in Oregon, not in Boskoop, The Netherlands. Available in the trade. Zone VI. (Group 2b)

**'Brevilobum'.** Hesse (1893). Germany. Leaf lobes short. No longer available.

**'Brocade'.** JDV I, 64; JDV II, 70. Another clone in the red Dissectum group, very close to 'Ornatum' in its leaf color, save that the autumn color tends to become scarlet or orange instead of orange-yellow. The branches are somewhat more pendulous. Young leaves are a pleasant dark purple but tend to become much greener in summer. This cultivar is not well known, and it differs but little from the more common cultivars. There is another cultivar also bearing the name 'Brocade' (see cultivars of *A. saccharum*). Zone VI. (Group 4b)

**'Burgundy Lace'.** Mulligan (1958). Washington, USA. JDV I, 76; JDV II, 82, photo. A splendid cultivar of US origin. It has beautiful, deeply divided leaves, 7-lobed, serrate along the entire margin, about 8–10 cm across. The shrubs grow moderately as high and wide, usually 4–5 m as a mature plant. The color holds very well in regions with a rather moist climate. In very dry regions it tends to become greenish in late summer. 'Sherwood Flame' is very similar but holds its color better. Though well known for many years in the United States, 'Burgundy Lace' was only introduced to Europe about 1972 and was given an Award of Merit in 1977 by the Royal Boskoop Horticultural Society. Only occasionally seen in gardens but readily available in the trade. (Group 3b)

**'Butterfly'.** Wada (1938). Japan. JDV I, 106; JDV II, 114, photo. Fine, attractive, silver-variegated shrub, not exceeding 2.5–3 m. It grows rather stiffly upright and is densely branched. The young shoots are thin, and stronger shoots branch a second time in the same season. The leaves are rather small, 5-lobed, and with large, silvery white margins (Plate 153). The lobes are irregular; almost all are different. There is no pink variegation, which makes it strikingly different from its nearest ally, 'Beni schichi henge'. In autumn the silvery tone changes to scarlet-magenta. 'Butterfly' is becoming more popular. It was given an Award of Merit in 1977 by the Royal Boskoop Horticultural Society. It is eminently suitable for very small gardens. It seldom reverts, but if reverting twigs develop they must be removed at once as they will eventually take over the entire plant. Possibly its original Japanese name is 'Kocho nishiki', which was published in 1882. Plants grown from cuttings are often short-lived, weak, and fragile. It must be grafted to obtain healthy plants. Zone VI. (Group 1c)

**'Carminium'**, see **'Corallinum'** (This name appears in the Fratelli Gilardelli (Italy) catalog of 1981 and is clearly identical with 'Corallinum'.)

**'Carneum'.** Siebold ex Wesmael (1890). Germany. A red-leaved cultivar. Apparently lost from cultivation.

**'Caudatum'.** Schwerin (1893). Germany. Leaf lobes caudate-acuminate. Probably identical with the species. Apparently not in cultivation.

**'Chiba'**, see **'Kashima'**

**'Chiba yatsubusa'**, see **'Kashima'**

**'Chichibu'**, see **'Kotohime'**

**'Chichibu yatsubusa'**, see **'Kotohime'**

**'Chikuma no'.** JDV II, 82. Medium-sized, treelike shrub. Leaves large, 15–20 cm across, dark purple-red, changing to dark olive-green in summer, with yellow-orange fall colors. A desirable plant for landscaping, but only rarely available. (Group 2b)

**'Chikushigata'**, see **'Tsukushigata'**

**'Chirimen kaede'**, see **'Tamukeyama'**

**'Chirimen momiji'**, see **'Tamukeyama'**

**'Chirimen nishiki'.** JDV I, 107; JDV II, 115, photo. This is a choice cultivar, about 2 m high, slow-growing and rather delicate. The leaves are very deeply divided, the lobes very narrow and coarsely toothed. The latter feature is in striking contrast to the others in the Linearilobum group, which have finely serrate or entire margins. The leaves show traces of variegation, but not strikingly, and most of the leaves are entirely green. Occasionally an entire lobe is creamy, but usually the variegations cannot be seen. Leaves on vigorous shoots have broader lobes, as is usual on young plants of this and other dwarfish cultivars. It is difficult to propagate and therefore extremely rare. Its name means "crêpe de Chine." Zone VI. (Group 5a)

**'Chishio'.** Yokohama Nurseries (1896). Japan. JDV I, 119; JDV II, 127, photo. One of the many cultivars having a brilliant red foliage when unfolding. This plant grows rather slowly and is densely branched, to 2.5–3 m. The leaves are smaller than the species, 5-lobed, and turn almost entirely green in summer. The autumn colors are orange-scarlet. Some have viewed this name as synonymous with 'Sanguineum'. The name 'Sanguineum' has been applied to several different clones, however, all with purple-red leaves. In our opinion it is best to drop the name 'Sanguineum' for the same reasons as pointed out (under 'Beni shidare') for 'Dissectum Atropurpureum' An alternative spelling is 'Shishio', and there is also a much improved clone named 'Chishio Improved'. The name 'Shishio' is also misused, especially in the United States, for the well-known cultivar 'Okushimo'. It is even applied sometimes to 'Shishigashira', due to other synonyms they have in common, such as 'Crispum'. Names like this are in fact not correct, but as there is no other name in synonymy, confusion is not as marked as it might be. The name 'Chishio' means "blood." True 'Chishio' is rarely met and almost never available in the trade. Zones VI–VII. (Group 1a or Group 6)

**'Chishio Improved'.** JDV I, 130; JDV II, 138, photo. This remarkable cultivar looks very much like 'Deshojo' or 'Shindeshojo'. It grows rather rapidly into a good shrub of about 3–4 m or more. Its thin, young wood is dark purple and the unfolding leaves are of a brilliant scarlet. After the leaves have matured, the color changes to an interesting mixture of blue and green. It must be planted in a sheltered position in the garden. Given the proper site it pleases everyone, especially in spring. It came from Japan under this name about 1965, but the name cannot be traced in the literature. Zone VI. (Group 1b)

**'Chitoseyama'.** *Japanese Maple List* (1882); JDV I, 77; JDV II, 83, photo. According to the description by Vertrees, this is a rather slow-growing shrub of about 3 m width. Plants acquired from him are quite like his description, with dark purple, 7-lobed leaves and serrate margins, turning a lighter red in summer and becoming scarlet in the autumn. In September a green undertone is apparent. Messrs. W. de Jong & Sons, Boskoop, The Netherlands, imported plants under this name from E. de Rothschild, Exbury Estate, Great Britain. Unfortunately, these plants are quite different from those obtained from the United States. The Rothschild plant is more or less spreading, not exceeding 2.5–3 m in height but growing much wider. The leaves are also deeply divided and olive-brown, turning olive-green, with an orange-yellow autumn color. It is a very attractive plant. This Rothschild cultivar is also described and offered in Hillier's *Manual*. Most of the plants in Europe sold under 'Chitoseyama' are certainly of this origin. The authoritative account by Nakamura et al. (1974) gives a description written by the Japanese expert Kobayashi on page 140, as follows: Leaves palmate, 9-lobed, narrow-lobed, deeply divided to the base. Brilliant purplish red. New leaves when opening are pale crimson, later becoming purplish red. The preceding makes it clear that the first described clone is correct. The cultivar from Exbury has to be renamed or correctly identified. Zone VI. (Group 3b)

**'Chizome'.** Mulligan (1958). Washington, USA. Lacks a description. The name means "spotted with blood."

**'Cinnabar Wooded'.** Kelsey & Dayton (1942). USA. See **'Sangokaku'.**

**'Cinnabarinum'**, see **'Sangokaku'**

**'Circumlobatum'.** Koidzumi (1911). Japan. Leaves with the lobes connivent at the bases, possibly related to *A. japonicum.* Apparently not in cultivation.

**'Compactum'.** R. Smith (1874). Great Britain. Lacks a description; no longer in cultivation.

**'Coonara Pygmy'.** Teese. Australia. JDV I, 95; JDV II, 101, photo. Densely branched, dwarf shrub, to 1.5 m or slightly more, of globular shape. The leaves are different in shape and size; leaves on young shoots are clearly 5-lobed, fresh green, and about 2 cm across. Young plants grow as neat, round specimens, perfectly suitable for a large rock garden or as a bonsai plant. The autumn color is a very attractive fiery orange. Sometimes the whole plant or parts of it tend to sudden dieback. This cultivar originated in Australia, at Arnold Teese's nursery in Victoria. It came to The Netherlands through Oregon and is sometimes available in Europe. Zone VI. (Group 6)

**'Coralliformis'**, see **'Corallinum'**

**'Corallinum'.** Hillier & Sons (before 1900). Ampfield, Great Britain. JDV I, 120; JDV II, 128, photo. Semidwarf shrub of outstanding beauty up to 3 m high but fragile and difficult to propagate. The new leaves have the striking scarlet color of cultivars such as 'Chishio' or 'Beni maiko', but the plant grows quite slowly and compactly (Plate 154). The new, dark pink leaves tend to burn in full sun. Later they turn green with occasional traces of pink variegation. There is a splendid specimen in the garden of the late Sir Harold Hillier, at Jermyns Lane in Ampfield. Another good specimen is in the Trompenburg Arboretum, Rotterdam, The Netherlands. The name 'Corallinum' has also been attached to the coral-bark maple, 'Sangokaku' or 'Senkaki', originally offered by Veitch in 1904. This confusion has persisted so strongly that it was still used by van Gelderen (1969). 'Corallinum' is quite rare and almost never available in the trade. It is very difficult to propagate, so production on a large scale is impossible. To add to the difficulties, scions are hardly ever available as the plant grows so slowly. Zone VI. (Group 6)

**'Corallinum'.** Veitch (1904). Great Britain. Not to be confused with the above cultivar, this name is used incorrectly for 'Sangokaku', which see.

**'Coral Pink'.** De Belder (1985). Belgium. A very slow-growing, upright shrub, sparsely branched. The leaves are strikingly coral-pink, turning to a yellow-pink in summer. The shape is typical of the species. This cultivar needs protection against full sun. It was found and selected by R. de Belder of the Kalmthout Arboretum, Belgium, about 1965 and named following a long period of observation. It is delicate and difficult to propagate. Rarely available in Europe. Zones VI–VII. (Group 6)

**'Coreanum'**, see **'Koreanum'**

**'Crested'.** Kelsey & Dayton (1942). USA. See **'Okushimo'.**

**'Crimson Prince'.** Princeton Nurseries (before 1989). Ohio, USA. A rather stiff, upright-growing shrubby tree to 6 m high. Leaves 5- (to 7-) lobed, bold, dark purple in spring, becoming a lighter color in summer but not turning green. In moist climates, the tree stays purple all summer. Said to be an improvement of the well-known 'Bloodgood'. (Group 1b).

**'Crimson Queen'.** Cascio (1965). USA. JDV I, 65; JDV II, 71, photo. This is a truly outstanding cultivar. It has both beauty and a neat habit, which make it fit for any but the smallest garden. The young leaves are of the darkest purple-red, which is maintained throughout the summer. In late summer the leaves turn to a good reddish purple, without traces of yellow or orange developing in the autumn. It has a weeping habit and grows much wider than high, its mature height being about 2 m. The leaves are finely cut, definitely finer than in 'Garnet', the cultivar closest in color. 'Crimson Queen' received a First Class Certificate in Boskoop, The Netherlands, from the Royal Boskoop Horticultural Society. It is one of the very best Japanese maples available today. (Group 4b)

**'Crippsii'.** Hillier & Sons (1928). Ampfield, Great Britain. A weak, small maple of about 1 m, with small, dirty green leaves of many shapes, about 2 cm across or less. It may be suitable for bonsai but has very little value as a garden plant. Very rarely seen. Zone VI. (Group 6)

**'Crispa'**, see **'Okushimo'**

**'Crispum'.** Von Siebold (1870). Germany. See **'Okushimo'** or **'Shishigashira'.**

**'Cristatum'.** Schwerin (1893). Germany. See **'Shishigashira'.**

**'Cristatum Variegatum'.** Bergman (1969). USA. See **'Higasayama'.**

**'Cuneatum'.** Schwerin (1893). Germany. A shrub with 7-lobed green leaves with cuneate bases. Probably no longer in cultivation.

**'Daimyo'**, see **'Taimin'**

**'Daimyo nishiki'.** Wada (1938). Japan. See **'Taimin nishiki'.**

**'Decompositum'.** Miquel (1867). France. See **'Koshimino'.**

**'Deshojo'.** JDV I, 121; JDV II, 129, photo. This cultivar has brilliantly colored red leaves when unfolding, which quickly turn pink touched with bluish green. In summer the rather small, 5-lobed leaves are green with a red tone. The autumn color is not remarkable. There are a number of cultivars with much the same character, such as 'Chishio Improved', 'Beni maiko', and 'Shindeshojo'. The wood is thin and very dark purple. Long shoots tend to die back in winter as they are slow to ripen sufficiently. This plant is well known in Japanese horticulture and widely used as bonsai material in that country. In the West it is a rare plant and much in demand by maple collectors and bonsai enthusiasts. Zones VI–VII. (Group 1b)

**'Digitatum Atropurpureum'.** Van Houtte (1885). Belgium. See **'Nicholsonii'.**

**'Dissectum'.** Thunberg (1784). JDV I, 63; JDV II, 69.

One of the best-known Japanese maples of the mushroom habit (Plate 155). The leaves are deeply divided and the lobes deeply incised, looking like fern leaves and very elegant. 'Dissectum' is a small tree at its best, to 5 m high and as wide. It also frequently grows as a giant "mushroom," to 5–8 m wide and to half that height. This type, generally available, is correctly called 'Dissectum'. The name 'Dissectum Viride' is also often used. The autumn color is brilliant yellow; in summer and spring the leaves are a soft green. The plant is excellent for early forcing, and can be a beauty at flower shows. There is little need to prune or trim as it grows regularly without any help. Thunberg called this garden-cultivated variety *A. dissectum,* as he regarded it as a species. It is, however, of pure garden origin and does not exist in the wild so does not deserve subspecific or varietal rank. It belongs, in fact, to subspecies *matsumurae.* The best we can do is designate it as the type for the group with deeply dissected leaves. The 'Dissectum' of Thunberg is no longer in cultivation; it is, however, the type of the Dissectum group. Many different clones of different origin erroneously carry the cultivar name of 'Dissectum'. Seedlings from 'Dissectum' or related cultivars sometimes produce plants with more or less dissected leaves though only a very low percentage have really good dissected leaves even when seed is harvested from an isolated specimen. Due to the enormous variability of *A. palmatum,* twigs occasionally revert or sport. Such branches usually produce leaves less deeply incised than the mother plant, and they must be removed. However, a novelty plant occurs in this way from time to time. (Group 4a)

**'Dissectum Atropurpureum'.** Hogg (1879). Great Britain. See also **'Ornatum'.** It is clear that the name 'Dissectum Atropurpureum' covers more than one clone of several origins. This is the reason Nicholson rebaptized the well-known cultivar as 'Ornatum'. It is still sold under that incorrect name. The expression 'Dissectum Atropurpureum' is frequently used in the United States to include all red-leaved cultivars with dissected leaves. Consequently, trinominal to quinquenominal name combinations such as *Acer palmatum dissectum atropurpureum* 'Crimson Queen' are in use. Such usage, however, is not correct and is in conflict with the *International Code of Nomenclature for Cultivated Plants* (1980).

**'Dissectum Atropurpureum Variegatum',** see **'Dissectum Variegatum'**

**'Dissectum Atrosanguineum'.** Wezelenburg (circa 1930). Hazerswoude, The Netherlands. See **'Dissectum Nigrum'.**

**'Dissectum Aureum'** (in Japanese catalogs), see **'Dissectum Flavescens'**

**'Dissectum Barrie Bergman'** (1965). See **'Barrie Bergman'.**

**'Dissectum Ever Red'.** Cascio (1965). USA. See **'Dissectum Nigrum'.**

**'Dissectum Flavescens'.** Hillier & Sons (1928). Ampfield, Great Britain. JDV I, 67; JDV II, 73, photo. A green-leaved cultivar in the Dissectum group of a somewhat irregular habit, with pendulous branches, sometimes growing 60–80 cm per year. The leaves are like 'Dissectum' but more yellow-green, and the autumn color is more orange (Plate 156). A beautiful variety, especially suitable for planting along a pond or in a rock garden for its unusual growth. Rather rare but available. (Group 4a)

**'Dissectum Garnet',** see 'Garnet'

**'Dissectum Inazuma'.** Wada (1938). Japan. See **'Inazuma'.**

**'Dissectum Matsukaze'.** Koidzumi (1911). Japan. See **'Matsukaze'.**

**'Dissectum Nigrum'.** Wada (1938). Japan. JDV I, 69; JDV II, 71, photo. A rather well-known cultivar, originating in Japan and introduced into The Netherlands under the name 'Dissectum Nigrum' and better known in the United States as 'Ever Red'. It is easily recognized by the silvery hairs on the young leaves; no other cultivar in the Dissectum group has this peculiar feature. A few hairs remain visible in the summer. The color is dark purple but lighter than 'Garnet' and somewhat buff. The growth habit of the plant is irregular, as it often develops only on one side. But this characteristic makes it quite suitable for planting along a pond or other sites constricted on one side. The name 'Ever Red' was erected by Cascio (1965) and is not in use in Europe. While still rather widely grown, 'Dissectum Nigrum' is slowly losing its popularity in favor of 'Crimson Queen', 'Garnet', etc. (Group 4b)

**'Dissectum Ornatum'.** Siesmayer (1888). Germany. See **'Ornatum'.**

**'Dissectum Ornatum Variegatum'.** Hillier & Sons. Great Britain. See **'Dissectum Variegatum'.**

**'Dissectum Palmatifidum'.** Hillier & Sons (1928). Great Britain. Most probably this cultivar, known and cultivated worldwide, is identical with 'Dissectum'. Some believe this name has been attached to the old cultivar 'Dissectum Paucum'. The name is often misspelled as 'Dissectum Palmatifidium'. In the United States this name is assigned to a sturdier 'Dissectum' clone, with leaves somewhat less deeply incised and a darker green. This clone is identical with the European 'Dissectum Paucum', a rather rare cultivar. It has good autumn color. The Japanese name is

'Washi no o' (*Japanese Maple List,* 1882). (Group 4a)

**'Dissectum Paucum'.** Dutch nurseries (before 1900). The Netherlands. JDV I, 69; JDV II, 76, photo. A robust cultivar, more upright than many of its relatives, somewhat sparsely branched. The leaves are dark green, 7-lobed, and not as deeply incised as usual. It often has a very beautiful autumn color. See **'Dissectum Palmatifidum'.** It has been in the trade for many years and the date of its introduction is not known. The common 'Dissectum', as well as 'Waterfall', may be considered by name as 'Washi no o'. This name has to be rejected as it is a homonym, both for 'Dissectum Palmatifidum' and 'Dissectum Paucum'. This name was published in 1940 by W. J. Hendriks in his manual *Onze Loofhoutgewassen,* a Dutch dendrology (first edition, 1940; second edition, 1957). (Group 4a)

**'Dissectum Pendulum Julian'.** Kingsville. USA. See **'Pendulum Julian'.**

**'Dissectum Pinnatifidum Roseo-pictum',** see **'Dissectum Roseo-marginatum'**

**'Dissectum Rhodophyllum'.** Pax (1886). Germany. Said to be a cultivar with purple, lacy leaves. Probably not in cultivation. (Group 4b)

**'Dissectum Roseo-marginatum'.** Lemaire (1867). France. JDV I, 71; JDV II, 77. An old cultivar with dissected leaves, green, flushed with red or occasionally some pink variegation that reverts easily. A rare variety. (Group 4c)

**'Dissectum Roseo-pictum'.** Lemaire (1857). France. See **'Dissectum Roseo-marginatum'.**

**'Dissectum Rubellum'.** Pax (1886) Germany. See **'Dissectum Rubrifolium'.**

**'Dissectum Rubrifolium'.** Miquel (1865). France. JDV I, 71; JDV II, 77. This cultivar is not particularly desirable. It has been in cultivation very many years, but there are now several better cultivars. Its leaves unfold a rather dark purple, soon turning a reddish, almost dirty green. In late summer they are a dark green that turns yellow to orange in autumn. 'Ornatum' is much more attractive and also has the better autumn color. It still grows in many old gardens but is seldom available in the trade. Zone VI. (Group 4b)

**'Dissectum Rubrum'.** Barron (1875). Great Britain. Very much like 'Dissectum Rubrifolium', but its summer leaves are greener and less deeply cut, having more the shape of 'Dissectum Paucum'. Only rarely available in the trade. Zone VI. (Group 4a/b)

**'Dissectum Ruth Murray'.** Murray (1969). USA. See **'Ruth Murray'.**

**'Dissectum Sessilifolium'.** Nicholson (1881). Great Britain. See **'Hagaromo'**

**'Dissectum Superbum'.** Wada (1938). Japan. Possibly this cultivar is available under a different name. It has black-purple leaves, finely dissected. (Group 4b)

**'Dissectum Tamukeyama',** see **'Tamukeyama'**

**'Dissectum Tinctum',** see **'Dissectum Rubrifolium'**

**'Dissectum Unicolor'.** Wada (1938). Japan. Leaf lobes lacy, yellow-green. Probably very close to or even identical with 'Dissectum Flavescens'. Not in the trade under this name. (Group 4a)

**'Dissectum Variegatum'.** Lawson (1874). Great Britain. JDV I, 73; JDV II, 79, photo. At first sight this slow-growing maple looks like 'Ornatum' with some variegation. It becomes a large plant, to 2 m high and at least as wide. The leaves are typical of 'Dissectum'—brown-red in spring, later greener, with pink and white variegations. Brown leaves tend to take over, and so the variegation disappears easily. A plant of more than 75 years in the gardens of the Research Station at Boskoop, The Netherlands, was over 3 m high and at least as wide, with only one heavy branch bearing variegated leaves. The other branches were very much like 'Ornatum'. Unfortunately, this large specimen died. This beautiful cultivar is propagated in modest quantities. 'Goshiki shidare' is similar, but slower growing. 'Goshiki shidare' has much more pink in its leaves and may be identical to 'Toyama nishiki' or 'Beni shidare Tricolor'. Zone VI. (Group 4c)

**'Dissectum Viride',** see **'Dissectum'**

**'Dissectum Waterfall'.** Tingle (1963). See **'Waterfall'.**

**'Dwarf Shishi'.** This plant is something of a mystery. Its origin is not known and the name has not previously been published. It is a very compact, densely branched shrub, about 1 m high and wide. The leaves are much smaller than typical *A. palmatum,* fresh green and 5-lobed. The autumn color is yellow. A good cultivar for bonsai but only rarely available. It is quite possible that this cultivar is identical with 'Shishi yatsubusa' in the late J. D. Vertrees' collection. The word "yatsubusa" means "dwarf." Zone VI. (Group 6)

**'Eddisbury'.** Morray & Sons (1970). Great Britain. A strong-growing upright shrub up to 6–7 m tall. The twigs and thinner branches are coral-red in winter, much like the well-known 'Sangokaku'. The leaves, however, are darker green and more leathery. Its fall color is less spectacular than that of 'Sangokaku', but it is a sturdier plant. Only rarely available in the trade. (Group 1a)

**'Effegi'.** Gilardelli (1975). Italy. See **'Fireglow'.**

**'Elegans'.** Smith (1874). Great Britain. JDV I, 77; JDV II, 83, photo. This is a vigorous, well-branched shrub or sometimes a multiple-stemmed tree. The leaves are of the Amoenum group shape, beautifully olive green when unfolding, later green and then turning a brilliant yellow. A beautiful cultivar and well worth a place in the garden. Rather common and readily available in the trade. (Group 2a)

**'Elegans Atropurpureum'.** Dickson (1887). Great Britain. See **'Hessei'.**

**'Elegans Purpureum'.** Nicholson (1881). Great Britain. See **'Hessei'.**

**'Elegans Purpureum'.** Schwerin (1893). Germany. See **'Nicholsonii'.**

**'Ellen'** Esveld (1992). Boskoop, The Netherlands. A well-growing shrub of the mushroom habit, (so far) not exceeding 1.5 m in height and 2 m in width. Rather dense branching. The leaves are very lacy and fresh green, 7-lobed, each lobe very finely dissected; the central veins of the lobes are rather long, up to 6–7 cm. It gives an airy and elegant impression, not unlike stylized snow flakes. Originated in a batch of open-pollinated seedlings of several 'Dissectum' types. Named after Mrs. Ellen van Gelderen–van Weely, daughter-in-law of the author. (Group 4a)

**'Enkan'.** Kobayashi. Japan. A dwarf form with dark red leaves of the Linearilobum group. Imported in 1991 from Japan to The Netherlands. (Group 5b)

**'Euchlorum'.** Van Houtte (1885). Belgium. Lacks a description; probably no longer in cultivation.

**'Ever Red'.** Cascio (1965). USA. See **'Dissectum Nigrum'.**

**'Ezo nishiki'**, see **'Yezo nishiki'**

**'Fichtenast'.** Schwerin (1893). Germany. See **'Matsugae'.**

**'Filiferum Purpureum'.** Kingsville (1963). USA. See **'Atrolineare'.**

**'Filigree'.** Spingarn (circa 1955). New York, USA. JDV I, 66; JDV II, 72, photo. One of the most attractive Japanese maples now available. It is a very beautiful plant, to 1 m tall and a little wider when mature. It grows slowly in a neat mushroom form. The leaves are finely and doubly dissected, giving them a very lacy look (Plate 157). The color is light green with a faintly visible variegation of white. Unfortunately it is rather difficult to propagate and so is not easily available. As it is a recent introduction, there are no adult specimens in collections. It seems to grow much smaller than other expressions of the mushroom type. It is a highly desirable plant. Zone VI. (Group 4a)

**'Fingerlobe'.** Kelsey & Dayton (1942). USA. See **'Linearilobum'.**

**'Fireglow'.** Fratelli Gilardelli (circa 1977). Omate, Italy. A cultivar recently developed in Italy at Fratelli Gilardelli and introduced into The Netherlands by Messrs. W. J. Spaargaren, Boskoop. The Royal Boskoop Horticultural Society gave this plant an Award of Merit in the summer of 1982. It is a vigorous shrub, rather upright and well branched. The leaves are much like 'Bloodgood' and of the same dark color. It seems to be an improvement of 'Bloodgood', especially in its good habit and ease of propagation. It is not yet generally available. The same cultivar has been released by Messrs. K. Wezelenburg & Sons, Hazerswoude, The Netherlands, under the name 'Effegi'. Fratelli Gilardelli seem to have another cultivar, quite different from this one, with red, dissected leaves, named 'Dissectum Fireglow'. This plant, not yet in the trade, has at present an illegitimate name so will have to be renamed. Zone VI. (Group 1b)

**'Fischergeraete'.** Schwerin (1893). Germany. See **'Hagaromo'.**

**'Flavescens'**, see **'Dissectum Flavescens'**

**'Flavescens'.** Veitch (1876). Great Britain. See **'Reticulatum'.**

**'Flushing'.** John Vermeulen, Inc. (1989). New Jersey, USA. A narrow but strongly growing shrub with deep purple leaves, not unlike the well-known 'Bloodgood'. Zones V–VI. (Group 1b)

**'Friderici-Guilelmi'.** Carrière (1867). France. See **'Dissectum Variegatum'.**

**'Frost in der Erde'.** Schwerin (1893). Germany. See **'Okushimo'.**

**'Furu nishiki'.** Bijhouwer (1928). The Netherlands. See **'Tsuri nishiki'.**

**'Ganseki momiji'**, see **'Arakawa'**

**'Garnet'.** Guldemond Bros. (1959). Boskoop, The Netherlands. This is a Dutch introduction and a plant of excellent qualities. It grows to a large shrub. In fact, it is one of the largest of the Dissectum group, reaching 4–5 m high and as wide. The leaves are attractively dark purple—Garnet Red on the *R.H.S. Horticultural Color Chart*—hence the name. The leaves are slightly less incised than in 'Crimson Queen', though the color is much the same. Young plants grow vigorously and tend to become somewhat open and leggy. Such plants must be trimmed in the nursery and also staked the first few years in the garden. Messrs. Guldemond discovered it as a chance seedling in a lot of seedlings, purchased in Italy about 1950 for root stocks. 'Garnet' received the Award of Merit in 1960 from the Royal Boskoop Horticultural Society. It is now cultivated in quantity and is generally available. The name 'Dissectum Garnet' was published after 1 January 1959, the cutoff date for cultivar names consisting of a mixture of Latin and non-Latin forms, and is thus illegitimate. (Group 4b)

**'Garyu'.** JDV I, 121; JDV II, 129, photo. A neat, small, slow-growing plant. Its leaves are small and delicate, but rather variable in size, from 3 to 6 cm across. Most are only 3-lobed, very deeply divided. The color is light green with a reddish hue. The name means "one's own style or manner." It is very difficult to propagate and so is practically never available. Zone VI. (Group 6–7)

**'Germaine's Gyration'.** Vandermoss (before 1990). USA. Cascading shrub with lacy, green leaves turning to yellow. Horizontal lateral branches twist to pleach at base. Introduced by Iseli Nursery, Eugene, Oregon, USA. (Group 4a)

**'Goshiki kotohime'.** JDV I, 95; JDV II, 101, photo. A choice cultivar, slow-growing to an upright shrub of about 1 m (Plate 157). It is the variegated form of 'Kotohime', also a slow grower. The leaves are very deeply divided, mostly 5-lobed, each lobe irregularly incised. Young growing tips are often pink; older leaves are dark green with irregular variegations. Older leaves are somewhat crinkled but never as markedly as in 'Shishigashira'. A rare cultivar. Not available in Europe. Zone VI. (Group 6)

**'Goshiki shidare'.** JDV I, 68; JDV II, 74, photo. A moderately cascading cultivar, closely related to 'Beni shidare Tricolor' and possibly the same. As there is insufficient material available for comparison, it is best to keep them separated at present. The finely dissected leaves are green with purple overtones and show variegations of pink, cream, and white (Plate 159). It is a slow-growing plant not exceeding 1–1.5 m. The autumn color is attractively purplish with variegations. It is rarely available, due to the difficulties of propagation. The wood is usually very thin and weak, which makes it difficult to graft. Zone VI. (Group 4c)

**'Greenet'.** Kelsey & Dayton (1942). USA. See **'Shigitatsu sawa'.**

**'Green Trompenburg'.** Esveld (1980). Boskoop, The Netherlands. A tall growing, treelike shrub, to 8 m, rather sparsely branched. The leaf lobes are convex, as in 'Trompenburg', and dark shining green. The autumn color is orange to yellow. This is an interesting plant; it gives added choice for landscaping. It originated in a large batch of seedlings, grown from open-pollinated seed, harvested in the Esveld Aceretum in Boskoop, The Netherlands. It is available in the trade. This name has been registered by J. D. Vertrees, but his information about the origin of this cultivar may be incorrect. The plant that originated at the Esveld Aceretum was called 'Groene Trompenburg', which means "Green Trompenburg". The red 'Trompenburg' was not sent to the United States before 1970. So it is not very likely that a green form was found as early as 1976. It is possible that Vertrees may have been mistaken when writing about his plant in the second edition of his work. He received quite a few scions and plants in the 1970s from Firma C. Esveld in The Netherlands. (Group 3a).

**'Hagaromo'.** Schwerin (1893). Germany. *Japanese Maple List,* 1882; JDV I, 122; JDV II, 130, photo. Upright shrub, not exceeding 5 m, and rather narrow. The leaves are almost sessile, hence the name 'Sessilifolium'—which has been a varietal name and also long in use as the cultivar name for this plant. 'Sessilifolium' as a cultivar name has to be rejected in favor of 'Hagaromo', as there are several other cultivars very close to this clone (e.g., 'Koshimino'). Said to have been occurred as a sport on true *A. palmatum,* it was regarded as a distinct species by Siebold and Zuccarini. It reverts to common *A. palmatum* from time to time. The leaves are broadly lanceolate and the leaf margins incised and irregular, thus giving a feathery and airy impression (Plate 160). Its garden value must not be overestimated, as it is mainly an aberration of *A. palmatum.* It can be found in a few collections and is sometimes available. Zone VI. (Group 7)

**'Hagerioni',** see **'Hazeroino'** or **'Hagaromo'** [This is a misspelling, and we cannot trace its proper use. It could be the green-leaved 'Hagaromo' ('Sessilifolium'), or it is also quite possible that it is the variegated 'Sessilifolium', which is correctly named 'Hazeroino'.]

**'Hamaotome'.** Yokohoma Nurseries. Japan. JDV I, 107; JDV II, 115. A shrubby Japanese cultivar up to 2 m, with yellow-green to whitish new leaves. The center of the leaf is lighter in color than its margins, becoming greener when mature. Leaves are 5–8 cm across, 7-lobed, and of thin texture. It is hardy but a little fragile. Very rare and not yet available. Zone VI. (Group 2c)

**'Hana izumi nishiki'.** Koidzumi (1911). Japan. See **'Kasen nishiki'.**

**'Hanami nishiki'.** JDV I, 96; JDV II, 102, photo. This choice cultivar grows very slowly, to 1.5 m, and is densely branched and rather fragile. The leaves are small, 5-lobed, and yellowish green with red-toned margins. Young grafts may produce rather long shoots, but this vigor disappears in the second year. Useful for bonsai. It is a rare plant as it was only recently introduced to the West. It seems to be more tender than most of the dwarf cultivars. The name means "flower viewing." Zones VI–VII. (Group 6)

**'Hanazono nishiki'.** *Japanese Maple List* (1882); JDV I, 107; JDV II, 115. This is a very rare cultivar with some variegations of cream and pink. According to Vertrees it must be an unattractive plant. Its closest relative, 'Karasugawa', is better known and also more beautiful. The name means "flower garden." Zones VI–VII. (Group 1c)

**'Harasume'**, see **'Harusame'**

**'Harusame'.** Wada (1938). Japan. JDV I, 107; JDV II, 115, photo. This plant is of greatest interest in the autumn. Its color is then a beautiful red with yellow-brown markings. It is a modest grower, about 3.5 m high and as wide. The leaves are 5- to 7-lobed. Vertrees's *Japanese Maples* contains a picture showing a variegated leaf. Half the leaf blade is white in this case, which Vertrees reports occurs from time to time. In The Netherlands we have never seen any variegation. 'Harusame' is also sold as 'Marusame', a misspelling. The name means "spring rain". Zone VI. (Group 2a)

**'Hatsushigure'.** Mulligan (1958). USA. Leaves lacy, vivid red, possibly still present in the Botanic Gardens of the University of Washington, Seattle. Not available in the trade. (Group 4b)

**'Hazeroino'.** Boom (1965). The Netherlands. JDV I, 122; JDV II, 130, photo. The only difference between this plant and 'Hagaromo' is the variegations present in this cultivar. The variegation is by no means heavy and is usually absent on stronger-growing shoots. Many years ago a large plant of this cultivar was present in the collection of the Research Station in Boskoop, The Netherlands. All plants now in the trade have been derived from this treelike shrub. When the Research Station was moved to a new locality many of the plants in this collection were sold into Italy, due to lack of space to maintain such immense specimens. Most of them survived the move, including the mother tree of this cultivar. This name has no meaning in Japanese. (Group 7)

**'Heptalobum'.** Rehder (1938). USA. JDV I, 50; JDV II, 56, photo. One of the best-known green-leaved cultivars, with regularly shaped leaves, always 7-lobed, hence its name. It grows into a mighty treelike shrub, easily to 8–10 m in favorable conditions. The autumn color is a clear yellow or occasionally orange-yellow. It is a heavy seed bearer. The seeds produce uniform, rather large-leaved seedlings, mostly with 7-lobed leaves. These plants conform to the description of *A. palmatum* ssp. *amoenum*. They are excellent for grafting purposes. It was formerly regarded as a natural variety but is now treated as a cultivar of subspecies *amoenum*. A very common synonym in the nursery trade is 'Septemlobum'. Plants under this name are invariably this cultivar. Often found in gardens and a rather common plant in nurseries and garden centers. (Group 2a)

**'Heptalobum Rubrum'.** Dutch nurseries (circa 1900). Origin not known. This old selection, in cultivation since the beginning of this century in Boskoop, The Netherlands, is quite similar to 'Heptalobum', but its leaves are dark purple-crimson when first unfolding, soon fading to a dull purple. In autumn they are a beautiful orange-red to reddish or, rarely, yellow (Plate 161). The leaf margins are more serrate than those of 'Heptalobum'. (Group 2b)

**'Herbstfeuer'.** Bärtels (1985). Germany. This seems to be a hybrid of *A. palmatum* with *A. circinatum*. The habit of the shrub is broad and densely branched, 5–6 m high and about as wide. The leaves are of a firm texture, 7-lobed, and dark green with an outstanding autumn color. It was found as a chance seedling by Andreas Bärtels, a German journalist and nurseryman. The plant looks very interesting and has been propagated, named, and introduced to the trade (released by Firma C. Esveld, Boskoop, The Netherlands). The name 'Herbstfeur' means "autumn fire." Zone V. (Group 2a)

**'Hessei'.** Schwerin (1893). Germany. JDV I, 77; JDV II, 83, photo. A medium-sized shrub, attaining 4–5 m in height. Its leaves are deeply divided with incised lobes. The spring color is a dark purple with a green undertone, which soon turns to a greenish brown in summer. The autumn colors are adequate, but there are better cultivars. In fact, its leaf color changes all the time during the growing season. It is better known by the synonym 'Elegans Purpureum'. It is in cultivation on a modest scale both in the United States and western Europe and is rather frequently found in gardens. (Group 2b)

**'Hibari'.** Koidzumi (1911). Japan. Leaf lobes narrow, blades green. Apparently not in cultivation.

**'Hichi henge'**, see **'Shichi henge'**

**'Higasayama'.** Yokohama Nurseries (1901). Japan. *Japanese Maple List*, 1882; JDV I, 108; JDV II, 116, photo. Tall, shrubby tree, to 7–8 m in height or occasionally more. It has a rather narrow, almost columnar, habit. The leaves are 7-lobed and the margins heavily variegated cream and pink (Plate 162). It is propagated in fair quantities in the United States, usually under an incorrect name, such as 'Roseo-marginatum', which is a quite different cultivar ('Kagiri nishiki'). It is also well known in Japan but is rather rare and only occasionally available in Europe. A magnificent tree grows in the Villa Taranto Gardens, Intra, Pallanza, Italy. This cultivar has one major drawback. It has a terrible tendency to revert to solid green as a young plant, in which case it is really ugly. Stock plants become full of strong-growing green twigs, so it is very difficult to find variegated scions. When reverted scions are grafted, the variegation ends abruptly and one has a common green *A. palmatum*. It is probably best to grow cultivars of this habit in pots or tubs as good, fertile soil leads more readily to reversion than a poor soil. Interestingly, the problem of reversion on the Dutch scale does not seem to occur in the United States. Zone VI. (Group 1c)

**'Hillieri'.** Harrison (1960). Great Britian. Said to be a selection of 'Atropurpureum'. Not available in the trade. The name is illegitimate and should be 'Hillier'.

**'Hina tayama'**, see **'Hyugayama'**

**'Hogyoku'.** *Japanese Maple List*, 1882. JDV I, 50; JDV II, 56, photo. A strong-growing cultivar, to 5 m high and 2–3 m wide. Its fresh green leaves are 5- to 7-lobed, the basal lobes being small. Its principal interest lies in its glowing orange-yellow autumn coloration, of which it is one of the best examples. It is an "easy" plant, growing happily and sturdy in most situations. Not common in collections and rarely available. (Group 2a)

**'Holland Select'**, see **'Inaba shidare'**

**'Hoshi kuzu'.** Vertrees (1979). Roseburg, Oregon, USA. JDV II, 102. A small shrub with small leaves of an unusual form. Some leaves are light green with breaks of variegation; others are totally colored. An interesting plant that deserves more attention. Found as a chance seedling from 'Kamagata'. Rarely available. (Group 6)

**'Hoshyadori'**, see ***A. mono* 'Hoshiyadori'**

**'Hupp's Dwarf'.** Hupp (1976). USA. JDV II, 103. A dwarf shrub, originating as a chance seedling, found by Barbara Hupp. It grows very slowly. The leaves are a rich green, with long, pointed lobes. The plant is comparable to cultivars such as 'Kotohime' or 'Mikawa yatsubusa'. The original plant is now at Maplewood Nursery, Roseburg, Oregon, and grows well. Not yet available in the trade. Zone VI. (Group 6)

**'Hyugayama'.** Kobayashi Nursery (1967). Japan. JDV I, 50; JDV II, 56. Another red-leaved cultivar, its leaves quickly turn to greenish purple. Not better than many other red-leaved clones, therefore seldom available in the trade. A seedling of 'Nomura'. Introduced in 1991 from Japan to The Netherlands. Zone VI. (Group 1b)

**'Ibo nishiki'.** JDV II, 84. This cultivar belongs to the group of rough-bark maples, like 'Nishiki gawa' or 'Arakawa'. Habit and leaves like the species. It develops a rough bark with age. Only rarely available in the trade. Zone VI. (Group 1a)

**'Ichigyo ji'.** Koidzumi (1911). Japan. *Japanese Maple List*, 1882; JDV I, 51; JDV II, 57, photo. This plant differs from the well-known 'Osakazuki' only in its autumn color: it is orange-yellow, and 'Osakazuki' is crimson. It is a rare plant and available only on a very limited scale. It probably deserves more attention, but better-known cultivars such as 'Heptalobum' or 'Hogyoku' fulfill the same functions in a garden. Zone VI. (Group 2a)

**'Iijima sunago'.** *Japanese Maple List*, 1882. JDV I, 109; JDV II, 117, photo. To us this is a rather unattractive cultivar. It grows to a large treelike shrub to 8 m. Almost immediately after unfolding, the large purplish leaves turn a dirty green. It has been praised in several publications, but only for its color in autumn, when it is attractive for a short time. "Sunago" means "dusted." Rarely available. (Group 3b)

**'Inaba shidare'.** Yokohoma Nurseries (1930). Japan. JDV I, 68; JDV II, 74, photo. A beautiful purple-leaved cultivar of the Dissectum group, imported from Japan, probably by Mr. Hohman. It was introduced into the trade by Henny's Nursery, Salem, Oregon, USA, who sold it along the Pacific Coast. It is a fast-growing, somewhat open shrub of the mushroom shape, about 2–2.5 m height and somewhat wider. Its leaves keep their color almost throughout the summer, save in very dry climates. The leaves are so close to those of 'Garnet' that young plants are easily confused and once confused cannot be sorted out again until more or less mature. Older plants have a distinctly different habit, more open and less cascading than 'Garnet'. This cultivar was introduced into western Europe by Messrs. K. Wezelenburg & Sons, Hazerswoude, The Netherlands. (Group 4b)

**'Inazuma'.** *Japanese Maple List*, 1882. JDV I, 78; JDV II, 84, photo. This cultivar is sometimes incorrectly listed as a "Dissectum" which is not at all the case. The leaves are very deeply divided, but the lobes are not serrate or incised as in the Dissectum group. The habit of the plant is also quite different. It grows into a large shrub or small tree to 10 m, higher than wide, and clearly belongs to subspecies *matsumurae.* The young leaves unfold a purple color, soon becoming olive green. The autumn colors are outstanding—in fact, one of the most spectacular selections! A good picture can be seen in Vertrees's *Japanese Maples.* It has been rated as "very good" in *Dendroflora,* 20. The name means "thunder." It is occasionally seen in gardens and will be more readily available in the future. (Group 3b)

**'Involutum'.** Siesmayer (1888). Germany. See **'Okushimo'.**

**'Irish Lace'.** Iseli Nursery (1991). Boring, Oregon, USA. Dissected leaves; no further description.

**'Iroha momiji',** see ***A. palmatum*** (Japanese designation for the species)

**'Iso chidori'.** *Japanese Maple List,* 1882. JDV I, 96; JDV II, 103, photo. Slow-growing cultivar with good green, rather small leaves, 5-lobed. The autumn color is yellow. Zone VI. (Group 6)

**Issai nishiki.** JDV I, 122/127; JDV II, 130, photo. This is not a published cultivar name but more a horticultural designation treated as a common name. "Issai" indicates that a plant develops its unique characteristic in one year (in this case, pinelike bark). "Nishiki" means rough in this context ("momiji" is the word for *A. palmatum).* Another common name for this cultivar, pine bark maple, is "Nishiki gawa." It is said to grow slowly but to develop a rough bark quickly. See **'Nishiki gawa'.** Zone VI. (Group 1a)

**'Ito shidare'.** Dickson (1887). Great Britain. All we know is that it must be a green-leaved cultivar, certainly cascading. No other information is available. Probably not in cultivation.

**'Iwato beni',** see ***A. palmatum*** ssp. ***palmatum***

**'Izu no odoriko'.** Kobayashi. Japan. No further description. Imported in 1991 from Japan to The Netherlands.

**'Jedo nishiki',** see **'Yezo nishiki'**

**'Jiro shidare'.** JDV II, 84. This is an outstanding, very different cultivar with long, pendulous, and cascading branches. The shrub may become 1.5–2 m high and will grow much wider. The leaves are 5-lobed, fresh green, turning to yellow in the autumn. The cascading habit, combined with 5-lobed leaves that are not dissected, is very unusual. The original plant was imported from Japan, supplied by Shibamichi Honten Co., Kawaguchi. Vertrees suggests that it is a seedling of *A. palmatum* subspecies *matsumurae.* This is not so; its position is in subspecies *palmatum.* Occasionally available in the trade. Zone VI. (Group 1a)

**'Kageori nishiki'.** Koidzumi (1911). Japan. JDV I, 109; JDV II, 117. This name has several misspellings. It is used for 'Shikageori nishiki', a cultivar of the Linearilobum group and also for 'Kagiri nishiki' (also misspelled 'Kagare nishiki'), belonging to the group with variegated palmate leaves.

**'Kagero'.** JDV I, 110, photo. One of the few yellow-variegated cultivars. Unfortunately, no trace of variegation can be seen in many cases, especially on young, well-grown shrubs. In any case it is a valuable plant, as its fresh green, 5- to 7-lobed leaves are quite attractive and the autumn colors beautiful. It grows into a dense shrub 4–5 m tall. Rather rare and only seldom seen in collections. (Group 1c)

**'Kagiri',** see **'Kagiri nishiki'**

**'Kagiri nishiki'.** Chikinsho (1710). Yokohama Nurseries (1896). Japan. JDV I, 110; JDV II, 117, photo. A well-known cultivar, almost always offered under the synonym 'Roseo-marginatum'. It is a strong-growing and upright shrub, to 8 m or occasionally more, rather densely branched. The leaves are small, but the leaf margins are white and pink variegated (not striped as in 'Higasayama'). It tends to revert to green and such shoots must be carefully removed. There are, unfortunately, several clones in the trade, all with the name 'Roseo-marginatum', as also is the case for 'Dissectum Atropurpureum' and 'Atropurpureum'. It is still possible to correct the name 'Roseo-marginatum' to 'Kagiri nishiki' as very little confusion has yet occurred, but when more of these plants are available, confusion is inevitable. Zone VI. (Group 1c)

**'Kakuremino'** ("invisible coat," "fairy's coat"), see **'Hagaromo'**

**'Kamagata'.** Vertrees (1970). Roseburg, Oregon, USA. JDV I, 97; JDV II, 103, photo. This is a very desirable, neat dwarf maple, selected and named by J. D. Vertrees, a distinguished "Acerologist." The leaves are very deeply divided, almost to the base, mostly 5-lobed, sometimes 3-lobed. The lobes are rather narrow and widely separated. The color is dark green with a purple overtone in spring, becoming light green in the summer and finally turning to brilliant shades of orange and yellow in the autumn (Plate 163). The growth is dense and branching. The Vertrees stock plant is now well over 1 m in height at about 25 years, having become denser with no sign of legginess. As this plant is of recent introduction, it is rare but will certainly become more popular when it is more readily available. Zone VI. (Group 6)

**'Karaori',** see **'Karaori nishiki'**

**'Karaori nishiki'.** Chikinsho (1733). Japan. JDV I,

110; JDV II, 118. A rather slow-growing shrub, to 4 m, of the same habit as 'Butterfly' but somewhat more vigorous. Its leaves are also like 'Butterfly', but in spring they are pinker. The autumn color is also different, lighter than 'Butterfly'. Single leaves of 'Butterfly' and 'Karaori nishiki' are hard to distinguish as they have the same type of variegation, but the latter cultivar has a somewhat more pink-brownish appearance than 'Butterfly'. A useful plant for the medium-sized garden. It seldom reverts, and while still uncommon in the trade is becoming more popular. Zone VI. (Group 1c)

**'Karasugawa'.** Angyo Maple Nursery (1930). Japan. JDV I, 111; JDV II, 119, photo. A rather narrowly growing shrub to 4–5 m (Plate 164). This is probably the most beautiful of all the variegated Japanese maples. It is, however, a difficult and fragile plant. It refuses to grow properly, must be grown out of full sun, and is not reliably hardy. It requires the best place in a well-sheltered garden. The variegation is abundantly pink and white on green. It belongs to a group near 'Versicolor', together with 'Oridono nishiki' and 'Asahi zuru'—both much hardier but less variegated. The wood is pink to red, almost like 'Sangokaku'. The leaves are 5-lobed, with irregular leaves due to the variegation. It is very difficult to propagate, as good, uninjured scions are seldom available. Very fine, very desirable, very difficult, and very seldom available. It can be grown in containers to make it easier to care for and so that in hot spells the plants can be moved to a cooler situation. Zones VI–VII. (Group 1c)

**'Karukaya'.** Koidzumi (1911). Japan. Belongs to the Linearilobum group, with leaf lobes almost linear to lanceolate and green. Very close to 'Shikageori nishiki'. Apparently not in cultivation. (Group 5a)

**'Kasagiyama'.** JDV I, 78; JDV II, 84, photo. A somewhat open-growing shrub or even small tree to 6–8 m. A very rare cultivar. The leaves are 7-lobed and of subspecies *matsumurae* shape. The color is an unusual brick red, greenish at the margins and veins. This peculiar color combination is also sometimes visible in 'Beni shigitatsu sawa'. Only very rarely available in the trade. Zone VI. (Group 3b)

**'Kasatoriyama',** see under ***A. sieboldianum*** cultivars

**'Kasen nishiki'.** *Japanese Maple List,* 1882. JDV I, 111; JDV II, 119, photo. Another slightly variegated cultivar, with leaves of the same shape as 'Oridono nishiki' or 'Asahi zuru'. An upright, shrubby tree, to 4–6 m tall. The variegation is not at all conspicuous and is often absent. Rarely available in the trade. Zone VI. (Group 1c)

**'Kashima'.** JDV I, 97; JDV II, 104, photo. A firm and tightly growing dwarf, well suited for bonsai as its habit is almost a bonsai. The tiny, 5-lobed leaves are much smaller than typical *A. palmatum* but of the same shape. It grows to 1.5–2 m tall and wide in many years. It has rather attractive colors in the autumn. A rare cultivar, much better known in the United States than in Europe. Also in the trade under the name 'Chiba'. (Group 6)

**'Kashima yatsubusa',** see **'Kashima'**

**'Katsura'.** JDV I, 98; JDV II, 110, photo. A splendid cultivar, both in spring with its almost orange young leaves, and in summer when the leaves are golden yellow. It is a shrubby and dense grower reaching about 6–7 m in height. It is usually much taller than wide. The leaves are small, 5-lobed, with a red hue in the orange-yellow range. This is one of our favorite plants. Vertrees writes that it is a dwarf, but its behavior in Europe is different, possibly due to a moister climate. It is well worth a place in the garden. Zone VI. (Group 1a)

**'Keiser'.** Buchholz Nursery (1990). Gaston, Oregon, USA. Dwarfish, upright-growing shrub with narrowly lobed leaves of the Linearilobum group, somewhat larger than those of 'Red Pygmy'. Not yet introduced to Europe. (Group 5b)

**'Kihachijo'.** Chikinsho (1733). Koidzumi (1911). Japan. JDV I, 51; JDV II, 57. This cultivar has remarkably firm and sturdy green leaves with 7–9 lobes about half the leaf length or slightly deeper, about 8 cm wide. This small tree will occasionally grow to 5–6 m tall, and about as wide. It has a very attractive golden yellow autumn color. The misspelling of the name as "Kihatsijo" can be traced to Koidzumi in his attempts to "latinize" certain Japanese words. 'Kihachijo' is an excellent garden plant and deserves to be planted on a larger scale than is now the case. A few good nurseries can supply it. (Group 3a)

**'Killarney'.** John Vermeulen, Inc. (1989). New Jersey, USA. A vigorous shrub. Leaves bright green in the spring, deepening in color in the summer. (Group 2a)

**'Kingsville Red'.** Kingsville Nurseries. Maryland, USA. JDV I, 51; JDV II, 57. Another purple-red-leaved *palmatum* of upright habit, about 8 m high, with 7-lobed leaves up to 10 cm long and wide. It is not present in Europe but seems to be a rather common red-leaved cultivar in USA. It is registered (Group 2b)

**'Kingsville Variegated'.** Kingsville Nurseries (H. Hohman) (circa 1955). Maryland, USA. JDV I, 112; JDV II, 119. Vertrees praises this cultivar rather highly as being a good, variegated sturdy plant. In Europe it displays hardly any trace of variegation and looks much like a common green *A. palmatum.* The few variegated leaves revert almost immediately to green. It possibly does better in a drier climate or a poor soil. It is no longer available, neither in the United States nor in Europe. (Group 1c)

**'Kinran'.** Chikinsho (1733). Japan. JDV I, 79; JDV II, 85, photo. A peculiar cultivar with interesting, deeply divided leaves of a mixed color between purple and green—in fact, quite attractive, but not universally appreciated. It is close to the old cultivar 'Hessei' with leaves about 8 cm across and lobes serrately toothed. The summer color is closer to green than purple, and in the autumn it turns a beautiful golden yellow. Its habit is about as high as wide, not exceeding 3–4 m. The name means "woven with golden strings". An interesting plant for specialists and collectors. It is available in the trade. (Group 3b)

**'Kinshi'.** Shibamichi Honten Co. (1984). Japan. This semidwarf shrub has been imported to The Netherlands. It is a neat and compact shrub, to 2 m. The leaves are green, deeply divided into 7 lobes, and with orange-yellow autumn colors. The name ("with golden threads") has only been found in the nursery catalogs of Japan. Rarely available in the trade. Zone VI. (Group 2a)

**'Kiri nishiki'.** Chikinsho (1710). Japan. JDV I, 68; JDV II, 74. A sturdy, green-leaved clone of the Dissectum group, not unlike 'Sekimori'. It can grow very vigorously and has a more or less weeping mushroom shape. The lobes are much less deeply dissected than in 'Dissectum' or its allies. It does not grow very high, about 1.5–2 m, but spreads to more than 3–4 m. According to Vertrees, it is more prostrate than other green-leaved Dissectum group cultivars. It is rare in the trade. (Group 4a)

**'Kiyohime'.** JDV I, 98; JDV II, 104, photo. This is a dense, well-branched shrub. Although a good dwarf plant, others are better. It reaches a height and width of 2 m. The leaves are small, dark green with a bluish undertone, distinctly 5-lobed, and with a red hue at the margins when young. It tends to die back a little on vigorous shoots but is nevertheless a useful plant, especially for bonsai. It is rather rare. Zone VI. (Group 1a)

**'Kocho nishiki'.** (*Japanese Maple List,* 1882), see **'Butterfly'**

**'Kocho no mai'.** (*Japanese Maple List,* 1882), see **'Butterfly'**

**'Kogane nishiki'.** JDV II, 57. This cultivar has 5- to 7-lobed, green leaves of the usual size for subspecies *palmatum.* It develops to a tall shrub useful for background purposes. The autumn color is orange. Its name means "golden brocade." Occasionally available in the trade. Zone VI. (Group 1a)

**'Kogane sakae'.** JDV II, 131. An unusual tree for the color of its bark, light green with yellow tones. This coloration is very different from other cultivars, except for 'Aoyagi' or 'Sangokaku'. Leaves are 4–10 cm across, 7-lobed, and green. Autumn colors range from orange to yellow. Its name means "golden prosperity." Only rarely available. (Group 2a)

**'Komon nishiki'.** Koidzumi (1911). Japan. *Japanese Maple List,* 1882; JDV I, 112; JDV II, 120, photo. A medium-sized shrub, probably to 2–2.5 m. The leaves are 5-lobed and of the same shape as the species. They have irregular yellow and yellow-green variegations, sometimes with spotting in the spring. Unfortunately, it also tends to revert, as do so many cultivars of this group. Rare in the trade. Also called 'Aureo-variegatum'. (Group 1c)

**'Komurasaki'.** *Japanese Maple List,* 1882. JDV I, 79; JDV II, 85. A purple-leaved cultivar of upright habit, holding its color fairly well. In August, however, it becomes dark green with a purple undertone. The leaves are rather deeply divided and of average size. Lobes deeply incised. It reaches about 2.5 m in height. Rarely available. (Group 3b)

**'Koreanum'.** JDV I, 51; JDV II, 57, photo. A very good green-leaved cultivar, with outstanding autumn colors, from golden yellow to crimson. It is a vigorously growing shrub, to 6–8 m, not unlike 'Osakazuki'. The leaves are fairly large, 6–7 cm long and about as wide. There is a problem with the nomenclature of this plant. It was originally described as variety *coreanum* Nakai (1914), as a naturally occurring variant of *A. palmatum* growing in Korea, on Cheju and Wanda islands. This variety is now a synonym of subspecies *amoenum.* Whether the cultivar now called 'Koreanum' was originally found in Korea cannot be traced. Vertrees states that this variety must not be treated as a cultivar, as it is indigenous to Korea. So far there is only one clone in the trade, bearing the name 'Koreanum'. Aside from the question of whether this plant belongs to the former *A. palmatum* var. *coreanum* (spelled with "c"), or not, it does seem that the cultivar name 'Koreanum' (spelled with "K") can be maintained for this clone. (Group 1a)

**'Koriba'.** Kobayashi. Japan. No description. Imported in 1992 to The Netherlands from Japan.

**'Koshibori nishiki'.** Wada (1938). Japan. JDV I, 112; JDV II, 120, photo. A finely twigged, small shrub, to 2–2.5 m. The leaves are small and 5-lobed, light green with minute yellow dots and red leaf margins when young. The variegation is not conspicuous and on rich soils the growth is so heavy that there are hardly any traces of the variegation. In fact, it is not a cultivar of first choice, but pot-grown it is acceptable for smaller gardens. Rare. Zone VI. (Group 1c)

**'Koshimino'.** Mulligan (1958). Washington, USA. JDV I, 123; JDV II, 131, photo. Very closely related to or identical with 'Hagaromo'. Vertrees has grown them side by side and concludes that they are indeed identical. He treated them separately, but merged them. (Group 7)

**'Kotohime'.** JDV I, 99; JDV II, 105, photo. Another dwarf. This sturdy, upright, small plant, to 1.5 m, has stiff branches on which the buds are closely set together. The small leaves are 5-lobed, but the outer lobes are often underdeveloped so that the leaves appear to be only 3-lobed. It shows a good autumn color, yellow to golden. Summer leaves are rather dark green with a yellowish new growth. It is certainly one of the most desirable dwarfs but only occasionally available. Propagating material is quite scarce, as the mother plants grow so slowly. Zone VI. (Group 6)

**'Kotoito komachi'.** Vertrees. Roseburg, Oregon, USA. JDV I, 123; JDV II, 131, photo. This was a chance seedling, discovered by the famous *Acer* grower J. D. Vertrees. It is a tiny plant, very thin-wooded; its leaves are threadlike, nicely red when unfolding, afterward an attractive green. It grows, of course, very slowly, and is extremely difficult to propagate. But it is a real gem in a sheltered place in a good rock garden. It will always be difficult to buy a plant. The name means "old harp string—beautiful little girl." It is not available in Europe. Zone VII. (Group 6)

**'Koto no ito'.** Wada (1938). Japan. JDV I, 90; JDV II, 96, photo. 'Koto no ito' is placed between the Palmatum and Linearilobum groups. It has the habit of most cultivars with linear leaves, that is, about 2.5 m high and rather upright. Its leaves are 7-lobed, fresh green, and with lobes narrower than those of the typical *A. palmatum*, but somewhat broader than the average Linearilobum. It is a nice plant, with good autumn colors. Occasionally seen in collections and nurseries. (Group 5a)

**'Kurabeyama'.** Koidzumi (1911). Japan. *Japanese Maple List*, 1882; JDV I, 79; JDV II, 85, photo. A little-known cultivar of medium size, about as high as wide: 2–3 m. Its leaves are rusty brown in spring, fresh dark green afterward, and deeply divided. It has beautiful autumn colors of yellow, speckled with crimson. Zone VI. (Group 3a)

**'Kurui jishi'.** *Japanese Maple List*, 1882. JDV I, 124; JDV II, 132, photo. This is a very nice dwarf plant, very slow growing and narrow, not exceeding 2 m in height (Plate 165). The leaves are very much like those of 'Okushimo' but slightly smaller in size and more revolute (rolled inward). The nodes are very close together and produce a very compact habit. Due to its slow growth it is rare, and it is difficult to propagate. Young plants sometimes produce shoots of 10–15 cm that can be used as scions. Zone VI. (Group 6)

**'Kushimiyano'.** Tingle (1967). USA. Lacks description.

**'Laceleaf'**, see **'Filigree'** (All members of the Dissectum group are called 'Laceleaf' in the United States.)

**'Laciniatum'.** Siesmayer (1888). Germany. See **'Tsuri nishiki'.**

**'Laciniatum Purpureum'.** Dutch nurseries. See **'Hessei'.**

**'Latifolium Atropurpureum'.** Nicholson (1881). Great Britain. See **'Sanguineum'.**

**'Latilobatum'.** Koidzumi (1911). Japan. Reported to have broadly deltoid leaf lobes, thus falling between true *A. palmatum* and the Linearilobum group. Apparently not in cultivation. Possibly it is a synonym for 'Koto no ito'. (Group 1a)

**'Lineare'.** Schwerin (1893). Germany. See **'Linearilobum'.**

**'Linearifolium'.** Mulligan. USA. See **'Linearilobum'.**

**'Linearilobum'.** Miquel (1867). France. JDV I, 90; JDV II, 96, photo. A clone cultivated in The Netherlands, widely planted, and available from several nurseries. This plant is almost certainly identical with 'Shinobuga oka'. It has bright green leaves, usually 7-lobed with very narrow lobes, often not much more than a broadened midvein. The very vigorously growing shoots occasionally have leaves with broader lobes. The autumn color is yellow. This cultivar can grow to 4–5 m tall and about 2–3 m wide. A good plant for the garden, as it does not dominate with its graceful leaves. Seedlings of this cultivar never produce linear leaves; all are palmate. The names 'Scolopendrifolium' and 'Shime no uchi' are also frequently used for this clone. See also 'Shinobuga oka'. (Group 5a)

**'Linearilobum Atropurpureum'.** Nicholson (1881). Great Britain. See **'Atrolineare'.**

**'Linearilobum Purpureum'.** Van Gelderen (1969). See **'Atrolineare'.**

**'Linearilobum Rubrum'.** Harrison (1960). Great Britain. See **'Atrolineare'.**

**'Little Princess'.** Russell (1990). Great Britain. Small, densely branched shrub; leaves 5- to 7-

lobed, light green, 3–4 cm wide. Little is known about the origin of this dwarfish cultivar. Possibly its original name is 'Mapi no machihime', but there is no documentation for this name, and it does not appear in Professor Yokoi's lists of maple names. Imported to The Netherlands from Great Britain in 1991. (Group 6)

**'Lobatum'.** Nicholson (1881). Great Britain. Old selection with wide leaf lobes. Perhaps no longer in cultivation.

**'Lozita'.** Vermeulen (1984). New Jersey, USA. A sturdy shrub up to 4–5 m in height. The 7-lobed leaves, 5–8 cm across, are a rich brown in summer, turning to scarlet in autumn. This cultivar's value is not yet known. (Group 2b)

**'Lutescens'.** Hillier & Sons (1928). Ampfield, Great Britain. JDV I, 52; JDV II, 58. Vigorous, treelike shrub, to 7–8 m. The leaves are of the same shape as such cultivars as 'Heptalobum' or 'Samidare', lustrous bright green in summer but yellowish in the spring. Its real glory is in the autumn, when its leaves turn to a rich golden yellow. It is only rarely seen. (Group 2a)

**'Luteum'**, see **'Lutescens'**

**'Machiyou'**, see **'Matsuyoi'**

**'Maiko'.** JDV I, 124; JDV II, 132, photo. The leaves of this attractive cultivar are bright green in summer and a beautiful yellow in the autumn. The petioles are reddish. The shape of the leaves is quite irregular, often deeply cleft, as are the lobes themselves. It is not quite a dwarf but remains a medium-sized, compact plant, growing to 2–2.5 m in height. The name is also spelled 'Maoka', 'Miaoka', etc., but all are identical with 'Maiko'; it means "dancing doll." The plant called 'Beni maiko' is not quite the red counterpart of 'Maiko'. The leaves are also shaped differently. 'Maiko' is still a rare plant but deserves more attention. (Group 1a)

**'Maimori'.** Japan. Origin not known. A dwarfish shrub up to 2 m in height and width, rather densely branched. The purplish green leaves, with some lighter green variegations, have 5–7 narrow lobes. This cultivar was recently added to the Esveld Aceretum, the Netherlands, and is not yet available. Zone VI. (Group 1a)

**'Mama'.** Chikinsho (1733). Japan. JDV I, 125; JDV II, 133, photo. No two leaves of this peculiar plant are alike. They are all 5-lobed, but beyond that they are all very different. The color is green, with yellowish young tips. It grows into a medium-sized, rather twiggy bush, 3–4 m tall. The name 'Mama', according to Vertrees, means "doing as one pleases" or "any which way," an apt description of the behavior of the leaves. It is a rare plant but is occasionally found in cultivation. Zone VI. (Group 1a)

**'Mapi no machihime'**, see **'Little Princess'**

**'Maragumo'**, see **'Marakumo'**

**'Marakum'**, see **'Marakumo'**

**'Marakumo'.** Bergman (1962). Pennsylvania, USA. JDV I, 113; JDV II, 120, photo. The leaves of this cultivar display a bright pinkish or orange coloration, shading from the margins to the center, not unlike 'Reticulatum' or 'Beni shigitatsu sawa' but in different tones. The leaf blades are covered with minute dots, so closely packed together that they seem to form a maculation. It is rather slow-growing and will not exceed a height of 3 m. Also spelled 'Marakum'. It is not in cultivation in Europe and is quite rare in the United States. (Group 1c)

**'Marginatum'.** Hereman (1868). Great Britain. See **'Reticulatum'.**

**'Marusame'**, see **'Harusame'**

**'Masukaga'**, see **'Masukagami'**

**'Masukagami'.** Chikinsho (1733). Japan. JDV I, 113; JDV II, 121, photo. A rare, slightly variegated cultivar, often bearing twigs that have reverted. The young leaves unfold crimson, soon turning to a reddish green with a subtle variegation of white or yellow (Plate 166). It will grow to 4 m. The leaves are 7-lobed and rather deeply divided. It needs some shade and also a soil that is not too rich. A very rare plant, it is seldom available in nurseries. Zone VI. (Group 2c)

**'Masumurasaki'.** Chikinsho (1719). Japan. JDV I, 80; JDV II, 86. A shrub of 6–7 m. This is another good red-leaved cultivar. The purplish leaves have no green undertone and keep their color well in the summer. Autumn color is not striking. Petioles are red. A good plant, but there are many similar cultivars. It is occasionally available in the trade. (Group 2b)

**'Matsugae'.** Schwerin (1893). Germany. JDV I, 113; JDV II, 121, photo. This cultivar is intermediate between 'Kagiri nishiki' and 'Butterfly'. The leaves are attractively variegated with dark pink and white, and rather irregularly 5-lobed. The plant does not grow strongly, only attaining a height of 3–4 m, and it is rather upright, always narrower than tall. Sometimes there is a tendency to revert; such shoots must be removed. Sometimes it is offered as 'Roseo-marginatum', but this name should be avoided for all cultivars of this type. Only rarely available. Zone VI. (Group 1c)

**'Matsukaze'.** Chikinsho (1710). Japan. JDV I, 80; JDV II, 86, photo. This cultivar is sometimes called 'Dissectum Matsukaze', a name that gives the impression of dealing with a member of the Dissectum group. This is not the case. The leaves are deeply divided to the bases, and the lobes are serrate but not so deeply incised as in typical Dissectum cultivars. It also has a different habit; it is not mushroom-shaped but grows into a large, spreading shrub, usually wider than high, to 4–5 m or more. Its main branches are somewhat pendulous. The color is bronze-red in spring, turning a rather unattractive green in summer (Plate 167). But its autumn color is spectacular, one of the most glorious crimson cultivars yet known. It is not suitable for a small garden. Van Gelderen (1969) mentioned in *Dendroflora* that this name was synonymous with true 'Dissectum'. This is incorrect. It is still rare in the trade and only occasionally seen in collections. (Group 3c)

**'Matsumurae'**, see ***A. palmatum*** ssp. ***matsumurae***

**'Matsuyoi'.** JDV II, 58. A large shrub with unusual foliage. The leaves are at first pale yellowish and turn to green when mature. Some leaves hang down, others are bent, or the lobes are twisted. It is rather broad, to 5 m wide. Rarely available in the trade. Zone VI. (Group 1a)

**'Mejishi'**, see **'Shishigashira'**

**'Mikasa'**, see **'Mikawa yatsubusa'**

**'Mikawa yatsubusa'.** JDV I, 99; JDV II, 105, photo. A real gem among the most dwarf maples (Plate 168). It is a very beautiful small plant, rather densely branched. The leaves are green with red coloration on the young growing tips. The leaves are delicately 5-lobed, with long apices. The new shoots are very densely set together, and the internodes are very short. This characteristic makes it hard to graft, so it is very rarely available. Zone VI. (Group 6)

**'Minus'.** Nicholson (1881). Great Britain. See **'Shishigashira'.**

**'Mioun'.** Tingle (1962). Maryland, USA. The leaves of this cultivar are red-purple and lacy. It has not been introduced into the trade. According to Vertrees it is not worth growing, as many seedlings are better. The name 'Dissectum Mioun' is illegitimate because, since 1959, Latin cannot be part of a cultivar name. (Group 4b)

**'Mirte'.** Esveld (1986). Boskoop, The Netherlands. Strong-growing shrub, to 6–8 m tall and about the same width. Leaves deeply incised, almost to the bases, margins serrate, softly pubescent when young, dark olive-green in spring, turning to very dark green in summer—a very conspicuous color, unusual in this group. Autumn color purplish olive-green. This cultivar was found in a batch of seedlings from seed of garden origin. Named after Mirte Yasemin van Gelderen, granddaughter of the author. (Group 3a)

**'Miyagino'.** *Japanese Maple List,* 1882; JDV I, 80; JDV II, 86. A green-leaved, rather vigorously growing shrub of about 4–5 m. The autumn color is excellent, a brilliant crimson. The leaves are of the Linearilobum group, but the lobes are somewhat wider than most cultivars in this group. It is not in cultivation in Europe and is available in the United States only on a very restricted scale. (Group 5a)

**'Mizu kuguri'.** Chikinsho (1773). Japan. JDV I, 100; JDV II, 110. Another beautiful small cultivar with 7-lobed leaves, green with pinkish hues in spring, darker green in summer. It reaches a height of 2–2.5 m after many years. A little-grown cultivar. (Group 6)

**'Momenshide'.** JDV I, 125; JDV II, 133, photo. This is very close to 'Hagaromo', one of the cultivars belonging to the Sessilifolium group. The lobes, however, are less deeply incised, and it does not grow as large as 'Hagaromo'. It may be a bud sport of 'Hagaromo'. It grows into a small tree of about 6 m. Not in cultivation in Europe. (Group 7)

**'Momiji'** (Japanese name for *A. palmatum.*)

**'Mon nishiki'.** Koidzumi (1911). Japan. A cultivar impossible to identify. Probably no longer in cultivation.

**'Mono'.** Bergman (1962). Pennsylvania, USA. The identification by Mr. Bergman is incorrect as the plant was *A. mono.*

**'Monzukushi'.** Chikinsho (1719). Japan. JDV I, 52; JDV II, 58. A good, green-leaved cultivar that turns a brilliant orange in autumn. A rather vigorous plant, attaining a height of about 5 m. Not very distinctive, but pleasant. (Group 1a)

**'Moonfire'.** Wolff (circa 1970). Pennsylvania, USA. JDV I, 52; JDV II, 58, photo. This fairly new cultivar is a significant rival to the well-known 'Bloodgood'. It has the same kind of leaves and coloration but displays a different hue of purple in summer, not unlike the beautiful 'Nuresagi'. In the autumn, it remains as dark purple as 'Bloodgood'. This cultivar has not been grown long enough to say which is better. It seems that 'Moonfire' has the same disadvantage as 'Bloodgood', that is, a tendency to become leggy. Heavy pruning encourages good branching. It also seems to grow less vigorously than 'Bloodgood' and will hardly become higher than 7 m. (Group 2b)

**'Mosen'**, see **'Chishio'**

**'Multifidum'.** Koch (1869). Germany. See **'Dissectum'.**

**'Muragumo'.** Mulligan (1958). Washington, USA. JDV I, 52; JDV II, 58. A good purple-leaved, upright shrub to 6 m. Unfolding leaves are almost crimson, but this color does not hold for long. In the autumn the intense red color returns. It is a good cultivar but little known. Not available in Europe. (Group 2b)

**'Murakumo'**, see **'Muragumo'**

**'Murasaki hime'.** JDV I, 100; JDV II, 106. A dwarf cultivar with purple leaves that are 5-lobed and divided to the center. The purple color changes to greenish in the summer, especially on leaves near the center of the plant. It is a somewhat fragile plant and very rarely seen. It is difficult to propagate. Mature plants do not exceed 1–1.25 m. Zone VI. (Group 6)

**'Murasaki kiyohime'.** JDV I, 100; JDV II, 106, photo. This is a better plant than the preceding. Its leaves are of the same shape but are yellow-green instead of purple. The lobes and margins are attractively colored when young. It is slow-growing but seems to be easier to maintain than 'Murasaki hime'. It branches densely and is suitable for bonsai culture, being about the same size as the latter. Its autumn color is golden yellow. Unfortunately, this fine cultivar is still very rare in the trade. Zone VI. (Group 6)

**'Murasaki take'.** Koidzumi (1911). Japan. Reported to have purple leaves, with incised lobes. Probably not in cultivation.

**'Mure hibari'.** Koidzumi (1911). Japan. *Japanese Maple List,* 1882; JDV I, 81; JDV II, 87, photo. The leaves of this cultivar are very deeply divided, almost like those of the Dissectum group, but the lobes are not as deeply incised. It grows to 4–5 m, with an upright habit. The leaves are of a good green, purplish when young. The autumn color is dark golden to crimson. The name means "a flock of skylarks." It is not widely known and only recently introduced into Europe. (Group 3a)

**'Murogawa'.** JDV I, 53; JDV II, 59. A strongly growing shrub with large, 7-lobed leaves that are purplish green in summer, later turning to a brilliant orange-red. Their veins are green, giving a multicolored effect. The branches of old plants cascade almost to the ground. This is a good plant for landscaping where no strong colors are required. Occasionally available in the trade. (Group 3a)

**'Musashino'**, see **'Nomura'**

**'Nana segawa'.** Chikinsho (1733). Japan. JDV I, 81; JDV II, 87, photo. This plant does not fit well into the group system used here. It lies between the Dissectum and Matsumurae groups, though it seems closer to the latter. Following Vertrees, it is a fairly large tree 3–4 m high, and also as wide, with purplish 7-lobed leaves that are deeply divided but without the incised lobes of the typical Dissectum group plant. The summer leaf is dark green, which turns to crimson in the autumn. It is named for a river. (Group 7)

**'Naruo nishiki'.** Wada (1938). Japan. JDV I, 114; JDV II, 121. This is an upright cultivar, to about 3 m. It must have variegated 5-lobed leaves, but according to Vertrees, it shows little or no variegation. Not in cultivation in Europe. (Group 1c)

**'Nicholsonii'.** Schwerin (1893). Germany. JDV I, 81; JDV II, 87, photo. One of the favorites of maple lovers. This cultivar grows into a medium-sized shrubby tree, to 5 m tall and as wide. It is rather heavily branched. The 7-lobed leaves unfold olive-green to olive-brown and are extremely attractive: in summer they turn green or olive-green and in autumn they are the most brilliant colors—golden yellow to brilliant crimson (Plate 169). Excellent, and readily available. (Group 3a)

**'Nigrum'.** Hillier & Sons (1928). Ampfield, Great Britain. JDV I, 53; JDV I,I 59. This cultivar forms a rather narrow shrub of about 3–4 m, not nearly so large as 'Atropurpureum' or 'Bloodgood'. The 5- to 7-lobed leaves are dark purple, of the same tone as 'Nuresagi' (Plate 170). There is not much autumn color. It is a useful plant for those gardens where 'Bloodgood' and its allies are too large. It is not widely available. Not to be confused with 'Dissectum Nigrum'. (Group 1b)

**'Nigrum Dissectum'**, see **'Dissectum Nigrum'**

**'Nimura'.** Dickson (1887). Great Britain. See **'Musashino'.**

**'Nishiki gasane'.** Yokohama Nurseries (1896). Japan. *Japanese Maple List,* 1882; JDV I, 114; JDV II, 121, photo. One of the very few golden-variegated Palmatum group cultivars, which is probably the only reason it is still in cultivation (Plate 171). It is in fact a hopeless plant. Young plants may grow vigorously but show no variegation. When variegation is present, it tends to burn badly in the sun, making ugly brown spots on the leaves. Cultivated in the shade it does not develop golden spots. It grows into a small shrub about 1.5 m high and wide. The leaves are 5-lobed and about 6 cm across. 'Sagare nishiki' is very similar, perhaps even identical. (Group 1c)

**'Nishiki gawa'.** JDV I, 125/127; JDV II, 135, photo. Vertrees calls this plant *A. palmatum* "Pine Bark Maple" which is not a valid cultivar name. As there is the epithet 'Nishiki gawa', it should be used. The bark of this cultivar is its distinctive feature. Even young plants develop a corky bark, with coarse, longitudinal creases. A shrubby tree to 6–8 m, its leaves and habit are like those of the species. It has a nice autumn color, but not spectacular. It can be used as a bonsai plant, with heavy pruning and trimming. Young plants can grow very vigorously but this new wood does not always ripen. 'Nishiki gawa' is the pine bark maple, or the Issai nishiki momiji maple, neither of which is a cultivar name. It is often referred to in the Japanese literature. Rarely found in the trade. (Group 1a)

**'Nishiki momiji'.** JDV I, 53; JDV II, 59. A small-leaved cultivar with normal green leaves and good autumn color, from orange to red. Not available in the trade. (Group 1a)

**'Nishiki sho'.** Kobayashi (before 1985). Japan. Nursery catalog. Another rough-bark form like 'Arakawa' and 'Nishiki gawa', but the roughness is of a different texture. (Group 1a)

**'Nokibata'.** Koidzumi (1911). Japan. Leaves pink; no further description. Probably no longer in cultivation.

**'Nomura'.** Yokohama Nurseries (1896). Japan. JDV I, 53; JDV II, 59, photo. A rather fast-growing cultivar, to 7 m tall and about 4–5 m wide. The bold leaves are dark purple in spring, with minute white pubescence. The pubescence quickly disappears and the leaf changes to a dull purple-green. The leaves are large, 7-lobed, 7–10 cm across, and of the Amoenum group. Its autumn color can be brilliant, crimson to glistening red. It is an old cultivar, also known under the name 'Noumura', and has been in cultivation in Japan for over 300 years. It is fairly widely available in both the United States and Europe and is often present in older collections. (Group 2b)

**'Nomura kaede'.** Yokohama Nurseries (1896). Japan. See **'Nomura'.**

**'Nomura nishiki'.** Yokohama Nurseries (1896). Japan. Said to have yellow-blotched leaves. Apparently no longer in cultivation.

**'Nomura shidare',** see **'Shojo shidare'**

**'Noshi',** see **'Komurasaki'**

**'Noumura',** see **'Nomura'**

**'Nou nishiki'.** Tingle (1967). USA. See **'Wou nishiki'.**

**'Novum'.** Mulligan (1958). USA. See **'Atropurpureum Novum'.**

**'Nuresagi'.** *Japanese Maple List,* 1882; JDV I, 54; JDV II, 60, photo. An excellent garden plant. It grows into a medium-sized shrub about 5 m tall and half that wide. The leaves are 5-lobed with 2 very small additional lobes, attractively dark purple, keeping their color well. The lobes terminate in tapered apices. There is a white pubescence when young, which soon disappears. The autumn color can be a glowing red. It is still rare but deserves to be much more widely known. Especially good for smaller gardens. The name means "the wet heron." (Group 1b)

**'Nusatoriyama'.** Hinkul (1956). Reported to have 7- to 9-lobed leaves, green with heavy variegations of cream and also occasionally entirely cream-colored. Possibly identical to *A. buergerianum.* 'Nusatoriyam'. No material is available for further study.

**'Obtusum'.** Koidzumi (1911). Japan. An obscure cultivar with obtuse-angled samara wings. Probably not in cultivation.

**'Octopus'.** Greer Gardens (1987). Eugene, Oregon, USA. A rather large, mushroom-shaped shrub, to 2.5 m, with cascading branches. The leaves are deeply dissected and are fiery red in spring and summer, later becoming greenish red. A new cultivar, not yet widely available. (Group 4b)

**'Ogashika',** see **'Saoshika'**

**'Ogi nagare',** see **'Ogi nagashi'**

**'Ogi nagashi'.** Bergman (1967). Maryland, USA. JDV I, 114; JDV II, 122, photo. A slightly variegated form, very close to the typical species, and as a young plant hardly distinguishable. Its autumn color is a deep golden yellow. It is not sufficiently distinctive to maintain in cultivation. (Group 1a)

**'Ogon sarasa'.** Mulligan (1958). Washington, USA. JDV I, 82; JDV II, 88. One of the cultivars with brick-red to purple-red leaves when unfolding in the spring. In the summer the leaves turn a bronze-green with a purple undertone. They are 7-lobed and deeply divided. It grows into a medium-sized shrub, to 5 m tall and 2–3 m wide. Its autumn color is beautiful but not spectacular. A good shrub for the medium-sized garden. The name means "gold calico cloth." (Group 3b)

**'Ogureyama',** see under *A. shirasawanum*

**'Ohsakazuki'.** Koidzumi (1911). Japan. See **'Osakazuki'.**

**'O jishi'.** JDV I, 126; JDV II, 134, photo. The leaves of this dwarf are very similar to those of the well-known 'Shishigashira' and can be described as resembling the small leaves of *Ribes alpinum.* A description of this leaf type may be found under 'Shishigashira'. It grows much slower than that cultivar, not more than 4–5 cm a year, to 2 m. It also has the same stiff, upright, densely branched habit. It is a very desirable plant, but unfortunately it is quite rare as it is difficult to propagate. (Group 6)

**'O kagami'.** Angyo Maple Nursery (1930). Japan. JDV I, 54; JDV II, 60, photo. Another excellent purple-leaved cultivar, its leaves deeply divided, the lobes only slightly serrated. The color holds well into summer and in autumn tends to change to crimson or scarlet. It grows into a small tree of about 4–5 m in height. It is still very rare, especially in Europe, but is becoming more popular. (Group 2b)

**'Okikoji nishiki'**, see **'Okukuji nishiki'**

**'Okukuji nishiki'.** JDV II, 122, photo. A small tree, very densely branched. Leaves variable in shape and well variegated, white and cream. It is not unlike 'Butterfly', though its color impression is slightly different. Now available in Europe. (Group 1c)

**'Okushimo'.** Chikinsho (1719). Japan. JDV I, 126; JDV II, 134, photo. Very beautiful dwarf form, rather well known in horticulture and also in the maple literature. Its nomenclature is very confused. It has been propagated and sold under various names such as 'Crispa', 'Crispum', 'Chishio', and 'Cristatum'. All these names must be rejected in favor of its oldest and only legitimate name—'Okushimo'. It grows into a small tree of about 4 m height and does not become wider than 1–1.5 m, that is, stiffly vase-shaped (Plate 172). Its leaves are very peculiar, radiating outward with every lobe ending in a tapering point. There are 7 lobes, divided to two-thirds of the size of the leaves. The color is dark green with a minute whitish pubescence when young. In the autumn it changes to a golden yellow to orange. It is not widely offered in the nursery trade, because it is not easy to grow. The name has been translated as "the pepper and salt leaf." (Group 1a or Group 6)

**'Omato'.** Angyo Maple Nursery (1930). Japan. JDV I, 55; JDV II, 61. Large-leaved cultivar, growing into a large, shrubby tree to 6–8 m tall and almost as wide. The leaves are 7-lobed, about 8–10 cm across, and orange-red when young but quickly turning a good green. It has the same splendid autumn colors as its close relatives 'Koreanum' and 'Heptalobum', but it is not as brilliant as 'Osakazuki', another ally. (Group 2a)

**'Omurayama'.** Wada (1938). Japan. JDV I, 82; JDV II, 88, photo. This splendid cultivar was one of the highlights of the Vertrees collection, but unfortunately the specimen has been lost. There is a good picture in the second edition of *Japanese Maples*. It was a cascading tree, to 7–8 m in height, not fully pendulous. The leaves have 7 slender lobes, closely held together, fresh green in summer; unfolding leaves have an orange hue. In autumn the leaves turn to a most brilliant combination of crimson and gold. Young plants do not show their pendulous character, but the habit is unique at maturity. It is not easy to propagate but is certainly worthwhile. Zone VI. (Group 3a)

**'Orange Dream'.** Gilardelli (before 1990). Italy. Slender, upright-growing shrub, well-branched, up to 8 m high. Bark fresh green, leaves 5-lobed, or sometimes 7-lobed, somewhat crinkled in juvenile state. Bright orange-yellow in spring, not unlike 'Katsura', turning to yellowish green in the autumn, later yellow. (Group 1a)

**'Orangeola'.** Greer Gardens (1988). Eugene, Oregon, USA. A fairly large shrub of weeping habit, not exceeding 2 m in height. The leaves are finely dissected, orange when young, turning to greenish yellow when mature, and persisting often until December. It is new to the trade and not yet widely available. (Group 4a)

**'Oregon Sunset'.** Portland Camellia Nursery (circa 1980). Oregon, USA. The outstanding feature of this newly introduced cultivar is its short, shrubby habit, to 4–5 m. The leaves are shining red, deeply divided into narrow lobes with serrate margins and that curve slightly downward like a relaxed hand. Its autumn color is outstanding, at least as good as 'Atropurpureum'. (Group 1b)

**'Orido nishiki'**, see **'Oridono nishiki'**

**'Oridono nishiki'.** Yokohama Nurseries (1896); Koidzumi (1911). *Japanese Maple List*, 1882; JDV I, 115; JDV II, 123, photo. One of the best of the variegated upright cultivars. It shows pink variegation in abundance, even on strongly growing young plants (Plate 173). The leaves are typical of *A. palmatum*. Very frequently, entire leaves are pink or white, and almost every leaf shows some variegation. It is much healthier and sturdier than 'Karasugawa' and also much better than 'Asahi zuru'. Some misspellings, such as 'Oridomo nishiki', are found in the literature. Confusion arose out of the very short description given by Koidzumi, in which he mentioned it as being "dotted gold." It grows as a shrub to 5–6 m. It belongs to the 'Versicolor' cultivars and does not revert as much as most. Since the old 'Versicolor' has almost disappeared in horticulture, 'Oridono nishiki' takes its place and has the added virtue of being better. Zone VI. (Group 1c)

**'Ornatum'.** Carrière (1867). France. JDV I, 69; JDV II, 75, photo. Very well-known, old cultivar, still quite common in the trade under the incorrect name 'Dissectum Atropurpureum'. As pointed out in the description of 'Beni shidare', 'Dissectum Atropurpureum' includes several cultivars and must be rejected in favor of 'Ornatum'. In German-speaking countries, and also in The

Netherlands, the old name 'Ornatum' is more widely used than in English-speaking countries. 'Ornatum' is one of the best of the Dissectum group available in horticulture. It has the typical mushroom shape and can grow into a mighty plant 4–5 m high and much wider (Plate 174). It can grow for many years—plants of more than 100 years of age are not uncommon. The leaves have the typical Dissectum group shape; they unfold dark purple, soon becoming rich brown-red. During the summer they slowly turn dark green with a reddish undertone. In October the brilliant golden yellow autumn colors appear, distinguishing it from its modern red-leaved allies, which all lack this feature. (Group 4b)

**'Ornatum Purpureum'**, see **'Ornatum'**

**'Ornatum Variegatum'**, see **'Dissectum Variegatum'**

**'Osakazuki'.** *Japanese Maple List,* 1882. JDV I, 55; JDV II, 61, photo. An old and very well-known cultivar and probably the best of all the *A. palmatum* cultivars for autumn color. The leaves turn a brilliant crimson red and display wonderfully for 2 weeks or more. The 7-lobed leaves are about 10 cm across, bright green in summer, olive-orange when first unfolding. Young plants maintain this coloration for many weeks when they are in full growth. It grows into a treelike shrub of 7–8 m, rather upright, but becoming wider with age. It is often found in parks and gardens and is readily available in nurseries or garden centers. (Group 2a)

**'Oshio beni'.** Yokohama Nurseries (1898). Japan. JDV I, 56; JDV II, 62. Several nurseries imported plants under this name from Japan. Unfortunately, the plants supplied by the Japanese nurseries were not always one and the same. Of course, they all had purple-brown leaves, but there were small differences. According to Vertrees the introduction under this name could easily be the same as the Dutch 'Atropurpureum' or another very similar cultivar. The name 'Oshio beni' is used fairly widely in the United States, but in Europe plants under this name have disappeared from the trade. Until this nomenclatural and taxonomic confusion is resolved, we offer the following description: A sturdy, upright, treelike shrub, to 6–8 m. The leaves are 5- to 7-lobed, dark purple in spring, becoming dull purple in summer. The autumn color is scarlet. See also 'Oshu beni'. (Group 2b)

**'Oshu beni'.** *Japanese Maple List,* 1882; JDV I, 56; JDV II, 62. According to Vertrees this is a round-topped, treelike shrub to 4 m. The leaves are 7-lobed, deeply divided, and with lanceolate lobes. Early foliage is bright red, soon becoming maroon-red and turning to a bronze-green in summer. The autumn color is deep red. Clearly this description is very different from the preceding cultivar. It is not in cultivation in Europe under this name, but possibly it is the true 'Oshio beni'. (Group 3b)

**'Oshu shidare'.** Chikinsho (1710); Yokohama Nurseries (1896). Japan. JDV I, 82; JDV II, 88, photo. A cascading, shrubby tree to 4–5 m in height, of the same shape as 'Omurayama'. It is a beautiful plant but not yet widely known. The leaves are dark purple in spring, in summer a deep bronze-purple with greenish undertones and later turning to scarlet. The leaves are very deeply divided, almost to the bases. The lobes are finely serrated. Leaves are 7–8 cm across. A good plant, but very rare. (Group 3b)

**'Otohime'.** JDV II, 106. A vigorous but compact shrub. The leaves, with exceptionally long petioles, are fresh green, turning to yellow in the autumn. Suitable for bonsai; in its general appearance like 'Kiyohime'. Not yet available in Europe. (Group 6)

**'Otome zakura'.** JDV II, 106, photo. A semidwarf tree with beautiful spring foliage. The leaves are of two types, large and small on the same plant. The color is flame red in spring, turning to pink later; in summer there is a green undertone. It is an interesting and attractive cultivar, and slowly available commercially. (Group 1b)

**'Palmatifidium'** (Misspelling of 'Palmatifidum'.)

**'Palmatifidum'.** Miquel (1870). France. See **'Dissectum Palmatifidum'.**

**'Paucum'.** Hendriks (1940). The Netherlands. See **'Dissectum Paucum'.**

**'Peaches and Cream'.** Teese (1980). Monbulk, Australia. JDV II, 122. One of the newer selections with variegated leaves. It forms a wide shrub, to 3 m. Leaves are rather densely arranged along the twigs and the variegation is of the same pattern as 'Shigitatsu sawa', with pink and salmon tones. Found as a seedling of 'Reticulatum' that had possibly been pollinated by 'Beni shigitatsu sawa'. Not yet available in Europe. Zone VI–VII. (Group 1c)

**'Pendulum'.** Wada (1938). Japan. This epithet has been attached to eight forms of the Dissectum group, each with Latin names given by Wada.

**'Pendulum Angustilobum Atropurpureum'.** Wada (1938). Japan. See **'Atrolineare'.**

**'Pendulum Atropurpureum'.** Wada (1938). Japan. See **'Atrolineare'.**

**'Pendulum Atropurpureum Superbum'.** Wada (1938). Japan. See **'Dissectum Superbum'.**

**'Pendulum Hatsushigure'.** Wada (1938). Japan. See **'Hatsushigure'.**

**'Pendulum Inazuma'.** Wada (1938). Japan. See **'Inazuma'.**

**'Pendulum Julian'.** Kingsville Nurseries (H. Hohman) (before 1950). Maryland, USA. JDV I, 70; JDV II, 76. A clone, imported into the United States from the Yokohama Nurseries in the 1930s by Henry Hohman. It is a distinct cultivar, very close to 'Ornatum' but differing from that cultivar in its more pendulous branches and slightly less dissected lobes. It certainly belongs to the 'Dissectum Atropurpureum' group. Its leaves are dark purple when unfolding, becoming dark bronze-green in late summer and turning to orange–golden yellow in the autumn. Good results are realized if grafted on standards of about 1 m. Originally spelled 'Pendula Julian'. (Group 4b)

**'Pendulum Matsukaze'.** Wada (1938). Japan. See **'Matsukaze'.**

**'Pendulum Nigrum'.** Wada (1938). Japan. See **'Dissectum Nigrum'.**

**'Pendulum Omurayama'.** Wada (1938). Japan. See **'Omurayama'.**

**'Pictum'.** Siebold (1864). Germany. A synonym of *A. truncatum,* which see in Chapter 7.

**'Pinebark Maple',** see **'Nishiki gawa'**

**'Pinkedge'.** Kelsey & Dayton (1942). USA. See **'Kagiri nishiki'.**

**'Pinnatifidum'.** Koch (1869). Germany. See **'Dissectum'.**

**'Pinnatum'.** Schwerin (1893). Germany. See **'Elegans'.**

**'Pixie'.** Buchholz Nursery (1990). Gaston, Oregon, USA. Dwarf, densely branched shrublet, leaves 5-lobed, small, dark purple-red. Rarely available in the United States. (Group 6)

**'Polychromum'.** Verschaffelt (1863). Belgium. See **'Dissectum Variegatum'.**

**'Pulchrum'.** Linden (1868). Lacks a description. Lost from cultivation.

**'Pulverulentum'.** Schwerin (1896). Germany. Shrub of the normal type, leaves finely dotted white. Probably no longer in cultivation. (Group 1c)

**'Purpureum'** sensu Krüssmann, see **'Deshojo'**

**'Purpureum'.** Lawson (1874). Great Britain. Slow-growing, upright shrub to 5–6 m, with 5- to 7-lobed leaves, dark purple when unfolding, later turning a dull purple-green. Autumn color scarlet. The plants cultivated under this name agree with this description and also with the description of 'Purpureum Superbum' from Hillier (1928). (Group 1b)

**'Purpureum Superbum'.** Hillier & Sons (1928). Great Britain. See **'Purpureum'.**

**'Red Dragon'.** Graham Roberts (1990). New Zealand. A strong-growing, shrubby tree with weeping branches and a mounding habit. Leaves dark purple, darker than 'Crimson Queen', and retaining color well into autumn. Rarely available in Europe. Zone VI. (Group 4b)

**'Red Filigree Lace'.** Curtis (circa 1965). Sherwood, Oregon, USA. JDV I, 70; JDV II, 76, photo. This dwarf Dissectum Group cultivar has the laciest leaves possible. It is hard to describe. As Vertrees notes, it must be seen to be properly appreciated. It is very lacy, dark red, and does not lose its color (Plate 175). In the autumn the fine leaves turn a bright crimson. The parent plant was a chance seedling, found by W. Curtis, a nurseryman. He presented the seedling to W. Goddard of Victoria, British Columbia, Canada. Goddard in turn cultivated it for a couple of years and then sold it to John Mitsch, a nurseryman in Aurora, Oregon. Mitsch sold it to the late Jean Iseli, a nurseryman in Boring, Oregon, who propagated it and introduced it into the trade. It is very slow growing and very difficult to propagate as its new wood is so limited, making it difficult to cut scions properly. Grafting on a short standard yields excellent plants. In spite of its slow growth it is a real gem, and it is hoped that it becomes generally available. Zone VI. (Group 4b)

**'Red Pygmy'.** Esveld (1969). Boskoop, The Netherlands. JDV I, 91; JDV II, 97, photo. The mother plants of this cultivar attained only about 2 m in 25 years. They form densely branched, vase-shaped plants. The leaves are linear, dark red in spring, later turning a blue-green and finally golden yellow in the autumn. Vigorous young shoots may produce leaves with broader lobes, as is usual for cultivars in this group. The plant was granted an Award of Merit by the Royal Boskoop Horticultural Society in 1969, the year of its introduction. The original material came from an unnamed plant in an old garden in northern Italy. It is definitely smaller than its close ally 'Atrolineare' and does not have the tendency for branch die-back. Readily available in the trade. (Group 5b)

**'Red Select'.** Vertrees (1978). USA. See **'Dissectum Nigrum'.**

**'Reticulatum'.** André (1870). France. See **'Shigitatsu sawa'.**

**'Rhodoneurum'.** Pax (1886). Germany. With red veins apparently similar to those of 'Rubricaule'. Virtually identical to some plants called 'Linearilobum' and related cultivars but much smaller. Lost from cultivation. (Group 5a)

**'Ribescifolium'**, see **'Shishigashira'**

**'Ribesifolium'.** Siesmayer (1888). Germany. See **'Shishigashira'.**

**'Rosco Red'.** Westbury (1962). USA. See **'Atropurpureum Novum'.**

**'Roseo-maculatum'.** Schwerin (1893). Germany. See **'Versicolor'.**

**'Roseo-marginatum'.** Schwerin (1893). USA. See **'Kagiri nishiki'.**

**'Roseo-pictum'.** Schwerin (1893). Germany. See **'Dissectum Variegtum'.**

**'Roseo-tricolor'.** Clark (1908). Great Britain. See **'Kagiri nishiki'.**

**'Roseo-versicolor'.** Siebold (1864). Germany. See **'Versicolor'.**

**'Roseum'.** Thibaut & Keteleer (1866). Great Britain. See **'Versicolor'.**

**'Rough Bark Maple'**, Vertrees (1977). USA. See **'Arakawa'.**

**'Rubellum'.** Pax (1886). Germany. See **'Dissectum Rubrifolium'.**

**'Rubricaule'.** R. Smith (1875). Great Britain. Imperfectly described. Leaves green, veins red. Apparently not in cultivation.

**'Rubrifolium'.** Pax (1886). Germany. See **'Dissectum Rubrifolium'.**

**'Rubrinerve'.** Schwerin (1893). Germany. See **'Rubricaule'.**

**'Rubrolatifolium'.** Schwerin (1893). Germany. See **'Sanguineum'.**

**'Rubrum'.** Huntington Gardens ex Mulligan (1958). USA. This tree is reported to have red, almost purple leaves. It is most unlikely that this is a clone of *A. japonicum,* as was reported. More likely it is an *A. palmatum* cultivar. To date there are no purple-leaved cultivars of *A. japonicum.*

**'Rubrum'.** Siebold (1864). Germany. JDV I, 56; JDV II, 62, photo. A very old cultivar, introduced by von Siebold, together with several other Japanese plants, into The Netherlands. He introduced it to Boskoop as *A. japonicum* 'Purpureum',—a name in use for many years. It is, however, clearly an *A. palmatum* with stiff and sturdy branches, growing much wider than high. The maximum height may be 4 m, but it grows out to a considerably greater width. The leaves are 7 lobed, dark purple in spring, soon turning brown-green or even dirty green. Its autumn color is a strong crimson. The lobes are sharply serrated, and the petioles are long and reddish. The cultivar under the name 'Daimyo nishiki' at Vertrees' nursery is very similar and may be identical. The name 'Sanguineum' must not be attached to this cultivar as is sometimes done. See also 'Sanguineum'. (Group 2b)

**'Ruby Lace'**, see **'Red Filigree Lace'**

**'Rufescens'.** Siesmayer (1888). Germany. JDV I, 5; JDV II, 626. A strong-growing shrub, to 6–8 m. New leaves unfold purple but turn dark green very quickly. The autumn color is orange to crimson. The 7-lobed leaves have the deeply divided leaves of the Matsumurae group. There is some confusion with this name, as 'Rufescens' has also been attached to a similar plant, but one that leafs out almost green instead of purple. The 'Rufescens' described here is a good plant, but 'Nicholsonii', one of its relatives, is better. Rare in the trade. (Group 3a/b)

**'Ruth Murray'.** Murray (1969). Very much like 'Dissectum Variegatum'. Not available in the trade. (Group 4c)

**'Ryokuryu'.** Kobayashi. Japan. A small shrub imported in 1991 from Japan to The Netherlands.

**'Ryumon nishiki'.** *Japanese Maple List,* 1882; JDV I, 115; JDV II, 123. Another variegated cultivar, with 5-lobed irregular leaves, dotted with white or yellowish markings; new growth with pinkish or reddish tones. In summer the variegation tends to disappear. It does not exceed 3 m in height and grows as a tall shrub. Not available in Europe. (Group 1c)

**'Ryuzu'.** JDV I, 100; JDV II, 110, photo. A compact little shrub, hardly becoming larger than about 1 m, and popular for bonsai culture. It has small, 5- to 7-lobed, pale green leaves, overlain with tones of pink or reddish; the margins are prominently serrate. The leaf nodes are closely set together. It is a desirable plant but difficult to graft, so it is very rare in the trade. Zones VI–VII. (Group 6)

**'Sagara nishiki'.** *Japanese Maple List,* 1882; JDV I, 115; JDV II, 123, photo. This cultivar is quite similar to 'Nishiki gasane'. It has 5-lobed leaves, often with 2 minor lobes, edged with yellow; occasionally entire leaves or parts of them are yellow. Unfortunately, it burns easily in the sun. It sometimes grows to 2 m but usually remains smaller. It is quite rare. According to M. Yokoi it is synomymous to 'Nishiki gasane'. Zone VI. (Group 1c)

**'Saintpaulianum'.** Schwerin (1896). Germany. See **'Nishiki gasane'.**

**'Saku'**, see **'Shigarami'**

**'Samari'.** Duncan & Davies catalog (1990). New Zealand. See **'Beni shigitatsu sawa'.**

**'Samidare'.** *Japanese Maple List,* 1882; JDV I, 57; JDV II, 63. A sturdy plant, growing into a large shrub, 5–6 m high and as wide. It has firm, almost leathery, rather large leaves, 10–12 cm across. They are 7-lobed, with serrate margins. The unfolding leaves have a slight tinge of pink but almost immediately turn a fresh green. The autumn colors can be very distinctive—golden yellow with crimson speckles. Its name means "early summer rain." A very useful plant for landscaping purposes, due to its resistance and hardiness. It is slowly becoming more popular. Zone V. (Group 2a)

**'Sangokaku'.** *Japanese Maple List,* 1882; Bean (1970); JDV I, 127; JDV II, 137, photo. A very popular shrub to 7–8 m, occasionally even to 10–12 m, with brilliant coral-red branches in winter (Plate 176). In summer this coloration is almost absent. The small, 5-lobed leaves are fresh green and turn a very attractive yellow in late autumn. Old branches lose their color, but a little pruning helps older plants develop new shoots, adding beauty to the tree. A more recently introduced cultivar with similar qualities is 'Beni kawa'. There is a green counterpart to 'Sangokaku'—'Aoyagi'. A combination of these two cultivars gives an especially attractive landscape effect. 'Sangokaku' was introduced into Europe by T. H. Lowinsky and put into the trade by the Sunningdale Nurseries, Great Britain, around 1920. It is also possible that it was independently introduced into Great Britain by the Daisy Hill Nurseries in Ireland. There is some confusion with the name 'Corallinum' as in older publications this name was used for 'Sangokaku'. 'Corallinum' is an entirely different plant. A name much in use, and more popular in Europe, is 'Senkaki', which is a synonym of 'Sangokaku'. The word 'Sangokaku' means "coral tower." Zone VI. (Group 1a)

**'Sangotsu'.** Dickson (1887). Great Britain. Reported to have pale green leaves, bronze-tinted. Probably not in cultivation.

**'Sanguineum'.** Lemaire (1867). France. JDV I, 57; JDV II, 63, photo. This name has been applied to so many different cultivars that it should not be used any longer. It is usually applied to a dark purple-leaved clone of 'Atropurpureum' and related cultivars. It is also in use for cultivars with much redder leaves, and even for clones with pinkish crimson leaves in early spring, such as 'Akaji nishiki', 'Deshojo', and 'Rubrum'.

**'Sanguineum Chishio'**, see note at **'Sanguineum'**

**'Sanguineum Seigai'**, see ***A. truncatum*** **'Akaji nishiki'**

**'Saoshika'.** *Japanese Maple List,* 1882; JDV I, 57; JDV II, 63, photo. This is a medium-sized shrub, to 2–3 m tall and as wide. Its leaves are 7-lobed and circular, almost starlike. They are pale green, later turning somewhat darker green. The lobe apices and margins are delicately reddish when young, which disappears when the leaves mature. It has a beautiful golden yellow autumn color. A desirable but not spectacular plant. Rare. (Group 1a)

**'Saotome'.** *Japanese Maple List,* 1882; JDV I, 58; JDV II, 64. A semidwarf, with 5-lobed, deeply divided leaves. Mature plants will hardly exceed 2 m. The leaves are small, about 4–5 cm across. Young growth makes a reddish impression, due to the red margins, that disappears later. Its name means "rice-planting girl." Not spectacular. (Group 1a)

**'Satzuki beni'.** JDV II, 64. A strong, upright, treelike shrub, to 7–8 m. The leaves are 7-lobed and of a strong texture, dark green, turning to a glistening scarlet in the autumn. Not yet available in the trade. (Group 2a)

**'Sazanami'.** Chikinsho (1733). Japan. JDV I, 83; JDV II, 89, photo. A shrub to 6 m tall and about 3–4 m wide. The leaves of this attractive cultivar are rather unusual. The leaf bases are almost horizontal, and the blades are distinctly 7-lobed, with sharp, pointed lobes. The margins are doubly serrated; the name means "ruffles." Leaves are dark green with red petioles. Unfolding leaves are orange-red, soon turning to green. In the autumn the colors change to dark golden to golden brown. An uncommon cultivar and only rarely available. Deserves more attention. (Group 3a)

**'Schichi henge'**, see **'Shichi henge'**

**'Schimeno uchi'**, see **'Shime no uchi'**

**'Scolopendrifolium'**, see **'Linearilobum'**

**'Scolopendrifolium Purpureum'**, see **'Atrolineare'**

**'Scolopendrifolium Rubrum'**, see **'Atrolineare'**

**'Scolopendrifolium Viride'**, see **'Linearilobum'**

**'Scottum Roseum'.** Fratelli Gilardelli (1981). Omate, Italy. Upright-growing shrub. Leaves variegated pink and white. The name is illegitimate although published in the catalog of Fratelli Gilardelli, as it was published in Latin form after 1 January 1959. As this cultivar has not been seen, it is unknown whether it is really different from 'Versicolor'. Zone VI. (Group 1c)

**'Seicha nishiki'.** Yokohama Nurseries (1898). Japan. JDV I, 104; JDV II, 112. This medium-sized shrub is reported to be a variegated cultivar, but its leaves are usually totally green. The leaves are 5- to 7-lobed, and their shape is normal. Occasionally there are some creamy yellow variegations, but it reverts easily. There are many cultivars much better than this one. Zone VI. (Group 1c)

**'Seigai'.** Koidzumi (1911). Japan. JDV I, 119; JDV II, 127, photo. Shrub to 4 m in favorable conditions, usually much smaller. Leaves rather small, always 5-lobed and brilliantly dark pink for about 4 weeks in the spring. Later the leaves change to bronze-green and finally become bluish green in summer. Recorded as early as 1710 (Chikinsho). It is suitable for bonsai culture. This cultivar is quite popular in the United States, where it is called 'Bonfire', but it is much better known as *A. truncatum* 'Akaji nishiki' (which see). Not to be confused with 'Seigen' (which see). Sometimes available in the trade. Zone VI. (Group 1b)

**'Seigen'.** Hinkul (1956). JDV I, 128; JDV II, 136. This is semidwarf like 'Tamahime' or 'Kiyohime' and produces a rounded, dense shrub of about 1.5 m. The leaves are 5-lobed, rather small, 4–5 cm across and closely set together. The young, unfolding leaves are bright crimson for a week or two, after which they turn a dull, light green, becoming yellow in the autumn. It is a desirable plant for bonsai culture. It must not be confused with 'Seigai' or 'Akaji nishiki'. 'Seigen' grows considerably larger, but has the same leaf form and color. It is a rare cultivar. Zones VI–VII. (Group 6)

**'Seikaiha'**, see **'Seigen'**

**'Seiryu'.** *Japanese Maple List*, 1882; *Dendroflora* 13/14; JDV I, 71; JDV II, 77, photo. This is the only upright-growing cultivar with leaves of the Dissectum group yet developed. It is unique in this respect. It grows into a broader, vase-shaped, small tree, to 5 m tall or more. Its branches are yellow-brown, long, and slender. Older plants tend to become somewhat broader but always keep the upright habit. The leaves are dark green and of the normal Dissectum shape (Plate 177). They turn to dark brown-purple in the autumn, another feature unique to this cultivar. 'Seiryu' won a Award of Merit from the Royal Boskoop Horticultural Society in 1977. It is now a popular cultivar and readily available. Zone VI. (Group 7)

**'Sekimori'.** Chikinsho (1719). Japan. JDV I, 72; JDV II, 78, photo. A strong, dark green member of the Dissectum group with the normal mushroom habit; it can grow to 3–4 m high and 5–6 m wide. The leaves are slightly larger than usual and are of the usual shape but have somewhat less incised lobes. It is very similar to 'Dissectum Paucum' and has an appearance described by Vertrees as "feathery," not "lacy." The autumn color is yellow and gives a fine display. Its autumn color is quite distinctive, and its bark is striped with white. Young plants require some pruning as they grow vigorously in the first years. It is rather uncommon in horticulture and may be a useful plant for grafting on standards, with its vigorous long weeping shoots. (Group 4a)

**'Sekka yatsubusa'.** JDV I, 101; JDV II, 110, photo. Another dwarf, to 2–3 m, with quite small leaves, 5-lobed and deeply divided. The leaves are closely set together and have a rusty overtone on darker green. The autumn color is yellow to orange. The outstanding feature of this cultivar is that many of the terminal shoots are quite flattened and fasciated. This dwarf is not widely known, and only incidentally in cultivation in Europe. Zone VI. (Group 6)

**'Seme no hane'.** JDV II,, 89. A vigorous shrub of moderate size. The leaves are very deeply divided, of a strong, light green with a rusty red undertone, and the lobes end in tapering points. Autumn colors are variable, from yellow to orange-red. It is rarely available in the trade. Zone VI. (Group 3a)

**'Senkaki'**, see **'Sangokaku'**

**'Senri'.** Koidzumi (1911). Japan. No adequate description. Leaves rose, turning green in summer. Probably not in cultivation.

**'Sensu agasi'** Koidzumi (1911). Japan. Leaf margins brown to rose. Probably not in cultivation. See also 'Ogi nagare'.

**'Septemlobum'**, see **'Heptalobum'**

**'Septemlobum Elegans'**, see **'Elegans'**

**'Septemlobum Osakazuki'**, see **'Osakazuki'**

**'Septemlobum Rubrum'**, see **'Rubrum'**

**'Septemlobum Sanguineum'**, see **'Rubrum'**

**'Sessilifolium'**, see **'Hagaromo'**

**'Shaina'.** Greer Gardens (1988). Eugene, Oregon, USA. A mutation or sport of 'Bloodgood' and of dwarfish habit. It grows upright and compact, and the growth slows with age. In later years the plant is dense and dwarfish. Leaves are 5-lobed, deeply cleft, and two-toned red, starting bright red and turning to maroon. (Group 1b)

**'Sharp's Pygmy'.** Sharp's Nursery (1985). Sandy, Oregon, USA. This is a dwarf cultivar, discovered by a friend of Sharp. It has small, palmate, 5-lobed leaves, bright green and with a very nice orange autumn color. The internodes are short. It grows about as wide as high and will not exceed 1 m. The original plants are about that size. It is easy to propagate from cuttings, but it is not known whether it is then short-lived. Zone VI. (Group 6)

**'Sherwood Flame'.** Curtis (circa 1970). Sherwood, Oregon, USA. JDV I, 84; JDV II, 89, photo. A remarkable cultivar, very much like 'Burgundy Lace'. In spring and summer it is impossible to distinguish them. In the late summer, however, 'Sherwood Flame' keeps its color, while 'Burgundy Lace' has a tendency to become "greener." This is especially evident in areas with a dry and hot summer. In the coastal climates of Belgium, The Netherlands, and Great Britain, there is practically no difference throughout the year, but in the Pacific Northwest of the United States and Canada, the difference is clearly visible. It becomes a large shrub 4–5 m tall and at least as wide. It was a chance seedling from 'Burgundy Lace', introduced by Will Curtis. A good plant for landscaping purposes and highly recommended. (Group 3b)

**'Shichi henge'.** JDV I, 58; JDV II, 64. This cultivar is almost identical to 'Musashino', but its leaf lobes are held more closely together. Not in cultivation in Europe. (Group 2b)

**'Shigarami'.** Chikinsho (1710). Japan. JDV I, 58; JDV II, 64, photo. An upright shrub to 3 m, rather openly branched. The 5–7 lobes are conspicuously colored dark purple on the otherwise green leaf blades. The dark color disappears as the summer progresses. It is very much like 'Tana', but the lobes of 'Shigarami' have darker and larger parts than that cultivar. The autumn color is a good yellow-brown, but not very distinctive. It is also known in the trade as 'Saku'. (Group 1a)

**'Shigare jama'.** Pax (1902). Germany. Reported to have dark red leaves, variegated rose. Probably not in cultivation.

**'Shigitatsu'**, see **'Shigitatsu sawa'**

**'Shigitatsu sawa'.** Yokohoma Nurseries (1896). Japan. *Japanese Maple List,* 1882; JDV I, 116; JDV II, 123, photo. A plant better known as 'Reticulatum' due to the reticulate pattern of the leaves, which have green veins with silvery or yellow-green interspaces (Plate 178). This cultivar lacks red, but when red is also present the plant is called 'Beni shigitatsu sawa'. Shrubby, but taller than wide, to 5 m. It is a fairly good garden plant, but somewhat fragile; the leaves tend to burn in hot sun. It is perfectly suitable as an exhibition plant and is really brilliant when young leaves are forced. It is very rarely available but was popular some decades ago. Zone VI. (Group 3c)

**'Shigure bato'.** Angyo Maple Nursery. (1930). Japan. JDV I, 84; JDV II, 90, photo. An unusual, slow-growing cultivar. The leaves are very deeply divided and 7-lobed. The lobes are rather strongly incised, but not as deeply as the typical cultivar of the Dissectum group. The shrubs grow to a height of about 2 m. Young leaves show an attractive red color, later turning to olive green, the margins remaining reddish. The autumn tints are golden yellow to golden brown. It is quite attractive but somewhat tender and fragile. It is also difficult to propagate. Extremely rare in the trade. Zone VI. (Group 3b)

**'Shigurezome'.** Chikinsho (1719). Japan; Koidzumi (1911). Japan. JDV I, 84; JDV II, 90. A very old cultivar but only rarely seen in horticulture. A medium-sized, treelike shrub, with 7-lobed leaves almost divided to the bases. As with so many cultivars of this group, the purple leaves fade quickly to a dull green, and the autumn color is an attractive crimson red. (Group 3b)

**'Shigurezono'**, see **'Shigurezome'**

**'Shikageori nishiki'.** Chikinsho (1719). Japan. JDV I, 116; JDV II, 124. This cultivar has a complicated nomenclature, as there are several synonyms such as 'Kageori nishiki' and 'Kagiri nishiki', although the latter is a variegated cultivar. 'Shikageori nishiki' is a vase-shaped shrub, to 5 m, with 7-lobed, purple-red leaves, incised halfway their centers. The color changes later to a not very conspicuous brown-green. There are many better cultivars. (Group 2b)

**'Shikushi gata'**, see **'Tsukushigata'**

**'Shime no uchi'**, see **'Linearilobum'**

**'Shindeshojo'.** JDV I, 129; JDV II, 137, photo. An excellent plant, close to such cultivars as 'Deshojo', and 'Chishio Improved'. It is a twiggy shrub, to 2–3 m, with dark purple young shoots. It is excellently suited for patios and small gardens, as it requires sheltered positions. The leaves are relatively small, 5-lobed, sometimes 7-lobed, 3–5 cm across. The color is an outstanding scarlet when unfolding, later turning a dull bluish green. It is much used for bonsai culture. The name means "a new Deshojo," indicating that it was a later selection. In countries with a cold climate this cultivar needs winter protection as new long shoots do not always ripen sufficiently to withstand low temperatures. Zones VI–VII. (Group 1b)

**'Shinobuga oka'.** *Japanese Maple List,* 1882; JDV I, 93; JDV II, 99, photo. A well-known cultivar but almost always labeled 'Linearilobum'. It has the typically narrow lobes of this group, fresh green, turning to orange-yellow. On long, vigorous shoots the lobes are distinctly broader, a quite normal feature of this group. The shrubby tree grows up to 5–6 m in very favorable conditions but usually does not reach this height. It can be found in many gardens, notably in the Maple Glade in the Westonbirt Arboretum, Tetbury, Great Britain. Possibly the plants in Europe labeled 'Shime no uchi' are identical to this cultivar. (Group 5a)

**'Shinonome'.** *Japanese Maple List,* 1882; JDV I, 84; JDV II, 90, photo. A little-known cultivar of about 3–4 m height and an erect habit. The leaves are 7-lobed and deeply divided, bright red when unfolding, becoming purple-red when mature. In summer the leaves turn green with a red overtone. Autumn colors are crimson to glistening red. A good garden plant for the small garden. The name means "dawn." (Group 3b)

**'Shiranami'.** Chikinsho (1710). Japan. JDV I, 85; JDV II, 91. A very old but rare cultivar, forming a dense, twiggy shrub to 3–4 m. The leaves are purple when unfolding, rapidly turning dark green and with yellow colors in autumn. The leaves are 5- to 7-lobed, deeply divided, and of medium size. It is rare and not available in Europe. (Group 3a)

**'Shishigashira'.** *Japanese Maple List,* 1882; JDV I, 129/130; JDV II, 137, photo. A compact, shrubby, but erect small tree, to 4–5 m tall with most interesting, heavily curled leaves, 5-lobed, and dark green. The leaves are very closely set together on short and thick twigs. It is rather well known in horticulture and very popular for bonsai culture. It is also increasingly popular for small Japanese gardens and as a pot plant. The leaves are almost of the same shape as those of *Ribes alpinum,* hence the synonymous name 'Ribesifolium' much in use in Great Britain (sometimes misspelled as 'Ribescifolium'). In The Netherlands it was propagated for years as 'Crispum' and later as 'Cristatum' [See van Gelderen (1969)]. The autumn colors appear very late, often 3–4 weeks later than in other cultivars. The leaves turn a peculiar purple-red with orange-red patterns. It is rather difficult to graft, as good scions are often lacking. Nevertheless, it is in cultivation at various nurseries. (Group 1a or 6)

**'Shishio Improved',** see **'Chishio Improved'**

**'Shishi yatsubusa'.** JDV II, 107. According to Vertrees, this is a very desirable dwarf plant. The leaves are densely set, palmate, with long tapering lobes. The autumn color is orange to yellow. It is reported to be popular with bonsai hobbyists. Difficult to propagate, as scions are often weak and limited. Occasionally available. Zone VI. (Group 6)

**'Shojo'.** Angyo Maple Nursery (1930). Japan. JDV I, 58; JDV II, 64, photo. One of the best purple-leaved cultivars. The leaves are very deeply colored and distinctly 7-lobed, the outer lobes being much smaller. The color holds very well in summer and the autumn color is a good crimson. The shrubby tree reaches a height of about 4 m but does not develop into a large plant. There are some difficulties with the name. 'Shojo' is the name of the red-faced orangutang, a character in many Japanese plays. Further, the word 'Shojo' is used for several red-leaved cultivars. About 1979 a clone under the name 'Shojo nomura' was imported into The Netherlands from Japan. This material seems identical with 'Shojo' as received from Vertrees in the United States. Plants with the name 'Shojo nomura' received from Vertrees are quite different from 'Shojo'. Up to this point it was easy, according to Vertrees in *Japanese Maples,* to consider the name 'Shojo' as correct. At the International Exhibition of Horticulture (Floriade), held in Amsterdam in 1982, however, the Japanese exhibit displayed a number of original *A. palmatum* cultivars, all properly labeled. Among them were five plants labeled 'Syoiou-noumura' (alternative spelling) that were absolutely identical with the recent Japanese importation under the name 'Shojo nomura'. It seems that 'Shojo' also belongs to this clone. It is difficult than to decide whether this name could be maintained. However, van Gelderen (1983) pointed out that the name 'Shojo' is the only valid name for this cultivar. It is to be hoped, therefore, that the later alternative names given by the Kawaguchi Trade Center will disappear from use. (Group 2b)

**'Shojo no mai'.** This plant, which came from J. D. Vertrees, is similar to 'Beni shichi henge', but the red-brown color at the leaf margins is even nicer than in that variety. It is a rapid grower, upright, with thin twigs rather heavily branched on 2-year-old wood. The 5-lobed leaves are small, whitish pink, and variegated with red-brown, irregular leaf margins. It is not mentioned in Vertrees' books on Japanese maples; we read of it in M. Yokoi's list. Zone VI. (Group 1c)

**'Shojo nomura'.** JDV I, 85; JDV II, 91. The description given by Vertrees is different from plants of this name received from Japan. Vertrees could not find a full description of this particular cultivar but stated in *Japanese Maples* that this plant is a good purple-red in spring, afterward turning to green with an undertone of bright orange-red. The leaves are deeply divided and have red petioles. The shrub forms a rather cascading tree to 4 m. As there is only a little material of this cultivar available in the West, it is difficult to decide whether this name is legitimate. (Group 2b)

**'Shojo shidare'.** JDV I, 72; JDV II, 78. This cultivar belongs to the 'Dissectum Atropurpureum' category, with brown-purple leaves turning to a dull green in late summer. It is a cascading cultivar around 3 m tall, so should be grafted on standards to achieve the best results. It is still rare and somewhat tender. Zone VI. (Group 4b)

**'Shuzanko'**, see ***A. palmatum*** ssp. ***amoenum***

**'Silver Lace'**, see **'Filigree'**

**'Sinuatum'**, see **'Yezo nishiki'**

**'Sotoyama'**, see **'Toyama'**

**'Sotoyama nishiki'**, see **'Toyama nishiki'**

**'Speciosum'.** Koidzumi (1911). Japan. Without description. Leaves golden brown in the autumn. Apparently not in cultivation.

**'Spiderleaf'.** Olmsted (1923). USA. See **'Ornatum'.**

**'Spring Fire'**, Krüssman (1970). See **'Corallinum'.**

**'Stalkless'.** Kelsey & Dayton (1942). USA. See **'Hagaromo'.**

**'Stella Rossa'.** Fratelli Gilardelli (1984). Italy. This is a new cultivar of Italian origin and has the same general habit as 'Inaba shidare'. It needs some staking when young to form neat plants. The leaves are very deeply dissected and dark wine-red, becoming lighter red in autumn. It is not yet generally available and it is not known whether it is really an improvement on the already existing comparable cultivars. Zone VI. (Group 4b)

**'Striatum'**, see **'Shigitatsu sawa'**

**'Suisei'.** Kobayashi (before 1990). Japan. Yellow-green, very finely dissected leaves, like 'Filigree'. No further description. Imported in 1991 from Japan to The Netherlands. Zone VI. (Group 4a)

**'Sulphureum'**, see **'Dissectum Flavescens'**

**'Sumi nagashi'.** Angyo Maple Nursery (1930). Japan. JDV I, 85; JDV II, 91, photo. This is a large-leaved cultivar, upright and forming a well-branched, treelike shrub of about 4–5 m. The leaves are distinctly 7-lobed and deeply divided, with serrate lobes. The leaf color is a rich dark purple in spring, becoming deep maroon in summer. The color holds well during the summer. Autumn colors are crimson and red. It is in cultivation in Europe on a restricted scale and is a good garden plant. It is indeed one of the best in the Matsumurae group. (Group 3b)

**'Sunrise'.** Kelsey & Dayton (1942). USA. See **'Aureum'.**

**'Sunset'.** Vertrees (1975). Roseburg, Oregon, USA. This umbrella-shaped, compact shrub is like other Dissectum group selections but is entirely unique in its colors. The saw-toothed (not doubly serrated) leaves are orange-yellow and orange over a green undertone. The colors develop best in full light. Not yet available in the trade. (Group 4a)

**'Superbum'**, see **'Atropurpureum Superbum'**

**'Taihai'**, see **'Osakazuki'**

**'Taimin'.** JDV I, 59; JDV II, 65. An old purple-leaved cultivar, of about 2 m in height, very rare in cultivation. It is not an outstanding clone; its variegated counterpart 'Taimin nishiki' is more desirable. Zone VI. (Group 2b)

**'Taimin nishiki'.** *Japanese Maple List,* 1882; JDV I, 116; JDV II, 124. A variegated red-leaved cultivar, derived from the preceding. It is a modest shrub to 2 m. The leaves are 5-lobed, occasionally remotely 7-lobed, and dark reddish purple with conspicuous pink variegations. It is a very charming plant, still quite rare in cultivation. Unfortunately, the variegation is not very stable. There are also plants under this name that do not bear variegated leaves. Some plants also differ in habit and are very close to *A. palmatum* 'Rubrum'. Occasionally they are labeled 'Daimyo nishiki', a misspelling for 'Taimin nishiki'. A comprehensive account of the history of this particular cultivar can be found in both editions of Vertrees' *Japanese Maples.* Zones VI–VII. (Group 3c)

**'Takao'.** Chikinsho (1710). Japan. JDV I, 59; JDV II, 65. Without description. With green leaves as in the species. Rather fast-growing vase-shaped bush. Leaves 5-lobed, green; yellow autumn color. Imported in 1991 from Japan. Zone VI. (Group 1c)

**'Takao momiji'**, see **'Takao'**

**'Takasago momiji'**, see ***A. duplicatoserratum*** (The name means "maple of Taiwan.")

**'Takinogawa'.** *Japanese Maple List,* 1882; Koidzumi (1911). Japan. This cultivar must not be confused with the *japonicum* cultivar of the same name. This one is a shrub to 5 m, bearing 7-lobed leaves with truncate bases. The lobes are narrow-oblong, caudate-acuminate, and narrowly cuneate at the bases. In cultivation in the United States. (Group 5a)

**'Tako kaede'**, see ***A. palmatum*** ssp. ***palmatum***

**'Tamahime'.** JDV I, 101; JDV II, 107, photo. A dwarf plant, forming a rounded shrub to 1.5–2 m wide and high. It is densely branched and suitable for bonsai. The small, 5-lobed leaves are of the normal shape of *A. palmatum,* but only 3–4 cm across. While it is a vigorous plant, it nevertheless gives the impression of a true dwarf. Occasionally offered in the trade. Zone VI. (Group 6)

**'Tama nishiki'.** (1930). JDV I, 117; JDV II, 125. An upright shrub, to 2–3 m. The leaves are 7-lobed and deeply divided, marked with white and yellow combinations in irregular and varied inconspicuous patterns; in the autumn these markings become brighter. A very rare plant. Not in cultivation in Europe. (Group 3c)

**'Tamaori nishiki'.** JDV II, 125. A medium-sized shrub to 3 m. The leaves are of the normal shape of *A. palmatum* but are variegated white with some pink. It tends to revert to entirely green, like other cultivars of this group. It is rare in the trade. (Group 1c)

**'Tamukeyama'.** Koidzumi (1911). Japan. Chikinsho (1710); JDV I, 73; JDV II, 79, photo. This is an excellent member of the Dissectum group, with crimson red leaves when unfolding that almost immediately turn to a dark purple. The color holds well during the summer, turning scarlet in autumn. The general impression is much like 'Crimson Queen' but the lobes are less "lacy." It grows somewhat leggy and will become about 3 m high and 5 m wide. This name has also been used as a synonym for 'Ornatum' but this is not correct. It is very good for grafting on standards, as its vigorous shoots cascade nicely. It is still unknown in the trade, but will become more popular. (Group 4b)

**'Tana'.** JDV I, 59; JDV II, 65, photo. A beautiful plant with interesting foliage. The leaves are light green, the lobe tips tinged heavily with purple. This color gradually shades into green. The leaves are 7-lobed and about 5–6 cm across. The plant grows rather upright into a treelike shrub, to 4 m. Its autumn colors are golden yellow with red. It is similar to 'Shigarami', but the latter has more deeply colored lobes.

The name 'Tanabate' has also been used for this cultivar but is incorrect. Zone VI. (Group 2a)

**'Tanabata'.** Pax (1902). Germany. See **'Atropurpureum'** and **'Tana'.**

**'Tatsu gashira'**, see **'Ryuzu'**

**'Tatsuta'.** Chikinsho (1710). Japan. JDV I, 60; JDV II, 62. An old cultivar described 300 years ago in Japan. It is a medium-sized shrub, to 3–4 m. The leaves unfold a very light green, turning a good clear green and then becoming scarlet and yellow in the autumn. They are 5- to 7-lobed, 7–8 cm across, and set widely apart along the shoot. This cultivar is not widely known but should be, as it is a good plant. Also known as 'Tatsutagawa'. (Group 2a)

**'Tatsutagawa'**, see **'Tatsuta'**

**'Tennyo no hoshi'.** JDV II, 107. A very twiggy, tall shrub, to 4–5 m. The leaves are small to medium-sized, 5 cm long. The lobes are very narrow and deeply incised, dark green with paler variegation. An interesting plant with unusual foliage. Available in the trade. Zone VI. (Group 1a)

**'The Bishop'.** Kingsville Nurseries (H. Hohman). Maryland, USA. JDV I, 49; JDV II, 55. A dull red cultivar of seedling origin. Not registered. Much better cultivars are available. Rarely seen in the trade. (Group 2b)

**'Threadleaf'.** Kelsey & Dayton (1942). USA. See **'Dissectum'.**

**'Thunbergii'**, see ***A. palmatum*** ssp. ***palmatum***

**'Tobiosho'.** Iseli Nursery (1991). Boring, Oregon, USA. A small tree with scarlet autumn colors. Leaves about 5 cm wide and appearing billowy. (Group 1a)

**'Tokonatsu'.** Koidzumi (1911). Japan. 7-lobed leaves with oblong, acuminate lobes. The name means "everlasting summer." Apparently not in cultivation.

**'Tokyo yatsubusa'**, see **'Kotohime'**

**'Toshi'**, see **'Azuma murasaki'**

**'Toyama'**, see **'Ornatum'**

**'Toyama nishiki'.** Dickson (1882). Great Britain. JDV I, 73; JDV II, 79, photo. A slow-growing member of the Dissectum group, not exceeding 1 m, with brown-red leaves, variegated with pink and white. Each leaf is differently colored and the finely dissected leaves droop more than related cultivars. It is tender in most regions. 'Dissectum Variegatum' makes a better plant. Zone VII. (Group 4c)

**'Toyo nishiki'**, see **'Toyama nishiki'**

**'Tricolor'.** Nicholson (1881). Leaves spotted red, pink, and white, but there is no further description. Apparently not in cultivation and probably a 'Versicolor' type. (Group 1c)

**'Trompenburg'.** Van Hoey Smith (1965). Rotterdam, The Netherlands. JDV I, 86; JDV II, 92, photo. A strong-growing, upright, shrubby tree, to 6–8 m tall. A chance seedling discovery by J. R. P. van Hoey Smith and named after his arboretum. Introduced by Firma C. Esveld, Boskoop, The Netherlands. This rather open cultivar has very attractive leaves, 7-lobed and deeply divided. The lobe margins roll down, almost forming a tube, which is a distinctive feature. No other cultivar possesses such convex, almost conduplicate, leaves, except for 'Green Trompenburg'. The color is dark purple, glistening, later turning to a rich brown-red (Plate 179). The autumn color is scarlet. It is an outstanding cultivar and becoming more popular, both in Europe and the United States. It is now widely available. (Group 3b)

**'Tsuchigumo'.** *Japanese Maple List,* 1882; Koidzumi (1911). Japan. JDV I, 131; JDV II, 138, photo. This is a very attractive, compact cultivar, but not really a dwarf, to 3 m. The young leaves are rusty red, very quickly turning to green, and autumn tints are crimson with yellow. The leaves are very different in shape, generally 7-lobed, the lobes are elongate, tapering gradually to sharp points. The overall impression is that the leaves are heavily curled. It is not well known but is well worth a place in small gardens. Zone VI. (Group 1a)

**'Tsukomo'**, see **'Tsukumo'**

**'Tsukubane'.** Koidzumi (1911). Japan. JDV I, 87; JDV II, 93, photo. A tall, upright, shrubby tree, to 7–8 m tall at maturity. The leaves are 7-lobed, divided to the center and crimson red when unfolding, almost immediately turning purple-red. The color does not hold well, becoming a deep greenish purple, difficult to describe. The autumn colors are orange to scarlet. It is an old cultivar, not widely known. In Europe a different plant is grown under this name; it is much closer to 'Heptalobum' or 'Koreanum'. Such plants are undoubtedly incorrectly named and should be avoided. The true cultivar bears outstandingly beautiful clusters of fruits on red stalks. The offspring is very uniform and close to subspecies *amoenum*. Can be used as understock. (Group 2b)

**'Tsukumo'.** Yokohama Nurseries (1936). Japan. JDV I, 102; JDV II, 107, photo. A delightful dwarf plant, no taller than 1–1.5 m and about as wide. Its small, 5-lobed leaves are set tightly together and are light green with reddish margins when young. The autumn color is golden yellow. This exquisite plant is very rare and difficult to propagate. Young plants grow extremely slowly. Zone VI. (Group 6)

**'Tsukushigata'.** *Japanese Maple List*, 1882; JDV I, 60; JDV II, 66, photo. This cultivar forms a large, spreading, treelike shrub, often as high as it is wide, to 4–5 m. The leaves are rather large, 6–8 cm across, 7-lobed but not deeply divided. The color is a rich purple, turning to a brown-purple, without any green undertone. The autumn color is a good scarlet. The leaf undersides are dark green. A quite attractive plant and long in cultivation. Sometimes offered under the name of 'Shikushi gata' or 'Chikischi gata'. (Group 2b)

**'Tsumabeni'.** *Japanese Maple List*, 1882; JDV I, 60; JDV II, 66, photo. A very fine plant, forming a rounded shrub to 2.5–3 m tall and almost as wide. The leaves are light green with attractive purple margins. The color becomes more intense as the leaves mature. It is rather difficult to propagate. A good landscape combination can be created using this cultivar and several Dissectum group cultivars or *A. shirasawanum* 'Aureum'. The name means "red nail." Only occasionally available, but worthwhile. Zones VI–VII. (Group 1c)

**'Tsumagaki'.** *Japanese Maple List*, 1882; JDV I, 61; JDV II, 67, photo. This plant is very similar to the preceding, but the leaves are of a different color, more yellow, and drooping. The margins are of an intense reddish purple, quite attractive. The autumn colors are golden yellow with crimson. Mature plants reach a height of only 2 m. This cultivar and 'Tsumabeni' are often confused, as the result of the similarity of names and leaves. An excellent plant for the small garden. Rare in cultivation. Has been shown at the International Exposition (Floriade) in Amsterdam (1982), mislabeled as 'Butterfly', which is an entirely different plant. Zones VI–VII. (Group 1c)

**'Tsuri nishiki'.** *Japanese Maple List*, 1882; JDV I, 87; JDV II, 93, photo. A very old cultivar, often met with in old collections under the name 'Laciniatum' or even 'Septemlobum'. It is now almost absent in nurseries but should be brought back into the trade. It is a small tree, to 5–6 m tall, with deeply divided green leaves having serrate margins. It is almost in the Linearilobum group but should more properly be included in the Matsumurae group. It has brilliant, golden crimson autumn colors. The leaves are quite sturdy. Zone VI. (Group 3a)

**'Uchiwa nagashi'.** Wada (1938). Japan. This is a plant in the Dissectum group with green leaves edged with red. Apparently no longer in cultivation. (Group 4a)

**'Ueno homare'.** JDV I, 88; JDV II, 94. Very close to a typical *A. palmatum*, growing into a small tree of 4–5 m in height. It has small, yellow to green, 5-lobed leaves, with a feathery appearance and is close to 'Katsura'. It is of recent introduction in the United States and Europe. (Group 1a)

**'Ueno yama'.** JDV II, 139, photo. An upright shrub of medium size. The typical palmate leaves are bright orange in spring, later turning to green, much like 'Katsura' but brighter. An excellent plant, unfortunately very rarely available. (Group 1a)

**'Ukigumo'.** JDV I, 117; JDV II, 125, photo. One of the cultivars to be either loved or hated. The extremely variegated leaves have very irregular patterns of white and pink in all possible combinations (Plate 180). The leaves are 5-lobed and about 5 cm across. Some people like it very much, others cannot stand such flamboyant variegation. It grows into a fairly dense shrub of about 2.5 m in height, and about as wide. Suitable for bonsai culture. The name means "floating clouds." It is not easy to graft, and young plants have a tendency to develop vigorous shoots with less variegation. However, the variegation appears the following year. Available on a restricted scale. Zone VI. (Group 1c)

**'Ukigumo nishiki'**, see **'Ukigumo'**

**'Ukon'**, see **'Aoyagi'**

**'Ukon nishiki'**, see **'Aoyagi'**

**'Umegae'.** *Japanese Maple List,* 1882; JDV I, 61; JDV II, 67, photo. Another purple-leafed, upright *A. palmatum;* to 5 m, but the leaves are smaller than usual, 4–6 cm across. The lobes are deeply divided and the margins very finely toothed. The color holds well until the end of the summer, turning crimson in the autumn. It is slow-growing and suitable for smaller gardens. An old cultivar, listed in Japanese catalogs for over 100 years, it is very rare in cultivation. (Group 2b)

**'Umegai'**, see **'Umegae'**

**'Utsusemi'.** *Japanese Maple List,* 1882; JDV I, 62; JDV II, 68, photo. An outstanding cultivar with bright green, bold leaves, 7-lobed, and of an almost leathery texture. The 2 basal lobes are much smaller than the others. Its autumn colors are purple to scarlet, dotted with orange. It grows into a medium-sized, treelike shrub, to 4 m tall and as wide. This fine cultivar deserves more attention, as it is suitable for smaller gardens. Its name means "skin of a grasshopper." Only occasionally available. (Group 2a)

**'Vanhouttei'.** Schwerin (1893). Germany. Leaves dark purple-red, bases cuneate. No further description. Probably lost from cultivation.

**'Variegatum'**, see **'Atropurpureum Variegatum'**

**'Versicolor'.** Van Houtte (1861). Belgium. JDV I, 118; JDV II, 126, photo. Today it is hard to say exactly which selection Van Houtte purchased under this name. There are at least a half dozen cultivars with irregularly variegated leaves. It might be advisable to treat this cultivar name the same way as with names like Linearilobum or Sessilifolium, as a group name. Even in the nursery center of Boskoop, The Netherlands, in earlier years two different clones were available under the same name. Plants under the name 'Versicolor' must be upright and have at least 5-lobed, palmate leaves, variegated white and pink.

**'Villa Taranto'.** Esveld (1967). Boskoop, The Netherlands. JDV I, 93; JDV II, 99, photo. A cultivar discovered as a nameless, semidwarf shrub in the Gardens of Villa Taranto, Pallanza, Italy. It has been named and introduced, in cooperation with the curator of the Gardens, by Firma C. Esveld. It is a modest, upright bush, growing to 2.5 m when mature. It has the same habit as 'Red Pygmy'. The leaves are 5-lobed with linear lobes, orange-crimson when unfolding, becoming orange-green almost immediately. In summer the leaves are of a good green and the autumn color is a beautiful golden yellow. The only element differing from 'Red Pygmy' is the coloring of the leaves (Plate 181). It is a very fine plant, and occasionally available in the trade. It is hard to propagate—for unknown reasons grafting results are always much poorer than with similar cultivars. Whether the mother plant is still alive is unknown, as it was in poor condition in 1967. Zone VI. (Group 5a)

**'Viride'**, see **'Dissectum'**

**'Volubile'.** Schwerin (1893). Germany. JDV I, 62; JDV II, 68, photo. An upright cultivar, forming trees to 5–6 m in height, very often multiple-stemmed. The leaves are 7-lobed, small, and regularly divided, each lobe with a narrow point. The bright green young leaves fade somewhat in color during the summer. The autumn tints are quite attractively orange and red. 'Aoyagi' is quite similar, but 'Aoyagi' adds its bright green twigs to its beauty. 'Volubile' is not distinctive in winter. It is a rare cultivar. (Group 1a)

**'Wabibito'**, see **'Wabito'**

**'Wabito'.** Chikinsho (1710). Yokohama Nurseries (1898). Japan. JDV I, 131; JDV II, 139, photo. A cultivar with very unusual leaves that make it difficult to place in any group. The leaves are 4–5 cm long and wide. The lobes are narrow and irregularly incised, dark green in summer and golden yellow in the autumn. It can grow into a fairly large shrub, to 3 m, but often remains much smaller. Traces of variegation are to be seen occasionally, but even the best-grown plants have no more than a touch of variegation at the margins. The name means "lonely man" or "lonely person." It has been known in Japanese horticulture for several hundred years. Sometimes available. (Group 7)

**'Waka momiji'.** Bergman (1969). Pennsylvania, USA. Reported to have pink and cream variegations. No further description. Probably identical with the following cultivar and belonging to the 'Versicolor' category. (Group 1c)

**'Waka momiji Variegated'.** JDV I, 118; JDV II, 126. This is an illegitimate name. The plant belongs to the 'Versicolor' category and grows into a treelike shrub of about 6 m. Probably identical with the preceding.

**'Wakehurst Pink'.** Wakehurst Place (1988). Great Britain. An openly branched shrub growing to 4 m in height and width. Leaves 7-lobed, lobes rather narrow; green with pinkish undertones in spring. Mature leaves have large pink blotches and "flames" all over. The original plant is growing in Wakehurst Place Gardens and was/is incorrectly labeled 'Roseo-marginatum'. Named and introduced in 1988 by Firma C. Esveld, Boskoop, The Netherlands. Zone VI. (Group 2c)

**'Washi no o'**, see **'Dissectum Palmatifidum'**

**'Waterfall'.** Kingsville Nurseries (H. Hohman) (1920). Maryland, USA. JDV I, 74; JDV II, 80, photo. A US introduction, very much like the Dutch 'Dissectum' and despite observation since the 1970s it is still uncertain as to whether they are identical or not. The leaves cannot be distinguished as they are of exactly the same shape and color in both summer and autumn; even the underlying tints are very much the same. Young plants seem to have a slightly more cascading character, but here also the difference is minor. We have the strong impression that this cultivar is nothing but 'Dissectum' rebaptized, a selection in cultivation for well over 120 years in The Netherlands. Now available in Europe and popular in the United States under the more sales appealing name 'Waterfall'. (Group 4a)

**'Watnong'.** Fincham (1991). Aurora, Oregon, USA. A cascading shrub with bright salmon-red foliage. (Group 4b)

**'Whitney Red'.** Whitney (1980). Oregon, USA. Another purple-leaved shrub; found in a batch of seedlings. The leaves are 7-lobed and rather large. (Group 2b)

**'Willow Leaf'.** Iseli Nursery (1991). Boring, Oregon, USA. A small, graceful shrub, to 3 m in height. Leaves dark purplish red, with narrow lobes, not unlike those of 'Red Pygmy'. Not yet introduced into Europe. (Group 5b)

**'Wilson's Pink Dwarf'.** Wilson (1980). California, USA. JDV II, 108, photo. A beautiful shrub of moderate size. The leaves are palmately 5-lobed, bright green in summer. In the spring the leaves unfold light pink to pinkish red. It is only very rarely available. (Group 6)

**'Wou nishiki'.** Mulligan (1958). Washington, USA. JDV I, 88; JDV II, 94, photo. This interesting cultivar bears leaves with 5–7 deeply divided and widely separated lobes. The color is green with margins tinted pink or brown-red, shading into the leaf. In summer these colors disappear and the leaf becomes bright green. Autumn colors are crimson to scarlet. An attractive, heavily branched upright shrub, to 3–4 m. Its leaf shape is rather peculiar, which makes it an attractive plant. Sometimes available. (Group 3a)

**'Yamamoto nishiki'**, see **'Sagara nishiki'**

**'Yamato nishiki'**, see **'Nishiki gasane'**

**'Yasemin'.** Esveld (1989). Boskoop, The Netherlands. Rather strong-growing, upright, shrubby tree, to 8–10 m tall. The leaves are large, 7- to 9-lobed, each lobe deeply incised and slightly dissected. The leaves have the general appearance of *A. japonicum* 'Aconitifolium', but of a dark purple, shining color (Plate 182). This combination of leaf color and shape is unique among the cultivars of *A. palmatum.* It has been selected from a large batch of open-pollinated seedlings, where all kinds of expressions occurred. It seems to have influence from nearby trees, like 'Bloodgood' for its color, 'Trompenburg' for its habit, and *A. japonicum* 'Aconitifolium' for its leaf shape. It is to be introduced to the trade in 1993. Named after Mirte Yasemin van Gelderen, granddaughter of the author. (Group 3b)

**Yatsubusa.** JDV I, 102; JDV II, 108, photo. This word means "dwarf" in Japanese and has been attached to several cultivars. The name should not be used as a cultivar name. A general description of Yatsubusa plants is given in Vertrees' *Japanese Maples.*

**'Yezo nishiki'.** JDV I, 62; JDV II, 68, photo. A good purple-leaved cultivar, which holds its color well in summer. The habit is broad-upright, about as high as wide, 4–5 m. The leaves are 7-lobed, 6–8 cm across, and of firm texture. The color is somewhat glistening and in autumn changes to a good scarlet. It is recommended for its superb habit, suitable for small gardens. Well-known old cultivar, present in several collections. (Group 2b)

**'Yoen'**, see **'Kagero'**

**'Yubae'.** Vertrees (1970). Roseburg, Oregon, USA. JDV I, 132; JDV II, 140, photo. A dark, purple-leaved, sturdy *A. palmatum,* to 5–6 m but with crimson-red variegations. Unfortunately, these variegations are not constant and they fully disappear in older plants. Vigorously growing plants show very little or no variegation. It is a beautiful plant bearing large dark purple leaves, partly 7-lobed. The name means "evening glow." Even without variegations it is a useful and attractive plant. (Group 2c)

**'Yugure'.** Koidzumi (1911). Japan. Chikinsho (1719); JDV I, 88; JDV II, 94, photo. A strong, upright shrub, to 5–6 m. Its leaves are 7-lobed and the lobe margins are finely serrate. The color is a good purple in the spring, soon becoming bronze-green. Its autumn color is the usual scarlet-crimson. A good plant in spring but not distinctive in summer. There is also some confusion in the material in Japan, due to incorrect labeling. The name means "twilight." Occasionally available in Europe. Zone VI. (Group 3b)

**'Yu jishi'**, see **'O jishi'**

**'Yuri hime'.** JDV II, 108. One of the most dwarfed

cultivars. The leaves are tightly packed together and light green, with little autumn color. Difficult to propagate, it is a rare plant and difficult to find in the trade. A gem for the rock garden. Zone VI. (Group 6)

**'Yushide'**, see **'Momenshide'**

## ACER PECTINATUM ssp. FORRESTII

**'Alice'.** Esveld (1981). Boskoop, The Netherlands. Shrub of moderate size, not exceeding 5–6 m in height and about the same width. Leaves 3-lobed, apices acuminate but less marked than in subspecies *forrestii,* 8–15 cm long and 4–7 cm wide, glossy, dark brown-green when young, somewhat rugose. In summer the mature leaves show a heavy pink variegation, which gives an elegant impression (Plate 183). Propagated and introduced by Firma C. Esveld, having been discovered as a chance seedling in a batch of seedlings of *A. pectinatum* ssp. *forrestii* collected in the Westonbirt Arboretum, Tetbury, Great Britain. Propagation by grafting on seedlings of any species of section *Macrantha.* Named after the late Mrs. Alice van Tright. 'Alice' was granted an Award of Merit by the Royal Boskoop Horticultural Society, named as *A. forrestii* 'Alice'. Available in the trade. Zone VI.

**'Sirene'.** Esveld (1988). The Netherlands. Shrub of moderate size, rather openly branched, to 6–7 m. The bark is reddish purple with rather inconspicuous white stripes. Leaves bold, 3-lobed, central lobes with longer apices but not tapered, 10–18 cm long, 4–8 cm wide, glossy, dark greenish purple when young, very dark green when mature. Autumn color reddish orange. Discovered in a seedbed of *A. pectinatum* ssp. *forrestii* from seed collected in the Esveld Aceretum. This cultivar is rather close to subspecies *forrestii* but is much darker in color in all respects. Propagated by grafting on any seedling of section *Macrantha.* Available in the trade. Zone VI.

**'Sparkling'.** Esveld (1989). Boskoop, The Netherlands. A more or less fastigiate tree to 8 m high and only 2–3 m wide. The leaves are fresh green and the central lobes much longer than the 2 outer ones (Plate 184). The fiery red petioles are a conspicuous feature. The contrast of leaf and petiole is striking and quite unusual for this species. Discovered in a batch of seedlings labeled *A. pectinatum* ssp. *forrestii.* Named after 15 years of observation on behalf of John Ravenscroft, Bridgemere Nurseries, Great Britain. Available in the trade. Zone VI.

## ACER PECTINATUM ssp. PECTINATUM

**'Rubrum'.** Dickson, Upton Nurseries (1880). Chester, Great Britain. Without description. Apparently no longer in cultivation.

## ACER PENSYLVANICUM

This maple has only a few cultivars, being remarkably uniform in its progeny. All cultivars are hardy in zone IV except for 'Erythrocladum'.

**'Albo-variegatum'.** Schwerin (1901). Germany. Leaves variegated white. It is quite uncertain whether this clone is still in cultivation. One can more or less regularly discover seedlings with white-variegated leaves in seed beds.

**'Aureo-marginatum'.** Schwerin (1901). Germany. Leaves variegated yellow. Probably no longer in cultivation, seedlings with yellow variegations are much scarcer than those with white.

**'Erythrocladum'.** Späth (1904). Berlin, Germany. Slow-growing small tree to 5–6 m with a very conspicuous salmon-red bark during the winter, especially on young wood. In summer this color disappears, turning to a dull greenish white. The leaves are smaller than those of the species, but similarly shaped. Difficult to propagate, even when grafted on seedling *A. pensylvanicum.* Occasionally available in the trade. Zone VI.

**'Select'.** Van der Bom (1969). The Netherlands. A medium-sized tree to 12 m. The leaves do not differ from *A. pensylvanicum.* The bark is conspicuously striped. Autumn color is brilliant golden yellow until late in the season. A strong-growing selection, easily cultivated. Must be propagated by budding or grafting on seedlings. A fine selection for street planting. Available in the trade in Europe.

## ACER PLATANOIDES

The Norway maple is a fairly uniform species, with one subspecies, the former *Acer turkestanicum.* During the 19th century many slightly different types were described as formae or even varieties, as was done with several other species such as *A. campestre, A. pseudoplatanus,* and *A. negundo.* These "cultivated varieties" have been sunk into synonymy or reduced to cultivar status. Many of the old cultivars are no longer grown or propagated. The cultivars are generally hardy in zones IV–V. After World War II a number of North American selections of the Norway maple were introduced, mainly selected for height, habit, and the form of their crowns. The other important goal was to obtain trees for street planting, able to withstand the unfavorable conditions that invariably occur in cities. E. H. Scanlon introduced a range of new selections, several of which are now propagated and cultivated on a large scale in both North America and Europe. They are commonly called Scanlon Tailored Trees.

Full bibliographic notes and descriptions may be found in the *Checklist of Cultivated Maples* III, *Acer platanoides,* compiled by Frank S. Santamour and A. Jacot McArdle (1982).

**'Acuminatum'.** Schwerin (1893). Germany. The leaf lobes of this tree are narrowly acuminate. Not available in the trade.

**'Adspermum'.** Schwerin (1893). Germany. This tree has larger leaves than the species. It is an indifferent cultivar.

**'Alberta Park'.** Ferrucci Nurseries (1990). New Jersey, USA. This is a large tree, a vigorous straight grower with a wide crown. Leaves of firm texture, somewhat leathery. The name is trademarked in the United States.

**'Albescens'.** Dieck (1885). Germany. The leaves of this old cultivar are creamy white at first, later turning reddish. As far as is known, it is no longer in cultivation.

**'Albo-dentatum'**, see **'Albo-marginatum'**

**'Albo-marginatum'.** Schwerin in Wesmael (1890). Germany. No description. Obviously bears white-variegated leaves, certainly not unlike 'Drummondii'. Probably not in cultivation.

**'Albo-mediatum'.** Schwerin (1890). Germany. No description. Probably not in cultivation.

**'Albo-variegatum'**, see **'Variegatum'**

**'Albo-variegatum Multicolor'**, see **'Multicolor'**

**'Albo-variegatum Quadricolor'**, see **'Quadricolor'**

**'Almira'.** Scanlon (1955). Ohio, USA. A dwarfish, flat-topped tree, growing to 5–6 m in height in 30 years. It was first discovered on a street in Cleveland, Ohio. The leaves are shining green. It grows slightly larger than the well-known 'Globosum'. It is a suitable tree for large containers and can be used where it is not possible to plant it in the soil. It is advisable to bud at soil level when propagating. The young shoots grow vigorously and after 2 years the crown can be formed. The name is trademarked in the United States, The Netherlands, and Belgium. It is available in the trade.

**'Argenteo-variegatum'**, see **'Variegatum'**

**'Argutum'.** Schwerin (1893). Germany. Leaf margins revolute. No longer known in cultivation.

**'Ascendens'**, see **'Erectum'**

**'Atropurpureum'**, see **'Schwedleri'**

**'Atropurpureum Globosum'**, see **'Faassen's Black'**

**'Aureo-marginatum'.** Milford (1874). Leaf margins yellow. This cultivar is probably no longer in cultivation.

**'Aureo-variegatum'**, see **'Flavo-variegatum'**

**'Bentleaf'.** Kelsey & Dayton (1942). USA. See **'Laciniatum'.**

**'Bicolor'.** Schwerin (1893). Germany. Leaves dotted with yellow spots, later turning to white. Apparently no longer in cultivation.

**'Bloodleaf'**, Kelsey & Dayton (1942). USA. See **'Reitenbachii'.**

**'Brevilobum'.** Schwerin (1896). Germany. Leaf lobes shallow. Hardly differs from the species.

**'Buntzelli'**, see **'Buntzleri'**

**'Buntzleri'.** Wittmarck (1880). Germany. Leaves reddish brown, flecked with orange, turning to golden yellow. Named after Max Buntzel, but originally described as 'Buntzleri'. Probably no longer in cultivation.

**'Cavalier'.** Scanlon (1969). Ohio, USA. Street tree of moderate size, about 10–12 m high in 40 years. The crown is round and compact. The leaves are of the same shape and size as the species. This is a good cultivar that deserves attention. US Plant Patent 2973 (1970). Not yet readily available in Europe, it is being propagated in a few Dutch nurseries. The name is trademarked in the United States, The Netherlands, and Belgium.

**'Charles Joly'.** Origin unknown (before 1990). The Netherlands(?). A weeping tree, branches pendent, horizontally. Leaves purplish red, somewhat more incised than the normal shape of the species. This newly introduced cultivar seems to be the weeping counterpart of 'Crimson King' and comparable clones. It was not possible to trace its origin, and it reached The Netherlands under several names such as 'Red Weeping Norway Maple' and also under the obviously misspelled name 'Karel Sjolivette'. Present in the Esveld Aceretum, Boskoop.

**'Chas. F. Irish'.** Scanlon (1951). Ohio, USA. A good tree with a somewhat open, round crown, with upswept branches to 15–20 m high. The leaves are of the usual form and color, hardly distinguishable from the species itself. It is named after

Charles F. Irish of Cleveland, Ohio. 'Irish' or 'Charles F. Irish' have been incorrectly used as the name of this cultivar. It is a well-known cultivar, available in both America and Europe. As it is one of the largest trees among cultivars of this species, it is suitable only for broad streets and boulevards. The name is trademarked in the United States, Belgium, and The Netherlands.

**'Clausum'.** Schwerin (1890). Germany. Lacks any description. Probably not in cultivation.

**'Cleveland'.** Scanlon (1948). Ohio, USA. A tree of moderate size, with an oval-shaped crown to 10–12 m high. The lateral branches are upswept. The leaves are bright green, of the same shape as the species. The young leaves are marbled with red. The main trunk is quite strong, and a good crown is built up with very little pruning. It is a valuable street tree, especially for somewhat narrower streets and smaller parks. Widely planted and cultivated in many towns and cities in America, and also to a lesser extent in Europe.

**'Cleveland Two'.** Scanlon (1973). Ohio, USA. This cultivar has a compact, dense crown and can be considered an improvement upon the original 'Cleveland'. It is also more conical and narrow. Recently introduced into Europe. The name is trademarked in United States, The Netherlands, and Belgium.

**'Coloratum'**, see **'Quadricolor'**

**'Column'**, see **'Columnare'**

**'Columnarbroad'.** J. Frank Schmidt & Son. Boring, Oregon, USA. A broader form of 'Columnare' traded under the name 'Parkway'. It is a fast-growing tree with a strong central leader and dense foliage, like the foliage of the species, turning to golden yellow in autumn. It branches well. Because of its pyramidal to oval shape, it is one of the best trees for street planting. Available in both the United States and Europe.

**'Columnare'.** Carrière (1878). France. A tree of fastigiate habit if grafted on a standard, but a multistemmed, fastigiate–columnar shrub 15–20 m high when grafted at soil level. The leaves are of the usual shape and size and are dark green. It is rather uncommon and only occasionally available. It deserves more attention, as there is always a need for columnar trees and shrubs.

**'Commune'.** Pax (1886). Germany. Leaf bases openly cordate. Probably not in cultivation.

**'Compactum'**, see **'Globosum'**

**'Crimped'.** Kelsey & Dayton (1942). USA. See **'Cucullatum'.**

**'Crimson King'.** Barbier & Co. (1937). France. Gulfstream Nursery Co. (1948). Virginia, USA. An excellent, purple- to red-leaved tree, quite common and generally available. It is of moderate size and has a regular, slightly oval habit. Mature trees of 25–30 years reach a height of about 12–15 m. The leaves are of a splendid crimson red when young, turning to dark purple when mature (Plate 185). The color is retained very well, but there is not much autumn color. The leaves are of the same shape and size as the species, somewhat less flat. The tree is valuable for its splendid flowerings, just before new leaves unfold. The original seedling was selected in 1937 in the nursery of Tips Brothers, Herck-de Stad, Belgium, together with many others. One of these, 'Faassen's Black', also well known, was growing in the same seed bed. 'Crimson King' was selected by Barbier & Co., a nursery in Orléans, France. It was introduced by Gulfstream Nursery Co., Wachapreague, Virginia, and the name was trademarked in 1947. This tree is the best of all red-leaved Norway maples.

**'Crimson Sentry'.** McGill & Son (1974). Fairview, Oregon, USA. This cultivar is a striking selection that originated as a sport of 'Crimson King'. It is smaller in every respect, profusely branched, and fastigiate of habit, not exceeding 8–10 m. The leaves are much smaller than those of 'Crimson King' but of the same shape and color. It is hard to transplant bareroot (when leaves are unfolding). It is a valuable addition to the range of trees particularly suitable for smaller gardens. US Plant Patent 3258 (1975). Not yet widely available.

**'Crimson Sunburst'**, see **'Faassen's Black'**

**'Crispum'.** Lauth (1781). Germany. Leaf margins crisped. Lost from cultivation.

**'Cucullatum'.** Carrière (1866). France. Leaves heavily crimped, the lobes lying on each other. Occasionally seen in collections and only very rarely available. This tree of about 10 m in height is not particularly beautiful, but it is peculiar and interesting.

**'Cultriforme'**, see *A. tataricum* cultivars

**'Cuneatum'.** Pax (1886). Germany. Leaf bases cuneate, margins crisped. Apparently no longer in cultivation.

**'Cuprescens'.** Wesmael (1890). Belgium. Lacks any description, but most probably with coppery leaves. Probably not in cultivation.

**'Cutleaf'.** Kelsey & Dayton (1942). USA. See **'Palmatifidum'.**

**'Deborah'.** Cannor Nurseries (1975). British Columbia, Canada. An upright tree with a rather heavy habit, to 15 m. The leaves are bright purple-red when young, later turning to green; the autumn color is attractively orange-yellow. It is not unlike 'Schwedleri' and in fact was selected from seedlings of that cultivar. 'Deborah' was found by J. Mathies and was registered in 1975 (Canadian Ornamental Plant Foundation). It is now also available in Europe. US Plant Patent 4944.

**'Decussatum'.** Van Houtte (1873). Belgium. Three-lobed, cruciform leaves. Lost from cultivation.

**'Dieckii'**, see *A.* × *dieckii* (Chapter 8)

**'Digitatum'**, see **'Palmatifidum'**

**'Digitatum Aureo-marginatum'**, see **'Aureo-marginatum'**

**'Dilaceratum'.** Dieck (1885). Germany. This small tree of 4–5 m in height has deformed, wrinkled leaves, each with a small, yellowish blotch, and with green shoots. It is extremely rare but can be seen in the garden of Castle Hulboka, where Alfred Rehder's father was head-gardener, near Brno, Slovakia. It will eventually be available in the trade as it has recently been reintroduced to The Netherlands.

**'Dilatilobum'.** Opiz (1852). Germany. Lacks a description. Probably not in cultivation.

**'Dissectum'.** Spach (1834). Germany. Deeply dissected leaves, opening brown-red, later turning to green. Possibly still in cultivation in some old gardens but quite rare.

**'Drummondii'.** Schwerin (1910). Germany. A tree of moderate size, 10–12 m high, with a rather broadly shaped crown (Plate 186). The leaves are of the same form and shape as the species and are very conspicuously variegated, with broad, creamy white margins, yellow when young. Occasionally, green shoots are produced that must be removed as soon as possible. This tree was released by Messrs. Drummond of Stirling, Great Britain, but without description. It is a beautiful tree, suitable for smaller gardens as well as larger ones. It is widely available in the trade.

**'Eagle Claw'.** Kelsey & Dayton (1942). USA. See **'Laciniatum'.**

**'Emerald Lustre'**, see **'Pond'**

**'Emerald Queen'.** McGill & Son (1963). Fairview, Oregon, USA. This tree is among the best cultivars for general use in parks, larger gardens, and streets. It is strongly growing, with a regular, densely branched crown, up to 15 m in height or more. The leaf shape is like that of the species but somewhat more "leathery." The young, unfolding leaves are pinkish. The autumn color is a good yellow. It was selected in 1959 by John McIntyre of Oregon and introduced by McGill. It is generally available in both North America and Europe.

**'Erectum'.** Slavin (1931). New York, USA. A pyramidal tree with short and stout lateral branches up to 12–15 m in height. Leaf shape as in the species, sometimes slightly smaller, bright green. Discovered by B. H. Slavin in a cemetery in Rochester, New York. It is still in cultivation on a limited scale.

**'Eurostar'.** Research Station De Dorschkamp, Wageningen (1990). The Netherlands. This large tree, up to 20 m tall with a central leader, makes a very good street tree. It is comparable to 'Emerald Queen', but its leaves are larger and the growth of this cultivar is faster. Fall color is golden yellow. It flowers very freely in April and is very attractive to bees. This new cultivar will be released in the near future. The name is trademarked and patented in The Netherlands.

**'Faassen's Black'.** Faassen-Hekkens (1946). Tegelen, The Netherlands. The origin of this tree is the same as 'Crimson King'. It was selected about 1937 and introduced after World War II. It differs from 'Crimson King' in the duller leaf surface and somewhat darker summer color but is identical in all other characteristics. It is difficult to say which one is the "better." It is in general cultivation and widely available.

**'Farlake's Green'.** Vermeer & Sons (1983). Opheusden, The Netherlands. This recently named selection has been in cultivation for several years. It has sturdy, green leaves of the same size as those of the species and is 18–20 m tall. Its characteristics fall between such well-known cultivars as 'Emerald Queen' and 'Summershade'. It was discovered and introduced by Messrs. G. Vermeer & Sons Nurseries. "Farlake" is a literal translation of the name Vermeer.

**'Flavo-variegatum'.** Hayne (1822). With yellow-variegated leaves. Probably lost from cultivation.

**'Geneva'.** Olmsted, Coville and Kelsey (1923). USA. Leaf lobes shallow, purple in the autumn. It is not available in the trade and is probably lost from cultivation.

**'Globe'.** Kelsey & Dayton (1942). USA. See **'Globosum'.**

**'Globosum'.** Van Houtte (1873). Belgium. A very well-known tree with a flat-topped crown, densely branched and globular. The crown develops this form with almost no pruning. A 25- to 30-year-old tree usually has a crown at least 3 m in diameter. The leaves are slightly smaller than usual, and young leaves are attractively olive green. It is propagated by budding on standards of *A. platanoides*. Generally available, it is widely planted in small gardens, shopping centers, and small parks.

**'Globosum Atropurpureum'**, see **'Faassen's Black'**

**'Goldsworth Crimson'**, see **'Goldsworth Purple'**

**'Goldsworth Purple'.** Slocock (1947). Great Britain. A moderately sized tree of 12–15 m in height with a spreading and somewhat irregular crown. The leaves are purplish red during the spring and summer, becoming duller in late summer. There are traces of a good autumn color after a dry summer. The original plant was presented to Wisley Gardens around 1937 by an unknown lady and introduced into the trade by W. C. Slocock Ltd. It is no longer widely available, as both 'Crimson King' and 'Royal Red' are better.

**'Greenlace'.** J. Frank Schmidt & Son (1968). Boring, Oregon, USA. A newly introduced form with dissected leaves, slightly different from those of 'Dissectum', 'Palmatifidum', and comparable cultivars. It was selected as a seedling and grows into a moderately sized tree of 10–12 m in height. US Plant Patent 2759 (1967).

**'Harlequin'**, see **'Drummondii'**

**'Heterophyllum Aureo-variegatum'.** Baudriller (1880). France. An old cultivar, still present in a few European collections. It is a small tree with a broadly columnar habit. The leaves are rather small, slightly deformed, and often only 3-lobed, with irregular yellow margins. It is no longer available in the trade.

**'Heterophyllum Variegatum'**, see **'Aureo-variegatum'**

**'Improved Columnar'**, see **'Olmsted'**

**'Incumbens'**, see **'Undulatum'**

**'Irregulare'.** Schwerin (1893). Germany. The leaves are often deformed. Lost from cultivation.

**'Jade Glen'.** J. Frank Schmidt & Son (1970). Boring, Oregon, USA. A fast-growing tree with a broad and more open crown than the usual Norway maple. The tree attains a height of about 15 m and can grow as wide. Fall color is yellow.

**'Jouinii'.** Schwerin (1910). Germany. The leaves have golden flecks. Probably no longer in cultivation.

**'Karel Sjolivetti'**, see **'Charles Joly'**

**'Laciniatum'.** Sutherland (1683). Great Britain. Leaves deeply cut, like a bird's claw. It is a small tree, 10–12 m tall. Although long in cultivation, it is rarely available.

**'Laciniosum'**, see **'Laciniatum'**

**'Lactescens'**, see ***A. platanoides***

**'Laetum'**, see ***A. platanoides*** and ***A. cappadocicum***

**'Latifolium'.** Dieck (1885). Germany. Tree of the usual shape, with very large leaves. Probably not in cultivation.

**'Lorbergii'**, see **'Palmatifidum'**

**'Lutescens'.** Schwerin (1890). Wesmael, Germany. Lacks a description; probably with yellowish leaves. Apparently not in cultivation.

**'Maculatum'.** Nicholson (1881). Great Britain. A plant purchased from Great Britain several years ago developed into a small tree of 8–10 m in height, rather sparsely branched. Leaves are the usual size for the species, but the basal lobes are occasionally very small or absent. The leaves are heavily blotched cream and yellow in spring, turning to light green. Good autumn color with yellow and orange tones. Flowers very freely but produces few viable seeds. Available in The Netherlands, and possibly still in Great Britain.

**'Marginatum Album'.** Simon Louis Frères (1900). France. The leaf margins are dotted with white. Lost from cultivation.

**'Meyering'.** Grootendorst (1969). Boskoop, The Netherlands. A medium-sized tree of 12–15 m in height with leaves of the usual shape and size. They are light bronze-red in spring, turning green during the summer, and showing very attractive autumn colors, orange-red to dark red. This cultivar originated in a Dutch nursery about 1958 and was named after J. Meyering, who discovered it in a batch of seedlings. It is available in Europe. It closely resembles 'Reitenbachii'.

**'Microphyllum'.** Ringstrand (1845). Great Britain. With smaller leaves than usual. Introduced by Rodger McClelland & Co., Great Britain. It is uncertain as to whether or not it is still available.

**'Miller's'**, see **'Superform'**

**'Miller's Superform'**, see **'Superform'**

**'Monstrosum'.** Schwerin (1890). Germany. Lacks a description. Apparently not in cultivation.

**'Multicolor'.** Schwerin (1896). Germany. According to Schwerin this is a sport of 'Reitenbachii' or 'Schwedleri'. It is of the same habit and with light-pink-variegated leaves, later becoming gray-rose. It is no longer available.

**'Nanum'**, see **'Pyramidale Nanum'**

**'Nanum Pyramidale'**, see **'Pyramidale Nanum'**

**'Natorp'.** Mulligan (1958). Washington, USA. A sport of 'Schwedleri' with a dwarfish habit; quite small-leaved. It is grown in the Arnold Arboretum, Jamaica Plain, Massachusetts, and the Morris Arboretum, Philadelphia, Pennsylvania, both in the United States. It has been abandoned by Natorp Corp., Cincinnati, Ohio, USA, due to its weak and slow growth.

**'Nigrum',** see **'Reitenbachii'**

**'Occulatum'.** Lawson Nursery Co. (1874). USA. Lacks a description. Probably not in cultivation.

**'Oekonomierat Stoll'.** Späth (1888). Berlin, Germany. This small tree of 6–8 m in height has almost 3-lobed leaves of a rather attractive color. It is a seedling of 'Schwedleri' and is also known as 'Stollii'. Available from time to time in the trade.

**'Olmsted'.** Scanlon (1955). Ohio, USA. A good, pyramidal tree, to 15–18 m in height, narrower than 'Cleveland' and comparable cultivars. The leaves are like those of the species or slightly smaller. The tree grows to about 10 m in 20 years' time. The original tree was discovered in Rochester, New York, USA, but named for Olmsted, Ohio, USA. It is now in general cultivation and is a handsome and useful tree for streets and squares, shopping centers, and small gardens. The name is trademarked in the United States, The Netherlands, and Belgium.

**'Oregon Pride'.** Pacific Coast Nurseries (1979). Oregon, USA. This highly interesting introduction has very deeply cut leaves, not unlike those of the old *A. platanoides* 'Dissectum' or 'Palmatifidum'. It is not yet available in Europe.

**'Palmatifidum'.** Tausch (1829). Germany. Tree of moderate size, 12–15 m in height, rather heavily branched. Leaves dissected to the bases, lobes slightly overlapping each other. It is often incorrectly labeled as 'Lorbergii'. It is an attractive and interesting cultivar that deserves more attention. It is available in the trade.

**'Palmatum',** see **'Dissectum'**

**'Parkway',** see **'Columnarbroad'**

**'Pendulum'.** Niemetz (1900). Germany. Tree with pendant branches and leaves of the normal shape and size. Originated in Timisoara, Romania. It is no longer propagated and is not available in the trade.

**'Pictum'.** Hesse (1892). Germany. Leaves dotted rose and white. Lost from cultivation.

**'Plenum'.** Schwerin (1901). Germany. Lacks a description. Probably not in cultivation.

**'Plicatum'.** Schwerin (1893). Germany. The leaf lobes apparently look like a fan but there is no further description. Probably not in cultivation.

**'Pond'.** J. Frank Schmidt & Son (1970). Boring, Oregon, USA. A vigorous growing tree, up to 15 m tall. It tends to branch out heavily as a young tree in the nursery. The shape of the crown is rounded and spreading. Leaves are medium green, and fall color is yellow, as is usual for Norway maple. In mountainous and cold regions, it is red. This cultivar is usually traded under the name 'Emerald Lustre', but its cultivar name is 'Pond'. It is trademarked in the USA.

**'Pseudotruncatum'.** Pax (1886). Germany. Leaf bases subtruncate. Probably not in cultivation.

**'Pubescens'.** Guinpel & Hayne (1820). Great Britain. Leaves pubescent beneath. Probably not in cultivation.

**'Pueckleri',** see **'Reichsgraf von Pueckler'**

**'Purple Heart'.** Scanlon (1951). Ohio, USA. One of the many red-leaved clones that stay colored throughout the growing season. Not generally available. Cultivars such as 'Crimson King' and 'Royal Red' are preferable.

**'Purpurascens',** see **'Schwedleri'**

**'Purpureum'.** Nicholson (1881). Great Britain. An old cultivar with dull red leaves in the spring, much like those of 'Reitenbachii'. It was propagated by Messrs. Van Houtte in Ghent, Belgium, at the beginning of the 20th century, but dropped in favor of 'Reitenbachii'.

**'Pygmaeum'.** Schwerin. Germany (1893). A very slow-growing form of shrubby appearance. The leaves are only 3–6 cm across and the yearly growth is hardly more than 10 cm. It is most probably no longer in cultivation. The dwarf form 'Pyramidale Nanum' is faster-growing and much better known.

**'Pyramidale',** see **'Pyramidale Nanum'**

**'Pyramidale Nanum'.** Van Houtte (1877). Belgium. A slow-growing, pyramidal, shrubby tree, to 4–5 m in height in 20 years (Plate 187). The internodes are short and old plants grow very slowly. The leaves, on very short side branches, are much smaller than in the species but of the same shape. Young plants grow rather quickly during the first 5 years. Sometimes rather long shoots, which should be removed, appear on fairly young plants. If not removed, short lateral branches reappear on these branches the following year. A very valuable little tree and occasionally available in the trade, often listed as 'Nanum'.

**'Quadricolor'.** Dieck (1885). Germany. Leaves with pink spots, later turning to white. Apparently no longer in cultivation.

**'Recurvum'.** Reinecke (1900). Germany. Tree, samaras recurved; no further description. Apparently no longer in cultivation.

**'Reichenbachii'**, see **'Reitenbachii'**

**'Reichsgraf von Pueckler'.** Schwerin (1893). Germany. A small tree with leaves maculated white, later turning to mottled pink, brown, and purple. Originated at Späth's nurseries in Berlin about 1885. It is usually called 'Pueckleri'. It is very rarely found in the trade.

**'Reitenbachii'.** Caspary (1874). Germany. Tree of average size, to 15 m in height, young leaves crimson to brown-red, later turning to dark green with the veins somewhat crimson. The seedling originated in the nursery of J. Reitenbach in Plicken, Russia, and was named by J. R. Caspary. It was introduced by L. Van Houtte, Ghent, Belgium, about 1880. Some exceptionally fine trees can be seen on the Esplanade in Helsinki, Finland. An attractive tree, but not distinctive, having been surpassed by 'Schwedleri'.

**'Rochester'**, see **'Olmsted'**

**'Roseo-bullatum'.** Schwerin (1893). Germany. With leaves that are rosy bullate. Lost from cultivation.

**'Royal Crimson'.** Scanlon (1967). Ohio, USA. A recently introduced red-leaved cultivar of controversial origin. It is considered to be a "selection," or better, a sport, from 'Crimson King', but with a better red color in the summer. Also, however, it is said to be a sport of 'Goldsworth Purple'. It is not possible to decide which origin is correct. Not in cultivation in Europe.

**'Royal Red'.** Pacific Coast Nursery (1963). Oregon, USA. A perfect tree of 15–20 m in height, with rich crimson-red and glossy leaves, staying dark red until autumn. The shape and color of the leaves are practically indistinguishable from those of 'Crimson King', at least in the coastal countries of western Europe. In North America, however, it tends to keep its color better than 'Crimson King', due to the very different climatic conditions. (See *A. palmatum* 'Burgundy Lace', compared with *A. palmatum* 'Sherwood Flame'.) It is in general cultivation and readily available.

**'Rubrum'.** Von Regel (1867). Russia. An old Russian clone from St. Petersburg, having green leaves that become redder in summer, which is an interesting feature, not often reported. As far as is known, this cultivar is no longer in cultivation.

**'Rufescens'.** Schwerin (1893). Germany. The leaves are red-brown when opening, turning green when mature. Not in cultivation.

**'Sanguineum'.** Schwerin (1910). Germany. The autumn color is crimson red. Probably no longer in cultivation.

**'Scanlon Gold'.** Scanlon (1976). Ohio, USA. A tree of average size (12–15 m), with fresh green leaves of the usual shape and size. Its autumn color is a conspicuous golden yellow. This tree was named by Hillier & Sons, Ampfield, Great Britain, in honor of E. H. Scanlon. It is still quite scarce in the trade.

**'Schwedleri'.** Koch (1869). Germany. A superb, distinctive tree, beginning with the spring unfolding of its purplish yellow flowers, after which its purple-red leaves appear, later turning to a purple-veined green. In autumn the leaves again turn to a purple tone. It is a rather large tree, 20–22 m, slightly larger than most cultivars of the species. It is still in general cultivation and is preferred by those who do not like the dark tones of 'Crimson King' or 'Royal Red'. Old trees can be seen in many European cities, used as street trees and also as shade trees in squares or along lake borders, such as Lago Maggiore or Lake Geneva.

**'Schwedleri Nigrum'**, see **'Crimson King'**

**'Sorbergii'**, see **'Palmatifidum'**

**'Stand Fast'.** Spongberg (1981). Massachusetts, USA. A dwarf tree which at 50 years is only about 80 cm high and 50 cm wide, with a trunk diameter of about 3 cm. This particular little tree was discovered in 1932 by Elsie Grant Lundquist of Kennett Square, Pennsylvania, USA. Longwood Gardens in that city intends to propagate this miniature cultivar. It is as yet uncertain that the dwarf characteristics will be retained in vegetatively propagated plants. Not yet available. Spongberg internationally registered this clone in 1985.

**'Stollii'**, see **'Oekonomierat Stoll'**

**'Summershade'.** Princeton Nurseries (1958). New Jersey, USA. A valuable columnar tree of rapid and upright growth, to 20 m tall, highly esteemed by landscapers. The leaves are large, somewhat leathery, and heat-resistant. It was selected as a seedling from open-pollinated *A. platanoides* 'Erectum'. US Plant Patent 1748 (1958). Generally available in the trade and useful as a street tree.

**'Superform'.** J. Frank Schmidt & Son (1968). Boring, Oregon, USA. A fast-growing tree with a straight trunk, 20–22 m high, quite similar to 'Summershade'. The leaves are large, lustrous green, and somewhat leathery. They unfold about 2 weeks earlier than 'Summershade'. This characteristic is not favored by the European nursery industry, as it shortens the selling season. It is, however, an excellent street tree. The original name, 'Miller's Superform', was changed when Schmidt took over Miller's nursery. It is widely available in America, in Europe on a restricted scale.

**'Umbraculiferum'.** Baron (1785). Great Britain. Lacks a description, probably with an umbrella-shaped crown. Apparently not in cultivation.

**'Undulatum'.** Dieck (1885). Germany. Leaf margins wavy, bases cordate. Not in cultivation.

**'Variegatum'.** Weston (1770). Lacks a description. Probably not in cultivation.

**'Walderseei'.** Späth (1904). Germany. Small tree of about 8–10 m in height, with speckled and dotted white leaves (Plate 188). A very handsome, uncommon cultivar, comparable to *A. campestre* 'Pulverulentum'. Sometimes shoots with green leaves appear; they must be removed. Slow-growing trees show more "silver" than vigorously growing young plants. It is rarely available in the trade. A fine specimen is in the Romberg Park, Dortmund, Germany.

**'Wittmackii'.** Schwerin (1893). Germany. Leaves at first coppery brown, later turning to green with yellow margins. No longer available in the trade.

**'Yellowrim'**, see **'Aureo-marginatum'**

**'Youngii'**, see **'Reitenbachii'**

---

## ACER PSEUDOPLATANUS

For the same reasons as those discussed under *Acer palmatum*, the cultivars of this species are divided into six groups:

GROUP 1. Leaves clearly 5-lobed, green.

Group 1a: Leaves symmetric, bases cordate

'Amry'
'Bruchem'
'Constant P.'
'Erectum'
'Erythrocarpum'
'Euchlorum'
'Jaspideum'
'Latialatum'
'Latifolium'
'Laxum'
'Negenia'
'Pyramidale'
'Rotterdam'
'Serotinum'
'Zenith'

Group 1b: Leaves irregularly shaped, surfaces rugose and "bullate"

'Concavum'
'Neglectum'
'Rugosum'

Group 1c: Leaves deeply divided

'Clausum'
'Palmatifidum'

GROUP 2. Leaves clearly 5-lobed, leaves variegated or red.

Group 2a: leaves green, but young growth bright red or purplish red

'Cupreum'
'Metallicum'
'Opulifolium'

Group 2b: Leaves yellowish, later greenish

'Flavescens'
'Lutescens'
'Worley'

Group 2c: Leaves maculated yellow, young leaves brown-red

'Aucubifolium'
'Aureo-variegatum'
'Brilliantissimum'
'Spring Gold'
'Striatum'

Group 2d: Leaves maculated sulphur yellow, young leaves bright red

'Leopoldii'
'Limbatum'
'Tricolor'
'Variegatum'
'Zebrinum'

Group 2e: Leaves mottled with yellow

'Bicolor'
'Luteo-virescens'

Group 2f: Leaves variegated, with purple undersides

'Nervosum'
'Nizettii'
'Prinz Handjéry'
'Pseudo-Nizetii'

GROUP 3. Leaves clearly 5-lobed, green, with purple undersides.

'Atropurpureum'
'Prince Camille de Rohan'
'Purpurascens'
'Spaethii' (syn. 'Atropurpureum')

GROUP 4. Leaves 3-lobed.

Group 4a: Leaves green

'Cruciatum'
'Rafinesquianum'
'Trilobatum'
'Vitifolium'

Group 4b: Leaves yellow

'Albertii'

Group 4c: Leaves light green, young growth yellowish

'Laetum'
'Spaethii' (Schwerin)

GROUP 5. Leaves triangular.

Group 5a: Leaves green

'Argutum'
'Opizii'

Group 5b: Leaves yellow

'Corstorphinense'

Group 5c: Leaves maculated white

'Annae'
'Discolor'
'Insigne'
'Pulverulentum'
'Simon Louis Frères'

GROUP 6. Leaves with aberrant forms, not fitting in the above groups.

'Crispum': with very wavy margins
'Heterophyllum'
'Purpureum Digitatum': deeply cleft
'Ternatum': deeply divided

**'Albertii'.** Dieck (1885). Germany. Leaves 3-lobed, especially juveniles, basal lobes small, orange to yellow, mature leaves speckled with white when in full sun. Described in 1892 from trees in the Dieck nursery in 1885. Probably lost from cultivation. (Group 4b)

**'Albo-marmoratum'.** Pax (1886). Germany. Leaves variably white-maculate. Probably no longer in cultivation.

**'Albo-variegatum',** see ***A. pseudoplatanus*** **f. variegatum**

**'Amry'.** De Dorschkamp (1984). Wageningen, The Netherlands. A street tree with rather erect branches, forming a broadly pyramidal crown. Leaves like the species. Selected as a chance tree in the Forestry Research Station "De Dorschkamp," Wageningen, The Netherlands. (Group 1a)

**'Annae'.** Schwerin (1893). Germany. Leaves almost triangular, with long lobes, maculated white, not speckled. Young leaves dark brown, maculations dark red at first, later pink but becoming white. Very rare and no longer available in the trade. (Group 5c)

**'Argenteovariegatum'.** Identical to 'Albo-variegatum'.

**'Argutum'.** Schwerin (1893). Germany. Leaves almost triangular, light green, with somewhat acuminate lobes, margins argutely serrate, not unlike those of *Acer rubrum.* (Group 5a)

**'Atropurpureum'.** Groinland (1862). Späth (1883). Germany. Tree of normal size, to 25 m in height, leaves dark green, of the same shape as the species, undersides intensely purple during the whole of the summer and autumn (Plate 188). This is a sturdy cultivar, frequently planted as a street tree. Its samaras are also dark purplish red. The famous Späth Nursery in Berlin introduced this tree as 'Atropurpureum' in 1883. For unknown reasons it became popular under its synonym 'Spaethii'. This name is often used in the nursery trade and was also proposed by H. J. Grootendorst (1969). The name 'Spaethii' has to be rejected in favor of the original 'Atropurpureum', as the true 'Spaethii', now lost from cultivation, is a quite different tree. The reasons offered by Grootendorst (1969) to maintain the name 'Spaethii' are illegitimate and thus invalid. It is essential to propagate this cultivar by budding on seedlings, despite the fact that a good percentage of its seeds come true. (Group 3)

**'Atropurpureum Spaethii'.** California gardens. See **'Atropurpureum'.**

**'Atrum'.** Wesmael (1890). See **'Atropurpureum'.**

**'Aucubifolium'.** Nicholson (1881). Great Britain. Tree of about 15 m in height, leaves of normal size, green, dotted with gold over the entire leaf. Originated about 1876 in the nurseries of Little & Ballantyne, Carlisle, Scotland. (Group 2c)

**'Aureo-variegatum'.** This is a confusing name as it has been given to several cultivars by different authors. J. Miller attached it in 1826 to a clone now called 'Flavo-variegatum' (Hayne, 1822). The cultivar 'Bicolor', introduced in 1885 by Dieck, has also been known under this name. (Group 2c)

**'Aureum'.** Wesmael (1890). Belgium. Lacks a description. Probably not in cultivation.

**'Aureum Tricolor'.** Wesmael (1890). Belgium. Lacks a description. Probably not in cultivation.

**'Bicolor'.** Späth (1880). Germany. Very much like 'Aucubifolium'; introduced in 1885 by the Dieck Nursery in Germany but named by Späth 5 years earlier. It is no longer possible to trace living plants for comparison so it seems better to name trees bearing normal green leaves dotted with yellow, pea-like flecks with the name 'Aucubifolium'. (Group 2e)

**'Brevialatum'.** Schwerin (1893). Germany. The same as the species, samaras 3 cm long, wings narrow. Probably not in cultivation.

**'Brilliant'.** Kelsey & Dayton (1942). USA. See **'Brilliantissimum'.**

**'Brilliantissimum'.** Clark (1905). Great Britain. Leaves conspicuously terra-cotta to orange when unfolding, later yellow-orange fading to light green. Leaf undersides green. It is very distinctive in spring (Plate 190). It is a slow-growing small tree, usually grafted on 120- or 180-cm standards of straight *A. pseudoplatanus.* Prone to sunburn. Its close relative, 'Prinz Handjery', grows faster and has purplish leaf undersides. If grown as a shrub it seldom reaches more than 2–3 m tall and wide. (Group 2c)

**'Bruchem'.** De Dorschkamp (1984). The Netherlands. Street tree with erect but not fastigiate branches, forming a slender crown, to 15–20 m in height. The leaves are of the shape of the species, dark green, and not prone to *Rhytisma* disease. Selected as a chance tree in a small wood near Bruchem, The Netherlands. Observed throughout 25 years and propagated and tested. It is recommended for narrower streets and requires no special conditions. (Group 1a)

**'Burettii'.** Willkomm (1879). A misspelling for *A. × durettii,* which see in Chapter 8.

**'Clausum'.** Schwerin (1893). Germany. Leaves 5-lobed as in the species, but the basal lobes much broader and connivent. Very rare and almost never obtainable. (Group 1c)

**'Concavum'.** Schwerin (1893). Germany. Small tree 5–6 m tall. Leaves 5-lobed, light green, yellow in the sun, leaf margins crisped and bubbled, often damaged by sunburn. Lost from cultivation. (Group 1b)

**'Constant P'.** De Dorschkamp (1984). Wageningen, The Netherlands. A tree for large parks and gardens, with a rather narrow, somewhat irregular crown, to 20 m in height. Leaves 5-lobed, somewhat leathery, with long petioles. Found in Bruchem, The Netherlands, and named after C. P. van Goor, Assistant Director of the Research Station for Forestry, De Dorschkamp. (Group 1a)

**'Corstorphinense'.** Sutherland (1883). Great Britain. Moderate to tall tree, to 15 m, leaves mostly 3-lobed or triangular, especially when young; clear yellow, later turning greener. Leafs out 7–10 days earlier than other cultivars of *A. pseudoplatanus.* Not prone to sunburn. Sometimes labeled 'Flavo-marginatum'—a wrong name, as this tree is not variegated. The leaves are entirely yellow. The original tree is still alive and grows in the zoo in Corstorphine, a suburb of Edinburgh, Scotland. Worth a place in large gardens and again becoming more readily available. Elwes and Henry, *Trees of Great Britain and Ireland* (vol. III), recount the following story: the original tree grows in the parish of Corstorphine on the outskirts of Edinburgh in the grounds of Sir Dick Lauder. At the foot of this tree the second Lord Forrester was murdered by his sister-in-law on August 26, 1679. He was involved in difficulties on account of a heavy fine laid on him by Cromwell. (Group 5b)

**'Crispum'.** Schwerin (1893). Germany. Leaves asymmetric and crisped, mostly 5-lobed, veins yellowish. Very rare and not in the trade. (Group 6)

**'Cruciatum'.** Schwerin (1893). Germany. Leaves 3-lobed, dark green, both basal lobes in a straight angle, like a cross. Probably not in cultivation. (Group 4a)

**'Cupreum'.** Behnsch (1885). Germany. Leaves of normal shape and size, green, young leaves coppery red. Very rare and not in the trade. (Group 2a)

**'Digitatum'.** Wesmael (1890). Belgium. Without description.

**'Discolor'.** Miller (1826). Great Britain. Leaves small and 3-lobed, yellow-pink when young, pure white afterward, main veins green, in summer speckled with green and white. Grows very weakly. Also known as 'Punctatum'. Probably no longer in cultivation. (Group 5c)

**'Dissectum'.** Van Houtte (1867). Belgium. See **'Palmatifidum'.**

**'Dittrichii'.** Ortmann ex Pax (1886). Germany. Samaras falcate. Probably not in cultivation.

**'Elegantissimum Variegatum',** see **'Lutescens'**

**'Erectum'.** Doorenbos (1955). The Hague, The Netherlands. Narrow tree of moderate size, 15–20 m tall, branches erect, leaves of the normal shape and size. Originated at The Hague in a planting at "Nachtegaalplein" (Nightingale Square). The late S. G. A. Doorenbos, a well-known Dutch dendrologist, selected this tree and introduced it into the trade. The name was first mentioned in the nursery catalog of Lombarts Nurseries, Zundert, in 1949, and validly published in the *Year Book of the Dutch Dendrological Society* 20 (1955). Scanlon also introduced a narrowly growing selection under this name in 1956; this must be rejected. Possibly both clones are in the trade in the United States under the same name. The Dutch 'Erectum' is a very useful selection fit for street plantings along narrow streets. It is generally available in the trade in Europe. (Group 1a)

**'Erythrocarpum'.** Vaillant (1727). France. This clone

is included in forma *erythrocarpum* (Carr.) Pax (1864). It has been found wild in the Bavarian Alps as well as in Switzerland and Austria. The cultivar 'Erythrocarpum' originated in a French nursery. This tree is the mother tree of all the plants now available in the European trade. The samara wings are conspicuously dark red, and the leaves are slightly smaller than in the species (Plate 191). The petioles are reddish. It is a handsome tree of 20–25 m in height and deserves more attention. (Group 1a)

**'Euchlorum'.** Späth (1878). Germany. Leaves dark green above, light gray-green beneath, yellow petioles. No longer available, but there is a fine specimen at Bergholt Place, Suffolk, Great Britain, measuring 25 m. (Group 1a)

**'Extra Fort'.** Van Houtte (1867). Belgium. Leaves purple beneath. See also **'Atropurpureum'.**

**'Fastigiatum'.** Eiselt (1960). Germany. Illegitimate name for fastigiate seedling because it was published with a Latin name after 1 January 1959. Not in the trade.

**'Fieberi'**, see **'Palmatifidum'**

**'Flavescens'.** Schwerin (1893). Germany. Leaves dull yellow, in the shade light green. A rather slow-growing tree. (Group 2b)

**'Flavo-marginatum'**, see **'Corstorphinense'**

**'Flavo-variegatum'.** Hayne (1822). Great Britain. Leaves variegated yellow; no further description. Not available in the trade.

**'Fructu-rubra'**, see **'Erythrocarpum'**

**'Globosum'.** Geelhaar (1911). Germany. Tree of moderate size, crown globose, leaves like the species. As far as we know not in cultivation.

**'Goldfleck'.** Kelsey & Dayton (1942). USA. See **'Corstorphinense'.**

**'Heterophyllum'.** Schwerin (1896). Germany. Tree of moderate size, 15–20 m high, leaves irregularly shaped, asymmetric, partly 4-lobed or even double leaves on one petiole, margins serrate. Apparently no longer in cultivation. (Group 6)

**'Hodgkinsii'.** Loudon (1838). Great Britain. Leaves blotched yellow. See also forma *variegatum* under *A. pseudoplatanus* in Chapter 7.

**'Insigne'.** Späth (1883). Germany. Leaves 3-lobed, rather small, reddish, later becoming whitish, mostly in the center of the leaf. Apparently no longer in cultivation. (Group 5c)

**'Jaspideum'.** Lavallée (1877). France. Tree of 15–20 m in height, leaves of normal shape and size, light green, shiny. Bark of both trunk and branches yellowish. In cultivation for many years (before 1875) in the Arboretum Segrez, France, it was introduced into cultivation in Germany by the Dieck Nurseries around 1895. (Group 1a)

**'Laciniatum'.** Loudon (1830). See **'Palmatifidum'.**

**'Laetum'.** Schwerin (1893). Germany. Leaves light green, 3-lobed, young leaves almost yellow. Probably no longer in cultivation. (Group 4c)

**'Latialatum'.** Pax (1886). Germany. Samaras 2.5 cm wide, erect. Apparently not in cultivation. (Group 1a)

**'Latifolium'.** Schwerin (1896). Germany. Big-leaved form, discovered in 1896 by Reuter at Potsdam, Germany. Apparently not in cultivation. (Group 1a)

**'Laxum'.** Schwerin (1896). Germany. Leaves of normal size and shape, petioles abruptly incurved so that they hang vertically on the tree. Probably not in cultivation. (Group 1a)

**'Leopoldii'.** Vervaene (1864). Belgium. Tree of normal size, 15–20 m high, leaves of the same size and shape as the species, but mottled white and yellow, young leaves pinkish. Named by Vervaene after King Leopold I of Belgium, this tree was much in vogue at the end of the 19th century. Seedlings with similar leaves occur from time to time but must not be confused with true 'Leopoldii'. Trees with variegated leaves sold under the name 'Variegatum' are usually 'Leopoldii'. A valuable tree, planted on a fairly wide scale. This cultivar has to be budded from verified trees. (Group 2d)

**'Leslie'.** Loudon (1838). Without description.

**'Limbatum'.** Schwerin (1901). Germany. Leaves green with yellow margins, fading to green at the center. Apparently no longer in cultivation. (Group 2d)

**'Lobatum'.** Nicholson (1881). Great Britain. Leaf lobes dissected. Probably not in cultivation.

**'Lombarts'.** Lombarts ex Vrugtman (1970). The Netherlands. See **'Atropurpureum'.**

**'Longifolium'.** Booth ex Loudon (1842). Germany. Leaf lobes long. Probably not in cultivation.

**'Luteo-virens'.** Pax (1902). See **'Luteo-virescens'.**

**'Luteo-virescens'.** Simon Louis Frères (1887). France. Leaves 5-lobed with light yellow maculations, light green in the center, young leaves yellowish, similar to 'Tricolor' but of different color. Probably lost from cultivation. (Group 2e)

**'Lutescens'.** Loddiges (1823). France. Leaves orange to yellow in the sun. Lost from cultivation. (Group 2b)

**'Lutescens Crispum'.** Wesmael (1890). Belgium. Without description, but most probably with light yellow, wrinkled leaves.

**'Lutescens Novum'.** Nicholson (1881). See **'Corstorphinense'.**

**'Luteum'.** Dickson (1887). See **'Corstorphinense'.**

**'Metallicum'.** Schwerin (1893). Germany. Leaves of the typical shape and size, shiny with a metallic hue, young leaves first yellow, later coppery, then olive, and at last green. Probably no longer available. (Group 2a)

**'Microphyllum'.** Dickson (1880). Great Britain. Small-leaved, no further description.

**'Nachtegaalplein'.** Doorenbos (1935). The Hague, The Netherlands. See **'Erectum'.**

**'Nanum'.** Wesmael (1890). Belgium. Without description.

**'Negenia'.** NAKB (1948). The Hague, The Netherlands. A street tree of good habit, 20–25 m high. Selected by the Dutch Selection Service for Horticulture (NAKB). Planted on a wide scale in The Netherlands and Belgium as street and landscape trees. Tolerates poor growing conditions and wind. It has the same ornamental value as the species, with leaves of typical shape and size. Sets very few seeds. Petioles are red. The original tree is still growing between Meteren and Waardenburg in The Netherlands, not far from the city of Nijmegen. Readily available. (Group 1a)

**'Neglectum'.** Schwerin (1893). Germany. Leaves very large, coarsely incised. Probably lost from cultivation. (Group 1b)

**'Nervosum'.** Schwerin (1893). Germany. Slow-growing tree with pyramidal habit, 12–15 m high, densely branched. Leaves small, 5-lobed, lobes acuminate, yellowish pink on the upper surfaces, green veins, orange to pinkish beneath. Second growth with leaves like the species. Very rare. (Group 2f)

**'Nizetii'.** Makoy (1887). France. Leaves not unlike those of 'Leopoldii', but the undersides are purple (Plate 192). Much rarer than 'Leopoldii'. Not closely related to 'Prinz Handjéry', as stated in Bean, *Trees and Shrubs Hardy in the British Isles.* (Group 2f)

**'Opizii'.** Ortmann (1852); Schwerin (1893). Germany. Leaves 3-lobed to triangular, leaf bases half-circular to cordate, leaf margins crenulate. Very rare. (Group 5a)

**'Opulifolium'.** Kirchner (1864). Germany. Tree 15 m high. Leaves 5-lobed, lustrous green above, whitish green beneath, smaller than those of the species, somewhat leathery, with long, red petioles. Pubescent dots at the vein axils. Young leaves purplish. Very rare and not available in the trade. (Group 2a)

**'Ovale'.** Nicholson (1881). Great Britain. Leaf lobes short. Probably not in cultivation.

**'Palmatifidum'.** Duhamel (1755). France. Leaves deeply divided, not unlike those of *A. heldreichii.* Probably no longer in cultivation. (Group 1c)

**'Pendulum'.** Loudon (1850). Great Britain. Branches pendulous. Probably no longer in cultivation.

**'Pendunculatum'.** Wesmael (1890). Belgium. Without description.

**'Prince Camille de Rohan'.** Bijhouwer (1927). Wageningen, The Netherlands. Strongly growing tree, dark gray-green leaves with purple undersides. Lobes rather deeply divided and not serrate. A rare cultivar and not very distinctive. Also called 'Purpureo-variegatum'. Belongs to forma *purpureum* (see *A. pseudoplatanus* in Chapter 7). (Group 3)

**'Prinz Handjéry'.** Späth (1883). Germany. Leaves 5-lobed, salmon-red to salmon-pink when unfolding, later turning pink and yellowish, and finally light green. Very spectacular, slow-growing, shrubby tree. The undersides of the leaves are purple and not green as in its close relative 'Brilliantissimum'. Widely grown and valuable plant for the small garden and readily available in the trade. Less prone to sunburn than 'Brilliantissimum'. Quite often grafted as a standard tree. Grafted at the base, it forms a dense shrub about 4–5 m high. (Group 2f)

**'Pseudo-Nizetii'.** Schwerin (1893). Germany. Similar to 'Nizetii' but has pale orange maculations on the young leaves, with golden dots above and purplish undersides. This plant is closer to 'Prinz Handjery' than to 'Nizetii', but both of them are faster-growing. (Group 2f)

**'Pubescens'.** Endlicher (1843). Austria. Without description.

**'Pulverulentum'.** Jacques & Herincq (1847). France. Leaves like 'Aucubifolium' but densely speckled and mottled with white. Long shoots bear pale orange young leaves that lack conspicuous markings. Not available in the trade. (Group 5c)

**'Punctatulum'.** Kuntze (1867). Germany. Leaves dotted yellow. See forma *variegatum* under *A. pseudoplatanus* in Chapter 7.

**'Punctatum'.** Baudriller (1880). France. Without description. See **'Discolor'.**

**'Purple leaf'.** Kelsey & Dayton (1942). USA. See **'Atropurpureum'.**

**'Purpurascens'.** Van Houtte (1867). Belgium. See forma *purpureum* under *A. pseudoplatanus* in Chapter 7. Most probably a seedling selection with purplish samaras. (Group 3)

**'Purpureo-variegatum'.** Barron (1875). See **'Prince Camille de Rohan'.**

**'Purpureum'.** Clarke (1828). See forma *purpureum.* Again, nothing but an individual from this natural group, with purple undersides of the leaves. Can frequently be found as a seedling. Not worthy of propagation. If a good cultivar with purple undersides is required, plant 'Atropurpureum'.

**'Purpureum Digitatum'.** Hesse (1898). Germany. Leaves ternate and purplish beneath. No further description. No longer available.

**'Purpureum Spaethii'**, see **'Atropurpureum'**

**'Purpureum Variegatum'.** Barron (1875). France. With leaves variegated purple, rose, and white. Originated in the Bois de Boulogne, Paris, France. Not in cultivation.

**'Pyramidale'.** McClelland ex Nicholson (1881). Great Britain. Nicholson (1881) reported this as being of a pyramidal habit. It is another fastigiate clone, certainly not identical with 'Erectum' as suggested by Krüssmann (1976a). Probably no longer in cultivation. (Group 1a)

**'Quadricolor'.** Schwerin (1893). Germany. See **'Simon Louis Frè**res'.

**'Rafinesquianum'.** Nicholson (1881). Great Britain. Leaves 3-lobed, blood red when unfolding but soon becoming green, glaucous beneath. Not available in the trade. (Group 4a)

**'Roseum'.** Wesmael (1890). Belgium. See forma *variegatum* under *A. pseudoplatanus* in Chapter 7.

**'Rotterdam'.** Vink (1944). Rotterdam, The Netherlands. Large tree, with a pyramidal crown when young, later more broadly upright. A very good street tree for poor growing conditions. Leaves like the species. Must be budded on seedlings. Selected in 1944 by the late H. W. Vink, Director of the Municipal Park Service of Rotterdam. (Group 1a)

**'Rubicundum'.** Schwerin (1910). Germany. Leaves speckled dark pink. See forma *variegatum* under *A. pseudoplatanus* in Chapter 7.

**'Rubro-maculatum'.** Pax (1886). Germany. Leaves variegated red on lower surfaces. Not in cultivation.

**'Rubro-purpureum'.** Saunders (1871). Great Britain. Leaves purple below. See **'Atropurpureum'.**

**'Rubrum'**, see **'Atropurpureum'**

**'Rugosum'.** Schwerin (1901). Germany. Leaves wrinkled, green, and 5-lobed. No longer available in the trade. (Group 1b)

**'Sanguineum'.** Kuntze (1967). Germany. See **'Rafinesquianum'.**

**'Scarletfruit'.** Kelsey & Dayton (1942). USA. See **'Erythrocarpum'.**

**'Scoticum'.** Miller (1826). See **'Corstorphinense'.**

**'Serotinum'.** Endlicher (1843). Austria. A tree, with leaves the size and shape of those of the species but unfolding much later in the season. Grows very quickly. Not available in the trade. (Group 1a)

**'Serratum'.** Schwerin (1893). Leaves not incised; no further description.

**'Simon Louis Frères'.** Deegen (1881). France. Slow-growing tree, often a mere shrub, to 10 m. Leaves 3-lobed, pale pink when unfolding, becoming white-variegated with only a very few green leaves. Occasionally available in the trade. Unusual cultivar but appealing. (Group 5c)

**'Spaethii'.** Schwerin (1893). Germany. Leaves green, lower surfaces with lemon-yellow spots. (Group 4c)

**'Spaethii'** of Dutch nurseries, see **'Atropurpureum'.** (Group 3)

**'Splendens'.** Lawson (1874). Great Britain. Without description.

**'Spring Gold'.** Verboom (1991). Boskoop, The Netherlands. This cultivar appeared as a sport in the well-known 'Brilliantissimum' and differs from the latter by its stronger growth. The leaves are very much like those of 'Brilliantissimum', also green underneath, and tending to become yellow somewhat earlier than 'Brilliantissimum'. When leaves unfold the two cultivars are quite alike. The leaves turn to green in summer and there is not much autumn color. It is now available in the trade and will possibly replace 'Prinz Handjéry' as it grows better and has a nicer color. (Group 2c)

**'Striatum'.** Kuntze (1867). Germany. Leaves striped yellow. Probably not in cultivation. (Group 2c)

**'Ternatum'.** Schwerin (1893). Germany. Leaves deeply divided to the bases, single leaflets sometimes stalked, lobes oblique, resembling those of *A. negundo.* Not known to be growing in any collection. Seems to be a very interesting cultivar. (Group 6)

**'Tricolor'.** Koch (1853). Germany. Rapidly growing tree to 15–20 m in height, leaves of the same size and shape as in the species but flecked red, white and green, not unlike 'Leopoldii' or 'Nizetii' but larger and stronger. Young leaves brown-red. Originated in the Muskau Arboretum, Germany, in the valley of the Neisse River. (Group 2d)

**'Tricolor Longifolium'.** Wesmael (1890). Belgium. Without description.

**'Trilobatum'.** Lavallée (1877). France. Leaves 3-lobed, larger than in the species, juvenile leaves with cordate bases. Originated in the Arboretum Ségrez, France. (Group 4a)

**'Umbraculiferum'.** Nicholson (1881). Great Britain. Without description.

**'Variegatum'.** See forma *variegatum* under *A. pseudoplatanus* in Chapter 7 and 'Corstorphinense' (Murray 1970c). (Group 2d)

**'Veiny'.** Kelsey & Dayton (1942). USA. See **'Nervosum'.**

**'Velutinum'.** Späth (1892). Germany. See **'Pyramidale'.**

**'Vink'.** Scanlon (1960). Ohio, USA. See **'Rotterdam'.**

**'Virescens Maculatum'.** Wesmael (1890). Belgium. Without description.

**'Virescens Pulverulentum'.** Wesmael (1890). Belgium. See **'Pulverulentum'.**

**'Virescens Variegatum'.** Wesmael (1890). Belgium. Without description.

**'Vitifolium'.** Opiz ex Tausch (1829). Germany. Leaves almost 3-lobed, bases deeply cordate. Probably not in cultivation. (Group 4a)

**'Webbianum'.** Nicholson (1881). Great Britain. Leaves variegated. No further description. Probably not in cultivation.

**'Worley'.** Willkomm (1879). Germany. Medium-sized tree 12–15 m in height. Leaves 5-lobed, beautifully golden yellow when young, later becoming pale green (Plate 193). Lobes somewhat serrate, more yellow than 'Corstorphinense'. Introduced into cultivation by Ohlendorff in 1893 (Hamburg, Germany) and not by Rosenthal as commonly thought. Frequently misspelled 'Worlei', 'Woorly', 'Woorley', 'Worleeii', 'Woorleeii', 'Worlee', and 'Worlei'. It is a good yellow-leaved tree and readily available in the trade. (Group 2b)

**'Zebrinum'.** Schwerin (1901). Germany. Very much like 'Nervosum' but with green rather than purple leaf undersides. Probably no longer in cultivation. (Group 2d)

**'Zenith'.** NAKB (1952). The Hague, The Netherlands. A fastigiate selection selected by the NAKB (see **'Negenia'**), but not introduced due to unsatisfactory growth as a young tree. 'Erectum' is better. (Group 1a)

## ACER PYCNANTHUM (Hana no ki)

Professor M. Yokoi (personal communication) mentioned two cultivar names: 'Hana no ki benefi' and 'Hana no ki shirofu'. Both names are without description or record. As "Hana no ki" refers to the species, the names are most probably 'Benefi' and 'Shirofu'.

## ACER RUBESCENS

Only one cultivar is so far recognized as belonging to this rare species.

**'Summer Surprise'.** Cave (circa 1987). New Zealand. It is not known whether this cultivar originated as a spontaneous seedling or as a mutation. Two small plants have developed from scions sent to The Netherlands in 1990. A photograph shows they have bold, somewhat crinkled, 3-lobed leaves with abundant white and pink variegation. Zone VII.

## ACER RUBRUM

Many cultivars have been introduced since World War II. All are hardy in zone IV. Full bibliographic notes may be found in *Checklist of Cultivated Maples* I, *Acer rubrum,* compiled by Frank S. Santamour and A. Jacot McArdle.

**'Ablaze'.** Sarcoxie Nurseries (1974). Illinois, USA. A tree with a broadly rounded crown of about the same size as that of the species. The leaves turn a brilliant red autumn color. Leaf fall occurs rather late in the season. This cultivar is in cultivation in North America but not in Europe.

**'Albo-variegatum'.** Schwerin (1901). Germany. Leaves spotted white. Probably lost from cultivation.

**'Armstrong'.** Scanlon (1951). Ohio, USA. A strongly growing tree with a fastigiate, almost columnar habit. The leaves are of about the same shape and size as those of the species. The original tree was discovered in 1947 by Newton Armstrong of Ohio. It is now in general cultivation. Unfortunately, its autumn color is not conspicuous in Europe. It is a very useful tree for narrow streets, because of its fastigiate habit and because it does not lift paving with its root system. It might be, according to K. R. Bachtell (1989), of hybrid origin (*A.* × *freemanii*).

**'Armstrong Two'.** Scanlon (1976). Ohio, USA. This newer clone is not yet in cultivation in European nurseries. According to its description by Scanlon in 1965 (as 'Armstrong II'), it has a lighter habit, narrower crotches, and more tightly ascending branches than 'Armstrong'. It might be, according to K. R. Bachtell (1989), of hybrid origin (*A.* × *freemanii*). Patented in the United States.

**'Aureo-variegatum'.** Wiegers (1809). Belgium. Leaves flecked gold. Probably not in cultivation.

**'Autumn Blaze'**, see under ***A.* × *freemanii***

**'Autumn Flame'.** Collins (1964). USA. This tree was released by McGill & Sons of Fairview, Oregon. It develops its well-colored autumn tints early and the leaves remain on the tree longer than those of the species but are of the same shape and size. US Plant Patent 2377 (1964). It is also in cultivation in Europe.

**'Autumn Glory'.** Davey Tree Expert Co. (1967). Ohio, USA. A rather heavily branched tree, also multistemmed and shrublike. The crown is spreading. The leaves are of the typical shape and size. It colors extremely well in red and orange autumn tones. It also colors well in Europe in climates with high humidity in the autumn. The mother tree was selected by M. W. Staples, Kent, Ohio. It is available in some specialized nurseries. US Plant Patent 2431 (1964).

**'Autumn Spire'.** University of Minnesota (1980). USA. A columnar selection with beautiful red colors in the autumn. Introduced to the trade by Bailey Nurseries, Minnesota.

**'Bowhall'.** Scanlon (1951). Ohio, USA. One of the better columnar cultivars, coloring well in the autumn. The parent tree was about 12 m high and only 4 m wide in 1982. The tree was named for the road along which it was first discovered in Olmsted, Ohio. Available in many nurseries, it seems to be one of the best of its kind, comparable with 'Armstrong', though the latter tends to grow larger.

**'Column'.** Kelsey & Dayton (1942). USA. See **'Columnare'.**

**'Columnare'.** Rehder (1900). Massachusetts, USA. A tree with a columnar habit. No longer in cultivation; it has been replaced by several newer cultivars, such as 'Armstrong' and 'Bowhall'.

**'Columnar Walters'.** Manbeck Nurseries (1975). Tennessee, USA. Another columnar cultivar, fast growing, with attractively colored leaves in the autumn. Introduced in 1958 as 'Columnare Walters', an invalid name. It was released by Princeton Nurseries, Princeton, New Jersey, USA, to the Arnold Arboretum, Jamaica Plain, Massachusetts, USA. It is not in cultivation in Europe.

**'Curtis'.** Pacific Coast Nurseries (1967). Oregon, USA. Another upright clone, with nicely colored leaves in the autumn. Probably not in cultivation in Europe.

**'Doric'.** Scanlon (1967). Ohio, USA. A narrowly columnar tree with branches at a 30-degree angle to the main trunk. The somewhat leathery leaves color extremely well in autumn. It is still a rare tree but in cultivation in Europe. It seems to be suitable for climates with a high humidity. US Plant Patent 2823 (1967). Trademarked in the United States, The Netherlands, and Belgium.

**'Drake'**, see **'V. J. Drake'**

**'Drummondii'**, see ***A. rubrum*** var. ***drummondii*** in Chapter 7.

**'Dwarf'.** Kelsey & Dayton (1942). USA. See **'Globosum'.**

**'Embers'.** Lake County Nursery (before 1990). Ohio, USA. Very hardy, vigorous-growing tree with a narrow habit, maturing to a rounded crown. The autumn colors are bright red. It is available only in the United States. The name is trademarked in the United States.

**'Excelsior'.** Handy Nurseries (1978). Portland, Oregon, USA. A fast-growing tree of pyramidal habit. It is not available in Europe. Related to cultivars such as 'Armstrong' and 'Bowhall'. Trademarked in the United States.

**'Floridanum'.** Lauche (1880). Germany. This old cultivar has red leaves in the autumn. Possibly it belongs to *A. saccharum.* It is very doubtful whether it is still in cultivation. Another clone with this name was mentioned by Reichert (1804), without description.

**'Franksred'**, see **'Red Sunset'**

**'Fulgens'.** Willkomm (1879). Germany. This old cultivar seems to have slightly tomentose leaf undersides and might be identical with *A. rubrum* var. *tomentosum.* Probably lost from cultivation.

**'Gerling'.** Scanlon (1956). Ohio, USA. This is one of the first selections made by Scanlon, chosen for its columnar habit. Older trees show a more broadly conical habit, with horizontal older branches, while younger trees are more conical or columnar. It is a beautiful tree, suitable for large gardens, municipal parks, and rather wide streets. The leaves are of the normal size and shape, but color rather poorly in the autumn. Named for Jacob Gerling, Rochester, New York, USA. It is already a rather common cultivar and available in Europe. The name is trademarked in the United States, The Netherlands, and Belgium.

**'Glaucum'.** Dieck (1885). Germany. The leaf undersides are more bluish than usual but otherwise hardly differ from the species. It is apparently no longer in cultivation.

**'Globosum'.** Parsons & Co. (1887). New York, USA. A dwarf and compact-growing cultivar; flowers scarlet. Probably lost from cultivation.

**'Indian Summer'**, see **'Morgan'**

**'Karpick'** Femrite Nursery (circa 1980). Oregon, USA. A tree with a very narrow crown and well adapted for street plantings. Its red twigs and lustrous green leaves are quite distinct. The tree grows up to 10 m tall, and its fall colors are variable—red, orange, yellow, or various intermediate shades.

**'Landsberg'.** Bailey Nurseries (1988). Minnesota, USA. Taken from a tree in the Brainerd area of northern Minnesota, this medium-sized tree with a good oval form and branching habit has excellent red color in the autumn. Bailey Nurseries call it "Firedance" maple. Not yet available in Europe.

**'Magnificum'.** Schwerin (1910). Germany. Supposedly has red leaf margins. Probably no longer in cultivation.

**'Morgan'.** Sheridan Arboretum (1972). Quebec, Canada. A beautiful tree with very good scarlet autumn color that appears even on young trees. Deserves more attention and is becoming more generally available, both in North America and Europe. The name in use in the United States is 'Indian Summer'. It might be, according to K. R. Bachtell, of hybrid origin (*A.* × *freemanii*).

**'Newton Armstrong'**, see **'Armstrong'**

**'Northwood'.** J. Frank Schmidt & Son (circa 1980). Boring, Oregon, USA. Tree up to 12–15 m tall with a broadly oval crown. The leaves are dark green and the usual size. The tree has been selected by the University of Minnesota from wild collected seed. It is a very hardy form. The fall colors are variable and not always too good.

**'October Glory'.** Princeton Nurseries (1961). New Jersey, USA. A very beautiful tree with a rather upright habit. Its leaves tend to stay on the tree longer than usual. The autumn color is very good, a rich crimson or dark orange-red. It colors well in unfavorable conditions. It grows too fast for small gardens but is suitable for plantings along main streets and small parks. Some protection against strong wind is useful. It is in general cultivation. US Plant Patent 2116 (1961). Trademarked.

**'Pallidiflorum'**, see ***A. rubrum*** var. ***pallidiflorum***

**'Palmatum'.** Späth (1892). Germany. See **'Pendulum'.**

**'Paul E. Tilford'**, see **'Tilford'**

**'Pendulum'.** Kirchner (1864). Germany. This very old cultivar from the Muskau Arboretum near Dresden has pendant branches. The large, palmate leaves suggest that it might belong to *A. saccharinum* rather than to *A. rubrum.* This cultivar is still present in Tilgate Arboretum, Great Britain, and it was also imported in 1990 to The Netherlands. Its proper position cannot yet be established as the author has not seen the leaves.

**'Phipp's Farm'.** Weston Nurseries (1977). Massachusetts, USA. Selected for its outstanding red autumn color. Not available in Europe, rare in America.

**'Pyramidale'.** Parsons & Co. (1887). New York, USA. Lacks a description, but most probably of pyramidal shape. Lost from cultivation.

**'Red Sentinal'.** Lacks description.

**'Red Sunset'.** Amfac Cole Nurseries (1966). Ohio, USA. Selected by J. Frank Schmidt & Sons, Portland, Oregon. This is an outstanding cultivar, growing into a moderately sized tree with somewhat larger leaves than usual. The autumn color is excellent and present even in young trees. It has a broadly pyramidal crown. It is now a widely planted tree in both North America and Europe. Trademarked.

**'Sanguineum'.** Lavallée (1887). France. Reported to have crimson red leaves in the autumn. Leaf undersides tomentose; bases cordate. Probably no longer in cultivation.

**'Scanlon'.** Scanlon (1956). Ohio, USA. A compactly branched, almost columnar tree with fresh green leaves of the usual form and size (Plate 194). The leaves turn a brilliant orange-crimson and purple in early autumn. It is a well-known cultivar, in cultivation both in Europe and America. US Plant Patent 1722 (1958). Trademarked.

**'Scarlet Sentinel'**, see **'Scarsen'**

**'Scarsen'.** J. Frank Schmidt & Son. Boring, Oregon, USA. A tree with a strong, upright-growing habit, which gives it an oval-rectangular outline and a bold appearance. Excellent for parks and street plantings. It grows up to 12–13 m tall, with dark green foliage. Its fall colors are yellow, orange, and red. The leaves are larger than the average red maple leaf and hold up well in summer heat. This cultivar is in the trade as 'Scarlet Sentinel', which is its trademarked name. US Plant Patent 3109.

**'Schlesingeri'.** Schwerin (1896). Germany. An old cultivar but still being grown in several nurseries. It has a splendid autumn color, varying from orange-yellow to darkest wine-red. The leaf margins are more wavy and serrate than in the species. It remains in cultivation in spite of the fact that so many newer cultivars have been selected. This particular cultivar was selected by C. S. Sargent from the garden of a Schlesinger somewhere in the United States. It was introduced into the trade by the famous Späth Nursery in Berlin.

**'Shade King'.** Handy Nursery Co. (1973). Portland, Oregon, USA. Vigorously growing tree to 20 m. The leaves are slightly larger than those of the species but of the usual shape, very dark green. Apparently not yet in cultivation in Europe. Trademarked.

**'Sir Charles Wager'.** Miller (1768). Identical to *A. saccharinum.*

**'Splendens'.** Koch (1869). Germany. See ***A. rubrum*** var. ***tomentosum*** in Chapter 7.

**'Tilford'.** Scanlon (1951). Ohio, USA. This is a large tree with a globose crown, about as wide as tall. The leaves are slightly smaller than usual, but of the normal shape. They color well but not as brilliantly as several other clones. The trunk is remarkably straight and smooth. Named after Paul E. Tilford of Wooster, Ohio. This tree needs much space for good development so is not suitable for small and moderately sized gardens. It is an easy grower on almost any nonalkaline soil. 'Tilford' and 'October Glory' are best suited for the coastal areas in Europe. It is available in the trade in both North America and Europe. Trademarked in the United States, The Netherlands, and Belgium.

**'Tomentosum'.** Identical to *A. rubrum* var. *tomentosum* [According to Späth (1896), this variety had exceptionally good colors in autumn. The leaf undersides are tomentose.]

**'Variegatum'.** Groinland (1862) Germany. With variegated leaves, almost certainly lost from cultivation. A small percentage of *A. rubrum* seedlings tend to have slightly variegated leaves but are insufficiently distinct to separate them.

**'V. J. Drake'.** J. Frank Schmidt & Son (1977). Boring, Oregon, USA. Said to have distinctly colored leaves, turning from green to a colored border through shades of blue-violet to red and yellow. US Plant Patent 3542 (1974). Not yet introduced into Europe.

**'Wageri'.** Koch (1869). Germany. This tall tree has pendulous branches. This particular cultivar has been lost from cultivation, but this variation of growth habit seems to appear regularly in seed beds of *A. rubrum* and might well be identical with *A. saccharinum.*

**'Wagneri'.** Koch (1869). See **'Wageri'.**

**'Woolly'.** Kelsey & Dayton (1942). USA. See ***A. rubrum*** var. ***tomentosum*** in Chapter 7.

## ACER RUFINERVE

This widely grown species has not produced many cultivars; in fact, only four are significant.

**'Albo-limbatum'.** Hooker f. (1869). Slightly slower-growing than the species, and the bark less conspicuously striped. The leaves are markedly variegated with white, especially the margins, which are irregularly whitish (Plate 195). Some leaves are speckled, others are fully green. It is very free-flowering but most of the fruits are sterile. While wild seedlings and those grown in seed beds frequently produce white-variegated plants, the true clone must be grafted on seedlings. It is generally available. The Japanese name is 'Hatsuyuki kaede'. Zone V.

**'Beni uri'.** JDV I, 157; JDV II, 164. Grows less strongly than the species. The leaves are large, 8–14 cm across, and not as triangular as in the species. They are green, variegated yellow, sometimes up to half the length of the lobes but usually less. The yellow flecks tend to some sunburning. These lighter colored parts of the leaves turn crimson in the autumn. It is a rare plant, difficult to propagate, and it has not yet been introduced into Europe. The name 'Beni uri' is occasionally incorrectly applied to *A. crataegifolium.* The variegated *A. crataegifolium* is correctly called 'Veitchii'.

**'Erythrocladum'.** Marshall ex Brimfield (1953). Great Britain. Slow-growing shrub with ruby red to orange-yellow young shoots, especially notable in winter. The color disappears completely in summer, turning to whitish yellow. It is less distinctive than *A. pensylvanicum* 'Erythrocladum'. The leaves are slightly smaller than those of the species, somewhat bold and wavy. They tend to sunburn in exposed situations. Difficult to propagate and to grow. Very rare in the trade. Zone VI.

**'Fuiri urihada kaede'**, see **'Albo-limbatum'**

**'Hatsuyuki'**, see **'Albo-limbatum'**

**'Hatsuyuki kaede'** (the Japanese name for 'Albo-limbatum')

**'Kyo nishiki'**, see **'Beni uri'**

**'Luteo-variegatum'.** Wada (1938). Japan. Leaves variegated yellow. Probably not in cultivation. Possibly identical to 'Albo-limbatum'.

**'Marginatum'**, see **'Albo-limbatum'**

**'Marmoratum'**, see **'Albo-limbatum'**

**'Shirayuki'.** JDV I, 157; JDV II, 164. Almost identical to 'Albo-limbatum' but slightly more yellowish.

**'Shufu nishiki'**, see **'Albo-limbatum'**

**'Uriha nishiki'**, see **'Albo-limbatum'**

**'Whitedot'.** Kelsey & Dayton (1942). USA. See **'Albo-limbatum'.**

**'Winter Gold'.** Teese (1974). Monbulk, Australia. JDV II, 164. This cultivar has the same habit and leaves as the species but differs in its unique golden yellow bark in winter. In the summer, the bark color is more greenish yellow. This cultivar dislikes chalky soils. Discovered by P. Douwsma, Olinda, Victoria, Australia, and introduced by Yamina Rare Plants Nurseries.

---

## ACER SACCHARINUM

The silver maple is a remarkably uniform species, with no recognized botanical subspecies or varieties. Nevertheless, variability occurs when plants are propagated from seed of garden origin. In particular, it is fairly easy to locate seedlings with more distinctly dissected leaves than is usual from seed collected in the wild. Although *A. saccharinum* has a rather poor reputation with landscapers and horticulturists, it is still planted on a fairly large scale. Its wood is weak and brittle, so it is easily damaged in storms. Further, the roots tend to heave paving and penetrate water pipes.

Fortunately, there are a number of valuable cultivars, all easily propagated by layering or grafting on seedlings of *A. saccharinum.* All are hardy in zone IV.

For full bibliography and descriptions see *Checklist of Cultivated Maples* IV, *Acer saccharinum,* by F. S. Santamour and A. Jacot McArdle (1982).

**'Albo-maculatum'.** Späth (1883). Germany. See **'Variegatum'.**

**'Albo-variegatum'.** Späth (1883). See **'Variegatum'.**

**'Arbusculum'.** Schwerin (1893). Germany. A shrubby clone with leaves like the species, coloring red in the autumn. Apparently no longer in cultivation.

**'Argenteum Striatum'.** Ellwanger & Barry (1875). USA. A clone with variegated leaves. Probably no longer in cultivation.

**'Asplenifolium'.** De Bie van Aalst (1925). Zundert, The Netherlands. A large tree, closely allied to 'Wieri Laciniatum'. The leaves spread less, are not so deeply incised, and frequently contain small holes. This cultivar has been in cultivation in The Netherlands at the Royal Nurseries De Bie van Aalst Ltd. since about 1925 as 'Asplenifolium' and sold as a substitute for 'Laciniatum Wieri'. The name 'Asplenifolium' was used in a survey of *Acer* (Grootendorst, 1969). De Bie van Aalst Ltd. no longer exists and the nursery has been liquidated. As a consequence, the mother plants of 'Asplenifolium' are no longer in existence. The name 'Asplenifolium' is in use, published in catalogs since 1925. A number of trees sold as 'Laciniatum Wieri' are in fact 'Asplenifolium' and accordingly are incorrectly labeled.

**'Aureo-variegatum'.** Willkomm (1879). Germany. Leaves variegated yellow. It originated in the gardens of Fürst Rohan in Sichnow, eastern Germany. Probably no longer in cultivation.

**'Aureum'.** Naperville Nursery (1934). Illinois, USA. Said to be a golden maple. As far as is known, it is no longer in collections or in cultivation.

**'Beebe Cutleaf Weeping'.** Cole Nursery Co. (1953). USA. This cultivar has a horizontal branching habit. The leaves are very similar to those of the species. It is a rare tree both in the United States and in Europe.

**'Bicolor'.** Schwerin (1901). Germany. The leaves have inconspicuous golden yellow spots. The color improves as the leaves mature. Very rarely seen in cultivation.

**'Blair'.** Marshall Nurseries (1939). USA. This tree with an upright habit originated in Blair, Nebraska. It is less subject to storm injury than the species. It is not known whether it is still in cultivation. Not available in Europe.

**'Born's Graciosa'**, see **'Born's Gracious'**

**'Born's Gracious'.** Van Gelderen (1992). Boskoop, The Netherlands. A graceful tree of slightly weeping habit. The leaves are deeply cut but shaped differently than those of 'Wieri Laciniatum'. It was discovered in 1948 in the nurseries of Georg Born in Rosenheim, Germany, as a chance seedling, and it proved to be very hardy in the extremely cold winter of 1956. Rudolf Schmidt in Rellingen, Germany, started to propagate it. G. Krüssmann published the name 'Born's Graciosa' in 1959, but this name was rejected by the registrar (Arnold Arboretum). As this illegitimate name is widely used in the German and Dutch nursery trades, we propose to change the name to 'Born's Gracious'. This change will not cause any confusion and is legitimate. See also note under 'Bruno'.

**'Bruno'.** About 1980 some scions were received with the name 'Bruno'. This name cannot be found in the literature, nor in any checklists. It looks very much like *A. saccharinum* 'Born's Gracious' so the labels obviously reflected a misspelling. Because this name has figured in the catalog of Firma C. Esveld, Boskoop, The Netherlands, 1984–1986, we include it here.

**'Chlorotinctum'.** Gebbers (1905). Germany. Leaves gray-green with a dark green, irregular margin, probably formed by chlorosis or a viral disease. This old cultivar is no longer available.

**'Citreo-variegatum'.** Schwerin (1893). Germany. Another variegated cultivar, the leaves being dotted with pale lemon. Apparently no longer in cultivation.

**'Columnare'.** Temple (1885). Identical to *A. saccharum* 'Newton Sentry' (Murray 1970c).

**'Crispum'.** Kelsey (1894). USA. Tree with irregularly cut and curled leaves. Lost from cultivation.

**'Crispum Novum'.** Ellwanger & Barry (1880). Great Britain. Small tree with deformed and crinkled leaves. Lost from cultivation.

**'Cuneatum'.** Pax (1886). Germany. Leaves 3- to 5-lobed with cuneate bases. Very rare and not available in the trade.

**'Curvatum'.** Schwerin (1893). Germany. Leaf lobes falcate. Most probably lost from cultivation.

**'Cutleaf'.** Kelsey & Dayton (1942). USA. See **'Laciniatum Wieri'.**

**'Dilaceratum'.** Schwerin (1901). Germany. Leaf margins irregularly torn, with gray or yellow streaks. Another selection that is probably no longer in cultivation.

**'Dissectifolium'.** Sudworth (1897). See **'Dissectum'.**

**'Dissectum'.** Pax (1886). Germany. Leaves deformed, small, with creamy edges. No longer in cultivation.

**'Elegant'**, see ***A.* × *freemanii***

**'Fasciatum'.** Carrière (1885). France. A monstrous selection with fasciated branches. Probably no longer in cultivation.

**'Fastigiatum'.** Dutch nurseries ex Grootendorst (1969). See **'Pyramidale'.**

**'Floridanum Macrophyllum'.** Nicholson (1881). Great Britain. Lacks a description. Possibly belongs to *A. saccharum.*

**'Golden'.** Jewell Nurseries (1947). Minnesota, USA. This is a sport of *A. saccharinum* with an attractively colored bark. Possibly in the trade in North America before 1947. The "Golden" silver maple, growing in the Arnold Arboretum, Jamaica Plain, Massachusetts, USA, is probably 'Lutescens'.

**'Hance's Variegated'.** Hance & Son (1879). USA. The leaves are regularly striped and splashed with creamy white throughout the growing season. Probably lost from cultivation.

**'Heterophyllum'.** Ellwanger & Barry (1881). See **'Heterophyllum Laciniatum'.**

**'Heterophyllum Laciniatum'.** Ellwanger & Barry (1880). Great Britain. Said to differ from 'Wieri Laciniatum' in that its leaves are more deeply incised. It is a fast-growing tree. No longer available under this name in the trade.

**'Improved'.** Mulligan (1958). Washington, USA. A name used without description for a plant in the Morton Arboretum, Lisle, Illinois, USA, with the reputation of being less brittle and breakable than the species. It has also been listed as 'Pyramidale', but note that it is not the same as 'Pyramidale' Späth (1885).

**'Juhlkei'.** Jurrissen (1886). The Netherlands. See **'Variegatum'.**

**Laciniatum.** Pax (1886). Germany. This is a grex name for all types with dissected leaves.

**'Laciniatum Beebe'.** Harkness (1964). See **'Beebe Cutleaf Weeping'.**

**'Laciniatum Wieri'.** Ellwanger & Barry (1875). Great Britain. A very widely grown, large, slightly flat-topped tree. Its leaves are deeply cut and the lobes deeply dissected. This cultivar is usually propagated by layering and is generally available. The wood is like that of the species, rather brittle. It is planted on a large scale in the suburbs, especially of Swiss cities, where it has been extremely popular since the 1960s. It is often sold under an incorrect name such as 'Wieri', 'Wageri', 'Wagneri', 'Asplenifolium', or 'Laciniatum'. The original tree was discovered by Wier. Ellwanger & Barry bought it from him and named it for him.

**'Lactescens'.** Schwerin (1892). Germany. Leaves speckled gray and white. Apparently no longer in cultivation.

**'Lee's Red'.** Sheridan Nursery (before 1989).

Ontario, Canada. Large tree, selected in southern Ontario and, according to its description, notable for its brilliant autumn colors. The leaves are not so deeply divided as those of *A. saccharinum* itself.

**'Longifolium'.** Späth (1882). Germany. Leaf lobes acuminate, bases cordate. Probably not in cultivation.

**'Lutescens'.** Späth (1883). Germany. This old cultivar is still in cultivation in a few nurseries and is available on a restricted scale. The tree grows somewhat slower than the species. The leaves are of the normal shape and size and are a good clear yellow in spring, turning light green when mature. Its autumn color is yellow. See also 'Golden'.

**'Luteum'.** Mulligan (1958). Washington, USA. See also 'Golden'.

**'Macrophyllum'.** Petzold & Kirchner (1864). Germany. Leaves very large. Apparently no longer in cultivation.

**'Monstrosum'.** Nicholson (1881). Great Britain. Lacks a description. Probably not in cultivation.

**'Nanum'.** Schwerin (1893). Germany. A shrubby and globose clone. It is quite uncertain whether this peculiarity is still growing in some collections. It is no longer available in the trade.

**'Nervosum'.** Wesmael (1890). Belgium. Lacks a description. Not in cultivation.

**'Northline'.** McBeath (1983). Ontario, Canada. An open-pollinated seedling (1970) originating in the Morden Research Station, Canada, grown by Dr. Skinner. It has a widely branching habit and grows slowly. It is distinguished from cultivars such as 'Sheridan' by its branch strength and hardiness.

**'Novum'**, see **'Crispum Novum'**

**'Palmatum'.** Zabel (1878). Germany. Leaves deeply cleft, nearly closed by the lobes. It is an old cultivar, certainly no longer available in the trade. There is a 7-m-tall male tree on the campus of the University of Florida, Gainesville, labeled *A. rubrum* 'Palmatum'. There is no question that this plant is a clone or variant of *A. saccharinum* whose leaves match the illustration of *A. saccharinum* 'Palmatum' in Krüssman in all respects, except size; those of the Gainesville tree are one-half to one-third the size of typical *A. saccharinum*.

**'Pavia'.** Petzold & Kirchner (1864). Germany. The upper surfaces of the leaves are somewhat wrinkled, not unlike the leaflets of a horse chestnut leaf. The name 'Pavia' was given by Messrs. Booth, nurserymen in Hamburg, Germany, and is cited in the old Arboretum Muskaw, a former property of the Princes of Orange-Nassau of The Netherlands. This cultivar is now lost from cultivation.

**'Pendulum'.** Van Houtte (1875). Belgium. A tree with a pendulous habit. Whether this particular clone is still grown is uncertain. Such trees are common in seedling populations and so are easily confused with the original clone.

**'Pipal'.** Cole Nursery Co (1957). USA. A sterile tree, leafing out rather early in the spring and holding its leaves until November. Named after F. Pipal, city forester of Omaha, Nebraska. It is not in general cultivation and not available in Europe.

**'Pseudoternatum'.** Schwerin (1893). Germany. The leaves seem to be trifoliate, which is in fact not the case. They are very deeply cleft into the bases. Apparently no longer in cultivation.

**'Pulverulentum'**, see **'Variegatum'**

**'Pyramidale'.** Späth (1885). Germany. A fast-growing tree, with a rather narrow columnar habit. Occasionally branches bend out of the crown and must be removed. The leaf is indistinguishable from that of the species. It is in cultivation in several European nurseries and still readily available. Not suitable for small gardens.

**'Rubellum'**, see **'Rubrum'**

**'Rubrum'.** Hillier & Sons (1928). Ampfield, Great Britain. Tree of normal shape and size. The leaves turn red in the autumn. Possibly still available.

**'Saira'.** Petzold & Kirchner (1864). Germany. An odd name, which appears in the old literature. It is probably nothing but a pale-leaved expression of *A. saccharinum*.

**'Sanguineum'.** Schwerin (1893). Germany. The young leaves are a good red in spring, turning to green when mature. This characteristic is sometimes seen in seedlings. The original cultivar may be lost to cultivation.

**'Schwerinii'.** Beissner (1902). Germany. An erect tree with deeply dissected leaves, very much like 'Laciniatum Wieri'. It seems to be a good selection but is no longer available. Possibly still present in old collections.

**'Serpentinum'.** Schwerin (1893). Germany. A tree of moderate size with thin, long, pendulous branches. No longer available.

**'Sheridan'.** Sheridan Nurseries (1980). Canada. This is a rather fast-growing selection, suitable for rather large gardens and public parks. It is a tree of regular habit, with fresh green leaves, hardly differing from the species. Comparable to trees such as 'Northline' or 'Silver Queen', it has a more widely branching habit and slower growth. Not yet available in Europe.

**'Silver Queen'.** J. Frank Schmidt & Son (1966). A good tree with an oval crown and upright spreading branches. Its form is more regular than that of the average silver maple. It has a good central leader and is suitable for large streets and parks. It is a male form, so does not bear any seed. The leaves are the usual shape and silvery beneath. The fall color is golden yellow.

**'Sir Charles Wager'.** Miller (1768). Identical to the species.

**'Skinneri'.** Naperville Nurseries (1934). Illinois, USA. Another tree with deeply incised leaves, closely related to 'Laciniatum Wieri'. It originated as a chance seedling in the nursery of J. H. Skinner in Topeka, Kansas.

**'Souvenir de Louis Van Houtte'**, see **'Aureovariegatum'**

**'Trefoil'**, see **'Tripartitum'**

**'Tricolor'.** Wesmael (1890). Belgium. Lacks a description. Apparently not in cultivation.

**'Trifoliatum'.** Wesmael (1890). Belgium. Lacks a description. Apparently not in cultivation.

**'Trilobatum'.** Schwerin (1901). Germany. Tree of moderate size, leaves distinctly 3-lobed. We know of no example of this plant still growing.

**'Tripartitum'.** Ellwanger & Barry (1880). Great Britain. A vigorous, upright tree, with deeply incised leaves. Probably lost from cultivation. Such types of garden origin, however, are frequently found in seed beds.

**'Variegatum'.** Zabel (1878). Germany. Lacks a description, but doubtless with variegated leaves. Probably not in cultivation.

**'Villosum'.** Ascherson (1860). Germany. With villose samaras. Probably no longer in cultivation.

**'Wagneri'.** Haage & Schmidt (1865). Germany. One of the many cultivars with deeply incised leaves. This name is occasionally used for 'Laciniatum Wieri' but it is slightly different in that the leaves are more deeply incised. Occasionally in the trade.

**'Wagneri Dissectum'**, see **'Wagneri'**

**'Wagneri Laciniatum'**, see **'Wagneri'**

**'Weeping'.** Kelsey & Dayton (1942). USA. See **'Pendulum'.**

**'Wieri'.** Wier (1873). See **'Laciniatum Wieri'.**

**'Wier's Cutleaf'**, see **'Laciniatum Wieri'**

**'Willis' Cutleaf'.** Willis Nursery Co. (1937). Kansas, USA. Leaves deeply dissected, shredded, illustrated in *American Nurseryman* 68(8) 1938, together with 'Laciniatum Wieri' and 'Skinneri'. It is uncertain whether this is still available. It is not grown in Europe.

**'Willisii'.** Willis (1939). See **'Willis' Cutleaf'.**

**'Yellow Bronze'.** Kelsey & Dayton (1942). USA. See **'Lutescens'.**

## ACER SACCHARUM

The sugar maple is a very variable species, which had resulted in species rank being assigned to several variants. These former species have been merged and are now classified as subspecies of *Acer saccharum.* Sugar maple inhabits a very large area in North America, so is adapted to a wide range of climates and conditions. Due to geographic variability in adaptations, several variations have been described as forms or cultivars while others have been selected for their growth characteristics. While common in North America, where it is a highly satisfactory landscape plant, this is not the case in Europe. Large, old trees exist in many European gardens, but the species is rare in general horticulture. It flowers irregularly and seed production is very low in Europe. Consequently, it is usually propagated by layering or from seedlings imported from North American nurseries. (See under *A. platanoides*). All cultivars are hardy in zone III.

Full bibliographic notes and more information can be found in the *Checklist of Cultivated Maples* II, *Acer saccharum,* compiled by Frank S. Santamour and A. Jacot McArdle (1982).

**'Alton Ogden'.** Scanlon (1951). Ohio, USA. Lacks a description, referred to as "lyre"-shaped. Probably not in cultivation.

**'Arrowhead'.** Carlton Plants (1961). Dayton, Ohio, USA. Tree, up to 20 m tall, with an upright habit and a strong leader. Leaves rather large, same shape as the species itself, dark green. Fall color is orange to red.

**'Bonfire'.** J. Frank Schmidt & Son (circa 1965). Boring, Oregon, USA. Tree up to 15 m tall, growing faster than most sugar maple selections. It is well adapted to various climatic conditions. Its fall colors are orange, orange-red, and red.

**'Brocade'.** Delendick (1983). New York, USA. A small tree or shrublike tree. Leaves deeply dissected, almost to the bases, lobes slightly overlapping (Plate 196). The leaves are large, about 15 cm across, dark green with a red petiole. The autumn color is golden yellow. It was first released as 'Dissectum' but later named 'Brocade' as the Latin name was illegitimate. Unfortunately, the name 'Brocade' had already been used for a cultivar of *A. palmatum,* but in the genus *Acer* the use of the same fancy name is allowed for another "cultivar class." This practice, in fact, should be avoided as there are so many words available to express the characteristics of a plant. 'Brocade' is still rare in the trade.

**'Cary'.** Brooklyn Botanic Garden (1965). New York, USA. Tree with a columnar habit, less narrow than some other newer selections. Rather slow-growing and densely branched. Leaves smaller than those of the species, narrowly bell-shaped. This tree was discovered by J. W. Ploetz, near Millbrook, New York, now the site of the Cary Arboretum of the New York Botanical Garden. Named for Mary Flagler Cary and introduced by the Brooklyn Botanic Garden. US Plant Patent 2581 (1965). Not available in Europe.

**'Coleman'.** Mulligan (1958). Washington, USA. According to D. Wyman (1959) this is a broad columnar tree to 15 m tall or more. It was discovered growing in Lake City, Minnesota, and selected by R. Nordine. It is not available in Europe.

**'Columnare'**, see **'Newton Sentry'**

**'Commemoration'.** Moller's Nursery (1981). Gresham, Oregon, USA. Selected by W. N. Wandell of Urbana, Illinois. Tree with a spreading crown, vigorously growing. Its leaves are leathery and very resistant to leaf tatter. It branches well. Fall colors appear early and are orange to red. US Plant Patent 5079.

**'Conicum'.** Fernald (1934). USA. See ***A. saccharum*** f. ***conicum.***

**'Cutleaf'**, see **'Sweet Shadow Cut-Leaf'**

**'Dissectum'**, see **'Brocade'**

**'Endownment'.** Hort. Research Institute. University of North Carolina, USA. Upright-growing tree with columnar habit, up to 15–18 m tall. Well suited for street plantings. The leaves are dark green, turning to bright yellow in the fall. US Plant Patent 4654.

**'Fairview'.** McGill & Son (1975). Fairview, Oregon, USA. Vigorously growing tree with a sturdy habit. Does not require staking. The leaves are of the typical shape, and emerald green. The color of the bark is much lighter than usual. Not available in Europe.

**'Flax Mill Majesty'.** J. Frank Schmidt & Sons (circa 1980). Boring, Oregon, USA. Large tree, up to 17–20 m tall with a broadly oval crown. Very vigorous grower, developing a heavy caliper and full branching at a relatively early age. Dark green leaves turn to orange or reddish in the fall. US Plant Patent 5273.

**'Flower'.** Mulligan (1958). Washington, USA. According to Donald Wyman (1959) it is a tree of a narrow habit, discovered in Manchester, Vermont. The original tree is on the property of H. C. Flower. Not available in Europe.

**'Globosum'.** Kingsville Nurseries (1947). Maryland, USA. An unusual form of sugar maple with a globose crown, broader than tall. The leaves are a beautifully golden orange in the autumn. Discovered at LaBar's Rhododendron Nursery near Stroudsburg, Pennsylavnia, and introduced and registered by H. J. Hohman, Kingsville, Maryland. It is rarely available in America, and not at all in Europe.

**'Goldspire'.** Princeton Nurseries (1973). New Jersey, USA. A tree with a more or less columnar crown, 10–12 m high and about 5–6 m wide. The leaves are lustrous green and somewhat leathery. Autumn color, orange-yellow. Thought to be a hybrid of 'Temple's Upright' and 'Newton Sentry'. US Plant Patent 2917 (1969). It is also available in Europe.

**'Greencolumn'.** B. Heard (1906). USA. This tree belongs to subspecies *nigrum,* sometimes called the black maple. It has been selected from a native stand in Iowa by B. Heard. It is an upright growing tree with an oval crown, up to 20 m tall, its leaves are large, light green, and fall color is always excellent—various shades of yellow to apricot orange. As the black maple is well adapted to dry conditions, this tree is quite useful in dry regions. US Plant Patent 3722.

**'Green Mountain'.** Princeton Nurseries (1964). New Jersey, USA. A broadly pyramidal tree, 10–12 m high and 6–8 m wide. Leaves dark green and leathery, turning orange and scarlet in the autumn as well as in unfavorable conditions. This is the best-known clone of all the sugar maples and has the most reliable fall color. It is widely planted. US Plant Patent 2339 (1964). Rarely available in Europe.

**'Laciniatum'.** Collins (1964). See **'Sweet Shadow Cut-Leaf'.**

**'Lanco Columnar'.** Siebenthaler Co. (1981). Ohio, USA. Another recently introduced columnar tree. Leaves dark green and very lustrous with very good autumn colors. US Plant Patent 4654 (1981). Not yet available in Europe.

**'Legacy'.** Moller's Nursery (1981). Gresham, Oregon, USA. A vigorously growing tree with a spreading habit, densely branched. Leaves dark green, leathery, and very lustrous. Autumn colors red to orange, resistant to leaf tatter. In favorable conditions the autumn colors are soft pink and salmon. Selected by W. N. Wandell of Urbana, Illinois. Not available in Europe. US Plant Patent 4979.

**'Louisa Lad'.** Van den Oever (1984). Haaren, The Netherlands. A fast-growing street tree with an openly oval crown. Leaves sea green with glaucous lower surfaces; 5-lobed, outer lobes underdeveloped. Autumn colors yellow to orange-red. Flowers yellowish and inconspicuous. Does not tolerate a chalky soil or stagnating water. Selected by Ton van den Oever Nurseries from a large batch of seedlings. Named after the estate "Louisa Hof," where the nurseries are situated.

**'Majesty'.** Flax Mill Nursery (before 1990). USA. A distinct cultivar, characterized by a perfectly ovoid crown at a very early age. A vigorous grower, abundantly branched, and with a straight leader. Leaves firm and somewhat leathery, turning orange-red in the autumn. Not available in Europe. US Plant Patent 5273.

**'Monstrosum'.** Raraflora Nurseries (1962). Pennsylvania, USA. Lacks a description and has an illegitimate Latin epithet. Apparently not in cultivation.

**'Monumental'.** Ellwanger & Barry (1893). Great Britain. Described as *A. saccharinum monumentalis,* an incorrect Latin trinomial for a selection of *A. saccharum.* It is said to be a compact and pyramidal tree with good, lustrous green foliage, the second growth producing crimson leaves and providing a striking contrast. Probably no longer in cultivation, but well worth searching for in old collections.

**'Monumentale'**, see **'Temple's Upright'**

**'Moraine'.** Siebenthaler Co. (1980). Ohio, USA. A rapidly growing tree with a conical crown. Leaves green, turning first a mottled golden crimson and orange, afterward blood red. Selected from seedlings in the Moraine Nursery as one of the best of many hundreds. Not susceptible to frost cracking of the bark. US Plant Patent 4534 (1980). Very rarely available in Europe.

**'Newton Sentry'.** Harkness (1954 + 1955). Rochester, New York, USA. A very narrow columnar tree, lacking a single central leader above 2 m (Plate 197). Major and minor branches vertically arranged. Short, stubby, lateral branches on the secondary branches. Leaves dark green and leathery in texture, margins wavy. There is a remarkable confusion between this cultivar and 'Temple's Upright', caused by an incorrect description by Harkness in *Baileya* (1954) as well as in *Hortus Third* and in *Trees for American Gardens* by Wyman (1965). An article by R. E. Weaver (1976) in *Arnoldia* illustrated the two cultivars with the names reversed. The type specimen of 'Newton Sentry', now about 100 years old, located in the Newton Cemetery in Massachussetts, is over 15 m high and about 4 m wide. As 'Newton Sentry' matures it develops several major leaders, and the lateral branches follow closely. This feature gives the tree its extremely narrow form. It has not become very popular, possibly due to its stick-like winter appearance for the first 25 years. It is not suitable as a hedging plant, as it lacks low branches. The autumn colors are typical, and the leaves are lost quite early. 'Temple's Upright' has a more elliptical and much wider growth habit with a central leader. Detailed information on this cultivar can be found in an article by M. Dathe (1983) in *Arnoldia,* which sets the record straight. It is a very rare tree in Europe and only occasionally available.

**'Pyramidal'.** Kelsey & Dayton (1942). Massachusetts, USA. This is a valid name, for while synonymous with 'Pyramidale', the latter name has not previously been used as an epithet in *A. saccharum.* This plant lacks a description but is undoubtedly a pyramidal selection. It is possible that 'Temple's Upright' was meant.

**'Rocky Mountains Glow'**, see **Schmidt'**

**'Sandborn'.** Mulligan (1958). Washington, USA. According to Wyman (1959) this is a narrow, columnar tree, without further description. It originated on Mrs. Sandborn's property in Concord, New Hampshire. Not available in Europe.

**'Schmidt'.** J. Frank Schmidt & Son. Boring, Oregon, USA. This slow-growing tree belongs to subspecies *grandidentatum.* It attains a height of about 7 m with age. The leaves are smaller and more leathery than those of the common sugar maple. The fall color is bright red. Its trademarked name is 'Rocky Mountains Glow'.

**'Seneca Chief'.** Schichtel's Nurseries (1979). New York, USA. A tree with a narrow, oval crown, densely branched. Leaves fresh green, turning yellow and orange in the autumn. Not available in Europe.

**'Senecaensis'.** Slavin (1950). USA. Originally considered as an interspecific hybrid between *A. saccharum* and the former species *A. leucoderme.* Since *A. leucoderme* has been reduced to subspecific rank under *A. saccharum,* Slavin's name *A.* × *senecaense* must also be reduced to cultivar status. This tree originated about 1919 at Durand Eastman Park, Rochester, New York. Leaves small, not unlike those of *A. saccharum* ssp. *grandidentatum*. It is not known whether this cultivar is still in cultivation.

**'Sentry'**, see **'Temple's Upright'**

**'Slavin's Upright'.** Harkness (1955). Rochester, New York, USA. An upright tree, with strongly ascending branches, of columnar habit. It is considered to belong to subspecies *nigrum* and was selected as a seedling from a tree near Salamanca, New York. The tree was first described, but not named, by Slavin in 1950. Not available in Europe.

**'Sweet Shadow Cut-Leaf'.** Powell Valley Nursery Co. (1962). Oregon, USA. Small tree, leaves very deeply cut, almost to the bases (Plate 198). The lobes, slightly overlapping each other, are again incised. The leaves are smaller than those of 'Brocade' and more dissected. It grows slowly and is very rare in Europe. US Plant Patent 2139 (1962). It is a very interesting small tree and should be more widely planted.

**'Temple's Upright'.** Harkness (1954). Rochester, New York, USA. A broadly columnar tree with a strong central leader, well into the crown (Plate 199). The major and minor branches ascend gradually but do not have short, stubby lateral branchlets; the secondary branches are similar to those of the species. 'Temple's Upright' presents an elliptical silhouette and is a first-class landscaping tree. The leaves are rather large, somewhat leathery in texture, and develop good color in the autumn. It is not known how or where Temple acquired his first scions or cuttings, or whether the original tree is still growing. It belongs to subspecies *nigrum*. It is rare in Europe but occasionally available.

**'Wright Brothers'.** Studebaker Nursery (1991). Ohio, USA. New selection; no further description available.

There is a very large group of code names, arising out of a Canadian selection program, not included in this survey. In 1968 the province of Ontario started a program to select potentially good specimen trees from native stands of sugar maple. Rather than assigning numbers to the trees selected they were given code names, usually indicating the place where each was growing. The names were frequently followed by a number, indicating more than one selected tree in that area. As far as is known, these plants are not available in the trade. Morsink and Jorgensen (1974) compiled these lists and made the information available in tabular form, briefly mentioning shape, branching, density, and estimated height and age. Of the 257 names originally identified, 50 have been vegetatively propagated. They are

| | |
|---|---|
| Agawa | Hopeville 2 |
| Amurlee 1 | Ingersoll |
| Auburn 2 | Kettleby |
| Balantyre 1 | Kirkwall 1 |
| Ballantrae 1 | Kirkwall 2 |
| Campbellford 1 | Middlemiss |
| Campbellford 2 | Midhurst |
| Centreville 3 | Mono Mills 1 |
| Christina 6 | Mono Mills 2 |
| Christina 7 | Morganston |
| Craighurst 2 | Mt. Albert 2 |
| Cristina 1 | Northland 1 |
| Crosby | Paris |
| Delta | Parkhill 1 |
| Desboro | Plattsville 1 |
| Edgar 1 | Princeton 2 |
| Garden Hill 1 | Rosemont 2 |
| Goodwood 1 | Selby |
| Goodwood 2 | Springbank 1 |
| Groveton 4 | Thamesford 5 |
| Harrowsmith 1 | Thamesford 8 |
| Harrowsmith 2 | Thamesford 9 |
| Hillsburgh 1 | Uxbridge 2 |
| Hilton Beach 1 | Wellesley 1 |
| Hilton Beach 2 | Wellesley 2 |

## ACER SHIRASAWANUM

This maple was poorly understood for many years. Investigations have made it better known, as several cultivars formerly assigned to *Acer japonicum* were transferred to this species by T. Delendick in 1984. Although it will take some time for these changes to be widely known and accepted by the horticultural world, Delendick's assignment is accepted here.

**'Aureum'.** Siesmayer (1888). Germany.
Synonyms:
'Flagelliforme Aureum'. Van Houtte (1885).
'Goldenmoon'. Kelsey & Dayton (1942). Massachusetts, USA.
'Kakure gasa'
'Kinkakure'
'Macrophyllum Aureum'. Nicholson (1881).
'Yellow Moon'. Pennsylvania, USA.
Compact, densely branched shrub, occasionally to 7–8 m high and sometimes (rarely) as wide. Bark ash gray, smooth. Leaves orbicular, 9- to 11-lobed, 7–10 cm across, incised to half the length of the blade, glabrous, golden yellow, darkening when mature, the margins often reddish. Occasionally the leaves are fully edged with scarlet, or

entire leaves turn scarlet and later turn a warm brown golden tone in autumn. Flowers are red, in small erect spikes, conspicuous on older trees. The seeds are borne in small clusters, also erect, which appear to lie on the leaves.

These features, and its glabrous leaves, make it necessary to transfer this cultivar to *A. shirasawanum,* as it fits with this species much better than with *A. japonicum.* It has been in cultivation in Japan for more than 200 years and has always heretofore been placed in *A. japonicum.* It was introduced into Europe by von Siebold about 1865 and introduced into the trade by L. Van Houtte circa 1870. This is a very well-known cultivar and one of the most outstanding. It is generally available in the trade. It is relatively difficult to propagate and grows slowly as a young plant. The leaves are prone to some sunburn in hot and dry sites. One of the largest specimens in the world, now about 135 years old, grows in Boskoop, The Netherlands, in the *Acer* collection of Firma C. Esveld; it is illustrated in JDV II, 165 and in the present volume (Plates 200, 201).

**'Aureum Oblongum'.** Wada (1938). Japan. Probably the same as the preceding cultivar. Not known in cultivation.

**'Autumn Moon'.** Vertrees (1985). Roseburg, Oregon, USA. JDV II, 166. Medium-sized, shrubby tree. Leaves 9- to 11-lobed and of the typical shape of the species. The rusty-colored lobes radiate in almost a circular pattern. Leaves may also be light green or rusty green. They make a most attractive impression and are of a firm texture (not thin as in the species). This cultivar was found as a chance seedling in a seedbed. It requires a sunny situation for best results. Not yet available in Europe.

**'Ezono o momiji'.** JDV I, 137; JDV II, 144. Large, shrubby tree, 5–6 m in height and often as wide. Leaves orbicular, of much the same shape as 'Aureum', light green in spring, darkening when mature. The shoots are of a firm and stout texture. The autumnal colors are mainly yellow. It is an attractive plant for large gardens. It has traditionally been placed under *A. japonicum,* but has been transferred to *A. shirasawanum* for the same reasons as pointed out for 'Aureum'. It is available in the trade. Zone V.

**'Junihitoe'.** JDV I, 138; JDV II, 145, photo. The name 'Junihitoe' is confusing. It is used in old Japanese nursery catalogs as the common name for the species. Henry Hohman of the Kingsville Nurseries, USA, carried it in his early listings, according to Vertrees. Koidzumi lists it as forma *typicum,* which is simply the species. M. Yokoi says it is synonymous with 'Ogureyama'. Vertrees uses this name for a small-leaved form, similar to *A. japonicum* 'Microphyllum', bearing orbicular, 11-lobed leaves on short petioles that hold the leaves horizontally. The autumn color is orange. As with 'Aureum', flowers and seeds are held erect. This clone must also be moved to *A. shirasawanum.* Plants recently imported from Japan into The Netherlands are indeed very similar to 'Microphyllum'.

**'Microphyllum'.** Siesmayer (1888). Germany. New York, USA. JDV I, 139; JDV II, 167. A rather small, treelike shrub, upright, to 5–6 m tall but not as wide. It is rather densely branched, with gray-brown or ash gray, smooth bark. Leaves orbicular, 9- to 11-lobed, of the same shape and size as those of 'Aureum', fresh green throughout the spring and summer, turning golden yellow in the autumn. Flowers red, in small, erect spikes; the fruits are borne in small, erect bunches, much as in 'Aureum' (Plate 202). For the reasons already pointed out, this cultivar, formerly in *A. japonicum,* is here transferred to *A. shirasawanum.* Delendick has pointed out that the name *microphyllum,* as a varietal epithet, must be dropped. Seedlings of the clonal form 'Microphyllum' are indistinguishable from true *A. shirasawanum.* The clone 'Microphyllum', which originated in the Coimbra Botanic Garden, Portugal—vegetatively propagated by grafting—has to be maintained as a cultivar. Seedlings are now produced by the hundreds and the grafted clone is easily available.

**'Murasame'.** Koidzumi (1911). Japan. A small-leaved selection, 11-lobed, leaves 5 cm across, bases deeply cordate, veins pilose beneath. Apparently not in cultivation.

**'Ogon itaya',** see **'Aureum'**

**'Ogureyama'.** JDV I, 140; JDV II, 147, photo. Very much like 'Microphyllum' in its general habit but less upright. The leaves are almost identical to 'Microphyllum', orbicular, 11-lobed and 6–8 cm across. The autumn color is orange-red to golden yellow. It is not yet in cultivation in Europe.

**'Palmatifolium'.** JDV I, 158; JDV II, 167, photo. This is a very beautiful selection of *A. shirasawanum* and has been in cultivation for many years. We have been unable to trace the name, as it is not mentioned in the literature. It might have been given by Koidzumi but is not mentioned in his work *Revisio Aceracearum Japonicarum.* A very old plant is growing in the Kalmthout Arboretum, Belgium, and in Hergest Croft Gardens, Great Britain. It is a large, treelike shrub, to 6 m tall or more and about as wide. The leaves, about 10 cm across, are 11-lobed and deeply incised, almost to the bases, with sharp, narrow apices. The leaf margins are serrate and roll slightly downward, giving a convex impression. The autumn colors are very brilliant, scarlet and orange to golden yellow. Unfortunately, the leaves drop rather quickly. It is a sturdy plant, adapting easily to all growing conditions. It is available in the trade. Zone V.

**'Sayo shigure'.** Koidzumi (1911). Japan. JDV I, 141; JDV II, 148. Small-leaved, close to 'Microphyllum', and of the same size. It is little grown. The leaves are dull green, 9-lobed with lightly toothed margins. It grows as a medium-sized shrub. Not in cultivation in Europe and very rare in the United States.

**'Susanne'.** H. J. Drath (1992). Barmstedt, Germany. A relatively fast-growing upright shrub with sturdy, stout branching. Young plants especially grow vigorously and form shoots up to 60 cm. The leaves are almost orbicular, 9- to 13-lobed, and pale linden-green with a yellow hue; later in the summer they have a delicate red edging and in autumn the entire leaf turns golden-brown. The flowers are like those of the species, and fruits are tightly packed together. This conspicuous cultivar, a seedling of the well-known *Acer shirasawanum* 'Aureum', was found by Drath and presented to the Thiensen Arboretum in Ellerhoop, Germany. It was named after the daughter of H. D. Warda, director of the arboretum, and has been introduced by Firma C. Esveld, Boskoop, The Netherlands.

**'Yezo meigetsu'**, see **'Microphyllum'**

## ACER SIEBOLDIANUM

*Acer sieboldianum* is a rather rare species, closely related to *A. palmatum*, and with few cultivars. Nevertheless, these few are very interesting and valuable. All are hardy in zone V.

**'Aiai gasa'**, a synonym for *A. sieboldianum*, which see in Chapter 7

**'Albiflorum'.** Koidzumi (1911). Japan. With white flowers rather than the yellow ones typical of *Acer*. Otherwise like the species. Probably not in cultivation.

**'Attaryi'**, see ***A. japonicum* 'Attaryi'**

**'Ayai gasa'**, see **'Aiai gasa'**

**'Hime uchiwa'**, a synonym for *A. sieboldianum* var. *microphyllum*, which see in Chapter 7

**'Kasatoriyama'.** JDV I, 158; JDV II, 167. A rather narrow, small tree of about 4–5 m in height. It is densely branched when mature. The leaves are circular, pale green, rather thin, 9- to 11-lobed, and with lobe apices ending abruptly in sharp points. Autumn colors are scarlet to golden yellow. It is a rare cultivar and not available in Europe.

**'Kinugasa yama'.** JDV I, 158; JDV II, 168, photo. A rapidly growing, small tree, to 6–8 m in height, rather strongly branched. Leaves green with a bluish tone and densely set with silky hairs, particularly when young. The petioles are also pubescent. This pubescence is a conspicuous feature of this cultivar, making it easy to recognize. The autumn colors are good, in the usual color range. A useful plant for larger gardens and easy to grow. Available in the trade. The name means "silk canopy", or "umbrella."

**'Ko uchiwa,'** see ***A. sieboldianum* var. *microphyllum***

**'Mikasa nishiki'.** Leaves 9-lobed, with small white dots. Probably not in cultivation.

**'Momiji gasa'.** JDV I 159; JDV II, 168. A small tree or only a shrub, of sturdy appearance, 3–4 m high. Leaves 9-lobed, with silky, whitish hairs covering both surfaces. The color is light green, which in combination with the pubescence gives the leaves a silvery appearance. The autumn color is mainly yellow. Formerly placed under *A. japonicum*. It is not in cultivation in Europe.

**'Momiji gasane'**, see **'Momiji gasa'**

**'Sayoginu'.** Wada (1938). Japan. Leaves small, turning vividly red in autumn. Not available in the trade.

**'Sode no uchi'.** JDV I, 159; JDV II, 168, photo. This is one of the few dwarf selections of *A. sieboldianum* and is a very attractive plant for rockeries or for bonsai. A rounded shrub of 2 m, it bears tiny leaves not exceeding 4 cm, usually smaller; 11-lobed, sometimes 9-lobed. The color is a fresh yellow-green, with a yellow to crimson autumn color. Unfortunately, it is rather difficult to propagate. Available in the trade.

**'Taiyu'.** Wada (1938). Japan. Leaves turning red in the autumn. No further description available. Not available in the trade.

**'Tortuosum'.** Maximowicz (1886). Russia. The branches spiral tortuously. Lost from cultivation.

## ACER TATARICUM ssp. GINNALA

This very common subspecies is frequently planted as background for large borders or massed park plantings. It is propagated by seed as it is only slightly variable. At the beginning of the 20th century, several selections were named and described. Not all of them can be viewed as distinct since identical plants are frequently found in every seedbed. A few continue to be grafted for their splendid autumn colors.

**'Albo-variegatum'.** Schwerin (1910). Germany. Leaves flecked white. This is a very common feature, obviating any need to grow it vegetatively.

**'Angustilobum'.** Schwerin (1896) Germany. Leaf lobes somewhat narrower than usual.

**'Aureo-variegatum'.** Späth (1894). Germany. Leaves variegated yellow.

**'Bailey Compact'.** Bailey Nurseries (1975). Minnesota, USA. Dense and compact in habit. Leaves turn a brilliant scarlet in the autumn. Suitable for cultivation in tubs. It was formerly named "Compact Amur Maple," not a legitimate cultivar name. Rarely available in the trade.

**'Coccineum'.** Nakai (1909). Japan. Samaras brilliant red, as is common in this subspecies.

**'Durand Dwarf'.** Harkness (1955). Rochester, Massachusetts, USA. A very compact shrub, originating as a witches' broom. The leaves are much smaller than usual, fresh green, and with a fiery red autumn color. An attractive plant but rarely available. Subject to sudden die-back. Not grown in Europe.

**'Fire'.** Esveld (1982–83). Boskoop, The Netherlands. A vigorously growing shrub, with long, slender shoots, densely branched. The leaves are of a firm texture, 3-lobed, the central lobes much longer than the basal ones. Color dark green with no trace of the variegation which is common in the subspecies. The autumn color is brilliantly scarlet, and the leaves hold for several weeks. This is a fine shrub and very reliable in its autumn color. Available in the trade.

**'Flame'.** Esveld (1982). Boskoop, The Netherlands. This and the preceding 'Fire' came nameless from Canada. A very hardy small tree or large shrub with a spreading branch pattern. It is a seed source selection and is an important improvement to seedling plants of *A. tataricum* ssp. *ginnala*.

**'Mondy'.** Monrovia Nurseries Ltd. California, USA. Large multistemmed shrub or small tree with 3-lobed leaves, dark green and somewhat leathery. Fall colors are red through orange to yellow-orange. Its trademarked name is 'Red Rhapsody'.

**'Pulverulentum'.** Schwerin (1896). Germany. Leaves powdery white, soon reverting to green. Apparently not in cultivation.

**'Red Rhapsody', see 'Mondy'**

## ACER TATARICUM ssp. TATARICUM

There are only a few cultivars of this rather common subspecies, most of them named many years ago. They are not at all distinctive and can be found in almost every seedbed. All the cultivars are hardy in zone IV.

**'Cordifolium'.** Wolf ex Pojarkova (1932). Russia. Identical to *A. tataricum* ssp. *tataricum.*

**'Crispatum'.** Pax (1886). Leaf margins crisped.

**'Crispum', see 'Crispatum'**

**'Cultriforme'.** Nicholson ex Schwerin (1903). Germany. No further description available.

**'Cuspidatum'.** Pax (1886). Germany. Leaf margins undulate.

**'Nanum'.** Dieck (1887). Germany. Densely branched shrub, dwarf and compact-growing.

**'Rubrum'.** Van Houtte (1873). Belgium. Leaves blood red when unfolding.

**'Variegatum'.** Wiegers (1809). Germany. Leaves variegated.

## ACER TRUNCATUM

This species is very closely related to *Acer mono,* and few cultivars formerly assigned to *A. mono* must be transferred here.

**'Akaji'.** Yokohama Nurseries (1896). Idential to *A. truncatum.* According to Hideo Suzuki, this name has been used since 1882 for a variegated form of *A. truncatum* and certainly not as a cultivar name of *A. palmatum,* as stated by Murray.

**'Akaji nishiki'.** Yokohama Nurseries (1896). Most probably the same as the preceding. Listed in the *Yokohama Catalogue* and possibly identical to *A. truncatum* 'Shuhunishiki'. Not known in cultivation under this name. According to M. Yokoi it might be identical to *A. palmatum* 'Seigai' (which see).

**'Akikaze'.** JDV I, 154, JDV II, 161, photo. A densely branched large shrub to 5 m, leaves 5-lobed, lobes somewhat irregular and wavy. Also known as *A. mono* var. *marmoratum,* but that is a different plant. The photo in Vertrees' *Japanese Maples* clearly shows *A. truncatum* leaves. Seedlings obtained from seed of Chinese origin, labeled *A. mono* var. *marmoratum,* also produced this type of plant. A tree, labeled *A. mono* var. *marmoratum,* growing in the Esveld Aceretum has *A. mono* leaves that are slightly more divided than usual. Murray placed *A. mono* as a subspecies under *A. truncatum*, an opinion not accepted in this book.

**'Akikaze nishiki'.** JDV I, 160; JDV II, 169, photo. A rather vigorous shrub to 4 m or more, well branched. The leaves are irregularly 5- to 7-lobed and rather heavily variegated with white (Plate 203). Sometimes a whole lobe or half the blade is completely white. Occasionally, complete green shoots appear and should be removed. It is a good plant that deserves more attention. Zone V.

**'Albo-variegatum',** a synonym of *A. mono* 'Hoshiyadori', which see

**'Albo-vittatum',** see **'Akikaze nishiki'** (This name, once used in Germany and listed in both German and Dutch nursery catalogs, has not been validly published.)

**'Aureum',** a synonym of *A. cappadocicum* 'Aureum', which see

**'Dissectum',** a synonym of *A. mono* 'Dissectum'

**'Luteo-variegatum',** a synonym of *A. cappadocicum* 'Aureum', which see

**'Shuen nishiki',** see **'Akikaze nishiki'**

**'Shufu nishiki',** see **'Akikaze nishiki'**

**'Shuhu nishiki',** see **'Akikaze nishiki'**

## ACER VELUTINUM

Virtually no cultivars have been derived from this species. Variety *glabrescens* (Boissier & Buhse) Murray (1969) is occasionally propagated vegetatively and a clone should be chosen for cultivar status. A selection has yet to be made and given a cultivar name. Plants so propagated are derived from trees grown from wild-collected seed.

**'Wolfii'.** Rehder (1938). Massachusetts, USA. This plant was first described as *A. insigne wolfii* by Schwerin (1905). Rehder reduced it to forma rank under *A. velutinum*. It has large, greenish leaves that are purplish red on their lower surfaces. It is named after E. Wolf of St. Petersburg, Russia. Not available.

## ACER × ZOESCHENSE

**'Annae'.** Schwerin (1908). Germany. A medium-sized tree to 10 m in height, densely branched. The crown is about as high as wide. Leaves dark purple at first, later turning to dark green, 3- to 5-lobed and somewhat wavy, 5–8 cm across. This beautiful tree is a forgotten gem that deserves more attention as a street tree or solitary in larger gardens. Propagated by layering.

**'Elongatum'.** Schwerin (1911). Germany. Leaves 3-lobed, lobes acuminate, margins wavy as in the preceding cultivar. Petioles reddish. Probably no longer in cultivation.

**'Friderici'.** Schwerin (1908). Germany. Flower buds creamy yellow, leaves golden yellow, petioles red. This cultivar is no longer available despite its attractive characteristics.

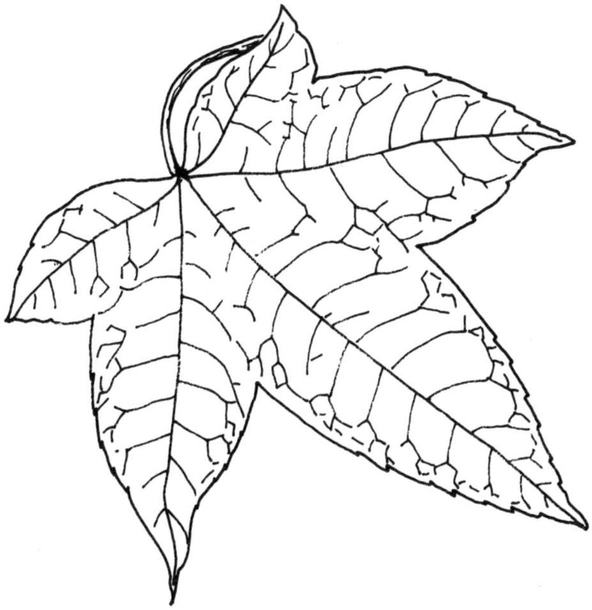

# Appendices

Appendix 1

# Japanese Names and Their Meanings

J. D. VERTREES

The following Japanese words, given with their English equivalents, are used in Japanese names for many maple cultivars. In a number of cases the translations are direct applications of meaning. For example, 'Beni shidare', a cultivar of *Acer palmatum,* comes from *beni,* meaning "red" and *shidare,* meaning "drooping, cascading." Hence, 'Beni shidare' is "the red, cascading" variety of *A. palmatum.* In other cases the English translation is a portion of or a combination of interpretations which cannot be applied literally. Many names are only abbreviated references to more complex meanings, as in the case of 'Tanabata', which refers to the Japanese Festival of the Stars (7 July). There is a delightful tale behind the name, but to understand the tale, readers must first understand that two constellations in the skies of Japan relate to this festival: one is called Kengyu (the young boy who cares for the cows), and the other is Kyokujo (the girl who weaves at the loom). The tale, as it was told to me, goes like this:

> Once upon a time there were two diligent young people, Kengyu and Kyokujo. Upon meeting for the first time, they immediately fell in love. Thereafter, the two did not work as hard as before but spent all their time walking together. When the gods noticed this, they became very angry and separated the two young people by a great river (i.e., the Milky Way). The young people could no longer be together, but the gods promised them that if they worked very hard they could see each other again once a year. So Kengyu and Kyokujo worked very hard throughout the year so they could see each other every 7 July. Thus began the Festival of the Stars—*Tanabata.*

***Aka*** = red
***Ao*** = green
***Aoba*** = green leaves
***Aocha*** = yellow green
***Arakawa*** = rough bark
***Asahi*** = rising sun
***Asahi zuru*** = swan of the dawn
***Beni*** = red
***Chirimen*** = Japanese crepe paper
***Gasane*** = piling one thing on another
***Gasumi*** or ***Kasumi*** = a mist or haze
***Goshiki*** = multicolored
***Hagaromo*** = cloth of an angel
***Hime*** = dwarf, princess
***Inazuma*** = thunder
***Ito*** = fine strings or thread
***Iwato*** = rock
***Kaede*** = one of the terms for maple, often applied to foreign maple species
***Kagami*** = mirror
***Kaku*** = tower
***Kakure*** = shade or shelter

***Kamagata*** = falcate
***Kara*** = ancient Chin or Chinese
***Kashi*** = filament
***Kin*** = gold
***Komachi*** = beautiful girl; dwarf
***Koto*** = an old harp
***Koto no ito*** = harp of string
***Kujaku*** = peacock
***Kumo no su*** = a spider's web
***Kyo*** = ancient capital, Kyoto city; beautiful dress, variegated leaf
***Kyohime*** = fairy tale princess
***Mai*** = dancing
***Maruba*** = round leaves
***Masu*** = wooden box used to drink sake
***Mejishi*** = mythical female lion
***Miyama*** = remote high mountain
***Miyasama kaede*** = prince's maple; an early plant of this kind was grown in Prince Fushina's garden
***Nishiki*** = variegated (literally, brocade or tapestry); fine dress
***Nishiki*** or ***Nishikisho*** = rough bark, like that of pine
***No*** = of
***Normura*** = beautiful
***Ojishi*** = mythical male lion
***Ryu*** = dragon
***Saku*** = fence
***Sango*** = coral
***Sarasa*** = a type of fabric with beautiful figures
***Sazanami*** = small source
***Sei*** = green
***Seiryu*** = blue dragon
***Sekka*** = dwarf (from witch's broom)
***Shidare*** = cascading, willowy, drooping
***Shigure*** = soft drizzle
***Shigure zono*** = colored rain
***Shime*** = a decoration used on New Year's Day
***Shime no uchi*** = within New Year's Day
***Shin*** = new
***Shira*** = white
***Shishigashira*** = lion's head (mythical lion)
***Shojo*** or ***Syojo*** = red-faced monkey; usually applied to a fictional monkey of Japanese drama, but can also mean a young girl.
***Tama*** = ball or gem
***Tamshime*** = jewel of a princess
***Tana*** = shelves, layers
***Tanabata*** = Festival of the Stars (7 July)
***Ten nyo*** = angel
***Toyama*** = name of a place
***Tsuchi*** = earth
***Tsuchigumo*** = spider on the ground
***Tsuma*** = nail
***Uchi*** = within
***Wabito*** = hermit
***Yama*** = mountain
***Yatsubusa*** = compact, dwarf
***Yezo nishiki*** = Yezo, a northern island of Japan
***Yu*** = evening
***Yuki*** = snow

Appendix 2

# New (Pinyin) and Old (Wade-Giles) Spellings of Selected Chinese Localities

D. M. VAN GELDEREN

| Pinyin | Wade-Giles |
|---|---|
| Anhui Province | Anhwei |
| Beijing | Peking |
| Chengdu | Chengtu |
| Chongqing | Chungking |
| Fujian Province | Fukien |
| Fuzhou | Foochow |
| Gansu | Kansu |
| Guangdong Province | Kwangtung |
| Guangxi Province | Kwangsi |
| Guangzhou | Canton |
| Guilin | Kweilin |
| Guizhou Province | Kweichow |
| Hainan Province | Hainan Island |
| Hangzhou | Hangchow |
| Hebei Province | Hopei |
| Heilongjiang Province | Heilungkiang |
| Henan | Honan |
| Hubei Province | Hupei |
| Hunan Province | Hunan |
| Jiangsu Province | Kiangsu |
| Jiangxi Province | Kiangsi (Changsi) |
| Jilin Province | Kirin |
| Kunming | Yunnan-fu |
| Lanzhou | Lanchow |

| Pinyin | Wade-Giles |
|---|---|
| Liaoning Province | Liaoning |
| Lijiang | Likiang |
| Nanjing | Nanking |
| Nei Monggol Province | Inner Mongolia |
| Ningxia | Ningsia |
| Qinghai Province | Tsinghai |
| Qinling Shan | Tsingling |
| Quingdao | Tsingtao |
| Shaanxi Province | Shenshi |
| Shandong Province | Shantung |
| Shanghai | Shanghai |
| Shanxi Province | Shansi |
| Sichuan Province | Szechwan |
| Taiwan | Formosa |
| Ukurundu | Manchuria |
| Xian | Sian |
| Xianggang | Hong Kong |
| Xinjiang Province | Sinkiang |
| Xizang Province | Tibet |
| Yichang | Ichang |
| Yunnan Province | Yunnan |
| Zhejiang Province | Chekiang |
| Zhongzhou | Chengchow |

Appendix 3

# Selected Sources of Maples

D. M. VAN GELDEREN

Although most nurseries stock some maples, the following nurseries and garden centers stock or can order more than the average range of maples.

*Australia*

Gaibor's Nursery
Great Western Highway
Wentworth Falls NSW 2782

Tristania Park Nurseries
28 Honour Ave
Macedon Vic 3440

Yamina Rare Plants
25 Moores Rd
Monbulk Vic 3793

*Belgium*

CECE
Monsieur B. Choteau
Av. Leopold IV 12
7130 Bray

*Denmark*

Plantekassen AB
S. Bergström
Jaegersborg Alle 170
2820 Gentofte

*England*

Bridgemere Garden World
Nantwich
Cheshire CW5 7QB

Hillier's Nurseries Ltd.
Ampfield House
Ampfield
Romsey
Hampshire SO5 9PA

Mallet Court Nursery
Currey Mallet
Taunton
Somerset TA3 6SY

P. Catt
Liss Forest Nursery
Petersfield Road
Greatham
Hampshire GU33 6EX

P. Chappell
Spinners
Boldre
Lymington
Hampshire SO4 8QU

*France*

Ets. F. Despalles SA
5, rue d'Alésia
75014 Paris

Jardins Ellebore
C. Geoffroy
Bois de Boulogne
75116 Paris

J. Hennebelle de Bonnières
La ferme Fleurie
Boubers sur Canches
62270 Frévent

Limousin Espaces Verts
Le Ponteix
87229 Feytiat

Pépinières Rhône-Alpes
R. N. 75
01440 Viriat

*Germany*

Baumschulen Schwendemann
Pestalozzistrasse 1
7630 Lahr

Joh. Wieting
Omorikastrasse 6
2910 Westerstede-Giesselhorst

W. Nagel
Hetzenbaumhöfe 4
7518 Bretten

W. Schmid
Gartencenter
Bei der Straubenmühle
7081 Hüttlingen

*New Zealand*

Blue Mountain Nurseries
99 Bushy Hill St
Tapanui

Peter Cave
Pukeroro RD 3
Hamilton

*Scotland*

P. A. Cox
Glendoick Gardencentre
Perth PH2 7NS

*Switzerland*

R. Haller AG
Baumschulen
4663 Aarburg, post Oftringen AG

Richard Huber AG
Baumschulen
5605 Dottikon AG

*The Netherlands*

Firma C. Esveld
Rijneveld 72
2771 XS Boskoop

*United States*

Buchholz & Buchholz Nursery
Route 1, Box 80
Gaston, OR 97119

Greer Gardens
1280 Goodpasture Island Road
Eugene, OR 97401

Iseli Nurseries
30590 S.E. Kelso Road
Boring, OR 97009

John Vermeulen & Son
Box 600
Neshanic Station, NJ 08853

Lake County Nursery
Route 84, Box 122
Perry, OH 44081

TCPlant
Tsai Cheng
23255 N.W. Evergreen St.
Hillsboro, OR 97124

# Appendix 4

# *Acer mono* and *Kalopanax septemlobus*[1]

DR. D. O. WIJNANDS

Prolonged discussion and uncertainty exist about the correct use of the name *Acer pictum* (e.g., Hunt 1977; Clarke 1988, 298). The problems concern its correct author citation, its accurate date of publication, its typification, and its legitimate taxonomic position, either in the Aceraceae or in the Araliaceae.

In 1784, two volumes, and possibly a third, were published dealing with the plants collected by C. P. Thunberg in Japan in 1775–1776. The first of these references was J. A. Murray's *Systema Vegetabilium,* 14th edition, which was published in May or June 1784 (Stafleu & Cowan 1981, 3:670). The second book was Thunberg's *Flora Japonica,* which was published in August 1784 (Stafleu & Cowan 1986, 6:317). Murray used the manuscript for *Flora Japonica,* containing Thunberg's new novelties from Japan, to compile his updated edition of Linnaeus' (1774) *Systema vegetabilium.* Thus there are very few discrepancies between these two books by Murray and Thunberg, and their texts of *Acer pictum* are identical.

The dating of the third publication, *Kaempferus illustratus seu explicatio illarum plantarum, quas Kaempferus in Iaponia collegit et in fasciculo quinto Amoenitatum Exoticarum adnotavit, secundum systema sexuale ad classes, ordines, genera et species iam redactarum; sectio secunda* (hereinafter referred to as *Kaempferus illustratus II*), poses a great problem. This work by Thunberg, comprising his interpretation of Kaempfer's *Flora Japonica,* was published in two parts. The first part appeared in 1780 in volume 3 of the journal *Nova Acta Regiae Societatis Scientiarum Upsaliensis,* and the second part was published in volume 4 of the same journal, the title page of which bears an imprint of 1784. Some authors (e.g., Hunt 1977), however, accept 1783 as the date of publication of volume 4. Accepting 1783 as the publication date of Thunberg's *Kaempferus illustratus II* gives it publication and nomenclatural priority over Murray's *Systema vegatibilium* (14th edition) and Thunberg's *Flora Japonica,* both published in 1784.

The publication details of Thunberg's *Kaempferus illustratus II* in volume 4 of *Nova Acta* can be gleaned from the minutes of the Royal Academy of Science of Uppsala. Judging from the printer's continuous numbering by signatures of the gatherings (excluding the preliminaries), volume 4 was printed and published as one unit. The issues of *Nova Acta* were published at irregular intervals; for example, volume 3 was published in 1780 and volume 5 was published in 1792. Accordingly, this irregular series was not a yearbook with an expected or regular pub-

[1]Rolf Du Rietz and Dr. Carl-Otto von Sydow gave essential support in establishing the publication data on *Kaempferus illustratus II.* Part of this study was supported by a grant from the Svenska Linne-Sallskapet. This study is part of the research project "Early relations in the field of natural history between Japan and The Netherlands," which is sponsored by the Ministry of Education of Japan.

lication at the end of any given year. The "Protocoll" of the "Vetenskaps Societeten" (= Minutes of the Academy of Sciences) of Uppsala, volume 2 (for the years 1732–1784), conserved in the University of Uppsala Library, Department of Manuscripts, contains relevant information.

In the minutes of the meeting of 25 October 1784 it was reported that volume 4 was completed, but the lists of Fellows and donated books, and the *Index auctorum* still had to be added. It can only be assumed that volume 4 was not published until late in 1784 (certainly after 25 October) or in 1785. In any case, its publication date is later than that of Thunberg's *Flora japonica,* published in August 1784. A copy of volume 4 of *Nova Acta* in the library of the Linnean Society of London is inscribed as having been received by J. E. Smith in 1785.

There is no question that the 14th edition of Murray's *Systema vegetabilium,* published in May or June 1784, has publication and nomenclatural priority, followed by Thunberg's *Flora japonica,* August 1784, and finally by Thunberg's *Kaempferus illustratus II,* post 25 October 1784.

*Acer pictum* was first published by Murray in *Systema vegetabilium* (May or June 1784), and again by Thunberg in *Flora japonica* (August 1784). The lectotype specimen of *A. pictum* Thunberg ex J.A. Murray is *UPS-THUNB 24084* (selected by D. O. Wijnands). However, this lectotype specimen is in very serious conflict with Thunberg's diagnosis of *A. pictum,* which was adopted by Murray (1784). The protologue mentions "Folio . . . alterna." This phrase alone would exclude *A. pictum* from the genus *Acer.* I interpret the designation of alternate leaves to be a failure by Thunberg to recognize the opposite phyllotaxy of the congested terminal cluster of leaves as represented in the lectotype specimen *UPS-THUNB 24084.*

Thunberg's (1805) later publication of a drawing of the cited lectotype specimen as *Acer pictum* cogently proves that he considered the specimen to be typical of his species, *A. pictum.* This lectotype clearly belongs to *A. mono,* but represents an ancient cultivar with finely white-spotted leaves, now called 'Marmoratum.' Thunberg's epithet, *pictum* (meaning "painted") could well have referred to the spotted leaves of the chosen lectotype.

Thunberg used a different plant and specimen in a different plant family for his *Acer pictum* in *Kaempferus illustratus II.* This plant represents *Kalopanax septemlobus* (Thunberg ex J. A. Murray) Koidzumi in the Araliaceae. Its basionym is *Acer septemlobus* Thunberg ex J. A. Murray, *Systema vegetabilium,* 14th edition, May or June 1784, and the selected lectotype specimen is *UPS-THUNB 24095.*

The taxonomic position of *Acer pictum* has now been resolved and is no longer ambiguous. *Acer pictum* Thunberg ex J. A. Murray (in *Systema vegetabilium,* 14th edition, 1784) is a synonym of *A. mono* Maximowicz (1857), and *A. pictum* Thunberg in *Kaempferus illustratus II* (in *Nova Acta,* volume 4, post October 1784) is a synonym of *Kalopanax septemlobus* (Thunberg ex J. A. Murray) Koidzumi (1925). *Acer pictum* Thunberg (post October 1784) is a later homonym of *A. pictum* Thunberg ex J. A. Murray (May or June 1784) and therefore an unacceptable name. *Kalopanax pictus* Nakai (1927) has been used incorrectly (e.g., Encke et al. 1984, 313). The correct name is *Kalopanax septemlobus* (Thunberg ex J. A. Murray) Koidzumi. The Nakai (1927) publication was based on *Acer pictum* Thunberg (post October 1784), an illegitimate name, and, according to the present rules of nomenclature, cannot be used as the basis of a new combination. Therefore, *Kalopanax pictus* should be attributed to Nakai alone.

The name *Acer pictum* Thunberg ex J. A. Murray is today never used for a maple. Depending on taxonomic opinion and judgment, the plant originally so named is now named either *A. mono* Maximowicz (1857) or *A. cappadocicum* Gleditsch ssp. *mono* (Maxim.) E. Murray (1982). In the latter case, E. Murray considered *A. mono* as conspecific with *A. cappadocicum* Gleditsch (1785) and *A. truncatum* Bunge (1833, 84). I do not agree. However, if these three taxa are indeed treated as conspecific then *A. pictum* Thunberg ex J. A. Murray (1784) undoubtedly has publication and nomenclatural priority over *A. mono* (1857), *A. cappadocicum* (1785), and *A. truncatum* (1833). Additional massive confusion would result.

There can be no question, however, that the name *Acer pictum,* because of being used incorrectly as the basionym of *Kalopanax pictus* in the Araliaceae, but not in its correct application as an *Acer,* should be rejected as a *nomen rejiciendum.* A formal proposal to reject the name *A. pictum* was published in *Taxon,* the journal of the International Association for Plant Taxonomy (Wijnands, 1990). If this proposal is accepted, the name *A. pictum* will never again be allowed to confuse and upset the nomenclature of any species of *Acer* or *Kalopanax.*

## SPECIES COLLATIONS

**ACER MONO** Maximowicz, *Bulletin de la classe Psychico-Mathématique de l'Académie Imperiale des Sciences de Saint Petersbourg,* 15:126. 1857.

### Synonyms

**A. PICTUM** Thunberg ex J. A. Murray, *Systema vegetabilium,* ed. 14, p. 912 (May/June 1784)—non Thunberg (post October 1784); Thunberg, *Flora Japonica,* p. 162 (August 1784); Thunberg, *Kaempferus illustratus II, Nova acta Regiae Societatis Upsaliensis,* 4:40 (post October 1784); Thunberg, *Dissertatio de Acere,* p. 7 (1793); Thunberg, *Icones plantarum Japonicarum,* vol. 5., t. 3 (1805) (drawn from the lectotype specimen UPS-THUNB 24084); Thunberg, *Plantarum Japonicarum novae species,* p. 7 (1824). Nomen rej. prop. (Wijnands 1990).

**A. TRUNCATUM** Bunge ssp. **MONO** (Maxim.) E. Murray, *Kalmia,* 1:7 (1969).

**A. CAPPADOCICUM** Gleditsch ssp. **MONO** (Maxim.) E. Murray, *Kalmia,* 12:17 (1982).

**A. MONO** Maxim. var. **MARMORATUM** Nicholson, *Gardeners' Chronicle,* n.s., 16:375 (1881) (= 'Marmoratum').

**KALOPANAX SEPTEMLOBUS** (Thunberg ex J. A. Murray) Koidzumi, *Botanical Magazine Tokyo 39:* 36. 1925.

Basionym: **ACER SEPTEMLOBUM** Thunberg ex J. A. Murray, *Systema vegetabilium,* ed. 14, p. 912 (May/June 1784); Thunberg *Flora Japonica,* p. 162 (August 1784); Thunberg, *Dissertatio de Acere,* p. 7 (1793); Thunberg, *Plantarum Japonicarum novae species,* p. 7 (1824).

Lectotype specimen: *UPS-THUNB 24095.*

### Synonyms

**ACER PICTUM** Thunberg, *Kaempferus illustratus II, Nova Acta Regiae Societatis Scientiarum Upsaliensis,* 4:36 (post October 1784)—non Thunberg ex J. A. Murray (May/June 1784).

**KALOPANAX PICTUS** Nakai, *Flora sylvatica Koreana,* 16:34 (1927).

## LITERATURE CITED

Bunge, A. A. von. 1833. *Enumeratio plantarum, quas in China boreali collegit.* Reprint. Mém. Sav. Etr. Acad. Sci. St. Petersburg.
Clarke, D. L. 1988. *Bean's trees and shrubs hardy in the British Isles, Supplement.* 8th rev. ed. London.
Encke, F., G. Buchheim, & S. Seybold. 1984. *Zander Handwörterbuch der Pflanzennamen.* 13th ed. Stuttgart.
Gleditsch, J. G. 1785. *A. cappadocicum* Gled. Vom Cappadocischen Ahorn. *Schriften der Berlinischen Gesellschaft Naturforschenden Freunde* 6:116, t. 2.
Hunt, D. R. 1977. *Kalopanax septemlobus. Curtis's Botanical Magazine* 81:141–143, t. 737.
Koidzumi, G. I. 1925. Contributiones ad cognitionem florae Asiae Orientalis. *Botanical Magazine Tokyo* 39:306.
Linnaeus, C. 1774. *Systema vegetabilium.* 13th ed. Gottingen.
Maximowicz, C. J. 1857. *A. tegmentosum* Maxim., *A. mono* Maxim. Ueber die Wichtigeren Bäume und Sträucher des Amurlandes. *Bulletin de la classe Psychico-Mathématique de l'Acaðemie Impériale des Sciences de Saint Petersbourg* 15:126.
Murray, E. 1969. *Acer* notes no. 1. *Kalmia* 1:1–8.
______. 1982. *Acer* notes no. 11. *Kalmia* 12:17.
Murray, J. A. 1784. *Systema vegetabilium.* 14th ed. Göttingen.
Nakai, T. 1927. *Flora sylvatica Koreana* 16:34. Seoul.
Nicholson, G. 1881. The Kew Arboretum. The maples. I–XVI. *The Gardeners' Chronicle,* n.s., 16:375–376.
Stafleu, G. A., and R. S. Cowan. 1981. *Taxonomic Literature,* 2nd ed., vol. 3. Utrecht, The Hague.
______. 1986. *Taxonomic Literature,* 2nd ed., vol. 6. Utrecht, Antwerpen, The Hague, Boston.
Thunberg, C. P. 1780. Kaempferus illustratus I. *Nova Acta Regiae Societatis Scientiarum Upsaliensis* 3:196–209.
______. 1784a. *Flora Japonica.* Leipzig.
______. 1784b. Kaempferus illustratus II. *Nova Acta Regiae Societatis Scientiarum Upsaliensis* 4:31–40.
______. 1793. *Dissertatio botanica de Acere.* Uppsala.
______. 1805. *Icones plantarum Japonicarum.* Vol. 5, t. 3. Uppsala.
______. 1824. *Plantarum Japonicarum novae species.* Uppsala.
Wijnands, D. O. 1990. Proposal to reject *Acer pictum* Thunb. ex Murr. (Aceraceae). *Taxon* 39:535–537.

Appendix 5

# Herbarium Abbreviations

| | |
|---|---|
| A | CAMBRIDGE: Arnold Arboretum, Harvard University, 22 Divinity Avenue, Cambridge, Massachusetts 02138, USA. |
| AAH | JAMAICA PLAIN: Arnold Arboretum, Harvard University, The Arborway, Jamaica Plain, Massachusetts 02130, USA. |
| B | BERLIN: Botanischer Garten und Botanisches Museum Berlin-Dahlem, Königin-luise Strasse 6-8, D-I Berlin 33 (Dahlem), Germany. |
| BM | LONDON: Natural History Museum, formerly British Museum (Natural History), Cromwell Road, London SW7 5BD, England. |
| BRNU | BRNO: Institute of Plant Biology and Herbarium, University of J. E. Purkyne, Kotlárská 2, 611 37 Brno, Slovakia. |
| CAL | CALCUTTA: Botanical Survey of India, Head Office at Calcutta, Central National Herbarium, Sibpore, Howrah, India. |
| CANT | GUANGZHOU: Department of Forestry, College of Agriculture of South China, Shekp'ai, Guangzhou, Guangdong, China. |
| DWC | WEST CHESTER: Darlington Herbarium, West Chester State College, West Chester, Pennsylvania 19380, USA. |
| E | EDINBURGH: Royal Botanic Garden, Edinburgh EH3 5LR, Scotland. |
| F | CHICAGO: John G. Searle Herbarium, Field Museum of Natural History, Roosevelt Road at Lake Shore Drive, Chicago, Illinois 60605, USA. |
| FI | FIRENZE: Herbarium Universitatis Florentinae, Museo Botanicao, Via Giorgio La Pira 4, I-50121 Florence, Italy. |
| G | GENEVE: Conservatoire et Jardin botaniques de la Ville de Genève, Case postale 60, CH-1292 Chambésy/GE, Switzerland. |
| HHBG | HANGZHOU: Hangzhou Botanic Garden, Hangzhou Zhejiang, China. |
| HK | HONG KONG: Herbarium, Agriculture and Fisheries Department, 393 Canton Road, 14/F Kowloon, Hong Kong. |
| HNWP | XINING: Northwest Plateau Institute of Biology, Academia Sinica, 57 Xiquan Street, Xining, Qinghai, China. |
| IBK | GUILIN: Guangxi Institute of Botany, Yenshan, Guilin, Guangxi, China. |
| IBSC | GUANGZHOU: Botanical Institute, Academia Sinica, Guangzhou, Guangdong, China. |
| ISTO | ISTANBUL: Istanbul Üniversitesi Orman Fakültesi, Orman botanigi kürsÿsü, Büyüjdere-Istanbul, Turkey. |
| K | KEW: The Herbarium, Royal Botanic Gardens, Kew, Richmond, Surrey TW9 3AB, England. |
| KUN | KUNMING: Kunming Institute of Botany, Academia Sinica, Helongtan, Kunming, Yunnan, China. |
| KYO | KYOTO: Department of Botany, Faculty of Science, Kyoto University, Sakyo-ku, Kyoto 606, Japan. |
| L | LEIDEN: Rijksherbarium, Schelpenkade 6, 2313 ZT Leiden, The Netherlands. |
| LBG | LUSHAN: Lushan Botanical Garden, P.O. Box 4, Lushan, Jiangxi, China. |
| LE | ST. PETERSBURG: Herbarium of the Department of Higher Plants, V. L. Komarov Botanical Institute of the Academy of Sciences of Russia, Prof. Popov Street 2, 197022 St. Petersburg, Russia. |

LECB ST. PETERSBURG: Herbarium of the Cathedra Botanica, St. Petersburg University, V. O. Quay of University 7/9, 199164 St. Petersburg, Russia.
LINN LONDON: The Linnean Society of London, Burlington House, Piccadilly, London W1V 0LQ, England.
LU GUANGZHOU: Herbarium, Lingnan University, Guanzhou, Guangdong, China.
M MUNICH: Botanische Staatssammlung, Menzingerstrasse 67, D-8000 Munich 19, Germany.
MO SAINT LOUIS: Herbarium, Missouri Botanical Garden, P.O. Box 299, St. Louis, Missouri 63166, USA.
MOAR PHILADELPHIA: Herbarium, Morris Arboretum, University of Pennsylvania, 9414 Meadowbrook Avenue, Philadelphia, Pennsylvania 19118, USA.
NA WASHINGTON: Herbarium, U.S. National Arboretum, Washington, DC 20002, USA.
NAP NAPOLI: Istituto Botanico della Università de Napoli, Via Foria 223, Naples, Italy.
NBV LEIDEN: Koninklijke Nederlandse Botanische Vereniging (Royal Botanical Society of The Netherlands), c/o Schelpenkade 6, 2313 ZT Leiden, The Netherlands.
NY NEW YORK: Herbarium, New York Botanical Garden, Bronx, New York 10458, USA.
P PARIS: Muséum National d'Historie Naturelle, Laboratoire de Phanérogamie, 16 rue Buffon, 75005 Paris, France.
PE BEIJING: Institute of Botany, Academica Sinica, Beijing, China.
PH PHILADELPHIA: Academy of Natural Sciences, 19th and the Parkway, Philadelphia, Pennsylvania 19103, USA.
S STOCKHOLM: Section for Botany, Swedish Museum of Natural History (Naturhistoriska riksmuseet), S-104 05 Stockholm 50, Sweden.
SBT STOCKHOLM: Bergius Foundation, S-104 05 Stockholm, Sweden.
SC WINSTON-SALEM: Salem Academy and College, Inc., Winston-Salem, North Carolina 27108, USA.
SH SHANGHAI: Herbarium, Institute of Botany, Academia Sinica, Shanghai, China (incorporated in PE).
SZ CHENGDU: The Herbarium of the Department of Biology, National Sichuan University, Chengdu, Sichuan, China.
TAIF TAIPEI: Taiwan Forestry Research Institute, Po-A Road Botanical Garden, Taipei, Taiwan.
TI TOKYO: Botanic Gardens Koishikawa, Hakusan 3-7-1, Bunkyo-ku, Tokyo 112, Japan.
TNS TOKYO: National Science Museum, Department of Botany, 3-23-1 Hyakunin-cho, Shinjuku-ku, Tokyo 160, Japan.
UPS UPPSALA: The Herbarium, University of Uppsala, P.O. Box 541, S-751 21 Uppsala, Sweden.
US WASHINGTON: U.S. National Herbarium, Department of Botany, Smithsonian Institution, Washington, DC 20560, USA.
VLA VLADIVOSTOK: Herbarium, Institute of Biology—Soils, Far Eastern Scientific Center of the Academy of Sciences of Russia, 159 G. Stoletiya Prospect, 690022 Vladivostok, Russia.
W WIEN: Naturhistorisches Museum, Botanische Abteilung, Burgring 7, Postfach 417, A-1014, Vienna, Austria.
WAG WAGENINGEN: Herbarium Landbouw Universiteit, Generaal Foulkesweg 37, Wageningen, The Netherlands.
WU WIEN: Institut für Botanik und Botanischer Garten der Universität, Rennweg 14, A-1030, Vienna, Austria.

# Hardiness Zone Maps

HARDINESS ZONE TEMPERATURE RANGES

| °F | ZONE | °C |
|---|---|---|
| below −50 | 1 | below −45 |
| −50 to −40 | 2 | −45 to −40 |
| −40 to −30 | 3 | −40 to −34 |
| −30 to −20 | 4 | −34 to −29 |
| −20 to −10 | 5 | −29 to −23 |
| −10 to 0 | 6 | −23 to −17 |
| 0 to 10 | 7 | −17 to −12 |
| 10 to 20 | 8 | −12 to −7 |
| 20 to 30 | 9 | —7 to −1 |
| 30 to 40 | 10 | −1 to 5 |

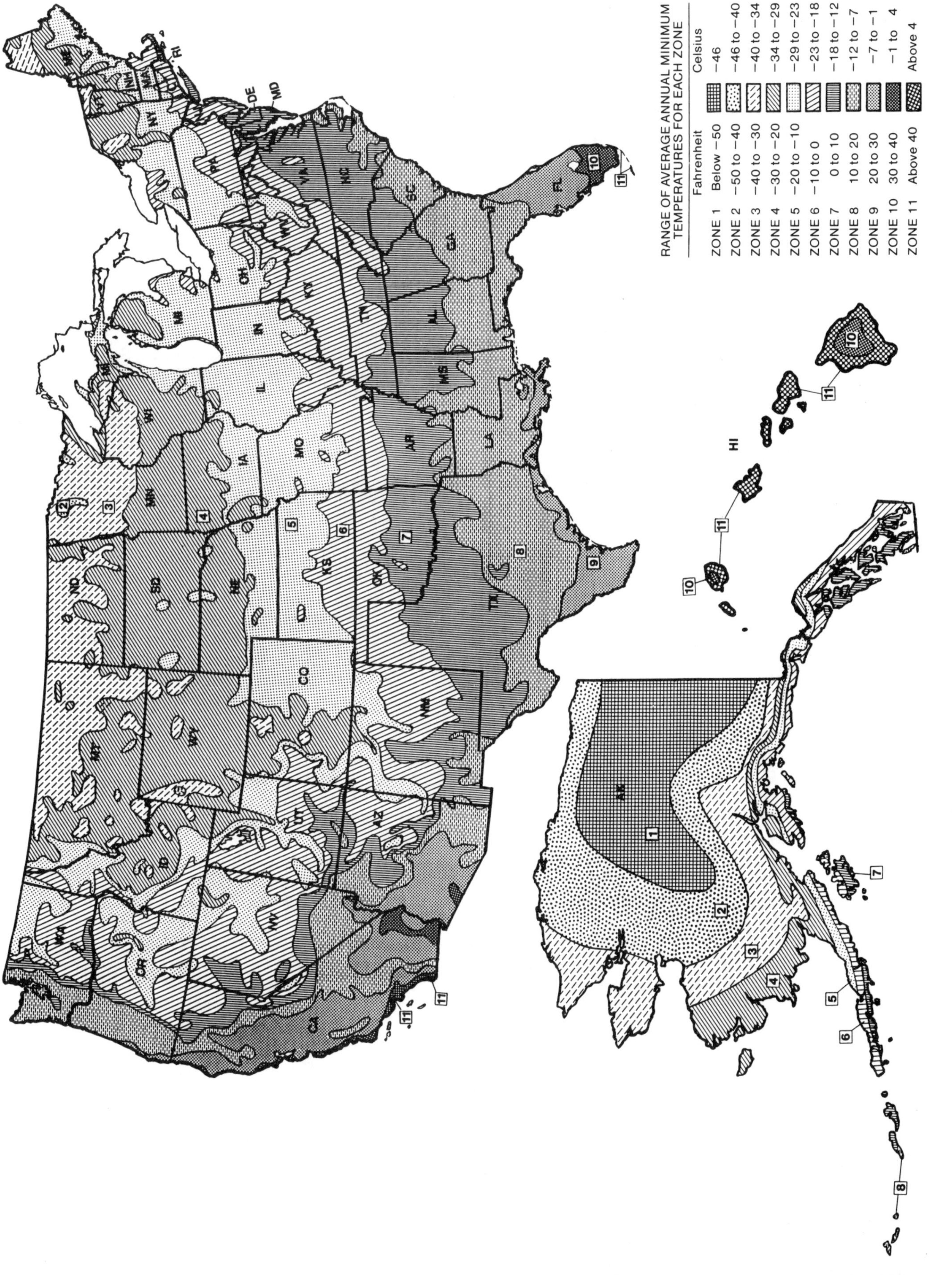
RANGE OF AVERAGE ANNUAL MINIMUM TEMPERATURES FOR EACH ZONE
Fahrenheit
Celsius
ZONE 1 Below −50 −46
ZONE 2 −50 to −40 −46 to −40
ZONE 3 −40 to −30 −40 to −34
ZONE 4 −30 to −20 −34 to −29
ZONE 5 −20 to −10 −29 to −23
ZONE 6 −10 to 0 −23 to −18
ZONE 7 0 to 10 −18 to −12
ZONE 8 10 to 20 −12 to −7
ZONE 9 20 to 30 −7 to −1
ZONE 10 30 to 40 −1 to 4
ZONE 11 Above 40 Above 4
HI

# Appendix 7

# Photograph Locations

The numbers in parenthesis at the end of each plate caption correspond to the following locations where photographs were taken:

1. Abbey Leix, County Laois, Ireland
2. Ahrensburg Research Station, Holstein, Germany
3. Arboretum Les Barres, Loiret, France
4. Arboretum Trompenburg, Rotterdam, The Netherlands
5. Arcadia Park, Los Angeles, California, USA
6. Arnold Arboretum, Jamaica Plain, Massachusetts, USA
7. Belmonte Arboretum, Wageningen, The Netherlands
8. Birr Castle, Earl of Rosse, County Offaly, Ireland
9. Borde Hill Gardens, Sussex, England
10. Botanical Garden, Hannover-Minden, Germany
11. Châteauneuf-sur-Loire, France
12. Dumbarton Oaks, Washington, DC, USA
13. Eastwood Hill Arboretum, North Island, New Zealand
14. Endsleigh Garden, Tavistock, Devon, England
15. Esveld Aceretum, Boskoop, The Netherlands
16. Fairchild Estate, Chevy Chase, Maryland, USA
17. Geographic Arboretum, Tervuren, Belgium
18. Hillier's Arboretum, Ampfield, England
19. Hof ter Saksen, Beveren, Belgium
20. Hørsholm Gardens and Arboretum, Hørsholm, Denmark
21. Kalmthout Arboretum, Kalmthout, Belgium
22. Kanopiste, Czech Republic
23. Kristick Nurseries, Wellsville, Pennsylvania, USA
24. Mallet Court Nursery, Somerset, England
25. Maplewood Nursery, Roseburg, Oregon, USA
26. Morris Arboretum, Philadelphia, Pennsylvania, USA
27. Novy Dvar, Slovakia
28. Parc des Eaux-Vives, Geneva, Switzerland
29. Parc d'Esneux, Esneux University, Belgium
30. Princeton Nursery, Princeton, New Jersey, USA
31. Research Station, Pruhonice Prague, Czech Republic
32. (Bernard de la) Rochefaucould garden, Fay-aux-Loges, Loiret, France.
33. Rombergpark, Dortmund, Germany
34. Royal Botanic Garden, Edinburgh, Scotland
35. Royal Botanic Garden, Vancouver, British Columbia, Canada
36. Royal Botanic Gardens, Kew, England
37. The Royal Horticultural Society Gardens, Wisley, Surrey, England
38. Strybing Arboretum, San Francisco, California, USA
39. Talbot Manor, King's Lynn, England
40. Tremeer Garden, Cornwall, England
41. University of Washington Arboretum, Seattle, Washington, USA
42. Vilmorin-Andrieux Arboretum, Verrieres, France
43. Von Gimborn Arboretum, Doorn, The Netherlands
44. Wakehurst Place, Sussex, England
45. Westfalenpark, Dortmund, Germany
46. Westonbirt Arboretum, Gloucestershire, England
47. Willamette Research Station, Aurora, Oregon, USA
48. Willowwood Arboretum, Gladstone, New Jersey, USA
49. Winkworth Arboretum, Godalming, England
50. Winterthur Gardens, Winterthur, Delaware, USA

# Glossary[1]

**Anemophily.** A state in which flowers are usually wind-pollinated.

**Clone.** Any group of individuals propagated vegetatively from a single ancestor and reproduced by layering, cuttings, or grafting.

**Cotype.** A second specimen from the same plant as the holotype.

**Cultivar.** A horticultural or garden variety that owes its continued existence to human activity. A cultivar name may include up to three words, each beginning with a capital letter, and is either enclosed in single quotation marks or preceded by cv. Validly published names given before 1 January 1959 stand, but to be legitimate after that date a cultivar name cannot be in Latin and it must be published with a description.

**Decussate.** Appearing in opposite pairs.

**Dichogamy.** Flowering in a female-male sequence.

**Duodichogamy.** Flowering in a male-female-male sequence.

**Entomophily.** A state in which flowers are usually pollinated by insects.

**Fasciated.** Abnormally large and flattened.

**Forma,** pl. **formae.** A taxonomic unit subordinate to a variety, often differing only in a single character (e.g., flower color).

**Geitonogamy.** A state in which flowers self-pollinate.

**Genus,** pl. **genera.** An assemblage of rather similar species distinguishable from other assemblages by usually well-marked characters. A monotypic genus consists of only one species with no near relatives.

**Grex.** A group of species or hybrids.

**Heterodichogamy.** Flowering in which the flowers are either all male or all female.

**Holotype.** The specimen used by the author of a name, or designated by the author, as the nomenclatural type.

**Hybrid.** A cross between different species or subspecies but not between minor variants of a species.

**Isotype.** A duplicate specimen of the holotype.

**Lectotype.** A specimen selected from the original material to serve as the nomenclatural type, either when the holotype was not designated at the time of publication, or when the holotype is missing.

**Lignified.** Woody.

**Monochasium,** pl. **monochasia.** A cyme reduced to single flowers on each rachis.

**Neotype.** A specimen selected to serve as the nomenclatural type of a taxon in a situation when all material on which the taxon was originally based is missing.

**Paratype.** A specimen other than the holotype that is cited with the original description.

**Parthenocarpic.** Development of seedless fruit without fertilization.

**Petioles.** Leaf stalks.

**Protandry.** A state of flowering in which male flowers precede female flowers.

**Protogyny.** A state of flowering in which female flowers precede male flowers.

**Species.** The basic unit in living organisms on which the whole of classification depends. Botanically a species is an assemblage of plants with a large number of constant characters in common that are maintained from generation to generation.

**Subspecies.** A rank probably best restricted to morphologically distinct populations within a species that are separated by geography or ecology. Subspecies may have evolved differently as a result of growing in different areas or habitats, but will normally be able to interbreed when given the opportunity.

**Sympatry.** A state in which two or more species share the same range without interbreeding.

**Syntype.** One of two or more specimens used

[1]Based in part on excerpts from *A Guide to the Naming of Plants* by David McClintock. Used with permission.

by an author when no holotype was designated, or in place of a holotype, or one of two or more specimens designated simultaneously as the type.

**Taxon.** A unit of classification of any rank, be it form, variety, species, subspecies, genus, family, or so forth.

**Topotype.** A specimen collected at the type locality where the holotype was originally collected.

**Type.** A dried plant in a herbarium documenting the published description of it by the author. See also cotype, holotype, isotype, lectotype, neotype, paratype, syntype, and topotype.

**Typical.** Used for any plant that represents the characteristics of a taxon (i.e., a typical specimen).

**Variety.** A botanical rank for assemblages differing slightly but distinctly from the species to which they belong, less markedly so than a subspecies. Varieties are found in the wild, usually throughout the range of a species. Although this term was once applied to horticultural and garden varieties, these are not correctly designated cultivars.

# Bibliography


Aas, G. von, et al. 1991. Der Diedorfer Exotenwald. *Mitt. Dtsch. Dendr. Ges.* 80:181–186.

Abel, M. H. 1899. Sugar as food. Farmers' Bulletin 93. Washington, DC: USDA.

Aberconway, Lord. 1961. *Acer Sangokaku. Gardener's Chronicle* III. 149(5):105.

Abrams, L. 1907. A new maple from southern California. *Torreya* 7:217–219.

Ackerman, W. L. 1957. After-ripening requirements for germination of *Acer truncatum* Bunge. In *Proceedings of the American Society for Horticultural Science* 69:570–573.

Adams, G. A., and C. T. Bishop. 1960. Constitution of an arabinogalactan from maple sap. *Canadian Journal of Chemistry* 38:2380.

Adanson, M. 1763. *Familles Naturelles des Plantes.* Paris: Vincent. Rpt. J. Cramer, Lehre, 1966.

Agris, G. N. 1978. *Plant Pathology.* New York: Academic Press.

Aitchison, J. E. T. 1880. The flora of the Kuram Valley, Afghanistan. *Botanical Journal, Linnean Society* 18:41.

Aiton, W. 1811. *Hortus Kewensis; or A Catalogue of the Plants Cultivated in the Royal Botanic Garden at Kew.* 2nd ed.

Akman, Y. 1973. Contribution à l'étude de la flore des montagnes de l'Amanus. II. *Comm. Fac. Sci. Univ. Ankara,* ser. C., sci. nat. 17C:21–42.

Albersheim, P. 1974. The primary cell wall and control of elongation growth. In *Plant Carbohydrate Biochemistry.* Ed. J. B. Pridham. New York: Academic Press.

______. 1975. The walls of growing plant cells. *Scientific American* 232 (April):80–95.

______. 1976. The primary cell wall. In *Plant Biochemistry.* Eds. J. Bonner and J. E. Varner. 3rd ed. New York: Academic Press.

Albersheim, P., et al. 1973. The structure of the wall of suspension-cultured sycamore cells. In *Biogenesis of Plant Cell Wall Polysaccharides.* Ed. F. Loewus. New York: Academic Press.

Alberti, F. R. 1951. Las especias del genero *Acer* cultivadas en la Argentina. *Revista Invest. de Agricultura* 5(4):483–522.

Alden, B. 1986. *Acer opalus* var. *reginae-amaliae* (Orph. ex Boiss.) B. Alden. In *Mountain Flora Greece.* Ed. A. Strid. 1:582.

Allen, D. C. 1979. Observations on biology and natural control of the orangehumped mapleworm, *Symmerista leucitys* (Lepidoptera: Notodontidae), in New York. *The Canadian Entomologist* 111:703–708.

Almstedt, M. F. 1933. *An Anatomical Study of the Inflorescences of Certain Species of Acer.* Ph.D. thesis, Cornell University, Ithaca, New York.

Alvord, C. T. 1863. The manufacture of maple sugar. *Report of the Commissioner of Agriculture for the Year 1862–1863.* Washington.

Ambrózy-Migazzi, J. Graf. 1922. Zur Etymologie des Ahorns. *Mitt. Dtsch. Dendr. Ges.* 32:251–252.

Amelinckx, F. 1953. Een Nieuwe Rode *Acer? Cultuur & Handel* 19:116.

American Phytopathological Society. 1979. Symposium on wood decay in living trees. Mechanisms of tree defense and wood decay. *Phytopathology* 69:1135–1160.

Ampofo, S. T., et al. 1976a. The role of the cotyledons in four *Acer* species and in *Fagus sylvatica* during early seedling development. *New Phytology* 76:31–39.

______. 1976b. The influence of leaves on cotyledon photosynthesis and export during seedling development in *Acer. New Phytology* 76:247–255.

Ananthakrishnan, T. N. 1984. *The Biology of Gall Insects.* London: Arnold.
Anderson, E., and L. Hubricht. 1938. The American sugar maples. I. Phylogenetic relationships, as deduced from a study of leaf variation. *Botanical Gazette* 100:312–323.
Anderson, J. F. 1960. *Forest and Shade Tree Entomology.* New York: Wiley.
Anderson, N. A. 1970. Propagating *Acer palmatum* by seed. *The Plant Propagator* 16(4):5.
Andra, C. J. 1855. Beiträge zur Kenntnis der Fossilen Flora Siebenburgens. *Abh. Geol. Reichsanst. Wien* Abth. 3(4):21.
André, E. F. 1870a. (no title). *Illustration Horticole* 17:98–99, 241, 244.
______. 1870b. (no title). *Illustration Horticole* 18:43, 46.
Andreae, J. 1991. Die Allee—Ein Lebendiges Gestaltungselement des Planers. *Mitt. Dtsch. Dendr. Ges.* 80:225–239.
Andrews, H. N., Jr. 1961. *Studies in Paleobotany.* New York: Wiley.
Angyo Maple Nursery. 1930. *Catalogue.* Tokyo.
Anstey, J. M. 1969. *Acers* from cuttings. *International Plant Propagators' Society Proceedings* 19.
Antonites, J. J. 1968. The mystery of moving maple seeds. *Home Gard.* 55:43.
Appel. 1933. Ahornwelke. *Mitt. Dtsch. Dendr. Ges.* 45:397–398.
Arends, J. C., and F. M. van der Laan. 1979. IOPB chromosome number reports. LXV. *Taxon* 28:637.
Aritomi, M. 1962. Studies on the chemical constituents in leaves of *Acer palmatum* Thunb. *J. Pharm. Soc. Japan* 82:1329–1331.
______. 1963. Chemical constituents in Aceraceous plants. I. Flavonoids in the leaves of *Acer palmatum* Thunb. *J. Pharm. Soc. Japan* 83:737–740.
______. 1964a. Chemical constituents in Aceraceous plants. II. Flavonoids in leaves of *A. carpinifolium, A. diabolicum, A. marmoratum,* and *A. negundo. J. Pharm. Soc. Japan* 84:360–362.
______. 1964b. Chemical constituents in Aceraceous plants. III. Flavonoids in leaves of *A. cissifolium.* Chem. Pharm. Bulletin 12:841–843.
Arno, S. F. 1977. *Northwest Trees.* Seattle, Washington: The Mountaineers.
Arnold, C. A. 1947. *An Introduction to Paleobotany.* New York: McGraw Hill.
Arthur, J. J., et al. 1981. Flooding and landfill gas effects on red and sugar maples. *Journal of Environmental Quality* 10:431–433.
Asayama, E. 1971. *Ornamental Plants in Colour.* 2 vols. Tokyo: Heibonsha.
Ascherson, P. F. A. 1860–1864. *Flora der Provinz Brandenburg.* Berlin.
Ashe, W. W. 1897. Possibilities of a maple sugar industry in western North Carolina. Geological Survey Paper no. 1:15.
______. 1918. Notes on trees and shrubs. Bulletin of the Charleston Museum 14:30.
______. 1922. Notes on trees and shrubs of southeastern North America. *Rhodora* 24:77–79.
Audubon, J. J. 1966. *The Birds of America.* New York: American Heritage Publ./Crown.
*Australian Dictionary of Biography.* 1851–1890. Vol. 5. Melbourne: Melbourne University Press.
Axelrod, D. I. 1966. The Eocene Copper Basin flora of northeastern Nevada. University of California Publication, geological science, 59:1–83.
Ayensu, E. S., et al. 1984. *Our Green and Living World.* Washington, DC: Smithsonian Institution.
Baas, I. 1932. Eine Frühdiluviale Flora im Mainzerbecken. *Zeitschr. Bot.* 26:289–371.
Baas, P., ed. 1982. *New Perspectives in Wood Anatomy.* The Hague: Nijhoff/Junk.
Baas-Becking, L. H. 1918. Das Arboretum der Landbouwhoogeschool in Wageningen. *Mitt. Dtsch. Dendr. Ges.* 27:189–195.
Bachtell, K. R. 1989. *Acer* × *freemanii*—A source for new shade tree selections. *International Plant Propagators' Society Proceedings* 38:509–514.
Baerg, W. J. 1947. The biology of the maple leaf scale. Arkansas Agricultural Experiment Station Bulletin 470.
Bailey, L. H. 1928. *The Standard Cyclopedia of Horticulture.* New York: Macmillan.
Baker, C. F. 1904. *West American Plants* 3:3.
Baker, F. S. 1945. *Forest Cover Types of Western North America.* Washington, DC: Society of American Foresters.
Baker, J. H. 1965. Relationships between salt concentrations in leaves and sap and the decline of sugar maples along roadsides. Massachusetts Agricultural Experiment Station Bulletin 553.
Baker, J. R. 1982. The Biology of Parasitic Protozoa. Studies in Biology 138. London: Arnold.
Balgooyen, W. P. 1978. Maple sugaring as a hobby. *Plants and Gardens* 33:14–17.
Banerji, M. L. 1961. Critical notes on *Acer campbellii* Hiern. *Journal of the Bombay Natural History Society* 58:305–307.

———. 1963. A new variety of *Acer oblongum* Wall. *Phytologia* 9:265–266.
Banerji, M. L., and S. Das. 1971. *Acers* in Nepal. *Industrial Forestry* 97(5):243–250.
———. 1972. Minor venation patterns in the Indian *Acers*. In *Advances in Plant Morphology*. Eds. Murty et al.
Banks, R. A. 1972. Some maples at Hergest Croft. *Int. Dendr. Soc. Yrbk.* 1971:8–13.
Banks, W. L. 1976. Tour of some Sussex gardens October 25–28, 1974. *Int. Dendr. Soc. Yrbk.* 1975:62–68.
———. 1977. I.D.S. South Wales tour May 20–May 23, 1976. *Int. Dendr. Soc. Yrbk.* 1976:75–80.
Banks, W. L., and J. Filer. 1988. I.D.S. tour Germany 4th–6th July, 1987. *Int. Dendr. Soc. Yrbk.* 1987:45–52.
Barbeau, M. 1946. Maple sugar: its native origin. *Transactions of the Royal Society of Canada*, 3rd ser., 60(2):75–86.
Barber, P., and C. E. Lucas Phillips. 1975. *The Trees Around Us*. London: Weidenfeld & Nicolson.
Barker, P. A. 1977. Canyon maple—a colorful mountaineer. *American Forestry* 83:22–25.
———. 1983. Some urban trees of California. *Metria*. In *4th Proceedings of the Pennsylvania State University*.
Barker, P. A., and D. K. Salunkhe. 1974. Maple syrup from bigtooth maple. *Journal of Forestry* 72:491–492.
Barker, P. A., et al. 1982. Variation in the breeding system of *Acer grandidentatum*. *Forest Science* 28(3):563–572.
Barnes, L. R. 1959. Formation of allantoin and allantoic acid from adenine in leaves of *Acer saccharinum* L. *Nature* 184:1944.
Barnes, P. 1989. Four days in Yakushima. *Journal of the Royal Horticultural Society* 114(12):598–604.
Baroni, E. 1901. Padre Giusepe Giraldi. Bull. della Soc. Bot. Ital. 7.
Barrett, J. W., ed. 1980. *Regional Sylviculture of the United States*. New York: Wiley.
Barron, W. 1875. *Catalogue of Conifers & Other Ornamental Plants*. Derby, England: Elvaston Nurseries.
Bärtels, A. 1973. *Gartengehölze*. Stuttgart, Germany: Ulmer.
Bartels, H. 1991a. Jahrestagung in Bremen vom 27.5 bis 1.6.89. *Mitt. Dtsch. Dendr. Ges.* 80:267–279.
———. 1991b. Studienreise 1989 in die Toskana. *Mitt. Dtsch. Dendr. Ges.* 80:280–296.
Bartels, H., et al. 1981. Erhebung über das Vorkommen Winterharter Freilandgehölze. I. Die Gärten und Parks mit Ihrem Gehölzbestand. *Mitt. Dtsch. Dendr. Ges.* 73.
———. 1982. Erhebung über das Vorkommen Winterharter Freilandgehölze. II. Die Gehölze mit Ihrer Verbreitung in den Gärten und Parks. *Mitt. Dtsch. Dendr. Ges.* 74.
Bartlett, J. M. 1933. Maple syrup. Maine Agricultural Experiment Station Bulletin 143.
Bartley, G. B., et al. 1981. Maple-syrup urine odor due to fenugreek ingestion. *New England Journal of Medicine* 308 (8):467.
Bartram, J., and F. Harper, eds. 1942. Diary of a journey. *Transactions of the American Philosophical Society*, n.s., 33:1.
———. 1977. Astringent tannins of *Acer* species. *Phytochemistry* 16:1421–1426.
———. 1978. Systematic aspects of the astringent tannins of *Acer* species. *Phytochemistry* 17:1945–1948.
Bateman, D. F. 1976. Plant cell wall hydrolysis by pathogens. In *Biochemical Aspects of Plant-Parasite Relationships*. Eds. J. Friend and D. R. Threlfall. New York: Academic Press.
Bate-Smith, E. C. 1962. The phenolic constituents of plants and their taxonomic significance. *Botanical Journal, Linnean Society* 58:39,95.
———. 1974. Systematic distribution of ellagitannins in relation to the phylogeny and classification of the angiosperms. In *Chemistry in Botanical Classification*. Eds. G. Bendz and J. Santesson. London: Academic Press.
Batra, S. W. T. 1985. Red maple (*Acer rubrum* L.), an important early spring food resource for honey bees and other insects. *Kansas Entomological Society Journal* 58:169–172.
Baudriller Nursery. 1880. *Catalogue Génerale Descriptif et Raisonné des Arbres Fruitiers Forestiers et d'Ornement*. (Gennes Anger, France).
Bauer, H. 1970. *Hitzeresistenz und $CO_2$-Gaswechsel von Tanne* (*Abies alba* Mill.) *und Bergahorn* (*Acer pseudoplatanus* L.). Ph.D. thesis, University of Innsbruck, Austria.
Bauer, H., et al. 1969. Der Einflusz und die Nachwirkung von Hitze-und Kältestress auf den $CO_2$-Gaswechsel von Tanne und Ahorn. *Ber. Dtsch. Bot. Ges.* 82:65–70.

Baumann, H. 1982. *Die griechische Pflanzenwelt in Mythos, Kunst und Literatur.* Munich: Hirmer.
Baumbach, von. 1924. Erfahrungen mit dem Anbau Fremdländischer Holzarten in der Provinz Hessen-Nassau. *Mitt. Dtsch. Dendr. Ges.* 34:19–32.
Beach, J. 1986. Thorp Perrow Arboretum. *Journal of the Royal Horticultural Society* 111:355–361.
Bean, W. J. 1934. *Handlist of Trees and Shrubs (excl. Coniferae) Cultivated in the Royal Botanic Gardens Kew.* 4th ed. London: H.M.S.O.
______. 1970. *Trees & Shrubs Hardy in the British Isles,* vol. 1. 8th ed. London: Murray.
______. 1988. *Trees & Shrubs Hardy in the British Isles.* Supplement. London: Murray.
Beart, J. E., et al. 1985. Plant polyphenolics—secondary metabolism and chemical defense: some observations. *Phytochemistry* 24(1):33–38.
Beauverd, G. 1920. In Schinz und Thellung, Gefässpflanzen. *Ber. Schweiz. Bot. Ges.* 26–29:226.
______. 1930. Une race d'*Acer opalus* Mill. à fruits pourpres. Bulletin de la Société Botanique de Suisse 21:268–270.
Beck, C. B. 1976. *Origin and Early Evolution of Angiosperms.* New York: Columbia University Press.
Beck, G. von Mannagetta and Lerchenau. 1892. *Flora von Niederösterreich.* Vienna.
______. 1895. Flora von Südbosnien und der Angrenzende Hercegovina. *Ann. Naturh. Hofmus.* 10:189–192. Vienna.
Beck, H. R. 1947. *Handbook of the Trees of the Northern States and Canada, East of the Rocky Mountains.* New York.
Becker, W. B. 1938. Leaf-feeding insects of shade trees. Massachusetts Agricultural Experiment Station Bulletin 353.
Bedwell, J. L., and T. W. Childs. 1938. *Verticillium* wilt of maple and elm in the Pacific Northwest. *Plant Disease Reporter* 22:22–23.
Beevers, L. 1976. *Nitrogen Metabolism in Plants.* London: Arnold.
Behnke, H. D., et al. 1985. *Progress in Botany,* vol. 47. Berlin: Springer Verlag.
Beissner, L. 1900. Reiseerinnerungen. *Mitt. Dtsch. Dendr. Ges.* 9:94–118.
______. 1902. Reiseerinnerungen. *Mitt. Dtsch. Dendr. Ges.* 11:104.
______. 1903. Reiseerinnerungen. *Mitt. Dtsch. Dendr. Ges.* 12:17–23.
______. 1904. Reiseerinnerungen. *Mitt. Dtsch. Dendr. Ges.* 13:124–147.
Belcher. 1964. *Acer saccharum* 'Laciniatum'. *American Nurseryman* 120:31.
Belder J. de. 1969. Yugoslav tour 1967. *Int. Dendr. Soc. Yrbk.* 1968:9–28.
Belder, R. de, and Lady Anne Palmer. 1968. I.D.S tour of Scotland 14th–26th May 1965. *Int. Dendr. Soc. Yrbk.* 1967:3–15.
Beldie, A. 1958. Aceraceae. In Sávulescu. *Flora Republicii Populare Romine* 6:220–248, 654–655. Bucharest.
Bell, E. A. 1981. The non-protein amino acids occurring in plants. In *Progress in Phytochemistry* 7. Eds. L. Reinhold et al. Oxford: Pergamon.
Bellair, G. A. 1905. Les négondos panachés. *Revue Horticole* 77:510–512.
Benezra, C., et al. 1985. *Plant Contact Dermatitis.* Toronto: Decker.
Bentham, G., and W. J. Hooker. 1862. *Genera Plantarum and Exemplaria Imprimis Herbariis Kewensis* 1:409. London.
Berchtold, F. Graf von, and J. S. Presl. 1825. *O Prirozenosti Rostlin* 2, t. 32.
Bergmann, F. W. 1962. *Raraflora* (catalogue).
______. 1967. *Raraflora* (catalogue).
Berrang, P., and D. F. Karnosky. 1983. *Street Trees for Metropolitan New York.* New York Botanical Garden, Institute of Urban Horticulture Publication no. 1.
Berry, E. W. 1923. *Tree Ancestors.* Baltimore.
______. 1930. Revision of the Lower Eocene Wilcox flora of the southeastern states. U.S. Geological Survey Prof. Paper 156:48, 98.
______. 1931. A flora of Green River age in Wind River Basin of Wyoming. U.S. Geological Survey Prof. Paper 165-B:72.
Bertram, A. 1933. Die Heimat der *Abies numidica* am Djebel Babor. *Mitt. Dtsch. Dendr. Ges.* 45:17.
Beskaravajnaja, M. A. 1958. Gibridy klena yasenelistnogo. *Lesnoe Khoziaistvo* 11:28–30.
Bialobok, S. 1971. Trees and shrubs of some parks in Poland. *Int. Dendr. Soc. Yrbk.* 1970:35–43.
Bialobok, S., and Z. Czubinski, eds. 1963–1971. *Atlas of Distribution of Trees and Shrubs in Poland.* 10 parts. Poznan: Zaklad Dendrologii I Arboretum Kórnickie, Polskiej Akademii Nauk.
Bidwell, R. G. 1974. *Plant Physiology.* New York: Macmillan.
Bier, J. E. 1959–1961. The relation of bark moisture content to the development of canker diseases caused by native, facultative parasites. *Canadian Journal of Botany* 37:229–238, 781–788; 39:1555–1561.

Biesboer, D. D. 1975. Pollen morphology of the Aceraceae. *Grana* 15:19–27.
Bijhouwer, P. T. P. 1926. *Acer pseudoplatanus* L. *Jaarboek Nederlandse Dendr. Ver.* 2:42–47.
______. 1927a. *Acer pseudoplatanus. Jaarboek Nederlandse Dendr. Ver.* 2:2–47.
______. 1927b. Losse Opmerkingen naar Aanleiding van Rehders Manual. *Jaarboek Nederlandse Dendr. Ver.* 3:105–109.
______. 1927c. *Acer palmatum* en Zijn Geschiedenis. *Jaarboek Nederlandse Dendr. Ver.* 3:51–69.
______. 1950–1951. Contrasts. *Jaarboek Nederlandse Dendr. Ver.* 18:51–60.
Billot, P. C. 1855. *Annotations à la flore de France et d'Allemagne.* Haguenau.
Binggeli, P. 1990. Detection of protandry and protogyny in sycamore (*Acer pseudoplatanus* L.) from infructescenses. *Watsonia* 18:17–20.
Black, M. E. 1981. *Acer macrophyllum.* Hills of Gold. University of Washington Arboretum Bulletin 44:35–38.
Blackburn, B. 1952. *Trees and Shrubs in Eastern North America.* New York: Oxford University Press.
Blake, J. L. 1852. *The Farmer at Home.* New York: Saxton.
Blakeman, J. P. 1981. *Microbial Ecology of the Phylloplane.* New York: Academic Press.
Blakeslee, A. F., and C. D. Jarvis. 1931. *Trees in Winter, Their Study and Identification.* New York.
Blocksma, M. 1989. *Reading the Numbers, A Survival Guide to the Measurements Numbers, and Sizes Encountered in Everyday Life (Firewood).* New York: Penguin.
Bloembergen, S. 1948. Aceraceae. *Flora Malesiana,* ser. 1, 4(1):2–4.
______. 1954. Addenda, corrigenda et emendanda. *Flora Malesiana,* ser. 1, 4(1):592.
Blonski, F. 1903. Acerum formae novae Ucrainicae. *Magyar. Bor. Lapok* 2:79–85.
Blöte–Obbes, M. 1953. *Boom en Struik in Bos en Veld.* Utrecht: de Haan.
Blue, A. 1914. Ahornzucker als ein Nebenerzeugnis des Waldes. *Mitt. Dtsch. Dendr. Ges.* 23:79.
Blume, K. L. von. 1845. *Jaarboek Kon. Nederlandse Mij. Aanmoed. Tuinbouw* 1844:84.
______. 1847. *Rumphia* 3:193, t. 167-B.
Blumer, S. 1967. *Echte Mehltaupilze (Erysiphaceae).* Jena: Fischer.
Blunt, W. 1971. *The Complete Naturalist: A Life of Linnaeus.* London: Collins.
______. 1978. *In for a Penny; A Prospect of Kew Gardens: Their Flora, Fauna and Falballas.* London: Hamish Hamilton.
Bock, K., et al. 1980. The structure of acertannin. *Phytochemistry* 19:2033.
Boden, F. 1924. Anbauversuche mit Ausländischen Holzarten im Akademischen Lehrrevier Freienwalde a. O. 1883–1921. *Mitt. Dtsch. Dendr. Ges.* 34:32–54.
Boehmer, G. R. 1760. In Ludwig's *Definitiones Generum Plantarum.* 3rd ed. Leipzig.
Boehringer, K. 1810. *Über Zuckererzeugung aus dem Safte der in den Oesterreichischen Staaten Wild Wachsenden Ahornbäume* Vienna.
Boerg, W. J., see Baerg, W. J.
Boerhave Beekman, W. 1939. *Hout van Oerwoud tot Interieur.* Deventer: Kluwer.
Boerner, F. 1924. Bemerkenswerte Gehölze im Botanischen Garten zu Dorpat, Estland. *Mitt. Dtsch. Dendr. Ges.* 34:224–228.
______. 1961. *Blütengehölze.* Darmstadt: Stichnote.
Bogenrieder, A., et al. 1983–1987. *Lexikon der Biologie.* 9 vols. Freiberg: Herder.
Boissier, E. P. 1838. *Elenchus Plantarum Novarum.* Geneva.
______. 1840. *Voyage Botanique dans le Midi de l'Espagne* 2:117. Paris.
______. 1846. *Diagnoses Plantarum Orientalium Novarum, I.* 6:28–29. Leipzig.
______. 1856. *A. heldreichii* Boiss. *Diagnoses Plantarum Orientalium Novarum, II.* 5:71–73.
______. 1867. *Flora Orientalis* 1:947–952. Geneva.
Boissier, E. P., and F. A. Buhse. 1860. Aufzählung der auf einer Reise durch Trans-Kaukasien und Persien Gesammelten Pflanzen. *Nouv. Mém. de la Soc. de Nat. de Moscou* 12. 46–47.
Boissier, E. P., and T. G. Orphanides. 1876. *Acer ricinifolius. Atti Congr. Firenze* 214.
Bolkhovshikh, et al. 1969. *Chromosome Numbers of Flowering Plants.* Leningrad: Acad. Sci., USSR, Botanicheskii Institut Komarov.
Bolle, C. 1894. Etwas über Ahorne. *Mitt. Dtsch. Dendr. Ges.* 3:32–37.
Bolton, Lord. 1949. The growth and treatment of sycamore in England. *Quarterly Journal of Forestry* (October):43–44.
Bom, P. J. van der. 1982. Amerikaanse Selectie van Straat-, Laan- en Parkbomen. *Dendroflora* 19:45–82.
Bonamy Nursery (Toulouse, France). 1852. *Acer negundo* 'Argenteo-variegatum'. *Revue Horticole* 24:364.
Bonn, M. 1986. Belgian tour October 18–21, 1985. *Int. Dendr. Soc. Yrbk.* 1985:30–37.
Boom, B. K. 1954–1955. Nomenclature, history and characteristics of some woody plants. (English

summary.) *Jaarboek Nederlandse Dendr. Ver.* 20:37–120.
———. 1956–1958. Nomenclature, history and characteristics of some woody plants. (English summary.) *Jaarboek Nederlandse Dendr. Ver.* 21:85–178.
———. 1982. *Nederlandse Dendrologie.* 12th ed. Wageningen: Veenman.
Boom, B. K., and H. Kleijn. 1966. *Bomen Hun Vorm en Kleur.* Amsterdam: Becht.
Borbàs, V. T. 1881. *Bèkèsvàrmegye Flòràja.* Budapest.
———. 1884. In Hirc, flora okolice bakarce. *Rad. Jugoslav. Akad.* 69:132.
———. 1885. A fehèr-fagy hegyi juhar. *Erdèszeti Lapok* 24:1046–1047.
———. 1887. *Vasvàrmegye Növèyföldrajza ès Flòràja.* Szombathely.
———. 1891. Species *Acerum* Hungariae atque Peninsulae Balcanae. *Termèszetrajzi Füzetek* 14:68–80.
Borkhausen, M. B. 1793. Flora der Oberen Grafschaft Catzenellenbogen nach den System vom Stande. *Rhein. Mag. zur Erweiterung der Naturk.* 1:493–497.
———. 1800. *Theor.-prakt. Handb. der Forstbot. und Forsttechnol.* Giessen.
Borman, F. H. 1982. The effects of air pollution on the New England landscape. *Ambio* 11:338–346.
Born, G. L. 1974. Root infection of woody hosts with *Verticillium albo-atrum.* Illinois Natural History Survey Bulletin 31:205–249.
Bornmueller, J. F. N. 1888. Beiträge zur Kenntnis der Flora des Bulgarischen Küstenlandes. *Bot. Centralbl.* 36:57.
———. 1894. Nachtrag zur "Florula Insulae Thasos." *Österr. Bot. Zeitschr.* 44:126–127.
———. 1898. Ein Beiträg zur Kenntnis der Flora von Syrien und Palastina. *Verh. Zool.-Bot. Ges. Wien* 48:570–572.
———. 1905. Beiträge zur Flora der Elbrusgebirge Nord-Persiens. Bull. Herb. Boiss. 2(5):643.
———. 1906. Plantae Straussianae. *Bot. Centralbl. Beih.* 19:223–224.
———. 1914. *A. monspessulanum* ssp. *microphyllum* (Boiss.) Bornm. Zur Flora des Libanon und Antilibanon. *Bot. Centralbl. Beih.* 89(1):142.
———. 1925. *Acer hyrcanum* ssp. *intermedium* (Panč.) Bornm. Beiträge zur Flora Mazedoniens. I. *Bot. Jahrb.* 59:451–455.
———. 1939. *Repert. Sp. Nov.* Beih. 89(1):142.
Bosc, L. A. G. 1821. Dictionnaire de la culture des arbres. *Encycl. Méth. Agric.* 7:373–379.
Boscawen, A. 1988. A spring visit to Bhutan. *Rhododendrons 1988–1989 with magnolias and camellias,* no. 41. London: The Royal Horticultural Society.
Bose, J. C. 1923. *Physiology of the Ascent of Sap.* New York: Longmans, Green & Co.
———. 1927. *Plant Autographs.* New York: Macmillan.
Boskoop, Koninklijke Vereniging van Boskoopse Culturen. 1962. *Japanese Acer.* Keuringsrapport. Boskoop.
Boulay, J. N. 1890. *Flore Pliocène des environs de Théziers.* Paris.
Bowen, P. R. 1930. A maple leaf disease caused by *Cristulariella depraedens.* Connecticut Agricultural Experiment Station Bulletin 316:625–647.
Bowles, E. A. 1914a. *My Garden in Spring.* London: T. C. and E. C. Jack. (Rpt. 1972. Newton Abbot, Devon: David & Charles.)
———. 1914b. *My Garden in Summer.* London: T. C. & E. C. Jack. (Rpt. 1972. Newton Abbot, Devon: David & Charles.)
———. 1914c. *My Garden in Autumn and Winter.* London: T. C. & E. C. Jack. (Rpt. 1972. Newton Abbot, Devon: David & Charles.)
Boyce, E. A., and T. D. Sydnor. 1983. Effect of varying levels of manganese and pH on the growth of three cultivars of *Acer rubrum. Journal of Arboriculture* 9(9).
Boyce, J. S. 1961. *Forest Pathology.* 3rd ed. New York: McGraw-Hill.
Boyd, J. M. 1990. *The Hebrides.* London: Collins.
Bradlow, F. R. 1965. *Baron von Ludwigsburg and the Ludwigsburg Garden.* Dordrecht: A. A. Balkema.
Bramwell, M., ed. 1976. *The International Book of Wood.* London: Mitchell Beazley.
Brandis, D. 1874. *The Forest Flora of Northwest and Central India.* London.
Braun, A. 1845. *Neues Jahrbuch Mineralogie* 172.
———. 1864. Sapindaceae subfam. Aceroideae. In *Flora der Provinz Brandenburg, der Altmark und des Herzogtums Magdeburg,* by P. Ascherson. 1:52. Berlin.
Braun, E. L. 1950. *Deciduous Forests of Eastern North America.* Philadelphia: Blakistone.
Braun, H. 1891. *Österr. Bot. Zeitschr.* 41:255–257.
Bretschneider, E. 1898. *History of European Botanical Discoveries in China.* Leipzig: Zentral-Antiquariat der DDR. Rpt. 1981.

Brickell, C. D. 1968. French tour 30th September–3rd October 1966. *Int. Dendr. Soc. Yrbk.* 1967:26–43.
______. 1970. West of England tour October 19th–24th 1967. *Int. Dendr. Soc. Yrbk.* 1969:8–18.
Brickell, C., ed. 1989. *The Royal Horticultural Society, Gardener's Encyclopedia of Plants and Flowers.* London: Dorling Kindersley.
Brickell, C. D., et al. 1980. *International Code of Nomenclature for Cultivated Plants—1980 (ICNCP).* Utrecht: Bohn, Scheltema & Holkema.
Brimfield Gardens Nursery. 1953. *Catologue.* Wethersfield, Connecticut.
Britton, N. L. 1889. Catalogue of plants found in New Jersey. *Final Rep. State Geol. New Jersey* 2:78.
Britton, N. L., and A. Brown. 1913. *An Illustrated Flora of the Northern United States and Canada.* Scribner. Rpt. 1970. New York: Dover.
Britton, N. L., and A. Shafer. 1908. *North American Trees.* New York.
Brizicky, K. 1963. Aceraceae in genera of Sapindales. *Journal of Arnold Arboretum* 44:481–494.
Brockmann, W. 1991. Reiseeindrücke Anatolien 1990. *Kurzmitt. Dtsch. Dendr. Ges.* 49:10–17.
Brockmann-Jerosch, H. 1936. Futterlaubbäume und Speisebäume. *Ber. Schweiz. Bot. Ges.* 46:594–613.
Broerse, C. P. 1953. Een paar goede *Acer campestre's. Boomkwekerij* 8:46.
Brongniart, A. T. 1828. *Prodrome d'une histoire des végétaux fossiles.* Paris.
Brookes, J. 1977. *The Small Garden.* London: Marshall Cavendish.
Brooks, J., et al. 1971. *Sporopollenin.* New York: Academic Press.
Brooks, R. R. 1987. *Serpentine and its Vegetation.* London: Croom Helm, London.
Browicz, K. 1978. *Chorology of Trees and Shrubs in South West Asia.* 1. Kornik.
Brown, E. G., and K. C. Short. 1969. The changing nucleotide pattern of sycamore cells during culture in suspension. *Phytochemistry* 8:1365–1372.
Brown, G. E. 1972. *The Pruning of Trees, Shrubs & Conifers.* London: Faber & Faber.
Brown, N. A. 1941. Tumors on elm and maple trees. *Phytopathology* 31:541–548.
Brown, N. C. 1919. *Forest Products.* New York: Wiley.
Brown, N. E. 1882. *Gardener's Dictionary.* Ed. G. W. Johnson. Supplement.
Brown, R. W. 1935. Miocene leaves, fruits and seeds from Idaho, Oregon and Washington. *Journal of Paleontology* 9:580.
______. 1937. Additions to some fossil floras of the western United States. U.S. Geological Survey Prof. Paper 186:179–181.
______. 1940. New species and changes of name in some American fossil floras. *Journal of the Washington Academy of Science* 30:351.
Brown, S. S., et al., eds. 1979. Maple syrup urine disease. In *Chemical Diagnosis of Disease.* Amsterdam: Elsevier.
Brown, V. K., et al. 1987. Plants and insects in early old-field succession: Comparison of an English site and an American site. *Biological Journal, Linnean Society* 31:59–74.
Browne, D. J. 1846. *The Trees of America.* New York: Harper & Brothers.
Bruce, H. 1969. Author's Note. In *The Gardens of Winterthur.* New York.
Bryan, A. H. 1910. Maple-sap syrup: its manufacture composition and effect of environment thereon. Farmers' Bulletin 134. Washington, DC: USDA.
Bryan, A. H., et al. 1937. Production of maple sirup and sugar. Farmers' Bulletin 1366. Washington, DC: USDA.
Buchenau, F. 1861. Morphologische Bemerkungen über Einige Acerineen. *Bot. Zeitschr.* 19:265, 273, 281.
Buchholz Nursery. 1989–1990. *Catalogue.* Gaston, Oregon.
Buckley, E. H. 1987. PCBs in the atmosphere and their accumulation in foliage and crops. In *Phytochemical Effects of Environmental Compounds.* Eds. J. A. Saunders et al. Vol. 21 of *Recent Advances in Phytochemistry.* New York: Plenum.
Budavari, S., et al. 1989. *The Merck Index.* 11th ed. Rahway, New Jersey: Merck.
Budischev. 1867. *Zap. Sib. Otd. Russk. Geogr. Obshch.* 9–10:107–108, 137, 437.
Buis, J. 1985. *Historia Forestis. (Dutch Forest History.)* Utrecht: Hes.
Bunge, A. A. von. 1833. *Acer truncatum* Bunge. Enumeratio plantarum, quas in China boreali collegit. Repr. *Mémoirs Sav. Etr. de l'Académie Imperiale des Sciences de St. Pétersbourg* 2:75–148.
______. 1847. Alexandri Lehmann reliquiae botanicae. *Arb. Naturfr. Ver. Riga* 1(2):192.
Burg, J. van den. 1981. *pH and Tree Growth.* Report 282. Wageningen: De Dorschkamp.
Burgh, J. van der. 1982. Pliocene flora of Lower Rhine Basin. *Rev. Paleobot. & Palynol.* 40.
______. 1987. Miocene floras of the Lower Rhenish Basin and their ecological interpretation. *Rev.*

*Paleobot. & Palynol.* 52:299.
Burkwood & Skipwith Ltd. Nursery. 1969. Guinea Maples. *Journal of the Royal Horticultural Society* 94: XX. (Advertisement)
Burman, N. L. 1768. *Flora Indica.* Leiden Amsterdam.
Burnham, L. 1988. Acquired taste, now the pear thrips is eating New England's sugar maples. *Scientific American* 259(5):20.
Burstall, S. W. 1972. Some notable trees in New Zealand. II. *Int. Dendr. Soc. Yrbk.* 1971:88.
Burton, J. H. 1952. The grafting of some maples. *International Plant Propagators' Society Proceedings* 2:71–73.
Bush, B. F. 1928. Notes on trees and shrubs of Missouri. *American Midland Naturalist* 11:116.
Butin, H. 1981. Die Weissfleckigkeit des Bergahorns—eine "Neue" Blattkrankheit. *Allg. Forstzeitschr.* 36:327–328.
______. 1983. *Krankheiten der Wald—und Parkbäume.* Stuttgart: Thieme.
Butin, H., and A. Wulf. 1987. *Asteroma pseudoplatani* sp. nov., Anamorphe zu *Pleuroceras pseudoplatani* (V. Tubeuf.) Monod. *Sydowia* 40:38–41.
Butkov, A. I. 1954. Generis *Acer* species nova e Pamiralaj. *Akad. Nauk Uzbek. Inst. Bot. Gerbar. Bot. Mater.* 14:5–6.
Butler, E. J., and S. G. Jones. 1955. *Plant Pathology.* London: Macmillan.
Cadevall y Diars, J. 1915. *Flora de Catalunya* 1:387–391.
Cain, St. A. 1944. *Foundations of Plant Geography.* New York: Harper & Brothers.
Caldicott, A. B., and G. Eglinton. 1973. Surface Waxes. *Phytochemistry* 3:163–194. Ed. L. P. Miller. New York: Van Nostrand Reinhard.
Calman, G. 1977. *Ehret, Flower Painter Extraordinary.* Oxford: Phaidon.
Cameron, K. 1977. *English Place-Names.* 3rd ed. London: Batsford.
Campbell, W. A. 1939. *Daedalea unicolor* decay and associated cankers of maples and other hardwoods. *Journal of Forestry* 37:974–977.
Campbell, W. A., and R. W. Davidson. 1939. Sterile conks of *Polyporus glomeratus* and associated cankers on beech and red maple. *Mycologia* 31:606–611.
______. 1940a. *Ustulina vulgaris* decay in sugar maple and other hardwoods. *Journal of Forestry* 38:474–477.
______. 1940b. Top rot in glaze-damaged black cherry and sugar maple on the Allegheny Plateau. *Journal of Forestry* 38:963–965.
Canadian Forestry Service, Forest Insect and Disease Survey. 1980– . *Forest Insects and Disease Conditions in Canada.* (formerly titled *Annual Report.*)
Candolle, A. P. de. 1819. *Théorie élémentaire de la Botanique.* 2nd ed. Paris.
______. 1824. *A. oblongum* Wall. ex DC. *Prodromus Systematis Naturalis Regni Vegetabilis* 1:593–596.
Candolle, R. de, and Radcliffe-Smith. 1981. Nathaniel Wallich. *Botanical Journal, Linnean Society* 83:325–348.
Cannell, M. G. R., and Last F. T. 1976. *Tree Physiology and Yield Improvement.* New York: Academic Press.
Cannon, H. L. 1971. The use of plant indicators in ground and water surveys, geological mapping, and mineral prospecting. *Taxon* 20(2/3):227–256.
Carcellar, M., et al. 1971. The influence of sucrose, 2, 4-D and kinetin on the growth, fine structure and lignin content of cultured sycamore cells. *Protoplasma* 73:367.
Carey, D. P. 1974. Production of Japanese maples by cuttings. *International Plant Propagators' Society Proceedings* 24.
Carl, C. M., and H. W. Yawney. 1969. The use of pentane to separate filled & empty sugar maple samaras. *Tree Planter's Notes* 20(3):24–27.
______. 1972. Multiple seedlings in *Acer saccharinum.* Bulletin of the Torrey Botanical Club 99:142–144.
Carlson, K. D. 1980. *Early Testing for Resistance to* Verticillium *Wilt and Potato Leafhopper Feeding in Norway and Sugar Maples.* Master's thesis, State University of New York, Syracuse.
Carlson, R. W. 1979. Reduction in the photosynthetic rate of *Acer, Quercus* and *Fraxinus* species caused by sulphur dioxide and ozone. *Environ. Pollut.* 18:159–170.
Caroselli, N. E. 1955. Investigations of toxins produced *in vitro* by the maple wilt fungus *Verticillium* sp. *Phytopathology* 45:183–184.
______. 1956. The effect of various soil amendments on maple wilt incited by *Verticillium* sp. *Phytopathology* 46:240. Abstr.
______. 1957. *Verticillium* wilt of maples. Rhode Island Agricultural Experiment Station Bulletin 335:1–84.

______. 1959. The relation of sapwood moisture content to the incidence of maple wilt caused by *Verticillium albo-atrum*. *Phytopathology* 49:496–498.
Carpenter, P. L., et al. 1975. *Plants in the Landscape.* San Francisco: Freeman.
Carr, L. 1896. The food of certain American Indians and their methods of preparing It. In *Proceedings of the American Antiq. Society,* n.s., 10:115–190.
Carr, R. 1814. *Catalogue of Trees, Shrubs and Herbaceous Plants, Indigenous to the United States of America: Cultivated and for Sale at Bartram's Botanic Garden, Kingsess, near Philadelphia.*
Carrière, E. A. 1852. Erable négundo à feuilles panachées. *Revue Horticole* 24:364.
______. 1864. Erable sycomore à fruits rouge. *Revue Horticole* 36:371.
______. 1865. *Production et Fixation des Variétés dans les Végétaux.* Paris.
______. 1866. Sur quelques plantes inédites ou rares. *Revue Horticole* 38:133.
______. 1867. Plantes nouvelles. *Revue Horticole* 39:280, 300, 380, 391–392.
______. 1878. *Acer platanoides columnaris* (sic). *Revue Horticole* 50:346.
______. 1886. *Acer colchicum tricolor. Revue Horticole* 58:371.
Carville, L. L. 1975. Propagation of *Acer palmatum* cultivars from hardwood cuttings. *International Plant Propagators' Society Proceedings* 25.
Caspary, J. X. R. 1880. *Schrift. Phys. Ökon. Ges. Königsberg* 21.
______. 1881. *Schrift. Phys. Ökon. Ges. Königsberg* 22. Bericht.
______. 1886. Einige Neue Pflanzenreste aus dem Samländischen Bernstein. *Schrift. Phys. Ökon. Ges. Königsberg* 27:7.
______. 1887. Einige Fossile Hölzer Preussens. *Schrift. Phys. Ökon. Ges. Königsberg* 28:38.
Castiglioni, L. 1790. *Viaggio Negli Stati Uniti dell' America Settentrionale* 2:171–185.
Catesby, M. 1730–1748. *The Natural History of Carolina, Florida and the Bahama Islands.* 2 vols. London.
Catesson, A. M. 1964. Origine, fonctionnement et variations cytologiques saisonnières du cambium de l'*Acer pseudoplatanus* L. *Annuel de Sciences Naturelles,* botany, 12th ser., 5:229–498.
______. 1966. Présence de phytoferritine dans le cambium et les tissus conducteurs de la tige de sycomore *Acer pseudoplatanus. Compte Rendue de l'Académie de Science (France)* 262:1070–1073.
______. 1974. Cambial cells. In *Dynamic Aspects of Plant Ultrastructure.* Ed. A. W. Robards. London: McGraw-Hill.
______. 1980. The vascular cambium. In *Control of Shoot Growth in Trees.* Ed. C. H. A. Little. IUFRO Workshop Proceedings, Maritimes Forest Research Centre, Fredericton, New Brunswick, Canada.
Catesson, A. M., & J. C. Roland. 1981. Sequential changes associated with cell wall formation and fusion in the vascular cambium. IAWA Bulletin, n.s., 2:151–162.
Catesson, A. M., et al. 1971. Etude d'activités phosphatasiques acides dans les cellules d'*Acer pseudoplatanus* cultivées en suspension. *Compte Rendue de l'Académie de Science (France)* 272:2078–2081.
Cecil, E., and V. Manners. 1907. *London Parks and Gardens.* London: Constable.
Chabert, A. 1910. Revision des érables de la Savoie. Bulletin de la Societé Botanique de France 57:10–18, 39–47.
Challinor Davies, V. 1986. The rescue of two Cornish gardens. *Journal of the Royal Horticultural Society* 111:30–35.
Chamberlain, A. F. 1891a. The maple amongst the Algonkian tribes. *American Anthropologist* 4:39–44.
______. 1891b. Maple sugar and the Indians. *American Anthropologist* 4:381–383.
Champion, J. G. 1851. Florula Honkongensis. *Journal of Botany, Kew Gardens,* Miscellaneous 3:312.
Chaney, R. W. 1920. The flora of the Eagle Creek Formation. *Contributions of the Walker Museum* 2:175–179. Chicago.
______. 1933. A Pliocene Flora from Shansi Province. Bulletin of the Geological Society of China 12:135–137.
Chang, C. S. 1990. A reconsideration of the *Acer palmatum* complex in China, Taiwan, and Korea. *Journal of Arnold Arboretum* 71:553–565.
Chapman, A. W. 1860. *Flora of the Southern United States.* New York.
Chapman, S. 1986. The Beale Arboretum. *Journal of the Royal Horticultural Society* 111:501–508.
Chasseraud, J. 1980. *L'arbre dans la Ville Paris.* Mairie de Paris, Direction des Parcs, Jardins et Espaces Verts.
Cheng, W. C. 1931. *Acer sinopurparescens* Cheng. In Chien & Cheng. A few new species of Chinese plants. *Contr. Biol. Lab. Sci. Soc. China,* botany ser., 6:62–65.
______. 1949. Some new trees from the living *Metasequoia* region. *Sci. Techn. China* 2:35–36.

Chénu, Dr. 1876. *Encyclopédie d'Histoire Naturelle.* III, part 2. Botanique. Paris: Librairie de Fermin-Didot.
Chesters, K. I. M., et al. 1967. Angiospermae. In *The Fossil Record.* Eds. W. B. Harland et al. Geological Society of London. 269–288.
Chien, S. S., and W. P. Fang. 1934. Geographical distribution of Chinese *Acer.* In *Pacific Science Congress Proceedings 1933* 4:3305–3310.
Chittenden, F. J., and P. M. Synge, eds. 1956. *Dictionary of Gardening: A Practical and Scientific Encyclopedia of Horticulture.* 2nd ed. 4 vols. London: Oxford University Press.
Chu, C. D., and G. G. Tang. 1984. *Acer lichuanense. Journal of Nanjing Institute of Forestry* 2:83.
Chugai Nursery Co. 1941. *Descriptive Catalogue of Seeds, Plants & Bulbs.*
Chun, F. 1948. New Chinese plants. *Acer bicolor. Journal of Arnold Arboretum* 29:420.
Chun, W. Y. 1932. *Acer sycopseoides* Chun. In Hooker's *Icon. Pl.* 32, t. 3160.
______. 1934. Contributions to the flora of Kwantung and Southeastern China. *Sunyatsenia* 1:264.
Clark, J. 1905. A variegated sycamore. *The Garden* 67:318.
______. 1908. Japanese maples. *Gardener's Chronicle* III. 44:273–274.
Clarke, D., see Bean, W. J.
______. 1935. *Acer monspessulanum* 'Red Fruited'. *Gardener's Chronicle* III. 97:342.
Clarke, G. C. S., and M. R. Jones. 1978. The northwest European pollen flora, 17. Aceraceae. *Rev. Paleobot. & Palynol.* 26:181–193.
Clegg, C. J., and G. Cox. 1978. *Anatomy and Activities of Plants.* London: Murray.
Coats, A. M., ed. 1969. *Quest for Plants; A History of Horticultural Explorers.* London: Studio Vista. New York: McGraw-Hill, 1970.
Cockerell, T. D. A. 1906. *Comptonia insignis.* Colorado University Studies 3:173.
______. 1908. Descriptions of Tertiary Plants. *American Journal of Science* 26:65–67.
Codrington, J. 1982. Some thoughts on trees in parks. *Int. Dendr. Soc. Yrbk.* 1981:96–98.
Coggeshall, R. C. 1957. Asiatic maples, their propagation from softwood cuttings. *Arnoldia* 17:45–55.
Coker and Totten. 1973. *Trees of the South Eastern States.* Rev. ed. (from original in 1934). Chapel Hill: University of North Carolina Press.
Cole Nursery. 1968. *Spring Catalogue.* Circleville, Ohio.
Colley, R. H. 1922. The maple wilt. *Experiment Station Record* 51:52–53.
Collingwood, G. H., and J. A. Cope. 1938. Maple sugar & syrup. New York State Agricultural Experiment Station Bulletin 297.
Collins, J. F., and H. W. Preston. 1912. *Illustrated Key to the Wild and Commonly Cultivated Trees.* New York: Holt.
Collins, W. H. 1964. New trees available in the trade. *American Nurseryman* 120:10, 31.
Collman, S. J. 1971. *Insect Pests of Ornamental Trees and Shrubs of the University of Washington Arboretum.* Master's thesis, University of Washington.
Conwentz, H. W. 1886. In Goeppert & Menge's *Die Flora des Bernsteins* 2:74.
Cook, A. J. 1887. *Maple Sugar and the Sugar Bush.* Ohio: Root.
Cooke, W. W., and J. L. Hills. 1891. Maple sugar. Vermont Agricultural Experiment Station Bulletin 26.
Cooper, J. I. 1979. *Virus Diseases of Trees and Shrubs.* Oxford: Institute of Terrestrial Ecology.
Copping, L., and H. E. Street. 1972. Properties of the invertases of cultured sycamore cells and changes in their activity during culture growth. *Physiol. Pl.* 26:346.
Cordell, G. A. 1978. Anticancer agents from plants. In *Progress in Phytochemistry* 5. Eds. L. Reinhold et al. Oxford: Pergamon.
Coré, H. W., et al. 1979. *Wood Structure and Identification.* Syracuse: Syracuse University Press.
Corner, E. J. H. 1964. *The Life of Plants.* London: Weidenfeld & Nicolson.
Correns, C. 1928. Bestimmung, Vererbung und Verteilung des Geschlechtes bei den höheren Pflanzen. In *Handbuch der Vererbungswissenschaft.* Eds. E. Bauer & M. Hartman. Berlin.
Cortesi, R. 1943. Contributions à l'anatomie des pétioles des *Acer.* Bulletin de la Societé Botanique de Suisse 53:102.
Coté, W. A., and D. C. Allen. 1973. Biology of the maple trumpet skeletonizer *Epinotia aceriella* (Lepidoptera: Olethreutidae) in New York. *The Canadian Entomologist* 105:463–470.
Cowan, J. M. 1952. *The journeys and plants introductions of George Forest VMH.* In *Quest for Plants; A History of Horticultural Explorers.* Ed. A. M. Coats. London: Studio Vista, 1969; New York: McGraw-Hill, 1970.
Cox, C. B., et al. 1976. *Biogeography.* Oxford: Blackwell.

Cox, E. H. M. 1961. *Plant Hunting in China.* London: Oldbourne.
Coxe, T. 1794. *A View of the United States of America.* Philadelphia: Hall.
Craib, W. G. 1920. *A. garrettii* Craib. Contributions to the flora of Siam. Kew Bulletin 301–302.
Crane, E. 1975. *Honey, a Comprehensive Survey.* London: Heinemann.
Crawley, M. J. 1983. *Herbivory. The Dynamics of Animal-Plant Interactions.* Oxford: Blackwell.
Cremers, C. M. 1970. Tour of Kent and Sussex, May 1968. *Int. Dendr. Soc. Yrbk.* 1969:30–35.
Critchfield, W. B. 1971. Shoot growth and heterophylly in *Acer. Journal of Arnold Arboretum* 52:240–266.
Crocketh, W. H. 1929. Vermont maple sugar. Comm. Agriculture Vermont Bur. Publ. Bull. 38.
Crockett, J. U. 1978. *Bomen.* (Translated from the English *Trees.*) Amsterdam: Time-Life.
Crockett, W. H. 1915. How Vermont maple sugar is made. Vermont Agricultural Experiment Station Bulletin 21.
Crok, C. 1881. Iets over Boskoopse Kwekerijen. II. *Sieboldia* 7(45):356.
Cronquist, A. 1968. *The Evolution and Classification of Flowering Plants.* London: Nelson.
______. 1973. *Basic Botany.* 3rd ed. New York: Harper & Row.
______. 1981. *An Integrated System of Classification of Flowering Plants.* New York: Columbia University Press.
Crouch, A. G. 1974. Arboretum at University of Exeter. *Int. Dendr. Soc. Yrbk.* 1973:52–56.
Cui, S. C., and J. X. Y. Cui. 1989. *Acer stenolobum* var. *monochladea. Acta Phytotaxonomica Sinica* 27(2):131.
Cummins, G. B., and Yhiratsuka. 1983. *Illustrated Genera of Rust Fungi.* Rev. ed. St. Paul, Minnesota: American Phytopathological Society.
Cunningham, I. S. 1984. *Frank N. Meyer, Plant Hunter in Asia.* Iowa: Iowa State University Press.
Curtis, W. J. 1969. Seed germination and culture of *Acer palmatum. International Plant Propagators' Society Proceedings* 19:142.
Cutler, D. F. 1978. *Applied Plant Anatomy.* London: Longman.
Cutler, D. F., and I. B. K. Richardson. 1981. *Tree Roots and Buildings.* London: Construction Press.
Cutler, D. F., et al., eds. 1982. *The Plant Cuticle.* London: Academic Press.
Cutler, D. F., et al. 1987. *Root Indentification Manual of Trees and Shrubs.* London: Chapman and Hall.
Cutting, H. A. 1886. The maple sugar industry. *Vermont Agricultural Report* 272–303.
Cypher, J., and D. E. Boucher. 1982. Beech/maple co-existence and seedling growth rates at Mont St. Hilaire, Quebec, Canada. *Canadian Journal of Botany* 60:1279–1284.
Czaninski, Y. 1977. Mise en évidence de cellules associées aux vaisseaux dans le xyléme de sycomore. *Journal de Microscopie* 13:137–140.
Czaninski, Y., & A. M. Catesson. 1970. Activités peroxydasiques d'origine diverses dans les cellules d'*Acer pseudoplatanus* (tissus conducteurs et cellules en culture). *Journal de Microscopie* 9:1089–1102.
Czeczott, H., and A. Skirgiello. 1961. *Aceraceae*—the fossil flora of Turov near Bogatynia. *Prace Muz. Ziemi* 4:51–73, 116–117.
Dahlgren, R. M. T. 1979. Gross-taxonomic evaluation in the angiosperms in relation to parasitism. *Symb. Bot. Uppsala* 23, 4:212.
______. 1980. A revised system of classification of the angiosperms. *Botanical Journal, Linnean Society* 80:91–124.
Dale, J. E., and F. L. Milthorpe. 1983. *The Growth and Functioning of Leaves.* New York: Cambridge University Press.
Dalla Torre, K. W. von, and L. von Sarnthein. 1909. *Flora der Gefürsteten Grafschaft Tirol* 6(2):790–793.
Dana, D. 1947. *Sugar Bush.* New York: Nelson.
Dansereau, P. 1945a. Herborisations Laurentiennes. I. *Nature Canada* 72:125–128.
______. 1945b. Les conditions de l'acériculture. Bulletin du Service de Biogéographie 1.
Dansereau, P., and A. LaFond. 1941. Introgression des caractères de l'*Acer saccharophorum* Koch, K. et de l'*Acer nigrum* Michx. *Contributions de l'Institut Botanique de l'Université de Montréal* 37:17–31.
Dansereau, P., and Y. Desmarais. 1947. Introgression in sugar maples. II. *American Midland Naturalist* 37:146–161.
Darling, C. A. 1923. Chromosome Behavior in *Acer platanoides* L. *American Journal of Botany* 10:450–457.
Darlington, C. D., and A. P. Wylie. 1955. *Chromosome Atlas of Flowering Plants.* 2nd ed. London: Allen & Unwin.

Darrall, N. M., and P. F. Wareing. 1981. The effects of nitrogen nutrition on cytokinin activity and free amino acids in *Betula pendula* Roth and *Acer pseudoplatanus* L. *Journal of Experimental Botany* 32:369–379.
Dathe, M. 1983. *Acer saccharum* 'Newton Sentry'. *Arnoldia,* summer issue.
Daubenmire, R. 1974. *Plants and Environment.* 3rd ed. New York: Wiley.
______. 1978. *Plant Geography.* New York: Academic Press.
David, Père A. 1845. Erables nouveaux peu connus. *Revue Horticole* 17:45–47.
Davidson, M. 1976. *The Sunday Express Weekend Gardening Book.* London: White Lion.
Davidson, R. W., and W. A. Campbell. 1944. Observations on gall of sugar maple. *Phytopathology* 34:132–135.
Davidson, R. W., and R. C. Lorenz. 1939. Species of *Eutypella* and *Schizoxylon* associated with cankers of maple. *Phytopathology* 28:733–745.
Davies, H. V., and N. J. Penfield. 1979. RNA and protein synthesis during afterripening of seeds of *Acer platanoides* L. *Zeitschr. Pflanzenphysiol.* 92:85–90.
Davies, J. 1979. *Douglas of the Forests.* Edinburgh: Hall Harris.
Davis, P. H., and V. H. Heywood. 1973. *Principles of Angiosperm Taxonomy.* New York: Krieger.
Davis, R., et al. 1982. *Catalogue of Eriophyid Mites* (Acari: Eriophyoidea). Warsaw: Warsaw Agricultural University Press.
Dawson, J. W. 1886. On the Mesozoic floras of the Rocky Mountain region of Canada. *Mémoirs du Compte Rendu de la Société Royale de Canada.* 4(3):16–22.
Dayton, W. A. 1945. A tricarpellary maple. In *Proceedings of the Biological Society, Washington* 58:27–28.
Deam, C. C. 1940. *Flora of Indiana.* Indianapolis.
De Belder, R. 1969. *Acer palmatum* 'Autumn Glory'. *Dendroflora* 6:25.
______. 1973. Visit to Yakushima. *Int. Dendr. Soc. Yrbk.* 1972:22–30.
De Boer, S. 1947. Het Stekken van *Acer. Jaarboek Nederlandse Dendr. Ver.* 16:116–118.
Deegen, F., Jr. 1886. Drei Buntfärbige Gehölzneuigkeiten für die Frühjahrs-Saison. *Ill. Monatsh. Gesamt-Inter. Gartenb.* 5:103.
Delaveau, P., and R.-R. Paris. 1968. Répartition des pigments flavoniques dans les feuilles panachées. *Compte Rendu Hebdomadaire des Séances de l'Académie de Science* 267:317.
Delendick, T. J. 1979. *Acer craibianum* (Aceraceae). A new name for a maple of southeast Asia. *Brittonia* 30:473–476.
______. 1980a. The correct name for the Nikko maple (Aceraceae). *Brittonia* 32:286–290.
______. 1980b. The correct name for the *Acer* of Malesia. *Reinwardtia* 9:395–401.
______. 1981. *A Systematic Review of the Aceraceae.* Ph.D. thesis, City University of New York.
______. 1982. Infrageneric nomenclature in *Acer* (Aceraceae). *Brittonia* 34:81–84.
______. 1983. Reconsideration of two intraspecific taxa of the full-moon maple, *Acer japonicum* (Aceraceae). *Brittonia* 36:49–58.
______. 1985. *Acer buergerianum* 'Jako Kaede'. Member of the Verbenaceae. *Taxon* 34:96–101.
______. 1990a. A survey of foliar flavonoids in the Aceraceae. *Mem. New York Botanical Garden* 54.
______. 1990b. The chemotaxonomy of the Aceraceae. *Int. Dendr. Soc. Yrbk.* 1990:22–41.
Dendrovski, R. 1973. Neue Beiträge zur Kenntnis der Arten *A. campestre* L. und *A. marsicum* Guss. *Godisen Zbornic Biol. (Skopje)* 25:185–203.
______. 1974a. *Acer marsicum* Guss. in der Flora Bulgariens. *Ann. de la Fac. des Sci. de l'Univ. de Skopje* 26.
______. 1974b. Einige Neue Formen der Gattung *Acer* L. *Extrait du Rec. des Trav. du Symp. à l'Occ. du 100-Anniv. de la prem. Dendrol. Yougoslav. de Jos Pančić.* Belgrade.
______. 1974c. *Acer obtusatum* f. *daisaretica. Naucni Skup. Odelje Prir.- Mat. Nauk.* 1(1):17.
Dennis, J. V. 1988. *The Great Cypress Swamps.* Baton Rouge: Louisiana State University Press.
Densmore, F. 1928. Uses of plants by the Chippewa Indians. *Bureau of American Ethnology 44th Annual Report* 275–397.
Dent, T. C. 1969a. *Relationships of Two Isolated Groups of Sugar Maple in Central Oklahoma.* Ph.D. thesis, University of Oklahoma.
______. 1969b. IOPB chromosome number reports. *Taxon* 18:433.
Desch, H. E., and J. M. Dinwoodie. 1981. *Timber: Its Structure, Properties and Utilisation* 6th ed. New York: Macmillan.
Deschênes, J. M. 1968. Acer saccharum *near and at the Periphery of its Range in New Jersey.* Ph.D. thesis, Rutgers University, New Jersey.
______. 1970. The history of the genus *Acer,* a review. *Nature Canada* 97:51–59.

Desfontaines, R. L. 1804. *Tableau de l'Ecole de Botanique du Musée d'Histoire Naturelle.* Paris.
Desmarais, Y. 1947. Taxonomy of the sugar maples. *American Journal of Botany* 34:606.
______. 1952. Dynamics of leaf variation in the sugar maples. *Brittonia* 7:347–387.
Dessureault, M., et al. 1985. Symposium maple decline in Quebec. *Phytoprotection* 66:69–99.
Detmers, F. 1919. Two new varieties of *Acer rubrum. The Ohio Journal of Science* 19:235–239.
Devonport, Viscount. 1988. Tour in Canada and N.W. America 27th Sept. to 16th Oct. 1987. *Int. Dendr. Soc. Yrbk.* 1987:52–67.
DeVos, C. 1887. *Handboek tot de Praktische Kennis der Voornaamste Boomen, Heesters & Coniferen.* 2nd ed. Amsterdam: M. M. Olivier.
______. 1890. *Supplement. Handboek tot de Praktische Kennis der Voornaamste Boomen, Heesters & Coniferen.* 2nd ed. Amsterdam: M. M. Olivier.
De Wit, H. C. D. 1954–1955. The planting of a maple tree in the Arboretum Belmonte, May 1955. *Jaarboek Nederlandse Dendr. Ver.* 20:34–36.
DeWolf, J. 1888. Maples from Japan. *Am. Garden* 9:139.
Dhar, U., and P. Kachroo. 1983. *Alpine Flora of Kashmir Himalaya.* Jodphur: Scientific Publ.
Dickinson, C. H., and J. A. Lucas. 1977. *Plant Pathology & Plant Pathogens.* Oxford: Blackwell.
Dickinson, C. H., and G. J. F. Pugh. 1974. *Biology of Plant Litter Decomposition.* New York: Academic Press.
Dickson, F., and A. Dickson. 1880. *Catalogue* for 1880–81. Chester, England.
______ 1881. *Catalogue* for 1881–82. Chester, England.
______. 1883. *Catalogue* for 1883–84. Chester, England.
Dickson, J., and Sons. 1882. *Catalogue.* Chester, England.
______. 1887. *Catalogue.* Chester, England.
Dieck, G. 1885. *Hauptcatalog der Obst—und Gehölzbaumschulen des Ritterguts Zöschen bei Merseburg.* Zöschen.
______. 1887. *Nachtrag I Hauptcatalog der Obst—und Gehölzbaumschulen des Ritterguts Zöschen bei Merseburg.* Zöschen.
Diels, F. L. E. 1900. Die Flora von Central-China. *Bot. Jahrb.* 29:380.
______. 1912. *A. pentaphyllum* Diels. Plantae Chinenses Forrestianae. *Notes of the Royal Botanic Garden, Edinburgh* 5:165.
______. 1931. *A. pentaphyllum* Diels. Miscellanea Sinensia. IV. *Notizbl. Bot. Gard. Berlin* 11:211–212.
Dietrich, A. G. 1832. In Willdenow's *Anleitung zum Selbststudium der Botanik.* 4th ed. Berlin.
Dietrich, D. N. F. 1840. *Synopsis Plantarum* 2:1281–1283.
Dimbleby, R. 1978. *Plants and Archaeology.* London: John Baker.
Dinsmore, J. E. 1931. In *Flora of Syria, Palestine and Sinai.* 2nd ed. Ed. G. E. Post. Beirut. 1:280–281.
Dippel, L. 1892. *Handbuch der Laubgehölzkunde.* II. Berlin: Parey.
Di Sanzo, C. P., and R. A. Rohde. 1969. *Xiphinema americanum* associated with maple decline in Massachusetts. *Phytopathology* 59:279–284.
Dix, N. J. 1974. Identification of a water-soluble fungal inhibitor in leaves of *Acer platanoides* L. *Ann. Bot.* 38:505–514.
Dixon, A. F. G. 1971. The role of aphids in wood formation. I. The effect of the sycamore aphid, *Drepanosiphum platanoides* (Schr.) (*Aphididae*), on the growth of sycamore, *Acer pseudoplatanus* L. *Journal of Applied Biology* 8:165–179.
Dochinger, L. S. 1956. New concepts of the *Verticillium* wilt disease of maple. *Phytopathology* 46:467.
Dochinger, L. S., and A. M. Townsend. 1979. Effects of roadside deicer salts and ozone on red maple progenies. *Environ. Pollut.* 19:229–237.
Docters van Leeuwen, W. M. 1957. *Gallenboek.* 2nd ed. Zutphen: Thieme.
______. 1982. *Gallenboek.* 3rd ed. Zutphen. Thieme. Revised and enlarged by A. A. Wiebes-Rijks et al.
Dodonaeus, R. 1583. *Stirpium historiae.* Pemptades sex. Antwerp: Plantijn.
Dohna, Countess U., et al. 1986. *Private Gardens of Germany.* London: Wiedenfeld & Nicolson.
Doing Kraft, H. 1954–1955. Natural habitat of *Cornus mas* L. (With English summary.) *Jaarboek Nederlandse Dendr. Ver.* 20:169–197.
Doing Kraft, H., and V. Westhoff. 1956–1958. De Plaats van de Beuk (*Fagus sylvatica*) in het Midden- en West-Europese Bos. (With English summary.) *Jaarboek Nederlandse Dendr. Ver.* 21:226–254.
Don, D. 1825. *Acer acuminatum* Wall. ex. Don. D. *Prodromus Florae Nepalensis.* London: Gale.
______. 1831. *A General History of Dichlamydus Plants.* I. London.
Dönig, G. 1991. Eine Neue und Sichere Veredlungsmethode auch für Liebhaber und Sammler

Dendrologischer Spezialitäten: Die Grün–Veredlung. *Mitt. Dtsch. Dendr. Ges.* 80:247–249.
Doorenbos, J. 1947. De Verspreiding van het Geslacht *Acer* in Europa. *Jaarboek Nederlandse Dendr. Ver.* 16:41–47.
Doorenbos, S. G. A. 1933. 41ste Jaarvergadering van de Deutsche Dendrologische Gesellschaft. *Jaarboek Nederlandse Dendr. Ver.* 9:47–58.
______. 1939. Zomerbijeenkomst 1939. Frederiksoord, Groningen en Weener. *Jaarboek Nederlandse Dendr. Ver.* 14:19–22.
______. 1956–1958. Hoe Ontwikkelden Zich de Bomen in het Zuiderpark te Den Haag Gedurende de Eerste Dertig Jaren? *Jaarboek Nederlandse Dendr. Ver.* 21:68–77.
______. 1969. *Acer pseudoplatanus* 'Nachtegaalplein'. *Dendroflora* 6:12.
Dorofeev, P. I. 1963a. Novye dannye o Plejstocenovych florach Belorussii i Smolenskoi Oblasti. *Mat. po Istorii Flory i Rastiteln. USSR* 4:5–180.
______. 1963b. *Treticnye Flory Zapadnoj Sibiri.* Leningrad.
______. 1970. *Treticnye Flory Urala.* Leningrad.
______. 1977. Simbuginskaja flora. In *Fauna i Flora Simbugino.* Moscow.
Douglas, D. 1914. *Journal, Kept by David Douglas During His Travels, 1823–1827.* London.
Dowden, A. O. 1975. *The Blossom on the Bough.* New York: Crowell.
Downs, A. A. 1938. Glaze damage in the birch-beech-maple-hemlock type of Pennsylvania and New York. *Journal of Forestry* 36:63–70.
Doyle, J. A. 1969. Cretaceous angiosperm pollen of the Atlantic Coastal Plain and its evolutionary significance. *Journal of Arnold Arboretum* 50:1–35.
Drilias, M. J., et al. 1982. Collar rot and basal canker of sugar maple. *Journal of Arboriculture* 8:29–33.
Drooz, A. T. 1985. Insects of eastern forests. USDA Forest Service Miscellaneous Publication 1426.
Druce, G. C. 1931. *Report of the Botany Society Exchange Club, British Isles* 9:259.
Drude, C. G. O. 1887. Sapindaceae 1. Acerinae. In *Handbuch der Botanik,* by A. Schenk. 3/2:390.
DuCane, E., and F. DuCane. 1908. *The Flowers and Gardens of Japan.* London: Adam & Charles.
Dudley, P. 1720. An account of the method of making sugar. *Transactions of the Royal Society of London.*
Dudley, T. R. 1984. Names for unassigned woody genera (1981–1983). Bulletin of the American Association of Botanic Gardens and Arboreta 18 (4):97–98.
______. 1986. International registrations of cultivar names for unassigned woody genera (1984). Bulletin of the American Association of Botanic Gardens and Arboreta 19(3):86–94.
Dudzik, K. R. 1988. Macro-microscopic anatomy: obtaining a composite view of barrier zone formation in *Acer saccharum.* IAWA Bulletin 9(1):183–186.
Duffey, E. 1980. *The Forest World. The Ecology of the Temperate Woodlands.* London: Orbis.
Duffield, J. W. 1943. Polyploidy in *Acer rubrum* L. *Chron. Bot.* 7:390–391.
Duhamel du Monceau, H. L. 1755. *Traité des Arbres et Arbustes.* Vol. 1. Paris.
______. 1809. *Traité des Arbres et Arbustes.* Vol. 4. Paris: Michel.
Duke, J. A. 1986. Folk anticancer plants containing antitumor compounds. In *Plants in Indigenous Medicine and Diet.* Ed. N. L. Etkin. Bedford Hills, New York: Redgrave.
Duke, J. A., and E. S. Ayensu. 1985. *Medicinal Plants of China.* Michigan: Reference.
Dulac, J. 1867. *Flore du Département des Hautes-Pyrénées.* Paris.
Dumbroff, E. B., and D. P. Webb. 1970. Factors influencing the stratification process in seeds of *Acer ginnala. Canadian Journal of Botany* 48:2009–2015.
Dumbroff, E. B., and D. C. W. Brown. 1976. Cytokines and inhibitor activity in roots and stems of sugar maple seedlings through the dormant season. *Canadian Journal of Botany* 54:191–197.
Dumbroff, E. B., and H. W. Elmore. 1977. Living fibres as a principal feature of the xylem in seedlings of *Acer saccharum* Marsh. *Ann. Bot.* 41:471–472.
Dumbroff, E. B., et al. 1979. Seasonal levels of abscisic acid in buds and atems of *Acer saccharum. Physiol. Pl.* 45:211–214.
Dumortier, B. C. J. 1827. *Florula Belgica.* Tournay.
Duncan, W. H., and M. B. Duncan. 1988. *Trees of the South-Eastern States.* Athens: University of Georgia Press.
Dunn, S. T. 1908. A botanical expedition to central Fokien. *Botanical Journal, Linnean Society* 38:358.
Dunn, S., and R. J. Townsend. 1954. Propagation of sugar maple by vegetative cuttings. *International Plant Propagators' Society Proceedings* 3:108–110.
DuRoi, J. P. 1771. *Die Harbkesche Wilde Baumzucht* 1:1–33. Braunschweig.
Duthie, J. F. 1908. *A. tutcheri* Duthie. Kew Bulletin 16.
Dwinell, L. D., and W. A. Sinclair. 1965. Effects of N, P, K, and inoculum density on *Verticillium* wilt

of American elm and sugar maple. *Phytopathology* 55:1056.
Easton, G. D., et al. 1969. A method of estimating *Verticillium albo-atrum* propagules in field soil and irrigation waste water. *Phytopathology* 59:1171–1172.
Eastop, V. 1979. *Sternorrynchia* as angiosperm taxonomists. *Symb. Bot. Uppsala* 23(4):13.
Eastop, V. F., and D. Hille Ris Lambers. 1976. *Survey of the World's Aphids.* The Hague: Junk.
Edlin, H. L. 1972. *Trees, Woods and Man.* The New Naturalist 32. London: Collins.
______. 1974. *Woodland Crafts in Britain.* Newton Abbott: David & Charles.
______. 1976. *The Natural History of Trees.* London: Weidenfeld & Nicolson.
Edlin, H. L., and M. Nimmo. 1956. *Treasury of Trees.* Manchester: Countrygoer Books
Edson, H. A. 1912. Micro-organisms of maple sap. Vermont Agricultural Experiment Station Bulletin 167.
Ehrhart, J. F. 1789. *Beiträge zur Naturkunde* 4:23–25.
Eichler, A. W. 1875. *Blütendiagramme* 1:350–354.
Eiselt, M. 1960. *Deutsche Baumschule* 12:129.
Elblova, M. 1979. *Das Ahorn-Sortiment im Arboretum Novy Dur bei Opava,* Ser. C (Dendrologie) 28(2):117–134.
Eley, M. 1973. East Bergholt Place, Suffolk. *Int. Dendr. Soc. Yrbk.* 1972:30–39.
Elias, T. S. 1980. *The Complete Trees of North America.* New York: Van Nostrand Reinhard.
Elias, T. S., and H. S. Irwin. 1976. Urban trees. *Scientific American* 235(5):111–118.
Ellacombe, C. 1982. *In a Gloucestershire Garden.* Rpt. from 1895. London: Century.
Ellenberg, H. 1979. Zeigerwerte der Gefäszpflanzen Mitteleuropas. *Scripta Geobotanica* 9.
Elliott, S. 1821. *A Sketch of the Botany of South Carolina and Georgia* 1:449–452
Ellis, W. H. 1963. *Revision of* Acer *Section* Rubra *of Eastern North America, excluding* Acer saccharinum L. Ph.D. thesis, University of Tennessee.
Ellwanger and Barry. 1881. New forms of the silver maple. *The Garden* 20:166–167.
Elmore, H. W., and E. B. Dumbroff. 1977. Living fibers in secondary xylem from the root and stem of sugar maple, *Acer saccharum* Marsh. In *Proceedings of the West Virginia Academy of Science* 49:9–10.
Elwes H. J., and A. Henry. 1908. *The Trees of Great Britain & Ireland* 3:630–686. Rpt. SPR, 1970.
Emanuel, D. A., et al. 1966. Maple bark stripper's disease. *New England Journal of Medicine* 274:1413.
Endlicher, S. F. L. 1836–1840. *Genera Plantarum Secundum Ordines Naturalis Disposita.* clas. 53:1055. Vienna.
______. 1843. *Catalogus Horti Academici Vindobonensis.* 2:372–374.
Endo, S. 1934. Some Japanese Cenozoic plants. *Jap. J. Geol. Geogr. Transactions* 11:239–253.
______. 1950. On the fossil *Acer* from Japan, Korea, and South Manchuria. I. Institute of Geology and Paleontology, Taihoku University, Short Paper 1:11–17.
______. 1951. On the fossil *Acer* from Japan, Korea, and South Manchuria. II. Institute of Geology and Paleontology, Taihoku University, Short Paper 3:52–58.
Engelhard, A. W. 1957. Host index of *Verticillium albo-atrum* (including *V. dahliae*). *Plant Disease Reporter Supplement* 244:23–49.
Engelhardt, H. 1881. Ueber Pflanzenreste aus den Tertiärablagerungen von Liebotitz. *Sitz-ber. Naturw. Ges. Isis Dresden* 1880:83.
Engler, A. 1905. Einfluss der Provenienz des Samens auf die Eigenschaften der Forstlichen Holzgewächse. Bergahorn (*Acer pseudoplatanus*). *Mitt. Schweiz. Centralanstalt für das Forstl. Versuchswesen* 8(2):225–236.
Engler H. G. A., and K. A. E. Prantl. 1907. *Die Natürlichen Pflanzenfamilien.* III. 5:267–268. Leipzig.
Enu-Kwesi, L., and E. B. Dumbroff. 1978. Changes in abscisic acid in the embryo and covering structures of *A. saccharum* during stratification. *Zeitschr. Pflanzenphysiol.* 86:371–377.
Erdmann, G. G., et al. 1988. Foliar nutrient variation and sampling intensity for *Acer rubrum. Canadian Journal of Forest Research* 18(1):134–139.
Erdtman, O. G. E. 1952. *Pollen Morphology and Plant Taxonomy,* Waltham, Massachusetts: Stockholm.
______. 1969. *Handbook of Palynology.* Copenhagen: Munksgaard.
Ern, H., and K. Browicz. 1983. *Acer campestre* in the Amanus Mountains, Turkey. *Arboretum Kornickie* 28:3–5.
Errico, P. 1957. Studio sistematico delle entita Italiane di *Acer opalus* Mill. *We bia* 12:41–120.
Erwin, D. C. 1969. Methods of determination of the systemic and fungitoxic properties of chemicals applied to plants with emphasis on control of *Verticillium* wilt with thiabendazole and benlate. *World Review of Pest Control* 8:6–22.
Esau, K. 1965. *Plant Anatomy.* 2nd ed. New York: Wiley.

______. 1977. *Anatomy of Seed Plants.* 2nd ed. New York: Wiley.
Essig, E. O., and F. Abernathy. 1952. *The Aphid Genus* Periphyllus. Berkeley: University of California Press.
Esveld, F. C. 1988–1989. *Catalogue* (Nurseries). Boskoop, The Netherlands.
Etkin, N. L. 1986. *Plants in Indigenous Medicine and Diet. Behavioral Approaches.* New York: Redgrave.
Ettingshausen, C. F. von. 1851. Die Tertiaeren-Floren der Oesterreichischen Monarchie. I. *Abh. Geol. Reichsanst. Wien* 2(1):22.
______. 1858. Zur Kenntnis der Fossilen Flora von Sotzka in Untersteiermark. *Sitz-ber. Math. Naturw. Akad. Wiss. Wien* 28:471–567.
______. 1867. Die Fossile Flora des Tertiärbeckens von Bilin I–III. *Denkschr. Math. Naturw. Kl. Akad. Wiss. Wien* 26.
______. 1868. *Sitz-ber. Math. Naturw. Akad. Wiss. Wien* 57:874.
______. 1869. Die Fossile Flora des Tertiär-Beckens von Bilin. III. *Denkschr. Math. Naturw. Kl. Akad. Wiss. Wien* 29:18–23, t. 44–45.
______. 1870. Beitrage zur Kenntnis der Tertiärflora Steiermarks. *Sitz-ber. Math. Naturw. Akad. Wiss. Wien* 60:79–80.
______. 1887. *Denkschr. Math. Naturw. Kl. Akad. Wiss. Wien* 53:125,170.
Evelyn, J. 1664. *Sylva.* London Council of the Royal Society. Facsimile rpt. 1973. Menston, Yorkshire: Scolar Press.
Everett, T. H. 1980. *The New York Botanical Garden Illustrated Encyclopedia of Horticulture.* 10 vols. New York: Garland.
Eyre, S. R. 1977. *Vegetation and Soils: A World Picture.* London: Arnold.
Faber, H. 1978. New York maple-sugar harvest ends, with indications of a 'Fair'. *The New York Times* (16 April):57.
Faegri, K., and J. Iversen. 1975. *Textbook of Pollen Analysis.* Oxford: Blackwell.
Faegri, K., and L. van der Pijl. 1979. *The Principles of Pollination Ecology.* 3rd ed. Oxford: Pergamon.
Fahn, A. 1967. *Plant Anatomy.* Oxford: Pergamon.
______. 1979. *Secretory Tissues in Plants.* New York: Academic Press.
Falk, J. P. 1786. *Beiträge zur Topographischen Kenntnis des Russischen Reiches* 2:79. St. Petersburg.
Fang, W. P. 1932a. Preliminary notes on Chinese Aceraceae. *Contr. Biol. Lab. Sci. Soc. China,* botany ser., 7(6):143–189.
______. 1932b. *A. pubipalmatum* Fang. Further notes on Chinese Aceraceae. *Contr. Biol. Lab. Sci. Soc. China,* botany ser., 8(2):162–182.
______. 1934. *Acer yuii* Fang. A new species of *Acer* from Szechuan. *Contr. Biol. Lab. Sci. Soc. China,* botany ser., 9(3):235–237.
______. 1937. A new Chinese *Acer. Sunyatsenia* 3:263–264.
______. 1939. A monograph of Chinese Aceraceae. *Contr. Biol. Lab. Sci. Soc. China,* botany ser., 11:1–346.
______. 1945. *Icones Plantarum Omeiensium* 2:128–142.
______. 1966. Revisio taxorum Aceracearum Sinicarum. *Acta Phytotaxonomica Sinica* 11(2):139–189.
______. 1979a. Praecursores florae Aceracearum Sinensium. *Acta Phytotaxonomica Sinica* 17(1):60–86.
______. 1979b. *Acer yaoshanicum. Acta Phytotaxonomica Sinica* 17(1):74.
______. 1981a. *Flora Reipublicae Popularis Sinicae.* Vol. 46. Beijing: Science Press.
______. 1981b. *Flora Tsinlingensis.* Vol I. Beijing: Science Press.
Fang, W. P., and S. Y. Liang. 1981a. *Acer cinnamomifolium* var. *microphyllum. Acta Phytotaxonomica Sinica* 19(1):116.
______. 1981b. *Acer fabri* var. *dolichophyllum. Acta Phytotaxonomica Sinica* 19(1):117.
Fang, W. P., et al. N.d. *Flora Sichuanica.* Chengdu Institute of Biology.
Farley, J. D., et al. 1971. Repeated germination and sporulation of microsclerotia of *Verticillium albo-atrum* in soil. *Phytopathology* 61:260–264.
Faust, H. 1963. *Waldbauliche Untersuchungen am Bergahorn* (A. pseudoplatanus). Ph.D. thesis, Hannover, Munden.
Fedde, F. K. G. 1913. *Acer bodinieri* Lév. *Repertorium Specierum Novarum Regni Vegetabilis* 10:433.
Fedorov, A. A., ed. 1969. *Chromosome Numbers of Flowering Plants.* Leningrad: Acad. Sci., USSR, Botanicheskii Institut Komarov.
Feininger, A. 1968. *Wunderbare Welt der Bäume und Wälder.* Vienna: Econ. Verlag.
Felt, E. P. 1924. *Manual of Tree and Shrub Insects.* Ed. L. H. Bailey. New York: Macmillan.
______. 1940. *Plant Galls and Gall-makers.* Ithaca, New York: Comstock.

Fenska, R. R. 1959. *The Complete Modern Tree Experts Manual.* New York: Dodd, Mead & Co.
Fentener van Vlissingen, P. 1896. *Onze Boomen en Heesters.* Leiden: Brill.
Fenton, F. A. 1939. Control of shade tree borers. Oklahoma Agricultural Experiment Station Circular 84.
Fergus, C. L. 1954. An epiphytotic of *Phyllosticta* leaf spot of maple. *Plant Disease Reporter* 38:678–679.
Ferguson, D. K. 1971. *The Miocene Flora of Kreuzau, West Germany.* Amsterdam: North Holland Publ. Co.
Fernald, M. L. 1934. A conical sugar maple. *Rhodora* 36:238–239.
______. 1942. Additions to the flora of Virginia. *Rhodora* 44:426–427.
______. 1945. Botanical specialties of Virginia. *Rhodora* 47:156–160.
______. 1949. Studies in eastern American plants. *Rhodora* 51:103.
Fernald, M. L., and A. C. Kinsey. 1943. *Edible Wild Plants of Eastern North America.* Cornwall on Hudson, New York: Idlewild Press.
Feron, J. 1979. It's almost time to tap the maples. *The New York Times* (4 March) 10:1, 15.
Filer, J. 1989. Gloucestershire tour May 19–23, 1988. *Int. Dendr. Soc. Yrbk.* 1988:49–54.
Finlay, M. C. 1935. *Our American Maples.* New York: Georgian.
Fiori, A. 1906. Flora Italica exsiccata. Eds. Fiori, Beguinot, and Pamapanini. *Nuovo Giorn. Bot. Ital.* 13:169.
______. 1909. *Flora Analitica d'Italia* 5:192–193. Eds. Fiori, Paoletti, and Beguinot.
Firsov, G. A. 1982. To the question of geography and systematics of the genus *Acer* (Aceraceae). *Botanicheskii Zhurnal* 67(8):1082–1090.
Fischer, F. E. L. von. 1812. *Catalogue du jardin des plantes de son excellence Monsieur le Compte, Alexis de Razoumoffsky, à Gorenki.* 2nd ed. Moscow.
Fischer, F. E. L. von, and C. A. Meyer. 1837. *A. hyrcanum* F. et M. *Index Sem. Hort. Petrop.* 4:31.
Fitschen, J. 1987. *Gehölzflora. Ein Buch zur Bestimmung der in Mitteleuropa Wildwachsenden und Angepflanzten Bäume und Sträucher.* 8th ed. Rev. by F. H. Meyer et al. Heidelberg, Wiesbaden: Quelle & Meyer.
Fitter, A. 1978. *An Atlas of the Wild Flowers of Britain and Northern Europe.* London: Collins.
Flemer, William, III. 1965. *Shade and Ornamental Trees in Color.* New York.
Fletcher, H. 1975. *A Quest of Flowers.* Edinburgh: Edinburgh University Press.
Fletcher, J., ed. 1978. *Dendrochronology in Europe* 127. Archeol. ser. no. 4. Greenwich: Nat. Marit. Mus.
Flohn, H. 1982. Climatic change and an ice-free Arctic Ocean. *Carbon Dioxide Review.* New York: Oxford University Press.
Follett, M. 1941. *A Drop in the Bucket.* Brattleboro, Vermont: Stephen Day.
Font y Quer, P., and W. H. P. Rothmaler. 1934. *Sched. Fl. Iber. Select. Cent.* 1:56.
Fontaine, F. J. 1954–1955. Zomerbijeenkomst 1955 op 22 en 23 Juli. *Jaarboek Nederlandse Dendr. Ver.* 20:21–29.
______. 1956–1958a. Zomerbijeenkomst 1956 op 29 en 30 Juni. *Jaarboek Nederlandse Dendr. Ver.* 21:36–44.
______. 1956–1958b. Zomerbijeenkomst 1957 op 5 en 6 Juli. *Jaarboek Nederlandse Dendr. Ver.* 21:45–51.
______. 1956–1958c. Zomerbijeenkomst 1958 op 11 en 12 Juli. *Jaarboek Nederlandse Dendr. Ver.* 21:52–55.
Forbes, F. B., and W. B. Hemsley. 1886. An enumeration of all the plants known from China. *Botanical Journal, Linnean Society* 23:140.
Forbes, R. D., ed. 1955. *Forestry Handbook.* New York: Ronald Press.
Fordham, A. F. 1969. *Acer griseum* and its propagation. *International Plant Propagators' Society Proceedings* 19:346–348.
Formanek, E. 1896. Zweiter Beitrag zur Flora von Serbien, Macedonien und Thessalien. *Verh. Naturfr. Ver. Brünn* 34:344–345.
Forrest, G. 1952. *The Journeys and Plant Introductions of George Forrest V.M.H.* London: Oxford University Press.
Forrest, M. 1990. Ornamental plants at University College Dublin. *Int. Dendr. Soc. Yrbk.* 1989:115–117.
Forster, H. von. 1918. Fürsprache für Einige Exoten. *Mitt. Dtsch. Dendr. Ges.* 27:229–244.
Fosberg, F. R. 1941. Notes on North American plants. *American Midland Naturalist* 26:690–695.
______. 1954. Notes on plants of the eastern United States. *Castanea* 19:26–28.

Foster, R. C. 1933. Chromosome numbers in *Acer and Staphylea. Journal of Arnold Arboretum* 14:386–393.
Fournier, J. P. 1937. *Les quatres flores de la France.* Paris: Lechevalier.
Fowden, L., and H. Pratt. 1972. Cyclopropylamino acids of the genus *Acer:* distribution and biosynthesis. *Phytochemistry* 12:1677–1681.
Fowells, H. A. 1965. *Silvics of Forest Trees of the United States.* Agriculture Handbook no. 271. Washington, DC: USDA Forest Service.
Fowler, M. W., and A. Clifton. 1974. Activities of enzymes of carbohydrate metabolism in cells of *Acer pseudoplatanus* L. maintained in continuous (chemostat) culture. *Eur. J. Biotechn.* 45:445.
______. 1975. Hexokinase activity in cultured sycamore cells. *New Phytology* 75:533.
Fowler, M. W., and G. Stepans-Sarkissian. 1985. Carbohydrate source, biomass productivity and natural product yield in cell suspension cultures. In *Primary and Secondary Metabolism of Plant Cell Cultures.* Eds. K. H. Neumann et al. Berlin.
Fox, H. M. 1949. *Abbé David's Diary.* Cambridge, Massachusetts.
Fox, W., and W. F. Hubbard. 1905. The Maple Sugar Industry. Bulletin no. 59. Washington, DC: USDA.
Franchet, A. R. 1879. Stirpes navae vel rariores florae Japonicae. Bulletin de la Société Botanique de France 26:84.
______. 1883. Plantes de Turkestan. *Annuelles des Sciences Naturelles et Botanique* 6 (15):246–247.
______. 1884. Plantae Davidianae ex Sinarum Imperio. *Nouvelles Archives du Musée d'Histoire Naturelle, Paris* 2(5):228–229.
______. 1885. Plantae Davidianae ex Sinarum Imperio. *Nouvelles Archives du Musée d'Histoire Naturelle, Paris* 2(8):212.
______. 1886. *A. paxii* Franch., Plantae Yunnanenses. Bulletin de la Societe Botanique de France 33:463–464.
______. 1894. *A. davidii* Franch., Plantes nouvelles de la Chine Occidentale. *J. Bot.* 8:294.
Franchet A. R., and P. A. L. Savatier. 1878. *Enumeratio Plantarum in Japonia Sponte Crescentium* 2:317–323. Paris.
François, L. E. 1982. Salt tolerance of eight ornamental tree species. *Journal of the American Society for Horticultural Science* 107:66–68.
Fraser, C. G. 1912. Induced hermaphroditism in *Acer negundo* L. *Torreya* 12:121–124.
Fraser, J., and A. Hemsley. 1917. *Johnson's Gardener's Dictionary and Cultural Instructor.* London.
Freeman, D. T., et al. 1980. Sex changes in plants: old and new observations and new hypotheses. *Oecologia* 47:222–232.
Freeman, O. M. 1941. A red maple, silver maple hybrid. *Journal of Heredity* 32:11–14.
French, W. J. 1969. *Eutypella* canker on *Acer* in New York. *New York State College of Forestry Technical Publication* 94.
Frey, W. 1980. Wald- und Gebüschverbreitung in Nordwest-Horasan (Nord Iran). *Beihefte zum Tüb. Atlas des Vordern Orients.* Reih. A. Naturw. Nr. 6. Wiesbaden: Ludwig Reichert.
Freyn, J. F., and P. E. E. Sintenis. 1902. In Freyn. Plantae Novae Orientales. *Bull. Herb. Boiss.* 2(2):843.
Friedrich, P. 1970. *Proto-Indo-European Trees.* Chicago: University of Chicago Press.
Friis, E. M., W. G. Chaloner, and P. R. Crane. 1987. *The Origins of Angiosperms and Their Biological Consequences.* Cambridge: Cambridge University Press.
Fryxell, P. A. 1957. Mode of reproduction in higher plants. *Botanical Review* 23:135–233.
Fukarek, P. 1969a. A short description of some trees & shrubs of the Balkan Peninsula. *Int. Dendr. Soc. Yrbk.* 1968:32–52.
______. 1969b. A list of the more important trees and shrubs of the western Balkan Peninsula. *Int. Dendr. Soc. Yrbk.* 1968:29–31.
Fukarek, P., and A. Celjo. 1959. Hybrides entre *Acer pseudoplatanus* et *A. heldreichii. Sumarstvo* 12:543–548.
Fuller, K. A. P., and J. M. Langdon. 1973. The house of Veitch. *Int. Dendr. Soc. Yrbk.* 1972:63–69.
Fürstenberg, F. von. 1904. Dendrologische Studien im Westlichen Canada. *Mitt. Dtsch. Dendr. Ges.* 13:19–36.
Gabriel, W. J. 1962. Inbreeding experiments in sugar maple (*Acer saccharum* Marsh.)—early results. In *Proceedings of the 9th Northeastern Forest Tree Improvement Conference* 8–12.
______. 1966. Onset and duration of stigma receptivity in sugar maple flowers. *Forest Science* 12:14–18.
______. 1967. Reproductive behaviour in sugar maple: self-compatibility, cross-compatibility,

agamospermy and agamocarpy. *Sylvae Genet.* 16(5/6):165–168.

______. 1968. Dichogamy in *Acer saccharum. Botanical Gazette* 129:334–338.

Gagnepain, F. 1948. *A. chapaeensis* Gagnep. In *Acers* Nouveaux d'Indochine. *Not. Syst. Paris* 13:192–195.

______. 1950. Supplement. Lecompte. *Flore Générale de l'Indochine.* Paris.

Gallagher, J. T. 1984. Tour of East Anglia. May 1983. *Int. Dendr. Soc. Yrbk.* 1983:7–12.

Gallagher, P. W., and T. D. Sydnor. 1981. *Variation in Wound-closure Rates Among* Acer rubrum *cultivars.* Ohio Agriculture Research and Development Center, Research Circular 263.

______. 1983a. Genetic variation in wound response among cultivars of *Acer platanoides* L. Ohio Agriculture Research and Development Center, Research Circular 274.

______. 1983b. Variation in wound response among cultivars of red maple. *Journal of the American Society for Horticultural Science* 108(5):744–746.

______. 1983c. Electrical resistance related to volume of discolored and decayed wood in silver maple. *HortScience* 18(5):762–764.

Gamble, J. S. 1908. *A. osmastonii* Gamble. Kew Bulletin 446.

Gams, H. 1925. *Acer.* In G. Hegi's *Illustrierte Flora von Mittel-Europa* 5(1):262–295.

Garbers, F. 1937. Überseeische Hölzer. *Mitt. Dtsch. Dendr. Ges.* 49:130–141.

Gardner, M. W., and C. E. Yarwood. 1978. Host list of powdery mildews of California. *California Plant Pathology* 42.

Garner, R. J. 1967. *The Grafter's Handbook.* 3rd ed. East Malling Research Station: Oxford University Press.

Garrett, S. D. 1977. *Pathogenic Root-Infecting Fungi.* New York: Cambridge University Press.

Garsault, F. A. P. de. 1764. *Les figures des plantes et animaux d'usage en médécine* 1: t. 113. Paris.

______. 1767. *Explication abrégé de 719 plantes.* Paris.

Gates, J. E., and D. M. Harman. 1980. White-tailed deer wintering area in a hemlock-northern hardwood forest. *Canada Field Naturalist* 94:259–268.

Gaudin, C. T. 1858. Mémoire sur quelques gisements de feuilles fossiles de la Toscane. *Neue Denkschr. All. Schweiz. Ges.* 16(3):38, t. 13.

Gebbers, C. 1905. *Acer saccharinum (= dasycarpum) chlorocinctum. Mitt. Dtsch. Dendr. Ges.* 14:209.

Gebhardt, E. 1924. *Acer platanoides* 'Globosum'. *Mitt. Dtsch. Dendr. Ges.* 34:385.

Geelhaar Baumschule (Nursery). 1911. *Mitt. Dtsch. Dendr. Ges.* 20:424.

Geisenheyner, L. 1918. Unsymmetrische Ahornfrüchte, eine Umkehrung und Ausnahme. *Mitt. Dtsch. Dendr. Ges.* 27:261–270.

Geissman, T. A., and D. H. G. Crout. 1969. *Organic Chemistry of Secondary Plant Metabolism.* San Francisco: Freeman, Cooper & Co.

Gelderen, D. M. van. 1969. Japanese *Acers. Dendroflora* 6:19–36.

______. 1979. *Acer palmatum,* Bruinbladige cultivars. *Dendroflora* 15/16:3–8.

______. 1983. *Acer palmatum,* Bruinbladige cultivars. *Dendroflora* 20:55–60.

______. 1989. A maple collection in Holland. *Int. Dendr. Soc. Yrbk.* 1988:95–110.

______. 1990. *Acer palmatum* in cultivation. *Int. Dendr. Soc. Yrbk.* 1990:20–22.

Gerard, J. 1633. *The Herbal of General History of Plants.* Rev. by T. Johnson. Facsimile 1975. New York: Dover.

Gerhold, H. D., and W. D. Bartoe. 1976. Performance testing tree cultivars in metropolitan environments. *Journal of Arboriculture* 2(12):212–227.

Gerhold, H. D., et al. 1979. Selecting and growing better landscape trees for northeastern United States: practices of arborists and nurserymen. Pennsylvania Agricultural Experiment Station Bulletin 829.

Gershenzon, J., and T. J. Mabry. 1983. Secondary metabolites and the higher classification of angiosperms. *Nord. J. Bot.* 3(1):5–34.

Gershoy, A., and W. J. Gabriel. 1961. A technique for germinating pollen of sugar maple. *Journal of Forestry* 59:210.

Gibbs, C. D. 1969. The effect of xylem age on volume yield and sugar content of sugar maple sap. USDA Forest Service Research Paper NE–141.

______. 1958a. The Mäule reaction, lignins, and the relationships between woody plants. In *The Physiology of Forest Trees.* Ed. K. V. Thimann. New York: Ronald.

______. 1958b. Patterns in the seasonal water content of trees. In *The Physiology of Forest Trees.* Ed. K. V. Thiman. New York: Ronald.

______. 1974. *Chemotaxonomy of Flowering Plants.* Vols. 1–4. Montreal: McGill-Queen's University Press.

Gilbert-Carter, H. 1922. *Guide to the University Botanic Garden Cambridge.* Cambridge: Cambridge University Press.
Gillespie, W. H., et al. 1978. Plant fossils of West Virginia. *West Virginia Geological and Economic Survey.*
Gilmore, M. R. 1919. Uses of plants by the Indians of the Missouri River region. *Bureau of American Ethnology 33rd Annual Report.*
Giono, J. 1988. *De Man die Bomen Plantte.* Utrecht: Van Arkel.
Gleditsch, J. G. 1773. *Pflantzenverzeichniss zum Nutzen und Vergnügen der Lust- und Baumgärtner.* Berlin.
______. 1785. *A. cappadocicum* Gled. Vom Cappadocischen Ahorn. *Schriften der Berlinischen Gesellschaft Naturforschenden Freunde* 6:116–121.
Gmelin, J. F. 1791. *Systema Naturae.* 13th ed. 2(1):615–617, 766.
Goblet d'Alviella, Comte. 1947. *Cahier Forestiers.* II. Brussel: P. Lechevalier, Paris et M. Lamertin.
Godet, J. D. 1980. *Bäume Mitteleuropas in den Vier Jahreszeiten.* Bern: Arboris.
Godman, R. M. 1957. Silvical characteristics of sugar maple. USDA Forest Service, Lake States Forest Experiment Station Paper 50.
Godwin, H. 1975. *History of the British Flora.* 2nd ed. Cambridge: Cambridge University Press.
Goeppert, J. H. R. 1852a. Beiträge zur Tertiärflora Schlesiens. *Palaeontographica* 2:279, t. 37–38.
______. 1852b. Über die Braunkohlenflora des Nordöstlichen Deutschlands. *Zeitschr. Dtsch. Geol. Ges.* 4:494.
______. 1855. *Die Tertiäre Flora von Schossnitz in Schlesien.* Görlitz.
Goeppert, J. H. R., and H. von Meyer. 1848. *Index Palaeontologicus* 1:6.
Goeschke. 1903. Meine Erfahrungen über das Verhalten Ausländischer Gehölze im Rauhen Oberschlesischen Klima. *Mitt. Dtsch. Dendr. Ges.* 12:71–77.
Goeze, E. 1914. Eine Dendrologische Rundschau. *Mitt. Dtsch. Dendr. Ges.* 23:116–133.
______. 1916. Liste der Seit dem 16. Jahrhundert bis auf die Gegenwart in die Garten und Parks Europas Eingeführten Bäume und Sträucher. *Mitt. Dtsch. Dendr. Ges.* 25:129–201.
Gogichaishvili, L. K. 1964. The morphology of maple pollen for the purpose of pollen analysis. *Trudy Tbilissk. Bot. Inst.* 23:241–245. Translated for the USDA Forest Service by Amerind. Publ. 293–302.
Goidànich, G. 1932. Verticilliosis of *Acer campestre* L. and some other cases of tracheomycosis in Italy. *Rev. Appl. Mycol.* 12:337–338.
______. 1934a. Verticilliosis of *Acer platanoides* L., *Acer pseudoplatanus* L., and *Maclura aurantiaca* L. *Rev. Appl. Mycol.* 13:811.
______. 1934b. La moria degli *Aceri. Italia Agric.* 71:1043–1055.
Goiran, A. 1890. *Acer campestre* L. forma *subserosus* (sic). *Nuovo Giorn. Bot. Ital.* 22:423–424.
Goldstein, J. L., et al. 1962. Factors affecting the production of leucoanthocyanins in sycamore cambial cells. *Archives of Biochemistry and Biophysics* 98:176–178.
Gonzalez, G. L. 1982. *La Guia de Incafo de los Arboles y Arbustos de la Pensular Iberica.* Madrid: Incafo.
Good, H. M., and C. D. Nelson. 1951. A histological study of sugar maple decayed by *Polyporus glomeratus* Peck. *Canadian Journal of Botany* 29:215–223.
Good, R. 1974. *The Geography of the Flowering Plants.* 4th ed. London: Longman.
Gordon, G. 1840. Report on the new species and varieties of hardy trees and shrubs raised in the horticultural society gardens. *London's Gardener's Magazine* 16:632.
______. 1872. The Bohemian maple (*Acer Loudoni*). *The Garden* 2:321–322.
______. 1873. *Acer lobatum. The Garden* 3:69.
______. 1874. The truncate-leaved maple. *The Garden* 5:274.
Gorer, R. 1971. *Multi-Season Shrubs and Trees.* London: Faber and Faber.
______. 1980. *Illustrated Guide to Trees.* London: Kingfisher.
Gosenthal and Hybler. 1905. *Acer Negundo* 'Schwerinii'. *Mitt. Dtsch. Dendr. Ges.* 14:211–212.
Goto, H. F. 1982. *Animal Taxonomy.* Studies in Biology 143. London: Arnold.
Gouchault, A. 1886. *Acer colchicum tricolor. Revue Horticole* 58:371.
Gouin, F. R. 1983. Girdling roots: fact or fiction? *International Plant Propagators' Society Proceedings* 33:428–432.
Graebener, L. 1914. Die Empfehlenswertesten Ziergehölze für einen Gröszeren Hausgarten. *Mitt. Dtsch. Dendr. Ges.* 23:104–106.
Graebner, K. O. R. P. P. 1926. In Graebner & Langer's *Ill. Gartenbau-Lexicon.* 4th ed. 1:15. Berlin.
Graham, A., ed. 1972. *Floristics and Paleofloristics of Asia and Eastern North America.* Amsterdam: Elsevier.

Grandtner, M. 1966. *La Végétation Forestière du Quebec Méridional.* Laval, Quebec, Canada: Presses Université.
Gravatt, G. F. 1926. Maple wilt. USDA Circular 382:1–13.
Gray, A. 1858. *Introduction to Structural and Systematic Botany.* 5th ed. New York.
______. 1861. A cursory examination of a collection of dried plants made by L. C. Ervendberg around Wartenberg . . . Huasteca, Mexico. In *Proceedings of the American Academy of Art and Science* 5:176.
Gray, S. F. 1821. *A Natural Arrangement of British Plants* 2:635–636.
Greene, E. L. 1902. New or critical species of *Acer. Pittonia* 5:1–4.
______. 1912. Some Californian maples. *Leaflets of Botanical Observations and Criticisms* 2:248–254.
Greene, S. 1954. Sugar weather in the Green Mountains. *National Geographic* (April):471–482.
Greenhalgh, G. N., and R. J. Bevan. 1978. Response of *Rhytisma acerinum* to air pollution. *Transactions of the British Mycological Society* 71:491–494.
Gregorova, B. 1975. Einflusz des Pericarps auf Keimung und Keimruhe der Bergahornfrüchte. *Lesnictvi* 21:611–620.
______. 1977. The fluctuations in the level of endogenous growth regulators in seeds of *Acer pseudoplatanus* L. in the course of stratification. *Biol. Pl.* 321–330.
Gregory, R. A. 1977. Cambial activity and ray cell abundance in *Acer saccharum. Canadian Journal of Botany* 55:2559–2564.
______. 1978. Living elements of the conducting secondary xylem of sugar maple (*Acer saccharum* Marsh.). International Association of Wood Anat. Bulletin 4:65–69.
Griffin, H. D. 1965. Maple dieback in Ontario. *Forestry Chronicle* 41:295–300.
Griffith, W. 1848. *Itinerary Notes of Plants Collected in the Khasyah and Boutan Mountains 1877–8 in Afghanistan and Neighbouring Countries 1939–41.* Calcutta: Bishops College Press. 2:148, 200.
Grigson, G. 1960. *The Englishman's Flora.* London: Phoenix House.
______. 1974. *A Dictionary of English Plant Names and Some Products of Plants.* London: Lane.
Grisebach, A. H. R. 1843. *Spicilegium Florae Rumeliae et Bithynicae* 1:154–156.
Groinland, J. 1862. Les plantes à feuilles bigarrées. *Revue Horticole* 34:88–91.
Groom, P. 1909. *Trees and Their Life Histories.* London: Cassell.
Grootendorst, H. J. 1969. *Acer.* Keuringsrapport van de Regelingscommissie Sierbomen N.A.K.B. *Dendroflora* 6:3–18.
Gross, G. G. 1980. The biochemistry of lignification. In *Advances in Botanical Research.* Vol. 8. Ed. H. W. Woolhouse. New York: Academic Press.
Grosser, D., and H. Schulz. 1986. Das Malteser Kreuz und Ähnliche Verfärbungsfiguren im Holz. *Mitt. Dtsch. Dendr. Ges.* 76:99–104.
Grout, B. W. W., et al. 1976. Aspects of growth and metabolism in a suspension culture of *Acer pseudoplatanus* L. grown on a glycerol carbon source. *Journal of Experimental Botany* 27:77–86.
Guard, A. T., and N. F. Anderson. 1964. A comparative study of the vegetative transitional and floral apex of *Acer pseudoplatanus. American Journal of Botany* 51:675.
Guedes, M. 1980. Endorhythmic development in *Choysia ternata* Kunth (Rutaceae), with a further elucidation of lamma shoots, as well as sylleptic and proleptic shoots. *Botanical Journal, Linnean Society* 80:243–255.
Guggenbühl, P. 1980. *Unsere Einheimischen Nutzhölzer.* Zürich: Stocker-Schmid.
Guichard Nursery. 1889. *Acer negundo* 'Guichardii'. *Revue Horticole Belge* 15:268.
Guimpel, F., and F. G. Hayne. 1820. *Abbildung der Deutschen Holzarten für Forstmänner und Liebhaber der Botanik* 2:278–284. Berlin.
Guldemond Nursery. 1960. *Acer palmatum* 'Dissectum Garnet'. *Deutsche Baumschule* 13:48.
Gunther, E. 1945. Ethnobotany of western Washington. In *The Knowledge and Use of Indigenous Plants by Native Americans.* Rev. ed. Seattle: University of Washington Press.
Gussone, G. 1826. *Plantae rariores quas in Itinere per Oras Ionii ac Adriatici.* Naples.
Haas, T. P. 1933. *Untersuchungen an der Gattung Acer.* Ph.D. thesis, Ludwig Maximil. Universität.
Haasis, F. W. 1963. Polycarpellate fruits in bigleaf maple. *Leafl. West Bot.* 10:29.
Haddock, E. A., et al. 1982a. The metabolism of gallic acid and hexahydroxydiphenic acid in plants. *J. Chem. Soc. Perkin Transactions* 1:2515–2524.
______. 1982b. The metabolism of gallic acid in plants. *J. Chem. Soc. Perkin Transactions* 1:2535–2545.
______. 1982c. The metabolism of gallic acid and hexahydroxydephenic acid in plants: biogenetic and molecular taxonomic considerations. *Phytochemistry* 21(5):1049–1062.
Hadfield, M. 1957. *British Trees.* London: Dent.

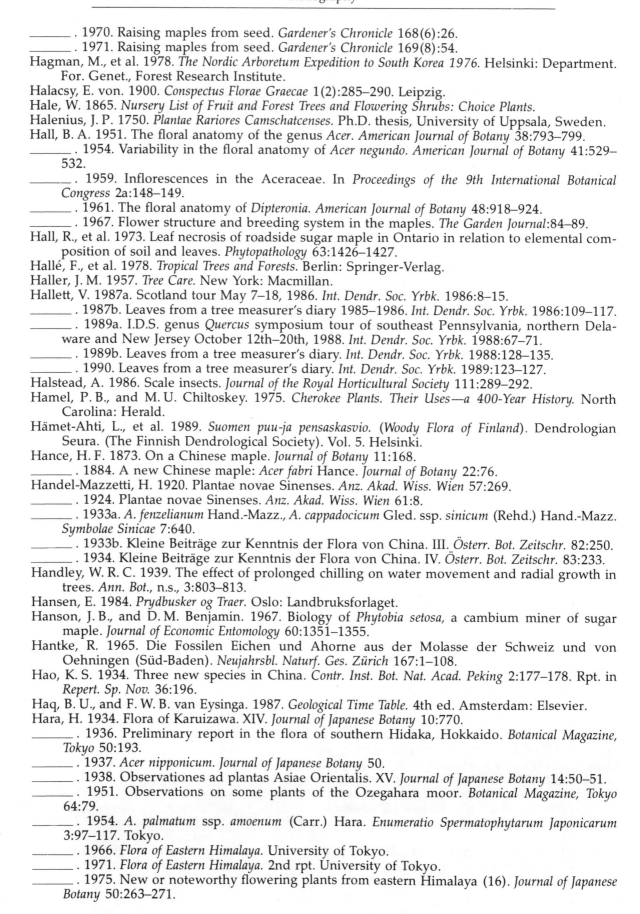

———. 1970. Raising maples from seed. *Gardener's Chronicle* 168(6):26.
———. 1971. Raising maples from seed. *Gardener's Chronicle* 169(8):54.
Hagman, M., et al. 1978. *The Nordic Arboretum Expedition to South Korea 1976.* Helsinki: Department. For. Genet., Forest Research Institute.
Halacsy, E. von. 1900. *Conspectus Florae Graecae* 1(2):285–290. Leipzig.
Hale, W. 1865. *Nursery List of Fruit and Forest Trees and Flowering Shrubs: Choice Plants.*
Halenius, J. P. 1750. *Plantae Rariores Camschatcenses.* Ph.D. thesis, University of Uppsala, Sweden.
Hall, B. A. 1951. The floral anatomy of the genus *Acer. American Journal of Botany* 38:793–799.
———. 1954. Variability in the floral anatomy of *Acer negundo. American Journal of Botany* 41:529–532.
———. 1959. Inflorescences in the Aceraceae. In *Proceedings of the 9th International Botanical Congress* 2a:148–149.
———. 1961. The floral anatomy of *Dipteronia. American Journal of Botany* 48:918–924.
———. 1967. Flower structure and breeding system in the maples. *The Garden Journal*:84–89.
Hall, R., et al. 1973. Leaf necrosis of roadside sugar maple in Ontario in relation to elemental composition of soil and leaves. *Phytopathology* 63:1426–1427.
Hallé, F., et al. 1978. *Tropical Trees and Forests.* Berlin: Springer-Verlag.
Haller, J. M. 1957. *Tree Care.* New York: Macmillan.
Hallett, V. 1987a. Scotland tour May 7–18, 1986. *Int. Dendr. Soc. Yrbk.* 1986:8–15.
———. 1987b. Leaves from a tree measurer's diary 1985–1986. *Int. Dendr. Soc. Yrbk.* 1986:109–117.
———. 1989a. I.D.S. genus *Quercus* symposium tour of southeast Pennsylvania, northern Delaware and New Jersey October 12th–20th, 1988. *Int. Dendr. Soc. Yrbk.* 1988:67–71.
———. 1989b. Leaves from a tree measurer's diary. *Int. Dendr. Soc. Yrbk.* 1988:128–135.
———. 1990. Leaves from a tree measurer's diary. *Int. Dendr. Soc. Yrbk.* 1989:123–127.
Halstead, A. 1986. Scale insects. *Journal of the Royal Horticultural Society* 111:289–292.
Hamel, P. B., and M. U. Chiltoskey. 1975. *Cherokee Plants. Their Uses—a 400-Year History.* North Carolina: Herald.
Hämet-Ahti, L., et al. 1989. *Suomen puu-ja pensaskasvio.* (*Woody Flora of Finland*). Dendrologian Seura. (The Finnish Dendrological Society). Vol. 5. Helsinki.
Hance, H. F. 1873. On a Chinese maple. *Journal of Botany* 11:168.
———. 1884. A new Chinese maple: *Acer fabri* Hance. *Journal of Botany* 22:76.
Handel-Mazzetti, H. 1920. Plantae novae Sinenses. *Anz. Akad. Wiss. Wien* 57:269.
———. 1924. Plantae novae Sinenses. *Anz. Akad. Wiss. Wien* 61:8.
———. 1933a. *A. fenzelianum* Hand.-Mazz., *A. cappadocicum* Gled. ssp. *sinicum* (Rehd.) Hand.-Mazz. *Symbolae Sinicae* 7:640.
———. 1933b. Kleine Beiträge zur Kenntnis der Flora von China. III. *Österr. Bot. Zeitschr.* 82:250.
———. 1934. Kleine Beiträge zur Kenntnis der Flora von China. IV. *Österr. Bot. Zeitschr.* 83:233.
Handley, W. R. C. 1939. The effect of prolonged chilling on water movement and radial growth in trees. *Ann. Bot.*, n.s., 3:803–813.
Hansen, E. 1984. *Prydbusker og Traer.* Oslo: Landbruksforlaget.
Hanson, J. B., and D. M. Benjamin. 1967. Biology of *Phytobia setosa,* a cambium miner of sugar maple. *Journal of Economic Entomology* 60:1351–1355.
Hantke, R. 1965. Die Fossilen Eichen und Ahorne aus der Molasse der Schweiz und von Oehningen (Süd-Baden). *Neujahrsbl. Naturf. Ges. Zürich* 167:1–108.
Hao, K. S. 1934. Three new species in China. *Contr. Inst. Bot. Nat. Acad. Peking* 2:177–178. Rpt. in *Repert. Sp. Nov.* 36:196.
Haq, B. U., and F. W. B. van Eysinga. 1987. *Geological Time Table.* 4th ed. Amsterdam: Elsevier.
Hara, H. 1934. Flora of Karuizawa. XIV. *Journal of Japanese Botany* 10:770.
———. 1936. Preliminary report in the flora of southern Hidaka, Hokkaido. *Botanical Magazine, Tokyo* 50:193.
———. 1937. *Acer nipponicum. Journal of Japanese Botany* 50.
———. 1938. Observationes ad plantas Asiae Orientalis. XV. *Journal of Japanese Botany* 14:50–51.
———. 1951. Observations on some plants of the Ozegahara moor. *Botanical Magazine, Tokyo* 64:79.
———. 1954. *A. palmatum* ssp. *amoenum* (Carr.) Hara. *Enumeratio Spermatophytarum Japonicarum* 3:97–117. Tokyo.
———. 1966. *Flora of Eastern Himalaya.* University of Tokyo.
———. 1971. *Flora of Eastern Himalaya.* 2nd rpt. University of Tokyo.
———. 1975. New or noteworthy flowering plants from eastern Himalaya (16). *Journal of Japanese Botany* 50:263–271.

Hara, H., and H. Kanai. 1958. *Distribution Maps of Flowering Plants in Japan.* I.

Hara, H., and M. Mizushima. 1954. Vegetation of the Ozegahara moor and its surrounding districts, central Japan. *Science Research of the Ozegahara Moor*:401–479.

Hara, H., et al. 1978–1982. *An Enumeration of the Flowering Plants of Nepal.* 3 vols. London: Natural History Museum.

Harborne, J. B. 1963. Distribution of anthocyanins in higher plants. In *Chemical Plant Taxonomy.* Ed. T. Swain. New York: Academic Press.

______. 1967. *Comparative Biochemistry of the Flavonoids.* New York: Academic Press.

______. 1970. *Phytochemical Phylogeny.* London: Academic Press.

______. 1975. Functions of flavonoids in plants. In *Chemistry and Biochemistry of Plant Pigments.* Ed. T. W. Goodwin. London: Academic Press.

______. 1988. *The Flavonoids. Advances in Research Since 1980.* London: Chapman & Hall.

Harborne, J. B., and T. J. Mabry. 1982. *Flavonoids: Advances in Research, 1975–1981.* London: Chapman & Hall.

Harkness, B. 1954. Habit forms of *Acer saccharum. Baileya* 2:99–102.

Harley, J. L. 1969. *The Biology of Mycorrhiza.* London: Leonard Hill.

Harley, J. L., and S. E. Smith. 1983. *Mycorrhizal Symbiosis.* New York: Academic Press.

Harley, J. L., and J. S. Waid. 1955. A method of studying active mycelia on living roots and other surfaces in the soil. *Transactions of the British Mycological Society* 38:104.

Harlow, W. M. 1942. *Trees of the Eastern United States and Canada.* New York: Whittlesey House.

______. 1959. *Fruit Key and Twig Key to Trees and Shrubs.* New York: Dover.

Harlow, W. M., and E. S. Harrar. 1958. *Textbook of Dendrology.* New York: McGraw-Hill.

Harrar, E. S. 1940. The Kimball maple. *Journal of Forestry* 38:726–728.

Harrar, E. S., and J. G. Harrar. 1962. *Guide to Southern Trees.* 2nd ed. New York: Dover.

Harries, H., and F. Barlocher. 1988. *Pseudospiropes* sp., a fungal epiphyte on living stems of striped maple (*Acer pensylvanicum*). *Canadian Journal of Botany* 66(9):1717–1722.

Harris, D. C. 1976. Propagation of Japanese maples by grafting. *International Plant Propagators' Society Proceedings* 26.

Harris, J. G. S. 1972. Maples in my garden. *Int. Dendr. Soc. Yrbk.* 1971:14–24.

______. 1973. Maples in Taiwan and Hongkong. *Int. Dendr. Soc. Yrbk.* 1972:59–62.

______. 1974. Propagation of *Acers. Int. Dendr. Soc. Yrbk.* 1973:57–62.

______. 1975. Maples from Japan. *Journal of the Royal Horticultural Society* 99:394–399.

______. 1983. An account of maples in cultivation. *The Plantsman* 5:35–58.

______. 1985. A day on Ullong-do (South Korea). University of Washington Arboretum Bulletin 48(2):8–10.

______. 1986. Land of the morning calm plants of South Korea. *Int. Dendr. Soc. Yrbk.* 1985:55–62.

Harrison, R. E. 1960. *Handbook of Trees and Shrubs for the Southern Hemisphere.* 2nd ed. Wellington.

Hart, J. A. 1980. The ethnobotany of the Flatfeet Indians of western Montana. *Botanical Museum Leaflets* 27:261–307.

Hart, R. 1976. Revegetation of a 70 year old sandpit in southern New Jersey. *Bartonia* 44:37–43.

Hart, C. and C. Raymond. 1973. *British Trees in Colour.* London: Michael Joseph.

Hartig, T. 1851. *Vollständige Naturgeschichte der Forstlichen Culturpflanzen Deutschlands.* Berlin.

Hartley, C. 1918. Stem lesions caused by excessive heat. *Journal of Agricultural Research* 14:595–604.

Hartmann, E. 1900. Ueber die Verbreitung der Ahornarten in Libanon. *Mitt. Dtsch. Dendr. Ges.* 9:8.

Hartmann, H. T. and D. E. Kester. 1968. *Plant Propagation.* Englewood Cliffs, New Jersey: Prentice-Hall.

Hartmann, K. 1905. Die Wälder der Insel Cypern. *Mitt. Dtsch. Dendr. Ges.* 14:167–193.

Hartwell, J. L. 1982. *Plants Used Against Cancer.* Laurence, Massachusetts: Quarterman.

Hartwig, K. G. 1905. Der Amerikanische Zucker-Ahorn (*Acer saccharum* Marsh. = *Acer saccharinum* Wgh.). Richtigstellung von Namen Verteilter Pflanzen. *Mitt. Dtsch. Dendr. Ges.* 14:209.

______. 1919. Dendrologisches aus Rudolstadt. *Mitt. Dtsch. Dendr. Ges.* 28:300–301.

Harvey, J. 1972. *Early Gardening Catalogues.* London: Phillimore.

Hasis, F. W. 1963. Polycarpellate fruits in bigleaf maple. *Leafl. West Bot.* 10:2.

Haskell, D. A., and S. N. Postlethwait. 1971. Structure and histogenesis of the embryo of *Acer saccharinum.* I. Embryo sa. and proembryo. *American Journal of Botany* 58:595–603.

Haslam, E. 1965. Galloylesters in the Aceraceae. *Phytochemistry* 4:495–498.

______. 1979. Vegetable tannins. In *Biochemistry of Plant Phenolics.* Eds. T. Swain et al. Vol. 12. *Recent Advances in Phytochemistry.* New York: Plenum.

______. 1986. Hydrobenzoic acids and the enigma of gallic acid. In *Recent Advances in Phytochemistry,* vol. 20. Ed. E. Conn. New York: Plenum.

———. 1989. *Plant Polyphenols. Vegetable Tannins Revisited.* New York: Cambridge University Press.

Haslam, E., and T. H. Lilley. 1985. New polyphenols for old tannins. In *Annual Proceedings of the Phytochemical Society of Europe* 25:237–256. Eds. C. F. van Sumere and P. J. Lea. Oxford: Clarendon.

Hasselquist, F. 1766. *Voyages and Travels in the Levant.* London: Published for Davies & Reymour.

Hasskarl, J. K. 1843. *Acer laurinum* Hassk. Adnotationes . . . Catalogo Horti Bogoriensis. In *Tijdschr. Nat. Gesch. Phys.* 10:138. Eds. Hoeven and de Vriese.

Hattori, S., and K. Hayashi. 1937. Studien über Anthocyane. II. Über die Farbstoffe aus den Roten Herbstblättern von Einigen *Acer*-Arten. *Acta Phytochemistry* 10:129–138.

Hatusima, S. 1954. New and noteworthy plants from southern Japan. *Journal of Japanese Botany* 29:230–238.

Hausen, B. 1981. *Woods Injurious to Human Health.* Berlin: De Gruyter.

Hayata, B. 1911. *A. caudatifolium* Hayata, *A. rubescens* Hayata. In Materials for a flora of Formosa. *J. Coll. Sci. Univ. Tokyo* 30:64–71, 449.

———. 1913. *Icones Plantarum Formosararum* 3:65–67.

Hayek, A. E. von. 1925. *A. campestre* ssp. *marsicum* (Guss.) Hayek. Prodromus Florae Peninsulae Balcanicae I. *Repert. Sp. Nov.* Beih. 30(1):601–607.

Hayne, F. G. 1822. *Dendrologische Flora der Umgegend und der Gärten Berlins.* Berlin.

Hayward, F. W. 1946a. Factors in the preparation of maple cream. New York State Agricultural Experiment Station Bulletin 720.

———. 1946b. The storage of maple syrup. New York State Agricultural Experiment Station Bulletin 719.

Hayward, F. W., and C. S. Pederson. 1946. Some factors causing dark-colored maple syrup. New York State Agricultural Experiment Station Bulletin 718.

Heale, E. L., and D. P. Ormrod. 1982. Effects of nickel and copper on *Acer rubrum, Cornus stolonifera, Lonicera tatarica,* and *Pinus resinosa. Canadian Journal of Botany* 58:2674–2681.

Heath, M. F., et al. 1971. Glycoprotein of the wall of sycamore tissue-culture cells. *Biochem. J.* 125:953.

Heer, O. 1853. Uebersicht der Tertiärflora der Schweiz. *Mitt. Naturf. Ges. Zürich* 3:146.

———. 1859. *Flora Tertiaria Helvetiae* 3:44–60, 197–199, 313.

———. 1869a. Flora fossilis Alaskana. *Sv. Vet.-Akad. Handl.* 8(4):37.

———. 1869b. Miocene Baltische Flora. *Beitr. Naturk. Preussens* 2:93.

———. 1877. Beiträge zur Fossilen Flora Spitsbergens. *Sv. Vet.-Akad. Handl.* 14(5):86–89.

———. 1878. Miocänische Flora Sacchalin. *Mémoirs de l'Academie Imperiale des Sciences de St. Petersbourg* 7(25):46–50.

———. 1883. Die Tertiäre Flora von Grönland. *Flora Foss. Arct.* 7:125–127.

Hegi, G. 1925. *Illustrierte Flora von Mittel-Europa* 5(1):262–295.

Hegnauer, R. 1989. *Chemotaxonomie der Pflanzen.* Vol. 8. Basel: Birkhauser.

———. 1990. *Chemotaxonomie der Pflanzen.* Vol. 9. Basel: Birkhauser.

Heichel, G. H., et al. 1972. Anthracnose causes diseases of regrowth on defoliated oak and maple. *Plant Disease Reporter* 56:1046–1047.

Hein, W. H. 1907. Some observations on the flowers of *Acer saccharinum. Plant World* 10:200–205.

Heine, E. W. 1966. Zur Kenntnis der Inhaltsstoffe der Aceraceae. IV. Prüfung auf Saponine mit der Haemolyse Test. *Pharmazie* 21:493.

Heine, H. 1977. I.D.S. Paris tour October 17–20, 1975. *Int. Dendr. Soc. Yrbk.* 1976:58–74.

———. 1978. Tour of New Zealand February 14th–March 9th, 1977. *Int. Dendr. Soc. Yrbk.* 1977:25–60.

———. 1979. Tour of New Zealand, part two, February 14th–March 9th, 1977. *Int. Dendr. Soc. Yrbk.* 1978:61–70.

———. 1986. Netherlands tour May 5–11, 1985. *Int. Dendr. Soc. Yrbk.* 1985:11–22.

Hellson, J. C., and M. Gadd. 1974. Ethnobotany of the Blackfoot Indians. Can. Ethnol. Service Paper no. 19, Natural Museum of Man.

Hellyer, A. 1981. *Ornamental Garden Shrubs.* Richmond: Collingridge.

Helmich, D. E. 1963. Pollen morphology in the maples (*Acer* L.). *Papers of the Michigan Academy of Science, Arts and Letters* 48:151–164.

Hendriks, W. J. 1926. Het Oosterpark te Amsterdam; Toepassing der Nomenclatuur. *Jaarboek Nederlandse Dendr. Ver.* 2:100–104.

———. 1929. De Zomerbijeenkomst in Zuid-Limburg. *Jaarboek Nederlandse Dendr. Ver.* 5:18–25.

———. 1935–1936a Zomerbijeenkomst 1934. *Jaarboek Nederlandse Dendr. Ver.* 10:16–22.

______. 1935–1936b. Zomerbijeenkomst 1935. *Jaarboek Nederlandse Dendr. Ver.* 11:15–26.
______. 1938. De Zomerbijeenkomst te Essen op 18, 19, 20 Augustus 1938. *Jaarboek Nederlandse Dendr. Ver.* 13:14–28.
______. 1952–1953. Zomerbijeenkomst op 16 en 17 Juli. *Jaarboek Nederlandse Dendr. Ver.* 19:17–20.
______. 1956–1958. The Arboretum Poortbulten in Oldenzaal. *Jaarboek Nederlandse Dendr. Ver.* 21:59–67.
______. 1957. *Onze Loofhoutgewassen.* Wageningen: Veenman.
Henry, A. 1899. *Travels and Adventures in Canada and the Indian Territories.* New York: Riley.
______. 1903. Chinese maples. *Gardener's Chronicle* III. 33:21–22.
______. 1908. See Elwes and Henry, 1908.
Henshaw, H. W. 1890. The Indian origin of maple sugar. *American Anthropologist* 3:341–351.
Hepper, J. N. 1982. *Kew Gardens for Science & Pleasure.* London: H.M.S.O.
Hepting, G. H. 1944. Sapstreak, a new killing disease of sugar maple. *Phytopathology* 34:1069–1076.
______. 1971. *Diseases of Forest and Shade Trees of the United States.* Agriculture Handbook no. 386. Washington, DC: USDA Forest Service.
Herder, F. G. T. M. 1867. *Acer platanoides* 'Rubrum'. *Gartenflora* 16:163.
Hereman, S. 1868. *Paxton's Botanical Dictionary.* New ed. London.
Herr, C. S. 1938. Maple syrup and sugar production in New Hampshire. Bulletin 52. University of New Hampshire Extension Service.
Herrick, G. T. 1988. Relationships between soil salinity, sap-sugar concentration and health of declining sugar maples (*Acer saccharum*). *Ohio Journal of Science* 88(5):192–194.
Herrick, G. W. 1923. The maple casebearer. Cornell University Agricultural Experiment Station Bulletin.
______. 1935. *Insect Enemies of Shade Trees.* Ithaca, New York: Comstock.
Heslop-Harrison, J. 1954. The experimental modification of sex expression in flowering plants. *Biological Reviews of the Cambridge Philosophical Society* 32:38–90.
______. 1972. Sexuality of angiosperms. In *Plant Physiology: A Treatise,*. vol. 4A. Ed. F. C. Steward. New York: Academic Press. 133–289.
Hessayon, D. G. 1983. *The Tree and Shrub Expert.* Waltham Cross: PBI Publ.
Hesse, H. A. 1898. *Katalog.*
______. 1903–1904. Neuheiten. In *Katolog.*
______. 1912. *Acer crassipes* Pax. *Mitt. Dtsch. Dendr. Ges.* 21:358.
______. 1914–1915. *Katolog.*
______. 1935–1936. *Preisliste.* Weener am Ems.
Hett, J. M. 1971. A dynamic analysis of age in sugar maple seedlings. *Ecology* 52:1071–1074.
Heusser, C. J. 1977. Quaternary palynology of the Pacific Slope of Washington. *Quaternary Research* 8:282–306.
Hey, F. 1924. Berg-Ahorn-Naturverjüngung im Wildpark Dülmen. *Mitt. Dtsch. Dendr. Ges.* 34:440.
Heybroek, H. M., et al., eds. 1982. *Resistance to Diseases and Pests in Forest Trees.* Wageningen: Pudoc.
Heyne, K. 1913. *De Nuttige Planten van Nederlandsch Indië.* Batavia: Ruygrok.
______. 1927. *De Nuttige Planten van Nederlandsch Indië.* 2nd ed. Buitenzorg: Departement van Landbouw, Nijverheid en Handel.
Heywood, V. H., ed. 1978. *Flowering Plants of the World.* London: Oxford University Press.
Hibben, C. R. 1959. *Relations of* Steganosporium ovatum *(Pers. ex Mér.) Hughes with Dieback of Sugar Maple (*Acer saccharum *Marsh.).* Master's thesis, Cornell University, Ithaca, New York.
Hibbs, D. E. 1978. *The Life History and Strategy of Striped Maple* (Acer pensylvanicum *L.*). Ph.D. thesis, University of Massachusetts.
Hibbs, D. E., and B. C. Fischer. 1979. Sexual and vegetative reproduction of striped maple. (*Acer pensylvanicum* L.). Bulletin of the Torrey Botanical Club 106:222–227.
Hieke, K. 1989. *Praktische Dendrologie.* 2 vols. Berlin: VEB Verlag.
Hiern, W. P. 1875. *A. campbellii* Hook. f. et Thoms, ex Hiern, *A. stachyophyllum* Hiern. In *The Flora of British India,* by J. D. Hooker. Kent: Reeve. 692–696.
Hille Ris Lambers, D. 1979. Aphids as botanists? *Symb. Bot. Uppsala* 11(4):114.
Hillier & Sons. 1928. *Catalogue of Trees and Shrubs.* Winchester.
Hillier, H. G. 1969. Planting of a large maple at Chelsea. *Journal of the Royal Horticultural Society* 94:342–344.
______. 1973. *Hillier's Manual of Trees & Shrubs.* 3rd ed.
______. 1979. The Hillier Arboretum, Romsey, Hampshire. *Int. Dendr. Soc. Yrbk.* 1978:7–16.
Hillis, W. E. 1977. Secondary changes in wood. In *Recent Advances in Phytochemistry,* vol. 11. Eds.

F. A. Loewus and V. C. Runeckles. London: Plenum.
______. 1987. *Heartwood and Tree Exudates.* Berlin: Springer-Verlag.
Hills, J. L. 1904. The maple sap flow. Vermont Agricultural Experiment Station Bulletin 104.
Himelick, E. B. 1969. Tree and shrub hosts of *Verticillium albo-atrum.* Illinois Natural History Survey, Biology Notes no. 66.
Hinkley, D. J. 1986. A connoisseur's guide to maples. University of Washington Arboretum Bulletin 49(1):12–17.
Hinkul, S. G. 1956. Iaponskii klen *Acer palmatum. Izv. Batum. Bot. Sada* 7:33–65.
Hinneri, S. 1982. Vaahtera (*Acer platanoides*) metsäpuuna. *Sorbifolia* 13(1):5–12.
Hirc, D. 1884. Flora Okolice Bakarske. *Rad. Jugosl. Akad.* 69:132.
Hisauchi, K. K. 1934. Some varieties of *Acer mono. Journal of Japanese Botany* 10:102–105.
Hitchcock, A. S. 1894. *A Key to the Spring Flora of Manhattan.* Kansas: Manhattan.
Hitchcock, C. L., and A. Cronquist. 1973. *Flora of the Pacific Northwest.* Seattle: University of Washington Press.
Hitchcock, J. A. 1904. Cost and profit in the sugar orchard. Vermont Agricultural Experiment Station Bulletin 292.
______. 1928, 1929. Economics of the farm manufacture of maple syrup and sugar. Vermont Agricultural Experiment Station Bulletin 285, 286.
______. 1937. The grazing of maple sugar orchards. Vermont Agricultural Experiment Station Bulletin 414.
Hodgkiss, H. E. 1930. The Eriphyidae of New York. Vol. 2. The maple mites. New York Agricultural Experiment Station Technical Bulletin 163.
Hoey Smith, J. R. P. van. 1983. True from seed? *Int. Dendr. Soc. Yrbk.* 1982:82–89.
______. 1984. Plaque for the Arboretum Trompenburg. *Int. Dendr. Soc. Yrbk.* 1983:34–36.
Hoffmann, E. 1959. *Der Ahorn. (Wald-, Park- und Straszenbaum).* Berlin.
Hoffman, H. 1871. Zur Geslechtsbestimmung. *Zeitschr. Bot.* 29:81–89, 97–109.
Hoffmannsegg, J. C. Graf von. 1842. In *Walpers. Repert. Bot. Syst.* 1:410.
Hogg, J. 1879. Japanese maples. *The Garden* 2:578–580.
Hoitink, H. A. J., et al. 1979. Resistance of maple cultivars and species to *Verticillium* wilt—preliminary report. Ornamental plants. A summary of research. Ohio Agriculture Research and Development Center, Research Circular 46–47.
Holdt, F. von. 1904. Der Baumwuchs unter Künstliche Bedingungen. *Mitt. Dtsch. Dendr. Ges.* 13:163–164.
Hollick, C. A. 1892. Additions to the paleobotany of the Cretaceous Formation on Staten Island. *Transactions of the New York Academy of Science* 12:35.
______. 1897. The Cretaceous clay marl exposure at Cliffwood, New Jersey. *Transactions of the New York Academy of Science* 16.
______. 1936. The Tertiary floras of Alaska. U.S. Geological Survey Prof. Paper 182:134–135.
Holmason, J. 1965. *Wholesale Pricelist.* Portland, Oregon: Pacific Company Nursery.
Holmes, F. W. 1976. *Verticillium* wilt of salt-injured sugar maple—preliminary study. In *Proceedings of the American Phytopathological Society* 3:305–306.
______. 1984. Effects on maples of prolonged exposure by artificial girdling roots. *Journal of Arboriculture* 10:40–44.
Holmes, G. D., and G. Buszewicz. 1958. The storage of seeds of temperate forest tree species. *Forestry Abstracts* 19:313–322, 455–476.
Holmgren, P. K., W. Keuken, and E. Schofield, compilers. 1981. *Index Herbariorum. Part I, The Herbaria of the World.* 7th ed. Utrecht/Antwerp: Bohn, Scheltema & Holkema; The Hague/Boston: W. Junk B.V.
Holub, J. L., and Z. Pouzar. 1967. A nomenclatural analysis of the generic names of phanerogams proposed by F. M. Opiz. *Folio Geobot. Phytotax.* 2:407.
Honda, M. 1931. Nuntia ad floram Japonicae. X. *Botanical Magazine, Tokyo* 45:43.
______. 1932. Nuntia ad floram Japonicae. XVI. *Botanical Magazine, Tokyo* 46:371–373.
Hooker, J. D. 1869. *Acer rufinerve* var. *albo-limbatum. Curtis's Botanical Magazine* 95, t. 5793.
Hooker, W. J. 1831. *Flora Boreali-Americana* 1:111–114. London.
______. 1847. *Acer Douglasii. London Journal of Botany* 6:77.
Hooker, W. J., and G. Arnott-Walker. 1833. *The Botany of Captain Beechey's Voyage.* London.
Hopkins, C. Y., et al. 1968. Fatty acids of Aceraceae seed oils. *Canadian Journal of Biochemistry* 46:999–1002.
Hopkins, D. M. 1967. *The Bering Land Bridge.* Stanford, California: Stanford University Press.

Hopkins, W. S., Jr. 1969. Palynology of the Eocene Kitsilano Formation, southwest British Columbia. *Canadian Journal of Botany* 47:1101–1131.
Hora, B. 1981. *The Oxford Encyclopedia of Trees of the World.* Oxford: Oxford University Press.
Horaninov, H. 1847. *Caractères essentiales.* Petropolis.
Horn, H. S. 1975. Forest Succession. *Scientific American* 232(May):90–98.
Hosie, R. C. 1973. *Native Trees of Canada.* Ottawa: Canadian Forest Servive, Department of the Environment.
Hottes, A. C. 1932. *The Book of Trees.* New York: De la Mare.
Hough, F. B. 1884. Report on the production of maple sugar in the United States and Canada. *Report on Forestry* 4:394–414.
Houston, D. R. 1981. Stress triggered tree diseases. The diebacks and declines. USDA Forest Service, n.s., INF–41–81.
______. 1985. Diebacks and declines of urban trees. In *Improving the Quality of Urban Life with Plants.* Eds. D. F. and S. L. Karnosky. New York Botanical Garden, Institute of Urban Horticulture Publication no. 2.
Houston, J. 1978. Maple syrup, a growth industry. *The New York Times* (19 March):7.
Houtzagers, G. 1954. *Houtteelt der Gematigde Luchtstreek.* Zwolle: Tjeenk Willink.
Houtzagers, G., et al. 1946. *Boomzaden.* Wageningen: Nederl. Boschbouw-Vereniging.
Howard, F. L., and N. E. Caroselli. 1939. A maple blight in Rhode Island. *Phytopathology* 29:11.
______. 1940. Bleeding canker of maple. *Phytopathology* 30:11.
Howes, F. N. 1953. *Vegetable Tanning Materials.* London: Butterworths.
Hradzina, G. 1982. Anthocyanins. In *Flavonoids: Advances in Research, 1975–1981.* Eds. J. B. Harborne & T. J. Mabry. London: Chapman & Hall.
Hsu, T. 1983. A new species of *Acer* from Emeishan. *Acta Bot. Yunn.* 5:281–282.
Hu, H. H. 1930. Notulae systematicae ad floram Sinensem. II. *Journal of Arnold Arboretum* 11:224.
______. 1931. Notulae systematicae ad floram Sinensem. III. *Journal of Arnold Arboretum* 12:154–155.
Hu, H. H., and R. W. Chaney. 1940. A Miocene flora from Shantung Province, China. Carnegie Institute, Washington, Publication 507:56–59.
Hu, H. H., and W. C. Cheng. 1948. New and noteworthy species of Chinese *Acer.* Bulletin Fan. Mem. Institute Biology, n.s., 1:199–212.
Hu, Y., and the Shanghai Botanic Garden. 1982. *Penjing, the Chinese Art of Miniature Gardens.* Beaverton, Oregon: Timber Press.
Huang, T. C. 1967. Pollen grains of Formosan plants. 2. *Taiwania* 13:15–110.
______. 1972. *Pollen Flora of Taiwan.* Nat. Taiwan University Botany Department Press.
Hubbard, W. F. 1906. Maple sugar and syrup. Farmers' Bulletin 252. Washington, DC: USDA.
Huber, B. 1935. Die Physiologische Bedeutung der Ring-und Zerstreutporigkeit. *Ber. Dtsch. Bot. Ges.* 53:711–719.
Hübner, O. 1904. Herbst-oder Frühjahrspflanzung? *Mitt. Dtsch. Dendr. Ges.* 13:170–171.
Hudler, G. W. 1984. Wound healing in bark of woody plants. *Journal of Arboriculture* 10:241–245.
Hudler, G. W., and M. A. Beale. 1981. Anatomical features of girdling root injury. *Journal of Arboriculture* 7:29–32.
Hudson, H. J. 1986. *Fungal Biology.* London: Arnold.
Hughes, S. J. 1976. Sooty moulds. *Mycologia* 68:693–820.
Huisman, O. C., and L. J. Ashworth Jr. 1976. Influence of crop rotation on survival of *Verticillium albo-atrum* in soils. *Phytopathology* 66:978–981.
Hultén, E. 1968. *Flora of Alaska.* Stanford, California: Stanford University Press.
Humphrey, B. E., and P. R. C. Dummer. 1966. Propagation of *Acer* by cuttings. *The Plant Propagator* 12(1):4–7.
Hunt, D. R. 1978a. *Acer capillipes. Curtis's Botanical Magazine* 182:113–115.
______. 1978b. *Acer griseum. Curtis's Botanical Magazine* 183:13–15.
Hunt, H. M. 1979. Summer, autumn and winter diets of elk in Saskatchewan. *Canadian Field Naturalist* 93:282–287.
Hunter, D. 1980. Maple bark (stripper's) disease. *The Diseases of Occupations.* 6th ed. London: Hodder & Stoughton.
Hussain, R. A., et al. 1988. Sweetening agents of plant origin: literature search for candidate sweet plants. *Economic Botany* 42(2):267–283.
Hussey, J. S. 1974. Some useful plants of early New England. *Economic Botany* 28:311–337.
Hutchinson, J. 1969. *Evolution & Phylogeny of Flowering Plants.* London: Academic Press.

Hutchinson, P. A. 1971. Propagation of *Acers* from seed. *International Plant Propagators' Society Proceedings* 21:233.
Hutnik, R. J., and H. W. Yawney. 1961. Silvical characteristics of red maple (*Acer rubrum*). Northeastern Forest Experiment Station Paper no. 142.
Huttleston, D. G. 1989. International registrations of cultivar names for unassigned woody genera. *HortScience* (243):430.
Huxley, A. 1974. *Plant and Planet.* London: Lane.
______. 1985. *Green Inheritance.* Garden City, New York: Anchor Press/Doubleday.
Hyams, E., and W. MacQuitty. 1969. *Great Botanical Gardens of the World.* London: Nelson.
Hyde, H. A., and K. F. Adams. 1958. *An Atlas of Airborne Pollen.* New York: Macmillan.
*ICBN,* see Voss et al. 1983.
*Iconographia Cormophytorum Sinicorum.* 1972. Peking.
*ICNCP,* see Brickell et al. 1980.
Ikuse, M. 1956. *Pollen Grains of Japan.* Tokyo: Hirokawa.
*Illustrated Woody Plants of Korea.* 1987. Seoul: Forest Research Institute, Forestry Administration, Republic of Korea.
Ilsink, L. K. J. 1987. *Darthuizer Vademecum.* Leersum: Darthuizer Boomkwekerijen.
*Index Kewensis.* 1896– . London: Oxford University Press.
Ingram, C. 1970. *A Garden of Memories.* London: Witherby.
______. 1975. Stray notes on a few maple species. *Int. Dendr. Soc. Yrbk.* 1976:28–30.
Inoue, T., et al. 1978. Studies on the constituents of Aceraceae plants. I. Constituents in the leaves and the stem bark of *Acer nikoense* Maxim. *J. Pharm. Soc. Japan* 98:41–46.
Instituto Botanico Boreali-Occidentali Academiae Sinicae Edita. 1981. *Flora Tsinlingensis,* vol. I. *Spermatophyta* (Part 3). Chengdu, Sichuan: Science Press.
International Association of Wood Anatomists. 1984. Special issue on discolored wood. IAWA Bulletin, n.s., 5:91–154.
*International Bonsai and Suiseki Exhibition.* 1980. Nippon Bonsai Association in Commemoration of the 10th Anniversary of Expo '70.
*International Code of Nomenclature for Cultivated Plants.* 1969. Regnum vegetabile 46. Utrecht.
Introductory dates of familiar trees, shrubs and vines. 1967. *Plants & Gardens,* Origins of American Horticulture Special Issue, 23(3):87.
Iqbal, M. 1990. *The Vascular Cambium.* New York: Wiley.
Irving, R. M. 1968. Study of dormancy, germination and growth of seeds and buds of *Acer negundo. Plant Physiology* 43:5–49.
Irving, R. M., and F. O. Lanphear. 1967. Dehardening and the dormant condition in *Acer* and *Viburnum.* In *Proceedings of the American Society for Horticultural Science* 91:699–705.
Isaac, I. 1967. Speciation in *Verticillium. Annual Review of Phytopathology* 5:201–222.
Iseli Nursery. 1991. *Catalogue.* Boring, Oregon.
Ishikura, N. 1972. Anthocyanins and the other phenolics in autumn leaves. *Phytochemistry* 11:2555–2558.
______. 1973. The changes in anthocyanin and chlorophyll content during the autumnal reddening of leaves. *Kumamoto Journal of Science,* sect. 2, biology, 11:43–50.
Ishikura, N., et al. 1984. Biosynthesis of gallic and ellagic acids with 14C-labeled compounds in *Acer* and *Rhus* leaves. *Botanical Magazine, Tokyo* 97:355–367.
Ito, T., and J. Matsumura. 1900. Tentamen Florae Lutchensis. I. *J. Coll. Sci. Univ. Tokyo* 12:387.
Ito, T., and J. Matsu Zakaya. 1911. *Momiji.* Tokyo: Kokoh. Geichikudo.
Itoh, J., and Y. Shinmura. 1976. A study on the shelterbelt establishment at Tokachi and Hikada districts, Hokkaido. Bulletin of the Hokkaido Forest Experiment Station 14:61–76.
Iwamiya, T., and T. Itoh. 1981. *Imperial Gardens of Japan.* New York: Weatherhill.
Jackson, A. B. 1927. *A Catalogue of Trees and Shrubs at Westonbirt.* London: Oxford University Press.
Jackson, B. D. 1895. *Index Kewensis* 1:21. London: Oxford University Press.
Jackson, R. M., and P. A. Mason. 1984. *Mycorrhiza.* Studies in Biology 159. London: Arnold.
Jacobs, H. 1979a. Sugar maple decline is treatable. *Arboretum Leaves* 21(1):4–5, 12–13.
______. 1979b. Syrup in your own back yard. *Arboretum Leaves* 21(2):22–25.
Jacobson, J. S., and A. C. Hill. eds. 1970. *Recognition of Air Pollution Injury to Vegetation: A Pictorial Atlas.* Air Pollution Control Association, Pittsburgh, Pennsylvania.
Jacques, H. A. 1847. *Manuel général des plantes, arbres et arbustes, ou flores des jardins de l'Europe* 1:252–257. Paris.
Jaeger, H., and L. Beissner. 1889. *Die Ziergehölze der Gärten und Parkanlagen.* 3rd ed. Weimar.

Jaennicke, F. 1904. Der Park in Historischer und Wissenschaftlicher Hinsicht mit Besonderer Berücksichtigung der Nordamerikanischen und Japanischen Waldbestände. *Mitt. Dtsch. Dendr. Ges.* 13:99–107.
Jakubovskaja, T. V. 1977. *Paleaografija Lichvinskogo Mezlednikov'ja Grodnenskogo Poneman'ja.* Minsk.
James, N. D. G. 1973. *A Book of Trees, An Anthology.* Royal Forestry Society.
______. 1990. *The Arboriculturalist's Companion.* 2nd ed. Oxford: Basil Blackwell.
Jamison, D. 1988. A visit to Montreal 25th to 27th September 1987. *Int. Dendr. Soc. Yrbk.* 1987:50–52.
______. 1990a. I.D.S. tour of Belgium and Holland. *Int. Dendr. Soc. Yrbk.* 1990:51–58.
______. 1990b. I.D.S. tour in Provence, 26th May–2nd June 1989. *Int. Dendr. Soc. Yrbk.* 1989:64–73.
Janick, J. 1986. *Horticultural Science.* 4th ed. New York: Freeman.
Janson, T. J. M. 1983. *Stadsbomen van Acer tot Zelkova.* Utrecht: Bomenstichting.
Jensen, K. F. 1983. Growth relationships in silver maple seedlings fumigated with $O_2$ and $SO_2$. *Canadian Journal of Forest Research* 13:298–302.
Jepson, W. L. 1910. *The Silva of California.* Berkeley.
Jeswiet, J. 1942. Suringar's Laatste Werk. Suringar en het Arboretum op den Ohrberg. *Nederlandse Dendr. Ver. Gedenkboek J. Vackenier Suringar* 9–22.
Jimbo, T. 1933. The diagnosis of the pollen of forest trees. I. *Sci. Rep., Taihoku Imperial University,* ser. 4, biology, 8:287–296.
Johnson, C. W. 1848. *The Farmer's Cyclopedia and Dictionary of Rural Affairs.* Philadelphia, Pennsylvania: Carey and Hart.
Johnson, H. 1973. *The International Book of Trees.* London: Mitchell Beazley.
______. 1981. Origins of Plants. *Sunday Telegraph Magazine* nos. 242–244.
Johnson, D. W., and J. E. Kuntz. 1979a. *Eutypella* canker of maple: ascospore discharge and dissemination. *Phytopathology* 69:130–135.
______. 1979b. *Eutypella parasitica:* ascospore germination and mycelial growth. *Canadian Journal of Botany* 57:624–628.
Johnson, P. S. 1976. Eight-year performance of interplanted hardwoods in southern Wisconsin oak clearcuts. USDA Forest Service Research Paper NC–126.
Johnson, S. A. 1906. The cottony maple scale. College of Agricultural Experiment Station Press Bulletin 27.
Johnson, W. T., and H. H. Lyon. 1976. *Insects that Feed on Trees and Shrubs.* Ithaca, New York: Cornell University Press.
______. 1988. *Insects that Feed on Trees and Shrubs.* 2nd ed. Ithaca, New York: Cornell University Press.
Jones, C. H. 1903. The exclusion of lead from maple sap. Vermont Agricultural Experiment Station Bulletin 439.
Jones, C. H., and J. L. Bradlee. 1933. The carbohydrate contents of the maple tree. Vermont Agricultural Experiment Station Bulletin 358.
Jones, C. H., et al. 1903. The maple sap flow. Vermont Agricultural Experiment Station Bulletin 103.
Jones, E. 1832a. *The Acer Saccharinum.* London: Colyer.
______. 1832b. *Review of Facts and Observations Made by Naturalists, Botanists, Historians and Travellers on the Properties and Productions of the Sugar Maple Tree.* London: Colyer.
Jones, E., and R. E. Hughes. 1984. A note on the ascorbic acid contents of some trees and woody shrubs. *Phytochemistry* 23:2366–2367.
Jones, M. A. 1920. Physical study of maple seeds. *Botanical Gazette* 69:127–152.
Jones, S. G. 1925. Life history and cytology of *Rhytisma acerinum* (Pers.) Fries. *Ann. Bot.* 39:41–75.
Jong, P. C. de. 1974. Esdoorns met een streepjes-bast. *Acer* L. Sectie Macrantha Pax. *Groen* 30:104–107.
______. 1976. *Flowering and sex expression in Acer* L. A biosystematic study. *Meded. Landb. Univ. Wageningen* 76(2):1–201.
______. 1977. *Acer* section *Macrantha. Dendroflora* 13/14:3–16.
______. 1986. *Catalogue of Plant Collections.* Utrecht: University Botanical Gardens.
______. 1989. The Von Gimborn Arboretum at Doorn (Netherlands). *Int. Dendr. Soc. Yrbk.* 1988:5–7.
______. 1990a. Taxonomy and distribution of *Acer. Int. Dendr. Soc. Yrbk.* 1990:6–10.
______. 1990b. Flowering and evolution of *Acer. Int. Dendr. Soc. Yrbk.* 1990:42–47.
Jordan, A. 1852. *Pugillus Plantarum Novarum.* Paris.

Jorgensen, N. 1978. *A Sierra Naturalist's Guide to Southern New England.* San Francisco, California: Sierra Club Books.

Joørstad, I. 1925. *The Erysiphaceae of Norway.* Oslo: Dybwad.

Jouin, E. 1907. *Acer spicatum laciniatum. Mitt. Dtsch. Dendr. Ges.* 16:257.

Jovanovic, B. 1973. *A. monspessulanum* L. subf. *cruciatum. Fl. SR Srbije* 5:612.

Jung, W., et al. 1972. Das Risz/Würm-Interglazial von Zeifen, Landkreis Laufen a.d. Salzach. *Abh. Math.-Naturw. Kl. K. Bayer. Akad. Wiss. München* N.F. 151:5–131.

Junghuhn, F. W. 1842. *Monatsber. Verh. Ges. Erdkunde Berlin* 3:96.

Juniper, B. E., and C. E. Jeffree. 1983. *Plant Surfaces.* London: Arnold.

Juniper, B. E., and R. Southwood. eds. 1986. *Insects and the Plant Surface.* London: Arnold.

Jupin, H., et al. 1975. Chloroplastes à empilements granaires anormaux appauvris en photosysteme I, dans le phloème de *Robinia pseudoacacia et d'Acer pseudoplatanus. Ztschr. Pflanzenphysiol.* 75:95–106.

Jussieu, A. L. de. 1789. *Genera Plantarum.* 1st ed. Paris. Rpt. 1964. Weinheim: J. Cramer.

———. 1811. Dixième mémoire sur les caractéres généraux des familles tirés des graines. *Annuel du Musée d'Histoire Naturelle de Paris* 18:477.

Kabulov, S. K. 1966. Polycarpellate fruits of some species of maple. (*Acer* L.). *Botanicheskii Zhurnal* 51:1617–1620.

———. 1970. Osobennosti sezonnogo razvitiya vidov Klena v Karakalpakia (Peculiarities of the seasonal development of maple species in Karakalpakia). *Bjull. Glavn. Bot. Sada* 76:22–26.

Kac, N. J., et al. 1965. *Atlas i Opredelitel'plodov i Semjan Vstrecajuscichsja v Cetverticnych Otlozenijach.* Moscow.

Kache, P. 1919. Die Besten der Neueren und Selteneren Laubgehölze. *Mitt. Dtsch. Dendr. Ges.* 28:213–254.

———. 1923. Zur Stichtung Unserer Gehölz-Sortimente. *Mitt. Dtsch. Dendr. Ges.* 33:198–205.

Kaempfer, E. 1712. *Flora Japonica.* Rpt. and commentary by W. Muntschick, 1993. Wiesbaden: Steiner.

Kalm, P. 1771. *Travels in North America.* 1st ed. Translated by Forster. London: Warrington.

———. 1772. *Travels in North America.* 2nd ed. Translated by Forster. London: Warrington.

Kamenická, A., and M. Rypak. 1977. Vplyv rôznych koncentracií kyseliny abscicovej na klícenie semien *Acer saccharinum* L. V zavislosti od teploty. *Biologia (Bratislava)* 32:815–819.

Kammerer, E. L. 1957. Autumn color high lights in foliage and fruits. Bulletin of Popular Information, Morton Arboretum 32(11):47–50.

Kammeyer, H. F. 1918. Zahlreiche Misteln auf Spitz-Ahorn. *Mitt. Dtsch. Dendr. Ges.* 27:290.

———. 1923. Pillnitz und Seine Dendrologischen Schätze. *Mitt. Dtsch. Dendr. Ges.* 33:195–197.

Kaniewski, K., and Z. Wazynska. 1970. Sklerenchymatous endocarp with hairs in the fruit of *Acer pseudoplatanus* L. Bulletin of the Academy of Polish.Science 2(18):413–420.

Kanitz, A. 1880. *Plantas Romaniae.* Claudiopoli (Cluj).

Kaplan, L., et al. 1990. The Boylston Street fishweir: revisited. *Economic Botany* 44(4):516–528.

Karley, S. L. M. 1972. *Acer*—unusual fruits. *Watsonia* 9:43.

Karnosky, D. F. 1979. Screening urban trees for air pollution tolerance. *Journal of Arboriculture* 5:159.

———. 1981. Chamber and field evaluations of air pollution tolerances of urban trees. *Journal of Arboriculture* 7:99–105.

Karr, A. L. 1976. Cell wall biogenesis. In *Plant Biochemistry* Eds. J. Bonner and J. E. Varner. 3rd ed. New York: Academic Press.

Karsten, G. K. W. H. 1880. *Deutsche Flora.* Berlin.

Kasapligil, B. 1977. A Late-Tertiary conifer-hardwood forest from the vicinity of Güvem Village, near Kizilcahamam, Ankara. Bulletin of Mineral Resources and Exploration, Inst. Turkey, foreign ed., 88:25–33.

Kavasch, B. 1980. Herbaria. The maples (Aceraceae). Artifacts. *Amerind. Archeol. Inst.* 8(3):6–7.

Kearney, T. H. 1939. New species, varieties and combinations. *Journal of the Washington Academy of Science* 29:486.

Keble Martin, W. 1986. *The New Concise British Flora.* London: Mermaid Books.

Keenan, J. 1952. George Forrest, 1873–1932. *Journal of the Royal Horticultural Society* 98:112–117.

Keenan, P. Q. 1957. On the application of the term cultivar to plants of wild origin. *Baileya* 5:101–105.

Keifer, H. H. 1946. A review of North American economic eriophyid mites. *Journal of Economic Entomology* 39:563–570.

Keifer, H. H., et al. 1982. *An Illustrated Guide to Plant Abnormalities Caused by Eriophyid Mites in North America.* Agriculture Handbook no. 573. Washington, DC: USDA Forest Service.
Keller, A. C. 1942. *Acer glabrum* and its varieties. *American Midland Naturalist* 27:491–500.
Kellman, M. C. 1977. *Plant Geography.* London: Methuen.
Kelly, J. W. 1972. *Introgressive Hybridization Between Red and Silver Maples.* Master's thesis, State University of New York, Geneseo.
Kelsey, H. P., and W. A. Dayton. 1942. *Standardized Plant Names.* Harrisburg, Pennsylvania.
Kerkkonen, M. 1959. Peter Kalm's North American journey. Its ideological background and results. *Studia Historia* 1. Helsinki.
Kerner, J. S. von. 1796. *Darstellung Vorzüglicher Ausländischer Baeume und Gestraeuche Welche in Deutschland im Freien Ausdauern.* Tübingen.
Kerner von Marilaun, A. 1890. *Pflanzenleben.* Leipzig: Bibliogr. Inst.
Kessler, K. J., Jr. 1972. Sapstreak disease of sugar maple. USDA Forest Service, Forest Pest Leaflet 128.
Kessler, K. J., Jr., and J. S. Hadfield. 1972. *Eutypella* canker of maple. USDA Forest Service, Forest Pest Leaflet 136.
*Kew Record of Taxonomic Literature.* 1971– . London: H.M.S.O.
Khushalani, I. 1963. Floral morphology and embryology of *Acer oblongum. Phyton* 10:275–284.
Kielbaso, J. J., and K. Ottman. 1976. Manganese deficiency—contributory to maple decline? *Journal of Arboriculture* 2:27–32.
King, G. 1896. New Indian trees. *J. Asiat. Soc. Bengal* 65(2):115.
King, J. E., and W. H. Allen Jr. 1977. A Holocene vegetation record from the Mississippi River Valley, southeastern Missouri. *Quaternary Research* 8:307–323.
King, P. J. 1976. Studies on the growth in culture of plant cells. XX. Utilization of 2, 4-dichlorophenoxyacetic Acid by steady-state cell cultures of *Acer pseudoplatanus* L. *Journal of Experimental Botany* 27:1053–1072.
Kingdon Ward, F. 1928. *Plant Hunting on the Edge of the World.* London: Cadogan Books. 1985 edition.
Kingsville Nurseries, Maryland. 1968. *List.* Henry J. Hohman.
Kirchheimer, F. 1928. Die Fossile Makroflora der Kieslgur von Beuern. *Notizbl. Ver. Erdk. Hess. Geol. Land. Darmstadt* 5(10):140.
Kirchner, G. 1859. Das Arboretum des Prinzlichen Parkes zu Muskau. *Wochenschr. Ver. Beförd. Gartenb. Preussen* 1859:348–350.
______. 1864. In *Arboretum Muscaviense.* Eds. E. Petzold and G. Kirchner.
Kirchner, W. C. G. 1898. Contribution to the fossil flora of Florissant, Colorado. *Transactions of the St. Louis Academy of Science* 8:181.
Kissena Nurseries. 1905. *Catalogue of Deciduous Trees and Shrubs, Rare Evergreens, Japanese Maples, Rhododendrons, Roses & Fruits.*
Kissena Nurseries, Parsons & Sons Co. Ltd. 1900. *Catalogue of Deciduous Trees and Shrubs, Rare Evergreens, Japanese Maples and Rhododendrons.*
Kitaibel, P. 1864. Additamenta ad floram Hungaricam. *Linnaea* 32:552.
Kitamura, S. 1972. *Acer rufinerve* Sieb. & Zucc. f. *angustifolium* Kitamura. *Acta Phytotaxonomica et Geobotanica* 25(2–3):42.
Kitamura, S., et al. 1963. *Garden Plants of Japan.*
Kitamura, S., and G. Murata. 1971. *Acer tschonoskii* subsp. *australe. Acta Phytotaxonomica et Geobotanica* 25(1):2.
______. 1972. New names and new conceptions adopted in our coloured illustrations of woody plants of Japan. I. *Acta Phytotaxonomica et Geobotanica* 25(2/3):33–44.
Kitamura, S., and S. Okamoto. 1983. *Colored Illustrations of Trees and Shrubs of Japan.* 52nd printing. Osaka: Hoikusha.
Kitanoff, B. 1936. Varku formit ot *Acer heldreichii* Orph. v Bálgariia. *Trav. Soc. Bulg. Sci. Nat. Sofia* 17:135–142.
Kjölby, V., et al. 1958. *Acer* (*Acer pseudoplatanus* L.). Copenhagen: Dansk Skovforening.
Klaehn, F. U. 1958. Some interesting aspects of flower morphology and flower ecology of various forest trees. In *Proceedings of the 5th Northeastern Forest Tree Improvement Conference.* 71–76.
______. 1959. Flower morphology and flower ecology with respect to forest tree breeding procedures. *Recent Advances in Botany, 9th Int. Bot. Congr. Montreal* 2(14):1666–1671. University of Toronto Press.
Klinkspoor, T. H. 1959–1961. Buitenplaatsen, die om Hun Bomen de Aandacht Vragen. *Jaarboek*

*Nederlandse Dendr. Ver.* 22:83–95.
Kneiff, F. 1915. Dendrologische Beobachtungen im Sommer 1915. *Mitt. Dtsch. Dendr. Ges.* 24:279–281.
Knoop, J. H. 1749. *Pomologia.* Chapter Beschrijving van de Plantagetuin of van de Wilde Boom- en Heestergewassen. Leeuwarden: Ferwerda & Tresling.
Knowlton, F. H. 1898. Catalogue of the Cretaceous and Tertiary plants of North America. Bulletin of the U.S. Geological Survey 152:25–27.
______. 1899. Geology of the Yellowstone National Park. U.S. Geological Survey Monograph 32(2):735–736.
______. 1902. Fossil flora of the John Day Basin, Oregon. Bulletin of the U.S. Geological Survey 204:72–78.
______. 1916. Fossil plants from Florissant. In *Proceedings of the U.S. Natural Museum* 51:282–283.
______. 1917. Geology and paleontology of Raton Mesa in Colorado-New Mexico. U.S. Geological Survey Prof. Paper 101:330, t. 101.
______. 1919. *Catalog of Mesozoic and Cenozoic Plants of North America.* Washington, DC.
______. 1922. Laramie flora of the Denver Basin. U.S. Geological Survey Prof. Paper 130:149–150.
______. 1926. Flora of the Latah Formation of Spokane, Washington. U.S. Geological Survey Prof. Paper 140:45–46.
Knuchel, H. and M. Schnyder. 1984. *Baumbuch.* (Stereoscopic photographs). Zürich: Tanner & Staehelin.
Knuth, P. 1904. *Handbuch der Blütenbiologie.* II. Aceraceae 1. Leipzig.
Knystautas, A. 1987. *The Natural History of the USSR.* London: Century.
Kobayashi, J. 1975. *Maples for Beginners.* Tokyo: Nihon Bungei Sha.
Kobendza, R. 1953. Observations on the biology of the blossoming of the silvery maple (*Acer saccharinum* L.). *Ann. Sect. Dendr. Soc. Bot. de Pologne* 9:175–181.
Koch, K. H. E. 1853. *Hortus Dendrologicus.* Berlin: Schneider.
______. 1864. *A. diabolicum* Blume ex. Koch, K. *A. pycnanthum* Koch, K. Pomaceae, Acerineae et Berberideae. In Miquel. *Ann. Mus. Bot. Lugd. Bat.* 1:248–253.
______. 1867. Gärtnerische Briefe über die Pariser Welt-Ausstellung. *Wochenschr. Ver. Beförd. Gartenb. Preussen* 10:172.
______. 1869. *Dendrologie.* I. Erlangen: Enke.
Koehne, E. 1893. *Deutsche Dendrologie.* Berlin: Parey.
Koide, N., et al. 1978. *The Master's Book of Bonsai.* New York: Kodansha.
Koidzumi, G. I. 1911a. Observations on the Aceraceae. *Botanical Magazine, Tokyo* 25:42–61, 97–113.
______. 1911b. Revisio Aceracearum Japonicarum. *J. Coll. Sci. Univ. Tokyo* 32(1):1–75.
______. 1914. *A. morifolium* Koidz., plantae novae Japonicae. I. *Botanical Magazine, Tokyo* 28:151.
______. 1916. Decades plantarum novarum. *Botanical Magazine, Tokyo* 30:327–329.
______. 1925. Contributiones ad cognitionem florae Asiae Orientalis. *Botanical Magazine, Tokyo* 39:306–307.
______. 1929. Contributiones ad cognitionem florae Asiae Orientalis. *Botanical Magazine, Tokyo* 43:382–383.
______. 1930a. *Florae Symbolae Orientali-Asiaticae.* Osaka.
______. 1930b. Contributiones ad cognitionem florae Asiae Orientalis. *Botanical Magazine, Tokyo* 44:99–100.
______. 1937. Contributiones ad cognitionem florae Asiae Orientalis. *Acta Phytotaxonomica et Geobotanica, Kyoto* 6:210.
Kökichi, M., et al. 1987. *The Gardens of Kyoto.* Kyoto: Kyoto Shoin.
Komarov, V. L. 1896. *Trav. Soc. Nat. St. Petersburg Bot.* 26:157.
______. 1901. *Acer triflorum* Komar. In Species Novae Florae Asiae Orientalis. *Acta Horti Petrop.* 18:340.
______. 1904. Flora Manshuriae. II. *Acta Horti Petrop.* 22:719–739.
Kooiman, H. N., and H. J. Venema. 1937. De catalogi van von Siebold en de introductie van planten uit Japan. *Jaarboek Nederlandse Dendr. Ver.* 12:124–126.
Koorders, S. H. 1912. *Exkursionsflora von Java.* Jena: Fischer.
______. 1918. *Atlas der Baumarten von Java.* Jena: Fischer.
Koppeschaar, W. F. 1942. Een Reis door Japan in 1911. *Nederlandse Dendr. Ver. Gedenkboek J. Vackenier Suringar* 132–150.
Kornas, J. 1972. Corresponding taxa and their ecological background in the forests of temperate Eurasia and North America. In *Taxonomy Phytogeography and Evolution.* Ed. D.H. Valentine. New York: Academic Press.

Kort, A. 1906. Les érables panachés. *Revue Horticole Belge Etranger* 32:197–199.
Köstler, J. N., et al. 1968. *Die Wurzeln der Waldbäume*. Berlin: Parey.
Kovata, J. von. 1856. Fossile Flora von Erdöbénye. *Arbeit Geol. Ges. Ungarn* 1:32.
Kozel, P. C. and M. Jansen. 1976. A new look at red maple. *American Nurseryman* 142:7, 70–72, 83.
Kozlowski, T. T. 1984. *Flooding and Plant Growth*. New York: Academic Press.
Kozlowski, T. T., et al. 1974. Transpiration rate of *Fraxinum americana* and *Acer saccharum*. *Canadian Journal of Forest Research* 4:259–267.
Kraeusel, R. 1921. Nachträge zur Tertiärflora Schlesiens. III. *Jahrb. Preuss. Geol. Landesanst.* 40(1):411–414.
Kraeusel, R., and H. Weyland. 1959. Kritische Untersuchungen zur Kutikular-analyse Tertiärer Blätter. IV. *Palaeontographica* B 105:102–122.
Kramer, K. 1974. Fossile Pflanzen aus der Braunkohlenzeit. *Mitt. Dtsch. Dendr. Ges.* 67:199–233.
Kramer, P. J., and T. T. Kozlowski. 1979. *Physiology of Woody Plants*. New York: Academic Press.
Krasnov, A. N. 1911. Primitiae florae Tertiariae Rossiae meridionalis. *Trav. Soc. Nat. Univ. Kharkov* 44:245.
Krause, C. R. 1978. Identification of four red maple cultivars with scanning electronic microscopy. *HortScience* 13:586–588.
Kreuzen, E. M. 1947. Opheusden en de Oorlog met Zijn Gevolgen. *Jaarboek Nederlandse Dendr. Ver.* 16:124–126.
Kriebel, H. B. 1957. Patterns of genetic variation in sugar maple. Ohio Agricultural Experiment Station Bulletin 791.
Krishtofovich, A. N. 1914. In Fedchenko's *Flora Aziatskoi Rossii* 5:57.
Krocker, A. J. 1814. *Flora Silesiaca Renovata* 3:367–371. Vratislava.
Kruckeberg, A. R. 1982. *Gardening with Native Plants of the Pacific Northwest*. Seattle: University of Washington Press.
Krüssmann, G. 1954. *Die Baumschule*. Berlin: Parey.
———. 1958. *Taschenbuch der Gehölzverwendung*. Berlin: Parey.
———. 1968. I.D.S. tour in western Germany 18th–26th June 1966. *Int. Dendr. Soc. Yrbk.* 1967:16–25.
———. 1976a. *Handbuch der Laubgehölze*. Berlin: Parey.
———. 1976b. Experiences and problems with trees in West Germany. *Int. Dendr. Soc. Yrbk.* 1975:80–84.
———. 1984. *Manual of Cultivated Broad-leaved Trees and Shrubs*. Beaverton, Oregon: Timber Press.
Krüssmann, G., and H. Heine. 1979. The "Golden Tour" to Cumbria and southern Scotland 12th–21st May 1978. *Int. Dendr. Soc. Yrbk.* 1978:85–100.
Kubler, H. 1983. Mechanism of frost crack formation in trees. A review and synthesis. *Forest Science* 29:559–568.
Kuck, L. 1982. *The World of the Japanese Garden*. New York: Weatherhill.
Kuiters, L. 1987. *Phenolic Acids and Plant Growth in Forest Ecosystems*. Ph.D. thesis, Free University of Amsterdam.
Kunijiro, Y., et al. 1972. A survey of anthocyanins in sprouting leaves of some Japanese angiosperms. Studies on anthocyanins LXV. *Botanical Magazine, Tokyo* 85:303–306.
Kuntze, C. E. O. 1867. *Taschen-Flora von Leipzig*. Leipzig.
———. 1891. *Revisio Generum Plantarum*. Leipzig.
Kupchan, S. M. 1975. Advances in the chemistry of tumor-inhibitory products. In *Recent Advances in Phytochemistry*, vol. 9. Ed. V. C. Runeckles. New York: Plenum.
Kupchan, S. M., et al. 1967. Tumor inhibitors. XXI. Active principles of *Acer negundo* and *Cyclamen persicum*. *J. Pharm. Sci.* 56:602–608.
Kuphaldt, G. 1915. Ausländische Gehölze in den Rigaer Gärten. *Mitt. Dtsch. Dendr. Ges.* 24:228–241.
Kurata, S., ed. 1964–1976. *Illustrated Important Forest Trees of Japan*. 5 vols. Tokyo: Japan Forestry Technical Association.
Kurz, W. S. 1872. New Birmese Plants. *J. Asiat. Soc. Bengal* 41:304.
Küster, E. 1919. Beiträge zur Kenntnis der Panaschierten Laubgehölze. *Mitt. Dtsch. Dendr. Ges.* 28:85–88.
———. 1923. Zur Kenntnis der Panaschierten Gehölze. V & VI. *Mitt. Dtsch. Dendr. Ges.* 33:183–188.
———. 1924. Zur Kenntnis der Panaschierten Gehölze. *Mitt. Dtsch. Dendr. Ges.* 34:136–139.
———. 1936. Beiträge zur Kenntnis der Panaschierten Gehölze. *Mitt. Dtsch. Dendr. Ges.* 48:166–171.

Kutani, N. 1951. On the chemical composition of aceritannin, crystalline tannin from the leaves of *Acer ginnala* Maxim. I, II. *Mem. Kumamoto Women's University* 3:57–66.

______. 1960. The chemical structure of aceritannin. Part I. Chem. Pharm. Bulletin 8:72.

Kuznetsov, N. I. 1891. *Zap. Russk. Geogr. Obshch.* 23(3):151.

Laar, H. J. van de. 1977. Keuringen 1977. Dendroflora 13–14:74.

Laar, H. J. van de. 1989. *Naamlijst van Houtige Gewassen.* 4th ed. Brochure no. 5. Boskoop: Proefstation voor de Boomkwekerij.

Lacasse, N. L., and A. E. Rich. 1964. Maple decline in New Hampshire. *Phytopathology* 54:1071–1075.

Lachance, D. 1971a. Discharge and germination of *Eutypella parasitica* ascospores. *Canadian Journal of Botany* 49:111–118.

______. 1971b. Inoculation and development of *Eutypella* canker of maple. *Canadian Journal of Forest Research* 1:228–234.

Lachance, D., and J. E. Kuntz. 1970. Ascocarp development of *Eutypella parasitica. Canadian Journal of Botany* 48:1977–1979.

Lafitau, J. F. 1724. *Moeurs des Sauvages Amériquains.* Paris: Hocherau.

Lake County Nursery. 1990. *Catalogue.* Perry, Ohio.

Lakon, G. 1917. Kleinere Teratologische Mitteilungen. 2. *Pflanzenkrankh.* 27:100–102.

Lamarck, J. B. A. P. M. de. 1786. *Acer spicatum* Lam. *Encyclopédie Méthodique Botanique.* II:381. (Paris, 1790)

Lamb, J. G. D. 1972. Vegetative propagation of Japanese maples at Kinsealy, Eire. *International Plant Propagators' Society Proceedings* 22.

Lamb, J. G. D., and F. J. Nutty. 1983–1984. Propagation techniques in the genus *Acer. The Plantsman* 5:186–192.

Lamotte, R. S. 1952. Catalogue of the Cenozoic plants of North America through 1950. *Memoirs of the Geological Society of America* 51:52–58.

Lamport, D. T. A. 1977. Structure, biosynthesis and significance of cell wall glycoproteins. In *Recent Advances in Phytochemistry,* vol. 11. Eds. F. A. Loewus and V. C. Runeckles. London: Plenum.

Lamport, D. T. A., and D. H. Northcote. 1960. Hydroxyproline in primary cell walls of higher plants. *Nature* 188:665–666.

Lamson, N. I., and H. C. Smith. 1976. Response to crop tree release: sugar maple, red oak, black berry, and yellow poplar saplings in a 9-year-old stand. USDA Forest Service Research Paper NE–394.

Lana, A. F., et al. 1980. A virus isolated from sugar maple. *Phytopathology* 97:214–218.

Lancaster, R. 1959. Many forms and uses rank maples high among shade trees. *American Nurseryman* 110(7):10–11, 88–94.

______. 1974. *Trees for Your Garden.* Calverton: Floraprint.

______. 1976. Maples of the Himalaya. *Journal of the Royal Horticultural Society* 101:589.

______. 1979a. *Acer* × *hillieri. The Plantsman* 1:124–127.

______. 1979b. *Acer* 'Summergold'. *Journal of the Royal Horticultural Society* 104:424.

______. 1979c. Some cultivars of hardy woody plants raised in the Hillier Arboretum and Nurseries. *The Plantsman* 1:67–73.

______. 1984a. Observations on *Acer. The Plantsman* 5:254–255.

______. 1984b. The Wudang Mountains of North West Hubeh. *Int. Dendr. Soc. Yrbk.* 1983:50–54.

______. 1986. Award plants 1985, part 3. *Journal of the Royal Horticultural Society* 111:561–566.

______. 1989a. Award plants 1988, part 3. *Journal of the Royal Horticultural Society* 114:500–504.

______. 1989b. *Travels in China, a Plantsman's Paradise.* Woodbridge, Suffolk: Antique Coll. Club.

______. 1990. *Acer* in the wild in Asia. *Int. Dendr. Soc. Yrbk.* 1990:50.

Lancucka-Srodoniowa, M. 1966. Tortonian flora from the "Gdow-Bay" in the south of Poland. *Acta Paleobot.* 7(1):3–135.

______. 1979. Macroscopic plant remains from the freshwater Miocene of the Nowy Sacz Basin (West Carpathians, Poland). *Acta Paleobot.* 20(1):1–116.

Landolt, E. 1977. *Ökologische Zeigerwerte zur Schweizer Flora.* Zürich: Geobot. Inst. ETH.

Láng, A. F. 1824. *Sylloge Plantarum Novarum Regensburg* I:187.

Lange, J. M. C. 1866. Pugillus plantarum imrimis Hispanicarum. *Vidensk. Meddel. Naturh. For. Kjobenhavn.* II. 7:120.

______. 1882. *Acer neglectum. Bot. Tidsskr.* 13:30.

Langenheim, J. H., and K. V. Thimann. 1982. *Botany.* New York: Wiley.

Langeron, M. 1899. Contributions à l'éude de la flore fossile de Sézanne. Bulletin de la Société d'Histoire Naturelle Autun 12:431–455.

______. 1901. Contributions à l'étude de la flore fossile de Sézanne. Bulletin de la Societe d'Histoire Naturelle Autun 13:356–370.
Lape, F. 1965. *A Garden of Trees and Shrubs. Practical Hints for Planning and Planting an Arboretum.* Ithaca, New York: Cornell University Press.
Larcher, W., et al. 1985. *Handbuch der Pflanzenkrankheiten, die Nichtparasitären Krankheiten. 5. Teil. Meteorol. Pfl. Pathol., Kälte und Frost.* Berlin: Parey.
Laubert, R. 1937. Beobachtungen über Krüppelblätter an Ahorn und Anderen Gewächse. *Mitt. Dtsch. Dendr. Ges.* 49:183–185.
Lauche, W. G. 1880. *Deutsche Dendrologie.* Berlin.
Lauener, L. A. 1967. Catalogue of the names published by Hector Léveillé. V. *Notes of the Royal Botanic Garden, Edinburgh* 27:265–292.
Lauth, T. 1781. *De Acere.* Strassbourg.
Lavallé, P. A. M. 1877. *Arboretum Segrezianum.* Baillière, Paris; London: Tindall and Cox.
Lawrence, G. M. H. 1965. *Taxonomy of Vascular Plants.* New York: Macmillan.
Lawrey, J. D. 1977. Trace metal accumulation by plant species from a coal strip-mining area in Ohio. Bulletin of the Torrey Botanical Club 104:368–375.
Lawson Seed and Nursery Co. 1874. *Catalog, IV. Forest Trees & Shrubs.*
Leaf, A. L. 1968. K, Mg, and S deficiencies in forest trees. In *Forest Fertilization: Theory and Practice.* Muscle Shoals: Tennessee Valley Authority.
Lear, M. 1990. The threatened temperate tree list. *Int. Dendr. Soc. Yrbk.* 1990:130–152.
Leathart, S. 1977. *Trees of the World.* London: Hamlyn.
Lebas, E. L. 1868. *Acer Wagneri laciniatus. Revue Horticole* 40:387–388.
Lecompte, P. H. 1912. *Flore Générale de l'Indo-Chine* 1:1054–1055. Paris: Musée Nationale d'Histoire Naturelle.
Ledebour, K. F. 1842. *Flora Rossica* 1:454–457.
Lee, C., and Son. 1881. *Acer Pseudo-Platanus* 'Webbianum'. *Gardener's Chronicle* III. 15:300.
Lee, S. 1978. A factor analysis study of the functional significance of angiosperm pollen. *Systematic Botany* 3:1–19.
Lee, S. C. 1935. *Forest Botany of China.* Shanghai: Commercial Press.
Lee, T. B. 1979. *Illustrated Flora of Korea.* Seoul: Hyang-mun Publ. (in Korean).
Lees-Milne, A., and R. Verey. 1987. *The New Englishwoman's Garden.* London: Chatto & Windus.
Leet, J. 1987. *Flowering Trees and Shrubs. The Botanical Paintings of Esther Heins.* New York: Abrams.
Legendre, P., and D. J. Rogers. 1972. Characters and clustering in taxonomy. *Taxon* 21:567–606.
Leith, I. D., and D. Fowler. 1987. Urban distribution of *Rhytisma acerinum* (Pers.) Fries (tar spot) on sycamore. *New Phytology* 108:175–181.
Lemaire, G. M. H. 1864. *Acer pseudoplatanus* var. 'Leopoldii'. *Illustration Horticole* 11, pl. 411.
______. 1867. *Illustration Horticole* 14, t. 523, 526.
Lemmon, K. 1968. *The Golden Age of the Plant Hunters.* London: Phoenix House.
Leopold, E. B. 1969. Late Cenozoic palynology. In *Aspects of Palynology.* Eds. R. H. Tschudy and R. A. Scott. New York: Wiley.
Leopold, E. B., and H. D. MacGinitie. 1972. *Development and Affinities of Tertiary Floras in the Rocky Mountains.*
Le Saint, A. M., and A. M. Catesson. 1966. Variations simultanées des teneurs en eau, en sucres solubles, en acides aminès et de la pression osmotique dans le phloème et le cambium de sycomore pendant les pèriodes de repos apparent et de la reprise de la croissance. *Compte Rendue de l'Académie de Science (France)* 263:1463–1466.
Lesquereux, L. 1868. Fossil plants from Nebraska. *The American Journal of Science* 2(46):100–101.
______. 1872. *Annual Report, U.S. Geological Survey, Terr. 1871,* Supplement 12.
______. 1876. New species of Tertiary fossil plants briefly described. *Annual Report, U.S. Geological Survey, Terr. 1874.*
______. 1878. Report on the fossil plants of the auriferous gravel deposits. *Memoirs of the Museum of Comparative Zoology, Harvard College* 6(2):26–27.
______. 1883. Contribution to the fossil flora of the Western Territories. *Annual Report, U.S. Geological Survey, Terr.* 8:83, 180, 234.
______. 1888. Bulletin of the Museum of Comparative Zoology, Harvard College 16:54.
______. 1889. Recent determination of fossil plants. In *Proceedings of the U.S. Natural Museum* 11:14–15.
______. 1892. The flora of the South Dakota Group. U.S. Geological Survey Monograph 17:156–158.
Levasseur and Son. 1898. *Acer Negundo californicum aureum. Revue Horticole* 70:327.

Léveillé, A. A. H. 1906. Les érables de Japon. Bulletin de la Société Botanique de France 53:587–593.
______. 1912. *Acer coriaceifolium* Lév. Decades Plantarum Novarum. *Repert. Sp. Nov.* 10:432–433.
______. 1913. Decades plantarum novarum. *Repert. Sp. Nov.* 12:185.
______. 1915. *Flore du Kouy Tchéou.*
______. 1917. *Catalogue des Plantes du Yun-nan.*
Levenson, J. B. 1981. The southern-mesic forest of southeastern Wisconsin: species composition and community structure. *Contributions in Biology and Geology* 41. Milwaukee Public Museum.
Lever, J. 1988. Zacheus. *Biovisie* 68(17):208.
Lewis, W. H., and M. P. F. Elvin-Lewis. 1977. *Medical Botany.* New York: Wiley.
Lewis, M., et al. 1905. A history of the expedition under the command of Captain Lewis and Clark 1804–1806. *Great American Explorers Series.*
Li, H. L. 1952. The genus *Acer* in Formosa and the Liu Kiu Islands. *Pacific Science* 6:288–294.
______. 1963a. *Woody Flora of Taiwan.* Philadelphia, Pennsylvania: Livingstone.
______. 1963b. *The Origin and Cultivation of Shade and Ornamental Trees.* Philadelphia: University of Pennsylvania Press.
______. 1977. *Flora of Taiwan.* Taiwan: Epoch Publications.
Li, Y. K. 1985. *Acer rubronervium. Guihaia* 5(1):7.
______. 1987a. *Acer guizhouense. Guihaia* 7(3):211.
______. 1987b. *Acer legousanicum. Guihaia* 7(3):212.
Liberty Hyde Bailey Hortorium. 1976. *Hortus third: A concise dictionary of plants cultivated in the United States and Canada.* 3rd ed. New York: Macmillan.
Lid, J. 1985. *Norsk, Svensk, Finsk Flora.* Oslo: Det Norske Samlaget.
Lindemann, E. von. 1875. Supplementus III ad Florulam Elizabethgradensem. Bull. Soc. Nat. Moscou 49(2):72.
Linden, J. J. 1868. Brussels Exposition. In *Index Bibliographique de l'Hortus Belgicus.* Gand.
Lindley, J. 1836. *A Natural System of Botany.* 2nd ed. London.
Lindley, J., and T. Moore, eds. 1876. *The Treasury of Botany.* London: Longmans, Green & Co.
Lindquist, O. H., and P. D. Syme. 1981. Insects and mites associated with Ontario forests. Canadian Forest Service Information Report O-X-333.
Line, L., and A. Sutton. 1981. *The Audubon Society Book of Trees.* New York: Abrams.
Ling, Y. 1951. Species novae vel non satis cognitae e flora Fukienensi. *Acta Phytotaxonomica Sinica, Peking* 1(2):201–203.
Linnaeus, C. 1737a. *Genera Plantarum.* 1st ed. Leiden.
______. 1737b. *Hortus Cliffortianus.* Amsterdam. Rpt. J. Cramer, Lehre, 1966.
______. 1742. *Genera Plantarum.* 2nd ed. Leiden.
______. 1753. *Species Plantarum.* 1st ed. Stockholm.
______. 1754. *Genera Plantarum.* 5th ed. Stockholm.
______. 1759. *Systema Naturae.* 10th ed. Holmiae.
______. 1763. *Species Plantarum.* 2nd ed. Holmiae.
______. 1767. *Acer sempervirens* L. *Mantissa Plantarum.*
Lipetz, J. 1970. Wound-healing in higher plants. *International Review of Cytology* 27:1–28.
Lippman, E. O. von. 1929. *Geschichte des Zuckers.* Berlin: Springer-Verlag.
Lippold, H. 1968. Die Europäische Arten der Gattung *Acer* aus der Sektion Platanoidea Pax emend. Momotani. *Wiss. Zeitschr. der Fr. Schiller Univ. Jena* Jrg. 17:341–347.
Lipsky, V. I. 1911. Die Baum- und Strauchvegetation in Turkestan. *Trudy Lesn. Opytn. Delu Ross. St. Petersburg* 30:20.
Lisitsina, G. N. 1984. The Caucasus—A centre of ancient farming in Eurasia. In *Plants and Ancient Man.* Eds. W. Van Zeist and W. A. Casparie. Rotterdam: Balkema.
Little, E. L. 1944. *Acer grandidentatum* in Oklahoma. *Rhodora* 46:445–450.
______. 1948. Notes on nomenclature of trees. *Phytologia* 2:457–463.
______. 1949a. Important forest trees of the United States. In *Trees.* Yearbook of Agriculture 1949. Washington, DC: USDA.
______. 1949b. Fifty trees from foreign lands. In *Trees.* Yearbook of Agriculture 1949. Washington, DC: USDA.
______. 1971. *Atlas of United States Trees.* Vol. 1, *Conifers and Important Hardwoods.* Washington, DC: USDA Forest Service.
______. 1977. *Atlas of United States Trees.* Washington, DC: USDA Superintendent of Documents.
______. 1983. North American trees with relationships in eastern Asia. *Annals of the Missouri Botanical Garden* 70:605–615.

______. 1984. *The Audubon Society Field Guide to North American Trees. Eastern Region.* New York: Knopf.
______. 1987. *The Audubon Society Field Guide to North American Trees. Western Region.* New York: Knopf.
Littlefield, L. J. 1981. *Biology of the Plant Rusts: an Introduction.* Ames: Iowa State University Press.
Liu, T. S. 1962. *Illustrations of Native and Introduced Ligneous Plants of Taiwan,* vol. 2. Taiwan: Nat. Taiwan University.
______. 1971. *A Monograph of the Genus Abies.* Taiwan: Dept. For. Coll. Agric. Nat. Taiwan University, Taipei.
Liverpool Botanic Garden. 1808. *A Catalogue of Plants in the Botanic Garden at Liverpool.*
Lloyd, C. 1970. *The Well-Tempered Garden.* London: Collins.
Lobkowitz Baumschule Eisenberg, Czechoslovakia. 1889. Misc. *Acer Platanoides smaragdinum aureo maculatum. Österr. Garten-Zeitung.* 14:123.
Loddiges, C. 1823. *Catalogue of Plants.* 13th ed. London.
______. 1826. *Catalogue of Plants.* 14th ed. London.
______. 1827. *Acer hybridum. Bot. Cabinet* 13: t. 1221.
______. 1836. *Catalogue of Plants.* 16th ed. London.
Loder, Sir Giles. 1985. Tour in Austria 11–21 August 1984. *Int. Dendr. Soc. Yrbk.* 1984:29–36.
Loeve, A. 1971. IOPB chromosome number reports. XXXIV. *Taxon* 20(5/6):790.
Loeve, A., and D. Loeve. 1954. *A. negundo* ssp. *interius* (Britton) A. and D. Loeve. Vegetation of a prairie marsh. Bulletin of the Torrey Botanical Club 81:33.
______. 1961. Chromosome numbers of central and northwest European plant species. *Opera Bot.* 5:1–581.
______. 1966. Cytotaxonomy of the alpine vascular plants of Mount Washington. *Univ. Color. Stud.* 24:1–74.
______. 1969. IOPB chromosome number reports. XX. *Taxon* 18:218, 433, 441.
Loeve, A., and O. T. Solbrig. 1964. IOPB chromosome number reports. I. *Taxon* 13:99–110.
Lojacono Pojero, M. 1909. *Flora Sicula.* Palermo.
Lombarts, P. 1984. Trees for towns. *Int. Dendr. Soc. Yrbk.* 1983:79–83.
Lorain, J. 1825. *Nature and Reason Harmonized in the Practice of Husbandry.* Philadephia, Pennnsylvania: Carey.
Lort-Phillips, V. 1988. The I.D.S. tour of southern Ireland April 25th–May 1st, 1987. *Int. Dendr. Soc. Yrbk.* 1987:14–26.
______. 1990. Gordon Castle, Morayshire, Scotland. *Int. Dendr. Soc. Yrbk.* 1990:112–115.
Lothian, N. 1979. Trees and tree planting in China. *Int. Dendr. Soc. Yrbk.* 1978:71–81.
______. 1980. Trees and tree planting in China. Part 2. *Int. Dendr. Soc. Yrbk.* 1979:89–96.
______. 1989. Unusual woody plants of the world. *Int. Dendr. Soc. Yrbk.* 1988:8.
Loudon, A. 1982. Too many deer for the trees? *New Scientist* (18 March):708–711.
Loudon, J. C. 1830. *Hortus Britannicus.* London.
______. 1838. *Arboretum et Fruticetum Britannicum.* London.
______. 1839. *Hortus Britannicus.* Supplement 2. London.
______. 1842. *Encyclopedia of Trees & Shrubs.* London.
______. 1844. *Arboretum et Fruticetum Britannicum.* 2nd ed. London.
______. 1850. *Hortus Britannicus.* New ed. London.
Loureiro, J. de. 1790. *Flora Cochinchinensis* 2:649. Lisbon.
Lovett Doust, J., and L. Lovett Doust. 1988. *Plant Reproductive Ecology.* New York: Oxford University Press.
Lovka, M., et al. 1971. IOPB chromosome number reports. XXXIV. *Taxon* 20:785–797.
Low, H. 1899. *Acer californicum aureum. Moller's Deutsche Gärtn. Zeitung*:377.
Lubbock, J. 1892. *A Contribution to Our Knowledge of Seedlings,* vol. I. New York: Appelton.
Ludwig, R. A. B. S. 1860. *Palaeontographica* 8:132,177.
Luesscher, H. 1910. Zweiter Nachtrag zur Flora des Kantons Solothurn. *Allg. Bot. Zeitschr. Karlsruhe* 16:73.
Lull, H. W. 1968. *A Forest Atlas of the Northeast.* USDA Forest Service, Northeastern Forest Experiment Station.
Lumis, G. P., et al. 1973. Sensitivity of roadside trees and shrubs to aerial drift of deicing salt. *HortScience* 8:475–477.
______. 1976. Roadside woody plant susceptibility to sodium and chloride accumulation during winter and spring. *Canadian Journal of Plant Science* 56:853–859.
Lundström-Baudais, K. 1984. Palaeo-ethnobotanical investigation of plant remains from a neolithic

lakeshore site in France: Clairvaux, Station III. In *Plants and Ancient Man.* Eds. W. Van Zeist and W. A. Casparie. Boston: Balkema.
Lyon, M. W. 1930. List of flowering plants and ferns in the Dunes State Park. *American Midland Naturalist* 12:39.
Mabberley, D. J. 1984. *Acer neapolitanum. Taxon* 33(3):454, 231.
______. 1987. *The Plant-Book. A Portable Dictionary of the Higher Plants.* Cambridge: Cambridge University Press.
Mabey, R. 1977. *Plants with a Purpose.* London: Collins.
McCain, A. H., et al. 1979. Plants resistant or susceptible to *Verticillium* wilt. University of California, Division of Agricultural Science Leaflet 2703.
McClintock, D. 1969. *A Guide to the Naming of Plants.* Horley, Surrey: The Heather Society.
______. 1981. Tour in Wiltshire and Gloucestershire, England Sept. 27 to Oct. 1, 1979. *Int. Dendr. Soc. Yrbk.* 1980:27–43.
______. 1983. Tour of northeast England 4 to 12 June 1982. *Int. Dendr. Soc. Yrbk.* 1982:33–40.
______. 1984a. Tour in Yugoslavia 27 May–9 June 1983. *Int. Dendr. Soc. Yrbk.* 1983:18–27.
______. 1984b. Dorset, Somerset and Wilts tour 1983, Oct. 21–24. *Int. Dendr. Soc. Yrbk.* 1983:28–33.
______. 1985. Tour in Jersey and Guernsey April 26–30, 1984. *Int. Dendr. Soc. Yrbk.* 1984:17–27.
______. 1986. AGM Orleans 6–9 June 1985. *Int. Dendr. Soc. Yrbk.* 1985:6–11.
______. 1989. Tour in Czechoslovakia and Hungary 24th June to 5th July 1988. *Int. Dendr. Soc. Yrbk.* 1988:55–67.
McCutchen, C. W. 1977. The spinning rotation of ash and tulip tree samaras. *Science* 197(4304):691–692.
McElhanney, T. A. 1935. *Canadian Woods: Their Properties and Uses.* Ottawa.
McGill, W. 1952. The selection of maple understock, budwood, and the timing and placements of the buds. *International Plant Propagators' Society Proceedings* 2:64–69.
McGill, W. E., and Son. 1964. *Acer rubrum* 'Autumn Flame'. *American Nurseryman* 120:31.
MacGinitie, H. D. 1933. The Trout Creek flora of southeastern Oregon. Carnegie Institute, Washington, Publication 416:61–63.
______. 1953. Fossil plants of the Florissant Beds, Colorado. Carnegie Institute, Washington, Publication 599:139–142.
______. 1974. An Early Middle Eocene Flora from the Yellowstone-Absaroka volcanic province, northwestern Wind River Basin, Wyoming. University of California Publication, geological science, 108.
McIntyre, A. C. 1932. Maple industry in Pennsylvania. Pennsylvania State Bulletin 280.
Mackenzie, K. K. 1926a. *Acer saccharum* Marsh. *Rhodora* 28:111–112.
______. 1926b. Technical name of sugar maple. *Rhodora* 28:233–234.
Macleod, J. 1894. Over de Bevruchting der Bloemen in het Kempisch Gedeelte van Vlaanderen. *Acer pseudoplatanus* L. *Bot. Jrb. Dodonea* 6:240.
McMahon, B. 1804. *A Catalogue of American Seeds.* Philadelphia, Pennsylvania.
McMillan Browse, P. D. A. 1971. Propagation of some *Acers. Gardener's Chronicle* 169(22):25.
______. 1979. *Hardy Woody Plants from Seed.* London: Grower.
______. 1990. Seed stratification—an individual exercise. Observations on the propagation of *Acer truncatum* Bunge from seed. *The Plantsman* 11(4):241–243.
McMillen, J. M. 1976. Control of reddish-brown coloration in drying maple sapwood. USDA Forest Service Research Note FPL–0231.
McNair, J. B. 1927. Sugar and sugar-making. Field Museum of Natural History Leaflet 13. Chicago.
McNeill, J. 1979. Structural value: a concept used in the construction of taxonomic classifications. *Taxon* 28:481–504.
Mader, D. L., and B. W. Thompson. 1969. Foliar and soil nutrients in relation to maple decline. In *Proceedings of the Soil Science Society of America* 33:794–800.
Maedler, K. 1939. Die Pliozäne Flora von Frankfurt am Main. *Abh. Senckenb. Naturf. Ges.* 446:112–119.
Maeglin, R. R., and L. F. Ohmann. 1973. Boxelder (*Acer negundo*): a review and a commentary. Bulletin of the Torrey Botanical Club 100:357–363.
Mägdefrau, K. 1953. *Paläobiologie der Pflanzen.* Jena: Fischer.
Mai, D. H. 1983. Studien an Endokarpien Europäischen und Westasiatischen Arten der Gattung *Acer* L. *Gleditschia* 10:37–57.
______. 1984. Die Endokarpien bei der Gattung *Acer* L. Eine Biosystematische Studie. *Gleditschia* 11:17–46.

Mai, D. H., and H. Walther. 1978. Die Floren der Haselbacher Serie im Weiszelster Becken (Bezirk Leipzig, DDR). *Abh. Staatl. Mus. Mineral. Geol. Dresden* 28:1–101.
Mairie de Paris, Direction des Parcs, Jardins et Espaces Verts. 1983. *Les Arbres Remarquables et Jardins de Paris* 37.
Majovsky, J. 1974. Index of chromosome numbers of Slovakian flora, part 4. *Acta Fac. Rerum Nat. Univ. Comenianae, Bot.* 23:1–23.
Makino, T. 1901. Observations on the flora of Japan. *Botanical Magazine, Tokyo* 15:113.
______. 1902. On *Acer pycnanthum* Koch. *Botanical Magazine, Tokyo* 16:87–94.
______. 1904. Observations on the flora of Japan. *Botanical Magazine, Tokyo* 18:114–115.
______. 1910. Observations on the flora of Japan. *Botanical Magazine, Tokyo* 24:74–75, 292–294.
______. 1912. Observations on the flora of Japan. *Botanical Magazine, Tokyo* 26:148.
______. 1940. *Illustrated Flora of Nippon.* Tokyo.
______. 1949. *Illustrated Flora of Japan.* Tokyo: Hokurya Kan.
Makino, T., and K. Nemoto. 1931. *Nippon Shokubutsu Sóran* (Flora of Japan).
Makins, F. K. 1967. *The Identification of Trees and Shrubs.* London: Dent.
Malmy, M., and P. Bouvet. 1942. Présence de québrachitol dans les feuilles d'*Acer pseudoplatanus* L. et d'*Acer platanoides* L. *J. Pharm. Chem.*, ser. 9, 2:5–10.
Maly, J. K. 1906. *Acer Bosniacum. Österr. Bot. Zeitschr.* 56:95–97.
______. 1908. Beitráge zur Kenntnis der Illyrischen Flora. Butlleti Inst. Catalana Hist. Nat. Barcelona 6:36.
Mamayev, S. A., and L. A. Semkina. 1971. The anthocyanin pigments in purple-leaved forms of certain trees and shrubs. *Rastitel'nie Resursi* 7:280–282 (in Russian).
Manenti, G. 1975. The structure of variegated leaves of *Acer negundo* L. *Israel Journal of Botany* 24:61–70.
Mani, M. S. 1964. *Ecology of Plant Galls.* The Hague: Junk.
______. 1978. *Ecology & Phytogeography of High-altitude Plants of the Northwest Himalaya.* London: Chapman & Hall.
Mani, U. V., et al. 1978. Arabinogalactanproteins (AGPs) from sycamore suspension cultures. In *Plant Research* 78:88–90.
Mansell, R. L., et al. Multiple forms and specificity of coniferyl alcohol dehydrogenase from cambial regions of higher plants. *Phytochemistry* 15:1849–1853.
Maramorosch, K., and S. P. Raychaudhuri, eds. 1981. *Mycoplasma Diseases of Trees and Shrubs.* New York: Academic Press.
Marcet, R. P. A. 1906. Notes pera la "Flora Montserratina." Butlleti Inst. Catalana Hist. Nat. Barcelona 6:36.
______. 1909. Notes pera la "Flora Montserratina." Butlleti Inst. Catalana Hist. Nat. Barcelona 9:85–87.
March, S. G. 1981. Tour of Japan April 26 to May 14, 1980. *Int. Dendr. Soc. Yrbk.* 1980:55–82.
______. 1988. Nymans and Highdown May 21st, 1986. *Int. Dendr. Soc. Yrbk.* 1987:8–14.
Marie-Victorin, Frère. 1942. Premières observations botanique sur la nouvelle route de l'Abitibi. *Contributions de l'Institut Botanique de l'Université de Montréal* 42:15–19.
______. 1944. Quelques entités phanérogamiques mineures de la flore du Quebec. *Nature Canada* 71:201–209.
______. 1964. *Flore Laurentienne.* Les Presses de l'Université de Montréal.
Marie-Victorin, Frère, and J. Rousseau. 1940. Nouvelles entitées de la flore phanérogamiques du Canada Oriental. *Contributions de l'Institut Botanique de l'Université de Montréal* 36:34.
Maries, C. 1881. Rambles of a plant collector. *The Garden.*
Marks, G. C., and T. T. Kozlowski. 1973. *Ectomycorrhizae.* New York: Academic Press.
Marshall, H. 1785. *Acer saccharum* Marsh. *Arbustrum Americanum* 1–4.
Marshall Nurseries (Lisle, Illinois). 1952. *Acer saccharinum* 'Blair'. Morton Arboretum Bulletin 27:22.
Marshall, R. 1953. *Brimfield Gardens Nursery Catalogue.*
Marshall, R. P., and A. M. Waterman. 1948. Common diseases of important shade trees. Farmers' Bulletin 1987. Washington, DC: USDA.
Martin, L. 1949. Red-fruited form of *Acer negundo. Canadian Field Naturalist* 63:213.
Martin, P. S., and C. M. Drew. 1969. Scanning electronic micrographs of southwestern pollen grains. *Journal of the Arizona Academy of Science, Tucson* 5:147–176.
Martineau, R. 1984. Insects harmful to forest trees. Agriculture Canadian Government Publications Centre. Ottawa: Supply Services.

Marvin, J. W. 1958. The physiology of maple sap flow. In *The Physiology of Forest Trees.* Ed. K. V. Thimann. New York: Ronald Press.
Marx, D. H., and N. C. Schenck. 1983. Potential of mycorrhizal symbiosis in agricultural and forest productivity. In *Challenging Problems in Plant Health.* Eds. T. Kommedahl and P. H. Williams. St. Paul: American Phytopathological Society.
Masamune, G. 1934. Floristic and geobotanical studies on the island of Yakushima. *Memoirs of the Faculty of Science and Agriculture, Taihoku Imperial University* 11.
Maskell, S. F. 1976. I.D.S. tour of eastern Ireland May 1975. *Int. Dendr. Soc. Yrbk.* 1975:69–79.
Massolongo, A. B. 1851. *Sopra le Piante Fossili dei Terreni Terziarj del Vicentino Osservazioni.* Padova.
______. 1853. Descrizione di alcune piante fossili Terziarie dell' Italia meridionale. *N. Ann. Sci. Nat. Bologna* 1853:196–197.
______. 1854. Prodromus florae fossilis Senogalliensis. *Giorn. Ist. Lombardo Sci.,* n.s., 5:215.
______. 1859a. *Studii sulla Flora Fossile e Geologia Stratigrafica del Senigalliese.* II. Imola.
______. 1859b. *Syllabus Plantae Fossilius.* Verona.
Masson, F. 1776. An account of three journeys from Cape Town. *Philos. Transactions of the Royal Society* 66.
Masters, M. T. 1877. *Acer Van Volxemii. Gardener's Chronicle* II. 7:72.
______. 1891. *Acer Volxemii. Gardener's Chronicle* III. 10:188–189.
Mathews, F. S. 1908. *Familiar Trees and Their Leaves.* New York: Appelton.
______. 1915. *Field Book of American Trees and Shrubs.* New York: Putnam.
Mathias, M. E., and E. M. McClintock. 1963. A checklist of woody ornamental plants of California. California Agricultural Experiment Station Extension Service Manual 32:3–4.
Matsumura, J. 1898. Notes on Liu Kiu and Formosan plants. *Botanical Magazine, Tokyo* 12:63.
Matsumura, Y. 1954. Maples of Japan. *Arb. Bulletin* 17:105–111.
Matthews, B. 1984. Why so many tree diseases? *Journal of the Royal Horticultural Society* 109:467–470.
Maurice Mason, L. 1985. The gardens at Talbot Manor and Larchwood, Norfolk. *Int. Dendr. Soc. Yrbk.* 1984:71–79.
Maurizio, A., and J. Louveaux. 1960. Pollens des plantes mellifères d'Europe. I. *Pollen & Spores* 2:159–182.
Maximov, N. A. 1938. *Plant Physiology.* New York: McGraw-Hill.
Maximowicz, C. J. 1857. *A tegmentosum* Maxim., *A. mono* Maxim. Ueber die Wichtigeren Bäume und Sträucher des Amurlandes. Bulletin de la classe Physico-Mathematique de l'Académie Impériale des Sciences de St. Pétersbourg 15:125–126.
______. 1859. Primitiae florae Amurensis. *Mémoirs Sav. Etr. de l'Acad*émie *Imp*é*riale des Sciences de St. P*étersbourg 9:65–68.
______. 1867. *Acer capillipes* Maxim., *A. mandshuricum* Maxim., *A. argutum* Maxim., *A. barbinerve* Maxim. Diagnoses breves plantarum novarum Japoniae et Mandshuriae. VI. Bulletin de l'Académie Impériale des Sciences de St. Pétersbourg 12:225–228.
______. 1872–1876. Diagnoses plantarum novarum Japoniae et Manshuriae. Melanges Biologiques Tires du Bulletin de l'Académie Impériale des Sciences de St. Pétersbourg 8, 9.
______. 1880. Diagnoses plantarum novarum Asiaticarum. III. Bulletin de l'Academie Impériale des Sciences de St. Pétersbourg 26:436–451.
______. 1882. Diagnoses plantarum novarum Asiaticarum. IV. Bulletin de l'Académie Impériale des Sciences de St. Pétersbourg 27:559–560, t. 27.
______. 1886. *A. tschonoskii* Maxim. Diagnoses plantarum novarum Asiaticarum. VI. Bulletin de l'Académie Impériale des Sciences de St. Pétersbourg 31:24–27.
______. 1888. *A. miyabei* Maxim. Diagnoses plantarum novarum Asiaticarum. VII. Bulletin de l'Académie Impériale des Sciences de St. Pétersbourg 32:485–486.
______. 1889. Plantae Chinenses Potanininae. *Acta Horti Petrop.* 11:105–109.
May, C. 1961. *Diseases of Shade and Ornamental Maples.* Agriculture Handbook no. 211. Washington, DC: USDA Forest Service.
Mayer, A. M., and A. Poljakoff–Mayber. 1975. *The Germination of Seeds.* 2nd ed. Oxford: Pergamon.
Mayer, A. M. and I. Marbach. 1981. Biochemistry of the transition from resting to germinating state in seeds. In *Progress in Phytochemistry,* vol. 7. Eds. L. Reinhold et al. Oxford: Pergamon.
Medikus, F. K. 1801. *Pflanzenanatomie.* Leipzig.
Medina, J. M. M. 1951. Breves recorridos botánicos por el Marruecos Espagnol. *Anal. Inst. Bot. A. J. Cavanilles Madrid* 10:360–364.
Medvedev, I. S. 1880. *Izv. Kavkazsk. Obshch. Liubit. Estestv.* 2:9.

Meehan, T. 1888. The varieties of Japanese maples. *American Garden* 9:140–141.
______. 1879a. Notes on *Acer rubrum.* In *Proceedings of the Academy of Natural Science, Philadelphia* 1878:122–123.
______. 1879b. The law governing sex. In *Proceedings of the Academy of Natural Science, Philadelphia* 1879:267–268.
______. 1889. Contributions to the life-histories of plants. III. In *Proceedings of the Academy of Natural Science, Philadelphia* 1888:391–394.
______. 1891. Contributions to the life-histories of plants. V. On the male and hermaphrodite flowers of *Aesculus parviflora.* In *Proceedings of the Academy of Natural Science, Philadelphia* 1890:274–275.
Meeuse, B. J. D. 1961. *The Story of Pollination.* New York: Ronald Press.
Meeuse, B. J. D., and S. Morris. 1984. *The Sex Life of Flowers.* London: Faber & Faber.
Mehra, P. V. et al. 1972. Cytological studies of Himalayan Aceraceae, Hippocastanaceae, Sapindaceae and Staphylaceae. *Sylvae Genet.* 21:96–102.
Meikle, R. D. 1977. *Flora of Cyprus.* The Bentham-Moxon Trust, The Royal Botanic Gardens, Kew.
Melle, P. J. van. 1947. Debuts of woody plants in cultivation. *Phytologia* 2:7.
Menninger, E. A. 1975. *Fantastic Trees.* New York: Viking. Rpt. Stuart, Florida: Hort. Books.
Menzies, A. 1792. *A Diary of His Journey in North West America.* Unpublished. See Naish 1989.
Merrill, E. D. 1906. New or noteworthy Philippine plants 2. Philippine Bur. Govt. Lab. Bulletin 35:36.
______. 1909. New or noteworthy Philippine plants 7. *Philippine J. Sci. Bot.* 4:285.
______. 1932. A fourth supplementary list of Hainan plants. *Lingnan Science Journal* 11:47.
______. 1941. The Upper Burma plants collected by Capt. F. Kingdon Ward on the Vernay-Cutting Expedition, 1938–39. *Brittonia* 4:107–110.
Merrill, E. D., and F. P. Metcalf. 1937. *A. confertifolium* Merr. & Metc. New Kwangtung plants. *Lingnan Science Journal* 16:167–168.
Messenger, A. S. 1984. Seasonal variations of foliar nutrients in green and chlorotic red maples. *Journal of Environmental Horticulture* 2:117–119.
Metcalf, F. P. 1932. Series Penninervia, *Acer lucidum* Metc., *A. sino-oblongum* Metc. *Acer* (Section Integrifolia Pax) for southeastern China. *Lingnan Science Journal* 11:193–210, t. 3.
______. 1933. Notes on Fang's Chinese Aceraceae. *Lingnan Science Journal* 12:135.
______. 1942. Additional notes on *Acer. Lingnan Science Journal* 20:219–226.
Meurman, O. 1933. Chromosome morphology, somatic doubling and secondary association in *Acer platanoides* L. *Hereditas* 18:145–173.
Meusel, H., et al. 1976. *Vergleichende Chorologie der Zentraleuropäischen Flora.* II. Jena.
Meyer, B. S., and D. B. Anderson. 1939. *Plant Physiology.* New York: Van Nostrand.
Meyer, C. A. 1831. *Verzeichniss* der Pflanzen ... in Caucasus und ... des Caspischen Meeres Gefunden. St. Petersburg.
Meyer, F. G. 1959. *Acer palmatum* 'Cinnabar Wooded'. USDA ARS 34–9:93.
Meyer, F. H. 1990. Turkish *Acer* species. *Int. Dendr. Soc. Yrbk.* 1990:48–49.
Meyer, F. H., et al. 1978. *Bäume in der Stadt.* Stuttgart: Ulmer.
Michaux, A. 1803. *Flora Boreali-Americana* 2:252–253. Paris.
Michaux, F. A. 1812. *Histoire des arbres forestiers de l'Amérique Septentrionale.* Paris.
______. 1817. *The North American Sylva.* 2 vols. Philadelphia: Dobson.
Mielke, J. L. 1935. *Verticillium* wilt of maple in California. *Plant Disease Reporter* 19:303.
Miki, S. 1941. On the change of flora in eastern Asia since Tertiary period. *Journal of Japanese Botany* 11:283.
Milborrow, B. V., ed. 1973. *Biosynthesis and its Control in Plants.* New York: Academic Press.
Millar Gault, S. 1986. The Windlesham Trophy. Prison Gardens. *Journal of the Royal Horticultural Society* 111:293–295.
Miller, J. 1826. *A Catalogue of Forest Trees.* Bristol.
Miller, P. 1752. *The Gardener's Dictionary.* 6th ed. London.
______. 1755. *Figures of the Most Beautiful, Useful, and Uncommon Plants Described in the Gardener's Dictionary.* London.
______. 1759. *The Gardener's Dictionary.* 7th ed. London.
______. 1768. *The Gardener's Dictionary.* 8th ed. London.
______. 1771. *The Gardener's Dictionary.* 6th ed. abridged. London.
Milton Nursery. 1964. *Acer platanoides* 'Miller's Superform'. *American Nurseryman* 120(3):10.
Minnigerode, L. Freiherr von. 1923. Starkes *Acer platanoides. Mitt. Dtsch. Dendr. Ges.* 33:225–226.

Minter, D. W., and P. F. Cannon. 1984. Ascospore discharge in some members of the *Rhytismataceae. Transactions of the British Mycological Society* 83:65–92.
Miquel, F. A. W. 1857. In Miquel and Groenewegen's *Catalogus Horti Botanici Amstelodamensis.* Amsterdam.
______. 1859. *Flora Indiae Batavae.* Amsterdam.
______. 1865. *A. sieboldianum* Miq., *A. buergerianum* Miq. prolusio florae Japonicae. *Ann. Mus. Bot. Lugd. Bat.* 2:86–90.
______. 1867a. Prolusio florae Japonicae. *Ann. Mus. Bot. Lugd. Bat.* 3:200.
______. 1867b. Sur les érables du Japon. *Arch. Néerl.* 2:467–479.
______. 1870. *A. palmatum* Thunb. In *Flora Japonica,* by P. F. von Siebold and J. G. Zuccarini. Leiden.
Mir, I. et al. 1975. Constituents of *Acer pentapomicum. Pakistan J. Sci. Industr. Res.* 18:91–92.
Mitsukashi, H. 1976. Medicinal plants of the Ainu. *Economic Botany* 30:209–217.
Mitchell, A. F. 1972. The snake-bark maples. *Quarterly Journal of Forestry* 65:1–20.
______. 1974a. *A Field Guide to Great Britain and Northern Europe.* London: Collins.
______. 1974b. Measure a tree in '73. *Int. Dendr. Soc. Yrbk.* 1973:23–29.
______. 1975a. *The Complete Guide to Trees of Great Britain and Northern Europe.* Limpsfield: Dragon's World.
______. 1975b. Measure a tree in '74. *Int. Dendr. Soc. Yrbk.* 1974:34–39.
______. 1976. Measure a tree in '75. *Int. Dendr. Soc. Yrbk.* 1975:28–36.
______. 1981. *The Gardener's Book of Trees.* London: Dent.
______. 1982. Leaves from a tree-measurer's diary 1981. *Int. Dendr. Soc. Yrbk.* 1981:89–93.
______. 1983. Leaves from a tree-measurer's diary 1981–2. *Int. Dendr. Soc. Yrbk.* 1982:57–62.
______. 1984. Leaves from a tree-measurer's diary. *Int. Dendr. Soc. Yrbk.* 1983:37–42.
______. 1985. Leaves from a tree-measurer's diary. *Int. Dendr. Soc. Yrbk.* 1984:85–91.
______. 1986a. Leaves from a tree-measurer's diary. *Int. Dendr. Soc. Yrbk.* 1985:106–111.
______. 1986b. The Garden at Cracknells. *Journal of the Royal Horticultural Society* 111:462–466.
Mitchell, A. F., and V. Hallett. 1988. Leaves from a tree-measurer's diary. *Int. Dendr. Soc. Yrbk.* 1987:113–131.
Mitchell, A. F., and D. More. 1987. *The Trees of North America.* New York: Facts on File.
Mitchell, A. F., et al. 1990. *Champion Trees in the British Isles.* Field Book 10, Forestry Commission. London: H.M.S.O.
Mitchell, J., and A. Rook. 1979. *Botanical Dermatology.* Vancouver: Greengrass.
Mitscher, L. A. 1975. Antimicrobial agents from higher plants. In *Recent Advances in Phytochemistry,* vol. 9. Ed. V. C. Runeckles. New York: Plenum.
Miyabe, K. 1895. *Acer lobelii* var. *platanoides. Botanical Magazine, Tokyo* 9:346.
Miyabe, K., and C. Suzaki. 1920–1922. *Ikones of the Essential Forest Trees of Hokkaido.* Published by the Hokkaido Government, 1920–1923. Rpt. Hokkaido University Press, 1984.
Miyabe, K., and M. Tatewaki. 1938. *Trans. Sapporo Nat. Hist.* 15:206.
Mizushima, M. 1956. Identity of some forms of *Acer mono. Journal of Japanese Botany* 31:285–286.
______. 1964. Materials for the distribution of vascular plants in Japan: *Acer capillipes* Maxim. *Journal of Japanese Botany* 39:347.
Moench, K. 1794. *Negundo aceroides. Methodus Plantas Horti Botanici et Agri Marburgensis* 334. Marburg.
Mohl, H. 1835. Sur la structure et les formes des graines de pollen. *Annuelles des Sciences Naturelles et Botanique,* ser. 2, 3:148–180, 220–236, 304–346.
Moldenke, H. N. 1937. *Saccharodendron Saccharum. Revista Sudam. Bot.* 5:2.
______. 1944. A contribution to our knowledge of the wild and cultivated flora of Ohio. I. *Castanea* 9:53.
Moller Nursery. 1965. *Catalogue.* Gresham, Oregon.
Molliard, M. 1903. *Acer lanceolatum.* Bulletin de la Sociéte Botanique de France 50:134–135.
Momotani, Y. 1961. Taxonomic study of the genus *Acer* with special reference to the seed proteins. I. Taxonomic characters. *Mem. Coll. Sci. Univ. Kyoto,* ser. B, 28(3):455–470.
______. 1962a. II. Analysis of protein. *Mem. Coll. Sci. Univ. Kyoto* 29(1):81–102.
______. 1962b. III. System of Aceraceae. *Mem. Coll. Sci. Univ. Kyoto* 29(3):177–189.
______. 1962c. Taxonomic significance of seed proteins with special reference to the system of the Genus *Acer.* In *Proceedings of the 27th Annual Meeting of the Botany Society of Japan.*
Monachino, J. 1960. The internal characteristics of winter buds. Bulletin of the Torrey Botanical Club 87:419–421.

Monnard, J. P. 1836. In *Synopsis Florae Helveticae,* by J. Gaudin. Turici.
Moor, M. 1974. Zwei Artenreiche Bestände des Lerchensporn-Ahornwaldes im Berner Jura. *Bauhinia, Zeitschr. Basl. Bot. Ges.* 5(2):95–100.
Moore, D. M., ed. 1982. *Green Planet: The Story of Plant Life on Earth.* New York: Cambridge University Press.
Moore, R. J., ed. 1971. *Index to Plant Chromosome Numbers for 1969.* Regnum vegetabile 77.
______. 1977. *Index to Plant Chromosome Numbers for 1973–1974.* Regnum vegetabile 96.
Moore, W. C. 1959. *British Parasitic Fungi.* Cambridge: Cambridge University Press.
Mori, O. 1962. *Typical Japanese Gardens.* Tokyo: Shibata.
Morot, L. 1900. *Journal Botanique* (Février).
Morren, E., and A. de Vos. 1887. *Index Bibliographique de l'Hortus Belgicus.* Gand.
Morse, F. W., and A. H. Wood. 1895. The composition of maple sap. New Hampshire Agricultural Experiment Station Bulletin 25.
Morsink, W. A. G., and E. Jorgensen. 1974. *Propagation and Selection of Sugar Maple* Acer saccharum *(Marsh) in Ontario.* Ontario Ministry of Natural Resources.
Mortensen, H. 1878. In J. Lange and Mortensen's Oversigt over de i Aarene 1872–78 i Denmark. *Bot. Tidsskr.* III. 10:253.
Morton Arboretum. 1952. *Acer saccharinum* 'Blair'. Morton Arboretum Bulletin 27:22.
Morwood, W. 1973. *Traveller in a Vanished Landscape.* New York: Clarkson N. Potter.
Mottier, D. M. 1883. Development of embryo sac in *Acer rubrum. Botanical Gazette* 18:375–377.
______. 1914. Mitosis in the pollen mother-cells of *Acer negundo* L., and *Staphylea trifolia* L. *Ann. Bot.* 28:115–133.
Mouillefert, P. 1895. *Traité des arbres et arbrisseaux forestiers.* Paris.
Mouterde, P. 1947. La végétation arborescente de pays du Levant. *Publ. Techn. Sci. Ecole Franc. d'Ingénieurs.* Beirut.
Muenscher, W. C. 1946. *Key to Woody Plants.* New York: Comstock.
Mulcahy, D. L. 1975. Differential mortality among cohorts in a population of *Acer saccharum* (Aceraeae) seedlings. *American Journal of Botany* 62:422–426.
Mulder ten Kate, M. J., and H. Karaca. 1990. Turkey's Black Sea region. *Int. Dendr. Soc. Yrbk.* 1990:64–68.
Mulhern, J., et al. 1979. Barrier zones in red maple: an optical and scanning microscope examination. *Forest Science* 25:311–316.
Muller, F. M. 1978. *Seedlings of the north-western European lowland.* The Hague: Junk.
Muller, J., and P. W. Leenhouts. 1976. A general survey of pollen types in sapindaceae in relation to taxonomy. In *The Evolutionary Significance of the Exine.* Eds. I. K. Ferguson and J. Muller. New York: Academic Press.
Müller, K. 1912. Über das Biologische Verhalten von *Rhytisma acerinum* auf Verschiedenen Ahornarten. *Ber. Dtsch. Bot. Ges.* 1912:385.
Muller, K. K., et al. 1974. *Trees of Santa Barbara.* Santa Barbara Botanic Garden, California.
Mulligan, B. O. 1954. An upright Oregon maple. University of Washington Arboretum Bulletin 17:112.
______. 1958. *Maples Cultivated in the United States and Canada.* Lancaster, Pennsylvania: American Association of Botanic Gardens and Arboreta.
______. 1971. Maples in the north western U.S.A. *Int. Dendr. Soc. Yrbk.* 1970:12–19.
______. 1974. A form of *Acer circinatum* with variegated leaves. *Baileya* 19:111–114.
______. 1977a. *Acer erianthum. Int. Dendr. Soc. Yrbk.* 1976:56–57.
______. 1977b. *Woody Plants in the University of Washington Arboretum, Washington Park.* Seattle: University of Washington Press.
______. 1981. A rare maple in the arboretum, *Acer tegmentosum.* University of Washington Arboretum Bulletin 44(4):15–16.
Mulloy, M. S. 1976. Variability in Japanese maples. American Rock Garden Society Bulletin 24.
______. 1977. Variability in Japanese maples. *Bonsai Journal* 11:56–58.
Munns, E. N. 1938. The distribution of important forest trees of the United States. USDA Miscellaneous Publication 287. Washington, DC.
Munting, A. 1696. *Beschrijving der Aardgewassen.* Leiden: Van der AA & Halma.
Murray, A. E. 1966. New combinations of Asiatic subspecies of *Acer.* Morris Arboretum Bulletin 17:51.
______. 1969a. *Acer* notes nos. 1–6. *Kalmia* 1:1–42.
______. 1969b. Aceraceae. In *Flora Iranica.* Ed. K. H. Rechinger. 61:1–11.

______. 1970a. *Acer* notes no. 7. *Kalmia* 2:1.
______. 1970b. Key to the subgenera of the genus *Acer. Kalmia* 2:2.
______. 1970c. *A Monograph of the Aceraceae.* Ph.D. thesis, Pennsylvania State University.
______. 1970d. Key to the sections and series of *Acer.* Subgenus *Acer. Kalmia* 2:3–4.
______. 1970e. Sections of the genus *Acer. Kalmia* 2:5–8.
______. 1970f. Series of the genus *Acer. Kalmia* 2:9–20.
______. 1970g. Addenda to a monograph of Aceraceae. Unpublished.
______. 1970h. Bibliography for *Acer* subgenera, sections and series. *Kalmia* 2:21–22.
______. 1970i. A checklist of species of *Acer. Kalmia* 2:22–45.
______. 1971a. *Acer,* infraspecific taxa. *Kalmia* 3:1–28.
______. 1971b. *Acer glabrum* ssp. *diffusum* (Greene) Murr., A. E. *Kalmia* 3(4):14.
______. 1974a. Himalayan maples. *Kalmia* 6:2.
______. 1974b. Key to the native maples of Pakistan (Western Himalayan species). *Kalmia* 6:3–8.
______. 1975a. Aceraceae. In *Flora of West Pakistan,* by E. Nasir and S.I. Ali.
______. 1975b. North American maples. *Kalmia* 7:1–20.
______. 1977. New Asiatic taxa in *Acer. Kalmia* 8:2–12.
______. 1978a. The genus *Dipteronia. Kalmia* 8:14–16.
______. 1978b. *Acer* notes no. 8. *Kalmia* 8:17–20.
______. 1979. Afrasian and European maples. *Kalmia* 9:2–39.
______. 1980a. *Acer* notes no. 9. *Kalmia* 10:2.
______. 1980b. Guatemalan maples. *Kalmia* 10:3–4.
______. 1980c. Mexican maples. *Kalmia* 10:5–8.
______. 1981a. *Acer* of North America. Key to the species. *Kalmia* 11:3–8.
______. 1981b. *Acer* notes no. 10. *Kalmia* 11:7.
______. 1982a. Infrageneric taxa in *Acer* (Aceraceae). *Kalmia* 12:2–16.
______. 1982b. *Acer* notes no. 11. *Kalmia* 12:17.
______. 1983a. *Acer* notes no. 12. *Kalmia* 13:2.
______. 1983b. Spermatophyte notes no. 2. *Kalmia* 13:3–21.
______. 1985a. *Index to all New Combinations of Papers in* Kalmia *Vols. 1–15. Kalmia* 15:19–22.
______. 1985b. Distributio Aceracearum Americae Borealis donatur. *Kalmia* 15:2–11.
______. 1985c. *Acer* notes no. 13. *Kalmia* 15:11.
Murray, J. A. 1784. *Systema Vegetabilium,* 14th ed. Stafleu & Cowan 1981, 3:670.
Myczkowski, S. 1973. Native tree species of the Tatra National Park. *Int. Dendr. Soc. Yrbk.* 1972:70–80.
Nadel, I. B., et al. 1977. *Trees in the City.* New York: Pergamon.
Nair, P. K. K. 1970. *Pollen Morphology of Angiosperms.* Delhi: Vikas.
Naish, J. 1989. Archibald Menzies: Surgeon and Botanist. *Int. Dendr. Soc. Yrbk.* 1988:123–128.
Naito, A. 1977. *Katsura: A Princely Retreat.* Tokyo: Kodansha.
Nakahara, S. 1982. Checklist of the armored scales (Homoptera: Diaspididae) of the conterminous United States. USDA, APHIS, Plant Protection and Quarantine.
Nakai, T. 1909. Flora Koreana. *J. Coll. Sci. Univ. Tokyo* 26:131–136.
______. 1914. Plantae novae Japonicae et Koreanae. *Botanical Magazine, Tokyo* 28:308.
______. 1915a. Praecursores ad floram sylvaticam Koreanam. *Botanical Magazine, Tokyo* 29:25–30.
______. 1915b. *Flora Sylvatica Koreana* 1:23.
______. 1917. Notulae ad plantas Japoniae et Koreae. XIII. *Botanical Magazine, Tokyo* 31:28.
______. 1918. Notulae ad plantas Japoniae et Koreae. XVII. *Botanical Magazine, Tokyo* 32:107.
______. 1919. Notulae ad plantas Japoniae et Koreae. XX. *Botanical Magazine, Tokyo* 33:59–60.
______. 1926. Notulae ad plantas Japoniae et Koreae. XXXIII. *Botanical Magazine, Tokyo* 40:584–585.
______. 1927. *Flora Sylvatica Koreana* 16:34.
______. 1931. Notulae ad plantas Japoniae et Koreae. XL. *Botanical Magazine, Tokyo* 45:123–127.
______. 1932. *A. mono* var. Mayrii (Schwer.) Sugimoto. Notulae ad Plantas Japoniae et Koreae. XLII. *Botanical Magazine, Tokyo* 46:608–614.
______. 1935. Notulae ad plantas Japoniae et Koreae. XLVI. *Botanical Magazine, Tokyo* 49:418.
______. 1937. *Acer* novum Japonicum. *Botanical Magazine, Tokyo* 51:364–366.
______. 1942. Notulae ad plantas Asiae Orientalis. XXII. *Journal of Japanese Botany* 18:608–614.
______. 1950. Notulae ad plantas Asiae Orientalis. XXXV. *Journal of Japanese Botany* 25:133.
Nakai, T., and G. Koidzumi. 1927. *Trees and Shrubs Indigenous in Japan Proper.* Tokyo: Seibido Shoten.
Nakamura, T., et al. 1974. *Momiji & Kaede.* Seibundo Shinkosha, Tokyo.

N.A.K.B., see Nederlandse Algemene Keuringsdienst voor Boomkwekerijgewassen.
Napierville Nursery. 1934. *General Price List.* Napierville, Ohio.
Narayanan, V., and R. Seshadri. 1969. Chemical components of *Acer rubrum* wood and bark: occurrence of procyanidin dimer and trimer. *Indian Journal of Chemistry* 7:213–214.
Natarajan, G. 1978. IOPB chromosome number reports. LXII. *Taxon* 27:526–531.
Nathorst, A. G. 1883. Nya bidrag till kännedomen om Spetsbergens Kärlväxter. *Sv. Vet.-Akad. Handl.* 20(2):60, 85.
______. 1888. Fossil Flora Japans. *Paleontology* 4:26.
Nearing, H., and S. Nearing. 1950. *The Maple Sugar Book.* New York: John Day.
Nederlandse Algemene Keuringsdienst voor Boomkwekerijgewassen. 1958. *Rassenlijst voor Loofhoutgewassen.* Boskoop, The Netherlands. 9–10.
Neely, D., and W. R. Crowley, Jr. 1974. Toxicity of soil-applied herbicides to shade trees. *HortScience* 9:147–149.
Negulescu, E. G., and A. Sávulescu. 1965. *Dendrologie.* 2nd ed. Bucharest: Agro-Silvica.
Neilreich, A. 1846. *Flora von Wien.* Vienna.
Neiswander, R. B. 1966. Insect and mite pests of trees and shrubs. Ohio Agriculture Research and Development Center, Research Bulletin 983.
Nelson, E. C. 1985. *Trees & Shrubs Cultivated in Ireland.* Dublin: Boethius.
______. 1987. A letter to Mr. Forsyth, Chelsea Physic Garden. *Int. Dendr. Soc. Yrbk.* 1986:107–109.
Nemoto, K. 1936. *Flora of Japan.* Tokyo.
Netolitzky, F. 1926. Anatomie der Angiospermen-Samen. Band X. *Handbuch der Pflanzenanatomie.* Ed. K. Linsbauer. Berlin: Borntraeger.
Neumann et al., eds. 1985. *Primary and Secondary Metabolism of Plant Cell Cultures.* Berlin: Springer-Verlag.
Neunzig, H. H. 1972. Taxonomy of *Acrobasis* larvae and pupae in eastern North America. USDA Technical Bulletin 1457.
Newberry, J. S. 1870. Notes on the later extinct floras of North America. *Ann. Lyc. Nat. Hist. N.Y.* 9:15, 57.
______. 1895. The flora of the Amboy Clays. U.S. Geological Survey Monograph 26:1–260.
______. 1898. The later extinct floras of North America. U.S. Geological Survey.
Newsom, S. 1960. *A Dwarfed Tree Manual for Westerners.* Tokyo: Tokyo News Service.
Newton, W. G., and D. C. Allen. 1982. Characteristics of trees damaged by sugar maple borer, *Glycobius speciosus* Say. *Canadian Journal of Forest Research* 12:738–744.
Nicholson, G. 1881. The Kew Arboretum. The maples. I–XVI. *Gardener's Chronicle,* n.s., 15:10, 42, 74–75, 136 137, 141, 172, 268, 299, 364, 499, 532, 564, 725, 788.
______. 1882. The Kew Arboretum. The maples. I–XVI. *Gardener's Chronicle,* n.s., 16:75, 136, 375, 590, 719, 750, 815.
Nicholson, B. E., and A. R. Clapham. 1975. *The Oxford Book of Trees.* London: Oxford University Press.
Nicholson, P. 1968. *V. Sackville-West's Garden Book.* London: Michael Joseph.
Nicotra, L. 1893. Note sopra alcune piante di Sicilia. *Malpighia* 7:83.
Nieuwland, J. A. A. 1910. *Negundo texana. American Midland Naturalist* 1:163.
______. 1911. Box-elders, real and so-called. *American Midland Naturalist* 2:129–142.
______. 1914. Critical notes on new and old genera of plants. I. *American Midland Naturalist* 3:181–183.
Niklas, K. J. 1979. An assessment of chemical features for the classification of plant fossils. *Taxon* 28:505–516.
______. 1980. Paleobiochemical techniques and their application to paleobotany. In *Progress in Phytochemistry,* vol. 6. Eds. L. Reinhold et al. New York: Pergamon.
Niklas, K. J., ed. 1981. *Paleobotany, Paleoecology, and Evolution.* 2 vols. New York: Praeger.
Niklas, K. J., and D. E. Giannasi. 1978. Angiosperm paleobiochemistry of the Succor Creek Flora (Miocene) Oregon. *American Journal of Botany* 65:943–952.
Niklfield, H. 1971. Bericht über die Kartierung der Flora Mitteleuropas. *Taxon* 20(4):545–571.
Nilsson, S. 1832. Fossila Växter Funna i Skåne och Beskrifne. *Sv. Vet.-Akad. Handl.* 1831:345.
Nitecki, M. H. 1982. *Biochemical Aspects of Evolutionary Biology.* Chicago: University of Chicago Press.
Nitsch, J. P., and C. Nitsch. 1965. Présence de phytokinines et autres substances de croissance dans la sève d'*Acer saccharum* et de *Vitis vinifera.* Bulletin de la Société Botanique de France 112:11–18.

Norberg, R. A. 1973. Autorotation, self-stability, and structure of single-winged fruits and seeds (samaras) with comparative remarks on animal flight. *Biological Reviews of the Cambridge Philosophical Society* 48(4):561–596.
Nordin, V. J. 1954. Studies in forest pathology XIII. Decay in sugar maple in the Ottawa-Huron and Algoma extension forest region of Ontario. *Canadian Journal of Botany* 32:221–258.
Nordine, R. M. 1962. Collection, storage and germination of maple seed. *International Plant Propagators' Society Proceedings* 2:62.
Northcote, D. H. 1963. Changes in the cell walls of plants during differentiation. *Symposium, Society for Experimental Biology* 17:157–174.
______. 1977. *Plant Biochemistry. II.* Vol. 13 of *International Review of Biochemistry.* Baltimore, Maryland: University Park Press.
Northcote, D. H., and F. P. B. Wooding. 1966. Development of sieve tubes in *Acer pseudoplatanus. Proceedings of the Royal Society of London* (B) 163:524–536.
Northen, H. T., and R. T. Northen. 1954. *The Secret of a Green Thumb.* London: Harrap.
Northington, D. K., and J. R. Goodin. 1984. *The Botanical World.* St. Louis: Times Mirror/Mosby.
Nozzolillo, C. 1972. The site and chemical nature of red pigmentation in seedlings. *Canadian Journal of Botany* 50:29–34.
Numata, M. 1975. *Flora & Vegetation of Japan.* Tokyo: Kodansha; Amsterdam: Elsevier.
Nuttall, T. 1818. *The Genera of North American Plants* 1:252–253. Philadelphia.
______. 1846. *The North American Sylva* 2:211–253. Philadelphia.
Oever, J. J. W. M. van den. 1990. *Catalogue.* Haaren: Van den Oever.
Ogata, K. 1964. On the varieties of *Acer mono* found in Japan. *Journal of Geobotany, University of Tokyo* 12:94–97; 13:15–18, 34–38.
______. 1965a. A dendrological study of the Japanese Aceraceae. Bull. Tokyo Univ. Forests no. 60:1–99.
______. 1965b. On *Acer pycnanthum. Journal of Geobotany, University of Tokyo* 13:102–109.
______. 1967. A systematic study of the Aceraceae. Bull. Tokyo Univ. Forests no. 63:89–206.
Oheimb, F. von. 1927. Meine Schönen Ahorne. *Mitt. Dtsch. Dendr. Ges.* 38:270–271.
Ohman, J. H. 1968. Decay and discoloration of sugar maple. USDA Forest Service, Forest Pest Leaflet 110.
Ohwi, J. 1953. New names and new combinations adopted in my "Flora of Japan." Bull. Nat. Sci. Mus. Tokyo 33:79.
______. 1965. *Flora of Japan.* Washington, DC: Smithsonian Institution.
Oldershausen, J. Freifrau von. 1928. Riesiges *Acer campestre. Mitt. Dtsch. Dendr. Ges.* 40:342.
Oliver, D. 1889. *Dipteronia sinensis.* In Hooker's *Icon. Pl.* 19, t. 1898.
Olmsted, F. L., et al. 1923. *Standardized Plant Names.* Salem, Massachusetts.
Olson, D. F., and W. J. Gabriel. 1974. Aceraceae—maple family: *Acer* L. In *Seeds of Woody Plants in the United States.* Agriculture Handbook. no. 450:187–194. Washington, DC: USDA Forest Service.
Olver, C. 1988. Tour of Turkey June 8th–21st, 1987. *Int. Dendr. Soc. Yrbk.* 1987:32–41.
Omar, W. 1962. The grafting of *Acer palmatum. International Plant Propagators' Society Proceedings* 12:256–257.
O'Neill, J. 1990. New Zealand Feb. 4th–March 4th, 1990. South Island. *Int. Dendr. Soc. Yrbk.* 1990:79–94.
Opiz, F. M. 1824a. *Naturalientausch* (1):6.
______. 1824b. *Naturalientausch* (6):48–49.
______. 1824c. Nachtrag zu Meinem Phanerogamischen Gewächsen Boheims. *Flora* 7(1):82–83.
______. 1825. *Naturalientausch* (9):114.
______. 1839. *Oekon. Neuigk. Verhandl.* 552.
______. 1852. *Seznam Rostlin Kvéteny Ceské* 42. Prague.
______. 1853. Nachtrag zu Meinem Seznam Rostlin Kvéteny Ceské. *Lotos* 3:63.
Orton, E. R. 1978. Single-node cuttings: a simple method for the rapid propagation of plants of selected clones of *Acer rubrum* L. *The Plant Propagator* 24:12–15.
Osti, L. 1989. *Abies nebrodensis. Int. Dendr. Soc. Yrbk.* 1988:80–81.
Oterdoom, H. J. 1980. *Maples in Japan.* Unpublished report of I.D.S. Tour Japan.
______. 1982. A visit to China. *Int. Dendr. Soc. Yrbk.* 1981:20–33.
______. 1988. *Acer griseum,* a remarkable tree. *Groen* 44(12):43–44.
______. Maples of the world. *Int. Dendr. Soc. Yrbk.* 1990:11–12.
______. 1990b. Paleobotany and evolution of the maples. *Int. Dendr. Soc. Yrbk.* 1990:12–13.

Otto, E. 1883. Neuheiten von Harten Gehölzarten. *Hamburger Garten- und Blumenzeitung* 39:511–512.

Ottolander, K. J. W., et al. 1879. *Flora & Pomona.* 2 vols. Groningen: Wolters.

Ottolander, T. 1884. *Het Enten van Vruchtbomen en Heesters.* Leiden: Brill.

Oudemans, J. J. M. 1980. I.D.S. tour in Greece 22 May–5 June 1979. *Int. Dendr. Soc. Yrbk.* 1979:98–107.

Pachter, I. J., et al. 1959. Indole alkaloids of *Acer saccharinum* (the Silver Maple), *Dictyoloma incanescens, Piptadenia colubrina,* and *Mimosa hostilis. Journal of Organic Chemistry* 24:1285–1287.

Packard, A. S. 1890. Insects injurious to forest and shade trees. USDA 5th Report of the Entomology Commission. Bulletin no. 7.

Packham, J. R., and D. J. L. Harding. 1982. *Ecology of Woodland Processes.* London: Arnold.

Paddock, E. F. 1961. Introgression between *Acer nigrum* and *Acer saccharum* in Ohio. *American Journal of Botany* 535.

Palamarev, E. 1979. *Acer hyrcanum* ssp. *intermedium. Fl. Nar. Rep. Bulgariya* 7:232.

Palmer, Lady Anne. 1974. A visit to Trewithen Garden, Grampound Road, Cornwall, March 1973. *Int. Dendr. Soc. Yrbk.* 1973:6–10.

______. 1977. Tour of southern Germany June 12–19, 1976. *Int. Dendr. Soc. Yrbk.* 1976:81–92.

______. 1985. Tour in Ireland April 12–17, 1984. *Int. Dendr. Soc. Yrbk.* 1984:6–17.

Palmer, Lady Anne, and A. Mitchell. 1972. The I.D.S. tour to western North America October 14th–November 4th, 1971. *Int. Dendr. Soc. Yrbk.* 1971:37–65.

Palmer, Lady Anne, and H. G. Hillier. 1975. I.D.S. Poland tour May 31th–June 12th, 1974. *Int. Dendr. Soc. Yrbk.* 1974:67–76.

Palmer, E. J., and J. A. Steyermark. 1938. Validation of combinations in Palmer & Steyermark's annotated catalogue of the flowering plants of Missouri. *Rhodora* 40:133.

Pals, J. P. 1984. Plant remains from Aartswoud, a Neolithic settlement in the coastal area (Holland). In *Plants and Ancient Man.* Eds. W. Van Zeist and W. A. Casparie. Rotterdam: Balkema.

Pampanini, R. 1910. Le piante vascolari raccolte del Rev. P.C. Silvestri nell' Hupeh. *Nuovo Giorn. Bot. Ital.* 17:421–422.

______. 1911. Le piante vascolari raccolte del Rev. P.C. Silvestri nell' Hupeh. *Nuovo Giorn. Bot. Ital.* 18:127.

Pančić, J. 1871. *Sumsko Drvetje i Siblje. Glasn. Srpsk. Uc. Drustv.* 30:149.

______. 1874. *Flora Principatus Serbiae.* Beograd.

Pantu, Z. C. 1910. *Contributiuni la Flora Bucuresti* 3:53.

Pape, Dr. 1926. Absterben eines Bestandes von Spitz-Ahorn. *Mitt. Dtsch. Dendr. Ges.* 37:353.

Papp, J. 1954. *Botanikai Közlemények* 45:268–271.

Parlatore, F. 1875. *Flora Italiana.* Firenze.

Parrish, M., and R. Wiedenmann. 1978. A growth study of three *Acer rubrum* cultivars. *American Nurseryman* 148:12, 104–106.

Parsa, A. 1951. *Flore de l'Iran.* Teheran.

Parsons & Sons Co. 1887. *Descriptive Catalogue of Hardy Ornamental Trees.* Flushing, New York: Kissena Nurseries.

Pattison, G. 1990. Trees held in the national collection of the N.C.C.P.G. *Int. Dendr. Soc. Yrbk.* 1990:122–129.

Pau Y Español, C. 1892. *Notas Botánicas á la Flora Española.* Madrid.

Paull, R. E., and R. L. Jones. 1978. Regulation of synthesis and secretion of fucose-containing polysaccharides in cultured sycamore cells. *Australian Journal of Plant Physiology* 6:457–467.

Pawsey, R. 1973. Amenity tree pathology, a neglected science. *New Scientist* (2 November):552.

Pax, F. 1885. Monographie der Gattung *Acer. Bot. Jahrb.* 6:287–347.

______. 1886. Monographie der Gattung *Acer. Bot. Jahrb.* 7:177–263.

______. 1889. *Acer oliverianum* Pax, *A. cordatum* Pax, *A. tenellum* Pax. In Hooker's *Icon. Pl.* 19, t. 1896–1897.

______. 1890. Nachträge und Ergänzungen zu der Monographie der Gattung *Acer. Bot. Jahrb.* 11:72–83.

______. 1893. Weitere Nachträge zur Monographie der Gattung *Acer. Bot. Jahrb.* 16:393–404.

______. 1902. Aceraceae. In *Das Pflanzenreich.* IV. By H. G. A. Engler. 163/8:1–89.

______. 1903. Ueber Bastardbildung der Ahornarten. *Mitt. Dtsch. Dendr. Ges.* 12:83–87.

Pax, F., and K. Hoffmann. 1922. *A. schneiderianum* Pax et Hoffm. In W. Limpricht. Botanische Reisen in den Hochgebirgen Chinas und Ost-Tibets. *Repert. Sp. Nov.* Beih. 12:435.

Payer, J. B. 1857. *Traité d'Organogène Végétale Comparée de la Fleur.* Paris.
Peace, T. R. 1962. *Pathology of Trees and Shrubs.* London: Clarendon.
Peattie, D. C. 1950. *A Natural History of Trees.* Boston: Houghton Mifflin, Boston.
Peck, C. J. 1977. Carpal anatomy of black maple (*Acer nigrum*) with emphasis on the transmitting tissue. Botanical Society of America Publication, misc. ser., 154:17.
Peel, A. J. 1974. *Transport of Nutrients in Plants.* London: Butterworths.
Pegg, G. F. 1974. *Verticillium* diseases. *Review of Plant Pathology* 53:157–182.
Penhallow, D. P. 1890. The Pleistocene flora of Canada. Bulletin of the Geological Society of America 1:327–330.
______. 1907. Contributions to the Pleistocene flora of Canada. *American Naturalist* 41:443–452.
Penny, J. S. 1969. Late Cretaceous and Early Tertiary Palynology. In *Aspects of Palynology: An Introduction to Plant Microfossils in Time.* Eds. R. J. Tschudy and R. A. Scott. New York: Wiley.
Perala, D. A., and E. Sucoff. 1965. Diagnosing potassium deficiency in American elm, silver maple, Russian olive, hackberry, and box elder. *Forest Science* 11:347–352.
Pereira Coutinho, A. X. 1895. Acerineae. *Bol. Soc. Brot.* 12:12–14.
Pereire A., and G. van Zuylen. 1983. *Private Gardens of France.* London: Weidenfeld and Nicolson.
Perez Iara, J. M. 1895. Florula Gaditana. *Anal. Soc. Españ. Hist. Nat.* 24:319.
Perkin, A. G., and Y. Uyeda. 1922. Occurrence of crystalline tannin in the leaves of the *Acer ginnala. Journal of the Chemical Society* 121:66–76.
Perkins, T., & Son (Nursery, Northampton). 1899. Neue Pflanzen. *Möllers Gärtner-Zeitung* 1899:351.
Perley, S. F. 1862. Maple sugar. *Maine Board of Agriculture Report* 47–56.
Perry, T. O. 1962. Racial variation in the day and night temperature requirements of red maple and loblolly pine. *Forest Science* 8:336–344.
______. 1971. Seasonal and genetic differences in fats, phenols, iso-enzymes, and pigments of red maple. *Forest Science* 17:209–212.
Perry, T. O., and C. W. Wang. 1960. Genetic variation in the winter chilling requirements for date of dormancy break for *Acer rubrum. Ecology* 41:785–790.
Persoon, C. H. 1805. *Synopsis Plantarum* 1:417–418.
Peterken, G. 1981. *Woodland Conservation and Management.* London: Chapman & Hall.
Peterson, L. O. T. 1958. The boxelder twig borer, *Proeoteras willingana* Kearfott, (Lepidoptera: Olethreutidae). *The Canadian Entomologist* 90:639–646.
Petzold and Kirchner. 1864. *Arboretum Muscavense.*
Pfeiffer, W. 1904. *Pflanzenphysiologie.* Leipzig: Engelmann.
Phillips, D. H., and D. A. Burdekin. 1982. *Diseases of Forest and Ornamental Trees.* London: Macmillan.
Phillips, I. D. J., et al. 1980. Effects of light and photoperiodic conditions on abscisic acid in leaves and roots of *Acer pseudoplatanus* L. *Planta* 149:118–122.
Phillips, R. 1980. *Trees in Britain, Europe and North America.* London: Pan.
Phillips, R., and G. G. Henshaw. 1977. The regulation of synthesis of phenolics in stationary phase cell cultures of *Acer pseudoplatanus* L. *Journal of Experimental Botany* 28:785–794.
Philipson, W. R., et al. 1971. *The Vascular Cambium.* London: Chapman & Hall.
Phytian, J. E. 1907. *Trees in Nature, Myth and Art.* Philadelphia: Jacobs.
Piearce, G. D. 1972. *Studies on* Verticillium *Wilt in Maples.* Thesis, Cambridge University.
Pielou, E. C. 1979. *Biogeography.* New York: Wiley.
Pieper, S. 1981. Analysen der Verzweigung von *Fraxinus excelsior* und *Acer pseudoplatanus. Dipl. Arb. Forstwiss. Fachber.* Univ. Göttingen.
Piggott, F. T. 1892. *Garden of Japan.* London: Allen.
Pims, S. 1966. *The Wood and the Trees. A Biography of Augustine Henry.* London: MacDonald.
Pinfield, N. J., and A. K. Stobart. 1972. Hormonal regulation of germination and early seedling development in *Acer pseudoplatanus* L. *Plants* 104:134–135.
Piper, C. V. 1906. *Flora of the State of Washington.* Washington, DC: Smithsonian Institution.
Pirone, P. P. 1978. *Tree Maintenance.* 5th ed. New York: Oxford University Press.
Pitcher, J. A. 1960. Heteroplastic grafting in the genera *Acer, Fraxinus, Picea* and *Abies. Proceedings of the 7th Northeastern Forest Tree Improvement Conference* 1959:52–58.
Pitkin, R. S. 1934. *Maple Sugar Time.* Brattleboro, Vermont: St. Day.
Plant, T. C. 1988–1989. *Catalogue.* Hillsboro, Oregon.
Plants and Gardens. 1967. *Introductory Dates of Familiar Trees, Shrubs and Vines* 23(3):87.
Plavsić, Svetislav. 1941. Über Neue und Seltene Pflanzenformen aus Mittelbosnien. II. *Österr. Bot. Zeitschr.* 90:213–223.

Pliny. 1968. *Naturalis Historia,* vol. 4. Translated by H. Rackham. Loeb Classical Library, Harvard University.

Plouvier, V. 1947. Sur la présence de québrachitol dans quelques Sapindacées et Aceracées. *Compte Rendu Hebdomadaire des Séances de l'Académie de Science* 224:1842–1844.

———. 1948. Sur la recherche du québrachitol et de l'allantoine chez les érables et la platane. *Compte Rendu Hebdomadaire des Séances de l'Académie de Science* 227:225–227.

———. 1963. Distribution of aliphatic polyols and cyclitols. In *Chemical Plant Taxonomy.* Ed. T. Swain. New York: Academic Press.

Plowman, A. B. 1915. Is the box elder a maple? A study of the comparative anatomy of *Negundo. Botanical Gazette* 60:169–192.

Plyuto, K. B. 1972. Results of phenological observations for maples in the Dniepropetrovsk Botanical Garden. *Ukrajins'ka Botanicheskii Zhurnal* 29:196–199. (Summary in English.)

Podtelok, M. P. 1972. Effect of physiologically active substances of maple, oak and ash roots and their role in seedling growth. In *Physiological-Biochemical Basis of Plant Interactions in Phytocenosis,* vol. 3. Ed. A. M. Grodzinsky. Kiev: Naukova Dumka. (In Russian.)

Pohl, F. 1937. Die Pollenerzeugung der Windblüter. *Beih. Bot. Zentralbl.* 56:365–470.

Poiret, J. L. M. 1823. *Tableau encyclopédique et méthodique des trois règnes de la nature.* Paris.

Pojàrkova, A. I. 1932. *Acer turcomanicum. Delect. Sem. Hort. Bot. Acad. Sci. USSR* 1933:3.

———. 1933a. Neue und Wenig Bekannte Arten der Gattung *Acer* L. *Acta Inst. Bot. Acad. Sci. USSR,* ser. 1, 1:143–155.

———. 1933b. Botanico-geographical survey of the maples of the USSR in connection with the history of the whole genus *Acer* L. *Acta Inst. Bot. Acad. Sci. USSR,* ser. 1, 1:225–374.

———. 1949. Aceraceae. In Komarov's *Flora USSR* 14:580–622, 746. Translated into English by Israel Program for Scientific Translation, Jerusalem, 1974.

———. 1976a. *Acer undulatum. Novosti Sist. Vyssh. Rast.* 13:216.

———. 1976b. *Acer libani. Novosti Sist. Vyssh. Rast.* 13:213.

Pollard, J. K., Jr. and T. Sproston. 1954. Nitrogenous constituents of sap exuded from the sapwood of *Acer saccharum. Plant Physiology* 59:894–900.

Pollard, E., et al. 1974. *Hedges.* The New Naturalist 58. London: Collins.

Poor, J. M., ed. 1984. *Plants That Merit Attention.* Vol. 1, *Trees.* Portland, Oregon: Timber Press.

Pope, D. G. 1977. Relationship between hydroxyproline-containing proteins secreted into the cell wall and medium by suspension-cultured *Acer pseudoplatanus* cells. *Plant Physiology* 59:894–900.

Porter, C. L. 1967. *Taxonomy of Flowering Plants.* San Francisco: Freeman.

Poskin, A. 1949. *Traité de Sylviculture.* Paris: J. Duculot, Gembloux et Librairie Agricole de la Maison Rustique.

Post, G. E., and J. E. Dinsmore. 1932. *Flora of Syria, Palestine and Sinai.* Vol. 1. Beirut.

Pottle, H. W., and A. L. Shigo. 1975. Treatment of wounds on *Acer rubrum* with *Trichoderma viride. European Journal of Forest Pathology* 5:274–279.

Potvin, F. 1978. Deer and browse distribution by cover type in the Cherry River wintering area, Quebec. *Nature Canada* 105:437–444.

Potvin, F., et al. 1981. Deer mortality in the Phénégamook wintering area, Quebec. *Canadian Field Naturalist* 95:80–84.

Pourret, P. E. de Figeac. 1788. Extrait de la cloris narbonensis. *Mémoires de l'Académie de Science du Toulouse* 3:305.

Powers, H. O. 1967. A blade tissue study of forty-seven species and varieties of Aceraceae. *American Midland Naturalist* 78:301–323.

Powers, J. L., and E. L. Cataline. 1940. Crystalline tannin from the bark of *Acer spicatum. Journal of Pharmaceutical Sciences* 29:209.

Praglowski, J. 1962. Notes on the pollen morphology of Swedish trees and shrubs. *Grana Palynology* 3(2):45–65.

Prance, G. T., and K. B. Sandved. 1985. *Leaves.* London: Thames & Hudson.

Presl, J. S., and K. B. Presl. 1822. *Deliciae Pragensis.* Prague.

Preston, R. J. 1965. *North American Trees.* Cambridge, Massachusetts: MIT Press.

Primack, R. B., and C. McCall. 1986. Gender variation in a red maple population: A seven year study. *American Journal of Botany* 73(9):1239–1248.

Princeton Nurseries (New Jersey). 1965. In Flemer's *Shade and Ornamental Trees in Color.* New York.

Privalov, G. F. 1965. Somatic radiomutations by *Acer negundo.* Bull. Mosk. Obshch. Isp. Pri. Biol. 70:153–160.

______. 1972a. Effect of combined treatment of seeds with mutagens and growth regulators on viability and growth of *Acer negundo* L. seedlings. *Genetika* 8:36–45. (In Russian).
______. 1972b. Studies of combined treatment of *Acer negundo* L. seeds with growth regulators and mutagens. In *Induced Mutations and Plant Improvement.* Vienna: International Atomic Energy Agency. 265–275.
Procházka, M., and C. Buzék. 1975. Maple leaves from the Tertiary of North Bohemia. *Rozpr. Ustredniho Ustavu Geol.* Svazek 1–86.
Prockter, N. J. 1976. *Simple Propagation.* London: Faber & Faber.
Proctor, M., and P. Yeo. 1973. *The Pollination of Flowers.* The New Naturalist 54. London: Collins.
Puckett, L. J. 1982. Acid rain, air pollution, and tree growth in southeastern New York. *Journal of Environmental Quality* 11:376–381.
Punt, W., and G. C. S. Clarke. 1980. *The Northwest European Pollen Flora.* II. Amsterdam: Elsevier.
Purpus, J. A. 1897. Besuch der Baumschulen von H.A. Hesse in Weener am Ems in Ostfriesland. *Mitt. Dtsch. Dendr. Ges.* 6:14.
______. 1900. *Acer glabrum* Torr. *Mitt. Dtsch. Dendr. Ges.* 9:44.
Pursh, F. T. 1814. *A. circinatum* Pursh. & *A. macrophyllum* Pursh. *Flora Americae Septentrionalis* 1:265–268.
Pynaert, E. C. 1881. Les érables de Japon. *Illustration Horticole* 28:139–140.
Quezel, P. and S. Santa. 1963. *Nouvelle Flore de l'Algérie.* Paris.
Raad, A. 1982. *Bomen in Stad en Dorp.* The Hague: Ver. Nederland Gem.
Raciborski, M. 1888. Klony Polskie. *Spraw. Kom Fizyjogr. Akad. Krakow* 23:50–55.
Rackham, O. 1976. *Trees and Woodland in the British Landscape.* London: Dent.
______. 1980. *Ancient Woodland.* London: Arnold.
Radde, G. 1899. *Die Vegetation der Erde. Plants in the Caucasus.* Part III. Rpt. 1976. Vaduz: Gantner.
Radde-Fomin, O. G. 1931. Über Einige Kaukasische Ahornarten aus dem *Acer monspessulanum* Zyklus. Bull. Jard. Bot. Kieff 12/13:71–74.
______. 1932. Do sistematiki deiakikh vidiv rodu *Acer* iz Turkestanu. *Zhurnal Bio-botanicheskii Tsiklu VUAN* 3/4:39–59.
______. 1934. Do sistematiki polimorfnogo vidu *Acer campestre. Zhurnal Institut Botanicheskii Tsiklu VUAN* 10:3–28.
Raff, J., and R. Keller. 1979. *Pflanzenschätze der Mainau.* Insel Mainau: Mainauverwaltung.
Rafinesque, C. S. 1808. Prospectus of two intended works in botany. *Medic. Repos. N.Y. Hex.* 2(5):352.
______. 1809. Prospectus of two intended works in botany. *Journal of Botany Desvaux* 2:170.
______. 1833. Florula Texensis. *Atlantic J.* 6:170.
______. 1836. *New Flora of North America.* Philadelphia, Pennsylvania.
Ramp, F. F., and S. N. Stephenson. 1988. Gender dimorphism in growth and mass partitioning by box-elder (*Acer negundo* L.). *American Midland Naturalist* 75(8):420–430.
Rankin, W. H. 1914. Thrombotic disease of maple. *Phytopathology* 4:395–396.
Raphael, S. 1989. *An Oak Spring Sylva. A Selection of the Rare Books on Trees in the Oak Spring Garden Library.* Uppderville, Virginia: Oak Spring Garden Library.
Rapley, B. A. 1974. Grafting maples from imported scions (New Zealand). *International Plant Propagators' Society Proceedings* 24.
Raven, P. H. and D. I. Axelrod. 1974. Angiosperm biogeography and past continental movements. *Annals of the Missouri Botanical Garden* 61:539–673.
Raven, P. H., et al. 1981. *Biology of Plants.* 3rd ed. New York: Worth.
Rechinger, K. H. 1929. Beitrag zur Kenntnis der Flora der Ägäischen Inseln und Ost-Griechenlands. *Ann. Naturh. Mus. Wien* 43:305–306.
______. 1969. *A. monspessulanum* ssp. *assyriacum* (Pójark.) Rechinger f., *A. monspessulanum* ssp. *persicum* (Pójark.) Rechinger f. In *Flora Iranica.* Ed. K. H. Rechinger. 61:1–11.
Record, S. J. M. 1934. *The Identification of the Timbers of Temperate North America.* New York.
Regel, E. A. von. 1857. Vegetations-skizzen des Amurlandes. Bulletin de la classe Physico-Mathématique de l'Académie Impériale des Sciences de St. Petersbourg 15:211–238.
______. 1861. Tentamen florae Ussuriensis. *Mémoirs de l'Académie Impériale des Sciences de St. Petersbourg* VII. 4(4):1–228.
______. 1886. *Acer Platanoides Compactum. Gartenflora* 35:117.
______. 1891. *Gartenflora.* Zeitschr. für Garten-und Blumenkunde 40.
Regel, E. A. von, and F. G. Herder. 1866. Plantae Semenovianae. Bull. Soc. Nat. Moscou 39(1):550–551.

Rehder, A. 1900a. *Acer saccharum* var. *rugelii* (Pax) Rehd. *Acer.* In *Cyclopedia of American Horticulture,* by L. H. Bailey. 1:12–16.
______. 1900b. Ein Ausflug nach Nord-Carolina. *Mitt. Dtsch. Dendr. Ges.* 9:15–20.
______. 1905. The maples of eastern continental Asia. In *Trees and Shrubs,* by C. S. Sargent. 1:131–181. Boston.
______. 1907. In *Trees and Shrubs,* by C. S. Sargent. 2:25–26. Boston.
______. 1911. *A. ceriferum* Rehd. In *Plantae Wilsonianae,* vol. 1. Ed. C. S. Sargent. Rpt. 1988. Portland, Oregon: Dioscorides Press. 89.
______. 1913a. *Acer saccharum* var. *schneckii* Rehd. In *Trees and Shrubs,* by C. S. Sargent. 2:255–256. Boston.
______. 1913b. Neue oder Kritische Gehölze. *Mitt. Dtsch. Dendr. Ges.* 22:258.
______. 1914. *A. cappadocicum* var. *tricaudatum* (Rehd. ex Veitch) Rehd. In *Standard Cyclopedia of Horticulture,* by L. H. Bailey. 1:195–205.
______. 1922. New species, varieties and combinations. *Journal of Arnold Arboretum* 3:216–219.
______. 1923. New species, varieties and combinations. *Journal of Arnold Arboretum* 4:115–116.
______. 1927. *Manual of Cultivated Trees and Shrubs.* New York: Macmillan.
______. 1933. New species, varieties and combinations. *Acer* sect. Macrantha. *Journal of Arnold Arboretum* 14:211–212.
______. 1936. *Acer skutchii* in Guatemala. *Journal of Arnold Arboretum* 17:350–351.
______. 1938. New species, varieties and combinations. *Journal of Arnold Arboretum* 19:80–87.
______. 1939. *Acer mono* var. *ambiguum* (Pax) Rehd. New species, varieties and combinations. *Journal of Arnold Arboretum* 20:416–417.
______. 1949. *Bibliography of Cultivated Trees and Shrubs.* Cambridge, Massachusetts: Harvard University. Rpt. Königstein: Koeltz.
______. 1986. *Manual of Cultivated Trees and Shrubs.* 2nd ed. New York: Macmillan.
Rehnelt, F. 1905. Dendrologische Notizen aus Giessen. II. *Acer rubrum dasycarpum. Mitt. Dtsch. Dendr. Ges.* 14:204–205.
Reichard, J. J. 1780. Botanische Bemerkungen. *Schriften der Berlinischen Gesellschaft Naturforschenden Freunde* 1:310–313.
Reichenbach, H. G. L. 1828. *Conspectus Regni Vegetabilis.* Leipzig.
______. 1832. *Flora Germanica Excursoria.* Leipzig.
______. 1834. *Das Pflanzenreich in Seinen Natürlichen Klassen Entwickelt.* Leipzig.
Reichert, J. F. 1804. *Hortus Reichertianus.* Weimar.
Reid, C., and E. M. Reid. 1907. The fossil flora of Tegelen sur Meuse, near Venlo in the Province of Limburg. Section 2. *Verh. Kon. Akad. Wetensch.*
______. 1915. The Pliocene floras of the Dutch-Prussian border. *Med. Rijksopsporingsdienst Delfstoffen* 6:1–178.
Reid, D. M., and W. J. Burrows. 1968. Cytokinin and gibberellin-like activity in the spring sap of trees. *Experientia* 24:189.
Reinecke, K. 1892. *Mitt. Thüring. Bot. Ver.* 2:11–12.
______. 1899. *Mitt. Thüring. Bot. Ver.* 13:119.
______. 1900. Bericht über die Herbst-Hauptversammlung in Erfurt. *Mitt. Thüring. Bot. Ver.* 15:14.
Reisæter, O. 1967. Dendrologi for Hagebruksstudentane i 2. àrsklasse ved Noregs Landbrukshøgskule i às 1967–1968.
Reisch, K. W. 1967. The maples. Lawn and ornamental research. Ohio Agriculture Research and Development Center, Research Summary 24.
Renaudin, J. P. 1981. Uptake and accumulation of an indole alkaloid, (14C)-tabernanthine, by cell suspension cultures of *Cataranthus roseus* (L.) Don, G. and *Acer pseudoplatanus* L. *Plant Sci. Letter* 22:59–69.
Rérolle, L. 1885. Etude sur les végétaux fossiles de Cardagne. *Revue des Sciences Naturelles, Montpellier,* ser. 3, 4:368–377.
Reynier, L. 1788. *Mémoires pour servir à l'histoire physique et naturelle de la Suisse.* Geneva, Switzerland.
Reynolds, E. F., ed. 1989. *Martindale, the Extra Pharmacopoeia.* 29th ed. London: The Pharmaceutical Press.
Rezek, E. 1988. *Acer platanoides* 'Cindy Lou'. American Conifer Society Bulletin 5:98–99.
Rice, E. L. 1974. *Allelopathy.* New York: Academic Press.
Rich, S., and G. S. Walton. 1979. Decline of curbside sugar maples in Connecticut. *Journal of Arboriculture* 5:265–268.

Richard, P. 1970. Atlas pollinique des arbres et de quelques arbustes indigènes du Quebec. IV. *Nature Canada* 97:241–306.
Richards, A. J., ed. 1978. *The Pollination of Flowers by Insects.* London: Academic Press.
Richards, P. W. 1976. *The Tropical Rain Forest.* Cambridge: Cambridge University Press.
Richardson, H. L. 1943. The Ice Age in West China. *Journal of the West China Border Society* 14B:1 ff.
Richardson, S. D. 1953. Studies on root growth of *Acer saccharinum.* II. Factors affecting root growth where photosynthesis is curtailed. In *Proc. Kon. Nederlandse Akad. Wetensch.*, ser. C, 56:366.
Richardson, S. D. 1956. Studies on root growth of *Acer saccharinum.* V. The effect of long term limitation of photosynthesis on root growth in first year seedlings. In *Proc. Kon. Nederlandse Akad. Wetensch.*, ser. C, 59:694.
Richens, R. H. 1983. *Elm.* New York: Cambridge University Press.
Richter, G. 1978. *Plant Metabolism, Physiology and Biochemistry of Primary Metabolism.* (Translated from German.) London: Croom Helm.
Ridley, H. N. 1930. *The Dispersal of Plants Throughout the World.* Kent: Reeve.
Rier, J. P., and A. L. Shigo. 1972. Some changes in red maple, *Acer rubrum,* tissues within 34 days after wounding in July. *Canadian Journal of Botany* 50:1783–1784.
Rikli, M. A. 1903. Eine Neue Form des Bergahorns. *Ber. Zürich. Bot. Ges.* 8:1–2.
Ringstrand, M. 1845. *Acer Platanoides microphylla. Bot. Not.* 1845:135.
Riou, P., and D. Delorme. 1940. *Nature Canada* 67:167–224.
Roach, B. A. 1977. A stocking guide for Allegheny hardwoods and its use in controlling intermediate cuttings. Northeastern Forest Experiment Station, Upper Darby, Pennsylvania, USDA Forest Service Research Paper NE–373.
Roberts, E. H., ed. 1972. *Viability of Seeds.* London: Chapman & Hall.
Roberts, R. 1978. Japanese maples. *Bonsai* 17:355.
Robinette, G. O., and S. Van Gieson. 1985. *Trees of the South.* New York: Van Nostrand Reinhard.
Robinson, F. B. 1941. *Tabular Keys for the Identification of the Woody Plants.* Champain, Illinois: Champain.
Robinson, H. 1974. *Pressed Plants as an Art.* London: Bell.
Robinson, P. M., et al. 1963. Isolation of the inhibitor varying with photoperiod in *Acer pseudoplatanus. Nature* 199:875–876.
Robinson, P. M., and P. F. Wareing. 1964. Chemical nature and biological properties of the inhibitor varying with photoperiod in Sycamore (*Acer pseudoplatanus*). *Physiol. Pl.* (Copenhagen) 17:314–323.
Robinson, S. 1866. *Facts for Farmers.* New York: Johnson.
Robinson, W. 1883. *Parks & Gardens of Paris.* London: Murray.
Rodger, McClelland, & Co. Nursery (Newry, England). 1881. *Acer Pseudo-Platanus* 'Pyramidale'. *Gardener's Chronicle* II. 15:300.
Rohrbach, Prof. Dr. 1930. Ausbleiben des Runzelschorfs beim Ahorn. *Mitt. Dtsch. Dendr. Ges.* 42:390–391.
Roloff, A. 1991. Ausgewählte Morphologische Aspekte der Kronenentwicklung: Architekturmodelle, Astordnungen und Blattanordnung. *Mitt. Dtsch. Dendr. Ges.* 80:87–110.
Romano, G. R., and Y. Y. Chen. 1970. An illustrated key to some fossilized postglacial climatic indicator pollens. *Taiwania* 15:227–244.
Roper, L. 1967a. The Sunday Times *Gardening Book.* London: Nelson.
______. 1967b. The landscaping of motorways. *Journal of the Royal Horticultural Society* 92:302–308.
______. 1968. Landscape design. *Journal of the Royal Horticultural Society* 93:499–509.
Rose, A. H., and D. H. Lindquist. 1982. Insects of eastern hardwood trees. Canadian Forest Service, Forest Technical Report 29.
Rosenthal, G. A. 1986. The chemical defenses of higher plants. *Scientific American* 254(1):76–81.
Ross, D. A. 1962. Bionomics of the maple leaf cutter, *Paraclemensia acerifoliella* Fitch, (Lepidoptera: Incurvariidae). *The Canadian Entomologist* 94:1053–1063.
Rosse, The Earl of. 1973. Dr. H. H. Hu's plant-hunting expeditions 1937–40. Part II. *Int. Dendr. Soc. Yrbk.* 1972:7–12.
Roth, A. W. 1827. *Enumeratio Plantarum Phanerogamarum in Germania* 1:168–169.
Rothe, T. 1896. *Acer Negundo aureum odessanum. Mitt. Dtsch. Dendr. Ges.* 5:1.
Rousseau, J. J. J. J. 1940. Histoire de la nomenclature de l'*Acer saccharophorum* Koch, K. (*A. saccharum* Marsh.). *Contributions de l'Institut Botanique de l'Université de Montréal* 35:1–66.
Rouy, G., and G. Foucaud. 1897. *Flore de France.* Paris.
The Royal Botanic Gardens, Kew. N.d. *Souvenir Guide.*

The Royal Botanic Gardens, Kew. 1894. *Hand-list of Trees and Shrubs Grown in Arboretum.* Richmond, Surrey, England.
Royal Dutch Geographical Society KNAG. 1938. *Atlas van Tropisch Nederland.* Facs. ed. 1990. Landsmeer: Antiquariaat Gemilang.
Ruark, G. A., et al. 1983. Soil factors related to urban sugar maple decline. *Journal of Arboriculture* 9:1–6.
Rubens, J. M. 1978. Soil desalination to counteract maple decline. *Journal of Arboriculture* 4:33–42.
Ruehle, J. L. 1967. Distribution of plant-parasitic nematodes associated with forest trees of the world. Southeastern Forest Experiment Station, USDA Forest Service.
Ruhe, W. 1936. Die Areale der Mitteleuropäischen *Acer*-Arten. In *Repertorium Specierum Novarum* Beiheft 89:95–106.
Ruprecht, F. J. 1870. Flora Caucasi. *Mémoirs de l'Académie Impériale des Sciences de St. Petersbourg* VII. 15:279–301.
Rush, B. 1792. *An Account of the Sugar Maple-Tree of the United States.* Philadelphia, Pennsylvania: Aitken.
Russell, J. 1984. Recent tree planting at Castle Howard. *Int. Dendr. Soc. Yrbk.* 1983:66–78.
______. 1987. Review of *Manual of Cultivated Broad-Leaved Trees and Shrubs,* by G. Krüssmann. *Int. Dendr. Soc. Yrbk.* 1986:131.
Rydberg, P. E. 1913. Rocky Mountain flora. Bulletin of the Torrey Botanical Club 40:54–56.
Sabeti, H. 1976. *Forests, Trees and Shrubs of Iran.* Tehran: Ministry of Agriculture and Natural Resources. (In Iranian.)
Sakai, A. K. 1978. *Ecological and Evolutionary Aspects of Sex Expression in Silver Maple (Acer saccharinum* L.). Ph.D. thesis, University of Michigan, Ann Arbor.
Sakai, S. 1987. Patterns of branching and extension growth of vigorous saplings of Japanese *Acer* species in relation to their regeneration strategies. *Canadian Journal of Botany* 65:1578–1585.
Sakai, A. K., and N. L. Oden. 1983. Spatial pattern of sex expression in silver maple. (*Acer saccharinum* L.): Morisita's index spatial autocorrelation. *American Naturalist* 122:489–508.
Saleh, N. A. M., et al. 1969. Local plants as potential sources of tannins in Egypt, Part IV (Aceraceae to Flacourtiaceae). *Qual. Pl. Mater. Veg.* 17:384–394.
Salisbury, E. 1961. *Weeds and Aliens.* New Naturalist 43. London: Collins.
Salisbury, R. A. 1796. *Prodromus Stirpium in Horto ad Chapel Allerton.* London.
Sanders, J. G. 1905. The cottony maple scale. USDA Bureau of Entomology Circular 64.
Sangster, A. G., and H. M. Dale. 1964. Pollen grain preservation of underrepresented species in fossil spectra. *Canadian Journal of Botany* 42:437–449.
Santamour, F. S., Jr. 1962. Chromosome number in striped and mountain maples. *Rhodora* 64:281–282.
______. 1965. Cytological studies in red and silver maples and their hybrids. Bulletin of the Torrey Botanical Club 92(2):127–134.
______. 1971. IOPB chromosome number reports. XXXII. *Taxon* 20:355.
______. 1982a. Cambial peroxydase isoenzymes in relation to systematics of *Acer.* Bulletin of the Torrey Botanical Club 109(2):152–161.
______. 1982b. Checklist of cultivated maples. *Journal of Arboriculture* (April, June, September, October).
______. 1984. Wound compartmentalization in cultivars of *Acer, Gleditsia,* and other genera. *Journal of Environmental Horticulture* 2:123–125.
______. 1988. New chromosome counts in *Acer. Rhodora* 90(862):127–131.
Santamour, F. S., Jr. and A. J. McArdle. 1982. Checklist of cultivated maples. I. *Acer rubrum* L. *Journal of Arboriculture* 8:110–112.
Santamour, F. S., Jr., et al., eds. 1976. Better trees for metropolitan landscapes. USDA Forest Service, General Technical Report NE–22.
Saporta, L. C. J. G. de. 1862. Etudes sur la végétation du Sud-Est de la France. *Annuelles des Sciences Naturelles et Botanique* 4(17):273.
______. 1863. Etudes sur la végétation du Sud-Est de la France. *Annuelles des Sciences Naturelles et Botanique* 4(19):84.
______. 1865a. Etudes sur la végétation du Sud-Est de la France. *Annuelles des Sciences Naturelles et Botanique* 4(3):128–130.
______. 1865b. Etudes sur la végétation du Sud-Est de la France. *Annuelles des Sciences Naturelles et Botanique* 5 (4):176–181.
______. 1866. Notice sur les plantes fossiles des calcaires concrétionnés de Brognon. Bulletin de la

Société Geologique de France 2(23):270.
______. 1867. Flore du Bassin à lignites de Manosque. *Annuelles des Sciences Naturelles* 5(8):101–105, t. 13.
______. 1869. Sur l'éxistence . . . la flore de Meximieux. Bulletin de la Société Geologique de France 26:763.
______. 1873. Forêts ensevelies sous les cendres eruptives de .... Cantal. *Annuelles des Sciences Naturelles et Botanique* 5 (17):402–406.
______. 1879. *Le Monde des Plantes avant l'Apparition de l'Homme.* Paris.
______. 1889. Flore fossile d'Aix-en-Provence. *Annuelles des Sciences Naturelles et Botanique* 7(10):90.
Saporta, L. C. J. G., and A. F. Marion. 1875. Recherches sur les végétaux fossiles de Meximieux. *Archives du Musée d'Histoire Naturelle de Lyon* 1:280–294.
Sargeaunt, J. 1920. *The Trees, Shrubs, and Plants of Virgil.* Oxford: Blackwell.
Sargent, C. S. 1884. *Report on the Forests of North America.* 10th census. Washington, DC: U.S. Departments of Commerce and Labor, Bureau of Census. 9:46–51.
______. 1889. Notes upon some North American trees. *Garden and Forest* 2:364.
______. 1891a. Notes upon some North American trees. *Garden and Forest* 4:147–148.
______. 1891b. *Silva of North America.* 14 vols. Boston: Houghton Mifflin. 2:79–113.
______. 1894. *Forest Flora of Japan.* Tokyo: Shokubusu Bunken Kanko-Kai. Rpt. 1939. Boston: Houghton Mifflin.
______. 1902. *Silva of North America* 13:7–11.
______. 1913. *Plantae Wilsonianae.* Vol. 1. Rpt. 1988. Portland, Oregon: Dioscorides Press.
______. 1919. *A. saccharum* var. *sinuosum* (Rehd.) Sarg. Notes on North American trees. IV. *Botanical Gazette* 67:233–241.
______. 1921. Notes on American trees. VIII. *Journal of Arnold Arboretum* 2:166.
______. 1922. *Manual of the Trees of North America.* 2nd ed. Boston: Houghton Mifflin. Rpt. 1961. New York: Dover.
______. 1828. *Acer Pseudo-Platanus* 'Purpureum'. *Gardener's Chronicle* II. 15:300.
______. 1871. *Acer Pseudo-Platanus* 'Rubro-purpureum'. *Gardener's Chronicle* 1871:1041.
Satake, Y., et al. 1989. *Wild Flowers of Japan: Woody Plants.* 2 vols. Tokyo: Heibonsha.
Sauter, J. J. 1974. Maple, a description of the mechanism of maple sap flow. In *McGraw-Hill Yearbook Science & Technology.* Eds. McGraw-Hill. New York: McGraw-Hill.
Sauter, J. J., et al. 1973. Studies on the release of sugar into the vessels of sugar maple (*Acer saccharum*). *Canadian Journal of Botany* 51:1–8.
Savage, S. 1945. *A Catalogue of the Linnean Herbarium.* London.
Savella, L. 1971. Top grafting of Japanese maples and dogwood. *International Plant Propagators' Society Proceedings* 21.
Sávulescu, T., and Rayss. 1958. *Flora Republicii Romine.* Bucharest.
Savonius, M. 1989. Kingsnorth Garden, Folkestone. *Journal of the Royal Horticultural Society* 114(4):170–173.
Scanlon, E. H. 1951. Ninety trees for changing street and home trends. *Trees* 11(5):10–11,22–23.
______. 1952. Presenting the new 'Charles F. Irish' Norway Maple. *Trees* 12(5):10–11.
______. 1953. Several aspects of contemporary street tree management. *Trees* 13(5):10–11,24.
______. 1960. *Trees* 20(3):12.
______. 1976. Seed source effects on sugar maple. *American Nurseryman* 143(1):13.
Schaefer, A. 1924. 'Winterhart'. Ein Wort über Theorie und Praxis. *Mitt. Dtsch. Dendr. Ges.* 34:378–379.
Schalk, P. H. 1990. *Acer pseudoplatanus* L. Zaad- en Nakomelingschaptoetsingen 1976–1987. *Rapport* 625.
______. 1991. Nieuwe Kloon Noorse Esdoorn. *Boomblad* 3(1):7.
Scharpf, R. F., and F.G. Hawksworth. 1974. Mistletoes on hardwoods in the United States. USDA Forest Service, Forest Pest Leaflet 147.
Schelle, E. 1912. Neue, Seltene und Interessante Gehölze. *Mitt. Dtsch. Dendr. Ges.* 21:219–222.
Schelle, E. 1915. Auswahl Wertvoller Zierbäume und Ziersträucher. *Mitt. Dtsch. Dendr. Ges.* 24:172–212.
______. 1924. Über Einige Dendrologisch Wichtige Gehölze. *Mitt. Dtsch. Dendr. Ges.* 34:344–347.
Schellens, R. 1931. Gewinnung von Ahornzucker in Deutschland. *Mitt. Dtsch. Dendr. Ges.* 43:427.
Scheller, H. 1980. Seltene Ahorn-arten—Kostbarkeiten der Gärten. *Gartenprax.* 12:534–538.
Schenk, J. A. von. 1887. *Handbuch der Botanik.* Wroclaw, Poland.
Schilling, N., et al. 1972. Formation of L-quebrachitol from D-bornesitol in leaves of *Acer pseudoplatanus. Phytochemistry* 11:1401–1404.

Schimper, W. P. 1874. *Traité de paléontologie végétale.* Paris.
Schinz, H., and R. Keller. 1914. *Flora der Schweiz.* 2nd ed. Zürich.
Schinz, H., and A. Thellung. 1920. Gefässpflanzen. *Ber. Schweiz. Bot. Ges.* 26/29:226.
Schippers, B., and W. Gams, eds. 1979. *Soil-Borne Pathogens.* New York: Academic Press.
Schmidt, F. 1792. *Oesterreichs Allgemeine Baumzucht.* Vienna.
______. 1868. Flora Sachalinensis. In Reisen im Amurlande und auf der Insel Sachalin. *Mémoirs de l'Académie Imperiale des Sciences de St. Petersburg.* 7th ser.
Schmidt, J., and Son Co. (Nursery). 1967. *Brochure. Acer Platanoides* 'Greenlace'.
Schmoe, F. W. 1925. *Our Greatest Mountain. A Handbook for Mount Rainier National Park.* New York: Putnam.
Schmutz, E. 1976. An amateur botanist on the Lesser Sunda Islands. Flora Malesiana Bulletin 29:2605–2609.
Schnack, F., ed. 1957. *Der Wald.* München: Kindler.
Schneider, C. K. 1907. *A. ukurunduensis* var. *multiserratum* (Maxim.) Schneid. *Illustriertes Handbuch der Laubholzkunde* 2:192–240. Jena: Fischer.
Schneider, C. K. 1909. *Illustriertes Handbuch der Laubholzkunde* 2:241–245. Jena: Fischer.
______. 1912. *Illustriertes Handbuch der Laubholzkunde* 2:1027–1029. Jena: Fischer.
______. 1922. In *Unsere Freiland-Laubgehölze,* by Silva Tarouca, G. Ernst, and C. Schneider. 2nd ed. Vienna: Hölder-Pichler-Tempsky.
Scholz, E. 1960. Blütenmorphologische und Biologische Untersuchungen bei *Acer pseudoplatanus* L. und *Acer platanoides* L. *Der Züchter* 30:11–16.
Schroeder, J. L. B. 1896. *Acer Negundo boreale. Mitt. Dtsch. Dendr. Ges.* 5:2
Schröter, C. 1936. Eine Exkursion von Nikko (Japan) zum Chuzen-ji See am 7. Oktober 1898. *Ber. Schweiz. Bot. Ges.* 46:505–516.
Schuepp, O. 1929. Untersuchungen zur Verschreibenden und Experimentellen Entwicklungsgeschichte von *Acer pseudoplatanus* L. *Jahrb. Wiss. Bot.* 70:743–804.
Schuette, H. A., and C. Sybil. 1935. Maple sugar: a bibliography of early records. *Transactions of the Wisconsin Academy of Science* 29:209–236.
Schulz, R. 1913. *Acer Pseudo-Platanus* L. var. *tripartitum. Verh. Bot. Ver. Brandenburg* 54:123.
Schur, P. J. F. 1866. *Enumeratio Plantarum Transsilvaniae.* Vienna.
Schütt, P., and E. B. Cowling. 1985. Waldsterben, a general decline of forests in central Europe: symptoms, development, and possible causes. *Plant Disease Reporter* 69:548–558.
Schwarz, E. 1937. Merkwürdige Wurzelbildung (*Acer pseudoplatanus*). *Mitt. Dtsch. Dendr. Ges.* 49:187–188.
Schwerin, F. Graf von. 1892. *Acer dasycarpum lactescens. Gartenflora* 42:501.
______. 1893. Die Varietäten der Gattung *Acer. Gartenflora* 42:161–714.
______. 1894. Ueber Einige zum Teil Neue Ahornarten. *Mitt. Dtsch. Dendr. Ges.* 3:45–52.
______. 1896a. Ueber Variation beim Ahorn. *Mitt. Dtsch. Dendr. Ges.* 5:31–46.
______. 1896b. Dritter Beitrag zur Gattung *Acer. Mitt. Dtsch. Dendr. Ges.* 5:77–81.
______. 1896c. *Acer Negundo pendulum. Gartenflora* 45:219.
______. 1898a. Der Persische Ahorn. *Mitt. Dtsch. Dendr. Ges.* 7:47–53.
______. 1898b. Zwei Pontische Ahorne. *Gartenflora* 47:120–125.
______. 1899. *Acer monspessulanum* 'Biedermannii'. *Gartenflora* 48:410.
______. 1900. Ueber Einführung und Akklimatisation Ausländischer Ahorn-Arten. *Mitt. Dtsch. Dendr. Ges.* 9:12–22.
______. 1901. *A. erianthum* Schwer. Neue Mitteilungen über den Ahorn. *Mitt. Dtsch. Dendr. Ges.* 10:58–65.
______. 1903. *Acer syriacum* var. *hermoneum.* In Beissner, Schelle & Zabel. *Handbuch der Laubholzbenennung.* Berlin.
______. 1904a. Pathologische Beobachtungen an Gehölzen. *Mitt. Dtsch. Dendr. Ges.* 13:107–114.
______. 1904b. *Acer ukurunduense* Fisch & May. *Mitt. Dtsch. Dendr. Ges.* 13:210.
______. 1905a. Bericht und Betrachtungen über die Resultate des Wiener Nomenklatur-Kongresses. *Mitt. Dtsch. Dendr. Ges.* 14:91–100.
______. 1905b. *Acer pseudoplatanus eythrocarpum. Mitt. Dtsch. Dendr. Ges.* 14:193–194.
______. 1905c. *Acer Bosci Spach* (tataricum × monspessulanum). *Mitt. Dtsch. Dendr. Ges.* 14:206.
______. 1905d. Ahorn-Runzelschorf, *Rhytisma acerinum* Fries. *Mitt. Dtsch. Dendr. Ges.* 14:206.
______. 1905e. *Acer insigne* 'Wolfii'. *Mitt. Dtsch. Dendr. Ges.* 14:210.
______. 1905f. Mangelhafte Veredelung bei *Acer. Mitt. Dtsch. Dendr. Ges.* 14:221.
______. 1906a. *Acer heldreichii purpuratum. Mitt. Dtsch. Dendr. Ges.* 15:212.
______. 1906b. Herbstrote Ahorne. *Die Gartenwelt* 12:17–19.

______. 1907. Ueber Pflanzeneinbürgerung. *Mitt. Dtsch. Dendr. Ges.* 16:148–157.
______. 1908. Zehn Neue Gehölzformen. *Mitt. Dtsch. Dendr. Ges.* 17:216.
______. 1910. Vierzehn Neue Gehölzformen. *Mitt. Dtsch. Dendr. Ges.* 19:287–289.
______. 1911. Einige Neue Gehölzformen. *Mitt. Dtsch. Dendr. Ges.* 20:322.
______. 1917a. Jahresversammlung. Baumreihen. *Mitt. Dtsch. Dendr. Ges.* 26:263–266.
______. 1917b. Ahorn-Baumschule. *Mitt. Dtsch. Dendr. Ges.* 26:269.
______. 1917c. Jahressammlung. Die Baumschule von L. Späth in Baumschulenweg. *Mitt. Dtsch. Dendr. Ges.* 26:274–277.
______. 1919a. Acht Beiträge zur Gattung *Acer.* Private Publication.
______. 1919b. Baumkronen als 'Windkugeln'. *Mitt. Dtsch. Dendr. Ges.* 28:181–182.
______. 1919c. *Acer platanoides* 'Reitenbachii'. *Mitt. Dtsch. Dendr. Ges.* 28:184–185.
______. 1921a. Unsymmetrische Früchte des *Acer saccharum. Mitt. Dtsch. Dendr. Ges.* 31:181–182.
______. 1921b. Der Ahorn-Runzelschorf, *Rhytisma acerinum* Fries. *Mitt. Dtsch. Dendr. Ges.* 31:186–188.
______. 1922. Neue Ahornformen. *Mitt. Dtsch. Dendr. Ges.* 32:258.
______. 1925. Über Rotblättrige Pflanzen. *Mitt. Dtsch. Dendr. Ges.* 35:156–163.
______. 1930. Kein *Acer pseudoplatanus pyramidale. Mitt. Dtsch. Dendr. Ges.* 42:368–369.
______. 1931. Beste Vermehrungsart der Japanischen Ahorne. *Mitt. Dtsch. Dendr. Ges.* 43:406.
______. 1932. Ahorne der Palmatum-Klasse Lieben Halbschatten. *Mitt. Dtsch. Dendr. Ges.* 44:381.
______. 1933. Rote Ahornallee. *Mitt. Dtsch. Dendr. Ges.* 45:340–341.
Scopoli, J. A. 1772. *Flora Carniolica.* 2nd ed. Vienna.
Searles, R. 1978a. Japanese maples—unequaled. Bonsai Bulletin 16(1):10–12.
______. 1978b. Japanese maples—unequaled. Part II—Dwarf and rough bark cultivars. Bonsai Bulletin 16(2):10–11.
Sears, P. B. 1930. Common fossil pollen of the Erie Basin. *Botanical Gazette* 89:95–106.
Seeger, R. 1923. Dendrologische Bemerkungen zur Flora des Karwendelgebirges. *Mitt. Dtsch. Dendr. Ges.* 33:234.
Seehaus, P. 1912. Riesige Ahorne in der Schweiz. *Mitt. Dtsch. Dendr. Ges.* 21:342–345.
Seely, H. M. 1878. *Profits of sugar making. Vermont Agricultural Report* 111–114.
Seki, M. S. 1912/13. *Wholesale List of Pure Japanese Plants, Bulbs, Seeds, and Orchids.* Tokyo.
Seśták, Z. 1985. *Photosynthesis During Leaf Development.* Boston: Junk.
Seward, A. C. 1966. *Plant Life Through the Ages.* New York: Hafner.
Seydel, von. 1915. Ein Weiszbunter Spitz-Ahorn, *Acer platanoides. Mitt. Dtsch. Dendr. Ges.* 24:275–276.
Sharma, G. K. 1975. Leaf surface effects of environmental pollution on sugar maple (*Acer saccharum*) in Montreal. *Canadian Journal of Botany* 53:2312–2314.
Sharon, E. M. 1973. Some histological features of *Acer saccharum* wood formed after wounding. *Canadian Journal of Forest Research* 3:83–89.
Shaw, E. A. 1977. *Saccharum* or *saccharophorum? Rhodora* 79:123–127.
Sheat, W. G. 1948. *Propagation of Trees, Shrubs and Conifers.* London: Macmillan.
Shenefeld, R. D., and D. M. Benjamin. 1955. Insects of Wisconsin forests. University of Wisconsin, College of Agriculture Circular 500.
Shigo, A. L. 1964. A canker on red maple caused by fungi infecting wounds made by the red squirrel. *Plant Disease Reporter* 48:794–796.
______. 1965. Decay and discoloration in sprout red maple. *Phytopathology* 55:957–962.
______. 1974. Relative abilities of *Phialophora melinii, Fomes connatus,* and *F. igniarius* to invade freshly founded tissues of *Acer rubrum. Phytopathology* 64:708–710.
______. 1976. Mineral stain. *The North Logger & Timber Processor* 24:18.
______. 1981. Proper pruning of tree branches. *Journal of the Royal Horticultural Society* 106:471–473.
______. 1982. Tree decay. *Plant Dis.* 66.
______. 1983. Tree defects: a photo guide. USDA Forest Service, General Technical Report NE–82.
______. 1984. How to assess the defect status of a stand. *New Journal of Applied Forestry* 1.
______. 1985. Compartmentalization of decay in trees. *Scientific American* 252(April):76–83.
______. 1986. *A New Tree Biology.* Durham, New Hampshire: Shigo and Trees.
______. 1989. *Tree Pruning. A Worldwide Photo Guide.* Durham, New Hampshire: Shigo and Trees.
Shigo, A. L., and E. M. Sharon. 1970. Mapping columns of discolored and decayed tissues in sugar maple, *Acer saccharum. Phytopathology* 60:232–237.
Shigo, A. L., and C. L. Wilson. 1977. Wound dressing on red maple and American elm: effectiveness after five years. *Journal of Arboriculture* 3(4):81–86.

Shimizu, T., et al. 1977. Changes in metabolite levels during growth of *Acer pseudoplatanus* cells in batch suspension culture. *Physiol. Pl.* 40:125–129.

______. 1981. Contributions to the flora of southeast Asia. VI. Taxonomy and phytogeography of some temperate species in Thailand. (2). *Acta Phytotaxonomica et Geobotanica* 32(1–4):37–46.

Shorland, F. B. 1963. The distribution of fatty acids in plant lipids. In *Chemical Plant Taxonomy.* Ed. T. Swain. New York: Academic Press.

Shortle, W. C., and A. L. Shigo. 1978. Effect of plastic wrap on wound closure and internal compartmentalization of discolored and decayed wood in red maple. *Plant Disease Reporter* 62(11):999–1002.

Shun-Ching Lee. 1935. *Acer sutchuenense* Franch. *For. Bot. of China* 55:740–779.

Shurtleff, M. C. 1980. The search for disease-resistant trees. *Journal of Arboriculture* 6:238–244.

Sibthorp, J., and J. E. Smith. 1809. *A. obtusifolium* Sibth. et Sm. *Florae Graecae Prodromus* 1(2):262–263.

Siebert, A., and A. Voss. 1894. *Vilmorin's Blumengärtnerei.* 3rd ed. Berlin.

Siebold, P. F. von. 1844. Kruidkundige Naamlijst van Oud en Nieuw Ingevoerde Japanse en Chinese Planten. *Jaarboek Nederlandse Mij. Aanmoed. Tuinbouw* 1844:23.

______. 1864. Brussels Exposition. In *Index Bibliographique de l'Hortus Belgicus.* Gent.

Siebold, P. F. von, and J. G. Zuccarini. 1845. Florae Japonicae familiae naturales. *Abh. Math.-Phys. Kl. K. Bayer. Akad. Wiss. München* 4(2):154–159.

______. 1870. *Flora Japonica sive Plantae.* Leiden.

Siehe, W. 1924. Bäume und Holzartige Sträucher Ciliciens nebst Angabe der Höhenlagen in Welchem Sie Vorkommen. *Mitt. Dtsch. Dendr. Ges.* 34:187–194.

Siesmayer, J. A. 1888. Die Japanischen Ahorn-Arten. *Müller's Gärtn. Zeitung.* 268–270.

Silva Tarouca, G. Ernst, and C. Schneider. 1931. *Unsere Freiland-Laubgehölze.* 3rd ed. Vienna: Hölder-Pichler-Tempsky.

Sim, T. R. 1919. *Flowering Trees and Shrubs for Use in South Africa.* Johannesburg: Speciality Press of South Africa.

Simmons, G. A. 1983. The obliquebanded leafroller and *Cenopis pettitana* infesting maple buds in Michigan. *Annuals of the Entomological Society of America* 66:1166–1167.

Simmons, J. 1986. A 7000 foot mountain with a five step snake, Guizhou. *Journal of the Royal Horticultural Society* 111:567–572.

Simonkai, L. T. 1908. *Conspectus Acerorum in Hungaria. Növ. Közlem.* 7:141–182.

Simon-Louis Frères (Nursery). 1886. *Catalogue 1886–1887*:21–22. Metz, France.

______. 1900. *Catalogue 1900–1901*:23–24.

Simpkins, I., et al. 1970. The growth of *Acer pseudoplatanus* cells in a synthetic liquid medium: response to the carbohydrate, nitrogenous and growth hormone constituents. *Physiol. Pl.* 23:385.

Simsíková, J. 1969. A new method to break dormancy of terminal buds of *Acer pseudoplatanus* L. *Acta Univ. Palckianae Olomuc. Fac. Rer. Nat.* 31:49–56.

Simson, B. W., and T. E. Timell. 1978. Polysaccharides in cambial tissues of *Populus tremuloides* and *Tilia americana.* I. isolation, fractionation and chemical composition of the cambial tissue. *Cellulose Chem. Techn.* 12:39–50.

Sinclair, W. A. 1967. Decline of hardwoods: possible causes. In *Proceedings of the International Shade Tree Conference* 42:17–32.

Sinclair, W. A., and G. W. Hudler. 1980. Tree and shrub pathogens new or noteworthy in New York State. *Plant Disease Reporter* 64:590–592.

Sinclair, W. A., et al. 1981. *Verticillium* wilt of maples: symptoms related to movement of the pathogen in stems. *Phytopathology* 71:340–345.

______. 1987. *Diseases of Trees and Shrubs.* Ithaca, New York: Cornell University Press.

Skelly, J. M. 1964. *The Nature and Occurrence of an Annual Canker of Acer saccharum* Marsh. in Pennsylvania. Master's thesis, Pennsylvania State University.

Skinner, J. H., & Co. (Nursery, Topeka, Kansas). 1938. *Acer saccharinum* 'Skinneri'. *American Nurseryman* 68:13.

Slavin, A. D. 1931. Several forms of native and naturalized trees. *American Midland Naturalist* 12:224–226.

Slavin, B. H. 1950. A new hybrid maple. *Nat. Hort. Magazine* 29:103–107.

______. 1954. The Seneca hybrid maple. *Phytologia* 5:1.

Slocock, W. C., Ltd. (Nursery). 1947. *Catalogue* 1947–48. Woking, Great Britain.

Small, J. K. 1895. *Acer leucoderme.* Bulletin of the Torrey Botanical Club 22:367–368.

______. 1903. *Flora of the Southeastern United States.* New York.
______. 1933. *Manual of the Southeastern Flora.* Chapel Hill, North Carolina.
Smiley, C. J. 1963. The Ellensburg flora of Washington. University of California Publication, geological science, 35:227–228, t. 13.
Smiley, F. J. 1921. A report upon the boreal flora of the Sierra Nevada of California. University of California Publication, botany, 9:261–262.
Smith, C. F., and C. S. Parron. 1978. An annotated list of Aphididae (Homoptera) of North America. North Carolina Agricultural Experiment Station Technical Bulletin 255.
Smith, C. J. 1980. *Ecology of the English Chalk.* London: Academic Press.
Smith, E. M. 1975. Tree stress from salts and herbicides. *Journal of Arboriculture* 1:201–205.
Smith, E. M., and C. H. Gilliam. 1980. Fertilization of container grown nursery stock. Ohio State University Cooperative Extension Bulletin 858.
Smith, E. M., and C. D. Mitchell. 1977. Manganese deficiency of red maple. *Journal of Arboriculture* 3:87–88.
Smith, G. 1985. New Zealand I.D.S. members' weekend. *Int. Dendr. Soc. Yrbk.* 1984:80–83.
Smith, H. C., et al. 1976. Reproduction 12 years after seed-tree harvest cutting in Appalachian hardwoods. USDA Forest Service Research Paper NE–379.
Smith, H. H. 1933. Ethnobotany of the forest Potawatomi Indians. Bulletin of the Public Museum, City of Milwaukee 7:1–230.
Smith, H. V. 1938a. *Engelhardtia Tuckeri. Papers of the Michigan Academy of Science* 23:226.
______. 1938b. *Quercus malheurensis.* Bulletin of the Torrey Botanical Club 65:560.
Smith, J. J. 1817. In *The North American Sylva,* by F. A. Michaux. 2 vols. Translated from French, with notes by J. J. Smith. Philadelphia: Dobson.
Smith, L. D. 1983. Major nutrient influence on *Verticillium dahliae* infections of *Acer saccharum. Journal of Arboriculture* 9:277–281.
Smith, L. D., and D. Neely. 1979. Relative susceptibility of tree species to *Verticillium dahliae. Plant Disease Reporter* 63:328–332.
Smith, P. 1990. Andalusia Tour, April 6 to 12, 1989. *Int. Dendr. Soc. Yrbk.* 1989:26–31.
Smith, R., & Co. (Nursery, Worcester, Great Britain). 1874. *Gardener's Chronicle* II. 1:674.
Smith, W. H. 1970. Root exudates of seedling and mature sugar maple. *Phytopathology* 60:701.
Smith, W. W. 1915. Diagnoses specierum novarum. *Notes of the Royal Botanic Garden, Edinburgh* 8:329.
______. 1917. Diagnoses specierum novarum. *Notes of the Royal Botanic Garden, Edinburgh* 10:8.
______. 1921. Diagnoses specierum novarum. *Notes of the Royal Botanic Garden, Edinburgh* 13:151.
Smithsonian Scientific Series. 1931. *Old and New Plant Lore.* Vol. 2.
Society of American Foresters. 1980. *Forest Cover Types of North America.* Washington, DC: Society of American Foresters.
Society of Gentlemen. 1790. *Remarks on the Manufacturing of Maple Sugar.* Philadelphia, Pennsylvania.
Sondergaard, P. 1985. Tour in Nepal October 26 to November 16, 1984. *Int. Dendr. Soc. Yrbk.* 1984:36–51.
Sonnerfeld, N. L. 1988. A guide to the vegetative communities at the Valley of the Giants, northwestern Oregon, USA. *Int. Dendr. Soc. Yrbk.* 1987:72–77. Rpt. from *Journal of Arboriculture* 11(3). 1987.
Spach, E. 1834. Revisio generis *Acerum. Ann. Sci. Nat. Bot.* II. 2:160–180.
Späth, F. L. 1879. Neuheiten aus dem Etablissement des Herrn Spaeth in Berlin. *Monatsschr. Ver. Beförd. Gartenb. Preussen* 22:20.
______. 1883a. In Neuheiten von Harten Gehölzarten, by E. Otto. *Hamburger Garten- und Blumenzeitung* 39:511–512.
______. 1883b. Neue Buntblätterige Ahorne. *Gartenzeitung* 1883:513.
______. 1887. Neue und Sehr Wenig Verbreitete Ziergehölze. *Spaeth Katalog* 69:7.
______. 1892. *Acer palmatum* 'Aokii'. *Gartenflora* 41:33.
______. 1896. Einige Neue und Seltene Gehölze der Späth'schen Baumschule. *Mitt. Dtsch. Dendr. Ges.* 5:23–25.
______. 1904. Zwei Neue Ahornformen. *Mitt. Dtsch. Dendr. Ges.* 13:199.
Speight, M., and M. Nicol. 1984. Horse-chestnut scale—a new urban menace? *New Scientist* (April) 5:40.
Spencer, D. M., ed. 1978. *The Powdery Mildews.* New York: Academic Press.
Spencer, J. B. 1913. The maple sugar industry in Canada. Canada Department of Agriculture

Bulletin 2B.
______. 1914. Die Ahornzucker-Industrie in Kanada. *Mitt. Dtsch. Dendr. Ges.* 23:54–78.
______. 1923. The maple sugar industry in Canada. Canada Department of Agriculture Bulletin 30.
Sperry, J. S., et al. 1988. Seasonal occurrence of xylem embolism in sugar maple (*Acer saccharum*). *American Journal of Botany* 75(8):1212–1218.
Spethmann, W. 1982. Stecklingsvermehrung von Laubbaumarten. *Allg. Forst- und Jagdztng* 153:13–24.
Spethmann, W. and K. Namvar. 1985. Der Bergahorn und die Gattung *Acer. Allg. Forstzeitschr.* 42. Sonderdruck.
Spoelberch, P. de. 1988. I.D.S. Council visit to the garden of Buckingham Palace Oct. 23, 1987. *Int. Dendr. Soc. Yrbk.* 1987:42–44.
Spongberg, S. A. 1981. Cultivar registration at the Arnold Arboretum. AABGA Bulletin 15(3):67–70.
______. 1990. *A Reunion of Trees.* Cambridge, Massachusetts: Harvard University Press.
Sporne, K. R. 1969. The ovule as an indicator of evolutionary status in angiosperms. *New Phytology* 68:555–566.
______. 1974. *The Morphology of Angiosperms.* London: Hutchinson University Library.
______. 1980. A re-investigation of character correlations among dicotyledons. *New Phytology* 85:419–449.
Sprague, T. A. 1929. The botanical name of the sugar maple. Kew Bulletin 1929:81.
Springer, L. A. 1927. *Acer Pseudo-platanus* L. *Jaarboek Nederlandse Dendr. Ver.* 3:84–88.
______. 1928a. Variabilität der Fruchtflügel bei *Acer pseudoplatanus. Mitt. Dtsch. Dendr. Ges.* 40:351.
______. 1928b. Het Vermenigvuldigen van Boomen en Struiken door Zaad. *Jaarboek Nederlandse Dendr. Ver.* 4:93–96.
______. 1930. *Acer campestre* L. var. *fastigiatum. Jaarboek Nederlandse Dendr. Ver.* 6:179–180.
______. 1933a. Kweekerijen—Dendrologie. *Jaarboek Nederlandse Dendr. Ver.* 9:141–145.
______. 1933b. *Acer kawakamii* Koidz. *Jaarboek Nederland Dendr. Ver.* 9:189–190.
St. Przedpelski Plock, Polonia Russia Nursery. 1909–1910. *Price List of Trees and Shrub Seeds.*
Stace, C. A. 1980. *Plant Taxonomy and Biosystematics.* London: Arnold.
Stafleu, F. A. 1967. *Taxonomic Literature.* Regnum vegetabile 52. Utrecht.
Stafleu, F. A., and R. S. Cowan. 1976– . *Taxonomic Literature.* 2nd ed. Regnum vegetabile. Utrecht: Bohn, Scheltema & Holkema.
Stainton, J. D. A. 1972. *Forests of Nepal.* London: Murray.
Standley, P. C. 1923. *Trees and Shrubs of Mexico. Contr. from the Nat. Herb.* 23:689–690. Rpt. 1982. Vaduz: J. Cramer.
Standley, P. C., and J. A. Steyermark. 1944. Studies of Central American plants. *Fieldiana Bot.* 23(2):60.
______. 1949. Flora of Guatemala. *Fieldiana Bot.* 24(6):1–440.
Stanley, R. G., and H. F. Linskens. 1974. *Pollen.* New York: Springer.
Stearn, W. T. 1966. *Botanical Latin.* London: Nelson.
______. 1986. *Acer negundo,* a puzzling plant name. *Journal of the Royal Horticultural Society* 111:529–530.
Stebbins, G. L. 1950. *Variation and Evolution of Plants.* New York: Columbia University Press.
______. 1974. *Flowering Plants. Evolution Above the Species Level.* Cambridge: Harvard University Press.
______. 1977. *Processes of Organic Evolution.* 3rd ed. Englewood Cliffs, New Jersey: Prentice-Hall.
Steenis, C. G. G. J. van. 1979. Plant-geography of East Malaysia. *Botanical Journal, Linnean Society* 79:97–178.
______. 1982b. Heterophylly and neoformation of leaves in sugar maple (*Acer saccharum*). *American Journal of Botany* 69:1277–1282.
______. 1984. Heterophylly in *Acer glabrum* Torr. In *35th Annual AIBS Meeting,* Abstract 137.
Steingraeber, D. A. 1982. Phenotypic plasticity of branching pattern in sugar maple (*Acer saccharum*). *American Journal of Botany* 69:638–640.
Stephens, Sir L., and Sir S. Lee. N.d. *Dictionary of National Biography,* part 1. Vol. 13, *From the Earliest Time to 1900.* Rpt. 1920–1922. London: Oxford University Press.
Stephyrtza, A. G. 1978. Contribution to the Pontian flora of Moldavia. *Botanicheskii Zhurnal* 63:785–796.
Sternberg, K. M. Graf von. 1823. *Versuch Einer Geognostisch-botanischen Darstellung der Flora der*

*Vorwelt* 3:39. Leipzig.
______. 1825. *Versuch Einer Geognostisch-botanischen Darstellung der Flora der Vorwelt,* Heft 4:42. Leipzig.
Steudel, E. G. von. 1821. *Nomenclator Botanicus.* 1:5. 1st ed. Stuttgart.
______. 1840. *Nomenclator Botanicus.* 1:11–12. 2nd ed. Stuttgart.
Stevens, O. A. 1975. Comparison of flowering records from Kansas and North Dakota. *Prairie Naturalist* 7:81–85.
Steward, F. C., et al. 1974. The labeling of cultured cells of *Acer* with 14Cproline and its significance. *Journal of Cell Biology* 60:695–701.
Stimart, D. P. 1981. Factors regulating germination of trifoliate maple seeds. *HortScience* 16:341–343.
Stinson, E. E., et al. 1967. Quebrachitol—A new component of maple sap and syrup. *Journal of Agricultural Food and Chemistry* 15:394–397.
Stokes, J. 1812. *A Botanical Materia Medica* 2:370–384. London.
Stokoe, W. J. 1959. *The Observer's Book of Trees and Shrubs.* London: Warne.
Stolberg-Stolberg, H. Graf von. 1919. Über Verwendung, Fortkommen und Nutzbarkeit der Fremdhölzer in Westfalen. *Mitt. Dtsch. Dendr. Ges.* 28:100–106.
Stone, E. L. 1968. Microelement nutrition of forest trees: a review. In *Forest Fertilization: Theory and Practice.* Muscle Shoals: Tennessee Valley Authority.
Stone, W. 1911. The plants of southern New Jersey. *Annual Report of the New Jersey State Museum for 1910* no. 544. Trenton, New Jersey.
Stott, P. 1981. *Historical Plant Geography.* London: Allen & Unwin.
Strassburger. 1976. *Textbook of Botany.* Translated from the 1971 German ed. London: Longman.
Street, H. E. ed. 1974. *Tissue Culture and Plant Science.* London: Academic Press.
Stróbl, P. G. 1885. Flora der Etna. *Österr. Bot. Zeitschr.* 35:404,432.
Strong, F. C. 1936. Maple wilt. Michigan Agricultural Experiment Station Quarterly Bulletin 18:225–227.
______. 1938. Prevalence of wilt diseases in maple and elm. Michigan Agricultural Experiment Station Quarterly Bulletin 21:96–99.
Students of Landscape Architecture. 1983. *Acer negundo*—Survey of its distribution in Montreal. Unpublished manuscript. University of Montreal, Quebec, Canada.
Stur, D. R. J. 1867. Beiträge zur Kenntnis der Flora der Süsswasserquarze. *Jahrb. Geol. Reichsanst. Wien* 17:175–178
Sudworth, G. B. 1893. Additions to the forest flora of North America. USDA Off. Secy. Report for 1892. Washington, DC: USDA.
______. 1897. Nomenclature of the arborescent flora of the United States. USDA Forest Service Bulletin 14:282–293.
______. 1927. Check list of the trees of the United States, their names and ranges. USDA Miscellaneous Circular 92.
Sullivan, J. B. 1983. Comparative reproductive biology of *Acer pensylvanicum* and *A. spicatum* (Aceraceae). *American Journal of Botany* 70:916–924.
Sutherland, J. 1683. *Hortus Medicus Edinburgensis.* Edinburgh: Heir of Andrew Anderson.
Suzuki and Iida (nurserymen). N.d. *Catalogue of Japanese Bulbs, Plants and Seeds.* New York.
Suzuki, H. no date. *Personal Correspondence and Translations 1972–77.* Japan: Kumagaya Saitamaken.
Swain, T. 1988. Evolution of flavonoid compounds. In *The Flavonoids: Advances in Research Since 1980.* Ed. J. B. Harborne. London: Chapman & Hall.
______. 1985. Plant phenolics, past and future. In *Annual Proceedings of the Phytochemistry Society of Europe* 25. Eds. C. F. van Sumere and P. J. Lea. Oxford: Clarendon Press.
Sy, A. P. 1908. History, manufacture and analysis of maple products. *J. Franklin Inst.* 166:249–280, 321–352, 433–445.
Synge, P. M. 1971. Tour to Dorset and Devon 4th–11th May 1970. *Int. Dendr. Soc. Yrbk.* 1970:60–75.
______. 1972. Autumn day tours. *Int. Dendr. Soc. Yrbk.* 1971:81–86.
______. 1973. Belgian tour October 13th–17th, 1972. *Int. Dendr. Soc. Yrbk.* 1972:88–98.
______. 1974a. South Russian tour 29th April–20th May 1973. *Int. Dendr. Soc. Yrbk.* 1973:62–84.
______. 1974b. Val de Loire tour 11th–17th October 1973. *Int. Dendr. Soc. Yrbk.* 1973:92–103.
______. 1975a. The Arboretum at Endsleigh. *Int. Dendr. Soc. Yrbk.* 1974:19–27.
______. 1975b. Southern Highlands tour, U.S.A. October 7th–22nd, 1974. *Int. Dendr. Soc. Yrbk.* 1974:77–92.
______. 1978. I.D.S. Tour in Holland September 29–October 5, 1976. *Int. Dendr. Soc. Yrbk.* 1977:61–71.

Szafer, W. 1947. The Pliocene flora of Kroszienko in Polonia. *Rozpr. Wydz. Matem. Przyr.* B 72 (1/2):1–375.

______. 1954. Pliocenska Flora Czorsztyna i jej Stosunek do Plejsocenu. *Prace Inst. Geol.* 11:1–238.

______. 1961. Miocenska Flora ze Strych Gliwic na Slasku. *Prace Inst. Geol.* 33:1–205.

Szirmai, J. 1972. An *Acer* virus disease in maple trees planted in avenues. *Acta Phytopathologia Acad. Sci. Hung.* 7:197–207.

Taggert, R. E. 1971. *Palynology and Paleoecology of the Miocene Sucker Creek Flora from the Oregon-Idaho Boundary.* Ph.D. thesis, Michigan State University, Ann Arbor.

Tait, W. A. 1986. A stream and its plants. *Journal of the Royal Horticultural Society* 111:5–10.

Takahashi, A., and M. Suzuki. 1988. Two new fossil woods of *Acer* and a new combination of *Prunus* from the Tertiary of Japan. *Botanical Magazine, Tokyo* 101:473–481.

Takeshi, N., and N. Akira. 1982. *Katsura,* A Princely Retreat. Tokyo: Kodansha.

Takhtajan, A. 1969. *Flowering Plants, Origins and Dispersal.* (Translated from Russian.) Edinburgh: Oliver & Boyd.

Takizawa, S. 1952. Chromosome studies in the genus *Acer. Journal of the Faculty of Science, Hokkaido Imperial University,* botany, 5(6):249–272.

Talbot de Malahide, Lord. 1970. Tour of Guernsey, Jersey and Brittany 16th–26th April 1969. *Int. Dendr. Soc. Yrbk.* 1969:36–56.

Tanai, T. 1952. Notes à propos de quelques plantes fossiles dans la groupe d'Ennichi. *Trans. Proc. Palaeont. Soc. Japan,* n.s., 8:234.

Tanai, T. 1971. The Miocene Sakipenpetsu flora from Ashibetsu Area, central Hokkaido. *Memoirs of the Natural Science Museum of Tokyo* 4:127–172.

______. 1972. Tertiary history of vegetation in Japan. In *Floristics and Paleofloristics of Asia and Eastern North America.* Ed. A. Graham. Amsterdam: Elsevier.

______. 1978a. Taxonomical reinvestigation of the Genus *Acer* L. based on vein architecture of leaves. *Journal of Japanese Botany* 53(3):65–83.

______. 1978b. Taxonomical investigations of the living species of the genus *Acer* based on vein architecture of leaves. *Journal of the Faculty of Science, Hokkaido Imperial University,* ser. 4, geology, 18:243–282.

Tanai, T., and N. Suzuki. 1960. Miocene maples from southwestern Hokkaido, Japan. *Journal of the Faculty of Science, Hokkaido Imperial University,* ser. 4, geology, 10:551–570.

Tang, G. 1984. A new species of *Acer* in China. *J. Nanjing Inst. For.* 2:83–85.

Tansley, A. G. 1968. *Britain's Green Mantle.* 2nd ed. London: Allen & Unwin.

Tarjan, A. C., and F. L. Howard. 1954. Detrimental effects of copper sprays to Norway maple in Rhode Island. *Plant Disease Reporter* 38:58.

Tate, R. L. 1980. Detection, description, and treatment of girdling roots on urban Norway maple trees. *Journal of Arboriculture* 6:168.

______. 1981. Characteristics of girdling roots on urban Norway maples. *Journal of Arboriculture* 7:268–270.

Tatewaki, M. 1960. Migration routes of the higher plants for the flora of Hokkaido. *Journal of Geobotany, University of Tokyo* 8:43–52.

Tattar, T. A. 1978. *Diseases of Shade Trees.* New York: Academic Press.

Tattar, T. A., and A. E. Rich. 1973. Extractable phenols in clear, discolored, and decayed woody tissues and bark of sugar maple and red maple. *Phytopathology* 63:167–169.

Tausch, I. F. 1829. Bemerkungen über *Acer. Flora* 12:545–554. Regensburg.

Taylor, D. 1974. The Essex landscape—a county council programme for replanting the countryside. *Int. Dendr. Soc. Yrbk.* 1973:36–44.

Taylor, G. S. 1983. *Cryptosporiopsis* canker of *Acer rubrum:* some relationships among host, pathogen, and vector. *Plant Disease Reporter* 67:984–986.

Taylor, G. S., and R. E. B. Moore. 1979. A canker of red maples associated with oviposition by the narrow-winged tree cricket. *Phytopathology* 69:236–239.

Taylor, R. 1976. *Acer circinatum. Davidsonia* 7 (3).

Taylor, W. R. 1920. A morphological and cytological study of reproduction in the Genus *Acer. Contributions, Botanical Laboratory, Morris Arboretum* 5(2):111–138.

Taylor, J. S., and E. B. Dumbroff. 1975. Bud, root, and growth-regulator activity in *Acer saccharum* during the dormant season. *Canadian Journal of Botany* 53:321–331.

Tehon, L. R., and E. Daniels. 1925. Notes on the parasitic fungi of Illinois. II. *Mycologia* 17:240–249.

Teixeira, C. 1949. Plantas fóssil do Plioceico do Alfeite. *Comun. Serv. Geol. Portugal* 30:43–48.

Tenore, M. 1813. *Ad Catalogum Plantarum Horti Regii Neapolitani.* First appendix. Naples. 75–76.

______. 1819. *Catalogus Plantarum Horti Regii Neapolitani.* Appendix altera. Naples. 69.

______. 1831. *Sylloge Plantarum Vascularium Florae Neopolitanae.* Naples.

______. 1845. *Catalogo delle Piante* ... Orto Botanico di Napoli. Naples.

Terazaki, T. 1932. *Nippon Shokubutsu Zukan* (Nippon Botany). Tokyo: Shun Yo Do.

Terraciano, N. 1872. *Relazione intorno alle peregrinazioni botaniche in terra di Lavoro.* Caserta.

Thakur, M. L. 1977a. Phenolic growth inhibitors isolated from dormant buds of sugar maple (*Acer saccharum* Marsh). *Journal of Experimental Botany* 28:795–803.

______. 1977b. Significance of phenolic compounds in dormant buds of sugar maple (*Acer saccharum* Marsh.). *Physiol. Pl.* 59(6, supplement):78.

Theophrastus. 1968. *Enquiry into Plants.* 2 vols. Translated by A. F. Hort. London: Heinemann; Cambridge, Massachusetts: Harvard University Press.

Thibaut & Keteleer Nursery. 1866. *Acer palmatum roseum. Revue Horticole* 38:379.

Thomas, K. 1984. *Man and the Natural World. Changing Attitudes in England 1500–1800.* London: Penguin.

Thompson, R. L., ed. 1971. *The Ecology and Management of the Red-cockaded Woodpecker.* U.S. Department of the Interior, Bureau of Sport Fishing and Wildlife.

Thomson, R. H. 1971. *Naturally Occurring Quinones.* New York: Academic Press.

Thuillier, J. L. 1799. *La flore des environs de Paris.* Paris.

Thunberg, C. P. 1783. *A. palmatum* Thunb. In Kaempferus Illustratus. *Nova Acta Regiae Societatis Scientiarum* (Uppsala) 4:36,40.

______. 1784. *Flora Japonica.* Leipzig.

______. 1793. *Dissertatio Botanica de Acere.* Uppsala.

______. 1795. *Travels in Europe, Africa and Asia 1770–1779.* 4 vols. London: Richardson.

Timberlake, C. F., and P. Bridle. 1975. The anthocyanins. In *The Flavonoids: Advances in Research Since 1980.* Ed. J. B. Harborne. London: Chapman & Hall.

Tingle Nursery. 1962. *Catalogue.* Pikesville, Maryland.

Tinus, R. W. 1981. Root system configuration is important to long tree life. *Plants Landscape* 4(1):1–5.

Tips Bros. Nursery (Herck-de-Stad, Belgium). 1953. *Cultuur en Handel* 19:116.

Tissut, M., and K. Egger. 1972. Les glycosides flavoniques foliaires de quelques arbres, au cours du cycle végétatif. *Phytochemistry* 11:631–634.

Tomaszewska, E. 1976. Growth regulators in *Acer platanoides* L. seeds. *Arboretum Kórnickie* 21:297–312.

Tomaszewski, M. 1960. The occurrence of p-hydroxybenzoic acid and some other simple phenolics in vascular plants. Bulletin of the Academy of Polish Science, ser. sci. biol. 8:61–65.

Tominari and Hayashi. 1971. *Nihon no ka boku.* (Ornamental Trees and Shrubs of Japan.) Tokyo: Kodansha.

Toogood, A. 1980. *Propagation.* London: Dent.

Torode, S. 1986. Dyffryn Gardens. With a note on some trees by Alan Mitchell. *Journal of the Royal Horticultural Society* 111:151–157.

Torrey, J. 1828. *Acer glabrum* Torr. Some account of a collection of plants ... by E. P. James. *Ann. Lyc. Nat. Hist. N.Y.* 2:172.

Torrey, J. ,and A. Gray. 1838. *A Flora of North America.* New York.

Torrey, J. G., and D. T. Clarkson. 1975. *The Development and Function of Roots.* New York: Academic Press.

Tournefort, J. P. de. 1700. *Institutiones Rei Herbariae.* Paris: Ed. Altera.

Towers, G. H. N., and R. D. Gibbs. 1953. Lignin chemistry and the taxonomy of higher plants. *Nature* 172:25–26.

Townsend, A. M. 1972. Geographic variation in fruit of *Acer rubrum.* Bulletin of the Torrey Botanical Club 99:122–126.

______. 1977a. Improving the adaptation of maples and elms to the urban environment. In *Proceedings of the 16th Meeting of the Canadian Tree Improvement Association* 2, University of Manitoba, Winnipeg. 27–31.

______. 1977b. Characteristics of red maple progenies from different geographic areas. *Journal of the American Society for Horticultural Science* 102:461–466.

Townsend, A. M., and L. S. Dochinger. 1974. Relationship of seed source and developmental stage to the ozone tolerance of *Acer rubrum* seedlings. *Atmospheric Environment* 8:957–964.

Townsend, A. M., and W. K. Hock. 1973. Tolerance of half-sib families of red maple to *Verticillium* wilt. *Phytopathology* 63(6):673–676.

Townsend, A. M., and B. R. Roberts. 1973. Effect of moisture stress on red maple seedlings from different seed sources. *Canadian Journal of Botany* 51:1989–1995.

Townsend, A. M., et al. 1979. Geographic variation in young red maple grown in north central United States. *Sylvae Genet.* 28:33–36.
______. 1982. Early patterns of flowering, winter injury, and flushing of red maple progenies grown in five locations. *Canadian Journal of Forest Research* 12:814–821.
T.R.A.D.A. (Timber Research & Development Association). 1979. *Timbers of the World.* 2 vols. Lancaster: Construction Press.
Traill, C. P. 1860. *The Canadian Settler's Guide.* London: Stanford.
Transeau, E. N., et al. 1940. *Textbook of Botany.* New York: Harper & Brothers.
Trattinnick, L. 1811. *Archiv der Gewächskunde* 1:1–4. Vienna.
______. 1812. *Ausgemahlte Tafeln aus dem Archiv der Gewächskunde* 1:1–25.
Trautvetter, E. R. 1856. Florula ochotensis phaenogama. In Middendorf's *Reise in den Aeussersten Norden und Osten Siberiens* 1(2):24.
Trelease, W. 1894. Sugar maples in winter. *Annual Report of the Missouri Botanical Garden* 5:88–106.
Tressler, C. J., and W. I. Zimmerman. 1942. Three years operation of an experimental sugar bush. New York State Agricultural Experiment Station Bulletin 699.
Trimble, G. R. 1967. Diameter increase in second-growth Appalachian hardwood stands—a comparison of species. USDA Forest Service Research Notes NE–75.
Trimble, G. R., et al. 1974. Some options for managing forest land in the Central Appalachians. USDA Forest Service, General Technical Report NE–12.
Troll, W. 1935. Vergleichende Morphologie der Fiederblätter. *Nova Acta Leop.* Bd. 2, Hft. 3/4, No. 4.
______. 1954. *Praktische Einführung in die Pflanzenmorphologie. Der Vegetative Aufbau.* Jena: Fischer.
______. 1957. *Praktische Einführung in die Pflanzenmorphologie. Die Blühende Pflanze.* Jena: Fischer.
______. 1964. Die Infloreszenzen. *Typologie und Stellung im Aufbau des Vegetationskörpers* 1:108–111.
Tromp, J. 1986. *'Boskoops Koninklijke'* 1861–1986. Boskoop: Kon. Ver. Bosk. Cult.
Tschewerda, M. 1924. Laubabwurf des Spitzahorns im Juli. *Mitt. Dtsch. Dendr. Ges.* 34:385.
Tsoong, P. C. 1954. A new *Acer* from China. Kew Bulletin 1954:83.
______. 1955. *Acer miatoanense. Acta Phytotaxonomica Sinica, Peking* 3:415.
Tsujimura, M. 1953. Chemical components of the leaves of *Acer aidzuense. Imp. Chem. Abstr.* 47:5498.
Tubbs, C. H. 1976. Effect of sugar maple root exudate on seedlings of northern conifer species. USDA Forest Service Research Notes NC–213.
Tubeuf, F. von. 1917. Gärtnerische Kultur der Mistel. *Mitt. Dtsch. Dendr. Ges.* 26:188–196.
Tucker, E. M. 1914–1933. *Catalogue of the Library of the Arnold Arboretum of Harvard University.* Cambridge, Massachusetts.
Tung, S. L. 1985. *Acer barbinerve* var. *chanbaischanense.* Bulletin of Botanical Research, Northeastern Forestry Institute 5(1):100.
Turner, W. 1551. *New Herball.* Part 1. London: Steven Mierdman.
______. 1562. *New Herball.* Part 2. Cologne: Arnold Birckman.
______. 1568. *New Herball.* Parts 1, 2, & 3. Cologne: Arnold Birckman Collen.
Turner, M. 1986. *Acer capillipes.* Front cover photograph *Journal of the Royal Horticultural Society* (November):111.
Turner, N. J. 1973. The ethnobotany of the Bella Coola Indians of British Columbia. *Syesis* 6:193–220.
Turner, N. C., and M. A. M. Bell. 1973. Ethnobotany of the Southern Kwakiutl Indians of British Columbia. *Economic Botany* 27:257–310.
Turner, N. C., and G. H. Heichel. 1977. Stomatal development and seasonal changes in diffuse resistance of primary and regrowth foliage of red oak (*Quercus rubra* L.) and red maple (*Acer rubrum* L.). *New Phytology* 78:71–81.
Turrill, W. B. 1959. *The Royal Botanic Gardens Kew. Past and Present.* London: Herbert Jenkins.
______. 1962. *Acer nikoense. Curtis's Botanical Magazine.* Table 387.
______. 1971. *British Plant Life.* London: Collins.
Tylkowski, T. 1985. The effect of storing silver maple samaras on the germinative capacity of seeds and seedlings growth. *Arboretum Kórnickie Rocnik.* XXIX. Warsaw-Poznań.
Udupa, K. N., and S. N. Tripathi. 1980. *Natürliche Heilkrafte. Früchte, Beeren, Gemüse, Gewürze.* Eltville am Rhein: Rheinhauer.
Ueda, Y. 1918a. On the application of leaves of *Acer ginnala* in Korea. *J. Chem. Ind. Tokyo* 21:211–219.
______. 1918b. *Acer ginnala;* application of leaves of (for dyeing, etc.) in Korea. *J. Soc. Chem. Ind.* 37:462.
______. 1961. *Jyuboku Daiju Setsu.* 3 vols. Tokyo: Arikae Shobo Bunkyo-ku.

Umbach, D. M., and D. D. Davis. 1984. Severity and frequency of $SO_2$-induced leaf necrosis on seedlings of 57 tree species. *Forest Science* 30:587–596.
Unger, F. J. A. N. 1842. In *Genera Plantarum Secundum Ordines Naturalis Disposita,* by S. F. L. Endlicher. Supplement 2. Vienna.
______. 1847. *Chloris Protogaea.* Leipzig.
______. 1850. *Genera et Species Plantarum Fossilium.* Vienna.
______. 1851. Die Fossile Flora von Sotzka. *Denkschr. Math. Naturw. Kl. Akad. Wiss. Wien* 2:175.
______. 1854. Die Fossile Flora von Gleichenberg. *Denkschr. Math. Naturw. Kl. Akad. Wiss. Wien* 7:180.
Uphof, J. C. T. 1927. Dendrologische Notizen aus dem Staate Florida. *Mitt. Dtsch. Dendr. Ges.* 38:158–173.
______. 1950–1951a. Een Overzicht der Rhododendrons van Noord-Amerika. *Jaarboek Nederlandse Dendr. Ver.* 18:61–67.
______. 1950–1951b. Virginische Cypressen in Hun Vaderland. *Jaarboek Nederlandse Dendr. Ver.* 18:69–73.
______. 1959. *Dictionary of Economic Plants.* Rpt. 1968. Lehre: J. Cramer.
Urstadt, Dr. 1929. Kreuzbildung im Innern eines Ahornstammes. *Mitt. Dtsch. Dendr. Ges.* 41:371.
Urusov, W. V. M. 1985. On the specific individualization of *Acer tschonoskii* and *Acer komarowii. Bot. J.* 70, part 5 of the Novosibirsk Forest Selection Laboratory of the Central Science Institute of Forest Genetics and Selection.
U.S.D.A. 1949. *Trees.* Yearbook of Agriculture. Washington, DC: USDA.
______. 1962. *After a Hundred Years.* Yearbook of Agriculture. Washington, DC: USDA.
U.S.D.A. Forest Service. 1948. Woody plant seed manual. Miscellaneous Publication no. 654. Washington, DC: USDA Forest Service.
U.S. Tariff Commission. 1930. *Maple Sugar and Maple Syrup.* Washington, DC.
Usher, G. 1974. *Dictionary of Plants Used by Man.* London: Constable.
Uyeda, Y., see Ueda, Y.
Uyeki, H. 1929. Four new ligneous plants from Corea and Manchuria. *J. Chosen Nat. Hist. Soc.* 9:20–21.
Vaillancourt, C. 1934. Erablieres. Agriculture Bulletin 134. Quebec, Canada.
Vaillant, S. 1727. *Botanicon Parisiense.* Leiden.
Vakhrameev, V. A., et al. 1970. *Paläozoische und Mesozoische Floren Asiens und die Phytogeographie dieser Zeit.* Jena: Fischer.
Valckenier Suringar, J. 1924. Die Nomenklatur der Amerikanischen Praktiker. *Mitt. Dtsch. Dendr. Ges.* 34:316–323.
______. 1929a. De Witte Strepen op den Stam van *Acer striatum (pennsylvanicum). Jaarboek Nederlandse Dendr. Ver.* 5:127.
______. 1929b. Nieuwe Planten. *Jaarboek Nederlandse Dendr. Ver.* 5:146–148.
______. 1930a. Nomenclaturalia. *Jaarboek Nederlandse Dendr. Ver.* 6:91–117.
______. 1930b. Die Weiszen Streifen am Stamm von *Acer pensylvanicum (A. striatum). Mitt. Dtsch. Dendr. Ges.* 42:390.
______. 1931. Nieuwe Soorten en Varieteiten. *Jaarboek Nederlandse Dendr. Ver.* 7:203–207.
______. 1932. Boeken en Tijdschriften. L. Späth. Späth-Buch, 1720–1930. 6 Mark. *Jaarboek Nederlandse Dendr. Ver.* 8:157–163.
Valckenier Suringar, J., and J. T. P. Bijhouwer. 1925. Overzicht van de Benamingskwesties onze Houtgewassen. *Jaarboek Nederlandse Dendr. Ver.* 1:20–80.
Valder, T. 1975. *Acer tonkinense. Journal of the Royal Horticultural Society* 100:497.
Valentine, F. A., and R. D. Westfall. 1979. Urban tree progeny tests of maples. *Journal of Arboriculture* 5:166–167.
Van Dersal, W. R. 1938. Native woody plants of the United States. USDA Miscellaneous Publication 303. Washington, DC.
Van der Meer, J. H. H. 1926. *Verticillium* wilt of maple and elm seedlings in Holland. *Phytopathology* 16:611–614.
Van Houtte, L. 1857. *Flores des Serres et des Jardins de l'Europe* 12:173.
______. 1861. *Flores des Serres et des Jardins de l'Europe* 14:273.
______. 1865. *Flores des Serres et des Jardins de l'Europe* 15:127.
______. 1867. *Catalogue.* Ghent.
______. 1868. *Flores des Serres et des Jardins de l'Europe* 17:117.
______. 1873. *Catalog* 152. Ghent.

———. 1875a. *Flores des Serres et des Jardins de l'Europe* 21:19.
———. 1875b. *Catalog* 165. Ghent.
———. 1876. *Catalog* 170. Ghent.
———. 1877. *Catalog* 175. Ghent.
———. 1885. *Catalog* 215. Ghent.
Van Klaveren, R. 1969. Growing *Acer palmatum* from cuttings. *International Plant Propagators' Society Proceedings* 19.
Van Volxem, J. 1882. *Acer campestre caucasicum. Gardener's Chronicle* II. 17:74.
Vaucher, H. 1990. *Baumrinden.* (Treebarks). Stuttgart: Enke.
Veendorp, H. 1937. Zomerbijeenkomst. *Jaarboek Nederlandse Dendr. Ver.* 12:22–32.
Veendorp, H., and L. G. M. Baas Becking. 1938. *Hortus Academicus Lugduno-Batavus.* Harlemi: Ex Typographia Enschedaiana.
Veitch, J. H. 1904. Far eastern maples. *Journal of the Royal Horticultural Society* 29:327–360.
———. 1906. *Hortus Veitchii.* London.
Veitch Nursery. 1867. *Catalog* 1867–68.
———. 1872. *Catalog* 1872–73.
———. 1876. *Catalog* 1876–77.
Velenovsky, J. 1881. Die Flora aus den Ausgebrannten Tertiären Letten von Vrŝovic bei Laun. *Abh. Böhm. Ges. Wiss. Prag.* VI. 11:38–39.
Venema, H. J. 1935–1936. De Houtige Gewassen der Eilanden van de Voormalige Zuiderzee. *Jaarboek Nederlandse Dendr. Ver.* 11:72–74.
———. 1937. Het Verblijf van Frederick Pursh in Noord-Amerika van 1799–1811. *Jaarboek Nederlandse Dendr. Ver.* 12:103–116.
Vermeulen & Son Inc. 1990. *Catalogue.* Neshanic Station, New Jersey.
Verney, P. 1976. *The Gardens of Scotland.* London: Batsford.
Verschaffelt, J. N. 1876. *Nursery Catalogue.* Ghent.
Versprille, B. 1989. Eindbeoordeling Plan Grootendorst. Med. Blad Nederlandse Dendr. Ver. (4):7–8.
Vertrees, J. D. 1972. Observations on the propagation of Asiatic maples. *International Plant Propagators' Society Proceedings* 22:192.
———. 1973. Maples of Japan. *American Horticulture* 52(2).
———. 1974. Maples. *American Horticulture* 53(3).
———. 1975. Japanese maples gain recognition. *American Nurseryman* 142(2).
———. 1978a. Notes on variants of *Acer circinatum. Int. Dendr. Soc. Yrbk.* 1979:82.
———. 1978b. *Japanese Maples.* Beaverton, Oregon: Timber Press.
———. 1979. Unusual maples for the landscape. *Pacific Horticulture* 40(4):15–19.
———. 1987. *Japanese Maples.* 2nd ed. Portland, Oregon: Timber Press.
———. 1988. Maplewood Nursery. *Int. Dendr. Soc. Yrbk.* 1987:107.
Vervaine Nursery. 1881. *Acer Pseudo-Platanus* 'Leopoldii'. *Gardener's Chronicle* II. 15:299.
Vierhapper, F. K. M. 1919. Beiträge zur Kenntnis der Flora Griechenlands. II. *Verh. Zool.-Bot. Ges. Wien* 69:108.
Vilanova y Piera, J. 1876. *La Creacion, Historia Natural* 7:170–171. Barcelona.
Villars, D. 1786. *Histoire des Plantes de Dauphiné* 1:259,333. Grenoble.
———. 1789. *Histoire des Plantes de Dauphiné* 3:802. Grenoble.
Visiani, R. de. 1860. Plantarum Serbicarum Pemptas 11. Venezia. Rpt. *Mém. Ist. Veneto Sci.* 9:165–175.
Viviani, V. 1833. Sur les restes de plantes fossiles. *Mémoires de la Société Géologique de France* 1:131.
Vlerk, I. M. van der, and F. Florschütz. 1950. *Nederlandse in het Ijstijdvak.* Utrecht: De Haan.
Vogel, E. F. de. 1980. *Seedlings of Dicotyledons.* Wageningen: Pudoc.
Vogler, P., et al. 1906. Kleine Botanische Beobachtungen. 1. Der Verlauf des Blühens von *Acer platanoides* L. im Stadtpark St. Gallen. *Jahrb. St. Galler Naturw. Ges.* 1905:343–353.
Vos, C. de. 1867. *Beredeneerd Woordenboek der Voornaamste Heesters en Coniferen.* Groningen: Wolters.
Voskuil, J., and J. R. P. van Hoey Smith. 1983. *Trees in Rotterdam.* Rotterdam: Arboretum Trompenburg.
Voss, A. 1894. *Vilmorin's Blumengärtnerei,* 3rd ed. Berlin.
Voss, E. G., et al. 1983. *International Code of Botanical Nomenclature.* Utrecht: Bohn, Scheltema & Holkema.
Vrugtman, F. 1968. Die Weniger Bekannten Ahorne im Botanischen Garten und Belmonte Arboretum. *Deutsche Baumschule* 20:9–10.

______. 1970. Notes on the *Acer* collection of the Botanical Gardens and the Belmonte Arboretum. Miscellaneous Paper 6. Landbouw University Wageningen.
Wada, K. (Hakoneya Nursery). 1938. *Catalog*. Numazushi, Japan.
Wagenführ, R., and C. Scheiber. 1985. *Holzatlas*. Leipzig: VEB.
Wahlenberg, G. 1820. *Flora Upsaliensis*. Uppsala.
Walker, E. H. 1976. *Flora of Okinawa and the Ryukyu Islands*. Washington, DC: Smithsonian Institution.
Walker, J. 1981. The Aerodynamics of the Samara. *Scientific American* 245(October):172–177.
Walker, J. W., and J. A. Doyle. 1976. The basis of angiosperm phylogeny: palynology. *Annals of the Missouri Botanical Garden* 62:664–723.
Wallich, N. 1830. *A. laevigatum* Wall., *A. sterculiaceum* Wall. *Plantae Asiaticae Rariores* 2:3–4.
______. 1831. *Plantae Asiaticae Rariores* 2:28.
Wallihan, E. F. 1944. Chemical composition in different parts of sugar maple trees. *Journal of Forestry* 42:684.
Wallroth, K. F. W. 1822. *Schedulae Criticae de Plantis Florae Halensis Selectis*. Halle.
Walpers, W. G. 1842. *Repertorium Botanicae Systematicae* 1:408–410. Leipzig.
Walter, T. 1788. *Flora Caroliniana*. London.
Walters, H. 1968. Aceraceae. *Flora Europaea* 2. Eds. Tutin, Heywood, et al. Cambridge: Cambridge University Press.
Walters, R. S. 1978. Tapholes drilled into frozen sugar maples close slowly. USDA Forest Service Research Notes NE–265.
Walters, R. S., and A. L. Shigo. 1978. *Tapholes in sugar maples:* what happens in the tree. USDA Forest Service, General Technical Report NE–47. Northeastern Forest Experiment Station, Broomall, Pennsylvania.
Walther, H. 1972. Studien über Tertiäre *Acer* Mitteleuropas. *Abh. Staatl. Mus. Mineral. Geol. Dresden* 19:1–309.
Walton, G. S. 1969. Phytotoxity of $NaCl_1$ and $CaCl_2$ to Norway maples. *Phytopathology* 59:1412–1415.
Wang, B. S., and B. D. Haddon. 1978. Germination of red maple seed. *Seed Science and Technology* 6(3):785–790.
Wang, C. W. 1961. *The Forests of China*. Cambridge, Massachusetts: Harvard University Press.
Wang, M. C. 1988. *Acer miaotaiense* var. *glabrum*. Bulletin of Botanical Research, Northeastern Forestry Institute 8(2):67.
Wang, M. C., and Z. Z. Yue. 1988. A new variety of *Acer* from Shaanxi. Bulletin of Botanical Research, Northeastern Forestry Institute 8(2):67.
Wangenheim, F. A. J. von. 1787. *Beytrag zur Teutschen Holzgerechten Forst-Wissenschaft*. Göttingen.
Ware, G. H. 1983a. Some ecological considerations for urban tree selection. *Morton Arboretum Quarterly* 13:1–4.
______. 1983b. *Acer saccharum* ssp. *nigrum*. *Metria*. Pennsylvania State University.
Wareing, P. F. 1969. Germination and dormancy. In *Physiology of Plant Growth and Development*. Ed. M. B. Wilkins. London: McGraw-Hill.
Wareing, P. F., and I. D. J. Phillips. 1975. *The Control of Growth and Differentiation in Plants*. Oxford: Pergamon.
Wargo, P. M. 1972. Defoliation-induced chemical changes in sugar maple roots stimulate growth of *Armillaria mellea*. *Phytopathology* 62:1278–1283.
______. 1975. Estimating starch content in roots of deciduous trees—a visual technique. USDA Forest Service Research Paper NE–313.
Wargo, P. M., and D. R. Houston. 1974. Infection of defoliated sugar maple trees by *Armillaria mellea*. *Phytopathology* 64:817–822.
Wargo, P. M., and C. G. Shaw III. 1985. *Armillaria* root rot: the puzzle is being solved. *Plant Disease Reporter* 69:826–832.
Warsow, G. 1903. Systematisch-anatomische Untersuchungen des Blattes bei der Gattung *Acer* mit Besonderer Berücksichtigung der Milchsaftelemente. *Beih. Bot. Centralbl.* 15:493–601.
Warstat. 1912. Alter Ahorn, *Acer platanoides*, in Ostpreussen. *Mitt. Dtsch. Dendr. Ges.* 21:342.
Watanabe, T., and K. Aso. 1963. The sugar composition of maple syrup. *Chemical Abstracts* 58:1620g.
Watari, S. 1936. Anatomical studies on the vascular system in the petioles of some species of *Acer*, with notes on the external morphological features. *Journal of the Faculty of Science, University of Tokyo*, sect. 3, 5:1–73.

Waterbolk, H. T. 1954. *De Praehistorische Mens en Zijn Milieu.* Assen: van Gorcum.
Weaver, R. E., Jr. 1976. Selected maples for shade and ornamental planting. *Arnoldia* 36:146–176.
Webb, D. P., and V. P. Agnihotri. 1970. Presence of fungal inhibitor in the pericarps of *Acer saccharum* fruits. *Canadian Journal of Botany* 48:2109–2116.
Webb, D. P., and E. B. Dumbroff. 1969. Factors influencing the stratification process in seeds of *Acer saccharum. Canadian Journal of Botany* 47:1555–1563.
Webb, D. P., and P. F. Wareing. 1972a. Seed dormancy in *A. pseudoplatanus. Journal of Experimental Botany* 23:813–829.
______. 1972b. Seed dormancy in *Acer:* endogenous germination inhibitors and dormancy in *Acer pseudoplatanus* L. *Planta* 104:115–125.
Webb, D. P., et al. 1973. Seed Dormancy in *Acer. Journal of Experimental Botany* 24:105–116.
Weber, K. O. 1852. Beitraege zur Naturgeschichte der Vorwelt. *Palaeontographica* 2:196–199.
Weberling, F. 1981. *Morphologie der Blüten und der Blütenstände.* Stuttgart: Ulmer.
Webster, A. D. 1916. *Tree Wounds and Diseases.* London: Williams & Norgate.
Wehmer, K. F. H. 1911. *Die Pflanzenstoffe Botanisch-systematisch Bearbeitet.* Jena.
Weir, J. G. 1932. Care of the sugar bush. Vermont Agricultural Extension Service Bulletin 71.
______. 1933. Suggestion for making high quality maple syrup. Vermont Agricultural Extension Service Bulletin 73.
Weiser, F. 1973. Beitrag zur Erklärung Blütenbiologische Fragen bei *A. pseudoplatanus* L. In *Int. Symp. Biol. of Woody Plants.* Ed. F. Bencat. Bratislava.
Weisz. 1912. Erfahrungen mit Ausländischen Gehölzen in den Augsburger Stadtwaldungen. *Mitt. Dtsch. Dendr. Ges.* 21:2–19.
Welch, D. S. 1934. The range and importance of Nectria canker on hardwoods in the Northeast. *Journal of Forestry* 32:997–1002.
Wells, J. S. 1968. *Plant Propagation Practices.* 3rd ed. New York: Macmillan.
Wells, S. D., and J. de Rue. 1927. The suitability of American woods for paper pulp. USDA Departmental Bulletin 1485. Washington, DC.
Welsh, K., et al. 1979. Progress on in vitro propagation of red maple. *International Plant Propagators' Society Proceedings* 29:382–387.
Wenderoth, G. W. F. 1831. Einige Bemerkungen über Verschiedene Neue Pflanzenarten des Botanischen Gartens in Marburg. *Schrift. Ges. Beförd. Gesammt. Naturw. Marburg* 2:250–251.
Wesmael, A. 1859. Notice sur quelques éspèces et variétés d'érables. *Belgique Hort.* 9:348–352. Liege.
______. 1890. Revue critique des éspèces du genre *Acer.* Bull. Soc. Roy. Hort. Belg. 29:17–65.
West, D. C., et al. 1981. *Forest Succession. Concepts and Application.* New York: Springer.
Westcott, C. 1964. *The Gardener's Bug Book.* New York: Doubleday.
Westhoff, V. 1950–1951. Plant communities with woody species ('lignosa') found in the Dutch dune areas and its inner border. *Jaarboek Nederlandse Dendr. Ver.* 18:9–49.
Westing, A. H. 1966. Sugar maple decline: an evaluation. *Economic Botany* 20:196–212.
______. 1969. Plants and salt in the roadside environment. *Phytopathology* 59:1174–1179.
Weston, R. 1770. *The Universal Botanist and Nurseryman.* London.
______. 1775. *The English Flora.* London.
Westveld, R. H. 1949. *Applied Silviculture in the United States.* New York: Wiley.
Wettstein, R. 1890. Beitrag zur Flora des Orientes. *Sitz-ber. Math. Naturw. Kl. K. Acad. Wiss. Wien* 98:384.
Wheeler, Q., and M. Blackwell., eds. 1984. *Fungus-Insect Relationships: Perspectives in Ecology and Evolution.* New York: Columbia University Press.
Wherry, E. T., et al. 1979. *Atlas of the Flora of Pennsylvania.* Morris Arboretum, University of Pennsylvania.
White, D. J. B. 1955. The architecture of the stem apex and the origin and development of the axillary bud in seedlings of *Acer pseudoplatanus. Ann. Bot.,* n.s., 19:437–449.
White, J. 1988. Westonbirt Arboretum. *Endeavour,* n.s., 12:71–75.
Whitley, B., and Milne. 1817. *A Catalogue of Plants.* London: Fulham Nursery.
Whitlock, R. 1979. *Historic Forests of England.* New York: Barnes.
Whittle, T. 1988. *The Plant Hunters.* New York: PAJ Publ.
Whone, H. 1990. *Touch Wood, A Journey Among Trees.* Otley: Smith Settle.
Wiegers, F. A. 1809. *Collection d'Arbres, Arbrisseaux, Plantes.* Malines.
Wier, D. B. 1877. *Acer saccharinum* 'Wieri'. *The Garden* 12:82.
Wijlen, T. van. 1984. *Bossenatlas van Nederland.* Baarn: Bigot & Van Rossum.

Wilde, J. 1933. *Acer monspessulanum* L., der Französische Ahorn, in der Pfalz. *Mitt. Dtsch. Dendr. Ges.* 45:84–87.
Wiley, H. W. 1884. The northern sugar industry. USDA Chemistry Division, Bulletin 3. Washington, DC.
Wilhelm, Prof. 1918a. Nebenblätter bei einem Ahorn. *Mitt. Dtsch. Dendr. Ges.* 27:203–204.
______. 1918b Trockener, Heiszer, Windiger Standort Schützt Nicht Immer vor Pilzentwicklung. *Mitt. Dtsch. Dendr. Ges.* 27:204–205.
Wilhelm, S., and J. B. Taylor. 1965. Control of *Verticillium* wilt of olive through natural recovery and resistance. *Phytopathology* 55:310–316.
Wilkins, M. B., ed. 1969. *Physiology of Plant Growth and Development.* New York: McGraw-Hill.
Wilkinson, G. 1973. *Trees in the Wild.* London: Stephen Hope.
Wilkinson, J. G. 1979. *Industrial Timber Preservation.* London: Associated Business Press.
Willdenov, K. L. 1796. *Berlinische Baumzucht.* Berlin.
______. 1806. *Species Plantarum* 4(2):983–992. Berlin.
Willemstein, S. C. 1987. *An Evolutionary Basis for Pollination Ecology.* Leiden Bot. Ser., vol. 10. Leiden: Brill.
Williams, S. W. 1849. Report on the indigenous medical botany of Massachusetts. *Transactions of the American Medical Association* 2:863–927.
Willis, J. C. 1980. *A Dictionary of the Flowering Plants and Ferns.* 8th ed. Cambridge: Cambridge University Press.
Willis Nursery Company. 1938. *Acer saccharinum* 'Willis' Cutleaf'. *American Nurseryman* 8:68.
Willits, C. O. 1950–1951. Crops from the maple trees. In *Crops in Peace and War.* Yearbook of Agriculture. Washington, DC: USDA.
______. 1958. Maple syrup producers manual. Agriculture Handbook no. 134. Washington, DC: USDA.
Willkomm, H. M. 1875. *Forstliche Flora von Deutschland und Oesterreich.* Leipzig.
______. 1879. *Laubhölzer, Zierbäume und Sträuche des Hochfürstlich von Rohan'schen Garten zu Sichrov.* Turnau.
______. 1886. *Forstliche Flora von Deutschland und Oesterreich,* 2nd ed. Leipzig.
Willkomm, H. M., and J. M. C. Lange. 1880. *Prodromus Florae Hispanicae* 3:560–563. Stuttgart.
______. 1893. *Supplementus Prodromi Florae Hispanicae.* Stuttgart.
Wilmanns, O., and R. Tüxen, eds. 1979. *Werden und Vergehen von Pflanzengesellschaften.* Vaduz: J. Cramer.
Wilson, B. F. 1966. Development of the shoot system of *Acer rubrum* L. *Harvard Forest Paper* 14:1–21.
______. 1966. Mitotic activity in the cambial zone of *Pinus strobus. American Journal of Botany* 53:364–371.
Wilson, E. H. 1925. *America's Greatest Garden. The Arnold Arboretum.* Boston: Stratford.
______. 1932. *Aristocrats of the Garden.* Boston: Stratford.
Wilson, E. O. 1989. Threats to biodiversity. *Scientific American* 261(3):60–66.
Wilson, K., and D. J. B. White. 1986. *The Anatomy of Wood.* London: Stobart.
Wilson, P., ed. 1968. *The Gardeners Yearbook 1969.* London: Collins.
Wilson, S. D., et al. 1949. The composition of the seeds of the maple tree (*Acer truncatum* Bunge). Peking Natural History Bulletin 17:217–221.
Wimmer, C. F., and H. E. Grabowski. 1827. *Flora Silesiae* 1. Vratislaviae.
Winch, F. E., Jr., and R. R. Morrow. 1967. Production of maple syrup and other maple products. Cornell Extension Bulletin no. 974.
Windholz, M., et al. 1983. *Merck Index.* 10th ed. Rahway, New Jersey: Merck.
Winstead, J. E. 1978. Trachaeid length as an ecotypic character in *Acer negundo* L. *American Journal of Botany* 65:811–812.
Wintershoven, J. R. 1795. *Handleiding v.d. Liefhebbers van Vreemde Plantzoenen.*
Wise, R. 1979. A New England autumn. *British Medical Journal* (15 December):1569.
Wit, H. C. D. de. 1967. *Plants of the World: Higher Plants* II. London: Thames & Hudson.
Witte, H. 1859–1860. *Catalogus Plantarum quae in Horto Botanico Academico Lugduno Batavo coluntur.* 4 vols.
______. 1860. *Les jardins Neérlandais.* Annales d'horticulture et de botanique ou flore des jardins du Royaumes des Pays-Bas. Vol. III. Leiden: Sijthoff.
Wittmack, M. C. L. 1880. *Acer platanoides* var. *aureo-variegatum* 'Buntzleri'. *Monatsschr. Ver. Beförd. Gartenbau Preussen* 1880:321.
______. 1883. Neue Buntblättrige Ahorne aus der L. Späth'schen Baumschule. *Gartenzeitg.* 1883:513.

Wittrock, V. B. 1886. Ueber die Geschlechtsverteilung bei *Acer platanoides* L. und Einige Andere *Acer*-Arten. *Bot. Zentralbl.* 25(2):55–68.
Wodehouse, R. P. 1935. *Pollen Grains: Their Structure, Identification and Significance in Science and Medicine.* New York: McGraw-Hill.
______. 1942. *Atmospheric Pollen.* Aerobiol. Publ. AAAS.
______. 1945. Hayfever plants. *Chron. Bot.*
Wolf, E. L. 1917. *Acer Pseudo-Platanus* L. *vinosum. Trudy Biuro Prikl. Bot.* Bulletin of Applied Botany 10:628–630.
Wolfe, H. R. 1955. Leafhoppers of the state of Washington. Washington Agricultural Experiment Station Circular 277.
Wolfe, J. A. 1960. *Early Miocene Floras of Northwest Oregon.* Ph.D. thesis, University of California, Berkeley.
______. 1966. Tertiary plants from the Cook Inlet region, Alaska. U.S. Geological Survey Prof. Paper 454-N.
______. 1972. *An interpretation of Alaskan Tertiary floras.* In *Floristics and Paleofloristics of Asia and Eastern North America.* Ed. A. Graham. Amsterdam: Elsevier.
______. 1981. Vicariance biogeography of angiosperms in relation to paleobotanic data. In *Vicariance Biogeography: A Critique.* Eds. G. Nelson and D. E. Rosen. New York: Columbia University Press.
Wolff, R. P. 1973. Success and failures in grafting Japanese maples. *International Plant Propagators' Society Proceedings* 23.
Wong, H. R., et al. 1983. Identification of three species of *Proteoteras* (Lepidoptera: Tortricidae) attacking shoots of Manitoba maple in the Canadian prairies. *The Canadian Entomologist* 115:333–339.
Woo, J. Y., and A. D. Partridge. 1969. The life history and cytology of *Rhytisma punctatum* on bigleaf maple. *Mycologia* 61:1085–1095.
Wood, A. 1861. *A Class-Book of Botany.* New York.
Wood, J. 1986. Tour of Czechoslovakia June 20–28, 1985. *Int. Dendr. Soc. Yrbk.* 1985:23–30.
Wooding, F. B. P., and D. H. Northcote. 1965. The fine structure and development of the companian cell of the phloem of *Acer pseudoplatanus. Journal of Cell Biology* 24:117–128.
Woods, K. D., and R. H. Whittaker. 1981. Canopy-understory interaction and the internal dynamics of mature hardwood and hemlock-hardwood forests. In *Forest Succession.* Eds. D. C. West et al. New York: Springer.
Wooton, E. O., and P. C. Standley. 1913. New plants from New Mexico. *Contributions of the U.S. National Herbarium* 16:146.
Wright, J. W. 1953a. Summary of tree-breeding experiments by the Northeastern Forest Experiment Station 1947–1950. Paper no. 56:8–15.
______. 1953b. Notes on the flowering of northeastern trees. Northeastern Forest Experiment Station Paper no. 60.
______. 1957. New chromosome numbers in *Acer* and *Fraxinus.* Morris Arboretum Bulletin 8:33–34.
Wu, C. Y. 1983. *Acer foveolatum. Acta Phytotaxonomica Sinica, Peking* 21(3):337.
Wu, C. Y., and T. Z. Hsu. 1983. *Acer caloneurum. Acta Phytotaxonomica Sinica, Peking* 21(3):339.
Wulf, A. 1988. *Pleuroceras platani* (V. Tubeuf). Monod. Erreger einer Blattbräune an Bergahorn (*Acer pseudoplatanus* L.) *Nachr. Blatt Dtsch. Pflanzenschutzd.* 40(5):65–70.
______. 1989a. Pilzkrankheiten an Ahornblättern. *Deutsche Baumschule* 41(3):122–124.
______. 1989b. Blattkrankheiten an Ahorn. *Gesunde Pflanzen* 41 (6):218–223. Inst. f. Pflanzenschütz im Forst. Biol Bundesanstalt f. Land-u. Forstwiss. Brunswick, Germany.
Wydler. 1857. *Flora.* In Monographie der Gattung *Acer,* by F. Pax. 1885. *Bot. Jahrb.* 6:310.
Wyman, D. 1954. Maples for park and garden use as they grow in the Arnold Arboretum. Arboretum Bulletin 17:113–115, 130.
______. 1963. *Acer Platanoides* 'Emerald Queen'. *Arnoldia* 23:116.
______. 1965. *Trees for American Gardens.* Rev. ed. New York: Macmillan.
______. *Wyman's Gardening Encyclopedia.* 1971. New York: Macmillan.
Xu, Z. R. 1986. *Acer changii. Acta Sci. Nat. Univ. Sunyatseni* 2:100.
Xu, Z. X. 1986a. *Acer cordatum* var. *jinggangshanense.* Bulletin of Botanical Research, Northeastern Forestry Institute 6(1):151.
______. 1986b. *Acer fabri* var. *tongguense.* Bulletin of Botanical Research, Northeastern Forestry Institute 6(1):152.
Yaltirik, F. 1967a. Aceraceae. In *Flora of Turkey,* by P. H. Davis. Edinburgh: Edinburgh University

Press. 2:509–519.
______. 1967b. Contribution to the taxonomy of woody plants in Turkey. *Notes of the Royal Botanic Garden, Edinburgh* 28:9–10.
______. 1971. The taxonomical study on the macro- and micromorphological characteristics of indigenous maples (*Acer* L.) in Turkey. *Istanbul Univ. Orman Fakült. Yayinlari* 179. (In Turkish).
______. 1990. Anatomic characteristics of woods in Turkish maples with relation to the humidity of the sites. *Int. Dendr. Soc. Yrbk.* 1990:49.
Yamabayashi, N. 1938. Identification of Corean woods. Bulletin of the Forest Experiment Station at Chosen 27:1–471, plate 1–60.
Yamauchi, F. 1962. Anatomical identification of the woods in Japanese *Acer. Miscellaneous Report of the Research Institute of Natural Resources* 58–59:3–11.
Yampolski, C., and H. Yampolski. 1922. Distribution of sex forms in the phanerogamic flora. *Bibl. Genet.* 3:1–62.
Yanagita, Y. 1929. Illustration of the seedling of forest trees. *J. Soc. For.* 371–375.
Yeoman, M. M., et al. 1977. Regulation of enzyme levels during the cell cycle. In *Regulation of Enzyme Synthesis and Activity in Plants.* Ed. H. Smith. New York: Academic Press.
Yinger, B. Y. 1990. Maples in Japan and Korea. *Int. Dendr. Soc. Yrbk.* 1990:14–20.
Yokohama Nursery. 1898. *Maples of Japan.* Yokohama, Japan.
______. 1914–1915. *Descriptive Catalogue.*
______. 1924. *Descriptive Catalogue.*
______. 1930–1931. *Descriptive Catalogue.*
Young, C. T. W. 1978. Sooty bark disease of sycamore. *Arboricultural Leaflet* 3. London: H.M.S.O.
Young, M. 1874. *Catalogue* Autumn 1874. Godalming, Great Britain.
______. 1973. Studies on the growth in culture of plant cells. XVI. Nitrogen assimilation during nitrogen-limited growth of *Acer pseudoplatanus* L. cells in chemostat culture. *Journal of Experimental Botany* 24:1171–1185.
Young, W., Jr. 1783. *Catalogue d'arbres, arbustes et plantes herbacées d'Amérique.* Paris. Rpt. 1916. Philadelphia.
Yu, D. 1983. *The Botanical Gardens of China.* Beijing: Science Press.
Yu, Z. X. 1983. *Acer buergerianum* var. *jiujiangense. Acta Phytotaxonomica Sinica, Peking* 21(4):368.
Yurtsev, B. A. 1972. *Phytogeography of northeastern Asia and the problem of Transberingian floristic interrelations.* In *Floristics and Paleofloristics of Asia and Eastern North America.* Ed. A. Graham. Amsterdam: Elsevier.
Zabel, H. 1878. *Systematisches Verzeichniss der in den Gärten der K. Preuss. Forstakademie zu Münden Kultivirten Pflanzen.* Münden.
______. 1887. *Acer Platanoides* L. var. *integrilobum. Gartenflora* 36:431.
______. 1904. Kleinere Dendrologische Beiträge. *Mitt. Dtsch. Dendr. Ges.* 13:58–68.
Zahner, R. 1970. Site quality and wood quality in upland hardwoods. In *Tree Growth and Forest Soils.* Eds. C. T. Youngberg and C. B. Davey. Oregon State University Press.
Zamiatnin, B. N. 1958. In Sokolov's *Dereviia i Kustarniki USSR* 4:405–499. Leningrad.
Zander, R. 1984. *Handwörterbuch der Pflanzennamen.* Stuttgart: Ulmer.
Ziegenfuss, T. T., and R. B. Clarkson. 1971a. A comparison of the soluble seed proteins of certain *Acer* species. *Canadian Journal of Botany* 49:1951–1957.
______. 1971b. The Electrophoretic and serologic patterns from seven taxa of *Acer.* In *Proceedings of the West Virginia Academy of Science* 42:39.
Zimm, L. A. 1918. A wilt disease of maples. *Phytopathology* 8:80–81. Abstr.
Zimmermann, G. 1982. *Zahlen Lexicon WALD.* Stuttgart: DRW-Verlag.
Zimmermann, M. H. 1983. *Xylem Structure and the Ascent of Sap.* Berlin: Springer.
Zimmermann, M. H., and C. L. Brown. 1974. *Trees, Structure and Function.* New York: Springer.
Zulver, S. 1963. *Trees.* Vest Pocket Nature Guides. Baltimore: Ottenheimer.

# Index of Maple Names

Where two or more page numbers are listed for a maple, the descriptive entry, if any, is boldfaced.

# Index of Maple Cultivars

This index facilitates the finding of a name where the species name is either not known or incorrect.